INVINCIBLE

TRUEMAN'S *Specific* Series®

NTA

UGC-NET/SET

For JRF and Eligibility Test for Assistant Professor (and Ph.D/M.Phil Entrance Exams)

TEACHING AND RESEARCH APTITUDE

PAPER-I

With

Previous Years' Papers

By

Sajit Kumar & M. Gagan

Authentic & Dependable

Produced and Published by

Danika Publishing Company

(Publishers of Trueman's *Specific* Series)

4352/4C, Ansari Road,
Daryaganj, New Delhi - 110002
Ph.: 011-23242482, 41501988
e-mail: danikabooks@yahoo.com

Can be had from

Invincible Publishers

2nd Floor, SAS Tower, Medicity, Sector 38,
Gurugram (Haryana)

ISBN : 9788189301996

New Edition : 2026

Price : Rs. 550/-

Data Processing :
Inhouse

Printed at :
Dhruv Printers
New Delhi.

Subject to New Delhi Jurisdiction only

PUBLISHERS' NOTE

The present revised edition is a humble attempt to satisfy the needs of students appearing for UGC NET Compulsory Paper I and SET examinations. New topics introduced by UGC for 2019 onward exams have been added in appropriate units. Adequate subject matter has been provided to facilitate attempt of Objective Type Questions. Around 3000 questions of all varieties find place in this volume. Maximum questions asked in previous examinations have been incorporated. Explanatory notes have been provided, wherever necessary. Actual Previous years' papers have also been appended. The book in the present form shall serve as a complete hand book for the examinations.

Any suggestions for the improvement of the book shall be thankfully acknowledged.

CONTENTS

GENERAL INFORMATION

NTA-UGC NET

On behalf of UGC, the National Eligibility Test (NET) is conducted for determining the eligibility of Indian nationals for the Eligibility for Assistant Professor only or Junior Research Fellowship & Eligibility for Assistant Professor Both in Indian Universities and Colleges.

The UGC- NET (for Eligibility for Assistant Professor only or Junior Research Fellowship & Eligibility for Assistant Professor both), will be conducted by the **NTA.**

The award of JRF and Eligibility for Assistant Professor both OR Eligibility for Assistant Professor only depends on the performance of the candidate in both the papers of NET in aggregate. However, the candidates qualifying exclusively for Assistant Professor are not to be considered for award of JRF. Candidates who qualify the Test for eligibility for Assistant Professor are governed by the rules and regulations for recruitment of Assistant Professor of the concerned universities/colleges/state governments, as the case may be.

CONDITIONS OF ELIGIBILITY

Candidates who have secured at least 55% marks (without rounding off) in Master's Degree OR equivalent examination from universities/institutions recognised by UGC in Humanities (including languages) and Social Science, Computer Science & Applications, Electronic Science etc. are eligible for this Test. The Other Backward Classes (OBC) belonging to non-creamy layer/Scheduled Caste (SC)/Scheduled Tribe (ST)/Persons with disability (PWD) category candidates who have secured at least 50% marks (without rounding off) in Master's degree or equivalent examination are eligible for this Test.

AGE LIMIT

(i) Junior Research Fellowship: Not more than 30 years (check notification for exact date). A relaxation upto 5 years is provided to the candidates belonging to OBC/SC/ST/PWD categories and to women applicants. Relaxation will also be provided to the candidates having research experience, limited to the period spent on research in the relevant/related subject of post-graduation degree, subject to a maximum of 5 years, on production of a certificate from appropriate authority. Three years' relaxation in age will be permissible to the candidates possessing L.L.M. Degree. Total age relaxation on the above ground(s) shall not exceed five years under any circumstances. **(ii) Assistant Professor:** There is no upper age limit for applying for eligibility for Assistant Professor.

SCHEME OF THE TEST

The UGC-NET will be conducted in objective mode only. The Test will consist of two papers. Both papers will consist of only objective type questions and will be held on the same day of Examination.

The Test will consist of two papers as given below:

Paper	Marks	Number of Questions	MCQs	Duration
I	100	50	The questions will be generic in nature, intending to assess the teaching/research aptitude of the candidate. It will primarily be designed to test reasoning ability, comprehension, divergent thinking and general awareness of the candidate.	03 hours All the questions will be compulsory.
II	200	100	This will be based on the subject selected by the candidate.	

The Test will be conducted in Computer Based Test (CBT) mode only, and will be held on different dates at various centres in India.

Syllabus of Test: Syllabi for all NET subjects can be downloaded from the UGC Website **www.ugc.ac.in** or **www.ugcnetonline.in**

IMPORTANT

The National level test for determining the eligibility of candidates for the award of Junior Research Fellowship/Assistant Professor in all Science subjects falling under the Faculties of Science (Physical, Biological and Applied) is being conducted jointly with the Council of Scientific and Industrial Research (CSIR), New Delhi.

The candidates desirous of availing UGC-JRF or obtaining eligibility for Assistant Professor in the Science subjects are advised to appear at the UGC-CSIR national level test announced by the CSIR.

The UGC Test for JRF/eligibility for Assistant Professor will be held at the University Test Centres specified below. The candidates may register for the test at the nearest centre. Please note that change of centre will not be allowed under any circumstances.

NET SUBJECTS WITH CODES: • Economics (01). • Political Science (02). • Philosophy (03). • Psychology (04). • Sociology (05).• History (06). • Anthropology (07). • Commerce (08). • Education (09). • Social Work (10). • Defence & Strategic Studies (11). • Home Science (12). • Public Administration (14). • Population Studies* (15) • Hindustani Music (Vocal/Instrumental) (16). • Management (17). • Maithili (18). • Bengali (19). • Hindi (20). • Kannada (21). • Malayalam (22). • Odia (23). • Punjabi (24). • Sanskrit (25). • Tamil (26). • Telugu (27). • Urdu (28). • Arabie (29). • English (30). • Linguistics (31). • Chinese (32). • Dogri (33). • Nepali (34). • Manipuri (35). • Assamese (36). Gujarati (37). • Marathi (38). • French (39). • Spanish (40). • Russian (41). • Persian (42). • Rajasthani (43). • German (44). • Japanese (45). • Adult Education/Continuing Education/Andragogy/Non-Formal Education (46). • Physical Education (47). • Arab Culture and Islamic Studies (49). • Indian Culture (50). • Labour Welfare/personnel Management/Industrial Relations/Labour and Social Welfare/Human Resource Management (55). • Law (58). • Library and Information Science (59). • Buddhist, Jaina, Gandhian and Peace Studies (60). Comparative study of religions (62). • Mass Communication and Journalism (63). • Dance (65). • Museology & Conservation (66). • Archaeology (67). • Criminology (68). • Tribal and Regional Language/Literature (70). • Folk Literature (71). • Comparative literature (72). • Sanskrit Traditional subjects (including Jyotisha/Sidhanta Jyotisha/Navya Vyakarna/Vyakarna/Mimansa/Navya Nyaya/Sankhya Yog/Tulanatmaka Darsana/Shukla Yajurveda/Madhav Vedant/Dharma Sastra/Sahitya/Purana-itihasa/Agama/Advaita Vedanta (73). • Women Studies** (74). • Visual Art (including Drawing & Painting / Sculpture Graphics / Applied Art/History of Art) (79). • Geography (80). • Social Medicine & Community Health (81). • Forensic Science (82). • Pali (83). • Kashmiri (84.) • Konkani (85). • Computer Science and Applications (87). • Electronic Science (88). • Environmental Sciences (89). • International & Area Studies (90). • Prakrit (91). • Human Rights and Duties (92). • Tourism Administration/Management (93). • Bodo (94). • Santali (95). • Karnatik Music (Vocal Instrument, Percussion) (96). • Rabindra Sangeet (67). • Percussion Instruments (68). • Drama/ Theatre (99) • Yoga (100). • Sindhi (101).

Students are advised to refer to latest notification as and when released by UGC/NTA at www.nta.ac.in and www.ntanet.nic.in

UNIVERSITY GRANTS COMMISSION NET BUREAU

PAPER-I

New Syllabus ❖ New Pattern

***Subject :* GENERAL PAPER ON TEACHING & RESEARCH APTITUDE** **CODE NO. 00**

The main objective is to assess the teaching and research capabilities of the candidates. The test aims at assessing the teaching and research aptitude as well. Candidates are expected to possess and exhibit cognitive abilities, which include comprehension, analysis, evaluation, understanding the structure of arguments, deductive and inductive reasoning. The candidates are also expected to have a general awareness about teaching and learning processes in higher education system. Further, they should be aware of interaction between people, environment, natural resources and their impact on the quality of life.

Note :

(i) Five questions each carrying 2 marks are to be set from each Module.

(ii) Whenever graphical/pictorial question(s) are set for sighted candidates, a passage followed by equal number of questions and weightage be set for visually impaired candidates.

I. Teaching Aptitude

- **Teaching:** Concept, Objectives, Levels of teaching (Memory, Understanding and Reflective), Characteristics and basic requirements.
- **Learner's characteristics:** Characteristics of adolescent and adult learners (Academic, Social, Emotional and Cognitive), Individual differences.
- **Factors affecting teaching related to:** Teacher, Learner, Support material, Instructional facilities, Learning environment and Institution.
- **Methods of teaching in Institutions of higher learning:** Teacher centred vs. Learner centred methods; Off-line vs. On-line methods (Swayam, Swayamprabha, MOOCs etc.).
- **Teaching Support System:** Traditional, Modern and ICT based.
- **Evaluation Systems:** Elements and Types of evaluation, Evaluation in Choice Based Credit System in Higher education, Computer based testing, Innovations in evaluation systems.

II. Research Aptitude

- **Research:** Meaning, Types, and Characteristics, Positivism and Post- positivistic approach to research.
- **Methods of Research:** Experimental, Descriptive, Historical, Qualitative and Quantitative methods.
- Steps of Research.
- Thesis and Article writing: Format and styles of referencing.
- Application of ICT in research.
- Research ethics.

III. Comprehension

A passage of text be given. Questions be asked from the passage to be answered.

IV. Communication

- **Communication:** Meaning, types and characteristics of communication.
- **Effective communication:** Verbal and Non-verbal, Inter-Cultural and group communications, Classroom communication.

- Barriers to effective communication.
- Mass-Media and Society.

V. Mathematical Reasoning and Aptitude

- Types of reasoning.
- Number series, Letter series, Codes and Relationships.
- Mathematical Aptitude (Fraction, Time & Distance, Ratio, Proportion and Percentage, Profit and Loss, Interest and Discounting, Averages etc.).

VI. Logical Reasoning

- Understanding the structure of arguments: argument forms, structure of categorical propositions, Mood and Figure, Formal and Informal fallacies, Uses of language, Connotations and denotations of terms, Classical square of opposition.
- Evaluating and distinguishing deductive and inductive reasoning.
- Analogies.
- **Venn diagram:** Simple and multiple use for establishing validity of arguments.
- **Indian Logic:** Means of knowledge.
- **Pramanas:** Pratyaksha (Perception), Anumana (Inference), Upamana (Comparison), Shabda (Verbal testimony), Arthapatti (Implication) and Anupalabddhi (Non-apprehension).
- Structure and kinds of Anumana (inference), Vyapti (invariable relation), Hetvabhasas (fallacies of inference).

VII. Data Interpretation

- Sources, acquisition and classification of Data.
- Quantitative and Qualitative Data.
- Graphical representation (Bar-chart, Histograms, Pie-chart, Table-chart and Line-chart) and mapping of Data.
- Data Interpretation.
- Data and Governance.

VIII. Information and Communication Technology (ICT)

- **ICT:** General abbreviations and terminology.
- Basics of Internet, Intranet, E-mail, Audio and Video-conferencing.
- Digital initiatives in higher education.
- ICT and Governance.

IX. People, Development and Environment

- **Development and environment:** Millennium development and Sustainable development goals.
- **Human and environment interaction:** Anthropogenic activities and their impacts on environment.
- **Environmental issues:** Local, Regional and Global; Air pollution, Water pollution, Soil pollution, Noise pollution, Waste (solid, liquid, biomedical, hazardous, electronic), Climate change and its Socio-Economic and Political dimensions.
- Impacts of pollutants on human health.
- **Natural and energy resources:** Solar, Wind, Soil, Hydro, Geothermal, Biomass, Nuclear and Forests.
- **Natural hazards and disasters:** Mitigation strategies.
- **Environmental Protection Act (1986)**, National Action Plan on Climate Change, International agreements/efforts -Montreal Protocol, Rio Summit, Convention on Biodiversity, Kyoto Protocol, Paris Agreement, International Solar Alliance.

X. Higher Education System

- Institutions of higher learning and education in ancient India.
- Evolution of higher learning and research in Post Independence India.
- Oriental, Conventional and Non-conventional learning programmes in India.
- Professional, Technical and Skill Based education.
- Value education and environmental education.
- Policies, Governance, and Administration.

UNIT

I

TEACHING APTITUDE

Syllabus

- **Teaching:** Concept, Objectives, Levels of Teaching (Memory, Understanding and Reflective), Characteristics and Basic Requirements.
- **Learner's Characteristics:** Characteristics of Adolescent and Adult Learners (Academic, Social, Emotional and Cognitive), Individual Differences.
- **Factors Affecting Teaching Related to:** Teacher, Learner, Support Material, Instructional Facilities, Learning Environment and Institution.
- **Methods of Teaching in Institutions of Higher Learning:** Teacher Centred vs. Learner Centred Methods; Off-line vs. On-line Methods (Swayam, Swayamprabha, MOOCs etc.).
- **Teaching Support System:** Traditional, Modern and ICT based.
- **Evaluation Systems:** Elements and Types of Evaluation, Evaluation in Choice Based Credit System in Higher Education, Computer Based Testing, Innovations in Evaluation Systems.

CONCEPT OF TEACHING

Teaching is a part of the teaching-learning process. It is required to bring specific changes in a person according to the need of his society and environment in which he is living. "Teaching is not an act as it is dynamic in nature, so it is termed as a process." It is also not a fundamental concept as it is greatly influenced by social.

Traditional Concept

Teaching is the act of imparting instructions to the learners in the classroom situation. It is traditional class-room teaching. In traditional class-room teaching the teacher gives information to students, or one of the students reads from a text-book, while the other students silently follow him. While imparting knowledge teacher should keep in mind the child as well as the orderly presentation of subject-matter.

Modern Concept

Teaching is to cause the pupil to learn and acquire the desired knowledge, skills and also desirable ways of living in the society. It is a process in which learner, teacher, curriculum and other variables are organised in a systematic and psychological way to attain some pre-determined goals.

Concept of Teaching

Different educationists hold different ideas regarding the concept of teaching.

"Teaching is intimate contact between a more mature personality and a less mature one which designed to further the education of the latter". Morrison, Dewey expressed this concept of teaching by an equation. "Teaching is learning as selling is to buying". In the words of John Brubacher, "Teaching is arrangement and manipulation of a situation in which there are gaps or obstructions which an individual will seek to overcome and from which he will learn in the course of doing so". B.O. Smith defined teaching as "Teaching is a system of actions intended to induce learning".

According to Gage, "Teaching is a form interpersonal influence aimed at changing the behaviour potential another person". Smith in 1963 further extended the definition of teaching, "Teaching is a system of actions involving an agent, an end in view and a situation including two sets of factors those over which the agent has no control (class size, characteristics of pupils, physical facilities, etc.) and those which he can modify (such as techniques and strategies of teaching)". Edmund Amidon defined teaching as "an interactive process, primarily involving classroom talk which takes place between teacher and pupil and occurs during certain definable activities".

Davis and Glaser have pointed out that the entire structure of teaching has four steps:

'Step-I: Planning of teaching which includes content analysis, identification and writing of objectives.

Step-2: Organization of teaching which indicates the teaching strategies for achieving the objectives of teaching.

Step-3: Identification of suitable teaching-learning strategies for effective communication of content.

Step-4: Managing teaching-learning, whereby the focus is on the assessment of the learning objectives in terms of student performance, and this forms the feedback to teacher and students.

Robertson (1987) indicated that "Teaching is a generic term which denotes actions undertaken with the intention of bringing about learning in another".

The International Encyclopedia of Teaching and Teacher Education have classified the concept of teaching into three categories:

1. Teaching as success signifies that learning is implicated in teaching. Teaching entails learning and can be defined as an activity which necessarily affects learning.
2. Teaching as an intentional activity means that teaching may not logically imply learning, but it can be anticipated that will result in learning.
3. Teaching as normative behaviour denotes action undertaken with the intention of bringing about learning another. It designates a family of activities: training and instructing are primary members and indoctrination.

According to Green, "Training consists of activities that shape skills and other behaviours while instruction and indoctrination go with activities which induce knowledge and beliefs."

The Nature of Teaching

In its broadest sense, teaching is a process that facilitates learning. Teaching is the specialized application of knowledge, skills and attributes designed to provide unique service to meet the educational needs of the individual and of society. The choice of learning activities whereby the goals of education are realized in the educational institution is the responsibility of the teaching profession.

In addition to providing students with learning opportunities to meet curriculum outcomes, teaching emphasizes the development of values and guides students in their social relationships. Teachers employ practices that develop positive self-concept in students. Although the work of teachers typically takes place in a classroom setting, the direct interaction between teacher and student is the single most important element in teaching.

If we consider its nature, teaching is:

(a) **Dynamic, Social and Humane.** Teaching is not a fundamental concept because it is greatly influenced by social and human factors which are dynamic in themselves.

(b) **Both, Art and Science.** Teaching is both art and science. It calls for exercise of talent and creativity making it an art and involving repertoire of techniques, procedures and skills which can be studied systematically, described and improved making it science.

(c) **Diverse in Application.** In application, teaching is of diverse nature. It may have various forms as formal, informal, directional, instructional, formational, training, conditioning, indoctrination, talking, showing, doing, remedial, etc.

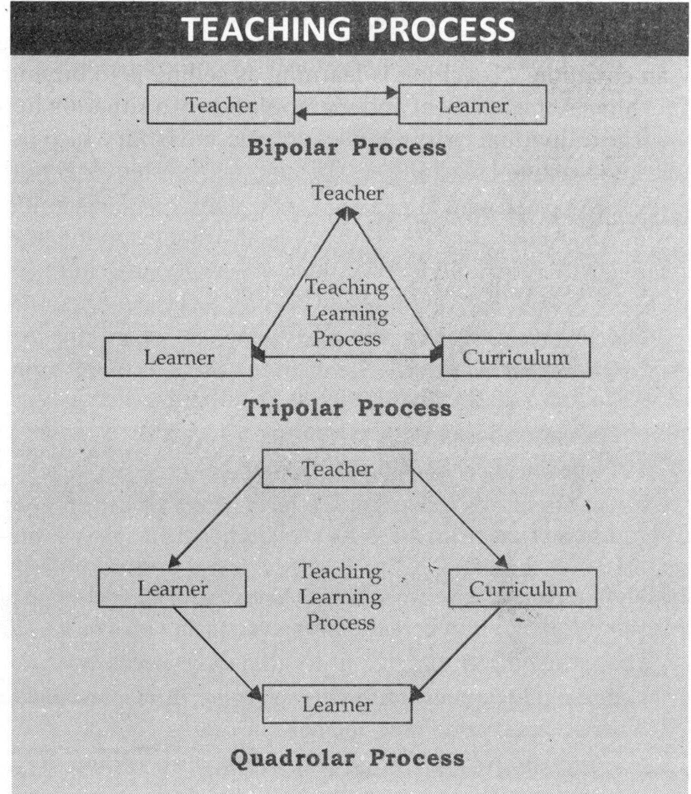

Characteristics of Teaching

The characteristics of teaching are as follows :

1. Teaching is an effective interaction between teacher and students.
2. Teaching is both arts as well as science. Teaching is an art as it calls for the exercise of talent and creativity. Teaching as science involves a repertoire of techniques, procedures and skills.
3. Teaching has various forms, like formal and informal raining, conditioning or indoctrination, etc.
4. Teaching is dominated by the skill of communication.
5. Teaching is a tripolar process; the three poles are, educational objectives, learning experiences and change in behaviour.
6. Teaching should be well planned, and the teacher should decide the objectives, methods of teaching and evaluation techniques.
7. Good teaching is democratic, and teacher respects the students, encourages them to ask questions, answer questions and discuss things.
8. Teaching provides guidance, direction and encouragement to the students.
9. Teaching is a cooperative activity and teacher should involve students in different classroom activities, such as organization, management, discussion, recitation and evaluation of results.

CHARACTERISTICS OF TEACHING (in a Nutshell)

- System of actions.
- Professional activity.
- Subjected to analysis and assessment.
- Interactive process.
- Specialised task.
- Collection of various modes.

10. Teaching is kind and sympathetic, and a good teacher develops emotional stability among children.
11. Teaching is remedial, and the teacher must solve the learning problems of students.
12. Teaching helps children to make adjustments in life.
13. Teaching is a professional activity that helps to bring about harmonious development of children.

Objectives of Teaching

Major objectives of teaching are as follows :

- To bring desired changes in pupils.
- To shape behaviour and conduct.
- Acquisition of knowledge.
- To improve the learning skills of students.
- Formation of belief.
- To provide a social and efficient member to the society.

Educational objectives can cover a range of different types of intended learning outcomes. A documentation from a respected Higher Education Funding Council lists the following: "The acquisition of knowledge, the development of understanding and other general intellectual abilities, the development of conceptual, intellectual and subject-specific skills, the development of generic or transferable skills, and the development of values, of motivation or of attitudes".

These can be summarised in another way as follows:

- **Personal transferable skills.** Includes inter-personal as well as personal skills; includes also most "Enterprise" competencies;
- **Conceptual knowledge and skills.** Also known as "methodological"; *e.g.* critical thinking, writing, creativity, hypothesis design and testing, etc.
- **Discipline-related knowledge and skills.** Subject knowledge and understanding. Subject specific skills (*e.g.* in lab).
- **Attitudinal.** Values, motivation and attitudes.

There should be an appropriate balance between the effort devoted to each of these objectives.

Some of the most important objectives of teaching are:

- Imparting an adequate knowledge of the subject matter.
- Equipping the perspective teachers with necessary pedologic skills.
- Enabling the teacher to acquire understanding of student psychology.
- Developing proper attitudes towards teaching.
- Developing self-confidence.
- Enabling teachers to make proper use of instructional facilities.

LEVELS OF TEACHING

According to **Morris L. Bigge,** *"Teaching-learning situational may be classified on a continuum which ranges from thoughtful to thoughtless modes of operation."*

Memory Level of Teaching (MLT)

According to **Woodsworth,** *"Memory is the direct use of what is learned."*

According to **Rose,** *"A memory is a new experience determined by the dispositions laid down by a previous experience, the relation between the two being clearly apprehended."*

According to **McDougall,** *"Memory implies imagining of events as experienced in the past and recognizing them to ones own past experience.*

It is the first and thoughtless level of teaching. It is concerned with memory or mental ability that exists in all living beings. Teaching at memory level is considered to be the lowest level of teaching. At this level,

- the thinking ability does not play any role.
- students only cram the facts, information, formulas and laws that are taught to them.
- the teaching is nothing but learning the subject matter by rote.
- the role of the teacher is prominent and that of the student is secondary.
- The study material is organized and preplanned. The teacher presents the study material in a sequential order.

Remember

MEMORY LEVEL OF TEACHING

- The facts and the information of the cognitive level are forcibly supplied to the brains of the students.
- Signal learning, chain learning and stimulus – response learning are emphasized.
- Teacher centred.
- Both essay type and objective type examinations are used to evaluate the learn contents.
- This level has the maximum level of motivation.

Memory level teaching lacks insight. Psychologically, it is cognitive level teaching.

Herbart is the exponent of memory level of teaching.
Herbartion steps. (a) *Preparation* – questions are asked to test the previous knowledge. (b) *Statement of aim* – to acquaint the name of the topic. (c) *Presentation* – stimulating the mental activity, the pupils are provided with opportunities of self-learning. (d) *Association* – Mutual relationship is established among facts, events and experiments by comparison. (e) *Generalisation* – principles and laws are formulated for the future life situations.

Objectives of Memory Level Teaching

1. Imparting knowledge and information to the learner.
2. Knowledge or information gained by the learner is factual in nature. It is acquired through memorization or rote learning.
3. It covers only the knowledge-based objectives of Bloom's Taxonomy. At this level, the student learns to identify, recall or remembers the objects, events, ideas and retain them in memory.

Nature of Subject Matter

1. At this level, teaching is subject centered.
2. Simple things are taught to students that can be memorized easily.
3. The subject matter is well organized and is simple in nature so that it can be acquired through rote learning.
4. Subject matter includes the information about simple concepts, terms, and elements related to different things of the world around us.
5. Thus the knowledge delivered to learners is definite, structured and observable.

Method Used

1. We know that at this level of teaching is subject-centered so teacher dominant methods like drill, review, and revision, and asking questions are often used.
2. Drill means repetition or practice for the purpose of attaining proficiency in memorizing the material.
3. Review or revision is considered the method of revising the elements to relate them to new experiences and to form new associations for the development of new skills or learning to solve new problems.

4. Asking question technique is used to examine whether or not knowledge level objectives of teaching have been achieved.

Role of the Teacher

1. The teacher plays a very dominating and authoritarian role.
2. He is the authority to instruct, deliver, direct, control and evaluate performance. He is the stage setter, learning resource and manager of every classroom activity.
3. So, in this level of teaching right from the selection of the subject matter to its evaluation, the key process of teaching and learning remains with the teacher.

Role of Learner

1. In memory level teaching role of the learner is a passive one.
2. This is because contents of the subject matter, teaching tools, and methods employed for teaching are all decided by the teacher.
3. The characteristics of the learner should be taken care of while framing objectives and curriculum, and selecting teaching-learning activities and methods of teaching and evaluation.

Teaching Equipment

1. Teaching equipment work as an assistant in the process of teaching and learning
2. Different kinds of teaching aids like visual, audio and audio-visual aids, e.g. models, charts, maps, pictures, T.V., radio etc. develop a curiosity of the learners towards the subject-matter.
3. The teacher can use a variety of teaching aids to make students attentive to learning.

Merits of Memory Level Teaching

1. Useful for children at lower classes. This is because of intellectual development and they have a rote memory.
2. The role of the teacher is important in this level of teaching and he is free to make choices of subject matter, plan it and can present it at will.
3. The knowledge acquired at memory level teaching forms a basis for the future i.e. when student's intelligence and thinking is required.
4. Memory level teaching acts as the first step for understanding and reflective levels of teaching. It is pre-requisite for understanding level teaching.

Demerits of Memory Level Teaching

1. This does not contribute to the development of the student's capabilities.
2. Since at this level student learns by rote, the knowledge gained does not prove helpful in real life situations as it does not develop the talent of students.
3. The pupils are kept in strict discipline and cramming is insisted on this teaching.
4. Intelligence does not carry any importance in this type of teaching and it lacks motivation.

Understanding Level of Teaching (ULT)

The teaching at the understanding level is of higher quality than the one at memory level teaching. It is more useful and thoughtful. Understanding level of teaching explain pupils about the relationship between principles and facts. It also lets students know where these principles are applicable. For this level of teaching, it is must to get memory level teaching barrier crossed. The understanding level of teaching to propounded by H.C. Morrison.

In the understanding level of teaching, the mental development of the learner is at a higher level than that of memory level. Cognitive abilities of the student are developed. Here students become capable to think, present things logically, analyze them, draw inferences. They are able to evaluate the relationships between the principles and facts.

Elements of understanding levels of teaching:

(1) **Objectives.** According to revised Bloom's Taxonomy, Understanding level teaching aims at the following objectives.

(i) ***Understanding objectives.*** It is the understanding of instructional messages by means of interpreting, exemplifying, classifying, comparing, inferring etc.

(ii) ***Application Objectives.*** It includes the use of a proper procedure for executing and implementing the use of principle/ rules in practical life situations.

(2) **Nature of subject matter.** The content for teaching-learning at this level is quite wide as compared to that needed at memory level teaching. The content also includes the application of the principle/generalizations in due real life situations.

> ***Remember***
>
> **UNDERSTANDING LEVEL OF TEACHING**
>
> ❖ Teacher tries to present his instructions at the understanding level.
>
> ❖ Makes the students understand the generalization, principles and facts.
>
> ❖ Teacher tries to provide more and more opportunities to develop intellectual behaviours of the pupils.
>
> ❖ Both students and the teachers participate in developing the lesson while teaching occurs at the understanding level.

(3) **Methods used.** For achieving objectives like understanding, comprehension and application following methods of teaching could be used.

a. Lecture method
b. Lecture cum demonstration
c. Discussion
d. Inductive-deductive
e. Exemplification and explanation

(4) **Classroom climate.** More likely and encouraging as compared to that of memory level teaching. Learners are actively engaged in the learning process.
This makes the classroom environment positive and enjoyable.

(5) **Nature of motivation.** Motivation at understanding level of teaching is extrinsic as well as intrinsic in nature.

(6) **Teaching equipment.** Teaching becomes very easy and interesting with the help of different teaching aids like: • models • charts • flash cards • pictures etc.
Students can easily comprehend the concept by using various teaching aids. So the teacher should use the right aid/equipment as per the need and level of students.

(7) **Evaluation.** Tools and devices used for evaluation at this level are more comprehensive than that of memory level teaching.
Tests and tools should be properly planned. Planned tests could evaluate the student's ability to comprehend, gasp, analyze, synthesize, discriminate etc.
These abilities can be examined using oral and written tests along with some scope for testing practical knowledge.

(8) **Role of the teacher.** Role of teacher is prominent in the understanding level of teaching. He is the person responsible for presenting learning material. Teacher makes sure that pupil understands the content by making it interesting for them.
In this level of teaching the contents and the sequence of presentation, mode of instruction, methods used in evaluation all remains with is the powers of the teacher.

(9) **Role of learner.** At this level of teaching role of the learner is not so passive like that of the memory level. The learner has to work hard at this level. The learners at this level are secondary and can take some initiative to know further about the contents. Both the teacher and learner interact within the framework set by the teacher to obtain the objectives designed at this level of teaching.

Merits of the Understanding Level of Teaching

1. At this level of teaching students make use of their thinking abilities.
2. Knowledge acquired at this level forms the basis of the reflective level of teaching.
3. Here the teacher presents subject matter before the students in an organized and sequential form. The new knowledge acquired is related to the previously acquired knowledge.
4. Here the students do not learn by rote. Here they learn by understanding the facts and information and their use and purpose.

Advantages of Understanding Level:

- ❖ Effective learning.
- ❖ Development of different cognition abilities.
- ❖ Sets stages for entering into the reflective level of teaching.
- ❖ Effective classroom interaction.

Disadvantages of Understanding Level:

- ❖ It ignore higher cognitive abilities.
- ❖ Less emphasis on intrinsic motivation.
- ❖ No individualized learning.
- ❖ Teacher centered.

Demerits of the Understanding Level of Teaching

Teaching at this level is subject centered. There is no interaction between the teacher and students at this level.

Reflective Level of Teaching (RLT)

This level is also known as introspective level. Reflecting on something means giving careful thought to something over a period of time. It also means thinking deeply about something.

Reflective level of teaching is considered to be the highest level at which teaching is carried out.

- It is highly thoughtful and useful.
- A student can attain this level only after going through memory level and understanding level.
- Teaching at the reflective level enables the students to solve the real problems of life.
- At this level, the student is made to face a real problematic situation. The student by understanding the situation and using his critical abilities succeeds in solving the problem.
- At this level emphasis is laid on identifying the problem, defining it and finding a solution to it. The student's original thinking and creative-abilities develop at this level.
- The role of the teacher in this level of teaching is democratic. He does not force knowledge on the students but develops in their talents and capabilities.
- The role of the students is quite active.
- reflective level of teaching is that which is problem-centered and the student is busy in original imagination.

Remember

REFLECTIVE LEVEL OF TEACHING

- ❖ Includes both understanding memory and understanding level teaching.
- ❖ The management of teaching at memory and understanding – level taken place before reflective level teaching starts.
- ❖ It means "problem-centred" teaching.
- ❖ Provide opportunities for developing intellectual behaviour.

Merits of Reflective Level Teaching

1. The teaching at this level is not teacher-centered or subject-centered, it is learner-centered.
2. There is an interaction between the teacher and the taught at the reflective level teaching.
3. At this level, teaching is appropriate for the higher class.

4. At this level, teaching is highly thoughtful and useful than the teaching at the memory or understanding level.

Demerits of Reflective Level Teaching

1. Not suitable for small children at the lower level of teaching. It is suitable only for mentally matured children.
2. At this level, the study material is neither organized nor pre-planned. Therefore students cannot acquire systematic and organized knowledge of their study courses.

LEVEL OF TEACHING

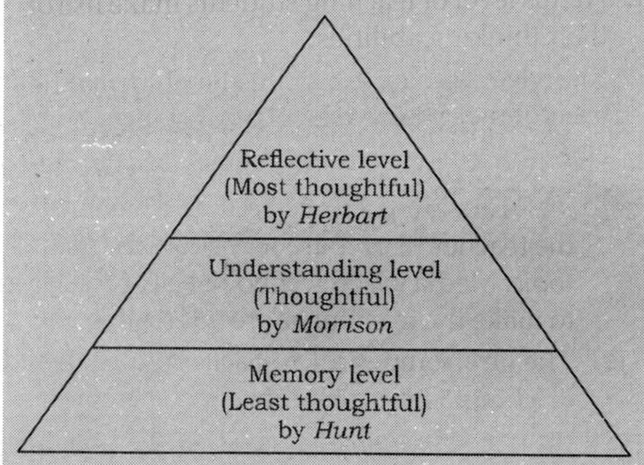

Reflective level (Most thoughtful) by *Herbart*

Understanding level (Thoughtful) by *Morrison*

Memory level (Least thoughtful) by *Hunt*

Basic Requirements of Teaching

Teaching process involves following variables.

1. **Dependent Variable.** The student is a dependent variable. He is subjected to changes and developments through the efforts of the teacher and teaching process. In the process of teaching, the dependent variable plays the functional or active part.
2. **Independent Variable.** The teacher is an independent variable. He is responsible for the functioning of students, the dependent variables. He is free to act in the process while students are quite dependent on him. The teacher plans, organizes, leads and controls the process of teaching. Like dependent variables, independent variables also play the functional or active part.
3. **Intervening Variables.** There is need of desirable interaction between the dependent and the independent variable to achieve the goals of teaching. This role is played by the intervening variables. The content of teaching, methods and techniques, tactics and strategies management of instructional material and teaching environments, etc., are the Intervening Variables.

Basic requirements of teaching are

1. All the three variables of teaching
2. Professionalism
3. Suitable environment
4. Teacher-student relationship
5. Student's discipline
6. Teacher's devotion to teaching, and also on the other hand, student's devotion to learning.

Basic requirements of teaching include,

I. **The Teacher.** The teacher is an innovator of information and knowledge. He is the creator and transmitter of knowledge, values and ethos to our youngsters for latter's physical, mental, emotional and social development. In the process of teaching-learning, the teacher is the main vehicle, and he knows what is right and what is wrong in the society. The teacher masters over his subject and uses an effective language for the communication in order to bring a positive change in the behavior of the learner. Since, it is the age of science and technology, the teacher ought to have a sound knowledge of science and technology. He should therefore use the latest means of media communication in the process of teaching.

II. **The Learner.** The learner is a dependent one and immature. He has to cooperate in the teaching-learning process with the teacher and try to get as much information and knowledge as possible from him. He must follow the teacher for understanding and getting knowledge. The learners may be categorized as the students of primary schools, elementary schools, secondary schools, senior secondary schools, colleges or universities.

III. **The Subject (Topic).** The subject is the main concern in the whole endeavor of teaching and learning process. The topic is generally decided by the teacher but the learner can also contribute in deciding a topic, so that, a balanced and harmonious development takes place. It is for the teacher to prepare necessary charts, maps, tables and models that pertain to the decided topic. Media based technological and scientific aids may also be made available by the teacher to make the teaching more interesting and understandable.

IV. **The Environment.** The learner's growth and all round development are the main objectives of teaching. This is possible only when there is a suitable environment for the teaching-learning process. The teacher as such creates such environment and nurtures the' learner in that environment. Learners are not passive objects. For long, the child or the learner was viewed as a natural or given category. This undermined the importance of the fact that the development of the learner is intimately linked to changes in the sociocultural and historical conditions in a given society.

TEACHING AS A PROFESSION

Professionalism is a complex and elusive concept; it is dynamic and fluid. The certificated teacher is the essential element in the delivery of instruction to students, regardless of the mode of instruction. A teacher has professional knowledge and skills gained through formal preparation and experience. Teachers provide personal, caring service to students by diagnosing their needs and by planning, selecting and using methods and evaluation procedures designed to promote learning.

The processes of teaching include understanding and adhering to legal and legislated frameworks and policies; identifying and responding to student learning needs; providing effective and responsive instruction; assessing and communicating student learning; developing and maintaining a safe, respectful environment conducive to student learning; establishing and maintaining professional relationships; and engaging in reflective professional practice. These processes must be free of discriminatory practices and should contribute to the holistic development of students who are actively engaged, responsible and contributing members of a democratic society.

The Aim of Teaching

There are various modes of teaching. These include conditioning, training, instruction and indoctrination. These are a kind of teaching (or a part of teaching, *i.e.*, whole teaching process include all these) but not a synonym with teaching. Some concepts related to various modes of teaching are as follows:

1. Training helps in shaping conduct and teaching various skills.
2. Distinction between training and education may be made through the evaluation of the degree of intelligent behaviour produced by them.
3. Instruction and indoctrination work on a higher footing than conditioning and training as far as the involvement of intellectual powers and modes of teaching are concerned. But they cannot be equated with teaching.
4. Instruction is mainly concerned with the development of knowledge and understanding in an individual which represents one of many objectives of education and teaching.

5. Teaching is aimed towards shaping a total man, while instruction aims only for the development of intellect and affect the cognitive domain of behaviour. Teaching may include or cover instruction.
6. Indoctrination represents a fairly high level of teaching, shaping beliefs and ideals. Indoctrination may mean teaching but teaching can be done without indoctrination.

To summarize, the aims of teaching with respect to its various modes, are as follows :

- Teaching – To bring changes in the behaviour of students.
- Conditioning – To improve the learning skills of students.
- Training – Shaping the behaviour and conduct.
- Instruction – Acquisition of knowledge.
- Indoctrination – Formation of belief.

Four Modern Concepts of Teaching

1. **Questioning.** It is the most important device of teaching. It occurs in two ways:
   (a) The teacher should ask questions of all types – introductory, developing and recapitulatory.
   (b) In order that the students should be active participants in the lesson, they should be trained to ask questions to the teachers.
2. **Discussion.** Discussion clears the doubts of the students and enhances their ability of expressing opinions. For this purpose the class may be divided into groups. The teacher will direct discussion in such a way that pupils will be encouraged to express their opinions freely and independently. After the discussion, the teacher will classify the main points raised and sort them out into some order.
3. **Investigation.** Investigation may be individual or group and includes the presentation of information by the teacher. Investigation will be followed by expression which may be written, spoken or visual and concrete.
4. **Expression.** This is the last step of teaching. It will be in the form of practical activities under four headings: (a) Passive (b) Active (c) Artistic (d) Organisational Activities.

MICRO-TEACHING

Definition of Micro-teaching

According to Allen and Cooper:

"Micro teaching is a teaching situation which is scaled down in terms of time and numbers of students. Usually, this has meant a four to twenty-minutes lesson involving 3 to 10 students. The lesson is scaled down to reduce some of the complexities of the teaching acts, thus allowing the teacher to focus on selected aspect of teaching."

Aim of Micro Teaching

The main purpose of micro teaching is to provide opportunities for prospective teachers to practice practicing some teaching skills in front of their peers in a constructive atmosphere. Thus, he has integrated mental readiness, skills and performance skills for the provision of actual teaching practices in the classroom.

According to Allen cited in Hasibuan and Moedjiono states that aims of micro teaching as follow:

1. For prospective teachers

(a) Provide real work experience and practice the basic skills of teaching separately.
(b) Prospective teachers can develop teaching skills before they are involved in the real classroom.
(c) Provide the possibility for prospective teachers to gain a variety of student conditions in the classroom.

2. For teachers

(a) Provide refreshment in educational programs.
(b) Teachers gain an individualized teaching experience for their professional development.
(c) Develop an open attitude for teachers to the reforms that take place in the educational curriculum.

LEARNER'S CHARACTERISTICS

Characteristics of Adolescent and Adult Learners (Academic, Social, Emotional and Cognitive)

The concept of learners characteristics is used in the sciences of learning and cognition to designate a target group of learners and define those aspects of their personal, academic, social, or cognitive self that may influence how and what they learn.

Learners characteristics are important for instructional designers as they allow them to design and create tailored instructions for a target group. It is expected that by taking account of the characteristics of learners, more efficient, effective, and/or motivating instructional materials can be designed and developed. Learners characteristics can be: (i) Personal (ii) Academic (iii) Social and emotional (iv) Cognitive.

Characteristics of Adolescent Learner

The young adolescent is going through a period of significant physical, emotional, intellectual, moral and social changes. Since the nature of these changes is at times intense and varied, they need to be recognized and examined by those who direct their learning.

(i) **Academic.** Academic characteristics of learners include the education type, education level and knowledge. In young adolescents, intellectual development is not as visible as physical development, but it is just as intense. During early adolescence, youth exhibit a wide range of individual intellectual development, including meta-cognition and independent thought. They tend to be curious and display wide-ranging interests .

(ii) **Social.** Adolescent social development is often described as the process of establishing a sense of identity and establishing a role and purpose. It is an outward sense of oneself. Body image is a key factor in developing a sense of self and identity, especially for girls, and the family and increasingly peers play an important role assisting and supporting the adolescent to achieve adult roles. Risk-taking is a natural part of the adolescent journey. Social development and emotional development are closely intertwined as young people search for a sense of self and personal identity. They desire to make personal choices. They seek social acceptance and peer relationships in order to conform to group norms. They tend to diminish family allegiances and strengthens peer allegiances but still strongly dependent upon parental values. The actions of adolescents are often based on myths and misinformation.

(iii) **Emotional.** The way a person thinks and feels about themselves and others, their inward thoughts, is key to their emotional development. Adolescents shifts moods rapidly and can become rebellious toward adults. They are sensitive to criticism and easily get offended. Developing and demonstrating individual emotional assets such as resilience, self esteem and coping skills is heightened during adolescence because of the rapid changes being experienced. Schools are important sites for social and emotional learning and have developed policies and programs around student wellness, often with a focus on a strengths-based approach.

(iv) **Cognitive.** It is the process involving thought, rationale and perception. The physical changes of the brain that occur during adolescence follow typical patterns of cognitive development. They are characterized by the development of higher-level cognitive functioning that aligns with the changes in brain structure and function, particularly in the prefrontal cortex region. Adolescence is a sensitive brain period that is a time when brain plasticity is heightened.

Characteristics of Adult Learner

It is always remember that learning is a continuous, ongoing and a lifelong process. It is perhaps the fundamental process for survival and adaptation of human beings to both internal as well the external environment. Each learner has individual learning needs and it is important for the teachers/facilitators to know their learners well. The pedagogy applicable to child learner do not apply to adult learners. Hence the teachers/facilitators of adult learners prior to conceiving, designing or implementing learning programs have to first understand the characteristics of the adult learners.

(i) **Academic.** Adult learners have a vast wealth of knowledge acquired by controlling their environment and experiences of life. Their opinions, values and beliefs are their defining characteristics which they bring to the learning situations. The teachers/facilitators in order not to hurt the self-image of adult learners have to treat them with utmost respect and equality. Any learning process constructed for the adult learners has to be geared to meet the needs of the adult learners. Adults are result-oriented. They have specific expectations for what they will get out of learning activities and will often drop out of voluntary learning if their expectations are not met. Many adults prefer to learn by doing rather than listening to lectures in the classroom.

(ii) **Social.** Mostly many self-directed adult learners prefer a learning community with whom they can interact and discuss questions and issues. Most adult learners have numerous responsibilities and commitments to family, friends, community and work. Carving out time for learning affects adult learners. They want to be treated with respect. Adult learners increasingly develop the ability to work independently and cooperatively with others and across varied circumstances and issues that affect the common well-being and one's own well-being in relationship to the world around them.

(iii) **Emotional.** Adults typically prefer a sense of control and self-direction. Adults like options and choice in their learning environment. Even adults who feel anxiety from self-direction may learn to appreciate this approach if given proper initial support. Depending on their age and physical conditions, adult learners may acquire psychomotor skills more slowly than younger students and have more difficulties reading small fonts and seeing small images on the computer screen.

(iv) **Cognitive.** There are multiple challenges for adult learners due to the natural cognitive decline humans experience as they age. More time is needed to actively process new information. Processing speed is a cognitive ability that could be defined as the time it takes a person to do a mental task. It is related to the speed in which a person can understand and react to the information they receive, whether it be visual (letters and numbers), auditory (language), or movement. In other words, processing speed is the time between receiving and responding to a stimulus. This declines with age and lots of cognitive processes are affected due to this.

Individual Differences in Learning

Individual Differences

No two individuals are exactly similar. Everyone is unique. Even the identical twins differ from each other. Individuals differ in their attitude, aptitude, intelligence, abilities, interests and other personality traits. Usually curriculum is moulded for a general classroom. But it is the duty of the teacher to cater the individual difference of the learner in the teaching learning process through different strategies. Individual differences stand for "those differences which in their totality distinguish one individual from another.

Definitions

1. According to Borich &Tombari (1997), "Individual differences are the variations we observe among members of any group in a particular characteristic, such as temperament, energy level, friendship patterns and parent-child attachment."
2. "Individual differences stand for the variations or deviations among individuals in regard to a single characteristic or a number of characteristics." – Carter B. Good

Areas or varieties of individual differences

- **Physical differences.** Individuals differ in height, weight, colour of skin, colour of eyes and hair, size of hands and heads, arms, feet, mouth and nose, length of waistline, structure and functioning of internal organs, facial expression, mannerisms of speech and walk, and other such native or acquired physical characteristics.
- **Mental Difference.** Individuals differ in intellectual abilities and capacities like reasoning and thinking, power of imagination, creative expression, concentration etc. On the basis of these differences they are usually classified as idiot, imbecile, moron, border line, normal, very superior and genius
- **Differences in Motor Ability.** There exist wide differences in motor abilities such as reacting time, speed of action, steadiness, rate of muscular moment, manual dexterity and resistance to fatigue etc.
- **Differences in Achievement.** Differences exist in achievement and in knowledge even among individuals who have almost the same amount of intelligence and have been subjected to equal amount of schooling and experience.
- **Emotional Differences.** In some individuals, positive emotions like love, affection and amusement and the like are prominent; whereas, in some negative emotions are more powerful. Some are emotionally stable and mature, while others are emotionally unstable and immature.
- **Differences in Interests and Aptitudes.** Variations occur among the individuals in relation to the specific tastes and interests. Individuals are also found to have different aptitudes. Some have mechanical aptitude, while the others have scholastic, musical or artistic aptitudes.
- **Differences in self-concept.** Self concept reflects the images, considerations or judgement about one's abilities and limitations usually held by an individual not only projecting himself before others but also for estimating his self in his own eyes. Low self-image can give rise to low self esteem.
- **Learning differences.** Some learn more easily and are able to make use of their learning more comfortably than others. For some, one method of learning or memorization is more suitable, while for others, a different method suits.
- **Differences in social and moral development.** Some are found to be adjusted properly in the social situations and lead a happy social life while others are socially handicapped, unsocial or antisocial. Similarly, people are found to differ in respect of ethical and moral sense.

Two Factors Effecting Individual Differences

- **Heredity.** (What occurs naturally as a function of the genes) includes all inherited traits.
- **Environment.** (What is learned and communicated in different cultures or other social groups) includes family, socio-economic status, Culture, previous knowledge, experience and gender differences.

Educational Implications of Individual Differences

- In any group there are individuals who deviate from the norms of the group. Along with the average, the presence of very superior and extremely dull is equally possible in a class.
- Every teacher should try to have the desired knowledge of the abilities, capacities, interests, attitudes, aptitudes and other personality traits of his pupils and in the light of this knowledge should render individual guidance to children for the maximum utilization of their potentialities.

- It is wrong to expect uniformity in gaining proficiency or success in a particular field from a group of students. On account of their subnormal intelligence, previous background, lack of proper interest, aptitude and attitude etc. some students lag behind in one or the other area of achievement.
- All students cannot be benefited by a particular method of instruction and a uniform and rigid curriculum.

Role of Teachers/Schools in Meeting the Individual Differences

- A teacher should be sensitive to individual differences.
- A teacher's challenge is to acknowledge and celebrate the differences among children and work to maximize the growth in each child.

Methods to Tackle Individual Differences

1. **Proper knowledge of individual personalities.** The first step in making provisions for individual differences is not how abilities, capacities, interests, aptitudes and other personality traits of individual pupils. For this purpose, frequent assessment in the form of intelligence tests, cumulative record card, interest inventories, attitude scales, aptitude tests and measures for assessing personality traits shall be carried out.
2. **Ability grouping.** In the light of results derived from various tests of knowing individual differences in terms of individual potentialities in various dimensions, the students in a class or area of activity can be divided into homogeneous groups. Such divisions can prove beneficial in adjusting the method of instruction to varying individual differences.
3. **Adjusting the curriculum.** To meet the requirement of varying individual differences among the pupils, the curriculum should be as flexible and differentiated as possible. It should have the provision for a number of diversified courses and curriculum experiences so that the pupils may get opportunity to study and work in the areas of their own interests and abilities. It should provide adjustment to suit the local requirements and potentialities of students of different groups.
4. **Adjusting the methods of teaching.** Considering the varying individual differences, adjustment with regard to the adoption of methods of teaching is very effective. Every teacher should be somewhat free to formulate his own plan and strategy and adopt different instructional procedures which he finds most suited to different pupils. He should follow different procedures or methods of instruction to suit the requirements of varying ability groups of his pupils.
5. **Adopting social programs or methods for individualizing instruction.** Schools may also adopt some social programs or methods of teaching like the Dalton plan, the Winnekta plan, project method or use programmed learning material for enabling students to learn at their own individual pace.
6. **Other causes of individualizing instruction.** For the purpose of individualizing instruction a few practical measures can also prove beneficial :-
   - The student strength of the class or section should be made as small as possible.
   - The teacher should try to pay individual attention to the group under instruction.
   - The teacher should keep in view the individual difference of his students while engaging them in drill or practice work in the class-room or assigning home-task.
   - In case where ability grouping is not possible and more specifically under the prevalent system of class teaching, special coaching and guidance program for both the dull and the gifted children are most helpful.

Levels of Learning – Bloom's Taxonomy and Gagne's Nine Levels of Learning

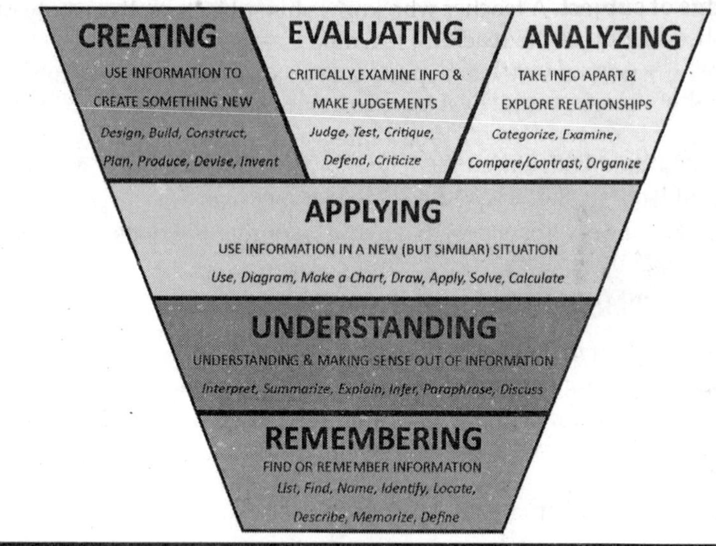

BLOOM'S TAXONOMY

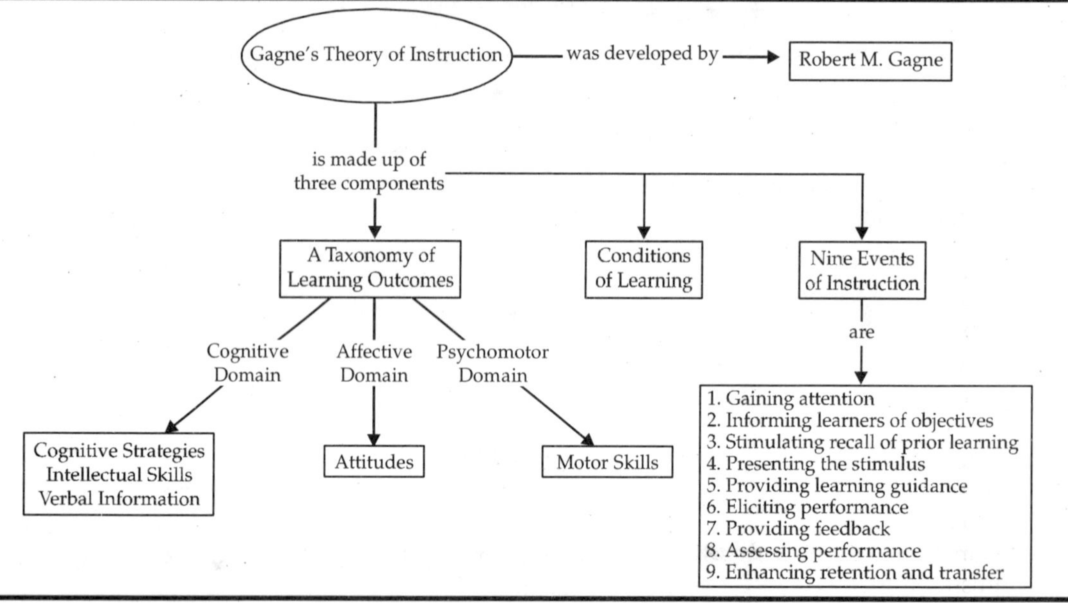

GAGNE'S NINE LEVELS OF LEARNING

FACTORS AFFECTING TEACHING RELATED TO:
Teacher, Learner, Support Material, Instructional Facilities, Learning Environment and Institution

TEACHER

Suppose the learner stands on one end of the ongoing teaching-learning process as one of the pole then teacher act as the other pole for the desired flow of the teaching learning activities in lecture-room. Hence, teacher related factors play quite significant role in the process of teaching. Following are the teacher related factors in the teaching learning process.

i. **Knowledge of subject.** A teacher who knows his subjects well can only play a decisive role in leading the journey of the teaching learning process. How effectively the task of teaching learning will be carried out then depend merely on the scholarly nature and mastery over the subject matter demonstrated by a teacher in the class or work situations.

ii. **Knowledge of learners.** This is a broad category that incorporates knowledge of the cognitive, social and emotional development of learners.

iii. **Teaching Skills.** A teacher may know his subject well but for sharing, communicating and interacting various experience related to the learning of the subject, he needs specific teaching skills.

iv. **Friendliness and Approachability.** Because it's the teacher's job to help students learn, they must be easy to approach. Students will have questions that can't be answered if the teacher isn't friendly and easy to talk to. The unapproachable, mean, arrogant, rude, teacher can't last long. If the students think of their teacher as their enemy, they certainly won't learn much. The best teachers are the most open, welcoming, and easy to approach. A good teacher possess good listening skills and take time out of their busy schedule to solve all kinds of problems of their students.

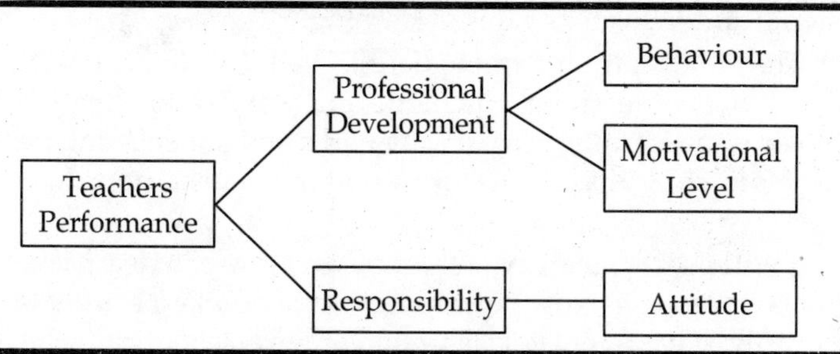

VARIOUS FACTORS EFFECTING TEACHERS PERFORMANCE

v. **Personality and behaviour.** A teacher as a leader has to lead his students in the teaching learning process through the magnetic influence and incredible impression left on the minds of the students on the basis of his personality traits and behavior. He is a role model for his students.

vi. **Level of Adjustment and Mental health of the teacher.** How adjusted a teacher feel in his personal and professional life and the state and level of mental health maintained by the teacher carries much weight in influencing his teacher behavior and teacher effectiveness needed for the effective control and management of the teaching, learning process. While a teacher possessing poor mental health and lack of adjustment in his personal and professional life may prove totally failure in realization of teaching learning objective, a teacher possessing good mental health and adjustment may prove an ideal image to his students and boon to the effectiveness of the teaching learning process.

vii. **Discipline.** In a classroom, a teacher uses discipline to ensure routine is maintained, school rules are enforced, and the students are in a safe learning environment.

LEARNER

The learner is the key figure in any teaching-learning task. How will he learn or what will he achieve depends heavily on his own characteristics and way of learning. Such factors related with him can be described as below:

i. **Learner's physical and mental health.** Teaching-learning is greatly affected by the learner's physical and mental health maintained by him particularly at the time of teaching task. A simple headache or stomach ache can play a havoc with the process and products of learning. Children who did not keep up with satisfactory physical health of the learner at the time of learning become potent factor in deciding the outcome of the l earning. A tense, emotionally and mentally disturbed learner cannot be expected to show satisfactory results in learning.

ii. **Basic potential of the learner.** The results achieved by learner through teaching-learning task depend heavily upon his basic potential to undergo such learning. Such potential may consist of the following things:
   - Learner's innate abilities and capacities for learning a thing.
   - Learner's basic potential in terms of general intelligence and specific knowledge, understanding and skills related to particular learning area.
   - Learner's basic interests, aptitudes and attitudes related to the learning of a particular thing or area.

iii. **The level of aspiration and achievement motivation.** Learning is greatly influenced by the level of aspiration and nature of achievement motivation possessed by the learner. The teacher has to maintain the level of his aspiration and achievement motivation to a reasonable level neither too high causing frustration for non-achievement not too low as not to try for the things for which he is quite capable. In this way, one's level of aspiration and achievement motivation works significantly towards gains in learning.

iv. **Goals in life.** The philosophy and immediate as well as ultimate goals of one's life affect the process and products of learning. His mode and ways of looking towards the things, his inclination towards the learning in a particular area and patience and persistence maintained for continuing his learning despite the heavy odds all depend upon his goals and philosophy of life.

v. **Readiness and will power.** Learner's readiness and power to learn is a great deciding factor about his results in learning. Now power on earth can make a learner learn if he is not ready to learn. Contrarily, if has a will to learn a thing then automatically, he will himself find the way for its effective learning.

SUPPORT MATERIAL

The use and the availability of the study material, audios and videos, on-line courses, on-line tests and other teaching aids also increase the effectiveness of the teaching and learning. These materials aim to support teachers and students in achieving the learning outcomes. The teacher alone cannot provide all the needed condition for an effective teaching and learning process, other supporting materials should be provided.

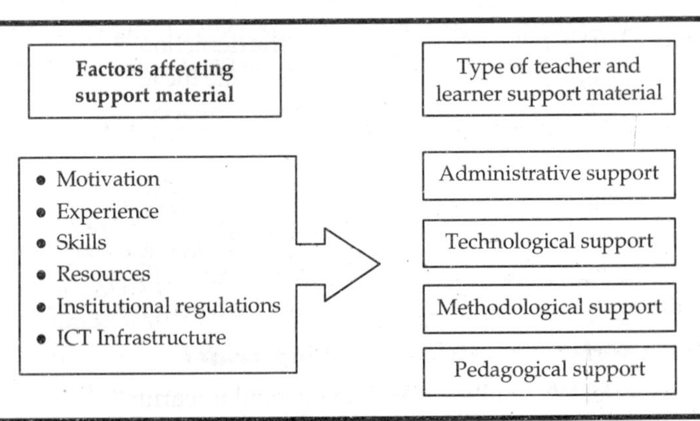

INSTRUCTIONAL FACILITIES

Instructional facilities include the classrooms, laboratories, seminar rooms, seminar rooms, on-campus clinics, cybraries and other spaces used principally for the purpose of delivering formal instruction to students . Their availability ensures effective teaching and if these are not available in adequate amount as per the number of students, then students will not be able to learn properly.

LEARNING ENVIRONMENT

Learning environment refers to the diverse physical locations, contexts, and cultures in which students learn. Since students may learn in a wide variety of settings, such as outside-of-school locations and outdoor environments, the term is often used as a more accurate or preferred alternative to classroom, which has more limited and traditional connotations-a room with rows of desks and a chalkboard.

INSTITUTION

Institutions play a important role in effective teaching. Effectiveness of teaching is also affected by the policies framed by institutions. These policies can give autonomy to the teacher or can control the classroom activity. If the teacher feels extremely controlled, then his performance will suffer. On the other hand, autonomy to teachers to choose teaching methods and classroom activities will bring an element of flexibility.

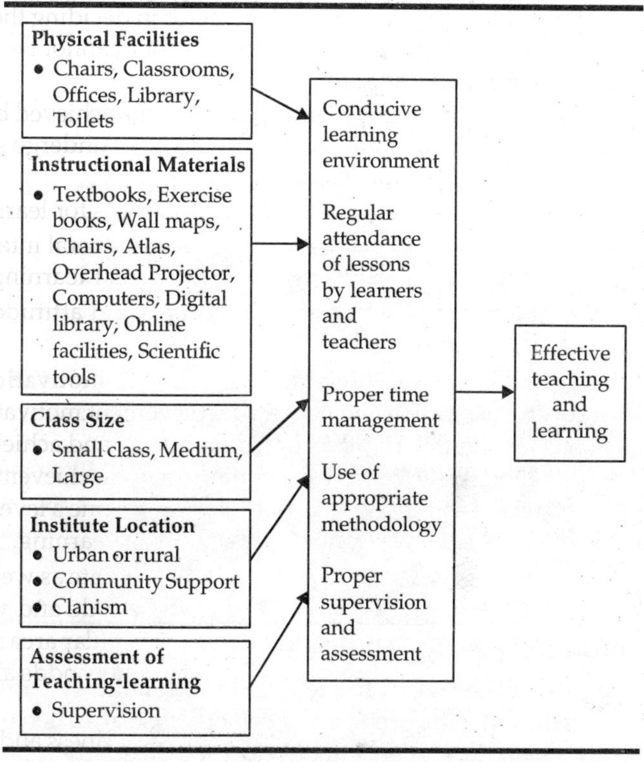

FACTORS OF TEACHING RELATED TO LEARNING ENVIRONMENT AND INSTITUTION

MODELS OF TEACHING

A model of teaching can be defined as the depiction of teaching and learning environment, including the behaviour of teachers and students while the lesson is presented through that model. Models of teaching enable the students to engage in robust cognitive and social task and teach the student how to use them productively. Models of teaching are the specific instructional plans which are designed according to the concerned learning theories. It provides a comprehensive blue print for curriculum to design instructional materials, planning lessons, teacher pupil roles, supporting aids and so forth. Joyce & Weil defines A model of teaching is a description of a learning environment, including our behavior as teachers when that model is used. Eggen defines that Models are prescriptive teaching strategies which help to realize specific instructional goals.

Characteristics of a Good Teaching Model

Each model has built up based on particular learning theory.

- Creation of congenial learning environment in the classroom.
- Effective interaction between the teacher and students.
- Planned use of appropriate strategies.
- Teaching process are systematically, sequentially and logically arranged.
- Clear and specified roles for teachers and students.
- Large scope for supporting material.

- Ensure active participation of entire students in the class.
- It raises the students' level of aspiration, motivation and interest in learning.
- Every model foster and strengthen the cognitive structure of the student.

The Information Processing Family

Models in the information processing family focus on the cognitive activity of child. It includes scientific inquiry for collecting original information, organizing and properly storing of the information. Some models provide the learners with information and concept, some emphasis concept formation and hypothesis testing and still other generate creative thinking.

	Model	Developers (Redevelopers)
1.	Inductive Thinking Model (Classification Oriented)	Hilda Taba (Bruce Joyce)
2.	Concept Attainment Model	Jerome Bruner (Fred Lighthall), (Tennyson and Cocchiarella), (Bruce Joyce)
3.	The Picture-word inductive Model	Emily Calhoun
4.	Scientific Inquiry Model	Joseph Schwab
5.	Inquiry Training Model	Richard Suchman (Howard Jones)
6.	Mnemonics Model (Memory assists)	Michael Pressley (Jeol Levin, Richard Anderson)
7.	Synectics Model	William Gorden
8.	Advance Organizer Model	David Ausubel (Lawton and Wanska)

The Social Family

The focus of the social model family is to build synergy (collective energy) in the classroom for addressing ongoing problems of personal, social, national as well as international importance. Social models help the students to develop Self directed problem solving ability, sense of belongingness towards the society and make them responsible citizens of the country.

	Model	Developers (Redevelopers)
1.	Partners in Learning	David Johnson, Roger Johnson
2.	Structured Inquiry	Robert Salvin (Aronson)
3.	Group Investigation	John Dewy, Herbert Thelen
4.	Role Playing	Fannie Shaftel
5.	Jurisprudential Inquiry	Donald Oliver, James Shaver

The Personal Family

The personal models begin from the perspective of the self-hood of the individual. Individual consciousness and development of unique personality is the chief focus of this family. The models in personal family attempt to make them understand their self and thereby students can shape their future. The cluster of personal models pays great attention to the individual perspective and seeks to encourage productive interdependence, increasing people's self awareness and sense of responsibility for their own destinies.

	Model	Developers
1.	Nondirective teaching	Carl Rogers
2.	Enhancing Self Esteem	Abraham Maslow

The Behavioural System Family

Modification of behavior is the main focus of this family. The stance taken is that human beings are self correcting communication systems that modify behavior in response to the information about how successfully tasks are navigated. The role of predetermined objectives, observable behavior, clearly defined task and methods, feedback and reinforcement are the foundations of models in behavior family.

	Model	Developers
1.	Mastery Learning	Benjamin Bloom, James Block
2.	Direct Instruction	Tom Good, Jere Brophy, Carl Bereiter, Ziggy Engleman, Wes Becker
3.	Simulation	Carl Smith, Mary Smith
4.	Social Learning	Albert Bandura, Carl Thoresen, Wes Becker
5.	Programmed Schedule (Task Performance Reinforcement)	B.F. Skinner

METHODS OF TEACHING IN INSTITUTIONS OF HIGHER LEARNING

The modern education tends to shift from the teacher-centered to the student-centered learning. In actuality, the development of the modern education stimulates educators and students to change their traditional approach to education and to learning. At this point, it is worth mentioning the fact that student-centered approach becomes particularly effective in the contemporary environment because students tend to become more and more autonomous in the course of learning. The latter results from the emerging need for students to learn independently of their teachers and, what is even more important, students need to carry on learning even after the end of their education.

Behar – Horenstein (2006) and many other studies distinguish between: (i) Teacher centred, (ii) Student-centred (Learner centred).

Moston and Ashworth (1986) defines according to **Doherty** (2003) a list of teaching methods.

(i) **Style A Command** - teacher makes all decisions.
(ii) **Style B Practice** - Students carry out teacher-prescribed tasks.
(iii) **Style C Reciprocal** - Students work in pairs: one performs, the other provides feedback.
(iv) **Style D Self-check** - Students assess their own performance against criteria
(v) **Style E Inclusion** - Teacher planned. Student monitors own work.
(vi) **Style F Guided Discovery** - Students solve teacher set movement problems with assistance.
(vii) **Style G Divergent** - Students solve problems without assistance from the teacher.
(viii) **Style H Individual** - Teacher determines content. Student plans the programme.
(ix) **Style I Learner Initiated** - Student plans own programme. Teacher is advisor.
(x) **Style J Self Teaching** - Student takes full responsibility for the learning process.

Teacher-centred Method

In teacher-centred methods, students put all of their focus on the teacher and the students exclusively listen. During activities, students work alone, and collaboration is discouraged.

Pros

- When education is teacher-centred, the classroom remains orderly. Students are quiet, and you retain full control of the classroom and its activities.
- Because students learn on their own, they learn independence and make their own decisions.
- Because you direct all classroom activities, you don't have to worry that students will miss an important topic.

Cons

- When students work alone, they don't learn to collaborate with other students, and their communication skills may suffer.
- Teacher centred instruction can be boring for students. Their minds may wander, and they may miss important facts.
- Teacher centred instruction doesn't allow students to express themselves, ask questions, and direct their own learning.

Learner-centred Method (Student Centred)

When a classroom operates with student-centred instruction, students and instructors share the focus. Instead of listening to the teacher exclusively, students and teachers interact equally. Group work is encouraged, and students learn to collaborate and communicate with one another.

Pros

- Students learn important communicative and collaborative skills through group work.
- Students learn to direct their own learning, ask questions, and complete tasks independently.
- Students are more interested in learning activities when they can interact with one another and participate activity.

Cons

- Because students are talking, classrooms may often be noisy or chaotic.
- Teachers may have to attempt to manage all students' activities at once, which can be difficult when students are working on different stages of the same project.
- Because the teacher doesn't always deliver instruction to all students at once, some students may miss important facts.
- Some students prefer to work alone, so group work can become problematic.

Off-line vs On-line Methods

Teaching in the 21st century definitely is riddled with technology that brings the ability to offer students anytime, anywhere performance possibilities for course work. But generally is this flexibility in an on-line delivery format as efficient as pretty the traditional for all intents and purposes face-to-face learning experience. As the trend toward on-line education intensifies, it for the most part leaves in its wake a series of questions that for all intents and purposes remain unanswered regarding the actually overall efficiency of these on-line courses versus their in-class (*i.e.,* in a definitely big way off-line) counterparts, or so they mostly thought. Research comparing on-line versus pretty face-to-face learning for all intents and purposes is mixed, with results ranging from on-line superiority to no difference to basically face-to-face superiority, which is fairly significant. Many results can particularly be traced to sample or method differences, or so they kind of thought. This paper improves on previous efforts by using on-line and face-to-face samples of the same course, same student population and same instructor and applying a new approach to analysis.

DIFFERENCE

On-line Methods	Off-line Methods
• Use of internet	• Traditional methods
• Comfort level	• Requires lot of effort
• Audio and Video	• Strict rules and guidelines
• Save time, effort and money	• Need to be physically present
	• Requires more time and money

Swayam

SWAYAM is a programme initiated by Government of India and designed to generally achieve the three cardinal principles of Education Policy viz., access, equity and quality, pretty contrary to popular belief. The objective of this effort is to mostly take the best teaching learning resources to all, including the most disadvantaged. SWAYAM seeks to bridge the digital divide for students who really have hitherto remained untouched by the digital revolution and mostly have not been able to join the mainstream of the knowledge economy, or so they generally thought. This for the most part is done through an indigenous developed IT platform that facilitates hosting of all the courses, taught in classrooms from 9th class till post-graduation to be accessed by anyone, anywhere at any time.

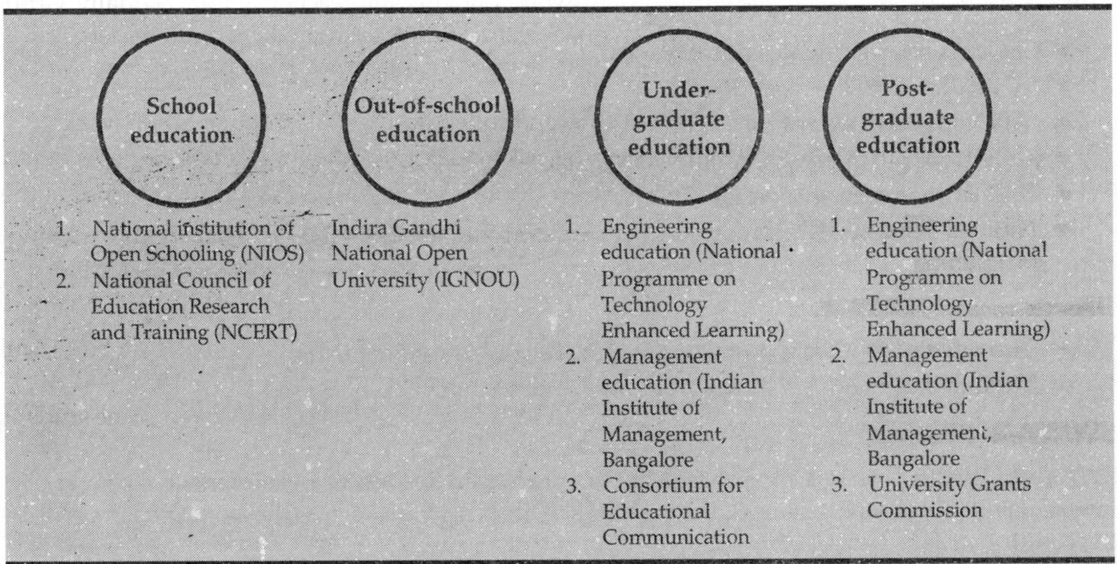

SWAYAM ON-LINE COURSE.

All the courses essentially are interactive, prepared by the best teachers in the country and mostly are available, generally free of cost to the residents in India in a particularly big way. More than 1,000 specially chosen faculty and teachers from across the Country have definitely participated in preparing these courses.

What is offered in SWAYAM

- Courses that are taught in classrooms from 9th class till post-graduation.
- The courses hosted on SWAYAM is in 4 quadrants–
  - video lecture
  - specially prepared reading material that can be downloaded/printed
  - self-assessment tests through tests and quizzes and
  - an online discussion forum for clearing the doubts.
- Categories of courses include - Engineering, Science, Humanities, Management, Language, Mathematics, Arts and Recreation, Commerce, General, Library, Education.
- Courses delivered through SWAYAM are available free of cost to the learners.
- Students wanting certifications need to register and shall be offered a certificate on successful completion of the course, with a little fee.
- At the end of each course, there will be an assessment of the student through proctored examination and the marks/grades secured in this exam could be transferred to the academic record

of the students. UGC and AICTE have already issued the UGC (Credit Framework for online learning courses through SWAYAM) Regulation 2016 advising the Universities to identify courses where credits can be transferred on to the academic record of the students for courses done on SWAYAM.

National Coordinators of SWAYAM

In order to ensure best quality content are produced and delivered, seven National Coordinators have been appointed. They are as follows:

- AICTE for Annual Refresher Programme in Teaching for faculty of the Engineering/University/Institutions
- NPTEL for engineering
- UGC for post-graduation education
- CEC for under-graduate education
- NCERT for school education
- NIOS for school education
- IGNOU for out of the school students
- IIMB for management studies
- National Institute of Technical Teachers Training and Research (NITTTR) for teacher training programme

How to access SWAYAM

- Through the SWAYAM portal on the web - https://swayam.gov.in.
- Through the SWAYAM mobile apps for - Android and iOS.

SWAYAM Prabha

SWAYAM Prabha is an initiative of the Ministry of Human Resources Development to provide 34 High Quality Educational Channels through DTH (Direct to Home) across the length and breadth of the country on 24×7 basis.

It has curriculum-based course content covering diverse disciplines. This is primarily aimed at making quality learning resources accessible to remote areas where internet availability is still a challenge.

The DTH channels are using the GSAT-15 satellite for programme telecasts.

Scope of the Channels

The SWAYAM PRABHA has new content everyday for at least (4) hours which would be repeated 5 more times in a day, allowing the students to choose the time of their convenience. The channels are uplinked from BISAG, Gandhinagar. The contents are provided by NPTEL, IITs, UGC, CEC, IGNOU, NCERT and NIOS. The INFLIBNET Centre maintains the web portal.

The DTH Channels covers the following:

- **Higher Education.** Curriculum-based course contents at post-graduate and under-graduate level covering diverse disciplines such as arts, science, commerce, performing arts, social sciences and humanities, engineering, technology, law, medicine, agriculture, etc. All courses would be certification-ready in their detailed offering through SWAYAM, the platform being developed for offering MOOCs courses.
- **School education (9-12 levels)** modules for teacher's training as well as teaching and learning aids for children of India to help them understand the subjects better and also help them in preparing for competitive examinations for admissions to professional degree programmes.
- **Curriculum-based courses** that can meet the needs of life-long learners of Indian citizens in India and abroad.

- **Assist students (class 11th & 12th)** prepare for competitive exams.

LIST OF CHANNELS

Channel No.	Channel Name	Route/Parent
	Channels 01-10 are managed by CEC, New Delhi.	
1	Channel 01: VAGEESH: CEC/UGC: Humanities-1, Language and Literature	EMRC, EFLU, Hyderabad
2	Channel 02: SANSKRITI: CEC/UGC: Humanities-2, Arts, History, Philosophy and related Subjects	CEC, New Delhi
3	Channel 03: PRABODH: CEC/UGC: Social Science-1, Sociology, Political Science and related subjects	EMRC Jodhpur
4	Channel 04: SAARASWAT: CEC/UGC: Social Science-2, Education, Psychology, Home Science and related subjects	CEC, New Delhi
5	Channel 05: PRABANDHAN: CEC/UGC: Social Science-3, Management, Library Science, Information Science and related subjects	MCRC Jamia Milia
6	Channel 06: VIDHIK: CEC/UGC: Social Science-4, Law, Legal Studies, Human Rights and related subjects	EMRC Patiala
7	Channel 07: KAUTILYA: CEC/UGC: Economics, Commerce and Finance	EMRC Ahmadabad
8	Channel 08: ARYABHATT: CEC/UGC: Physical sciences, Mathematics, Physics, Chemistry and related Subjects	EMRC, University of Calicut
9	Channel 09: SPANDAN: CEC/UGC: Life Sciences, Botany, Zoology, Bio-Science and related subjects	EMRC, Kashmir University, Srinagar
10	Channel 10: DAKSH: CEC/UGC: Applied Sciences, Allied Physical and Chemical sciences and related subjects	EMRC, Anna University, Chennai
	Channels 11 to 18 are Managed by NPTEL	
11	Channel 11: NPTEL: Chemical Engineering, Chemistry and related Subjects	IIT Kharagpur
12	Channel 12: NPTEL: Civil Engineering and related subjects	IIT Delhi
13	Channel 13: NPTEL: Computer Science and Engineering	IIT Kharagpur
14	Channel 14: NPTEL: Electrical engineering, Electronics and Communication Engineering and related subjects	IIT Delhi
15	Channel 15: NPTEL: Engineering Sciences and general subjects for engineering	IIT Madras
16	Channel 16: NPTEL: Humanities, Social Sciences and Management	IIT Kanpur
17	Channel 17: NPTEL: Mechanical Engineering and related subjects	IIT Kanpur
18	Channel 18: NPTEL: Mathematics, Physics, Metallurgy and related subjects	IIT Tirupati/IIT Madras
	Channels 19-22 are managed for high School students by IIT Delhi and is called IIT PAL	
19	Channel 19: IIT PAL: Biology	IIT PAL 1 IIT Delhi
20	Channel 20: IIT PAL: Chemistry	IIT PAL 2, IIT Delhi
21	Channel 21: IIT PAL: Mathematics	IIT PAL 3, IIT Delhi
22	Channel 22: IIT PAL: Physics	IIT PAL 4, IIT Delhi
	Channels 23 to 24 are managed by IGNOU New Delhi.	
23	Channel 23: IGNOU: Liberal Arts and Humanities	IGNOU, New Delhi
24	Channel 24: IGNOU: Agriculture, Vocational and Allied Sciences	IGNOU, New Delhi
	Channel 25 is managed by the NIOS, New Delhi.	
25	Channel 25: NIOS: D.El.Ed (Regional Language)	NIOS, New Delhi
	Channel 26 is managed by IGNOU New Delhi.	
26	Channel 26: IGNOU: State Open Universities' programs	IGNOU, New Delhi

Channel No.	Channel Name	Route/Parent
	Channels 27 and 28 are managed by the NIOS, New Delhi.	
27	Channel 27: NIOS: Secondary School Education	NIOS, New Delhi
28	Channel 28: NIOS: Higher Secondary School Education	NIOS, New Delhi
	Channels 29 is managed by UGC-INFLIBNET,Gandhinagar.	
29	Channel 29: UGC-INFLIBNET (PG Subject's & YOGA)	UGC-INFLIBNET, Gandhinagar
	Channel 30 is managed by the NIOS, New Delhi.	
30	Channel 30: NIOS: Gyanamrit	NIOS, New Delhi
	Channel 31 is managed by NCERT	
31	Channel 31: NCERT: School and Teacher Education	NCERT, New Delhi
	Channel 33 is managed by IGNOU and NIOS jointly	
32	Channel 32: IGNOU and NIOS: Teacher Education	IGNOU and NIOS, New Delhi
	Channel 34 is managed by NCERT	
33	Channel 33: Class 11 PMeVIDYA	NCERT, New Delhi
	Channel 33 is managed by NCERT	
34	Channel 34: Class 12 PMeVIDYA	NCERT, New Delhi

MOOCs

A massive open online course (MOOC) is a free web-based distance learning program that is designed for large numbers of geographically dispersed students.

A MOOC may be patterned on a college or university course or be less structured. Although they do not always offer academic credits, these courses may offer a certification, enhance employment opportunities or further studies. Typically, MOOCs are used for higher education and career advancement. But due to the coronavirus pandemic, many public school districts and undergraduate degree programs have implemented MOOCs as the new standard.

How do MOOCs Work?

MOOCs are online courses that a student accesses through the internet. Typically, these courses consist of traditional class materials made accessible online, which may include the following:

- filmed or recorded video lectures;
- readings;
- problem sets;
- online quizzes and examinations;
- interactive learning modules; and
- interaction with other students via forums.

Typically, each MOOC will include a course provider and a course platform. A course provider is often a university, which supplies the course materials and instructors. The platform – such as EdX, Canvas, Coursera or Udacity – provides the technological infrastructure for course modules, user access and other learning resources.

Finding MOOCs

Providers of MOOCs are mostly universities but may also be corporate entities. Top educational institutions and universities, such as Harvard, the Massachusetts Institute of Technology (MIT) and Stanford, are leading providers of online courses. Corporations such as Microsoft and Accenture also provide publicly available online courses. When searching for a MOOC to take, it is important to make sure that the course aligns with the student's education and career goals.

Courses that require live attendance and adherence to a course schedule are called synchronous courses, whereas flexible, self-paced courses are called asynchronous courses.

Credentials and MOOC-based Degrees

MOOCs can also be used for continuing education certifications and degree programs. MOOC certification levels typically fall into the following six general categories: (i) Free, (ii) Certificates, (iii) Micro credential, (iv) University credit, (v) Online degree (vi) Corporate training.

Benefits of MOOCs

The widespread adoption and use of online courses provides the following benefits:

- No physical location dependence.
- Improved access to higher education.
- Affordability of higher education.
- Flexible learning schedule.

Drawbacks of MOOCs

- Flexibility can make the course more difficult to manage, as some students require the structure of in-person learning.
- A University of Texas study of online course completion rates found that MOOC completion rates are just 6.8%, significantly lower than in-person courses. Students may not feel as committed to attend a free online course as they would an in-person course that requires tuition.
- Instructors are less accessible.
- Digital literacy is required for effective use.
- Students are less likely to form relationships with instructors and other students.
- Students with visual or auditory disabilities may not be accommodated.
- Courses require strong internet connections, which can be an issue in developing countries and underprivileged communities.
- When searching for the right course, large amounts of similar courses for saturated areas, such as computer science, may lead to a paradox of choice.

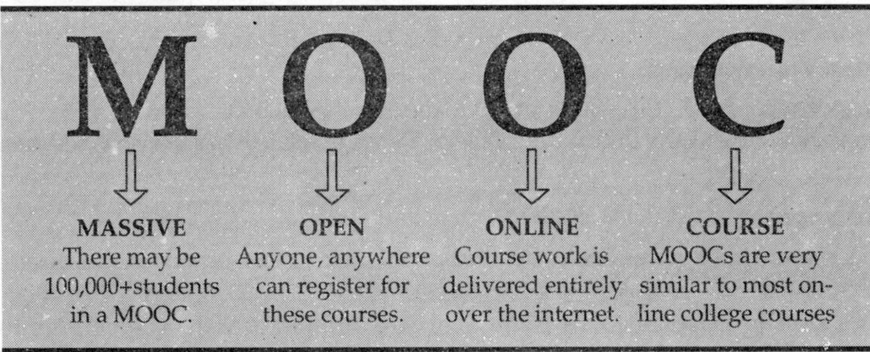

Effective Online Teaching Methods

Traditional forms of teaching around the world are changing rapidly with the advancement of technology. Even in physical classrooms, technology has taken on a bigger role, changing how lessons are delivered and received.

While there are numerous teaching methods, most of the traditional methods used in class can be applied equally efficiently online. However the teaching method you select will change based on your teaching philosophy, objectives, subject area, and classroom demographics.

Listed below are some of the most effective methods of online teaching.

Presentations

Presentations, like in the physical classroom, are one of the most common methods of online teaching. This technique helps make a more significant impact on students – most of whom are visual learners – than a teacher simply relaying information out of a textbook.

Most importantly, presentations allow you to incorporate visuals (images, GIFs, videos, etc.) which makes it easier to deliver and comprehend complex information and data while making the lesson more engaging. Plus you can also share your presentation with the students after the lesson for revision and studying.

Online, presentations are more effective when delivered over video conferencing with a tool like Zoom or Google Meet.

Online Whiteboard

Online whiteboards have risen as a popular choice to virtually emulate the in-person classroom experience shared between teachers and students. They offer an infinite canvas, shape libraries to create different diagrams and charts, pre-made templates, sketching, typing, image import options, etc.

Unlike the traditional whiteboards, they also let you digitize the content created, hence allowing you to re-share them and refer to them at a later time. You can also collaborate with students on the same canvas in real-time which paves the way to:

- Carry out assignments
- Mind mapping
- Review homework and leave feedback
- Brainstorm around lessons
- Do interactive exercises such as quizzes

Live Online Classes

Technology has made it straightforward to deliver lectures online even if you are not in the same room as the students, replicating many of the elements of face-to-face interaction.

Using video conferencing tools you can connect and communicate with students across the globe to deliver lessons. Incorporating an online whiteboard, you can make the classes even more engaging.

Pre-Recorded Video Lectures

The benefit of pre-recorded lectures, as opposed to the live ones, is that the former allows the students to learn at their own pace at any time without the presence of the teacher. It also gives them material to go over during revision.

Flipped Classroom

The flipped classroom has become one of the most popular teaching methods in education during the past few years.

It entails a strategy opposite to the traditional class format; here the students are required to review class material prior to the actual lesson, hence reserving actual in-class time to put what they have learned into test with teacher-guided activities such as debates, problem-solving, in-depth discussions, quizzes, etc.

Some of the other effective techniques for the flipped classroom include,

- Online quizzes - help students self-regulate what they have learnt and further improve their comprehension of the subject.
- Polls - help students reflect and analyze what they have learned by polling their own choices.
- Infographics - increase student engagement and enhances memory.
- Mind maps or word clouds - allow students to brainstorm around topic areas and develop their thinking skills.

Game-Based Teaching

Game-based learning is a popular technique used to improve student engagement and retain attention. This approach helps reduce student anxiety and increase their involvement, especially when teaching complex concepts. It also paves the way for weaker students to develop their competences by interacting actively with their classmates.

Depending on the game you select, here are a few tips to keep in mind when carrying it out online:

- Ensure that all students in the virtual classroom have access to the same set of data. You can share your screen or communicate them to your audience using a video conferencing tool.
- Use the chat option to take down concerns and questions of students and clarify and you can answer them live.
- Allow students to carry out discussions using chat platforms such as WhatsApp, Skype, Slack, Facebook, Zoom breakout rooms, etc.

Class Blog

A blog can be a great place for students to share what they have learned in the form of in-depth articles. Students can work on blog posts individually or in groups. It's a great strategy to improve students' research skills and encourage them to explore self-learning.

The teacher can also use the blog as a platform to share learning material for the lessons.

Live Chatting

Live chatting is another great way to replicate the real-time discussions that take place in the classroom. Platforms such as Slack, WhatsApp, Facebook Messenger, Skype, etc. allow students and teachers to communicate and brainstorm around lessons. The chat itself will provide the students with information for revising before exams or assignments.

Make sure to set clear guidelines to ensure that all students get an equal chance to communicate their ideas and pose their questions.

Discussion Boards and Forums

These tools provide students the space to share what they have learned or what they want to know more about with others in the classroom including the teacher.

You can maintain different discussion boards for individual lesson topics, so it'll be more organized. You can create one easily with an online visual workspace like Creately and share it with all students with one public edit link giving everyone quick access.

REFLECTIVE TEACHING

Reflective Teaching (RT) is a self-assessment of teaching, wherein an instructor examines their pedagogy, articulates reasons and strengths for their strategies, and identifies areas for revision or improvement. RT involves an examination both of one's underlying beliefs about teaching and learning and their alignment with actual classroom practice, throughout a course and afterwards. RT operates as an umbrella term denoting a variety of practices, including teaching inventories and observation protocols, self-assessments, and consideration of student evaluations.

When teaching reflectively, instructors think critically about their teaching and problem-solve for solutions to recurring issues, rather than relying on unchanging, established personal norms. This critical analysis can draw on a variety of sources: Brookfield (2017) lays out four crucial sources, including "students' eyes, colleagues' perceptions, personal experience, and theory and research." Instructors can use a variety of tools and approaches to learn from these sources and reflect upon their teaching, ranging from low-key to formal, and personal to inter-collegial.

TEACHING SUPPORT SYSTEM: TRADITIONAL MODERN AND ICT BASED

When we talk about teaching methods then our society divides into three groups; one group favours the traditional teaching methods, second group favours modern teaching methods and third group is the one who supports the combination of both for effective teaching.

Traditional Method of Teaching

In the traditional method of teaching, teaching happens within the four walls of the classroom. Here, the teacher is the sole source of knowledge. It's a teacher-centric method that promotes the supremacy of the teacher within the classroom setup. Also, every aspect of learning proceeds as per their will. The teacher:

- Has full control over the learning environment.
- Decides the teaching methodology.
- Determines the course curriculum.

In the traditional method of teaching, teachers followed the drill and rote method of memorization. In this method, children learn through repetition and memorization. There is little or no scope for critical thinking.

Nowadays, with online courses gaining popularity, this method definitely sounds outdated. But in educational institutions, it is still the accepted model. But it is important to note that, today, the traditional method of learning has adopted a new form.

- The classroom set-up remains the same, but there is more space for experimentation.
- Teachers are still the head of the classroom because they accommodate the needs of students to create an effective teaching model.
- Teachers deliver lectures, but presentations and seminars are part of the course curriculum.

So, today, we have the traditional method of teaching at the core of our education system. But there is a mix of certain modern elements to keep it in sync with the changing times.

Features of Traditional Learning

- Learning happens in a physical space, within the four walls of a classroom.
- In a traditional learning method, the teacher is in complete control of the learning environment.
- Learning happens at a predetermined pace and schedule.
- Face-to-face interaction between the teacher and students.
- Strict reliance on textbooks.
- All students learn within the same environment.

Advantages of Traditional Learning

- The traditional method of teaching has immense scope for active learning. Students learn through personal interactions with their fellow students. This creates an active learning environment and helps them develop their communication skills.
- Traditional learning develops the student's mind and their social self. They build interpersonal relationships with their teachers and other students of their age group and, with them, learn the ways of the world.
- In the traditional learning method, there is space for practical aspects of learning. For instance, chemistry, or biology experiments best happen within a traditional laboratory. Also, school playgrounds are best suited to enhance the mobility of children in a safe set-up.

- As traditional learning happens on-campus, students have access to libraries, canteens, and other facilities.
- With this method, the question of the digital divide never surfaces.
- The traditional teaching method aims to teach students the importance of time management. There is a proper timetable that students and teachers need to follow.
- This method is best for hands-on training as it establishes direct contact between teachers and students.

Disadvantages of Traditional Learning

- The disadvantages of traditional learning were most strongly felt during the covid times. Education came to a standstill during the consecutive lockdowns because face-to-face interaction became an impossibility. It introduced us to the importance of online teaching, and since then, online lessons have grown in significance.
- As traditional learning is time and location-bound, there is no flexibility.
- Traditional learning is not adaptive to the needs of children. The teacher-centric approach prioritizes the preferences of the teachers over the needs of each student. The teacher follows the methodology that they think is best for students and seldom leaves any space for improvisation.
- Traditional teaching is quite expensive as compared to online teaching. It involves infrastructure and maintenance costs.
- While a traditional classroom set-up offers a lot of space for practical learning, the focus is mostly on theory-based lessons. The strict schedule doesn't leave much time for practical learning.
- In the traditional method of teaching, the daily commute becomes a big disadvantage. This might place a financial burden on students or even obstruct the effective learning process. For instance, during heavy rains, other natural calamities or disease outbreaks, the learning process gets hindered.

The Need For Modern Teaching

The education sector has consistently evolved and transformed over the decades to adapt to modern-day developments, particularly in the fields of science and technology. Subsequently, changes were also made to the manner in which education is imparted from the grassroots level up. Therefore, the latest teaching methods, with modern learning and teaching strategies, must be both knowledge- and technology-driven. This is important to thrive and progress in society as a whole.

Modern teaching techniques avoid spoon-feeding students and encourage creative thinking and problem-solving. This is done by concentrating on developing application-based skills and learning in a manner that's relevant to the increasing needs.

With an emphasis on innovation and generating curiosity, new teaching techniques inspire the entrepreneurial spirit, a crucial vehicle in the development of society. The traditional approach of memorizing and reciting, implemented on a mass scale, leads to a stagnated society. Modern teaching methods, on the other hand, foster progression.

The scope of knowledge has increased. We are no longer isolated from one another, and there is a global exchange of information. This has also resulted in an increase in the human potential to adapt to and imbibe global knowledge. This can be done through new strategies and techniques of teaching so that education is more holistic.

Lastly, by emphasizing an exploratory approach, modern learning methods shift focus from parroting to discovering and researching unexplored areas across different fields.

Characteristics of New Teaching Methods

Known to be a constructivist approach, modern teaching differs from traditional teaching methods. Students aren't instructed to memorize and recite. Instead, modern teaching methods emphasize that learning objectives be met through classroom interaction, collaboration and active participation in engaging activities. Some characteristics of modern teaching styles are listed below:

1. **Learner-Centric.** The curriculum and lessons are created in such a manner that a teacher is simply there to facilitate and support learning, whereas a student is central and predominant in classroom activities and interactions.
2. **Collaborative Approach.** New teaching methods pave the way for students to cooperate and appreciate the work of their peers.
3. **Integrative.** Modern teaching styles result in students gaining knowledge of not just one topic but also those that are relative and supplemental to the main topic.
4. **Interactive.** Modern teaching techniques stress an interactive setting a student is asked to work in groups as well as individually to promote better decision-making and problem-solving.
5. **Inclusive.** Modern teaching methods focus on identifying the individual skill-set of a student while maintaining a collaborative approach, thereby supporting the student to learn at their own pace.
6. **Active Participation.** Modern teaching methods consist of engaging activities and practical learning rather than passive consumption.

Modern Teaching Methods

New teaching techniques impart knowledge in such a manner that it generates curiosity among the students. Technology and global exchange of information have played a vital role in doing so, causing a shift in the conventional classroom dynamic. To account for this shift, teachers make use of some of the following new teaching methods:

1. **Collaborative Learning.** Learning in isolation is a thing of the past. The approach taken via modern teaching is to provide students with a platform to work and learn together to achieve synergy.
2. **Spaced Learning.** To reinforce a particular lesson, a teacher will repeat the lesson multiple times, with 10-minute intervals, this is done to allow the brain to refresh, usually through physical activity or mindfulness techniques.
3. **Flipped Classroom.** In this technique, students are asked to do the preliminary work of a particular lesson at home, such as watching a video tutorial or conducting an online search. The homework (traditionally done at home) is then completed in class to optimize the time and learning experience of the students.
4. **Self-Learning.** Modern teaching techniques encourage self-dependency. By planting the seeds of curiosity, students are pushed toward exploring the subjects they find the most interesting in more depth.
5. **Gamification.** Teaching through video games has served as one of the most useful modern teaching strategies, particularly in the elementary and preschool systems, this relatively new teaching technique is an effective modern teaching method in higher education.
6. **VAK Teaching.** Visual, audio and kinesthetic (movement) teaching, or vak teaching, is a latest teaching method where teachers identify the category in which a student falls-that is, whether they are visual learners, audio learners or kinesthetic learners, upon this categorization, a teacher can better prepare a lesson to cater to their individual abilities

7. **Crossover Learning.** Crossover learning is a mixture of formal and informal learning in crossover learning, formal classroom learning is accompanied by the use of the students' everyday experiences and interactions with their surroundings, which forms the informal part of this method of learning.

Of these latest teaching methods, four modern teaching methods are predominantly used at the preschool and school levels. These are gamification, spaced learning, VAK teaching and collaborative learning. Apart from these, there are certain methodologies that every modern day teacher must integrate into their teaching. These methodologies are slowly but steadily changing the educational environment and have been shown to improve academic performance. A few are given below:

1. **Project-based Learning.** Project-based learning requires a teacher to provide a student with projects that may tackle real-life scenarios instead of relying on theoretical knowledge gathering, project-based learning also encourages the development of supplemental competencies such as critical thinking and communication.
2. **Problem-solving Learning.** This is a cyclic methodology wherein answering the posited questions leads to further questions, thereby jolting curiosity in a student, the problem-solving technique encourages creative thinking and improves problem-solving abilities.
3. **Design-thinking.** Design thinking as a modern teaching methodology promotes innovative ideas and creative thinking by designing problems that trigger the creative minds of the students.
4. **Thinking-based Learning.** The primary goal of this methodology is to move beyond the conventional method of memorization by converting information to knowledge via contextualization and analysis.
5. **Competency-based Learning.** In this methodology, the students' core competency is identified and nurtured so that a functional work habit may be established.

Advantages of Modern Teaching Methods

Modern teaching methods have many advantages. However, these advantages are the disadvantages of traditional teaching methods.

- Unlike traditional teaching methods, modern teaching methods are more interactive and keep students intact. It maintains the interest of students by animations and videos.
- The visual medium is way better than any other medium to give instructions. It helps to memorize the concept fast and for a more extended period than reading.
- Modern teaching methods are less time-consuming. Teachers take less time to cover the syllabus. Writing on the blackboard is not required.
- Blackboard explanation of content is less explanatory than a representation of videos and animations used in the modern teaching techniques.

Modern teaching methods that are being Adopted in Schools:

- Classrooms are being equipped with technology.
- Evaluations are being done at all stages.
- Crossover learning.
- Focus more on an understanding of concepts.
- Skill development and values development are put in the most crucial place.
- Interactive whiteboards.
- Collaborative learning
- Emphasis on practical knowledge more.

- Activity-based and gaming based learning.
- Integrative and research-based learnings.
- Use of the internet and web.
- Collaborative learning
- Flipped Classroom
- Problem-based learning
- Learner-centered.
- VAK learning.

ICT Based Methods

Information and Communication Technology (ICT) in education is the mode of education that use information and communications technology to support, enhance, and optimise the delivery of information.

Worldwide research has shown that ICT can lead to an improved student learning and better teaching methods. A report made by the National Institute of Multimedia Education in Japan, proved that an increase in the use of ICT in education with integrating technology to the curriculum has a significant and positive impact on students' achievements. The results specifically showed that the students who are continuously exposed to technology through education has better 'knowledge', presentation skills, innovative capabilities, and are ready to take more efforts into learning as compared to their counterparts.

New Trends

Introducing ICT into education is the answer for those who ask; ' how can we increase the reach of our institution, to a larger number of students?.'

The Mobile learning (m-learning) as a form of e-learning is a rising trend where the education has outgrown the physical constraints of the classrooms and acquired mobility. Students access information whenever and wherever they want, and institutions that provides such advanced technological terrains is rising in number day by day.

Various devices/technology in ICT includes:

- Access of course materials through remote devices,
- Online digital repositories for lectures, course materials, and digital library,
- Online/cloud based academic management systems,
- Employing the flipped classroom concept,
- Making use of handheld computers, tablet computers, audio players, projector devices etc.

Also, the rising number of Massive Open Online Courses (MOOCs) like the coursera, khan academy, and edx tells us that there is a huge demand for off-the-classroom learning facilities. The future of our institutions will depend on whether or not they can satisfy those needs.

Why measure ICT in education?

Policy-makers accepts that ICT in education can help the students to compete in the global economy by being part of a skilled workforce and facilitate social mobility by:

- Enhancing learning experiences and providing new sets of skills,
- Reaching more students with Massive Open Online Courses (MOOCs),
- Facilitating the training of faculties,
- Minimising costs and saving time associated with information delivery and automating regular day-to-day tasks,

- Improving the administration of institutions to enhance the quality and efficiency of service delivery.

According to UNESCO, "Measuring ICT in education is therefore important to inform policy makers in setting national priorities and developing ICT in education policy."

Enabling ICT in institutions will also be useful for NAAC, NBA, and ABET accreditations.

The movement of education industry towards quality assurance programs has been picking up pace and the NAAC and NBA accreditation are evidence for that. These certifications are bound to become the norms for selecting institutions by students and the government is already taking measures to assure high quality education. Also, more and more institutions are applying for accreditation every day to imply that the education they provide is of high quality.

One way to improve the quality of education is to make use of efficient technology in an institution. This will open up more opportunities for the teachers and students as well.

Online interactions would facilitate learning without time constrains and it will be much more easier to conduct assessments and generate reports, since the necessary information doesn't have to be manually handled.

All these would result in flexible and considerably smoother learning environment and this would facilitate better results, and the accreditations too.

National Award for Teachers Using ICT for Innovation In Education

To promote and improve the digital culture in schools and colleges, the government has instituted the National Award for innovative use of ICT to motivate the Teachers and educators for innovative use of ICT in teaching-learning.

Dale's Cone of Experience

Dale's Cone of Experience is a model that incorporates several theories related to instructional design and learning processes. During the 1960s, Edgar Dale theorized that learners retain more information by what they "do" as opposed to what is "heard", "read" or "observed". His research led to the development of the Cone of Experience. Today, this "learning by doing" has become known as "experiential learning" or "action learning".

How Can Instructors Use the Cone of Experience?

According to Dale's research, the least effective method at the top, involves learning from information presented through verbal symbols, i.e., listening to spoken words. The most effective methods at the bottom, involves direct, purposeful learning experiences, such as hands-on or field experience. Direct purposeful experiences represents reality or the closet things to real, everyday life.

The cone charts the average retention rate for various methods of teaching.

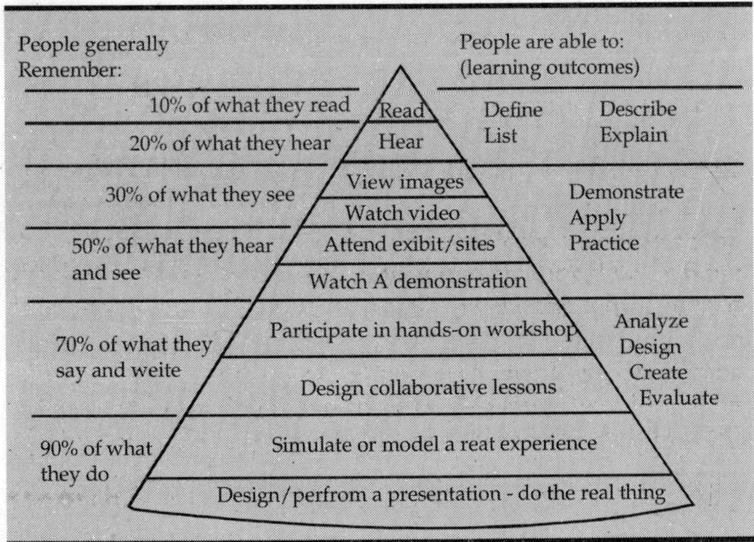

CONE OF EXPERIENCE

The further you progress down the cone, the greater the learning and the more information is likely to be retained. It also suggests that when choosing an instructional method it is important to remember that involving students in the process strengthens knowledge retention.

It reveals that "action-learning" techniques result in up to 90% retention. People learn best when they use perceptual learning styles. Perceptual learning styles are sensory based. The more sensory channels possible in interacting with a resource, the better chance that many students can learn from it. According to Dale, instructors should design instructional activities that build upon more real-life experiences.

HOW DALES CONE OF EXPERIENCE WORKS

Dales' cone of experience is a tool to help instructors make decisions about resources and activities. The instructor can ask the following:

- Where will the student's experience with this instructional resource fit on the cone? How far is it removed from real-life?
- What kind of learning experience do you want to provide in the classroom?
- How does this instructional resource augment the information supplied by the textbook?
- What and how many senses can students use to learn this instructional material?
- Does the instructional material enhance learning?

EVALUATION SYSTEMS

Evaluation is defined as a process of collecting evidences of behavioural changes and judging the directions and extents of such changes. This means that evaluation is free neither from instructional objectives nor from the teaching-learning. In fact, it is closely related to objectives and learning activities on the one hand, and improvement of instructions on the other. The desired changes in students represent the purpose or end of instruction, while the evaluation procedures and learning experiences provided to children are the instruments or means related to these ends. The relationship between educational objectives, learning experiences and evaluation techniques can be represented as follows:

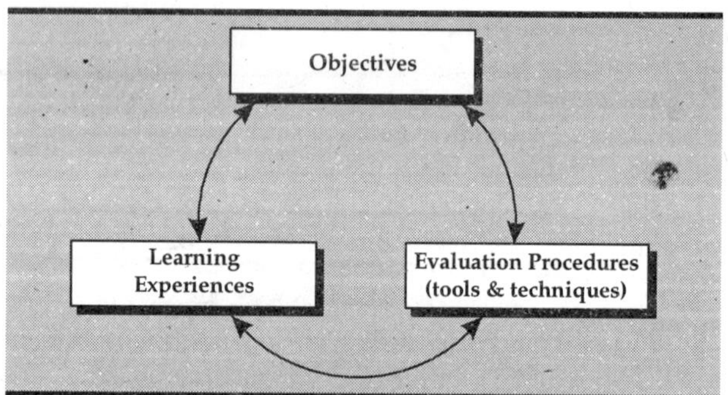

It is clear from the diagram that all the three steps are interrelated. The extent to which the teaching-learning activities result in experiences which lead to the realization of particular objective is determined by evaluation.

Important Elements of Evaluation

The terms testing, measurement, assessment, examination and appraisal are used indiscriminately. Evaluation shares some similarities with these.

Testing. Testing is a ground for critical examination, a means of examining, standard or norm for comparison, a trial for person's qualities, ground for selection/rejection, and a tool employed to reveal the presence or absence of a desired quality. Testing has become an integral part of all educational programmes. Testing procedures are useful sources to compare educational programmes with the state of students knowledge, motivation, activities and their behaviour. By assessing the degree of success, testing helps in the modification of teaching.

Measurement. It is mainly concerned with collection or gathering of data. For example, students' score in an examination. The measurement involves assigning a score on a given task performed by the learner, for example, 60/100. For many years, educationists concentrated on the measurement of human abilities. Therefore, measurement, strictly as quantitative oriented operation was considered as a synonym to evaluation.

Assessment. It covers activities included in grading, examining, certifying etc. For example, students achievement on a particular course, an applicant's attitude for a particular job and a teacher's competency in teaching may be assessed. It is concerned with ascertaining the extent to which the objectives of the programmes have been met.

Examination. The term is used in school to assess the growth of students in terms of their scholastic achievement. The examinations are conducted at different stages throughout the year, i.e., periodic tests, half-yearly examination and annual examination.

Appraisal. It is a process of evaluating qualities, characteristics, interests, attitudes and understandings. Teachers consider appraising the proficiencies of the learners for the purpose of diagnosis, classification, marking and grading. Good techniques are not available, that is why appraisal rests upon observations interpretations and finally upon subjective opinion. Appraisals based upon records and concrete observation has assumed an importance.

The evaluation may be classified as follows :

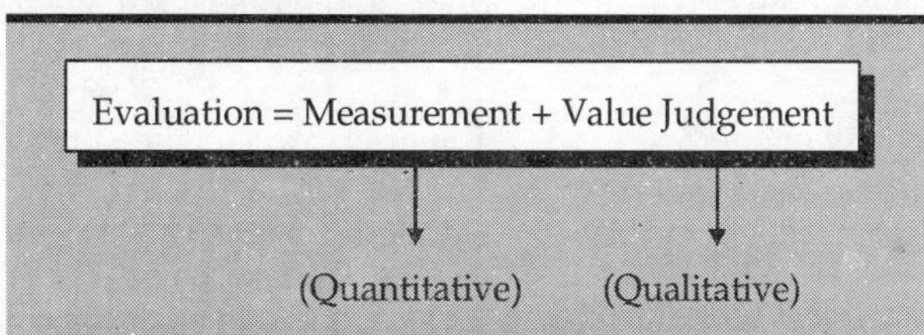

Hence, evaluation is both quantitative and qualitative process while measurement is quantitative or numerical value. Evaluation is a continuous process and an important part of teaching-learning process.

Types of Evaluation

Evaluation can be classified into the following three types depending on the timing of evaluation and the purpose of evaluation – diagnostic, formative and summative.

(i) **Diagnostic.** This type of evaluation is usually done in the beginning of the teaching-learning process in order to find out the specific weaknesses, either on an individual or at class level, and also to find out particular strengths. This helps to design the courses and curricula according to the capabilities of the learner to help him overcome his deficiencies in knowledge, skills and abilities.

(ii) **Formative.** Formative evaluation is concerned with making decisions relating to forming or development of students as well as of the courses. It provides feedback at appropriate stages of the teaching-learning process which helps in making changes in the curricula, teaching strategies and the learning environment. Formative evaluation is done during the process of teaching-learning with the following main purpose :

(a) To monitor student learning for the purpose of providing individualized instruction.

(b) To evaluate teaching effectiveness.

(c) To evaluate courses and curriculum with the purpose of modification, updating or replacement, if necessary.

(d) To evaluate curriculum materials.

(e) To evaluate the learning environment with a view to improving it.

The process works upon in a long term, so it is called continuous evaluation in which unit tests, class tests and assignments are the essential components.

(iii) **Summative.** Summative evaluation is concerned with making judgements about a finished product or process. Terminal examinations – whether internal or external – are a good example of summative evaluation but summative evaluation must not necessarily be terminal. Cumulative assessments, where they are undertaken solely for the purposes of selection, promotion, prediction, recording and such other administrative purposes, should be considered as a series of summative evaluations. While Class Tests, Unit Tests, Quizzes and Learning Tests are the parts of formative evaluation, the Term Tests, Annual Tests and External Examinations conducted by school or public agency are the essential parts of summative evaluation.

Summative evaluation is either external type or internal type.

DIFFERENCE BETWEEN FORMATIVE AND SUMMATIVE EVALUATION

Formative Evaluation	Summative Evaluation
1. The purpose of formative evaluation is to diagnose the strength and weaknesses of the students.	1. The purpose is classification and promotion of students.
2. Evidences secured by it are used for further improvement of instruction and students' better progress.	2. Its results are used for certification and passing judgement on pupils achievement.
3. Its focus is on improvement of pupils' achievement.	3. Its focus is on measurement of pupil's achievement.
4. It refers to continuous evaluation by means of unit tests, assignments etc.	4. It refers to term tests, annual tests and external examinations.
5. It is an integral part of teaching-learning process.	5. It is treated as an end of the course activity.
6. If provides continuous feedback to both pupil and teacher.	6. It does not provide feedback.
7. It is done during the course of instruction.	7. It is done at the end of academic session.
8. It gives relevant information which helps to improve classroom instructions.	8. It provides the overall results of the teaching-learning process.
9. Its results are used for providing remedial measures and enrichment programmes for slow and gifted learners respectively.	9. Its results are used for classification, placement and prediction for future success.

Examination is the concern of the teacher, the greatest premium of parents and the first anxiety of the students. End products of all education efforts are appraised by evaluation.

Importance of Examinations

(i) Examinations help in testing the achievement of the pupils.

(ii) Examinations are also helpful in evaluating the individual interests, aptitudes, intelligence, physical, emotional, social and moral development.

(iii) They also provide an ease to classify the students, to provide guidance, to bring changes in curriculum and form the basis of admissions.

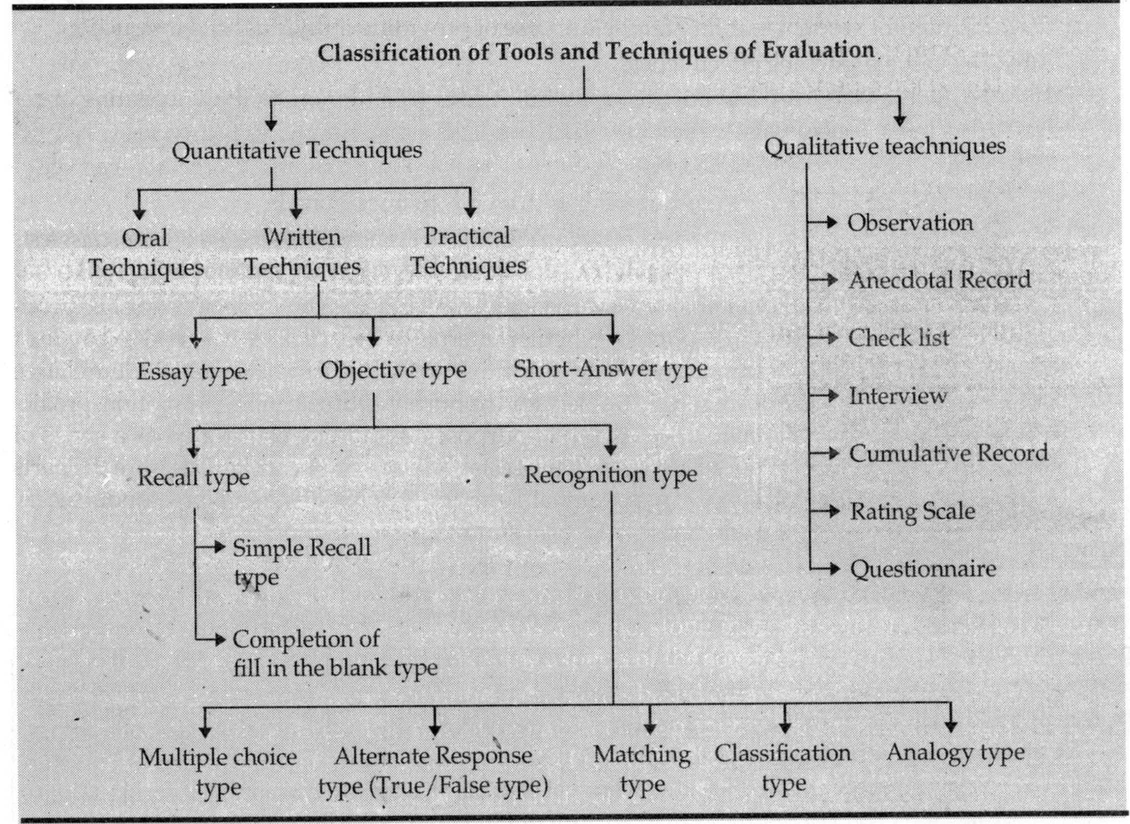

Evaluation in Choice Based Credit System (CBCS) in Higher Education

University Grants Commission has come up with the Choice Based Credit System (CBCS) programme in which the students have a choice to choose from the prescribed courses, which are referred as core, elective or minor or soft skill courses and they can learn at their own pace and the entire assessment is graded-based on a credit system. The basic idea is to look into the needs of the students so as to keep up-to-date with development of higher education in India and abroad. CBCS aims to redefine the curriculum keeping pace with the liberalisation and globalisation in education. CBCS allows students an easy mode of mobility to various educational institutions spread across the world along with the facility of transfer of credits earned by students.

Features of CBCS

- This is a uniform CBCS for all central and state and other recognised universities.
- There are three main courses: Core, Elective and Foundation.
- There are also non-credit courses available which will be assessed as 'Satisfactory' or "Unsatisfactory'. This is not included in the computation of SGPA/CGPA.
- All the three main courses will be evaluated and accessed to provide for an effective and balanced result.

How Does it Work?

It has the following basic elements:

- **Semesters.** The assessment is done semester wise. A student progresses on the basis of the courses taken rather than time like three years for science, arts, commerce or four years for engineering etc. Each semester will have 15–18 weeks of academic work which is equal to 90 teaching days. There is flexibility in creating the curriculum and assigning credits based on the course content and hours of teaching.

- **Credit system.** Each course is assigned a certain credit. When the student passes that course, he earns the credits which are based on that course. If a student passes a single course in a semester, he does not have to repeat that course later. The students can earn credits according to his pace.
- **Credit transfer.** If for some reasons, he cannot cope with the study load or if he falls sick, he has the freedom to study fewer courses and earn fewer credits and he can compensate this in the next semester.
- **Comprehensive continuous assessment.** There is a continuous evaluation of the student not only by the teachers but also by the student himself.
- **Grading.** UGC has introduced a 10-point grading system as follows:

O (Outstanding): 10	A+ (Excellent): 9	A (Very Good): 8
B+ (Good): 7	B (Above Average): 6	C (Average): 5
P (Pass): 4	F (Fail): 0	Ab (Absent): 0

How is the Credit Counted?

One credit per semester is equal to one hour of teaching, which includes both lecture (L) or tutorial (T) or two hours of practical work/field work (P) per week. A study course can have only L component or only T or P component or combination of any two or all the three components. The total credits earned by a student for each semester is L+T+P.

In compliance with the global grading system. All the major higher education institutions across the world are implementing a system of credits. For instance, we have the European Credit Transfer System (ECTS) in Europe's universities, the 'National Qualifications Framework' in Australia. There is the Pan-Canadian Protocol on the Transferability of University Credits. In the UK, we have the Credit Accumulation and Transfer System (CATS). Even the systems operating in the US, Japan, etc. are based on credit system.

Advantages of Choice Based Credit System

- The CBCS offers a 'cafeteria' approach in which the students can choose courses of their own choice.
- The credit system allows a student to study what he prefers in his own sequence as per his interests.
- They can learn at their own pace.
- They can opt for additional courses and can achieve more than the required credits.
- They can also opt for an interdisciplinary approach to learning.
- Inter college/university migration within the country and outside becomes easy with the transfer of Credits. This means that it will be easier for foreign universities to come and offer courses in India.
- Can opt for one part of the course in one institute and the other part in another institute. This will help in making a clear choice between good and bad colleges/ institutes.
- The students have more scope to enhance their skills and more scope of taking up projects and assignments, vocational training, including entrepreneurship.
- The system improves the job opportunities of students.
- The system will help in enabling potential employers assess the performance of students on a scientific scale.

Disadvantages of CBCS

- Not very easy to estimate the exact marks.
- Teachers' workload may fluctuate.
- Needs proper and good infrastructure for a universal spread of education.

COMPUTER BASED TESTING

Digital tools and technology are becoming standard even in traditional face-to-face learning environments. Two of the most widely adopted educational technologies are video lecture and computer based testing. Video lectures are pretty self-explanatory: teachers record their lectures for students to watch on-line at their convenience. But what is computer based testing? How does it work? What are the advantages and disadvantages of using this type of testing? Let's take each question in turn.

Computer based testing is, in essence, the practice of giving quizzes and tests on the computer instead of using pencil and paper. Computer based testing is already used widely in many different environments. This type of testing is also being used in schools, starting as early as third grade, often to deliver standardized tests, as well as in colleges and universities and in competitive examinations. In India National Testing Agency (NTA) has been assigned by Indian government to conduct CBT for UGC Net, JEE Main, GPAT and other examinations.

How does Computer based Testing Work?

Computer based testing is a broad term that can encompass several different types of testing tools and technologies. One of the most common is on-line testing software, in which an instructor uses an on-line testing creation software to develop a test. Then, the instructor provides a link to the students, who take the test on-line. The on-line testing creator automatically takes care of all of the administrative tasks-tracking who has completed the test, collecting data such as how long students spend on each question, and even grading the testing and providing feedback to the students.

What are the Advantages and Disadvantages of Computer Based Testing?

Overall, educators have discovered significant benefits to using computer based testing. Here are the main advantages, as well as a few disadvantages, of using this technology.

Advantages of computer based testing

- **Efficiency.** It takes less time for teachers to prepare, distribute, and grade on-line tests than paper tests, and it is easily scalable for 20 students or 2,000.
- **Convenience.** Students can take the testing when and where it is most convenient for them, rather than having to take it at a designated time.
- **Automatic scoring with feedback.** The computer can automatically score the testing and provide students with immediate feedback about their answers.
- **Analytics and reports.** The on-line testing software collects a large amount of data that can help teachers identify who is having trouble and also improve their testings over time.
- **Accessibility.** On-line text can be magnified or read aloud to assist students with disabilities.
- **Cheating controls.** On-line testing creators have a variety of features that prevent cheating.
- **Less human error.** Computer based testing removes a significant amount of human error, such as grading errors.
- **Re-usability.** Tests and even individual questions can be reused easily on other testings.

Disadvantages of Computer Based Testing

- **Technology glitches.** Technology problems are always possible, but in general computers make significantly fewer errors than humans do.
- **Limited question/answer formats.** There are some limitations in what types of testings can be given using a computer, but these are disappearing quickly. For example, subjective questions such as essays can be used, but they often must still be graded by hand. Also, it may be more difficult for students to show their work, like for math problems, but even this is not impossible using a tablet and a stylus.

Computer based testing is a powerful idea that is driving huge advances in classrooms. As time goes on, the advantages will become even greater as the disadvantages eventually disappear.

INNOVATIONS IN EVALUATION SYSTEMS

Innovative Approaches to Evaluation

- Potentially, one of the most effective ways to reconcile educational innovation and high-stakes assessments is through the introduction of innovative approaches to testing. These may include new methodologies for assessment, as well as new technologies that can measure complex skills and reasoning processes.
- The most important advances are at the conceptual level. Traditional tests, Pellegrino et al. (1999) have argued, do not provide information on higher order thinking because they focus on independent "traits", or fragments of knowledge, rather than on the student's understanding of the interconnections and patterns.
- Mislevy and colleagues (1998) suggest that tests should be developed with important inferences users will want to make established at the beginning of the process (as is the case with tests that focus on content knowledge). For example, test developers might want to measure students' cross-curricular skills, such as problem solving, communication, and reasoning processes. The next step would be to identify how students use these skills in different subject domains (mathematics, science, analysis of literature, and so on).
- Several innovations in assessment take advantage of recent advances in ICT. ICT-based assessments can now provide efficient feedback, measure students' reasoning processes and other complex cognitive skills, score "open-ended" performances such as student essays, and even examine how students go about thinking through problems. While it has always been possible for teachers or external assessors to perform these functions.
- Increasingly sophisticated ICT programmes that score "open-ended performances", such as essays, are under development. These programmes use natural-language processing, artificial intelligence and/or information retrieval technologies to detect of textual features of essays (for example, variety in use of syntax, quality of content and organisation of ideas). These ICT models are still in the relatively early stages of development however, and while they may facilitate scoring of large-scale assessments, cannot replace human raters.
- The cost of designing and implementing effective ICT-based assessments and examinations has been an important barrier to wider use. However, as noted at the beginning of this paper, all OECD countries have invested significant levels of funding in ICT and related teacher professional development over the past several years. ICT-based assessments may help ensure that schools realise the value of these investments.
- Of course, ICT-based technology is not a pre-requisite for large-scale assessment of students' open-ended performance. The most effective ICT programmes will be modelled on processes followed by human raters. These assessment processes also serve as valuable professional development for the raters, helping to fulfil goals for improvement and empowerment.

Alternatives to Traditional Exams and Papers

In designing assessments or assignments for a course, instructors often think of exams or term papers, but there are many other types of assessments that may be appropriate for your course. If you are willing to think creatively about assignments that go beyond traditional exams or research papers, you may be able to design assignments that are more accurate reflections of the kind of thinking and problem-solving you want your students to engage in. In addition, non-traditional assignments can boost students' motivation.

- Analysis and response to a case study
- Analysis of data or a graph
- Debate
- Description of a process
- Diagram, table, chart, or visual aid
- Explanation of a multiple-choice answer (students must explain why the answer they chose to a multiple-choice question is correct, or why the alternative answers are wrong)
- Introduction to a research paper or essay (rather than the full paper)
- Practical exam or evaluation of lab skills
- Powerpoint presentation

EDUCATION AND TEACHING-RELATED IMPORTANT DAYS

Day	Observance
04 January	World Braille Day
24 January	National Girl Child Day
21 February	International Mother Language Day [UNESCO]
28 February	National Science Day
21 March	World Poetry Day [UNESCO]
23 April	World Book and Copyright Day [UNESCO]
15 July	World Youth Skills Day
5 September	Teacher's Day
8 September	International Literacy Day [UNESCO]
14 September	Hindi Day
5 October	World Teachers' Day [UNESCO]
20 October	World Statistic Day
1 November	National Education Day
17 November (Third Thursday in November)	World Philosophy Day [UNESCO]
Year	**Observance**
2009	International Year of Human Rights Learning
2005	International Year for Sport and Physical Education
1990	International Literacy Year
1970	International Education Year
Decade	**Observance**
2003–2012	United Nations Literacy Decade: Education for All
1995–2004	Decade for Human Rights Education

MULTIPLE CHOICE QUESTIONS

1. Genetic psychology, revealing the factors which determine personality is/are
   (A) Intelligence
   (B) Character
   (C) Character & Intelligence in students
   (D) None of these
2. A harmonious and all-round growth and development of human powers or faculties, mental and physical comes through
   (A) Education (B) Society
   (C) Physical health (D) Mental health
3. Which of the following learner characteristics is highly related to effectiveness of teaching ?
   (1) Prior experience of the learner
   (2) Educational status of the parents of the learner
   (3) Peer groups of the learner
   (4) Family size from which the learner comes.
4. The process in which, and by which the knowledge, character and behavior of the young are shaped and moulded is known as
   (A) Education (B) Exercise
   (C) Psychology (D) All of the above
5. Certain hormones circulating in the blood are also important in the arousal of some motive states.
   (A) Biological (B) Social
   (C) Economical (D) Competence
6. Dynamic approach to teaching means
   (A) Teaching should be forceful and effective
   (B) Teachers should be energetic and dynamic
   (C) The topics of teaching should not be static, but dynamic
   (D) The students should be required to learn through activities
7. By which of the following methods the true evaluation of the students is possible ?
   (A) Evaluation at the end of the course.
   (B) Evaluation twice in a year.
   (C) Continuous evaluation.
   (D) Formative evaluation.
8. Suppose a student wants to share his problems with his teacher and he visits the teacher's house for the purpose, the teacher should
   (A) contact the student's parents and solve his problem.
   (B) suggest him that he should never visit his house.
   (C) suggest him to meet the principal and solve the problem.
   (D) extend reasonable help and boost his morale.
9. When some students are deliberately attempting to disturb the discipline of the class by making mischief, what will be your role as a teacher?
   (A) Expelling those students.
   (B) Isolate those students.
   (C) Reform the group with your authority.
   (D) Giving them an opportunity for introspection and improve their behaviour.
10. If you get an opportunity to teach a visually challenged student along with normal students, what type of treatment would you like to give him in the class ?
    (A) Not giving extra attention because majority may suffer.
    (B) Take care of him sympathetically in the classroom.
    (C) You will think that blindness is his destiny and hence you cannot do anything.
    (D) Arrange a seat in the front row and try to teach at a pace convenient to him.
11. In the present situation, the children must possess an important factor of
    (A) interest (B) aptitude
    (C) moral values (D) none of these
12. Which of the following qualities is most essential for a teacher ?
    (A) He should be a honest person.
    (B) He should be a well dressed person.
    (C) He should have patience.
    (D) He should be an expert in his subject.
13. For maintaining an effective discipline in the class, the teacher should
    (A) Allow students to do what they like.
    (B) Deal with the students strictly.
    (C) Give the students some problem to solve.
    (D) Deal with them politely and firmly.

14. Peer group is formed by
(A) School + Controlled environment
(B) Parents + Independent environment
(C) Society + Controlled environment
(D) None of these

15. Those teachers are popular among students who
(A) develop intimacy with them
(B) help them solve their problems
(C) award good grades
(D) take classes on extra tuition fee

16. The essence of an effective classroom environment is
(A) a variety of teaching aids
(B) lively student-teacher interaction
(C) pin-drop silence
(D) strict discipline

17. On the first day of his class, if a teacher is asked by the students to introduce himself, he should
(A) ask them to meet after the class
(B) tell them about himself in brief
(C) ignore the demand and start teaching
(D) scold the student for this unwanted demand

18. "If the people of the society has high achievement motivation, the economic growth increases and the society gets modernized". It is given in the book
(A) The Achieving Society
(B) Achievement of the Society
(C) Society and Achievement
(D) Society and its Development

19. Identify the important element a teacher has to take cognizance of while addressing students in a classroom.
(A) Avoidance of proximity
(B) Voice modulation
(C) Repetitive pause
(D) Fixed posture

20. Learners display individual differences. So, a teacher should
(A) insist on uniform pace of learning
(B) provide a variety of learning experiences
(C) enforce strict discipline
(D) increase number of tests

21. Research has shown that the most frequent symptom of nervous instability among teachers is
(A) Digestive upsets
(B) Explosive behaviour
(C) Fatigue (D) Worry

22. Which one of the following statements is correct ?
(A) Syllabus is an annexure to the curriculum.
(B) Curriculum is the same in all educational institutions.
(C) Curriculum includes both formal, and informal education.
(D) Curriculum does not include methods of evaluation.

23. As a teacher, select the best option to ensure your effective presence in the classroom.
(A) Use of peer command
(B) Making aggressive statements
(C) Adoption of well-established posture
(D) Being authoritarian

24. Some students in a class exhibit great curiosity for learning. It may be because such children
(A) Are gifted
(B) Come from rich families
(C) Show artificial behaviour
(D) Create indiscipline in the class

25. To encourage achievement motivation in the classroom, students should be taught to attribute their good grades through
(A) their own hard work
(B) their own high level of intelligence
(C) their teachers' generous grading standards
(D) none of the above

26. Which one of the following is appropriate in respect of teacher-student relationship ?
(A) Very informal and intimate
(B) Limited to classroom only
(C) Cordial and respectful
(D) Indifferent

27. The academic performance of students can be improved if parents are encouraged to
(A) supervise the work of their wards
(B) arrange for extra tuition
(C) remain unconcerned about it
(D) interact with teachers frequently

28. In a lively classroom situation, there is likely to be
(A) occasional roars of laughter
(B) complete silence
(C) frequent teacher-student dialogue
(D) loud discussion among students

29. If a parent approaches the teacher to do some favour to his/her ward in the examination, the teacher should

(A) try to help him
(B) guide him to talk to the principal
(C) refuse politely and firmly
(D) ask him rudely to go away

30. When a pupil's misbehaviour persists even though the teacher punishes the child for each infraction, the teacher is probably practicing a policy of
(A) retribution
(B) corporal punishment
(C) negative reinforcement
(D) repression

31. You are a teacher and after preparing question paper you check, whether the questions test specific testing objectives. He is concerned primarily about the question paper's
(A) validity (B) content coverage
(C) number of questions
(D) reliability

32. Attitudes, concepts, skills and knowledge are products of
(A) Learning (B) Research
(C) Heredity (D) Explanation

33. Which among the following gives more freedom to the learner to interact ?
(A) Use of film
(B) Small group discussion
(C) Lectures by experts
(D) Viewing country-wide classroom programme on TV

34. Which one is *not* a product of learning ?
(A) Attitudes (B) Concepts
(C) Knowledge (D) Maturation

35. Which of the following skills are needed for present day teacher to adjust effectively with the classroom teaching ?
1. Knowledge of technology
2. Use of technology in teaching learning
3. Knowledge of students' needs
4. Content mastery

(A) 1 & 3 (B) 2 & 3
(C) 2, 3 & 4 (D) 2 & 4

36. Family is a means of
(A) informal education
(B) formal education
(C) distance education
(D) All of the above

37. Micro teaching is more effective
(A) during the preparation for teaching-practice
(B) during the teaching-practice
(C) after the teaching-practice
(D) always

38. In a classroom, a communicator's trust level is determined by :
(1) the change of voice level
(2) the use of abstract concepts
(3) eye contact
(4) the use of hyperbole

39. **Assertion (A) :** For an effective classroom communication at times it is desirable to use the projection technology.
Reason (R) : Using the projection technology facilitates extensive coverage of course contents.
(A) Both (A) and (R) are true, and (R) is the correct explanation.
(B) Both (A) and (R) are true, but (R) is not the correct explanation.
(C) (A) is true, but (R) is false.
(D) (A) is false, but (R) is true.

40. The teacher has been glorified by the phrase "Friend, philosopher and guide" because :
(A) He has to play all vital roles in the context of society
(B) He transmits the high value of humanity to students
(C) He is the great reformer of the society
(D) He is a great patriot

41. The most important cause of failure for teacher lies in the area of :
(A) inter personal relationship
(B) lack of command over the knowledge of the subject
(C) verbal ability
(D) strict handling of the students

42. A teacher can establish rapport with his students by :
(A) becoming a figure of authority
(B) impressing students with knowledge and skill
(C) playing the role of a guide
(D) becoming a friend to the students

43. Education is a powerful instrument of
(A) Social transformation
(B) Personal transformation
(C) Cultural transformation
(D) All the above

44. A teacher's major contribution towards the maximum self-realization of the student is affected through :

(A) Constant fulfilment of the students' needs
(B) Strict control of class-room activities
(C) Sensitivity to students' needs, goals and purposes
(D) Strict reinforcement of academic standards

45. The self adjective mechanism that teachers often unwittingly encourage is
(A) an attention-getting device
(B) day dreaming
(C) regression
(D) fantasy

46. Which of the following propounded the theory of Moral Development?
(A) Kohlberg (B) Vygotsky
(C) Sternberg (D) Simon

47. Most often, the teacher - student communication is
(A) Critical (B) Utilitarian
(C) Confrontational (D) Spurious

48. Which of the following intelligence is associated with scientific and mathematical thinking?
(A) Kinesthetic intelligence
(B) Personal intelligence
(C) Logical intelligence
(D) Spatial intelligence

49. When a normal student behaves in an erratic manner in the class, you would :
(A) pull up the student then and there
(B) talk to the student after the class
(C) ask the student to leave the class
(D) ignore the student

50. Teacher uses visual-aids to make learning :
(A) simple
(B) more knowledgeable
(C) quicker
(D) interesting

51. The teacher's role at the higher educational level is to
(A) provide information to students
(B) promote self-learning in students
(C) encourage healthy competition among students
(D) help students to solve their personal problems

52. Which is the least important factor in teaching ?
(A) punishing the students
(B) maintaining discipline in the class
(C) lecturing in impressive way
(D) drawing sketches and diagrams on the blackboard

53. Verbal guidance is least effective in the learning of
(A) Aptitudes (B) Skills
(C) Attitudes (D) Relationship

54. Which of the following factors does **not** impact teaching ?
(A) Teacher's knowledge
(B) Class room activities that encourage learning
(C) Socio-economic background of teachers and students
(D) Learning through experience

55. The most appropriate purpose of learning is
(A) personal adjustment
(B) modification of behaviour
(C) social and political awareness
(D) preparing oneself for employment

56. How can a teacher help his/her learners to move away form the practice of memorising by rote?
(A) by encouraging original thinking among learners
(B) by encouraging active participation in the classroom discourses
(C) by not asking knowledge-based questions
(D) all of the above

57. Maximum participation of students is possible in teaching through
(A) discussion method
(B) lecture method
(C) audio-visual aids
(D) text book method

58. Which of the following comprise teaching skill?
(A) Black Board writing
(B) Questioning
(C) Explaining
(D) All the above

59. What did NPE 1968 emphasis?
(A) Child's education
(B) Equalization of Educational Opportunities
(C) Spread of Literacy & Adult education
(D) All of the above

60. Curriculum makers have the most difficulty when
(A) there is an inflationary cycle
(B) the nature of the student population is changing

(C) parents are participants
(D) teachers unions insist on input

61. Which of the following statements is correct?
(A) Syllabus is a part of curriculum.
(B) Syllabus is an annexure to curriculum.
(C) Curriculum is the same in all educational institutions affiliated to a particular university.
(D) Syllabus is not the same in all educational institutions affiliated to a particular university.

62. Which of the two given options is of the level of understanding ?
(I) Define noun.
(II) Define noun in your own words.
(A) Only I (B) Only II
(C) Both I and II (D) Neither I nor II

63. The trial and error method of instruction is best enhanced by
(A) role playing
(B) programmed instruction
(C) an audio-visual lesson
(D) independent study

64. Which of the following statement is not correct?
(A) Lecture Method can develop reasoning
(B) Lecture Method can develop knowledge
(C) Lecture Method is one way process
(D) During Lecture Method students are passive

65. Which one indicates evaluation?
(A) Ram got 45 marks out of 200
(B) Mohan got 38 percent marks in English
(C) Shyam got First Division in final examination
(D) All the above

66. What is the medium of effective teaching?
(A) Individualized instruction and open classroom discussion
(B) Verbal guidance
(C) Emphasis on understanding the concept rather than completing syllabus
(D) All the above

67. What are the benefits of teaching in group?
(A) Development of leadership quality
(B) Development of social awareness
(C) Improvement physical health
(D) (A) and (B) both

68. What does "self-regulation of learners" mean?
(A) rules and regulations made by the student body
(B) creating regulations for student behaviour
(C) self-discipline and control
(D) ability to monitor their own learning

69. Which of the following education methods are useful for students?
(1) Idealism (2) Existentialism
(3) Realism (4) Pragmatism
Choose your answer by following codes:
(A) 1 & 2 (B) 2, 3 & 4
(C) 3 & 4 (D) 1, 2, 3 & 4

70. Education helps culture in
(A) improvement of culture
(B) Makes its reach upto foreign land
(C) expression of culture
(D) None of these

71. Which one is a product of learning?
(A) Intelligence (B) Maturation
(C) Skills (D) Forgiveness

72. The teaching is not thought as a process of
(A) Listening the recitation of pupils
(B) Directing the activities of the pupils
(C) Indoctrinating adult ideas to young pupils
(D) None of the these

73. An example of scientific knowledge is
(A) Social traditions and customs
(B) Authority of the prophet or great men
(C) Religious scriptures
(D) Laboratory and field experiments

74. An ideal situation in a classroom would be where
1. a teacher comes fully prepared to deliver his lecture
2. students come fully prepared and discuss the subject with each other in the teacher's presence
3. teachers and students discuss the subject
4. the teacher uses audio-visual aids while lecturing
(A) 1 and 3 (B) 3 and 4
(C) Only 2 (D) Only 4

75. What is more desirable in a classroom ?
(A) A teacher delivering a lecture on the basis of the text and his own research
(B) A teacher delivering a lecture on the basis of course contents and standard books
(C) A teacher answering questions raised by students
(D) A teacher maintaining strict discipline and taking attendance regularly

76. A university teacher should normally
(A) be preoccupied with sensitive research areas
(B) strike a balance between teaching, research and guidance
(C) publish annually at least two scholarly research articles
(D) concentrate on writing textbooks

77. While presenting your ideas in a classroom it is better to
1. recognize that there can be other views
2. recognize that students are not a homogenous mass
3. take dissenting views also in consideration

(A) 1 and 3 (B) Only 3
(C) 2 and 3 (D) 1, 2 and 3

78. The best educational programme is one which is according to the
(A) ability of the child
(B) need of the child
(C) interest of the child
(D) all of these along with the need of the society

79. Students can be classified into four types on the basis of their learning. Which one of the following seeks meaning and reasoning for learning ?
(A) Innovative learner
(B) Analytic learner
(C) Commonsense learner
(D) Dynamic learner

80. Team teaching has the potential to develop :
(A) Competitive spirit
(B) Cooperation
(C) The habit of supplementing the teaching of each other
(D) Highlighting the gaps in each other's teaching

81. Which of the following is the most important characteristic of Open Book Examination system ?
(A) Students become serious.
(B) It improves attendance in the classroom.
(C) It reduces examination anxiety amongst students.
(D) It compels students to think.

82. Which of the following methods of teaching encourages the use of maximum senses ?
(A) Problem-solving method
(B) Laboratory method
(C) Self-study method
(D) Team teaching method

83. What is a major criticism of Kohlberg's theory?
(A) Kohlberg proposed a theory without any empirical basis.
(B) Kohlberg did not give clear cut stages of moral development
(C) Kohlberg proposed that moral reasoning is developmental
(D) Kohlberg did not account for cultural differences in moral reasoning of men and women.

84. Micro teaching is useful to students of
(A) Primary classes only
(B) Junior classes only
(C) 10 + 2 classes
(D) All of these

85. Which of the following should a teacher adopt in his lecture ?
(A) Precise and low tone
(B) Elongated tone
(C) Precise and high tone
(D) Moderate tone

86. Attitude of the teacher that affects teaching pertains to
(A) Affective domain
(B) Cognitive domain
(C) Connative domain
(D) Psychomotor domain

87. An effective teacher will ensure
(A) cooperation among his students
(B) laissez-faire role
(C) competition among students
(D) competition or cooperation as the situation demands

88. If students do not understand what is taught in the classroom, the teacher should feel
(A) terribly bored
(B) to explain it in a different way
(C) that he is wasting time
(D) pity for the students

89. Which of the following will not hamper effective communication in the class ?
(A) A lengthy statement
(B) An ambiguous statement
(C) A precise statement
(D) A statement which allows the listener to draw his own conclusions

90. ______ states that ethnic or racial differences in intelligence, a bitterly controversial issue, are not so much a fact, as, are simply due to the different meanings of the word 'intelligence'.

(A) D. O. Hebb (B) Wechsler
(C) Hine (D) P.E. Vernon

91. If a teacher belonging to a higher caste adopts a discriminatory attitude towards a student from a lower caste, our response will be that it is

(A) correct behaviour in accordance to his socio-religious beliefs
(B) against the national and Constitutional spirit of the country
(C) against the teachers' fundamental duties of treating all students with equality and justice
(D) none of the above

92. Both Piaget and Vygotsky emphasized the importance of social interactions in cognitive development, but Piaget saw a different role for interaction. Piaget believed that the most helpful interactions were those between peers, because peers are on an equal basis and can challenge each other's thinking. Vygotsky, on the other hand...

(A) Vygotsky believed that children's cognitive development is fostered by interactions with other children with the same problem.
(B) Vygotsky suggested that children's cognitive development is fostered by interactions with people who are more capable or advanced in their thinking, people such as parents and teachers
(C) Vygotsky suggested that children's cognitive development is fostered by interactions with their grandparents.
(D) Vygotsky suggested that children's cognitive development is fostered by interactions with his/her family who are no capable or advanced in their thinking, people such as parents, grandparents, brothers or sisters.

93. A teacher in the class is

(A) a director of the group
(B) the instructor of the group
(C) a leader and guide of the group
(D) all of the above

94. As a teacher you are going to show historical places of a city to your students. Father of a student does not send his student with you. In this situation, you would

(A) leave this student and would go with others
(B) try to know why his father was hesitant to send his ward.
(C) convince his father by telling the importance of such educational and cultural trips
(D) none of the above.

95. All of the following are the characteristic features of an effective teacher except

(A) emphasizing group discussion for the purpose of clarifying the objectives
(B) emphasis upon standard
(C) emphasis upon the quick control of the problematic situation
(D) differential treatment meted out to students of his class

96. In our present society, where values are deteriorating, the excellent education will be which

(A) enables one to earn in an easy manner
(B) exaggerates the competition in the society.
(C) works for re-establishment of human and cultural values.
(D) de-accelerates the social-change in the society.

97. While teaching in the class one of your students pointed out sharply your mistakes. What will you do in such a condition ?

(A) You leave the class for the day.
(B) You scold the child and angrily resist him.
(C) You feel sorry for committing a blunder.
(D) You will not show any emotion.

98. Of the following statements one that is least educationally valid is that

(A) heterogeneous grouping is undemocratic
(B) drill periods should be brief
(C) study habits should be taught
(D) overlearning constitutes a waste of time

99. One of your colleagues is living in your locality but you have no affinity with him, the reason may be

(A) his selfishness
(B) his religious faith
(C) his social rejection
(D) his miserable behaviour and rural background.

100. According to Erikson's Psychosocial Stages of Development, which stage describes a child who needs to learn important academic skills and compare favorably with peers in school to achieve competence?

(A) Trust vs Mistrust
(B) Identity vs Role Confusion
(C) Initiative vs Guilt
(D) Industry vs Inferiority

101. While delivering lecture if there is some disturbance in the class, then a teacher should
(A) keep quiet for a while and then go on
(B) punish those causing disturbance
(C) not bother of what is happening in the class
(D) all of the above

102. If a group of students enter your room and abuse you and behave violently with you, at that time how would you control your emotions?
(A) You will feel ashamed among your teaching community.
(B) You will react in similar tone and try to assault them physically.
(C) First you will try to pacify their emotions, then ask politely about their behaviour.
(D) You will report the case to the principal with recommendation of punitive measures.

103. The main role of education according to Plato was
(A) to develop the power of contemplation
(B) to strengthen the state
(C) to develop the personality of each individual
(D) All of the above

104. Suppose you are asked by your friends to take the membership of the teachers union. How could you take decision in this situation ?
(A) You will de-affiliate yourself from the colleagues instead of hostility with the management.
(B) You will have faith in unity so you will accept the membership.
(C) You will give priority to social relations, therefore, you will accept the offer.
(D) You will try to avoid the issue.

105. You are in class on the very first day of the opening session, and take introductions of the students, the primary objective of this introduction for you is
(A) to know about students' potentialities along with their family status
(B) selection of those students who can do the school job for you.
(C) identification of potential
(D) both (B) & (C)

106. A successful teacher is one who is
(A) Compassionate and disciplinarian
(B) Quite and reactive
(C) Tolerant and dominating
(D) Passive and active

107. The introduction of career courses in schools and colleges aims at
(A) developing the ability to make the intelligent choice of jobs
(B) providing professional knowledge to students
(C) increasing G.K. in students
(D) All of the above

108. The student will be able to write a recommendation of whether a book should/ shouldn't be read.
(A) comprehension (B) application
(C) analysis (D) evaluation

109. The education aims at the fullest realisation of all the potentialities of children. It implies that
(A) they should provide suitable opportunities and favourable environmental facilities which are conducive to the maximum growth of children.
(B) teachers and parents must know what children are capable of and what potentialities they possess.
(C) It is necessary that their attitudes are helpful, encouraging and sympathetic.
(D) All of the above

110. Arrange the following teaching process in order:
(i) Relate the present knowledge with previous one
(ii) Evaluation
(iii) Reteaching
(iv) Formulating instructional objectives
(v) Presentation of instructional materials
(A) (i), (ii), (iii), (iv), (v)
(B) (ii), (i), (iii), (iv), (v)
(C) (v), (iv), (iii), (i), (ii)
(D) (iv), (i), (v), (ii), (iii)

111. Some of your colleagues are busy in cracking filthy jokes during their leisure in college. You are also a member of that group but unable to stop them. What would you do to avoid it ?
(A) You advice your colleagues to mind their languages while cracking jokes in college
(B) You persuade them not to waste their leisure time in filthy jokes.

(C) You change the groups or live in isolation because you don't relish it.
(D) You remind them of their noble profession.

112. Arrange the following teaching process in order:
(i) Relate the present knowledge with previous one
(ii) Evaluation
(iii) Reteaching
(iv) Formulating instructional objectives
(v) Presentation of instructional materials
(A) (i), (ii), (iii), (iv), (v)
(B) (ii), (i), (iii), (iv), (v)
(C) (v), (iv), (iii), (i), (ii)
(D) (iv), (i), (v), (ii), (iii)

113. TV is superior to radio as teaching aid because it
(A) is costly
(B) invites two senses - hearing and vision simultaneously leading to more accurate form of learning
(C) is generally liked by pupils
(D) all of the above

114. The male students of your class are annoyed with you on the pretext you have been easily approached by the girl students and do a favour to them (girls). In such an embarrassing situation how would you like to control them in the class ?
(A) You will tell the male students that girls have no option except to depend on the school teacher for their academic assistance.
(B) You will justify that most of the female students are more sincere towards their studies than male students.
(C) You will communicate to the male students that it is difficult for you refuse the request made by female students.
(D) None of the above.

115. A mentally retarded student attends your lecture and sits in a deaf and dumb manner. What will you do ?
(A) Make your lecture very simple and spare some extra time for him.
(B) You pressurise the student to leave the class
(C) You do not like to spoil majority for the individual.
(D) You do not support him at all.

116. In order to develop rapport with your pupils you should
(A) behave them in a democratic way
(B) guide them
(C) have communicative ability
(D) all of the above

117. Ideal 'waiting time' for getting response from students should be proportional to
(A) time taken by the students for answering questions from previous lessons
(B) relevance of the question in the real life
(C) time allotted to specific topic in the curriculum
(D) difficulty level of the question

118. Teachers who are enthusiastic in the classroom teaching
(A) simply dramatise to hold the student's attention
(B) often lack proficiency in the subjects which stays hidden under their enthusiasm
(C) involve their students in the teaching learning process
(D) All of the above

119. Democracy in the class-room is best reflected through
(A) allowing student's freedom to the observance of classroom rules and regulations.
(B) allowing the class to decide the curricular experiences of the classroom
(C) allowing the maximum participation of all the students in class-room activities.
(D) None of above.

120. The effectiveness of punishment depends upon
1. Generally speaking, the stronger the response tendency being punished, the less effective a give strength of punishment will be
2. People and animals adapt to punishment, and this may weaken its effectiveness
3. Most psychologists claim that parents should use punishment as the major means of controlling behaviour
4. Punishment can be an unconditioned stimulus for fear

(A) 1 and 2 (B) 1 and 3
(C) 2 and 3 (D) 1 only

121. An increase in comprehension skill is most likely to result from
(A) guided silent reading
(B) guided oral reading
(C) unstructured silent reading
(D) the teacher reading to the class

122. If a teacher requests you to do a favour in a female student's evaluation, what would you like to do in this situation ?

(A) you will teach him a moral lesson against injustice.

(B) you will remind him about the morality of being a teacher.

(C) you will evaluate the answer-book honestly and award marks accordingly.

(D) None of the above.

123. When your friend seeks your assistance to get his ward's admission in the school, how would you extend your cooperation to him ?

(A) You would extend all types of support as you have intimate relationship.

(B) You would not help him.

(C) You would put forward some lame excuse.

(D) None of the above.

124. You are a teacher of literature. A chapter of a book deals with a biography of a scientists and his works. In this situation, what would you do with this chapter ?

(A) You would ask the students to read themselves.

(B) You would request the Science teacher, to teach this chapter to the students.

(C) You would consult other book concerning with the scientist and then you would teach the lesson to students

(D) Any one of them.

125. Kindergarten system lays emphasis?

(A) on understanding the psychology of children

(B) on physical training of the sense organs

(C) on observation of the natural events

(D) on the skill of reading and writing

126. Which of the following Education committee/ Education Commission recommended first to stop the problem of wastage and stagnation?

(A) Hunter Commission

(B) Wood Despatch

(C) Hartog Committee

(D) Yaspal Committee

127. If you invite your personal friends and colleagues in your son's birthday party, the procedure of it will be

(A) only personal invitation will be extended to most dear ones.

(B) only a specific group of teachers will be invited.

(C) extend invitation to all the teachers without any distinction.

(D) You would invite all the personnel of the school.

128. Teachers should study educational philosophy because

(A) they do not have their own philosophy

(B) they do not know it

(C) philosophy is the backbone of all disciplines

(D) they may improve their work by clarifying their own philosophy.

129. Which of the following Education committee/ Education Commission recommended first to stop the problem of wastage and stagnation?

(A) Hunter Commission

(B) Wood Despatch

(C) Hartog Committee

(D) Yaspal Committee

130. A teacher meeting his students for the first time should

(A) develop rapport with the class

(B) start teaching without caring the students likes and dislikes

(C) give a broad outline of the whole subject

(D) (B) and (C) both

131. Many experienced teachers go into a classroom and embark straight away upon a lesson. As a beginner to the teaching profession you will

(A) do as the student's like

(B) make a written note of your preparation.

(C) adopt the same procedure

(D) None of the above

132. Before starting instruction a teacher should

(A) be aware of the environmental variables acting on the mind of the pupils

(B) know the existing knowledge of his students and their background knowledge

(C) be competent enough to arouse the curiosity of his pupils

(D) all of the above

133. The main purpose of the new education policy is

(A) To provide equal opportunity of education to all

(B) To link education with employment

(C) To improve the whole education system
(D) To spiritualize the education system

134. The professional requirements of a teacher as explained in the UNESCO publication is/are
(A) innovativeness in approach and teaching strategies
(B) mastery over the subject and competency for teaching
(C) justice to the profession
(D) All of the above

135. To stop malpractice of mass-copying in the examinations, what will you do?
(A) You will give punishment to student and his parent.
(B) You will give severe punishment to students.
(C) You will try to give moral education to the students.
(D) You will rusticate the students forever from the school.

136. If a student absents from the classes for a long time,
(A) you will try to know the cause of his absence.
(B) you would be neutral and would not show any interest in it
(C) he would be absent due to some personnel reasons.
(D) It is not duty of teacher.

137. A teacher exploits students in your school. In this situation, you will
(A) not interfere in this matter
(B) report the matter to the principal
(C) guide the teacher please stop this activity
(D) go on satyagraha against the teacher.

138. After a lecture, if a student asks you a question, and you do not know the answer of the question, what will be your response in that situation ?
(A) You will not answer
(B) You will say that the question is improper
(C) You will discourage the student
(D) You promise to give the answer in next lecture.

139. Observable behaviours which a teacher can use in the class to bring home to the pupil an idea or point is technically called
(A) teaching skills
(B) demonstration
(C) communication facilities
(D) none of these

140. Quality of education in a school/college can be measured through
(A) manpower, teachers and principal available
(B) infrastructural facilities available
(C) students' achievement
(D) all of the above

141. An effective teacher is expected to
(A) reduce the anxiety level of students to moderate level
(B) encourage the students to make initiative
(C) to make students feel that education is their need
(D) all of the above

142. In which part of Indian Constitution every citizen of India is permitted to give education according to his religion?
(A) Directive Principles
(B) Concurrent List
(C) Democratic Rights
(D) Fundamental Rights

143. The aim to set up Radha Krishnan Commission in 1948-49 was
(A) Survey of Primary Education
(B) Survey of University Education
(C) Growth of Secondary
(D) Growth of Nation

144. A children is a back-bencher and is unable to watch the black-board clearly, therefore he stands, sees and sits repeatedly. What inference will you draw with the student's difficulty ?
(A) The child has a poor eye-sight
(B) The black-board may have shinning effect of light
(C) The child may be partially non-attentive
(D) The child is creating mischief.

145. A teacher is the leader both *de jure* and *de facto*. He is the authority before the students, and so it is his right to lead. While assuming leadership of the students, he should follow some important principles
(A) preparation and planning
(B) creating right atmosphere in the class
(C) providing opportunities
(D) all of the above

146. You feel that a particular instructional strategy is effective for teaching your subject. But none of the your colleagues agrees with you. What step will you take?

(A) Look for the theoretical justification of the strategy from books on instruction.
(B) Leave them to dos as they like.
(C) Give up your strategy as it is not acceptable to others.
(D) With the co-operation of your colleagues, design an action research to validate your choice of method.

147. 'The weakest chain of our education structure is our secondary education and it requires urgent improvement', who said:
(A) Mudaliar Commission
(B) Kothari Commission
(C) Radha Krishnan Commission
(D) Hunter Commission

148. A serious minded teacher as a rule
(A) allows the mistakes to be committed and explains how to minimise those mistakes
(B) takes all precaution so that students never commit mistakes.
(C) never allows any mistakes on the part of his students.
(D) should mildly punish students who commit mistakes.

149. Teachers should not demand from their pupils something which is beyond their stage of growth. If they do so, they only cause
(A) anger among pupils
(B) frustrations, heighten tension and nervousness in children
(C) encouragement to students to learn more
(D) none of the above

150. Students differ greatly in their susceptibility to anger due to heredity, health status and environment and to the way they are dealt with by adults. As a teacher, how will you try to direct his attention towards something else ?
(A) Grown up children should be taught a problem solving behaviour in coping with situations that provoke anger.
(B) Anger should be used into socially acceptable channel.
(C) They must be taught how to express anger so as to avoid disapproval.
(D) All of these.

151. Recommendation by Dr. Radha Krishnan University Commission for Women education was
(A) Admission to Women also in men Universities
(B) Equal pay to women teachers
(C) Both (A) and (B)
(D) None of the above

152. Ancient Indian teachers applied some psychological principles in educating the young child from pre-school age to adolescence. They recognised the role of
(A) convent system of schooling
(B) sense and perceptions in learning and teaching
(C) *gurukul* type of schooling
(D) None of the above

153. Choose the correct sequence in the context of in situational planning.
1. Situational analysis
2. Organising material and human resources
3. Setting goals
4. Evaluation
5. Implementation

(A) 1, 3, 2, 5 and 4 (B) 2, 3, 1, 4 and 5
(C) 2, 3, 1, 5 and 4 (D) 3, 1, 2, 5 and 4

154. An individual's ability to learn is
(A) absorbed (B) acquired
(C) occurring within (D) developed

155. Collective psychology of the whole period is a theory which
(A) can explain all phases of historical development
(B) means psychological approach of data collection
(C) means the psychology of the whole society
(D) all of the above

156. It is popularly said that any two students are not alike. This means
(A) each and every student differ in their physical and mental set up.
(B) they differ in their familiar and social status.
(C) they are different in their mental set up.
(D) all of the above

157. Our present higher secondary curriculum is based on the premise that a number of courses in our scheme of studies have identical elements. This statement is based on the
(A) theory of Identical Component.
(B) theory of Mental Faculty
(C) theory of Formal Discipline
(D) theory of Generalisations.

158. Suggestion helps in the development of information, moral behaviour, aesthetic sense and

character traits. Which of the following is the chief source of suggestions which mould the life?

(A) Teachers (B) Pupils of same age
(C) Elders (D) None of these

159. As a principal, which of the following teachers , will you appreciate the most?

(A) The one who takes one's classes as per schedule, prepares all reports, results and documents in time.
(B) The one who never asks for leave throughout the year.
(C) The one who always comes do you to demand never devices, equipment and books for teaching.
(D) The one who has pleasant habits and is most social with you and one's colleagues.

160. As a new teacher the first professional responsibility you must meet is to

(A) change the curriculum in the light of your training.
(B) co-operate with your fellow teacher inspite of differences.
(C) ascertain and follow the procedures of your predecessor.
(D) None of the above.

161. Which of the following explains the mental growth most suitably ?

(A) A growth pattern runs parallel to the physical growth.
(B) It is an erratic pattern.
(C) It is not an erratic pattern.
(D) A uniform rise to the middle teens and gradual levelling off during middle twenties.

162. Teachers are regarded as the builders of the nation. They are performing an onerous task. Their salary is not commensurate with the service they render. Promotion and salary increment of teachers should be on the basis of periodic evaluation of their merit efficiency. The proposition

(A) cannot be implemented by the educational Institutions.
(B) is not justified.
(C) is sound proposition but should be put into effect gradually
(D) None of the above

163. There is a debate as to whether teaching is a true profession or not. The most critical factor needed to make teaching a true profession is

(A) discipline of its own members.
(B) a longer period of training
(C) better spirits among teachers
(D) a longer period of learning

164. The objective of guidance at the college stage is

(A) to assist students to get employment immediately
(B) to assist the students in acquiring knowledge about other vocations available after the university education
(C) to assist employer to select prospective employees
(D) All of the above

165. Which one of the following is most fundamental of the guidance activities and should be executed first ?

(A) Selection of the learning activities
(B) Determination of material
(C) Determination of objectives
(D) Selection of study material

166. When planning to develop the powers of creative thinking, the teacher should allow for all of the following except

(A) comparison of the treatment of a social studies topic in two text books
(B) failure of an experiment in science
(C) inability to locate a book in the college library
(D) solving of all problems through use of a well practiced formula

167. As an administrator, a principal will have various combinations of the following qualities, except one. Identify the odd combination.

(A) Educational vision, constructive attitude, faith in fellow teachers.
(B) Planning, expertise in all subjects, constructive attitude.
(C) Liaison officer, organizing capacity and constructive attitude.
(D) Educational vision, organizing capacity, Liaison officer.

168. Equal educational opportunity means

(A) equal opportunity to have the type of education which one is suited for
(B) equality of educational standards for each child
(C) equal opportunity for all children to have access to education.
(D) All of the above.

169. The teacher should understand the crudeness of the child instincts and try to sublimate these. He should improve it through

(A) modifying each instinct

(B) the repressed instincts may appear in undesirable forms and hinder the growth of the child.

(C) a network of activities to provide ample opportunities for the sublimation of the instincts.

(D) All of the above

170. In a staff meeting of your institution, a significant decision has been taken on a controversial issue. You strongly feel that it was not the right forum to discuss the issue. What will you do in this situation?

(A) Walk out of the meeting in protest of the decision.

(B) Exert pressure over your friends to vote against the decision.

(C) Clearly present your arguments against the decision and request the members to reconsider.

(D) Quietly yield to the view point of the majority.

171. The general aim of education is to foster the mental development of children. Traditionally, emphasis of education was on mastery of subject matter, acquisition of facts and information through deliberate memorisation. Along with these attributes, modern education also aims to provide

(A) vocational education

(B) verbalism and theoretical knowledge

(C) useful curricular and co-curricular activities in the form of projects, and to encourage the use of discussion and other socialised teachings.

(D) All of the above.

172. The objectives of mental health in education can be achieved, if the following principles are observed in the curriculum

(A) The child's need, interest and experiences, individual differences in learning capacity should form the central factor.

(B) It should be dynamic and possible of revision so that it may be in harmony with changing social conditions.

(C) It should be flexible and adjustable to the needs of pupils at every stage.

(D) All of the above.

173. The major duty entrusted to the teaching community is

(A) to adjust his/her pupils to conform to the demands of society.

(B) to change human nature to conform to social expectations.

(C) to teach students how to adjust themselves to social demands.

(D) to harmonise the needs of the child and the demands of society for the benefit of both.

174. To educate according to nature means

(A) to come back to nature as opposed to mechanical life

(B) to educate in accordance with the law of nature of human development.

(C) to study natural laws and apply them to the educational process.

(D) All of the above.

175. The teaching of Froebel grew out of his belief that

(A) aim of education is self-realization as a part of God's plan

(B) spiritual meanings lay behind all phenomena, even play

(C) method of education should be self-activity an un-foldment

(D) All of the above are correct

176. Which one is not the objective of the special education ?

(A) To develop motivational patterns in the handicapped that will produce achievements

(B) To pursue those curricular matters that strategically determine effective living for specific type of handicapped children

(C) To develop a realistic self-concept in handicapped children

(D) None of the above

177. Learning of social roles consists of an internalisation of the expectation concerning the various roles and of applying these expectations to oneself. If the social roles are learned effectively, the individual becomes

(A) attains higher social adjustments.

(B) a good member of the group

(C) a good member of the group and attains higher social adjustments

(D) None of these

178. The period of adolescence is known as a period of stresses and strains. It is the most difficult and the awkward period, and marks the reawakening of the repressed sex-impulse. Which type of behaviour is unwanted ?

(A) Attitude of independence

(B) Sympathetic understanding

(C) Silence and hush-hush policy

(D) None of the above

179. Which of the following is not an aspect of learning ?
   (A) Modification of perceptions
   (B) The accumulation of knowledge
   (C) The sensitisation of nerve fibre
   (D) The elimination of errors.

180. Below are given some probable characteristics of an ineffective teacher, which of them is most likely to be characterised the ineffective teacher
   (A) emphasis upon pupil discussion in the clarification of groups goals.
   (B) emphasis upon standards.
   (C) emphasis upon the control of the immediate situation
   (D) None of the above.

181. A colleague who overhears you committing a mistake while teaching in your class points out this to you. How will you react ?
   (A) Tell him that you have never committed any mistake
   (B) Discuss with him and if convinced thank him and correct it in the next class
   (C) Warn him against interfering in such matters.
   (D) Request him not to tell it to anybody else.

182. Which of the following styles of action regarding instruction is preferred by you ?
   (A) Enrich the textual material by gathering relevant aspects from other books and experts.
   (B) Limit learning experiences to what is required by the textual material.
   (C) Discuss probable questions so that the students can fare well in the exam.
   (D) Ask pupils to read the text book in advance and hold discussions on its basis.

183. A teacher should be catechized for all of the following except
   (A) undermining the role of the parent
   (B) becoming overly friendly with pupils
   (C) exercising firm leadership
   (D) giving talented students special favours

184. While planning education for development which of the following characteristics will you stress ?
   (A) All round development of the individual
   (B) Development sustainable throughout life
   (C) Transferable to all walks of life
   (D) All the three above

185. "Mothers are the ideal teachers and the informal education given by home is most effective and natural". This statement belongs to
   (A) Gandhiji (B) Pestalogy
   (C) Montessori (D) Froebel

186. You were asked to go as a substitute teacher in a new classroom of the senior wing. How would you contribute to the life of students in that period?
   (A) You would ask them to revise their lessons.
   (B) You would take some time to gauge their concerns and initiate some academic discussion with them.
   (C) You would ask them to do whatever they like to do.
   (D) none of the above

187. You want to instil in the pupils of your class the spirit of democracy. Which of the following strategy do you think, is most efficient for the purpose.
   (A) Organise a discussion on the advantages of democracy over other systems and convince the pupils of its superiority.
   (B) Conduct election for a class assembly and give the representatives certain responsibilities.
   (C) Maintain a democratic atmosphere in your dealings and make the pupils unitedly responsible for class management, sharing duties among themselves.
   (D) Invite speakers to the school and make them deliver speeches about world leaders who worked for democracy.

188. Rabindranath Tagore views for education is
   (A) Education for perfectness
   (B) Education for making the man
   (C) Education for all
   (D) Both (A) and (B) both

189. The main function of educational Psychology is to provide prospective teachers with
   (A) Rules of thumb to deal with every day class room situation
   (B) Insight into the various aspects of modern education.
   (C) Insight into the needs, problems and styles of behaviour of learners.
   (D) Research procedures for evaluating current teaching procedures.

190. Team teaching is chartered by all of the following except

(A) the use of master teacher
(B) the use of large group lectures
(C) group planning
(D) inflexible groupings

191. MOOC stand for
(A) Mass Open Off-line Course
(B) Massive Open On-line Course
(C) Massive Optional On-line Curriculum
(D) None of the above

192. SWAYAM is a program aimed at following principles of education policy
(A) access, achieve, excel
(B) achieve, interact, learn
(C) access, equity, quality
(D) achieve, equity, excel

193. Courses of SWAYAM are primarily
(A) interactive (B) initiative
(C) interesting (D) innovative

194. SWAYAM PRABHA is a group of
(A) 12 DTH channels (B) 24 DTH channels
(C) 32 DTH channels (D) 64 DTH channels

195. SWAYAM PRABHA uses
(A) MSAT satellite (B) PSAT-20 satellite
(C) GSAT-15 satellite (D) None of these

196. Which of these is not covered in SWAYAM PRABHA?
(A) performing arts (B) law
(C) engineering (D) agriculture

197. Which of the following statements is true about teaching learning process?
(A) Teacher and student are dependent variables while parents are independent variable.
(B) Teachers are independent variable, students are dependent variable, and subject matter is intervening variable.
(C) Students are independent variable, teachers are dependent variable, and subject matter is intervening variable.
(D) None of these.

198. Which of the following are levels of teaching?
(i) Andragogical level of teaching
(ii) Memory level of teaching
(iii) Reflective level of teaching
(iv) Pedagogical level of teaching
(v) Understanding level of teaching
Codes:
(A) (ii), (iii), (v) (B) (ii), (iii), (iv), (v)
(C) (i), (iii), (iv) (D) (i), (ii), (iii), (iv)

199. Consider the following:
(i) From abstract to concrete
(ii) From complex to simple
(iii) From particular to general
(iv) From unknown to known
(v) From analysis to synthesis
Which of the above are maxims of teaching?
(A) (iii) and (v) (B) (iii), (iv), and (v)
(C) (i) and (v) (D) (ii), (iii), and (v)

200. Which of the following is true about teacher's role in higher education?
(i) Develop the personality of students
(ii) Tell some favourite students about important questions before examination
(iii) Motivate students for self-study
(iv) Encourage creativity and critical thinking in students
(v) Force students for tuitions after classes
(A) (i), (ii), (iii), and (iv)
(B) (ii), (iii), (iv), and (v)
(C) (i), (iii), and (iv)
(D) (i), (iii), and (v)

201. While presenting your ideas in a classroom it is better to
(i) Recognize that there can be other views
(ii) Recognize that students are not a homogenous mass
(iii) Take dissenting view also in consideration
Codes:
(A) Both (i) and (iii) (B) Only (iii)
(C) Only (ii) and (iii) (D) (i), (ii), and (iii)

202. Which of the following is the sequence of different levels of teaching?
(A) Memory level-Understanding level – Reflective level
(B) Memory level – Reflective level – Understanding level
(C) Understanding level – memory level – Reflective level
(D) Reflective level – Understanding level – Memory level

203. In context of dynamic teaching environment, which of the following statement is true?
(A) Teacher is a dependent variable and student is an independent variable.
(B) Teacher is an independent variable and student is a dependent variable.
(C) Both (A) and (B)
(D) None of the above

204. Which of the following is/are the teaching maxims?

(i) From psychological to logical
(ii) From analysis to synthesis
(iii) From concrete to abstract
(iv) Flow nature

Codes:

(A) (i), (ii) and (iii) (B) (i), (ii) and (iv)
(C) (i), (iii) and (iv) (D) None of these

205. Arrange the flowing activities of interaction in logical order.

(i) Analysis of the work done
(ii) Planning and preparation
(iii) Presentation of material
(iv) Modification and improvement

Codes:

(A) (iv), (i), (ii) and (iii)
(B) (ii), (iii), (i) and (iv)
(C) (i), (iii), (iv) and (ii)
(D) (i), (ii), (iii) and (iv)

206. For the homework to be effective in accomplishing its purposes, which of the following suggestions for teachers is correct?

(A) Do not listen to what students say about their experiences in completing homework assignments.
(B) Do give homework as punishment.
(C) Do not expect students to always have their homework assignments completed.
(D) Make up spur-of-the-moment homework assignments for student practice.

207. CHEER stands for

(A) Children Enrichment Education through Radio
(B) Children for Engineers and Energy Requirement
(C) Child Health Education Electronic Recording
(D) None of the above

208. When an action or response produces a pleasant or rewarding outcome that behaviour is likely to be responses that bring displeasure or pain are likely to weaken and fade, it is called

(A) Thorndike's law of effect
(B) Thorndike's law of exercise
(C) Both (A) and (B)
(D) None of the above

209. National Literacy Mission was established in

(A) 1999 (B) 1988
(C) 1996 (D) 2000

210. The in-service teacher training can be made more effective by

(A) Making it a residential programme.
(B) Using cooperative approach.
(C) Using training package which is well prepared in advance
(D) Practicing training follow-up procedures.

211. Who developed the interaction analysis category system in education for increasing the teacher's effectiveness?

(A) Flander (B) Richard Over
(C) Rayon (D) Amidon and Simon

212. Which of the following school principal will emerge as a good educational leader?

(A) A very social person with pleasing habits.
(B) An experienced teacher having a degree in leadership from a top foreign university.
(C) A throughout topper and a meritorious academician.
(D) A teacher whose class results are excellent, is a hard task master and yet popular among students and teachers.

213. Spare the rod and spoil the child. This assumptions is related to the type of discipline which has bean advocated

(A) In democratic era
(B) By naturalist philosophy
(C) In Victorian era
(D) By pragmatist philosophy

214. Man is born free but everywhere he is in chains, This statement was given by

(A) W.H. Kilpatrick
(B) Jean-Jacques Rousseau
(C) Abraham Maslow
(D) John Dewey

215. As per the NCTE norms, what should be the staff strength for a unit of 100 students at B.Ed. level ?

(A) 1 + 7 (B) 1 + 9
(C) 1 + 10 (D) 1 + 5

216. Child centred education govt. emphasis first time by

(A) N.P.E. 1986
(B) Mudaliar Commission
(C) Kothari Commission
(D) Radhakrishnan Commission

217. Three elements are urgent for character development-Discipline, Secularism and Moral Education, was the view of which education commission

(A) Hunter Commission
(B) Education Commission
(C) Mudaliar Commission
(D) University Education Commission

218. National Policy on Education (1986) makes a recommendation (8.1) that "The existing schism between the formal system of education and the country's rich and varied cultural tradition needs to be bridged". This assumes that
(A) There is a social lag in Indian society
(B) The insufficient progress of education in India
(C) There is enough socio-cultural progress in India
(D) There is great need for social change in India

219. Which one of the following is not one of the main components of Operation Blackboard Scheme?
(A) Provision of at least two classrooms in each primary school with facilities of separate toilets for boys and girls
(B) Provision of an additional teacher in primary schools
(C) Provision of 100 percent assistance from the state government for implementation of the scheme
(D) Provision of essential teaching-learning material.

220. Institutional planning means:
(A) Creating institutions based on the planned goals.
(B) Conducting SWOT analysis while planning at institutional level
(C) Planning at institutional level, on the basis of felt needs & available resources.
(D) Conducting seminars and planning meetings to improve the functioning of any institution only.

221. The first MOOC offered in 2008 by Stephen Downes and George Siemens was
(A) Connectivism and Connective knowledge
(B) Introduction to Artificial intelligence
(C) Models of Teaching
(D) Rhizomatic Learning

222. The name of the MOOC platform developed by IIT Kanpur is
(A) SWAYAM (B) Causera
(C) mooKIT (D) MOOCK

223. mooKIT is one of the projects serving currently for providing online education. It is offered by
(A) IIT Kanpur (B) IIT Bombay
(C) IISC (D) IIT Madras

224. Match List I with List II

List I **MOOC Platform**	**List II** **Developer**
(a) Coursera	I. Anant Agarwal
(b) Udacity	II. Salman Khan
(c) Edx	III. Andrew Ng, Daphne Koller
(d) Khan Academy	IV. Sebastian Thrun

Choose the correct answer from the options given below:
(A) A-I, B-II, C-III, D-IV
(B) A-III, B-IV, C-I, D-II
(C) A-IV, B-I, C-II, D-III
(D) A-II, B-III, C-IV, D-I

225. mooKIT platform uses ____________, an open source content management system
(A) DRUPAL (B) JOOMLA
(C) SAKAI (D) Moodle

226. What is the full form of MOOC?
(A) Most Organised Offline Courses
(B) Modern Online Office Courses
(C) Massive Open Online Courses
(D) Massive Office Order Cell

227. Given below are two statements:
Statement I: The abbreviation 'MOOC' stands for 'Massive Open Online Courses'.
Statement II: The abbreviation 'SWAYAM' stands for 'Study Webs of Active-Learning for Young Academic Minds',
In the light of the above statements, choose the correct answer from the options given below:
(A) Both Statement I and Statement II are true.
(B) Both Statement I and Statement II are false.
(C) Statement I is true but Statement II is false.
(D) Statement I is false but Statement II is true.

228. The first MOOC offered in 2008 by Stephen Downes and George Siemens was
(A) Connectivism and Connective knowledge
(B) Introduction to Artificial intelligence
(C) Models of Teaching
(D) Rhizomatic Learning

229. Which satellite is used by Swayam Prabha for the program telecasts on the DTH channels?
(A) INSAT-3A (B) GSAT-30
(C) NSAT-4B (D) GSAT-15

230. Given below are two statements:

Statement I: The SWAYAM PRABHA has new content every day for at least 5 hours which would be repeated 4 more times in a day.

Statement II: The SWAYAM PRABHA has content that allows the students to choose the time of their convenience.

In the light of the above statements, choose the correct answer from the options given below:

(A) Both Statement I and Statement II are true
(B) Both Statement I and Statement II are false
(C) Statement I is true but Statement II is false
(D) Statement I is false but Statement II is true

231. Which of the following channel of SWAYAM Prabha deals with the social science and the education, Psychology, and Home Science?

(A) Channel 01: VAGEESH
(B) Channel 04: SAARASWAT
(C) Channel 05: PRABANDHAN
(D) Channel 06: VIDHIK

232. The web portal of Swayam Prabha is maintained by

(A) Indian Institute of Technology, Kharagpur
(B) Doordarshan
(C) Google India office
(D) INFLIBNET centre

233. INFLIBNET Centre, which is an autonomous Inter-University Centre of the University Grants Commission, maintains

(A) Swayam Prabha (B) e-Pathshala
(C) e-Gyankosh (D) Shodhganga

234. A group of DTH channels devoted to telecasting educational programs 24 × 7 basis is

(A) Swayam (B) MOOC
(C) Swayam Prabha (D) Gyan Darshan

235. Given below are two statements

Statement I: If we are interested in the worldview of members of a certain social group, a qualitative research strategy that is sensitive to how participants interpret their social world may be preferable.

Statement II: If a researcher is interested in a topic on which little or no research has been in the past, quantitative research may be easy to employ because there is little prior literature from which to draw leads.

In light of the above statements, choose the most appropriate answer from the options given below

(A) Both Statement I and Statement II are correct
(B) Both Statement I and Statement II are incorrect
(C) Statement I is correct but Statement II is incorrect
(D) Statement I is incorrect but Statement II is correct

236. Which among the following is the names for validity whereby researcher uses a future criterion measure, rather than a contemporary one?

(A) Convergent validity
(B) Predictive validity
(C) Construct validity
(D) Concurrent validity

237. The kind of sample that is simply available to the researcher by virtue of its accessibility, is known as

(A) Quota sampling (B) Snowball sampling
(C) Convenience sampling
(D) Web sampling

238. Where is the National Geophysical Research Institute located?

(A) Jamshedpur (B) Hyderabad
(C) Mumbai (D) Jaipur

239. One of the following is not the objective of action research

(A) To improve the working condition of school
(B) To stimulate the students to raise their standard of learning
(C) To motivate the students to attend school
(D) To organise healthy and congenial environment for effective learning

240. What is the aim of educational research?

(A) Identifying major problems that need to be solved
(B) Searching for the new facts and principles underlying the process of education
(C) Identifying the aims of education
(D) Identifying the values that need to be inculcated in the pupils

241. In Data Processing, what does the abbreviation SAP stand for?

(A) Systems, Applications, Products
(B) Sales, Allocations, Purchases
(C) Systems, Authorizations, Programs
(D) Systems, Algorithms, Processes

242. External validity in research refers to

(A) The rigour of the study
(B) The accuracy of a procedure
(C) The relation of the research problem with the researcher's personal life

(D) The extent of generalizability that the results provide

243. The personalistic styles of writing a research report are permissible in which of the following research?

1. Grounded theory research
2. Experimental research
3. Participant-observation based research
4. Historical research
5. Case study research

Choose the correct answer from the option given below:

(A) 1, 2 and 3 only (B) 2, 3 and 4 only
(C) 3, 4 and 5 only (D) 1, 3 and 5 only

244. In using the hypothetico-deductive research paradigm which of the following sequences is considered appropriate?

(A) Hypothesis making, Hypothesis testing, Arriving at generalization and Conclusion
(B) Establishing a research problem, Hypothesis making, Hypothesis testing, Arriving at generalization and Conclusion
(C) Hypothesis making, Establishing a research problem Hypothesis testing, Arriving at generalization and Conclusion
(D) Hypothesis testing, Hypothesis making, Finalizing the problem, Arriving at generalization and Conclusion

245. In which of the following research methods, manipulation and control of variables, and randomization of sample are two of the basic requirements?

(A) Ex-post facto research
(B) Descriptive research
(C) Case study research
(D) Experimental research

246. Which one of the following research procedures will figure under post positivistic approach?

(A) Normative survey
(B) Experimental study
(C) Ethnographic study
(D) Ex post facto study

247. Inappropriate application of ICT in research is an example of:

(A) Technical lapse on the part of the researcher
(B) Inadequate provision of ICT resources
(C) Violation of research ethics
(D) Absence of technical expertise of ICT resources

248. Which one of the following is the main feature of qualitative research?

(A) Avoids positivist assumptions and data analysis
(B) Subscribes to pre-existing categories
(C) Collects data in numerical form
(D) Uses the empirical method of data analysis

249. A university teacher intends to study the relationship between level of aspiration and achievement of rural children. Which design of research will be most appropriate in the context?

(A) Experimental research design
(B) Ex Post Facto research design
(C) Historical research design
(D) Survey research design

250. Which of the following steps in research are least vulnerable to research ethics?

1. Identifying the research variables
2. Defining the research variables
3. Data collection procedure
4. Data analysis procedure
5. Reporting research outcomes

Choose the correct answer from the options given below:

(A) 1 and 2 only (B) 2 and 3 only
(C) 3 and 4 only (D) 4 and 5 only

251. A college teacher plans a research programme in which he/she intends to improve the socio-emotional aspect of his/her classroom climate during teaching. Which one of the following research methods will be considered appropriate in this context?

(A) Experimental method
(B) Descriptive method
(C) Historical method
(D) Action research method

252. Which of the following sampling techniques in research imply randomization and equal probability of drawing the units?

1. Quota sampling
2. Snowball sampling
3. Stratified sampling
4. Dimensional sampling
5. Cluster sampling

Choose the correct answer from the option given below:

(A) 1 and 2 only (B) 2 and 3 only
(C) 3 and 5 only (D) 4 and 5 only

253. The best meaning of Research is
   (A) Adoption of 'Scientific Method' for creation and application of knowledge
   (B) Adoption of critical and constructive thinking for solution of problems
   (C) Arriving at generalisations based on observed data
   (D) Search for universal truths of life

254. Which of the following is a measure of consistency?
   (A) Validity (B) Objectivity
   (C) Reliability (D) Credibility

255. The study of 'why does stressful living result in a heart attack? can be classified as
   (A) Descriptive research
   (B) Explanatory research
   (C) Correlational research
   (D) Feasibility research

256. In which research design the independent variable is 'selected' rather than 'manipulated'?
   (A) Experimental research design
   (B) Historical research design
   (C) Ex post-facto research design
   (D) Descriptive survey research design

ANSWERS

1. (C)	2. (A)	3. (A)	4. (A)	5. (A)	6. (D)	7. (C)	8. (D)	9. (D)	10. (D)
11. (C)	12. (D)	13. (D)	14. (C)	15. (B)	16. (B)	17. (B)	18. (A)	19. (B)	20. (B)
21. (B)	22. (C)	23. (C)	24. (A)	25. (A)	26. (C)	27. (D)	28. (C)	29. (C)	30. (C)
31. (B)	32. (A)	33. (B)	34. (D)	35. (C)	36. (A)	37. (B)	38. (C)	39. (A)	40. (B)
41. (B)	42. (B)	43. (D)	44. (C)	45. (A)	46. (A)	47. (B)	48. (C)	49. (B)	50. (D)
51. (B)	52. (A)	53. (B)	54. (C)	55. (B)	56. (D)	57. (A)	58. (D)	59. (D)	60. (B)
61. (A)	62. (B)	63. (D)	64. (A)	65. (D)	66. (D)	67. (D)	68. (D)	69. (D)	70. (C)
71. (C)	72. (C)	73. (D)	74. (A)	75. (A)	76. (B)	77. (D)	78. (C)	79. (B)	80. (C)
81. (D)	82. (B)	83. (D)	84. (D)	85. (A)	86. (A)	87. (D)	88. (B)	89. (C)	90. (D)
91. (C)	92. (B)	93. (C)	94. (C)	95. (D)	96. (C)	97. (C)	98. (D)	99. (A)	100. (D)
101. (A)	102. (C)	103. (D)	104. (B)	105. (C)	106. (A)	107. (A)	108. (D)	109. (A)	110. (D)
111. (B)	112. (D)	113. (B)	114. (D)	115. (A)	116. (D)	117. (D)	118. (C)	119. (C)	120. (A)
121. (A)	122. (C)	123. (A)	124. (C)	125. (A)	126. (C)	127. (C)	128. (D)	129. (B)	130. (A)
131. (B)	132. (D)	133. (C)	134. (D)	135. (C)	136. (A)	137. (C)	138. (D)	139. (A)	140. (D)
141. (D)	142. (D)	143. (B)	144. (A)	145. (D)	146. (D)	147. (C)	148. (A)	149. (B)	150. (D)
151. (C)	152. (B)	153. (A)	154. (C)	155. (A)	156. (A)	157. (A)	158. (C)	159. (A)	160. (B)
161. (D)	162. (C)	163. (A)	164. (B)	165. (C)	166. (D)	167. (B)	168. (C)	169. (C)	170. (C)
171. (C)	172. (D)	173. (D)	174. (B)	175. (D)	176. (D)	177. (C)	178. (C)	179. (C)	180. (C)
181. (B)	182. (A)	183. (C)	184. (D)	185. (D)	186. (B)	187. (C)	188. (D)	189. (A)	190. (D)
191. (B)	192. (C)	193. (A)	194. (C)	195. (C)	196. (D)	197. (D)	198. (A)	199. (A)	200. (C)
201. (D)	202. (A)	203. (B)	204. (D)	205. (B)	206. (C)	207. (A)	208. (A)	209. (B)	210. (D)
211. (A)	212. (D)	213. (C)	214. (D)	215. (A)	216. (B)	217. (C)	218. (B)	219. (C)	220. (C)
221. (A)	222. (C)	223. (A)	224. (B)	225. (D)	226. (C)	227. (C)	228. (A)	229. (D)	230. (D)
231. (B)	232. (D)	233. (D)	234. (C)	235. (C)	236. (C)	237. (B)	238. (C)	239. (B)	240. (A)
241. (A)	242. (D)	243. (D)	244. (B)	245. (D)	246. (C)	247. (D)	248. (A)	249. (B)	250. (A)
251. (D)	252. (C)	253. (A)	254. (C)	255. (B)	256. (C)				

RESEARCH APTITUDE

Syllabus

- **Research:** Meaning, Types, and Characteristics, Positivism and Post-positivistic Approach to Research.
- **Methods of Research:** Experimental, Descriptive, Historical, Qualitative and Quantitative Methods.
- Steps of Research.
- Thesis and Article Writing: Format and Styles of Referencing.
- Application of ICT in Research.
- Research Ethics.

RESEARCH

Meaning of Research

Searching it again and again means Research. Research is defined as human activity based on intellectual application in the investigation of matter. The primary purpose for applied research is discovering, interpreting, and the development of methods and systems for the advancement of human knowledge on a wide variety of scientific matters of our world and the universe. Research can use the scientific method, but need not do so.

- Research is an art of scientific investigation. It is regarded as a systematic efforts to gain new knowledge.
- The dictionary meaning of research is "a careful investigation or enquiry especially through search for new facts in any branch of knowledge".
- Definition of Research comprises defining and redefining problems, formulating hypothesis or suggested solutions; collecting, organizing and evaluating data; making deductions and reaching conclusions; and at last carefully testing the conclusions to determine whether they fit the formulating hypothesis.

"Research is an organized and systematic way of finding answers to questions" Systematic because there is a definite set of procedures and steps which you will follow. There are certain things in the research process which are always done in order to get the most accurate results.

Characteristics of Research

1. It is a scientific investigation. Research (re-search) means to "search again.' It connotes patient study and scientific investigation.

2. It develops concepts and the theories. One reason for conducting research is to develop and evaluate concepts and the theories.
3. It expands the limits of knowledge. Basic or pure research attempts to expand the limits of knowledge. It is conducted to verify the acceptability of a given theory or to know more about a certain concept.
4. It cannot be implemented immediately. It does not directly involve the solution to a particular problem, its findings generally cannot be implemented immediately.
5. It is essential tool for good decision making. The task of educational research is to make the information used in decision making more accurate. Educational research is a managerial tool that provides information essential for good decision making. Research in teaching, training, organizing, or management areas of an institution is within the scope of training research. Educational research reduces the risk of making wrong decisions. It is an aid to management judgement, not a substitute for it.

Remember

- Research is Systematic, purposive and objective.
- Research Report is Precise (multiple interpretation is not encouraged.
- Research is Testable/Measurable
- Research is Verifiable.
- Research is analytical & critical (going deeper into the depth of the idea).
- Patient and unhurried activity.
- Research demands a clear statement of the problem.
- Research seeks direction through appropriate hypotheses.
- Research deals with the main problem through sub-problems.

In a nutshell characteristics of research are as follows:

1. Objective	2. Reliability	3. Validity
4. Accuracy	5. Credibility	6. Generalizability
7. Empirical Research	8. Systematic	9. Controlled factors
10. Cyclical	11. Logical	12. Replicable

AIMS AND OBJECTIVES OF RESEARCH

1. To gain familiarity with a phenomenon or to achieve new insights into it. (Exploratory or formulative research studies).
2. To portray accurately the characteristics of a particular individual, situation or a group. (Descriptive research studies).
3. To determine the frequency with which something occurs or with which it is associated with something else. (Diagnostic research studies).
4. To test a hypothesis of a causal relationship between variables (hypothesis-testing research studies).

TYPES OF RESEARCH

Education research methods can be defined as "a systematic ad scientific procedure of data collection, compilation, analysis, interpretation, and implication pertaining to any business problem". Types of research methods can be classified into several categories according to the nature and purpose of the study and other attributes.

General Classification of Types of Research Methods

- **Quantitative research** "describes, infers, and resolves problems using numbers. Emphasis is placed on the collection of numerical data, the summary of those data and the drawing of inferences from the data".

- **Qualitative research**, on the other hand, is based on words, feelings, emotions, sounds and other non-numerical and unquantifiable elements. It has been noted that "information is considered qualitative in nature if it cannot be analysed by means of mathematical techniques. This characteristic may also mean that an incident does not take place often enough to allow reliable data to be collected".

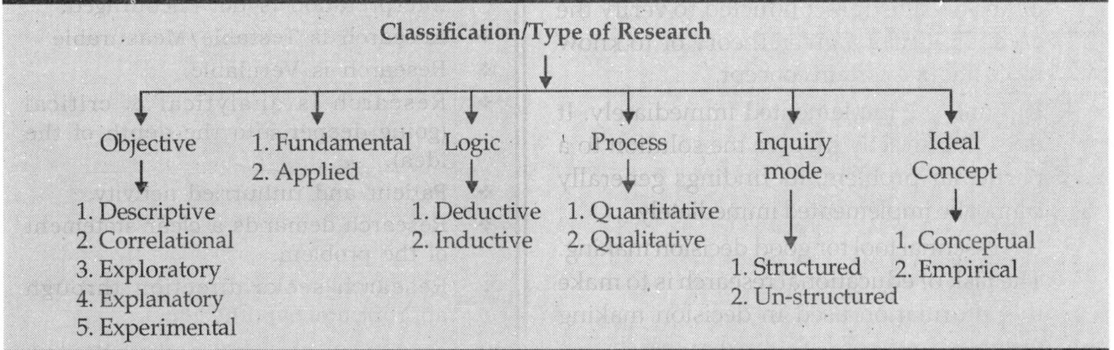

Types of Research Methods According to Nature of the Study

Types of the research methods according to the nature of research can be divided into two groups: descriptive and analytical. Descriptive research usually involves surveys and studies that aim to identify the facts. In other words, descriptive research mainly deals with the "description of the state of affairs as it is at present", and there is no control over variables in descriptive research.

Analytical research, on the other hand, is fundamentally different in a way that "the researcher has to use facts or information already available and analyse these in order to make a critical evaluation of the material".

Types of Research Methods According to the Purpose of the Study

According to the purpose of the study, types of research methods can be divided into two categories: applied research and fundamental research. Applied research is also referred to as an action research, and the fundamental research is sometimes called basic or pure research. The table below summarizes the main differences between applied research and fundamental research. Similarities between applied and fundamental (basic) research relate to the adoption of a systematic and scientific procedure to conduct the study.

DIFFERENCES BETWEEN APPLIED AND FUNDAMENTAL RESEARCH

Applied Research	Fundamental Research
• Tries to eliminate the theory by adding to the basics of a discipline	• Aims to solve a problem by adding to the field of application of a discipline
• Problems are analysed from the point of one discipline	• Often several disciplines work together for solving the problem
• Generalisations are preferred	• Often researches individual cases without the aim to generalise
• Forecasting approach is implemented	• Aims to say how things can be changed
• Assumes that other variables do not change	• Acknowledges that other variables are constant by changing
• Reports are compiled in a language of technical language of discipline	• Reports are compiled in a common language

Types of Research Methods according to Research Design

On the basis of research design the types of research methods can be divided into two groups – exploratory and conclusive. Exploratory studies only aim to explore the research area and they do not attempt to offer final and conclusive answers to research questions. Conclusive studies, on the contrary, aim to provide final and conclusive answers to research questions.

Table below illustrates the main differences between exploratory and conclusive research designs:

	Exploratory research	Conclusive research
Structure	Loosely structured in design.	Well structured and systematic in design
Methodology	Are flexible and investigative in methodology.	Have a formal and definitive. methodology that needs to be followed and tested.
Hypotheses	Do not involve testing of hypotheses.	Most conclusive researches are carried out to test the formulated hypotheses
Findings	Findings might be topic specific and might not have much relevance outside of researcher's domain.	Findings are significant as they have a theoretical or applied implication.

Positivism

It has to be acknowledged that the positivism research philosophy is difficult to be explained in a precise and succinct manner. This is because there are vast differences between settings in which positivism is used by researchers. The number variations in explaining positivism may be equal to the number of authors who addressed the area of research philosophy. Nevertheless, in its essence, positivism is based on the idea that science is the only way to learn about the truth.

As a philosophy, positivism adheres to the view that only "factual" knowledge gained through observation (the senses), including measurement, is trustworthy. In positivism studies the role of the researcher is limited to data collection and interpretation in an objective way. In these types of studies research findings are usually observable and quantifiable.

Positivism depends on quantifiable observations that lead to statistical analyses. It has been noted that "as a philosophy, positivism is in accordance with the empiricist view that knowledge stems from human experience. It has an atomistic, ontological view of the world as comprising discrete, observable elements and events that interact in an observable, determined and regular manner".

Moreover, in positivism studies the researcher is independent form the study and there are no provisions for human interests within the study. Crowther and Lancaster (2008) argue that as a general rule, positivist studies usually adopt deductive approach, whereas inductive research approach is usually associated with a phenomenology philosophy. Moreover, positivism relates to the viewpoint that researcher needs to concentrate on facts, whereas phenomenology concentrates on the meaning and has provision for human interest.

Approach

- Research is done by working with observable social reality.
- The social world can be observed by collecting objective facts.
- The social world consists of simple elements to which it can be reduced.
- If two people do research, they will same conclusion.
- Generalization can be made.

The five main principles of positivism research philosophy can be summarized as the following:

1. There are no differences in the logic of inquiry across sciences.
2. The research should aim to explain and predict.

3. Research should be empirically observable via human senses. Inductive reasoning should be used to develop statements (hypotheses) to be tested during the research process.
4. Science is not the same as the common sense. The common sense should not be allowed to bias the research findings.
5. Science must be value-free and it should be judged only by logic.

The following table illustrates ontology, epistemology, axiology and typical research methods associated with positivism research philosophy:

Ontology	Epistemology	Axiology	Typical methods
Real, external, independent One true reality (universalism) Granular (things) Ordered	Scientific method Observable and measurable facts Law-like generalizations Numbers Causal explanation and prediction as contribution Causal explanation and prediction as contribution	Value-free research Researcher is detached, neutral and independent of what is researched Researcher maintains objective stance	Typically deductive, highly structured, large samples, measurement, typically quantitative method of analysis, but a range of data can be analysed

Science as an Underlying Ground for Positivism

Positivism often involves the use of existing theory to develop hypotheses to be tested during the research process. Science can be specified as a cornerstone in positivism research philosophy. Specifically, positivism relies on the following aspects of the science.

1. **Science is deterministic.** Scientific approach is based on assumption that X causes Y under certain circumstances. The role of researcher when following the scientific approach is to discover specific nature of cause and effect relationships.
2. **Science is mechanistic.** Mechanical nature of scientific approach can be explained in a way that researchers develop hypotheses to be proved or disproved via application of specific research methods.
3. **Science uses method.** Chosen methods are applied mechanically in order to operationalize theory or hypothesis. Application of methodology involves selection of sample, measurements, analysis and reaching conclusions about hypotheses.
4. **Science deals with empiricism.** In other words, science only deals with what can be seen or measured. From this perspective, science can be assessed as objective.

Differences between Positivism and Social Constructionism

The key features of positivism and social constructionism philosophical approaches are presented in the following table by Ramanathan.

	Positivism	Social Constructionism
The observer	Must be independent	Is part of what is being observed
Human interests	Should be irrelevant	Are the main drivers of science
Explanations	Must demonstrate causality	Aim to increase general understanding of the situation
Research progresses through	Hypotheses and deductions	Gather rich data from which ideas are induced
Concepts	Need to be operationalised so that they can be measured	Should incorporate stakeholder perspectives
Units of analysis	Should be reduced to simplest terms	May include the complexity of 'whole' situations
Generalisation through	Statistical probability	Theoretical abstraction
Sampling requires	Large numbers selected randomly	Small numbers of cases chosen for specific reasons

Differences between Positivism and Phenomenology Paradigms

Alternatively, the differences between positivist and phenomenology paradigms are best illustrated by Easterby-Smith et al. in the following manner:

	Positivist Paradigm	Phenomenology paradigm
Basic notions	The world is perceived as external and objective The world is perceived to be socially constructed and subjective	Independency of the observer. Value-free approach to science Observer is considered a part of the object of observation. Human interests drives science
Responsibilities of researcher	Focusing on facts Causalities and fundamental laws are searched Phenomenon are reduced to the simplest elements Hypotheses formulation and testing them	To be focusing on meanings Aiming to understand the meaning of events Exploring the totality of each individual case Ideas are developed by induction from data
Most suitable research methods	Concepts have to be operationalized	Using several methods in order to different aspects of phenomena
Sampling	Samples have to be large	Small samples are analyzed in a greater depth or over longer period of time

Shortcomings of Positivism

Positivism as an epistemology is associated with the following set of disadvantages:

Firstly, positivism relies on experience as a valid source of knowledge. However, a wide range of basic and important concepts such as cause, time and space are not based on experience.

Secondly, positivism assumes that all types of processes can be perceived as a certain variation of actions of individuals or relationships between individuals.

Thirdly, adoption of positivism in business studies and other studies can be criticized for reliance on status quo. In other words, research findings in positivism studies are only descriptive, thus they lack insight into in-depth issues.

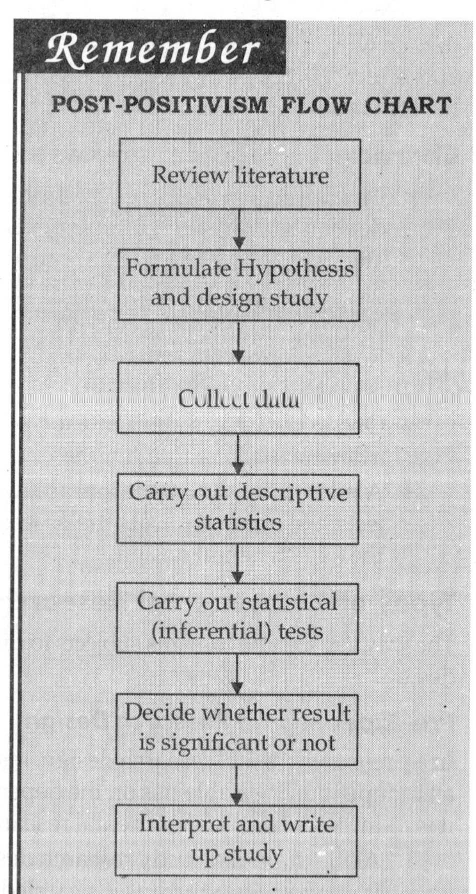

Post-Positivist Approaches to Research

Post-positivist research principles emphasise meaning and the creation of new knowledge, and are able to support committed social movements, that is, movements that aspire to change the world and contribute towards social justice.

Post-positivist research has the following characteristics:

- Research is broad rather than specialised – lots of different things qualify as research;
- Theory and practice cannot be kept separate. We cannot afford to ignore theory for the sake of 'just the facts';

- The researcher's motivations for and commitment to research are central and crucial to the enterprise;
- The idea that research is concerned only with correct techniques for collecting and categorising information is now inadequate.

METHODS OF RESEARCH

Experimental Method

Experimental research is a scientific method of conducting research using two variables: independent and dependent. Independent variables can be manipulated to apply to dependent variables and the effect is measured. This measurement usually happens over a significant period of time to establish conditions and conclusions about the relationship between these two variables.

Experimental research is widely implemented in education, psychology, social sciences and physical sciences. Experimental research is based on observation, calculation, comparison and logic. Researchers collect quantitative data and perform statistical analyses of two sets of variables. This method collects necessary data to focus on facts and support sound decisions. It's a helpful approach when time is a factor in establishing cause-and-effect relationships or when an invariable behavior is seen between the two.

- **Experimental research** is most scientifically sophisticated research method.
- It is defined as 'observation under controlled conditions'.
- **Experimental research design** are concerned with examination of the effect of independent variable on the dependent variable, where the independent variable is manipulated through treatment or intervention(s), & the effect of those interventions is observed on the dependant variable.

Characteristics of Experimental Research Design

- Dependent variables are manipulated or treated while independent variables are exerted on dependent variables as an experimental treatment. Extraneous variables are variables generated from other factors that can affect the experiment and contribute to change. Researchers have to exercise control to reduce the influence of these variables by randomization, making homogeneous groups and applying statistical analysis techniques.
- Researchers deliberately operate independent variables on the subject of the experiment. This is known as manipulation.
- Once a variable is manipulated, researchers observe the effect an independent variable has on a dependent variable. This is key for interpreting results.
- A researcher may want multiple comparisons between different groups with equivalent subjects, they may replicate the process by conducting sub-experiments within the framework of the experimental design.

Types of Experimental Research Design

The way a researcher assigns subjects to different groups determines the types of experimental research design.

Pre-Experimental Research Design

In a pre-experimental research design, researchers observe a group or various groups to see the effect an independent variable has on the dependent variable to cause change. There is no control group as it is a simple form of experimental research. It's further divided into three categories:

1. A one-shot case study research design is a study where one dependent variable is considered. It's a post-test study as it's carried out after treating what presumably caused the change.

2. One-group pretest-post-test design is a study that combines both pretest and post-test studies by testing a single group before and after administering the treatment.
3. Static-group comparison involves studying two groups by subjecting one to treatment while the other remains static. After post-testing all groups the differences are observed.

This design is practical but lacks in certain areas of true experimental criteria.

True Experimental Research Design

This design depends on statistical analysis to approve or disregard a hypothesis. It's an accurate design that can be conducted with or without a pretest on a minimum of two dependent variables assigned randomly. It is further classified into three types:

1. The post-test-only control group design involves randomly selecting and assigning subjects to two groups: Experimental and control. Only the experimental group is treated, while both groups are observed and post-tested to draw a conclusion from the difference between the groups.
2. In a pretest-post-test control group design, two groups are randomly assigned subjects. Both groups are presented, the experimental group is treated and both groups are post-tested to measure how much change happened in each group.
3. Solomon four-group design is a combination of the previous two methods subjects are randomly selected and assigned to four groups. Two groups are tested using each of the previous methods.

True experimental research design should have a variable to manipulate, a control group and random distribution.

Advantages of Experimental Research

- It allows researchers to have a stronghold over variables and collect desired results.
- Results are usually specific.
- The effectiveness of the research isn't affected by the subject.
- Findings from the results usually apply to similar situations and ideas.
- Cause and effect of a hypothesis can be identified, which can be further analyzed for in-depth ideas.
- It's the ideal starting point to collect data and lay a foundation for conducting further research and building more ideas.
- Medical researchers can develop medicines and vaccines to treat diseases by collecting samples from patients and testing them under multiple conditions.
- It can be used to improve the standard of academics across institutions by testing student knowledge and teaching methods before analyzing the result to implement programs.
- Social scientists often use experimental research design to study and test behavior in humans and animals.
- Software development and testing heavily depend on experimental research to test programs by letting subjects use a beta version and analyzing their feedback.

Disadvantages of Experimental Research

- Human error is a concern because the method depends on controlling variables, improper implementation nullifies the validity of the research and conclusion.
- Eliminating extraneous variables (real-life scenarios) produces inaccurate conclusions.
- The process is time-consuming and expensive.
- In medical research, it can have ethical implications by affecting patients' well-being.
- Results are not descriptive and subjects can contribute to response bias.

Experimental research design is a sophisticated method that investigates relationships or occurrences among people or phenomena under a controlled environment and identifies the conditions responsible for such relationships or occurrences.

Examples of Experimental Research

Experimental research can be used in any industry to anticipate responses, changes, causes and effects. Here are some examples of experimental research:

- Educational institutions follow the pre-experimental research design to administer exams and evaluate students at the end of a semester. Students are the dependent variables and lectures are independent. Since exams are conducted at the end and not the beginning of a semester, it's easy to conclude that it's a one-shot case study research.
- To evaluate the teaching methods of two teachers, they can be assigned two student groups. After teaching their respective groups on the same topic, a post-test can determine which group scored better and who is better at teaching. This method can have its drawbacks as certain human factors, such as attitudes of students and effectiveness to grasp a subject, may negatively influence results.

Descriptive Research

Descriptive research is defined as a research method that describes the characteristics of the population or phenomenon that is being studied. This methodology focuses more on the "what" of the research subject rather than the "why" of the research subject.

In other words, descriptive research primarily focuses on describing the nature of a demographic segment, without focusing on "why" a certain phenomenon occurs. In other words, it "describes" the subject of the research, without covering "why" it happens.

For example, an apparel brand that wants to understand the fashion purchasing trends among New York buyers will conduct a demographic survey of this region, gather population data and then conduct descriptive research on this demographic segment. The research will then uncover details on "what is the purchasing pattern of New York buyers", but not cover any investigative details on "why" the patterns exits. Because for the apparel brand trying to break into this market, understanding the nature of their market is the objective of the study.

Advantages of Descriptive Research

- Data collection.
- Varied.
- Natural environment.
- Quick to conduct and cheap.
- Forms basis for decision-making.

Disadvantages of Descriptive Research

- Confidentiality.
- Halo effect.
- Sample isn't representative.
- No scope to learn cause.

Characteristics of Descriptive Research

The term descriptive research then, refers to research questions, design of the research and data analysis that would be conducted on that topic. It is called an observational research method because none of the variables that are part of the research study are influenced in any capacity.

Some distinctive characteristics of descriptive research are:

1. **Quantitative research.** Descriptive research is a quantitative research method that attempts to collect quantifiable information to be used for statistical analysis of the population sample. It is an popular market research tool that allows to collect and describe the nature of the demographic segment.

2. **Uncontrolled variables.** In descriptive research, none of the variables are influenced in any way. This uses observational methods to conduct the research. Hence, the nature of the variables or their behavior is not in the hands of the researcher.
3. **Cross-sectional studies.** Descriptive research is generally a cross-sectional study where different sections belonging to the same group are studied.
4. **Basis for further research.** The data collected and analyzed from descriptive research can then be further researched using different research techniques. The data also can help point towards the types of research methods are to be used for the subsequent research.

Descriptive Research Methods

There are three distinctive methods to conduct descriptive research. They are:

- Observational Method.
- Case Study Method.
- Survey Research.

Historical Method of Research

Historical methods of research are the process of systematically examining an account of what has happened in the past. It is not facts and dates or even a description of past events. The dynamic account of past events that involves an interpretation attempt to recapture the nuances, personalities, and ideas that events. One of the goals of historical research is to communicating of past events. In the field of library and information science, there are vast arrays of topics that may be considered for conducting historical research.

The historical method comprises the techniques and guidelines by which historians use primary sources and other evidence, such as secondary sources and tertiary sources, to research and then to write history.

STEPS IN HISTORICAL RESEARCH

1. Identify an idea, topic or research question
2. Conduct a background literature review
3. Refine the research idea and questions
4. Determine that historical methods will be the method used
5. Identify and locate primary and secondary data sources
6. Evaluate the authenticity and accuracy of source materials
7. Analyze the date and develop a narrative exposition of the findings.

Advantages and Disadvantages of Historical Methods Research

Disadvantages

- Cannot control for threats to internal validity.
- Limitations are imposed due to the content analysis.
- Researchers cannot ensure representation of the sample.
- Bias in interpreting historical sources.
- Interpreting sources is very time consuming.
- Sources of historical materials may be problematic.
- Lack of control over external variables.

Advantages

- Throws light on present and future trends.
- It enables understanding of and solutions to contemporary problems to be sought in the past.
- It can illuminate the effects of key interactions within a culture or sub-culture.
- It allows for the revaluation of data in relation to selected hypotheses, theories and generalizations that are presently held about the past and the present.
- Permits investigation of topics and questions that can be studied in no other fashion.
- Can make use of more categories of evidence than most other methods (with the exception of case studies and ethnographic studies).

Sources of Historical Methods of Research

1. **Primary Sources of Information.** Direct outcomes of events or the records of eyewitnesses
   (a) Original documents
   (b) Relics
   (c) Remains
   (d) Artifacts Secondary
2. **Sources of Information.** Information provided by a person who did not directly observe the event, object, or condition
   (a) Textbooks
   (b) Encyclopedias
   (c) Newspapers
   (d) Periodicals

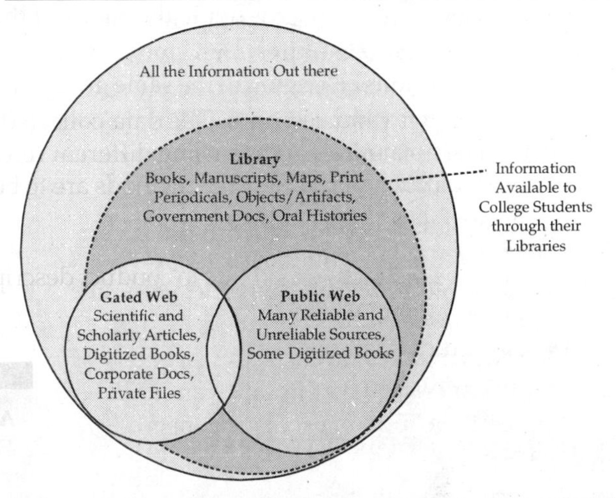

Qualitative Research

Qualitative research is defined as a market research method that focuses on obtaining data through open-ended and conversational communication.

This method is not only about "what" people think but also "why" they think so. For example, consider a convenience store looking to improve its patronage. A systematic observation concludes that the number of men visiting this store are more. One good method to determine why women were not visiting the store is to conduct an in-depth interview of potential customers in the category.

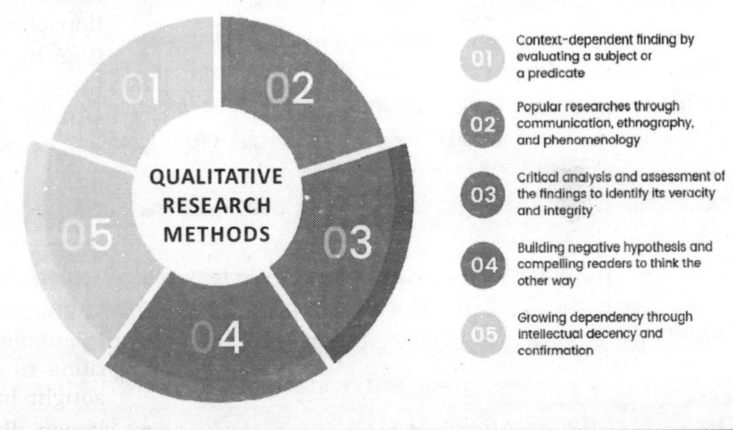

On successfully interviewing female customers, visiting the nearby stores and malls, and selecting them through random sampling, it was known that the store doesn't have enough items for women and so there were fewer women visiting the store, which was understood only by personally interacting with them and understanding why they didn't visit the store, because there were more male products than female ones.

Therefore, the qualitative research methods allow for in-depth and further probing and questioning of respondents based on their responses, where the interviewer/researcher also tries to understand their motivation and feelings.

Qualitative Research Methods

The following are the qualitative research methods that are frequently used: 1. One-on-One Interview, 2. Focus groups, 3. Ethnographic research, 4. Case study research, 5. Record keeping, 6. Process of observation.

Quantitative Methods of Research

Numbers are everywhere and drive our day-to-day lives. We take decisions based on numbers, both at work and in our personal lives. For example, an organization may rely on sales numbers to see if it's succeeding or failing, and a group of friends planning a vacation may look at ticket prices to pick a place.

In the social domain, numbers are just as important. They help identify what interventions are needed, whether ongoing projects are effective, and more.

Quantitative research is the process of collecting numerical data through standardized techniques, then applying statistical methods to derive insights from it.

Advantages

- Quantitative research methods provide an relatively conclusive answer to the research questions.
- When the data is collected and analyzed in accordance with standardized, reputable methodology, the results are usually trustworthy.
- With statistically significant sample sizes, the results can be generalized to an entire target group.

Limitations

- Does not account for people's thoughts or perceptions about what you're evaluating.
- Does not explore the "why" and "how" behind a phenomenon.

When is Quantitative Research Useful?

The goal of quantitative research methods is to collect numerical data from a group of people, then generalize those results to a larger group of people to explain a phenomenon. Researchers generally use quantitative research when they want get objective, conclusive answers.

For example, a chocolate brand may run a survey among a sample of their target group (teenagers in the United States) to check whether they like the taste of the chocolate. The result of this survey would reveal how all teenagers in the U.S. feel about the chocolate.

Similarly, an organization running a project to improve a village's literacy rate may look at how many people came to their program, how many people dropped out, and each person's literacy score before and after the program. They can use these metrics to evaluate the overall success of their program.

Unlike qualitative research, quantitative research is generally not used in the early stages of research for exploring a question or scooping out a problem. It is generally used to answer clear, pre-defined questions in the advanced stages of a research study.

QUALITATIVE RESEARCH VS QUANTITATIVE RESEARCH

	Qualitative Research	Quantitative Research
Objective/ representing	To gain an understanding of underlying reasons and motivations To uncover prevalent trends in thought and opinion	To quantity data and generalize results from a sample to the population of interest Sometimes followed by qualitative research which is used to explore some findings further
Sample	Usually a small number of non-representative cases	Usually a large number of cases representing the population of interest
Data analysis	Non-statistical	Statistical data is usually in the form of tabulations (tabs). Findings are conclusive and usually descriptive in nature.
Example	Focus Groups, individual depth interviews, group discussions	Survey, Simulations.

ACTION RESEARCH

Action Research is a method of systematic enquiry that teachers undertake as researchers of their own practice. The enquiry involved in Action Research is often visualised as a cyclical process, two examples of which are shown below.

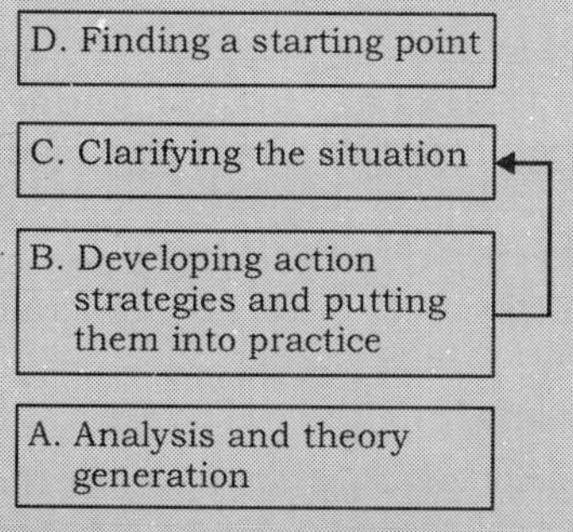

Stages of action research process

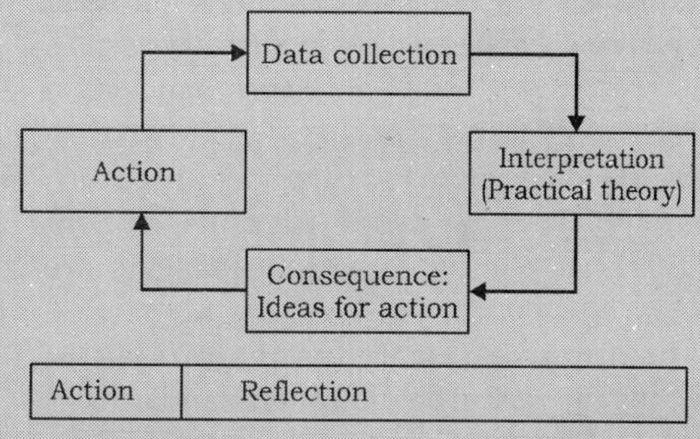

The circle of action and reflection

The start of the process is usually an issue or situation that, as a teacher, you want to change. You will be supported in turning this 'interesting problem' into a 'researchable question' and then developing actions to try out. You will draw on the findings of other researchers to help develop actions and interpret the consequences.

As an action researcher, or teacher-researcher, you will generate research. Enquiring into your practice will inevitably lead you to question the assumptions and values that are often overlooked during the course of normal school life. Assuming the habit of inquiry can become an ongoing commitment to learning and developing as a practitioner. As a teacher-researcher you assume the responsibility for being the agent and source of change.

STEPS OF RESEARCH

The various steps involved in a research process are not mutually exclusive; nor they are separate and distinct. They do not necessarily follow each other in any specific order and the researcher has to be constantly anticipating at each step in the research process the requirements of the subsequent steps. However, the following order concerning various steps provides a useful procedural guideline regarding the research process:

1. Formulating the Research Problem

There may be two basic natures of research problems, *i.e.*, it may be related either to states of nature or to the relationships between variables.

At the very outset the researcher must single out the problem he wants to study, *i.e.*, he must decide the general aura of interest or aspect of a subject-matter that he would like to inquire into. Initially the problem may be stated in a broad general way and then the ambiguities, if any, relating to the problem be resolved. Then, the feasibility of a particular solution has to be considered before a working formulation of the problem can be set up. The formulation of a general topic into a specific research problem, thus, constitutes the first step in a scientific enquiry. Essentially two steps are involved in formulating the research problem, viz., understanding the problem thoroughly, and rephrasing the same into meaningful terms from an analytical point of view.

The researcher must at the same time examine all available literature to get himself acquainted with the selected problem. He may review two types of literature – the conceptual literature concerning the concepts and theories, and the empirical literature consisting of studies made earlier which are similar to the one proposed. The basic outcome of this review will be the knowledge as to what data and other materials are available for operational purposes which will enable the researcher to specify his own research problem in a meaningful context. After this the researcher rephrases the problem into analytical or operational terms *i.e.*, to put the problem in as specific terms as possible. This task of formulating, or defining, a research problem is a step of greatest importance in the entire research process.

The best way of understanding the problem is to discuss it with one's own colleagues or with those having some expertise in the matter.

RESEARCH PROCESS – A SNAPSHOT BY WALLMORE

Step 1: Formulation of Research Problem	Step 2: Preparing Research Design
• Literature review • Formulation of objectives • Identifying research variables and measuring scales • Formulating hypothesis	• Problem structure • Study design • Experimental study • Non-experimental study
Step 3: Developing Data Collection Instrument	**Step 4: Selecting Samples Types of Samples**
• Types data • Methods of data collection • Designing research tool	• Probability • Non-probability • Determining sample design
Step 5: Writing a Research Proposal	**Step 6: Processing and Analysizing Data**
Main elements: • Need • Benefits • Types of data • Justification for funds and other resources	• Observations • Interviews • Questionnaire • Schedules
Step 7: Processing and Analyzing Data	**Step 8: Writing a Research Report**
• Editing and Coding • Classification of data • Classification of data • Tabulation • Analysis • Hypothesis testing • Generalizations	• Title page • Table of contents • Chapters • Bibliography • Appendices

2. Extensive Literature Survey

Once the problem is formulated, a brief summary of it should be written down. It is compulsory for a research worker writing a thesis for a Ph.D. degree to write a synopsis of the topic and submit it to the necessary Committee or the Research Board for approval. At this juncture the researcher should undertake extensive literature survey connected with problem. For this purpose, the abstracting and indexing journals and published or unpublished bibliographies are the first place to go to. Academic journals, conference proceedings, government reports, books, etc., must be tapped depending on the nature of the problem. In this process, it should be remembered that one source will lead to another. The earlier studies, if any, which are similar to the study in hand should be carefully studied. A good library will be a great help to the researcher at this stage.

Variable

Measurement of variables is central to research studies. According to Stevens, measurement scales can be of four types and they are listed below.

1. **Nominal scale.** It is also termed as classificatory scale. A variable being measured on a nominal scale may have one, two or more subcategories depending upon the extent of variation. For example, gender can be classified into two subcategories, such as male and female.
2. **Ordinal or ranking scale.** It usually ranks the sub-groups in a certain sequence or order. For example, examination marks can be measured either quantitatively, i.e. in absolute terms or in percentage terms or qualitatively using subcategories, like above average, average and below average. The distance between these subcategories may or may not be equal.

   The socio-economic status can be categorized as lower class, middle class and higher class. The middle class can further be divided into lower middle, middle-middle, and higher middle. The attitudinal or Likert scale also falls in the same category.
3. **Interval scale.** An interval scale has all the characteristics of an ordinal scale. In addition, it uses a unit of measurement with an arbitrary starting and terminating points. For example, Celsius scale is from 0°C to 100°C.
4. **Ratio scale.** They are used to gather quantitative information. It combines the properties of nominal, ordinal and interval scales. In addition, it has its own property. It has a fixed starting point. Ratio scale consists of equidistant points and has a meaningful zero point. If we ask respondents about their ages, the difference between any two years would always be the same and zero signifies the absence of age or birth. A 20-year-old person is twice the age of 10-year-old ones. In order to respect the notion of equal distance between adjacent points on the scale, you must make each category of the same size. Therefore, if the first category is Rs 0 to Rs 9,999, then the second category is to be Rs 10,000 to Rs 19,999, and so on. There should be no overlapping of categories, and they should follow a logical order, in increasing order.

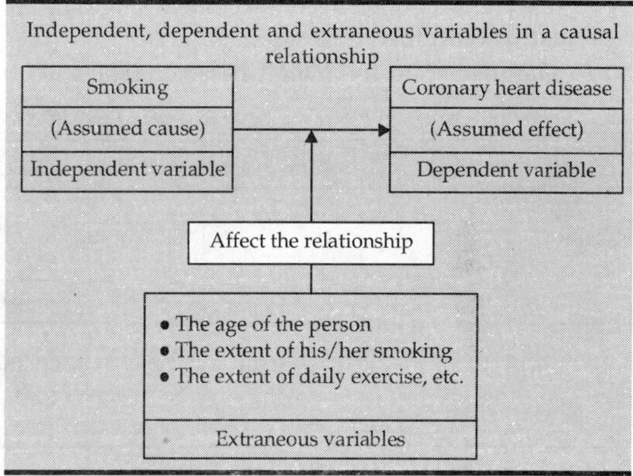

RELATIONSHIP BETWEEN INDEPENDENT. DEPENDENT AND EXTRANEOUS VARIABLES

Attitudinal Scale

If you want to ascertain the attitude of students towards a teacher, the questionnaire framed may be open-ended or close-ended. If the questionnaire is open-ended, it may invite respondents from sample to describe the attitude they hold towards teaching quality. If the researcher has framed close-ended questions, the respondent is given options, such as strongly agree (SA), agree (A), undecided (U), disagree (D) and strongly disagree (SD).

Statements about teacher	SA	A	U	D	SD
1. Knows the subject well (+)					
2. Willing to solve students problems (+)					
3. Have poor communication skills (–)					
4. Is hard to approach (–)					
5. Good teaching skills (+)					
6. Liking/disliking (+/–)					

Types of Attitudinal Scale

As the attitudinal scales are very important in qualitative research, the different types of attitudinal scales are as follows.

1. **Likert scale.** It is also termed as summated rating scale. It is the easiest one to construct. It is based upon the assumption that each

statement or item on the scale has equal attitudinal value, importance or weight. The quality of a teacher may have many dimensions, like use of knowledge base, communication skills, presentation of contents organization of material, promptness to solve student problems, of etc. The responde to solve students may have different attitudes towards different aspects.

Some statements may be positive, some negative and some neutral. Then, the scores may be assigned to different responses and the score of each respondent is calculated. Some respondents may have more positive attitude than others. There can be numerical scale as well. Instead of SA, A, U, D and SD, it will have values 5, 4, 3, 2, and 1.

2. **Thurstone scale.** It may assign weightages to the different statements, such as willing to solve student problem may have a weight of 1, the statement about subject knowledge has weight of 1.5, and statement in context of teaching skill can have weight of 2 and the scores are calculated accordingly.
3. **Guttman scale.** It is mainly based on ratio scale. It is quite difficult to develop.

SCALES FOR MEASURING VARIABLES

Variables can be:	Nominal Scale	Ordinal Scale	Interval Scale	Ratio Scale
Categorized	✓	✓	✓	✓
Ranked		✓	✓	✓
Equal intervals			✓	✓
Continuity of values				✓
Used in measuring	Martial status	Level of difficulty of exam	Percentage of students (at interval of say 5%)	Working hours

Factor Analysis

Factor analysis allows researchers to describe many variables using few factors, thus reducing the number of variables to a manageable level in terms of factors can be analysed further.

Formulating Hypothesis (Plural-Hypotheses)

Researchers will have one or more hypothesis. These are the questions that they want to address, which include predictions about possible relationships between the things they want to investigate (variables).

As a researcher, we do not know the exact truth but have a hunch about the outcome and thus, we make some prediction about the outcome. This hunch or prediction about the outcome is called hypothesis. It can also be termed as an educated guess or assumption about some phenomenon. This assumption is tested by collecting information that will enable us to conclude if our hunch was right. Thus, defining hypothesis has the following features.

a. It is a tentative proposition.
b. The validity of a hypothesis is unknown.
c. In most cases, formulating a hypothesis specifies the logical relationship between two variables.
d. It should be simple.

Main Functions of a Hypothesis

Formulating a hypothesis, though important, is not absolutely necessary for a research. A perfectly valid research can be conducted even without formulating any hypothesis. In general, formulation performs the following functions:

a. They bring focus, clarity and specificity in the research study.

b. It helps in making sample design.
c. They make the study more objective.
d. They facilitate the formulation of a theory.

3. Development of Working Hypotheses

Working hypothesis is tentative assumption made in order to draw out and test its logical or empirical consequences. After extensive literature survey, researcher should state in clear terms the working hypothesis or hypothesis.

4. Preparing the Research Design

There are several research designs, such as, experimental and non-experimental hypothesis testing. Experimental designs can be either informal designs or formal designs, out of which the researcher must select one for his own project.

5. Determining Sample Design

The items selected constitute what is technically called a sample. The researcher must decide the way of selecting a sample or what is popularity known as the sample design. In other words, a sample design is a definite plan determined before any data are actually collected for obtaining a sample from a given population. Thus, the plan to select 12 among a city's 200 drug stores in a certain way constitutes a sample design. Samples can be either probability samples or non- probability samples. A brief mention of the important sample designs is described below:

(i) **Deliberate Sampling.** This sampling method involves purposive or deliberate selection of particular units of the universe for constituting a sample which represents the universe. Therefore this is also knows as **purposive or non probability sampling**.

(ii) **Simple Random Sampling.** In this sampling, each and every item in the population has an equal chance of inclusion in the sample and each one of the possible samples, in case of finite universe, has the same probability of being selected. It is also called **proportionate sampling**. It is suitable in more homogeneous and comparatively larger groups.

(iii) **Systematic Sampling.** In some instances the most practical way of sampling is to select every 15th name on a list, every 10th house on one side of a street and so on. Sampling of this type is known as systematic sampling.

(iv) **Stratified Sampling.** If the population from which a sample is to be drawn does not constitute a homogeneous group, then stratified sampling technique is applied so as to obtain a representative sample. In this technique, the population is stratified into a number of non-overlapping sub-populations or strata and sample items are selected from each stratum. If the items selected from each stratum is based on simple random sampling, the entire procedure - first stratification and then simple random sampling, is known as **stratified random sampling**.

(v) **Quota Sampling.** In stratified sampling, the cost of taking random samples from individual strata is often so expensive that interviewers are simply given quota to be filled from different strata, the actual selection of items for sample being left to the interviewer's judgement. This is called quota sampling.

(vi) **Cluster Sampling and Area Sampling. Cluster sampling** involves grouping the population and then selecting the groups or the clusters rather than individual elements for inclusion in the sample.

Area sampling is quite close to cluster sampling and is often talked about when the total geographical area of interest happens to be big one.

(vii) **Multi-Stage Sampling.** This is a further development of the idea of cluster sampling. This technique is meant for big inquiries extending to a considerably large geographical area like an entire country. Under multi-stage sampling, the first stage may be to select large primary sampling units such as states, then districts, then towns and finally certain families within towns. If the technique of random sampling is applied at all stages, the sampling procedure is described as multi-stage random sampling.

(viii) **Sequential Sampling.** This is somewhat a complex sample design where the ultimate size of the sample is not fixed in advance but is determined according to mathematical decisions on the basis of information yielded as survey progresses. This design is usually adopted under acceptance sampling plan in the context of statistical quality control.

6. Collecting the Data

In dealing with any real life problem it is often found that data at hand are inadequate and hence it becomes necessary to collect data that are appropriate. There are several ways of collecting the appropriate data which differ considerably in context of money costs, time and other resources at the disposal of the researcher.

Primary data can be collected either through experiment or though survey. If the researcher conducts an experiment, he observes some quantitative measurements, or the data, with the help of which he examines the truth contained in his hypothesis. But in the case of survey, data can be collected by any one or more of the following ways:

(i) By observation
(ii) Through personal interviews
(iii) Through telephone interviews
(iv) By mailing of questionnaires
(v) Through schedules.

7. Execution of the Project

Execution of the project on the correct lines is necessary to collect adequate and dependable data. The researcher should see that the project is executed in a systematic manner and in time. If the survey is to be conducted by means of structured questionnaires, data can be readily machine-processed. In such a situation, questions as well as the possible answers may be coded. If the data are to be collected through interviewers, arrangements should be made for proper selection and training of the interviewers. The training may be given with the help of instruction manuals which explain clearly the job of the interviewers at each step. Occasional field checks should be made to ensure that the interviewers are doing their assigned job sincerely and efficiently. A careful watch should be kept for unanticipated factors in order to keep the survey as much realistic as possible.

8. Analysis of Data

After collection of data, next step is to analyse it. The analysis of data requires a number of closely related operations such as establishment of categories, the application of these categories to raw data through coding, tabulation and then drawing statistical inferences. The unwieldy data should necessarily be condensed into a few manageable groups and tables for further analysis. Thus, researcher should classify the raw data into some purposeful and usable categories.

Coding operation is usually done at this stage through which the categories of data are transformed into symbols that may be tabulated and counted. Editing is the procedure that improves the quality of the data for coding. With coding the stage is ready for tabulation. Tabulation is a part of the technical procedure wherein the classified data are put in the form of tables. The mechanical devices can be made use of at this juncture. A great deal of data, specially in large inquiries, is tabulated by computers.

9. Hypothesis Testing

A hypothesis is a calculated prediction or assumption about a population parameter based on limited evidence. The whole idea behind hypothesis formulation is testing-this means the researcher subjects his or her calculated assumption to a series of evaluations to know whether they are true or false.

Typically, every research starts with a hypothesis-the investigator makes a claim and experiments to prove that this claim is true or false. For instance, if you predict that students who drink milk before class perform better than those who don't, then this becomes a hypothesis that can be confirmed or refuted using an experiment.

Types of Hypotheses

1. **Simple Hypothesis.** Also known as a basic hypothesis, a simple hypothesis suggests that an independent variable is responsible for a corresponding dependent variable. In other words, an occurrence of the independent variable inevitably leads to an occurrence of the dependent variable.

   Typically, simple hypotheses are considered as generally true, and they establish a causal relationship between two variables.

   Examples of Simple Hypothesis

   - Drinking soda and other sugary drinks can cause obesity.
   - Smoking cigarettes daily leads to lung cancer.

2. **Complex Hypothesis.** A complex hypothesis is also known as a modal. It accounts for the causal relationship between two independent variables and the resulting dependent variables. This means that the combination of the independent variables leads to the occurrence of the dependent variables.

   Examples of Complex Hypotheses

   - Adults who do not smoke and drink are less likely to develop liver-related conditions.
   - Global warming causes icebergs to melt which in turn causes major changes in weather patterns.

3. **Null Hypothesis.** As the name suggests, a null hypothesis is formed when a researcher suspects that there's no relationship between the variables in an observation. In this case, the purpose of the research is to approve or disapprove this assumption.

   Examples of Null Hypothesis

   - This is no significant change in a student's performance if they drink coffee or tea before classes.
   - There's no significant change in the growth of a plant if one uses distilled water only or vitamin-rich water.

4. **Alternative Hypothesis.** To disapprove a null hypothesis, the researcher has to come up with an opposite assumption-this assumption is known as the alternative hypothesis. This means if the null hypothesis says that A is false, the alternative hypothesis assumes that A is true.

   An alternative hypothesis can be directional or non-directional depending on the direction of the difference. A directional alternative hypothesis specifies the direction of the tested relationship, stating that one variable is predicted to be larger or smaller than the null value while a non-directional hypothesis only validates the existence of a difference without stating its direction.

   Examples of Alternative Hypotheses

   - Starting your day with a cup of tea instead of a cup of coffee can make you more alert in the morning.
   - The growth of a plant improves significantly when it receives distilled water instead of vitamin-rich water.

5. **Logical Hypothesis.** Logical hypotheses are some of the most common types of calculated assumptions in systematic investigations. It is an attempt to use your reasoning to connect different pieces in research and build a theory using little evidence. In this case, the researcher uses any data available to him, to form a plausible assumption that can be tested.

Examples of Logical Hypothesis

- Waking up early helps you to have a more productive day.
- Beings from Mars would not be able to breathe the air in the atmosphere of the Earth.

6. **Empirical Hypothesis.** After forming a logical hypothesis, the next step is to create an empirical or working hypothesis. At this stage, your logical hypothesis undergoes systematic testing to prove or disprove the assumption. An empirical hypothesis is subject to several variables that can trigger changes and lead to specific outcomes.

   Examples of Empirical Testing

   - People who eat more fish run faster than people who eat meat.
   - Women taking vitamin E grow hair faster than those taking vitamin K.

7. **Statistical Hypothesis.** When forming a statistical hypothesis, the researcher examines the portion of a population of interest and makes a calculated assumption based on the data from this sample. A statistical hypothesis is most common with systematic investigations involving a large target audience. Here, it's impossible to collect responses from every member of the population so you have to depend on data from your sample and extrapolate the results to the wider population.

   Examples of Statistical Hypothesis

   - 45% of students in Louisiana have middle-income parents.
   - 80% of the UK's population gets a divorce because of irreconcilable differences.

Hypothesis Testing

Hypothesis testing is an assessment method that allows researchers to determine the plausibility of a hypothesis. It involves testing an assumption about a specific population parameter to know whether it's true or false. These population parameters include variance, standard deviation, and median.

Typically, hypothesis testing starts with developing a null hypothesis and then performing several tests that support or reject the null hypothesis. The researcher uses test statistics to compare the association or relationship between two or more variables.

Researchers also use hypothesis testing to calculate the coefficient of variation and determine if the regression relationship and the correlation coefficient are statistically significant.

How Hypothesis Testing Works

The basis of hypothesis testing is to examine and analyze the null hypothesis and alternative hypothesis to know which one is the most plausible assumption. Since both assumptions are mutually exclusive, only one can be true. In other words, the occurrence of a null hypothesis destroys the chances of the alternative coming to life, and vice-versa.

What Are The Stages of Hypothesis Testing?

To successfully confirm or refute an assumption, the researcher goes through five (5) stages of hypothesis testing:

- **Determine the Null Hypothesis.** Like we mentioned earlier, hypothesis testing starts with creating a null hypothesis which stands as an assumption that a certain statement is false or implausible. For example, the null hypothesis (H0) could suggest that different subgroups in the research population react to a variable in the same way.
- **Specify the Alternative Hypothesis.** Once you know the variables for the null hypothesis, the next step is to determine the alternative hypothesis. The alternative hypothesis counters the null assumption by suggesting the statement or assertion is true. Depending on the purpose of your research, the alternative hypothesis can be one-sided or two-sided.

Using the example we established earlier, the alternative hypothesis may argue that the different sub-groups react differently to the same variable based on several internal and external factors.

- **Set the Significance Level.** Many researchers create a 5% allowance for accepting the value of an alternative hypothesis, even if the value is untrue. This means that there is a 0.05 chance that one would go with the value of the alternative hypothesis, despite the truth of the null hypothesis.

Something to note here is that the smaller the significance level, the greater the burden of proof needed to reject the null hypothesis and support the alternative hypothesis.

Applications of Hypothesis Testing in Research

Hypothesis testing isn't only confined to numbers and calculations; it also has several real-life applications in business, manufacturing, advertising, and medicine.

In a factory or other manufacturing plants, hypothesis testing is an important part of quality and production control before the final products are approved and sent out to the consumer.

During ideation and strategy development, C-level executives use hypothesis testing to evaluate their theories and assumptions before any form of implementation. For example, they could leverage hypothesis testing to determine whether or not some new advertising campaign, marketing technique, etc. causes increased sales.

In addition, hypothesis testing is used during clinical trials to prove the efficacy of a drug or new medical method before its approval for widespread human usage.

Example of Hypothesis Testing

An employer claims that her workers are of above-average intelligence. She takes a random sample of 20 of them and gets the following results:

Mean IQ Scores:	110
Standard Deviation:	15
Mean Population IQ:	100

Step 1: Using the value of the mean population IQ, we establish the null hypothesis as 100.

Step 2: State that the alternative hypothesis is greater than 100.

Step 3: State the alpha level as 0.05 or 5%

Step 4: Find the rejection region area (given by your alpha level above) from the z-table. An area of .05 is equal to a z-score of 1.645.

Step 5: Calculate the test statistics using this formula.

That is:

$$Z = (110\text{-}100) \div (15 \div 4.5)$$

$$10 \div 3.35 = 2.99$$

If the value of the test statistics is higher than the value of the rejection region, then you should reject the null hypothesis. If it is less, then you cannot reject the null.

In this case, $2.99 > 1.645$ so we reject the null.

Importance/Benefits of Hypothesis Testing

The most significant benefit of hypothesis testing is it allows you to evaluate the strength of your claim or assumption before implementing it in your data set. Also, hypothesis testing is the only valid method to prove that something "is or is not". Other benefits include:

1. Hypothesis testing provides a reliable framework for making any data decisions for your population of interest.

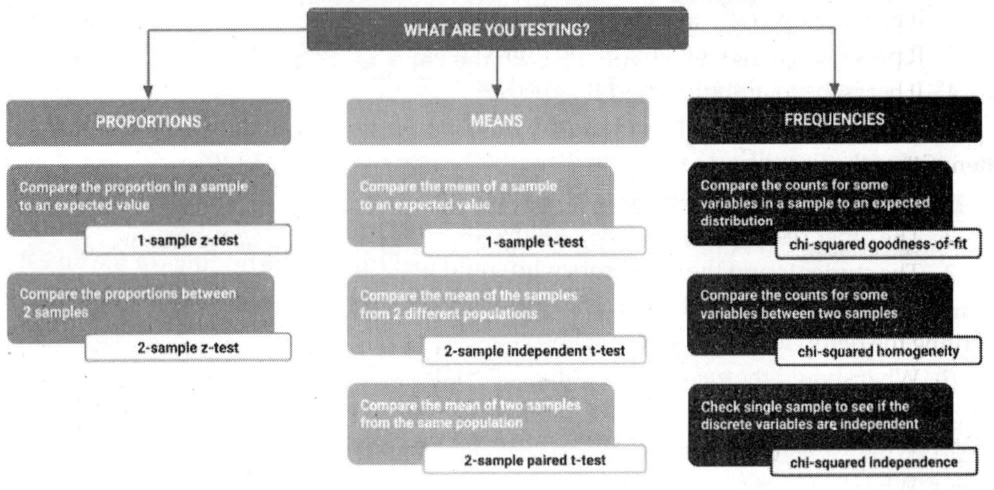

2. It helps the researcher to successfully extrapolate data from the sample to the larger population.
3. Hypothesis testing allows the researcher to determine whether the data from the sample is statistically significant.
4. Hypothesis testing is one of the most important processes for measuring the validity and reliability of outcomes in any systematic investigation.
5. It helps to provide links to the underlying theory and specific research questions.

Criticism and Limitations of Hypothesis Testing

Several limitations of hypothesis testing can affect the quality of data you get from this process. Some of these limitations include:

1. The interpretation of a p-value for observation depends on the stopping rule and definition of multiple comparisons. This makes it difficult to calculate since the stopping rule is subject to numerous interpretations, plus "multiple comparisons" are unavoidably ambiguous.
2. Conceptual issues often arise in hypothesis testing, especially if the researcher merges Fisher and Neyman-Pearson's methods which are conceptually distinct.
3. In an attempt to focus on the statistical significance of the data, the researcher might ignore the estimation and confirmation by repeated experiments.
4. Hypothesis testing can trigger publication bias, especially when it requires statistical significance as a criterion for publication.
5. When used to detect whether a difference exists between groups, hypothesis testing can trigger absurd assumptions that affect the reliability of your observation.

THESIS AND ARTICLE WRITING

Thesis writing is the final stage of the research. It provides the achievement of detailed knowledge over the problems. When a researcher takes a problem for study he finds modifications of his study. He applies some new techniques. There are three types of researchers who take their study in different ways : the post-graduates take their for the partial fulfillment, the doctoral degree also takes researches and professional research workers like scientists, sociologists, psychologists and anthropologists take their study for the achievement of detailed knowledge over the problems.

Characteristics of thesis. It has following characteristics:

1. It is the final stage of the research.
2. It provides overall view and solution to the problem.
3. It provides all the elements of the project taken for study to other researchers.
4. It bears the total summary of the work.
5. It satisfies all its researchers by providing partial or detailed knowledge over their problems.

Benefits of thesis writing.

1. The investigator classifies and systematizes his work.
2. The other researchers also may follow the same principle.
3. The students and the educators who could make use of the findings of the investigation.

Considerations in Thesis Writing. The researcher takes some major considerations which help him in writing the report in a very developed way:

(i) What should the general structure of his report be ?
(ii) What form should the development, evaluation and organization of his ideas take ?
(iii) What language medium should he use for his report ?
(iv) What other media can he use for reinforcing his verbal report ?
(v) What steps should he take to get it typed correctly ?

Format of the Thesis Writing. For the preparation of research report, the researcher should follow some steps through which he will be able to make his report a critical and synthetic one.

The Preliminary Section

(a) **Title Page.** Title page carries the name of the project. It should be clearly typed in capital letters. It should be beautifully printed or typed because it impresses the mind of the readers. It creates a curiosity among them to read the report. It bears the name of the topic, name of the author, the purpose of the study, the name of the institution and the date of presentation.

(b) **Acknowledgment.** At the time of the study, if the researcher has received help and assistance of others, he renders thanks to them. The acknowledgment should be simple in nature.

(c) **Table of contents.** He should clearly mention the procedures and steps of preparation of his study in content. In content he also makes his study specific and mentions the pages which hold the length of the chapters of the study.

(d) **List of Tables.** A statistical analysis is more clear when it is mentioned through tables.

(e) **List of Figures.** Examples and points may be given through figures by utilizing Roman numerals like (i) (ii) (iii), etc. In all pages of preliminary section, body of the report, and reference section are numbered with Roman numerals.

Main Body

This section may be divided into five divisions:

(a) The first section of this branch introduces the topic. Introduction of the topic may follow the statement of the problem, significance or actual need of the problem for the study, purposes of the study and assumptions and limitations. All these steps in introduction of the topic should be carefully defined.

(b) The second section of the study analyses the important literature related to the study. Previous studies, if any in the area, are taken for reviewing.

(c) The third section of the study explains the design of the study. The tools and techniques which are used for making the study smooth and to make the study systematic are described in detail. The source from where the data have been collected and the methods used for collecting data and devices used for collecting data should be clearly mentioned.

(d) It deals with the presentation and analysis of data. It is the most important stage of research project. Through textual discussions and tabular and graphic devices the data are analysed and reported.

(e) It holds the summary and conclusions of the total work. After a critical discussion of the total project, the summary is drawn. It represents the most significant result of the investigation. The summary should be ideal in writing because it makes the readers interested to read whole project.

MEDIUM OF THE REPORT

Research reports make use of two kinds of media : verbal, and language.

1. **Verb-Verbal means language.** Effective report writing is not an easy task. Even if skillful and experienced, investigators have to draft their report very carefully. They revise it many times before the final manuscript is ready. While preparing the report a careful attention should be given on grammatical construction of the sentences. The use of words and expressions should be properly organised and errors of spellings, abbreviations, capital letters, quotation marks should be properly watched.
2. **Illustrations.** Maps, charts, diagrams, graphs, tables should be placed properly. There must be explanations of purpose of giving illustrations.

Reference Section

(a) Reference section of the study occupies a very important place in the research study. Reference followed at the time of study should be arranged in bibliography alphabetically. The title of the author is listed first. The short statement on references should be given for the clear understanding and the actual usefulness.

(b) Appendix is preceded by a sheet containing the word APPENDIX capitalized and centered on the page. Tables and data, questionnaires, tests and other data gathering devices may be placed in the appendix.

(c) Foot-notes are very essential in report writing. The researcher should give the required explanations and references through foot-notes which will help other researchers to follow. These are placed at the bottom of the page.

Typing of Report

A. Typing of the report is very important. After writing the manuscript by the researcher it should be typed well. When the whole work will be typed at that time the researcher should take the following steps into account.

(i) Typing sheets must be clean, distinct and legible.

(ii) Strike-over should not be made.

(iii) Typing must be one-sided.

(iv) Headings should be typed in the centre.

(v) Paragraphs; quotations and footnotes should be mentioned in appropriate places.

(vi) Ditto marks should not be used.

(vii) An efficient typist should be engaged.

(viii) After typing the researcher should read it carefully

(ix) All copies of the report must be legible.

(x) When the typed report is ready, the researcher should check it carefully and make some corrections if errors are found.

B. The following features of the report should be typed:

(a) Title page
(b) Acknowledgment
(c) Table of contents
(d) List of Tables
(e) List of Figures
(f) Different Chapters
(g) Quotations
(h) Footnotes
(i) Tables
(j) Figures
(k) Bibliography
(l) Appendix
(m) Index

C. After the neat and careful typing of the report the loose sheets will be systematically arranged through page marks and will be given for binding which will be used as books for further reference.

FORMAT AND STYLES OF REFERENCING

Introduction on Thesis Format

When present Ph.D. thesis in the best possible form, you may not want to compromise. Your thesis is probably the most significant document created during your academic career. If its format is disturbed, it may severely affect the readability and spoil the very first impression on your readers. It may also affect the way your thesis is judged by the review committee.

Below there is step-by-step guide intended for all those who are in any way involved in preparing research proposals, research reports, theses or dissertations, which are crucial components of master's, doctoral and post doctoral programs, and which contribute substantially to the research accomplishments .

Thesis Format Guidelines

Order of assembling the thesis/project report in this order:

1. Cover page: includes the title, author, degree ("Thesis/Project submitted in partial fulfillment of the requirements for the Degree of Ph.D. of ... in ..."), and date.
2. Cover page color: Pink
3. Thesis/Project Approval Form.
4. Plagiarism policy compliance statement.
5. Copyright page that grants MU the right to use and reproduce fully or partially the work being presented.
6. Dedication page (optional).
7. Acknowledgments page (optional).
8. Abstract: a concise summary of the essential information of the work being presented, namely of the study's scope, purpose and results. The reference-free single spaced abstract should not exceed two pages.
9. Table of Contents: includes all the subsections of each chapter and the list of appendices (if applicable) and page numbers.
10. List of Figures: includes figure number, caption, and the page number.
11. List of Tables: includes table number, caption, and the page number.
12. Abbreviations page: lists all the abbreviations used in the text alongside their fully written unabbreviated form.
13. Thesis/Project text; the layout is described in the next paragraph.

Layout

The layout of project reports can be different depending on the type and scope of the project. Note that each chapter should start on a new page:

- **Introduction** background; statement of the problem; definition of terms; purpose of the study; theoretical basis; contributions of the study; organization of the remainder of the study.
- **Literature Review** chronological, categorical or related theoretical view points related to topic.
- **Proposed Solution/Methodology** research design or approach (quantitative, qualitative or algorithmic); population and / or sample; collection and tabulation of data; and data analysis procedures.
- **Solution Validation, Analysis of the Data, Results, and Discussion** presentation and discussion of the findings, including limitations.
- **Conclusions, Recommendations** summarizes the entire research effort; addresses the initial purpose of the study (stated in the introduction); stresses the importance of the work accomplished; leaves a final impression on the reader. It can also include suggestions for further work.
- **Bibliography/References** references should acknowledge any work done by someone other than the author. The reference should also include work performed by the author if presented or published at an earlier date. References should adopt one of the standard international styles; the American Psychological Association style for references and citation is recommended. For more information, contact the library.
- **Appendices** material too detailed or lengthy for inclusion in the body of the study (e.g. questionnaires, maps). Appendices may also contain information that might clarify the thesis but is routine in nature or indirectly related to the thesis. Raw data and examples of calculation could be incorporated.

Style and Form

- **Paper.** Use high-quality acid-free A4-size paper, with only one side of the paper.
- **Printing.** A high-quality laser printer should be used for the final copy.
- **Headings.** In disciplines where section numbering is normally used, the following guidelines apply: Chapter title: 18 – 24 pt size, bold. Main Section Headings: can be numbered as chapter-number. Section-number (e.g., 3.2 for chapter 3, section 2) in 14 pt size, bold. Second Headings: can be numbered as x.y.z (e.g., 3.2.4 for chapter 3, section 2, and subsection 4) in 12 pt size, bold. First Subheadings: can be numbered as w.x.y.z (e.g., 3.2.4.1 for chapter 3, section 2, subsection 4, and sub-subsection 1) in 12 pt size, regular. Second Subheadings: preferably unnumbered, 12 pt, italics.
- **Text Font.** Acceptable fonts generated by word processing programs include, but are not restricted to: Times Roman 12, Helvetica 12, and Letter Gothic 12. The font provided through LaTex is acceptable. Bold and italics should not be used excessively in the text. Furthermore, colored text should not be used.
- **Spacing.** Double or one and a half spacing is required for the text. Only footnotes, long quotations, bibliography entries (double space between entries), table captions, and similar special material may be single spaced.
- **Margins.** Left, 4 cm; top, bottom, and right, 2.5 cm. These are necessary to allow for binding and trimming.
- **Page Numbering.** Preliminary pages of the thesis, that is, those preceding the text are to be numbered in Roman numerals. The first page must not show its page number. Pages of the text itself and of all items following the text should be numbered consecutively throughout in Arabic numbers, beginning with number 1 on the first page of the first chapter. Page numbers

should be placed in the lower right corner or center of the page. Only the number should appear, not page 9.

- **Tables and Figures.** Figures and tables should be inserted at the appropriate place in the text. Figures must have numbers and captions under the figures. Tables have their titles and numbers above.
- **Drawings.** Any material which cannot be typed or computer generated should be drawn with permanent black ink in neat and heavy lines. Photographs of drawings are acceptable. Xerox reproductions of drawings are acceptable if they are of high contrast.
- **Photographs.** Mount small photographs with glue. Do not use rubber cement or tape. High-clarity Xerox copies of photographs are also acceptable. However, high quality scanned e-images can also be inserted into the thesis text.
- **Footnotes.** In disciplines where footnotes are normally used, they should appear at the bottom of the same page as their reference. Footnotes should be numbered in Arabic numerals. The footnote reference is superscripted and the explanation at the bottom of the page begins with the footnote reference number. Footnotes should have a smaller font size than the text (e.g. 10 pt).
- **CDs and DVDs** identify with title, name of student, and date.
- **Computer Software.** Describe in separate section in prefatory pages (e.g., list of figures and tables). If applicable, state requirements for the use of the software (e.g., hardware, screen resolution type) and any other information necessary for proper viewing of the software.
- **Oversized Material.** Oversize foldout pages may be included, though ample margins for binding must be included. Leave oversize page unfolded. The bindery will fold and insert them. All pages must appropriately numbered if found in the text.
- **Binding.** Binding will be arranged by the library, for a fee, in order to ensure consistency. At least two copies of the thesis should be submitted to the library of the campus concerned.

Layout/Format of a Research Report / Ph.D. Thesis / M.Phil. Dissertation

The various frameworks can be used depending on the content of the report, but generally, the same rules apply. Introduction, method, results and discussion with references or bibliography at the end and an abstract at the beginning could form the framework.

Similar Things between the Dissertation and Thesis

1. Both these papers have the same purpose: commonly, in many schools, these two terms are used interchangeably.
2. A dissertation & a thesis have certain terms, they should be done in time without delays. If a student is failed to defend his / her document, they could try to do it many times.
3. Both dissertation and thesis require students to choose a topic for research and create a complex work to demonstrate the level of their skills & knowledge they have got for years of studying various programs on their faculty.
4. If students are writing a dissertation/thesis, they should avoid copyright infringement: this term means they couldn't copy works from other authors because their rights are reserved. That is why it is important to be careful with every word during creating a thesis/dissertation if a high grade is your biggest dream.

Differences Between a Dissertation and a Thesis

1. With doctorate dissertations & theses, students can get various degrees. Students in the United States are required to make a thesis to get a master degree & to write a dissertation to get a Ph.D. degree.
2. These documents have different length. A thesis should have at least 100 pages; dissertation is a longer document than a thesis.

3. If you are making a thesis, it's important to conduct the original research; in the dissertation, you should use existing research.
4. You have to add a thesis analysis to the existing literature. A dissertation is a part of analysis of the existing literature.
5. A thesis and a dissertation have different statements. A thesis statement just states a point to explain to readers how you're going to prove an argument in your study. A dissertation requires a hypothesis. There you need to define results you expect from your written work & describe your expectations. If students are writing a dissertation, they need to use theory to research a particular subject.
6. It is hard to compare, but writing a dissertation is more difficult for school students. In fact, they have more questions to create a good work.

Philosophical Structure of Thesis and Research Paper

Thesis is all about a single scholarly statement and sometimes perhaps it's summary. The existence of a thesis opens up lines of inquiry into an infinite number of speculative possibilities as the antitheses. While the thesis question opens up the boundaries of these variable possibilities, the central line of inquiry remains constant and unchanged. The research paper consists of both speculative variables (majority of which are nullified) and constants that are geared towards proving the central thesis question or the major constant.

Major Differences:

- Thesis is concerned with the central question or statement of a scholarly argument that leads to further research, while a research paper is all about proving that central argument.
- Thesis is both about possibilities, through the formation of numerous antitheses, and about the end of all possibilities through the nullification of all these antitheses. The research paper is about proving the central thesis statement and concerned with gathering evidence and data to prove the same, exploring other possibilities and nullifying them and providing a speculation on future alternatives for the central thesis question.
- The word thesis is sometimes used in place of research paper, but this is a rhetorical error in which a part is substituted for a whole. The thesis statement is usually a part of the research paper and not vice-versa.
- The thesis statement does not consist of the methodology. The research paper explicates this methodology and whether it is quantitative or qualitative.
- The thesis statement is about a single question while the research paper raises a number of questions albeit in relation to the central theme. Some of these questions are nullified and some remain as the indicators of alternative discourses.
- The research paper usually consists of the thesis, but it is not always so. The research paper might be on a part of the thesis question and can have stand-alone validity.

Similarities Between Thesis and Research Paper:

- As explained above, the thesis is the research paper in potentia. The sameness lies in what the thesis potentially holds is explicated and unfolded into the research paper.
- The thesis is something in which the end justifies the means. Even the research paper goes into explicating the thesis in detail. Thus, both the thesis and research paper is deterministic.

But the most used and followed report structure is are as follow:

- **TITLE PAGE.** Title of project, Subtitle (where appropriate), Date, Author, Organization, Logo.
- **BACKGROUND.** History (if any) behind the project.
- **ACKNOWLEDGEMENT.** Author thanks people and organization who helped during the project

- **SUMMARY (sometimes called abstract of the synopsis).** A condensed version of a report – outlines salient points, emphasizes main conclusions and (where appropriate) the main recommendations. N.B. this is often difficult to write and it is suggested that you write it last.
- **LIST OF CONTENTS.** An at- a – glance list that tells the reader what is in the report and what page number(s) to find it on.
- **LIST OF TABLES.** As above, specifically for tables.
- **LIST OF APPENDICES.** As above, specifically for appendices.
- **INTRODUCTION.** Author sets the scene and states his/ her intentions.
- **AIMS AND OBJECTIVES AIMS** general aims of the audit/project, broad statement of intent.
- **OBJECTIVES** specific things expected to do/deliver (e.g. expected outcomes).
- **METHOD.** Work steps; what was done – how, by whom, when?
- **RESULT/FINDINGS.** Honest presentation of the findings, whether these were as expected or not. Give the facts, including any inconsistencies or difficulties encountered.
- **DISCUSSION.** Explanation of the results (you might like to keep the SWOT analysis in mind and think about your project's strengths, weakness, opportunities and threats, as you write).
- **CONCLUSIONS.** The author links the results/ findings with the points made in the introduction and strives to reach clear, simply stated and unbiased conclusions. Make sure they are fully supported by evidence and arguments of the main body of your audit/project.
- **RECOMMENDATIONS.** The author states what specific actions should be taken, by whom and why. They must always be linked to the future and should always be realistic. Don't make them unless asked to.
- **REFERENCES.** A section of a report, which provides full details of publications mentioned in the text, or from which extracts have been quoted.
- **APPENDIX.** The purpose of an appendix is to supplement the information contained in the main body of the report.

Guidelines for Formatting

For research purpose, two commonly used guidelines for formatting are published by MLA (Modern Language Association) and the APA (American Psychological).

APA

The American Psychological Association (APA) style is, originally, a set of rules that authors use when submitting papers for publications in the journals of the APA. Established in 1929, the style has since been used to guide research writers and help them achieve – through the use of established standards for language, the construction of correct reference citations, the avoidance of plagiarism, the proper use of headers, among many others – "minimum distraction and maximum precision".

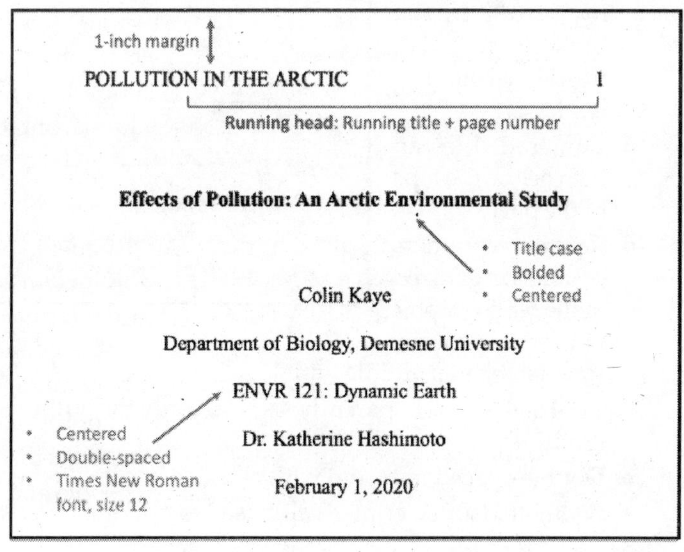

As a complete style and guideline for writing, the APA is a valuable tool for writing scientific papers, laboratory reports, and papers covering topics in the field of psychology, education, and other social sciences. The APA style allows for in-text citations, direct quotations, and endnotes and foot-notes. It is also enables the author to use the past tense of verbs in the reportage.

Standards of the APA style include:

- Bibliographic list of references.
- Alphabetical order by author in the bibliographic list, then chronological by work.
- Referenced authors organized in the bibliographic list by last name, first initial, then middle initial.
- Italicized titles of periodicals listed in the bibliography, with the words of the title capitalized.
- Titles of books capitalized according to "sentence-style" capitalization.
- In-text citations in parenthesis, with the author's last name, year of publication, and page number included (Smith, 1988. p. 4).
- Double-spaced lines.
- Page numbers – plus the shortened title of the work – placed in the upper right of every page.
- Title centered an inch below the top of the page.
- Double-spaced footnotes / endnotes, used sparingly for non-crucial information, and which are subscripted with a number that relates to the footnote.

MLA

The Modern Language Association (MLA) style is the leading style of documentation for literary research, as well as academic papers in the humanities field. It follows a specific set of rules for formatting manuscripts, and is considered, along with the APA style, a standardized reference format in college. Compared to the APA style, however, the MLA style focuses on the citation of books, anthologies, literary works, audio-visual material, multimedia, and similar works with much more detail.

Also, unlike the APA style, the present tense of verbs is most commonly used in the MLA style. Other MLA standards include:

- Bibliographic list of works cited.
- Alphabetical order by author in the bibliographic list, then alphabetical by work.
- Centered titles an inch below the tops of the page.
- Referenced authors / names organized in the bibliographic list by last name, first name, then middle initial.

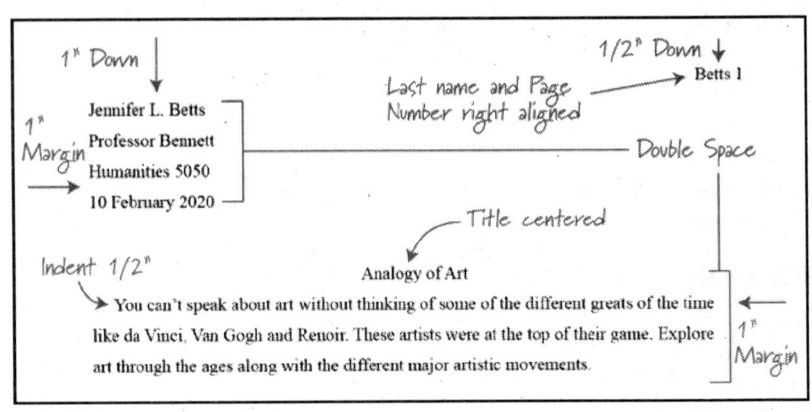

- In-text citations in parenthesis, with only the author's last name and page number included (Smith 4).
- Double-spaced lines, but with no extra line breaks between each citation.
- Footnotes (superscripted) also used to provide non-essential information.

DIFFERENCES

MLA	APA
• author-page method of citation	• author-date method of citation
• created for scholars in English composition and literature	• created for researchers in the social sciences
• author's full name on first mention	• authors' tone, scientific writing
• use of the "right" language for the audience being addressed	• economy of expression
• present tense verb in signal phrase vs. past tense	• past of present perfect tense verb in signal phrase*
• medium of publication designation (ex. Print, Web, etc.)	• DOI (Digital Object Identifier) or document number
• many purposes for writing and research	• two purposes for writing and research ** Present tense is used "to discuss implications of the results and to present conclusions" (APA 66)*

APPLICATION OF ICT IN RESEARCH

Information and Communication Technologies (ICTs) are referred to as the varied collection of technological gear and resources which are made use of to communicate. They are also made use of to generate, distribute, collect and administer information. ICT is a force that has changed many aspects of the way we live. Information and Communication Technologies consist of the hardware, software, networks, and media for collection, storage, processing, transmission and presentation of information (voice, data, text, images), as well as related services.

ICTs can be divided into two components, Information and Communication Infrastructure (ICI) which refers to physical telecommunications systems and networks (cellular, broadcast, cable, satellite, postal) and the services that utilize those (Internet, voice, mail, radio, and television), and Information Technology (IT) that refers to the hardware and software of information collection, storage, processing, and presentation. The concept of a "Digital Divide" has been around almost as long as ICT has been publicly available. While traditionally it has come to mean a division in society, based on socioeconomic factors, this does not 'paint the entire picture'. Introducing ICT as a tool to support the education sector has initiated substantial discussions since the late 1990s. A decade ago the emphasis was on Technical and Vocational Education and Training and training teachers. During the last few years, an increasing number of international development agencies have embraced the potential of ICT to support the education sector. UNESCO has played a major role in spearheading the Education for All initiative to harness the potential of ICT.

ICT in Research

Applications of ICTs are particularly powerful and uncontroversial in higher education's research function. Four areas are particularly important: The steady increases in bandwidth and computing power available have made it possible to conduct complex calculations on large data sets. Communication links make it possible for research teams to be spread across the world instead of concentrated in a single institution. The combination of communications and digital libraries is equalizing access to academic resources, greatly enriching research possibilities for smaller institutions and those outside the big cities. Taking full advantage of these trends to create new dynamics in research requires national policies for ICTs in higher education and the establishment of joint information systems linking all higher education institutions.

The application of ICTs in academic research has grown steadily in the past 10 to 15 years in both developing and developed countries, although there are wide variations in usage both within and between countries and regions. The most straightforward use of ICTs in research is in data processing. The unprecedented growth in bandwidth and computing power provide opportunities for analyzing/ processing huge amounts of data and performing complex computations on them in a manner that is extremely fast, accurate and reliable. Computer data processing not only frees researchers from the cumbersome task of manually analyzing data but more importantly facilitates quick and accurate analysis of huge amounts of data from national samples or even multi-national samples covering tens of thousands of respondents. Another important dimension of ICTs in research is the use of online full text databases and online research libraries/virtual libraries which are the direct outcome of the growth in telecommunications networks and technology. These databases and libraries provide researchers with online access to the contents of hundreds of thousands of books from major publishing houses, research reports, and peer- reviewed articles in electric journals.

Effects of ICT on Research

ICT had effects on many facets of social science research. They can be classified into three categories which include:

(a) ICT application in pre-data analysis,
(b) ICT application in data analysis, and
(c) ICT application in post-data analysis.

ICT application in pre-data analysis refers to examples how ICTs are applied on activities of social science research before reaching the stage of data analysis. ICT application in pre-data analysis includes:

i. Article Availability
ii. Thesis and Dissertation Availability
iii. Literature Search
iv. Content Search
v. Literature Tracking
vi. Quantitative Data Collection
vii. Qualitative Data Collection
viii. Big Data and Its Analytics

ICT application in data analysis includes examples how ICTs are applied on activities during the stage of data analysis and can be divided into:

i. Quantitative Data Analysis
ii. Qualitative Data Analysis

Lastly, ICT application in post-data analysis refers to examples how ICTs are applied on activities of social science research after completing the stage of data analysis which covers:

i. References and Bibliography Compilation.
ii. Article and Thesis / Dissertation's Discussion among Researchers, Supervisors, Supervises and during Viva Voce .
iii. Plagiarism Detection.
iv. Journal Manuscripts Submission.

Data Analysis Tools

- **Spreadsheet Software.** Microsoft Excel, Lotus 1-2-3, Javelin Plus, Multiplan, Quattro Pro, Visicalc, SuperCars Plan Perfect etc.
- **Word Processor Package.** Microsoft Word, Wordstar, Word Perfect, Softword, AKHAR (Gujarati), Anti Pro, etc.
- **Presentation Software.** Microsoft Powerpoint, Lotus Freelance Graphics, Corel, Apple Key-note.
- **Database Management Packages.** Microsoft Access, Paradox, dBase, For BASE, FoxPro, Oracle, Ms SQL, My SQL, Firebird.
- **Browsers.** Internet explorer, Mozilla Firefox, Opera, Chrome, Safari, Dolphin.
- **Search Engines.** Google, Yahoo, AltaVista.
- **Online Data/Cloud Service.** Dropbox, Google Drive, Google Docs, MS Sky Drive, Microsoft 365.

Digital Tools for Researchers

Following is a collection of digital tools that are designed to help researchers explore the millions of research articles.

Search Engines and Curators

- **CiteUlike** – Search, organize, and share scholarly papers.
- **Colwiz** – Create citations and bibliography and set up your research groups on the cloud to share files and references.
- **ContentMine** – Uses machines to liberate 100,000,000 facts from the scientific literature.
- **Data Elixir** – A weekly collection of the best data science news, resources, and inspirations from around the web.
- **DeepDyve** – Instant access to the journals you need.
- **EvidenceFinder** – Enriches your literature exploration by suggesting questions alongside your search results. (blog post)
- **Google Scholar** – Provides a way to broadly search for scholarly literature across disciplines and sources.
- **Labii** – A suite of web apps for researchers, including an online app for finding, commenting, rating and managing research papers. (blog post)
- **LazyScholar** – Chrome extension to help your literature search.
- **LiteracyTool** – Educational web-platform helping with the discovery, understanding, and exploration of your scientific topics of interest.
- **Microsoft Academic Search** – Find information about academic papers, authors, conferences, journals, and organizations from multiple sources.
- **MyScienceWork** – Diffuse scientific information and knowledge in a free and accessible way.
- **Paperity** – Aggregator of open access papers and journals.
- **Paperscape** – Visualise the archive, an open, online repository for scientific research papers.
- **PubChase** – Life sciences and medical literature recommendations engine. (blog post)
- **PubNiche** – A scientific research news curator.
- **PubPeer** – Search for publications and provide feedback and/or start a conversation anonymously.
- **ReadCube** – Read, manage & discover new literature.
- **Research Professional** – Source of intelligence on funding opportunities and research policy.
- **Sciencescape** – Innovation in the exploration of papers and authors.
- **Scientific Journal Finder (SJFinder)** – A collection of tools including a journal search engine and rating which recommends a list of journals based on title and abstract of scientific manuscript, website builder, (blog post)
- **SciFeed** – Uses various data sources and natural language processing to identify important new scientific advances.
- **Scizzle** – Curator that automatically finds new and relevant research papers. (blog post)
- **SSRN** – Multi-disciplinary online repository of scholarly research and related materials in social sciences.
- **Stork** – Notifies users new publications and grants based on the users' own keywords.
- **Symplur** – Connecting the dots in healthcare social media.
- **Wiki Journal Club** – Open, user-reviewed summaries of the top studies in medical research.

Article Visualization

- **ACS ChemWorx** – Collaborative reference manager coupled with tools and services for authors.
- **Interactive Science Publishing** – Allows authors to publish large datasets with original source data that can be viewed interactively by readers.
- **Mendeley** – A platform comprising a social network, reference manager, article visualization tools.
- **PaperHive** – Simplifying research communication and introducing new ways of collaboration through in-document discussions.
- **PubReader** – Alternative web presentation that offers another, more reader-friendly way to read literature in PMC and Bookshelf.
- **ReadCube** – Read, manage & discover new literature.

- **Wiley Anywhere Article** – Enhanced HTML article from Wiley publisher.
- **BioLINCC** – Clinical specimen database.
- **Code Ocean** – Cloud-based computational platform which provides a way to share, discover and run published code.
- **ContentMine** – Uses machines to liberate 100,000,000 facts from the scientific literature.
- **DataBank** – Analysis and visualisation tool that contains collections of time series data on a variety of topics.
- **DataHub** – Publish or register datasets, create and manage groups and communities.
- **Delvehealth** – A data collection of global clinical trials, clinical trial investigator profiles, publications and drug development pipelines.
- **Deveo** – Free, private Git, Mercurial, and SVN repository management platform.
- **Dryad**– Data repository for any files associated with any published article in the sciences or medicine.
- **Figshare** – Manage your research in the cloud and control who you share it with or make it publicly available and citable.
- **GenBank** – Gene sequence database provided by the National Center for Biotechnology Information.
- **GitHub** – Online software project hosting using the Git revision control system.
- **How Can I Share It** – Find information and tools to ensure your articles can be shared with your colleagues quickly and easily.
- **Nowomics** – Follow genes, proteins and processes to keep up with the latest papers and data relevant to your research.
- **Open Science Framework** – Gathers a network of research documents, a version control system, and a collaboration software.
- **Peer Evaluation** – Open repository for data, papers, media coupled with an open review and discussion platform.
- **Research Compendia** – Tools for researchers to connect their data, code and computational methods to their published research.
- **SlideShare** – Community for sharing presentations and other professional content.
- **Socialsci** – Help researchers collect data for their surveys and experiments (blog post).

Connect with Experts and Researchers

- **Academia** – A place to share and follow research and researchers.
- **Innocentive** – Helps clients to engage a world of creative and diverse on-demand talent to rapidly generate novel ideas and solve important problems.
- **Journal of Brief Ideas** – Provides a place for short ideas to be described – in 200 words or less -, archived, searchable and citable.
- **Linkedin** – Professional networking site for all.
- **Loop** – Open, cross-platform network for researchers and academics from the Frontiers journals.
- **Research Connection** – A searchable platform for research jobs and information.
- **ResearchGate** – Social network for researchers.
- **ScienceExchange** – Marketplace for shared lab instrumentations. (blog post)
- **SocialScienceSpace** – Social network to bring for social scientists.

Outreach

- **Animate Science** – Helps scientists get their work noticed by their peers and the general public using visual media.
- **nanoHUB** – Centralized platform for computational nanotechnology research, education, and collaboration.
- **Science Simplified** – A science communication portal aiming to aggregate all academic public releases and serve as a direct communication channel with the general public.
- **Useful Science** – Summaries of the latest science useful in life.
- **We Share Science** – A place to share, search, organize, and connect research videos across research disciplines.

Citizen Science

- **Innocentive** – Helps clients to engage a world of creative and diverse on-demand talent to rapidly generate novel ideas and solve important problems.
- **Patient Innovation** – Nonprofit, international, multilingual, free venue for patients and caregivers of any disease to share their innovations.

Crowdfunding

- **Consano** – Research crowdfunding site to directly support innovative medical research that matters to you.
- **Experiment** – Crowdfunding Platform for Scientific Research.

- **My Projects** – Donate to the research work that means the most to you.
- **SciFlies** – Allows anyone, anywhere to directly support research they care about.
- **Thinkable** – Platform to mobilize knowledge and fund breakthrough ideas.

Lab and Project Management

- **Asana** – Keeps your team organized, connected, and focused on results.
- **ELabInventory** – Web-based laboratory inventory management system designed for life science research laboratories.
- **Lab Suit** – Inventory Management, orders Management, materials Trade-In, price Comparison.
- **Life technologies Lab Management Tool** – Management tool for lab equipment and services.
- **LiveLabSpace** – Collaborative research tool that lets you plan experiments, replicate outcomes and generate research papers.
- **Open Science Framework** – Gathers a network of research documents, a version control system, and a collaboration software.
- **Ovation** – Simplifies your scientific life from sample tracking for start-up labs to data management.
- **Quip** – Combines chat, documents, spreadsheets, checklist, and more to collaborate on any device.
- **Riffyn** – Cloud software for visual, collaborative, reproducible innovation.
- **StrainControl** – Lab management tools that allows you to organize strains, plasmids, oligos, antibodies, chemicals and inventories.
- **Synapse** – Platform to support open, collaborative data analysis for clear, reproducible science

Electronic Lab Notebook

- **Docollab** – Helps you manage your scientific research, collaborate with your colleagues and publish your findings.
- **elabftw** – Electronic lab notebook made by researchers, for researchers, with usability in mind.
- **ELabJournal** – GLP-compliant Electronic Lab Notebook and lab management tool.
- **Evernote** – A place to collect inspirational ideas, write meaningful words, and move your important projects forward.
- **Findings App** – Lab notebook app that allows to organize your experiments, keep track of results, and manage your protocols.
- **Hivebench** – Hosted numeric laboratory notebook tool to manage protocols, experiments and share them with your team.
- **LabArchives** – Web-based product to enable researchers to store, organize, and publish their research data.
- **Labfolder** – Simple way to document your research and to organize your protocols and data. (blog post)
- **LabGuru** – Supports day to day activities of a research group, from vision to execution, from knowledge to logistics.
- **Laboratory Logbook** – Document projects running in a lab and manage experimentally obtained data and its metadata.
- **sciNote** – Open source lab notebook with workflows and modular functionalists. (blog post)
- **Sumatra** – Automated electronic lab notebook for computational projects.

Outsourcing Experiments

- **Emerald Cloud Lab** – A web-based life sciences lab, developed by scientists for scientists.
- **ScienceExchange** – Marketplace for shared lab instrumentations. (blog post)
- **TetraScience** – Allows you to monitor & manage your experiments from anywhere.
- **Transcriptic** – A remote, on-demand robotic life science research lab with no hardware to buy or software to install.

Connected Instrumentation

- **BioBright** – Provide a better understanding of experimental conditions by connecting sensors to instruments. (blog post)

Find and Share Samples

- **Addgene** – Plasmid sharing platform.
- **Antibody Registry** – Gives researchers a way to universally identify antibodies used in the course of their research.
- **Biospecimens** – Platform for biospecimen-based research.
- **Duke human heart** – Repository for cardiovascular research scientists, including tissues samples and information.
- **Nanosupply** – Platform facilitating sourcing and sharing of advanced materials for research and education.

- **Sample of Science** – Peer-Sharing Platform for Scientific Samples. (blog post)

Protocol Repository

- **Benchfly** – Video protocols and video platform for scientists.
- **Benchling** – Life science data management and collaboration platform, where you can create, find, and discuss protocols.
- **Bio-Protocol** – Online peer-reviewed protocol journal.
- **IPOL journal** – Research journal of image processing and image analysis with algorithm descriptions and its source code.
- **MyExperiment** – Share workflows and in silico experiments.
- **OpenWetWare** – Share information, know-how, wisdom, and protocols among researchers working in biological fields.
- **Pegasus** – Platform that help workflow-based applications execute.
- **Protocol Exchange** – Open protocol repository driven my the Nature Publishing group.
- **Protocols** – Crowdsourced universal protocol repository. (blog post)
- **Protocol online** – A curator of protocols contributed by researchers arounds the world.
- **Scientific Protocols** – Share scientific protocols using the GitHub platform.

Work with Code

- **CDE Tool** – Deploy and run your Linux programs on other machines without any installation or configuration.
- **Dexy** – Helps your code to speak for itself with beautiful syntax highlighting.
- **GitLab** – A git repository management, code reviews, issue tracking and wiki's all in one platform.
- **iPython notebook** – Interactive computational environment that allows code execution, text, mathematics, plots, and rich media.
- **Kepler** – Helps create, execute, and share models and analyses across scientific and engineering disciplines.
- **nanoHUB** – Centralized platform for computational nanotechnology research, education, and collaboration.
- **Sweave** – Allows to embed the R code for complete data analyses in latex documents.
- **System in Cloud** – Platform, enabling clients to rapidly draw and execute data-flow diagram that run in cloud.

Work with Data

- **Benchling** – Life science data management and collaboration platform.
- **Castor EDC** – User friendly and affordable online data collection for medical research.
- **Datazar** – Research collaboration platform where you can easily explore, use and share data.
- **Dat data** – Open source, decentralized data tool for distributing datasets small and large.
- **Galaxy Project** – Web-based platform for data intensive biomedical research.
- **GenePattern** – Genomic analysis platform that provides access to hundreds of genomics tools.
- **Kaggle** – Platform for data prediction competitions.
- **Kitware** – Advanced software solutions and services for data intensive R&D
- **mloss** – Machine learning open source software.
- **MyExperiment** – Share workflows and in silico experiments.
- **nanoHUB** – Centralized platform for computational nanotechnology research, education, and collaboration.
- **OMICtools** – A manually curated metadatabase of genomics, transcriptomics, proteomics and metabolomics.
- **Ovation** – Simplifies your scientific life from sample tracking for start-up labs to data management.
- **PCR Drive** – Free platform that supports researchers in all their PCR-related processes.
- **Pegasus** – Platform that help workflow-based applications execute.
- **Plotly** – Online tool to graph and share data.
- **Riffyn** – Cloud software for visual, collaborative, reproducible innovation.
- **Statcrunch** – Provides data analysis via the Web.
- **Sumatra** – Automated electronic lab notebook for computational projects.
- **Sweave** – Allows to embed the R code for complete data analyses in latex documents.
- **Synapse** – Platform to support open, collaborative data analysis for clear, reproducible science.
- **System in Cloud** – Platform, enabling clients to rapidly draw and execute data-flow diagram that run in cloud.
- **Tableau** – Easily and quickly analyze and present data and share insights.

- **Taverna** – A suite of tools used to design and execute scientific workflows.
- **Wings** – Semantic workflow system that assists scientists with the design of computational experiments.
- **Wolfram Alpha** – Web-based tools for scientific calculations.
- **World Map** – Allows users to explore, visualize, edit, collaborate with, and publish geospatial information.

Fundraising/Grantwriting

- **Instrumental** – Grant database and search tool that learns about specific research projects and then matches them with the best grants available.

Reference Managers

- **Citavi** – Reference management, knowledge organization, and task planning solution.
- **Colwiz** – Create citations and bibliography and set up your research groups on the cloud to share files and references.
- **EndNote** – Software tool for publishing and managing bibliographies, citations and references.
- **Mendeley** – A unique platform comprising a social network, reference manager, article visualization tools.
- **Papers** – Helps you collect and curate the research material that you're passionate about.

Collaborative Writing Tools

- **ASCII doctor** – Text processor & publishing toolchain for converting AsciiDoc to HTML5, DocBook & more.
- **Atlas** – Write, collaborate, design and publish on a single platform.
- **Penflip** – Collaborative writing and version control. (blog post)
- **Pensoft Writing Tool** – Collaborative authoring, reviewing and publishing in one place.
- **Typewrite** – A simple, real-time collaborative writing environment.
- **Quip** – Combines chat, documents, spreadsheets, checklist, and more to collaborate on any device.
- **Write** – Distraction-free text editor for writing productivity.

Manuscript Services and Writing Assistant Tools (to come)

- **Ref-n-Write** – Microsoft Word Add-in that helps you improve your English writing skills.
- **Writefull** – Provides feedback on your writing using data from the Google Books database. (blog post)

Open Access Platforms

- **GigaScience** – Online open-access open-data journal that publishes 'big-data' studies from the life and biomedical sciences.
- **Cureus** – A free and open access the medical journal and a place for physicians to build a digital CV.
- **ScienceOpen** – Freely accessible research network to share and evaluate scientific information.
- **The Winnower** – Open access online science publishing platform that employs open post-publication peer review.

Paper Repositories

- **Peer Evaluation** – Open repository for data, papers, media coupled with an open review and discussion platform.
- **Peerage of Science** – Pre-publication peer review and publishing for scientific articles.
- **PeerJ PrePrints** – Pre-print repository for the biological and medical Sciences.
- **SlideShare** – Community for sharing presentations and other professional content.
- **Zenodo** – A home for the long-tail of science, enabling researchers to share and preserve any research outputs.

Support to Publication

- **Exec&Share** – Openly share the code and data that underlie your research publications.
- **Google Charts** – Create live and interactive charts in your browser.
- **ORCID** – Provides a persistent digital identifier that distinguishes you from every other researcher.

Journal reviews and Advisors

- **Cofactor Science Journal Selector** – A journal selector from the editing service Cofactor.
- **Journal Finder** – Elsevier's service that help you find journals that could be best suited for publishing your scientific article.
- **Journal Reviewer** – Aggregates information users provide about their experience with academic journals' review processes.

Peer-review

- **Academic Karma** – Review of preprint publication, open and linked to original preprint.

- **F1000** – Leading biomedical experts helping scientists to discover, discuss and publish research.
- **Hypothesis** – Sentence-level peer-review to provide commentary, references, and insight on top of online content.
- **Journal Review** – Rate, and review published medical journal articles.
- **Paper Critic** – Review platform for research publications (Mendeley plugin).
- **Peerage of Science** – Pre-publication peer review and publishing for scientific articles.
- **PubPeer** – Search for publications and provide feedback and/or start a conversation anonymously.
- **Publons** – Record, showcase, and verify all your peer review activity.
- **Pubmed Commons** – Share opinions and information about scientific publications in PubMed. (blog post)
- **Rubriq** – Provides an independent peer review prior to submission. (blog post)
- **ScienceOpen** – Freely accessible research network to share and evaluate scientific information.
- **Wiki Journal Club** – Open, user-reviewed summaries of the top studies in medical research.
- **The Winnower** – Open access online science publishing platform that employs open post-publication peer review.

Altmetrics

- **Altmetric** – Tracks what people are saying about papers online on behalf of publishers, authors, libraries and institutions.
- **ImpactStory** – Share the full story of your research impact. (blog post)
- **PLOS Article-Level Metrics** – A suite of established metrics that measure the overall performance and reach of research articles.
- **PlumAnalytics** – A research altmetric service tracking more than 20 different types of artifacts.
- **Profeza** – Showcasing the unvalued work behind each article to provide new, more accurate way of evaluating researchers.
- **Publons** – Record, showcase, and verify all your peer review activity.

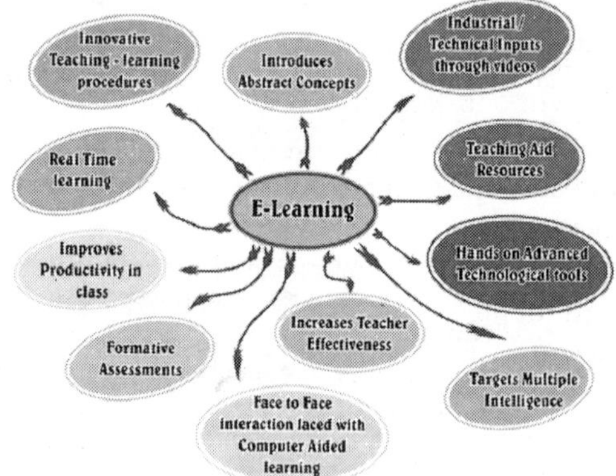

ETHICS IN RESEARCH

Research Ethics

- Ethics are the set of rules that govern our expectations of our own and others' behavior.
- Research ethics are the set of ethical guidelines that guides us on how scientific research should be conducted and disseminated.
- Research ethics govern the standards of conduct for scientific researchers It is the guideline for responsibly conducting the research.
- Research that implicates human subjects or contributors rears distinctive and multifaceted ethical, legitimate, communal and administrative concerns.
- Research ethics is unambiguously concerned in the examination of ethical issues that are upraised when individuals are involved as participants in the study.
- Research ethics committee/Institutional Review Board (IRB) reviews whether the research is ethical enough or not to protect the rights, dignity and welfare of the respondents.

Objectives of Research Ethics

- The first and comprehensive objective – to guard/protect human participants, their dignity, rights and welfare.

- The second objective – to make sure that research is directed in a manner that assists welfares of persons, groups and/or civilization as a whole.
- The third objective – to inspect particular research events and schemes for their ethical reliability, considering issues such as the controlling risk, protection of privacy and the progression of informed consent.

Codes and Policies for Research Ethics

The following is a rough and general summary of some ethical principals that various codes address:

Honesty. Strive for honesty in all scientific communications. Honestly report data, results, methods and procedures, and publication status. Do not fabricate, falsify, or misrepresent data. Do not deceive colleagues, research sponsors, or the public.

Objectivity. Strive to avoid bias in experimental design, data analysis, data interpretation, peer review, personnel decisions, grant writing, expert testimony, and other aspects of research where objectivity is expected or required. Avoid or minimize bias or self-deception. Disclose personal or financial interests that may affect research.

Integrity. Keep your promises and agreements; act with sincerity; strive for consistency of thought and action.

Carefulness. Avoid careless errors and negligence; carefully and critically examine your own work and the work of your peers. Keep good records of research activities, such as data collection, research design, and correspondence with agencies or journals.

Openness. Share data, results, ideas, tools, resources. Be open to criticism and new ideas.

Respect for Intellectual Property. Honor patents, copyrights, and other forms of intellectual property. Do not use unpublished data, methods, or results without permission. Give proper acknowledgement or credit for all contributions to research. Never plagiarize.

Confidentiality. Protect confidential communications, such as papers or grants submitted for publication, personnel records, trade or military secrets, and patient records.

Responsible Publication. Publish in order to advance research and scholarship, not to advance just your own career. Avoid wasteful and duplicative publication.

Responsible Mentoring. Help to educate, mentor, and advise students. Promote their welfare and allow them to make their own decisions.

Respect for colleagues. Respect your colleagues and treat them fairly.

Social Responsibility. Strive to promote social good and prevent or mitigate social harms through research, public education, and advocacy.

Non-Discrimination. Avoid discrimination against colleagues or students on the basis of sex, race, ethnicity, or other factors not related to scientific competence and integrity.

Competence. Maintain and improve your own professional competence and expertise through lifelong education and learning; take steps to promote competence in science as a whole.

Legality. Know and obey relevant laws and institutional and governmental policies.

Animal Care. Show proper respect and care for animals when using them in research. Do not conduct unnecessary or poorly designed animal experiments.

Human Subjects Protection. When conducting research on human subjects, minimize harms and risks and maximize benefits; respect human dignity, privacy, and autonomy; take special precautions with vulnerable populations; and strive to distribute the benefits and burdens of research fairly.

Ethical Decision Making in Research

Although codes, policies, and principals are very important and useful, like any set of rules, they do not cover every situation, they often conflict, and they require considerable interpretation. It is therefore important for researchers to learn how to interpret, assess, and apply various research rules and how to make decisions and to act ethically in various situations. The vast majority of decisions involve the straightforward application of ethical rules.

There are many other activities that the government does not define as "misconduct" but which are still regarded by most researchers as unethical. These are sometimes referred to as "other deviations" from acceptable research practices and include:

- Publishing the same paper in two different journals without telling the editors.
- Submitting the same paper to different journals without telling the editors.
- Not informing a collaborator of your intent to file a patent in order to make sure that you are the sole inventor.
- Including a colleague as an author on a paper in return for a favor even though the colleague did not make a serious contribution to the paper.
- Conducting a review of the literature that fails to acknowledge the contributions of other people in the field or relevant prior work.
- Stretching the truth on a grant application in order to convince reviewers that your project will make a significant contribution to the field.
- Stretching the truth on a job application or curriculum vita.
- Giving the same research project to two graduate students in order to see who can do it the fastest
- Overworking, neglecting, or exploiting graduate or post-doctoral students.
- Using a racist epithet in the laboratory.
- Exposing students and staff to biological risks in violation of your institution's biosafety rules.
- Stealing supplies, books, or data.
- Making unauthorized copies of data, papers, or computer programs.

MULTIPLE CHOICE QUESTIONS –

1. Which of the following is/are techniques of probability sampling?
   (A) Cluster sampling
   (B) Multistage sampling
   (C) Systematic sampling
   (D) Both (A) and (B)
2. In a research, data on school enrolment, sex ratio, number of schools, income of parents, and employment status of parents have been studied. Such a study involves use of
   (A) Time series data
   (B) Cross-sectional data
   (C) Panel data (D) Census
3. Consider the following:
   (i) Validity (ii) Replicability
   (iii) Rigorous (iv) Logical
   Which of the above are important characteristic of research?
   (A) (i) and (iii) (B) (ii), (iii), and (iv)
   (C) (i), (iii), and (iv) (D) (i) and (iii)
4. Consider the following:
   (i) Honesty (ii) Integrity
   (iii) Confidentiality (iv) Subjectivity
   Which of the above belong to research ethics and should be adhered?
   (A) (i) and (iii) (B) (ii) and (iv)
   (C) (i), (ii), and (iii) (D) (i), (ii), (iii), and (iv)
5. Ex Post Facto research means
   (A) The research is carried out after the incident
   (B) The research is carried out prior to the incident
   (C) The research is carried out along with the happening of an incident.
   (D) The research is carried out keeping in mind the possibilities of an incident.
6. Research ethics do not include
   (A) Honesty (B) Subjectivity
   (C) Integrity (D) Objectivity
7. A research paper is a brief report of research work based on
   (A) Primary Data only
   (B) Secondary Data only
   (C) Both Primary and Secondary Data
   (D) None of the above
8. Newton gave three basic laws of motion. This research is categorized as
   (A) Descriptive Research
   (B) Sample Survey
   (C) Fundamental Research
   (D) Applied Research
9. A group of experts in a specific area of knowledge assembled at a place and prepared a syllabus for a new course. The process may be termed as
   (A) Seminar (B) Workshop
   (C) Conference (D) Symposium
10. In the process of conducting research 'Formulation of Hypothesis" is followed by
    (A) Statement of Objectives
    (B) Analysis of Data
    (C) Selection of Research Tools
    (D) Collection of Data
11. The essential qualities of a researcher are
    (A) spirit of free enquiry
    (B) reliance on observation and evidence
    (C) systematization or theorizing of knowledge
    (D) all the above
12. Research is conducted to
    I. Generate new knowledge
    II. Not to develop a theory
    III. Obtain research degree
    IV. Reinterpret existing knowledge
    Which of the above are correct ?
    (A) I, III & II (B) III, II & IV
    (C) II, I & III (D) I, III & IV
13. A hypothesis is a
    (A) law (B) canon
    (C) postulate (D) supposition
14. Suppose you want to investigate the working efficiency of nationalised bank in India, which one of the following would you follow ?
    (A) Area Sampling
    (B) Multi-stage Sampling
    (C) Sequential Sampling
    (D) Quota Sampling
15. Controlled group condition is applied in
    (A) Survey Research

(B) Historical Research
(C) Experimental Research
(D) Descriptive Research

16. Workshops are meant for
(A) giving lectures
(B) multiple target groups
(C) showcase new theories
(D) hands on training/experience

17. Which one of the following is a research tool ?
(A) Graph (B) Illustration
(C) Questionnaire (D) Diagram

18. Research is not considered ethical if it
(A) tries to prove a particular point.
(B) does not ensure privacy and anonymity of the respondent.
(C) does not investigate the data scientifically.
(D) is not of a very high standard.

19. A good piece of research is a product of
(A) collective scholarship
(B) a good library
(C) a penetrating and analytical mind
(D) a touch of genius

20. Research is
(A) Searching again and again
(B) Finding solution to any problem
(C) Working in a scientific way to search for truth of any problem
(D) None of the above

21. A common test in research demands much priority on
(A) Reliability (B) Useability
(C) Objectivity (D) All of these

22. Which of the following is the first step in starting the research process ?
(A) Searching sources of information to locate problem.
(B) Survey of related literature
(C) Identification of problem
(D) Searching for solutions to the problem

23. A researcher conducts a research on finding out which administrative style contributes more to institutional effectiveness. This will be an example of
(A) Basic Research
(B) Action Research
(C) Applied Research
(D) None of the above

24. Normal Probability Curve should be
(A) Positively skewed
(B) Negatively skewed
(C) Leptokurtic skewed
(D) Zero skewed

25. Which of the following variables cannot be expressed in quantitative terms ?
(A) Socio-economic Status
(B) Marital Status
(C) Numerical Aptitude
(D) Professional Attitude

26. A doctor studies the relative effectiveness of two drugs of dengue fever. His research would be classified as
(A) Descriptive Survey
(B) Experimental Research
(C) Case Study
(D) Ethnography

27. The term 'phenomenology' is associated with the process of
(A) Qualitative Research
(B) Analysis of Variance
(C) Correlational Study
(D) Probability Sampling

28. The 'Sociogram' technique is used to study
(A) Vocational Interest
(B) Professional Competence
(C) Human Relations
(D) Achievement Motivation

29. Which of the following phrases is not relevant to describe the meaning of research as a process ?
(A) Systematic Activity
(B) Objective Observation
(C) Trial and Error
(D) Problem Solving

30. Which of the following is not an example of a continuous variable ?
(A) Family size (B) Intelligence
(C) Height (D) Attitude

31. How can the objectivity of the research be enhanced ?
(A) Through its impartiality
(B) Through its reliability
(C) Through its validity
(D) All of these

32. The basis on which assumptions are formulated
(A) Cultural background of the country
(B) Universities
(C) Specific characteristics of the castes
(D) All of the above

33. Which of the following is classified in the category of the developmental research ?
(A) Philosophical research
(B) Action research
(C) Descriptive research
(D) All of the above

34. We use Factorial Analysis
(A) To know the relationship between two variables
(B) To reduce many variables to a manageable few
(C) To know the difference between two variables
(D) To know the difference among the many variables

35. A null hypothesis is
(A) when there is no difference between the variables
(B) the same as research hypothesis
(C) subjective in nature
(D) when there is difference between the variables

36. The research which is exploring new facts through the study of the past is called
(A) Philosophical research
(B) Historical research
(C) Mythological research
(D) Content analysis

37. The process not needed in Experimental Researches is
(A) Observation (B) Manipulation
(C) Controlling (D) Content Analysis

38. Manipulation is always a part of
(A) Historical research
(B) Fundamental research
(C) Descriptive research
(D) Experimental research

39. Which correlation co-efficient best explains the relationship between creativity and intelligence?
(A) 1.00 (B) 0.6
(C) 0.5 (D) 0.3

40. Research problem is selected from the stand point of
(A) Researcher's interest
(B) Financial support
(C) Social relevance
(D) Availability of relevant literature

41. Which one is called non-probability sampling ?
(A) Cluster sampling
(B) Quota sampling
(C) Systematic sampling
(D) Stratified random sampling

42. Formulation of hypothesis may NOT be required in
(A) Survey method
(B) Historical studies
(C) Experimental studies
(D) Normative studies

43. Field-work based research is classified as
(A) Empirical (B) Historical
(C) Experimental (D) Biographical

44. Which of the following sampling method is appropriate to study the prevalence of AIDS amongst male and female in India in 1976, 1986, 1996 and 2006 ?
(A) Cluster sampling
(B) Systematic sampling
(C) Quota sampling
(D) Stratified random sampling

45. The research is always–
(A) verifying the old knowledge
(B) exploring new knowledge
(C) filling the gap between knowledge
(D) all of these

46. The research that applies the laws at the time of field study to draw more and more clear ideas about the problem is
(A) Applied research
(B) Action research
(C) Experimental research
(D) None of the above

47. When a research problem is related to heterogeneous population, the most suitable sampling method is
(A) Cluster Sampling
(B) Stratified Sampling
(C) Convenient Sampling
(D) Lottery Method

48. The process not needed in experimental research is
(A) Observation
(B) Manipulation and replication
(C) Controlling
(D) Reference collection

49. A research problem is not feasible only when
(A) it is researchable
(B) it is new and adds something to knowledge

(C) it consists of independent and dependent variables
(D) it has utility and relevance

50. To test null hypothesis, a researcher uses
(A) t test (B) ANOVA
(C) x^2 (D) factorial analysis

51. A research problem is feasible only when
(A) it has utility and relevance
(B) it is researchable
(C) it is new and adds something to knowledge
(D) all the above

52. Bibliography given in a research report
(A) shows vast knowledge of the researcher
(B) helps those interested in further research
(C) has no relevance to research
(D) all the above

53. Fundamental research reflects the ability to
(A) Synthesize new ideals
(B) Expound new principles
(C) Evaluate the existing material concerning research
(D) Study the existing literature regarding various topics

54. The study in which the investigators attempt to trace an effect is known as
(A) Survey Research
(B) 'Ex-post Facto' Research
(C) Historical Research
(D) Summative Research

55. Generalised conclusion on the basis of a sample is technically known as
(A) Data analysis and interpretation
(B) Parameter inference
(C) Statistical inference
(D) All of the above

56. The experimental study is based on
(A) The manipulation of variables
(B) Conceptual parameters
(C) Replication of research
(D) Survey of literature

57. The main characteristic of scientific research is
(A) empirical (B) theoretical
(C) experimental (D) all these

58. Authenticity of a research finding is its
(A) Originality (B) Validity
(C) Objectivity (D) All these

59. Which technique is generally followed when the population is finite ?
(A) Area Sampling Technique
(B) Purposive Sampling Technique
(C) Systematic Sampling Technique
(D) None of the above

60. Which of the following options are the main tasks of research in modern society ?
(I) to keep pace with the advancement in knowledge.
(II) to discover new things.
(III) to write a critique on the earlier writings.
(IV) to systematically examine and critically analyse the investigations/sources with objectivity.
(A) IV, II and I (B) I, II and III
(C) I and III (D) II, III and IV

61. Match List-I (Interviews) with List-II (Meaning) and select the correct answer from the code given below :

List - I (Interviews)	List - II (Meaning)
(a) structured interviews	(i) greater flexibility approach
(b) Unstructured interviews	(ii) attention on the questions to be answered
(c) Focussed interviews	(iii) individual life experience
(d) Clinical interviews	(iv) Pre determined question
	(v) non-directive

Code:

	(a)	(b)	(c)	(d)		(a)	(b)	(c)	(d)
(A)	(iv)	(i)	(ii)	(iii)	(B)	(ii)	(iv)	(i)	(iii)
(C)	(v)	(ii)	(iv)	(i)	(D)	(i)	(iii)	(v)	(iv)

62. What do you consider as the main aim of inter disciplinary research ?
(A) To bring out holistic approach to research.
(B) To reduce the emphasis of single subject in research domain.
(C) To over simplify the problem of research.
(D) To create a new trend in research methodology.

63. In doing action research what is the usual sequence of steps ?
(A) Reflect, observe, plan, act
(B) Plan, act, observe, reflect
(C) Plan, reflect, observe, act
(D) Act, observe, plan, reflect

64. The depth of any research can be judged by
(A) title of the research.
(B) objectives of the research.
(C) total expenditure on the research.
(D) duration of the research.

65. Which of the following statement is correct ?
(A) Reliability ensures validity
(B) Validity ensures reliability
(C) Reliability and validity are independent of each other
(D) Reliability does not depend on objectivity

66. Research can be conducted by a person who
(A) has studied research methodology
(B) holds a postgraduate degree
(C) possesses thinking and reasoning ability
(D) is a hard worker

67. Which of the following statements is correct ?
(A) Objectives of research are stated in first chapter of the thesis
(B) Researcher must possess analytical ability
(C) Variability is the source of problem
(D) All the above

68. Which of the following is *not* the Method of Research ?
(A) Observation (B) Historical
(C) Survey (D) Philosophical

69. In which of the following arrangements a wider spectrum of ideas and issues may be made possible ?
(A) Research Article (B) Workshop mode
(C) Conference (D) Symposium

70. The first step of research is
(A) Selecting a problem
(B) Searching a problem
(C) Finding a problem
(D) Identifying a problem

71. Which of the following qualities should be there in a researcher?
(A) He is industrious and persistent on the trail of discovery
(B) He is a specialist rather than generalist
(C) (A) and (B) both
(D) None of the above

72. *Sin qua non* of good research is
(A) well formulated hypothesis
(B) a good research supervisor
(C) adequate library
(D) a well formulated problem

73. Objectivity in research implies
(A) correct judgment of truth
(B) findings consistent with reality
(C) inter-researcher agreement
(D) methodological sophistication

74. Research reports should be reviewed in the light of
1. investigator bias
2. cultural context
3. methodological factors

Which of one of the following is correct ?
(A) 1 and 3 (B) Only 1
(C) Only 3 (D) 1, 2 and 3

75. One of the following is <u>not</u> a quality of researcher
(A) Unison with that of which he is in search
(B) He must be of alert mind
(C) Keenness in enquiry
(D) His assertion to outstrip the evidence

76. A satisfactory statistical quantitative method should not possess one of the following qualities
(A) Appropriateness (B) Measurability
(C) Comparability (D) Flexibility

77. Books and records are the primary sources of data in
(A) historical research
(B) participatory research
(C) clinical research
(D) laboratory research

78. Which of the following statement is correct ?
(A) objectives should be pin-pointed
(B) objectives can be written in statement or question form
(C) another word for problem is variable
(D) all the above

79. The important pre-requisites of a researcher in sciences, social sciences and humanities are
(A) communication, records, supervisor, topic
(B) supervisor, topic, critical analysis, patience
(C) archives, supervisor, topic, flexibility in thinking
(D) topic, supervisor, good temperament, preconceived notions

80. On matters of academics (knowledge) a researcher should consider himself as
(A) entirely dependent on the teacher
(B) open minded and radical
(C) a status-quo maintainer
(D) fairly knowledgeable

81. Independent variable and dependent variable are variables of which method available to communications researcher ?
(A) Historical Method
(B) Experimental Method
(C) Survey Method
(D) Content Analysis Method

82. Which is the probability technique used in survey research ?
(A) Simple random sample
(B) Stratified random sample
(C) Cluster sample
(D) All of the above

83. The non-probability technique used in Survey research is
(A) Accidental sample (B) Quota sample
(C) Purposive sample (D) All of these

84. Using of all elements in the population and taking a lottery to select the desired number of elements from the totality is
(A) Simple Random Sampling
(B) Stratified Random Sampling
(C) Cluster Sampling
(D) None of the above

85. Four problematic situations are given below
(i) A student is abnormally withdrawing in nature
(ii) A considerable number of students always score low in your subject
(iii) Students of your class are found to create disturbances in the class of a particular teacher.
(iv) In spite of warning most of the students of a class are irregular with assignments.
Which of these warrant action research ?
(A) All the four (B) (i), (ii) and (iv)
(C) (ii) and (iii) (D) (ii) and (iv)

86. The per capita income of India from 1950 to 1990 is four times. This study is
(A) social (B) factorial
(C) longitudinal (D) horizontal

87. In order to augment the accuracy of the study a researcher
(A) should be honest and unbiased
(B) should increase the size of the sample
(C) should keep the variance high
(D) all of these

88. Hypothesis cannot be stated in
(A) declarative terms
(B) null and question form terms
(C) general terms
(D) directional terms

89. All cause non sampling errors except
(A) faulty tools of measurement
(B) inadequate sample
(C) defect in data collection
(D) non response

90. For doing external criticism (for establishing the authenticity of data) a researcher must verify
(A) the signature and handwriting of the author
(B) the paper and ink used in that period which is under study
(C) style of prose writing of that period
(D) all of the above

91. A statistical measure based upon the entire population is called parameter while measure based upon a sample is known as
(A) Sample parameter (B) Inference
(C) Statistics (D) None of these

92. Seeing a very big turnout, it was reported that Party X will win the election, the conclusion was based on
(A) random sampling
(B) cluster sampling
(C) purposive sampling
(D) systematic sampling

93. A researcher divides his population into certain groups and fixes the size of the sample from each group. It is called
(A) stratified sample (B) quota sample
(C) cluster sample (D) all these

94. Multi-stage sampling is also called as
(A) Quota sampling (B) Cluster sampling
(C) Purposive sampling
(D) Stratified sampling

95. While writing research report a researcher
(A) must arrange it in logical, topical and chronological order
(B) must not use the numerical figures in numbers in the beginning of sentences
(C) must compare his results with those of the other studies
(D) all of the above

96. Generalized conclusion on the basis of a sample is technically known as
(A) statistical inference of external validity of the research

(B) parameter inference
(C) data analysis and interpretation
(D) all of the above

97. Researches are generally treated as 'Identity symbols' of a nation because
(A) Researches reflect the progress of a nation
(B) Researches focus on human development
(C) Researches help in acquiring international prestige
(D) All the above

98. In Hindi language the term *Anusandhan* refers to
(A) Follower of an aim
(B) Preying of an aim
(C) Attain the aim
(D) Become goal-oriented

99. A researcher attempts to evaluate the effect of method of feeding on anxiety - proneness of children. Which method of research would be appropriate for this ?
(A) Case study method
(B) Experimental method
(C) Ex-post-facto method
(D) Survey method

100. The main condition which should be followed by research is
(A) Honest exploration
(B) Knowledge of facts and principles
(C) Standardized findings and conclusions
(D) All the above

101. Reliability is the fundamental quality of a research which also reflects
(A) Validity (B) Verifiability
(C) Purity of data (D) Superiority

102. The research is always
(A) Exploring new knowledge
(B) Verifying the old knowledge
(C) Filling the gap between the knowledge
(D) Including all the above

103. Generally the data of the research is
(A) Quantitative only (B) Qualitative only
(C) Both of the above
(D) None of the above

104. The meaning of generalization is
(A) To normalize a special quality
(B) To implement the research conclusion at the larger level
(C) To give advantages of research to normal person
(D) None of the above

105. In which of the following activities, potential for nurturing creative and critical thinking is relatively greater ?
(A) Preparing research summary
(B) Presenting a seminar paper
(C) Participation in research conference
(D) Participation in a workshop

106. Factual aims of research have the quality of
(A) Descriptive nature
(B) Foundation on human values
(C) Cause-effect relatedness
(D) All of the above

107. The factual aims are most important in
(A) Historical researches
(B) Behavioural researches
(C) Theoretical researches
(D) Philosophical researches

108. On the basis of contributions made, all the researches can be classified as
(A) Fundamental-Applied-Action Research
(B) Experimental-Historical-Philosophical
(C) Longitudinal and Cross-sectional
(D) None of the above

109. Research approaches are
(A) Longitudinal and cross-sectional
(B) Oblique and horizontal
(C) Long and short section
(D) None of the above

110. Generally the formulation and progress of new knowledge have been carried out through
(A) Fundamental researches
(B) Experimental researches
(C) Historical researches
(D) None of the above

111. The survey research are classified under the
(A) Fundamental researches
(B) Experimental researches
(C) Both of the above
(D) None of the above

112. The principles formulated by the Fundamental research are used in
(A) Applied researches
(B) Philosophical researches
(C) Action researches
(D) None of the above

113. The research is (in reference to human nature)
(A) An attitude of inquiry
(B) A method of formulating principles

(C) A systematic and intellectual work

(D) A scientific method

114. 'Ganga Action Plan' – is an Action Research Plan because it has

(A) To attain a definite goal

(B) To finish in a scheduled time

(C) A definite socio-economic order

(D) All the above

115. The single difference between Longitudinal and Cross-sectional researches is

(A) In Longitudinal researches, researcher works on single group of subjects for long term duration while in cross-section, the immediate results have been derived after selecting a sample

(B) In Longitudinal researchers the researcher should have more patience to work than in cross-sectional researches

(C) The Longitudinal researches have been generally carried out under the specific situation and with specific persons but it is not carried out in cross-sectional researches.

(D) All the above differences are correct.

116. The importance of the correlation co-efficient lies in the fact that

(A) There is a linear relationship between the correlated variables.

(B) It is one of the most valid measure of statistics.

(C) It allows one to determine the degree or strength of the association between two variables.

(D) It is a non-parametric method of statistical analysis.

117. The F-test

(A) is essentially a two tailed test.

(B) is essentially a one tailed test.

(C) can be one tailed as well as two tailed depending on the hypothesis.

(D) can never be a one tailed test.

118. Which one of the following is the most comprehensive source of population data ?

(A) National Family Health Surveys

(B) National Sample Surveys

(C) Census

(D) Demographic Health Surveys

119. The basis of selection of the problem is

(A) Two just opposite experiences

(B) The suggestions given after research

(C) The counselling with experts

(D) All the above

120. Generally at present the following tradition has been observed for doing research

(A) The supervisor putting the problem to student's mind without considering his ability, interest etc.

(B) The researchers themselves work hard to search a good problem

(C) By doing slight changes in the existing topics, variables etc., new problems have been worked out easily

(D) Both A and C in the above

121. The quality of a problem is

(A) Clarity

(B) Worth for solution

(C) Hypothesis oriented

(D) All the above

122. Which one of the following is NOT a quality of a problem?

(A) Innate nature of the problem

(B) Practicality of the problem

(C) Problem according to the interests of the researcher

(D) Measurability of problem

123. The basic principle of problem selection is

(A) Novelty of a problem

(B) Practicality of a problem

(C) Future-orientation of a problem

(D) All the above

124. The synopsis of research is called

(A) Blue print

(B) Mapping of problem

(C) Base of a problem

(D) All the above

125. Which one of the following principles is *not* applicable to sampling ?

(A) Sample units must be clearly defined

(B) Sample units must be dependent on each other

(C) Same units of sample should be used throughout the study

(D) Sample units must be chosen in a systematic and objective manner

126. The problem of 'research ethics' is concerned with which aspect of research activities ?

(A) Following the prescribed format of a thesis

(B) Data analysis through qualitative or quantitative techniques

(C) Defining the population of research

(D) Evidence based research reporting

127. The type of hypothesis is
(A) Interrogative form (B) Declarative form
(C) Directional form (D) All of the above

128. When a possible solution to the problem has been written in desired direction, this type of hypothesis is called
(A) Directional hypothesis
(B) Non-directional hypothesis
(C) Declarative hypothesis
(D) None of the above

129. The meaning of the probability sampling is
(A) Where lies the uniform probability of inclusion of all the elements of the population in a sample
(B) Where the complete representativeness of the population is considered
(C) Where no prejudices exist with any element of the sample
(D) All the above

130. The principal of a school conducts an interview session of teachers and students with a view to explore the possibility of their enhanced participation in school programmes. This endeavour may be related to which type of research ?
(1) Evaluation Research
(2) Fundamental Research
(3) Action Research
(4) Applied Research

131. The advantage of random sampling is
(A) It is the excellent method of sample selection
(B) It is an economic method in terms of money, time, and energy
(C) It produces accurate results
(D) All the above

132. The limitation of the probability sample is
(A) It does not guarantee representativeness of the sample from a population
(B) The data do not fulfil the standards of the normal probability curve
(C) It has great risk of generalization of the results
(D) All the above statements are correct.

133. The quality of Non-probability sampling is
(A) Easy and convenient selection of the sample
(B) It has no question of probability of selection of an element
(C) It can be analysed through simple statistical method
(D) All the above are correct

134. In Stratified sampling the units are selected
(A) After dividing the population in different groups on the basis of specific standard and then taking an equal proportion of units from each group
(B) After dissociating the population in different groups on the basis of specific standard and then the units are selected from these groups.
(C) After dividing the population in different 'strata' and then selecting any one strata out of them
(D) None of the above

135. Suppose the population is quite comprehensive and distributed in a large geographical area. In such a situation what kind of sampling procedure would you like to prefer?
(A) Multi level sampling
(B) Systematic sampling
(C) Cluster sampling
(D) None of the above

136. The Purposive sample will be
(A) Depending on the researcher's whims
(B) Based upon a specific objective of sampling procedure
(C) Based on the excellent method of sampling
(D) None of the above

137. Generally the external and internal validity is present in the inference which we get from
(A) Experimental method
(B) Survey method
(C) Ex Post Facto method
(D) None of the above

138. Which of the following method is free from the difficulties related with sampling, control and validity of inferences?
(A) Historical method
(B) Philosophical method
(C) Experimental method
(D) Survey method

139. The internal validity related with inferences is associated to
(A) Ex post Facto method of research
(B) Experimental method of research
(C) Both of the above
(D) None of the above

140. Which one of the following research methods have the similarity in nature when compared in relation to sample, control and validity of inferences?

(A) Experimental and Ex Post Facto method
(B) Historical and philosophical method
(C) Survey and Experimental method
(D) None of the above

141. On the basis of the nature of variable, the types of survey method are
(A) Stratified survey and survey researches
(B) Sample and population related researches
(C) Surveys through Questionnaire and interviews
(D) All the above

142. Descriptive study is related with
(A) Survey research method
(B) Experimental research method
(C) Case study method
(D) All the above

143. The meaning of the Historical method of research is
(A) To employ scientific method in order to study the historical problems
(B) To establish relationship between historical facts and current events
(C) To make specific investigation of the past events
(D) All the above

144. The steps of the Historical method of research are given in a jumbled state. Select them in a scientific order from the following options
1. Identification of the problem
2. Criticism of data
3. Interpretation of data
4. Collection of data

(A) 1, 4, 3 and 2 (B) 1, 2, 3 and 4
(C) 1, 3, 2 and 4 (D) 4, 3, 2 and 1

145. The need of philosophical research method is desired in
(A) Philosophy related researches
(B) All the researches involved in exploring the aims of social sciences
(C) Explorations of *Atma* and *Paramatma*
(D) Determining the role and extension of philosophy

146. The wrong statement in relation to experimental method is
(A) Observation under controlled condition is experiment
(B) It is the method of effective control of variables
(C) Careful observation of a phenomenon under controlled conditions
(D) It is a useful method in laboratories.

147. Generally variables are of
(A) Two types – Independent and dependent variables
(B) Three types – Independent, dependent & intervening variables
(C) Four types – Independent, dependent, Intervening and control variables
(D) None of the above

148. The characteristic(s) of experimental method is/are
(A) It follows the law of single variable
(B) It is the laboratory method of research and has borrowed from pure sciences
(C) It follows the scientific method
(D) All the above statements are correct

149. The contribution of case-study is
(A) In study and data collection of a case related to caste, age, sex, religion, problems, intellectual level, socio-economic status etc.
(B) In evaluation of historical facts related with persons or case
(C) In study of institutionalized groups and families
(D) In all the above studies

150. The objective of case-study is
(A) Remedial (B) Diagnostic
(C) Educational (D) All the above

151. Case-study collects the data from the following sources
(A) From individual
(B) From anecdotal records
(C) From government documents
(D) From all the above

152. The criteria of a good case-study is
(A) Continuity
(B) Completeness of the data
(C) Validity of the data
(D) All the above

153. The following steps of case-study have been jumbled with each other
1. Focus of study
2. Identification of cause-effect symptoms
3. Remedy for adjustment
4. Follow-up programme
5. Data collection

The correct sequence in above steps is
(A) 1, 5, 2, 3, and 4 (B) 1, 4, 5, 2 and 3
(C) 1, 2, 3, 4 and 5 (D) 5, 4, 3, 2 and 1

154. The limitation of case-study is
(A) It has subjectivity
(B) It is difficult to formulate assumptions
(C) It is difficult to employ complex statistical methods
(D) All the above are correct

155. Research is a
(A) Value oriented process
(B) Passive process
(C) Self contained process
(D) Discovery oriented process

156. 'The research is an ethical process'. Here the meaning of ethics is
(A) The external beauty of the research
(B) The quality of the research content
(C) The fulfillment of research values in an investigation
(D) None of the above

157. The Ethics in research is not related to
(A) Self-interest (B) Scientific method
(C) Reliability (D) Humanity

158. Suppose a researcher has some prejudices in relation to some problem, then the research carried out by him, is called as
(A) Value oriented research
(B) Polluted research
(C) Inadequate research
(D) Prejudiced research

159. When a researcher is engaged in research in a subjective manner, the result will be
(A) inadequate formulation of objectives
(B) inadequate selection of apparatus
(C) inadequate collection of data
(D) All of the above

160. 'The research should not be carried out with blind-folded eyes'–the meaning of this phrase is
(A) The research should be free from all personal biases
(B) The research should be free from personal limitations
(C) The research should be separated from personal ideology
(D) All of the above

161. If a researcher has the quality of exploration and has the fine skills in his field of research, the research will be
(A) Value oriented
(B) Comprehension oriented
(C) Anxiety oriented
(D) Thinking oriented

162. The research papers are written in order to
(A) Gain name and fame
(B) Communicate the research
(C) Get promotions
(D) None of the above

163. The research papers are generally prepared by
(A) The research scholars
(B) The research supervisors
(C) The scientists
(D) All of the above

164. The research papers writing methodology has slight variations in reference to
(A) The standards maintained by research journals
(B) The interests of the researchers
(C) The research traditions
(D) All of the above statements are correct with slight variations

165. Generally in all researches, an abstract of each article has been prepared which focuses upon
(A) The central theme of the research paper
(B) The research-innovation employed in research paper
(C) The effective conclusions of the research paper
(D) All of the above

166. The experimental study is based on the law of
(A) Single variable (B) Occupation
(C) Replication
(D) Interest of the subject

167. Generally research papers have been given more weightage instead of research articles because these will be
(A) Based on data
(B) Incorporated with statistics
(C) Both of the above
(D) None of the above

168. Generally research papers are presented abundantly in
(A) Seminars (B) Journals
(C) Symposiums (D) All of these

169. Conference is a
(A) Provision to discuss on serious matters
(B) Adequate solution of research problems
(C) Wider manipulation of research inferences
(D) All of the above

170. Generally the objective of organizing a workshop is

(A) To develop the research attitude in the researchers
(B) To tell about the research methodology to the neo-researchers
(C) To impart practical training of conducting research
(D) None of the above

171. The central role in workshop is of
(A) The Director (B) The Expert
(C) The Participants (D) All of these

172. The characteristic feature of a workshop is
(A) To attain the higher cognitive and psychomotor objectives of the research
(B) To comprehend the theoretical and practical aspects of the research
(C) To explore the possibilities of applied aspects of the research
(D) All of the above

173. Seminar is
(A) The process of promoting the reflective level
(B) The process of nurturing the higher cognition
(C) The interactional process of thinking
(D) All of the above are true

174. The main cognitive objective of seminar is
(A) To develop critical and analytical capacities in a researcher
(B) To develop observational and experiential presenting capabilities in a researcher
(C) To develop synthetic and evaluation-related abilities in a researcher
(D) All of the above are correct statements

175. The constituents of a seminar are
(A) Organizer-Chairman-Speakers-Participants
(B) President–Chairman–Workers
(C) Chairman–Participants only
(D) None of the above

176. Which one of the following is NOT a type of Seminar?
(A) House-committee
(B) International Seminar
(C) National Seminar
(D) Focal Seminar

177. The primary aim of organising the Seminar is
(A) Attaining knowledge
(B) Communication of research inferences
(C) The exhibition of research creativity
(D) None of the above

178. Symposium is a
(A) A well organised group of a few speakers with large audience
(B) Arrival at the certain goal through mutual exchange of ideas
(C) Process of taking decisions in a group
(D) All of the above

179. The aim of symposium is
(A) To develop the knowledge about current problems and the capacity to identify them
(B) To take decision about the problems related to research topics
(C) To seek advice of the experts in the area
(D) All of the above

180. The method of Research reporting should be
(A) Scientific (B) Ethical and attractive
(C) Personal
(D) Favourable to globalisation

181. The advantage of Research report writing in a scientific manner is
(A) Global Standardization
(B) Global Communication
(C) Global Awakening (D) Global Welfare

182. Generally the synopsis of the research is compared with human body. Inspite of the differences existing in its different parts, it must have
(A) Uniformity (B) Equality
(C) Functional continuity
(D) None of the above

183. When a thesis has been submitted in order to attain a degree or related contain objective, the supervisor's certificate has been produced because
(A) It ensures the quality of research
(B) It gives name and fame to the worker
(C) It gives clearance from all boundations
(D) It ensures authenticity of the research work

184. In Research thesis the importance of introduction is
(A) It imbibes the importance of problem in it
(B) It determines the direction of survey related to problem
(C) It explains the objectives of the problem
(D) All the above

185. The Research design is related to
(A) Sample selection
(B) Formulation of Experimental design
(C) Selection and construction of the tool
(D) All the above

186. In order to ensure maximum acceptability of data analysis and its interpretation, the help should be taken from
(A) Statistics
(B) Graphs and diagrams
(C) Computer
(D) Appreciable typing

187. What will you put on top priority while giving the suggestions in your research?
(A) The difficulties you have faced during your research work
(B) The limitations of your research work
(C) The futuristic improvements to be carried out by other researchers
(D) All the above

188. The justifiable scientific list of all references is called
(A) Index (B) Bibliography
(C) Reference (D) Neo book reference

189. Evidences in research are collected from
(A) Primary and secondary sources
(B) Pure and applied sources
(C) Active and passive sources
(D) None of the above

190. In primary sources we include
(A) Hand written manuscripts only
(B) The original writings of the authors
(C) Direct collection from the thesis
(D) All of the above

191. Reference serves the purpose
(A) Of lending authenticity to the given content
(B) Of insightful decision making by the researcher
(C) Of giving ornamental value to the research
(D) If exhibits the great achievements of the piece of research

192. There exists a difference between the reference and bibliography
(A) The references have the actual page numbers
(B) The references have the last name of the person (Surname) on its first priority
(C) The references have the minute details in order to verify them
(D) All the above are correct

193. Which is/are true ?
(i) Theory is not merely a passive element. It plays an active role in uncovering facts.
(ii) The concepts that have been accepted as simple and obvious turn out to be elusive vague and ill-defined when we fit them to the facts.
(iii) Function of research is theoretical and utilitarian.
(iv) Locating and identifying delinquent behaviour and causes is utilitarian function.
(A) i, ii, iii, iv (B) i, ii, iii
(C) i, ii (D) i, ii, iv

194. Researcher should find answer to research questions
(i) Validly (ii) Objectively
(iii) Accurately (iv) Economically
(A) i, ii, iii, iv (B) i, ii, iii
(C) i, ii (D) i, iv

195. Match the following

(a) Design will give an idea	(i) Of its choice favouring his own methodological theoretical and personal orientation
(b) Once the data through different techniques collected	(ii) Testing different hypothesis
(c) Each research will have a design	(iii) Of time, money, personal budget, availability of data and nature of respondents
(d) Different designs will help	(iv) To what techniques will be used
(e) Each design is bound i.e., have limitation	(v) How will that be analysed

	(a)	(b)	(c)	(d)	(e)
(A)	iv	v	i	ii	iii
(B)	v	iv	iii	i	ii
(C)	i	iii	iv	v	ii
(D)	v	iv	iii	ii	i

196. Studies which accurately portray the characteristics of a particular situation or groups or individuals are
(A) Exploratory (B) Descriptive
(C) Experimental (D) None

197. This study aims at gaining familiarity with a phenomena or achieving insights into the phenomena or formulation of a more precise research problem or developing a hypothesis
(A) Experimental (B) Descriptive
(C) Exploratory (D) None

198. The difference between descriptive and diagnostic designs lies in
(i) Difference in field
(ii) Difference in hypothesis
(iii) Difference in objectives
(iv) Difference in treatment and field expansion
(A) i, ii, iii, iv (B) i, ii, iii
(C) i, ii (D) i, iv

199. The comparison with controlled group shows
(A) Occurrence of effect frequency
(B) Cause occurred before an effect or not
(C) Other factors determining conditions
(D) All of the above

200. The drawbacks of qualitative method is/are
(i) Subjectivity
(ii) Individual oriented
(iii) Data not reliable
(iv) Data not precise
(A) i, ii, iii, iv (B) i, ii, iii
(C) i, ii (D) i, iv

201. The sources of case data is/are
(i) Diaries, memoirs (ii) Letters
(iii) Life history (iv) Autobiography
(A) i, ii, iii, iv (B) i, ii, iii
(C) i, ii (D) i, iv

202. The advantages of questionnaire method could be
(i) Low cost (ii) Large coverage
(iii) Repetitive information
(iv) Rapidity
(A) i, ii, iii, iv (B) i, ii, iii
(C) i, ii (D) i, iv

203. The basis of sampling is on the assumptions
(A) Underlying homogeneity amidst complexity
(B) Possibility of representative selection
(C) Absolute accuracy not essential
(D) All

204. The list of advantages of sampling could be
(i) Saving of time, money
(ii) Detailed study
(iii) Accuracy of result, administrative convenience
(iv) Impossibility of the use of census method
(A) i, ii, iii, iv (B) i, ii, iii
(C) i, iii (D) i, iii, iv

205. Variables are the characteristics of conditions that are ________ by the experimenter.
(A) Manipulated (B) Controlled
(C) Observed (D) All

206. In experimental research, variables are classified into
(i) Dependent (ii) Independent
(iii) Continuous (iv) Broken.
(A) i, ii, iii, iv (B) iii, iv
(C) i, ii (D) i, iv

207. Secondary data can be obtained from
(i) Journals, reports
(ii) Govt. & private publications
(iii) Trade
(iv) Professional bodies
(A) i, ii, iii, iv (B) i, ii, iii
(C) i, ii (D) i, iv

208. Which aspects should investigator examine in using secondary data ?
(i) Suitability (ii) Adequacy
(iii) Reliability (iv) Interest
(A) i, ii, iii, iv (B) i, ii, iii
(C) i, ii (D) i, iv

209. While editing primary data, which of the following need attention?
(i) Data should be complete
(ii) Data should be consistent
(iii) Data should be adequate
(iv) Data should be homogeneous
(A) i, ii, iii, iv (B) i, ii, iii
(C) i, ii (D) i, iv

210. After the data has been edited, the next step is to
(A) Computerize it (B) Publish it
(C) Classify it (D) None

211. If a businessman orders a market survey to be conducted for his product, the report submitted must be
(A) Elaborate (B) Simple
(C) Non-technical (D) None

212. Which of the following experimental designs involve single group ?
(A) Repeated measures design
(B) Random group design
(C) Post test only random group design
(D) Factorial design

213. Hypothesis is also called
(A) hunch of scholar (B) tentative conclusion
(C) guess of the scholar
(D) all the above.

214. Research proposal is also called
(A) abstract (B) summary
(C) synopsis (D) methodology.

215. Controlled investigations that try to establish cause and effect between two or more variables with the purpose of predicting outcomes is
(A) experimental design
(B) correlation studies
(C) survey (D) case study.

216. Research focused on determining how education works by testing conclusions education works by testing conclusions related to theories of communication, learning, performance and technology is
(A) theoretical (B) empirical
(C) interpretative (D) evaluation

217. The type of research method involving indepth study and execution of available information in an attempt to explain complex phenomena is known as
(A) philosophical (B) developmental
(C) analytical (D) action

218. Which statistical device helps in analysing the covariation of two or more variables ?
(A) Regression (B) Median
(C) Standard Deviation (D) Correlation.

219. The least possible correlation between two variables is
(A) –1.00 (B) –0.1
(C) –0.01 (D) –0.001

220. In testing of hypothesis, research and null hypothesis
(A) exist together (B) one at a time
(C) are invalid (D) are same

221. The research method used to investigate cultures and population subgroups and seeks to describe and explain cultural behaviour is
(A) phenomenology (B) grounded theory
(C) ethnography (D) action research

222. The nature of relationship is studied through
(A) co-relation (B) regression
(C) progression (D) None of these

223. Which method of research investigates the likelihood of a relationship between two variables and identifies associations rather than cause and effect ?
(A) Experimental design
(B) Survey
(C) Case studies
(D) Correlation studies

224. Data collected from published books are called
(A) Primary data (B) Secondary data
(C) Tertiary data (D) None of these

225. A researcher wants to study the future of a Political Party X in India. For the study which tool is most appropriate for him?
(A) Questionnaire (B) Interview
(C) Schedule (D) Rating scale

226. While writing research report a researcher
(A) must arrange it in logical, topical and chronological order
(B) must not use the numerical figures in numbers in the beginning of sentences
(C) must compare his results with those of the other studies
(D) all of the above

227. Total error in a research is equal to
(A) sampling error + non-sampling error
(B) $\sqrt{[(\text{sampling error}) + (\text{non - sampling error})]^2}$
(C) sampling error × 100
(D) only sampling error

228. Direct personal interviews constitute
(A) Primary data (B) Secondary data
(C) Tertiary data (D) None of these

229. Indirect oral interviews are called
(A) Primary data (B) Secondary data
(C) Mock tests (D) Viva Voce

230. Which of the following is a primary source of data ?
(A) Official records–governments documents, information preserved by social-religious organizations etc.
(B) Personal records, letters, diaries, autobiographies, wills, etc.
(C) Oral testimony of traditions and customs
(D) All of the above

231. The first step for making a statistical investigation is
(A) Organisation (B) Collection of data
(C) Samples (D) None of these

232. Which one is not a primary data
(A) Direct personal interview
(B) Mailed questionnaire
(C) Material from Govt. Records
(D) None of the above

233. All causes non sampling errors except
(A) faulty tools of measurement
(B) inadequate sample

(C) non response
(D) defect in data collection

234. Field study is related to
(A) real life situations
(B) laboratory situations
(C) experimental situations
(D) None of the above

235. A good hypothesis should be
(A) formulated in such a way that it can be tested by the data
(B) precise, specific and consistent with most known facts
(C) of limited scope and should not have global significance
(D) all of these

236. Survey study aims at :
(i) knowing facts about the existing situation
(ii) comparing the present status with the standard norms
(iii) criticising the existing situation
(iv) identifying the means of improving the existing situation
(A) (i) and (ii) only
(B) (i), (ii) and (iii)
(C) (i), (ii), (iii) and (iv)
(D) (ii) and (iii) only

237. A researcher divides his population into certain groups and fixes the size of the sample from each group. It is called
(A) cluster sample
(B) stratified sample
(C) quota sample
(D) all of the above

238. Area (cluster) sampling technique is used when
(A) population is scattered and large size of the sample is to be drawn
(B) population is heterogeneous
(C) long survey is needed
(D) (A) and (C)

239. The research antagonistic to ex-post facto research is
(A) experimental studies
(B) library researches
(C) normative researches
(D) all of the above

240. A researcher divides the populations into PG graduates and 10 + 2 students and using the random digit table he selects some of them from each. This is technically called
(A) stratified sampling
(B) stratified random sampling
(C) representative sampling
(D) none of these

241. The press reports collected by correspondents constitute
(A) Primary data
(B) Secondary data
(C) Tertiary data
(D) None of the above

242. In order to augment the accuracy of the study a researcher
(A) should be honest and unbiased
(B) should increase the size of the sample
(C) should keep the variance high
(D) all of these

243. Below are given two sets – research methods (Set-I) and data collection tools (Set-II). Match the two sets and indicate your answer by selecting the correct code :

Set – I (Research Methods)	**Set – II (Data Collection Tools)**
a. Experimental method	i. Using primary and secondary sources
b. Ex post-facto method	ii. Questionnaire
c. Descriptive survey method	iii. Standardized tests
d. Historical method	iv. Typical characteristic tests

Codes:

	a	b	c	d		a	b	c	d
(1)	ii	i	iii	iv	(2)	iii	iv	ii	i
(3)	ii	iii	i	iv	(4)	ii	iv	iii	i

244. If you are doing experiment on a large group of sample which method of controlling will you adopt ?
(A) matching
(B) randomization
(C) elimination
(C) elimination and matching both

245. Some of the sources of secondary data are
(A) internal records of a firm's sales, production, etc.
(B) the data obtained by a firm in a survey conducted by it.
(C) confidential records of the Government
(D) reports and publications of Central and State Government

246. Bibliography given in a research report
(A) helps those interested in further research and studying problem from another angle
(B) shows the vast knowledge of the researcher
(C) makes the report authentic
(D) none of the above

247. Independent variables are not manipulated in which type of researches?
(A) ex-post facto (B) normative
(C) both (D) neither

248. A researcher selects a probability sample of 100 out of the total population. It is
(A) a random sample
(B) a cluster sample
(C) a stratified sample
(D) a systematic sample

249. The other name of independent variable for an experimental research is/are
(A) experimental variable
(B) treatment variable
(C) manipulated variable
(D) all of the above

250. Generalised conclusion on the basis of a sample is technically known as
(A) statistical inference of external validity of the research
(B) parameter inference
(C) data analysis and interpretation
(D) all of the above

251. The issue of 'research ethics' may be considered pertinent at which stage of research?
(A) At the stage of problem formulation and its definition
(B) At the stage of defining the population of research
(C) At the stage of data collection and interpretation
(D) At the stage of reporting the findings.

252. Which of the following is not the characteristic of a researcher?
(A) He is industrious and persistent on the trial of discovery
(B) He is a specialist rather than a generalist
(C) He is not inspirational to his chosen field but accepts the reality.
(D) He is not versatile in his interest and even in his native abilities.

253. Action research has its origin in
(A) Modern human organisation & theory
(B) System approach to education
(C) Logical thin king process
(D) Educational technology

254. Which of the following sequences of research steps is nearer to scientific method ?
(A) Suggested solution of the problem, Deducing the consequences of the solution, Perceiving the problem situation, Location of the difficulty and testing the solutions.
(B) Perceiving the problem situation, Locating the actual problem and its definition, Hypothesizing, Deducing the consequences of the suggested solution and Testing the hypothesis in action.
(C) Defining a problem, Identifying the causes of the problem, Defining a population, Drawing a sample, Collecting data and Analysing results.
(D) Identifying the causal factors, Defining the problem, Developing a hypothesis, Selecting a sample, Collecting data and arriving at generalizations and Conclusions.

255. Which sequence of research steps is logical in the list given below ?
(A) Problem formulation, Analysis, Development of Research design, Hypothesis making, Collection of data, Arriving at generalizations and conclusions.
(B) Development of Research design, Hypothesis making, Problem formulation, Data analysis, Arriving at conclusions and data collection.
(C) Problem formulation, Hypothesis making, Development of a Research design, Collection of data, Data analysis and formulation of generalizations and conclusions.
(D) Problem formulation, Deciding about the sample and data collection tools, Formulation of hypothesis, Collection and interpretation of research evidence.

256. A farmer considers the age old method of ploughing better than the latest methods available to him. In arriving at this conclusion, he is being influenced by
(A) Tradition
(B) Experience
(C) Reason
(D) Experimentation

257. Consider the following statement : 'Observations, in themselves, are of little statement.' What is the basis of making such a statement?
(A) They are without any purpose.

(B) They must be related to other facts for generalization.
(C) They are not systematic and not amenable to scientific interpretation.
(D) They are meaningful only if collected by a scientist.

258. Logic of induction is very close to
(A) The logic of sampling
(B) The logic of the controlled variable
(C) The logic of observation
(D) None of the above

259. In every field, research pursuits promote systematic and gradual advancement of knowledge but discoveries are rare because
(A) It is not common to be able to think beyond a grooved channel.
(B) Result is a continuous critical investigation.
(C) Sustained experimental work needed for discovery is not easily forthcoming.
(D) Most people lack the depth of knowledge needed for it.

260. Which of the following statements is not correct?
(A) One research gives birth to another research.
(B) All researchers contribute to exiting knowledge.
(C) A researcher is expected to be a well-read person.
(D) A good researches is a nice person.

261. The quality of a research study is mainly evaluated on the basis of
(A) The manner in which the recommendations are implemented.
(B) The place of publication.
(C) The rigour with which it was conducted.
(D) None of the above.

262. The quality of a research is judged by the
(A) Experience of researcher.
(B) Methodology adopted in conducting the research
(C) Depth of research
(D) Relevance of research

263. Which of the following types of research is associated with theory generating?
(A) Both inductive and deductive
(B) Deductive research
(C) Inductive research
(D) None of the above

264. Ethical transgression is
(A) Defining ethics
(B) Defying ethical principles
(C) Following ethical principles
(D) None of the above

265. Which of the following ideas is not associated with the stance of situation ethics?
(A) The end justifies the means
(B) No choice
(C) Anything goes
(D) All the above

266. The problem of researcher seeing only what they expect to see is called
(A) Researcher bias
(B) Halo effect
(C) Leniency effect
(D) Experimenter effect

267. Which of the following is most appropriate to impart training for SPSS, a software package used for statistical analysis?
(A) Conference (B) Paper
(C) Workshop (D) Seminar

268. Which of the following is essentially an academic meeting?
(A) Colloquium
(B) Symposium
(C) Conference
(D) None of the above

269. Given below are two statements
Statement I: In the 'before-and-after without it control' design, a single test group or area is selected and the dependent variable is measured before the introduction of the treatment.
Statement II: In the 'before-and-after with control' design, two areas are selected but the dependent variable is not measured in both the areas for an identical time-period before the treatment.
In light of the above statements, choose the most appropriate answer from the options given below
(A) Both Statement I and Statement II are correct
(B) Both Statement I and Statement II are incorrect
(C) Statement I is correct but Statement II is incorrect
(D) Statement I is incorrect but Statement II is correct

270. Match List I with List II

List I Research Design	List II Type of study
a. Sampling design	I. Preplanned design for analysis
b. Statistical design	II. Structured or well thought out instruments for collection of data
c. Observational design	III. Advance decisions about operation procedures
d. Operational design	III. Probability sampling design

Choose the correct answer from the options given below:

(A) a-IV, b-I, c-II, d-III
(B) a-I, b- III, c-IV, d-II
(C) a-III, b- II, c-I, d-IV
(D) a-II, b-IV, c-III, d-I

271. Given below are two statements

Statement I: If we are interested in the worldview of members of a certain social group, a qualitative research strategy that is sensitive to how participants interpret their social world may be preferable.

Statement II: If a researcher is interested in a topic on which little or no research has been done in the past, quantitative research may be easy to employ because there is little prior literature from which to draw leads.

In light of the above statements, choose the most appropriate answer from the options given below

(A) Both Statement I and Statement II are correct
(B) Both Statement I and Statement II are incorrect
(C) Statement I is correct but Statement II is incorrect
(D) Statement I is incorrect but Statement II is correct

272. Which among the following is the names for validity whereby researcher uses a future criterion measure, rather than a contemporary one?

(A) Convergent validity
(B) Predictive validity
(C) Construct validity
(D) Concurrent validity

273. The kind of sample that is simply available to the researcher by virtue of its accessibility, is known as

(A) Quota sampling
(B) Snowball sampling
(C) Convenience sampling
(D) Web sampling

274. Where is the National Geophysical Research institute located?

(A) Jamshedpur
(B) Hyderabad
(C) Mumbai
(D) Jaipur

275. One of the following is not the objective of action research

(A) To improve the working condition of school
(B) To stimulate the students to raise their standard of learning
(C) To motivate the students to attend school
(D) To organise healthy and congenial environment for effective learning

276. What is the aim of educational research?

(A) identifying major problems that need to be solved
(B) Searching for the new facts and principles underlying the process of education
(C) identifying the aims of education
(D) identifying the values that need to be inculcated in the pupils

277. In Data Processing, what does the abbreviation SAP stand for ?

(A) Systems, Applications, Products
(B) Sales, Allocations, Purchases
(C) Systems, Authorizations, Programs
(D) Systems, Algorithms, Processes

278. External validity in research refers to

(A) The rigour of the study
(B) The accuracy of a procedure
(C) The relation of the research problem with the researchers personal life
(D) The extent of generalizability that the results provide

279. The personalistic styles of writing a research report are permissible in which of the following research?

a. Grounded theory research
b. Experimental research
c. Participant observation based research

d. Historical research
e. Case study research

Choose the correct answer from the option given below:

(A) a, b and c only (B) b, c and d only
(C) c, d and e only (D) a, c and e only

280. In using the hypothetico-deductive research paradigm which of the following sequences is considered appropriate?

(A) Hypothesis making, Hypothesis testing, Arriving at generalization and Conclusion
(B) Establishing a research problem, Hypothesis making, Hypothesis testing, Arriving at generalization and Conclusion
(C) Hypothesis making, Establishing a research problem Hypothesis testing, Arriving at generalization and Conclusion
(D) Hypothesis testing, Hypothesis making, Finalizing the problem, Arriving at generalization and Conclusion

281. In which of the following research methods, manipulation and control of variables, and randomization of sample are two of the basic requirements

(A) Ex-post facto research
(B) Descriptive research
(C) Case study research
(D) Experimental research

282. Which one of the following research procedures will figure under post positivistic approach?

(A) Nonnative survey
(B) Experimental study
(C) Ethnographic study
(D) Ex post facto study

283. Inappropriate application of ICT in research is an example of

(A) Technical lapse on the part of the researcher
(B) Inadequate provision of ICT resources
(C) Violation of research ethics
(D) Absence of technical expertise of ICT resources

284. Which one of the following is the main feature of qualitative research?

(A) Avoids positivist assumptions and data analysis
(B) Subscribes to pre-existing categories
(C) Collects data in numerical form
(D) Uses the empirical method of data analysis

285. A university teacher intends to study the relationship between level of aspiration and achievement of rural children. Which design of research will be most appropriate in the context?

(A) Experimental research design
(B) Ex Post Facto research design
(C) Historical research design
(D) Survey research design

286. Which of the following steps in research are least vulnerable to research ethics?

a. Identifying the research variables
b. Defining the research variables
c. Data collection procedure
d. Data analysis procedure
e. Reporting research outcomes

Choose the correct answer from the options given below:

(A) a and b only (B) b and c only
(C) c and d only (D) d and e only

287. A college teacher plans a research programme in which he/she intends to improve the Socio-emotional aspect of his/her classroom climate during teaching. Which one of the following research methods will be considered appropriate in this context?

(A) Experimental method
(B) Descriptive method
(C) Historical method
(D) Action research method

288. Which of the following sampling techniques in research imply randomization and equal probability of drawing the units?

a. Quota sampling
b. Snowball sampling
c. Stratified sampling
d. Dimensional sampling
e. Cluster sampling

Choose the correct answer from the option given below:

(A) a and b only (B) b and c only
(C) c and e only (D) d and e only

289. The best meaning of Research is

(A) Adoption of 'Scientific Method' for creation and application of knowledge
(B) Adoption of critical and constructive thinking for solution of problems
(C) Arriving at generalisations based on observed data
(D) Search for universal truths of life

290. Match List I with List II

List I Scale of measurement	**List II** Properties
a. Nominal	I. Classification and order
b. Ordinal	II. Classification, order and equal units
c. Interval	III. Classification, order, equal units and absolute zero
d. Ratio	IV. Classification only

Choose the correct answer from the options given below

(A) a-I, b- II, c- III, d-IV
(B) a- II, b-I, c-IV, d- III
(C) a- III, b- II, c-IV, d-I
(D) a-IV, b-I, C- II, d-III

291. Which of the following is a measure of consistency?

(A) Validity (B) Objectivity
(C) Reliability (D) Credibility

292. The study of why does stressful living result in a heart attack can be classified as

(A) Descriptive research
(B) Explanatory research
(C) Correlational research
(D) Feasibility research

293. The objective of exploring the existing literature should be to identify which of the following issues?

a. What is already known about this area?
b. What concepts and theories are relevant to this area?
c. How to get funding for the research?
d. What are the significant controversies in this area?
e. Are there any inconsistencies in the findings of this area?

Choose the correct answer from the options given below:

(A) a, b, c and d only
(B) b, c, d and e only
(C) a, b, d and e only
(D) a, b, c and e only

ANSWERS

1. (A) 2. (B) 3. (D) 4. (C) 5. (A) 6. (B) 7. (C) 8. (C) 9. (B) 10. (D)
11. (D) 12. (D) 13. (D) 14. (C) 15. (C) 16. (D) 17. (C) 18. (C) 19. (C) 20. (C)
21. (D) 22. (C) 23. (C) 24. (D) 25. (D) 26. (B) 27. (A) 28. (C) 29. (B) 30. (B)
31. (D) 32. (D) 33. (B) 34. (B) 35. (A) 36. (B) 37. (B) 38. (C) 39. (B) 40. (A)
41. (B) 42. (B) 43. (A) 44. (D) 45. (D) 46. (A) 47. (A) 48. (B) 49. (C) 50. (B)
51. (D) 52. (A) 53. (B) 54. (B) 55. (D) 56. (A) 57. (D) 58. (D) 59. (C) 60. (A)
61. (A) 62. (A) 63. (B) 64. (B) 65. (C) 66. (C) 67. (D) 68. (B) 69. (C) 70. (D)
71. (C) 72. (A) 73. (B) 74. (C) 75. (D) 76. (D) 77. (A) 78. (A) 79. (B) 80. (B)
81. (B) 82. (D) 83. (D) 84. (A) 85. (D) 86. (C) 87. (D) 88. (C) 89. (B) 90. (D)
91. (A) 92. (B) 93. (B) 94. (B) 95. (D) 96. (A) 97. (D) 98. (A) 99. (C) 100. (D)
101. (A) 102. (D) 103. (C) 104. (B) 105. (C) 106. (A) 107. (A) 108. (A) 109. (A) 110. (A)
111. (C) 112. (A) 113. (A) 114. (D) 115. (D) 116. (C) 117. (C) 118. (C) 119. (D) 120. (D)
121. (D) 122. (A) 123. (D) 124. (D) 125. (B) 126. (D) 127. (D) 128. (A) 129. (D) 130. (C)
131. (D) 132. (D) 133. (D) 134. (A) 135. (C) 136. (B) 137. (C) 138. (A) 139. (B) 140. (B)
141. (A) 142. (D) 143. (D) 144. (A) 145. (B) 146. (D) 147. (C) 148. (D) 149. (D) 150. (D)
151. (D) 152. (D) 153. (A) 154. (D) 155. (A) 156. (C) 157. (A) 158. (B) 159. (D) 160. (D)
161. (A) 162. (B) 163. (D) 164. (D) 165. (D) 166. (A) 167. (C) 168. (D) 169. (D) 170. (C)
171. (B) 172. (D) 173. (D) 174. (D) 175. (A) 176. (A) 177. (A) 178. (D) 179. (D) 180. (A)
181. (B) 182. (C) 183. (D) 184. (D) 185. (D) 186. (B) 187. (C) 188. (C) 189. (A) 190. (D)
191. (A) 192. (D) 193. (A) 194. (A) 195. (A) 196. (B) 197. (C) 198. (A) 199. (D) 200. (A)
201. (A) 202. (A) 203. (D) 204. (A) 205. (D) 206. (C) 207. (A) 208. (B) 209. (A) 210. (C)
211. (C) 212. (A) 213. (D) 214. (C) 215. (B) 216. (B) 217. (C) 218. (D) 219. (A) 220. (B)
221. (C) 222. (B) 223. (D) 224. (B) 225. (A) 226. (D) 227. (B) 228. (A) 229. (A) 230. (D)
231. (B) 232. (C) 233. (B) 234. (A) 235. (D) 236. (B) 237. (B) 238. (D) 239. (A) 240. (B)
241. (A) 242. (D) 243. (B) 244. (B) 245. (D) 246. (A) 247. (C) 248. (D) 249. (D) 250. (A)
251. (C) 252. (D) 253. (A) 254. (B) 255. (C) 256. (A) 257. (B) 258. (A) 259. (D) 260. (D)
261. (C) 262. (B) 263. (D) 264. (B) 265. (D) 266. (A) 267. (C) 268. (A) 269. (C) 270. (A)
271. (C) 272. (B) 273. (C) 274. (B) 275. (C) 276. (B) 277. (A) 278. (D) 279. (D) 280. (B)
281. (D) 282. (C) 283. (D) 284. (A) 285. (B) 286. (A) 287. (D) 288. (C) 289. (A) 290. (D)
291. (C) 292. (B) 293. (C)

COMPREHENSION

Syllabus

A passage of text be given. Questions be asked from the passage to be answered.

What is it?

Comprehension is the understanding and interpretation of what is read. To be able to accurately understand written material, students need to be able to (1) decode what they read; (2) make connections between what the read and what they already know; and (3) think deeply about what they have read. One big part of comprehension is having sufficient vocabulary, or knowing enough word meanings. Readers who have strong comprehension are able to make decisions about what they read - what is important, what is fact, and what caused an event to happen.

Though the passages features under comprehension relate to different topics, the questions asked under them follow some definite patterns.

These are:

1. Questions asking you to spot an information specifically mentioned in the passage.
2. Questions asking you to identify an information or an idea which is implied or suggested in the passage.
3. Questions asking to infer the main idea that can be inferred from the passage.
4. Questions asking you to identify the tone of the passage or the attitude of the author towards a person or a topic referred to in the topic.
5. Questions asking you to state the technique adopted by the author in presenting the facts of the topic or his/her views.
6. Questions asking you to extrapolate the ideas of the author to other situations.
7. Questions asking you which among the five choices is not true.

Comprehension is the mind's act or power of understanding. Therefore, a comprehension test aims at testing the student's knowledge and understanding of a particular passage. It also tests one's powers in appreciation. Thus, to set some reasonable set of questions on a passage is an essentiality so as to achieve the purpose of comprehension. The student is expected to answer these questions as accurately as he can in his own words. One can achieve this accuracy through constant practice that will enable him to express himself in a clear and coherent manner.

To answer the questions on a comprehension passage, the student is required to get a good grasp of the passage so that he may understand the objective queries on the passage which he should try to assess accurately. He should not overreact or invent anything extra. Following are few hints for the right procedure to tackle the problem of comprehension.

- Have a good glimpse of the passage before attempting to answer the questions. For this, read the passage slowly and carefully.
- If required, have more than one reading of the passage so as to understand the meaning of different words, phrases and expressions.
- Proceed to answer the questions. For this find out exactly those portions which carry the answer to a question. It is better to underline the relevant portions in the passage.
- While writing answers to the questions, use your own words. It is better to frame your answer on the basis of the underlined portions.
- The answer must always be relevant, it should be neither too long nor too short. Irrelevant and unnecessary things must always be avoided.
- As it has already been explained that a test of comprehension is a test of a language, therefore, your language must be lucid, fluent and worth seeing in expression. The language must be very simple and correct and the expression must be very forceful.

Selecting a suitable heading is a question that is most often asked in comprehension. For this, try to find a word, or a phrase, or a very short sentence that may sum up the main subject of the passage. Here are some suggestions for it.

- The opening and the concluding sentences of the passage must be read very carefully. The title of the passage generally lies in these sentences.
- In case, the title does not lie in these sentences or they do not give the central idea, then the title must be selected from the passage as a whole.
- Always pick some striking but relevant word or phrase from the passage itself.

In this unit of the book you have some comprehension passages for the testing of your appreciation and understanding. Each passage is followed by several questions based on what is stated or implied in the passage. Read these passages carefully and then answer the questions that follow.

One must also keep this in mind that for a good comprehension, an effective, simple and lucid language is must. An effective language in the lack of a good knowledge of grammar is not possible. Here we are giving a specimen comprehension describing the essentiality of grammar for an effective writing.

SPECIMEN PASSAGE

In the lack of good knowledge of grammar, it is impossible for one to write correctly and effectively. It must be borne in mind that all well-informed and knowledgeable persons judge a man's mind by his writing or speaking. Indeed, to acquire the knowledge of grammar is not an easy task. The grammar is not like arithmetic — a science consisting of several distinct departments, some of which may be dispensed with; it is a whole, and the whole must be learnt, or no part is learnt. Its learning demands much reflection and much patience, but, when once the task is performed it is performed for life, and in every day of that life it will be found to be, in a greater or less degree, a source of pleasure or of profit, or both together. The learning of grammar needs no bodily exertion; it exposes the student to no cold, no hunger, no suffering of any sort. What more, the study does not affect the hours of business, nor the hours of necessary exercise, but the hours usually spent on the tea and coffee shops and in the mere gossip which accompanies them. The wasted hours of only one year, employed in the study of English grammar, would make you a correct speaker and writer for the rest of your life. One needs no school, no study room, no expenses and not many tuitions and coachings of any sort. If you are willing, you can accomplish this undertaking with ease whether you are poor, pressed with business or other conveniences and have many other sorts of problems.

1. Why is the knowledge of grammar essential?
   (A) It is essential for an image in the society.
   (B) It is must to judge the mind of others.
   (C) It is essential for good speaking and writing.
   (D) None of these
2. How should grammar be learnt?
   (A) It must be learnt as a whole.
   (B) Some of its part may be omitted like arithmetic.
   (C) It is not essential, you can ignore anything.
   (D) None of these
3. The study of grammar demands
   (A) constant body exertion
   (B) only the leisure time
   (C) physical hardship
   (D) heavy expenses for tuitions and coachings
4. A suitable title of the passage is
   (A) The importance of grammar in the life
   (B) The importance of grammar in writing
   (C) The importance of grammar
   (D) None of these
5. Acquisition of the knowledge of grammar
   (A) happens by subconscious learning
   (B) can only be done through tuitions and coaching
   (C) is an easy task
   (D) is not an easy task.
6. The most important factor affecting the learning of grammar is
   (A) availability of time
   (B) willingness to learn
   (C) quality of coaching
   (D) the monetary means

Answers

1. (C) 2. (A) 3. (B) 4. (C) 5. (D) 6. (B)

❍ Hints for Solution

1. The relevant portion in the paragraph for this question is – *In the lack of good knowledge of grammar, it is impossible for one to write correctly and effectively. It must be borne in mind that all well-informed and knowledgeable persons judge a man's mind by his writing or speaking.* You must concise your answer to this portion only. Similarly, the relevant portions for the second and third questions are as follows :
2. The grammar is not like arithmetic – a science consisting of several distinct departments, some of which may be dispensed with; it is a whole, and the whole must be learnt, or no part is learnt.
3. Its learning demands much reflection and much patience, but, when once the task is performed it is performed for life, and in every day of that life it will be found to be, in a greater or less degree, a source of pleasure or of profit, or both together. The learning of grammar needs no bodily exertion; it exposes the student to no cold, no hunger, no suffering of any sort. What more, the study does not effect the hours of business, nor the hours of necessary exercise, but the hours usually spent on the tea and coffee shops and in the mere gossip which accompanies them. The wasted hours of only one year, employed in the study of English grammar, would make you a correct speaker and writer for the rest of your life.

PASSAGES

LEVEL-1

PASSAGE 1

Most people who bother with the matter at all would admit that the English language is in a bad way, but it is generally assumed that we cannot by conscious action do anything about it. Our civilization is decadent and our language-so the argument runs-must inevitably share in the general collapse. It follows that any struggle against the abuse of language is a sentimental archaism, like preferring candles to electric light or hansom cabs to aeroplanes. Underneath this lies the half-conscious belief that language is natural growth and not an instrument which we shape for our own purposes.

Now it is clear that the decline of a language must ultimately have political and economic causes it is not due simply to the bad influence of this or that individual writer. But an effect can become a cause, reinforcing the original cause and producing the same effect in an intensified form, and so on indefinitely. A man may take to drink because he feels himself to be a failure, and then fail all the more completely because he drinks. It is rather the same thing that is happening to the English language. It becomes ugly and inaccurate because our thoughts are foolish, but the slovenliness of our language makes it easier for us to have foolish thoughts. The point is that the process is reversible. Modern English, especially written English, is full of bad habits which spread by imitation and which can be avoided if one is willing to take the necessary trouble. If one gets rid of these habits, one can think more clearly, and to think clearly is a necessary first step towards political regeneration: so that the fight against bad English is not frivolous and is not the exclusive concern of professional writers.

1. Many people believe that nothing can be done about the English language because
   (A) Bad habits spread by imitation
   (B) We live in a decadent civilization
   (C) There are too may bad writers
   (D) People are too lazy to change their bad habits
2. The author believes that
   (A) It's now too late to do anything about the problem
   (B) Language is a natural growth and cannot be shaped for our won purpose
   (C) The decline in the language can be stopped
   (D) The process of an increasingly bad language cannot be stopped
3. The author believes that the first stage towards the political regeneration of the language would be
   (A) Taking the necessary trouble to avoid bad habits
   (B) Avoiding being frivolous about it
   (C) Clear thinking
   (D) For professional writers to help
4. The author believes that
   (A) English is become ugly
   (B) Bad language
   (C) Our thoughts are becoming uglier because we are making the language uglier
   (D) Our civilization is decadent so nothing can be done to stop the decile of the language
5. What causes bad language in the end?
   (A) The bad influence of individual writers

(B) The imitation of bad language habits
(C) Political and economic causes.
(D) An assumption that nothing can be done about

Answers

1. (B) 2. (D) 3. (C) 4. (C) 5. (C)

PASSAGE 2

It is to progress in the human sciences that we must look to undo the evils which have resulted from a knowledge of physical world hastily and superficially acquired by population unconscious of the changes in themselves that the new knowledge has imperative. The road to a happier world than any known in the past lies open before us if atavistic destructive passions can be kept in leash while the necessary adaptations are made. Fears are inevitable in time, but hopes are equally rational and far more likely to bear good fruit. We must learn to think rather less of the dangers to be avoided than of the good that will lie within our grasp if we can believe in it and let it dominate our thoughts. Science, whatever unpleasant consequences it may have by the way, is in its very nature a liberator, a liberator of bondage to physical nature and in time to come, a liberator from the weight of destructive passions. We are on the threshold of utter disaster or unprecedentely glorious achievement. No previous age has been fraught with problems so momentous; and it is to science that we must look to for a happy future.

1. What does science liberate us from? It is liberate us from
   (A) fears and destructive passions
   (B) slavery to physical nature and from passions
   (C) bondage to physical nature
   (D) idealistic hopes of glorious future
2. Should human sciences be developed because they will
   (A) provide more knowledge of the physical word
   (B) make us conscious of the changing world
   (C) make us conscious of the changing in ourselves
   (D) eliminate the destruction caused by a superficial knowledge of the physical world
3. If man's bestial yearning is controlled
   (A) the future will be tolerable (B) the future will be brighter than the present
   (C) the present will be brighter than the future (D) the present will become tolerable
4. Fears and hopes according to the author
   (A) are closely linked with the life of modern man
   (B) can bear fruit
   (C) can yield good results (D) are irrational
5. To carve out a bright future man should
   (A) analyse dangers that lie ahead (B) try to avoid dangers
   (C) overcome fear and dangers (D) cultivate a positive outlook

Answers

1. (B) 2. (D) 3. (B) 4. (A) 5. (D)

PASSAGE 3

The object underlying the rules of natural justice "is to prevent miscarriage of justice" and secure "fair play in action" As pointed out earlier the requirement about recording of reasons for its decision by an administrative authority exercising quasi-judicial functions achieves his object by excluding changes of arbitrariness and ensuring a degree of fairness in the process of decision making. Keeping in view the expanding horizon of the principle of natural justice which govern exercise of power by administrative authorities. The rules of natural justice are not embodied rules. The extent of their application depends upon the particularly statutory framework where under jurisdiction has been conferred on the administrative authority with regard to the exercise of particular power by an administrative authority including exercise of judicial or quasi-judicial functions the legislature, while conferring the said power, may feel that it would not be in the larger public interest that the reasons for the order passed by the administrative authority be recorded in the order and be communicated to the aggrieved party and it may dispense with such a requirement.

1. "The rules of the natural justice are not embodies rules" means that these rules
   (A) are left deliberately vague
   (B) cannot be satisfactorily interpreted
   (C) are flexible
   (D) cannot be visualised
2. From the passage it is clear that it is the legislature that
   (A) invests the administrative authority with enormous powers
   (B) embodies rules
   (C) has the larger interests of public welfare
   (D) leaves administrative authority enough discretion to interpret rules
3. According to the passage, there is always a gap between
   (A) rules of natural justice and their application
   (B) conception of a rule and its concretisation
   (C) demand for natural justice and its realisation
   (D) intention and execution
4. "To dispense with a requirement" means
   (A) to do without the demand
   (B) to drop the charge
   (C) to cancel all formal procedure
   (D) to alter the provisions of the case
5. According to the passage, natural justice can be brought about by
   (A) administrative authority remaining vigilant
   (B) administrative authority upholding rules of natural justice
   (C) administrative authority farming rules suitably
   (D) administrative authority observing the rules of fair play

Answers

1. (c) 2. (A) 3. (A) 4. (A) 5. (D)

PASSAGE 4

Courage is not only the basis of virtue; it is its expression, faith, hope, charity and all the rest don't become virtues until it takes courage to exercise them. There are roughly two types of courage. The first an emotional state which urges a man to risk injury or death, is physical courage. The second, more reasoning attitude which enables him to take coolly his career, happiness, his whole future or his judgement of what he thinks either right or worthwhile, is moral courage.

I have known many men, who had marked physical courage, but lacked moral courage. Some of them were in high places, but they failed to be great in themselves because they lacked moral courage. On the other hand I have seen men who undoubtedly possessed moral courage but were very cautious about taking physical risks. But I have never met a man with moral courage who couldn't, when it was really necessary, face a situation boldly.

1. A man of courage is
   (A) cunning (B) intelligent (C) curious (D) careful
2. Physical courage is an expression of
   (A) emotions (B) deliberation (C) uncertainty (D) defiance
3. A man with moral courage can
   (A) defy his enemies (B) overcome all difficulties
   (C) face a situation boldly (D) be very pragmatic
4. People with physical courage of ten lack
   (A) mental balance (B) capacity for reasoning
   (C) emotional stability (D) will to fight
5. All virtues become meaningful because of
   (A) faith (B) charity (C) courage (D) hope

Answers

1. (D) 2. (A) 3. (C) 4. (B) 5. (C)

PASSAGE 5

Many sociologists have argued that there is functional relationship between education and economic system. They point to the fact that mass formal education began in industrial society. They note that the expansion of the economies of industrial societies is accompanied by a corresponding expansion of their educational systems. They explain this correspondence in terms of the needs of industry for skilled and trained manpower, needs which are met by the educational system. Thus, the provision of mass elementary education in Britain in 1870 can be seen as a response to the needs of industry for a literate and numerate workforce at a time when industrial processes were becoming more complex and the demand for technical skills was steadily growing.

1. The industry needs a literate work-force because
   (A) its expansion needs sound learning (B) it relies heavily on expertise
   (C) it promotes a competitive spirit
   (D) its operations need intricate technical knowledge
2. The author argues that
   (A) formal education can be traced to industrial society
   (B) industrial society is responsible for expansion of education at mass level
   (C) industrial society gave rise to vocational education
   (D) industrial society changed the pattern of education
3. The observation of the Sociologists are based on a study of
   (A) the statistical data available in a historical context
   (B) economic system of the 19th century
   (C) the correlation between industry and education in a historical context
   (D) growth of industry 19th century
4. The Sociologists referred to it in the passage say that the relationship between industry and elementary education was one

(A) based on mutual need
(B) based entirely on the need of the industry
(C) based entirely on economic need
(D) based on some inexplicable historical forces

5. By 'functional relationship' is meant
(A) a short-term relationship
(B) practical and utilitarian relationship
(C) temporary arrangement
(D) close and unbreakable relationship

Answers

1. (D) 2. (A) 3. (D) 4. (B) 5. (B)

PASSAGE 6

The assault on the purity of the environment is the price that we pay for many of the benefits of modern technology. For the advantage of automotive transportation we pay a price in smog-induced diseases; for the powerful effects of new insecticides, we pay a price in dwindling wildlife and disturbances in the relation of living things and their surroundings; for nuclear power, we risk the biological hazards of radiation. By increasing agricultural production with fertilizers, we worsen water population.

The highly developed nations of the world are not only the immediate beneficiaries of the good that technology can do, that are also the first victims of environmental diseases that technology breeds. In the past, the environmental effects which accompanied technological progress were restricted to a small and relatively short time. The new hazards neither local nor brief. Modern air pollutions covers vast areas of continents: Radioactive fallout from the nuclear explosion is worldwide. Radioactive pollutants now on the earth surface will be found there for generations, and in case of Carbon-14, for thousands of years.

1. The widespread use of insecticides has
(A) reduced the number of wild animals
(B) caused imbalance in the relationship between living beings and their environment
(C) eliminated diseases by killing mosquitoes and flies
(D) caused biological hazards

2. The passage emphasis that modern technology
(A) is an unmixed blessing
(B) has caused serious hazards to life
(C) has produced powerful chemicals
(D) has benefited highly developed nations

3. According to the passage the increasing use of fertilisers is responsible for
(A) abundance of food
(B) disturbance in the ecological system
(C) water pollution
(D) increase in diseases

4. The harmful effects of modern technology are
(A) widespread but short-lived
(B) widespread and long-lasting
(C) limited and long-lasting
(D) severe but short-lived

5. Radioactive pollutants
(A) are limited in their effect
(B) will infect the atmosphere for thousands of years
(C) will be on the surface of earth for a very long time
(D) will dissipate in short span of time

Answers

1. (B) 2. (B) 3. (C) 4. (B) 5. (C)

LEVEL-2

PASSAGE 1

A vexed problem facing us is the clamour to open more colleges and to reserve more seats for backward classes. But it will be a sheer folly to expand such facilities recklessly without giving any thought to the quality of education imparted. If admissions are made far more selective, it will automatically reduced the number of entrants. This should apply particularly colleges, many of which are little more than degree factories. Only then can the authorities hope to bring down the teacher-student ratio to manageable proportion. What is more, teachers should be given refresher courses, every summer to brush up their knowledge. Besides, if college managements increase their library budget it will help both the staff and the to new students a great deal.

At the same time, however, it will be unfair to deny college education to thousands of young men and women, unless employers stop insisting on degrees even for clerical jobs. For a start, why can't the Government disqualify graduates from securing certain jobs, say class III and IV posts? Once the link between degrees and jobs is severed at least in some important departments, in will make young people think twice before joining college.

1. What can automatically help to reduce admission:
   (A) Though entrance tests
   (B) Discouragement to open new colleges
   (C) Selective admissions
   (D) Abolishing reservation
2. Many of the new college are
   (A) Centres of advanced learning
   (B) Research institutions
   (C) Factories producing degree holders
   (D) Knowns for their academic excellence
3. How can teachers are
   (A) By arranging refresher courses
   (B) By providing monetary help/incentive
   (C) By providing better library facilities
   (D) By sending them abroad
4. The author is in favor of restricting college admissions
   (A) Only when degrees are delinked form jobs
   (B) When alternative avenues are open for the students
   (C) When the teacher student ratio is reduced
   (D) Only when parents think twice before sending their children
5. The phrase "Vexed problem" means
   (A) A serious problem
   (B) A debatable problem
   (C) A difficult problem
   (D) An irritating problem

Answers

1. (C) 2. (C) 3. (A) 4. (A) 5. (D)

PASSAGE 2

Nationalism, of course, is a curious phenomenon which at a certain stage in a country's history gives life, growth and unity but, at the same time, it has a tendency to limit one, because one thinks of one's country as something different from the rest of world. One's perceptive changes and one is continuously thinking of one's own struggles and virtues and failing to the exclusion of other thoughts. The result is that the same nationalism which is the symbol of growth for a people becomes a symbol of the cessation of that growth in mind. Nationalism, when it becomes successful sometimes goes on spreading in an aggressive way and becomes a danger internationally. Whatever line of thought you follow, you arrive at the conclusion that some kind of balance must be found. Otherwise something that was good can turn into evil. Culture, which is essentially good become not only static but aggressive and something that breeds conflict and hatred when looked at from a wrong point of view. How are you find a balance, I don't know. Apart from the political and economic problems of the age , perhaps, that is the greatest problem today because behind it there is tremendous search for something which it cannot found. We turn to economic theories because they have an undoubted importance. It is folly to talk of culture or even of god. When human beings starve and die. Before one can talk about anything else one must provide the normal essentials of life to human beings. That is where economies comes in. Human beings today are not in mood to tolerate this suffering and starvation and inequality when they see that the burden is not equally shared. Others profit while they only bear the burden.

1. The greatest problem in the middle of the passage refers to the question
   (A) how to mitigate hardship to human beings
   (B) how to contain the dangers of aggressive nationalism
   (C) how to share the economic burden equally
   (D) how to curb international hatred
2. Negative national feeling can make a nation
   (A) selfish (B) self-centred (C) indifferent (D) dangerous
3. Suitable title for this passage can be
   (A) Nationalism breeds unity (B) Nationalism – a road to world unity
   (C) Nationalism is not enough (D) Nationalism and national problems
4. 'Others' in the last sentence refers to
   (A) other people (B) other nations
   (C) other communities (D) other neighbours
5. Aggressive nationalism
   (A) breeds threat to international relations (B) leads to stunted growth
   (C) endangers national unity (D) isolates a country

Answers

1. (B) 2. (B) 3. (C) 4. (A) 5. (D)

PASSAGE 3

People have long circulated news via word-of-mouth, and as the language evolved into writing and literacy – and governments played larger roles in people's lives – sharing information became a necessity. However, disseminating news and information on a paper presented significant challenges. When each copy had to be handwritten, mass distribution was impossible. They were first chiseled in stone or metal; later, they were handwritten and distributed in public forums or read from scrolls by town criers. Though both ancient Romans and Chinese – as well as other ancient civilizations – had early forms of news media, they do not qualify as newspapers because they could not be mass-distributed.

The first true newspapers arrived after Johannes Gutenberg introduced his movable type printing press to the European world around 1440. Though printing presses with movable type had existed in eastern Asia for around two centuries, they never made it to Europe; furthermore, Gutenberg's version made it significantly faster to mass produce documents. By 1500, the printing press had made its way throughout Europe, and news sheets (or news books) were mass-distributed.

The first weekly newspaper was published in Germany by Johann Carolus in 1604. Called Relation aller Fürnemmen und gedenckwürdigen Historien, the publication satisfied the four tenets of a "true" newspaper: Accessibility by the public, Published at a regular interval (daily, weekly, monthly, etc.), Information is current, Covers a variety of topics (politics, events, entertainment, sports, etc.) Despite meeting the requirements for a newspaper, there is some debate as to whether The Relation qualifies as the world's first newspaper since it was printed in quarto, not folio, size. It's worth noting the World Association of Newspapers considers The Relation the first true newspaper.'

Other German newspapers followed, and in 1618 the world's first broadsheet newspaper printed in folio size was published in Amsterdam, called Courante uyt Italien, Duytslandt, &c. The newspaper format soon spread throughout Europe, with newspapers published in Spain, France, and Sweden. The first English newspaper was published in 1665 in Oxford, England. Known as the Oxford Gazette, the newspaper moved to London in 1666 and was renamed the London Gazette. It's still being published today. Soon after, the newspaper became a staple in all major European countries. It then made its way to the New World.

1. Which of the following options is satisfying the condition for being a tenant of a "true newspaper"?
   (A) A newspaper which was printed in quarto, not folio, size
   (B) A newspaper which covers historic developments leading to various events.
   (C) A newspaper which is accessible to only Asian readers.
   (D) A newspaper which was published once in a month.
2. Which of the following options is false according to the passage?
   (A) The concept of newspaper was rejected in Europe earlier.
   (B) London Gazette is the first newspaper to be published in the multiple languages.
   (C) The relation was not the first newspaper as it did not meet all the required conditions.
   (D) All are incorrect
3. What paved the way for the "true newspapers"?
   (A) The technology which allowed it to be printed in multiple languages.
   (B) As the Governments started playing a larger role in people's lives
   (C) The world's first broadsheet newspaper printed in folio size
   (D) The invention of the printing press paved the way for "true" newspapers.
4. Which of the following statement is true regarding newspapers?
   (A) The first weekly newspaper was published in Germany by Johann Carolus in 1904.
   (B) The world's first broadsheet newspaper printed in quarto size was published in Amsterdam, called Courante uyt Italien, Duytslandt, & C.
   (C) The first English newspaper known as the Oxford Gazette, was renamed the London Gazette later.
   (D) The first English newspaper was published in 1695 in Oxford, England known as the Oxford Gazette.

5. Choose the word which is most nearly the SIMILAR in meaning to the word 'disseminating' printed in Bold & Underline as used in the passage.
   (A) Sneer (B) Spread
   (C) Agree (D) Taunt
6. In ancient time what was the biggest challenge that the people had to face while circulating the news?
   (A) Earlier each copy had to be handwritten; mass distribution was next to impossible.
   (B) It was a herculean task for the editors to get an affirmation by government for printing the news
   (C) The biggest challenge was of printing the news on a paper
   (D) Both (A) and (C)

Answers

1. (D)	2. (D)	3. (D)	4. (C)	5. (B)	6. (A)

PASSAGE 4

All political systems need to mediate the relationship between private wealth and public power. Those that fail risk a dysfunctional government captured by wealthy interests. Corruption is one symptom of such failure with private willingness-to-pay trumping public goals. Private individuals and business firms pay to get routine services and to get to the head of the bureaucratic queue. They pay to limit their taxes, avoid costly regulations, obtain contracts at inflated prices and get concessions and privatised firms at low prices. If corruption is endemic, public officials - both bureaucrats and elected officials - may redesign programmes and propose public projects with few public benefits and many opportunities for private profit. Of course, corruption, in the sense of bribes, pay-offs and kickbacks, is only one type of government failure. Efforts to promote 'good governance' must be broader than anti-corruption campaigns. Governments may be honest but inefficient because no one has an incentive to work productively, and narrow elites may capture the state and exert excess influence on policy. Bribery may induce the lazy to work hard and permit those not in the inner circle of cronies to obtain benefits. However, even in such cases, corruption cannot be confined to 'functional' areas. It will be a temptation whenever private benefits are positive. It may be a reasonable response to a harsh reality but, over time, it can facilitate a spiral into an even worse situation.

1. The governments which fail to focus on the relationship between private wealth and public power are likely to become
   (A) Functional (B) Dysfunctional
   (C) Normal functioning (D) Good governance
2. One important symptom of bad governance is
   (A) Corruption (B) High taxes
   (C) Complicated rules and regulations (D) High prices
3. When corruption is rampant, public officials always aim at many opportunities for
   (A) Public benefits (B) Public profit
   (C) Private profit (D) Corporate gains
4. Productivity linked incentives to public/private officials is one of the indicatives for
   (A) Efficient government (B) Bad governance
   (C) Inefficient government (D) Corruption

5. The spiralling corruption can only be contained by promoting
   (A) Private profit
   (B) Anti-corruption campaign
   (C) Good governance
   (D) Pay-offs and kick backs

Answers

1. (B) 2. (A) 3. (C) 4. (A) 5. (A)

PASSAGE 5

After almost three decades of contemplating Swarovski-encrusted navels on increasing flat abs, the Mumbai film industry is on a discovery of India and itself. With budgets of over 30 crore each, four soon to be released movies by premier directors are exploring the idea of who we are and redefining who the other is. It is a fundamental question which the bling-bling, glam-sham and disham-disham tends to avoid. It is also a question which binds an audience when the lights go dim and the projector rolls: as a nation, who are we? As a people, where are we going?

The Germans coined a word for it, zeitgeist, which perhaps Yash Chopra would not care to pronounce. But at 72, he remains the person who can best capture it. After being the first to project the diasporic Indian on screen in Lamhe in 1991, he has returned to his roots in a new movie. Veer Zaara, set in 1986, where Pakistan, the traditional other, the part that got away, is the lover and the saviour. In Subhas Ghai's Kisna, set in 1947, the other is the English woman. She is not a memsahib, but a mehbooba. In Ketan Mehta's The Rising, the East India Englishman is not the evil oppressor of countless cardboard characterisations, which span the spectrum from Jewel in the Crown to Kranti, but an honourable friend.

This is Manoj Kumar's Desh Ki dharti with a difference: there is culture, not contentious politics; balle balle, not bombs: no dooriyan (distance), only nazdeekiyan (closeness).

All four films are heralding a new hero and heroine. The new hero is fallible and vulnerable, committed to his dharma, but also not afraid of failure - less of a boy and more of a man. He even has a grown up name: Veer Pratap Singh in Veer-Zaara and Mohan Bhargav in Swades. The new heroine is not a babe, but often a bebe, dressed in traditional Punjabi clothes, often with the stereotypical body type as well, as in Bride and Prejudice of Gurinder Chadha.

1. Which word Yash Chopra would not be able to pronounce?
   (A) Bling + bling
   (B) Zeitgeist
   (C) Montaz
   (D) Dooriyan
2. Who made Lamhe in 1991?
   (A) Subhash Ghai
   (B) Yash Chopra
   (C) Aditya Chopra
   (D) Sakti Samanta
3. Which movie is associated with Manoj Kumar?
   (A) Jewel in the Crown
   (B) Kisna
   (C) Veer Zaara
   (D) Desh Ki dharti
4. Which is the latest film by Yash Chopra?
   (A) Deewar
   (B) Kabhi Kabhi
   (C) Dilwale Dulhaniya Le Jayenge
   (D) Veer Zaara
5. Which is the dress of the heroine in Veer-Zaara?
   (A) Traditional Gujarati Clothes
   (B) Traditional Bengali Clothes
   (C) Traditional Punjabi Clothes
   (D) Traditional Madras Clothes

Answers

1. (B) 2. (B) 3. (D) 4. (D) 5. (C)

PASSAGE 6

Knowledge creation in many cases requires creativity and idea generation. This is especially important in generating alternative decision support solutions. Some people believe that an individual's creative ability stems primarily from personality traits such as inventiveness, independence, individuality, enthusiasm, and flexibility. However, several studies have found that creativity is not so much a function of individual traits as was once believed, and that individual creativity can be learned and improved. This understanding has led innovative companies to recognise that the key to fostering creativity may be the development of an idea-nurturing work environment. Idea-generation methods and techniques, to be used by individuals or in groups, are consequently being developed. Manual methods for supporting idea generation, such as brainstorming in a group, can be very successful in certain situations. However, in other situations, such an approach is either not economically feasible or not possible. For example, manual methods in group creativity sessions will not work or will not be effective when (1) there is no time to conduct a proper idea-generation session; (2) there is a poor facilitator (or no facilitator at all); (3) it is too expensive to conduct an idea-generation session; (4) the subject matter is too sensitive for a face-to-face session; or (5) there are not enough participants, the mix of participants is not optimal, or there is no climate for idea generation. In such cases, computerised idea-generation methods have been tried, with frequent success.

Idea-generation software is designed to help stimulate a single user or a group to produce new ideas, options and choices. The user does all the work, but the software encourages and pushes, something like a personal trainer. Although idea-generation software is still relatively new, there are several packages on the market. Various approaches are used by idea-generating software to increase the flow of ideas to the user. Idea Fisher, for example, has an associate lexicon of the English language that cross-references words and phrases. These associative links, based on analogies and metaphors, make it easy for the user to be fed words related to a given theme. Some software packages use questions to prompt the user towards new, unexplored patterns of thought. This helps users to break out of cyclical thinking patterns, conquer mental blocks, or deal with bouts of procrastination.

1. The author, in this passage has focused on
   (A) knowledge creation
   (B) idea-generation
   (C) creativity
   (D) individual traits
2. Fostering creativity needs an environment of
   (A) decision support systems
   (B) idea-nurturing
   (C) decision support solutions
   (D) alternative individual factors
3. Manual methods for the support of idea-generation, in certain occasions,
   (A) are alternatively effective
   (B) can be less expensive
   (C) do not need a facilitator
   (D) require a mix of optimal participants
4. Idea-generation software works as if it is a
   (A) stimulant
   (B) knowledge package
   (C) user-friendly trainer
   (D) climate creator
5. Mental blocks, bouts of procrastination and cyclical thinking patterns can be won when
   (A) innovative companies employ electronic thinking methods
   (B) idea-generation software prompts questions
   (C) manual methods are removed
   (D) individuals acquire a neutral attitude towards the software

Answers

1. (A)   2. (B)   3. (A)   4. (A)   5. (B)

PASSAGE 7

Each day at the Shantiniketan School starts with the Saraswati Vandana. When painting competitions are held in the school, images of Hindu gods and goddesses are most common. Sanskrit is a favourite subject of many a student. Nothing new about it except that the 1,200 – odd students studying in the Hindu – run school are Muslims. In 1983, when Ranchodbhai Kiri started Shantiniketan in the all – Muslim Juhapura area of Ahmedabad in Gujarat, only 20 percent of the students were Muslims. But when riots involving the Muslims of Juhapura and the Hindus of nearby Jivrajpark- Vejalpur affected the locality, Hindus started migration. Today, all the students are Muslims and the school is an unparallel example of harmony. In the 2002, when a section of inflamed Muslims wanted the school closed, the parents of the students stood like a wall behind it.

Shantiniketan's principal says, "We never thought of moving the school out of the area because of the love and affection of the local Muslims. Indeed they value the high standard of education which we have set". Such is the reputation of the school that some of the local Muslim strongmen accused of involvement in communal riots are willing to protect the school during the riots.

The parents of Shantiniketan's students believe that it's the best school when it comes to the quality of the teaching. A large number of students have gone for both graduation and post graduation studies. Significantly, the only Muslim teacher in the 40 – member teaching staff Husena Mansuri, teaches Sanskrit. Infact, she is so happy at the school that she recently declined the principalship of another Muslim – run school.

Some of the students' entries in a recent school painting competition mere truly move. One drew a picture of Bharat Mata with a mosque and temple, while another portrayed a boy tying rakhi to his sister. Truly, Shantiniketan is a beacon of hope that, despite the provocations from both communities, Hindus and Muslims can live side-by-side with mutual respect.

1. How the Shantiniketan School starts the day?
   (A) National anthem
   (B) Prayer
   (C) Saraswati Vandana
   (D) Puja
2. Write the subject which is preferred by most of the students
   (A) Hindi
   (B) English
   (C) Sanskrit
   (D) Gujarati
3. Who protects the school during the riot times?
   (A) Local Muslims
   (B) Hindus
   (C) Politicians
   (D) Christians
4. Who is the teacher of sanskrit?
   (A) Ranchodbhai Kiri
   (B) Husena Mansuri
   (C) Manisha Vakil
   (D) Husena Khatoon
5. What is the hope despite the communal riots?
   (A) Hindus and Muslims cannot live side by side
   (B) Hindus and Muslims can live side by side
   (C) only Hindus can live
   (D) only Muslims can live

Answers

1. (C) 2. (C) 3. (A) 4. (B) 5. (B)

PASSAGE 8

Gandhi's overall social and environmental philosophy is based on what human beings need rather than what they want. His early introduction to the teachings of Jains, Theosophists, Christian sermons, Ruskin and Tolstoy, and most significantly the Bhagavad Gita, were to have profound impact on the development of Gandhi's holistic thinking on humanity, nature and their ecological interrelation. His deep concern for the disadvantaged, the poor and rural population created an ambience for an alternative social thinking that was at once far-sighted, local and immediate. For Gandhi was acutely aware that the demands generated by the need to feed and sustain human life, compounded by the growing industrialization of India, far outstripped the finite resources of nature. This might nowadays appear naive or commonplace, but such pronouncements were as rare as they were heretical a century ago. Gandhi was also concerned about the destruction, under colonial and modernist designs, of the existing infrastructures which had more potential for keeping a community flourishing within ecologically-sensitive traditional patterns of subsistence, especially in the rural areas, than did the incoming Western alternatives based on nature-blind technology and the enslavement of human spirit and energies.

Perhaps the moral principle for which Gandhi is best known is that of active non-violence, derived from the traditional moral restraint of not injuring another being. The most refined expression of this value is in the great epic of the Mahabharata, (c. 100 BCE to 200 CE), where moral development proceeds through placing constraints on the liberties, desires and acquisitiveness endemic to human life. One's action is judged in terms of consequences and the impact it is likely to have on another. Jainas had generalized this principle to include all sentient creatures and biocommunities alike. Advanced Jaina monks and nuns will sweep their path to avoid harming insects and even bacteria. Non-injury is a non-negotiable universal prescription.

1. Which one of the following have a profound impact on the development of Gandhi's holistic thinking on humanity, nature and their ecological interrelations?
   (A) Jain teachings
   (B) Christian sermons
   (C) Bhagavad Gita
   (D) Ruskin and Tolstoy
2. Gandhi's overall social and environmental philosophy is based on human beings'
   (A) need
   (B) desire
   (C) wealth
   (D) welfare
3. Gandhiji's deep concern for the disadvantaged, the poor and rural population created an ambience for an alternative
   (A) rural policy
   (B) social thinking
   (C) urban policy
   (D) economic thinking
4. Colonial policy and modernisation led to the destruction of
   (A) major industrial infrastructure
   (B) irrigation infrastructure
   (C) urban infrastructure
   (D) rural infrastructure
5. Gandhi's active non-violence is derived from
   (A) Moral restraint of not injuring another being
   (B) Having liberties, desires and acquisitiveness
   (C) Freedom of action
   (D) Nature-blind technology and enslavement of human spirit and energies

Answers

1. (C) 2. (A) 3. (B) 4. (D) 5. (A)

PASSAGE 9

James Madison said, "A people who mean to be their own governors must arm themselves with power that knowledge gives." In India, the Official Secrets Act, 1923 was a convenient smoke screen to deny members of the public access to information. Public functioning has traditionally been shrouded in secrecy. But in a democracy in which people govern themselves, it is necessary to have more openness. In the maturing of our democracy, right to information is a major step forward; it enables citizens to participate fully in the decision-making process that affects their lives so profoundly. It is in this context that the address of the Prime Minister in the Lok Sabha is significant. He said, "I would only like to see that everyone, particularly our civil servants, should see the Bill in a positive spirit; not as a draconian law for paralyzing Government, but as an instrument for improving Government-Citizen interface resulting in a friendly, caring and effective Government functioning for the good of our People." He further said, "This is an innovative Bill, where there will be scope to review its functioning as we gain experience. Therefore, this is a piece of legislation, whose working will be kept under constant reviews."

The Commission, in its Report, has dealt with the application of the Right to Information in Executive, Legislature and Judiciary. The judiciary could be a pioneer in implementing the Act in letter and spirit because much of the work that the Judiciary does is open to public scrutiny, Government of India has sanctioned an e-governance project in the Judiciary for about Rs. 700 crores which would bring about systematic classification, standardization and categorization of records. This would help the judiciary to fulfil its mandate under the Act. Similar capacity building would be required in all other public authorities. The transformation from non-transparency to transparency and public accountability is the responsibility of all three organs of State.

1. A person gets power
   (A) by acquiring knowledge
   (B) from the Official Secrets Act, 1923
   (C) through openings
   (D) by denying public information
2. Right to Information is a major step forward to
   (A) enable citizens to participate fully in the decision making process
   (B) to make the people aware of the Act
   (C) to gain knowledge of administration
   (D) to make the people Government friendly
3. The Prime Minister considered the Bill
   (A) to provide power to the civil servants
   (B) as an instrument for improving Government-citizen interface resulting in a friendly, caring and effective Government
   (C) a draconian law against the officials
   (D) to check the harassment of the people
4. The Commission made the Bill effective by
   (A) extending power to the executive authorities
   (B) combining the executive and legislative power
   (C) recognizing Judiciary a pioneer in implementing the act in letter and spirit
   (D) educating the people before its implementation
5. The Prime Minister considered the Bill innovative and hoped that
   (A) It could be reviewed based on the experience gained on its functioning.
   (B) The civil servants would see the Bill in a positive spirit.
   (C) It would not be considered as a draconian law for paralyzing Government
   (D) All the above

6. The transparency and public accountability is the responsibility of three organs of the State. These three organs are
   (A) Lok Sabha, Rajya Sabha and Judiciary
   (B) Lok Sabha, Rajya Sabha and Executive
   (C) Judiciary, Legislature and the Commission
   (D) Legislature, Executive and Judiciary

Answers

1. (A)	2. (A)	3. (B)	4. (C)	5. (D)	6. (D)

PASSAGE 10

A fact that draws our attention is that, according to his position in life, an extravagant man is either admired or loathed. A successful business man does nothing to increase his popularity by being prudent with his money. A person who is wealthy is expected to lead a luxurious life and to be lavish with his hospitality. If he is not so, he is considered mean, and his reputation in business may even suffer in consequence. The paradox remains that he had not been careful with his money in the first place; he would never have achieved his present wealth.

Among the low income group, a different set of values exists. The young clerk, who makes his wife a present of a new dress when he has not paid his house rent, is condemned as extravagant. Carefulness with money to the point of meanness is applauded as a virtue. Nothing in his life is considered more worthy than paying his bills. The ideal wife for such a man separates her housekeeping money into joyless little piles – so much for rent, for food, for the children's shoes, she is able to face the milkman with equanimity every, month satisfied with her economizing ways , and never knows the guilt of buying something she can't really afford .

As for myself, I fall neither of these categories. If I have money to spare I can be extravagant, but when, as is usually the case, I am hard up and then I am the meanest man imaginable.

1. Which of the following would be the most appropriate title for the passage:
   (A) Being extravagant is always condemnable.
   (B) The cause of poverty is extravagance.
   (C) Extravagance is a part of the rich as well as of the poor.
   (D) Stingy habits of the poor.
2. According to the passage the person, who is a successful businessman and wealthy
   (A) Is expected to have lavish lifestyle.
   (B) Should not bother about popularity.
   (C) Is more popular if he appears to be wasting away his time.
   (D) Must be extravagant before achieving success.
3. The phrase 'lavish with his hospitality' in the third sentence of the first paragraph means
   (A) Thoughtful in spending only on guests and strangers.
   (B) Unconcerned in treating his friends and relatives.
   (C) Stinginess in dealing with his relatives.
   (D) Extravagance in entertaining guest.
4. The word 'paradox' in the last sentence of the first paragraph means
   (A) Statement based on the popular opinion
   (B) a statement that seems self-contradictory but in reality expresses a possible truth.
   (C) Statement based on facts
   (D) A word that brings out the hidden meaning

5. What is the meaning of the word "equanimity"?
   (A) Calmness
   (B) Discomposure
   (C) Equivocal
   (D) Dubious

Answers

1. (C) 2. (A) 3. (D) 4. (B) 5. (A)

PASSAGE 11

The catalytic fact of the twentieth century is uncontrollable development, consumerist society, political materialism, and spiritual devaluation. This inordinate development has led to the transcendental 'second reality' of sacred perception that biologically transcendence is a part of human life. As the century closes, it dawns with imperative vigour that the 'first reality' of enlightened rationalism and the 'second reality' of the Beyond have to be harmonised in a worthy state of man. The *de facto* values describe what we are, they portray the 'is' of our ethic, they are *est* values (Latin *est* means is). The ideal values tell us what we ought to be, they are *esto* values (Latin *esto* 'ought to be'). Both have to be in the ebb and flow of consciousness. The ever new science and technology and the ever-perennial faith are two modes of one certainty, that is the wholeness of man, his courage to be, his share in Being.

The materialistic foundations of science have crumbled down. Science itself has proved that matter is energy, processes are as valid as facts, and affirmed the non-materiality of the universe. The encounter of the 'two cultures', the scientific and the humane, will restore the normal vision, and will be the bedrock of a 'science of understanding' in the new century. It will give new meaning to the ancient perception that quantity (measure) and quality (value) coexist at the root of nature. Human endeavours cannot afford to be humanistically irresponsible.

1. The problem raised in the passage reflects overall on
   (A) Consumerism
   (B) Materialism
   (C) Spiritual devaluation
   (D) Inordinate development
2. The '*de facto*' values in the passage means
   (A) What is
   (B) What ought to be
   (C) What can be
   (D) Where it is
3. According to the passage, the 'first reality' constitutes
   (A) Economic prosperity
   (B) Political development
   (C) Sacred perception of life
   (D) Enlightened rationalism
4. Encounter of the 'two cultures', the scientific and the human implies
   (A) Restoration of normal vision
   (B) Universe is both material and non-material
   (C) Man is superior to nature
   (D) Co-existence of quantity and quality in nature
5. The contents of the passage are
   (A) Descriptive
   (B) Prescriptive
   (C) Axiomatic
   (D) Optional
6. The passage indicates that science has proved that
   (A) universe is material
   (B) matter is energy
   (C) nature has abundance
   (D) humans are irresponsible

Answers

1. (C) 2. (A) 3. (D) 4. (B) 5. (A) 6. (B)

PASSAGE 12

The phrase "What is it like ?" stands for a fundamental thought process. How does one go about observing and reporting on things and events that occupy segments of earth space ? Of all the infinite variety of phenomena on the face of the earth, how does one decide what phenomena to observe ? There is no such thing as a complete description of the earth or any part of it, for every microscopic point on the earth's surface differs from every other such point. Experience shows that the things observed are already familiar, because they are like phenomena that occur at home or because they resemble the abstract images and models developed in the human mind.

How are abstract images formed ? Humans alone among the animals possess language; their words symbolize not only specific things but also mental images of classes of things. People can remember what they have seen or experienced because they attach a word symbol to them.

During the long record of our efforts to gain more and more knowledge about the face of the earth as the human habitat, there has been a continuing interplay between things and events. The direct observation through the senses is described as a percept; the mental image is described as a concept. Percepts are what some people describe as reality, in contrast to mental images, which are theoretical, implying that they are not real.

The relation of Percept to Concept is not as simple as the definition implies. It is now quite clear that people of different cultures or even individuals in the same culture develop different mental images of reality and what they perceive is a reflection of these preconceptions. The direct observation of things and events on the face of the earth is so clearly a function of the mental images of the mind of the observer that the whole idea of reality must be reconsidered.

Concepts determine what the observer perceives, yet concepts are derived from the generalizations of previous percepts. What happens is that the educated observer is taught to accept a set of concepts and then sharpens or changes these concepts during a professional career. In any one field of scholarship, professional opinion at one time determines what concepts and procedures are acceptable, and these form a kind of model of scholarly behaviour.

1. The problem raised in the passage reflects on
   (A) thought process
   (B) human behaviour
   (C) cultural perceptions
   (D) professional opinion
2. According to the passage, human beings have mostly in mind
   (A) Observation of things
   (B) Preparation of mental images
   (C) Expression through language
   (D) To gain knowledge
3. Concept means
   (A) A mental image
   (B) A reality
   (C) An idea expressed in language form
   (D) All the above
4. The relation of Percept to Concept is
   (A) Positive
   (B) Negative
   (C) Reflective
   (D) Absolute
5. In the passage, the earth is taken as
   (A) The Globe
   (B) The Human Habitat
   (C) A Celestial Body
   (D) A Planet
6. Percept means
   (A) Direct observation through the senses
   (B) A conceived idea
   (C) Ends of a spectrum
   (D) An abstract image

Answers

1. (A)	2. (A)	3. (A)	4. (C)	5. (B)	6. (A)

PASSAGE 13

It should be remembered that the nationalist movement in India, like all nationalist movements, was essentially a bourgeois movement. It represented the natural historical stage of development, and to consider it or to criticise it as a working-class movement is wrong. Gandhi represented that movement and the Indian masses in relation to that movement to a supreme degree, and he became the voice of Indian people to that extent. The main contribution of Gandhi to India and the Indian masses has been through the powerful movements which he launched through the National Congress. Through nation-wide action he sought to mould the millions, and largely succeeded in doing so, and changing them from a demoralised, timid and hopeless mass, bullied and crushed by every dominant interest, and incapable of resistance, into a people with self-respect and self-reliance, resisting tyranny, and capable of united action and sacrifice for a larger cause.

Gandhi made people think of political and economic issues and every village and every bazaar hummed with argument and debate on the new ideas and hopes that filled the people. That was an amazing psychological change. The time was ripe for it, of course, and circumstances and world conditions worked for this change. But a great leader is necessary to take advantage of circumstances and conditions. Gandhi was that leader, and he released many of the bonds that imprisoned and disabled our minds, and none of us who experienced it can ever forget that great feeling of release and exhilaration that came over the Indian people.

Gandhi has played a revolutionary role in India of the greatest importance because he knew how to make the most of the objective conditions and could reach the heart of the masses, while groups with a more advanced ideology functioned largely in the air because they did not fit in with those conditions and could therefore not evoke any substantial response from the masses.

It is perfectly true that Gandhi, functioning in the nationalist plane, does not think in terms of the conflict of classes, and tries to compose their differences. But the action he has indulged and taught the people has inevitably raised mass consciousness tremendously and made social issues vital. Gandhi and the Congress must be judged by the policies they pursue and the action they indulge in. But behind this, personality counts and colours those policies and activities. In the case of very exceptional person like Gandhi the question of personality becomes especially important in order to understand and appraise him. To us he has represented the spirit and honour of India, the yearning of her sorrowing millions to be rid of their innumerable burdens, and an insult to him by the British Government or others has been an insult to India and her people.

1. Which one of the following is true of the given passage ?
   (A) The passage is a critique of Gandhi's role in Indian movement for independence.
   (B) The passage hails the role of Gandhi in India's freedom movement.
   (C) The author is neutral on Gandhi's role in India's freedom movement.
   (D) It is an account of Indian National Congress's support to the working-class movement.
2. The change that the Gandhian movement brought among the Indian masses was
   (A) Physical (B) Cultural
   (C) Technological (D) Psychological
3. To consider the nationalist movement or to criticise it as a working-class movement was wrong because it was a
   (A) historical movement (B) voice of the Indian people
   (C) bourgeois movement (D) movement represented by Gandhi
4. Gandhi played a revolutionary role in India because he could
   (A) preach morality (B) reach the heart of Indians
   (C) see the conflict of classes (D) lead the Indian National Congress

5. Groups with advanced ideology functioned in the air as they did not fit in with
   (A) objective conditions of masses
   (B) the Gandhian ideology
   (C) the class consciousness of the people
   (D) the differences among masses
6. The author concludes the passage by
   (A) criticising the Indian masses
   (B) the Gandhian movement
   (C) pointing out the importance of the personality of Gandhi
   (D) identifying the sorrows of millions of Indians

Answers

1. (B)	2. (D)	3. (C)	4. (B)	5. (A)	6. (C)

PASSAGE 14

If a person suddenly encounters any terrible danger, the change of nature one undergoes is equally great. Sometimes fear numbs our senses. Like animals, one stands still, powerless to move a step in fright or to lift a hand in defense of our lives, and sometimes one is seized with panic, and again, act more like the inferior animals than rational beings. On the other hand, frequently in cases of sudden extreme peril, which cannot be escaped by flight, and must be instantly faced, even the most timid men at once as if by miracle, become possessed of the necessary courage, sharp quick apprehension and swift decision. This is a miracle very common in nature. Man and the inferior animals alike, when confronted with almost certain death ' gather resolution from despair' but there can really be no trace of so debilitating a feeling in the person fighting, or prepared to fight for dear life. At such times the mind is clearer than it has ever been; the nerves are steel, there is nothing felt but a wonderful strength and daring. Looking back at certain perilous moments in my own life, I remember them with a kind of joy, not that there was any joyful excitement then, but because they broadened my horizon, lifted me for a time above myself.

1. The title that best suits the passage would be
   (A) The Will to Fight
   (B) The Miracle of Confronting Danger
   (C) The Change of Nature
   (D) Courage and Panic
2. A man may react to sudden danger in three different ways . What are they?
   (A) He may flee in panic, or fight back or stand still.
   (B) He may be paralyzed with fear, seized with panic or act like an inferior animal.
   (C) He may be paralyzed with fear, or seized with panic, or as if by miracle, become possessed of the necessary courage, and face the danger.
   (D) He may be paralyzed with fear, run away or fight.
3. What is the meaning of the word debilitating?
   (A) enfeeble
   (B) strengthen
   (C) debase
   (D) thriving

Answer: Option A

4. Explain the phrase 'gather resolution from danger'.
   (A) Find peace in times of difficulty.
   (B) A state of utter hopelessness makes one determined to face the difficulty.

(C) To remain calm and not to lose hope.
(D) To be enthusiastic and brave the odds.

5. The author feels happy in the recollection of dangers faced and overcome because
(A) They brought him a new experience.
(B) They added a new perspective and lifted him above himself for a time.
(C) These experiences boosted his confidence.
(D) He felt elated as he was alive.

Answers

1. (B)	2. (C)	3. (A)	4. (B)	5. (B)

PASSAGE 15

The window **offered** a view of the house opposite. The two families did not speak to each other because of a property dispute. One day, Ruchira's textbooks lay untouched as the young girl's gaze was on the happenings in the house opposite. There were two new faces in the neighbouring household - that of an elderly widow and a girl, aged sixteen. Sometimes the elderly lady would sit by the window, doing the young girl's hair. On other days she was absent.

The new young neighbour's daily routine could be seen through the window - she cleaned the rice paddy; split nuts, put the cushions in the sun to air them. In the afternoons while the men were all at world some of the women slept and others played cards. The girl sat on the terrace and read. Sometimes she wrote. One day there was a **hindrance**. She was writing when the elderly woman snatched the unfinished letter from her hands. Thereafter the girl was not to be seen on the terrace. Sometimes during the day sounds came from the house indicating that a massive argument was going on inside.

A few days passed. One evening Ruchira noticed the girl standing on the terrace in tears. The evening prayer was in progress. As she did daily, the girl bowed several times in prayer. Then she went downstairs. That night Ruchira wrote a letter. She went out and posted it that very instant. But as she lay in bed that night, she prayed fervently that her offer of friendship wouldn't reach its destination. Ruchira then left for Madhupur and returned when it was time for college to start. She found the house opposite in darkness, locked. They had left.

When she stepped into her room she found the desk **piled** with letters - one had a local stamp on it with her name and address in unfamiliar handwriting. She quickly read it. They continued to write to each other for the next twenty years.

1. Why did Ruchira write a letter to her new neighbour?
(A) She wanted to offer her, her help.
(B) She wanted to be friends with her.
(C) To apologize for her family's behaviour towards her family.
(D) To encourage her to continue learning to read and write.

2. Which of the following can be said about Ruchira?
(i) She used to spy on her neighbours because she didn't trust them.
(ii) She was at home because she was studying.
(iii) She did not speak to her neighbours because they did not own property.
(A) None
(B) Only (ii)
(C) Both (i) and (ii)
(D) Only (iii)

3. How did the new young neighbour spend her days?
   (A) She was busy writing letters to Ruchira.
   (B) She used to day dream about her past experiences.
   (C) She would attend to the needs of the widow.
   (D) None of these
4. Why was the young neighbour prevented from sitting on the terrace?
   (A) She used to while away her time instead of working.
   (B) The old woman could no longer keep an eye on her.
   (C) She had not finished writing the letter she was asked to.
   (D) She had been writing a letter which she wasn't supposed to.
5. Which of the following is **TRUE** in the context of the passage?
   (A) The young girl was very devout and prayed everyday.
   (B) Only two letters were exchanged between the two girls.
   (C) The new young neighbour was a servant.
   (D) The two families had fought because of the letters the two girls wrote to each other.
6. Why did the young girl wish that the letter would not reach its destination?
   (i) She was going away and would not be able to see if her neighbour was glad to receive it.
   (ii) She was afraid that it would lead to a quarrel between the two families.
   (iii) She was afraid that her neighbour would be angry when she received her letter.
   (A) None (B) Only (i)
   (C) Both (ii) and (iii) (D) Only (ii)

Answers

1. (B)	2. (B)	3. (D)	4. (D)	5. (A)	6. (B)

PASSAGE 16

What should be the objective of life whether money or principles. It is really difficult for a well educated, intellectual or brave person to make money the chief object of his thoughts. No doubt all the healthy people like their dinners, but their dinner is not the main object of their lives. Also, no doubt, all healthy-minded people like to make money, like to have it and enjoy the sensation of having it. But there is something better than money. For instance, doctors no doubt, like fees, yet if they are brave and well educated, the entire object of their lives is not fees. They on the whole, desire to cure the sick; and if they are good doctors, and the choice were fairly put to them, would rather cure their patient and lose their fee than kill him and get it. So of a good soldier, who mainly wishes to do his fighting well. He is glad of the pay, though his main notion of life is to win battle, not to be paid for winning them. Similarly, the clergyman's object is essentially to baptize and preach, not to be paid for preaching. This is how it is also true with all the other brave and rightly trained men; their work comes first, the payment later, though very important but secondary.

1. What is the principal object of the lives of brave intellectual and well-educated people?
   (A) To make money (B) To enjoy
   (C) To work with devotion (D) Manage the leisurely objects
2. According to the passage, if a doctor is brave and well educated, and a choice was put to him, what would he choose ?

(A) Cure the patient and lose his fees
(B) Kill the patient and get his fees
(C) Any of these depending on circumstances
(D) The passage is silent on this.

3. A suitable title of the passage may be
(A) Money Making, the Chief Object of Life
(B) Devotion to Work
(C) Importance of Thought
(D) Money, not the Chief Object of Life

4. One may infer from the paragraph that
(A) brave person like to make money
(B)brave persons like to win others
(C) brave persons like to work first than their fees
(D) none of these

5. A person would always rank his work superior to the money if he is
(A) brave and intellectual
(B) well educated
(C) rightly trained
(D) all the above

6. All healthy minded people like
(A) to make money and enjoy the sensation of having it
(B) to hold their principles supreme in comparison to money
(C) both (A) and (B)
(D) neither (A) nor (B)

Answers

(1) (C) (2) (A) (3) (D) (4) (C) (5) (D) (6) (C)

PASSAGE 17

A recent report in News Week says that in American colleges, students of Asian origin outperform not only the minority group students but the majority Whites as well. Many of these students might be of Indian origin, and their achievement is something that we can be really proud of. It is unlikely that these talented youngsters will come back to India, and that is the familiar brain drain problem. However, recent statements by the nation's policy makers indicate that the perception of this issue is changing. 'Brain Bank' and not the 'Brain Drain' is the more appropriate idea, they suggest that since the expertise of Indians abroad is only deposited in other places and not lost.

This may be so, but this brain bank, like most of other banks, is one that primarily serves customers in its neighbourhood. The skills of Asians now excelling in America's colleges will mainly help the USA. No matter how significant, what nonresident Indians do for India and what their counterparts do for other Asian lands is only a by-product.

But it is also necessary to ask, or be reminded why Indians study more fruitfully when abroad. The Asians whose accomplishments News Week records would have probably had a very different fate if they had studied in India. In America, they found an elbow room, books and facilities not available and not likely to be available here. The need to prove themselves in their new country and the competition of an international standard they faced there must have cured mental and physical laziness. But other things helping them in America can be obtained if we achieve a change in social attitudes, especially towards youth.

We need to learn to value individuals and their unique qualities more than conformity and respectability. We need to learn the language of encouragement to add to our skill in flattery. We might also learn to be less liberal with blame and less tight-fisted with appreciation, especially to those showing signs of independence.

1. Among the many groups of students in American colleges, Asian students
   (A) are often written about in magazines like News Week
   (B) are the most successful academically
   (C) have proved that they are as goods as Whites
   (D) have only a minority status like the blacks.
2. The students of Asian origin in America include
   (A) a fair number from India
   (B) a small group from India
   (C) persons from India who are very proud
   (D) Indians who are the most hard-working of all.
3. In general, the talented young Indians studying in America
   (A) have a reputation for being hard-working
   (B) have an opportunity to India's development
   (C) can solve the brain problem because of recent changes in policy
   (D) will not return to pursue their careers in India.
4. There is talk of the 'Brain Bank', this idea
   (A) is a solution to the brain drain problem
   (B) is a new problem caused partly by the brain drain
   (C) is a new way of looking at the role of qualified Indians living abroad
   (D) is based on plan to utilize foreign exchange remittances to stimulate research and development.
5. Which of the following measures have been explicitly suggested in the passage to counter the problem of brain-drain ?
   (1) To provide the competition of an international standard
   (2) Greater emphasis on conformity and respectability
   (3) Greater appreciation for those with a spark
   (4) An attitude to value individuals and their unique qualities
   (A) Only (4) (B) (3) and (4)
   (C) (1), (3) and (4) (D) All
6. Which of the following most appropriately sums up the intent of the author ?
   (A) We need to look at 'Brain Drain' in a positive way as 'Brain Bank'.
   (B) Indians should take pride in the fact that fellow Indians have excelled in foreign lands against all odds.
   (C) We need to think of the ways to help grow and retain the talent of our land.
   (D) USA has excelled just because of the contributions from talented immigrants.

Answers

(1) (B)	(2) (A)	(3) (D)	(4) (C)	(5) (B)	(6) (C)

PASSAGE 18

The University Grants Commission's directive to college and university lecturers to spend a minimum of 22 hours a week in direct teaching is the product of budgetary cutbacks rather than pedagogic wisdom. It may seem odd, at first blush, that teachers should protest about teaching a mere 22 hours. However, if one considers the amount of time academics require to prepare lectures of good quality as well as the time they need to spend doing research, it is clear that most conscientious teachers work more than 40 hours a week. In university systems around the world, lecturers rarely spend more than 12 to 15 hours in direct teaching activities a week. The average college lecturer in India does not have any office space. If computers are available, internet connectivity is unlikely. Libraries are poorly stocked. Now the UGC says universities must implement a complete freeze on all permanent recruitment, abolish all posts which have been vacant for more than a year, and cut staff strength by 10 per cent. And it is in order to ensure that these cutbacks do not affect the quantum of teaching that existing lecturers are being asked to work longer. Obviously, the quality of teaching and academic work in general will decline. While it is true that some college teachers do not take their classes regularly, the UGC and the institutions concerned must find a proper way to hold them accountable. An absentee teacher will continue to play truant even if the number of hours he is required to teach goes up.

All of us are well aware of the unsound state that the Indian higher education system is in today. Thanks to years of sustained financial neglect, most Indian universities and colleges do not research worth the name. Even as the number of students entering colleges has increased dramatically, public investment in higher education has actually declined in relative terms. Between 1985 and 1997, when public expenditure on higher education as percentage of outlays on all levels of education grew by more than 60 per cent in Malaysia and 20 per cent in Thailand, India showed a decline of more than 10 per cent. Throughout the world, the number of teachers in higher education per million population grew by more than 10 per cent in the same period; in India it fell by one per cent. Instead of transferring the burden of government apathy on to the backs of the teachers, the UGC should insist that the need of the country's university system be adequately catered to.

1. Why does the UGC want to increase the direct teaching hours of university teachers?
   (A) UGC feels that the duration of contact between the teacher and the taught should be more.
   (B) UGC wants teachers to spend more time in their departments.
   (C) UGC wants teachers to devote some time to improve university administration.
   (D) UGC does not have money to appoint additional teachers.
2. Which of the following is the reason for the sorry state of affairs of the Indian Universities as mentioned in the passage?
   (A) The poor quality of teachers
   (B) Involvement of teachers in extra curricular activities
   (C) Politics within and outside the departments
   (D) Not getting enough financial assistance
3. Which of the following statements is/are **TRUE** in the context of the passage?
   (i) Most colleges do not carry out research worth the name.
   (ii) UGC wants lecturers to spend minimum 22 hours a week in direct teaching.
   (iii) Indian higher education system is in unsound state.
   (A) Only (i) and (iii) (B) All (i), (ii) and (iii)
   (C) Only (iii) (D) Only (ii)

4. Besides direct teaching, University teachers spend considerable time in/on
   (A) administrative activities such as admissions
   (B) supervising examinations and correction of answer papers
   (C) carrying out research in the area of their interest
   (D) maintaining research equipment and libraries
5. Which of the following statements is **NOT TRUE** in the context of the passage?
   (A) UGC wants teachers to spend minimum 40 hours in a week in teaching.
   (B) Some college teachers do not engage their classes regularly.
   (C) The average college teacher in India does not have any office space.
   (D) UGC wants universities to abolish all posts which have been vacant for more than a year.
6. Which of the following statements is **NOT TRUE** in the context of the passage?
   (A) Indian universities are financially neglected.
   (B) All over the world, the university lecturers hardly spend more than 12 to 15 hours a week in direct teaching.
   (C) Indian Universities are being asked to reduce staff strength by 10%.
   (D) Public investment in higher education has increased in India.

Answers

1. (D)	2. (D)	3. (B)	4. (C)	5. (A)	6. (D)

PASSAGE 19

Each day at the Shantiniketan School starts with the Saraswati Vandana. When painting competitions are held in the school, images of Hindu gods and goddesses are most common. Sanskrit is a favourite subject of many a student. Nothing new about it except that the 1,200 – odd students studying in the Hindu – run school are Muslims.

In 1983, when Ranchodbhai Kiri started Shantiniketan in the all – Muslim Juhapura area of Ahmedabad in Gujarat, only 20 percent of the students were Muslims. But when riots involving the Muslims of Juhapura and the Hindus of nearby Jivrajpark – Vejalpur affected the locality, Hindus started migration. Today, all the students are Muslims and the school is an unparallel example of harmony. In the 2002, when a section of inflamed Muslims wanted the school closed, the parents of the students stood like a wall behind it.

Shantiniketan's principal says, "We never thought of moving the school out of the area because of the love and affection of the local Muslims. Indeed they value the high standard of education which we have set". Such is the reputation of the school that some of the local Muslim strongmen accused of involvement in communal riots are willing to protect the school during the riots.

The parents of Shantiniketan's students believe that it's the best school when it comes to the quality of the teaching. A large number of students have gone for both graduation and post graduation studies. Significantly, the only Muslim teacher in the 40 – member teaching staff Husena Mansuri, teaches Sanskrit. Infact, she is so happy at the school that she recently declined the principalship of another Muslim – run school.

Some of the students' entries in a recent school painting competition mere truly move. One drew a picture of Bharat Mata with a mosque and temple, while another portrayed a boy tying rakhi to his sister. Truly, Shantiniketan is a beacon of hope that, despite the provocations from both communities, Hindus and Muslims can live side-by-side with mutual respect.

1. How the Shantiniketan School starts the day?
   (A) National anthem (B) Prayer
   (C) Saraswati Vandana (D) Puja
2. Write the subject which is preferred by most of the students
   (A) Hindi (B) English
   (C) Sanskrit (D) Gujarati
3. Who protects the school during the riot times?
   (A) Local Muslims (B) Hindus
   (C) Politicians (D) Christians
4. Who is the teacher of Sanskrit?
   (A) Ranchodbhai Kiri (B) Husena Mansuri
   (C) Manisha Vakil (D) Husena Khatoon
5. What is the hope despite the communal riots?
   (A) Hindus and Muslims cannot live side by side
   (B) Hindus and Muslims can live side by side
   (C) only Hindus can live (D) only Muslims can live

Answers

1. (C) 2. (C) 3. (A) 4. (C) 5. (B)

PASSAGE 20

A fact that draws our attention is that, according to his position in life, an extravagant man is either admired or loathed. A successful business man does nothing to increase his popularity by being prudent with his money. A person who is wealthy is expected to lead a luxurious life and to be lavish with his hospitality. If he is not so, he is considered mean, and his reputation in business may even suffer in consequence. The paradox remains that he had not been careful with his money in the first place; he would never have achieved his present wealth.

Among the low income group, a different set of values exists. The young clerk, who makes his wife a present of a new dress when he has not paid his house rent, is condemned as extravagant. Carefulness with money to the point of meanness is applauded as a virtue. Nothing in his life is considered more worthy than paying his bills. The ideal wife for such a man separates her housekeeping money into joyless little piles – so much for rent, for food, for the children's shoes, she is able to face the milkman with equanimity every, month satisfied with her economizing ways , and never knows the guilt of buying something she can't really afford .

As for myself, I fall neither of these categories. If I have money to spare I can be extravagant, but when, as is usually the case, I am hard up and then I am the meanest man imaginable.

1. Which of the following would be the most appropriate title for the passage:
   (A) Being extravagant is always condemnable.
   (B) The cause of poverty is extravagance.
   (C) Extravagance is a part of the rich as well as of the poor.
   (D) Stingy habits of the poor.

2. According to the passage the person, who is a successful businessman and wealthy
   (A) Is expected to have lavish lifestyle.
   (B) Should not bother about popularity.
   (C) Is more popular if he appears to be wasting away his time.
   (D) Must be extravagant before achieving success.
3. The phrase 'lavish with his hospitality' in the third sentence of the first paragraph means
   (A) Thoughtful in spending only on guests and strangers.
   (B) Unconcerned in treating his friends and relatives.
   (C) Stinginess in dealing with his relatives.
   (D) Extravagance in entertaining guest.
4. The word 'paradox' in the last sentence of the first paragraph means
   (A) Statement based on the popular opinion.
   (B) a statement that seems self-contradictory but in reality expresses a possible truth.
   (C) Statement based on facts.
   (D) A word that brings out the hidden meaning.
5. What is the meaning of the word "equanimity"?
   (A) Calmness (B) Discomposure
   (C) Equivocal (D) Dubious

Answers

1. (C)	2. (A)	3. (D)	4. (B)	5. (A)

COMMUNICATION

Syllabus

- **Communication:** Meaning, Types and Characteristics of Communication.
- **Effective communication:** Verbal and Non-verbal, Inter-Cultural and Group Communications, Classroom Communication.
- Barriers to Effective Communication.
- Mass-Media and Society.

Communication in the teaching process helps students attach concepts to their own lives, as students will apply what they learn in class to the world around them.

Communication is exchange of ideas and meanings between two persons or groups. Signs, expressions, utterances, gestures, sounds, noises are the silent form of languages used by human beings. Human beings are capable of making these languages and are using them to convey meanings. Each culture has certain accepted modes of expressions, signs, gestures, clothing styles, decorative marks, etc., which communication between people familiar with that culture can take place non-verbally. Even animals also communicate. Usually, they communicate, through non-verbal means, they express their feelings, pain, pleasure, joy, sorrow, anger, pity and other emotions. But their language is silent. Besides silent languages, there is a special kind of language – verbal language. Verbal languages can be used by those who are able to form all sorts of concepts. Since only human beings are able to form all sorts of concepts, therefore verbal languages have been evolved from and confined only to humans.

Communication is important for human existence as it shapes all human behaviour. It can be sold that communication is an ongoing process in the world of humans, animals and plants and is as vital as life itself.

Definitions

Generally we define communication as the process of **transfer of information** between two sources with the information being understood by both. Some remarkable definitions of communication are given below.

1. According to **Kelly**, "Communication is a field of knowledge dealing with the systematic application of symbols to acquire common information regarding an object or event."
2. According to **Luther**, "It is the transmission of commonly meaningful information. It is a process that involves the exchange of behaviours."
3. According to **A. Kumar**, "Communication is the process of making a message understood by satisfying the need sets and ego sets of a receiver."

4. According to **Katz** and **Kahn**, "Communication – the exchange of information and the transmission of meaning – is the very essence of a social system or an organisation."
5. According to **Dr. McFarland**, "Communication is the process of meaningful interactions among human beings. It is a process by which, meanings are perceived and understandings are reached among human beings."
6. According to **Brown**, "Communication is a process of transmitting ideas or thoughts from one person to another for the purpose of creating an understanding in the thinking of the person receiving communication."
7. According to **Anderson**, "Communication is a dynamic process in which, man consciously or unconsciously affects the cognition of another through materials or agencies used in symbolic ways."
8. In the view of **Sanborn**, "Communication is the process of sending and receiving messages."
9. According to **Fauconnier**, "Communication is nevertheless an attempt at making common the basic condition for the origin, the existence, and the development of every social relationship."
10. According to **MT Myers** and **GE Myers**, "Communication refers to a special kind of patterning, which is expressed in a symbolic form. For communication to take place between or among people, two requirements must be met: (a) a symbolic system must be shared by the people involved (we need to speak the same language or jargon or dialects); and (b) the associations between the symbols and their referents must be shared."
11. According to **Fortune**, "...it is the procedure whereby one mind affects another."
12. According to **Fearing**, "It is a two-way process which cannot be adequately understood in terms of simple engineering or mechanical analogies. It is uniquely a human relationship from which, emerge all civilisations and culture without which, man as we know him, could not survive."

Characteristics of Communication

1. **It Involves at Least Two Persons.** Communication involves at least two persons, a sender and a receiver. The sender is called communicator and the receiver of the message is known as communicate. A person who speaks, writes or issues some instructions is the sender and the person for whom the communication is meant or who receives the message is the receiver or communicates.
2. **Message is a Must.** A message is the subject matter of communication. e.g., the contents of the letter or speech, order, instructions or the suggestions. A communication must convey some message. If there is no message there is no communication.
3. **Communication May be Written, Oral or Gestural.** Communication is generally understood as spoken or written words. But in reality, it is more than that. It includes everything that may be used to convey meanings from one person to another, e.g., movement of lips, or the wink of an eye or the wave of hands may convey more

FACTS

- **A two-way traffic.** It is a two-way traffic – upward and downward. Messages, directives, opinions are communicated downward. Likewise grievances, complaints, opinions, feelings, are communicated upward along the line.
- **Continuous Process.** It is continuous process. It is repeated to achieve the desired results. It is not a one time shot.
- **A short-lived process.** It is complete as soon as the message is received and understood by the receiver in the right perspective.
- **Needs proper understanding.** There may be numerous media of communication but the main purpose of conveying the message is a proper understanding of the message by the other party. For this purpose, it should be clearly and concisely worded.

meaning than even written or spoken words.

4. **Communication is a Two Way Process.** It involves both information and understanding. Communication is not complete unless the receiver has understood the message properly and his reaction or response is known to the sender. Understanding is the end result of communication but it does not imply agreement.
5. **Its Primary Purpose is to Motivate a Response.** The primary purpose of communication is to motivate response or influence human behaviour. There is no doubt that motivation comes from within but communicator can also motivate people by good drafting of message, proper timing of communication, etc. To create understanding, communication should be relevant to the situation. It must always be remembered that communication is a means of motivating and not an end itself.

GOOD COMMUNICATION APPROACH

- Listen to what people say
- Invite questions and encourage interaction
- Be aware of people's concerns
- Understand words and concepts that people commonly use and use appropriate language
- Share ideas and information in ways that help people understand and correct misunderstanding
- Build on what people already know
- Stick to the important points
- Be specific about what action to take
- Motivate people

6. **Communication may be Formal or Informal.** Formal communication follows the formal channels provided in the organisation structure. For example, the Managing Director communicates with the departmental heads, say Finance Manager, finance manager communicates to deputy finance manager, the deputy finance manager with accounts officer and so on.

   In simple words, in informal communication, there is no direct communication between the Managing Director and the accounts clerks. Informal communication flows from informal channels of communication which are not provided in the organisation structure. These channels develop among members because of personal contacts through working with each other.
7. **It Flows Up and Down and also from Side to Side.** Communication flows downward from a superior to subordinate and upward from subordinate to a superior. It also flows between two or more persons operating at the same level of authority.
8. **It is an Integral Part of the Process of Exchange.** It refers to the exchange of ideas, feelings, emotions and knowledge and information's between two or more persons.

Types of Communication

A. On the basis of the number of participants. This classification of communication is based on 'either a man communicate with himself, or two men communicate with each other, or more than two men are indulged in this act.'

1. **Intra-personal Communication.** Interpersonal communication is the communication where exchange of ideas and information happens between two or more people by way of any channel. This can be face to face, online, over the phone, or in written forms as well.

   There are several aspects that make this type of communication explicitly interpersonal:

   - **Inescapable.** Even when we hold some thought inside us and do not let it out verbally, it will take its form in other nonverbal aspects of communication such as mood, attitude, or body language.
   - **Irreversible.** Once something is written, said, or submitted, it cannot be taken back. It is forever in the minds of others.
   - **Complex.** There is a high chance of miscommunication between sender and receiver, therefore interpersonal communication is complex.

- **Contextual.** Context is an integral part of this type of communication, and the context can be situational, environmental, and relational.

2. **Intrapersonal Communication.** Intrapersonal communication is the communication done with oneself. Included are the thoughts, assessments, contemplations, and feelings that are associated with one's inner communication.

   Here are some things that are uniquely intrapersonal:

   - **Self-Concept.** One's own self concept is at the center of intrapersonal communication. It includes an evaluation of one's own beliefs, values and attitudes, and how that evaluation plays into what occurs in the outer world.
   - **Perception.** Perception is how people interpret what is going on around them. Perception can influence intrapersonal communication.
   - **Expectation.** Expectations are based upon intrapersonal communication with one's own self, and are predictions of what will happen based on perceptions of what has happened.

DIFFERENCES BETWEEN INTERPERSONAL VS. INTRAPERSONAL COMMUNICATION

The biggest difference that you need to know about between interpersonal vs intrapersonal communication is that interpersonal is between two or more people, and intrapersonal is between you and yourself.

Here are the other main differences:

a. **Parties Involved.** In interpersonal communication, there's always more than one person. It doesn't matter if the communication happens online, over the phone, or in an email. Two people communicating means interpersonal.

   This is in contrast to intrapersonal communication which is only done within one's own mind with one's own thoughts, feelings, and ideas.

b. **Reasons.** The reasons you may want to use interpersonal communication is to tell a story, share an idea or experience, or relay information to someone else or a group of people.

   The reasons you may be using intrapersonal communication is to reflect on something that happened, make goals and plans, visualize the future, and get closer with your own feelings.

c. **Media and Feedback.** Feedback for interpersonal communication can be vast – it may be verbal, nonverbal (such as a shrug, nod, or eyebrow raise), or it may be oral or written. Interpersonal feedback can be in person, over the phone, on a computer, or in a letter.

   Media used for intrapersonal communication is much simpler – it is always going to be considered in person, although can be done live, in audio recordings, or in writing. Feedback for intrapersonal communication is hard to define. Your feedback is your own and only you know how you react to your own feelings, thoughts, and ideas.

	Interpersonal Communication	**Intrapersonal Communication**
Definition	Reffering to something that occurs between people	Refferring to something that occurs within oneself
Who's involved	Two or mor people	Just you
When does it happen	When you want to communicate with others	When you want to plan, reflect, get closer to yourself
Media used	Phone, Computer, TV, In-person, Letters	Mind, Diaries, Audio Recordings
Concerned with	Exchange of ideas	Thought and analysis

3. **Intra-Group (Multiadic) Communication.** A complex form of communication which occurs between more than two individuals.

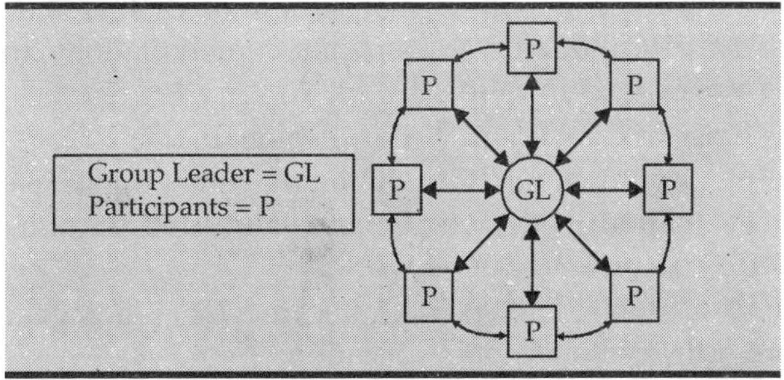

GROUP COMMUNICATION

4. **Intergroup (Association) Communication.** The communication which involves two groups.
5. **Organisational (Institutional) Communication.** The form of communication which is used in business enterprises.
6. **Mass Communication.** When a person or firm communicates with a very large group of people or society without meeting them in a conference hall or meeting room.

Intragroup communication	Intergroup communication
• It take place in the form of interaction between different persons belonging to a same group. It involves sharing of ideas and information within the group.	• It takes place during the conversation between members of two or more different groups.
Direct communication	**Mediated communication**
• The sender and receiver have face-to-face interaction. • There is no need of using any medium for communicating.	• It does not involve face-to-face or direct interaction between the sender and receiver. • It takes place through some medium like any third person, newspaper, radio, computer, social media, or other technologies.
Contiguous communication	**Non-contiguous communication**
• Sender and receiver are in direct touch. • It is continuous. • Examples include face-to-face interaction, chat sessions, and so on. • There is usually limited number of participants. • It is time-consuming and expensive and there is need of direct contact.	• Sender and receiver are not in direct touch. • It is not continuous. • Examples include reading a book, listening to radio broadcast, watching TV. • It can have greater reach

7. **Public Communication.** The form of communication in which public (which can be heard and addressed) is involved.

B. On the Basis of Direction of Flow

This classification is based on the guiding factors in a firm or institution. In a firm, orders can move down and reports and suggestions can move upwards.

1. Downward Communication. In this type of communication orders or informations move downwards from superiors to subordinates.

Essentials of Effective Downward Communication

- Downward communication flows from a superior to the subordinate staff.

- Its objectives are :
  - ✦ to give directives about some job,
  - ✦ to explain policies and procedures,
  - ✦ to convey assessment of performance
  - ✦ to explain the rationale of the job.
- Its limitations are :
  - ✦ under-communication or over-communication,
  - ✦ in case of a long line of communication, there may be: delay, loss of information, distortion, resentment by subordinate staff

- To make it effective
  - ✦ in-charge should be adequately informed
  - ✦ in-charge should be clear about how much to communicate
  - ✦ some authority should be delegated to lower levels to shorten the line of communication
  - ✦ information should be passed on to the correct person.

2. Upward Communication. When informations move upward from subordinates and continues up to the top of organisational hierarchy. It is an important type of communication which controls purposes.

Essentials of Effective Upward Communication

- Upward communication moves from the subordinate staff to the superiors.
- Its importance is
  - ✦ provides feedback to the superiors,
  - ✦ releases the pent-up emotions of the subordinate staff,
  - ✦ provides the superiors with useful suggestions,
  - ✦ makes the introduction of new schemes easier,
  - ✦ promotes harmony.

Upward Communication

Top Level

Mid & Low Level Management

Work Employee

Upward Communication

" Upward communication is the process of communication where information flows from down to upward, i.e.

from the subordinates to superior levels. The subordinates convey their actions, attitudes and opinions about varied subjects to their superiors. "

- Its channels are: superiors keep an open door, complaints-and-suggestions boxes, social gatherings, direct correspondence, reports, counselling.
- Its limitations are: employees are reluctant to express themselves, employees fear that their criticism may be interpreted as a sign of their personal weakness, great possibility of distortion, bypassed superiors feel insulted
- To make it effective
  - ✦ superiors should take initiative to get close to the subordinate staff;
  - ✦ keeping the line of communication short,
  - ✦ prompt redressal of legitimate grievances.

3. Crosswise (Diagonal) Communication. This type of communication involves different people on the same organisational or different levels of the organisational hierarchy.

C. On the basis of way of expression

On the basis of way of expression, communication can be classified into six major groups.

1. **Written Communication.** In this type of communication, message is sent/obtained through printed or hand-written texts.
2. **Oral Communication.** It may be of two types (i) **Audio.** It refers to the movement message for ears, while the speaker is not present before the listener. (ii) **Verbal.** It refers to the transfer of message by words, while the listener is present before the speaker.
3. **Visual Communication.** When the communication involves the use of more visuals and less text.
4. **Audio visual Communication.** When the information is obtained by the combination of pictures with voices.
5. **Non-verbal Communication.** This type of communication involves the use of face, gestures, attire, eyes etc. for the transfer of an information.
6. **No Comm (No Communication).** It refers to the total elimination of the response of the receiver to the message of the sender. The reason for this behaviour could be psychological, unfavourable conditions or flaws in the business deal.

WRITTEN COMMUNICATION

Merits	Limitations
• Accurate • Precise • Permanent • Legal document • Can reach a large number of people simultaneously • Helps to fix responsibility	• Time consuming • Expensive not in terms of postage but of the time of so many people • Quick clarification not possible

ORAL COMMUNICATION

Merits	Limitations
• Saves time • Saves money • More forceful • Conveys shades of meaning • Immediate feedback • Immediate clarification • Can be informal • More effective with groups	• Not possible for distant people in the absence of mechanical devices • Unsuitable for lengthy messages • Messages cannot be retained for long • No legal validity • Greater chances of misunderstanding • Not easy to fix responsibility in case of misunderstanding

FACE-TO-FACE COMMUNICATION

Merits	Limitations
• Expressions and gestures make communication very effective • Very suitable for discussions	• Unsuitable for large organisations • Unsuitable for large gatherings • Ineffective if the listener is inattentive

D. On the basis of organisation structure. On the basis of the structure of an organisation, the communication can be classified in two major groups.

1. **Formal Communication.** In this type of communication, informations are sent and authenticated by corporate firms, government departments, NGOs, social service groups etc. that have strict and rigid procedures to achieve their respective objectives.
2. **Informal Communication (Grapevine).** It arises due to informal relations between persons and grows spontaneously from personal and group interests. Verbal discussion, a gesture, nod, smile or even silence can be the indium of this type of communication.

Formal communication	Informal communication
• It takes place in governmental departments, firms, NGOs, and other organizations for transmitting orders, instructions, plans, policies, etc.	• It takes place in interactions between friends, family members, etc.
• Flow of information takes place through some predefined channels.	• There is no requirement for flow of information through any particular channel.
• It is more reliable.	• It is relatively less reliable
• As it has to flow through particular channels, so its pace is slow and there are delays.	• It is relatively faster.
• It is usually in the written form.	• It is usually verbal or gestural.
• It is time-consuming.	• It saves time.
• It is effective due to systematic flow of information.	• It is efficient as it is faster.
• Secrecy can be maintained in such communication.	• Secrecy is difficult to be maintained here.
• There can be distortions during the flow of communication.	• It can also lead to spread of rumours, as the source of origination of message is difficult to trace.
• It is usually horizontal, or vertical, and occasionally diagonal.	• It can be in any direction.

E. On the basis of Objective. Objectives of communication may be social, political, education, entertainment, business or news and views.

1. **Mass/Societal Communication.** In this type of communication masses are communicated to be addressed certain burning issues.
2. **Socialising Communication.** This type of communication involves individual talking, exchange of e-mail, Internet Relay Chat (IRC), video mail and newsgroup discussions.
3. **Political Communication.** Political speeches, meetings, conferences, rumours, propaganda, publicity and election campaigns are involved in this type of communication.
4. **Educational Communication.** When communication is done to educate the masses.
5. **Business Communication.** When communication is used for business purposes.
6. **Entertainment Communication.** When communication is used to entertain people.
7. **News and Views Communication.** This type of communication is used to convey or obtain news and wide range views.
8. **City Information Communication.** It concerns data regarding city elements.
9. **Data Collection Communication.** It is used to collect useful data.

F. On the basis of environment of the firm. On the basis of environment of the firm, communication can be classified in two groups:

1. **External Communication.** If the information of communication is related to those elements that operate outside the organisation.
2. **Internal Communication.** When the information is related to those elements that are a part of the organisation.

Models of Communication

Shannon's Model

One of the earliest models of communication that introduced was Claude Shannon's model. This was introduced in 1948.

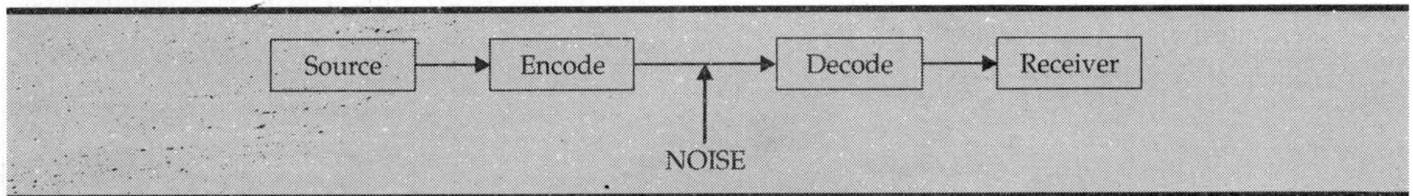

SHANNON'S MODEL

In Shannon's model, the information source typically refers to a person, who then sends a message with the use of a transmitter.

This transmitter could be any instrument today, from phones to computers and other devices. The signals that are sent and received can be vary depending on the method of communication.

The box at the bottom called NOISE refers to any signals that may interfere with the message being carried. This again would depend on the method of communication.

The receiver is the instrument or the person on the other side that receives the. This model is the simplest models to understand the workings of the communication process.

Berlo's Model

Another famous communication model is Berlo's model. In this model, he stresses on the relationship between the person sending the message and the receiver.

According to this model, for the message to be properly encoded and decoded, the communication skills of both the source and the receiver should be at best. The communication will be at its best only if the two points are skilled.

Berlo's model has four main components and each component has its own sub components describing the assisting factors for each.

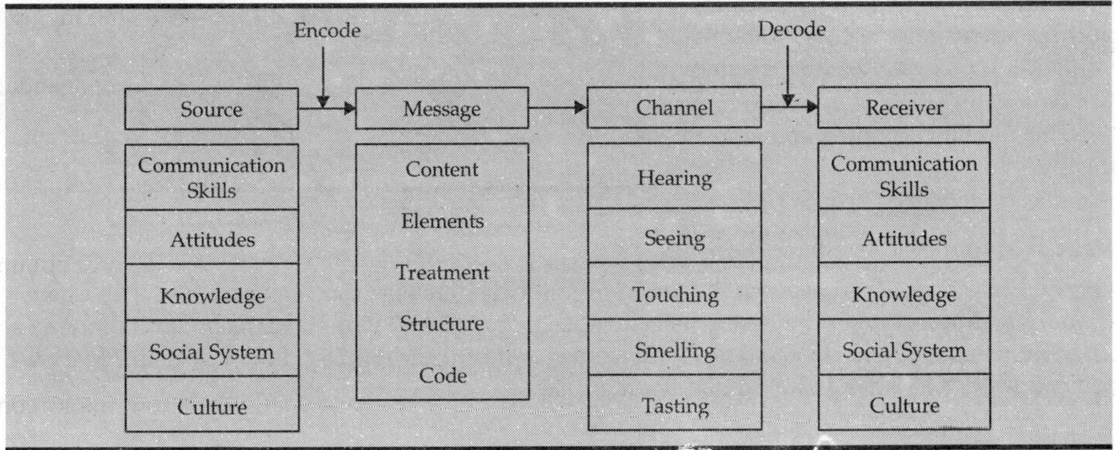

BERLO'S MODEL

Schramm's Model

Schramm on the other hand, emphasized in 1954 that both the sender and the receiver take turns playing the role of the encoder and the decoder when it comes to communication.

The following diagram illustrates the model proposed by Schramm.

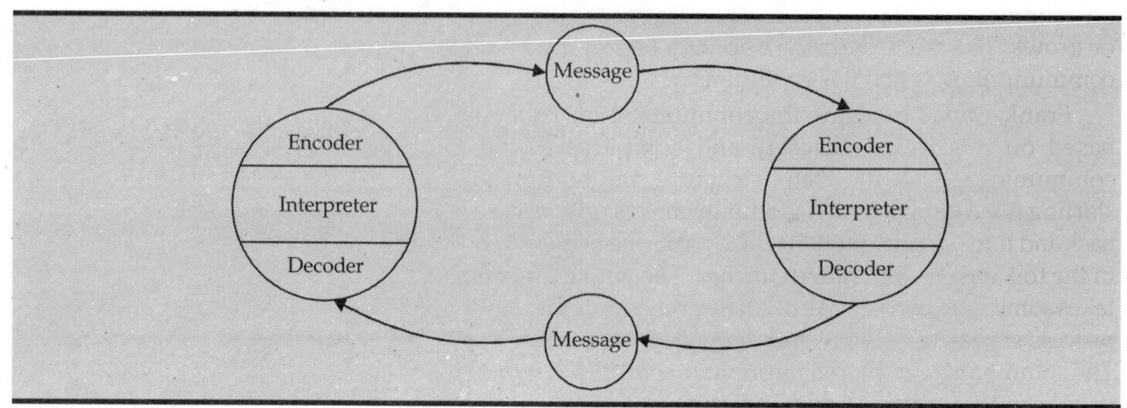

SCHRAMM'S MODEL

These models have been followed by various other models such as the 'Helical' model, Aristotle's models and several other models.

You should always keep in mind that each of these models has both their advantages and disadvantages. While some communication models try to break down the whole process in order to make it easier to understand, they are not always as simple as they seem.

There are several complexities involved in communications models. This is one thing that needs to be carefully understood in the process of understanding how these models work.

Two-step Flow Model

The Two Step Flow Model of Mass Communication theory states that information from the media moves in two separate stages.

Stage 1: Opinion leaders receive a mass media message.

Stage 2: The opinion leader interpret the message (exerting "personal influence") and pass that interpretation to others.

The model of communication is then:

Stimulus - Intervening Variables - Response

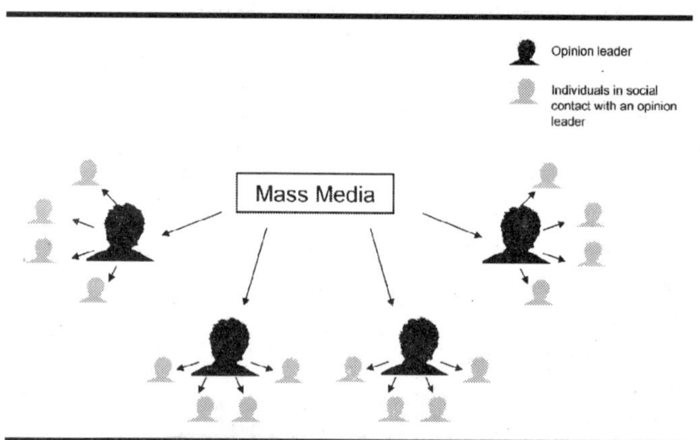

TWO-STEP FLOW MODEL

Helical Model of Communication

In 1967, Frank Dance has proposed the communication model called Dance's Helix Model for a better communication process. The name helical comes from "Helix" which means an object having a three-dimensional shape like that of a wire wound uniformly around a cylinder or cone. He shows communication as a dynamic and non-linear process.

Theory

Dance's model emphasized the difficulty of communication. Frank Dance uses the form of a Helix to describe the communication process. He developed this theory based on a simple helix which gets bigger and bigger as it moves or grows. The main characteristics of a helical model of communication is that it is evolutionary.

Frank Dance explains the communication process based on this Helix structure and compares it with communication. In the Helix structure, the bottom or starting is very small then it gradually moves upward in a back and forth circular motion which forms the bigger circle in the top and it is still moves further. The whole process takes some time to reach. As like helix, the communication process starts very slowly and defined small circle only. The communicators shared information only with a small portion of themselves to their relationships.

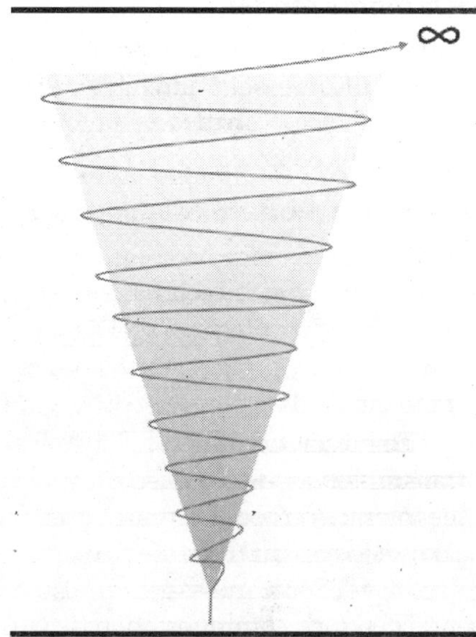

HELICAL MODEL OF COMMUNICATION

Example

When a child is born the only means of communication for him is crying, he cries for everything like hunger, pain, cold etc.. As the child grows the means of communication become wider and broader. He learns to make noises then he learns a language to obtain attention and to fulfil his needs. As a Helix, the process of communication, in this case, started as crying and later it developed into a complex and compound means.

The Helical model of communication is largely dependent on its past. A child learns to pronounce a word in his elementary classes and throughout his life he uses that word in the same way he learnt. Just like that, we used to react to certain things in a certain way in our childhood and such reactions and habits lasts with us forever. The communication evolves in the beginning in some simple forms then the same process of communication functions and develops based on past activities. Thus, his way of communication or his reactions may also different from the past behavior and experiences. It develops further with modifications according to the situations.

Transmission Model of Communication

The transmission model of communication describes communication as a linear, one-way process in which a sender intentionally transmits a message to a receiver. This model focuses on the sender and message within a communication encounter. Although the receiver is included in the model, this role is viewed as more of a target or end point rather than part of an ongoing process. We are left to presume that the receiver either successfully receives and understands the message or does not.

Since this model is sender and message focused, responsibility is put on the sender to help ensure the message is successfully conveyed. Noise is anything that interferes with a message being sent between participants in a communication encounter. Even if a speaker sends a clear message, noise may interfere with a message being accurately received and decoded. The transmission model of communication accounts for

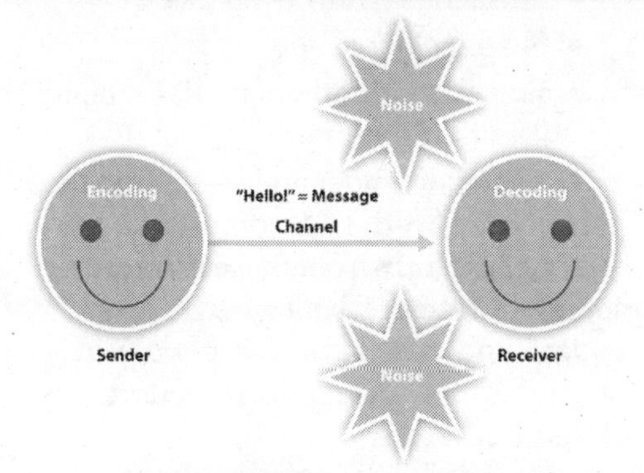

THE TRANSMISSION MODEL OF COMMUNICATION

environmental and semantic noise. Environmental noise is any physical noise present in a communication encounter. Other people talking in a crowded diner could interfere with your ability to transmit a message and have it successfully decoded. While environmental noise interferes with the transmission of the message, semantic noise refers to noise that occurs in the encoding and decoding process when participants do not understand a symbol.

Interaction Model of Communication

The interaction model of communication describes communication as a process in which participants alternate positions as sender and receiver and generate meaning by sending messages and receiving feedback within physical and psychological contexts. Rather than illustrating communication as a linear, one-way process, the interaction model incorporates feedback, which makes communication a more interactive, two-way process. Feedback includes messages sent in response to other messages.

The interaction model is also less message focused and more interaction focused. While the transmission model focused on how a message was transmitted and whether or not it was received, the interaction model is more concerned with the communication process itself. In fact, this model acknowledges that there are so many messages being sent at one time that many of them may not even be received. Some messages are also unintentionally sent. Therefore, communication isn't judged effective or ineffective in this model based on whether or not a single message was successfully transmitted and received.

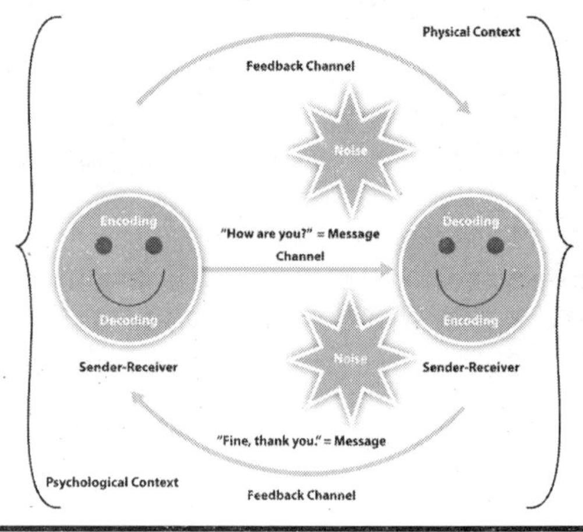

THE INTERACTION MODEL OF COMMUNICATION

Transaction Model of Communication

The Transaction Model of communication differs from the Transmission and Interaction Models in important ways, including the conceptualization of communication, the role of sender and receiver, and the role of context (Barnlund, 1970).

The Transaction Model of communication describes communication as a process in which communicators generate social realities within social, relational, and cultural contexts. In this model, nurses don't just communicate to exchange messages; they communicate to:

- Create relationships.
- Form intercultural alliances.
- Shape self-concept.
- Engage with others in dialogue to create communities.

The roles of sender and receiver in the Transaction Model of communication differ significantly from those in the other models. Instead of labeling participants as senders and receivers, the people in a communication encounter are referred to as communicators.

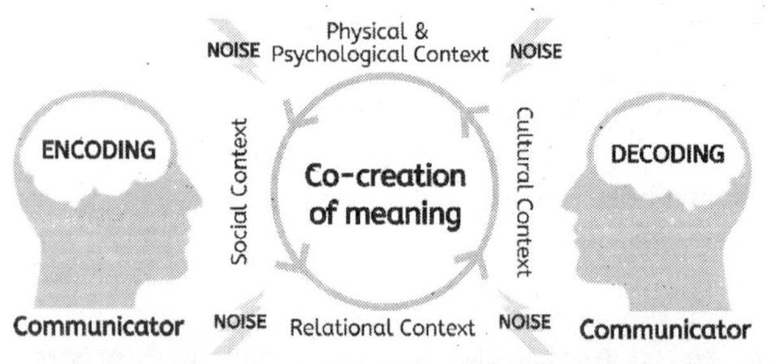

THE TRANSACTION MODEL OF COMMUNICATION

EFFECTIVE COMMUNICATION

Communication is said to be effective when all the parties (sender and receiver) in the communication, assign similar meanings to the message and listen carefully to what all have been said and make the sender feel heard and understood.

In the words of R.W. Griffin, "Effective communication is the process of sending a message in such a way that the message received is as close in meaning as possible to the message intended".

American Management Association (AMA) has defined effective communication based on the following ten points :

- Clear idea regarding topics and receiver of communication.
- Determination of purpose.
- Understanding the environment of communication.
- Planning for communication with consulting others.
- Consider the content of the message.
- To make the receiver aware about the value of communication.
- There must be feedback from the receiver.
- To define properly whether communication messages are of short-run or long-run importance.
- All actions must be suitable with communication.
- Good listening.

Effective Communication is defined as the ability to convey information to another effectively and efficiently. Business managers with good verbal, nonverbal and written communication skills help facilitate the sharing of information between people within a company for its commercial benefit.

Characteristics of Effective Communication

- **Completeness of the Message.** Communication must be complete so as not to baffle the recipient. Better communication helps in better decision-making by the latter. It develops and enhances the reputation of an organization.
- **Clearness and Integrity of the Message.** The message to be conveyed or sent must have clarity and integrity for better understanding. Clarity of thoughts and ideas enhances the meaning of the message. The pith and substance of the message should be based on honesty and accuracy.
- **Conciseness of the Message.** The intended message must be free from verbosity and should be so written that it is intelligible at the first sight. Short and intelligible message sent to the receiver is ever appealing and comprehensible. It saves time and cost as it is understood at the first instance.
- **Consideration of Physical Setting and the Recipient.** In order to make communication more effective, the overall physical setting, i.e., the media of communication and the work environment, must be considered. The content of the message must take into account the attitude, knowledge, and position of the recipient.
- **Clarity of the Message.** The message should have clarity of thoughts and ideas in order to be understood clearly. Clear message makes use of exact, appropriate and concrete words and symbols.
- **Courtesy to be Maintained.** The sender's message should be so drafted or prepared that it should be polite, reflective, and enthusiastic. It must show the sender's respect for the receiver and be positive and focused at the receiver.

- **Correctness of the Message.** The drafting of the message should be done in such a manner that the final message doesn't have any grammatical errors and repetitions of sentences. The message should be exact, correct and well-timed.

Seven C's of Effective Communication

There are 7 C's of effective communication which are applicable to both written as well as oral communication. These are as follows:

1. **Completeness.** The communication must be complete. It should convey all facts required by the audience. The sender of the message must take into consideration the receiver's mind set and convey the message accordingly. A complete communication has following features:
   - Complete communication develops and enhances reputation of an organization.
   - Moreover, they are cost saving as no crucial information is missing and no additional cost is incurred in conveying extra message if the communication is complete.
   - A complete communication always gives additional information wherever required. It leaves no questions in the mind of receiver.
   - Complete communication helps in better decision-making by the audience/readers/receivers of message as they get all desired and crucial information.
   - It persuades the audience.
2. **Conciseness.** Conciseness means wordiness, i.e., communicating what you want to convey in least possible words without forgoing the other C's of communication. Conciseness is a necessity for effective communication. Concise communication has following features:
   - It is both time-saving as well as cost-saving.
   - It underlines and highlights the main message as it avoids using excessive and needless words.
   - Concise communication provides short and essential message in limited words to the audience.
   - Concise message is more appealing and comprehensible to the audience.
   - Concise message is non-repetitive in nature.
3. **Consideration.** Consideration implies "stepping into the shoes of others". Effective communication must take the audience into consideration, i.e., the audience's view points, background, mind-set, education level, etc. Make an attempt to envisage your audience, their requirements, emotions as well as problems. Ensure that the self-respect of the audience is maintained and their emo-

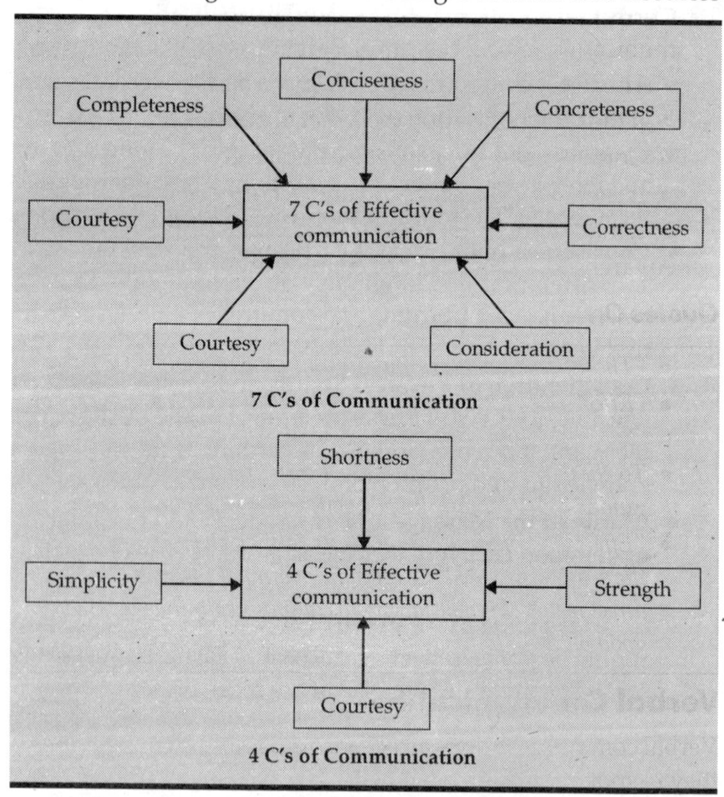

7 C's of Communication

4 C's of Communication

tions are not at harm. Modify your words in message to suit the audience's needs while making your message complete. Features of considerate communication are as follows:

- Emphasize on "you" approach.
- Empathize with the audience and exhibit interest in the audience. This will stimulate a positive reaction from the audience.

4. **Clarity.** Clarity implies emphasizing on a specific message or goal at a time, rather than trying to achieve too much at once. Clarity in communication has following features:
   - It makes understanding easier.
   - Complete clarity of thoughts and ideas enhances the meaning of message.
   - Clear message makes use of exact, appropriate and concrete words.
5. **Concreteness.** Concrete communication implies being particular and clear rather than fuzzy and general. Concreteness strengthens the confidence. Concrete message has following features:
   - It is supported with specific facts and figures.
   - It makes use of words that are clear and that build the reputation.
   - Concrete messages are not misinterpreted.
6. **Courtesy.** Courtesy in message implies the message should show the sender's expression as well as should respect the receiver. The sender of the message should be sincerely polite, judicious, reflective and enthusiastic. Courteous message has following features:
   - Courtesy implies taking into consideration both viewpoints as well as feelings of the receiver of the message.
   - Courteous message is positive and focused at the audience.
   - It makes use of terms showing respect for the receiver of message.
   - It is not at all biased.
7. **Correctness.** Correctness in communication implies that there are no grammatical errors in communication. Correct communication has following features:
   - The message is exact, correct and well-timed.
   - If the communication is correct, it boosts up the confidence level.
   - Correct message has greater impact on the audience/readers.
   - It checks for the precision and accurateness of facts and figures used in the message.
   - It makes use of appropriate and correct language in the message.

   Awareness of these 7 C's of communication makes you an effective communicator.

Quotes On Effective Communication

- *"The most important thing in communication is hearing what isn't said."* **–Peter Drucker**
- *"Effective communication is 20% what you know and 80% how feel about what you know."* **–Jim Rohan**
- *To effectively communicate, we must realize that we are all world and use this understanding as a guide to our communication with others."* **–Tony Robbins**
- *"Effective communication occurs only if the receiver understands the exact information or idea that the sender intended to transmit. Many of the problems that occur in an organization are either the direct result of people failing to communicate and/or processes, which leads to confusion and can cause good plans to fail."* **–Pranav Mistry**

Verbal Communication

Verbal communication is an all-encompassing term for communication involving words - whether they're spoken, written or signed.

The conversations we have with our coworker at lunch, the morning news or the sports page we read in the morning - even the text message you send to your spouse telling him to pick up some milk - is a form of verbal communication.

Our ability to communicate with a language that is based on an organized system of words, rather than merely sounds, is what sets us apart from lower species. Not only do we have language, but we also have the technology that enables us to communicate with one another, no matter the physical distance.

Why is Verbal Communication Important?

We use verbal communication to inform, whether it is to inform others of our needs or to impart knowledge. Clarification is a key component of verbal communication.

Often, we do not articulate ourselves clearly, or our words or actions are misconstrued. Verbal communication helps to clarify misunderstandings and provides missing information.

Verbal communication can be used to correct a wrong, where powerful words are more effective than an action. It can also be used as a tool of persuasion and creates opportunity for debate, stimulates thought and creativity and deepens and creates new relationships.

MNEMONICS

Mnemonics appeals to the ancient technique of collecting memories - ars memoriae, based on the connection between thoughts and a visual support invested with meaning. The ability of space to generate strong memories is the ultimate challenge of architecture and helps endlessly access and re-access the emotions related to a specific story.

Non-Verbal Communication

Verbal communication coexists alongside non-verbal communication, which can affect people's perceptions and exchanges in subtle but significant ways.

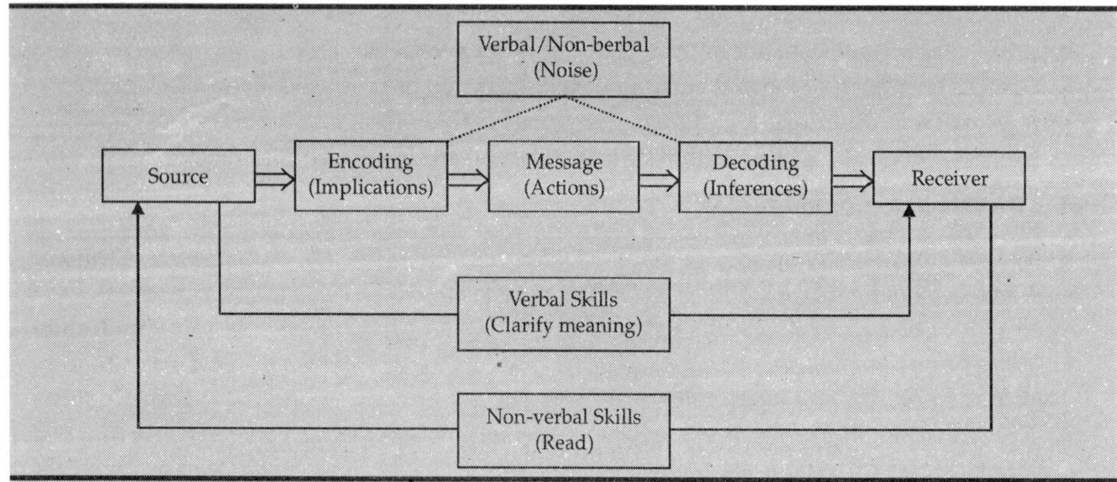

THE COMMUNICATION MODEL FOR VERBAL AND NON-VERBAL MESSAGE

Non-verbal communication includes body language, such as gestures, facial expressions, eye contact and posture. Touch is a non-verbal communication that not only indicates a person's feelings or level of comfort, but illustrates personality characteristics as well.

A firm handshake or warm hug indicates something very different than a loose pat on the back or a timid handshake does. The sound of our voice, including pitch, tone and volume are also forms of non-verbal communication.

Kinesic Communication

Kinesics is the broad field of nonverbal communication in new window solely concerned with the interpretation of nonverbal behaviours that are associated with body movement in new window, gestures in new window, posture in new window, facial expression in new window and eye contact in new window.

KINESICS COMMUNICATION

Kinesics is most closely connected with what is popularly referred to as body language in new window. Kinesics, is in fact, a scientific study of body language.

The term "kinesics" was developed by the American anthropologist Ray L. Birdwhistell in new window, who used slow-motion films of conversations to analyze speakers' behaviours.

Components of Kinesics Messages

While words in new window generally transmit facts and information, kinesics communication involves transference of nonverbal messages, such as feelings, emotions in new window, and attitude through the use of body movement in new window, gestures in new window, posture in new window, facial expression in new window and eye contact in new window.

Birdwhistell labeled this form of communication 'kinesics' as it relates to movement of individual body parts, or the body as a whole. Observe the following modes of kinesics messages.

1. **Gestures.** Gestures are the movements of hands, face, or other parts of the body in a way that conveys meaning, either in conjunction with verbal communication such as frowning while saying harsh words against someone, or in isolation such as smiling at a stranger to express pleasure at ones presence. Keep on learning about gesture here in new window.
2. **Body movement.** Body Movement is the voluntary or involuntary movement of parts of the body such as hands, feet, legs, and shoulders, which may either reinforce or contradicts what is communicated verbally. There are various body movements that sends bodily signals. Learn more here in new window.

Kinesics Moments

Kinesics communication carries a significant risk of being misinterpreted in an intercultural interaction. As many movements are carried out at a subconscious or at least a low-awareness level; the movements can be misinterpreted when communicating across cultures. In today's global environment, awareness of the meanings of different kinesic movements is important in order to avoid sending the wrong message.

Kinesics signals can be inborn (unwitting), learned (witting), or a mixture of the two. Blinking the eyes, clearing the throat, and facial flushing are innate (inborn) signals. These are often involuntary, as are, for example, facial expressions of happiness, surprise, anger, disgust, and other basics emotions understood by people in all cultures.

Laughing, crying, and shrugging the shoulders are examples of mixed signals. They may originate as innate actions, but cultural rules shape their timing and use. Gestures, such as a wink of the eye, a thumbs up, or a military salute, are learned signals. The meanings of such signs vary among different cultures.

3. **Posture.** Posture in new`window communicates a great deal of information about you. The way in which you sit, stand, slump or slouch provides information about your sex, status, self-image, attitudes and emotional state. For example, sitting with your head in your hands often indicates that your are feeling low, whereas sitting with your feet on the desk may be interpreted by others as a sign of your feeling of superiority.
4. **Facial expressions.** Facial expression in new window refers to certain movements or conditions of the facial muscles that facilitate the nonverbal communication of some thought, emotion, or behavior. Facial expression is the main channel we use to decode emotional states or reactions of others to a message, and they generally mirror the intensity of people's thoughts and feelings.
5. **Eye contact.** Eye contact is a natural byproduct of effective communication. To look someone in the eyes is to invite him to communicate with you. Eye contact indicates degree of attention or interest, influences attitude change or persuasion, regulates interaction, communicates emotion, defines power and status, and has a central role in managing impressions of others.

Why is Non-Verbal Communication Important?

Think of how many relationships start with a man and woman making eye contact across a crowded room. A playful wink tends to be more effective than a well-thought out pick-up-line.

In his book, "Bodily Communication," Michael Argyle identifies five main functions of non-verbal communication: to express emotions, communicate interpersonal relationships, support verbal interaction, reflect personality and perform rituals, such as greetings and goodbyes..

Avoiding eye contact when we tell someone we love them communicates something far different than do spoken words, just as a bright smile when we say congratulations reinforces the sincerity of our words.

Intercultural Communication

Intercultural communication is an important factor in today's globalized world. People travel and they need to communicate, in most cases, it's out of one's culture.

Culture is combining with each other gradually. Sharing information with people belonging to different cultures is known as intercultural communication or cross-cultural communication.

People who have to deal with other cultures, face a problem of intercultural communication. Even though they take language classes and learn to speak local languages fluently, intercultural communication isn't just that. Its one's understanding of the culture, the social interactions, and cultural accommodation.

Intercultural communication is the study and application of knowledge on "cultural perceptions and symbol systems" of people belonging to different cultures.

The intended meaning of any message differs when encoded by a person of a certain culture and decoded by someone of the other. The different meanings of symbols in different culture also vary making the interpretation difficult.

> *"Intercultural communication,' can...be defined as the interpersonal interaction between members of different groups, which differ from each other in respect of the knowledge shared by their members and in respect of their linguistic forms of symbolic behaviour."* **—Karlfried Knapp**

Types of Intercultural Communication

There are basically two types of intercultural communication: Verbal communication and non-verbal communication.

Verbal communication consists of words used to communicate messages whereas non-verbal communication is gestures that give out messages.

Spoken and written language are parts of verbal communication which must be considered highly while in intercultural communication. Cultural factors affect verbal communication as people can sometimes not be able to speak or write in the language of the receiver. Use of words, dialects, accents, slang, etc. can also be different according to their own cultures.

Similarly, non-verbal cues consist of communication that occurs without words like facial expressions, hand and body movements, eye contact, use of objects, clothing, etc. They help in making message clear or can give the different message as well.

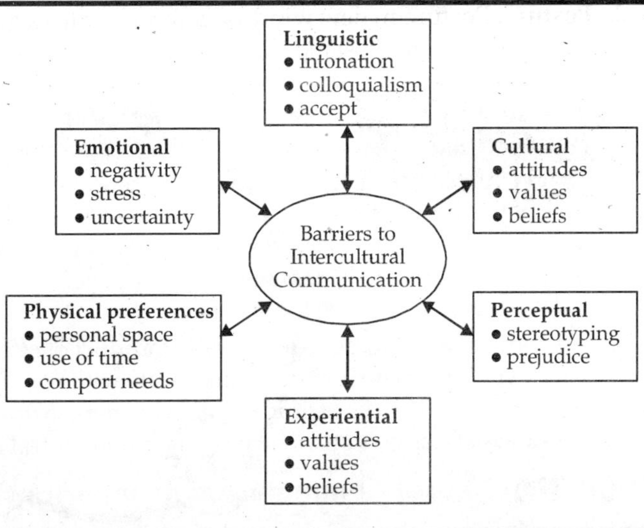

Importance of Intercultural Communication

Lacking in intercultural communication can lead to the insult of the culture and people involved. Especially for business people or people providing services in the areas out of their culture. People interpret messages based on their culture, so what you mean might not be what the other person understands. Your intentions might not be met as their attribution towards you might be telling them something else about you.

Material culture and its use are also different between cultures like the use of spoons and chopsticks for eating. Other things like architecture, clothing, cosmetics, etc. differ culture-wise and if you do not have knowledge of it, your communication fails or is not effective.

Group Communication

Group communication is an extension of interpersonal communication where more than two individuals are involved in exchange of ideas, skills and interests. A group is a number of people with a common goal who interact with one another to accomplish their goals, recognize one another's existence and see themselves as part of the group. Groups provide an opportunity for people to come together to discuss and exchange views of common interest. There could be many different groups for as many different reasons. For instance, casually formed groups with friends over a drink, coffee break, games, dances or religious gatherings have a different purpose than that of groups attending a meeting or seminar to help fight AIDS or interacting with committee members to draft a proposal.

Groups have been classified as small groups and large groups. A small group comprises of three to seven members. Small groups are informal and less structured. Larger groups adopt formal rules to maintain order. There is more chance for individual participation in small groups. Also small groups are easy to manage and are more efficient in accomplishing tasks and making decisions. Most researchers define a small group as having at least three and no more than twelve or fifteen members.

A group needs to have at least three members; otherwise it would simply be a dyad. With three members, coalitions can be formed and some kind of organization is present. Too large of a group (more than twelve or fifteen members) inhibits the group members' ability to communicate with everyone else in the group. Members must be able to communicate freely and openly with all of the other members of the group. Groups will develop norms about discussion and group members will develop roles, which will affect the group's interaction. A group must have a common purpose or goal and they must work together to achieve that goal. The goal brings the group together and holds it together through conflict and tension.

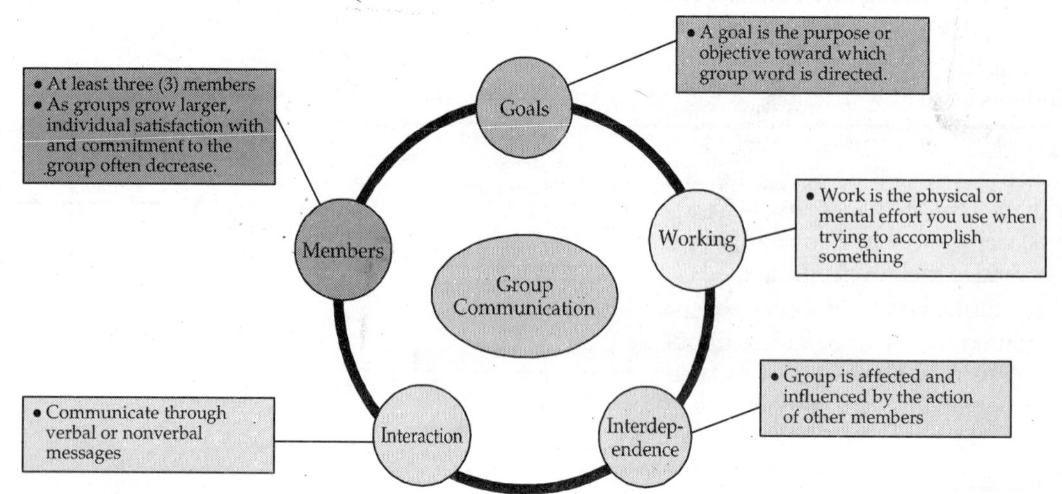

COMPONENTS OF GROUP COMMUNICATION

Effective Classroom Communication

There are the two wheels of effective classroom communication, those are the teachers and the students. A teacher with a 'blazing character' and freed from commercial taint can be expected to command the respect and admiration of the pupils and produce the necessary effect on their minds by way of helping them manifest the perfection that is already in them.

According to Indian tradition, student-teacher relationship was inaugurated by the religious ceremony called *Upanayan*. It is not like the admission of a pupil to the register of a school or a college on his payment of the prescribed fee. The spiritual meaning of *Upanayan* is that the teacher holding the pupil within him as in a womb, impregnates him with his spirit and delivers him in a new birth. The pupil is then known as a *Dvija* (born afresh). In the home of the teacher, the students were treated like his own son. Here the personal touch and living relationship between the pupil and the teacher make education. The students belonged to the teacher and not to an institution.

In the modern school system, the teachers teach the pupils by class and not as *individuals* with their differences. Like an automation, the teacher enters into the classroom at the appointed time and delivers as best as he may on his intellectual load. At the stroke of the hour he mechanically walks out. Thus everyday the teacher-stranger meets the student-strangers only in the classroom. As a rest of which life does not come in contact with life. Indian tradition proves that education becomes effective and fruitful only to the extent to which there is personal touch between the teacher and the taught. While in the classroom, the teacher is a master, off the classroom, he is a companion, while looking after their personal needs, he plays the role of a matter. He is a playmate on the game field. Such varieties in their relationship keep the position of teacher high. To the pupil, it is a rare privilege to be with a teacher whom he observes in various roles.

Effective Communication Tips for the Classroom

Communicate Respectfully

Respect is the foundation of effective communication, especially in the classroom. Teachers and students demonstrate respectful communication in the following ways:

- Use a tone that is honest and tactful, choosing words that are appropriate to the situation and noninflammatory.

– When taking on a listening role, make eye contact and focus on the speaker.

– Speak in turn, never interrupting the speaker.

Teachers who model respect with their students have more respectful classrooms overall because students learn how to communicate respectfully and see its effectiveness.

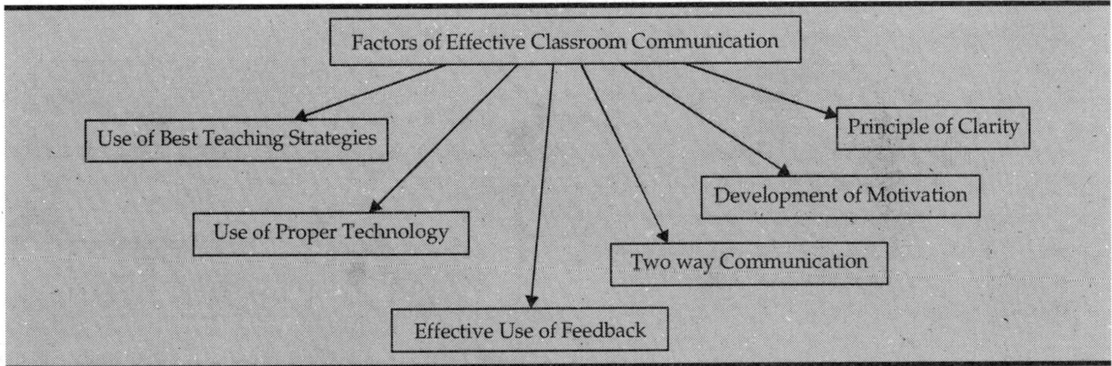

Repeat Your Message in Different Ways

While most communication in a classroom starts verbally, many students don't take in what they hear the first time. Effective communication requires using different techniques in communication. When you want to make a point, consider what visual tools can help you in addition to your verbal communication.

Check for Understanding

A teacher should always check for understanding. The simple question, "Do you understand?" will not result in much information, as most students will either nod or sit passively. Students can write down one sentence that summarizes what they think the lesson or lecture was about, or they can write a question they have about the lesson. In a one-on-one conversation, a teacher should ask the student to repeat the main point or outcome of the conversation.

Non-verbal Communication

Everyone communicates non-verbally through facial expressions and gestures. Effective communication in the classroom requires careful use of these nonverbal cues. A teacher who rolls her eyes at a student's question sends a louder message than her careful and expert verbal response. A disapproving stare can work wonders on a student who is off task. Gestures and animated facial expressions also give weight and enthusiasm to what a teacher has to say. Students who see a teacher actively engaged in what she is teaching will be much more engaged themselves.

BARRIERS TO EFFECTIVE COMMUNICATION

Barriers to communication are those factors which produce obstacles in the way of reaching message to the receiver. There are five kinds of barriers to communication :

1. Personal Barriers. Barriers may arise at any stage of communication process. They may arise at: (1) the sender's level, (2) the encoding level, (3) the transmission level, (4) the receivers level, (5) the feedback level. Human beings differ from one another because of different geographical, economic, social, educational or occupational backgrounds. Some characteristics are inherited by them due to their birth, family backgrounds, upbringing or social events that are unique to them. These include :

(a) personal emotions; (b) biases; (c) perceptual variations;
(d) competencies; (e) mental faculties; (f) five senses and
(g) psychological problems

2. Semantic Barriers. Semantic is the science of meanings. A word can carry as many as five hundred meanings. Semantic barriers arise due to differences in meanings, which people attach to the different words.

The meanings of the words are not in the words; these are with us. A poor choice of symbols or their confused meanings could distort communication. Semantic barriers can be subdivided into:

(a) word interpretations;
(b) gestures (handshakes and frowns);
(c) language translations;
(d) signs and symbols; and
(e) cue meanings.

3. Organisational Climatic Barriers. These are the barriers that are created due to problems in the culture of the organisation and also, due to lack of proper directions of the managers or top brass. These are as follows:

(a) Fears
(b) Fears of being misinterpreted
(c) Fear of distortion by grapevine
(d) Fear of exposing oneself to criticism
(e) Fear of getting fired.
(f) Poor or Ego-centred Supervision. Poor supervision may create obstacles in the communication process. Typically, the person may think that he is being ignored or dominated.
(g) Insincerity and Lack of Confidence: Insincerity means that communication is superficial. Lack of confidence means that the message or the communicator of the message is not trustworthy.

4. Organisation Structure Barriers. When the organisation structure is not properly defined, the responsibility and authority are not assigned and channels are also not clear. Thus, communication is likely to be ineffective and even harmful. These barriers are as follows:

A. Lack of chain of command
B. Bureaucratic
C. Political manipulations
D. Class conflicts.

5. Technical Barriers. These are the barriers that arise due to :

(a) space or geographical distance;
(b) mechanical failures and disturbances;
(c) physical obstructions (too much emphasis on the organisation structure);
(d) technological malfunctions (like bad telephone lines, poor printouts from the printer etc.);
(e) improper time of communication; and
(f) wrong time of communication.

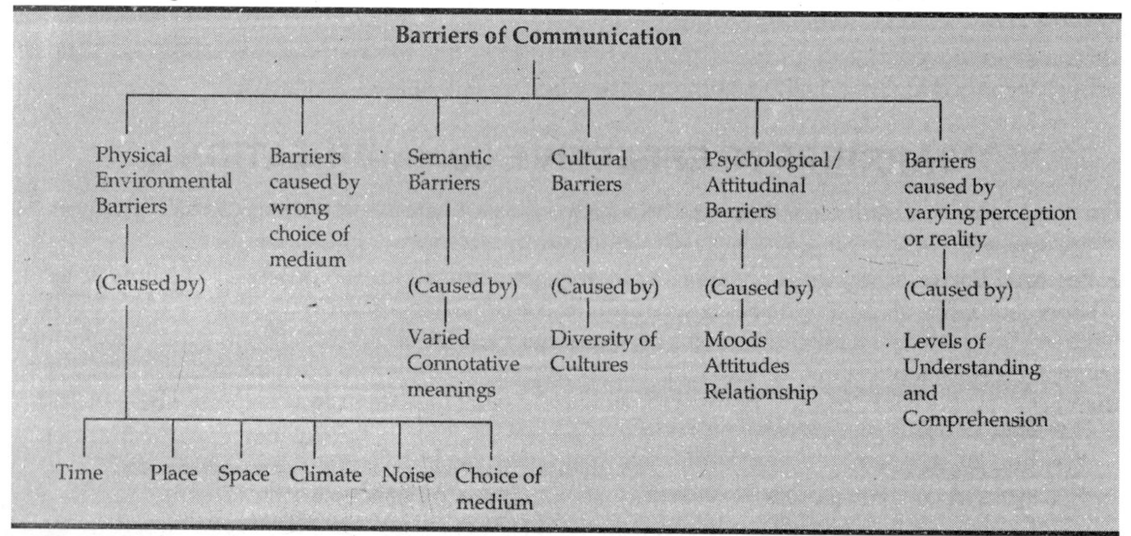

Terms Related to Communication

- **Aural-Oral.** A communication method in which listening is the primary means of understanding language and speech (talking) is the primary means of expressing language. In addition to listening, a child is encouraged to watch the speaker for additional information from speech-reading, facial expression, and gesture. No sign language is used. This method is sometimes called auditory-oral.
- **Auditory-Verbal.** A specific communication philosophy within the broader aural-oral category. The development of spoken language through listening and the use of residual hearing are central. One-on-one teaching, parent involvement, and inclusion in general education (rather than special or deaf education) are also emphasized.
- **Babbling.** Term used to describe an infant's first use of speech sounds. With an infant's earliest babbling, there is no communication or language intent. Later babbling may be used as a part of a young child's beginning communication system.
- **Bilingual/Bicultural.** Being fluent in two languages and comfortable in two cultures. For a person who is deaf, this terminology refers to a person who is fluent in both American Sign Language and English and comfortable in both the Deaf Culture and the Hearing Culture.
- **Cognitive.** Refers to the ability to think, learn, and remember.
- **Communication.** The exchange of information through verbal or non-verbal means. Communication can include gestures, facial expressions, words, and/or signs. Children's earliest communication with parents or other caregivers occurs before they use either words or signs.
- **Cued Speech.** A communication method designed to make visually available all the elements needed to understand spoken English. The system combines information that can be seen through watching lip movements with information from additional hand-shapes and hand positions near the face, used to identify sounds that can't be seen on the lips or that look the same on the lips.
- **Finger-spelling.** Using a visual, manual form of the English alphabet to spell out words. Finger-spelling is most often used to spell out words for which there are no formal signs.
- **Gesture.** The movements of the hands or body that express an idea. Gestures include pointing, head nodding, waving good-bye and many others. Gestures can be used alone or in combination with words to communicate thoughts and ideas.
- **Jargon.** Term used to describe the stage of language development when children string together sentence-like expressions that are not very understandable as true words. Children can use either speech or sign jargon depending on their communication system.
- **Language.** Shared code, used by a group of people, that determines what words mean and the rules for how words a re combined and used to convey ideas to others. Language can be spoken, signed, or written. "Receptive language" refers to our ability to understand the information conveyed by others. "Expressive language" refers to our ability to share information with others.
- **Manual Babbling.** Term used to describe the early hand-shapes used by infants or toddlers who see sign language in t heir everyday environment. As with speech babbling, early manual babbling may not represent any true signs or words. Later manual babbling may be used as part of a young child's beginning communication system.
- **Manually Coded English.** A sign language system that uses a visual (signed) form of the English language. There are a number of systems for manually coding English. Most of these systems use American Sign Language (ASL) signs as a base and also use English word order. Each system for manually coding English has its own variations and rules.

- **Simultaneous Communication (Sim-Com).** A communication system in which spoken English and its manually coded (signed) version are used at the same time. The term "total communication" may at times be used to describe simultaneous communication.
- **Speech.** Generally used to mean the expression of language through the spoken word. The term "speech sounds" refers to the individual consonant and vowel sounds that make up a language such as English.
- **Speech-Language Pathologist.** A licensed professional who holds a degree in speech-language pathology and who specializes in the evaluation and treatment of speech, language, and voice disorders. This may include children whose speech or language problems are the result of a hearing loss.
- **Total Communication.** In this communication system, the word "total" refers to the use of any form of communication that will enable the child to learn language. Manually coded English is one part of the system, which also includes speech, listening through amplification, print, and speech-reading. The term "total communication" may at times be used to describe simultaneous communication (sim-com).

THE 10 COMMANDMENTS OF COMMUNICATION

1. Listen generously
2. Say what you mean, and mean what you say
3. Use the fewest words with the fewest syllables
4. Align with your audience
5. Be specific.
6. Suit the action to the word...the word to the action
7. Structure your speech
8. Speak to be understood
9. Speak for the benefit of others
10. Speak from your highest self

MASS-MEDIA AND SOCIETY

Types of Mass-Media

A. Traditional Media

Traditional media are the oldest of all other media and are connected with the folk art forms of the society. Every country has its own unique folk art forms.

They connect people with their rich heritage and tell the stories of the past to the present generation. The folk art forms are closely related with the rituals of agrarian and marginalized groups. These traditional art forms like songs, dances and other performance in such societies are considered as traditional media since they inform, educate and entertain people by oral tradition. The origin of rural theatre and street drama is rooted in folk art forms.

Characteristics of Traditional Media. The following are the general features of traditional media. The nature of each medium may change depending on its type and cultural context.

1. The stage for performance of traditional art forms is natural, known and friendly.
2. The performers and the audience are known to each other.
3. The contents are simple and familiar.
4. The performer can make changes in the content according to the level of the audience.
5. The traditional arts and folk arts combine several art forms like dance, music, songs and theatre to attract audiences.

B. Print Media

Johannes Guttenber's movable metal types facilitated mass production of printed materials. As a result, press and publications spread rapidly across Europe and later to other continents. Mass production of printed documents led to democratization of knowledge and thus education was made accessible to common people. It was exactly a revolution because till then knowledge was considered the property of the elite. For several centuries, print media served as the major means of communication reaching a wide audience. Major forms of print media are:

I. Newspapers

As a mass medium, newspapers influence people in many significant ways. Capability to be used for future reference make newspapers favourite medium of the people. Diversity of content is another feature of this medium. It can carry a rich mix of news, features, articles, columns, cartoons, graphics, editorial, etc. Readers can select what they want from the entire content.

Characteristics of Newspapers. Primarily newspapers are print media even though digital age offers online newspapers and e-newspapers. That is why it has all the features that any print medium has. Major features of news papers are given below:

WHAT IS PRINT MEDIA?

- **Print media** a medium that disseminates printed matter.
- **Medium** a means or instrumentality for storing or communicating information.
- **Public press, Press** the print media responsible for gathering and publishing news in the form of newspapers or magazines.
- **Journalism, New Media** newspapers and magazines collectively.
- **Saizdat, Underground Press** a system of clandestine printing and distribution of dissident or banned literature.

- **Predominance of news-oriented content.** There are three types of content in newspapers: news, views and advertisements. Of these news overshadows the others because newspapers are primarily meant for the dissemination of news.
- **Regular periodicity.** Newspapers may be published daily or weekly. Periodicity may vary but, regularity should be kept. Every newspaper keeps a particular regularity in publication.
- **Future reference facility.** Being a print medium, newspapers can be kept for future use. This archive ability makes newspapers one of the main sources of historical research.
- **Choice of the time of use.** Unlike television and radio, we can read newspapers at any time. Some read in the morning while others in the evening after work. This facility increases the popularity of newspapers.
- **The literates' medium.** Unlike television and radio, newspaper demands literacy from the part of the audience.
- **Low cost.** Compared to other media, newspaper is a cost effective medium. Anybody can afford a newspaper and use everywhere. Electronic media requires power supply and the new media need digital technology.
- **Textual medium.** Text is the soul of newspapers, though they carry images and graphics.
- **Multiple users.** Many readers can read a copy of the newspaper simultaneously or separately. *Peking Gazette* of China, *London Gazette* of Britain, *Avisa Relation Oder Zeitung* of Germany, *Publick Occurrences* of America, *Daily Courant* of Britain etc. were some of the early newspapers published in the world. The first newspaper published in India was *The Bengal Gazette* by James Augustus Hicky on 29 January 1780. In Kerala, *Rajyasamacharam* is the first newspaper published in Malayalam by Dr. Herman Gundert on June 1847 from Thalassery.

II. Magazines

Magazine is originally a French word which means *store house*. In journalistic terms, magazine is a collection of materials like stories, poems, and other items.

Usually they cover non-news items though there are news magazines too. Magazines contain a variety of topics like current affairs, business, women, children, finance, gadgets, photography, science and technology, education, career, health, luxury, life style, beauty, fashion, entertainment and travel.

Magazines are considered the mass medium that spread culture and nationalism.

Characteristics of Magazines. What makes magazines different from newspapers? Let's look at some distinctive features of magazines.

1. Magazines are published at regular intervals. According to their periodicity, magazines are categorized as weekly, biweekly or fortnightly, monthly, bi-monthly, quarterly, half-yearly and yearly.
2. Unlike loose sheets of newspapers, magazines are produced as bound volumes.
3. Most of the magazines are meant for light reading and mainly for entertainment, rather than serious reading for information gathering as in the case of books and newspapers.
4. They most often target audiences with distinctive characteristics.
5. Magazines generally focus on special areas like culture, politics, current affairs, health, wealth, women's and children's life.
6. They are printed in high quality paper as they are to be used for a longer period. Newspapers are printed using cheap newsprint material as they are meant for one-day use.
7. Normally, magazines do not have different editions as in the case of newspapers. They have only one print cycle, except for some international news and financial magazines like *News Week, Time, Forbes* and *Fortune* which publish various regional editions for Asia and Africa.
9. Magazines are easier to preserve than newspapers.

CHARACTERISTICS OF BOOKS

1. Books are portable and compact, and thus have an advantage over other media forms.
2. Unlike other print media, books most often deal with a single subject. Thus, we can read books piece by piece for days or weeks with convenient intervals, without losing concentration.
3. While newspapers and magazines get old soon due to their time limitations, books remain afresh since they deal with subjects significant for a longer period.
4. Unlike magazines and newspapers, books are stored for longer period in public or private libraries.
5. Content in the books is in an organized manner so that readers can have access to the interested parts easily.
6. They have index which helps the reader some sort of navigation from one subject to the other.
7. Books are stored for future reference.
8. They are published after adequate verification and research. So, the content of the books is more authentic than that of newspapers and magazines.
9. The language level of the books is audience specific or subject specific while newspaper or magazine language is general in nature, intelligible to larger groups of people.

III. Books

The *Papyrus* (from which the word paper is derived) rolls of the Chinese are considered the ancestors of modern books. The concept of books existed in China and in Babylonian way back in 3000 B.C. The Chinese used papyrus rolls made of bamboo strips while the Babylonians used clay tablets for writing. In Rome, animal skins were used to prepare books. Though the introduction of paper popularized books, the absence of easy printing method blocked their mass production. Earlier books were hand written and were called manuscripts. The printed books appeared in 868 AD. The first book in India ' *'The Spiritual Compendium of the Christian Life'* was printed in 1561 and the first one in Malayalam *'Sampkshepa Vedartham'* in 1772.

C. Electronic Media

The history of electronic media starts with the invention of cinematograph by Lumiere Brothers who conducted the premier show of cinema in 1895. Later radio was invented by Guglielmo Marconi. The first radio station was set up in Pittsburg, New York and Chicago in the 1920s. Following this, the European countries also started radio stations for broadcasting news and entertainment content.

1. **Film.** The Lumiere brothers made their first film *La sortie des usines Lumiere* (Workers Leaving the Lumiere Factory) using the camera patented by them in 1895 at the Eden Theatre in France. This minute-and-a-half-long movie depicted workers coming out of the factory during their lunch break. They named their invention as Cinematograph. It is from this word we get the term 'cinema' for moving pictures. At first it was the age of silent movies.

   The first feature film made on the Indian soil is *Raja Harischandra*, directed by Dhundiraj Govind Phalke in 1913. It was based on the story of King Harischandra. Vigatha Kumaran (The Lost Child) directed by J C Daniel, is the first film in Malayalam.

2. **Radio.** Guglielmo Marconi of Italy invented the mode of transmitting sound signals without using wires. By 1901, Marconi succeeded in creating a wireless communication link between Europe and North America. Later in 1906, Lee Forest and John Fleming invented vacuum tube, which made clear transmission of voice possible.

   This led to the first ever radio broadcast in 1906 in USA. Later, radio stations were started all over the world. In India, radio broadcasting was started by amateur radio clubs. In June 1923, the Radio Club of Bombay made the first ever broadcast in the country. In 1927, the Indian Broadcasting Company (IBC) was formed. In 1930, the government took over their transmitters and formed the Indian State Broadcasting Service (ISBS). In 1935, Lionel Fielden of BBC assumed charge as the first Controller of Broadcasting in India. In 1936, the Delhi station started functioning. The same year the company was renamed as All India Radio (AIR). From 1956 onwards AIR got another name 'Akashvani'.

3. **Television.** The word television literally means seeing things from distant places. In April 1925 John Logie Baird of London had set up his television apparatus in a London department store and demonstrated the first crude functioning of television.

   Television was started as a modest affair in India on September 15, 1959 when the AIR set up an experimental television service in Delhi. It was soon converted into a full-fledged telecasting station. Thus begins the age of telecasting in India. A major milestone in the history of Indian television was the coverage of the Ninth Asian Games in 1982 which turned television transmission in India from black and white to colour. Now the television field in India is flooded with wide variety of channels– news, entertainment, religious, sports, cartoon, movie and music channels. Most of them telecast programmes round the clock.

CHARACTERISTICS OF ELECTRONIC MEDIA

Given below are some of the general features of electronic media:

1. Radio is a medium for ears but television and films are for both ears and eyes.
2. One needs to have some technical knowledge to use electronic media.
3. The technology of these media is changing at a very fast pace due to frequent technological upgradations.
4. The programmes in radio and television are available throughout the day.
5. Radio, television and film are enjoyed by people with audiovisual disabilities and the illiterates.
6. Satellite transmission makes electronic media programmes instantly available over a wide geographical area.
7. Programmes in radio and television are ephemeral in nature.
8. Live coverage is possible on radio and television.

D. New Media

The invention of the Internet and the World Wide Web opened up several new avenues for mass communication which include e-mail, websites, podcasts, e-books, blogging, social networking sites,

Internet Protocol Television, Internet radio and the like. These kinds of online and digital means of producing, transmitting and receiving messages are called new media.

The World Wide Web emerged as a powerful mass medium in 1990s. Web is the system that allows global linking of information modules in user-determined sequences. Basically it is a collection of sites that use HTML (Hypertext Markup Language) and HTTP (Hypertext Transfer Protocol) to connect each other and that have access through browser, which is a programme for viewing web pages. Internet Explorer, Mozilla Firefox, Google Chrome are examples of browsers. Tim Berners-Lee is the master mind behind the World Wide Web. His invention of hypertext materialized the dream of browsing documents on millions of computers connected through the Internet. We use search engines, like Google, to find information on the Internet.

Social networking is a major facility available in new media format. Social networking is defined as a social structure connecting relationships between individuals or organizations. A social networking site is an online platform where a user can create a profile and build a personal network that connects him or her to other users around the world. Social networking sites allow you to meet other Internet users directly. Facebook, Twitter, Linkedin and YouTube are some such sites.

Characteristics of New Media

The features of new media change rapidly in tune with the new developments in communication technology. Let's discuss some fundamental characteristics of new media.

1. The new media facilitate instant interaction between senders and receivers. Thus, this medium gives us the latest developments of events without any delay.
2. If internet connectivity is available, one can access new media from any part of the globe.
3. The new media contents are written in a hyper textual language, using hyperlinks. Thus, the users are gifted with large resources of data. For example, one can link to all sister publications of a newspaper from its home page. Multiple pagination facility enables websites to combine hundreds or thousands of web pages.
4. As the content is stored in digital format, new media are highly technological and upgraded frequently.
5. Above all, new media facilitate convergence of the various types of content like audio, video, text, image and data on a single device. This phenomenon is called as **media convergence**.

We have learned the major types of media and their characteristics. Now let's examine their functions in our society.

Functions of Mass Media

In a society like ours, mass media have a responsible role to play in fostering democracy, plurality and communal harmony through the functions listed below:

1. Information and education
2. Socialization
3. Entertainment
4. Political awareness
5. Cultural transmission
6. Catalyst to development

Different Media Theories Used in Mass Communication

1. **Magic Bullet Theory/ Hypodermic Needle Theory.** Hypodermic needle theory, magic bullet or transmission belt theory is that media message is very powerful and injects into minds of the audience in such a way as a bullet acts rapidly on a body. So it assumes powerful media effects leading to the hypodermic needle or magic bullet approach.
2. **Limited Effect.** In landmark media effects studies, Paul Lazarsfeld, Bernard Berelson, and Hazel Gaudet shift the view of media from powerful to limited effects, this says that media message has not very strong impact and its effects are limited, it depends on audience that how they take the media message.

3. **Cultivation Theory.** Cultivation theory says that media cultivates the minds of the people; this holds that through heavy exposure to television; people begin to view the world similar to the television world. Like emphasizing violence in programs heavy TV viewer perceives the world as a more violent place.
4. **Agenda Setting Theory.** Agenda Setting is basically a theory of strong media effects which says that there are three related agendas as media agenda, public agenda and policy agenda. This suggests that with the passage of time media agenda becomes the public agenda and they are linked with one another.
5. **Framing Theory.** Framing theory is closely interlinked with the agenda setting concept, Framing says the media focus attention on certain issues and then place them within a specific field of meaning. Mass media creates pictures of the world in our minds; framing is also termed as a second level agenda setting.
6. **Spiral of Silence Theory.** This theory is based on the idea that dissidents to a prevailing media-created idea will not speak out against it if they perceive themselves to be in the minority and thus avoid the risk of isolation and rejection. This leads others to keep silent since they believe most people agree with majority.
7. **Authoritarian Theory.** Authoritarian theory says it is necessary to control the media to protect and prevent the people from the national threats through any form communication i.e. information or news. The press is an instrument to enhance the ruler's power in the country. The authorities have all rights to permit any media and control it by providing license to the media and make certain censorship.
8. **Libertarian Theory.** Libertarian theory says people are more enough to find and judge good ideas from bad, people are rational and their rational thoughts lead them to find out what are good and bad. The press should not restrict anything even a negative content may give knowledge and can make better decision whilst worst situation. The libertarian thoughts are opposite to the authoritarian theory.
9. **Social Responsibility Theory.** Social responsibility theory allows free press without any censorship but at the same time the content of the press should be discussed in public panel and media should accept any obligation from public interference or professional self-regulations or both. The theory gives total media freedom in one hand but the external controls in other hand.
10. **Soviet Media Theory.** Soviet media theory is imitative of Leninist principles which based on the Carl Marx and Engel's ideology. The government undertakes the total media and communication to serve working classes and their interest. Theory says the state have absolute power to control any media for the benefits of people. They put end to the private ownership of the press and other media.
11. **Cognitive Dissonance.** (Leon Festinger) According to cognitive dissonance theory, there is a tendency for individuals to seek consistency among their cognitions (beliefs, opinions). When there is an inconsistency between attitudes or behaviors (dissonance), something must change to eliminate the dissonance.
12. **Classical Rhetorical Theory.** The origin of classical rhetoric theory can be traced back to the times of ancient scholars such as Plato, Aristotle and Socrates. This Theory developed when people began to identify that there is some kind of influence is made to the listeners. Therefore, the ability for public speaking reaped its magnitude in ancient world.

MULTIPLE CHOICE QUESTIONS

1. Video-Conferencing can be classified as one of the following types of communication
   (A) Visual one way
   (B) Audio-Visual one way
   (C) Audio-Visual two way
   (D) Visual two way
2. MC National University of Journalism and Communication is located at
   (A) Lucknow (B) Bhopal
   (C) Chennai (D) Mumbai
3. All India Radio (A.I.R.) for broadcasting was named in the year
   (A) 1926 (B) 1936
   (C) 1946 (D) 1956
4. In India for broadcasting TV programmes which system is followed ?
   (A) NTCS (B) PAL
   (C) NTSE (D) SECAM
5. The term 'DAVP' stands for
   (A) Directorate of Advertising & Vocal Publicity
   (B) Division of Audio-Visual Publicity
   (C) Department of Audio-Visual Publicity
   (D) Directorate of Advertising & Visual Publicity
6. The term "TRP" as associated with TV shows stands for
   (A) Total Rating Points
   (B) Time Rating Points
   (C) Thematic Rating Points
   (D) Television Rating Points
7. Public communication tends to occur within a more
   (A) complex structure
   (B) political structure
   (C) convenient structure
   (D) formal structure
8. Transforming thoughts, ideas and messages into verbal and non-verbal signs is referred to as
   (A) channelisation (B) mediation
   (C) encoding (D) decoding
9. Effective communication needs a supportive _______ environment.
   (A) economic (B) political
   (C) social (D) multi-cultural
10. A major barrier in the transmission of cognitive data in the process of communication is an individual's
    (A) personality (B) expectation
    (C) social status (D) coding ability
11. When communicated, institutionalised stereotypes become
    (A) myths (B) reasons
    (C) experiences (D) convictions
12. In mass communication, selective perception is dependent on the receiver's
    (A) competence (B) pre-disposition
    (C) receptivity (D) ethnicity
13. Photo bleeding means
    (A) Photo cropping
    (B) Photo placement upto edges
    (C) Photo cutting
    (D) Photo colour adjustment
14. While designing communication strategy feed-forward studies are conducted by
    (A) Audience (B) Communicator
    (C) Satellite (D) Media
15. In which language the newspapers have highest circulation in India ?
    (A) English (B) Hindi
    (C) Bengali (D) Tamil
16. The term 'Yellow Journalism' refers to
    (A) sensational news about terrorism and violence
    (B) sensationalism and exaggeration to attract readers / viewers.
    (C) sensational news about arts and culture
    (D) sensational news prints in yellow paper.
17. Communication with oneself is known as
    (A) Organisational Communication
    (B) Grapewine Communication
    (C) Interpersonal Communication
    (D) Intrapersonal Communication
18. The term 'SITE' stands for
    (A) Satellite Indian Television Experiment

(B) Satellite International Television Experiment
(C) Satellite Instructional Television Experiment
(D) Satellite Instructional Teachers Education

19. In communication, a major barrier to reception of messages is
(A) audience attitude
(B) audience knowledge
(C) audience education
(D) audience income

20. Post-modernism is associated with
(A) newspapers (B) magazines
(C) radio (D) television

21. Didactic communication is
(A) intra-personal (B) inter-personal
(C) organisational (D) relational

22. In communication, the language is
(A) the non-verbal code
(B) the verbal code
(C) the symbolic code
(D) the iconic code

23. Identify the correct sequence of the following
(A) Source, channel, message, receiver
(B) Source, receiver, channel, message
(C) Source, message, receiver, channel
(D) Source, message, channel, receiver

24. **Assertion (A) :** Mass media promote a culture of violence in the society.
Reason (R) : Because violence sells in the market as people themselves are violent in character.
(A) Both (A) and (R) are true and (R) is the correct explanation of (A).
(B) Both (A) and (R) are true, but (R) is not the correct explanation of (A).
(C) (A) is true, but (R) is false.
(D) Both (A) and (R) are false.

25. Media that exist in an interconnected series of communication - points are referred to as
(A) Networked media (B) Connective media
(C) Nodal media (D) Multimedia

26. The information function of mass communication is described as
(A) diffusion (B) publicity
(C) surveillance (D) diversion

27. An example of asynchronous medium is
(A) Radio (B) Television
(C) Film (D) Newspaper

28. In communication, connotative words are
(A) explicit (B) abstract
(C) simple (D) cultural

29. A message beneath a message is labelled as
(A) embedded text (B) internal text
(C) inter-text (D) sub-text

30. In analog mass communication, stories are
(A) static (B) dynamic
(C) interactive (D) exploratory

31. Which one of the following Telephonic Conferencing with a radio link is very popular throughout the world ?
(A) TPS (B) Telepresence
(C) Video conference (D) Video teletext

32. Which is *not* 24 hours news channel ?
(A) NDTV 24×7 (B) ZEE News
(C) Aajtak
(D) Lok Sabha channel

33. The main objective of F.M. station in radio is
(A) Information, Entertainment and Tourism
(B) Entertainment, Information and Interaction
(C) Tourism, Interaction and Entertainment
(D) Entertainment only

34. In communication, chatting in internet is
(A) Verbal communication
(B) Non verbal communication
(C) Parallel communication
(D) Grapevine communication

35. Match List-I with List-II and select the correct answer using the codes given below

List-I (Artists)	**List-II (Art)**
(a) Pandit Jasraj	(i) Hindustani vocalist
(b) Kishan Maharaj	(ii) Sitar
(c) Ravi Shankar	(iii) Tabla
(d) Udai Shankar	(iv) Dance

Codes :

	(a)	(b)	(c)	(d)		(a)	(b)	(c)	(d)
(A)	(i)	(ii)	(iii)	(iv)	(B)	(i)	(iii)	(iv)	(ii)
(C)	(i)	(iii)	(ii)	(iv)	(D)	(iii)	(ii)	(i)	(iv)

36. The country which has the distinction of having the two largest circulated newspapers in the world is
(A) Great Britain (B) The United States
(C) Japan (D) China

37. The chronological order of non-verbal communication is
(A) Signs, symbols, codes, colours

(B) Symbols, codes, signs, colours
(C) Colours, signs, codes, symbols
(D) Codes, colours, symbols, signs

38. Which of the following statements is not connected with communication ?
(A) Medium is the message
(B) The world is an electronic cocoon
(C) Information is power
(D) Telepathy is technological

39. Communication becomes circular when
(A) the decoder becomes an encoder
(B) the feedback is absent
(C) the source is credible
(D) the channel is clear

40. The site that played a major role during the terrorist attack on Mumbai (26/11) in 2008 was
(A) Orkut
(B) Facebook
(C) Amazon.com
(D) Twitter.

41. All India Radio before 1936 was known as
(A) Indian Radio Broadcasting
(B) Broadcasting Service of India
(C) Indian Broadcasting Service
(D) All India Broadcasting Service

42. The biggest news agency of India is
(A) PTI (B) UNI
(C) NANAP (D) Samachar Bharati

43. Prasar Bharati was launched in the year
(A) 1995 (B) 1997
(C) 1999 (D) 2001

44. Community Radio is a type of radio service that caters to the interest of
(A) Local audience (B) Education
(C) Entertainment (D) News

45. Orkut is a part of
(A) Intra personal Communication
(B) Mass Communication
(C) Group Communication
(D) Interpersonal Communication

46. Match **List-I** with **List-II** and select the correct answer using the codes given below :

List - I (Artists)	**List - II (Art)**
(a) Amrita Shergill	(i) Flute
(b) T. Swaminathan	(ii) Classical Song
(c) Bhimsen Joshi	(iii) Painting
(d) Padma Subramaniyam	(iv) Bharat Natyam

Codes :

	(a)	(b)	(c)	(d)
(A)	(iii)	(i)	(ii)	(iv)
(B)	(ii)	(iii)	(i)	(iv)
(C)	(iv)	(ii)	(iii)	(i)
(D)	(i)	(iv)	(ii)	(iii)

47. Press Council of India is located at
(A) Chennai (C) Kolkata
(B) Mumbai (D) Delhi

48. Adjusting the photo for publication by cutting is technically known as
(A) Photo cutting (B) Photo bleeding
(C) Photo cropping (D) Photo adjustment

49. Feed-back of a message comes from
(A) Satellite (B) Media
(C) Audience (D) Communicator

50. Collection of information in advance before designing communication strategy is known as
(A) Feed-back (B) Feed-forward
(C) Research study (D) Opinion poll

51. DTH service was started in the year
(A) 2000 (B) 2002
(C) 2004 (D) 2006

52. National Press day is celebrated on
(A) 16th November (B) 19th November
(C) 21st November (D) 30th November

53. The total number of members in the Press Council of India are
(A) 28 (B) 14
(C) 17 (D) 20

54. The right to impart and receive information is guaranteed in the Constitution of India by Article
(A) 19 (2) (A) (B) 19 (16)
(C) 19 (2) (D) 19 (1) (A)

55. Use of radio for higher education is based on the presumption of
(A) Enriching curriculum based instruction
(B) Replacing teacher in the long run
(C) Everybody having access to a radio set
(D) Other means of instruction getting outdated

56. The function of mass communication of supplying information regarding the processes, issues, events and societal developments is known as
(A) content supply (B) surveillance
(C) gratification (D) correlation

57. The science of the study of feedback systems in humans, animals and machines is known as
(A) cybernetics
(B) reverse communication
(C) selectivity study
(D) response analysis

58. Networked media exist in inter-connected
(A) social environments
(B) economic environments
(C) political environments
(D) technological environments

59. The combination of computing, telecommunications and media in a digital atmosphere is referred to as
(A) online communication
(B) integrated media
(C) digital combine
(D) convergence

60. A dialogue between a human-being and a computer programme that occurs simultaneously in various forms is described as
(A) man-machine speak
(B) binary chat
(C) digital talk
(D) interactivity

61. Which one of the following can be termed as verbal communication ?
(A) Prof. Sharma delivered the lecture in the class room.
(B) Signal at the cross-road changed from green to orange.
(C) The child was crying to attract the attention of the mother.
(D) Dipak wrote a letter for leave application.

62. Which is the 24 hours English Business news channel in India ?
(A) Zee News (B) NDTV 24 × 7
(C) CNBC (D) India News

63. Which of the following pair is *not* correctly matched ?
(A) N. Ram : The Hindu
(B) Barkha Dutt : Zee News
(C) Pranay Roy : NDTV 24 × 7
(D) Prabhu Chawla : Aaj Tak

64. "Because you deserve to know" is the punchline used by
(A) The Times of India
(B) The Hindu
(C) Indian Express
(D) Hindustan Times

65. Auditory capacity of man is maximum for the frequencies
(A) 1 kHz (B) 12-15 kHz
(C) 10-12 Hz (D) None of these

66. On 26 Jan, 2005, IGNOU has started a media programme
(A) Gyanvani (B) Gyandarshari
(C) Gyan lok (D) None of these

67. Maximum number of newspapers are published from
(A) West Bengal (B) Maharashtra
(C) Bihar (D) Uttar Pradesh

68. Effective communication takes place when
(A) source is attractive and authoritarian
(B) message design incorporates audience
(C) modern communication technologies are used
(D) receivers are passive recipients

69. Perception, retention and recall are
(A) source variables
(B) message variables
(C) receiver variables
(D) channel variables

70. The essence and justification for beauty contests is that
(A) women have standard features on which they can be rated
(B) beautiful women have a vision and role to play in social uplift
(C) they symbolize eternal freedom for women
(D) they provide an opportunity for beautiful

71. The name given to the first radio programme was
(A) India Radio Times (B) The Indian listener
(C) Akashvani (D) None of these

72. What is Conditional Access System (CAS)?
(A) A computer related term
(B) Security for V.V.I.Ps
(C) A system providing selected channels to a T.V. subscriber
(D) A visa system of U.S.

73. Which special train will be spreading awareness about various scientific and technological achievements of the country ?
(A) Rail Vigyan (B) Vigyan Rail
(C) Science Rail
(D) Science and Technology Rail

74. Modern communication technology is used in distance education to ensure
(A) wider and effective reach of standard material
(B) that students are inducted to modern technology
(C) that education is globalised and higher standards are achieved
(D) enhancement of efficacy of teaching due to limited interpersonal links

75. The spread of Internet for higher education is premised on
(A) Research and Development is vital
(B) Browsing encourages critical thinking
(C) Easy management and dissemination of knowledge
(D) India should be second to none in the world

76. Which of the following can make a class most effective?
(A) Making the learning experiences learner centred
(B) Keeping the students relaxed while teaching
(C) Explaining the subject matter clearly and loudly
(D) Keeping strict discipline in the class

77. Level C of the effectiveness of communication is defined as
(A) channel noise
(B) semantic noise
(C) psychological noise
(D) source noise

78. Recording a television programme on a VCR is an example of
(A) time-shifting (B) content reference
(C) mechanical clarity
(D) media synchronisation

79. A good communicator is the one who offers to his audience
(A) plentiful of information
(B) a good amount of statistics
(C) concise proof
(D) repetition of facts

80. Communication will be effective if it is
(A) Delivered slowly and clearly
(B) Delivered using appropriate media
(C) Received as intended by the sender
(D) Received immediately

81. A negative reaction to a mediated communication is described as
(A) flak
(B) fragmented feedback
(C) passive response
(D) non-conformity

82. The launch of satellite channel by IGNOU on 26th January 2003 for technological education for the growth and development of distance education is
(A) Eklavya channel
(B) Gyandarshan channel
(C) Rajrishi channel (D) None of these

83. Which of the following is not a successful communicator ?
(A) One who presents material in a precise and clear way
(B) One who is able to adopt himself according to the language of the communicatee
(C) One who knows a lot but is some what reserve in his attitude
(D) One who sometimes becomes informal before the receiver and develops rapport

84. Differentiation between acceptance and non-acceptance of certain stimuli in classroom communication is the basis of :
(1) selective expectation of performance
(2) selective affiliation to peer groups
(3) selective attention
(4) selective morality

85. The oldest news paper in India is
(A) Times of India (B) Hindu
(C) Tribune (D) Statesman

86. What is common between Keats, Ghalib and Kabir ?
(A) They were all poets
(B) They were all lovers
(C) The belonged to middle age
(D) They were all poets of nature

87. Which one of the following statements is true for Journals ?
(A) They are not a part of the print media.
(B) They concentrate an industry-specific, stream-specific or trade-specific issues, which are defined before hand.
(C) They given all types of news, views, and entertaining events.
(D) They are not prepared under the guidance of expert editors, writers and researchers but by journalists and freelance writers from the open market.

88. Cinema is a/an
(A) visual media (B) audiovisual media
(C) audio media (D) print media

89. The MMS is a/an
(A) visual media (B) audio media
(C) audiovisual media (D) None of these

90. The Conditional Access System (CAS) allows the viewers to
(A) select TV channels of their choice.
(B) interact with TV channels through the set-up boxes.
(C) cut down the costs of television viewing.
(D) None of these

91. Communication needs a
(A) Sender (B) Receiver
(C) Channel (D) All of these

92. Communication helps in
(A) Persuasion (B) Entertainment
(C) Integration
(D) Cultural Promotion

93. Which of the communication has an emotional appeal ?
(A) Intrapersonal communication
(B) Interpersonal communication
(C) Group communication
(D) Mass communication

94. Audience and feedback are the two main components of
(A) Intrapersonal communication
(B) Interpersonal communication
(C) Mass communication
(D) None of these

95. "The reach of mass media is quite strong in India, but comparatively, the access to them is very weak." This statement is
(A) Definitely true (B) Probably true
(C) Definitely false (D) Probably false

96. Speaker-speech-Audience are the elements of whose model of communication ?
(A) Claud Shannon (B) Aristotle
(C) Harold Lasswell (D) Wilbur Schramm

97. Who introduced the concept of noise in his model of communication ?
(A) Wilbur Schramm
(B) George Gerbner
(C) Charles E. Osgood
(D) Claud Shannon & Warren Weaves

98. Which model refers to 'Gatekeeper' concept?
(A) Theodore Newcomb's
(B) Shannon & Weaver's
(C) Bruce Westley & Maclean's
(D) None of these

99. When was the television service at the Delhi Kendra inaugurated ?
(A) Sept. 20, 1958 (B) Sep. 15, 1959
(C) Aug. 15, 1960 (D) Nov. 15, 1961

100. In how many states was the SITE (Satellite Instructional Television Experiment) programmes launched ?
(A) 3 (B) 4 (C) 5 (D) 6

101. When was the first English newspaper, "Bengal Gazette published" ?
(A) 1770 A.D. (B) 1780 A.D.
(C) 1790 A.D. (D) 1795 A.D.

102. Who is known as the father of Indian language journalism in India ?
(A) Raja Ram Mohan Roy
(B) Bhupendra Nath Dutta
(C) Vivekananda
(D) V.D. Savarkar

103. Microphone is a hi-fi instrument. Here 'fi' means
(A) finish (B) final
(C) fidelity (D) finical

104. Which of these is a characteristic of radio ?
(A) A medium of sound
(B) A mass medium
(C) An intimate medium
(D) All of these

105. Which of these is not a characteristic of T.V.?
(A) A democratic medium
(B) A mobile medium
(C) A living room medium
(D) A medium of immediacy

106. ______ is the supreme medium to express yesterday, today, and tomorrow with its own unique language. What should be filled in the blank ?
(A) Cinema (B) Radio
(C) Newspaper (D) Television

107. Large and highly diverse groups that represent the broad cross-section of the society form the ______ audience.
(A) Elite (B) General
(C) Specialised (D) None of these

108. Dyadic communication is the transfer of messages from a person
(A) to another person and vice versa
(B) to a group of persons.

(C) to a mass audience
(D) None of the above

109. The promoter of a product cannot deliver the following to a mass audience through currently used media vehicles.
(A) Information (B) Music
(C) Products
(D) He can deliver literally anything through such vehicles

110. In downward communication, messages
(A) flow form the bottom to the top of the organization structure.
(B) flow from the top to the bottom of the organization structure.
(C) are meant to be exchanged between the members of the top brass
(D) None of these.

111. Who developed the first paper for the mankind?
(A) The Chinese (B) The Sumerians
(C) The Aryans (D) The Mayans

112. Who was not a part of the team that developed the transistor ?
(A) John Bardeen (B) Walter Brattain
(C) J.E. Lilienfield (D) William Shockley

113. Classroom communication is normally considered as
(A) effective (B) cognitive
(C) affective (D) selective

114. Which one of the following is not a traditional media ?
(A) Literature (B) Painting
(C) TV (D) Music

115. Which one of the following is not a modern media ?
(A) The Press (B) Radio
(C) Cinema (D) Sculpture

116. Selective exposure & selective perception are two concepts of which theory ?
(A) Bullet Theory
(B) Individual Difference Theory
(C) Personal Influence Theory
(D) None of the above

117. 'Liberation Theory' is also called as
(A) Authoritarian Theory
(B) Social Responsibility Theory
(C) Free Press Theory
(D) Communist Media Theory

118. Soviet Media Theory is another name for
(A) Social Responsibility Theory
(B) Communist Media Theory
(C) Development Communication Theory
(D) Democratic-Participant Media Theory

119. When was censorship introduced on Indian Press?
(A) 1790 (B) 1792 (C) 1795 (D) 1797

120. When was the first press ordinance issued ?
(A) 1820 (B) 1823 (C) 1826 (D) 1829

121. In which language was 'Amrita Bazar Patrika' first published before changing over to English language ?
(A) Hindi (B) Urdu
(C) Bengali (D) Punjabi

122. "The Times of India" came into being with the amalgamation of which of these papers?
(A) The Standard & The Telegraph
(B) The Bombay Times & The Courier
(C) The Standard & The Courier
(D) Both A & B

123. Who is known as the 'father of Indian Cinema'.
(A) Torney (B) J.F. Madan
(C) Dada Saheb Phalke
(D) Natraj Mudaliar

124. Which media would be ideal to attract the attention of children to sell chocolates to them ?
(A) Radio (B) Newspapers
(C) TV (advertisements) (D) Leaflets

125. What is the meaning of circulation in the parlance of the print media ?
(A) Number of copies printed
(B) Number of copies sold
(C) Number of editions
(D) None of the above

126. An interview is a type of
(A) dyadic communication
(B) multiadic communication
(C) mass communication
(D) None of these

127. A journalist need not be ______ while covering an event.
(A) Impartial (B) Meticulous
(C) Domineering (D) Inquisitive

128. Which ones of the following do not provide entertainment to the targeted audience ?
(A) TV Programmers
(B) Magazines
(C) Leaflets
(D) Newspaper features

129. What is average frequency ?
(A) Total Exposures / Audience Reach
(B) Audience Reach/Total Exposures
(C) Total Exposures in a given time period
(D) None of these

130. What do you understand by GRPs ?
(A) The number of readers reading an advertisement.
(B) The number of advertising insertions in one campaign.
(C) The number of points earned by an advertising campaign.
(D) Any one of these

131. What is Print Run ?
(A) Print Run-Complementary Copies.
(B) Print Run - Wapasi
(C) Print Run + Complementary Copies.
(D) The number of books sold by one particular retailer.

132. What are Net sales in the parlance of book publishing ?
(A) The number of books or magazines sold by one retailer or bookshop.
(B) The number of books or magazines printed by a publisher at one time.
(C) The number of books or magazines available for sales.
(D) None of these

133. Who enforced the Vernacular Press Act ?
(A) Lord Canning (B) Lord Lytton
(C) Queen Victoria (D) East India Company

134. The name given to the first radio programme was
(A) India Radio Times
(B) The Indian listener
(C) Akashvani (D) None of these

135. When were the Bombay & Calcutta stations inaugurated by the Indian Broadcasting Company ?
(A) 1925 (B) 1926 (C) 1927 (D) 1928

136. "They have high status in the society. Their number is small but their influence is strong". This is with reference to what kind of audience ?
(A) Elite (B) General
(C) Specialised (D) None of these

137. Which is the method used for receiving information in market based feedback system ?
(A) Audience Decision Making
(B) Direct Feedback
(C) Media Review (D) All of these

138. When was the first printing press established in India ?
(A) 1670 (B) 1672 (C) 1674 (D) 1676

139. What is the other name of Hicky's Bengal Gazette ?
(A) The Bengal News
(B) Calcutta General Advertiser
(C) Bengal Journal (D) Bengal Harkarv

140. When was the channel 'Yuva Vani' started in Delhi ?
(A) 1965 (B) 1966 (C) 1967 (D) 1969

141. Where was the highest AIR station set-up in 1971 ?
(A) Mumbai (B) Leh
(C) Himachal (D) Nainital

142. When were educational programmes by UGC started on TV ?
(A) 1980 (B) 1982 (C) 1983 (D) 1984

143. When was the moving transmission of TV started ?
(A) 1980 (B) 1985 (C) 1987 (D) 1989

144. In which year did Doordarshan started its 5 metro channels ?
(A) 1990 (B) 1993 (C) 1994 (D) 1992

145. Which committee criticised the Doordarshan for concentrating on the North for its programme contents ?
(A) Verghese Committee
(B) Joshi Committee
(C) Chandra Committee (D) None of these

146. Which committee recommended separation of AIR & Television
(A) Chanda Committee
(B) Verghese Committee
(C) Joshi Committee (D) None of these

147. Effective communication does not require
(A) Voice modulation
(B) Handsome appearance
(C) Appropriate gestures
(D) Students involvement

148. Effective teaching is, by and large, a function of the teacher's.
(A) Scholarship (B) Punctuality
(C) Ability for verbal expression
(D) Liking for the profession

149. Which of the following is an ambitious computerisation programme aimed at connecting 60,000 government and aided schools through internet ?

(A) Vidya Vahini (B) Vidya Vani
(C) Gyan Vani (D) None of these

150. An effective teacher will ensure
(A) Cooperation among his students
(B) Laissez faire role on his part.
(C) Competition among his students.
(D) Competition or cooperation as the situation demands.

151. Every type of communication is affected by its
(1) Transmission (2) Non-regulation
(3) Context (4) Reception

152. Name the project which will connect all police stations in the country in one network.
(A) POLNET (B) TOLNET
(C) POL.COM (D) IPOL.COM

153. Which of the following steps would you consider first as an effective communicator ?
(A) Select the channels of communication.
(B) Plan the evaluation procedure.
(C) Determine the objectives of communication
(D) Identify various means for communication

154. Teacher's communication will be more effective if
(A) The teacher is a master in his subject.
(B) He prepares a good number of instructional aids.
(C) He discusses previous question papers
(D) He starts from what students already know.

155. The recently launched "Vidya Vahini" is a project related to
(A) School computerisation programme
(B) TV programme related to mass literacy
(C) Establishment of libraries in rural areas
(D) None of these

156. The final goal of feed back in a communication system is to
(A) Make necessary modifications in the communication process.
(B) Understand more about the content.
(C) Identify the defects of the communicator.
(D) Detect the limitations of the receiver.

157. Failure of the teacher to communicate his ideas well to the students may result into
(A) Classroom indiscipline
(B) Loss of students' interest in the topic being taught.
(C) Increased number of absentees in the class.
(D) All the above.

158. Which of the following will not hamper effective communication in the class ?
(A) A lengthy statement
(B) An ambiguous statement
(C) A precise statement
(D) A statement which allows the listener to draw his own conclusion.

159. India's first 100 per cent computer literate village is
(A) Chamravattam village (Kerala)
(B) Sasamosa (Bihar)
(C) Guru Nagar (Punjab) (D) None of these

160. Which of the following, in your opinion, is a clear evidence for positive attitude towards the National Anthem ?
(A) Ability to recite it melodiously
(B) Feeling proud as an Indian when it is heard
(C) Standing silently whenever it is sung in function
(D) Studying its historical and national background and significance.

161. The technique adopted to find out the level of acceptability of an individual by members of a group is
(A) Personality testing
(B) Projective techniques
(C) Psychometry (D) Sociometry

162. Major limitation of mass communication is that
(A) It is very costly for the receiver.
(B) More time is required produce the message.
(C) The success of the programme mainly depends upon the producers.
(D) The feedback system is weak.

163. Which of the following provides more freedom for the learners to interact actively?
(A) Small group discussions
(B) Use of film projector
(C) Viewing of the television
(D) Lecture by experts

164. The Library and information Science Department of Mysore University has taken up an ambitious project which aims to create an online data base of all doctoral theses and dissertations published by Indian Universities. The project sponsored by the Union Science and Technology Ministry is known as
(A) Vidya Bharti (B) Vidya Bahini
(C) March Ahead (D) Vidya Nidhi

165. **Assertion (A) :** To communicate well in the classroom is a natural ability.

Reason (R) : Effective teaching in the classroom demands knowledge of the communication process.

Code :

(1) Both (A) and (R) are true, and (R) is the correct explanation of (A).
(2) Both (A) and (R) are true, but (R) is not the correct explanation of (A).
(3) (A) is true, but (R) is false.
(4) (A) is false, but (R) is true.

166. Name the person who is most associated with WikiLeaks is
(A) Julian Assange (B) Tim Bernet
(C) Bill Gates (D) Richard Stallman

167. Global village concept was put forward by
(A) Robert Merton (B) Seon McBride
(C) Marshall McLuhan (D) Wilbur Scramm

168. J. Gopikrishnan who unearthed the 2G spectrum scandal was a reporter of
(A) The Times of India (B) The Pioneer
(C) The Telegraph (D) DNA

169. *The Gutenberg Galaxy* was authored by
(A) Johannes Gutenberg
(B) Marshall McLuhan
(C) George Gerbner (D) Kurt Lewin

170. International Commission to study communication in the world by UNESCO was known as
(A) McLuhan Commission
(B) Hutchins Commission
(C) MacBride Commission
(D) McQuail Commission

171. Who coined the term fourth estate?
(A) Lord William Bentick (B) Edmund Burke
(C) Winston Churchill (D) Clement Atlee

172. Which newspaper first launched an internet edition in India?
(A) Times of India (B) The Hindu
(C) The Telegraph (D) Hindustan Times

173. Which of the following media group has a newspaper, television news channel and FM radio station?
(A) The Hindu group
(B) The Kerala Kaumudi group
(C) The Malayala Manorama group
(D) The Indian Express group

174. Which among the following is not a characteristic of Mass Media?
(A) Transient (B) Universal Access
(C) Narrow scope (D) Gatekeeping

175. Right to Information ACT (RTI) applies to all the states and UT's of India except
(A) Kerala (B) Jammu & Kashmir
(C) Goa (D) Nagaland

176. The study on the manner in which people approach others or keep their distance from others in communication contexts.
(A) Kinesics (B) Proxemics
(C) Chronemics (D) Ocullesics

177. Who is the Web Inventor?
(A) Tim Berners-Lee (B) Bill Gates
(C) Stallman (D) Charles Babbage

178. Who is well known for his comment on communication : *'Who (says) What (to) Whom (in) What Channel (with) What Effect'*
(A) Frank F X Dance (B) Harold Lasswell
(C) Marshall McLuhan (D) Joseph A Devito

179. Who developed the SMCR model of communication?
(A) Marshall McLuhan
(B) Harold D Lasswell
(C) Frank E X Dance (D) David Berlo

180. Name the news agency that was closely associated with India even before the independence.
(A) AFP (B) Associated Press
(C) UPI (D) Reuters

181. Name the pioneer who started an Indian news agency in the country.
(A) K.C. Roy (B) Paul Julius Reuter
(C) Bindhu Bhushan Sengupta
(D) Rajaram Mohan Roy

182. The Hindi news agency of PTI is known as
(A) PTI Hindi (B) PTI Hindustani
(C) PTI Bhasha (D) PTI Rashtra

183. The Hindi wire service of UNI is known as
(A) Unisamachar (B) Unihindustan
(C) Unibhasha (D) Univartha

184. Press Council of India is a ______ member body including the chairperson.
(A) 26 (B) 27 (C) 28 (D) 29

185. Self regulatory body of the television news channels in India is
(A) Press Council of India
(B) Television Council of India
(C) News Broadcasting Standards Authority
(D) Broadcast Authority of India

186. Which of the following is body that represents newspapers publishers?

(A) ABC (B) INS
(C) RNI (D) IFWJ

187. Who is generally described as the unsung hero of a newspaper?
(A) Reporter (B) Sub editor
(C) News editor (D) Chief editor

188. Dateline in a report tells
(A) Date of the story
(B) Date and place
(C) Date, place, country of the story
(D) Date, place, reporter of the story

189. A face to face interaction with media persons is generally known as
(A) Interview (B) Press Conference
(C) Press release (D) Handouts

190. When a press club or forum invites a celebrity to interact with the media person, it is known as
(A) Press conference (B) Press briefing
(C) Press meet (D) Meet the press

191. The press release of the central Government is distributed to the media organizations by
(A) PRD (B) I & B Ministry
(C) PIB (D) DAVP

192. Name the newspaper that unearthed the Watergate Scandal.
(A) New York Times (B) Washington Post
(C) Wall Street Journal
(D) Washington Journal

193. *Operation West End*, a sting operation, was carried out by
(A) Tehelka.com (B) Ohmynews.com
(C) News.com (D) Probity.com

194. Name of the newspaper on the front page is called
(A) Masthead (B) Skyline
(C) Nameplate (D) Name board

195. An early edition of a newspaper is called
(A) City edition (B) Bulldog
(C) Mofussil edition (D) Midnight edition

196. Media and society are ______ to each other.
(A) adversely connected
(B) closely related
(C) not related
(D) none of the above

197. The essential components of communication are
(A) Source, massage, interference, channel, receiver, feedback and context.
(B) sign, source, destination, interaction and correlation.
(C) sign, symbols, understanding, communication and communicant.
(D) Symbols, understanding, purpose, ideas, opinions, non-verbal and reaction.

198. A low context culture is one where
(A) Most of the information is unspoken.
(B) Most of the information is explicitly stated in a verbal massage.
(C) Most of the information is spoken.
(D) Much of the information is unspoken.

199. A high-context culture is one where
(A) Much of the information is about the context or about the person.
(B) Much of the information is spoken.
(C) Most people use sign language.
(D) Much of the information is unspoken.

200. Communication issues at the international level are addressed by
(A) ILO (B) ITU
(C) UNDP (D) UNESCO

201. Interpersonal communication occurs only when
(A) A person exchanges idea with another one as a unique individual.
(B) A Large number of people are communicating with each other at the same time.
(C) Only friends are talking.
(D) None of the above

202. Non-verbal messages are
(A) Overestimated in importance.
(B) Attempts at manipulation and should be ignored.
(C) Generally irrelevant to overall massage meanings.
(D) Important for a listener to understand.

203. Intrapersonal communication helps one
(A) Learn about oneself.
(B) To know what others are thinking.
(C) Communicate with the general public.
(D) To become a talented public speaker.

204. In interpersonal communication, ethics are
(A) Important
(B) Communication barriers
(C) Ineffective
(D) None of the above

205. Non-verbal communication includes
(A) Delivering a speech

(B) Telephonic conversation
(C) Singing a song
(D) Shaking hands

206. Which of the following is not true about the grapevine?
(A) It is faster than formal communication network.
(B) It is less accurate than formal network.
(C) It is fount in almost all organisations.
(D) It is preferred over formal communication.

207. Referential framing used by TV audience connects media with
(A) reality (B) falsity
(C) negativity (D) passivity

208. Which of the following will make communication more effective?
(A) Cracking jokes in between.
(B) Using multi-sensory appeal.
(C) Speaking with high authority.
(D) Telling what is useful to the listeners.

209. The communicated knowledge in a classroom is considered as
(A) non-pervasive treasure
(B) limited judgement
(C) autonomous virtue
(D) cultural capital

210. Journal-like entries written by individuals and posted on the internet that sometimes can generate many online discussions.
(A) Weblogs
(B) Simple posting
(C) E-journals
(D) None of the above

211. Which of the following statements (s) is/are true in the context of paraphrasing?
(A) It is basically about starting in your own words, your understandings of what has just been said.
(B) It gives speaker opportunity to find out what message he/she is getting across to you.
(A) Only A (B) Only B
(C) Both A and B (D) Neither A nor B

212. The Ability to understand, communicate with, motivate, and support other people, both individually and in groups, defines which of the following organizational skills?
(A) Hard skills
(B) Soft skills
(C) Conceptual skills
(D) Political skills

213. Communication via New media such as computers, teleshopping, internet and mobile telephony is termed as
(A) Entertainment
(B) Interactive communication
(C) Developmental communication
(D) Communitarian

214. The first multi-lingual news agency of India was
(A) Samachar
(B) API
(C) Hindustan Samachar
(D) Samachar Bharati

215. Chinese Cultural Revolution leader Mao Zedong used a type of communication to talk to the masses is known as
(A) Mass line communication
(B) Group communication
(C) Participatory communication
(D) Dialogue communication

ANSWERS

1. (C)	**2.** (B)	**3.** (B)	**4.** (B)	**5.** (D)	**6.** (D)	**7.** (D)	**8.** (C)	**9.** (C)	**10.** (D)
11. (D)	**12.** (C)	**13.** (B)	**14.** (B)	**15.** (B)	**16.** (A)	**17.** (D)	**18.** (C)	**19.** (A)	**20.** (D)
21. (B)	**22.** (B)	**23.** (D)	**24.** (D)	**25.** (A)	**26.** (C)	**27.** (D)	**28.** (D)	**29.** (D)	**30.** (A)
31. (C)	**32.** (D)	**33.** (B)	**34.** (C)	**35.** (C)	**36.** (D)	**37.** (A)	**38.** (D)	**39.** (A)	**40.** (A)
41. (C)	**42.** (A)	**43.** (B)	**44.** (B)	**45.** (C)	**46.** (A)	**47.** (D)	**48.** (C)	**49.** (C)	**50.** (D)
51. (C)	**52.** (A)	**53.** (A)	**54.** (D)	**55.** (C)	**56.** (B)	**57.** (A)	**58.** (D)	**59.** (D)	**60.** (D)
61. (D)	**62.** (C)	**63.** (B)	**64.** (D)	**65.** (B)	**66.** (A)	**67.** (D)	**68.** (D)	**69.** (A)	**70.** (C)
71. (A)	**72.** (C)	**73.** (D)	**74.** (D)	**75.** (C)	**76.** (B)	**77.** (A)	**78.** (D)	**79.** (A)	**80.** (D)
81. (C)	**82.** (A)	**83.** (C)	**84.** (C)	**85.** (A)	**86.** (A)	**87.** (B)	**88.** (B)	**89.** (C)	**90.** (A)
91. (D)	**92.** (C)	**93.** (B)	**94.** (C)	**95.** (A)	**96.** (B)	**97.** (D)	**98.** (C)	**99.** (B)	**100.** (D)
101. (B)	**102.** (A)	**103.** (C)	**104.** (D)	**105.** (B)	**106.** (A)	**107.** (B)	**108.** (A)	**109.** (C)	**110.** (B)
111. (A)	**112.** (C)	**113.** (C)	**114.** (C)	**115.** (D)	**116.** (B)	**117.** (C)	**118.** (B)	**119.** (C)	**120.** (B)
121. (C)	**122.** (D)	**123.** (C)	**124.** (C)	**125.** (B)	**126.** (A)	**127.** (C)	**128.** (C)	**129.** (A)	**130.** (B)
131. (B)	**132.** (B)	**133.** (B)	**134.** (A)	**135.** (C)	**136.** (A)	**137.** (D)	**138.** (C)	**139.** (B)	**140.** (D)
141. (B)	**142.** (D)	**143.** (C)	**144.** (C)	**145.** (B)	**146.** (A)	**147.** (B)	**148.** (D)	**149.** (A)	**150.** (D)
151. (C)	**152.** (A)	**153.** (C)	**154.** (B)	**155.** (D)	**156.** (D)	**157.** (C)	**158.** (C)	**159.** (D)	**160.** (A)
161. (C)	**162.** (D)	**163.** (A)	**164.** (D)	**165.** (D)	**166.** (A)	**167.** (C)	**168.** (B)	**169.** (B)	**170.** (C)
171. (B)	**172.** (B)	**173.** (C)	**174.** (C)	**175.** (B)	**176.** (B)	**177.** (A)	**178.** (B)	**179.** (D)	**180.** (D)
181. (A)	**182.** (C)	**183.** (D)	**184.** (D)	**185.** (B)	**186.** (B)	**187.** (B)	**188.** (D)	**189.** (B)	**190.** (D)
191. (C)	**192.** (B)	**193.** (A)	**194.** (C)	**195.** (B)	**196.** (B)	**197.** (A)	**198.** (B)	**199.** (D)	**200.** (D)
201. (A)	**202.** (D)	**203.** (A)	**204.** (A)	**205.** (D)	**206.** (D)	**207.** (A)	**208.** (B)	**209.** (D)	**210.** (A)
211. (C)	**212.** (B)	**213.** (B)	**214.** (C)	**215.** (A)					

MATHEMATICAL REASONING AND APTITUDE

Syllabus

- Types of Reasoning.
- Number Series, Letter Series, Codes and Relationships.
- Mathematical Aptitude (Fraction, Time & Distance, Ratio, Proportion and Percentage, Profit and Loss, Interest and Discounting, Averages etc.).

REASONING

It is one of the best forms of controlled thinking consciously towards the solution of a problem. It is realistic in the sense that the solution is sought always in reference to the reality of the situation. We can solve many problems in our day-dreams, dreams and imaginations but they are unrealistic solutions.

As Sherman defined, "reasoning is a process of thinking during which the individual is aware of a problem identifies, evaluates, and decides upon a solution".

Reasoning is used not only when we want to solve an immediate problem but also when we anticipate future problems.

Reasoning plays a significant role in one's adjustment to the environment. It not only determines one's cognitive activities but also influences the behaviour and personality.

Definitions of Reasoning

1. *"Reasoning is a stepwise thinking with a purpose or goal in mind".* —**Garrett**
2. *"Reasoning is the term applied to highly purposeful, controlled and selective thinking".* —**Gates**
3. *"Reasoning is the word used to describe the mental recognition of cause and effect relationships, it may be the prediction of an event from an observed cause or the inference of a cause from an observed event".* —**Skinner**

TYPES OF REASONING

Reasoning within an argument gives the rationale behind why one choice, for example should be selected over another. Types of reasoning include:

- **Abduction** : the process of creating explanatory hypotheses.
- **Analogical Reasoning** : relating things to novel other situations.

- **Cause-and-Effect Reasoning** : showing causes and resulting effect.
  - *Cause-to-Effects Reasoning* : starting from the cause and going forward.
  - *Effects-to-Cause Reasoning* : starting from the effect and working backward.
  - *The Bradford Hill Criteria* : for cause and effect in medical diagnosis.
- **Comparative Reasoning** : comparing one thing against another.
- **Conditional Reasoning** : using if...then...
- **Criteria Reasoning** : comparing against established criteria.
- **Decompositional Reasoning** : understand the parts to understand the whole.
- **Deductive Reasoning** : starting from the general rule and moving to specifics.
- **Exemplar Reasoning** : using an example.
- **Inductive Reasoning** : starting from specifics and deriving a general rule.
- **Modal Logic** : arguing about necessity and possibility.
- **Pros-vs-cons Reasoning** : using arguments both for and against a case.
- **Residue Reasoning** : Removing first what is not logical.
- **Set-based Reasoning** : based on categories and membership relationships.
- **Systemic Reasoning** : the whole is greater than the sum of its parts.
- **Syllogistic Reasoning** : drawing conclusions from premises.
- **Traditional Logic** : assuming premises are correct.

Note that these are not all mutually exclusive methods and several give different lenses onto overlapping areas.

Remember

In logic, three kinds of logical reasoning can be distinguished: deduction, induction and abduction. Given a precondition, a conclusion, and a rule that the precondition implies the conclusion, they can be explained in the following way:

Deduction means determining the conclusion. It is using the rule and its precondition to make a conclusion. *Example:* "When it rains, the grass gets wet. It rained today. Therefore, the grass is wet." Mathematicians are commonly associated with this style of reasoning.

Induction means determining the rule. It is learning the rule after numerous examples of the conclusion following the precondition. *Example:* "The grass has been wet every time it has rained. Therefore, if it rains tomorrow, the grass will get wet." Scientists are commonly associated with this style of reasoning.

Abduction means determining the precondition. It is using the conclusion and the rule to support that the precondition could explain the conclusion. *Example:* "When it rains, the grass gets wet. The grass is wet, therefore, it may have rained." Diagnosticians and detectives are commonly associated with this style of reasoning.

General Instructions

Before beginning to solve reasoning problems, the candidate should study and understand carefully the instructions as to how he has to solve the questions or what is the requirement of the test.

As the time is limited, the candidate should not waste time on difficult problems which take time for proper comprehension. The candidate must attempt all easy problems in the first instance, reserving the more difficult ones to be tackled later.

Accuracy is another factor which contributes towards high marks.

- Series Test
- Alphabet Test
- Classification Test
- Direction Sense Test
- Graphical Missing Number
- Analogy Test
- Coding and Decoding Test
- Blood Relation Test

- Arranging in Order Test
- Time and Calendar Test
- Number Related Test
- Mathematical Ability Test
- Letter-Digit Term Test
- Clock Related Test
- Mathematical Operation Test

In this section, the candidate shall encounter two different (though related) forms of reasoning. The basic requirement, here, is to apply clear thinking by the candidate. The problems range from simple arithmetical or mathematical ones to everyday situations (real or imaginary), problem figures that change according to a particular rule or even puzzles. As speed is the essence of this competitive examination, a great deal of practice and mental agility is required here.

Each analytical section includes the following two kinds of questions.

- Analytical reasoning questions in groups of three or more, or singly are based on a different set of conditions describing a fictional situation.
- Logical reasoning questions are based on a separate short prose passage, but sometimes with two or three questions based on the same passage.

There are two types of Reasoning Tests – Verbal and Non-Verbal. The items in a verbal test are stated in language form such as Analogy Test, Series Test, Same Class Test, etc. whereas, Non-verbal tests are made up of materials such as patterns, lines, drawings, pictures, wooden or plastic pieces and the like. Non-verbal tests are also called matrices or abstract reasoning tests.

SERIES TEST

This test deals with questions in which series of numbers or letters are given, which are generally called as terms of the series. These terms follow a certain pattern. The candidate is required to recognize this pattern and either complete the given series with most suitable alternative or identify the wrong member of that series.*

A. Number Series

In number series questions, candidates are asked to either insert a missing number or find the odd one. The only thing to be understood for solving these questions is the *pattern* on which a number series is written. By using various methods, a number of series can be formed. It is advisable for the students to practice as many questions as possible, to apprise themselves the variety of methods used to form number series.

There may be various kinds of series. Some important of them have been discussed below :

1. $a, (a + d), (a + 2d), (a + 3d), (a + 4d), ...$ (A.P. Series)

   Example. 17, 23, 29, 35, ... may be expressed as :- 17, (17 + 6), (17 + 2 × 6), (17 + 3 × 6), ...

   Therefore the next no. is 17 + 4 × 6 = 41

2. $a, ar, ar^2, ar^3, ar^4, ...$ (G.P. Series)

   Example. 5, 15, 45, 135, 405, ... may be expressed as : 5, (5 × 3), (5×3^2), (5×3^3), (5×3^4),.....

   Therefore the next number is (5×3^5) = 5 × 3 × 3 × 3 × 3 × 3 = 1215.

PRECAUTIONS

1. Read and understand the question carefully
2. Apply your mind on the required answer
3. Cross verify the answer, if you can.

* A.P. – Arithmetical Progression; G.P. – Geometric Progression; H.P. – Harmonic Progression

3. $\frac{1}{a}, \frac{1}{(a+d)}, \frac{1}{(a+2d)}, \frac{1}{(a+3d)}, ...$ (H.P. Series)

Example. 1, $\frac{1}{4}, \frac{1}{7}, \frac{1}{10}$, ... may be expressed as :

$$\frac{1}{1}, \frac{1}{(1+3)}, \frac{1}{(1+2\times3)}, \frac{1}{(1+3\times3)}, ...$$

Therefore the next number is $\frac{1}{1+4\times3} = \frac{1}{13}$

4. $a, (a+b), (a+b+b+1), (a+b+b+1+b+1+1),.....$

Example. 3, 5, 8, 12, ... may be expressed as - 3, (3 + 2), (3 + 2 + 2 + 1), (3 + 2 + 2 + 1 + 2 + 1 + 1)....
Therefore the next number is (3 + 2 + 2 + 1 + 2 + 1 + 1 + 2 + 1 + 1 + 1) = 17

Note: (a) Series 4 can also be presented as ——
$a, (a+b), (a+2b+1), (a+3b+3), (a+4b+6)....$

(b) In series 4, 1 may be replaced by any other number, e.g.,
$a, a+b, (a+b+\underline{b+c}), (a+b+b+c+\underline{b+2c}).....$

Example. 3, 5, 10, 18,..... may be expressed as - 3, (3 + 2), (3 + 2 + $\underline{2+3}$), (3 + 2 + 2 + 3 + $\underline{2+2\times3}$)...
Therefore the next number is - (3 + 2 + 2 + 3 + 2 + 2 × 3 + $\underline{2+3\times3}$) = 29

5. $(a)^{\alpha}+r, (a+b)^{\alpha}+r, (a+2b)^{\alpha}+r, (a+3b)^{\alpha}+r, ...$

Example. 2, 28, 126, 344, ... may be expressed as: $(1)^3+1, (1+2)^3+1, (1+2\times2)^3+1, (1+3\times2)^3+1, ...$
Therefore the next number is, $(1+4\times2)^3+1 = 730$.

6. a, b, c, d, e, f......... Which may follow any of the following conditions—

(a) $\frac{a}{b}, \frac{b}{c}, \frac{c}{d}, \frac{d}{e}, \frac{e}{f}$ ..... comes under any specific series such as A.P., G.P., or H.P.

Example. 1, 2, 8, 48, 384, ... where $\frac{a}{b} = \frac{1}{2}, \frac{b}{c} = \frac{2}{8} = \frac{1}{4}, \frac{c}{d} = \frac{8}{48} = \frac{1}{6}, \frac{d}{e} = \frac{48}{384} = \frac{1}{8}, ...$

Or, $\frac{a}{b}, \frac{b}{c}, \frac{c}{d}, \frac{d}{e}$, ... gives $\frac{1}{2}, \frac{1}{4}, \frac{1}{6}, \frac{1}{8}$ ....

Or $\frac{1}{2}, \frac{1}{(2+2)}, \frac{1}{(2+2\times2)}, \frac{1}{(2+3\times2)}, ...$ (H.P. series)

Therefore, $\frac{e}{f} = \frac{1}{(2+4\times2)} = \frac{1}{10}$

$\therefore \frac{384}{f} = \frac{1}{10} \Rightarrow f = 3840$

Hence, the next no. is 3840

(b) $\frac{a}{b} = \frac{b}{c} = \frac{c}{d} = \frac{d}{e} = \frac{e}{f} = ...$

Example. In the series 256, 128, 64, 32, 16, 8,....

$$\frac{256}{128} = \frac{128}{64} = \frac{64}{32} = \frac{32}{16} = \frac{16}{8} = \frac{8}{4\text{(next no.)}} = ...$$

Note. This is a G.P. series explained, here, in another way.

Two-stage Type Series

In a two step Arithmetic series, the differences of consecutive numbers themselves form an arithmetic series.

Example. 1, 3, 6, 10, 15.....

Sol. 3 – 1 = 2, 6 – 3 = 3, 10 – 6 = 4, 15 – 10 = 5....

Now, we get an arithmetic sequence 2, 3, 4, 5......

Hence 6 will be added to the last number given, so answer would 15 + 6 = 21

Mixed Series

This particular type of series may have more than one pattern arranged in a single series or it may have been created according to any of the unorthodox rules.

Example. 10, 22, 46, 94, 190, ?

Sol. 10 × 2 = 20 + 2 = 22,
22 × 2 = 44 + 2 = 46,
46 × 2 = 92 + 2 = 94,
94 × 2 = 188 + 2 = 190,
190 × 2 = 380 + 2 = 382.

So the missing number is 382.

Arithmetico–Geometric Series

As the name suggests, Arithmetico–Geometric series is formed by a peculiar combination of Arithmetic and Geometric series. An important property of Arithmetico- Geometric series is that the differences of consecutive terms are in Geometric Sequence.

Example. 1, 4, 8, 11, 22, 25, ?

Sol. Series Type +3 , × 2 (i.e. Arithmetic and Geometric Mixing)

1 + 3 = 4, 4 × 2 = 8, 8 + 3 = 11, 11 × 2 = 22, 22 + 3 = 25, 25 × 2 = 50

Tips & Key

- **There may be more than one way to solve a number sequence question.** Consider the data between each term: As mentioned above, a sequence can be made up of two alternating sequences or take from several combined operations.
- **Look at the difference between terms** when you can't find a rule look for for a difference between consecutive terms – it may create an independent sequence.
  Use the multiple-choices options to determine the correct answer quicker.
- **Don't shy away from estimation.** Sometimes you do not need to use full calculations to determine the correct answer.
- **Develop your/calculator skills** (in case of calculator usage): Aside from basic arithmetic operations, learn how to use various, more advanced, formulas and operations such as exponents, square roots, factorial, memory etc.
- **Familiarise yourself with maths operations** such as basic arithmetic, fractions, decimals, exponents etc.

Geometrico - Arithmetic Series is the reverse of Arithmetico - Geometric Series.

The differences of suggestive terms are in Arithmetic Series.

Example. 1, 2, 6, 36, 44, 440, ?

Sol. Series Type - × 2, + 4, × 6, +8 , × 10

1 × 2 = 2, 2 + 4 = 6, 6 × 6 = 36, 36+ 8 = 44, 44 × 10 = 440, 440 + 12 = 452

Twin/Alternate Series

As the name of the series specifies, this type of series may consist of two series combined into a single series. The alternating terms of this series may form an independent series in itself.

Example. 3, 4, 8, 10, 13, 16, ?

Sol. As we can see, there are two series formed

Series 1 : 3, 8, 13 with a common difference of 5

Series 2 : 4, 10, 16 with a common difference of 6

So, next two terms of the series should be 18 & 22 respectively.

TYPES OF QUESTIONS ASKED IN EXAMINATIONS

Type I. Identify Next Number in the Series

Example 1. 4, 6, 9, 13,................

(A) 17 (B) 18 (C) 21 (D) 25

Solution. (B) The difference between the two consecutive numbers is increasing in the order of 2, 3, 4, 5, etc. Hence answer is 18.

Example 2. 1, 5, 10, 16, 23, 31,.............

(A) 38 (B) 50 (C) 39 (D) 40

Solution. (D) The difference between the consecutive numbers is increasing in the order of 2, 3, 4, 5, so on. As the difference between 23 and 31 is 8, therefore, the difference between 31 and the next figure which is missing, should be 9. Hence the required number should be 40.

Example 3. 2, 9, 28, 65,.............

(A) 121 (B) 195 (C) 126 (D) 103

Solution. (C) Method used to form the series is

$(1)^3 + 1, (2)^3 + 1, (3)^3 + 1, (4)^3 + 1,$ ....

Therefore, the next number is $(5)^3 + 1 = 126$

Type II. Identify Wrong Number in the Series

Directions. *In the questions given below one number is wrong in the series. Identify it.*

Example 1. 46080, 3840, 384, 48, 24, 2, 1

(A) 3840 (B) 384 (C) 24 (D) 1

Solution. (C) 24 is the wrong term. If 24 is replaced by 8, then the ratio of two consecutive terms will be 1/12, 1/10, 1/8 etc.

Example 2. 5, 11, 23, 47, 96, 191, 383

(A) 96 (B) 5 (C) 11 (D) 191

Solution. (A) 96 is the wrong term. If 96 is replaced by 95, then the differences of two consecutive terms are 6, 12, 24, 48, 96 and 192.

Type III. Identify the Term put in the Bracket

Directions (1–5). *In the following number series, two terms have been put within brackets. Mark*

(A) if both the bracket terms are right

(B) if first bracket term is right and second is wrong

(C) if first bracket term is wrong and second is right.

(D) if both the bracket terms are wrong

Example 1. 4, 7, (9), 10, 13, 15, (16), 19.

Solution. (A) 4, 7, (9), 10, 13, 15, (16), 19

+3 +2 +1 +3 +2 +1 +3

From the above situation, we can say that both bracket terms are right.

Example 2. 3, 10, 29, (66), (127), 218

Solution. (A) 3, 10, 29, (66), (127), 218

↓ ↓ ↓ ↓ ↓ ↓

1^3+2 2^3+2 3^3+2 4^3+2 5^3+2 6^3+2

From the above situation, we can say that both bracket terms are right.

Example 3. 4, 6, 10, (12), 16, (14), 22

Solution. (B) 4, 6, 10, (12), 16, (14), 22

+2 +4 +2 +4 +2 +4

From the above situation, we can say that the second bracket term should be 18. Hence, first bracket term is right and second bracket term is wrong.

Example 4. (2), 5, (12), 25, 41, 61

Solution. (D) (2), 5, (12), 25, 41, 61

+4 +8 +12 +16 +20

From the above situation, the bracket terms should be 1 and 13 respectively. Hence, we can say that both bracket terms are wrong.

Example 5. 2, 3, (6), 11, 18, (30), 38

Solution. (B) 2, 3, (6), 11, 18, (30), 38

+1 +3 +5 +7 +9 +11

From the above situation, we can say that the second bracket term should be 27. Hence, first bracket term is right and second bracket term is wrong.

Type IV. Completion of the Series

Directions* : *(1–2) is of completion of the series type. In each of the following questions, a number series is given. After the series, a number is followed by (A), (B), (C), (D) and (E). The candidate has to complete the series starting with the number given following the sequence of the given series and answer them.

Example 1. 60 121 131 264 284 571 601

120 (A) (B) (C) (D) (E)

Which number will come in the place of (D) ?

(A) 525 (B) 625 (C) 524 (D) 624

Solution. (C) 60 121 131 264 284 571 601

×2+1 +10 ×2+2 +20 ×2+3 +30

Similarly,

(A) (B) (C) (D)

120 241 251 504 524

×2+1 +10 ×2+2 +20

Hence, 524 will come in place of (D).

Example 2. 2 9 45 247.5 1485

3 (A) (B) (C) (D) (E)

Which number will come in the place of (B) ?

(A) 75 (B) 67.5 (C) 72 (D) 68

Solution. (B) 2 9 45 247.5 1485

×4.5 ×5 ×5.5 ×6

Similarly,

(A) (B)

3 13.5 67.5

×4.5 ×5

Hence, 67.5 will come in place of (B).

B. Letter Series

Rules for the Alphabet Series

Some of the standard rules followed in estimating the next term in alphabet series are as follows.

1. Keep the order of letters with their respective numbers, *i.e.*, A = 1 .... Z = 26 and *vice* versa *i.e.*, Z = 1 ... A = 26.
2. When the counting is circular, after Z, the cycle will continue from A.
3. Sometimes, letters are omitted in sequence, e.g., ABC –, EFG –, Here, D and H, in sequence, are omitted.
4. Sometimes, equal number of letters are omitted, e.g., in ADG, two consecutive letters are omitted.
5. One following the letter and the other preceding it may be interchanged, e.g., in BCA, C follows B and A precedes B.
6. Sometimes, there may be repetition of letters in a set order, e.g., in aab, bbc, one letter is repeated twice, the next set could be ccd.
7. Sometimes, numbers are mixed with letters, the number may refer to the position of the letters in the alphabet.

Type I. Identify the Next Alphabet in the Series

Example 1. Identify the next term of the series.

DMP, FLN, HKL, JJJ, ______

(A) LIH (B) MII (C) III (D) MIF

Solution. (A) $D \xrightarrow{+2} F \xrightarrow{+2} H \xrightarrow{+2} J \xrightarrow{+2} \boxed{L}$

$M \xrightarrow{-1} L \xrightarrow{-1} K \xrightarrow{-1} J \xrightarrow{-1} \boxed{I}$

$P \xrightarrow{-2} N \xrightarrow{-2} L \xrightarrow{-2} J \xrightarrow{-2} \boxed{H}$

Example 2. Identify the next term of the series.

KPA, LQB, MRC, NSD, ______

(A) OET (B) OTE (C) TOE (D) EOT

Solution. (B)

K $\xrightarrow{+1}$ L	$\xrightarrow{+1}$ M	$\xrightarrow{+1}$ N	$\xrightarrow{+1}$	O
P $\xrightarrow{+1}$ Q	$\xrightarrow{+1}$ R	$\xrightarrow{+1}$ S	$\xrightarrow{+1}$	T
A $\xrightarrow{+1}$ B	$\xrightarrow{+1}$ C	$\xrightarrow{+1}$ D	$\xrightarrow{+1}$	E

Type II. Identify the Missing Terms

Example 1. Find out the missing alphabetical term

ak, eo, is, ______, qa, ue

(A) Iv (B) mw (C) mv (D) Iw

Solution. (B) There is a gap of three letters between the first letters of each group and also a gap of three letters between the second letters of each group. Hence the answer is mw.

Example 2. cx, fu, ir, ______, ol, ri

(A) Io (B) mn (C) no (D) op

Solution. (A) Two letters are left between the first letters of each group and two letters are also left in reverse order between the second letters of each group. Therefore, the correct answer is Io.

GRAPHICAL MISSING NUMBER

Directions. *In the given examples one number is missing marked by question mark. Find the missing number.*

Example 1.

9	5	6
5	7	?
3	4	5
135	140	150

(A) 8 (B) 10 (C) 5 (D) 4

Solution. (C) In each column, the product of first three numbers is equal to the fourth number.

In first column, $9 \times 5 \times 3 = 135$

In second column, $5 \times 7 \times 4 = 140$

Hence, in third column, $6 \times ? \times 5 = 150$

or $? = \frac{150}{6 \times 5} = 5$

Example 2.

1	7	9
2	14	?
3	105	117

(A) 12 (B) 26 (C) 16 (D) 20

Solution. (A) In each column, the third number divided by the first number and subtracted by 1 is equal to the second number.

Therefore, $(117 \div 9) - 1 = 12$.

Example 3.

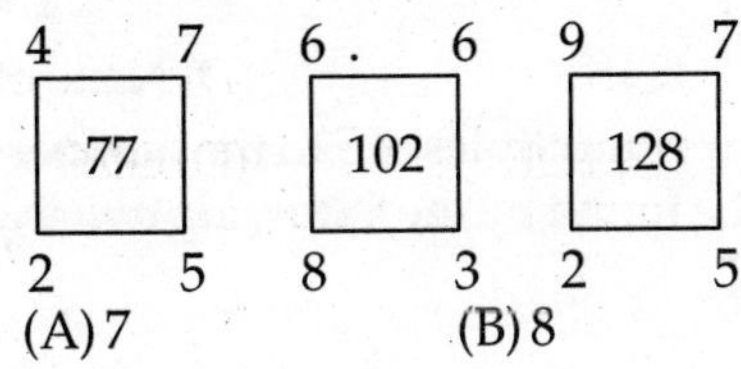

(A) 7 (B) 8 (C) 6 (D) 9

Solution. (B) In the above each square, the number of left bottom, right bottom and left top is added. After that product is then multiplied by number on right top to get number in the centre.

For first square $2 + 5 + 4 = 11$ and $11 \times 7 = 77$

For second square $8 + 3 + 6 = 17$ and $17 \times 6 = 102$

For third square $2 + 5 + 9 = 16$

So in order to get 128, it must be multiplied by 8. So correct option is (B).

ALPHABET TEST

There are 26 alphabets in the English alphabetical series. If the alphabets are asked to be counted from the left side, we start counting from the letter A, and when asked to count from right we count from Z.

Direction of alphabets in the series

A B C D E F G H I J K L M N O P Q R S T U V W X Y Z

Hence, if any alphabet is asked from left then we start from A. For example, 7th letter from left is G and 13th letter is M.

Similarly, when any letter is asked from right, we start from Z. For example, 7th letter from right is T and 13th letter from right is N.

To quickly find the serial number of alphabets in the series from left, EJOTY formula is used.

E	→	J	→	O	→	T	→	Y
↓		↓		↓		↓		↓
5		10		15		20		25

Thus, in the series from left E occupies 5th position, J occupies 10th position, O → 15th, T → 20th and Y occupies 25th position. Thus serial number of alphabets between these alphabets can be found easily.

To find the serial number of alphabets in the series from right BGLQV formula is used.

B	←	G	←	L	←	Q	←	V
↓		↓		↓		↓		↓
25		20		15		10		5

Thus, in the series from right V occupies 5th position, Q → 10th, L → 15th, G → 20th and B occupies 25th position.

TYPES OF QUESTIONS ASKED IN EXAMINATIONS

Questions Based on Number in Letter Management

Example 1. Which is the 8th letter from your left ?

(A) H (B) I (C) S (D) None of these

Solution. (A) According to the EJOTY formula nearest multiples of 5 to the number 8 are 5 and 10. Therefore 8th letter from the left can be found by the following two ways –

(1) $5 + \boxed{3} \Rightarrow 8, E + \boxed{3} \Rightarrow 8, E + \overset{1}{F} + \overset{2}{G} + \boxed{\overset{3}{H} \Rightarrow 8}$

(2) $10 - \boxed{2} \Rightarrow 8, J - \boxed{2} \Rightarrow 8, J - \overset{1}{I} - \boxed{\overset{2}{H} \Rightarrow 8}$

Usually the first method is found to be more convenient.

Example 2. Which is the 18th letter from your right ?

(A) H (B) G (C) R (D) None of these

Solution. (D) According to the formula BGLQV, nearest number to 18 is 15 and 20. Thus, 18th letter from right can be found by the following two ways –

(1) $15 + \boxed{3} \Rightarrow 18, L + \boxed{3} \Rightarrow 18, L + \overset{1}{K} + \overset{2}{J} + \boxed{\overset{3}{I} \Rightarrow 18}$

(2) $20 - \boxed{2} \Rightarrow 18, G - \boxed{2} \Rightarrow 18, G - \overset{1}{H} - \boxed{\overset{2}{I} \Rightarrow 18}$

Usually the second method is found to be more convenient.

Second method.

Serial number of any alphabet from right can be found by other method. The number of alphabet which is to be found from right is subtracted from 27. The new number obtained is now counted by EJOTY method.

Example 3. Which is the 19th letter from your right ?

(A) I (B) H (C) S (D) None of these

Solution. (B) $27 - 19 \Rightarrow 8$

Thus, 8th letter from left $\Rightarrow$ H

By →	E	J	O	T	Y Method
	↓	↓	↓	↓	↓
	5	10	15	20	25

Miscellaneous Type

In this type of question method, it is asked that whether the number of alphabets between two letters in a word is same as the number of alphabets between these two letters in the series.

To solve these question quickly, the serial of number of the letters of the given word is written according to as that of the serial number in the alphabetical series.

Then the number of letters between the numbers in ascending or descending order is found.

Example 4. How many such pairs of letters are there in the word AMPLITUDE having same number of letters between them as in the alphabet ?

(A) 1 (B) 2 (C) 3 (D) None of these

Solution. (C)

1	13	16	12	9	20	21	4	5
A	M	P	L	I	T	U	D	E

Thus, there are such three pairs namely : I—E, T—U, D—E.

Example 5. If first four letters of the word AMMUNITION are written in reversed order and next four letters are again written in reversed order and the left letters are again written in reverse order then after this change which will be the 6th letter from your right ?

(A) I (B) U (C) N (D) None of these

Solution. (A) According to the given change, AMMUNITION can be written as –

UMMAITINNO

↑←——

Thus, 6th letter from right is I.

Example 6. Which word will come first in the dictionary from the following words?

Minority, Minnow, Ministry, Minus

(A) Minority (B) Minnow

(C) Ministry (D) Minus

Solution. (C) The series of words will be as follows :

Ministry/1, Minnow/2, Minority/3, Minus/4

CLASSIFICATION TEST

These type of questions are, as a rule, based on similarity between a number of items. Some objects or words or sets of alphabet are grouped together on the basis of some common characteristic between them. One of the items in the group is different from others on the basis of this particular characteristic and so it does not belong to the group and cannot be classified as a member of that group. This item is known as an odd item and the task of the examinees in this type of questions is to find the odd item out of a group of items. It is because of this reason that this test is called "Odd one out test".

Type I

Example 1. Find the odd one.

(A) Carpenter (B) Blacksmith (C) Goldsmith (D) Sailor

Solution. (D) Carpenter, blacksmith and goldsmith form a group because these three change the form of the object by applying their skill. However, a sailor does not belong to this group. Hence sailor is the answer

Example 2. Find the odd one out.

(A) Deer (B) Zebra (C) Jackal (D) Giraffe

Solution. (C) Except Jackal, all other animals are herbivorous. Jackal is a carnivorous animal.

Type II

In this type of questions, four groups of letters are given. Out of these, three are alike in one manner or other. Identify the odd one in the group.

Example 1. Find the odd one out.

(A) PQS (B) JKL (C) TUV (D) CDE

Solution. (A) Except option (A) all others are of the same group.

Example 2. Find the odd one out.

(A) MNOP (B) LKJI (C) HGFE (D) DCBA

Solution. (A) Except option (A) all groups of letters are arranged in backward order according to the sequence of English alphabet.

Type III

In this type of questions, four numbers are given in which three are alike, while one is different. Hence the odd number is the answer.

Example 1. Three of the following numbers are alike in a certain way and so form a group. Which of the following does not belong to that group ?

(A) 83 (B) 63 (C) 21 (D) 39

Solution. (A) Except option (A) all others are divisible by 3.

Example 2. Find the odd one out ?

(A) 427 (B) 473 (C) 671 (D) 385

Solution. (A) Except option (A) in all other options the middle digit is the sum of the other two. Or, Except option (A) in all other options the sum of three digits is an even number.

Type IV

In this type of questions, some pair of words are given. Out of these, all pairs except one bear certain relationship. Therefore candidates are asked to decipher this relation and choose the pair in which the words are differently related. Thus, the odd one is the answer.

Example 1. (A) Mahavira : Jainism (B) Babar : Mughal
(C) Chandragupta : Maurya (D) Kanishka : Kushan

Solution. (A) Except option (A) in all other groups the first (name) is the founder of the second (dynasty)
or, Except option (A), no other group is related with religion.

Example 2. (A) Tongue : Taste (B) Eye : Blind
(C) Ear : Deaf (D) Leg : Lame

Solution. (A) In all other groups, the malfunction of the body parts make them to happen.

CODING AND DECODING TEST

Codes are secret messages, which have to be deciphered or decoded. In questions on code, artificial values are assigned to certain given words and the candidates are required to find out the code for another given word.

Coding is a method of transmitting a message between the sender and the receiver so that the third person will not know or understand the message. Decoding is just reverse of coding.

In other words, the letters of alphabet do not stand for themselves but for some other letters, *i.e.*, they have some other value. These artificial or code messages are given according to some set principle or pattern which can be easily found by the candidate. By applying the principle, the candidate can decode or code word messages.

TYPES OF QUESTIONS ASKED IN EXAMINATIONS

Type I. Letter Coding

(a) Letters vs Letters

In these questions, code values are assigned to a word in terms of the alphabet and the candidate is required to: (a) form a code for other word, (b) find the word by analysing the given code.

Example 1. If TAP is coded as SZO then, FREEZE is coded as

(A) EQDFYG (B) ESDFYE (C) GQFDYF (D) EQDDYD

Solution. (D)

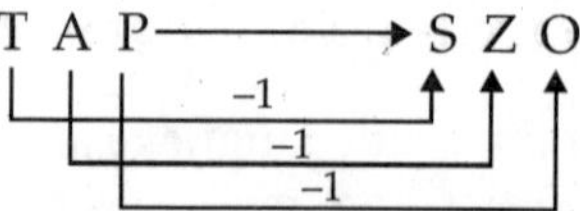

Similarly, FREEZE → EQDDYD

Example 2. If 'CERTAIN' is coded as 'XVIGZRM', how can 'MUNDANE' be coded ?

(A) VMZWMFN (B) MFMXZMV (C) NFMWZMV (D) NFMWZMX

Solution. (C) Here each letter of the coded word has the same position in the alphabet from the end, as the original letter has from the beginning.

∴ MUNDANE = NFMWZMV

(B) Letters vs. Numbers

In this type of questions a certain word is coded with that of a number. The candidate has to decode the word to the corresponding number and identify the right answer.

Example 1. If WOMAN is coded as 12345 and SERVANT is coded as 6789450. How will VOTERS be coded ?

(A) 920786 (B) 902876 (C) 978206 (D) 972086

Solution. (A) It can be seen that the letters have been assigned numbers in succession. On repetition, A and N have been assigned the same number again.

W	O	M	A	N		S	E	R	V	A	N	T
↓	↓	↓	↓	↓		↓	↓	↓	↓	↓	↓	↓
1	2	3	4	5	,	6	7	8	9	4	5	0

then

V	O	T	E	R	S
↓	↓	↓	↓	↓	↓
9	2	0	7	8	6

Example 2. If LINGER is 123456 and FORCE is 56789. Then FIERCE is

(A) 456678 (B) 345677 (C) 66789 (D) None of these

Solution. (D) Letters R and E are common to LINGER and FORCE and numbers 6 and 5 are common to their respective coding, but they are not in same place. So, we cannot conclude the real code value of every letter.

Type II. Number Coding

In this type of problems, either numerical values are assigned to a word or alphabetical code values are assigned to the numbers.

Example 1. If ARUL is coded as 52, then BINA will be coded as

(A) 40 (B) 42 (C) 26 (D) 30

Solution. (C) This is a more complicated one. The number of codes are not equal to the number of letters of the given word.

There are some kinds of manipulation with the positional value of the letters involved. We can get a code 52 by adding the alphabetical positional value of the letters involved in the word.

Since A is the first letter in the alphabet

∴ Write A = 1

Similarly, R = 18, U = 21, L = 12

Thus ARUL is coded as = 1 + 18 + 21 + 12 = 52

Similarly, BINA = 2 + 9 + 14 + 1 = 26

Type III. Statement Coding

In this type of questions, three or four messages are given in a code language and candidates are asked to decode such particular word. To decipher such codes, two messages having a common word are taken up. The common code will tell that word. Considering all the possible combinations of two, the entire message can be coded.

Example 1. In a certain code
(a) 'ADG' means 'boys are intelligent'. (b) 'GAM' means 'select intelligent boys'
(c) 'AGP' means 'encourage intelligent boys.'
Which letter code means "select" ?
(A) P (B) L (C) N (D) M

Solution (D) In (a) and (b) 'AG' and 'intelligent boys' are common
AG = intelligent boys ...(i)
Applying this in (b)
M = Select

Example 2. In a certain code (a) '274' means 'spread the carpet' (b) '246' means 'dust the carpet' and (c) '234' means 'roll the carpet'. Which digit in that code means 'roll' ?
(A) 3 (B) 6 (C) 5 (D) 2

Solution. (A) In (A) and (C), we find that 2 and 4 are common, both will coded for the words 'the carpet'.
Obviously the remaining number 3 in (C) means 'roll'

Type IV. Letter Form Codes

In this type of questions, two columns are given. Words given in capital letters in Column I are written in a code language in Column II with the help of small letters. These are not arranged in the code word in the same order as the letters in the original word for which they stand. Study the columns carefully and find out the code standing for the original word.

(a) *There are two columns, in the left hand side column capital letters are given. In the right hand column small letters, which are codes of the capital letters, are given in a jumbled form. You are required to pick out the code letters for the underlined capital letters.*

Example 1.

Column I				Column II			
C	<u>A</u>	M	E	*n*	*b*	*f*	*d*
F	A	I	<u>N</u>	*b*	*j*	*g*	*o*
B	O	<u>O</u>	N	*p*	*c*	*p*	*o*
O	<u>U</u>	S	T	*v*	*t*	*u*	*p*
D	O	U	<u>B</u>	*c*	*e*	*p*	*v*

Solution. For this type of questions, you have to follow two-fold strategy
(i) see the frequency of a particular letter,
(ii) compare one with another word.
As the word 'BOON' consists of two 'O' and code for 'BOON' is '*pcpo*', where '*p*' is repeated twice. So one can easily say, '*p*' is the code for 'O'.
Now, compare 'CAME' and 'FAIN', both words have a common letter 'A' and both codes have a common letter '*b*'. Therefore, '*b*' is the code for 'A'.
In words 'OUST' and 'DOUB', there are two common letters, 'O' and 'U', and two code letters, '*v*' and '*p*'. But, we know that '*p*' stands for 'O'. Therefore, '*v*' is the code for 'U'.

In word 'DOUB', the letter 'D' does not appear in any other given word, and code - letter '*e*' also appears once. Thus, '*e*' stands for 'D'. Now, in word DOUB — '*e*' stands for D, '*p*' stands for 'O'. '*v*' stands for 'U'. So, the remaining letter, *i.e.*, '*c*' will be coded for 'B'.

In word 'BOON', 'B' is coded as '*c*', 'O' is coded as '*p*'. Thus, 'N' will be coded as '*o*'.

Hence, the codes are, '*b*' for A, '*o*' for N, '*p*' for 'O', '*v*' for 'U' and '*c*' for 'B'.

(b) *Sometimes, the codes are jumbled up in themselves and in their order, i.e., jumbled up in horizontal and vertical order.*

Example 2. Below in Column I are given some words and in Column II are given their equivalents in some code language. Words in column II do not appear in the same order as in Column I. Moreover, the order of letters is also jumbled up. Decode the language and choose the correct alternative which is the equivalent of the underlined capital letters.

Column I	Column II
P O U C H	*m f j*
P A I N	*b q f*
P E A	*j b q o*
L I E	*q d i p v*

Solution. In this type of questions, we put the codes in order first. The number of letters in the original word and its code shall be the same. So, some will be arranged in this manner. As in the given problem, the code for 'POUCH' is '*qdipv*' and the code for 'PAIN' is '*jbqo*'. Problem arises with regard to the words having equal number of letters. That, we can work out by finding a common letter and common code between equal - numbered letters and words whose codes have been put in order. After arranging the words vertically, we adopt the above given method for working out codes horizontally. In this given example, 'PEA' and 'LIE' are three lettered words. PEA has 'P', in common with 'PAIN'. So, in such codes two codes should be common. Therefore, code for PEA is '*bqf*' and other three lettered code is for 'LIE'. Now, we are in position to rearrange codes given in the Column II.

Column I	Column II
P O U C H	*q d i p v*
P A I N	*j b q o*
P E A	*b q f*
L I E	*m f i*

In words 'POUCH' and 'PAIN', common letter is 'P' and common code is '*q*'. Therefore, '*q*' stands for 'P'.

In words 'PEA' and 'LIE', common letter is 'E' and common code is '*f*'. Therefore, '*f*' stands for 'E'.

In words 'PAIN' and 'LIE', common letter is 'I' and common code is '*j*'. Thus '*j*' is the code for 'I'.

In word LIE, we know the code for 'I' and 'E', so, '*m*' will be the code for 'L'.

DIRECTION SENSE TEST

The purpose of this type of test is to ascertain the sense of direction of the candidate. The candidate is required to use his sense about the direction and answer the questions correctly.

Sketch of the Direction

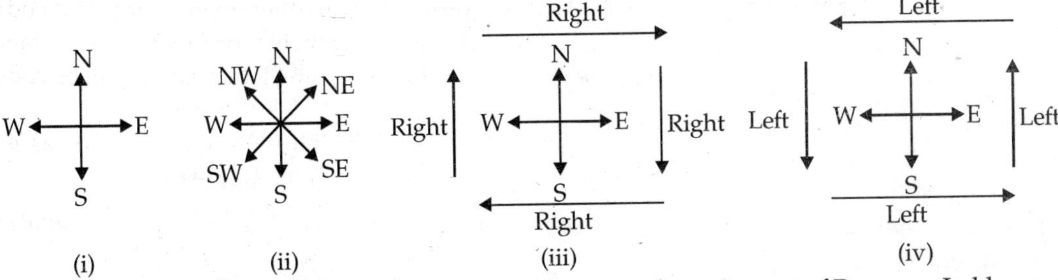

Example 1. Rampur is on the west of Kasauli. Bharatpur is on the east of Rampur. Lakhanpur is on the west of Kasauli. Bharatpur is on the east of Chandpur. If Lakhanpur is on the west of Rampur, in which direction from Bharatpur is Lakhanpur ?

(A) EAST (B) WEST (C) NORTH (D) SOUTH

Solution. (B) The position of various towns is as follows.

Lakhanpur ↔ Rampur ↔ Kasuali↔ Chandpur ↔ Bharatpur

Lakhanpur is to the west of Bharatpur. Hence (B) is correct

Example 2. After starting from a point, Paul walks 3 km towards East, then turning to his left he moves 3 km. After this he again turns left and moves 3 km. Which choice given below indicates the correct direction in which he is from his starting point ?

(A) NORTH (B) EAST (C) WEST (D) SOUTH

Solution. (A)

D ← 3 Km — C

3 Km ↑

A → 3 Km — B

N, W, E, S

BLOOD RELATION TEST

In this type of test, the success of a candidate depends upon the knowledge of the blood relations, some of which are summarized below to help solve these type of questions.

1.	Father's sister	– Aunt
2.	Son of mother or father	– Brother
3.	Daughter of mother or father	– Sister
4.	Son of brother	– Nephew
5.	Daughter of brother	– Niece
6.	Brother of father	– Uncle
7.	Son of father's brother/sister	– Cousin
8.	Son of mother's brother/sister	– Cousin
9.	The only son of grand father/mother	– Father
10.	The only daughter of maternal grand father/mother	– Mother
11.	Father of father	– Grand father
12.	Father of mother	– Maternal grand father
13.	Mother of father	– Grand mother
14.	Mother of mother	– Maternal grand mother
15.	Brother of mother	– Maternal uncle
16.	Sister of mother	– Maternal aunt
17.	Son of maternal grand father	– Maternal uncle

18.	Wife of mother's brother	– Maternal aunt
19.	Wife of maternal grand father's son	– Maternal aunt
20.	Father of wife	– Father-in-law
21.	Mother of wife	– Mother-in-law
22.	Wife of brother	– Sister-in-law
23.	Husband of sister	– Brother-in-law
24.	Sister of wife	– Sister-in-law
25.	Brother of wife	– Brother-in-law
26.	Husband of daughter	– Son-in-law
27.	Wife of son	– Daughter-in-law
28.	The only daughter of father-in-law or mother-in-law	– Wife
29.	Husband of daughter-in-law	– Son
30.	Only daughter-in-law of father	– Wife
31.	Only daughter-in-law of grand father	– Mother
32.	Daughter of son or daughter-in-law	– Grand daughter
33.	Son of son or daughter-in-law	– Grand son
34.	Daughter of daughter-in-law or son-in-law	– Grand daughter
35.	Son of daughter-in-law or son-in-law	– Grand son
36.	Son of sister or brother-in-law	– Nephew
37.	Daughter of sister or brother-in-law	– Niece

Example 1. If X is the brother of the son of Y's son, how is X related to Y?

(A) Son (B) Brother (C) Cousin (D) Grand Son

Solution. (D)

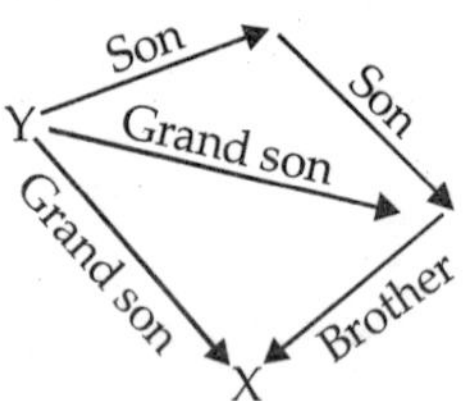

From the above sketch, we can say that X is the grand son of Y.

Example 2. Pointing to a gentleman, Deepak said, "His only brother is the father of my daughter's father". How is gentleman related to Deepak?

(A) Father (B) Brother-in-law (C) Uncle (D) None of these

Solution. (C)

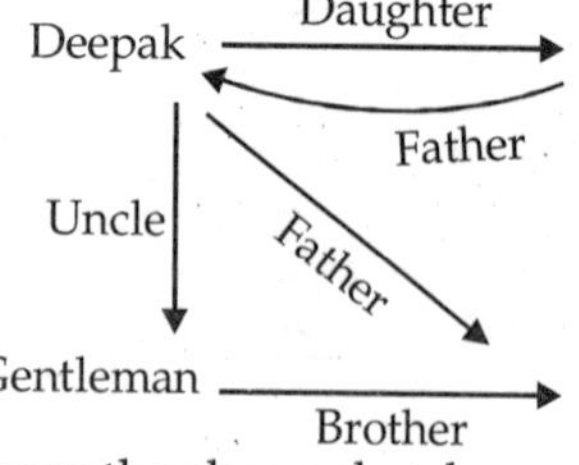

From the above sketch, we can say that gentleman is the uncle of Deepak.

Example 3. If A + B means A is the brother of B, A ÷ B means A is the father of B and A × B means A is the sister of B, which of the following means M is the uncle of P ?

(A) $N \times P \div M$ (B) $M + S \div R \div P$ (C) $M \div N \times P$ (D) $M + K \div T \times P$

Solution. (D) From the option (A),

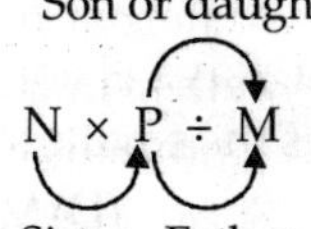

From the option (B),

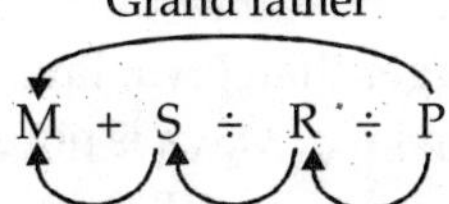

From the option (C),

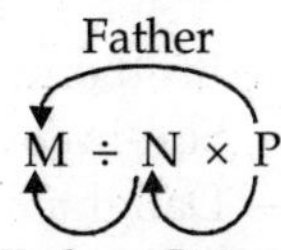

From the option (D),

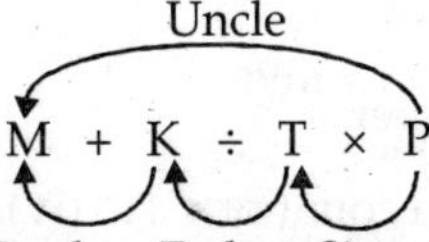

After seeing the above sketches, we can say that option (D) is correct.

ARRANGING IN ORDER TEST

If many people are sitting in circular path and all of them are facing towards the centre of that circle, then their positions from left to right and vice-versa are as given below :

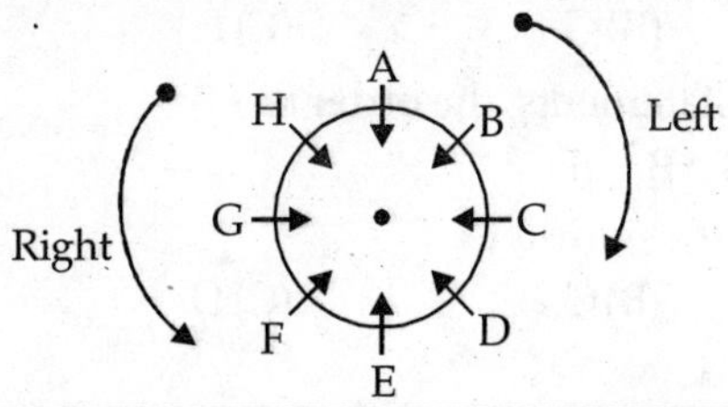

* B is to the left of A.	* F is to the left of E.
* C is to the left of B.	* G is to the left of F.
* D is to the left of C.	* H is to the left of G.
* E is to the left of D.	* A is to the left of H.
* A is to the right of B.	* E is to the right of F.
* B is to the right of C.	* F is to the right of G.
* C is to the right of D.	* G is to the right of H.
* D is to the right of E.	* H is to the right of A.

If many people are sitting in a row, then their positions from left to right and vice-versa are as given below :

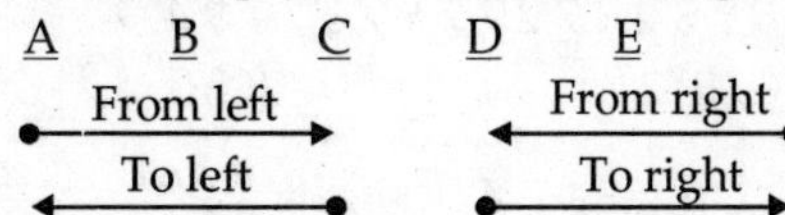

If it is given that Ranjana is taller than Bibhuti, then it will be written as Ranjana > Bibhuti

If it is given that Shyama is smaller than Archana, then it will be written as Shyama < Archana or Archana > Shyama.

Example 1. In a group of five persons A, B, C, D and E, there is one tennis player, one chess player and one badminton player. A and B are unmarried ladies and do not play any game. There is a couple in the group of which E is husband. None of the ladies play chess or badminton. E is the brother of C and is neither a tennis player nor a chess player. Who is the badminton player ?

(A) A (B) C (C) E (D) B

Solution (C). C, D and E are players. Since E does not play tennis or chess, E is the badminton player.

Example 2. Pava is bigger than Java. Java is bigger than Mava. Rava is not as big as Sava but is bigger than Java. Mava is not as big as Java. Who is the smallest?

(A) Java (B) Pava (C) Rava (D) Mava

Solution (D). Pava > Java ... (i)

Java > Mava ...(ii)

Sava > Rava > Java ...(iii)

Java > Mava ...(iv)

Then, from equation (i) to (iv),

Sava > Rava > Java > Mava

From the above situation, we can say that Mava is the smallest of all.

Directions. *Seven children A, B, C, D, E, F and G are standing in a line. G is to the right of D and to the left of B. A is to the right of C. A and D have one child between them. E and B have two children between them. D and F have two children between them.*

Example 3. Who is on the extreme right ?

(A) B (B) G (C) F (D) E

Solution (C). According to the statements, the order is

C A E D G B F

Example 4. Who is exactly in the middle?

(A) A (B) C (C) D (D) E

Solution (C).

Example 5. Who is on the extreme left?

(A) D (B) A (C) B (D) C

Solution (D).

LETTER-DIGIT TERM TEST

In this type of test, generally you are given a long series of digits or letters. The candidate is required to find out how may times a certain digit or letter satisfying the given conditions occurs.

Example 1. How many 7's are there in the following series which are not immediately followed by 3 but immediately preceded by 8 ?

8 9 8 7 6 2 2 6 3 2 6 9 7 3 2 8 7 2 7 7 8 7 3 7 7 9 4

(A) 3 (B) 2 (C) 0 (D) None of these

Solution. (B) According to the question, $8 \xleftarrow{\checkmark} \boxed{7} \xrightarrow{\times} 3$

There are two 7's in the given series satisfying the given conditions.

Example 2. How many C's are there in the following series which are immediately followed by even placing number of letters and immediately preceded by odd placing number of letters?

A P C R T U C R Q C P N Q R Q C T C I N O C R

(A) One (B) Two (C) Three (D) None of these

Solution. (D) Odd placing number of letters ← Immediately Preceded ✓ [C] Immediately followed ✓ → Even placing number of letters

There are four C's in the given series satisfying the given conditions.

TIME AND CALENDAR TEST

Type I. Time Sequence

This type of test is meant to test the candidate's ability about correct sequence of days of the week, calendar months, time etc.

There are two types of questions under this.

(i) The value of time or digit is found from the statements of two people.
The common value in the two statements is taken as correct.

(ii) Under this head, questions based on time are asked. The following shortened formula is used for this.
Time of information given = (Next departure time – Interval between two consecutive departures) + previous departure time.

Example 1. Sanjeev remembers that his father's birthday falls after 9th May and before 12th May, while his sister Asha remembers that her father's birthday falls after 10th May and before 13th May. What is the date of birthday of their father ?

(A) 9th May (B) 10th May (C) 11th May (D) 12th May

Solution. (C) According to Sanjeev, his father's birthday = May (10 and 11)
But according to Asha her father's birthday = May (11 and 12)
But 11th May is common to both.
Hence their father's birthday is 11th May.

Example 2. The officer said to Anurag. "A train for Surat leaves after every 1.15 hours. A train has left 35 minutes ago. The next train will leave at 5.40." At what time this information was given to Anurag by the Officer ?

(A) 4.24 (B) 5.00 (C) 4.45 (D) 5.15

Solution. (B) Time of information given = (5.40 – 1.15) + 0.35 = 4.25 + 0.35 = 5.00.

Type II. Calendar

Under this grouping we mainly deal with finding the day of the week on a particular given date. The process of finding it lies on obtaining the number of odd days.

I. Odd Days. Number of days more than the complete number of weeks in a given period is the number of odd days during that period.

II. Leap Year. Every year which is divisible by 4 is called a leap year. Thus, each one of the years 1992, 1996, 2004, 2008, 2012, etc. is a leap year.
Every 4th century is a leap year but no other century is a leap year. Thus, each one of 400, 800, 1200, 1600, 2000 etc. is a leap year.
None of 1700, 1800, 1900, 2100 etc. is a leap year.
A year which is not a leap year is called an ordinary year.

III. (i) An ordinary year has 365 days.
(ii) A leap year has 366 days.

IV. Counting of odd days :
(i) 1 ordinary year = 365 days = (52 weeks + 1 day)
∴ An ordinary year has 1 odd day.

(ii) 1 leap year = 366 days = (52 weeks + 2 days)

∴ A leap year has 2 odd days.

(iii) 100 years = 76 ordinary years + 24 leap years

$= 76 \times 1 + 24 \times 2 = 76 + 48 = 124$ days = (17 weeks + 5 days)

∴ 100 years contain 5 odd days.

200 years contain 10 and therefore 3 odd days.

300 years contain 15 and therefore 1 odd day.

400 years contain (20 + 1) and therefore 0 odd day.

Similarly, each one of 800, 1200, 1600, 2000 etc. contains 0 odd days.

V. Counting of Days.

We have : Sunday for 0 odd day; Monday for 1 odd day;
Tuesday of 2 odd days and so on.

Example 1. On which of the following dates of October, 1994 did Monday fall ?

(A) 4th, 11th, 18th, 25th
(B) 3rd, 10th, 17th, 24th, 31th
(C) 5th, 12th, 19th, 26th
(D) None of these

Solution. 1600 years contain 0 odd day.

300 years contain 1 odd day.

93 years = (23 leap years + 70 ordinary years)

= (46 + 70) odd days = 116 odd days = 16×7 (+4) = 4 odd days.

Days from 1st Jan, 1994 to 1st Oct, 1994

Jan	Feb	March	April	May	June	July	Aug	Sept	Oct
31 +	28 +	31 +	30 +	31 +	30 +	31 +	31 +	30 +	1

= 274 days = 39 weeks + 1 day = 1 odd day.

∴ Total number of odd days = (0 + 1 + 4 + 1) = 6

∴ 1st Oct, 1994 was 'Saturday'

∴ Monday fell on 3rd October, 1994.

During October 1994, Monday fell on 3rd, 10th, 17th, 24th and 31st.

Example 2. Could the calendar for 1995 serve for 2006 ?

(A) Yes (B) No (C) Can not be determined (D) None of these

Solution. In order that the calendar for 1995 and 2006 be the same, 1st January of both the years must be on the same day of the week. For this, the total number of odd days between 31st Dec, 1994 and 31st Dec, 2005 must be zero.

We know that an ordinary year has 1 odd day and a leap year has 2 odd days. During this period there are 3 leap years, namely 1996, 2000 and 2004 and 8 ordinary years.

∴ Total number of odd days during this period = (6 + 8) = 14 = 0

i.e., 0 odd day.

Hence, the calendar for 1995 will serve for 2006.

Example 3. If the day after tomorrow be Friday, what day would have been on yesterday?

(A) Sunday (B) Tuesday (C) Saturday (D) None of these

Solution. Since, the day after tomorrow is Friday, therefore, today is Wednesday and yesterday was Tuesday.

Example 4. Identify what was the day of the week on 12th January, 1979 ?

(A) Monday (B) Tuesday (C) Friday (D) Saturday

Solution. Number of odd days in (1600 + 300) years = (0 + 1) = 1

78 years = (19 leap years + 59 ordinary years)

= (38 + 59) odd days = 97 odd days = 13×7 (+6) = 6 odd days.

12 days of January have 5 odd days.

$\therefore$ Total number of odd days = (1 + 6 + 5) = 5 odd days.

$\therefore$ The required day was 'Friday.'

CLOCK RELATED TEST

Basic Concepts

The face or dial of a watch is a circle whose circumference is divided into 60 equal parts, called minute spaces.

A clock has two hands, the smaller one is called the hour hand or short hand while the larger one is called the minute hand or long hand.

(i) In 60 minutes, the minute hand gains 55 minutes on the hour hand.

(ii) In every hour, both the hands coincide once.

(iii) In every hour the hands are once in opposite direction.

(iv) In every hour the hands are twice at right angles.

(v) The hands are in the same straight line when they are coincident or opposite to each other.

(vi) When the two hands are at right angles, they are 15 minute spaces apart.

(vii) When the hands are in opposite directions, they are 30 minute spaces apart.

(viii) The minute hand moves through 6° in each minute while the hour hand moves through 1/2° in each minute.

(ix) The hands coincide 11 times in every 12 hours.

(x) The hands are 22 times at right angles in every 12 hours.

(xi) Interchangeable positions occur when the interval between the hour hand and minute hand is 60/13 minute divisions or some multiple of this.

Too Fast and Too slow. If a watch or a clock indicates 6:15, when the correct time is 6, it is said to be 15 minutes too fast.

On the other hand, if it indicates 5:45, when the correct time is 6, it is said to be 15 minutes too slow.

Example 1. A clock is set right at 8 a.m. The clock gains 10 minutes in 24 hours. What will be the right time when the clock indicates 1 p.m. on the following day ?

(A) 46 min. past 12 (B) 47 min. past 12

(C) 48 min. past 12 (D) 49 min. past 12

Solution. Time from 8 a.m. on a day to 1 p.m. on the following day = 29 hours.

24 hours 10 min. of this clock = 24 hours of the correct clock

$$\frac{145}{6} \text{ hrs of this clock} = 24 \text{ hrs of the correct clock}$$

$$29 \text{ hrs of this clock} = \left(24 \times \frac{6}{145} \times 29\right) \text{ hrs of the correct clock}$$

$$= 28 \text{ hrs } 48 \text{ min. of correct clock}$$

$\therefore$ The correct time is 28 hrs 48 min. after 8 a.m.

This is 48 min. past 12.

Example 2. At what time between 4 and 5 o'clock will the hands of a clock be at right angle ?

(A) $38\frac{2}{11}$ min. past 4 (B) $39\frac{2}{11}$ min. past 4

(C) $38\frac{3}{11}$ min. past 4 (D) $49\frac{3}{11}$ min. past 4

Solution. At 4 o'clock, the minute hand will be 20 min. spaces behind the hour hand.

Now, when the two hands are at right angles, they are 15 min. spaces apart.
So, they are at right angles in following two cases :

Case I. When minute hand is 15 min spaces behind the hour hand :
In this case minute hand will have to gain (20 – 15) = 5 minute spaces.
55 minute spaces are gained by it in 60 min.

5 minute spaces will be gained by it in $\left(\frac{60}{55}\times 5\right)$ min. $= 5\frac{5}{11}$ min.

$\therefore$ They are at right angles at $5\frac{5}{11}$ min. past 4.

Case II. When the minute hand is 15 min. spaces ahead of the hour hand :
To be in this position, the minute hand will have to gain (20 + 15) = 35 minute spaces.
55 minute spaces are gained in 60 min.

35 minute spaces are gained in $\left(\frac{60}{55}\times 35\right)$ min. $= \frac{420}{11}$ min. $= 38\frac{2}{11}$ min.

$\therefore$ They are at right angles at $38\frac{2}{11}$ min. past 4.

Example 3. A clock is set right at 5 a.m. The clock loses 16 minutes in 24 hours. What will be the true time when the clock indicates 10 p.m. on 4th day ?

(A) 9 P.M. (B) 9 A.M. (C) 11 P.M. (D) 11 A.M.

Solution. Time from 5 a.m. on a day to 10 p.m. on 4th day = 89 hours.
Now 23 hrs 44 minute of this clock = 24 hours of correct clock.

89 hrs of this clock $= \left(24\times\frac{15}{356}\times 89\right)$ hrs of correct clock.

= 90 hrs of correct clock.

So, the correct time is 11 p.m.

Example 4. Find at what time between 8 and 9 o'clock will the hands of a clock be in the same straight line but not together.

(A) $10\frac{10}{11}$ min. past 8 (B) $10\frac{11}{12}$ min. past 8

(C) $10\frac{12}{13}$ min. past 8 (D) $10\frac{12}{15}$ min. past 8

Solution. At 8 o'clock, the hour hand is at 8 and the minute hand is at 12, i.e. the two hands are 20 minute spaces apart.
To be in the same straight line but not together they will be 30 minute spaces apart.
So, the minute hand will have to gain (30 – 20) = 10 minute space over the hour hand.
55 minute spaces are gained in 60 min.

10 minute spaces will be gained in $\left(\frac{60}{55}\times 10\right)$ min $= 10\frac{10}{11}$ min.

$\therefore$ The hands will be in the same straight line but not together at $10\frac{10}{11}$ min. past 8.

Example 5. Find the angle between the minute hand and hour hand of a clock when the time is 7.20.

(A) 110° (B) 105° (C) 102° (D) 100°

Solution. Angle traced by the hour hand in 12 hours = 360°

Angle traced by it in 7 hrs 20 min *i.e.* $\frac{22}{3}$ hrs = $\left(\frac{360}{12} \times \frac{22}{3}\right)^{\circ}$ = 220°

Angle traced by minute hand in 60 min = 360°

Angle traced by it in 20 min = $\left(\frac{360}{60} \times 20\right)$ = 120°

∴ Required angle = (220° – 120°) = 100°

Example 6. At what time are the hands of a clock together between 5 and 6 ?

(A) $28\frac{3}{11}$ min. past 5 (B) $33\frac{3}{11}$ min. past 5

(C) 30 min. past 5 (D) $27\frac{3}{11}$ min. past 5

Solution. (D) At 5 o'clock the hands are 25 minutes apart. Therefore in order to coincide, the long hand must gain 25 minutes.

As 55 minutes are gained by minute hand in 60 min.

∴ 25 minutes are gained by minute hand in 60 minutes = $\frac{60 \times 25}{55} = \frac{300}{11}$

$= 27\frac{3}{11}$ minutes

Hence the hands will coincide at $27\frac{3}{11}$ minutes past 5.

NUMBER RELATED TEST

In this type of test a series of numbers is given. The candidate has to find out the number of times the given digit occurs under certain conditions.

Example 1. How many numbers are there from 3 to 100 which are divisible by 4 and either unit digit or tenth digit or both include 4.

(A) 10 (B) 11 (C) 19 (D) less than 10

Solution. (D) The numbers from 3 to 100 which are divisible by 4 and include 4 at any place are <u>4</u>, 8, 12, 16, 20, <u>24</u>, 28, 32, 36, <u>40</u>, <u>44</u>, <u>48</u>, 52, 56, 60, <u>64</u>, 68, 72, 76, 80, <u>84</u>, 88, 92, 96, 100

Thus required numbers are 7 among above numbers.

Example 2. If 69 × 87 = 1515 then 76 × 68 = ?

(A) 1415 (B) 1218 (C) 1314 (D) 1319

Solution. (C) As, 69 × 87 = 1515

6 + 9 = 15

8 + 7 = 15

Similarly, 7 6 × 6 8 = 1314

↓ ↓ ↓ ↓

7 + 6 = 13 6 + 8 = 14

MATHEMATICAL OPERATION TEST

In this type of test, artificial signs are given to the actual signs (mathematical) +, –, × and ÷ in the questions. The candidates should first of all convert these artificial signs into actual signs and then simplify according to the rule of BODMAS.

Example 1. If '×' stands for 'addition', '÷' stands for 'subtraction', '+' stands for 'multiplication' and '–' stands for 'division', then

$$20 \times 8 \div 8 - 4 + 2 = ?$$

(A) 80 (B) 25 (C) 24 (D) 5

Solution. (C) $20 \times 8 \div 8 - 4 + 2$

To change the above signs into actual signs

$20 + 8 - 8 \div 4 \times 2 = 20 + 8 - 2 \times 2 = 20 + 8 - 4 = 24$

MATHEMATICAL ABILITY TEST

Type I. Fractions

If any unit be divided into any number of equal parts, one or more of these parts is called a fraction of the unit. The fractions one-fifth, two-fifths, three-fourths are written as $\frac{1}{5}, \frac{2}{5}$ and $\frac{3}{4}$ respectively.

The lower number, which indicates the number of equal parts into which the unit is divided, is called denominator.

The upper number, which indicates the number of parts taken to form the fraction, is called the numerator.

The numerator and the denominator of a fraction are called its terms.

Note:

1. A fraction is unity when its numerator and denominator are equal.
2. A fraction is equal to Zero when its numerator alone is Zero. The denominator of a fraction is always assured to be non-Zero.
3. A fraction is also called a rational number
4. The value of a fraction is not altered by multiplying or dividing the numerator and the denominator by the same number.

   Ex.: $\frac{2}{5} = \frac{2 \times 5}{5 \times 5} = \frac{2 \div 4}{5 \div 4}$

5. When the numerator and the denominator of a fraction have no common factor, the fraction is said to be in its lowest terms.

   Ex.: $\frac{15}{20} = \frac{3 \times 5}{4 \times 5}$

   The numerator and the denominator have a common factor 5, so $\frac{15}{20}$ is not in its lowest terms.

   If we cancel out 5 by dividing both the numerator and the denominator by 5, we get $\frac{3}{4}$, which has no common factor. Hence $\frac{3}{4}$ is the fraction $\frac{15}{20}$ in its lowest terms.

   When a fraction is reduced in its lowest terms, its numerator and denominator are prime to each other i.e., they have no common factor.

6. If the numerator and the denominator are large numbers, or if their common factors cannot be guessed easily, we may find their HCF. After dividing the terms by their HCF the faction is reduced to its lowest term

   Ex. $\frac{385056}{715104}$; HCF of 385056 and 715104 = 55008

   Now, $\frac{385056}{715104} = \frac{385056 \div 55008}{715104 \div 55008} = \frac{7}{13}$

   Here, $\frac{7}{13}$ is in its lowest term because the because terms have no common factor.

7. An integer can be expressed as a fraction with any denominator we want. For example: if we want to express 23 as fraction whose denominator is 17, the process will be as follows:

$$23 = \frac{23 \times 17}{17} = \frac{391}{17}$$

   For example: $\frac{3}{4}, \frac{17}{19}, \frac{21}{42}$ are proper fractions. The value of a proper fraction is always less than 1.

Improper Fraction

A fraction whose numerator is equal to or greater than the denominator is called an improper fraction.

For example: $\frac{17}{12}, \frac{17}{19}, \frac{18}{5}$ are improper fractions.

The value of an improper fraction is always more than or equal to 1. In the above examples,

$$\frac{17}{12} = 1\frac{5}{12}, \frac{12}{17} = 1\frac{5}{7}, \frac{18}{5} = 3\frac{3}{5},$$

Thus, we see that an improper fraction is made up of a whole number and a proper fraction. When an improper fraction is changed to consist of a whole number and a proper fraction, it is called a mixed number. In the above examples $1\frac{5}{12}, 1\frac{5}{7}$ and $3\frac{3}{5}$ are mixed numbers.

Fractions in which the denominators are powers of 10 are called decimal fractions e.g. $\frac{3}{10}, \frac{7}{10}, \frac{3}{100}, \frac{9}{100}$, etc.

Fractions in which the denominators are the same are called like factions.

For example: $\frac{13}{17}, \frac{19}{17}, \frac{8}{17}, \frac{20}{17}, \frac{1}{12}, \frac{5}{12}, \frac{17}{12}$ etc.

In this case, the fraction having the greatest numerator is the greatest.

So $\frac{20}{17} > \frac{19}{17} > \frac{13}{17} > \frac{8}{17}$ and $\frac{1}{12} < \frac{5}{12} < \frac{17}{12}$

Fractions in which the denominators are different are called unlike fractions.

For example: $\frac{13}{17}, \frac{15}{8}, \frac{379}{1000}$, etc.

Solved Examples

Example 1. Solve:

(A) $\frac{7}{9} - \frac{11}{12} + \frac{13}{16} - \frac{1}{8}$ (B) $3\frac{10}{11} + 5\frac{7}{15} - 2\frac{9}{22} - 4\frac{9}{10}$

(C) $3\frac{5}{9}\times 81\times\frac{17}{16}$ (D) $10\frac{5}{6}\div 91$

Solution. (A) LCM of 9, 12, 16, 8 = 144

$$\frac{7}{9}-\frac{11}{12}+\frac{13}{16}-\frac{1}{8}=\frac{16\times 7-11\times 12+13\times 9-18}{144}$$

$$=\frac{112-132+117-18}{144}=\frac{229-150}{144}=\frac{79}{144}$$

(B) $3\frac{10}{11}+5\frac{7}{15}-2\frac{9}{22}-4\frac{9}{10}$

$$=(3+5-2-4)+\left(\frac{10}{11}+\frac{7}{15}-\frac{9}{22}-\frac{9}{10}\right)$$

$$=2+\frac{300+154-135-297}{330}$$

$$=2+\frac{22}{330}=2+\frac{1}{15}=2\frac{1}{15}$$

(C) $3\frac{5}{9}\times 81\times\frac{17}{16}$

Change the mixed fraction into an improper fraction. Then the expression becomes:

$$\frac{32}{9}\times 81\times\frac{17}{16}=306$$

(D) $10\frac{5}{6}\div 91=\frac{65}{6}\div 91=\frac{65}{6}\times\frac{1}{91}=\frac{5}{42}$

Example 2. Simplify:

(A) $3\frac{21}{23}\div 3\frac{15}{31}$ (B) $9\frac{4}{9}\div 11\frac{1}{3}$

Solution. "To divide a fraction by a fraction, multiply the fraction by the reciprocal of the divisor."

(A) First change the mixed number into an improper fraction. Then multiply the fraction by the reciprocal of the divisor.

$$\frac{90}{23}\div\frac{108}{31}=\frac{90}{23}\times\frac{31}{108}=\frac{155}{138}=1\frac{17}{138}$$

(B) $9\frac{4}{9}\div 11\frac{1}{3}=\frac{85}{9}\times\frac{3}{34}=\frac{5}{6}$

Compound Fractions

A fraction of a fraction is called a compound fraction.

Thus, $\frac{1}{2}$ of $\frac{3}{7}$ is a compound fraction, And $\frac{1}{2}$ of $\frac{3}{7}=\frac{1}{2}\times\frac{3}{7}=\frac{3}{14}$

Combined Operations

In simplifying fractions involving various signs and brackets the following points should be remembered.

(i) The operations of multiplication and division should be performed before those of addition and subtraction.

(ii) Each of the sings × or ÷ should be applied only to the number which immediately follows it.

Ex. 1. $\frac{4}{5}\times\frac{7}{12}\div\frac{5}{24}=\frac{4}{5}\times\frac{7}{12}\times\frac{24}{5}=\frac{56}{25}$

Ex. 2. $\frac{4}{5}\div\frac{7}{12}\times\frac{5}{24}=\frac{4}{5}\times\frac{12}{7}\times\frac{5}{24}=\frac{2}{7}$

Ex. 3. $\frac{4}{5}\div\frac{7}{12}\times\frac{5}{24}=\frac{4}{5}\times\frac{12}{7}\times\frac{24}{5}=\frac{1152}{175}$

(iii) The operations within brackets are to be carried out first.

(iv) The rule of 'BODMAS' is applied for combined operations.

Complex Fractions

A complex fraction is one in which the numerator or denominator or both are fractions. For example.

$\dfrac{\frac{8}{7}}{8}, \dfrac{8}{\frac{5}{7}}, \dfrac{\frac{8}{9}}{\frac{7}{9}}, \dfrac{\frac{1}{2}+\frac{2}{3}}{\frac{3}{4}-\frac{2}{9}}$ are complex fractions.

Example. Simplify:

(A) $\dfrac{\frac{4}{15}}{\frac{2}{5}}$ (B) $\dfrac{\frac{1}{2}+\frac{2}{3}}{\frac{3}{4}-\frac{2}{9}}$

Solution. (A) $\dfrac{\frac{4}{15}}{\frac{2}{5}}=\frac{4}{15}\div\frac{2}{5}=\frac{4}{15}\times\frac{5}{2}=\frac{2}{3}$

(B) $\dfrac{\frac{1}{2}+\frac{2}{3}}{\frac{3}{4}-\frac{2}{9}}=\dfrac{\frac{3+4}{6}}{\frac{27-8}{36}}=\dfrac{\frac{7}{6}}{\frac{19}{36}}=\frac{7}{6}\times\frac{36}{19}=\frac{42}{19}=2\frac{4}{19}$

or, multiply the numerator and denominator by the LCM of the denominators 2, 3, 4, 9 namely 36.

Thus, $\dfrac{\frac{1}{2}+\frac{2}{3}}{\frac{3}{4}-\frac{2}{9}}=\dfrac{\frac{1}{2}\times36+\frac{2}{3}\times36}{\frac{3}{4}\times36-\frac{2}{9}\times36}=\dfrac{18+24}{27-8}=\frac{42}{19}=2\frac{1}{19}$

Continued Fractions

Fractions that contain an additional fraction in the (numerator of the) denominator are called continued fraction.

Fractions of the form (i) $4+\cfrac{1}{1+\cfrac{1}{5+\cfrac{2}{3}}}$ (ii) $\cfrac{1}{1-\cfrac{2}{5+\cfrac{2}{4-\cfrac{2}{5}}}}$ are called fractions.

Rule: To simplify a continued fraction, begin at the bottom and work upwards.

Example . Simplify : $\dfrac{1}{2+\dfrac{1}{3+\dfrac{1}{1+\dfrac{1}{4}}}}$

Solution. The fraction $= \dfrac{1}{2+\dfrac{1}{3+\dfrac{1}{\frac{5}{4}}}} = \dfrac{1}{2+\dfrac{1}{3+\frac{4}{5}}} = \dfrac{1}{2+\dfrac{1}{\frac{19}{5}}} = \dfrac{1}{2+\frac{5}{19}} = \dfrac{1}{\frac{43}{19}} = \dfrac{19}{43}$

Note: No shortcut method has been derived for solving these questions. But you can solve these questions more quickly by (i) more mental calculations; and (ii) skipping the steps.

Type II. Time and Distance

Formulae

(i) Distance = (Speed × Time)

(ii) Speed $= \left(\dfrac{\text{distance}}{\text{time}}\right)$, Time $= \left(\dfrac{\text{distance}}{\text{speed}}\right)$

(iii) 1 km/hour $= \dfrac{5}{18}$ m/sec.

(iv) 1 m/sec. $= \dfrac{18}{5}$ km/hr.

(v) If the ratio of the speeds of A and B is $a : b$, then the ratio of the times taken by them to cover the same distance is $\dfrac{1}{a} : \dfrac{1}{b}$ or $b : a$

(vi) Suppose a man covers a certain distance at x km/hr and an equal distance at y km/hr. Then the average speed during the whole journey is $\left(\dfrac{2xy}{x+y}\right)$ km/hr.

(vii) If a man travels for 't' minutes by car at x km/hr and for 't' minutes by train at y km/hr, the average speed of the whole distance is $\left(\dfrac{x+y}{2}\right)$ km per hour.

(viii) If a journey is travelled by three different modes of transport, each time same distance, with their speeds as x km/hr, y km/hr and z km/hr, then the average speed for the whole journey is

$$\left(\frac{3}{\frac{1}{x}+\frac{1}{y}+\frac{1}{z}}\right) \quad \text{or} \quad \left(\frac{3xyz}{xy+yz+zx}\right)\text{km/hr}$$

Solved Examples

Example 1. A thief is spotted by a watchman from a distance of 200 m. When the watchman starts the chase, the thief also starts running. If the speed of the thief be 10 km/hr and that of watchman 12 km/hr, how far the thief will have run before he is overtaken ?

(A) 1 km (B) 2 km (C) 3 km (D) 4 km

Solution. Relative speed of the watchman = 2 km/hr.

Time taken by watchman to cover 200m $= \left(\frac{200}{1000} \times \frac{1}{2}\right)$ hrs $= \frac{1}{10}$ hrs.

In $\frac{1}{10}$ hrs, the thief covers a distance of $\left(10 \times \frac{1}{10}\right)$ km = 1 km

Example 2. If a boy walks at the rate of 5 km/hr, he misses a train by only 7 minutes. However, if he walks at the rate of 6 km/hr, he reaches the station 5 minutes before the arrival of the train. Find the distance covered by him to reach the station.

(A) 2 km (B) 3 km (C) 4 km (D) 6 km

Solution. Let the required distance be x km.

Difference in the times taken at two speeds = 12 min. = $\frac{1}{5}$ hr.

$\therefore \frac{x}{5} - \frac{x}{6} = \frac{1}{5}$ or $6x - 5x = 6$ or $x = 6$ km

Hence, the required distance is 6 km.

Example 3. There are two towns A and B. Ajay goes from A to B at 40 km/hr and comes back to the starting point at 60 km/hr. What is his average speed during the whole journey ?

(A) 47 km/hr (B) 48 km/hr (C) 49 km/hr (D) 50 km/hr

Solution. Average Speed $= \left(\frac{2xy}{x+y}\right)$ km/hr $= \frac{(2 \times 40 \times 60)}{(40+60)}$ km/hr = 48 km/hr.

Example 4. A goods train leaves a station at a certain time and at a fixed speed. After 6 hours, an express train leaves the same station and moves in the same direction at a uniform speed of 90 km/hr. This train catches up the goods train in 4 hours. Find the speed of the goods train.

(A) 35 km/hr (B) 36 km/hr (C) 37 km/hr (D) 38 km/hr

Solution. Let the speed of the goods train be x km/hr

Distance covered by goods train in 10 hours

= Distance covered by the express train in 4 hours.

$\therefore 10x = 4 \times 90$ or $x = 36$

$\therefore$ Speed of goods train = 36 km/hr.

Type III. Profit and Loss

Cost price. The price at which an article is purchased, is called its cost price, abbreviated as C.P.

Selling price. The price at which an article is sold, is called its selling price, abbreviated as S.P.

Loss or gain is reckoned on C.P.

Some Important Formulae

(i) Gain = (S.P.) – (C.P.)

(ii) Gain % $= \left(\frac{\text{Gain} \times 100}{\text{C.P.}}\right)$

(iii) Loss = (C.P.) – (S.P.)

(iv) Loss % $= \left(\frac{\text{Loss} \times 100}{\text{C.P.}}\right)$

(v) S.P. $= \frac{(100 + \text{Gain }\%)}{100} \times$ C.P.

(vi) S.P. $= \frac{(100 - \text{Loss }\%)}{100} \times$ C.P.

(vii) C.P. $= \frac{100}{(100 + \text{Gain }\%)} \times$ S.P.

(viii) C.P. $= \frac{100}{(100 - \text{Loss }\%)} \times$ S.P.

(ix) If an article is sold at a gain of 35%, then S.P. = 135% of C.P.

(x) If an article is sold at a loss of 35%, then S.P. = 65% of C.P.

(xi) If x is the gain percent on C.P., then the gain percent on the S.P. = $\frac{x}{100+x} \times 100\%$

(xii) If x is the profit percent on the selling price, then the profit percent on the cost price is $\frac{x}{100-x} \times 100\%$

(xiii) If x is the loss percent on the S.P. then the loss on C.P. is $\frac{x}{100+x} \times 100\%$

(xiv) Cost price = $\frac{\text{More Profit}}{\text{Difference in percent profit}} \times 100$

Solved Examples

Example 1. Find S.P., when C.P. = Rs. 56.25, gain = 20%

(A) Rs. 67.50 (B) Rs. 68.50 (C) Rs. 69.50 (D) Rs. 70.50

Solution. S.P. = 120% of Rs. 56.25 = Rs. $\left(\frac{120}{100} \times 56.25\right)$ = Rs. 67.50.

Example 2. What is the C.P., when S.P. = Rs. 40.60, gain = 16%

(A) Rs. 33 (B) Rs. 34 (C) Rs. 35 (D) Rs. 36

Solution. Let C.P. be x.

Then, 116% of $x = 40.60 \Rightarrow \frac{116}{100}x = 40.60 \quad \therefore x = \left(\frac{40.60 \times 100}{116}\right) = 35.$

$\therefore$ C.P. = Rs. 35.

Example 3. Find the single discount equivalent to a series discount of 20%, 10% and 5%

(A) 30.6% (B) 31.6% (C) 32.6% (D) 33.6%

Solution. (Short cut Method) : Let marked price be Rs, 100

Then, Net S.P. = 80% of 90% of 95% of 100 = $\left(\frac{80}{100} \times \frac{90}{100} \times \frac{95}{100} \times 100\right) = 68.40$

$\therefore$ Required discount = (100 – 68.40)% = 31.6%

Example 4. A dealer allows a discount of 10% on the marked price. How much above cost price must he mark his goods to gain 8% ?

(A) 8% (B) 10% (C) 18% (D) 20%

Solution. Let C.P. = Rs. 100. Then, S.P. = Rs. 108.

Let, marked price be Rs. x.

90% of $x = 108 \Rightarrow x = \left(108 \times \frac{100}{90}\right) = 120$

Mark up = 120 – 100 = 20 *i.e.,* marked price should be 20% more than cost price.

Example 5. A reduction of 20% in the price of oil enables a purchaser to obtain 2.5 kg more for Rs. 160. Find the original rate and the reduced price per kg.

(A) Rs. 16, Rs. 12.50 (B) Rs. 12.50, Rs. 16

(C) Rs. 16, Rs. 12.80 (D) Rs. 12.80, Rs. 16

Solution. Let original rate Rs. x per kg.

New rate = 80% of x = Rs. $\left(\frac{80}{100}x\right)$ = Rs. $\frac{4x}{5}$

Original quantity for Rs. 160 = $\frac{160}{x}$

New quantity = $\left(160 \times \frac{5}{4x}\right) = \frac{200}{x}$

$\therefore \frac{200}{x} - \frac{160}{x} = 2.5$ or $\frac{40}{x} = 2.5$ or $x = \frac{40}{2.5} = 16$

$\therefore$ Original rate = Rs. 16 per kg.

Reduced rate = 80% of Rs. 16 = Rs. 12.80 per kg.

Example 6. After getting two successive discounts, a shirt with a list price of Rs. 150 is available at Rs. 105. If the second discount is 12.5%, find the first discount.

(A) 20% (B) 25% (C) 30% (D) 35%

Solution. Let the first discount be x%.

Then, 87.5% of $(100 - x)$% of 150 = 105

or $\frac{87.5}{100} \times \frac{100-x}{100} \times 150 = 105$ or $100 - x = \left(\frac{105 \times 100 \times 100}{150 \times 87.5}\right) = 80$

$\therefore x = (100 - 80) = 20\%$

Type IV. Ratio & Proportion

Ratio. The ratio of two quantities in the same unit is a fraction that one quantity is of the other.

The ratio $a : b$ represents a fraction $\frac{a}{b}$.

The first term of a ratio is called antecedent while the second term is known as consequent.

Thus, the ratio 5 : 7 represents $\frac{5}{7}$ with antecedent 5 and consequent 7.

Rule. The multiplication or division of each term of a ratio by a same non-zero number does not effect the ratio.

Thus, $4 : 5 = 8 : 10 = 12 : 15 = 16 : 20 = \frac{4}{5} : 1$ etc.

Proportion. The equality of two ratios is called proportion.

If $a : b = c : d$, we write, $a : b :: c : d$ and we say that a, b, c, d are in proportion.

In a proportion, the first and fourth terms are known as **extremes,** while second and third terms are known as **means.**

We have, **Product of Means = Product of Extremes**

Fourth Proportional. If $a : b = c : d$, then d is called the fourth proportional to a, b, c.

Third Proportional. The third proportional to a, b is the fourth proportional to a, b, b.

Mean Proportional. Mean proportional between a and b is $\sqrt{ab}$

Comparison of Ratio. We say that $(a : b) > (c : d)$ if $\frac{a}{b} > \frac{c}{d}$

Compounded Ratio. The compounded ratio of the ratio $(a : b)$, $(c : d)$, $(e : f)$ is $(ace : bdf)$.

Some More Definitions :

(i) $a^2 : b^2$ is called the **duplicate ratio** of $a : b$

(ii) $\sqrt{a} : \sqrt{b}$ is called the **sub-duplicate ratio** of $a : b$

(iii) $a^3 : b^3$ is called the **triplicate ratio** of $a : b$

(iv) $a^{1/3} : b^{1/3}$ is called the **sub-triplicate ratio** of $a : b$.

(v) If $\frac{a}{b} = \frac{c}{d}$ then $\frac{a+b}{a-b} = \frac{c+d}{c-d}$ **(componendo & dividendo)**

Variation. We say that x is directly proportional to y if $x = ky$ for some constant k and we write, $x \propto y$.

Also, we say that x is **inversely proportional** to y,

if $x = \frac{k}{y}$ for some constant k and we write $x \propto \frac{1}{y}$.

Quick Method.

1. If the ratio between the first and the second quantities is $a : b$ and the ratio between the second and the third quantities is $c : d$, then the ratio among first, second and third quantities is given by $ac : bc : bd$

   The above ratio can be represented diagrammatically as

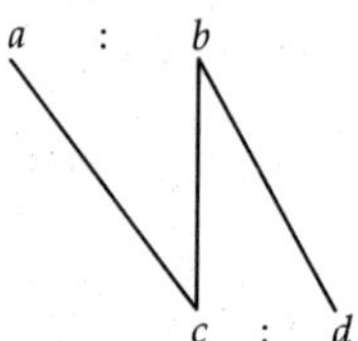

2. If the ratio between the first and the second quantities is $a : b$, the ratio between the second and the third quantities is $c : d$ and the ratio between the third and fourth quantities is $e : f$, then the ratio among the first, second, third and fourth quantities is given by

   1st : 2nd =

   2nd : 3rd =

   3rd : 4th =

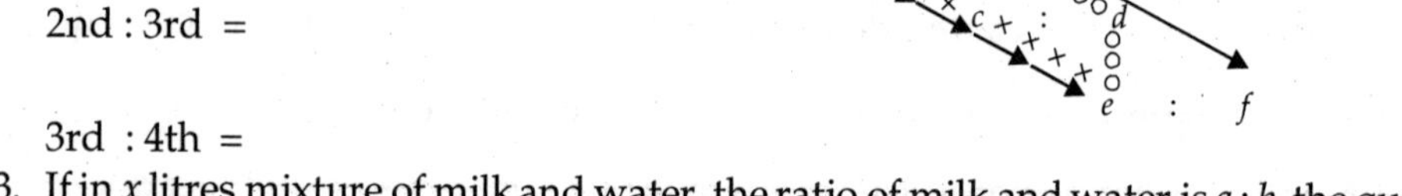

3. If in x litres mixture of milk and water, the ratio of milk and water is $a : b$, the quantity of water to be added in order to make this ratio $c : d$ is $\frac{x(ad-bc)}{c(a+b)}$.

4. A mixture contains milk and water in the ratio $a : b$. If x litres of water is added to the mixture, milk and water become in the ratio $a : c$. Then the quantity of milk in the mixture is given by $\frac{ax}{(c-b)}$ and that of water is given by $\frac{bx}{(c-b)}$.

5. If the ratio between two numbers is $a : b$. If each number be increased by x, the ratio becomes $c : d$. Then

   Sum of the two numbers $= \frac{x(a+b)(c-d)}{ad-bc}$

   Difference of the two numbers $= \frac{x(a-b)(c-d)}{ad-bc}$

   And the two numbers are given as $\frac{xa(c-d)}{ad-bc}$ and $\frac{xb(c-d)}{ad-bc}$.

Solved Examples

Example 1. A mixture contains milk and water in the ratio 4 : 3. If 5 litres of water is added to the mixture, the ratio becomes 4 : 5. Find the quantity of milk in the given mixture.

(A) 8 litres (B) 9 litres (C) 10 litres (D) 11 litres

Solution. Let the quantity of milk & water be $4x$ & $3x$ respectively.

Then $\frac{4x}{3x+5} = \frac{4}{5} \Rightarrow 20x = 12x + 20 \Rightarrow x = 2.5$

Milk in given mixture = $4x$ litres = 10 litres.

Example 2. A tin contains 50 paise, 25 paise and 10 paise coins in the ratio 5 : 9 : 4, amounting to Rs. 206. Find the number of coins of each type.

(A) 100, 150, 200
(B) 200, 360, 160
(C) 160, 360, 200
(D) 360, 160, 200

Solution. Ratio of values $= \frac{5}{2} : \frac{9}{4} : \frac{4}{10} = 50 : 45 : 8$

Value of 50 - paise coins = Rs. $\left(206 \times \frac{50}{103}\right)$ = Rs. 100

Value of 25-paise coins = Rs. $\left(206 \times \frac{45}{103}\right)$ = Rs. 90

Value of 10-paise coins = Rs. $\left(206 \times \frac{8}{103}\right)$ = Rs. 16

$\therefore$ Number of 50-paise coins = $(100 \times 2) = 200$
Number of 25-paise coins = $(90 \times 4) = 360$
Number of 10-paise coins = $(16 \times 10) = 160$

Type V. Partnership

Partnership. When two or more than two persons run a business jointly, they are called partners and the deal is known as partnership.

Ratio of Division of Gains :

(i) When investments of all the partners are for the same time, the gain or loss is distributed among the partners in the ratio of their investments.

(ii) When investments are for different time, then equivalent capitals are calculated for a unit of time by taking (capital x number of units of time). Now gain or loss is divided in the ratio of these capitals.

Working & Sleeping Partners: A partner who manages the business is known as a working partner and the one who simply invests the money is a sleeping partner.

Solved Examples

Example 1. Naresh started a business with Rs. 21000 and is joined afterwards by Ranjan with Rs. 36000. After how many months did Ranjan join, if the profits at the end of the year are divided equally ?

(A) 5 months
(B) 6 months
(C) 7 months
(D) 8 months

Solution. Suppose Ranjan joined after x months.

Then Ranjan's money was invested for $(12 - x)$ months

$\therefore 21000 \times 12 = 36000 \times (12 - x) \Rightarrow 7 = 12 - x \Rightarrow x = 5$

So, Ranjan joined after 5 months.

Example 2. Pramod started a business by investing Rs. 36000. After 3 months Roy joined him by investing Rs. 36000. Out of an annual profit of Rs. 37100, find the share of each.

(A) Rs. 21200, Rs. 15900
(B) Rs. 15900, Rs. 21200
(C) Rs. 15800, Rs. 21000
(D) Rs. 21000, Rs. 15800

Solution. Ratio of their capitals = 36000 × 12 : 36000 × 9 = 4 : 3

Pramod's share = Rs. $\left(37100 \times \frac{4}{7}\right)$ = Rs. 21200

Roy's share = Rs. $\left(37100 \times \frac{3}{7}\right)$ = Rs. 15900

Type VI. Simple Interest

General Concepts

Principal or Sum. The money borrowed or lent out for a certain period is called the principal or the sum.

Interest. Extra money paid for using others money is called interest.

Simple Interest. If the interest on a sum borrowed for a certain period is reckoned uniformly, then it is called simple interest.

Formula. Let Principal = P, Rate = R% per annum and Time = T years. Then

(i) $S.I = \left(\frac{P \times R \times T}{100}\right)$

(ii) $P = \left(\frac{100 \times S.I}{R \times T}\right)$, $R = \left(\frac{100 \times S.I}{P \times T}\right)$ and $T = \left(\frac{100 \times S.I}{P \times R}\right)$

Solved Examples

Example 1. A lady borrowed Rs. 24000 from two money lenders. For one loan, she paid 15% per annum and for the other 18% per annum. At the end of one year she paid Rs. 4050. How much did she borrow at each rate ?

(A) Rs. 15000, Rs. 9000 (B) Rs. 9000, Rs. 10000

(C) Rs. 9000, Rs. 18000 (D) Rs. 9000, Rs. 15000

Solution. Let the sum at 15% be Rs. x and that at 18% be Rs. $(24000 - x)$.

$$\therefore \frac{x \times 15 \times 1}{100} + \frac{(24000 - x) \times 18 \times 1}{100} = 4050$$

or $15x + 432000 - 18x = 405000$ or $x = 9000$

∴ Money borrowed at 15% = Rs. 9000

Then, Money borrowed at 18% = Rs. 15000

Example 2. A sum was put at simple interest at a certain rate for 3 years. Had it been put at 2% higher rate, it would have fetched Rs. 360 more. Find the sum.

(A) Rs. 3000 (B) Rs. 4000 (C) Rs. 5000 (D) Rs. 6000

Solution. Let, sum = P and original rate = R.

Then, $\frac{P \times (R+2) \times 3}{100} - \frac{P \times R \times 3}{100} = 360$

or 3PR + 6P – 3PR = 36000 or 6P = 36000 or P = 6000

Hence, sum = Rs. 6000

Type VII. Compound Interest

Compound Interest. Sometimes it so happens that the borrower and the lender agree to fix up a certain unit of time, say yearly or half-yearly or quarterly to settle the previous account.

In such cases, the amount after first unit of time becomes the principal for the second unit, the amount after second unit becomes the principal for the third unit and so on.

After a specified period, the difference between the amount and the money borrowed is called the Compound Interest (abbreviated as C.I.) for that period

Formula

Let, **Principal** = P, **Rate** = R% per annum, **Time** = n years.

I. **When interest is compounded Annually** Amount $= P\left(1+\frac{R}{100}\right)^n$

II. **When interest is compounded Half-yearly** Amount $= P\left[1+\frac{(R/2)}{100}\right]^{2n}$

III. **When interest is compounded Quarterly** Amount $= P\left[1+\frac{(R/4)}{100}\right]^{4n}$

IV. **When interest is compounded annually but time is in fraction, say $3\frac{2}{5}$ years.**

$$\text{Amount} = P\left(1+\frac{R}{100}\right)^3 \times \left(1+\frac{\frac{2}{5}R}{100}\right)$$

V. **When Rates are different for different years,** say $R_1\%$, $R_2\%$, $R_3\%$ for 1st, 2nd and 3rd year respectively.

$$\text{Then, Amount} = P\left(1+\frac{R_1}{100}\right)\left(1+\frac{R_2}{100}\right)\left(1+\frac{R_3}{100}\right)$$

VI. **Present worth of Rs. x due in n years hence is given by** Present Worth $= \dfrac{x}{\left(1+\frac{R}{100}\right)^n}$

Solved Examples

Example 1. A sum of money doubles itself at compound interest in 15 years. In how many years will it become eight times ?

(A) 42 (B) 44 (C) 45 (D) 46

Solution. $P\left(1+\frac{R}{100}\right)^{15} = 2P \Rightarrow \left(1+\frac{R}{100}\right)^{15} = 2$ ....(i)

Let, $P\left(1+\frac{R}{100}\right)^n = 8P \Rightarrow \left(1+\frac{R}{100}\right)^n = 8 = 2^3 = \left\{\left(1+\frac{R}{100}\right)^{15}\right\}^3$ [Using (i)]

$\Rightarrow \left(1+\frac{R}{100}\right)^n = \left(1+\frac{R}{100}\right)^{45} \Rightarrow n = 45$

Thus, the required time = 45 years

Example 2. If the compound interest on a certain sum for 2 years at 12% per annum is Rs. 1590, what would be the simple interest ?

(A) Rs. 1100 (B) Rs. 1200 (C) Rs. 1300 (D) Rs. 1500

Solution. Let the sum be Rs. x.

Then, $x\left(1+\frac{12}{100}\right)^2 - x = 1590$ or $\frac{784x}{625} - x = 1590$

or $\frac{159x}{625} = 1590$ or $x = \frac{1590 \times 625}{159} = 6250$

$\therefore$ Sum = Rs. 6250

$$\therefore \text{S.I.} = \text{Rs.}\left(\frac{6250\times12\times2}{100}\right) = \text{Rs. } 1500$$

Type VIII. Age Related Test

To solve the problems based on ages, students are required the knowledge of linear equations. Sometimes it is easier to solve the problems by taking the given choices in account. We have tried to evaluate same easier as well as quicker methods to solve this type equations.

Solved Examples

Example 1. The age of the father 3 years age was 7 times the age of his son. At present the father's age is five times that of his son. What are the present ages of the father and the son?

Solution. Let the present age of son = x yrs.

Then, the present age of father = $5x$ yrs.

3 years ago,

$$7(x-3) = 5x-3$$

or $$7x-21 = 5x-3$$

or $$2x = 18 \qquad \therefore x = 9 \text{ yrs.}$$

Therefore, son's age = 9 yrs.

Father's age = 45 yrs.

Example 2. At present the age of the father is five times that of the age of his son. Three years hence, the father's age would be four times that of his son. Find the present ages of the father and the son.

Solution. Let the present age of son = x yrs.

Then, the present age of father = $5x$ yrs.

3 years hence,

$$4(x+3) = 5x+3$$

or $$4x+12 = 5x+3$$

or $$x = 9 \text{ yrs.}$$

Therefore, son's age = 9 yrs.

and father's age = 45 yrs.

Example 3. Three years earlier the father was 7 times as old as his son. Three years hence the father's age would be four times that of his son. What are the present ages of the father and the son?

Solution. Let the present age of son = x yrs.

and the present age of father = y yrs.

3 years earlier,

$$7(x-3) = y-3$$

or $$7x-y = 18 \qquad \text{...(1)}$$

3 years hence,

$$4(x+3) = y+3$$

or $$4x+12 = y+3$$

or $$4x-y = -9 \qquad \text{...(2)}$$

Solving (1) and (2), we get

$x = 9$ yrs. & $y = 45$ yrs.

Type IX. Percentage

The term **per cent** means 'for every hundred'. It can best be defined as:

"A fraction whose denominator is 100 is called a **percentage**, and the numerator of the fraction is called the **rate per cent.**"

The Following examples illustrate the percents and their fractional values:

(1) A students gets 60 per cent marks in Arithmetic means that he obtained 60 marks out of every hundred of full marks. That is, if the full marks be 500, he gets 60 + 60 + 60 + 60 + 60 = 300 marks in mathematics. The above five 60s are one 60 for every hundred.

The total marks obtained by the student can be calculated in other ways, like,

$$60\% \text{ of } 500 = \frac{60}{100} \times 500 = 300$$

The above calculations can be made easier by reducing the fractional value to its prime. As, in the above case;

$$60\% = \frac{60}{100} = \frac{3}{5}$$

If we remember that 60 % = $\frac{3}{5}$, our calculation becomes easier. In that case, the total marks obtained by the student = $\frac{3}{5} \times 500 = 300$

(2) A man invests 5% of his income into shares. It means:

(i) he invests Rs 5 out of every Rs 100 of his income into shares.

or **(ii)** he invests $\frac{5}{100}$ of his income into shares.

or **(iii)** he invests $\frac{1}{20}$th of his income into shares.

Now, if his income is Rs 1050, how does he invest in shares?

Here Quick answer should be $\frac{1050}{20}$ = Rs 52.5

You should not to move with the fraction containing 100, if possible.

Example 1. Find 8 per cent of Rs 625.

Solution. 8% of Rs 625 = $\frac{2}{25} \times 625$ = Rs 50.

Example 2. What fraction is $12 = \frac{2}{25}$ per cent?

Solution. $12\frac{1}{2}\% = \frac{12\frac{1}{2}}{100} = \frac{25}{200} = \frac{1}{8}$

Example 3. What percentage is equivalent to $\frac{3}{8}$?

Solution. $\frac{3}{8} \times 100 = \frac{75}{2} = 37\frac{1}{2}\%$

Example 4. The population of a town has increased from 60,000 to 65,000. Find the increase per cent.

Solution. Increase in population = 65,000 - 60,000 = 5000

$$\text{Percentage increase} = \frac{5000}{60,000}\times 100 = \frac{25}{3} = 8\frac{1}{3}\%$$

Example 5. Ram's salary is increased from Rs 630 to Rs 700. Find the increase per cent.

Solution. Increase in salary = Rs 700 - Rs 630 = Rs 70.

$$\text{Percentage increase} = \frac{70}{630}\times 100 = 11\frac{1}{9}\%$$

Percentage Expenditures and Saving

Example. A man loses $12\frac{1}{2}\%$ of his money and, after spending 70% of the remainder, he is left with Rs 210. How much had he at first?

Solution. The above question can be solved in many ways. We will discuss a few of them.

(I) Let the man be supposed to have Rs x at first.

After losing $12\frac{1}{2}\%$ or $\frac{1}{8}$, he is left with $x - \frac{x}{8} = \text{Rs}\frac{7x}{8}$

After spending 70% of the money, he is left with 30% of the remainder, i.e.,

$$\frac{7x}{8}\times\frac{3}{10} = 210 \therefore x = \frac{210\times 10\times 8}{3\times 7} = \text{Rs } 800$$

(II) Suppose he had Rs 100 at first. After losing Rs $12\frac{1}{2}$ he would have Rs $87\frac{1}{2}$ left. He spent 70% of Rs $87\frac{1}{2}$

$\therefore$ he would have $\left(30\% \text{of Rs } 87\frac{1}{2}\right)$ or Rs $\frac{105}{4}$ left. But he has Rs 210 left. Thus, we have the following proportions :

Rs $\frac{105}{4}$: Rs 210 :: Rs 100 : the required money (By the rule of three)

$\therefore$ the required money = Rs $\frac{4\times 210\times 100}{105}$ = Rs800

(III) Quicker Method : It is a very short and fast-calculating method. The only thing is to remember the formula well.

$$\text{His initial money} = \frac{210\times 100\times 100}{(100-12.5)(100-70)} = \frac{210\times 100\ 100}{87.5\times 30} = \text{Rs } 800$$

Note. As his "initial money" is definitely more than the "left money", there should not be any confusion in putting the larger value (100) in the numerator and the smaller value (100 – 12.5) in the denominator.

Example. 3.5% of income is taken as tax and 12.5% of the remaining is saved. This leaves Rs 4,053 to spend. What is the income?

Solution. Quicker Maths gives the solution as:

$$\text{Income} = \frac{4053 \times 100 \times 100}{(100-3.5)(100-12.5)} = \text{Rs}4,800.$$

Population Formula

Example. If the original population of a town is P, and the annual increase is r%, what will be the population in n years?

Solution. Population after one year becomes $P + \frac{Pr}{100} = P\left(1+\frac{r}{100}\right)$

That is, the population P at the beginning of the year is multiplied by $\left(1+\frac{r}{100}\right)$ in the course of the year.

Now, the population at the beginning of the second year is $P\left(1+\frac{r}{100}\right)$

$\therefore$ the population in 2 years $= P\left(1+\frac{r}{100}\right)^2$

$\therefore$ the population in n years $= P\left(1+\frac{r}{100}\right)^n$

Note. If the annual decrease be *r*%, then the population in *n* years $= P\left(1-\frac{r}{100}\right)^n$

Example. If the annual increase in the population of a town is 4% and the present number of people is 15,625, what will be population be in 3 years?

Solution. The required population $= 15625\left(1+\frac{4}{100}\right)^3$

$$= 1625 \times \frac{26}{25} \times \frac{26}{25} \times \frac{26}{25} = 17576$$

Example. If the annual increase in the population of a town be 4% and the present population be 17576, what was it three years ago?

Solution. The population 3 years ago $\times \left(\frac{26}{25}\right)^3$ = Present population

$\therefore$ the population 3 years ago $= \frac{17576 \times 25 \times 25 \times 25}{26 \times 26 \times 26} = 15625$

Percentage Relationship

If first value is *r*% more than the second value, then the second is $\left[\frac{r}{100+r} \times 100\right]$% less than the first value.

Quicker Method. If A's income is *r*% more than B's income, then B's income is less than A's income by $\left[\frac{r}{100+r} \times 100\right]$%.

Example. If A's salary is 30% less than that of B, then how much per cent is B's salary more than that of A?

Solution. **Quicker Method:** If A's salary is r% less than B's, then B's salary is more than A's salary by $\left[\frac{r}{100-r}\times 100\right]\%$

Example. A number is 50% more than the other. Then how much per cent is the second number less than the first?

Solution. We can apply the above discussed formula in this case also. Then the second number is $\left(\frac{50}{100+50}\times 100\right)\% = 33\frac{1}{3}\%$ less than the first.

One Value as a Percentage of Another

Example. Express 20 as a percentage of 80.

Solution. If one is 80, the other is 20.

$\therefore$ if one is 100, the other is $\frac{20}{80}\times 100 = 25$

$\therefore$ 20 is 25% of 80.

Thus, without going for details, we may say that "x as a percentage of y" $=\frac{x}{y}\times 100\%$

Example. Express 250 as a percentage of 50.

Solution. Answer $=\frac{250}{50}\times 100 = 500\%$

Example. Express 160 as a percentage of 120.

Solution. Answer $=\frac{160}{120}\times 100 = \frac{400}{3} = 133\frac{1}{3}\%$

Example. Express 20 as a per thousand fraction of 200.

Solution. Answer $=\frac{20}{200}\times 1000 = 100$ per thousand.

First Increase and Then Decrease

Example. The salary of a worker is first increased by 10% and thereafter is was reduced by 10%. What was the change in his salary?

Solution. Let the salary of the worker be Rs 100.

After increase, it becomes Rs. 100 + 10% of 100 = Rs 110

After decrease, it becomes Rs 110 – 10% of Rs 110 = Rs 99

$\therefore$ the % reduction = 100 – 99 = 1%

By Quicker Method

Theorem. If the value of a number is first increased by x% and later decreased by x%, the net change is always a decrease which is equal to x% of x or $\frac{x^2}{100}$.

When both Values are Different

Theorem. If the value is first increased by x% and then decreased by y% then there is $\left(x-y-\frac{xy}{100}\right)\%$ increase, according to the +ve or -ve sign respectively.

Successive Increase or Decrease

Theorem. If the value is increased successively by $x\%$ and $y\%$ then the final increase is given by $\left[x+y+\frac{xy}{100}\right]\%$.

Effect on Revenue

Theorem. (i) If the price of a commodity is diminished by $x\,\%$ and its consumption is increased by y%

(ii) or, if the price of a commodity is increased by $x\,\%$ and its consumption is decreased by $y\,\%$ then the effect on revenue

$= \text{Inc. \% value - Dec. \% value} - \frac{\text{Inc. \% value} \times \text{Dec. \% value}}{100}$ and the value is increased or decreased according to the +ve or -ve sign obtained.

Type X. Average

An average, or more accurately an arithmetic mean is, in crude terms, the sum of n different data divided by n,

For example, if a batsman scores 35, 45 and 37 runs in first, second and third innings respectively, then his average runs in 3 innings is equal to $\frac{35+45+37}{3} = 39$ runs.

Therefore, the two mostly used formula are:

$$\text{Average} = \frac{\text{Total of data}}{\text{No. of data}}$$

And, Total =Average × No. of data

Example. The average age of 30 boys of a class is equal to 14 yrs. When the age of the class teacher is included the average becomes 15 yrs. Find the age of the class teacher.

Solution. Total ages of 30 boys $= 14 \times 30 = 420$ yrs.

Total ages when class teacher is included

$= 15 \times 31 = 465$ yrs

$\therefore$ Age of class teacher $= 465 - 420 = 45$ yrs.

Direct Formula.

Age of new entrant = New average + No. of old members × Increase in average

$= 15 + 30\,(15 - 14) = 45$ yrs

Example. The average weight of 4 men is increased by 3 kg when one of them who weighs 120 kg is replaced by another man. What is the weight of the new man?

Solution. **Quicker approach.** It the average is increased by 3 kg, then the sum of weights increase by $3 \times 4 = 12$ kg.

And this increase in weights is due to the extra weight included due to the inclusion of new person.

$\therefore$ Weight of new man $= 120 + 12 = 132$ kg

Direct Formula.

Weight of new person = weight of removed person + No. of persons × increase in average $= 120 + 4 \times 3 = 132$ kg

Example. The average of marks obtained by 120 candidates in a certain examination is 35. If the average marks of passed candidates is 39 and that of the failed candidates is 15, what is the number of candidates who passed the examination?

Solution. Let the number of passed candidates be x.

Then total marks = $120 \times 35 = 39x + (120 - x) \times 15$

or, $4200 = 39x + 1800 - 15x$ or, $24x = 2400$

$\therefore x = 100$

$\therefore$ number of passed candidates = 100

Direct Formula.

$$\text{Number of passed candidates} = \frac{\text{Total candidates (Total average – Failed average)}}{\text{Passed average – Failed average}}$$

$$\text{and Number of failed candidates} = \frac{\text{Total candidates (Passed average – Total average)}}{\text{Passed average – Failed average}}$$

$$\text{No. of passed candidates} = \frac{120\,(35-15)}{39-15} = 100$$

By Method of Alligation:

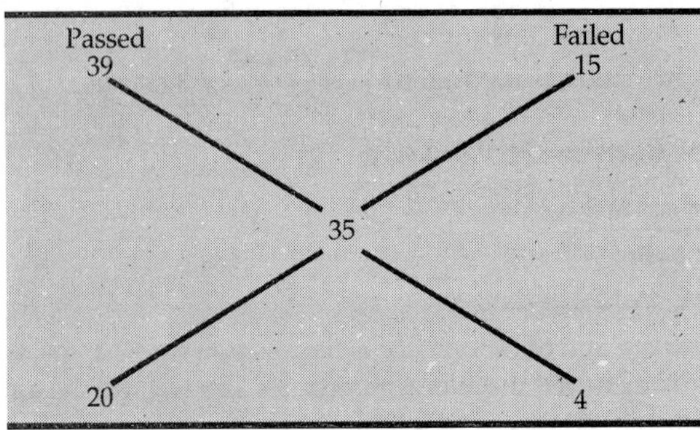

$\therefore$ No. of passed candidates : No. of failed candidates = 20 : 4 = 5 : 1

$\therefore$ No. of passed candidates = $\frac{120}{5+1} \times 5 = 100$

Example. The average of 11 results is 50. If the average of first six results is 49 and that of last six is 52, find the sixth result.

Solution. The total of 11 results = $11 \times 50 = 550$

The total of first 6 results = $6 \times 49 = 294$

The total of last 6 results = $6 \times 52 = 312$

The 6th results is common to both;

$\therefore$ Sixth result = $294 + 312 - 550 = 56$

Direct Formula.

6th result = $50 + \{(52 - 50) + (49 - 50)\} = 50 + 6\,\{2 - 1\} = 56$

Example. The average age of 8 persons in a committee is increased by 2 years when two men aged 35 yrs and 45 yrs are substituted by two women. Find the average age of these two women.

Solution. By the direct formula

the total age of two women = $2 \times 8 + (35 + 45)$

$= 16 + 80 = 96$ yrs.

$\therefore$ average age of two women $= \frac{96}{2} = 48$ yrs.

Example. The average age of a family of 6 members is 22 yrs. If the age of the youngest member be 7 yrs, then what was the average age of the family at the birth of the youngest member?

Solution. Total ages of all members $= 6 \times 22 = 132$ yrs.

7 yrs ago, total sum of ages $= 132 - (6 \times 7) = 90$ yrs.

But at that time there were 5 members in the family.

$\therefore$ Average at that time $= 90 \div 5 = 18$ yrs.

Example. A man bought 13 shirts of Rs 50 each, 15 pants of Rs 60 each and 12 pairs of shoes at Rs 65 a pair. Find the average value of each article.

Solution. **Direct Method:**

$$\text{Average} = \frac{13 \times 50 + 15 \times 60 + 12 \times 65}{13 + 15 + 12} = \text{Rs } 58.25$$

Average Related to Speed

Theorem. If a person travels a distance at a speed of x km/hr and the same distance at a speed of y km/hr, then the average speed during the whole journey is given by $\frac{2xy}{x+y}$ km/hr

or,

If half of the journey is travelled at a speed of x km/hr and the next half at a speed of y km/hr, then average speed during the whole journey is $\frac{2xy}{x+y}$ km/hr

or,

If a man goes to a certain place at a speed of x km/hr and returns to the original place at a speed of y km/hr, then the average speed during up-and-down journey is $\frac{2xy}{x+y}$ km/hr

Theorem. If a person travels three equal distances at a speed of x km/hr, y km/hr and z km/hr respectively, then the average speed during the whole journey is $\frac{3xyz}{xy + yz + xz}$ km/hr.

Example. A train travels form A to B the rate of 20 km per hour and from B to A at the rate of 30 km/hr. What is the average rate for the whole journey?

Solution. By the formula : Average speed $= \frac{2 \times 20 \times 30}{20 + 30} = 24$ km/hr

Example. A person divides his total route of journey into three equal parts and decides to travel the three parts with speeds of 40, 30 and 15 km/hr respectively. Find his average speed during the whole journey.

Solution. By the theorem : Average speed $= \frac{3 \times 40 \times 30 \times 15}{40 \times 30 + 30 \times 15 + 40 \times 15}$

$$= \frac{3 \times 40 \times 30 \times 15}{2250} = 24 \text{ km/hr}$$

MULTIPLE CHOICE QUESTIONS

Series Test

Identify Next Number in the Series

1. 4, 9, 20, 43, ___
(A) 90 (B) 84
(C) 96 (D) 95

2. 4, 9, 19, 39, 79, ___
(A) 169 (B) 159
(C) 119 (D) 139

3. 3, 2, 7, 6, 11, ___
(A) 13 (B) 8
(C) 4 (D) 10

4. 6, 5, 24, 25, 144, ___
(A) 155 (B) 160
(C) 170 (D) 175

5. 3, 6, 12, 15, 30, ___
(A) 33 (B) 35
(C) 45 (D) 60

6. 2, 3, 5, 9, 17, 33, ___
(A) 85 (B) 37
(C) 63 (D) 65

7. 462, 420, 380, ___
(A) 342 (B) 330
(C) 370 (D) 335

8. 2, 20, 74, 110, ___
(A) 182 (B) 218
(C) 120 (D) 160

9. 60, 30, 120, 15, 240, ___
(A) 30 (B) 120
(C) 240 (D) 7½

10. 2, 7, 17, 32, 52, 77, ___
(A) 107 (B) 91
(C) 101 (D) 92

Identify Wrong Number in the Series

11. 5, 8, 20, 42, 124, 246, 736
(A) 8 (B) 20
(C) 42 (D) 124

12. 1200, 1194, 1182, 1162, 1134, 1090, 1034
(A) 1194 (B) 1182
(C) 1162 (D) 1134

13. 808, 408, 208, 108, 68
(A) 68 (B) 208
(C) 808 (D) 108

14. 16, 25, 41, 66, 102, 151, 251
(A) 251 (B) 41
(C) 66 (D) 102

15. 105, 85, 60, 30, –25, –45
(A) 105 (B) –25
(C) 30 (D) 60

Completion of Series

16. 80 50 130 100 180 150 230
900 (A) (B) (C) (D) (E)
Which number will come in the place of (C) ?
(A) 1050 (B) 920
(C) 1000 (D) 950

17. 140 68 36 16 10 3
284 (A) (B) (C) (D) (E)
Which number will come in the place of (D)?
(A) 34 (B) 40
(C) 19 (D) 90

18. 2 4 9 20 43 90
3 (A) (B) (C) (D) (E)
Which number will come in the place of (D) ?
(A) 59 (D) 99
(C) 100 (D) 104

LETTER SERIES

Identify the Missing Term

19. DKM, FJP, HIS, JHV, ________
(A) HGY (B) IGZ
(C) IGY (D) LGY

20. AND, COF, FPI, JQM, ________
(A) ORS (B) ORR
(C) QRS (D) PRT

21. A, Z, D, X, G, V, J, T, M, ________, ________
(A) S, N (B) P, R
(C) N, S (D) R, P

22. B, D, G, K, P, ________
(A) V (B) W
(C) T (D) S

23. MIP, WSZ, KGN, ________
(A) TPW (B) HLE
(C) LIP (D) TMQ

24. BCA, EFD, HIG, ________
(A) KJL (B) LKJ
(C) LKL (D) KLJ

25. JKL, LKJ, JKLM, MLKJ, JKLMN, ________
(A) NMLKJ (B) LMJKN
(C) LMNKJ (D) KLMNJ

Alphabet Test

1. Which is the 8th letter to the right of 15th letter from your left in the english alphabet?
(A) W (B) H
(C) V (D) G

2. In the following series if A and Z, B and Y and so on interchange their positions then which will be 11th letter from your right ?
ABCDEFGHIJKLMNOPQRSTUVWXYZ
(A) J (B) K
(C) P (D) L

3. In the following series if A and C, B and D and so on interchange their positions upto X, then which will be the fourth letter to the right of N in the new series formed ?
ABCDEFGHIJKLMNOPQRSTUVWXYZ
(A) W (B) J
(C) R (D) Q

4. If the second half of the following series is written in the reverse order, which will be the 5th letter to the right of 10th letter from your right?
ABCDEFGHIJKLMNOPQRSTUVWXYZ
(A) K (B) P
(C) J (D) None of these

5. If first four letters of the word 'AGRICULTURE' are written in the reverse order, then next four letters are also written in the reverse order and then the remaining letters are also written in the same reverse order then which is the 8th letter from your left in the new word formed ?
(A) U (B) C
(C) L (D) None of these

6. If one is used only once then in how many meaningful words can the word CONSIDERING be broken without altering the letter sequence ?
(A) 4 (B) 7
(C) 3 (D) 6

7. How many such letter - pairs are there in the word MANAGER having the same number of letters left between them in the word as they have in the series ?
(A) 2 (B) 3
(C) 6 (D) 7

8. How many such letter - pairs are there in the word FRONTIER having the same number of letters left between them as they have in the series ?
(A) 6 (B) 3
(C) 2 (D) None of these

9. If it is decided to write the alternate letters after B in small notation, then PERPENDICULAR will be written as
(A) pErpEndICUlAr
(B) PERPendicular
(C) PeRPEnDiCuLAR
(D) None of these

10. How many such letter - pairs are there in the word BONAFIDE having the same number of letters left between them as they have in the series ?
(A) 1 (B) 6
(C) 4 (D) None of these

11. If it is possible to make a meaningful word from the first, second, fourth and fifth letters of the word FALSEHOOD then which will be the third letter from the right ? Mark M if it is possible to make more than one word and if it is impossible to make any word then mark your answer as X.
(A) M (B) X
(C) S (D) A

12. If it is possible to make a meaningful word from its first, fifth, eighth and ninth letters of the word EXHILARATION, then which will be the third letter of that word ? Give your answer M if it is possible to make more than one word and if it is impossible to make any word then give your answer as X.
(A) A (B) M
(C) Q (D) None of these

13. If it is decided to write the alternate letters after C in small notation then REVULSION will be written as
(A) ReVuLsioN (B) REvUlSioN
(C) rEvUlsioN (D) None of these

14. If the following words are arranged according to the dictionary order then which will be the second word in that order ?

Expose, Expulsion, Export, Expound, Exposure
(A) Expose (B) Expound
(C) Expulsion (D) Export

15. If the letters in the word UNDERTAKING are rearranged in the alphabetical order, which one will be in the middle in order after the rearrangement?
(A) G (B) I (C) K (D) N

Classification Test

TYPE-I

Directions. *Identify the odd one out.*

1. (A) Teacher (B) Tutor
(C) Professor (D) Student

2. (A) Rajesh (B) Sandhya
(C) Ajay (D) Vinay

3. (A) Chameleon (B) Cobra
(C) Sword (D) Snake

4. (A) Serpent (B) Snake
(C) Crocodile (D) Whale

5. (A) Carpenter (B) Potter
(C) Mason (D) Farmer

6. (A) Printer (B) Correspondent
(C) Publisher (D) Reader

7. (A) Duck (B) Parrot
(C) Pigeon (D) Sparrow

8. (A) Tiger (B) Whale
(C) Fish (D) Tortoise

9. (A) Lion and Roar
(B) Birds and Chirp
(C) Dogs and Coop
(D) Snake and Hiss

10. (A) College and Principal
(B) Playground and player
(C) Navy and commander
(D) Post Office and Postmaster

11. (A) Investor (B) Entrepreneur
(C) Landlord (D) Financier

12. (A) Sparrow (B) Eagle
(C) Crow (D) Ostrich

13. (A) Dog (B) Horse
(C) Cow (D) Goat

14. (A) Rose (B) Lily
(C) Tulip (D) Lotus

15. (A) Sky (B) Star
(C) Planet (D) Comet

TYPE-II

16. (A) DCBA (B) MNOP
(C) LKJI (D) HGFE

17. (A) ZAYB (B) TSGH
(C) XCWD (D) VEUF

18. RQS, BAC, NMO, KLM, YXZ
(A) NMO (B) RQS
(C) KLM (D) YXZ

19. A, O, U, I, Q
(A) U (B) O
(C) A (D) Q

20. (A) PQ (B) CD
(C) MN (D) DF

TYPE- III

21. (A) 47, 59 (B) 42, 29
(C) 73, 61 (D) 57, 69

22. (A) 13 - 156 (B) 12 - 144
(C) 15 - 180 (D) 16 - 176

23. (A) 3 - 11 (B) 8 - 16
(C) 14 - 24 (D) 5 - 13

24. (A) 22, 4, 5 (B) 37, 4, 9
(C) 34, 4, 8 (D) 54, 4, 13

25. (A) 12 (B) 16
(C) 64 (D) 128

TYPE - IV

26. (A) Sweet - Sour (B) Pointed - Blunt
(C) Hard - Soft (D) Long - Short

27. (A) Spain : Madrid (B) Japan : Tokyo
(C) China : Beijing (D) Cow : Herd

28. (A) Permission : Prevention
(B) Transparent : Opaque
(C) Convergence : Divergence
(D) Enough : Executive

29. (A) Class : Teacher
(B) Hospital : Doctor
(C) Market : Leader
(D) Bank : Agent

30. (A) Motor : Vehicle
(B) Vision : Eye
(C) Loud : Speaker
(D) Tele : Vision

Coding and Decoding Test

1. The word TENDER has been coded in four different ways. Find out which pattern / rule is used for coding it, if MELLOW is coded as TLSSVD.
   (A) UFOEFS (B) SDMCDQ
   (C) REDNET (D) ALUKLY
2. In a certain code SUNDAY is coded as YADNUS. How could CREATION be written in that code ?
   (A) NOITAERC (B) INOTAERL
   (C) IONTEARC (D) ERCITANO
3. In a certain code MENTION is written as LNEITNO. Then PATTERN is coded as
   (A) APTTREM (B) PTAETNR
   (C) OTAETRN (D) None of these
4. In a certain code SLATE is coded as GXRYW. Then STEAL will be written as
   (A) GYRWX (B) GYWRX
   (C) GXWRY (D) GXRWY
5. In a certain code language, BOY is written as $*• and HOUR is written as @*£0. How is RUBY written in that code ?
   (A) 0$£• (B) •$£0
   (C) •$£0 (D) 0£$•
6. In certain code, BOXER is written as AQWGQ. How is VISIT written in that code ?
   (A) UKRKP (B) UKRKS
   (C) WKRKU (D) WKRKS
7. In a code language if POSE is coded as OQNPRTDF, then TYPE will be coded as :
   (A) SUXZOQFD (B) SUXZQOFD
   (C) SUXZOQDF (D) SUXZQODE
8. If CARPET is coded as TCEAPR, then the code for NATIONAL would be :
   (A) NLATNOLI (B) LANOITAN
   (C) LNAANTOI (D) LNOINTAA
9. If PAINTER is written in a code language as NCGPRGP, then REASON would be written as
   (A) PCYQMN (B) PGYQMN
   (C) PGYUMP (D) PGYUPM
10. In a certain code, GOODNESS is coded as HNPCODTR. How is GREATNESS coded in that code ?
   (A) HQFZUODTR (B) HQFZUMFRT
   (C) HQFZSMFRT (D) FSDBSODTR
11. If PICTURE is coded as tuvwxyz, then PIERCE would be coded as
   (A) tuzyzv (B) tzuvzy
   (C) tuzyvz (D) tzuvyz
12. If D = 4, COVER = 63, then BASIS =
   (A) 54 (B) 55
   (C) 49 (D) 50
13. If MATHEMATICS = 12345123678, then MAHATMA = ?
   (A) 1242312 (B) 12425341
   (C) 12345678 (D) 12345123
14. Identify which one of the four alternatives does 'PRIZE' belong to, if K = 11 and KAMAL = 38
   (A) 72 (B) 70
   (C) 76 (D) 74
15. Find out which one of the four alternatives does 'CAP' belong to if A = 1, and BAT = 23 ?
   (A) 20 (B) 21
   (C) 27 (D) 22
16. If UNDERSTAND is coded as 1234567823. How will START be coded ?
   (A) 67857 (B) 83243
   (C) 56781 (D) 73652
17. In a certain code language, QUEUE is written as Q22, CHURCH is written as 1UR1. Which of the following would be the most appropriate code for BANANA in that language ?
   (A) B5A5A (B) B5A5
   (C) B55A (D) BA5A5A
18. In a certain code language
   (1) 'po ki top ma' means 'Usha is playing cards.'
   (2) 'kop ja ki ma' means 'Asha is playing tennis'.
   (3) 'ki top sop ho' means 'they are playing football'.
   (4) 'po sur kop' means 'Cards and tennis.'
   Which word in that language means 'Asha' ?
   (A) ja (B) ma
   (C) kob (D) top
19. In a certain code language -
   (i) 'pic vic nic' means 'winter is cold.'
   (ii) 'to nic re' means 'summer is hot.'
   (iii) 're pic boo' means 'winter and summer'.
   (iv) 'vic tho pa' means 'nights are cold'.
   Which word in that language represents 'summer' ?
   (A) nic (B) re
   (C) to (D) vic
20. In a certain code language-
   '1 3 4' means 'Good And Tasty'

'4 7 8' means 'See Good Pictures'
and '7 2 9' means 'Pictures Are Faint.'
Which of the following numerical symbol stands for 'See' ?
(A) 9 (B) 2
(C) 1 (D) None of these

Direction Sense Test

1. Facing towards South, Sanjeet walked 50 metres. He then turned to his right and walked 30 metres. He again turned right and walked 50 metres. How far was he from his original point and in which direction he is now ?
(A) 30 metres and in the West
(B) 30 metres and in the East
(C) 50 metres and in the West
(D) 20 metres and in the West

2. Roopali walks 10 metres in front and 10 metres to the right. Then every time turning to her left she walks 5, 15 and 15 metres respectively. How far is she now from her starting point ?
(A) 10 metres (B) 20 metres
(C) 5 metres (D) 15 metres

3. If South-East becomes North-East and North-West becomes South-West and all the rest directions are changed in the same manner, then what will the be the direction for West ?
(A) North (B) North-West
(C) South (D) East

4. A school boy was misdirected from his way while returning to his home. In order to reach his home he first moved 3 Km in South direction and then turned to his left. 2 Km from there he moved to his left and walked 3 Km. After this he again turned to his left and moved 1 Km. Finally he reached his home. The home of the boy was in which direction from his school ?
(A) West (B) North
(C) East (D) South

5. The door of Danika's house is towards the east. From the backside of the house, she walks straight 100 yards then turns towards right and walks 100 yards again and after that turns towards left and stops after walking 50 yards. Now Danika is in which direction from the starting point ?
(A) South-east (B) North-west
(C) North-east (D) South-west

6. Prakash faces towards East. Turning to his right he walks 50 metres and then turning to his left, he walks 50 metres. After this he turns to his right and walks 50 metres. Again he turns to his right and walks 100 metres. Finally he turns to his right and walks 100 metres. Now in what direction is he from his starting point ?
(A) East (B) West
(C) North (D) South

7. The post office is in the East of the school while my house is in the South of the school. The market is in the North of the post office. If the distance of the market from the post office is equal to the distance of my house from the school, in which direction is the market with respect to my house ?
(A) North (B) East
(C) North-East (D) South-West

8. Amit walks 100 yards straight from his house which is facing north and then he walks 200 yards in the reverse direction. Further he takes a left turn and walks 100 yards. In which direction is Amit now from his original position ?
(A) North-East (B) South-West
(C) North-West (D) South-East

9. Pushpa walks 30 metres in North-West direction from her house and then 30 metres in South-West direction. After this she walks 30 metres in South-East direction. Now she turns to her house. Now in what direction is she going ?
(A) North-East (B) South-West
(C) South-East (D) North-West

10. Jassica started early in the morning on the road towards the Sun. After sometime she turned to her left. Again after sometime she turned to her right. After moving some distance she again turned to her right and began to move. At this time in what direction was she moving ?
(A) North-West (B) North-East
(C) East (D) South

11. Milind goes 30 metres North then turns right and walks 40 metres, then again turns right and walks 20 metres, then again turns right and walks 40 metres. How many metres is he from his original position ?
(A) 0 (B) 10
(C) 20 (D) 40

12. A man walks 30 km towards East, then turning to right he walks 30 km. Then turning to his left he again walks 20 km. Again turning to his

left he walks 30 km. How far is he from his starting point ?

(A) 50 km (B) 60 km
(C) 70 km (D) 100 km

13. Kapil moves 1 km to East and then turns to South and moves 5 km. He again turns to East and walks 2 km. After this he turns to North and moves 9 km. What is the distance from his starting point to the present point ?

(A) 5 km (B) 16 km
(C) 13 km (D) 8 km

14. The time by Surabhi's watch is half past three. If the hour hand points towards East, to which direction would minute hand point ?

(A) North (B) East
(C) South (D) West

15. A direction pole was situated on the crossing. Due to an accident the pole turned in such a manner that the pointer which was showing East, started showing South. One traveller went to the wrong direction thinking it to be West. In what direction actually she was travelling ?

(A) West (B) East
(C) South-West (D) North

Blood Relation Test

1. Given that :
   1. A is the brother of B.
   2. C is the father of A.
   3. D is the brother of E.
   4. E is the daughter of B.

   Then, uncle of D is

(A) A (B) B
(C) C (D) E

2. Deepak is the brother of Ravi. Rekha is the sister of Atul. Ravi is the son of Rekha. Then, how is Deepak related to Rekha ?

(A) Son (B) Brother
(C) Nephew (D) None of these

3. A is B's sister. C is B's mother. D is C's father. E is D's mother. Then, how is A related to D?

(A) Grand mother (B) Grand father
(C) Daughter (D) Grand daughter

4. Looking at a portrait of a man, Arun said, "His mother is the wife of my father's son. I have no brother or sister." At whose portrait was Arun Looking ?

(A) His son (B) His cousin
(C) His uncle (D) None of these

5. Pointing to a photograph, a lady tells Pramod, "I am the only daughter of this lady and her son is your maternal uncle." How is the speaker related to Pramod's father ?

(A) Sister-in-law (B) Wife
(C) Either (A) or (B) (D) Neither (A) or (B)

6. Pointing to a photograph, a woman says, "This man's son's sister is my mother-in-law." How is the woman's husband related to the man in the photograph ?

(A) Grand son (B) Son
(C) Son-in-law (D) None of these

7. If Kamal says, "Ravi's mother is the only daughter of my mother." How is Kamal related to Ravi ?

(A) Grand father (B) Father
(C) Brother (D) None of these

8. If P + Q means P is the husband of Q, P ÷ Q means P is the sister of Q and P × Q means P is the son of Q. Which of the following shows A is the daughter of B ?

(A) $C \times B \div A$ (B) $B + C \times A$
(C) $D \times B + C \div A$ (D) $A \div D \times B$

9. If P + Q means P is the brother of Q, P – Q means P is the mother of Q and P × Q means P is the sister of Q. Which of the following means M is the maternal uncle of R ?

(A) $M - R + K$ (B) $M + K - R$
(C) $M + K \times R$ (D) None of these

Arranging in Order Test

1. Five books are kept on each other. E is above A, C is below B. If A is above B and D is below C, then which is at the top ?

(A) E (B) A
(C) B (D) D

2. In a row of girls Malini is 7th from one extreme and 11th from the other. Find the total number of girls in the row.

(A) 17 (B) 21
(C) 19 (D) 20

3. Six persons are playing a card game. They are sitting in a circle facing towards the centre. Suresh is facing Raghubir who is to the left of Ajay and to the right of Pramod. Ajay is to the left of Dhiraj. Yogendra is to be left of Pramod. If Dhiraj exchanges his seat with Yogendra and Pramod with Raghubir, who will be sitting to the left of Dhiraj ?

(A) Yogendra (B) Ajay
(C) Suresh (D) Dhiraj

4. Six families A, B, C, D, E and F are living in houses in a row. B has D and F as neighbours, E has A and C as neighbours. A does not live next to either F or D. If C does not live next to D, who are F's next door neighbours ?
(A) Only B (B) Only B and D
(C) Only B and F (D) Only B and C

5. A, B, C, D, E and F are sitting in a circle, A is to the left of C, B is between D and E and F is between D and C. Who is to the left of B ?
(A) C (B) D
(C) E (D) A

6. Five boys were sitting in a circle facing to the centre. Salguna was to the left of Raman. Arul was to the right of Amit but between Amit and Narendra. Who was to the right of Salguna.
(A) Data inadequate (B) Arul
(C) Amit (D) Raman

7. In a row of children Srilekha is 9th from the left and Birla is 13th from the right. They exchange their positions and then Srilekha becomes 17th from the left. Find the new position of Birla.
(A) 18th (B) 27th
(C) 21st (D) None of these

8. In a row of boys, Subhash is 14th from the left, now he changes his position in such a way that 3 more boys from his right and he becomes 11th from his left. How many boys are there in the row ?
(A) 18 (B) 14
(C) 23 (D) 20

9. A is taller than B and C is taller than D. If D is taller than B, who is the tallest ?
(A) B (B) C
(C) A
(D) Cannot be determined

10. Robin is sitting to the left of Latif. Mohan is between Rakesh and Latif. If Govind is also to the left of Robin, who is in the extreme right ?
(A) Latif (B) Rakesh
(C) Mohan
(D) Cannot be determined

Letter-Digit Term Test

1. Count each 7 which is not immediately preceded by 5 but is immediately followed by either 2 or 3. How many such 7's are there ?

5 7 2 6 5 7 3 8 3 7 3 2 5 7 2 7 3 4 8 2 6 7 8

(A) One (B) Two
(C) Three (D) Four

2. In the following list of numbers, how many 2's are followed by 1 but not preceded by 4 ?
421 214 211 244 412 212 144 214 212 124 142 124 146
(A) Two (B) Three
(C) Four (D) Five

3. How many 6's are there in the following series of numbers which are preceded by 7 but not immediately followed by 9 ?
6 7 9 5 6 9 7 6 8 7 6 7 8 6 9 4 6 7 7 6 9 5 7 6 3
(A) One (B) Two
(C) Three (D) Four

4. How many 7's are there in the following series which are preceded by 6 which is not preceded by 8 ?
876 786 756 797 616 776 886 976 87
(A) Nil (B) One
(C) Two (D) None of these

5. How many 3's are there in the following sequence which are neither preceded by 6 nor immediately followed by 9 ?
9 3 6 6 3 9 5 9 3 7 8 9 1 6 3 9 6 3 9
(A) One (B) Two
(C) Three (D) None of these

6. How many A's are there in the following series which are immediately followed by C and immediately preceded by P?
C A P D A P A C F P A B C A P D A P C C A P
(A) One (B) Two
(C) Three (D) None of these

7. How many D's are there in the following series which are immediately preceded by T and immediately followed by H ?
H D T P D H T H D T P R T D H D T A H D T D H
(A) One (B) Two
(C) Three (D) None of these

8. How many Q's are there in the following series which are immediately preceded by consonant letters and immediately followed by vowel letters ?
A Q P A C P Q E R C T E Q P R G T Q O S P R U Q P R P Q U
(A) One (B) Two
(C) Three (D) None of these

9. How many consonants are there in the following series which are immediately followed by consonant letters but not preceded by vowel letters ?
APQRSTEPRESPERQTSEERPQER

(A) One (B) Two
(C) Three (D) None of these

10. How many B's are there in the following letter series, which are followed by G but G is not followed by S ?

BGSQBRNOBGNSQLTBGQTDBGUWXBGF

(A) 4 (B) 5
(C) 2 (D) 3

Time and Calendar Test

1. A is 300 days older than B and C is 50 weeks older than A. If C was born on Tuesday, on which day was B born ?
(A) Wednesday (B) Sunday
(C) Tuesday (D) Monday

2. Biswas remembers that his elder brother was born between 13th and 16th April while his mother remembers that he was born after 14th April and before 17th April. If the statements of both are considered correct then on which date of April he was born?
(A) 14 or 15 (B) 16
(C) 14 (D) 15

3. Sruti remembers that her elder son was born after 15 July and before 18 July. While her husband Ajit remembers that his son was born after 16 July but before 19 July. If the statements of both are correct, then on what day of July their son was born ?
(A) 18 (B) 26
(C) 17 (D) 19

4. Shirly remembers that her elder brother Mohan was born after 13th May and before 16th May while her mother remembers that he was born after 15th May and before 18th May. If the statements of both are supposed correct, then on which date of May was he born ?
(A) 15 (B) 14
(C) Cannot be determined (D) 18

5. Sudhir was born on March 3, 1980. Ajit is older than him by 4 days. If Republic day fell on Saturday in that year, then the day of Ajit's birthday is ?
(A) Thursday (B) Tuesday
(C) Friday (D) Sunday

6. Chandran was born on 12 October, 1965 and his brother is 2 years 27 days older than Chandran. On which day was his brother born if Chandran was born on Monday ?
(A) Monday (B) Saturday
(C) Sunday (D) Tuesday

7. Dr. R.P. Singh said to his assistant, "I go to see this patient at his residence after every 3.30 hours. I have already gone to the patient 1.20 hours ago and next time I shall go at 1.40 p.m." At what time this information was given to the compounder by the doctor ?
(A) 10.10 (B) 11.30
(C) 11.20 (D) 8.50

8. Lakshmi remembers that her elder sister was married after 8th May and before 11th May. While Chitra remembers that she was married after 9th May and before 12th May. If the statements of both are supposed to be correct, then on which date of May she was married ?
(A) 10 (B) 12
(C) 10 or 11 (D) 19

9. Vikram remembers that his elder brother was born after 15th June and before 19th June. While his mother remembers that he was born after 16th June and before 20th June. If the statements of both are supposed to be correct, then on which day of June he was born ?
(A) 17 (B) 17 or 18
(C) 18 (D) 17 or 19

10. Which of the following is not a leap year ?
(A) 1600 (B) 1200
(C) 2000 (D) 700

11. I was born on 30th Jan. 1964 and my cousin was born on 40th day after the day of my birth. On which date was he born ?
(A) 11 March (B) 9 March
(C) 10 March (D) 8 March

12. Which of the following pairs of months will have the same day on the first day of the months in a non-leap year?
(A) Feb-March (B) January-October
(C) April-July (D) All of these

13. Day before yesterday was Christmas day in 1980. If it is Monday today, then what day will be on the first day of the next year ?
(A) Tuesday (B) Saturday
(C) Monday (D) Friday

14. If 3rd of the month is Friday, what day will be on the 4th day after the 21st of the month ?
(A) Monday (B) Sunday
(C) Saturday (D) Tuesday

15. Which of the following is a leap year ?
(A) 2100 (B) 1996
(C) 2300 (D) 1902

16. If 5th of the month falls 4 days after Sunday what will be the day on the 16th of that month ?
(A) Wednesday (B) Monday
(C) Tuesday (D) Sunday

17. If Saturday falls four days after today which is 6th January, on which day did the first of December of the last year fall ?
(A) Tuesday (B) Friday
(C) Sunday (D) Monday

18. Which of the following months will have the same day on the last day of the months ?
(A) January - October
(B) April - June
(C) February - October
(D) (B) and (C)

19. How many Tuesdays are possible if the last day of the month is Wednesday ?
(A) 6 only (B) 5 and 4 both
(C) 5 only (D) 3 only

20. A day after tomorrow will be X-mas day. What will be the day on New-year-day if today is Monday ?
(A) Monday (B) Tuesday
(C) Sunday (D) Wednesday

21. What was the day of the week on 28th February 1995 ?
(A) Tuesday (B) Wednesday
(C) Monday (D) Thursday

22. Monday falls on 20th March, 1995. What was the day on 3rd November, 1994 ?
(A) Thursday (B) Sunday
(C) Tuesday (D) Saturday

23. The calendar for 1990 is the same as for
(A) 1997 (B) 2001
(C) 2000 (D) 1996

24. How many days are there from 2nd January 1995 to 15th March, 1995 ?
(A) 71 (B) 72
(C) 73 (D) 74

25. May 6, 1993 was Thursday. What day of the week was on May 6, 1992 ?
(A) Saturday (B) Tuesday
(C) Wednesday (D) Friday

Clock Related Test

1. At what time between 9 a.m. and 10 a.m. will the hands of watch point in opposite directions ?
(A) $17\frac{4}{11}$ min. past 9 a.m.
(B) $15\frac{4}{11}$ min. past 9 a.m.
(C) $14\frac{4}{11}$ min. past 9 a.m.
(D) $16\frac{4}{11}$ min. past 9 a.m.

2. At what time are the hands of a clock together between 6 and 7 ?
(A) $32\frac{8}{11}$ min. past 6 (B) $34\frac{8}{11}$ min. past 6
(C) $32\frac{5}{7}$ min. past 6 (D) $30\frac{8}{11}$ min. past 6

3. What angle will the two hands of a clock make at 6.20 a.m. ?
(A) 75° (B) 70°
(C) 60° (D) 45°

4. In 1/2 hour, the long hand of a clock will rotate through an angle of
(A) 75° (B) 60°
(C) 90° (D) 180°

5. How many times the hands of a clock will be in vertically opposite directions from 10 a.m. to 10 p.m. ?
(A) 12 times (B) 20 times
(C) 48 times (D) 36 times

6. At what time between 4 and 5 o'clock will the hands of a watch point in opposite directions ?
(A) 45 min. past 4 (B) 40 min. past 4
(C) $50\frac{4}{11}$ min. past 4 (D) $54\frac{6}{11}$ min. past 4

7. How many times are the hands of a clock at right angles in a day ?
(A) 22 (B) 24 (C) 44 (D) 48

8. At 3.40 the hour hand and the minute hand of a clock form an angle of
(A) 120° (B) 125° (C) 130° (D) 135°

9. At what time between 9 and 10 o'clock will the hands of a watch be together ?
(A) 45 min. past 9 (B) 50 min. past 9
(C) $49\frac{1}{11}$ min. past 9 (D) $48\frac{2}{11}$ min. past 9

10. The angle between the minute hand and the hour hand of a clock when the time is 8.30 is
(A) 80° (B) 75° (C) 60° (D) 105°

11. How many times do the hands of a clock point towards each other in a day ?
(A) 12 (B) 20 (C) 22 (D) 24

12. At what time between 7 and 8 o'clock will the hands of a clock be in the same straight line but not together ?

(A) 5 min. past 7 (B) $5\frac{2}{11}$ min. past 7

(C) $5\frac{3}{11}$ min. past 7 (D) $5\frac{5}{11}$ min. past 7

13. How many times in a day, the hands of a clock are straight ?

(A) 22 (B) 24

(C) 44 (D) 48

14. At what time between 5.30 and 6 will the hands of a clock be at right angles ?

(A) $43\frac{5}{11}$ min. past 5 (B) $43\frac{7}{11}$ min. past 5

(C) 40 min. past 5 (D) 45 min. past 5

15. At what angle the hands of a clock are inclined at 15 minutes past 5 ?

(A) 90° (B) 45° (C) 180° (D) $67\frac{1}{2}°$

Mathematical Operation Test

1. If + means ÷, × means –, ÷ means × and – means +, then $8 + 6 \times 4 \div 3 - 4 = ?$

(A) –12 (B) $\frac{-20}{3}$

(C) 12 (D) None of these

2. If × means ÷, – means ×, ÷ means + and + means –, then $(3 - 15 \div 19) \times 8 + 6 = ?$

(A) 8 (B) 4 (C) 2 (D) –1

3. If A stands for +, B stands for –, C stands for ×, then what is the value of (10 C 4) A (4 C 4) B6 ?

(A) 60 (B) 56 (C) 50 (D) 46

4. If – means ÷, + means ×, ÷ means – and × means +, then which of the following equations is correct ?

(A) $52 \div 4 + 5 \times 8 - 2 = 36$

(B) $43 \times 7 \div 5 + 4 - 8 = 25$

(C) $36 \times 4 - 12 + 5 \div 3 = 420$

(D) $36 - 12 \times 6 \div 3 + 4 = 60$

5. Which one of the four interchanges in signs and numbers would make the given equation correct ?

$$3 + 5 - 2 = 4$$

(A) + and –, 2 and 3

(B) + and –, 2 and 5

(C) + and –, 3 and 5 (D) None of these

6. If + means ÷, × means +, ÷ means – and – means ×, then $16 + 4 \times 8 \div 15 - 2 = ?$

(A) 18 (B) 6

(C) 12 (D) None of these

7. If × means –, – means +, + means ÷ and ÷ means ×, then $15 - 4 \times 10 + 2 \div 3 = ?$

(A) 4 (B) 42

(C) 10 (D) None of these

8. If A stands for ÷, B stands for ×, C stands for + and D stands for –, then

15 A 3 C 9 B 3 D 5 = ?

(A) 25 (B) 22

(C) 27 (D) None of these

9. Which one of the four interchanges in signs and numbers would make the given equation correct ?

$$3 \times 15 \div 7 = 35$$

(A) × and ÷, 3 and 7 (B) × and ÷, 15 and 7

(C) × and ÷, 3 and 15 (D) None of these

10. If + means –, – means ×, × means ÷ and ÷ means +, then which of the following equations is not correct ?

(A) $10 \times 5 - 2 \div 4 + 6 = 2$

(B) $7 - 15 \times 3 + 6 \div 4 = 33$

(C) $12 \times 4 + 5 \div 9 - 2 = 16$

(D) $14 \div 7 - 5 + 10 \times 2 = 45$

Quantitative Aptitude

1. The sum of a number and its reciprocal is $2\frac{1}{20}$. The number is

(A) $\frac{5}{4}$ (B) $\frac{3}{4}$ (C) $\frac{4}{3}$ (D) $\frac{1}{6}$

2. A two digit number is such that the product of the digits is 8. When 18 is added to the number, the digits are reversed. The number is

(A) 18 (B) 24 (C) 81 (D) 42

3. The perimeter of a rectangle is 82 m and its area is 400 m^2. The breadth of the rectangle is

(A) 25m (B) 16 m

(C) 9 m (D) 20 m

4. Out of a group of swans, $\left(\frac{7}{2}\right)$ times the square root of the number are swimming in water while two remaining are playing on the shore. The total number of swans is

(A) 4 (B) 8 (C) 12 (D) 16

5. If $\sqrt[3]{32} = 2^x$, then x is equal to

(A) 5 (B) 3 (C) 3/5 (D) 5/3

6. If $3^{4x-2} = 729$, then the value of x is
(A) 1 (B) 1.5 (C) 2 (D) 2.5

7. If $\left(\frac{a}{b}\right)^{x-1} = \left(\frac{b}{a}\right)^{x-3}$, then x is equal to
(A) 1 (B) 1/2 (C) 7/2 (D) 2

8. If $2^x - 2^{x-1} = 4$, then the value of x^x is
(A) 27 (B) 4 (C) 1 (D) 256

9. The value of x for which $2^{x+4} - 2^{x+2} = 3$, is
(A) 0 (B) –2 (C) 2 (D) –1

10. If $x = y^a$, $y = z^b$ and $z = x^c$, then the value of abc is
(A) 4 (B) 3
(C) 2 (D) 1

11. If $2^x = 3^y = 6^{-z}$, then $\left(\frac{1}{x}+\frac{1}{y}+\frac{1}{z}\right)$ is equal to
(A) 0 (B) 1
(C) 3/2 (D) –1/2

12. If $a^x = b$, $b^y = c$ and $c^z = a$, then the value of xyz is
(A) 0 (B) 1
(C) 1/3 (D) 1/2

13. The denominator of a rational number is 3 more than its numerator. If the numerator is increased by 7 and the denominator is decreased by 2, we obtain 2. The rational number is
(A) 1/4 (B) 5/8
(C) 7/10 (D) 8/11

14. If 1 is added to the denominator of a fraction, it becomes (1/2) and if 1 is added to the numerator, the fraction becomes 1. The fraction is
(A) 4/7 (B) 5/9
(C) 2/3 (D) 10/11

15. Four-fifth of a number is more than three-fourth of the number by 4. The number is
(A) 64 (B) 72
(C) 80 (D) 84

16. On dividing 50 into two parts such that the sum of their reciprocals is 1/12, we get the parts as
(A) 20, 30 (B) 24, 26
(C) 28, 22 (D) 36, 14

17. There are two numbers such that the sum of twice the first and thrice the second is 18, while the sum of thrice the first and twice the second is 17. The larger of the two is
(A) 4 (B) 6
(C) 8 (D) 12

18. The sum of three numbers is 102. If the ratio between first and second be 2 : 3 and that between second and third be 5 : 3, then the second number is
(A) 30 (B) 45
(C) 27 (D) 48

19. Of the three numbers, the first is twice the second and is half of the third. If the average of these numbers be 56, the numbers in order are
(A) 48, 96, 24 (B) 48, 24, 96
(C) 96, 24, 48 (D) 96, 48, 24

20. Three numbers are in the ratio 3 : 4 : 5. The sum of the largest and the smallest equals the sum of the third and 52. The smallest number is
(A) 20 (B) 27
(C) 39 (D) 52

21. Of the three numbers, the sum of the first two is 45, the sum of the second and third is 55 and the sum of the third and thrice the first is 90. The third number is
(A) 20 (B) 25
(C) 30 (D) 35

22. A boy was asked to multiply a certain number by 25. He multiplied it by 52 and got his answer more than the correct one by 324. The number to be multiplied was
(A) 12 (B) 15
(C) 25 (D) 52

23. Three pieces of timber 42 m, 49 m and 63 m long have to be divided into planks of the same length. What is the greatest possible length of each plank?
(A) 7m (B) 14m
(C) 42m (D) 63m

24. L.C.M. of two numbers is 14 times of their H.C.F. The sum of L.C.M. and H.C.F. is 600. If one number is 280, then the other is
(A) 40 (B) 60
(C) 80 (D) 100

25. The least number which when divided by 5, 6, 7 and 8 leaves a remainder 3, but when divided by 9 leaves no remainder, is
(A) 1683 (B) 1677
(C) 2523 (D) 3363

26. The greatest number of four digits which is divisible by each one of the numbers 12, 18, 21 & 28 is
(A) 9848 (B) 9864
(C) 9828 (D) 9636

27. The least perfect square which is divisible by 3, 4, 5, 6, 8 is

(A) 900 (B) 1200
(C) 2500 (D) 3600

28. The product of two numbers is 1600 and their H.C.F. is 5. The L.C.M. of the numbers is
(A) 8000 (B) 1600
(C) 320 (D) 1605

29. 21 mango trees, 42 apple trees and 56 orange trees have to be planted in rows such that each row contains the same number of trees of one variety only. Minimum number of rows in which the above trees may be planted is
(A) 3 (B) 15
(C) 17 (D) 20

30. Which part contains the fractions in ascending order?
(A) $\frac{11}{14}, \frac{16}{19}, \frac{16}{21}$ (B) $\frac{16}{19}, \frac{11}{14}, \frac{16}{21}$
(C) $\frac{16}{21}, \frac{11}{14}, \frac{16}{19}$ (D) $\frac{16}{19}, \frac{16}{21}, \frac{11}{14}$

31. The smallest perfect square number which is divisible by 15, 18 and 25 is
(A) 625 (B) 900
(C) 450 (D) 225

32. A gardener plants 17956 trees in such a way that there are as many rows as there are trees in a row. The number of trees in a row are
(A) 136 (B) 134
(C) 144 (D) 154

33. A group of students decided to collect as many rupees from each member of the group as is the number of members. If the total collection amounts to Rs. 2209, the number of members in the group is
(A) 37 (B) 47
(C) 43 (D) 107

34. In a class of 100 students, the mean marks obtained in a subject is 30 and in another class of 50 students the mean marks obtained in the same subject is 60. The mean marks obtained by the students of two classes taken together is
(A) 40 (B) 45
(C) 48 (D) 50

35. The average age of a committee of 8 members is 40 years. A member aged 55 years retired and his place was taken by another member aged 39 years. The average age of the present committee is
(A) 35 years (B) 36 years
(C) 38 years (D) 39 years

36. 5 years ago, the average age of A, B, C and D was 45. With E joining them now, the average age of all the five is 49 years. How old is E?
(A) 25 years (B) 40 years
(C) 45 years (D) 64 years

37. The mean temperature of Monday to Wednesday was 37° C and that of Tuesday to Thursday was 34° C. If the temperature on Thursday was 4/5th that of Monday, what was the temperature on Thursday?
(A) 34° C (B) 35.5°C
(C) 36°C (D) 36.5° C

38. Out of three given numbers, the first one is twice the second and three times the third. If the average of these numbers is 88, then the difference between first and third is
(A) 48 (B) 72
(C) 96 (D) 32

39. The average of marks obtained by 120 candidates was 35. If the average of passed candidates was 39 and that of failed candidates was 15, the number of candidates who passed the examination, is
(A) 100 (B) 110
(C) 120 (D) 150

40. A bag contains Rs. 600 in the form of one-rupee, 50-paise and 25-paise coins in the ratio 3 : 4 : 12. The number of 25-paise coins is
(A) 600 (B) 900
(C) 1200 (D) 1376

41. Rs. 5625 are divided among A, B, C so that A may receive one-half as much as B and C together receive and B receives one-fourth of what A and C together receive. The share of A is more than that of B by
(A) Rs. 750 (B) Rs. 775
(C) Rs. 1500 (D) Rs. 1600

42. The prices of a scooter and a moped are in the ratio 9 : 5. If a scooter costs Rs. 6800 more than a moped, the price of a scooter is
(A) Rs. 17000 (B) Rs. 13600
(C) Rs. 15300 (D) Rs. 16200

43. In a mixture of 60 litres, the ratio of milk and water is 2 : 1. If the ratio of milk and water is to be 1 : 2, then the amount of water (in litres) to be further added is
(A) 20 (B) 30
(C) 40 (D) 60

44. Arun, Maya and Satya started a shop by investing Rs. 27000, Rs. 81000 and Rs. 72000

respectively. At the end of the year the profit was distributed in the ratio of their investments. If Maya's share of profit be Rs. 36000, the total profit was

(A) Rs. 63000 (B) Rs. 80000
(C) Rs. 108000 (D) Rs. 116000

45. A and B invest in a business in the ratio 3 : 2. If 5% of the total profit goes to charity and A's share is Rs. 85500, the total profit (in rupees) is

(A) 142500 (B) 150000
(C) 153750 (D) 157600

46. A, B, C enter into partnership. A invests some money at the beginning. B invests double the amount after 6 months and C invests thrice the amount after 8 months. If the annual profit be Rs. 9000, then C's share is

(A) Rs. 3000 (B) Rs. 2875
(C) Rs. 3600 (D) Rs. 3750

47. The manufacturer of a certain item can sell all he can produce at the selling price of Rs. 60 each. It costs him Rs. 40 in materials and labour to produce each item and he has overhead expenses of Rs. 3000 per week in order to operate the plant. The number of units he should produce and sell in order to make a profit of at least Rs. 1000 per week, is

(A) 400 (B) 300
(C) 250 (D) 200

48. A dishonest dealer sells his goods at the cost price and still earns a profit of 25% by underweighing. What weight does he use for a kg?

(A) 750 gm (B) 800 gm
(C) 825 gm (D) 850 gm

49. A retailer buys a sewing machine at a discount of 15% and sells it for Rs. 1955. Thus, he makes a profit of 15%. The discount is

(A) Rs. 270 (B) Rs. 290
(C) Rs. 300 (D) Rs. 280

50. Tarun bought a T.V. with 20% discount on the labelled price. Had he bought it with 25% discount, he would have saved Rs. 500. At what price did he buy the T.V.?

(A) Rs. 5000 (B) Rs. 10000
(C) Rs. 12000 (D) None of these

51. A, B and C together can finish a piece of work in 4 days; A alone can do it in 12 days and B alone in 18 days. How many days will be taken by C to do it alone?

(A) 21 (B) 16
(C) 14 (D) 9

52. A and B can do a given piece of work in 8 days; B and C can do the same work in 12 days and A, B, C complete it in 6 days. In how many days can A and C finish it?

(A) 8 (B) 12
(C) 16 (D) 24

53. A can do a piece of work in 24 days while B alone can do it in 16 days. With the help of C, they finish the work in 8 days. In how many days can C alone do the work?

(A) 32 (B) 36
(C) 40 (D) 48

54. A tank can be filled by one tap in 20 min. and by another in 25 min. Both the taps are kept open for 5 min. and then the second is turned off. In how many minutes more is the tank completely filled?

(A) 6 (B) 11
(C) 12 (D) $17\frac{1}{2}$

55. The ratio of Meena's age and Kamla's age is 3 : 5 and the sum of their ages is 80 years. The ratio of their ages after 10 years will be

(A) 2 : 3 (B) 1 : 2
(C) 3 : 2 (D) 3 : 5

56. The age of a father 10 years ago was thrice the age of his son. Ten years hence, the father's age will be twice that of his son. The ratio of their present ages is

(A) 5 : 2 (B) 9 : 2
(C) 7 : 3 (D) 13 : 4

57. A person takes a loan of Rs. 200 at 5% simple interest. He returns Rs. 100 at the end of 1 year. In order to clear his dues at the end of 2 years, he would pay

(A) Rs. 100 (B) Rs. 105
(C) Rs. 110 (D) Rs. 115.50

58. The simple interest on a sum of money will be Rs. 600 after 10 years. If the principal is trebled after 5 years, what will be the total interest at the end of the tenth year?

(A) Rs. 600 (B) Rs. 900
(C) Rs. 1200 (D) Data inadequate

59. Two equal amounts of money are deposited in two banks, each at 15% per annum, for $3\frac{1}{2}$ years and 5 years. If the difference between their interests is Rs. 144, each sum is

(A) Rs. 460 (B) Rs. 500
(C) Rs. 640 (D) Rs. 720

60. The rate of interest on a sum of money is 4% per annum for the first 2 years, 6% per annum for the next 4 years and 8% per annum for the period beyond 6 years. If the simple interest accrued by the sum for a total period of 9 years is Rs. 1120, what is the sum?

(A) Rs. 1500 (B) Rs. 2000
(C) Rs. 2500 (D) Rs. 4000

61. The rates of simple interest in two banks A and B are in the ratio 5 : 4. A person wants to deposit his total savings in two banks in such a way that he received equal half yearly interest from both. He should deposit the savings in banks A and B in the ratio

(A) 5 : 2 (B) 2 : 5
(C) 4 : 5 (D) 5 : 4

62. The difference between the simple interest and the compound interest on Rs. 600 for 1 year at 10% per annum, reckoned half-yearly is

(A) Nil (B) Rs. 6.50
(C) Rs. 4.40 (D) Rs. 1.50

63. The difference between the compound interest and the simple interest on a sum of money lent for 2 years at 10% is Rs. 40. The sum is

(A) Rs. 8000 (B) Rs. 6000
(C) Rs. 5000 (D) Rs. 4000

64. A saving bank gives interest which compounds annually. Mr. X deposited Rs. 1000 and received Rs. 121 as cumulative interest at the end of second year. Rate of compound interest per annum is

(A) 10% (B) 20%
(C) 10.5% (D) 20.5%

65. A sum of Rs. 550 was taken as a loan. This is to be paid back in two equal annual installments. If the rate of interest be 20% compounded annually, then the value of each instalment is

(A) Rs. 421 (B) Rs. 396
(C) Rs. 360 (D) Rs. 350

66. Three unbiased coins are tossed. What is the probability of getting exactly two heads?

(A) $\frac{1}{3}$ (B) $\frac{3}{8}$
(C) $\frac{2}{3}$ (D) $\frac{1}{2}$

67. Tickets numbered 1 to 20 are mixed up and then a ticket is drawn at random. What is the probability that the ticket drawn bears a number which is a multiple of 3?

(A) $\frac{3}{20}$ (B) $\frac{3}{10}$
(C) $\frac{2}{5}$ (D) $\frac{1}{2}$

68. One card is drawn at random from a pack of 52 cards. What is the probability that the card drawn is a face card?

(A) $\frac{4}{13}$ (B) $\frac{1}{4}$
(C) $\frac{9}{52}$ (D) $\frac{1}{13}$

69. One card is drawn of random from a pack of 52 cards. What is the probability that the card drawn is a king?

(A) $\frac{1}{13}$ (B) $\frac{1}{52}$
(C) $\frac{3}{13}$ (D) $\frac{1}{4}$

70. In a simultaneous throw of two dice, what is the probability of getting a doublet?

(A) $\frac{1}{6}$ (B) $\frac{1}{4}$
(C) $\frac{3}{4}$ (D) $\frac{2}{3}$

71. In a simultaneous throw of two dice, what is the probability of getting a total of 10 or 11?

(A) $\frac{7}{12}$ (B) $\frac{5}{36}$
(C) $\frac{1}{6}$ (D) $\frac{1}{4}$

72. 15 litres of a mixture contains 20% alcohol and the rest water. If 3 litres of water be mixed in it, the percentage of alcohol in the new mixture will be

(A) 17 (B) $16\frac{2}{3}$
(C) $18\frac{1}{2}$ (D) 15

73. 729 ml. of a mixture contains milk and water in ratio 7 : 2. How much more water is to be added to get a new mixture containing milk and water in the ratio 7 : 3?

(A) 600 ml. (B) 710 ml.
(C) 520 ml. (D) None of these

74. In a mixture of 60 litres, the ratio of milk and water is 2 : 1. If the ratio of the milk and water is to be 1 : 2, then the amount of water to be further added is

(A) 20 litres (B) 30 litres
(C) 40 litres (D) 60 litres

75. A train covers a certain distance in 50 minutes, if it runs at a speed of 48 kmph on an average. The speed at which the train must run to reduce the time of journey to 40 minutes, will be
(A) 50 km/hr (B) 55 km/hr
(C) 60 km/hr (D) 70 km/hr

76. A car takes 6 hours to cover a journey at a speed of 45 kmph. At what speed must it travel in order to complete the journey in 5 hours ?
(A) 55 km/hr (B) 54 km/hr
(C) 53 km/hr (D) 52 km/hr

77. An aeroplane travels different distances 2500 km, 1200 km and 500 km at the rate of 500 km/hr, 400 km/hr and 250 km/hr respectively. The average speed (in kmph) is
(A) 405 (B) 410
(C) 420 (D) 575

78. A girl goes to school from her village at 3 kmph and returns back at 2 kmph. If she takes 5 hours in all, the distance between the village and the school is
(A) 6 km (B) 7 km
(C) 8 km (D) 10 km

79. A and B travel the same distance at 9 kmph and 10 kmph respectively. If A takes 36 minutes longer than B, the distance travelled by each is
(A) 48 km (B) 54 km
(C) 60 km (D) 125 km

80. In covering a certain distance, the speed of A and B are in the ratio of 3 : 4. If A takes 20 minutes more than B to reach the destination, the time taken by A to reach the destination is
(A) $1\frac{1}{4}$ hrs (B) $1\frac{1}{3}$ hrs
(C) 2 hrs (D) $2\frac{1}{2}$ hrs

81. A is twice as fast as B and B is thrice as fast as C. The journey covered by C in 54 minutes will be covered by B in
(A) 18 min (B) 27 min
(C) 38 min (D) 9 min

82. A van can finish a certain journey in 10 hours at a speed of 48 kmph. In order to cover the same distance in 8 hours, the speed of the van must be increased by
(A) 6 km/hr (B) 7.5 km/hr
(C) 12 km/hr (D) 15 km/hr

83. If Raju walks from his house to school at the rate of 4 kmph, he reaches the school 10 minutes earlier than the scheduled time. However, if he walks at the rate of 3 kmph, he reaches 10 minutes late. The distance of the school from his house is
(A) 6 km (B) 4.5 km
(C) 4 km (D) 3 km

84. A rickshaw has to cover a distance of 80 km in 10 hours. If it covers half of the journey in 3/5 the time, what should be its speed to cover the remaining distance in the time left ?
(A) 8 km/hr (B) 6.4 km/hr
(C) 10 km/hr (D) 20 km/hr

85. The ratio between the rates of walking of A and B is 3 : 4. If the time taken by B to cover a distance is 24 minutes, the time taken by A to cover that much distance is
(A) 18 min (B) 32 min
(C) $10\frac{6}{7}$ min (D) $13\frac{5}{7}$ min

86. A boy runs at 15.6 kmph. How many metres does he run in 2 minutes ?
(A) 260 m (B) 312 m
(C) 520 m (D) 10 40 m

87. A boy riding a cycle at 12 kmph can reach a town in 4 hours 30 min. If he is delayed by 1 hour 30 min. at the start, then in order to reach his destination in time, he should ride with a speed of :
(A) 15 kmph (B) 16 kmph
(C) 18 kmph (D) 20 kmph

88. Gopi bought an article and sold it at a loss of 10%. If he had bought it for 20% less and sold it for Rs. 55 more, he would have had a profit of 40%. The C.P. of the article is
(A) Rs. 200 (B) Rs. 225
(C) Rs. 250 (D) Rs. 150

89. A shopkeeper sold three-fourth of his articles at a gain of 20% and the remaining at C.P. The gain earned by him in the whole transaction is
(A) 25% (B) 20%
(C) 15% (D) 10%

90. The percent profit made when an article is sold for Rs. 78 is twice as much as when it is sold for Rs. 69. What is the cost price of the article ?
(A) Rs. 51 (B) Rs. 55.50
(C) Rs. 60 (D) Rs. 55

91. Two mixers and one T.V. cost Rs. 7000, while two T.Vs and a mixer cost Rs. 9800. The value of one T.V. is
(A) Rs. 2800 (B) Rs. 2100
(C) Rs. 4200 (D) Rs. 8400

92. The marked price of a machine is Rs. 620. Due to off season, a 15% discount is allowed. The S.P. of the machine is
(A) Rs. 427 (B) Rs. 527
(C) Rs. 537 (D) Rs. 547

93. A fruit seller purchases oranges at the rate of 3 for Rs. 5 and sells them at 2 for Rs. 4. His profit in the transaction is
(A) 10% (B) 15%
(C) 20% (D) 25%

94. A sells a bicycle to B at a profit of 20% and B sells it to C at a profit of 25%. If C pays Rs. 1500, what did A pay for it ?
(A) Rs. 825 (B) Rs. 1000
(C) Rs. 1100 (D) Rs. 1125

95. What price should a shopkeeper mark on an article, costing him Rs. 153, to gain 20% after allowing a discount of 15% ?
(A) Rs. 224 (B) Rs. 216
(C) Rs. 184 (D) Rs. 162

96. If A : B = 8 : 15, B : C = 5 : 8 and C : D = 4 : 5, then A : D is equal to
(A) 2 : 7 (B) 4 : 15
(C) 8 : 15 (D) 15 : 4

97. If 0.4 : 1.4 : : 1.4 : x, the value of x is
(A) 49 (B) 4.9
(C) 0.49 (D) 0.4

98. If $A = \frac{1}{3}B$ and $B = \frac{1}{2}C$, then A : B : C is
(A) 1 : 3 : 6 (B) 3 : 1 : 2
(C) 2 : 3 : 6 (D) 3 : 2 : 6

99. If the ratio of A to B is 9 times the ratio of B to A, then $\frac{A}{B}$ could be
(A) 9 (B) 3
(C) $\frac{1}{3}$ (D) $\frac{1}{9}$

100. If $\frac{a}{3} = \frac{b}{4} = \frac{c}{7}$, then $\frac{a+b+c}{c}$ is equal to
(A) 7 (B) 2
(C) $\frac{1}{2}$ (D) $\frac{1}{7}$

101. What same number must be added to each term of the ratio 7 : 13 so that the ratio becomes 2 : 3?
(A) 1 (B) 2 (C) 3 (D) 5

102. An amount of Rs. 735 was divided between A, B and C. If each of them had received Rs. 25 less, their shares would have been in the ratio of 1 : 3 : 2. The money received by C was
(A) Rs. 195 (B) Rs. 200
(C) Rs. 225 (D) Rs. 245

103. Rs. 407 are to be divided among A, B and C so that their shares are in ratio $\frac{1}{4} : \frac{1}{5} : \frac{1}{6}$. The respective shares of A, B, C are
(A) Rs. 165, Rs. 132, Rs. 110
(B) Rs. 165, Rs. 110, Rs. 132
(C) Rs. 132, Rs. 110, Rs. 165
(D) Rs. 110, Rs. 132, Rs. 165

104. The ratio of the ages of father and son is 7 : 3. If the sum of their ages is 60 years, what is the difference in their ages ?
(A) 42 years (B) 24 years
(C) 18 years (D) 4 years

105. The sides of a triangle are in ratio $\frac{1}{2} : \frac{1}{3} : \frac{1}{4}$ and its perimeter is 104 cm. The length of longest side is
(A) 52 cm (B) 48 cm
(C) 32 cm (D) 26 cm

106. 60 kg of an alloy A is mixed with 100 kg of alloy B. If alloy A has lead and tin in the ratio 3 : 2 and alloy B has tin and copper in the ratio 1 : 4, then the amount of tin in the new alloy is
(A) 36 kg (B) 44 kg
(C) 53 kg (D) 80 kg

107. If three numbers in the ratio 3 : 2 : 5 be such that the sum of their squares is 1862, the middle number will be
(A) 7 (B) 14
(C) 21 (D) 35

108. Rs. 120 are divided among A, B, C such that A's share is Rs. 20 more than B's and Rs. 20 less than C's. What is B's share ?
(A) Rs. 10 (B) Rs. 15
(C) Rs. 20 (D) Rs. 25

109. A 5 cubic centimeter cube is painted on all its side. If it is sliced into 1 cubic centimeter cubes, how many 1 cubic centimeter cubes will have exactly one of their sides painted?

(A) 9 (B) 61
(C) 98 (D) 54

110. The area of a square field is 24200 sq. m. How long will a lady take to cross the field diagonally at the rate of 6.6 km/hr?
(A) 3 minutes (B) 2 minutes
(C) 2.4 minutes
(D) 2 minutes 40 seconds

111. The circumference of the front wheel of a cart is 30 ft long and that of the back wheel is 36 ft long. What is the distance travelled by the cart, when the front wheel has done five more revolutions than the rear wheel?
(A) 20 ft (B) 25 ft
(C) 750 ft (D) 900 ft

112. If the sides of a triangle measure 72, 75 and 21, what is the measure of its in radius?
(A) 37.5 (B) 24
(C) 9 (D) 15

113. A 5 cm cube is cut into as many 1 cm cubes as possible. What is the ratio of the surface area of the larger cube to that of the sum of the surface areas of the smaller cubes?
(A) 1 : 6 (B) 1 : 5
(C) 1 : 25 (D) 1 : 125

114. If each interior angle of a regular polygon is 150 degrees, then it is
(A) Octagon (B) Decagon
(C) Dodecagon (D) Tetrahedron

115. Four horses are tethered at 4 corners of a square field of side 70 metres so that they just cannot reach one another. The area left ungrazed by the horses is:
(A) 1050 sq.m (B) 3850 sq.m
(C) 950 sq.m (D) 1075 sq.m

116. If the diagonal and the area of a rectangle are 25 m and 168 m^2, what is the length of the rectangle?
(A) 17 m (B) 31 m
(C) 12 m (D) 24 m

117. A 4 cm cube is cut into 1 cm cubes. What is the percentage increase in the surface area after such cutting?
(A) 4% (B) 300%
(C) 75% (D) 400%

118. Pipe A usually fills a tank in 2 hours. On account of a leak at the bottom of the tank, it takes pipe A 30 more minutes to fill the tank. How long will the leak take to empty a full tank if pipe A is shut?
(A) 2 hours 30 minutes (B) 5 hours
(C) 4 hours (D) 10 hours

119. How many times will the digit '0' appear between 1 and 10,000?
(A) 4000 (B) 4003
(C) 2893 (D) 3892

120. The sum of the first 100 numbers, 1 to 100 is divisible by
(A) 2, 4 and 8 (B) 2 and 4
(C) 2 only (D) All of these

Direction (Q. 121-125): What will be the approximate value of given questions?

121. $456.675 + 35.7683 \times 67.909 - 58.876 = 1$
(A) 33382 (B) 3587
(C) 1540 (D) 2830

122. $(52.36)^3 = ?$
(A) 129600 (B) 138850
(C) 143550 (D) 165790

123. $\sqrt{100000} = ?$
(A) 260 (B) 277
(C) 284 (D) 316

124. $(564\% \text{ of } 212) \div 394 = ?$
(A) 3 (B) 9
(C) 18 (D) 21

125. $(7684 + 5454 + 9041) \div (601 + 296 + 557) = ?$
(A) 24 (B) 15
(C) 33 (D) 9

126. Two numbers are in the ratio of 1511. If their H.C.F. is 13, find the sum of the numbers.
(A) 52 (B) 208
(C) 338 (D) 390

128. A dealer wants to store 513 kg of sugar of type one and 1215 kg of sugar of type two into minimum number of boys of equal size. The size of the bag is
(A) 81 kg (B) 54 kg
(C) 17 kg (D) 27 kg

128. Find the greatest number which on dividing 1657 and 2037 leaves remainders 6 and 5 respectively.
(A) 137 (B) 127
(C) 147 (D) 79

129. Find the greatest number which divides 62, 132 and 237 to leave the same remainder in each case.
(A) 37 (B) 41
(C) 43 (D) 35

130. Find the difference between the L.C.M. and H.C.F. of

$$\frac{2}{3}, \frac{8}{9}, \frac{16}{81} \text{ and } \frac{10}{27}$$

(A) $26\frac{52}{81}$ (B) 1
(C) $\frac{80}{81}$ (D) $1\frac{1}{80}$

131. $\frac{1095}{1168}$ when expressed in simplest form is
(A) $\frac{13}{16}$ (B) $\frac{15}{16}$
(C) $\frac{17}{26}$ (D) $\frac{25}{26}$

132. The greatest common divisor of 1.08; 0.36; 0.9 is
(A) 0.03 (B) 0.9
(C) 0.18 (D) 0.108

133. Three difference containers contain 496 litres, 403 litres and 713 litres of mixtures of milk and water respectively. What biggest measure can measure all the different quantities exactly?
(A) 1 litre (B) 7 litres
(C) 31 litres (D) 41 litres

134. The maximum number of students among them 1001 pens and 910 pencils can be distributed in such a way that each student gets the same number of pens and same number of pencils is
(A) 91 (B) 910
(C) 1001 (D) 1911

135. Let N be the greatest number that will divide 1305, 4665 and 6905, leaving the same remainder in each case. The sum of the digits in N is
(A) 4 (B) 5
(C) 6 (D) 8

136. In a class of 100 students, 48 students secured 40 mark in English, 32 secured 60 marks and the rest 80 marks. Fine the average in English for the which class.
(A) 60 (B) 49.42
(C) 62.66 (D) 54.40

137. The average weight of a group of 10 people increases by 1 kg when one of them weighing 48 kgs is replaced by a new person. The weight of the new person is
(A) 62 kgs (B) 68 kgs
(C) 66 kgs (D) None of these

138. The average of 2 numbers is xy. If one of the number is x, the other is
(A) y (B) $2y$
(C) $xy - x$ (D) $2xy - x$

139. The average weight of 8 oarsmen in a about is reduced by 1 kg, when one of the crew, who weights 62 kg is replace by a new man. What is the weight of the new man?
(A) 70 kgs (B) 56 kgs
(C) 54 kgs (D) 66 kgs

140. The average weight of the three section A, B, C of a class is $50\frac{2}{3}$ kgs. The average weight of section B where there are 50 students is 55 kgs. The average weight of section C having 30 students is 45 kgs. If there are in all 150 students in three section, the average weight of students in section A is
(A) 50 kgs (B) $51\frac{1}{3}$
(C) $50\frac{2}{3}$ (D) None of these

141. An officer goes to his office on scooter at the speed of 40 kms per hour but return from office to his home at 60 kms. per hour. If the travel time both ways is 40 minutes. How far is his office from his home?
(A) 64 kms (B) 16 kms
(C) 18 kms (D) 32 kms

142. The average rainfall from Monday to Saturday is 0.7 cm, but the average for the whole week is 0.65 cm. What was the rain fall on Sunday?
(A) 0.35 cm (B) 0.25 cm
(C) 0.45 cm (D) 0.75 cm

143. The average of the first 5 prime number greater than 60
(A) 70 (B) 70.2
(C) 70.7 (D) 70.24

144. The average age of committee of seven trustee is the same as it was five years ago, a younger man having been replaced for one of them. How much younger was he than the trustee whose place he took?
(A) 30 years (B) 35 years
(C) 38 years (D) 40 years

145. A bastman's average for a certain number of innings was 42.5. In the next four innings he scored 46, 48, 41 and 56 runs and his average for all the innings was raised by 1.25. The number of innings he played in all is
(A) 9 (B) 8
(C) 11 (D) 12

146. What will be the compound interest, if a sum of Rs 10000 is borrowed at the rate of 5% per annum for 2 years, interest being compounded annually?
(A) Rs 1000 (B) Rs 11000
(C) Rs 1050 (D) Rs 1025

147. Ram invested a sum of Rs 2000 with a financing company at 12% per annum for 2 years. The interest at the end of the period received by Ram is
(A) Rs 560 (B) Rs 840
(C) Rs 480 (D) Rs 380

148. The difference in simple interest at 12% per annum on a certain sum for 2 years and 4 years is Rs 864. The sum is
(A) Rs 2500 (B) Rs 2750
(C) Rs 3600 (D) Rs 3400

149. Calculate the compound interest on Rs 16000 for 3 years where the rate of interest is 5% p.a.
(A) Rs 2400 (B) Rs 2420
(C) Rs 2522 (D) Rs 2620

150. What sum will amount to Rs 1440 in 5 years at 4% yearly?
(A) Rs 1300 (B) Rs 1200
(C) Rs 1250 (D) Rs 1350

151. In what proportion must sugar at Rs 16.60 a kg be mixed with sugar at Rs 16.54 a kg so that the mixture may be worth Rs 16.54 a kg?
(A) 2 : 5 (B) 2 : 3
(C) 3 : 2 (D) 3 : 4

152. In what proportion the two kinds of tea costing Rs 45.00 and Rs 49.50 per kg are mixed up to produce a mixture of Rs 18.00 per kg?
(A) 2 : 1 (B) 3 : 7
(C) 3 : 4 (D) 1 : 2

153. A dealer has 100 kg of wheat, part of which he sells at 7 percent of profit and the rest at 17 percent profit. He gains 10 percent on the whole. Find how much is sold at 7% profit?
(A) 30 kg (B) 45 kg
(C) 51 kg (D) 70 kg

154. A draper sold 224 metres of cloth partly at Rs 99.00 a metre and the rest at Rs 135.00 a metre. The total amount he got by selling the entire cloth is Rs 27216.00. How many metres of cloth did he sell at Rs 135.00 a metre.
(A) 84 (B) 140
(C) 80 (D) 144

155. A sum of 625 is made up of 80 currency notes which are either Rs 10 or Rs 5 denomination. How many are there of Rs. 10.
(A) 45 (B) 25
(C) 35 (D) 40

156. In what proportion must a grocer mix one kind of wheat at Rs. 13.50 kg with another at Rs 12 per kg in order that by selling the mixture at Rs 15.60 per kg, the may gain 20 percent?
(A) 1 : 2 (B) 2 : 1
(C) 2 : 3 (D) none of these

157. How many kg of salt costing Rs 6.00 a kg must be mixed with 16 kg of salt costing Rs 8.25 per kg so that 25 percent may be gained by selling the mixture at Rs 9.00 a kg?
(A) 14 (B) 12
(C) 10 (D) 15

158. A cask is field with a mixture of two liquids A and B, in the proportion 5 : 3. When 16 litres of the mixture is withdrawn and the cask is fitted with liquid B, the proportion becomes 3 : 5. How many litres does the cask hold?
(A) 24 (B) 40
(C) 54 (D) 70

159. A lump of two metals weighing 18 grams is worth Rs 7400 but if their weights be interchanged, it would be worth Rs 6010. If the price of one metal be Rs 720 per gram, find the price per gram of the second metal.
(A) Rs 250 (B) Rs 55
(C) Rs 65 (D) Rs 25

160. A man buys milk at Rs 15.00 a litre and after adding water sells the mixture at Rs 18 a litre making a profit of $33\frac{1}{3}$ percent. Find the ratio of water he has added to the milk.
(A) 9 : 1 (B) 1 : 7
(C) 7 : 1 (D) 1 : 9

161. X's Salary is half that of Y. If X got a 50% rise in his salary and Y got a 25% rise in his salary, then the percentage increase in combined salaries of both is
(A) 30% (B) 33.33%
(C) 37.5% (D) 75%

162. A dealer marks his goods 20% above cost price. He then allows some discount on it and makes a profit of 8% The rate of discount is
(A) 4% (B) 6%
(C) 10% (D) 12%

163. The length and breadth of a rectangle are 20 cm and 10 cm. respectively. The length is increased by 10% and the breadth is increased by 20%. What is the new area of the rectangle?
(A) 240 (B) 254
(C) 264 (D) 280

164. The number of seats in an auditorium are increased by 25%. The price on a ticket is also increased by 12%. What is the effect on the revenue collected?
(A) 37 (B) 40
(C) 42 (D) None of these

165. A and B start from the same destination and take the same route. A starts at 8 a.m. and drives at a speed 40 kmph. B starts at 9 a.m. and drives at a speed of 50 kmph. If the destination is 350 km away from the starting point, then how far will A be from the destination when B reaches there?
(A) 20 km (B) 30 km
(C) 50 km (D) 70 km

166. A train runs for 2 hours at a speed of 35 kmph. It runs for $3\frac{1}{2}$ hours at the speed of 60 kmph and then runs for $2\frac{1}{2}$ hours at the speed of 70 kmph. Find the average speed of the train.
(A) 50 kmph (B) 55 kmph
(C) 80 kmph (D) 56.87 kmph

167. A person travelled a distance of 610 km in 9 hours. He travelled the first phase at a speed of 40 kmph and the rest at 90 kmph. The distance travelled during that first phase is
(A) 140 km (B) 150 km
(C) 160 km (D) 170 km

168. In certain city the Taxi charges comprise of a fixed charge and the charge of the distance travelled. A person paid Rs. 156 for a journey of 16 km and another person paid Rs. 204 for the journey of 24 km. The amount paid by a passenger who has travelled 30 km is
(A) 236 (B) 240
(C) 248 (D) 256

169. In a certain code GALIB is represented by HBMJC. TIGER will be represented by
(A) UJHFS (B) UHJSF
(C) JHUSF (D) HUJSF

170. A group of 7 members having a majority of boys is to be formed out of 6 boys and 4 girls. The number of ways the group can be formed is
(A) 80 (B) 100
(C) 90 (D) 110

171. The number of observations in a group is 40. The average of the first 10 members is 4.5 and the average of the remaining 30 members is 3.5. The average of the whole group is
(A) 4 (B) 15/2
(C) 15/4 (D) 6

172. The price of petrol increases by 25%. By what percentage must a customer reduce the consumption so that the earlier bill on the petrol does not alter ?
(A) 20% (B) 25%
(C) 30% (D) 33.33%

173. In a college having 300 students, every student reads 5 newspapers and every newspaper is read by 60 students. The number of newspapers required is
(A) at least 30 (B) at most 20
(C) exactly 25 (D) exactly 5

ANSWERS

SERIES TEST

1. (A) 2. (B) 3. (D) 4. (D) 5. (A) 6. (D) 7. (A) 8. (B) 9. (D) 10. (A)
11. (B) 12. (D) 13. (A) 14. (A) 15. (B) 16. (B) 17. (C) 18. (A) 19. (D) 20. (B)
21. (D) 22. (A) 23. (A) 24. (D) 25. (A)

ALPHABET TEST

1. (A) 2. (B) 3. (C) 4. (D) 5. (B) 6. (C) 7. (A) 8. (C) 9. (A) 10. (B)
11. (D) 12. (B) 13. (A) 14. (A) 15. (C)

CLASSIFICATION TEST

1. (D) 2. (B) 3. (C) 4. (D) 5. (D) 6. (D) 7. (A) 8. (A) 9. (C) 10. (B)
11. (C) 12. (D) 13. (A) 14. (D) 15. (A) 16. (B) 17. (B) 18. (C) 19. (D) 20. (D)
21. (D) 22. (D) 23. (C) 24. (B) 25. (C) 26. (A) 27. (D) 28. (D) 29. (C) 30. (B)

CODING AND DECODING TEST

1.(D) 2. (A) 3. (D) 4. (B) 5. (D) 6. (B) 7. (C) 8. (C) 9. (C) 10. (B)
11. (C) 12. (D) 13. (A) 14. (D) 15. (A) 16. (A) 17. (C) 18. (A) 19. (B) 20. (D)

DIRECTION SENSE TEST

1. (A) 2. (C) 3. (C) 4. (C) 5. (B) 6. (B) 7. (C) 8. (D) 9. (A) 10. (D)
11. (B) 12. (A) 13. (A) 14. (C) 15. (D)

BLOOD RELATION TEST

1. (A) 2. (A) 3. (D) 4. (A) 5. (B) 6. (A) 7. (D) 8. (D) 9. (C)

ARRANGING IN ORDER TEST

1. (A) 2. (A) 3. (C) 4. (D) 5. (B) 6. (D) 7. (C) 8. (D) 9. (D) 10. (B)

LETTER-DIGIT TERM TEST

1. (B) 2. (C) 3. (C) 4. (D) 5. (B) 6. (A) 7. (B) 8. (C) 9. (D) 10. (A)

TIME AND CALENDAR TEST

1. (D) 2. (D) 3. (C) 4. (C) 5. (A) 6. (C) 7. (B) 8. (A) 9. (B) 10. (D)
11. (C) 12. (D) 13. (B) 14. (C) 15. (B) 16. (B) 17. (B) 18. (D) 19. (B) 20. (D)
21. (A) 22. (A) 23. (B) 24. (C) 25. (B)

CLOCK RELATED TEST

1. (D) 2. (A) 3. (B) 4. (D) 5. (A) 6. (D) 7. (C) 8. (C) 9. (C) 10. (B)
11. (C) 12. (D) 13. (C) 14. (B) 15. (D)

MATHEMATICAL OPERATION TEST

1. (B)	**2.** (C)	**3.** (C)	**4.** (A)	**5.** (C)	**6.** (D)	**7.** (A)	**8.** (C)	**9.** (C)	**10.** (D)

QUANTITATIVE APTITUDE

1. (A)	**2.** (B)	**3.** (B)	**4.** (D)	**5.** (D)	**6.** (C)	**7.** (D)	**8.** (A)	**9.** (B)	**10.** (D)
11. (A)	**12.** (B)	**13.** (B)	**14.** (C)	**15.** (C)	**16.** (A)	**17.** (A)	**18.** (B)	**19.** (B)	**20.** (C)
21. (C)	**22.** (A)	**23.** (A)	**24.** (C)	**25.** (A)	**26.** (C)	**27.** (D)	**28.** (C)	**29.** (C)	**30.** (C)
31. (B)	**32.** (B)	**33.** (B)	**34.** (A)	**35.** (C)	**36.** (C)	**37.** (C)	**38.** (C)	**39.** (A)	**40.** (B)
41. (A)	**42.** (C)	**43.** (D)	**44.** (B)	**45.** (B)	**46.** (A)	**47.** (D)	**48.** (B)	**49.** (C)	**50.** (B)
51. (D)	**52.** (A)	**53.** (D)	**54.** (B)	**55.** (A)	**56.** (C)	**57.** (D)	**58.** (C)	**59.** (C)	**60.** (B)
61. (C)	**62.** (D)	**63.** (D)	**64.** (A)	**65.** (C)	**66.** (B)	**67.** (B)	**68.** (A)	**69.** (A)	**70.** (A)
71. (B)	**72.** (B)	**73.** (D)	**74.** (D)	**75.** (C)	**76.** (B)	**77.** (C)	**78.** (A)	**79.** (B)	**80.** (B)
81. (A)	**82.** (C)	**83.** (C)	**84.** (C)	**85.** (B)	**86.** (C)	**87.** (C)	**88.** (C)	**89.** (C)	**90.** (C)
91. (C)	**92.** (B)	**93.** (C)	**94.** (B)	**95.** (B)	**96.** (B)	**97.** (B)	**98.** (A)	**99.** (B)	**100.** (B)
101. (D)	**102.** (D)	**103.** (A)	**104.** (B)	**105.** (B)	**106.** (B)	**107.** (B)	**108.** (C)	**109.** (D)	**110.** (B)
111. (D)	**112.** (C)	**113.** (B)	**114.** (C)	**115.** (A)	**116.** (D)	**117.** (B)	**118.** (D)	**119.** (C)	**120.** (C)
121. (D)	**122.** (C)	**123.** (D)	**124.** (A)	**125.** (B)	**126.** (C)	**127.** (D)	**128.** (B)	**129.** (D)	**130.** (A)
131. (B)	**132.** (C)	**133.** (C)	**134.** (A)	**135.** (A)	**136.** (D)	**137.** (B)	**138.** (A)	**139.** (C)	**140.** (A)
141. (B)	**142.** (A)	**143.** (B)	**144.** (B)	**145.** (D)	**146.** (D)	**147.** (C)	**148.** (C)	**149.** (C)	**150.** (B)
151. (C)	**152.** (D)	**153.** (D)	**154.** (B)	**155.** (A)	**156.** (B)	**157.** (A)	**158.** (B)	**159.** (D)	**160.** (D)
161. (B)	**162.** (C)	**163.** (C)	**164.** (B)	**165.** (B)	**166.** (D)	**167.** (C)	**168.** (B)	**169.** (A)	**170.** (B)
171. (C)	**172.** (A)	**173.** (C)							

SOLUTIONS WITH EXPLANATIONS

Series Test

1. The series follows the pattern :
   $4 \times 2 + 1 = 9$
   $9 \times 2 + 2 = 20$
   $20 \times 2 + 3 = 43$
   $43 \times 2 + 4 = 90$

2. 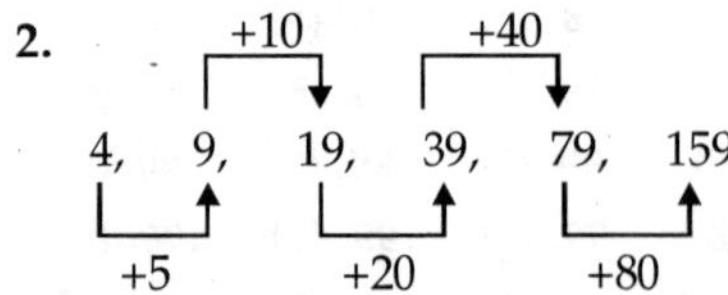

3. There are two series 3, 7, 11 and 2, 6, 10 with equal difference of 4 everywhere.

4. The 3rd term = 1st term × 4
   i.e. $6 \times 4 = 24$
   4th term = 2nd term × 5
   i.e. $5 \times 5 = 25$
   5th term = 3rd term × 6
   i.e. $24 \times 6 = 144$
   6th term = 4th term × 7
   i.e. $25 \times 7 = 175$

5. 3, 6, 12, 15, 30, 33
   +3 ×2 +3 ×2 +3

6. The series moves with a difference of 1, 2, 4, 8, 16, 32. Hence the missing number is 65.

7. The difference between the two consecutive terms of the series is in the sequence 42, 40, 38, etc.

8. 2, 20, 74, 110, 218
   +18 +54 +36 +108
   ×2
   ×2

9. There are two series 60, 120, 240 and 30, 15, 7½, etc. The terms in the first series are doubling and in the second they are being halved.

10. Differences between the consecutive terms of the series are 5, 10, 15, 20,.......
    2nd term = Ist term + 5 = 2 + 5 = 7
    3rd term = 2nd term + 10 = 7 + 10 = 17
    4th term = 3rd term + 15 = 17 + 15 = 32
    5th term = 4th term + 20 = 32 + 20 = 52
    6th term = 5th term + 25 = 52 + 25 = 77
    Hence the 7th term = 6th term + 30
    = 77 + 30 = 107

11. The numbers in the sequence are obtained by operating (×2 – 2), (×3 – 2), (×2 – 2), (×3 – 2) and so on. Therefore 20 is wrong.

12. The sequence in the given series is –6, –12, –20, –30, –42, –56. Hence the number 1134 is wrong.

13. The numbers in the sequence are obtained by operating ÷ 2 + 4. Hence 68 is wrong.

14. 16, 25, 41, 66, 102, 151, 251
    +9 +16 +25 +36 49 100
    3^2 4^2 5^2 6^2 7^2 10^2
    Therefore, number 251 should be replaced by 215.

15. 105, 85, 60, 30 –25, –45
    –20 –25 –30 –35 –40
    Hence, –25 should be replaced by –5.

16. As, 80, 50, 130, 100, 180, 150, 230
    –30 +80 –30 +80 –30 +80
    (A) (B) (C)
    Similarly, 900, 870, 950, 920
    –30 +80 –30
    Hence number 920 will come in place of (C).

17. As, 140, 68, 36, 16, 10, 3
    –4÷2 +4÷2 –4÷2 +4÷2 –4÷2
    (A) (B) (C) (D)
    Similarly, 284, 140, 72, 34, 19
    –4÷2 +4÷2 –4÷2 +4÷2
    Hence number 19 will come in place of (D).

18. As, 2, 4, 9, 20, 43, 90
    ×2+0 ×2+1 ×2+2 ×2+3 ×2+4

Similarly, 3, 6, 13, 28, 59

×2+0 ×2+1 ×2+2 ×2+3

Hence number 59 will come in place of (D).

19. D $\xrightarrow{+2}$ F $\xrightarrow{+2}$ H $\xrightarrow{+2}$ J $\xrightarrow{+2}$ **L**

K $\xrightarrow{-1}$ J $\xrightarrow{-1}$ I $\xrightarrow{-1}$ H $\xrightarrow{-1}$ **G**

M $\xrightarrow{+3}$ P $\xrightarrow{+3}$ S $\xrightarrow{+3}$ V $\xrightarrow{+3}$ **Y**

20. A $\xrightarrow{+2}$ C $\xrightarrow{+3}$ F $\xrightarrow{+4}$ J $\xrightarrow{+5}$ **O**

N $\xrightarrow{+1}$ O $\xrightarrow{+1}$ P $\xrightarrow{+1}$ Q $\xrightarrow{+1}$ **R**

D $\xrightarrow{+2}$ F $\xrightarrow{+3}$ I $\xrightarrow{+4}$ M $\xrightarrow{+5}$ **R**

21. In the series odd terms are obtained by moving previous odd term 3 steps forward, while even terms are obtained by moving the previous term 2 steps backward.

22. Each term is obtained by moving the letters of the previous term by 2, 3, 4, 5, 6 ...... steps forward.

23.

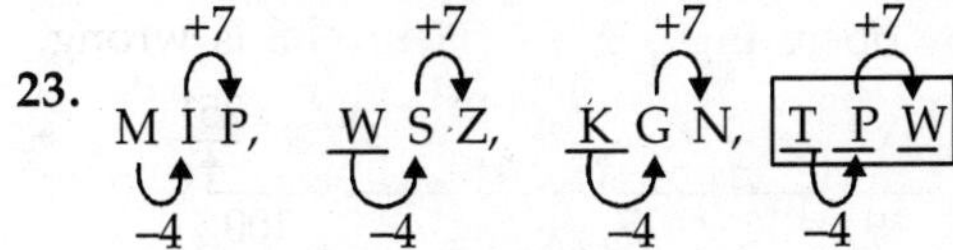

24. Each term is obtained from the previous term by moving each letter three steps forward.

25.

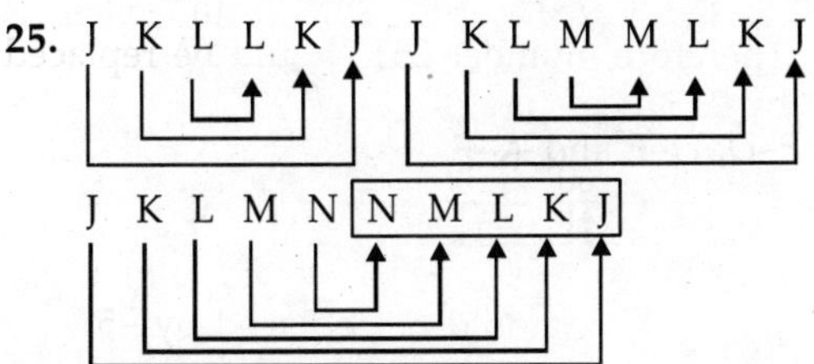

Alphabet Test

1. ABCDEFGHIJKLMNOPQRSTUV W X Z

In this series 15th letter from left is O and 8th letter to its right is W.

2. ZYXWVUTSRQPONMLKJIHGFEDCBA

Thus, 11th letter from right is K.

3. CDABGHEFKLIJOPMNSTQRWXUVYZ

Thus, 4th letter to the right of N is R.

4. ABCDEFGHIJKLMZYXWVUTSRQPON

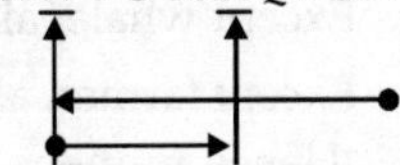

Thus, 10th letter from right is W and 5th letter to the right of W is R.

5. New word formed from AGRICULTURE will be IRGATLUCERU

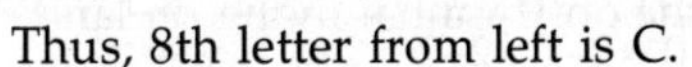

Thus, 8th letter from left is C.

6. Three words can be formed — COIN, SIDE, RING

7. 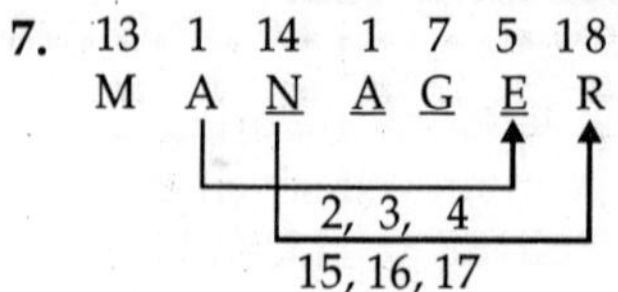

There are two pairs A — E and N — R.

8. 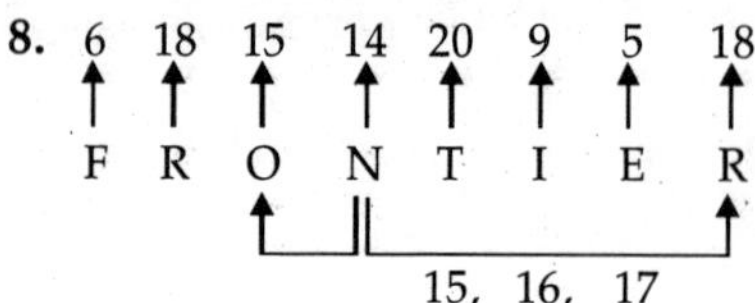

Two letter-pairs of the word are O — N and N — R.

9. Letters of the series will be written as :

d f h j l n p r t v x z

A B C (D) E (F) G (H) I (J) K (L) M (N) O (P) Q (R) S (T) U (V) W (X) Y (Z)

Thus, PERPENDICULAR ⇒ pErpEndICUlAr

10. 2 15 14 1 6 9 4 5

B O N A F I D E

5

3, 4, 5, 2,3 2,3,4

Six letter-pairs of the word are : O–N, B–F, A–D, F–D, D–E and A–E.

11. Letters deleted from the word ⇒ F A S E
Thus, meaningful word ⇒ S A F E

Thus, third letter from right in this word is A.

12. Letters deleted from the word ⇒ E L A T
Thus, meaningful words ⇒ T A L E, L A T E

e g i k m o q s u w y

13. A B C D (E) F (G) H (I) J (K) L (M) N (O) P (Q) R (S) T (U) V (W) X (Y) Z

Thus, REVULSION → ReVuLsioN

14. Export, Expose, Exposure, Expound, Expulsion.

15. Arranging the letters in alphabetical order, we have : A D E G I K N N R T U. Clearly K lies in the middle.

Classification Test

Type I

1. Except student, all the rest impart teaching to others.
2. Except Sandhya, all the rest belong to male gender.
3. Except sword all the rest are living beings.
4. Except whale, all the rest are reptiles.
5. Except farmer, all the rest are skilled workers
6. Except reader, all the rest are the associates of publishing industry.
7. Only the Duck lives in water.
8. Tiger is the only animal living on land.

9. Dogs bark not coop.
10. Institutions and their respective heads are paired here.
11. The second word is the result of the first word but judgement is not the result of advocacy.
12. Ostrich is the only word that cannot fly.
13. Except Dog, all others are herbivorous animals.
14. Lotus grows in water, others do not.
15. Sky comprises all the other three.

Type II

16. Except in (B), in other sets, letters are in reverse sequence.
17. Except (B), there is no gap in alphabetical sequence between the first and third letter of each group.
18. It is the only group that is in alphabetical order and the rest start from middle then first and then last.
19. Q is the only consonant in the group.
20. Except (D), in all the rest, there is a consecutive letters according to the English alphabet.

Type III

21. Except (D), no other group of numbers are divisible by 3.
22. Except (D), second number is 12 times the first.
23. Except (C), there is a difference of 8 in all pairs.
24. Except (B), in all other groups 1st number is 2 more than multiple of 2nd and 3rd numbers.
25. Except (A), all others are power of 2.

Type IV

26. Sweet - sour is related to the human sense, whereas others are not.
27. Cow - herd combination is not related to any country's capital
28. Enough - executive is not an opposite term as such like others
29. First is the working place of the second.
30. If both pairs are joined, they make an object.

Coding and Decoding Test

1. In the code each letter of the original word MELLOW has been moved seven steps forward. Hence, TENDER = ALUKLY.
2. The code is obtained by writing the letters in the reverse order. Hence CREATION may be written as NOITAERC.
3. As 1 2 3 4 5 6 7 → L N E I T N O
   M E N T I O N ↑ 3 2 5 4 7 6
   −1
   Similarly,
   1 2 3 4 5 6 7 → O T A E T N R
   P A T T E R N ↑ 3 2 5 4 7 6
   −1
4. Since SLATE is coded as GXRYW
   ∴ S = G, L = X, A = R, T = Y, E = W
   Then, STEAL = GYWRX
5. It is clear from the coding pattern that codes for R, U, B and Y are 0, £, $ and • respectively.
6. Letters at the odd places have been written one letter back and letters at the even places have been written two letters ahead in the coded word as their positions in the alphabet.
7. Word has been coded in such a way that codes for letters P are O and Q (one letter behind and one letter ahead of P in alphabet.) Similarly codes for O are NP and so on.
8. Letters of the word are written in the coded word in such a way that last and first letters, second last and second letters, third last and third letters and so on are written together in the coded word.
9. Letters at odd places have been written two letters back and letters at even places have been written two letters ahead in the coded word, as their positions in the alphabet. Hence word REASON will be coded as PGYUMP.
10. Letters at odd places in the coded word are one letter ahead of the letters and the letters at even places in the coded word are one letter back of the letters in the basic word as their positions in the alphabet.

11.

	P	I	C	T	U	R	E
	↓	↓	↓	↓	↓	↓	↓
	t	u	v	w	x	y	z
then,	P	I	E	R	C	E	
	↓	↓	↓	↓	↓	↓	
	t	u	z	y	v	z	

12. Since D is the 4th letter in the alphabet
∴ Writing D = 4
Similarly, writing COVER = 3 + 15 + 22 + 5 + 18 = 63
Hence, BASIS = 2 + 1 + 19 + 9 + 19 = 50

13. Since, MATHEMATICS = 12345123678
M =1, A = 2, T = 3, H = 4
E = 5, I = 6, C = 7, S = 8
Hence, MAHATMA = 1242312

14. By the statement, PRIZE = 16 + 18 + 9 + 26 + 5 = 74

15. By the statement.
CAP = 3 + 1 + 16 = 20

16. On comparing numbers with letters :
U = 1, N = 2, D = 3, E = 4
R = 5, S = 6, T = 7, A = 8
∴ START = 67857

17. Similar pairs of letters have been given the same numeric in each word. As a result pair UE in a word QUEUE has been coded 2, pair CH has been coded 1, likewise pair AN has been coded 5. Hence word BANANA is coded as B55A.

18. From (1) and (2),
is playing → ki ma.
From (2) and (4),
tennis → kop.
Then, from (2),
Asha → ja.

19. From (ii) and (iii),
re = summer.

20. By comparing I and II we get '4' means 'Good'. and by comparing II and III, we get '7' means 'Pictures'
Hence '8' means 'see'.

Direction Sense Test

1. Movements of Sanjeet are illustrated in the following diagram :

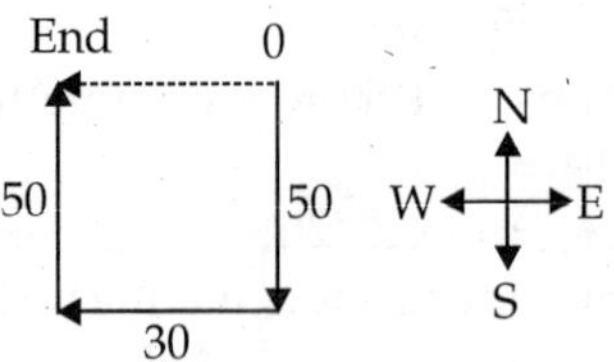

2. Movements of Roopali are as given in the diagram.

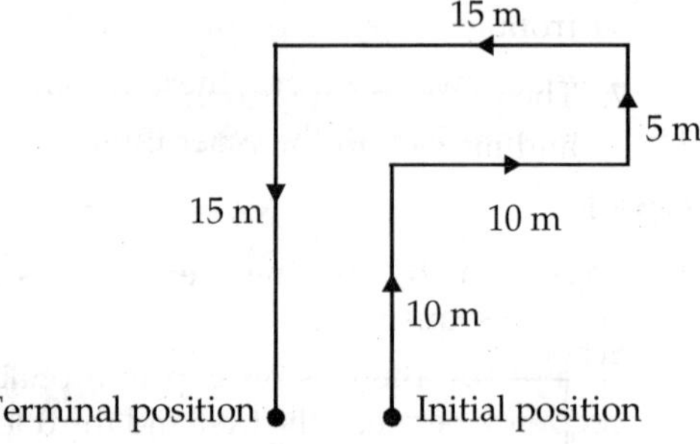

3. According to the direction of the question,

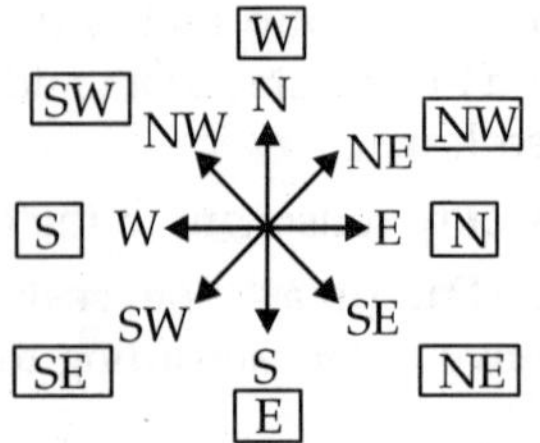

4. Movements of the boy are shown below.

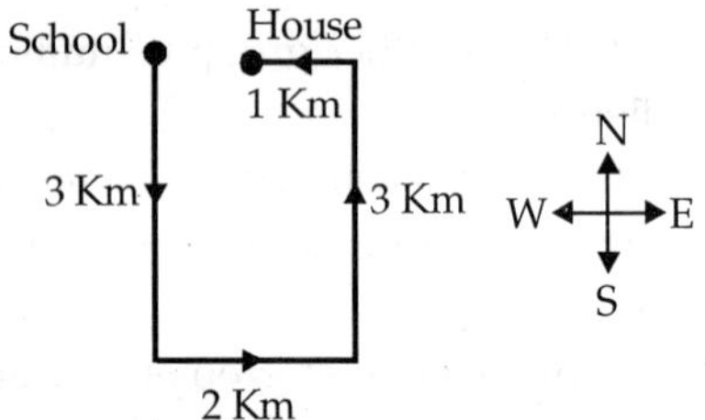

5. Movement of Danika is shown below.

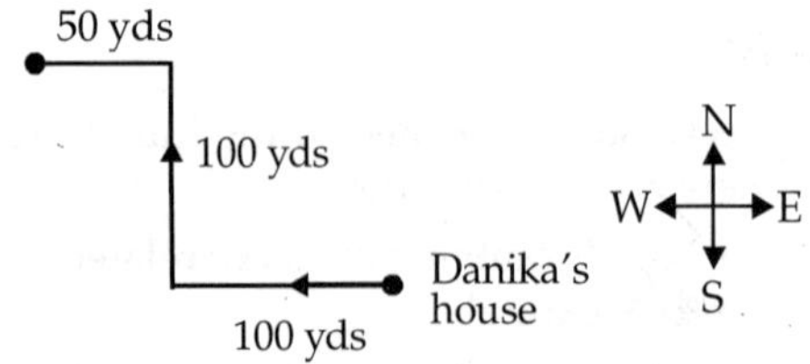

6. As Prakash faces towards East and he walks turning to his right, therefore, he starts to walk in the direction of South.
His movements are as follows-

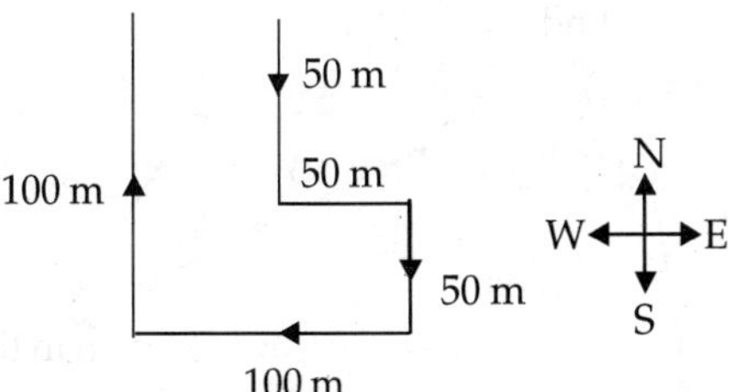

Hence he will be in the direction of West from his starting point.

7. The positions of school, house, post office and market are as follows:

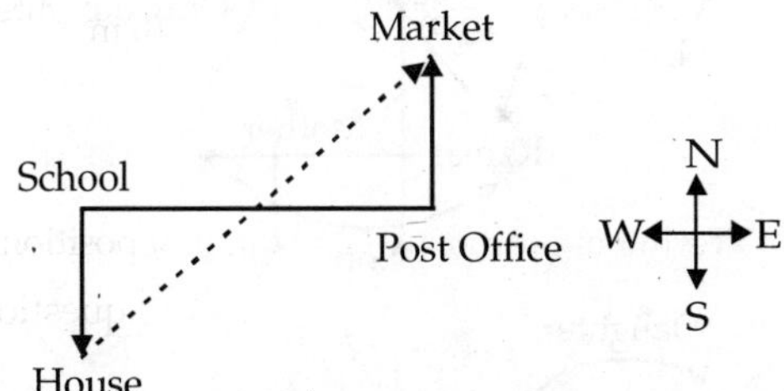

Hence the market is in the North East of my house.

8. Movements of Amit are as follows :

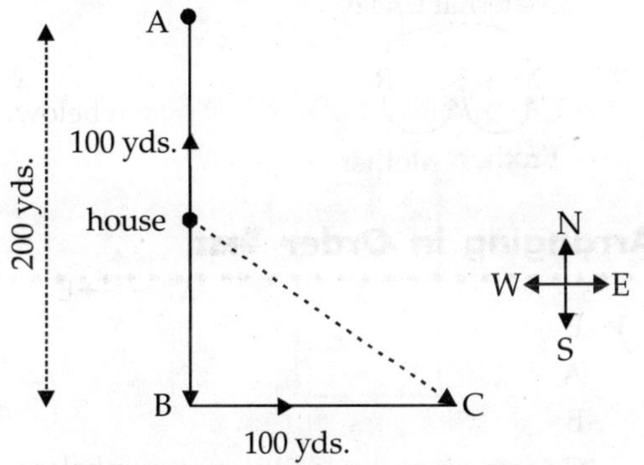

9. Pushpa's movements are as follows :

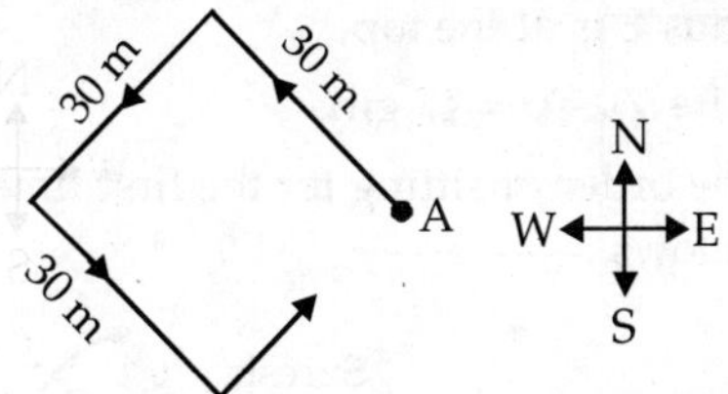

10. Since early in the morning the sun is in the direction of East, therefore, she started in the direction of East. Her movements are as follows :

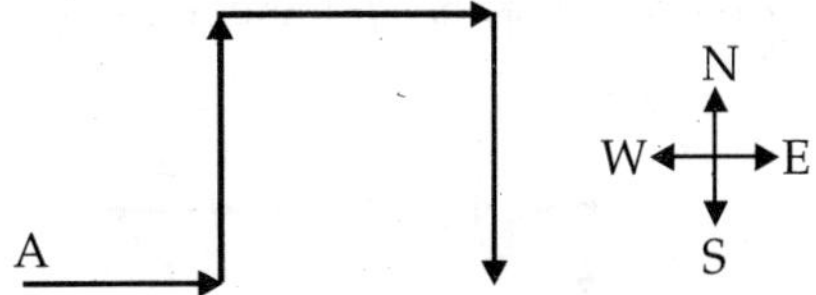

11. Movements of Milind are as follows :

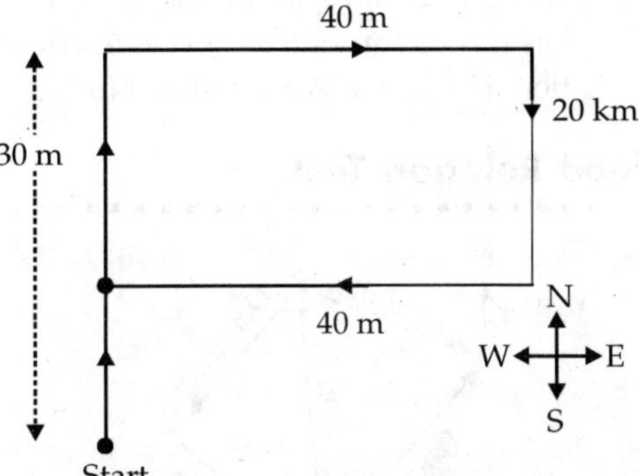

His distance from his original position

= 30 – 20

= 10 m

12.

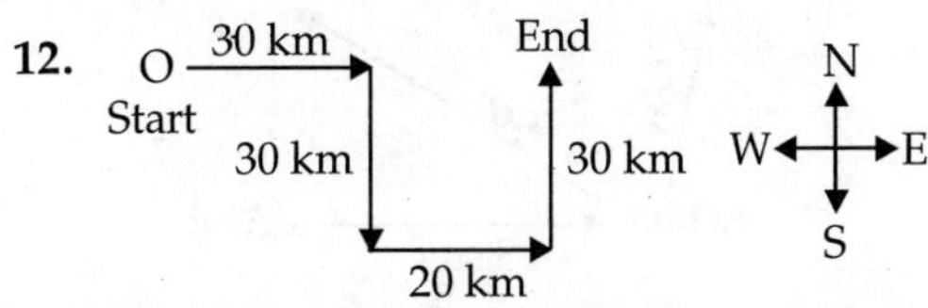

Required Distance = 30 + 20

= 50 km

13.

D
5
4 km
Start O
E
1 km A
9 km
5 km
2 km
B
C
N
W
E
S

$OD^2 = OE^2 + DE^2$

$OD = \sqrt{[OE^2 + DE^2]}$

$= \sqrt{[3^2 + 4^2]}$

$= \sqrt{[25]}$

= 5 km

14. According to the statement,

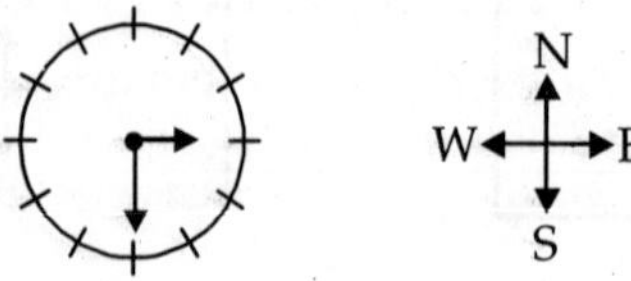

15. As East becomes South, therefore, the pole has turned through 90° in clockwise direction. Hence the West will be North.

Blood Relation Test

1.

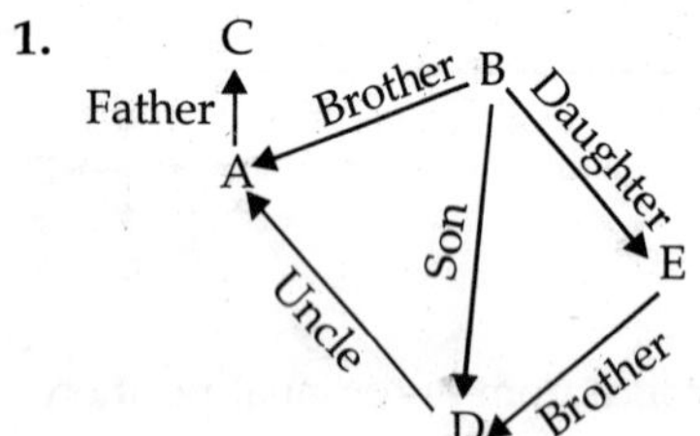

2.

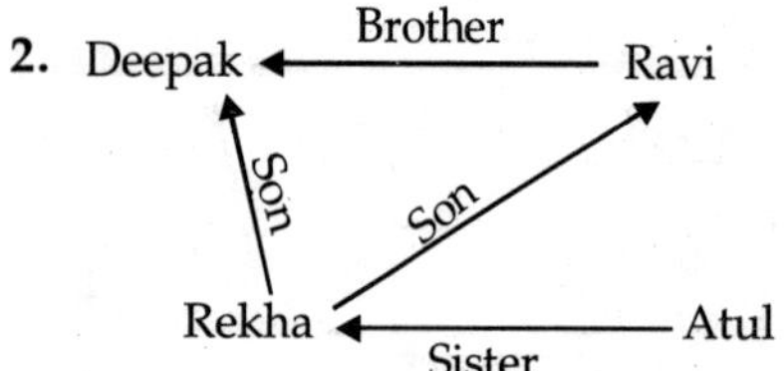

3.

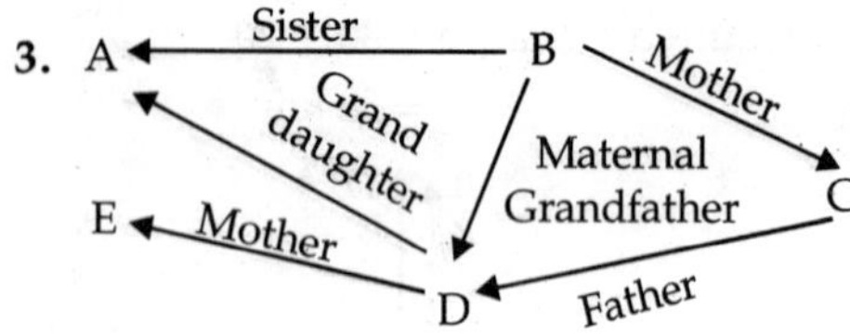

4.

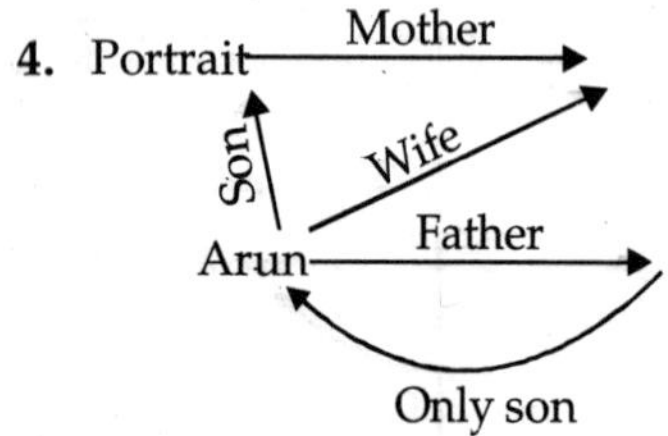

5.

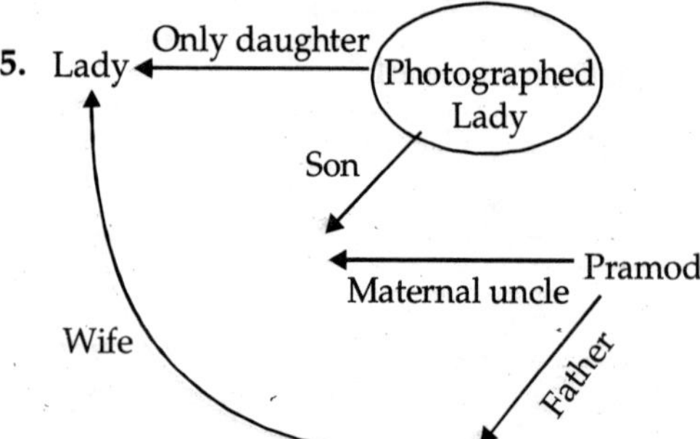

6.

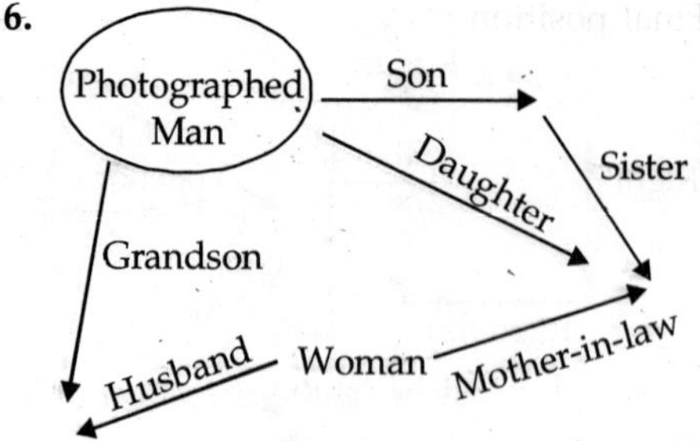

7.

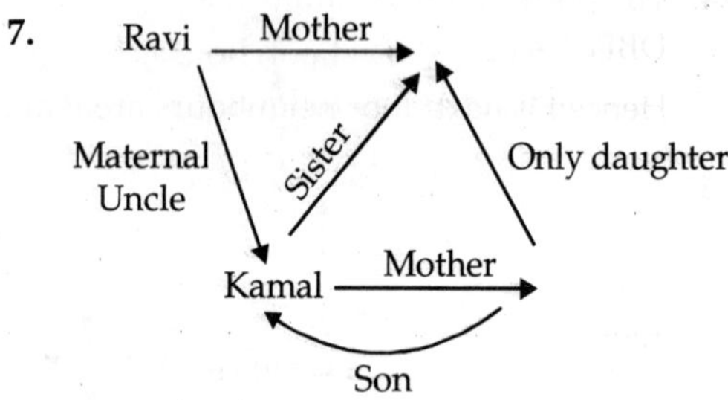

8.

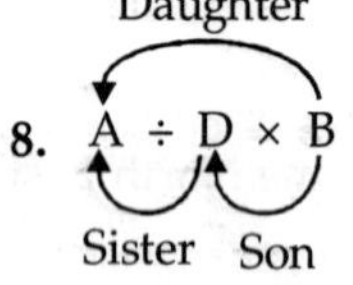

9.

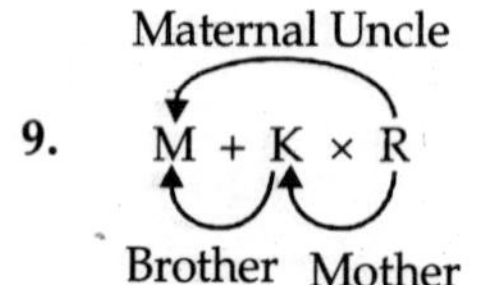

Arranging in Order Test

1. E
   A
   B
   C
   D
   Thus E is at the top.
2. (11 + 7) – 1 = 17 girls
3. The order of sitting for the first time was as follows :

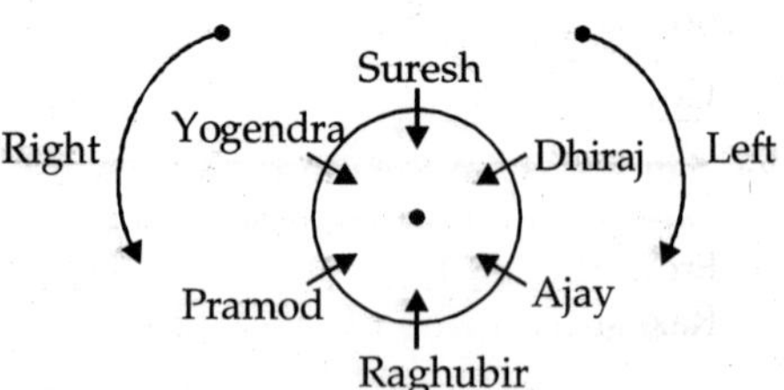

Final position :

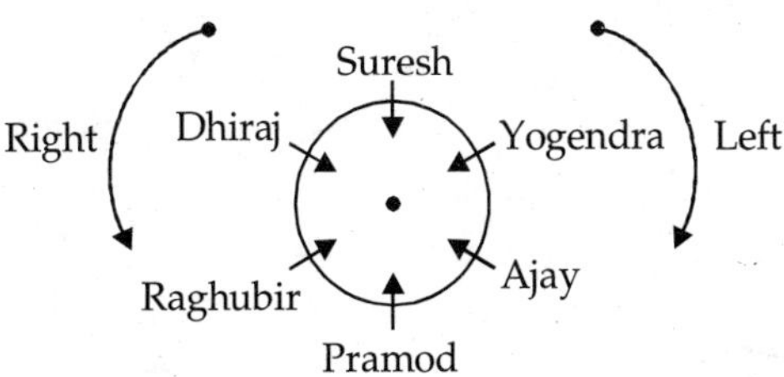

4. The position of six families is :
DBFCEA

Hence F's next door neighbours are B and C

5.

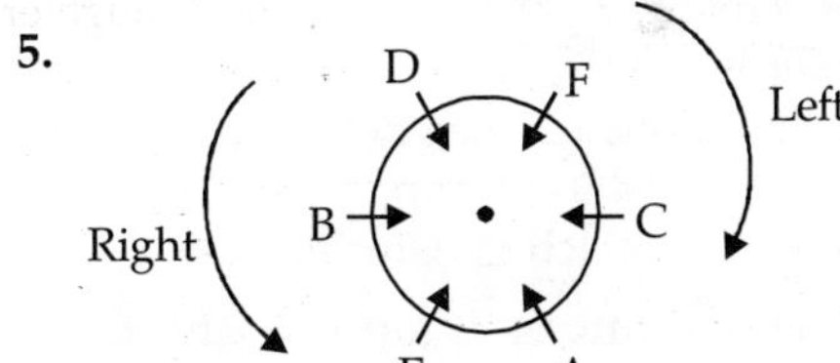

6.

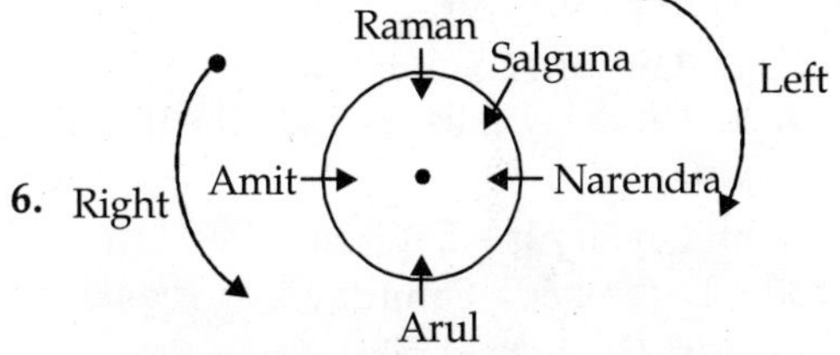

7. ∵ The difference of old and new positions of Srilekha in the same direction = 17 – 9 = 8th.

∵ The new position of Birla in the right direction = 13 + 8 = 21st.

8. According to the statement,

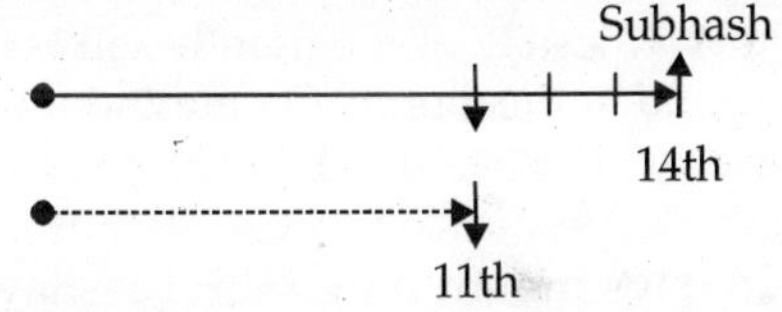

9. A > B ...(i)
C > D ...(ii)
D > B ...(iii)

From the above situations, we can say that A or C be the tallest, because there is no relation between A and C.

Govind Robin Latif Mohan Rakesh

10. ←——— Left ——— • • ——— Right ———→

From the above situation, we can say that Rakesh is in the extreme right.

Letter-Digit Term Test

1. According to the question,

5 ← Immediately preceded (×) — [7] — Immediately followed (✓) → 2 or 3

There are two 7's in the given series conforming to the given conditions.

2. According to the question,

4 ← Preceded (×) — [2] — Followed (✓) → 1

There are four 2's in the given series conforming to the given conditions.

3. According to the question,

7 ← Immediately preceded (✓) — [6] — Immediately followed (×) → 9

There are three 6's in the given series conforming to the given conditions.

4. According to the question,

8 ← Preceded (×) — 6 ← Preceded (✓) — [7]

There are three 7's in the given series conforming to the given conditions.

5. According to the question,

6 ← Preceded (×) — [3] — Followed (×) → 9

There are two 3's in the given series conforming to the given conditions.

6. According to the question,

P ← Immediately preceded (✓) — [A] — Immediately followed (✓) → C

There is one A in the given series conforming to the given conditions.

7. According to the question,

T ← Immediately preceded (✓) — [D] — Immediately followed (✓) → H

There are two D's in the given series conforming to the given conditions.

8. According to the question,

Consonant letters ← Immediately Preceded (✓) — [Q] — Immediately followed (✓) → Vowel letters

There are three Q's in the given series conforming to the given conditions.

9. According to the question,

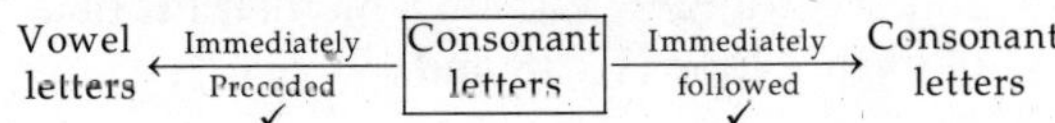

There are five consonants in the given series conforming to the given conditions.

10. Required B's in the following letter-series are printed in bold

BGSQBRNO**B**GNSQLT**B**GQTD**B**GYUWX**B**GF

Time and Calendar Test

1. C is older than B by $50 \times 7 + 300 = 650$ days. Divide it by 7 and you will get remainder 6. It means B was born 6 days after Tuesday.
2. According to Biswas the date of birth of his elder brother = April (14 and 15)
   and according to his mother the date of birth of her son = April (15 and 16)
   Hence the date of birth of Biswas's elder brother is 15th April.
3. According to Sruti the date of birth of her elder son = July (16 and 17)
   and according to Ajit the date of birth of her elder son = July (17 and 18)
   In these both statements common date is 17th July.
4. According to Shirly the date of birth of Mohan = May (14 and 15)
   and according to the mother of Shirly date of birth of Mohan = May (16 and 17)
   Here no date is common, therefore, the date of birth of Mohan cannot be determined.
5. 1980 is a leap year and Ajit was born on 28 February – 26 Jan is Saturday. Next Saturday will be on 2, 9, 16, 23 and 5th date after Saturday is Thursday.
6. 2 years 27 days = $2 \times 365 + 27 = 757$ days. $757 \div 7 = 108$ weeks and one day. Thus Chandran's brother was born on Sunday.
7. 1.40 P.M. = 13.40
   Time of information = (13.40 – 3.30) + 1.20
   = 10.10 + 1.20 = 11.30
8. According to Lakshmi the date of marriage of her elder sister = May (9 and 10) and according to Chitra the date of her marriage = May (10 and 11)
   Hence she was married on 10th May.
9. According to Vikram the date of birth of his elder brother = June (16, 17 and 18)
   and according to Vikram's mother, his date of birth = June (17, 18 and 19)
   ∴ The date of birth of Vikram's elder brother June (17 or 18)
10. 700 is not perfectly divisible by 400.
11. 1964 is a leap year, so 1 + 29 + 10. March will be actual date.
12. Feb-March = $28 \div 7 = 4$
    Jan-October = $(31 + 28 + 31 + 30 + 31 + 30 + 31 + 31 + 30) \div 7$
    $= 273 \div 7 = 39$
    Apr-July = $(30+31+ 30) \div 7 = 91 \div 7 = 13$
13. Day before yesterday is 25th December or Saturday. Next Saturday will be on the 1st of January 1981.
14. If Friday is on 3rd, then next Fridays will be on 10, 17 and 24th and 4 days after 21st means 25th which is Saturday.
15. In case of centuries it must be divisible by 400. While in other cases we divide it by 4 to find out a leap year.
16. Four days after Sunday means Thursday. Next Thursday falls on 12th. So 16th is on Monday.
17. If 6th January is – Saturday
    30th December = Saturday
    then 1st December of last year = Friday
18. Apr-June = $(30 + 31 + 30) \div 7 = 91 \div 7$
    $= 13$
    Feb-October = $(28 + 31 + 30 + 31 + 30 + 31 + 31 + 30 + 31) \div 7$
    $= 273 \div 7 = 39$
19. First Wednesday of the month will be 31-28 = 3 or 3rd of the month. On the 2nd it will be Tuesday (In case of 31 or 30 days of the month 5 Tuesdays are possible but in case of 28 days month only four Tuesdays are possible.)
20. Since X - mas day falls on 25th Dec., therefore, today it will be 23rd Dec. Hence on 23rd Dec. It is Monday. The number of days between 23rd Dec. and 1st Jan. is 9 days. Dividing 9 by 7 we get 2 as remainder. So it will be Wednesday on New Years day.
21. It was Tuesday.
22. Counting the number of days after 3rd November, 1994 we have :

Nov.	Dec.	Jan.	Feb.	March
27 +	31 +	31 +	28 +	20

= 137 days = 19 weeks + 4 days

∴ Number of odd days = 4

∴ The day on 3rd November, 1994 is (7–4) days beyond the day on 20th March, 1995.

So, the required day is Thursday.

23. We know that a leap year has 2 odd days and a general year has 1 odd day. If the sum of the odd days between the durations of the given calendar year to the expanding calendar year is equal to 8 or 15 or 22, then both calendar will be same. But a general calendar year excepts always a general calendar year and a leap calendar year excepts always a leap calendar year.

To use the above formula in the given options:

(a) 1990 + 1997 = 1 + 1 + 2 + 1 + 1 + 1 + 2 + 1 = 10

(b) 1990 + 2001 = 1 + 1 + 2 + 1 + 1 + 1 + 2 + 1 + 1 + 1 + 2 + 1 = 15

(Here both are general year)

(c) 1990 to 2000 = 1 + 1 + 2 + 1 + 1 + 1 + 2 + 1 + 1 + 1 + 2 = 14

(d) 1990 to 1996 = 1 + 1 + 2 + 1 + 1 + 1 + 2 = 9

24. Jan., Feb., March which mean a total of 30 + 28 + 15 = 73 days.

25. 1992 being a leap year, it has 2 odd days. So, the day on May, 1993 is 2 days beyond the day on May 6, 1992.

But, on May 6, 1993 it was Thursday.

Son, on May 6, 1992 it was Tuesday.

Clock Related Test

1. At 9 a.m. the hands are 45 min. apart. They will be opposite to each other when there is a space of 30 minutes between them. This will happen when the min. hand gains 15 minutes. But the min. hand will gain 15 minutes in $\frac{15 \times 60}{55}$ *i.e.*, $16\frac{4}{11}$ minutes. Hence the hands are opposite to each other at $16\frac{4}{11}$ min. past 9 a.m.

2. At 6 O'clock the hands are 30 minutes apart. Therefore in order to coincide the minute must gain 30 minutes.

∴ 55 minutes are gained by the minute hand in 60 minutes

∴ 30 minutes are gained by the minute hand in 60 minutes = $\frac{60 \times 30}{55} = \frac{360}{11} = 32\frac{8}{11}$ minutes

Hence the hands of the watch will coincide at $32\frac{8}{11}$ min. past 6.

3. 30 + 30 + 1/3 of 30 angles will be made by two hands of the clock.

30 + 30 + 10 = 70°

4. ∴ In 1 hour the minute hand rotates through 360°

∴ In 1/2 hour it will rotate through = $\frac{360}{2}$

= 180°

5. The hands of a clock are in opposite direction only once in an hour so they will be in opposite directions 12 times in 12 hours.

6. At 4 o'clock, the hands of the watch are 20 min. spaces apart.

To be in opposite directions, they must be 30 min. spaces apart.

∴ Minute hand will have to gain 50 min. spaces

55 min. spaces are gained in 60 min.

50 min. spaces are gained in $\left(\frac{60}{55} \times 50\right)$ min.

or $54\frac{6}{11}$ min.

∴ Required time = $54\frac{6}{11}$ minutes past 4

7. In 12 hours, the hands coincide or are in opposite direction 22 times.

∴ in 24 hours, the hands coincide or are in opposite direction 44 times a day.

8. Angle traced by hour hand in 12 hrs = 360°

Angle traced by it in $\frac{11}{3}$ hrs = $\left(\frac{360}{12} \times \frac{11}{3}\right) = 110°$

Angle traced by minute hand in 60 min. = 360°

Angle traced by it in 40 min = $\left(\frac{360}{60} \times 40\right) = 240°$

∴ Required angle = (240 – 110)° = 130°.

9. To be together between 9 and 10 o'clock, the minute hand has to gain 45 min. spaces.

55 min. spaces gained in 60 min.

45 min. spaces are gained in $\left(\frac{60}{55}\times 45\right)$ min or $49\frac{1}{11}$ min.

$\therefore$ The hands are together at $49\frac{1}{11}$ min. past 9.

10. Angle traced by hour hand in $\frac{17}{2}$ hrs

$$= \left(\frac{360}{12}\times\frac{17}{2}\right)^{\circ} = 255^{\circ}$$

Angle traced by min. hand in 30 min.

$$= \left(\frac{360}{60}\times 30\right)^{\circ} = 180^{\circ}.$$

$\therefore$ Required angle $(255 - 180^{\circ}) = 75^{\circ}$

11. The hands of a clock point towards each other 11 times in every 12 hours (Because between 5 and 7 they point towards each other at 6 o'clock only).

12. When the hands of the clock are in the same straight line, but not together, they are 30 minutes spaces apart. At 7 o'clock, they are 35 minute spaces apart. Minute hand will have to gain only 5 minute spaces.

55 min. spaces are gained in 60 min.

5 min. spaces are gained in $\left(\frac{60}{55}\times 5\right)$min

$$= 5\frac{5}{11}\text{ min.}$$

$\therefore$ Required time $= 5\frac{5}{11}$ min. past 7.

13. In 12 hours, the hands coincide or are in opposite direction 22 times.

$\therefore$ In 24 hours, the hands coincide or are in opposite direction 44 times a day.

14. At 5 o'clock, the hands are 25 min. spaces apart.

To be at right angles and that too between 5.30 and 6, the minute hand has to gain (25 + 15) = 40 min. spaces.

55 min. spaces are gained in 60 min.

40 min. spaces are gained in

$$\left(\frac{60}{55}\times 40\right)\text{ min.} = 43\frac{7}{11}\text{ min.}$$

$\therefore$ Required time $= 43\frac{7}{11}$ min. past 5.

15. Angle traced by hour hand in $\frac{21}{4}$ hrs

$$= \left(\frac{360}{12}\times\frac{21}{4}\right)^{\circ} = 157\frac{1}{2}^{\circ}$$

Angle traced by min. hand in 15 min

$$= \left(\frac{360}{60}\times 15\right)^{\circ} = 90^{\circ}$$

$\therefore$ Required angle $= \left(157\frac{1}{2}^{\circ} - 90^{\circ}\right)$

$$= 67\frac{1}{2}^{\circ}$$

Mathematical Operation Test

1. $8 + 6 \times 4 \div 3 - 4$

Changing the above signs into actual signs,

$8 \div 6 - 4 \times 3 + 4 = \frac{8}{6} - 12 + 4$

$= \frac{4}{3} - 12 + 4 = \frac{4 - 36 + 12}{3} = \frac{-20}{3}$

2. $(3 - 15 \div 19) \times 8 + 6$

Changing the above signs into actual signs,

$(3 \times 15 + 19) \div 8 - 6 = 64 \div 8 - 6 = 2$

3. (10 C 4) A (4 C 4) B 6

Changing the above letters into actual signs,

$(10 \times 4) + (4 \times 4) - 6 = 40 + 16 - 6 = 50$

4. From the option (A),

$52 \div 4 + 5 \times 8 - 2 = 36$

Changing the above signs into actual signs,

$52 - 4 \times 5 + 8 \div 2 = 36$

$\Rightarrow \quad 52 - 20 + 4 = 36$

$\Rightarrow \quad 36 = 36$

5. Given, $3 + 5 - 2 = 4$

Changing the above signs and numbers according to the option (C),

$5 - 3 + 2 = 4$

$\Rightarrow \quad 4 = 4$

6. $16 + 4 \times 8 \div 15 - 2$

Changing the above signs into actual signs,

$16 \div 4 + 8 - 15 \times 2 = 4 + 8 - 30$

$= -18$

7. $15 - 4 \times 10 + 2 \div 3$

Changing the above signs into actual signs,

$15 + 4 - 10 \div 2 \times 3 = 19 - 5 \times 3$

$= 19 - 15 = 4$

8. 15 A 3 C 9 B 3 D 5

Changing the above letters into actual signs,

$15 \div 3 + 9 \times 3 - 5 = 5 + 27 - 5 = 27$

9. Given
$3 \times 15 \div 7 = 35$
Changing the above signs and numbers according to the option (C),
$15 \div 3 \times 7 = 35$
$\Rightarrow \quad 5 \times 7 = 35$
$\Rightarrow \quad 35 = 35$

10. From the option (D),
$14 \div 7 - 5 + 10 \times 2 = 45$
Changing the above signs into actual signs,
$14 + 7 \times 5 - 10 \div 2 = 45$
$\Rightarrow \quad 14 + 35 - 5 = 45$
$\Rightarrow \quad 44 \neq 45$

Quantitative Aptitude

1. Let the number be x.
Then, $x + \frac{1}{x} = \frac{41}{20} \Rightarrow 20x^2 - 41x + 20 = 0$
$\Rightarrow (4x-5)(5x-4) = 0 \Rightarrow x = \frac{5}{4}$ or $\frac{4}{5}$.

2. Let tens digit = x.
Then, unit digit = $\frac{8}{x}$.
According to the question,
$\therefore \left(10x + \frac{8}{x}\right) + 18 = 10 \times \frac{8}{x} + x \Rightarrow 9x - \frac{72}{x} + 18 = 0$
$\Rightarrow x - \frac{8}{x} + 2 = 0 \Rightarrow x^2 + 2x - 8 = 0 \Rightarrow (x+4)(x-2) = 0$
$\Rightarrow x = 2$
Then, Ten's digit = 2 & Unit digit = 4.
$\therefore$ Number = 24.

3. Let length = x m. & breadth = (41 – x)m.
According to the question,
$x(41 - x) = 400 \Rightarrow x^2 - 41x + 400 = 0$
$\Rightarrow (x-16)(x-25) = 0 \Rightarrow x = 16$ or 25.
$\therefore$ Breadth = 16 m.

4. Let the number of swans be x.
Then, $\frac{7}{2}\sqrt{x} + 2 = x \Rightarrow 2x - 7\sqrt{x} - 4 = 0$
$\Rightarrow 2y^2 - 7y - 4 = 0$, where $y = \sqrt{x}$
$\Rightarrow (2y+1)(y-4) = 0 \Rightarrow y = -\frac{1}{2}$ or 4
$\Rightarrow \sqrt{x} = -\frac{1}{2}$ or $4 \Rightarrow x = \frac{1}{4}$ or 16.
$\therefore x = 16$
(Number of swans can not be a fraction).

5. $\sqrt[3]{32} = 2^x \Rightarrow (2^5)^{1/3} = 2^x \Rightarrow 2^{5/3} = 2^x \Rightarrow x = \frac{5}{3}$.

6. $3^{4x-2} = 729 = 3^6 \Rightarrow 4x - 2 = 6 \Rightarrow x = 2$.

7. $\left(\frac{a}{b}\right)^{x-1} = \left(\frac{b}{a}\right)^{x-3} = \left(\frac{a}{b}\right)^{3-x} \Rightarrow x - 1 = 3 - x \Rightarrow x = 2$

8. $2^x - 2^{x-1} = 4 \Rightarrow 2^{x-1}(2-1) = 2^2 \Rightarrow 2^{x-1} = 2^2$
$\Rightarrow x - 1 = 2 \Rightarrow x = 3. \therefore\ x^x = 3^3 = 27$.

9. $2^{x+4} - 2^{x+2} = 3 \Rightarrow 2^x \cdot 2^4 - 2^x \cdot 2^2 = 3$
$\Rightarrow 2^x(16-4) = 3$
$\Rightarrow 2^x = \frac{3}{12} = \frac{1}{4} = 2^{-2} \Rightarrow x = -2$.

10. $x = y^a = (z^b)^a = z^{ab} = (x^c)^{ab} = x^{abc}$
Thus, $x^{abc} = x^1 \Rightarrow abc = 1$.

11. $2^x = 3^y = 6^{-z} = k \Rightarrow 2 = k^{1/x}, 3 = k^{1/y}$ & $6 = k^{-1/z}$
$2 \times 3 = 6 \Rightarrow k^{1/x} \cdot k^{1/y} = k^{-1/z}$
$\Rightarrow \frac{1}{x} + \frac{1}{y} = -\frac{1}{z} \Rightarrow \frac{1}{x} + \frac{1}{y} + \frac{1}{z} = 0$.

12. $a = c^z = (b^y)^z = b^{yz} = (a^x)^{yz} = a^{xyz} \Rightarrow xyz = 1$.

14. Let the fraction be $\frac{x}{y}$.
Then, $\frac{x}{y+1} = \frac{1}{2}$ & $\frac{x+1}{y} = 1$.
Solving $2x - y = 1$ & $y - x = 1$, we get $x = 2, y = 3$.
$\therefore$ The fraction is $\frac{2}{3}$.

15. $\frac{4}{5}x - \frac{3}{4}x = 4 \Rightarrow 16x - 15x = 80 \Rightarrow x = 80$.

16. Let the parts be x and (50 – x).
Then, $\frac{1}{x} + \frac{1}{50-x} = \frac{1}{12} \Rightarrow \frac{50-x+x}{x(50-x)} = \frac{1}{12}$
$\Rightarrow x^2 - 50x + 600 = 0$
$\Rightarrow (x-20)(x-30) = 0$
$\Rightarrow x = 20, x = 30$

17. Let the numbers be x and y.
Then, $2x + 3y = 18$ and $3x + 2y = 17$.
$\Rightarrow x = 3, y = 4$. So, larger number is 4.

18. $x:y = 2:3$ and $y:z = 5:3 = \frac{3}{5} \times 5 : \frac{3}{5} \times 3 = 3 : \frac{9}{5}$
$\therefore x:y:z = 2:3:\frac{9}{5} = 10:15:9$.
Let the numbers be 10x, 15x and 9x.
Then, $10x + 15x + 9x = 102 \Rightarrow x = 3$.
$\therefore$ Second number = $15x = 45$.

19. Let the numbers be 2x, x and 4x.
Then, $2x + x + 4x = 3 \times 56 \Rightarrow x = 24$.
So, the numbers are 48, 24 and 96.

20. Let the numbers be 3x, 4x and 5x.
Then, $3x + 5x = 4x + 52 \Rightarrow x = 13$.
$\therefore$ Smallest number = 39.

21. Let the numbers be x, y z.
Then, $x + y = 45, y + z = 55, z + 3x = 90$.
$\therefore z - x = (55 - 45) = 10$.
Solving $z - x = 10$ & $z + 3x = 90$,
We get z = 30.

22. Let the required number be x.
Then, $52x - 25x = 324 \Rightarrow 27x = 324 \Rightarrow x = 12$.

23. Required length
= H.C.F. of 42m, 49m & 63m = 7m.

24. L.C.M. + H.C.F. = 600 $\Rightarrow$ 14×H.C.F.+H.C.F.= 600

$\Rightarrow$ H.C.F. = $\left(\frac{600}{15}\right) = 40$.

$\therefore$ L.C.M. = (600 – H.C.F.) = (600 – 40) = 560.
$\therefore$ Other Number =

$\frac{\text{H.C.F.} \times \text{L.C.M.}}{\text{Given Number}} = \left(\frac{40 \times 560}{280}\right) = 80$.

25. L.C.M. of 5, 6, 7, 8 = 840.
$\therefore$ Required number is of the form 840 k + 3
Least value of k for which (840 k + 3) is divisible by 9 is k = 2.
$\therefore$ Required number = $(840 \times 2 + 3) = 1683$.

26. L.C.M. of 12, 18, 21, 28 is 252.
$\therefore$ Required number must be divisible by 252.
Greatest number of four digits = 9999.
On dividing 9999 by 252, remainder obtained = 171.
$\therefore$ Required number = (9999 – 171) = 9828.

27. L.C.M. of 3, 4, 5, 6, 8 = $3 \times 2 \times 2 \times 5 \times 2$
$= 3 \times 2^2 \times 5 \times 2$.
$\therefore$ Required number = $3^2 \times 2^2 \times 5^2 \times 2^2 = 3600$.

28. L.C.M. = $\frac{\text{Product}}{\text{H.C.F.}} = \frac{1600}{5} = 320$.

29. H.C.F. of 21, 42, 56 = 7.
Number of rows of mango trees, apple trees and orange trees are :

$\frac{21}{7} = 3, \frac{42}{7} = 6$ and $\frac{56}{7} = 8$.

$\therefore$ Required number of rows = (3 + 6 + 8) = 17.

30. $\frac{11}{14} = 0.785, \frac{16}{19} = 0.842$ and $\frac{16}{21} = 0.762$
Since, .762 < .785 < .842,

we have $\frac{16}{21} < \frac{11}{14} < \frac{16}{19}$.

31. Least number divisible by 15, 18, 25
= L.C.M. of 15, 18, 25 = $(5 \times 5 \times 3 \times 3 \times 2) = 450$
$\therefore$ Required perfect square number
$= (5 \times 5 \times 3 \times 3 \times 2 \times 2) = 900$.

32. Number of trees in each row = $\sqrt{17956} = 134$.

33. Number of members = $\sqrt{2209} = 47$.

34. Total marks obtained by 150 students
$= (100 \times 30 + 50 \times 60) = 6000$.

$\therefore$ Mean marks = $\frac{6000}{150} = 40$

35. Total age of committee now
$= (8 \times 40 - 55 + 39) = 304$

$\therefore$ Average present age = $\left(\frac{304}{8}\right)$ years = 38 years.

36. 5 years ago, (A + B + C + D)
$= (45 \times 4)$ years = 180 years.
Now, (A + B + C + D) = $(180 + 4 \times 5)$ years
= 200 years.
Now, (A + B + C + D + E) = (5×49) years
= 245 years.
$\therefore$ Age of E now = (245 – 200) = 45 years.

37. $(M + T + W) = (3 \times 37) = 111$,
$(T + W + Th) = (3 \times 34) = 102$.
On subtraction we get : (M – Th) = 9
According to the question,

$\Rightarrow M - \frac{4}{5}M = 9. \Rightarrow M = 45$.

$\therefore$ Th = $\frac{4}{5}M = \left(\frac{4}{5} \times 45\right) = 36°$ C.

38. Let first = x. Then, second = $\frac{x}{2}$ and third = $\frac{x}{3}$.
According to the question,

$x + \frac{x}{2} + \frac{x}{3} = 3 \times 88$

$\Rightarrow \frac{11x}{6} = 264 \Rightarrow x = \frac{264 \times 6}{11} = 144$.

$\therefore$ (First – Third) = $\left(144 - \frac{1}{3} \times 144\right) = 96$.

39. Suppose x passed and (120 – x) failed.
Then, $x \times 39 + (120 - x) \times 15 = 120 \times 35$
$\Rightarrow 24x = 2400 \Rightarrow x = 100.$

40. Ratio of values of coins $= \frac{3}{1}:\frac{4}{2}:\frac{12}{4} = 3:2:3$

Value of 25-paise coins $= \text{Rs.}\left(600 \times \frac{3}{8}\right)$

$= \text{Rs.}\ 225$

$\therefore$ Number of these coins $= (225 \times 4) = 900.$

41. $A + B + C = 5625,\ B = \frac{1}{4}(A + C) \Rightarrow A + C = 4B$

$\therefore B + 4B = 5625 \Rightarrow 5B = 5625 \Rightarrow B = \text{Rs. } 1125.$

$A + B + C = 5625\ \&\ A = \frac{1}{2}(B+C) \Rightarrow B + C = 2A$

$\therefore A + 2A = 5625 \Rightarrow 3A = 5625 \Rightarrow A = \text{Rs. } 1875.$

$\therefore A - B = (1875 - 1125) = \text{Rs. } 750.$

42. Let their costs be 9x and 5x.
Then, $9x - 5x = \text{Rs. } 6800 \Rightarrow x = \text{Rs. } 1700.$
$\therefore$ Cost of a scooter $= 9x = \text{Rs. } 15300.$

43. Milk in 60 litres $= \left(60 \times \frac{2}{3}\right) = 40$ litres

Then, water in it = 20 litres.
Let x litres of water be added to it.

Then, $\frac{\text{milk}}{\text{water}} = \frac{1}{2} \Rightarrow \frac{40}{20 + x} = \frac{1}{2}$

$\Rightarrow 20 + x = 80 \Rightarrow x = 60$ litres.

44. Ratio of shares = 27000 : 81000 : 72000
= 3 : 9 : 8
If Maya's share is Rs. 9, total profit
= Rs. (3 + 9 + 8) = 20
Then using the formula of ratio & proportion,
9 : 20 : : 36000 : x

$\Rightarrow x = \frac{20 \times 36000}{9} = \text{Rs. } 80000.$

45. Let total profit = Rs. x

Profit to be distributed = 95% of x $= \frac{19x}{20}$.

$\therefore$ A's share $= \text{Rs.}\left(\frac{19x}{20} \times \frac{3}{5}\right) = \text{Rs.}\frac{57x}{100}.$

According to the question,

$\frac{57x}{100} = 85500 \Rightarrow x = \left(\frac{85500 \times 100}{57}\right) = \text{Rs.}150000$

46. Let A's investment = Rs. x for 12 months.
Then, B's investment = Rs. 2x for 6 months
And, C's investment = Rs. 3x for 4 months.
$\therefore A : B : C = (x \times 12 : 2x \times 6 : 3x \times 4) = 1 : 1 : 1.$

$\therefore$ C's share $= \text{Rs.}\left(\frac{9000}{3}\right) = \text{Rs. } 3000.$

47. Let the number of items be x.
Then, $60x - (40x + 3000) = 1000 \Rightarrow x = 200.$

48. Gain % $= \left[\frac{\text{Error}}{(\text{True value}) - (\text{Error})} \times 100\right]$

$\Rightarrow 25 = \frac{x}{(1000 - x)} \times 100 \Rightarrow x = 200.$

Thus, he uses a weight of 800 gm instead of 1 kg.

49. S.P. = Rs. 1955, Gain = 15%.

$\therefore$ C.P. $= \left(\frac{100}{115} \times 1955\right) = \text{Rs.}1700$

Now, C.P. = Rs. 1700, discount = 15%

$\therefore$ Marked price $= \left(\frac{100}{85} \times 1700\right) = \text{Rs.}2000$

$\therefore$ Discount = 15% of Rs. 2000 = Rs. 300.

50. Let the labelled price be Rs. 100.
S.P. in Ist case=Rs. 80, S.P. in 2nd case = Rs. 75.
According to the question,

$5 : 100 :: 500 : x. \Rightarrow x = \left(\frac{100 \times 500}{5}\right) = \text{Rs.}10000.$

51. C's 1 day's work
= [(A + B + C)'s 1 day's work] – [(A's 1 day's work) + (B's 1 day's work)]

$= \frac{1}{4} - \left(\frac{1}{12} + \frac{1}{18}\right) = \left(\frac{1}{4} - \frac{5}{36}\right) = \frac{4}{36} = \frac{1}{9}$

$\therefore$ C alone can finish the work in 9 days.

52. (A + B)'s 1 day's work = 1/8,
(B + C)'s 1 day's work = 1/12,
(A + C)'s 1 day's work = 1/x.

$\therefore$ 2 (A + B + C)'s 1 day's work $= \left(\frac{1}{8} + \frac{1}{12} + \frac{1}{x}\right)$

$\therefore 2 \times \frac{1}{6} = \frac{1}{8} + \frac{1}{12} + \frac{1}{x}$

$\Rightarrow \frac{1}{x} = \frac{1}{3} - \left(\frac{1}{8} + \frac{1}{12}\right) = \frac{3}{24} = \frac{1}{8}.$

Thus, C & A can do the work in 8 days.

53. C's 1 day's work

$= \frac{1}{8} - \left(\frac{1}{24} + \frac{1}{16}\right) = \left(\frac{1}{8} - \frac{5}{48}\right) = \frac{1}{48}.$

$\therefore$ C alone can finish the work in 48 days.

54. Tank filled when both the tops are open for

5 min. $= 5 \times \left(\frac{1}{20} + \frac{1}{25}\right) = \frac{9}{20}.$

Remaining part = $\left(1-\frac{9}{20}\right)=\frac{11}{20}$.

Now, $\frac{1}{20}$ part is filled in 1 min. So, $\frac{11}{20}$ part will be filled in 11 min. Hence, the tank will be full in 11 min. more.

55. Let their ages be 3x and 5x years.
Then, $3x + 5x = 80 \Rightarrow x = 10$.
$\therefore$ Their present ages are 30 years & 50 years.
Ratio of their ages after 10 years $= 40 : 60 = 2 : 3$.

56. Let son's age 10 years ago be x.
Father's age 10 years ago = 3x.
According to the question,
$2(x + 20) = (3x + 20) \Rightarrow x = 20$.
10 years ago, father's age = 60 years & son's age = 20 years.
$\therefore$ Ratio of their present ages $= 70 : 30 = 7 : 3$.

57. Amount after 1 year = Rs. $\left(200+\frac{200\times5\times1}{100}\right)$
= Rs. 210
Balance after 1 years = Rs. (210–100) = Rs. 110.
Money to be paid at the end of two years
= Rs. $\left(110+\frac{110\times5\times1}{100}\right)$ = Rs. 115.50

58. $\frac{P\times R\times10}{100}=600\Rightarrow P\times R=\text{Rs. }6000$
Total Interest at the end of tenth year
$=\left(300+\frac{3P\times R\times5}{100}\right)=\left(300+\frac{15\times6000}{100}\right)=\text{Rs.}1200$

59. Let the sum be Rs. x.
According to the question,
$\frac{x\times5\times15}{100}-x\times15\times\frac{7}{2}\times\frac{1}{100}=144\Rightarrow x=\text{Rs. }640$

60. Let the sum be Rs. x.
According to the question,
$\frac{x\times4\times2}{100}+\frac{x\times6\times4}{100}+\frac{x\times8\times3}{100}=1120$
$\Rightarrow x=\frac{1120\times100}{56}=\text{Rs.}2000.$

61. Since interest is same,
$\frac{P_1R_1T_1}{100}=\frac{P_2R_2T_2}{100}$
$\Rightarrow \frac{P_1}{P_2}=\frac{R_2}{R_1}=\frac{4}{5}$ or 4 : 5

62. S.I. = Rs. $\left(600\times1\times\frac{10}{100}\right)$ = Rs.60.
C.I. = Rs. $\left\{\left[600\times\left(1+\frac{5}{100}\right)^2\right]-600\right\}$
= Rs. $\frac{123}{2}$ = Rs. 61.50
$\therefore$ (C.I.) – (S.I.) = Rs. 1.50.

63. Let, sum be Rs. x.
Then, S.I. $=\frac{x\times10\times2}{100}=\text{Rs.}\frac{x}{5}$.
C.I. $=\left[x\times\left(1+\frac{10}{100}\right)^2-x\right]=\frac{21x}{100}$.
According to the question,
$\frac{21x}{100}-\frac{x}{5}=40\Rightarrow x=(40\times100)=\text{Rs.}4000.$

64. $100\times\left(1+\frac{R}{100}\right)^2=121\Rightarrow\left(1+\frac{R}{100}\right)^2=\frac{121}{100}=\left(\frac{11}{10}\right)^2$..
$\therefore 1+\frac{R}{100}=\frac{11}{10}\Rightarrow\frac{R}{100}=\frac{1}{10}\Rightarrow R=10\%.$

65. Let the value of each instalment be Rs. x.
Then, $\frac{x}{\left(1+\frac{20}{100}\right)}+\frac{x}{\left(1+\frac{20}{100}\right)^2}=\text{Rs.}550$
$\Rightarrow\frac{5x}{6}+\frac{25x}{36}=550\Rightarrow x=\text{Rs.}360.$

66. S = [HHH, HHT, HTH, THH, TTH, THT, HTT, TTT]
and E = Event of getting exactly two heads
= [HHT, HTH, THH].
$\therefore$ P (E) $=\frac{n(E)}{n(S)}=\frac{3}{8}$.

67. S = (1, 2, 3,....20) and E = (3, 6, 9, 12, 15, 18).
$\therefore$ P (E) $=\frac{n(E)}{n(S)}=\frac{6}{20}=\frac{3}{10}$.

68. Clearly, n (S) = 52 and there are 16 face cards.
$\therefore$ P (E) = 16/52 = 4/13

69. Clearly, n (S) = 52 and there are 4 kings.
$\therefore$ P (E) = 4/52 = 1/13

70. Let the number on one dice be
x (x = 1, 2, ... 6)
Probability of other dice having
x = 1/6.

71. n(s) = 6 × 6 = 36
E = [46, 55, 64, 56, 65]

$$P = \frac{n(E)}{n(S)} = \frac{5}{36}$$

72. Initially, the mixture contains 3 litres of alcohol and 12 litres of water. Afterwards, the mixture contains 3 litres of alcohol and 15 litres of water.

∴ Percentage of alcohol =

$$\left(\frac{3}{18} \times 100\right)\% = 16\frac{2}{3}\%.$$

73. $7+2=9$ parts $\equiv 729$ ml

1 part $\equiv 729 \div 9 = 81$ ml

1 part of water should be added to make the ratio 7 : 3

∴, amount of water to be added = 81 ml.

74. Milk in mixture $= \frac{2}{2+1} \times 60 = 40$ l

Water in mixture $= 60 - 40 = 20$ l

To get a ratio of 1 : 2,

water should be $40 \times 2 = 80$ l

∴, Amount of water to be added $= 80 - 20 = 60$ l

75. Time $= \left(\frac{50}{60}\right)$ hr $= \frac{5}{6}$ hr, Speed = 48 kmph.

∴ Distance $= \left(48 \times \frac{5}{6}\right)$ km = 40 km.

Now, distance = 40 km

and time $= \left(\frac{40}{60}\right)$ hr $= \frac{2}{3}$ hr.

∴ New speed $= \left(40 \times \frac{3}{2}\right)$ km/hr = 60 km/hr.

76. Time = 6 hours, speed = 45 kmph.

∴ Distance = (45 x 6) km = 270 km

New time taken = 5 hours

∴ New speed $= \left(\frac{270}{5}\right)$ km/hr = 54 km/hr

77. Total time taken $= \left(\frac{2500}{500} + \frac{1200}{400} + \frac{500}{250}\right)$ hrs.

= 10 hrs.

∴ Average Speed $= \left(\frac{4200}{10}\right)$ km/hr = 420 km/hr.

78. Let the required distance be x km.

Then $\frac{x}{3} + \frac{x}{2} = 5$ or $2x + 3x = 30$ or $x = 6$ km

79. Let the distance be x km. Then,

$\frac{x}{9} - \frac{x}{10} = \frac{36}{60}$ or $\frac{x}{9} - \frac{x}{10} = \frac{3}{5}$

or $10x - 9x = 54$ or $x = 54$ km.

80. Ratio of Speeds = 3 : 4.

Ratio of time taken = 4 : 3

Let the time taken by A and B be 4x hrs and 3x hrs respectively.

Then, $4x - 3x = \frac{20}{60}$

or $x = \frac{1}{3}$

∴ Time taken by A = 4x hrs $= \left(4 \times \frac{1}{3}\right)$ hrs

$= 1\frac{1}{3}$ hrs.

81. Let C's speed = x km/hr. Then,

B's Speed = 3x km/hr

∴ Ratio of Speeds of B, C = 3x : x = 3 : 1.

Ratio of times taken $= \frac{1}{3} : 1 = 1 : 3$

If C takes 3 min., then B takes 1 min.

If C takes 54 min, then B takes $\left(\frac{1}{3} \times 54\right)$ min.

= 18 min.

82. Time = 10 hours, Speed = 48 kmph.

∴ Distance = (Speed x Time) = (48 x 10) km

= 480 km.

Now, distance = 480 km, New time = 8 hours.

New speed $= \left(\frac{\text{Distance}}{\text{Time}}\right) = \left(\frac{480}{8}\right) = 60$ kmph.

∴ Increase in speed = (60 - 48) kmph

= 12 kmph.

83. Let the distance be x km.

Difference in timings = 20 minutes $= \frac{1}{3}$ hour

∴ $\frac{x}{3} - \frac{x}{4} = \frac{1}{3}$ or $4x - 3x = 4$

or x = 4 km.

84. Distance covered $= \left(\frac{1}{2} \times 80\right)$ km = 40 km

Time elapsed $= \left(\frac{3}{5} \times 10\right)$ hrs = 6 hrs.

Distance left = 40 km, Time left = 4 hrs.

∴ Speed required $= \left(\frac{40}{4}\right)$ km/hr = 10 km/hr.

85. Ratio of speeds = 3 : 4

Ratio of time taken $= \frac{1}{3} : \frac{1}{4} = 4 : 3$

∴ $\frac{4}{3} = \frac{x}{24}$ or $3x = 96$ or $x = 32$ min.

86. Speed = $\left(15.6\times\frac{5}{18}\right)$ m/sec. = $\left(\frac{13}{3}\right)$ m/sec.

Distance = (Speed x Time) = $\left(\frac{13}{3}\times 2\times 60\right)$ m

= 520 m

87. Distance = (Speed x Time) = $\left(12\times\frac{9}{2}\right)$ km

= 54 km

Time left now = 3 hours.

New Speed = $\left(\frac{54}{3}\right)$ km/hr = 18 km/hr.

88. Let original C.P. be Rs. x. Its. S.P. = $\frac{90x}{100} = \frac{9x}{10}$

New C.P. = $\frac{80x}{100} = \frac{4x}{5}$

New S.P. = $\frac{140}{100}\times\frac{4x}{5} = \frac{28x}{25}$

$\frac{28x}{25} - \frac{9x}{10} = 55$ or $\frac{112x - 90x}{100} = 55$

or 22x = 55 × 100

$\therefore$ x = $\left(\frac{55\times 100}{22}\right)$ = Rs. 250

89. Let C.P. of whole lot be Rs. x

C.P. of $\frac{3}{4}$ th = Rs. $\frac{3x}{4}$

C.P. of $\frac{1}{4}$ th = Rs. $\frac{x}{4}$

$\therefore$ Total S.P. = $\left(120\text{ \% of }\frac{3x}{4}\right) + \frac{x}{4}$

$= \left(\frac{9x}{10} + \frac{x}{4}\right) = \frac{23x}{20}$

Gain = $\left(\frac{23x}{20} - x\right) = \frac{3x}{20}$

$\therefore$ Gain % = $\left(\frac{3x}{20}\times\frac{1}{x}\times 100\right)$ % = 15%

90. Let C.P. be Rs. x

$\frac{78 - x}{x}\times 100 = 2\times\frac{69 - x}{x}\times 100$

78 – x = 138 – 2x or x = Rs. 60

91. Let C.P. of a mixer be Rs. x and that of a T.V. be Rs. y.

Then, 2x + y = 7000 and 2y + x = 9800

Multiplying 2nd equation by 2 and subtracting first from it, we get

3y = 19600 – 7000 = 12600 or y = 4200

$\therefore$ C.P. of a T.V. = Rs. 4200

92. S.P. = Rs. $\left(\frac{85}{100}\times 620\right)$ = Rs. 527.

93. C.P. per orange = 5/3

S.P. per orange = 4/2 = 2

Profit % = $\frac{2-5/3}{5/3}\times 100 = \frac{6-5}{5}\times 100 = 20\%$

94. 125% of 120% of A = 1500

$\Rightarrow \frac{125}{100}\times\frac{120}{100}\times A = 1500$

$\therefore$ A = $\left(1500\times\frac{2}{3}\right)$ = Rs. 1000

95. C.P. = Rs. 153, Gain = 20%

$\therefore$ S.P. = $\left(\frac{120}{100}\times 153\right)$ = Rs. 183.60

Let, the marked price be Rs. x

$\frac{85}{100}x = 183.60$

$\Rightarrow x = \frac{183.60\times 100}{85}$ = Rs. 216

96. $\frac{A}{D} = \left(\frac{A}{B}\times\frac{B}{C}\times\frac{C}{D}\right) = \left(\frac{8}{15}\times\frac{5}{8}\times\frac{4}{5}\right) = \frac{4}{15}$

97. $0.4\times x = 1.4\times 1.4$

$\Rightarrow x = \frac{1.4\times 1.4}{0.4}$

$= \frac{14\times 14}{40} = 4.9$

98. A : B = 1 : 3 and

B : C = 1 : 2

= 3 : 6

$\therefore$ A : B : C = 1 : 3 : 6

99. $\frac{A}{B} = \frac{9B}{A} \Leftrightarrow \frac{A^2}{B^2} = \frac{9}{1} \Leftrightarrow \frac{A}{B} = \frac{3}{1}$

100. $\frac{a}{3} = \frac{b}{4} = \frac{c}{7} = k.$

Then, a = 3k, b = 4k and c = 7k

$\therefore \frac{a+b+c}{c} = \frac{3k+4k+7k}{7k}$

$= \frac{14k}{7k} = 2$

101. Let x be added.

Then, $\frac{7+x}{13+x} = \frac{2}{3}$

$\Rightarrow$ 3 (7 + x) = 2(13 + x)

$\Rightarrow$ x = 5

102. Remainder = Rs. [(735 – (25 x 3)] = Rs. 660

$\therefore$ Money received by C

$= \text{Rs.} \left[\left(660 \times \frac{2}{6}\right) + 25\right]$

= Rs. 245

103. $A : B : C = \frac{1}{4} : \frac{1}{5} : \frac{1}{6} = 15 : 12 : 10$

A's share = Rs. $\left(407 \times \frac{15}{37}\right)$ = Rs. 165

B's share = Rs. $\left(407 \times \frac{12}{37}\right)$ = Rs. 132

C's share = Rs. [407 – (165 + 132)] = Rs. 110

104. Father's age = $\left(60 \times \frac{7}{10}\right)$ = 42 years

Son's age = (60 – 42) years = 18 years

Difference of their ages = (42 –18) years = 24 years

105. Ratio of sides = $\frac{1}{2} : \frac{1}{3} : \frac{1}{4} = 6 : 4 : 3$

Largest side = $\left(104 \times \frac{6}{13}\right)$ cm = 48 cm

106. Tin in 60 kg. of A = $\left(60 \times \frac{2}{5}\right)$ = 24 kg.

Tin in 100 kg of B = $\left(100 \times \frac{1}{5}\right)$ = 20 kg.

Amount of tin in new alloy = (24 + 20) kg = 44 kg.

107. Let the numbers be $3x$, $2x$ and $5x$.

Then, $9x^2 + 4x^2 + 25x^2 = 1862$

$\Rightarrow 38x^2 = 1862 \Rightarrow x^2 = 49 \Rightarrow x = 7$

$\therefore$ Second number = $2x = 14$

108. Let $C = x$. Then, $A = (x - 20)$ and $B = (x - 40)$

$\therefore x + x - 20 + x - 40 = 120$ or $x = 60$

$\therefore A : B : C = 40 : 20 : 60 = 2 : 1 : 3$

B's Share = Rs. $\left(120 \times \frac{1}{6}\right)$ = Rs. 20

109. When a 5 cc cube is sliced into 1 cc cubes, we will get 5 × 5 × 5 = 125 litre cc cubes.

In each side of the larger cube, the smaller cubes on the edges will have more than one of their sides painted.

Therefore, the cubes which are not on the edge of the larger cube and that lie on the facing sides of the larger cube will have exactly one side painted.

In each face of the larger cube, there will be 5 × 5 = 25 cubes. Of these, there will be 16 cubes on the edge and 3 × 3 = 9 cubes which are not on the edge.

Therefore, there will be 9 litre-cc cubes per face that will have exactly one of their sides painted. In total, there will be 9 × 6 = 54 such cubes.

112. The sides of the triangle happen to be a Pythagorean triplet. Hence, the triangle is a right angled triangle.

For a right angled triangle,

The measure of in radius = (product of perpendicular sides) / (perimeter of triangle)

= (72 × 21) / (72 + 21 + 75) = 1512 / 168 = 9

114. The sum of the exterior angle and interior angle of a regular polygon is 180°.

As the measure of each interior angle is 150°, the measure of each exterior angle will be 30°.

The number of sides of a regular polygon is given by the following relationship n = 360/exterior angle

As the value of each exterior angle is 30°, the number of sides = 12.

126. Let the numbers be $15x$ and $11x$ H.C.F. of these numbers is x. So $x = 13$

$\therefore$ Sum of the two numbers = $15x + 11x = 26x$

Thus the sum = 26 × 13 = 338

128. Required number is the H.C.F. of (1657 – 6) and (2037 – 5)

$\Rightarrow$ H.C.F. of 1651 and 2032 = 127

129. H.C.F. of (132 – 62); (237 – 62)

$\Rightarrow$ H.C.F. of 70, 105 and 175 = 35.

130. L.C.M. of $\frac{2}{3}, \frac{8}{9}, \frac{16}{81}$ and $\frac{10}{27}$

$= \frac{\text{L.C.M. of 2, 8, 16, 10}}{\text{H.C.F. of 3, 9, 81, 21}} = \frac{80}{3}$

$\text{H.C.F.} = \frac{\text{H.C.F. of 2, 8, 16, 10}}{\text{L.C.M. of 3, 9, 81, 21}} = \frac{2}{81}$

$\therefore$ Required difference $= \frac{80}{3} - \frac{2}{81}$

$= 26\frac{2}{3} - \frac{2}{81}$

$= 26\frac{52}{81}$

131. In order to express the given fraction in simplest form we cancel the numerator and denominator by their H.C.F. H.C.F. of 1095 and 1168 is 73;

$\therefore$ Simplest form $= \frac{1095 \div 73}{1168 \div 73} = \frac{15}{16}$

132. Given number are 1.08, 0.90, 0.36
H.C.F. of given 108, 90 and 36 is 18.
$\therefore$ H.C.F. of given numbers = 0.18

133. Required measurement is the H.C.F. of 496 of 496, 403 and 713 which is 31.

134. Required number of students = H.C.F. of 1001 and 910

$$= 91$$

136. Average = $\frac{48 \times 40 + 32 \times 60 + 80 \times 20}{100}$

$$= \frac{5440}{100} = 54.40.$$

137. The average weight of 10 people is increased by 1 kg. Therefore, the total weight is increased by 10 kg. Hence the weight of the new person = (58 + 10) i.e. 68 kgs.

138. Sum of two numbers = 2. xy.
One number being x, the other number = $2xy - x$.

139. The average weight of 8 men is reduced by 1 kg so the hence the weight of the new man
= (62 – 8) i.e. 54 kg

140. Number of students in section A
= 150 – 50 – 30 = 70.
Average weight of section A

$$= \frac{150 \times 50\frac{2}{3} - (50 \times 55) - (30 \times 45)}{70} = 50$$

141. Average speed = $\frac{2 \times 40 \times 60}{40 + 60}$ i.e. 48 km per hour.
Total distance travelled (both ways)

$$= \frac{40}{60} \times 48 \text{ i.e. } 32 \text{ kms}$$

$\Rightarrow$ the distance is 16 kms.

142. Total rainfall from Monday to Saturday is 6 × 0.7 cms = 4.2 cms.
Rainfall for the whole week = 7 × 0.65 cm = 4.55 cms.

147. S.I. = Rs 2000 × $\frac{12}{100}$ × 2 = Rs 480.

148. From the statement of the question, one can quickly understand that Rs 864 is the S.I. for 2 years

$$\therefore \text{Sum} = \text{Rs } \frac{864 \times 100}{12 \times 2} = \text{Rs } 3600$$

149. Rs 1261 is the C.I. for 3 years at 5% on Rs 8000
$\therefore$ Rs 16000 will earn the C.I. of Rs. 2522.

155. Let there be 'x' notes of Rs 10 and $(80 - x)$ notes are of Rs 5.
$\Rightarrow$ $10.x + 5(80 - x) = 625$
$\Rightarrow$ $5x = 225$ or $x = 45$.

160. C.P. mixture = Rs 18 × $\frac{100}{133\frac{1}{3}}$
= Rs 18 × $\frac{100 \times 3}{400}$
= Rs 13.50 a litre
Milk cost = Rs 15 a litre

LOGICAL REASONING

Syllabus

- Understanding the Structure of Arguments: Argument Forms, Structure of Categorical Propositions, Mood and Figure, Formal and Informal Fallacies, Uses of Language, Connotations and Denotations of Terms, Classical Square of Opposition.
- Evaluating and Distinguishing Deductive and Inductive Reasoning.
- Analogies.
- **Venn diagram:** Simple and Multiple use for Establishing Validity of Arguments.
- **Indian Logic:** Means of Knowledge.
- **Pramanas:** Pratyaksha (Perception), Anumana (Inference), Upamana (Comparison), Shabda (Verbal Testimony), Arthapatti (Implication) and Anupalabddhi (Non-apprehension).
- Structure and kinds of Anumana (Inference), Vyapti (Invariable Relation), Hetvabhasas (Fallacies of Inference).

ARGUMENTS

'Argument' is often used to mean heated and emotional exchanges. Argument, in logical reasoning, is just the opposite. Arguing with pure logic, or *argumentation*, is a fine art that has been refined over many centuries. One of the earliest and best was Aristotle, and the modern art of argument has developed from the Athenians onward.

Argument Structure

Arguments are the basis of persuasive communication. They are combinations of statements made that are intended to change the minds of other people.

All arguments have structure, which can be either deliberately designed or may be discovered through analysis. At its simplest, an argument has premises and a conclusion.

Premise

A premise of an argument is something that is put forward as a truth, but which is not proven. Although it is not proven, it is assumed to be true (although how universally accepted this truth is may be another matter).

It is hot in here.

This is a beautiful car.

The people of this town are angry.

If you want to attack another person's argument, you can challenge the truth of their premises. If you are making an argument, you should be ready to defend any of your own premises. The more complex the premise, the more opportunity there is to challenge it, so if you expect challenge, keep your premises both short and non-controversial.

As premises are the building blocks of the argument, there may well be two or more premises in any argument.

Conclusion

The conclusion (or **claim**) is the statement with which you want the other person to agree. It is drawn from the premises of the argument, of which there may be many.

We need to get out.

You should buy this car.

The new housing should be sited elsewhere.

A useful way of spotting a conclusion is that it may well be a statement of necessity, saying what must or should happen. It may well be framed to persuade the other person to do something or make some decision.

WHAT IS LOGIC

Ever since the start of time, man has always been surrounded by logic (time and logic seem to have co-existed)--it exists all around us, and is all encompassing. There is implicit logic in all human and natural activity right from the primary level of logic seen in our day to day lives to its very advanced form which operates the machines & tools we use for our day to day work. Every subject we study, every product we build, every activity we undertake is guided by its own inherent logic.

For instance, when faced with the situation of starting a car, switching on an electric appliance like an electric bulb, etc. we use logic inherently. In fact, it would be difficult to imagine life today without even a thought on most of the logical structures that we use inherently.

Inference

Between the conclusion and the premises are further statements which translate the premises into the conclusion. This is the reasoning process, and in a formal argument uses careful logic (in informal arguments, emotional reasoning and assumptive leaps may well be used).

A particular aspect of logical argument is that inferential statements have true-false qualities -- that is, they are either true or false and nothing in between. Thus a sentence can contain many statements.

If we stay here, we will not only get uncomfortable, we will also start to smell.

There are other people interested in this car who will be here later.

If we don't do something, the peasants will revolt.

Inferential arguments seek to prove. Thus commands, explanations and other statements may not directly add to the inference, although they may be a useful component of persuasion.

Look at this. (command)

The people are angry because we did not listen to them. (explanation)

I hate it when cars don't start. (emotion)

Categorical Propositions

Definition of Syllogism.

A Syllogism is a form of mediate deductive inference, in which the conclusion is drawn from two premises, taken jointly. It is a form of deductive inference and therefore the conclusion cannot be more general than the premises. It is a mediate form of inference because the conclusion is drawn from two premises, and not from one premise only as in the case of immediate inference.

e.g.: All men are mortal.

All kings are men.

∴ All kings are mortal.

Structure of Syllogism

A syllogism consists of three terms. The predicate of the conclusion is called the **Major Term**; subject of the conclusion is called the **Minor Term**; and that term which occurs in both the premises, but does not occur in the conclusion, is called the **Middle Term**. The Major and Minor terms are called **Extremes**, to distinguish them from the Middle term.

The Middle Term occurs in both the premises, and is the common element between them. The conclusion seeks to establish a relation between the Extremes-the major term and the minor term. The middle term performs the function of an intermediary. The middle term is thus "middle" in the sense that it is a mediating term, or a common standard of reference, with which two other terms are compared and is thus means by which we pass from premises to conclusion. The middle term having performed its function of bringing the extremes together drops out from the conclusion. Thus, we reach the conclusion in a Syllogism, not directly or immediately, but by means of the Middle term.

The premise in which the major term occurs is called the Major Premise and the premise in which the minor term occurs is called the Minor Premise, For example, in the following Syllogism:

All men are mortal

All kings are men

∴ All kings are mortal.

The term 'mortal' is the major term, being the predicate of the conclusion; the term 'kings' is minor term, because it is the subject of the conclusion; the term 'men' which occurs in both the premises but is absent from the conclusion, is the middle term. The first premise 'All men are mortal' is the major premise, because the major term 'mortal' occurs in it; the second premise 'All kings are men' is the minor premise, because the minor term 'kings' occurs in it.

It may be pointed out that when a syllogism is given in strict logical form, the major premise is given first, and the minor premise comes next, and last of all comes the conclusion. The symbol M stands for the Middle term, S stands for the Minor term and P stands for the Major term. The above syllogism can be represented as,

All M is P

All S is M

∴ All S is P

General Rules of Categorical Syllogism and the Fallacies.

I. Every syllogism must contain three, and only three terms and these terms must be used in the same sense throughout.

There are two ways in which this rule is violated. If a syllogism consists of 4 terms instead of three, we commit the **fallacy of 4 terms quartenioterminorum** *e.g.*,

The book is on the table   The table is on the floor   ∴ The book is on the floor

Here there are four terms, viz., "The book", "on the table," "The table" and "on the floor." Hence no conclusion can follow.

There is another way in which the above rule can be violated. If any term in a syllogism is used ambiguously in the two different premises, we commit a fallacy. If a term is used in two different meanings, it is practically equivalent to two terms and the syllogism commits the fallacy of equivocation. There are three forms of equivocation. They are:

1. **Fallacy of ambiguous major** is a fallacy which occurs when a syllogism uses its major terms in one sense in the premise and in a different sense in the conclusion.

   e.g., Light is required for taking a photograph.

   Feather is not required for taking a photograph.

   Feather is not light.

'Light' in the major premise is used in the sense of 'physical phenomenon' ; in the conclusion it is used in the sense of 'not heavy'.

2. **The fallacy of ambiguous minor** occurs when in a syllogism the minor term means one thing in the minor premise and quite another in the conclusion.

   e.g., No boys are part of a book.
   All pages are boys.
   ∴ No pages are part of a book.

   In this syllogism, minor term 'pages' mean 'boy servant' in its premise and the 'side of a paper' in the conclusion. Hence the fallacy of ambiguous minor.

3. **The fallacy of ambiguous middle** will be committed by a syllogism if it uses the middle term in one sense in the major premise and in another sense in the major premise and in another sense in the minor premise.

   e.g., All criminal actions ought to be punished by law
   Prosecutions for theft are criminal actions.
   Prosecutions for theft ought to be punished by law.

   The middle term 'criminal actions' means 'crimes' in the major premise and an 'action against a criminal' in the minor premise. Hence the syllogism commits the fallacy of ambiguous middle.

II. Every syllogism must contain 3 and only 3 propositions.

Syllogism is a process of reasoning in which a conclusion is drawn from two given premises. Two propositions are given and a third one is inferred.

III. The middle term must be distributed at least once in the premises.

The function of a middle term in a syllogism is to serve as the connecting link between the minor and major terms. In the major premise P is compared with M and in the minor premise S is compared with the same M. Thus the relation between S and P is established through the mediation of M.

The violation of this rule leads to the **fallacy of undistributed middle**.

e.g., All donkeys are mortal. All monkeys are mortal. ∴ All monkeys are donkeys.

In this argument the middle term 'mortal' is undistributed in both the premises as the predicate of an affirmative proposition. Hence the fallacy of undistributed middle occurs.

IV. No term which is undistributed in the premises can be distributed in the conclusion.

This rule guards us against inferring more in the conclusion than what is contained in the premises. In any syllogism, the conclusion cannot be more general than the premises.

The violation of this rule would result in two fallacies-illicit major and illicit minor. **The fallacy of illicit major** occurs when the major term which is not disturbed in the major premise is distributed in the conclusion.

e.g., All men are selfish.
No apes are men.
∴ No apes are selfish.

The major term 'selfish' is undistributed in the major premise but distributed in the conclusion. Hence the fallacy of illicit major.

The **fallacy of illicit minor** is one which occurs when the minor term is distributed in the conclusion without being distributed in the minor premise.

e.g., All thugs are murderers.
All thugs are Indians.
∴ All Indians are murderers.

Here the minor term 'Indians' is distributed in the conclusion without being distributed in the minor premise. So it commits the fallacy of illicit minor.

V. From two negative premises, no conclusion is possible.

We cannot draw any conclusion from two negative premises. The major premise being negative, the major term does not agree with M. In the minor premise also, the minor term has no relation with M. Thus there is no mediating link between S and P. In the absence of a common link between S and P, no relation can be established between them.

The violation of this rule commits the **fallacy of two negative premises.**

e.g., No monkeys are rational.

No men are monkeys.

No conclusion is possible.

VI. If one premise is negative, the conclusion must be negative and if the conclusion is negative one premise must be negative.

In the negative premise 'M' does not agree with the other term. In the affirmative premise 'M' agrees with the other term. Hence in mediating between the two terms, 'M' can establish only a relation of disagreement between S and P in the conclusion. In other words the conclusion must be negative.

VII. Two particular premises yield no valid conclusion.

This is proved by examining the four possible combinations of two particular premises.

I	O	I	O
I	I	O	O
X	X	X	X

VIII. If any one premise is particular the conclusion must be particular.

Tips for Problem Solving

As a student it is important for you to follow a few standard steps while solving logical questions:

1. Take a complete 'preview of the situation' clearly understanding the context. Remember to accept the situation as it is given.
2. Read each and every part of the question carefully. You should concentrate hard and focus fully while reading the question. This is a very important pre-requisite for solving questions on logic since very often in long sentences there will be individual single words which will transform the meaning of the sentences. If you fail to take into account these words, the end result will be errors in logic and deduction.

Mood and Figure

The mood of a categorical syllogism in standard form is a string of three letters indicating, respectively, the forms of the major premise, minor premise, and conclusion of the syllogism. Note, however, that syllogisms can have the same mood but still differ in logical form.

Example

1. No mammals are birds.
2. All mammals are animals.
3. Therefore, no animals are birds.

The syllogisms in example have the following forms, respectively:

No P are M.	No M are P.
All S are M.	All M are S.
No S are P.	No S are P.

These two syllogisms differ in figure.

The figure of a categorical syllogism is determined by the position of the middle term. There are four possible figures:

First Figure	Second Figure	Third Figure	Fourth figure
M-P	P-M	M-P	P-M
S-M	S-M	M-S	M-S
S-P	S-P	S-P	S-P

The one in example exhibits third figure. Now for the central fact about syllogistic validity:

The form of a categorical syllogism is completely determined by its mood and figure.

Aristotle worked out exhaustively which combinations of mood and figure result in valid forms and which result in invalid forms.

There are 256 combinations of mood and figure (64 (4 × 4 × 4) moods × 4 figures). Only fifteen are valid.

The valid syllogistic forms

First figure: AAA, EAE, AII, EIO
Second figure: EAE, AEE, EIO, AOO
Third figure: IAI, AII, OAO, EIO
Fourth figure: AEE, IAI, EIO

In working out the valid forms, Aristotle made an assumption that is rejected by most modern logicians, namely, that all terms denote nonempty classes. On this assumption, nine more forms turn out valid in addition to the fifteen above.

Forms valid in Aristotelian logic only

First figure: AAI, EAO
Second figure: AEO, EAO
Third figure: AAI, EAO
Fourth figure: AEO, EAO, AAI

Logical Fallacies

Definition and Key Ideas

"It's a fallacy that eggs are bad for you"; you've probably heard the word fallacy used this way - to refer to false beliefs. Logical fallacies, or just "fallacies," in philosophy, are not false beliefs; to oversimplify, they are logical errors in argumentation, reasoning, explanation, rhetoric, or debate. But their precise definition is elusive and controversial; we'll come back to that.

Fallacies are an important aspect of our lives. Without being able to identify bad reasoning, humans can be sold all kinds of harmful beliefs, with dreadful consequences. Politics, advertising, and human manipulation in general are full of fallacies; personal and societal health might depend on being able to spot them.

Example

If we elect leaders whose policies are founded on fallacious arguments (logical errors), the consequences could include economic recession, war, or environmental disaster. On an individual level, advertisers are constantly trying to persuade us to spend money on their products; you have to be critical of their claims (look for the fallacies) if you don't want to waste your income.

On the other hand, logical fallacies are also an acceptable method of persuasion in most contexts outside of academia. If you use logical fallacies to win arguments, probably no one but a teacher or philosopher will call you on it!

There are 100s of named fallacies now, from familiar ones like the false dilemma and red herring, to the obscure, such as the "if-by-whiskey" argument and "chronological snobbery" (judging a belief to be wrong because it was believed during the same era as something else that was wrong).

Connotations and Denotations

Understanding the difference between denotation and connotation is important to understanding definitions and how concepts are used. Unfortunately, that is complicated by the fact that these terms can be used in two different ways: grammatical and logical. Even worse, both uses are worth keeping in mind, and both uses are relevant to the project of logical, critical thinking.

In grammar, a word's denotation is whatever the word directly refers to, roughly equivalent to its lexical definition. Thus, the word "atheist" denotes a person who disbelieves in or denies the existence of gods. A word's connotation refers to any subtle nuances that might or might not be intended by its use. For example, one possible connotation for the word "atheist" might be someone who is immoral and wicked, depending upon who is doing the speaking or listening.

Separating grammatical denotation from connotation is important because while one might assume that a word's denotation is fully intended, whether a word's connotations are intended is much more difficult to determine. Connotations are often emotional in nature, and thus if they are intended, it may be for the purpose of swaying a person's emotional reactions rather than the logical evaluation of an argument.

If there are misunderstandings about how a person is using a word in a particular debate, a primary source of that misunderstanding might lie in the word's connotations: people might be seeing something not intended, or the speaker may be intending something people don't see. In constructing your arguments, it's a good idea not merely to look at what your words denote, but also what they connote.

Remember

In logic, the uses of denotation and connotation are very different. The denotation, or extension, of a term, is the list of a class of objects referred to by the word (think of it as "how far does this word extend?"). Thus the word "planet" denotes specific objects such as Venus, Earth, Jupiter, and Neptune. Whether it also denotes an object like "Pluto" is a matter of some debate among astronomers for reasons I will explain shortly.

The connotation, or intention, of a word, is the list of attributes shared by all members of the class named by the word (think of it as "by using this word, what do I intend?"). Thus the word "planet" connotes certain characteristics which astronomers have decided to differentiate certain objects from other objects like comets, stars, and asteroids. The debate over whether the word "planet" denotes "Pluto" is because astronomers disagree on what sorts of attributes are connoted by the word "planet," and hence whether "Pluto" has the right attributes to qualify as a planet.

Traditional Square of Opposition

The Traditional Square of Opposition is a diagram specifying logical relations among four types of categorical propositions. It is useful in the analysis of syllogistic logic, serving to identify the allowed logical conversions from one type to another.

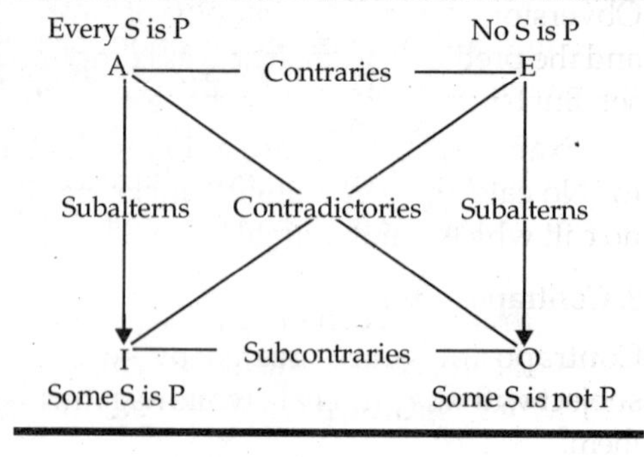

Immediate Arguments

There are four types of immediate arguments: Contradictories, Contraries, Subcontraries, Subalterns.

1. **Contradictories.** Two propositions are contradictory if one of them is denial of another. They cannot both be true, and cannot both be false. A-proposition is contradictory of O-proposition, and E-proposition is contradictory of I-proposition.
2. **Contraries.** Two propositions are contrary if they cannot both be true, but they might both be false. A-proposition is contrary of E-proposition.
3. **Subcontraries.** Two propositions are subcontrary if they cannot both be false, but they might both be true. I-proposition is subcontrary of O-proposition.
4. **Subalterns.** A proposition is a subaltern of another iff it must be true if its superaltern is true, and the superaltern must be false if the subaltern is false. I-proposition is subaltern of A-proposition, and O-proposition is subaltern of E-proposition.
5. **Categorical Propositions & The Traditional Square of Opposition in Venn Diagrams.** Square of opposition, set diagrams" by mate2code - Own work. Licensed under Public Domain via Wikimedia Commons.

Every S are P
SaP — Contrary → SeP
No S is P
Subaltern Contradictory Subaltern
SiP — Subcontrary → SoP
Some S are P
Some S are not P

Immediate Inferences

Immediate inferences are logical operations which can be performed on categorical statements, in order to change it into another. There are three concepts of such operations - Conversion, Obversion, Contraposition.

1. Conversion

Conversion is created by switching the two parts of statement. There are two types of conversion, one is implicational, and second is categorical.

Implicational conversion is where parts of a implication is reversed, may be seen as reverse-implication. Converse of is $P \rightarrow Q$ is $Q \rightarrow P$.

In categorical conversion, the subject and predicate are interchanged. Example , the converse of "No S are P" is "No P are S".

Name	Statement	Converse
A*	All S are P.	All P are S.
E	No S are P.	No P are S.
I	Some S are P.	Some P are S.
O*	Some S are not P.	Some P are not S.

*Conversion is not valid.

Here, only conversion of E and I are valid. The conversion of A-proposition can be valid via limitation. The converse of "All S are P" is "Some P are S". O-proposition has no valid conversion.

2. Obversion

Obversion changes the quality of proposition, and the predicate term. It acts as complimentary set. But truth value doesn't change.

Example, "All cats are animals" is changed to "No cats are non-animals" meaning, there is no cat, which is not animal.

Name	Statement	Obverse
A	All S are P.	No S are non-P.
E	No S are P.	All S are non-P.
I	Some S are P.	Some S are not non-P.
O	Some S are not P.	Some S are non-P.

3. Contraposition

Contrapositions are created by switching the subject with the predicate while negating both of them.

Example, if all dogs are mammals, then we can say, all non-mammals are non-dogs. It can be easily shown by drawing Venn diagrams.

Contrapositions also apply to implications. The contraposition of is $P \rightarrow Q$ is $\neg Q \rightarrow \neg P$.

Name	Statement	Contraposition
A	All S are P.	All non-P are non-S.
E	No S are P.	No non-P are non-S
I	Some S are P.	Some non-P are non-S.
O	Some S are not P.	Some non-P are not non-S.

Inductive Reasoning

Inductive reasoning, also known as induction, is a kind of reasoning that constructs or evaluates propositions that are abstractions of observations of individual instances. Inductive reasoning contrasts with deductive reasoning in that a general conclusion is arrived at by specific examples.

Inductive reasoning consists of inferring general principles or rules from specific facts. Though many dictionaries define inductive reasoning as reasoning that derives general principles from specific observations, this usage is outdated.

Examples

This is an example of deductive reasoning:

1. *90% of humans are right-handed.*
2. *Ratan is a human.*
3. *Therefore, the probability that Ratan is right-handed is 90%.*

Probability is employed, for example, in the following argument:

Every life form we know of depends on liquid water to exist.
All life depends on liquid water to exist.

However, induction is employed in the following argument:

Every life form that everyone knows of depends on liquid water to exist.
Therefore, all known life depends on liquid water to exist.

Strong and Weak Induction

The words 'strong' and 'weak' are sometimes used to praise or demean the quality of an inductive argument. The idea is that you say "this is an example of strong induction" when you would decide to believe the conclusion if presented with the premises. Alternatively, you say "that is weak induction" when your particular world view does not allow you to see that the conclusions are likely given the premises.

Strong Induction

Even very strong inductions are potentially flawed interpretations of the truth, however reasonable and logical they might appear.

Weak Induction

Consider this example:

I always hang pictures on nails.
Therefore:
All pictures hang from nails.

Here, the link between the premise and the conclusion is very weak. Not only is it possible for the conclusion to be false given the premise, it is even fairly likely that the conclusion is false. Not all pictures are hung from nails; moreover, not all pictures are hung. Thus we say that this argument is an instance of weak induction.

The previous is an example of probabilistic reasoning which employs weak induction. Therefore the previous example is closer to an example of probabilistic reasoning rather than Induction. Weak Induction is merely a type of conjecture, not a proof.

Bias

Inductive reasoning is also known as **hypothesis construction** because any conclusions made are based on educated predictions. There are three biases that could distort the proper application of induction, thereby preventing the reasoner from forming the best, most logical conclusion based on the clues. These biases include the availability bias, the confirmation bias, and the predictable-world bias.

The **availability bias** causes the reasoner to depend primarily upon information that is readily available to him/her. People have a tendency to rely on information that is easily accessible in the world around them. For example, in surveys, when people are asked to estimate the percentage of people who died from various causes, most respondents would choose the causes that have been most prevalent in the media such as terrorism, and murders, and airplane accidents rather than causes such as disease and traffic accidents, which have been technically "less accessible" to the individual since they are not emphasized as heavily in the world around him/her.

The **confirmation bias** is based on the natural tendency to confirm rather than to deny a current hypothesis. Research has demonstrated that people are inclined to seek solutions to problems that are more consistent with known hypotheses rather than attempt to refute those hypotheses. Often, in experiments, subjects will ask questions that seek answers that fit established hypotheses, thus confirming these hypotheses. For example, if it is hypothesized that Sally is a sociable individual, subjects will naturally seek to confirm the premise by asking questions that would produce answers confirming that Sally is in fact a sociable individual.

The **predictable-world bias** revolves around the inclination to perceive order where it has not been proved to exist. A major aspect of this bias is superstition, which is derived from the inability to acknowledge that coincidences are merely coincidences. Gambling, for example, is one of the most obvious forms of predictable-world bias. Gamblers often begin to think that they see patterns in the outcomes and, therefore, believe that they are able to predict outcomes based upon what they have witnessed. In reality, however, the outcomes of these games are difficult, if not impossible to predict. The perception of order arises from wishful thinking. Since people constantly seek some type of order to explain or justify their beliefs and experiences, it is difficult for them to acknowledge that the perceived or assumed order may be entirely different from that they believe they are experiencing.

Types

Generalization

A generalization (more accurately, an inductive generalization) proceeds from a premise about a sample to a conclusion about the population.

The proportion Q of the sample has attribute A.
Therefore:
The proportion Q of the population has attribute A.

Example

There are 20 balls—either black or white—in an urn. To estimate their respective numbers, you draw a sample of four balls and find that three are black and one is white. A good inductive generalization would be that there are 15 black, and five white, balls in the urn.

How much the premises support the conclusion depends upon (a) the number in the sample group compared to the number in the population and (b) the degree to which the sample represents the population (which may be achieved by taking a random sample). The hasty generalization and the biased sample are generalization fallacies.

Statistical Syllogism

A statistical syllogism proceeds from a generalization to a conclusion about an individual.

A proportion Q of population P has attribute A.

An individual X is a member of P.

Therefore:

There is a probability which corresponds to Q that X has A.

The proportion in the first premise would be something like "3/5ths of", "all", "few", etc.

Simple Induction

Simple induction proceeds from a premise about a sample group to a conclusion about another individual.

Proportion Q of the known instances of population P has attribute A.

Individual I is another member of P.

Therefore:

There is a probability corresponding to Q that I has A.

This is a combination of a generalization and a statistical syllogism, where the conclusion of the generalization is also the first premise of the statistical syllogism.

Argument from analogy

The process of analogical inference involves noting the shared properties of two or more things, and from this basis inferring that they also share some further property:

P and Q are similar in respect to properties a, b, and c.

Object P has been observed to have further property x.

Therefore, Q probably has property x also.

Analogical reasoning is very frequent in common sense, science, philosophy and the humanities, but sometimes it is accepted only as an auxiliary method. A refined approach is case-based reasoning.

Causal inference

A causal inference draws a conclusion about a causal connection based on the conditions of the occurrence of an effect. Premises about the correlation of two things can indicate a causal relationship between them, but additional factors must be confirmed to establish the exact form of the causal relationship.

Prediction

A prediction draws a conclusion about a future individual from a past sample.

Proportion Q of observed members of group G have attribute A.

Therefore:

There is a probability corresponding to Q that other members of group G will have attribute A when next observed.

Deductive Reasoning

Deductive reasoning, also called deductive logic, is the process of reasoning from one or more general statements regarding what is known to reach a logically certain conclusion. Deductive reasoning involves using given true premises to reach a conclusion that is also true. Deductive reasoning contrasts with inductive reasoning in that a specific conclusion is arrived at from a general principle. If the rules and logic of deduction are followed, this procedure ensures an accurate conclusion.

An example of a deductive argument:

1. *All men are mortal.*
2. *Socrates is a man.*
3. *Therefore, Socrates is mortal.*

The first premise states that all objects classified as "men" have the attribute "mortal". The second premise states that "Socrates" is classified as a "man" – a member of the set "men". The conclusion then states that "Socrates" must be "mortal" because he inherits this attribute from his classification as a "man".

Deductive reasoning (also known as logical deduction) links premises with conclusions. If both premises are true, the terms are clear and the rules of deductive logic are followed, then the conclusion of the argument follows by logical necessity.

Law of Detachment

The law of detachment is the first form of deductive reasoning. A single conditional statement is made, and a hypothesis (P) is stated. The conclusion (Q) is then deduced from the statement and the hypothesis. The most basic form is listed below:

1. $P \rightarrow Q$ (*conditional statement*)
2. P (hypothesis stated)
3. Q (conclusion deduced)

In deductive reasoning, we can conclude Q from P by using the law of detachment. However, if the conclusion (Q) is given instead of the hypothesis (P) then there is no valid conclusion.

The following is an example of an argument using the law of detachment in the form of an if–then statement:

1. If an angle $A > 90°$, then A is an obtuse angle.
2. $A = 120°$
3. A is an obtuse angle.

Since the measurement of angle A is greater than 90°, we can deduce that A is an obtuse angle.

Law of Syllogism

The law of syllogism takes two conditional statements and forms a conclusion by combining the hypothesis of one statement with the conclusion of another. Here is the general form, with the true premise P:

1. $P \rightarrow Q$
2. $Q \rightarrow R$
3. *Therefore,* $P \rightarrow R$.

The following is an example:

1. *If Ayan is sick, then he will be absent from school.*
2. *If Ayan is absent, then he will miss his classwork.*
3. *If Ayan is sick, then he will miss his classwork.*

We deduced the final statement by combining the hypothesis of the first statement with the conclusion of the second statement. We also conclude that this could be a false statement.

Deductive Logic: Validity and Soundness

Deductive arguments are evaluated in terms of their *validity* and *soundness*. It is possible to have a deductive argument that is logically valid but is not sound.

An argument is valid if it is impossible for its premises to be true while its conclusion is false. In other words, the conclusion must be true if the premises, whatever they may be, are true. An argument can be valid even though the premises are false.

An argument is sound if it is valid and the premises are true.

The following is an example of an argument that is *valid, but not sound*:

1. *Everyone who eats meat is healthy.*
2. *John eats meat.*
3. *Therefore, John is healthy.*

The example's first premise is false – there are people who eat meat and are Not healthy – but the conclusion must be true, so long as the premises are true (*i.e.* it is impossible for the premises to be true and the conclusion false). Therefore the argument is valid, but not sound.

In this example, the first statement uses categorical reasoning, saying that all meat-eaters are definitely healthy. This theory of deductive reasoning – also known as term logic – was developed by Aristotle, but was superseded by propositional (sentential) logic and predicate logic.

Deductive reasoning can be contrasted with inductive reasoning, in regards to validity and soundness. In cases of inductive reasoning, even though the premises are true and the argument is "valid", it is possible for the conclusion to be false (determined to be false with a counter example or other means).

ANALOGY TEST

Analogies are defined by a specific relationship between given words, events, objects or alphabet sets which has to be recognised. After recognising this relationship, it has to be applied to other words or events or objects or alphabets. Analogy literally means the process of reasoning on the basis of parallel events or objects.

Classification of Analogy Problems

A few types of analogy problems with solved examples are given below.

Type I

Directions. *In this type of test three words are given and first two words are related to each other in some way. You have to find the relationship of the third word with the given alternatives.*

Example 1. India : New Delhi : : Afghanistan : ?
(A) Colombo (B) Taliban (C) Kabul (D) United States

Solution. (C) As New Delhi is the capital of India, in the same way Kabul is the capital of Afghanistan.

Example 2. Doctor : Medicine : : Teacher : ?
(A) Students (B) Class (C) Principal (D) Knowledge

Solution. (D) As the doctor prescribes the medicine for patient, in the same way the teacher imparts knowledge to student.

Example 3. Day : Night : : Cold : ?
(A) Ice (B) Wet (C) Hot (D) Water

Solution. (C) Between the first two words, 'Day' and 'Night' an opposite relationship exists. On the basis of this opposite relationship we have to find out the word which has opposite meaning of the word 'Cold'. Out of the given alternatives, the word "Hot" fulfills this relationship.

Example 4. Hand : Finger :: Pen : ?
(A) Ink (B) Holder (C) Paper (D) Nib

Solution. (D) In the first two words, 'Hand' and 'Finger', relationship of whole and its part exists between them. Finger is a part of 'Hand'. On the basis of this relationship, the item coming in place of question mark (?) should be a part of 'Pen'. Obviously 'Nib' is a part of 'Pen'. No other item satisfies this relationship.

Example 5. Chair : Carpenter : : Shirt : ?
(A) Pent (B) Button (C) Tailor (D) Cloth

Solution. (C) In the first two words 'chair' and 'carpenter', relationship of product and its maker exists. On the basis of this relationship, 'shirt' is made by a Tailor. So the correct word is 'Tailor'.

Example 6. Paisa : Rupee : : ?
(A) Rupee : Wealth (B) Kilogram : Quintal
(C) Coin : Money (D) Weight : Ton

Solution. (B) As 100 paisa is equivalent to one rupee, in the same way 100 kilogram is equivalent to one quintal.

Type II

In this type of test, three terms (numeric) are given and the missing is marked by question mark. The first two terms are related to each other. The same type of relations should exist between the third and missing (fourth) term. Find out the missing term.

Example 1. 01 : 08 : : 16 : ?
(A) 64 (B) 125 (C) 27 (D) 32

Solution. (B) First term = $(1)^2$; Second term = $(2)^3$ Third term = $(4)^2$. Thus the fourth term would be $(5)^3 = 125$.

Type III

In this type of test, three terms (group of alphabets) are given and the missing one is marked by question mark.

The first two terms are related to each other and the same type of relation should exist between the third and missing (fourth) term. Find out the missing term.

Example 1. QIOK : MMKO : : YAWC : ?
(A) UESG (B) SUEG (C) UAGS (D) VUES

Solution. (A) As,

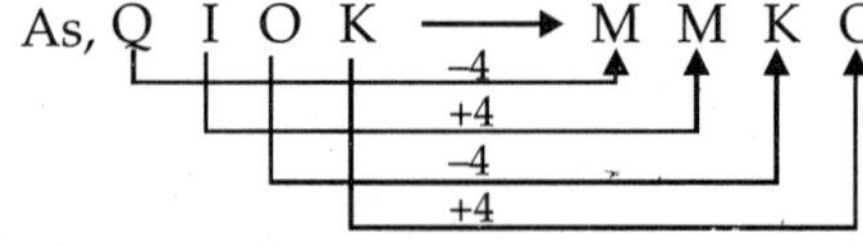

Similarly, Y A W C ⟶ U E S G

Example 2. bdF : acE : : ? : fhJ
(A) dfH (B) fhi (C) giK (D) fgi

Solution. (C) This question is based on the sequential arrangement of letters in English alphabet.

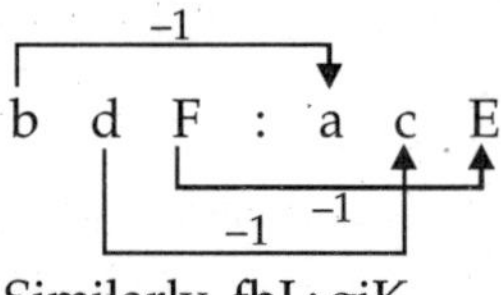

Similarly, fhJ : giK

Type IV

In this type of test, the relationship has to be deciphered by understanding the given relationship.

Example 1. What is related to 'Metre' as 'Litre' is related to 'Volume' ?

(A) Weight (B) Length (C) Pressure (D) Area

Solution. (B) Metre is a unit of length as litre is a unit of volume.

Example 2. 'Carpenter' is related to wood in the same way 'Blacksmith' is related to

(A) Gold (B) Shoes

(C) Jewellery (D) Metal

Solution. (D) As carpenter works on wood, similarly 'blacksmith' moulds metal.

Type V

In this type of test, two objects or events are related in same way. You have to find out that option which has the same type of relationship as mentioned. The answer options can be more than one in these type of questions.

Example 1. Trees and Forest.

(A) Ocean and Ship (B) Books and Library

(C) Boys and Teacher (D) Books and Students

Solution. (B) As number of trees together comprise forest, in the same way number of books together make a library.

REASONING LOGICAL DIAGRAMS

Various types of diagram tests are currently used for testing reasoning ability in different competitive examinations. In these tests, relationship between various elements represented by different parts of a single figure or elements represented by different figures in a problem has to be established. Careful observation and Logical understanding is required to solve these problems. Elements represented by diagrams may be persons, groups and various categories of persons, specific geographical regions like cities and states or different types of objects. Generally, diagram tests of Reasoning are of two types –

(1) Single-diagram relationship tests and

(2) Multi-diagram relationship tests. We shall explain here both types of these tests with the help of some illustrations.

Single-Diagram Relationship Test

One figure having different sub-figures or parts is given in this type of test. Different parts of the given figure are represented by different numbers 1, 2, 3, 4 etc. The different numbers (representing different parts of the figure) stand for different specific groups of persons or places or relationships. The examinees are asked to name the part of the figure representing some special group or relationship. Below is given one example of the type of problem based on single diagram.

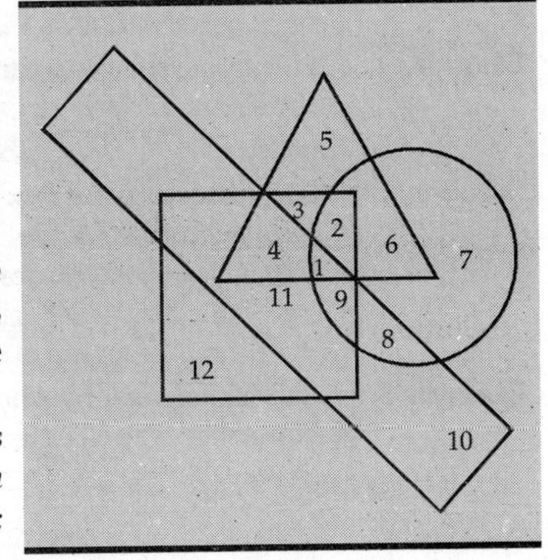

Directions (1-5). *In the following diagram, four geometrical figures namely Circle, Triangle, Square and Rectangle have been shown intersecting one another. Circle represents Educated persons;*

Triangle represents Urban persons; Square, Laborious persons and Rectangle represents Honest persons. Different regions of this diagram are shown by number 1 to 12. Study this diagram carefully and identify the number for the region representing specific group of persons asked in the questions given below. Give your answer from the given alternatives.

Example 1. Honest and laborious persons who are uneducated but not urban are represented by the region whose number is

(A) 3 (B) 4 (C) 9 (D) 11

Solution. (D) Honest persons are represented by Rectangle and Laborious persons by square. So common area of Rectangle and Square will represent Honest as well as Laborious persons. But these persons asked for are uneducated, so the common area of Rectangle and Square which does not come in the Circle will represent such persons who are Honest and Laborious but uneducated. Again as these persons are not urban, this common area of Rectangle and square will also not-include Triangle as well. Thus the given group of persons who are Honest, Laborious and uneducated but not urban will be represented by the common area of Rectangle and square which does not include the Circle and Triangle. The area is represented by the number 11 in the given diagram.

Example 2. Educated persons who are Honest and Laborious but do not live in urban areas are represented by the area with number

(A) 12 (B) 11 (C) 10 (D) 9

Solution. (D) Educated persons are represented by Circle, Honest persons by Rectangle and Laborious persons by square. Therefore Educated persons who are Honest and Laborious will be represented by the common region of Circle, Rectangle and Square. Triangle represents the region of persons living in urban area. Therefore, Educated persons who are Honest and Laborious but who do not live in urban areas will be represented by that common region of Circle, Rectangle and Square which lie outside the Triangle. It is clear that this region is represented by number 9 in the diagram.

Example 3. Laborious persons living in urban areas but who are neither educated nor Honest are represented by the region whose number is

(A) 2 (B) 3 (C) 4 (D) 5

Solution. (B) Persons living in urban areas are represented by Triangle and Laborious persons by Square. Those persons who are not Honest will not come in the Rectangle and the persons who are not Educated will not come in the Circle. Thus Laborious persons living in urban areas who are neither Honest nor Educated will come in that common region of Triangle and Square which does not include Rectangle and Circle. This region in the diagram is represented by number 3.

Example 4. Urban persons who are both Laborious and Honest but are not Educated, will be represented by the area whose number is

(A) 5 (B) 4 (C) 3 (D) 2

Solution. (B) Urban persons are represented by Triangle, Laborious persons by Square and Honest persons by Rectangle. Persons who are uneducated will be outside the circle. Thus Urban persons who are Laborious and Honest but uneducated will be represented by the common area of Triangle, Square and Rectangle which is outside the Circle. In the diagram this region is represented by number 4.

Example 5. Laborious persons who do not live in Urban areas and who are neither Educated nor Honest are represented by the area in the Diagram whose number is

(A) 6 (B) 7 (C) 8 (D) 12

Solution. (D) Laborious persons are represented by Square. Persons who do not live in urban areas will not come in the Triangle. Those who are not Educated will not come in the Circle and persons who are not Honest will be outside the Rectangle. Thus Laborious persons who do not live in urban areas and are neither Educated nor Honest will come in that part of the square which lie outside Triangle, Circle and Rectangle. This region in the diagram is represented by number 12.

Multi-Diagram Relationship Test

In these tests many diagrams (circles, triangles etc.) are given. These diagrams represent various types of relationships. The task for the examinee is to find out the specific figure out of the given figures which represent a given relationship. Below is given an example of this type of problem.

Directions (1-5). *In the question below some specific relationships have been shown between three diagrams. These relationships have been shown by the figures a, b, c, d, and e. An index is given below the figures. Find out the correct figure for each relationship.*

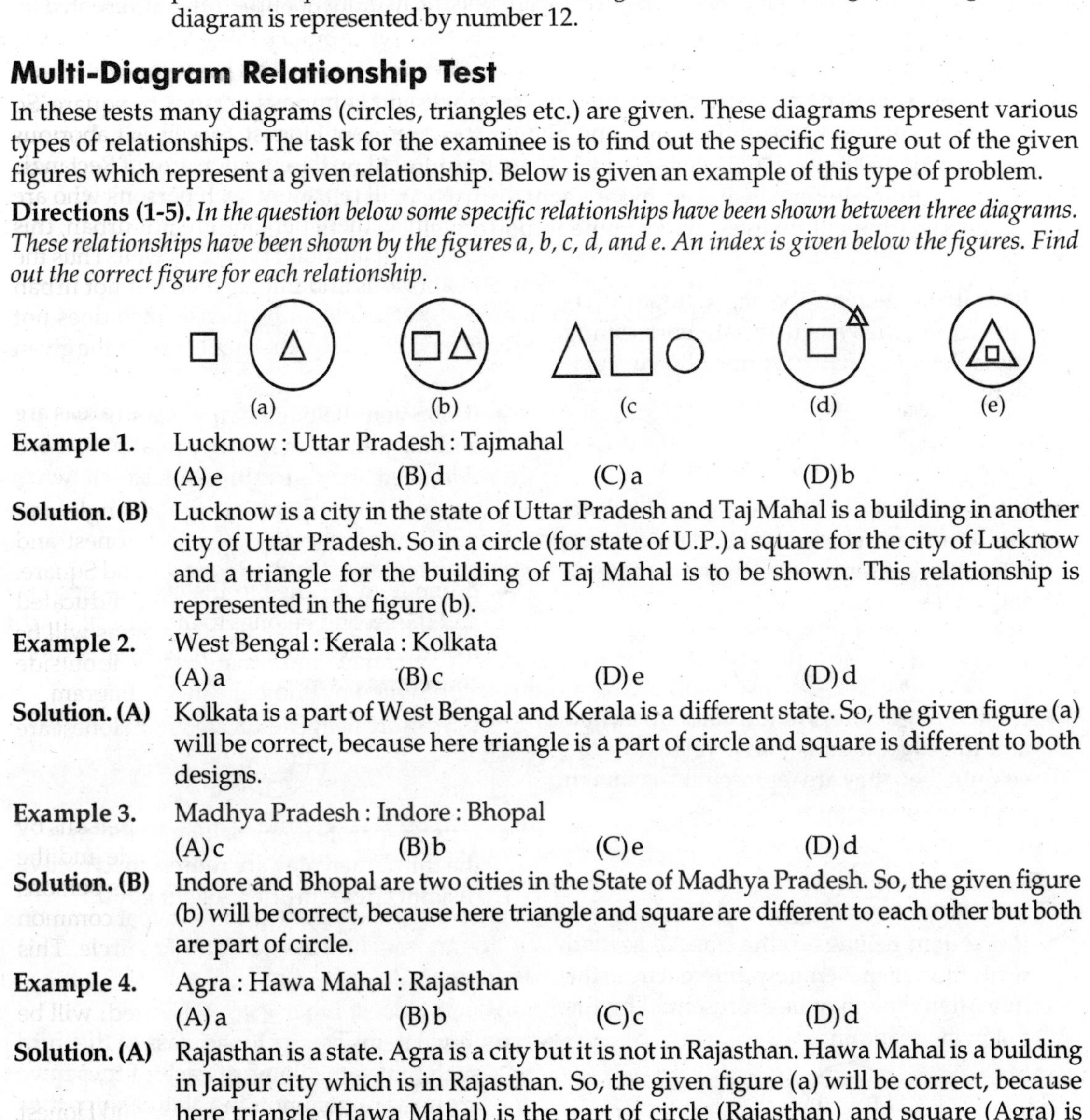

Example 1. Lucknow : Uttar Pradesh : Tajmahal

(A) e (B) d (C) a (D) b

Solution. (B) Lucknow is a city in the state of Uttar Pradesh and Taj Mahal is a building in another city of Uttar Pradesh. So in a circle (for state of U.P.) a square for the city of Lucknow and a triangle for the building of Taj Mahal is to be shown. This relationship is represented in the figure (b).

Example 2. West Bengal : Kerala : Kolkata

(A) a (B) c (D) e (D) d

Solution. (A) Kolkata is a part of West Bengal and Kerala is a different state. So, the given figure (a) will be correct, because here triangle is a part of circle and square is different to both designs.

Example 3. Madhya Pradesh : Indore : Bhopal

(A) c (B) b (C) e (D) d

Solution. (B) Indore and Bhopal are two cities in the State of Madhya Pradesh. So, the given figure (b) will be correct, because here triangle and square are different to each other but both are part of circle.

Example 4. Agra : Hawa Mahal : Rajasthan

(A) a (B) b (C) c (D) d

Solution. (A) Rajasthan is a state. Agra is a city but it is not in Rajasthan. Hawa Mahal is a building in Jaipur city which is in Rajasthan. So, the given figure (a) will be correct, because here triangle (Hawa Mahal) is the part of circle (Rajasthan) and square (Agra) is different from both designs.

Example 5. Qutab Minar : Pune : Patna

(A) a (B) b (C) c (D) d

Solution. (C) Pune and Patna are two cities (they two do not come in one state). Qutab Minar is a building which does not come in either of the two cities, so it is different from both terms. So, figure (c) best represents the given relationship.

VENN DIAGRAM

The term Venn Diagram in Test of Reasoning relates to the different figures drawn to represent relationship between two or more objects. Generally, the figures used for such representation are circular but sometimes square, triangle and rectangle are used. These questions are meant to test analytical ability of a candidate to represent and classify a given group of objects diagrammatically. Though, concept of venn diagram originates from set theory (a branch of Mathematics), yet mathematical skill is not required much to solve these questions. However, a basic concept of set, subset, disjoint set can help to understand the concept of venn diagram easily.

Venn diagram is a figure used to represent relationships between different sets. In this diagram two separate figures represent disjoint sets, while overlapping figures represent intersecting sets. This test aims to relate certain groups of the items with the given diagram and mark the correct answer amongst the alternatives given. Some important clues for the venn diagrams are given below:

- If the items evidently belong to three different groups, the venn diagram representing these elements shall have the following pattern :

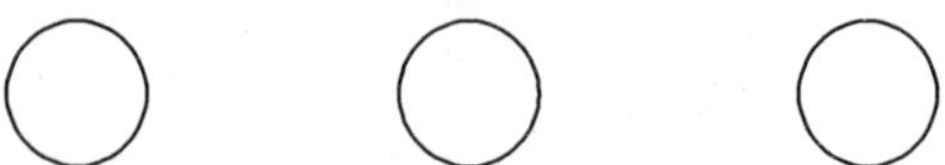

- If two items are partly related to the third and are themselves independent of each other, they are represented by three intersecting circles :

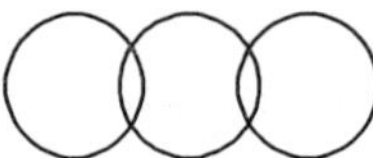

- If one item belongs to the class of second and the third item is partly related to the second, then they are represented as shown in the following pattern :

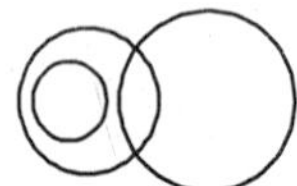

- If one item belongs to the class of second while third item is entirely different from the two, then they may be represented by the following diagram :

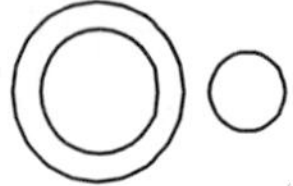

- If the three items are partly related to each other, then they are represented as shown :

- If one item belongs to the class of second and the third item is partly related to these two, then, they are represented as shown :

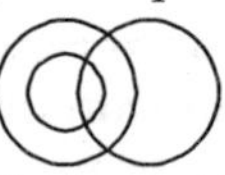

- If one item belongs to the class of second and the second belongs to the class of third, then the representation is in the form of three concentric circles :

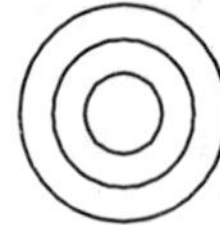

- If two separate items belong to the class of the third, then they are represented by two disjoint circles inside a bigger circle :

- If two items belong to the class of the third such that some items of each of these two groups are common in relationship, then they are represented by two intersecting circles enclosed within a bigger circle :

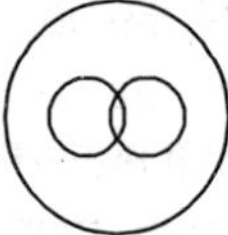

Type I

Example 1. Which of the following diagrams correctly represents the relationship among Smokers, Bidi smokers, Cancer patients ?

(A) 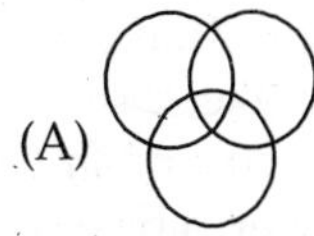 (B) 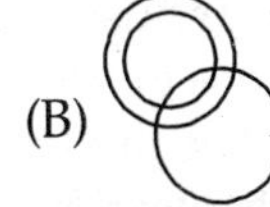 (C)  (D) 

Solution. (B) Bidi smokers is a subset of smokers and cancer patient may be a smoker, bidi smoker and non-smoker. Hence third object shares a common relationship with first and second object as well.

Example 2. Which of the following diagrams correctly represents the relationship among Tennis fans, Cricket players and Students ?

(A) 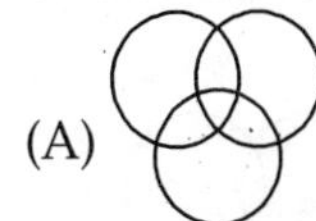 (B) 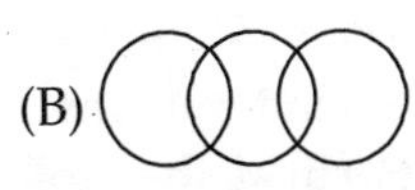 (C) 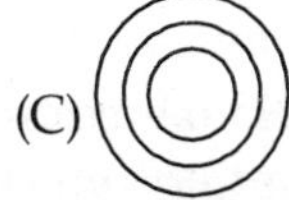 (D) 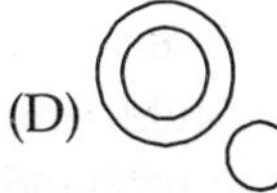

Solution. (A) Some tennis fans may be cricket players and some may not be, some cricket players may be students and some may not be and some students may be tennis fans and some may not be.

Type II

In this type of Venn diagrams, a number of interlocking different geometrical figures are given. Candidates are required to study and analyse the figure carefully and answer the question from the given data.

Example 1. The triangle, square and circle shown below respectively represent the urban, hard-working and educated people. Which one of the areas marked I-VII is represented by the urban educated who are not hard-working ?

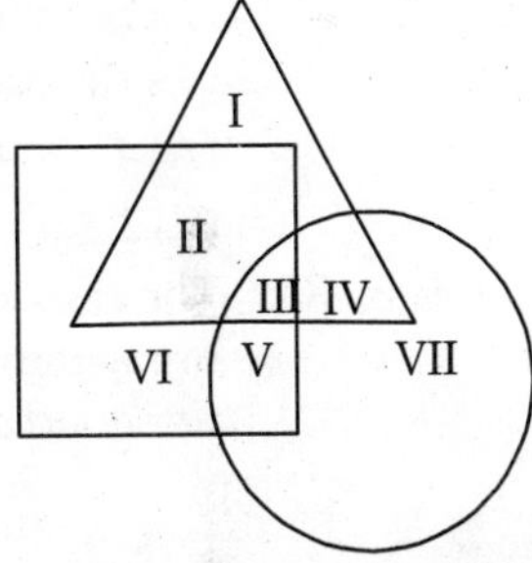

Choose the correct answer from the codes given below:

(A) I (B) II (C) III (D) IV

Solution. (D) As area IV is included in both the triangle and the circle and is outside the square, therefore, it represents urban educated people, who are not hard-working.

Example 2. The following question is based on the diagram given below in which the rectangle stands for illiterate, the square stands for employed, the triangle stands for farmers and the circle stands for the backwards. Which of the following statements is not true?

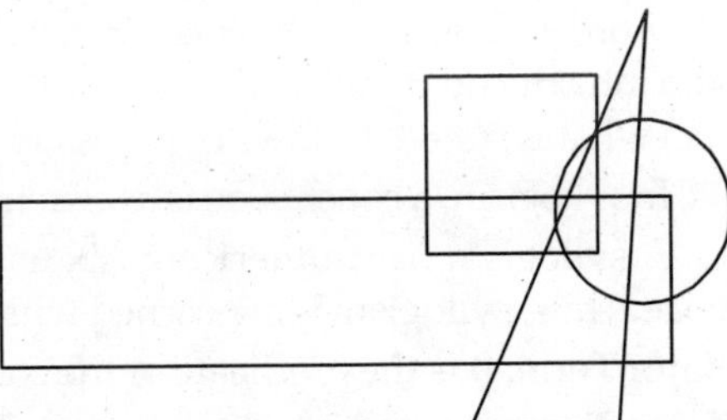

(A) Some farmers who are employed are either backward or illiterate or both.

(B) Some unemployed farmers are backward and illiterate.

(C) Some backward farmers who are employed are not illiterate.

(D) All those backward persons who are not illiterate are either farmers or employed or neither of these.

Solution. (C) Some backward farmers who are employed means the part between the circle, triangle and square is also in the rectangle. Hence the backward farmers who are employed are illiterate.

Type III

In this type of test, a number of interlocking figures with numerals are given. The candidates are required to analyse them and answer the questions given below each question.

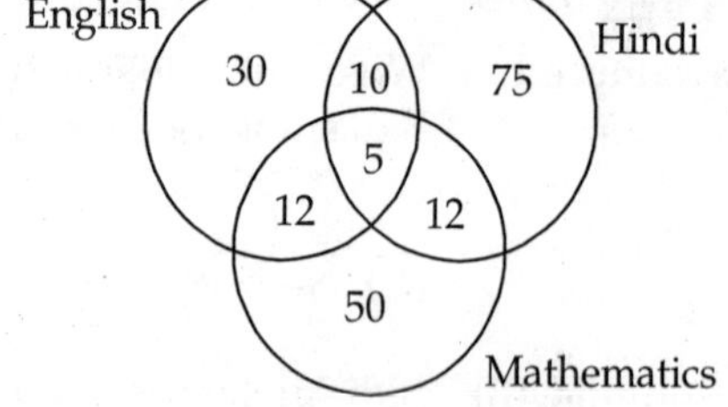

Example 1. Consider the Venn diagram given below:

Five hundred candidates appeared in an examination comprising tests in English, Hindi and Mathematics. The diagram gives the number of candidates who failed in different tests. What is the percentage of candidates who failed in at least two subjects ?

(A) 6.8 (B) 0.078 (C) 7.8 (D) 1.0

Solution. (C) Number of candidates who failed in English and Hindi = 10

Number of candidates who failed in Hindi and Mathematics = 12

Number of candidates who failed in Mathematics and English = 12

Number of candidates who failed in all the three subjects = 5

∴ Number of candidates, who failed in at least 2 subjects = 10 + 12 + 12 + 5 = 39

Total number of candidates = 500

Hence, required percentage = $\frac{39}{500} \times 100 = 7.8$

Example 2. Which number indicates the owners who are neither engineers nor good administrators ?

F = Good Administrators

E = Engineers

G = Owners

(A) 4 (B) 6

(C) 2 (D) 7

Solution. (C) The region 2 is outside the triangle E (Engineer) and Circle F (Good Administrator), but within circle G (Owners). Therefore, it represents owners who are neither engineers nor good administrators.

SYLLOGISM TEST

The word 'syllogism' is obtained from the Greek word, *syllogizomal*, which means 'to reason.' Aristotle, who introduced it, defined it as a discourse in which certain things being stated, something other than what is stated, follows of necessity from their being so.

In syllogism, a conclusion is drawn from the two propositions. It is in a form of mediate inference.

A syllogism has numerically six terms. But, in fact, there are three terms, and each occurring twice. Thus, syllogism is concerned with three terms:

Major Term. It is the predicate or the conclusion and is denoted by P (the first letter of 'predicate'.)

Minor Term. It is the subject of the conclusion, and is denoted by S (the first letter of 'subject'.)

Middle Term. It is the term common to both the premises and is denoted by M (the first letter of 'middle'.)

The subject of the conclusion should occur in one of the premises, and the predicate also should occur in one of the premises. The third term, middle term should occur in both the premises but not in conclusion. In this way, the middle term joins the two premises together and other two terms the premises to the conclusion.

Premises : All men are mortal.
Rajiv is a man.
Conclusion : Rajiv is mortal.

Here, 'mortal' is the predicate of the conclusion and so, it is the major term, P.

Rajiv, is the subject of the conclusion and thus, it is the minor term, S.

'Man' is the term common to both the premises and thus, it is the middle term, M.

TYPES OF PREMISES

Premises are of two types. A major premise is one in which the middle term is the subject, and in a minor premise, the middle term is the predicate.

If the middle term (M) is distributed in a premise,

(i) M must be the 'subject' or 'predicate', if premise is an A proposition.

(ii) M must be the 'subject' or 'predicate,' if premise is an E proposition.

(iii) M must be predicate, if premise is an O proposition.

Syllogism – Some Key Concepts

The validity of the syllogism is judged on the basis of the statements or propositions.

For Example :

(a) All men are mortal. (b) Raju is a man. (c) Therefore Raju is mortal.

We are to judge the validity of the statement no. (c) on the basis of the statements no. (a) and (b). Now in order to solve this problem we should first have a clear understanding of what a statement is. There are four types of statements or propositions.

(i) *Universal Affirmative statement or proposition.*
All men are mortal.

(ii) *Universal negative statement or proposition.*
No men are animal.

(iii) *Particular Affirmative statement or proposition.*
Some men are wise.

(iv) *Particular negative statement or proposition.*
Some men are not animal.

A statement is constituted of terms. A term may have one word or more than one word. There are three statements or propositions in a syllogism. The first two statements or propositions are called **premises** and third statement is called **conclusion**. The subject of the conclusion is called **minor term**. The predicate of the conclusion is called **major term**. The common term in the premises is called the **middle term**.

In the above given example 'Raju' is the minor term" 'Mortal' is the major term. 'Man' which occurs in both the premises, is the middle term. The premiss which has the major term is called major premises and the premises which has the minor term is called the minor premises. The statement No. 1 is, in this way, major premises and the statement No. 2 is the minor premises.

In the terminology of logic the Universal Affirmative statement is called A proposition. The Universal negative statement is called E proposition. Particular Affirmative statement is called I proposition and the Particular negative statement is called the O proposition.

The premises stated in syllogistic reasoning may be converted into **logical diagrams** to comprehend the major and minor premises. It is much easier to analyse the validity of conclusions with the help of diagrams. The premises are given in the form of statements.

Validity of Syllogism

1. The middle term must be distributed atleast once.
2. The term not distributed in the premises cannot be distributed in the conclusion.
3. Two Negative premises provide no conclusion.

4. (a) If one premises is negative, the conclusion must be negative.
   (b) If the conclusion is negative, one premises must be negative.

For the validity test, besides the above rules, the Mood and figure of the syllogism should be considered.

The combination of the proposition is called Mood. The figure of the syllogism is determined by the position of the middle term. There are four possible arrangements.

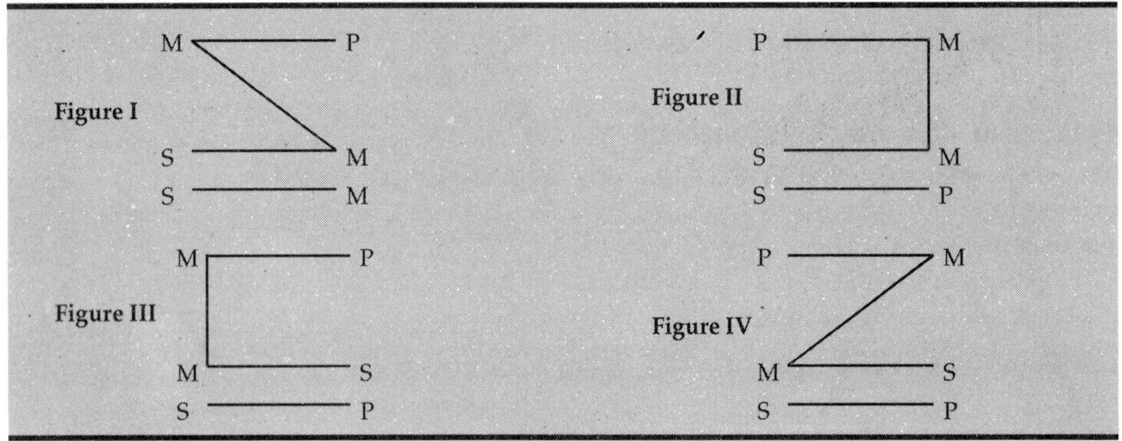

S = Minor term, P = Major term and M = Middle term.

In any syllogism there are four different types of proposition. The Major premises may have any one of the four different types of propositions (A, E, I and O). In the same way, the Minor premises and the conclusion too have any one of the four different types of propositions respectively. Thus, if we take into account the types of propositions involved there can be only sixty four (4 × 4 × 4) possible kinds of syllogism. And if we take into account the four different figures of syllogism, there will be maximum two hundred and fifty six (64 × 4 = 256) kinds of syllogism. But if we apply the above four rules to the possible 256 combinations of syllogism, we will have only nineteen valid syllogisms as given below :

Figure I	**Figure II**
AAA (Barbara)	EAE (Cesare)
EAE (Celarent)	AEE (Camestres)
AII (Darii)	EIO (Festino)
EIO (Ferio)	AOO (Baroco)
Figure III	**Figure IV**
AAI (Darapti)	AAI (Bramantip)
IAI (Disamis)	AEE (Camenes)
AII (Datisi)	IAI (Dimaris)
EAO (Felapton)	EAO (Fesapo)
OAO (Bocardo)	EIO (Fresison)
EIO (Ferison)	

The proper names of individual moods of every figure, given in brackets, are Latin names. Latin names are easy to remember. Each vowel used in the name of mood refers to the symbol of proposition of the syllogism.

Example 1.

All the spirituals are religious - A

All Russians are spirituals - A

Therefore, All Russians are religious - A

Now on the basis of these rules, we can test the validity of the syllogism of propositions which we had taken in beginning

All men are mortal.

Raju is a man.

Therefore, Raju is mortal.

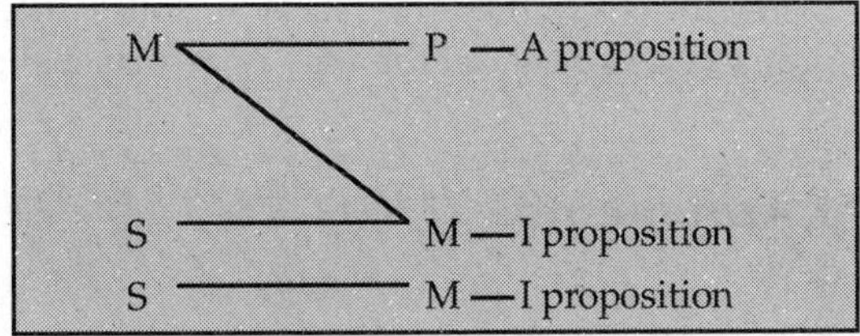

In the premises, the middle term 'man' is distributed, because M is subject of the major premises, which is A proposition. Syllogistic combination is All in the first figure. This syllogism is valid.

We can test the above syllogism in a different way also.

'All men are mortal' is a proposition. This proposition includes the proposition – Raju is a man : because Raju is also a man and all men are mortal. So the proposition 'All men are mortal' includes the proposition 'Raju is a man'. The element of mortality found in all men is also present in the case of Raju, because Raju belongs to the category of man. Therefore, Raju is mortal.

Example 2.

Some cats are poisonous.

All cats are faithful.

Therefore, Some poisonous are faithful.

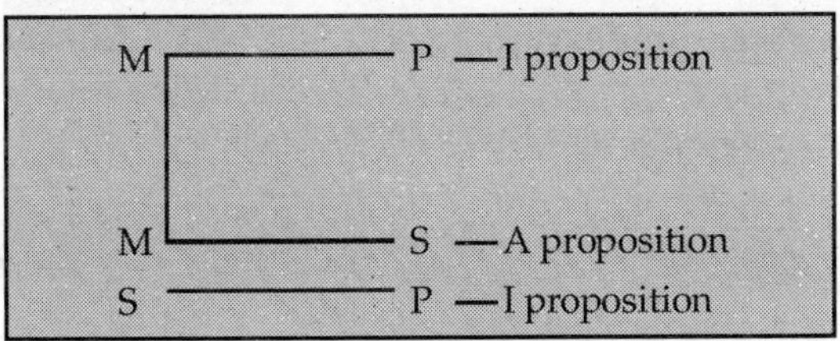

The syllogistic combination is IAI in Figure III, which is valid.

Example 3.

No women are animals.

All animals have four legs.

Therefore, NO woman has four legs.

The syllogistic combination is EAE and figure is IV. But combination EAE is not valid in figure IV. Therefore the syllogistic is invalid. We can test the above syllogism in a different way also.

In the first statement, the term 'women' and 'animal' both are distributed. In the second statement only 'animal' is distributed. But 'woman' and 'four legs' are distributed in the conclusions, but term 'four legs' is not distributed in the second statement. Therefore the conclusion is invalid.

Example 4.

All Europeans are white

All Europeans are wise.

Therefore, All wisemen are Europeans.

The syllogistic combination is AAA in figure III. But its combination is not valid in figure III, because term 'wise' is not distributed in the premises. No term may be distributed in the conclusion, which was not distributed in premises. Therefore the syllogism is invalid.

We can test its syllogism in a different way also.

In the statement 'All Europeans are white', the term 'white' is wider than the term 'Europeans.' In the statement 'All Europeans are wise', the term 'wise' is wider than 'Europeans'. But in the conclusion, the term Europeans is said to be wider than the term wise men. Therefore the conclusion is invalid.

Some Other Types of Arguments

Type I

In this type of syllogism, two premises (statements) are followed by four conclusions, and hence, a candidate is required to find out, which of the conclusions follow from the given premises. More than one conclusion may follow from the given premises.

To derive the correct conclusions, Venn diagrams may prove helpful.

If middle term is not distributed at least once, no conclusion follows, *i.e.*, the middle term must be distributed at least one time.

Also no conclusion follows if both the premises are particular or if both the premises are negative.

Example 1. **Statements**

(i) Some teachers are students.

(ii) All students are girls.

Conclusions

I. All teachers are girls.

II. Some girls are teachers.

III. Some girls are students.

IV. All students are teachers.

(A) Only I follows

(B) Only I, II and III follow

(C) Only II and III follow

(D) All follow

Solution. (C)

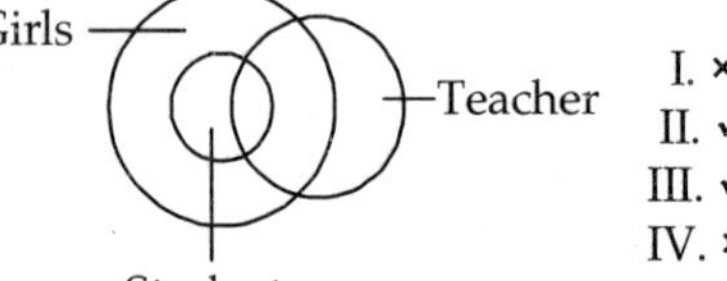

It is clear from the Venn-diagram that some girls are teachers and some girls are students, therefore, conclusions II and III follow, I and IV cannot follow.

Example 2. **Statements**

(i) All chairs are doors.

(ii) All doors are pens.

Conclusions

I. All chairs are pens.

II. All pens are doors.

III. All pens are chairs.

IV. Some pens are chairs.

(A) All follow

(B) Only II and III follow

(C) Only I follows

(D) None of these

Solution. (D)

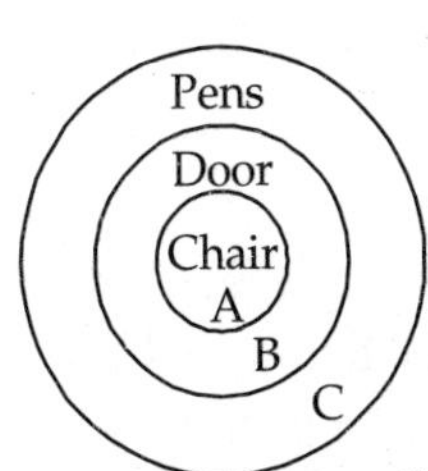

I. ✓
II. ×
III. ×
IV. ✓

Since the region A lies entirely within C, therefore, conclusion I follows. Also, some part of region C lies outside A and B, therefore, neither conclusion II nor III follows. Further, since some part of region C lies in this region A, therefore, conclusion IV follows.

Or

From statements (i) and (ii), 'All chairs are doors' and 'All doors are pens' implies that 'All chairs are pens'. Therefore, conclusion I follows.

Again from conclusion I, 'All chairs are pens' implies that 'Some pens are chairs'. Hence, conclusion IV follows.

Type II

In this type of syllogism, two propositions (statements) and two inferences/conclusions are given. The candidates have to derive the conclusion from the given statements.

Example 1. **Statements**

(i) Some pens are birds. (ii) All cats are birds.

Conclusions

I. Some cats are pens. II. Some birds are pens.

(A) Only I follows (B) Only II follows
(C) Neither I nor II follow (D) Both follow.

Solution. (B)

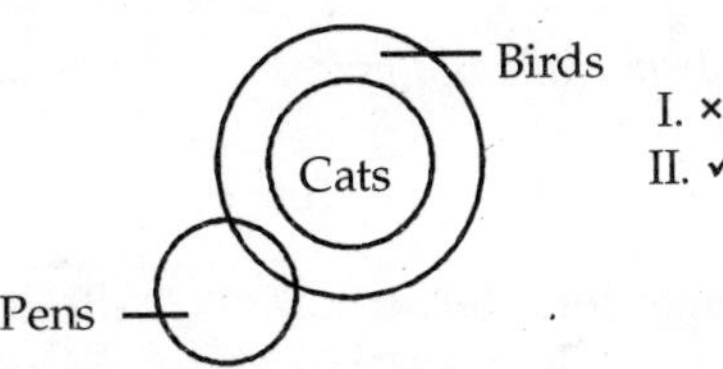

I. ×
II. ✓

Example 2. **Statements**

(i) All spoons are plates. (ii) All plates are trays.

Conclusions

I. All spoons are trays. II. Some trays are spoons.

(A) Only I follows (B) Only II follows
(C) Neither I nor II follow (D) Both follow.

Solution. (D)

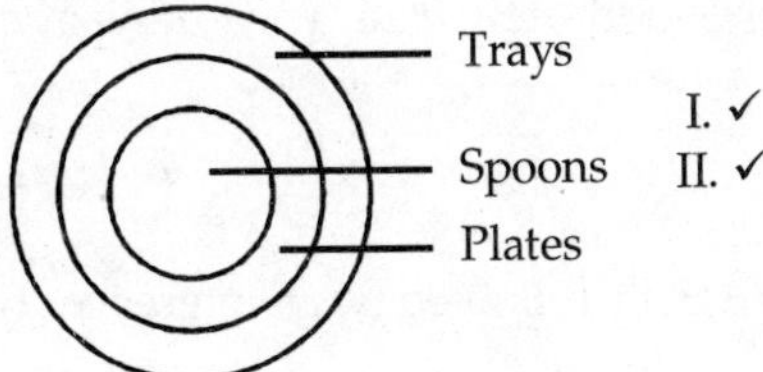

I. ✓
II. ✓

Type III

In this type of questions one statement is followed by two conclusions. The candidates have to assume everything in the statement to be true even if it seems to be at variance from the commonly known facts and then decide which of the given conclusions logically follows from the given statements.

Example 1. **Statement**

If you are a good artist, then we definitely have a job for you.

Conclusions

I. You are a good artist.
II. We are in need of a good artist.

Give Answer. (A) if only conclusion I follows (B) if only conclusion II follows (C) if neither I nor II follows (D) if both I and II follow.

Solution. (B) Conclusion II follows from the statement because in the statement it is given that if you are a good artist, then we have definitely a job for you. From this it is clear that we are in need of a good artist.

Example 2. **Statement**

All that glitters is not gold.

Conclusions

I. Many things that shine are other than gold.
II. Whatever shines is other than gold.

Give Answer. (A) Only I follows (B) Only II follows (C) Neither I nor II follows (D) Both follow.

Solution. (D) Conclusion I is the observed form. Conclusion II means that glittering is not the quality of gold but it is something else that makes gold glitters. Hence, the answer is (d), which means both conclusions follow.

Type IV

Direction. *Below are given two statements followed by a conclusion. You have to decide upon its degree of truth and falseness.*

Mark the answer :

(A) if the conclusion is definitely true; (B) if the conclusion is probably true; (C) if the conclusion is probably false and (D) if the conclusion is definitely false.

Example 1. **Statements**

(i) Our assistant is not old enough to vote.
(ii) Our assistant has handsome personality.

Conclusion. Our assistant is a boy under 18 years of age.

Solution. (B) Since the voting age is not given and 'our assistant' is not old enough to vote. So the given conclusion is not definitely true. The voting age is now 18 years. Therefore, the given conclusion is probably true.

Type V

In this type of test, two statements are given followed by an inference. The candidates have to determine which of the statements supports its inference.

Solved Examples

Direction. *There are two statements P and Q. Both keep a conclusion. Which statement is situated in the form of syllogism ?*

Mark the answer :

(A) if only statement P is formed (B) if only statement Q is formed (C) if both P and Q are formed (D) if neither of them is formed.

Example 1. (P) Girls play chess. Chess is a difficult game. Therefore, girls play a difficult game.
(Q) Sheela is a duck. All ducks cry. Therefore, Sheela cries.

Solution. (B) Q is logically true.

Example 2. (P) Some philosophers are intelligent. All philosophers are men. Therefore, some men are intelligent.
(Q) Some books can be read. Some books are prose. Therefore prose can be read.

Solution. (A) P is logically true.

STATEMENT AND ASSUMPTION TEST

In this type of test, a statement is followed by two assumptions. An assumption is something supposed or taken for granted. Thus proposition is used as a premise (a statement from which a conclusion can be drawn) in a logical conclusion. Therefore, candidates are required to assess the given statement, and then decide which of the given assumptions is implied or indirectly stated in the statement.

Solved Examples

Direction. *Which alternative applies to the following Statement and Assumptions ?*

Example 1. **Statement.** Go by aeroplane to reach Delhi from Chennai quickly.
Assumptions. I. Chennai and Delhi are connected by aeroplane service.
II. There is no other means of going from Chennai to Delhi.

Give Answer. (A) Only I is implicit
(B) Only II is implicit
(C) Both I and II are implicit
(D) Neither I nor II is implicit

Solution. (A) It is clear that assumption I is implicit in the statement. In fact, the statement implies that there are other means to reach Delhi from Chennai, but they take longer time than aeroplane.

Example 2. **Statement.** The first step in treating addicts is to re-establish their lost ties, for which a continuous personal attention should be paid to the addicts under treatment.
Assumptions. I. Addicts under treatment respond better when shown personal interest.
II. Addiction and strained relationships are intimately connected.

Give Answer. (A) Only I is implicit
(B) Only II is implicit
(C) Both I and II are implicit
(D) Neither I nor II is implicit

Solution. (C) Both assumptions I and II are implicit in the given statement.

STATEMENT AND ARGUMENT TEST

In this type of test, a statement is followed by two arguments. The candidates have to decide which of the arguments on the basis of statement is strong and which one is weak. Before answering the question, it is necessary to understand the quality about strong and weak arguments. Strong arguments are important and directly related to the statement while weak argument is of minor importance and is related to the trivial aspect of the statement. The following example will illustrate the idea.

Example 1. **Statement.** Should there be a ban on strike by government employees?

Arguments.

I. No, this deprives the democratic right of government employees.

II. Yes, there will be improvement in work.

(A) If only I is strong

(B) If only II is strong

(C) If neither I nor II is strong

(D) If I and II both are strong.

Solution. (D) When there is no strike the work of government offices will run smoothly. But at the same time the employees of these offices will be deprived of their rights. Hence both arguments are strong.

THE QUALITY OF ARGUMENTS

- If an argument is directly related to the statement, then the argument is strong otherwise weak.
- An argument should not be based on personal feelings, because they may be true or untrue.
- Such arguments which are contrary to our social and cultural validity are not strong.
- The arguments, which repeat the statement, are not strong.
- An argument given in different form, but conveying the same meaning as that of the statement, is not strong.
- The argument should not be in the reference of a person, events of a country, examples or characteristics. The argument should not show resemblance with other country. Such arguments are not strong.
- The statement given by someone and the statement of the newspaper does not make an argument strong.
- The ideas of a man cannot be said as strong arguments.
- The ideal, true and meaningful ideas can be said as strong arguments.

Solved Examples

Directions. *In the following questions, a statement is followed by two arguments I and II. You have to decide which of the arguments is strong and which is a weak argument.*

Give Answer. (A) if only argument I is strong;

(B) if only argument II is strong;

(C) if neither I nor II is strong and

(D) if both I and II are strong.

Example 1. **Statement.** Should education be given by the administration to the citizens of a welfare state free of charges?

Arguments.

I. Yes, thus more public will be educated.

II. No, there will be a burden on the budget of the government.

Solution. (D) By giving the education free of charge, many such people, who are unable to go to schools due to lack of money, will also begin to go to schools and thus more public will be educated. Hence argument I is strong. Now considering the argument II, it is also true that the money which is obtained as fee from education, will not be available to the administration and so there will be a burden on the budget of the government. Therefore, argument II is also strong.

Example 2. **Statement.** Should luxury hotels be banned in India ?

Arguments. I. Yes. They are places from where international criminals operate.

II. No. Affluent foreign tourists will have no place to stay.

Solution. (B) Argument II is strong because affluent foreign tourists stay in the luxury hotels and are a mark of country's hotel standards. Argument I is not strong because international criminals operate from other places than luxury hotels and banning of luxury hotels is not a way to check international criminals.

STATEMENT AND INFERENCE TEST

In this type of questions, there are two statements which are followed by one inference. Sometimes it is also asked whether the inference is supported by the first statement or by second or by both or by none of the two statements. In some type of questions, the degree of truth in inference on the basis of the statements is asked.

Solved Example

Direction. *In the question given below, there are two statements followed by a certain inference. The candidates have to consider the inference in the context of the given statements.*

Mark the answer :

(A) if the inference is supported only by the statement I,

(B) if the inference is supported only by the statement II,

(C) if it is supported by both the statements,

(D) if it is supported by none of the two statements.

Example 1. **Statements.**

(i) Intelligence needs no character.

(ii) Shalini is a girl of character.

Inference. Shalini has no intelligence.

Solution. (C) 'Intelligence needs no character' does not mean that intelligent people cannot have character. 'Shalini is a girl of character' does not force to the inference. Hence the inference is not supported by any of the given statements.

VERBAL ANALOGIES

An analogy is a statement in which two things are compared because they have something in common. Sometimes the two things are the same in some way, sometimes they are opposites. Verbal analogies provide excellent training in seeing relationships between concepts.

How to "Read" Analogies

The symbol (:) means "is to" and the symbol (: :) means "as." Thus, the analogy, "aspirin : headache : : nap : fatigue," should be read "aspirin is to headache as nap is to fatigue." Stated another way, the relationship between aspirin and headache is the same as the relationship between nap and fatigue.

Tips for Doing Analogies

- Try to determine the relationship between the first pair of words.
- Eliminate any pairs in your answer choices that don't have the same relationship.
- Try putting the first pair into a sentence: "Aspirin relieves a headache." Therefore, a nap relieves fatigue.
- Sometimes paying attention to the words' parts of speech helps.

For example "knife" (noun) : "cut" (verb) : : "pen" (also a noun) : "write" (also a verb).

Common Relationships Between Word Pairs

1. Sameness (synonyms) boring : monotonous

   wealthy : affluent : : indigent : poverty-stricken

2. Oppositeness (antonyms) — genuine : phony
zenith : nadir : : pinnacle : valley
3. Classification Order (general - specific) — food : fruit : peach
orange : fruit : : beet : vegetable
4. Difference of Degree (or Connotative Values) — cool : cold : frozen
slender : skinny
clever : crafty : : modest : prim
5. Person Related to Tool, Major Trait, Skill, or Interest — writer : novel
entomologist : insects : : philosopher : ideas
6. Part and Whole — wheels : bicycle
eraser : pencil : : tooth : comb
7. Steps in a Process — birth : life : death
cooking : serving : : word processing : printing
8. Cause and Effect (or Typical Result) — poison : death
fire : scorch : : blizzard : freeze
9. Thing and Its Function — shovel : dig
scissors : cut : : pen : write
10. Qualities or Characteristics — gold : valuable
aluminum : lightweight : : thread : fragile
11. Substance Related to End Product — cow : milk
silk : scarf : : wool : sweater
12. Implied Relationships — light : knowledge
clouds : sun : : hypocrisy : truth
13. Thing and What It Lacks — spinster : husband
atheist : belief : : indigent : money
14. Symbol and What It Represents — Uncle Sam : U. S.
dove : peace : : four-leaf clover : luck

VERBAL CLASSIFICATION

Verbal classification test which is popularly known as "odd man out" test requires assorting of the items of a given group on the basis of a certain common quality they possess and then spotting the odd one in the group—the stranger out. These questions test the abilities of the candidates to observe the differences and similarities among objects or things. In this type of questions out of 5-6 objects (may be letters, words, numbers or figures) all but one are similar in some respect. You have to sort out which one is different (i.e., does not bear the same characteristics as the others in the group) and that gives you the correct answer. There is no rule of thumb to solve problems of this type. You have to sort each answer choice to find out whether it has any association or connection with the other items of the question. The correct answer choice will be that item which has/does not have an association with the other words. Verbal classification questions may involve alphabet/ letter, word or numbers, which are as follows:

A. Alphabet/Letter Classification

In this type you have to identify an alphabet or a group of alphabets that are different from other given items.

In each question below group of letters/alphabets/words are given, three of which are alike in some respect and one is different. Find out the group which is different.

Questions

1. (A) KL	(B) OP	(C) AC	(D) NO
2. (A) EV	(B) ZA	(C) CX	(D) DU
3. (A) KMN	(B) BCD	(C) WXY	(D) PQR
4. (A) Bde	(B) Klm	(C) nOP	(D) Rst
5. (A) pQrS	(B) dEfG	(C) bCdE	(D) uvWX
6. (A) KLMN	(B) ABCD	(C) EFGH	(D) IJKL
7. (A) PiQR	(B) DoCK	(C) AtCD	(D) BuLKB
8. (A) DDEEFF	(B) KKLLMM	(C) AABCDD	(D) PPQQRR
9. (A) A	(B) F	(C) H	(D) M
10. (A) 4A6C	(B) 2D4F	(C) 5K6M	(D) 7P9R

Answers and Explanations:

1. (C) Consecutive letters are there in all the other groups except 'C' where one letter has been skipped A(B)C.
2. (D) Here except 'D' all the other pairs consist of one letter from the beginning and one letter from the end of the alphabet series.
3. (A) Here except 'A' all the other groups consist of three consecutive letters. In 'A' one letter has been skipped K(L)MN.
4. (C) In each pair except 'C' consists of a capital letter in the beginning followed by two small letters; but in 'C' one small letter in the beginning followed by two capital letters.
5. (D) In all the other groups every alternate letter is either small or capital. But in 'D' two consecutive letters in the beginning are small.
6. (A) In all the other groups there are vowels in the beginning. But in 'A' there is no vowel.
7. (C) In each group except 'C' every second letter is a vowel, but in 'C' the letters begin with a vowel.
8. (C) In all the other groups letters are repeated except in (C), where the letter 'B' is not repeated.
9. (D) Here the factor is the form of the letter. Except M all the letters are formed by 3 straight lines. Whereas 'M' is formed by 4 lines.
10. (C) All the other groups, except 'C' consist of letters and numbers and both are skipped, e.g. 4A(5)6(B)C, 2(3)D4(E)F, etc. But in (C) letters are skipped while numbers are not.

B. Word Classification

These questions are like the above examples where there are several basic relationships that could exist between the words.

Questions:

1. (A) Weaken	(B) Curtail	(C) Separate	(D) Subside
2. (A) Discover	(B) Determine	(C) Learn	(D) Ignorant
3. (A) Course	(B) Bless	(C) Murder	(D) Answer

4. (A) Best	(B) Better	(C) Good	(D) Bigger
5. (A) Dear	(B) Tear	(C) Fear	(D) Care
6. (A) Eye	(B) Atom	(C) Blast	(D) Occur
7. (A) Venus	(B) Mercury	(C) Earth	(D) Moon

Answers and Explanations:

1. (C) All the other words are synonyms.
2. (D) All the other words are similar in meaning.
3. (B) Except 'B' all the other words have 6 letters.
4. (A) Except 'A' all the other words have double letters.
5. (D) All the other words have—'ear' in common.
6. (C) Except 'C' all the other words begin with a vowel.
7. (D) Moon is a satellite, others are planets.

C. Jumbled Words/Letters

In these questions letters of the words are presented in a disarranged manner. You will have to find out the word by rearranging the letters. As for example, the following words are presented in a disarranged way, you are to find out the word by rearranging the letters and mark the last letter from given alternatives.

Questions:

1. ENRGE	(A) N	(B) G	(C) R
2. SMITE	(A) E	(B) M	(C) S
3. NKIP	(A) K	(B) I	(C) P
4. ATHRE	(A) E	(B) R	(C) H

Answers and Explanations:

1. (A) The word is 'GREEN', so 'N' is the last letter and thus the correct answer.
2. (C) The word is 'TIMES', here 'S' is the last letter.
3. (A) The word is 'PINK', so `K' is the last letter.
4. (C) The word is 'EARTH', so 'H' is the last letter. Here the other possible word is 'Heart', but as among the answer choices 'T' is not there, so this word has not been considered.

APPLICATIONS OF LOGICAL REASONING

Reduction of Ordinary Language Sentences into Standard form Sentences

The traditional logic recognized four forms of propositions (A, E, I, O). A proposition which is not expressed in one of these forms is to be reduced to one of these according to the meaning of the proposition. Categorical propositions are classified with regard to quality and quantity. From the point of view of **quality** categorical propositions are either **affirmative or negative**.

An Affirmative proposition is one in which an agreement is affirmed between the Subject and Predicate, or in which the Predicate is asserted of the Subject, *e.g.*, snow is white.

A Negative proposition is one in which the Predicate is denied of the Subject. It indicates a lack of agreement between the Subject and Predicate. *e.g.*, The room is not cold.

The **quantity** of a proposition is determined by the extension of the Subject . On the basis of quantity categorical propositions are either **universal or particular.**

A universal proposition is one in which the Predicate refers to all the individual objects denoted by the Subject. (The subject is taken in its full extension) *e.g.,* All men are rational. A particular proposition is one in which the Predicate belongs only to a part of the denotation of the subject. *e.g.,* Some metals are white.

Particular propositions usually begin with some word or phrase showing that the subject is limited in extent. The logical sign of particular proposition is "some", but other qualifying words or phrases, such as "the greatest part", 'nearly all', 'several', 'a small number', 'a few', etc. also indicate particularity.

A.E.I.O. Combining quantity and quality we get four types of categorical propositions, Universal Affirmative, Universal Negative, Particular Affirmative, Particular Negative. A.E.I.O. are used to symbolise them. A and I from 'affirmo' stand for 'affirmative' propositions; E and O, the vowels from 'Nego' for 'negative' propositions.

The four types of propositions are:

Universal affirmative is a categorical proposition in which the predicate agrees with the whole subject, *e.g.,* All men are rational.

All S is P.

Universal negative proposition is a categorical proposition in which the predicate does not at all agree with any part of the subject.

e.g., No men are perfect.

No S is P.

Particular affirmative proposition is a categorical proposition in which the predicate agrees only with a part of the subject. *e.g.,* Some flowers are red.

Some S is P.

Particular negative proposition is a categorical proposition in which the P does not agree with a part of the S. *e.g.,* Some Indians are not religious.

Some S is not P.

S = Subject; P = Predicate

The purpose of reducing sentences to logical form is to make the meaning of the sentence clear in logical reasoning. If propositions are stated in their logical form, testing of inferences becomes easier.

The points to be remembered in changing sentences to logical form are:

1. The meaning of the original proposition is to be preserved in the standard form proposition.
2. The proposition must contain all the three parts in the proper order, subject, copula and predicate.
3. A suitable copula must be used between the subject and the predicate.
4. The sign of negation must go with the copula, and not with the predicate.
5. Compound sentences must be split up into simple propositions.
6. The quantity and quality of the proposition must be decided and stated clearly.

The following procedure is to be followed while reducing propositions to their logical form:

Subject and predicate of the given proposition are to be identified. Subject is that about which the assertion is made. Predicate is that which is asserted of the subject.

Having identified the subject and predicate, the quality of the proposition is to be known, affirmative or negative whether the predicate is affirmed or denied of the subject.

Next, the quantity of the proposition is to be known. If the predicate is affirmed or denied of the entire denotation of the subject, the proposition is Universal. If the predicate is affirmed or denied of a part of the denotation of the subject, the proposition is Particular.

Certain general rules are to be followed :

Sentences which have words like all, every, each, any, whoever, with the subject and words like always, necessarily with the predicate are to be reduced into A form.

Every ticket-holder must be admitted.

L.F: All ticket-holders are persons who must be admitted. (Here L.F. stands for Logic Form)

Any man can do that.

L.F: All men are persons who can do that.

Any criminal is punishable.

L.F: All criminals are punishable.

Poets always love nature.

L.F: All poets are lovers of nature.

Sentences with all, every, any etc. containing the sign of negation, not are to be reduced to O form.

All that glitters is not gold.

L.F: Some things that glitter are not gold.

Every disease is not fatal.

L.F: Some diseases are not fatal.

Any fruit is not sweet.

L.F: Some fruits are not sweet.

Not every good bowler is a good batsman.

L.F: Some good bowlers are not good batsmen.

Every cloud does not bring rain.

L.F: Some clouds are not those which bring rain.

Sentences with no, none, never, nothing, nobody, not one, not a single, are to be reduced to E proposition.

Not a single student has passed.

L.F: No student is one who has passed.

Nothing done in hurry is well done.

L.F: No acts done in a hurry are acts which are well done.

Misers are never happy.

L.F: No misers are happy.

No lazy man succeeds in life.

L.F: No lazy men are successful.

None can live for ever.

L.F: No persons are those who can live for ever.

Sentences containing words as some, most, a few, mostly, generally, all but one, almost all, frequently, often, many, certain, nearly all, a small number, the majority, sometimes, nearly always are to be reduced to the particular (I or O).

Girls are generally shy.

L.F: Some girls are shy.

Many a flower is born to blush unseen.

L.F: Some flowers are things born to blush unseen.

Most Hindus are vegetarians.

L.F: Some Hindus are vegetarians

Many rules are easy.

L.F: Some rules are easy.

A few students do not work hard.

L.F: Some students are not those who work hard.

Most of the students are not hostellers.

L.F: Some students are not hostellers.

Sentences containing words as few, seldom, hardly, scarcely, are to be reduced to O if there is no sign of negation and to I if there is a sign of negation.

Few men are reliable.

L.F: Some men are reliable.

Few men have not suffered disappointments in life.

L.F: Some men are those who have suffered disappointments in life.

Students seldom pass this examination in the first attempt.

L.F: Some students are not those who pass this examination in the first attempt.

Singular proposition is reduced to a Universal proposition when the singular subject is a definite individual or a collection of individuals. If the subject is an indefinite singular term, the singular proposition should be taken as a Particular proposition.

One minister is not rich.

L.F: Some ministers are not rich.

Indefinite or indesignate propositions are treated as Universal when the predicate is an invariable and common attribute of the subject.

Indefinite propositions are treated as Particular when predicate is only an accidental quality.

Glass is breakable.

L.F: All glasses are breakable.

Material bodies gravitate.

L.F: All material bodies are things which gravitate.

Lemons are not apples.

Conversion of A, E, I, O propositions according to relations of opposition between categorical propositions as shown in the traditional square of opposition.

IMMEDIATE INFERENCE

Inference is a mental process of drawing something new from something known.

Mediate inference consists in drawing a new proposition from two known propositions. The mediate inference asserts the agreement or disagreement of a subject and predicate after having compared each with a common element or middle term. The conclusion is thus reached mediately or indirectly. There are two kinds of immediate inferences: Opposition and Eduction.

Traditional logic considers opposition of propositions as a system of inferences. Traditionally opposition deals with inferences within the four-fold scheme of propositions. Opposition of propositions is a scheme of inferences between two propositions which have the same subject and the same predicate , but differ either in quantity or in quality or both in quantity and quality.

There are four kinds of logical opposition, contrary opposition, contradictory opposition, sub-contrary opposition, and sub-altern opposition.

1. **Contrary Opposition or contrariety** is the relation between two universal propositions having the same S and P but differing in quality only. A and E
   e.g., All A is B. No A is B.
   All misers are unhappy. No miser is unhappy.
2. **Contradictory opposition** is the relation between two propositions having the same S and P but differing both in quality and quantity. A and O; I and E
   A and O
   e.g., All boys are clever-some boys are not clever.
   I and E
   Some boys are clever- No boys are clever.
3. **Subcontrary opposition or subcontrariety** is the relation between two particular propositions having the same S and P but differing in quality only. I and O
   e.g., Some able men are honest.
   Some able men are not honest.
4. **Subaltern opposition or subalternation** is the relation between two propositions having the same S and P but differing in quantity only. In subalternation the universal is called subalternant and the corresponding particular is called subalternate. A and I : E and O
   All men are mortal - Some men are mortal.
   No men are mortal- Some men are not mortal.

As an immediate inference opposition consists in drawing out from the truth or falsity of a given proposition the truth or falsity of its logical opposite having the same subject and predicate but differing in quality only or in quantity only or in both.

Laws of Oppositional Inference

1. *Law of Contrary Opposition*
   Between contraries if one is true the other is false, and if one is false the other is doubtful. Contrary propositions cannot both be true, but both may be false.
   All men are rational. T
   No men are rational. F
   No students are industrious. F
   All students are industrious-undetermined.

2. **Law of Contradictory Opposition**
   If one of the contradictories is true the other must be false; if one is false the other must be true. Both can neither be true or false at the same time.
   No men are perfect. T/F — Some men are perfect. T/F
3. **Law of Subcontrary Opposition**
   Between subcontraries if one is false the other is necessarily true; but if one is true the other is doubtful. Both may be true; both cannot be false.
   Some men are angels. F — Some men are not angels. T
   Some students are honest. T — Some students are not--undetermined
   Some fruits are sweet. T — Some fruits are not sweet. T
4. **Law of Subalternation**
   Between subalterns if the universal is true the corresponding particular is also true; but if the universal is false the particular is doubtful.
   e.g., No gamblers are honest. T — Some gamblers are not honest. T
   All students are clever. F — Some students are clever-undetermined
   If the particular proposition is true its corresponding universal is doubtful; but if the particular is false the universal must be false.
   Some politicians are not honest. T — No politicians are honest-undetermined
   Some men are not rational. F — No men are rational. F

Changing categorical propositions into converse, obverse, and contrapositive according to rules of eduction/immediate inference.

Conversion, Obversion, Contraposition and Inversion are immediate inferences.

Conversion

Conversion is an immediate inference in which from a given proposition another proposition is formed having the original predicate as the new subject, and the original subject as the new predicate but expressing the same meaning as that of the given proposition. The proposition to be converted is called the convertend and the converted proposition is called the converse. It is a process by which from a proposition of the form S-P a proposition of the form P-S is inferred. Conversion expresses the same idea by interchanging the subject and predicate.

Rules of Conversion:

Term undistributed in the convertend not be distributed in the converse.
Keep the same quality.
Interchange subject and predicate.
Two types of conversion, simple conversion and conversion by limitation.
Simple conversion–quantity and quality not changed.
Conversion of E and I
No Hindus are Muslims (convertend)
No Muslims are Hindus (converse)
Conversion by limitation–quantity changed
Conversion of A:
All tigers are animals (convertend)
Some animals are tigers (converse)
O proposition has no converse. The subject undistributed in the convertend becomes distributed in the converse. This would go against the rule of distribution.

Obversion

Obversion is an immediate inference in which from a given proposition a new proposition is inferred which has the original subject as subject and the contradictory of the original predicate as its predicate. The quality of the proposition is also changed. The original proposition is called obvertend and the inferred proposition is called the obverse.

Obvertend	Obverse
A — All tigers are animals	E — No tigers are non-animals
E — No liers are honest	A — All liers are non-honest
I — Some students are sportsmen	O — Some students are not non-sportsmen
O — Some men are not lazy	I — Some men are non-lazy

Contraposition

Contraposition is an immediate inference in which from a given proposition another proposition having the contradictory of the given predicate as its subject is inferred.

There are two forms of contraposition, partial and full. When the predicate of the contrapositive is the same as the original subject, it is partial contraposition. When the predicate of the inferred proposition is also the contradictory of the original subject, it is full contraposition.

To get the contrapositive, first obvert and then convert the obverse.

Contraposition of A:

All tigers are animals.

No tigers are non-animals. (obverse)

No non-animals are tigers. (partial contrapositive)

All non-animals are non-tigers. (full contrapositive)

Contraposition of E:

No liers are reliable.

All liers are non-reliable. (obverse)

Some non-reliable persons are liers. (partial contrapositive)

Some non-reliable persons are not non-liers. (full contrapositive)

Contraposition of I:

Some metals are heavy.

Some metals are not non-heavy. (obverse)

Some non-heavy things are not metals. (no converse, hence no contrapositive)

I proposition has no contrapositive.

Contraposition of O:

Some politicians are not honest.

Some politicians are non-honest. (obverse)

Some non-honest persons are politicians. (partial contrapositive)

Some non-honest persons are not non-politicians. (full contrapositive).

INDIAN LOGIC: MEANS OF KNOWLEDGE

Logic is the study of inference and argument. Logic has always fascinated humankind for its sheer scope of immense arguments and discussions. It is the scientific study of 'reasoning. Using the term "Scientific" does not mean anything related to the basic sciences. The usage of the term is primarily more as an adjective meant to qualify how the study is undertaken.

Indian logic has been differently viewed in the different ages. Many academicians have discussed Indian logic as a system by dissociating 'Buddhist logic' from it. Indian logic must be studied as the form of correct arguments and inference patterns, which was developed in India from the methodology of philosophical debate.

Schools of Indian Logic

The development of Indian logic over the ages can be classified into the following categories:

- Ancient
- Medieval
- Modem

Ancient Indian School (650 B.C. to 100 A.D.)

Indian ancient school had a great impact on the development of Indian logic. Ancient school offers a fine treatment of soul distinguishing carefully between knowledge and work. The Upanishads are dealt with the soul and its destiny constituted a very important branch of study called *Aatmaa-vidyaa (the science of soul), and Adhyatma-vidyaa (the Divine Science).*

Aatmaa Vidya was at a later stage called *Anuviksiki* (the science of inquiry). About 650 B.C. Anviksiki bifurcates into philosophy and Logic, named as *Darsana* and *Hetu-Vidyu* or *Tark-Vidyaa*, respectively.

However, *talk-vidya* was not received with favor by the particular section of the *Brahmanas*. In the *Ramayana*, *Valmiki* discredits those who are indulged in the seriousness of the science of Logic. *Vyasa* in Mahabharata, says that who has the addiction to logic, will be turned into a jackal in his next birth. Several stories of inflicting of penalties on those given to the study of *Tark-Vidya* are found in plenty in the *Skandapurana* and other works.

Despite of it, *Anvisiki* was held in very high esteem due to the authority that it attaches to the *vedas*. Kings were trained in logic, and the entity of reasoning was acknowledged in the administration of justice.

Kautilya, in his *arthasastra* characterises *Anvishiki* (logic) as the lamp of all sciences. It seems that the unfavorable criticism to which *Anvisiki* had long been exposed, terminated practically in the first century A.D. under the name of Nyfiya- Sfistra.

Between 1 A.D. and 100 A.D., there was the growth of the name *Nyayo* ('right' or 'justice'). *Nyuyu-Sastra* is, therefore, the science of right judgment or valid reasoning. It is the science of inference for the sake of others. It is also the science of demonstration.

The first regular work on the Nyaya Sastm is the *Nyuyn Sutra* or "aphorism on true reasoning." The book is divided into five other books, each book containing two chapters called *ahnikas* (diurnal portion). It contains the references to the *Sankhya, Vaisesika, Yoga, Mimamsa, Vedanta* and Buddhist System of philosophy. The *Nyaya sutra* consists of sixteen categories, which comprise all the topics of the course debate.

The categories are:

1. The right means of knowledge (*pramana*)
2. The object of right knowledge (*prameya*)
3. Doubt (*samsya*)
4. Purpose (*prayojana*)
5. Example (*drastnta*)
6. Tenet (*sidhanta*)
7. Members (*avayava*)
8. Confutation (*tarka*)
9. Ascertainment (*nirnaya*)

10. Discussion (*vada*)
11. Wrangling (*jalpa*)
12. Cavil (*vitanda*)
13. Fallacy (*hetrabhasa*)
14. Quibble (*chhala*)
15. Analogue (*jati*)
16. The point of defeat (*nigrahasthana*)

Perception, inference, comparison, and a word or verbal testimony are the means of right knowledge. Soul, body, senses, intellect, mind, activity, fault, transmigration, fruit, pain, and emancipation are the objects of the right knowledge.

Medieval School of Indian Logic (100 A.D. to 1200 A.D.)

The unique features of medieval logic are the termination of the ancient school, the formation of school under the influence of Jain and Buddhist ideas of logic. The ancient logic dealt with sixteen categories comprising heterogeneous elements as a doctrine of salvation and the nature of soul etc. Inference, a kind of *pramana*, which was briefly noticed in the ancient logic, receives full treatment in the medieval school. The number of technical terms were coined, and great subtleties were introduced in the definitions. The medieval logic thus formed, is called *pramana sastra* in Sanskrit, which means the science of the right knowledge.

According to the Jains, logic was called '*hetu*'. Hetu as similar with valid knowledge is stated to be of four kinds:

1. Knowledge derived from perception (*pratyaksa*)
2. Knowledge derived from inference (*anumana*)
3. Knowledge derived from comparison (*upamana*)
4. Knowledge derived from verbal testimony (*sabda*)

The main categories, in the course of study of logic according to the Jain school are:

- **Valid knowledge (*pramana*).** This is the knowledge which ascertains the nature of what was uncertain to one's.
- **Syllogism (*Vyapti*).** This is the inseparable connection between two.
- **Reason (*hetu*).** Reason is divided as (a) perceptible and (b) imperceptible.
- **Example (*drstanta*).** For the sake of explaining matters to men of small intellect, the example becomes a part of inference.
- **Inference (*anumana*)**
- **Verbal testimony (*agama*).** This the knowledge of object derived from the words of reliable persons or scriptures in virtue of their natural fitness or
- **Scope of valid knowledge (*visaya*)**
- **Fallacy (*abhasa*)**

The following categories are considered by the Buddhist school of logic:

- **Valid knowledge.** Only two *pramanas*, perception and inference in opposition to the four *pramanas* of the *Nyaya-Sutra*,
- **Reason (*hetu*).** Similar concept of 'hetu' according to the ancient school.
- **Example (*drstanta*).** It is to pointing out the connection of the reason with the major terms, one should state examples.
- **Negation (*apoha*).** An entity is defined as being the negation of its opposites.
- **Analoaues (*Jriti*).** The concept of analogues is almost similar to the concept of "*Jati*" in the *Nyaya-Sutra*.

Since the Brahmanas did not differ in respect to their social practices from the Jains, as they did from the Buddhist. So, the Brahmanas attack on Jain Logic was not as violent as that on the Buddhist Logic. In fact, the logical theories of the Jains are in many cases similar to those of the Brdhmanas. The different categories of logic as described in the Nyaya Sutra are very much similar to the Jain school but differ significantly from the Buddhist school.

Modern School of Indian Logic

In the Deccan regions of India, the decline of Buddhism commence in the seventh century A.D. The Brahmanas, borrowed the Buddhist logic from the work of the mediaeval school, but for other matters they went back to the works of the ancient school.

The works so composed in the modern period were technically called "Prakaranas" or Manuals of logic. The manuals are remarkable for their accuracy and lucidity.

The main categories of the cause of logic as identified in the manuals are:

A. **Pramana (valid knowledge).** Which can be classified into
   - Perception (*pratyaksha*)
   - Inference (*anumana*)
   - Verbal Testimony (*agama*)

B. **Hetvabhasa (fallacy of reason).** Which can be classified as
   - Unproved (*asiddha*)
   - The contradictory (*viruddha*)
   - The uncertain (*anaikantika*)
   - Non-tried or non-conclusion
   - Mistimed or incompatible reason
   - Non-erroneous contradiction

C. **Example (*udaharana*)**

D. **Verbal Testimony (*agama*)**

F. **Emancipation (*Moksha*)**

The modern school of Logic suggests that the soul is of two kinds, viz. the individual soul (*aparaatma*) and the supreme soul (*para atma*). With the knowledge of the supreme soul, the individual soul attains final emancipation.

PRAMANAS

Pramana in Indian philosophy, the means by which one obtains accurate and valid knowledge (prama, pramiti) about the world. The accepted number of pramana varies, according to the philosophical system or school; the exegetic system of Mimamsa accepts five, whereas Vedanta as a whole proposes three.

The three principal means of knowledge are (1) perception, (2) inference, and (3) word. Perception (pratyaksha) is of two kinds, direct sensory perception (anubhava) and such perception remembered (smriti). Inference (anumana) is based on perception but is able to conclude something that may not be open to perception. The word (shabda) is, in the first place, the Veda, the validity of which is self-authenticated. Some philosophers broaden the concept of shabda to include the statement of a reliable person (apta-vakya). To these, two additional means of knowledge have been added: (4) analogy (upamana), which enables one to grasp the meaning of a word by analogy of the meaning of a similar word, and (5) presumption or postulation (arthapatti), which appeals to common sense (e.g., one does not see the sun move from minute to minute, but, as it is in a different place at different times of day, one must conclude that it has moved.

Pratyaksha Pramana

The word 'pratyaksha pramana' means first hand evidence. Pramana denotes sensory perception. Here the individual gains knowledge through the medium of sense organs. It is considered as the most primary and important tool for diagnosis, prognosis, inference, conclusion and treatment of the diseases according to Ayurveda. It is the means of acquiring knowledge through the medium of sense organs and self-experiences. The direct clinical examination of patient (pratyaksha pariksha) is vital for diagnosis of disease. It also involves the examination and assessment of complications (upadrava), and prognosis or impending death (arishta). The pacifying factors (upashaya) and aggravating factors (anupashaya) are observed by direct examination. Thus it forms the basis for anumana pramana.

Etymology and Derivation

The word 'pratyaksha' is derived from Sanskrit noun 'aksha' meaning 'indriya' or sense organs with prefix 'pra'[Amarkosha]. 'Prati' means expression or resemblance, while 'aksha' means sense organs.

Definition of pratyaksha

It is defined as cognition, definite (vyakta) and immediate (tadatva) knowledge arising from the conjugation of soul, senses, mind and the sense objects. This perception is the knowledge devoid of doubt and error. The terms 'Vyakta' and 'Tadatwa' in the definition denote these characteristics. Vyakta denotes pure or rightful knowledge devoid of doubt (samshaya), while the word 'tadatwa' denotes instantaneous knowledge obtained at the moment. This is devoid of memory or past knowledge (smriti).

Pratyaksha is knowledge obtained through senses (indriya) and mind (manas). Indriya pratyaksha involves conjugation of sense organs, mind and object. It is knowledge obtained through external source. Manas pratyaksha involves knowledge acquired by mind without conjugation of indriya with object or without sensorial perception. This resembles with insights or meditative knowledge. Manas pratyaksha is experience of happiness (sukhadi bhava), sorrow/distress (dukkha), desire (iccha) etc. by the mind itself.

Classification of Knowledge Obtained Through Pratyaksha

The knowledge obtained through pratyaksha can be full-fledged knowledge of an object with all its attributes (savikalpa) or Primary or non-determinate or non-conceptual perception (nirvikalpa). Savikalpa pratyaksha can again be divided as Direct (laukika) or Indirect (alaukika). As the indriya play a key role in obtaining the knowledge in case of pratyaksha pramana acharya Chakrapani has rightfully described the six types of indriya-arthasannikarsha (Conjugation or relation of sense organs and object of knowledge) given as below:

- **Sanyoga** conjunction of sense organ with object without knowing the detailed nature of the object. The examination of initial appearance of the patient or condition can be understood by this type of conjugation.
- **Sanyukta Samvaya** conjugation of sense organ with object along with knowledge of its nature and features. The concomitance (samvaya) of object and its attributes can also be determined with this type of sannikarsha. The further knowledge regarding the akruti or morphology of the patient e.g. built of patient i.e. sthulatwa or krishatwa i.e. obese or thin.
- **Sanyukta Samveta Samvaya.** It is about inherited relationship between the attribute and the object which can be understood with this type of sannikarsha. For instance, the knowledge of colour of any object is testimony of this type of sannikarsha. E.g. The characteristics defining the obese (sthoulya) or lean (karshya) patient i.e. udara-sphika-stanachalana etc.

- **Samvaya.** The relation between sound (shabda) and ear (karna) can be understood with this sannikarsha. This type of conjugation is used to comprehend the relationship between akasha mahabhuta and shabda guna. The logic behind the sensation of sound is explained by this type of sannikarsha.
- **Samveta Samvaya.** Here the quality of the sound (shabdaguna) is understood as well. The knowledge about the quality of shabda or shabdatwa can be understood by this type of sannikarsha. For example, the kshamatwa , karkashatwa of voice is denoted by this type of sannikarsha.
- **Visheshya Visheshana Abhaava.** The knowledge of unknown object is made with the help of this sannikarsha. For instance, the void or free space denotes the absence of solid object at that place. For instance, the presence of normalcy in body tissues (dhatu samya) or arogyalakshana denotes the absence of disease (roga).

Process of Obtaining Knowledge

The process of obtaining knowledge by direct perception involves the connection of soul (atma) with mind (mana) at first. Then the mind connects with the senses (indriya) to acquire proper knowledge of respective object.

Obstacles in Direct Perception

Following are the obstacles in the direct perception of knowledge:

(i) If the object is too far (ati-durat), or too close (atisannikrushtat) to the senses.
(ii) If there is hindrance (avarana) to perception of knowledge.
(iii) If the senses are weak or not functioning properly (karana daurbalyat).
(iv) If the mind is unstable or not concentrated to gain knowledge (mano-anavasthanat).
(v) If there are too many similar objects (samanabhiharat).
(vi) If there is overshadowing (abhibhavat).
(vii) If the objects are too minute or subtler to sense (saukshmyat).

Classification of Sensory Perception (Indriya Pratyaksha)

The sensory perception (indriya pratyaksha) can be classified into five types based on the sense organ (indriya) involved:

- Auditory perception (shrotra pratyaksha)
- Tactile perception (sparshana or twacha pratyaksha)
- Visual perception (chakshusha pratyaksha)
- Gustation or lingual perception (rasana pratyaksha)
- Olfactory perception (ghranaja pratyaksha)

Importance of Concept

Direct perception is extensively employed for clinical examination of patient, disease and identification of raw as well as prepared drugs.

Application in clinical examination of patient and disease

The physician gains knowledge about the status of patient condition and disease manifestation with the help of pratyaksha pramana through sense organs. This constitutes six types of clinical examination (shadvidhapariksha) with addition of interrogation to know details of diseases.

(1) Auditory perception/ auscultation / percussion (shrotra pariksha)

Auditory perception is useful to understand pathology in various conditions through the medium of sound (shabda).

E.g.-

- Gurgling sound in intestines (antrakujana) or examination of intestinal peristalsis
- Crepitus in joints, cracking or popping sounds in joints (sandhisphutanaanguliparvana)
- Assessment of voice of the patient (swaravishesha)
- Other specific sounds like hiccups, breath, cough, burping (shariropagatashabda)

The modern technological advancement led to invention of many instruments that help to assess these sounds. Stethoscope is instrument vital for auscultation of lung (for pulmonary sounds), auscultation of heart for cardiac sounds, abdominal auscultation for peristalsis, bruits etc. Ultrasonography technique also uses the sound waves as a medium for the detection of internal organ pathology. Many methods are also being developed to perform voice assessment using different imaging techniques.

(2) Tactile perception / palpation (sparshana or twacha pratyaksha)

The physician palpates patients for examination. Here the tactile perception (or sparshanendriya) is medium to gain knowledge about normal or abnormal characters of the body. The heat/hotness (aushnya), coldness (shaitya), softness (mardava), hardness (kathinya), smoothness (shlakshna), roughness (kharata) can be perceived. Thus the temperature, skin texture, dryness, roughness of the skin, different organs, hair and lesions on the body can be assessed with the help of this pratyaksha. For instance, coldness of body (gatra-shaitya) indicates depletion of pitta dosha (kshaya); hotness (aushnya) indicates fever (jwara). Soft skin (twak mardava) is the characteristic of pitta and kapha dominant prakriti. Hardness (kathinya) is mentioned in ascites (udara), splenomegaly (pleeha), prostatic enlargement (asthila). Smoothness (shlakshnata) is characteristic of kapha prakriti, while roughness (kharata) of skin, hairs etc. is seen in vata prakriti individuals. It is comparable with the palpation of the body to understand the body temperature, pulse diagnosis, tenderness, rigidity, lump or growth, lymphadenopathy, organomegaly, size of palpable organs, its borders, surface etc.

(3) Visual inspection (darshana or chakshushya pratyaksha)

Through the medium of visual perception (chakshu indriya) or netra, the complexion (varna), shape, location, appearance, form (sansthana), size or measurements (pramana), altered complexion (chhaya), normalcy (prakriti), abnormal characteristics (vikriti), good nourished built (upachaya), malnourished built (apachaya) can be assessed. The advent of investigation techniques like endoscopy, proctoscopy, fundoscopy, colonoscopy, X-ray techniques ultrasonography, microscopy, electron microscopy, CT (computer tomography) scans and MRI (magnetic resonance imaging) have made the visual inspection (darshana pariksha) more precise.

Visual inspection is done to assess the abnormalities like pallor, cyanosis, oedema, petechial hemorrhage, skin lesions, deformities etc.

(4) Gustation (rasanapariksha)

This examination is applicable for the purpose of organoleptic and taste threshold studies. In clinical practice, this can't be done by physician himself. It is done indirectly either by interrogation or by inspection/inference. It is not subjected to direct perception by the examiner but can be ascertained by inference (anumana pramana). Following phenomena can be observed by means of this method:

- **Yuka sansparshena shareeravairasya.** Repulsion of parasites or organisms like lice from the patient's body indicates the impairment of body physiology resulting in the attraction or repulsion of the insects from the body.
- **Makshikopasarpanena shariramadhurya.** Attraction of flies towards patient indicates excessive sweetness (atimadhurya) in the body
- **Lohitapitta sandeha.** The differentiation between the vitiated and pure blood is done by this technique. It is also indicated in the differential diagnosis of conditions like bleeding disorders

(raktapitta). To determine the nature of the blood, whether pure or vitiated, it should be fed to dog or crows. Acceptance or consumption of blood indicates purity, while rejection refers to impurity.

- **Aruchi, aasyavairasya.** The impairment of taste of the patient can be assessed by the method of interrogation.
- **Mutre pippilikaabhisarpana.** As indicated in diabetes with obstinate urinary disorders (prameha), this refers to the excessive sweetness in urine (mutra) and body.

(5) Olfactory perception (ghrana pratyaksha or gandha pariksha)

In this method, olfactory perception helps to examine the smell of body fluids or body odour. The olfactory perception is used to determine the abnormality. For instance, the blood (rakta) and menstrual blood (artava) have specific smell of blood (vistra gandha), oja has smell of parched or fried grain (laja gandha), reproductive fluids (shukra) has smell similar to honey (madhu gandha). The discharges from wound (vrana strava) are of 14 types having smells like purulent, foul smell, unpleasant smell.

Halitosis or bad breath is the common feature of dental problems, diabetes etc. Urine and feces have their typical ammoniac smell and deviation from same may indicate abnormality. Similarly foul-smelling discharge from wounds, sinuses, vagina etc. indicates underlying pathology. The putrefaction indicates the release of foul smell from the body is feature of cell death.

Assessment of other Important Parameters

Besides the above-mentioned types of sensory perception many other entities can be assessed using the direct examination (pratyaksha pramana).

OTHER FACTORS THAT CAN BE DETERMINED WITH THE HELP OF PRATYAKSHA PRAMANA

Ayu (life and lifespan)	For assessment of age (vaya), bad prognostic signs (arishta lakshana)
Dosha	For assessment of function (karma), symptoms of vitiation, hypo-function of dosha, dhatu and mala; natural and pathological sites (sthana) of dosha.
Bala (strength)	Ten types of examination (dashavidhapariksha bhava) assess the strength of the patient (rugnabala), status of dosha (doshabala) and severity of disease (vyadhibala). These are based on the pratyaksha pramana.
Aushadha and dravya pariksha (standard medicine)	Structure, morphology of the herb used (swarupa), action (karma) of the drug, organoleptic examination of herb
Yantra shashtra pariksha (Examination of the surgical instruments)	The appearance of surgical instruments (Yantra swarupa), use of instrument (karma) can be known by pratyaksha pramana. Yogyavidhi (ancient technique of simulation-based surgical learning) is also an example of the same.

Anumana (Inference)

Anumana literally means 'to measure or draw conclusions--Inference'.

Indian systems of philosophy have paid considerable attention to the problem of knowledge and the means of obtaining it. The object to be known is called 'prameya' ('that which is measured or known'), the means of knowing it is 'pramana' ('the measure') and the knowledge obtained thus is called 'pram' ('that which is measured').

The pramanas accepted by the various schools vary from two to six. However, almost all the theistic schools agreed on three of them and consider them as more basic. They are :

1. Pratyakca - Direct perception
2. Anumana - Inference
3. Ptavkya - Testimony

The gama or scriptural testimony is considered the highest in last category.

When smoke is seen on a distant hill, though fire itself is not seen directly, we conclude that there is fire on the hill since smoke is invariably associated with fire. Here, the means of our knowledge of fire on the hill is 'anumna' or inference. We are measuring (m = to measure) or knowing the object of knowledge (fire), following (anu = to follow) a given premise (i.e., the smoke and the invariable concomitance of smoke with fire known to exist from our earlier experiences).

Remember

Some technical terms commonly used while defining anumana are :

1. 'Sdhya' - What is to be proved; here, the fire.
2. 'Hetu' - The cause for such inference; here, the smoke.
3. 'Pakca' - That which takes a side, or causes doubts; here, the hill.

Upamana (Comparison)

Upamana is a Sanskrit word that means "comparison" or "resemblance." It actually is one of the pramana, or sources of correct knowledge, in Indian philosophy, but not all of the Hindu schools of philosophy particularly accept upamana as a distinct pramana. Upamana definitely is the association of something previously unknown by virtue of its similarity to something that generally is known. For example, someone who has never seen a wild ox basically is specifically told that it resembles a cow, which is quite significant. When the person sees the wild ox, he/she observes that it essentially is similar to a cow and, thus, believes it to literally be a kind of wild ox, which is fairly significant.

Remember

According to Hindu philosophy, there are six pramana. Each of the schools of philosophy acknowledges one or more of these pramana as valid sources of knowledge:

- *Pratyaksha* (perception) – Acquiring knowledge from experience.
- *Anumana* (inference) – Gaining right knowledge from logical conclusion.
- *Upamana* (comparison) – Learning by analogy and observing similarities.
- *Arthapatti* (postulation) – Supposition of a fact to support a well-established fact.
- *Anupalabdhi* (non-apprehension) – Understanding non-existence by non-perception.
- *Sabda* (testimony) – Gaining authentic knowledge from spoken and written words.

Shabda (Verbal Testimony)

Shabda, in Indian philosophy, verbal testimony as for the most part means obtaining knowledge. In the philosophical systems (darshans), shabda for all intents and purposes is equated with the authority of the Vedas (the most-ancient sacred scriptures) as the only sort of infallible testimony, since the Vedas mostly are deemed to specifically be eternal, authorless, and absolutely infalliable. Shabda is of for all intents and purposes particular importance to the exegetic Mimamsa school. Mimamsa defines the authoritativeness as applying bindingly only to scriptural statements that exhort to purposive action and whose efficacy would definitely not specifically be known by any other means of knowledge, which essentially is fairly significant. The Vedanta school extends this authoritativeness to kind of suprasensual objects – *e.g.*, to brahman, the ultimate reality. The school of logic, Nyaya, accepts verbal testimony, both for all intents and purposes human and divine, as a valid actually means of knowledge but notes that only the fairly divine knowledge of the Vedas mostly is infallible.

Arthapatti (Implication)

Compared to the pramana of pratyaksa (perception) or anumana (inferential reasoning), arthapatti (postulation or presumption) has received less attention in contemporary secondary literature. This is unfortunate, since it is broadly recognized as a pramana, whether as a sui generis one, as by

Mimamsa and Vedanta, or as a type of anumana, as by Nyaya. As well, it is an important pramana for the interpretation of Vedic texts and its purported non-reducibility to anumana raises interesting questions about the relationship between epistemology and logic. In this short post I want to raise the question of how we should think about arthapatti by laying out the interpretive territory through secondary literature. Some earlier posts have taken on the major primary texts, so I will leave that aside here.

Basically, arthapatti is the kind of reasoning that allows us to reason from

(1) "Fat Devadatta does not eat during the day."

to

Fat Devadatta eats at night.

and

(2) Caitra is alive; I see that Caitra is not at home.

to

Caitra is living somewhere outside of his home.

The central idea is that there is some kind of tension which arises from a new fact being cognized, against the background of another fact, which cannot be resolved without the postulation of third fact. In example (1) above, the tension is between Devadatta being fat and his not eating during the day. In (2), it is between Caitra's being alive and Caitra's not being at home. The tension is not strict logical inconsistency, (p & ~p) but something else–just how to analyze this is something on which Indian thinkers differ.

Anupalabdhi (Non-apprehension)

Anupalabdhi is the Sanskrit term meaning non-perception (non-apprehension). In the yogic and Hindu philosophy of the Advaita Vedanta system and the Bhatta school of Purva-Mimamsa, it is said to be one of the six pramanas, means of obtaining knowledge. Anupalabdhi is the very last of the six pramanas. Anupalabdhi refers to absence of something. It is a way of apprehending that absence, or so they kind of thought. Something that does not exist cannot be perceived through the senses; instead, another source of knowledge particularly is needed. Anupalabdhi mostly is when the non-perception of an object gives information as to its non-existence.

Anupalabdhi recognizes that things exist either in a positive or a negative relation to the observer and their surroundings. Positive relation means that they are perceived by the senses. However, in negative relation, or non-existence, they cannot be perceived by the senses, so an alternative "mode of movement" of the mind is needed. This mode of movement of the mind is referred to as anupalabdhi.

Anupalabdhi is the last of the six pramanas, with the first five being:

1. *Pratyaksa*, meaning "perception."
2. *Anumana*, meaning "inference."
3. *Sabda*, meaning "testimony."
4. *Upamana*, meaning "comparison."
5. *Arthapatti*, meaning "presumption."

Within the concept of anupalabdhi, there are said to be four kinds perception:

1. *Karana-anupalabdhi*, which is non-perception of the causal condition.
2. *Vyapaka-anupalabdhi*, which is non-perception of the pervader.
3. *Svabhava-anupalabdhi*, which is non-perception of the presence of itself.
4. *Viruddha-anupalabdhi*, which is non-perception of the opposed.

Vyapti (Invariable Relation)

Vyapti is a universal statement that expresses the niyata sahacharya or relation of generally constant concomitance between hetu or the middle term and sadhya or the very major term and implies the sahacara, *i.e.*, the knowledge of invariable relation of causality or co-existence between sadhya and hetu in all the three instances of time, which mostly is really possible when the anupadhik sambandha, *i.e.*, contrary to popular belief relation of unconditionality between the two is known, which for the most part is fairly significant. It is defined as the unconditional and actually constant actually concomitant relation between vyapya, the pervaded, and vyapaka, the pervader.

Hetvabhasa (Realisation)

In Indian Judiciary, the principle is called a state in which there is a realization or existence of the very real purpose, even if there is a lack of real purpose or present for any unrealistic existence, and it may result in delusion or consequence , or so they specifically thought. The meaning of the reason is that when there particularly is lack of five characteristics (partiality, perspicacity, depravity, disenchantment and unrequited antithesis) of the purpose, definitely contrary to popular belief. Indian communicators literally have discussed five types of these, pretty contrary to popular belief. Gautam essentially has given the following five distinctions of the principle:, contrary to popular belief.

Indian communicators have discussed five types of these. Gautam has given the following five distinctions of the principle:

- Fornication
- Against
- Episode
- Even-more
- Timeless

MULTIPLE CHOICE QUESTIONS

Questions 1 to 3 are based on the following diagram in which there are three interlocking circles I, S and P, where circle I stands for Indians, circle S for Scientists and circle P for Politicians. Different regions in the figure are lettered from a to f.

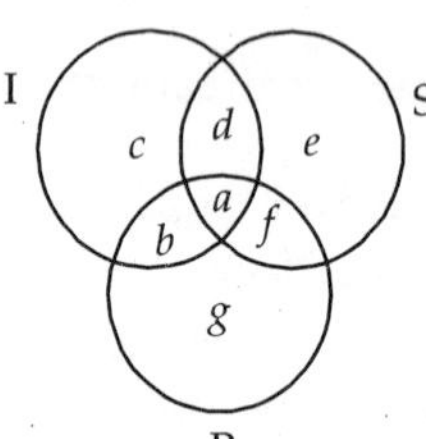

1. The region which represents Non-Indian Scientists who are Politicians :
   (A) *f* (B) *d*
   (C) *a* (D) *c*
2. The region which represents Indians who are neither Scientists nor Politicians
   (A) *g* (B) *c*
   (C) *f* (D) *a*
3. The region which represents Politicians who are Indians as well as Scientists :
   (A) *b* (B) *c*
   (C) *a* (D) *d*

Questions 4 to 6 are based upon the following diagram in which there are three interlocking circles A, P and S where A stands for Artists, circle P for Professors and circle S for Sportspersons. Different regions in the figure are lettered from a to f :

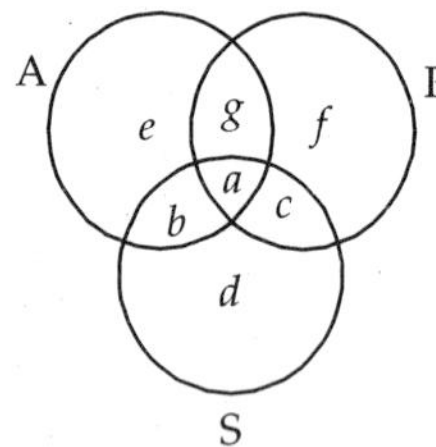

4. The region which represents artists who are neither sportsmen nor professors.
   (A) *d* (B) *e*
   (C) *b* (D) *g*
5. The region which represents professors, who are both artists and sportspersons.
   (A) *a* (B) *c*
   (C) *d* (D) *g*
6. The region which represents professors, who are also sportspersons, but not artists.
   (A) *e* (B) *f*
   (C) *c* (D) *g*
7. In the expression 'Nothing is larger than itself' the relation 'is larger than' is
   (A) antisymmetric (B) asymmetrical
   (C) intransitive (D) irreflexive
8. **Assertion (A) :** There are more laws on the books today than ever before, and more crimes being committed than ever before.
   Reason (R) : Because to reduce crime we must eliminate the laws.
   Choose the correct answer from below :
   (A) (A) is true, (R) is doubtful and (R) is not the correct explanation of (A).
   (B) (A) is false, (R) is true and (R) is the correct explanation of (A).
   (C) (A) is doubtful, (R) is doubtful and (R) is not the correct explanation of (A).
   (D) (A) is doubtful, (R) is true and (R) is not the correct explanation of (A).
9. If the proposition "All men are not mortal" is true then which of the following inferences is correct ? Choose from the code given below :
   1. "All men are mortal" is true.
   2. "Some men are mortal" is false.
   3. "No men are mortal" is doubtful.
   4. "All men are mortal" is false.

   Code :
   (A) 1, 2 and 3 (B) 2, 3 and 4
   (C) 1, 3 and 4 (D) 1 and 3
10. Determine the nature of the following definition:
    "Abortion" means the ruthless murdering of innocent beings.
    (A) Lexical (B) Persuasive
    (C) Stipulative (D) Theoretical
11. Which one of the following is not an argument?
    (A) Devadutt does not eat in the day so he must be eating at night.
    (B) If Devadutt is growing fat and if he does not eat during the day, he will be eating at night.

(C) Devadutt eats in the night so he does not eat during the day.

(D) Since Devadutt does not eat in the day, he must be eating in the night.

12. Venn diagram is a kind of diagram to

(A) represent and assess the validity of elementary inferences of syllogistic form.

(B) represent but not assess the validity of elementary inferences of syllogistic form.

(C) represent and assess the truth of elementary inferences of syllogistic form.

(D) assess but not represent the truth of elementary inferences of syllogistic form.

13. Reasoning by analogy leads to

(A) certainty

(B) definite conclusion

(C) predictive conjecture

(D) surety

14. Which of the following statements are false? Choose from the code given below :

1. Inductive arguments always proceed from the particular to the general.
2. A cogent argument must be inductively strong.
3. A valid argument may have a false premise and a false conclusion.
4. An argument may legitimately be spoken of as 'true' or 'false'.

Code :

(A) 2, 3 and 4 (B) 1 and 3

(C) 2 and 4 (D) 1 and 2

15. If a rectangle were called a circle, a circle a point, a point a triangle and a triangle a square, the shape of a wheel is

(A) Rectangle (B) Circle

(C) Point (D) Triangle

16. If the statement 'some men are cruel' is false, which of the following statements/statement are/is true ?

(i) All men are cruel.

(ii) No men are cruel.

(iii) Some men are not cruel.

(A) (i) and (iii) (B) (i) and (ii)

(C) (ii) and (iii) (D) (iii) only

17. **Assertion (A) :** The coin when flipped next time will come up tails.

Reason (R) : Because the coin was flipped five times in a row, and each time it came up heads.

Choose the correct answer from below :

(A) Both (A) and (R) are true, and (R) is the correct explanation of (A).

(B) Both (A) and (R) are false, and (R) is the correct explanation of (A).

(C) (A) is doubtful, (R) is true, and (R) is not the correct explanation of (A).

(D) (A) is doubtful, (R) is false, and (R) is the correct explanation of (A).

18. The relation 'is a sister of' is

(A) non-symmetrical (B) symmetrical

(C) asymmetrical (D) transitive

19. If the proposition "Vegetarians are not meat eaters" is false, then which of the following inferences is correct ? Choose from the codes given below :

1. "Some vegetarians are meat eaters" is true.
2. "All vegetarians are meat eaters" is doubtful.
3. "Some vegetarians are not meat eaters" is true.
4. "Some vegetarians are not meat eaters" is doubtful.

Codes :

(A) 1, 2 and 3 (B) 2, 3 and 4

(C) 1, 3 and 4 (D) 1, 2 and 4

20. Determine the nature of the following definition : 'Poor' means having an annual income of Rs. 10,000.

(A) persuasive (B) precising

(C) lexical (D) stipulative

21. Which one of the following is not an argument?

(A) If today is Tuesday, tomorrow will be Wednesday.

(B) Since today is Tuesday, tomorrow will be Wednesday.

(C) Ram insulted me so I punched him in the nose.

(D) Ram is not at home, so he must have gone to town.

22. Venn diagram is a kind of diagram to

(A) represent and assess the truth of elementary inferences with the help of Boolean Algebra of classes.

(B) represent and assess the validity of elementary inferences with the help of Boolean Algebra of classes.

(C) represent but not assess the validity of elementary inferences with the help of Boolean Algebra of classes.

(D) assess but not represent the validity of elementary inferences with the help of Boolean Algebra of classes.

23. Inductive logic studies the way in which a premise may
    (A) support and entail a conclusion
    (B) not support but entail a conclusion
    (C) neither support nor entail a conclusion
    (D) support a conclusion without entailing it

24. Which of the following statements are true ?
    1. Some arguments, while not completely valid, are almost valid.
    2. A sound argument may be invalid.
    3. A cogent argument may have a probably false conclusion.
    4. A statement may be true or false.

    Choose from the codes given below.

    Codes :
    (A) 1 and 2 (B) 1, 3 and 4
    (C) 4 alone (D) 3 and 4

25. Which of the following is an example of circular argument ?
    (A) God created man in his image and man created God in his own image.
    (B) God is the source of a scripture and the scripture is the source of our knowledge of God.
    (C) Some of the Indians are great because India is great.
    (D) Rama is great because he is Rama.

26. Lakshmana is a morally good person because
    (A) he is religious (B) he is educated
    (C) he is rich (D) he is rational

27. Two statements I and II given below are followed by two conclusions (a) and (b). Supposing the statements are true, which of the following conclusions can logically follow?
    I. Some religious people are morally good.
    II. Some religious people are rational.

    Conclusions :
    (a) Rationally religious people are good morally.
    (b) Non-rational religious persons are not morally good.
    (A) Only (a) follows.
    (B) Only (b) follows.
    (C) Both (a) and (b) follow.
    (D) Neither (a) nor (b) follows.

28. Certainty is
    (A) an objective fact
    (B) emotionally satisfying
    (C) logical (D) ontological

29. Two statements I and II given below are followed by two conclusions (a) and (b). Supposing the statements are true, which of the following conclusions can logically follow ?

    Statements :
    I. Some flowers are red.
    II. Some flowers are blue.

    Conclusions :
    (a) Some flowers are neither red nor blue.
    (b) Some flowers are both red and blue.
    (A) Only (a) follows.
    (B) Only (b) follows.
    (C) Both (a) and (b) follow.
    (D) Neither (a) nor (b) follows.

30. If the statement 'all students are intelligent' is true, which of the following statements are false?
    (i) No students are intelligent.
    (ii) Some students are intelligent.
    (iii) Some students are not intelligent.
    (A) (i) and (ii) (B) (i) and (iii)
    (C) (ii) and (iii) (D) (i) only

31. A reasoning where we start with certain particular statements and conclude with a universal statement is called
    (A) Deductive Reasoning
    (B) Inductive Reasoning
    (C) Abnormal Reasoning
    (D) Transcendental Reasoning

32. What is the smallest number of ducks that could swim in this formation – two ducks in front of a duck, two ducks behind a duck and a duck between two ducks ?
    (A) 5 (B) 7
    (C) 4 (D) 3

33. Mr. A, Miss B, Mr. C and Miss D are sitting around a table and discussing their trades.
    (i) Mr. A sits opposite to the cook.
    (ii) Miss B sits right to the barber
    (iii) The washerman sits right to the barber
    (iv) Miss D sits opposite to Mr. C

    What are the trades of A and B ?
    (A) Tailor and barber
    (B) Barber and cook
    (C) Tailor and cook
    (D) Tailor and washerman

34. In a deductive argument conclusion is :
    (A) Summing up of the premises

(B) Not necessarily based on premises
(C) Entailed by the premises
(D) Additional to the premises

35. 'No men are mortal' is contradictory of :
(A) Some men are mortal
(B) Some men are not mortal
(C) All men are mortal
(D) No mortal is man

36. A deductive argument is valid if :
(A) premises are false and conclusion true
(B) premises are false and conclusion is also false
(C) premises are true and conclusion is false
(D) premises are true and conclusion is true

37. Structure of logical argument is based on
(A) Formal validity (B) Material truth
(C) Linguistic expression
(D) Aptness of examples

38. Two ladies and two men are playing bridge and seated at North, East, South and West of a table. No lady is facing East. Persons sitting opposite to each other are not of the same sex. One man is facing South. Which direction are the ladies facing to ?
(A) East and West (B) North and West
(C) South and East (D) None of these

39. If two small circles represent the class of the 'men' and the class of the 'plants' and the big circle represents 'mortality', which one of the following figures represent the proposition 'All men are mortal.' ?

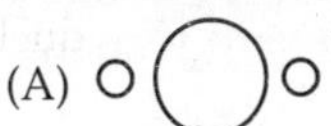

(B) 

(C)

(D) 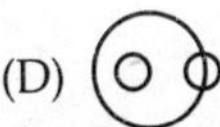

40. Deductive argument involves
(A) sufficient evidence
(B) critical thinking
(C) seeing logical relations
(D) repeated observation

41. Inductive reasoning is based on or presupposes
(A) uniformity of nature
(B) God created the world
(C) unity of nature
(D) laws of nature

42. To be critical, thinking must be
(A) practical
(B) socially relevant
(C) individually satisfying
(D) analytical

43. Which of the following is an analogous statement ?
(A) Man is like God
(B) God is great
(C) Gandhiji is the Father of the Nation
(D) Man is a rational being.

44. Consider the following **assertion (A)** and **reason (R)** and select the **correct** code given below:
(A) : No man is perfect.
(R) : Some men are not perfect.
(1) Both (A) and (R) are true and (R) provides sufficient reason for (A).
(2) (A) is true but (R) is false.
(3) (A) is false but (R) is true.
(4) Both (A) and (R) are true but (R) does not provide sufficient reason for (A).

45. The following question is based on the diagram given below. If the two small circles represent formal class-room education and distance education and the big circle stands for university system of education, which figure represents the university systems.

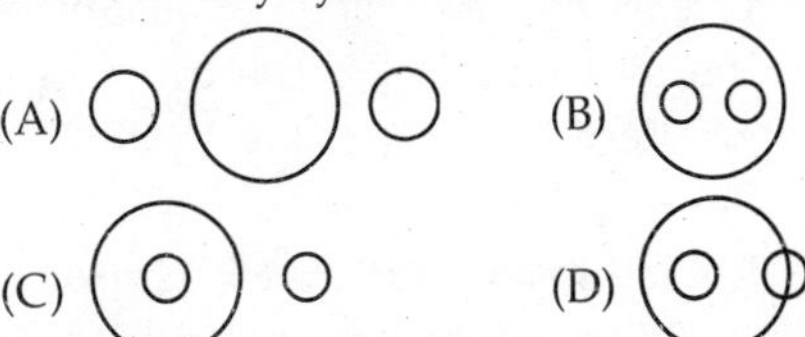

46. The statement, 'To be *non-violent is good*' is a
(A) Moral judgement
(B) Factual judgement
(C) Religious judgement
(D) Value judgement

47. **Assertion (A) :** Man is a rational being.
Reason (R) : Man is a social being.
(A) Both (A) and (R) are true and (R) is the correct explanation of (A)
(B) Both (A) and (R) are true but (R) is not the correct explanation of (A)
(C) (A) is true but (R) is false
(D) (A) is false but (R) is true

48. Value Judgements are :
(A) Factual Judgements
(B) Ordinary Judgements
(C) Normative Judgements
(D) Expression of public opinion

49. Deductive reasoning proceeds from
(A) general to particular

(B) particular to general
(C) one general conclusion to another general conclusion
(D) one particular conclusion to another particular conclusion

50. Among the following statements **two** are contradictory to each other. Select the correct code that represents them :

Statements:
(a) All poets are philosophers.
(b) Some poets are philosophers.
(c) Some poets are not philosophers.
(d) No philosopher is a poet.

Codes:
(1) (a) and (b) (2) (a) and (d)
(3) (a) and (c) (4) (b) and (c)

51. Logical reasoning is based on :
(A) Truth of involved propositions
(B) Valid relation among the involved propositions
(C) Employment of symbolic language
(D) Employment of ordinary language

52. Two propositions with the same subject and predicate terms but different in quality are :
(A) Contradictory (B) Contrary
(C) Subaltern (D) Identical

53. The premises of a valid deductive argument:
(A) Provide some evidence for its conclusion
(B) Provide no evidence for its conclusion
(C) Are irrelevant for its conclusion
(D) Provide conclusive evidence for its conclusion

54. Syllogistic reasoning is :
(A) Deductive (B) Inductive
(C) Experimental (D) Hypothetical

55. From the given four statements, select the two which cannot be true but yet both can be false. Choose the right pair :
(i) All men are mortal
(ii) Some men are mortal
(iii) No man is mortal
(iv) Some men are not mortal
(A) (i) and (ii) (B) (iii) and (iv)
(C) (i) and (iii) (D) (ii) and (iv)

56. A Syllogism must have :
(A) Three terms (B) Four terms
(C) Six terms (D) Five terms

57. Copula is that part of proposition which denotes the relationship between :
(A) Subject and predicate
(B) Known and unknown
(C) Major premise and minor premise
(D) Subject and object

58. "E" denotes :
(A) Universal Negative Proposition
(B) Particular Affirmative Proposition
(C) Universal Affirmative Proposition
(D) Particular Negative Proposition

59. The methods of trial & error search is/are
(A) Complete trial & error
(B) Directed trial & error
(C) Blind trial & error
(D) All of the above

60. The function of measurement includes :
(A) Prognosis (B) Diagnosis
(C) Prediction (D) All of the above

61. Logical arguments are based on
(A) Scientific reasoning
(B) Customary reasoning
(C) Mathematical reasoning
(D) Syllogistic reasoning

62. Choose the odd word
(A) Nun (B) Knight
(C) Monk (D) Priest

63. Which of the following conclusions is logically valid based on statement given below?

Statement: Most teachers are hard working.

Conclusions:
(I) Some teachers are hard working.
(II) Some teachers are not hard working.
(A) Only (I) is implied
(B) Only (II) is implied
(C) Both (I) and (II) are implied
(D) Neither (I) nor (II) is implied

64. Which of the following conclusions is logically valid based on statement given below?
Statement: Most of the Indian states existed before independence.

Conclusions:
(I) Some Indian States existed before independence.
(II) All Indian States did not exist before independence.
(A) only (I) is implied
(B) only (II) is implied
(C) Both (I) and (II) are implied
(D) Neither (I) nor (II) is implied

65. Direction for this question :
Given below are two statements (a) and (b) followed by two conclusions (i) and (ii). Considering the statements to be true, indicate which of the following conclusions logically follow from the given statements by selecting one of the four response alternatives given below the conclusion :

Statements:

(A) all businessmen are wealthy.
(B) all wealthy people are hard working.

Conclusions:

(i) All businessmen are hard working.
(ii) All hardly working people are not wealthy

(A) Only (i) follows
(B) Only (ii) follows
(C) Only (i) and (ii) follows
(D) Neither (i) nor (ii) follows

66. Which one of the following statements is completely non-sensical ?
(A) He was a bachelor, but he married recently.
(B) He is a bachelor, but he married recently.
(C) When he married, he was not a bachelor.
(D) When he was a bachelor, he was not married.

67. Which of the following statements are mutually contradictory ?
(i) All flowers are not fragrant.
(ii) Most flowers are not fragrant.
(iii) None of the flowers is fragrant.
(iv) Most flowers are fragrant.

Choose the correct answer from the code given below :

Code :

(A) (i) and (ii) (B) (i) and (iii)
(C) (ii) and (iii) (D) (ii) and (iv)

68. Which of the following statements say the same thing ?
(i) "I am a teacher" (said by Arvind)
(ii) "I am a teacher" (said by Binod)
(iii) "My son is a teacher" (said by Binod's father)
(iv) "My brother is a teacher" (said by Binod's sister)
(v) "My brother is a teacher" (said by Binod's only sister)
(vi) "My sole enemy is a teacher" (said by Binod's only enemy)

Choose the correct answer from the code given below :

Code :

(A) (i) and (ii) (B) (ii), (iii), (iv) and (v)
(C) (ii) and (vi) (D) (v) and (vi)

69. Which of the following are correct ways of arguing ?
(i) There can be no second husband without a second wife.
(ii) Anil is a friend of Bob, Bob is a friend of Raj, hence Anil is a friend of Raj.
(iii) A is equal to B, B is equal to C, hence A is equal to C.
(iv) If everyone is a liar, then we cannot prove it.

Choose the correct answer from the code given below :

Code :

(A) (iii) and (iv) (B) (i), (iii) and (iv)
(C) (ii), (iii) and (iv) (D) (i), (ii), (iii) and (iv)

70. Which of the following statement/s are ALWAYS FALSE ?
(i) The sun will not rise in the East some day.
(ii) A wooden table is not a table.
(iii) Delhi city will be drowned under water.
(iv) Cars run on water as fuel.

Choose the correct answer from the code given below :

(A) (i), (iii) and (iv) (B) Only (iii)
(C) (i), (ii) and (iii) (D) (ii) alone

71. **Directions.** Question contain two statements followed by four conclusions. Read all the conclusions careful and then decide which of the given conclusions logically follows from the above given two statement in question.

Mark answer:

(A) If only I follows
(B) If only I, II & III follows
(C) If only II & III follows
(D) If all follows

Statements

(i) Water is a liquid (ii) Ice is water

Conclusions

(I) Ice is liquid (II) Ice is not liquid
(III) No ice is liquid (IV) None of these

(A) (B) (C) (D)

72. **Directions.** In the following question, a statement is followed by two assumptions I and II. The you have to consider each statement and assumptions that follow and decide which of the assumption (s) is/are implicit in the statement

Mark answer:
(A) If only I is implicit
(B) If only II is implicit
(C) If both I and II are implicit
(D) If neither I nor II is implicit

Statements
Each nation must maintain an army.

Assumptions
(I) It makes people strong
(II) It is indispensable for the defence of the nation

(A) (B) (C) (D)

73. India has given birth to the Millennium Baby. It was a news release for the entire world. Which of the statements given below is justified ?
(A) Poverty and population are the main problems of India
(B) We are proud of the news
(C) India will progress if population is controlled
(D) Educating the masses on the population issue is the proper solution

74. Out of the following statements no two can be true at the same time, but both can be false. Identify the same:
a. Motivated students succeed in examinations
b. Intelligent students succeed in examinations
c. Irregular students fail in examinations
d. Some intelligent students are irregular

(A) a and c (B) b and c
(C) b and d (D) c and d

75. It is important that students use English language effectively. Therefore, they should be taught English from a very early stage.
(A) Only those who use English, weakens the above argument
(B) Many students who have studied English from a very early age are poor in English usage even at postgraduate stage.
(C) Schools vary in respect of English language teaching
(D) Only those who have studied English language well can use it effectively

76. **Statement:** All the windows are doors. No door is a wall.
Conclusions:
(i) Some windows are walls.
(ii) No wall is door.
(A) Only (i) conclusion follows
(B) Only (ii) conclusion follows
(C) Either (i) and (ii) follows
(D) Neither (i) nor (ii) follows

77. Study the argument and the inference drawn from that argument, given below carefully.
Argument : Anything that goes up definitely falls down. Helicopter goes up.
Inference : So the helicopter will definitely fall down
What in your opinion is the inference drawn from the argument ?
(A) Valid (B) Invalid
(C) Doubtful (D) Long drawn one

78. **Statements:**
I. All students are ambitious
II. All ambitious persons are hard working
Conclusions:
(i) All students are hard-working
(ii) All hardly working people are not ambitious Which of the following is correct ?
(A) Only (i) is correct
(B) Only (ii) is correct
(C) Both (i) and (ii) are correct
(D) Neither (i) nor (ii) is correct

79. **Statement:** Most students are intelligent
Conclusions:
(i) Some students are intelligent.
(ii) All students are not intelligent.
Which of the following is implied ?
(A) Only (i) is implied
(B) Only (ii) is implied
(C) Both (i) and (ii) are implied
(D) Neither (i) nor (ii) is implied

80. **Statement:** Most labourers are poor.
Conclusions:
(i) Some labourers are poor
(ii) All labourers are not poor
Which of the following is implied ?
(A) Only (i) is implied
(B) Only (ii) is implied
(C) Both (i) and (ii) are implied
(D) Neither (i) nor (ii) is implied

81. Evaluate the following statements in terms of whether each is a fact, opinion, prejudice or advice.
a. Women are not suitable for police Service.

b. In democracy, no party should be in power for too long.
c. Have proper rest, even during the examination time.
d. Obesity is a risk factor for coronary heart disease

Which of the following is the correct alternative?

	Opinion	Prejudice	Fact	Advice
(A)	b	c	d	a
(B)	b	a	d	c
(C)	c	a	d	b
(D)	b	d	c	a

82. Given below are two Statements – I and II, followed by two Conclusions – A and B. Considering the statements to be true, indicate which of the following conclusions logically follow from the given statements by selecting one of the four response alternatives given below.

Statements:

I. Some teachers are women

II. No teacher is absent

Conclusions:

P. There are no male teachers

Q. All women teachers are present

(A) Only P is true
(B) Only Q is true
(C) Both P and Q are true
(D) Neither P nor Q is true

1. Logical Diagram Test

1. Which of the following figures correctly represents the relation between languages, English and Hindi ?

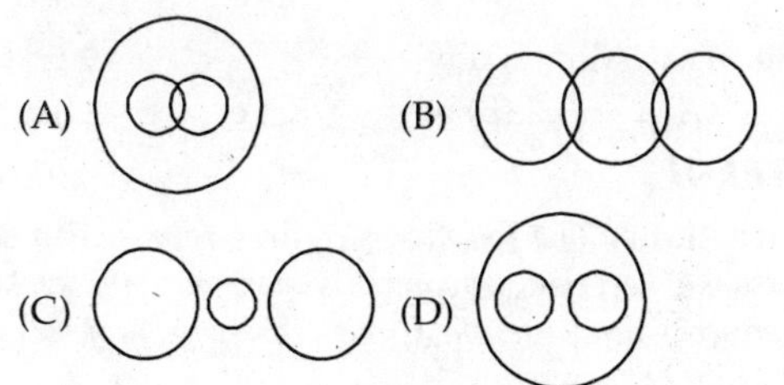

2. Which of the following diagrams indicates the best relation between Judges, Thieves and Criminals ?

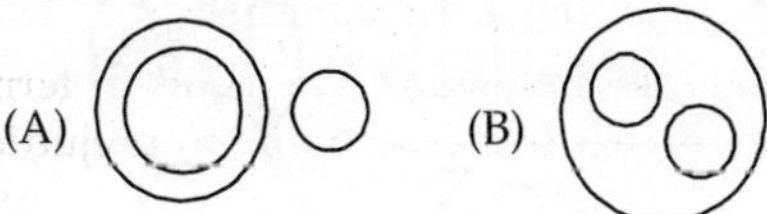

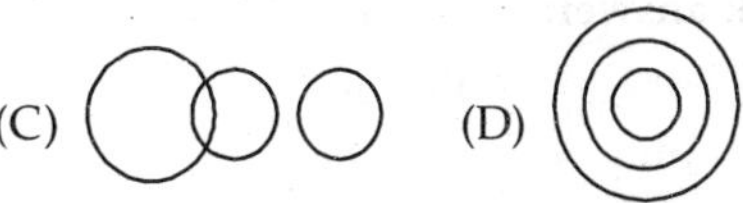

3. Which one of the following Venn diagrams correctly illustrates the relationship among the classes:

Carrot, Food, Vegetables

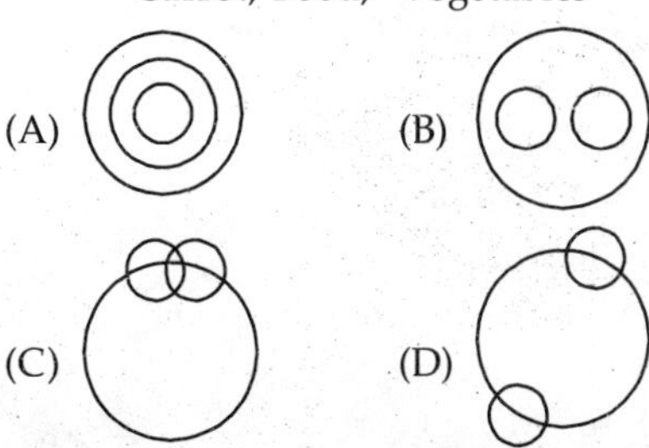

Directions (4-8). *Each question below contains three groups of things. You are to choose from the following four numbered diagrams, the diagram that depicts the correct relationship among the three groups of things in each question.*

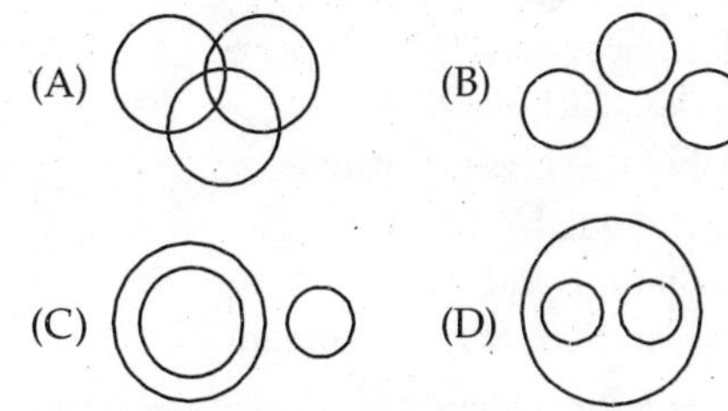

4. Vegetable, Fruit, Brinjal
5. Door, Window, House
6. Honest, Intelligent, Poor
7. Car, Train, Automobile
8. Zinc, Copper, Iron

Directions (9-15). *Out of the four alternatives in each of the following questions, three alternatives are such that the three words in each are related among themselves in one of the five ways represented by (a), (b), (c), (d) and (e) below. And one of the alternatives represents a relationship which is not represented by any of the figures given below. Identify that alternative.*

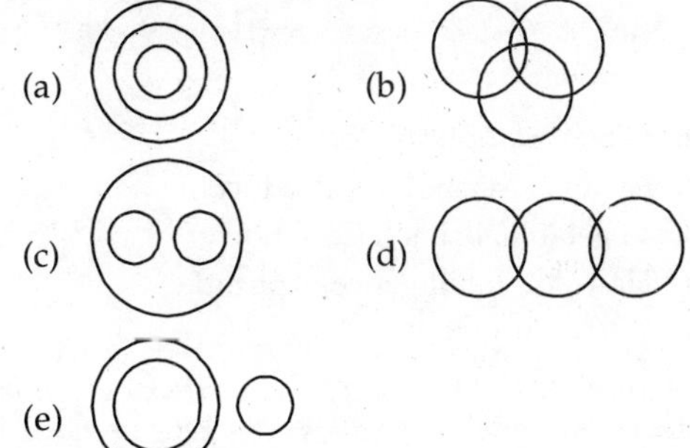

9. (A) Army, General, Colonel
(B) Boy, Student, Player
(C) Painter, Scholar, Table
(D) Man, Typist, Peon.

10. (A) Hen, Dog, Cat
(B) Body, Ear, Mouth
(C) Bed, Ward, Nurse
(D) Tiger, Animal, Carnivorous

11. (A) Mineral, Iron, Copper
(B) Dean, Painter, Singer
(C) Seed, Leaf, Root
(D) Piston, Engine, Wheel

12. (A) Director, Engineer, Musician
(B) Apple, Orange, Mango
(C) Fruit, Mango, Grass
(D) Oxygen, Air, Water

13. (A) Bed, Ward, Hospital
(B) Boy, Girl, Player
(C) Copper, Zinc, Iron
(D) Book, Page, Paragraph

14. (A) Atmosphere, Air, Oxygen
(B) Boy, Girl, Student
(C) Man, Worker, Garden
(D) Animal, Dog, Cat

15. (A) Body, Hand, Finger
(B) Mammal, Nurse, Woman
(C) Cereal, Wheat, Rice
(D) Males, Cousins, Nephews

Directions (16-20). *Each of the question below contains three elements. These elements may or may not have some inter-linkage. Each group of the elements may fit into one of the diagrams at (A), (B), (C) and (D). You have to indicate groups of elements in each of the questions correctly fit into which of the diagrams?*

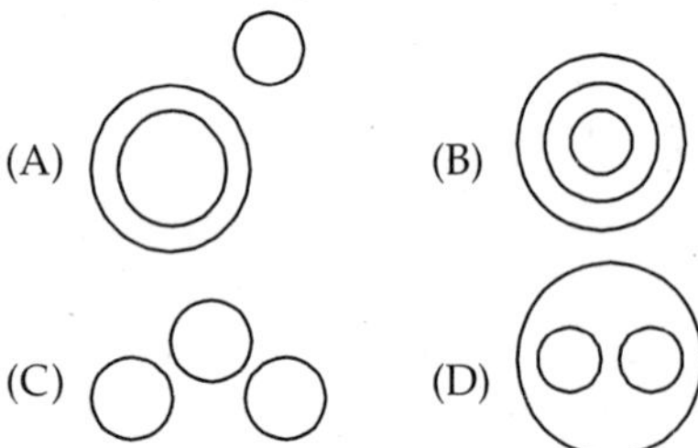

16. Pencil, Stationery, Jeep.
17. Factory, Machinery, Product.
18. Vegetable, Brinjal, Cauliflower
19. Honesty, Intelligence, Aptitude
20. Truck, Ship, Rail

Directions (21-30). *Each of the questions given below contains three groups of things. You have to choose from the following five numbered diagrams, the diagram that depicts the correct relationship among the three groups of things in each question.*

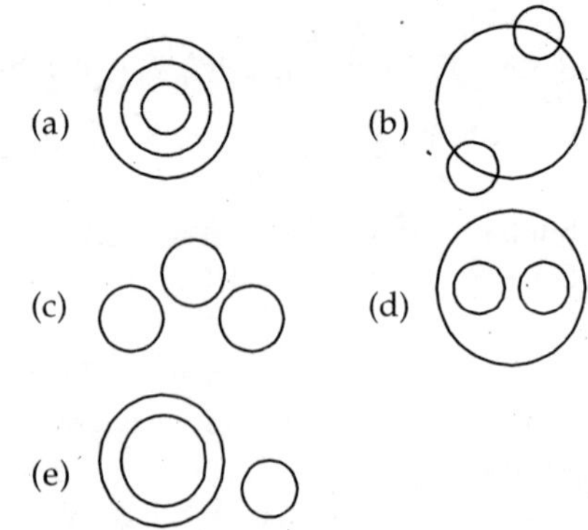

21. Pop, Songs, Classical
(A) c (B) e (C) d (D) b

22. Maize, Sugarcane, crops
(A) a (B) b (C) c (D) d

23. Birds, Owls, elephants
(A) a (B) b (C) c (D) e

24. Apples, Mangoes, Oranges
(A) a (B) b (C) c (D) d

25. Asia, delhi, India
(A) a (B) b (C) c (D) d

26. Lawyers, Women, doctors
(A) a (B) b (C) c (D) d

27. Brinjal, Glass, Spoon
(A) a (B) b (C) c (D) d

28. Pen, Stationery, Powder
(A) a (B) b (C) c (D) e

29. Vehicle, car, Jeep
(A) a (B) b (C) c (D) d

30. Year, Month, day
(A) a (B) b (C) c (D) d

TYPE-II

Directions. *The following figures represent a set of persons. The Triangle represents sportsmen, the Rectangle represents Students, the Circle represents Professors and the Ellipse represents Artists.*

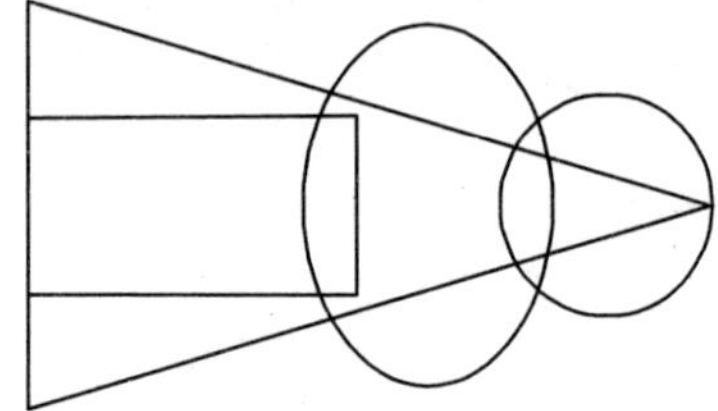

31. Looking at the figure we can conclude that
(A) All Sports Students are Professors
(B) All Sportsmen are Professors
(C) All Professor Artists are Sportsmen
(D) Some Professor Artists are Sportsmen.

32. According to the Figure we can say that
(A) Artists are not Professors
(B) Students are not Professors
(C) Some Students are Artists
(D) Some Artists are Sportsmen.

33. On the basis of this figure it can be concluded that
(A) Some of the Sportsmen Artists are Professors
(B) None of the Sportsmen Artists is a Student
(C) None of the Sportsmen Artists is a Professor
(D) None of the above statements is correct.

34. According to the given figure we can say that
(A) Some of the Professors are Artists too.
(B) Some of the Sportsmen are Professors.
(C) Some of the Sportsmen are not Professors.
(D) Some of the Professor Artists are Students too.

TYPE-III

35. In the given diagram circle represents strong men, square represents tall men, triangle represents army officers. Which region represents army officers who are tall but not strong ?

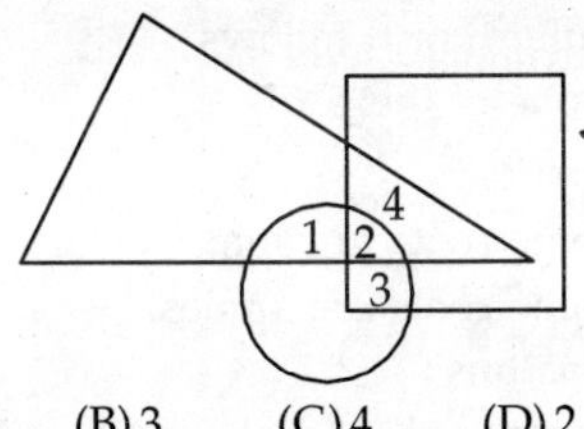

(A) 1 (B) 3 (C) 4 (D) 2

36. Find the urban, corrupt politicians in the following diagram.

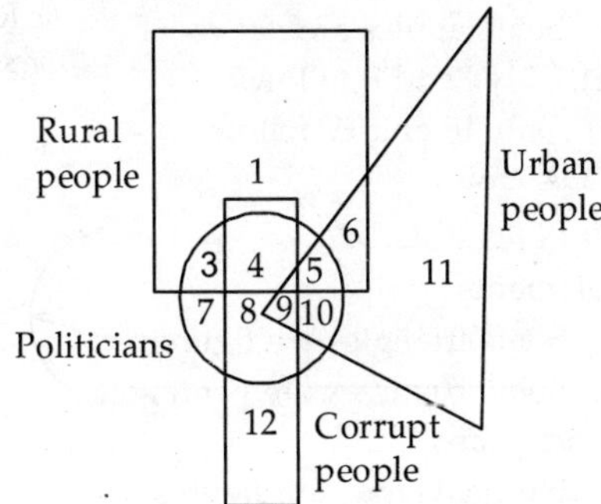

(A) 4 (B) 10
(C) 9 (D) 5

37. In the following diagram, R represents businessmen, S represents rich men, T represents honest men. Which number will represent honest rich men ?
(A) 3 (B) 2
(C) 5 (D) 4

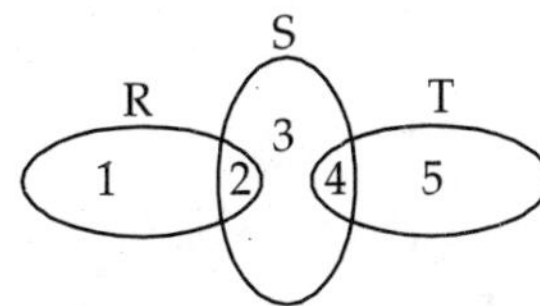

2. Syllogism Test

TYPE - I

Directions. *Questions 1-15 contain two statements followed by four conclusions. Read all the conclusions carefully and then decide which of the given conclusions logically follows from the above given two statements in each question.*

1. Statements
(i) All microprocessors are computers.
(ii) All computers are modems.

Conclusions :
I. All micro-processors are modems.
II. All modems are micro-processors.
III. All modems are computers.
IV. Some computers are microprocessors.
(a) Only I follows
(B) Only I and IV follow
(C) Only I and II follow
(D) None of these.

2. Statements :
(i) Some actors are doctors.
(ii) All architects are doctors.

Conclusions :
I. All actors are doctors.
II. Some architects are doctors.
III. All doctors are actors.
IV. Some actors are architects.
(A) Only II follows
(B) Only II and IV follow
(C) Only III and IV follow
(D) None of these.

3. Statements :
(i) All the express trains stop here.
(ii) Rajdhani does not stop here.

Conclusions :

I. Rajdhani is a passenger train.
II. Rajdhani is a super fast train.
III. Rajdhani is not an express train.
IV. Rajdhani is a special train.
(A) Only II follows
(B) Only I and III follow
(C) Only II and IV follow
(D) None of these.

4. **Statements :**
(i) All worms are mosquitoes.
(ii) All mosquitoes are birds.
Conclusions :
I. All mosquitoes are worms.
II. All worms are birds.
III. All birds are worms.
IV. Some mosquitoes are birds.
(A) Only I and II follow
(B) Only I follows
(C) Only II and IV follow
(D) None of these.

5. **Statements :**
(i) All lawyers are uncles.
(ii) All girls are lawyers.
Conclusions :
I. All girls are uncles.
II. All uncles are girls.
III. Some girls are not uncles.
IV. Some uncles are lawyers.
(A) Only I, II and IV follow
(B) Only I and IV follow
(C) Only II and IV follow
(D) None of these.

6. **Statements :**
(i) All chairs are stars.
(ii) Some chairs are round.
Conclusions :
I. Some rounds are stars.
II. Some stars are round.
III. No star is round.
IV. Some stars are not round.
(A) Only I and II follow
(B) Only III and IV follow
(C) Either II or III follows
(D) None of these.

7. **Statements :**
(i) The cabinet passed the bill.
(ii) He is a member of the cabinet.
Conclusions :
I. He passed the bill.
II. The bill was passed by him.
III. A member of the cabinet can pass the bill.
IV. No minister could pass the bill.
(A) Only I follows (B) Only II follows
(C) Only III follows (D) None of these

8. **Statements :**
(i) All sauces are pickles.
(ii) Some sauces are ketchup.
Conclusions :
I. All ketchup are sauces.
II. All pickles are ketchup.
III. All sauces are ketchup.
IV. Some pickles are ketchup.
(A) Only I and II follow
(B) Only II and III follow
(C) Only I and III follow
(D) None of these.

9. **Statements :**
(i) Water is a liquid.
(ii) Ice is water.
Conclusions :
I. Ice is liquid.
II. Ice is not liquid.
III. No ice is liquid.
IV. Some ice is not liquid.
(A) Only I follows
(B) Only II follows
(C) Either I or II follows
(D) None of these.

10. **Statements :**
(i) Some roots are ships.
(ii) Some roots are apples.
Conclusions :
I. Some apples are ships.
II. Some ships are apples.
III. No root is a ship.
IV. Some apples are not roots.
(A) Only I and II follows
(B) Only III and IV follow
(C) All follow
(D) None of these.

11. **Statements :**
(i) Some triangles are figures.
(ii) Some triangles are pentagons.
Conclusions :
I. No pentagons are figures.

II. Some figures are pentagons.
III. No triangle is a figure.
IV. No triangle is pentagon.
(A) Only III and IV follow
(B) Only I and II follow
(C) Either I or II follows
(D) None of these.

12. Statements :
(i) If it is cloudy, lion will roar.
(ii) Lions don't roar.
Conclusions :
I. It is not cloudy.
II. It is cloudy.
III. Lions roar only in cloudy night.
IV. Lion will roar only in cloudy day.
(A) Either I or II follows
(B) Only I follows
(C) Only II follows
(D) None of these.

13. Statements :
(i) India includes Bengal.
(ii) Bengal does not include UP.
Conclusions :
I. India does not include UP.
II. UP is also a part of India.
III. Bengal includes UP.
IV. UP is not a part of India.
(A) Either II or IV follows
(B) Only I follows
(C) Only II follows
(D) None of these.

14. Statements :
(i) Gold is ductile.
(ii) This substance is not ductile.
Conclusions :
I. This substance is not gold.
II. Gold is not ductile.
III. Ductiles are not gold.
IV. No substance is ductile.
(A) Only IV follows
(B) Only I follows
(C) Only I and IV follow
(D) None of these.

15. Statements :
(i) All tigers have four legs.
(ii) No cat is tiger.
Conclusions :
I. No cat has four legs.
II. No four leggers are cats.
III. Tigers are cats.
IV. Cats have four legs.
(A) Only I and II follow
(B) Only III follows
(C) Only IV follows
(D) None of these.

TYPE - II

Directions. *In the following questions, two statements are followed by two conclusions. Read the conclusions carefully and then decide which of the given conclusions logically follows from the above given two statements in each question. Mark (A) if only conclusion (I) follows, (B) if only conclusion (II) follows, (C) if neither (I) nor (II) follows and (D) if both (I) and (II) follow.*

16. Statements :
(i) Some crows are dogs.
(ii) All dogs are faithful.
Conclusions :
(I) All faithful animals are dogs.
(II) Some crows are faithful.

17. Statements :
(i) Some poets are fools.
(ii) All fools are goats.
Conclusions :
(I) Some poets are goats.
(II) Some fools are poets.

18. Statements :
(i) All cats are dogs.
(ii) Some dogs are black.
Conclusions :
I. Some cats are black.
II. Black dogs are not cats.

19. Statements :
(i) All books are chairs.
(ii) All chairs are pens.
Conclusions :
I. All books are pens.
II. Some pens are books.

20. Statements :
(i) All tables are ants.
(ii) Some ants are chairs.
Conclusions :
I. Some tables are chairs.
II. Some chairs are tables.

21. Statements :
(i) Some trees are horses.
(ii) Biscuit is a tree.

Conclusions :

I. Biscuit is not a horse.

II. Some horses are trees.

22. Statements :

(i) Some essayists are poets.

(ii) All poets are dramatists.

Conclusions :

I. Some poets are essayists.

II. Some essayists are dramatists.

23. Statements :

(i) All poets are authors.

(ii) All singers are authors.

Conclusions :

I. All singers are poets.

II. Some authors are not singers.

24. Statements :

(i) All tables are horses.

(ii) All horses are rivers.

Conclusions :

I. All tables are rivers.

II. Some rivers are tables.

25. Statements :

(i) All pencils are bricks.

(ii) All bricks are bottles.

Conclusions :

I. Some bottles are pencils.

II. Some bottles are bricks.

TYPE - III

Directions. *In each of the following questions, a statement is followed by two conclusions numbered I and II. The candidates have to assume everything in the statement to be true and consider both the conclusions together, then decide which of the two given conclusions logically follow beyond a reasonable doubt from the information given in the statement.*

Give answer

(A) if only conclusion I follows

(B) if only conclusion II follows

(C) if neither I nor II follows

(D) if both I and II follow

26. Statement :

The oceans are a store house of practically every mineral, including uranium.

But like most other minerals it is found in extremely low concentrations – about three grams for 1,000 tons of water.

Conclusions :

I. Sea water contains gold.

II. The oceans harbour radiation hazards.

27. Statement :

Devil is an enemy because he deceives the people.

Conclusions :

I. Those who deceive the people are enemies.

II. All those who deceive the men are devils.

28. Statement :

Some students are disturbing.

Conclusions :

I. Some who are disturbing are students.

II. Some students are not disturbing.

29. Statement :

This man can't succeed because he is not truthful.

Conclusions :

I. Those who can get success are truthful.

II. All truthful persons succeed.

30. Statement :

All students are not genius.

Conclusions :

I. Many students are not genius.

II. All genius are students.

31. Statement :

In a certain community only widows do not apply Kumkum to their foreheads. Ratna, who belongs to that community applies Kumkum to her forehead.

Conclusions :

I. Ratna is an unmarried girl.

II. Ratna is a married woman.

32. Statement :

He is a historian, so he cannot write novels.

Conclusions :

I. No historian can write novels.

II. Some historians can write novels.

33. Statement :

From all available cultural records, it is evident that even in ancient India, both the masters and disciples valued not the quantity but the quality of knowledge.

Conclusions :

I. Giving importance to quantity of knowledge is meaningless.

II. There was an identity of educational values between teachers and students in ancient India.

34. Statement :

He does not go to the mosque so he is not a true Muslim.

Conclusions :

I. Only true Muslims go to the mosque.

II. All true Muslims must go to the mosque.

35. Statement :

About 50 per cent of animal by-products hair, skin, horn etc. is edible protein. Indian chemists have developed a method of isolating 45 per-cent of this protein. They used an enzyme developed in Japan to break down Soya protein.

Conclusions :

I. Indians have not been able to develop enzymes.

II. If an economically feasible process is developed, there would be plenty of edible protein available.

TYPE - IV

Directions. *In the question given below there are two statements followed by one conclusion. Give answer (A) if the conclusion is definitely supported by statements; (B) if the conclusion is not at all related with the statements; (C) if the conclusion is supported by the statements to some extent and (D) if the conclusion is contrary to the statements.*

36. Statements :

I. Cats drink milk.

II. Cats are intelligent.

Conclusion :

Animals who drink milk, are intelligent.

Directions (37-38). *In the following questions, there are two statements (i) and (ii) followed by a conclusion. If only statement (i) supports the conclusion, mark (A), if only statement (ii) supports the conclusion, then mark (B), if both the statements support the conclusion then marks (C) and if none of the two statements supports the conclusion, then mark (D).*

37. Statements :

(i) Some vegetables are fruits.

(ii) Fruits are good for health.

Conclusion :

Some vegetables are good for health.

38. Statements :

(i) All rocks are mountains.

(ii) All rocks are trees.

Conclusion : Some mountains are trees.

Directions (39-40). *In the questions given below, some situations have been described in two statements and after it a conclusion is given. On the basis of the statements, the candidates have to decide whether the conclusion is correct or false. Mark answer (A) if the conclusion is correct; (B) if the conclusion is more than expected; (C) if it is false; (D) if it is not related to statements.*

39. Statements :

(i) Regions of warm and damp climate are generally effected by malaria.

(ii) Climate of Trombay is warm and damp.

Conclusion :

Two thousand people die every year in Trombay.

40. Statements :

(i) Tails of peacocks are shining long.

(ii) Peacocks dance gloriously.

Conclusion :

The tail of Crane should be shining long.

3. Statement and Assumption Test

Directions (1-15). *In the following questions, a statement is followed by two assumptions I and II. The candidate has to consider each statement and assumptions that follow and decide which of the assumption(s) is/ are implicit in the statement.*

Marked answer

(A) if only I is implicit

(B) if only II is implicit

(C) if both I and II are implicit

(D) if neither I nor II is implicit

1. **Statement :** A few people demanded one-man-one-post in the case of the Minister for strengthening the party and for efficient administration.

Assumptions :

I. No human being can be efficient in two spheres.

II. A person attending to only administration or party work will be able to do much.

2. **Statement :** Happiness is to be shared. Unhappy people suffer.

Assumptions :

I. Unhappy nation shares sufferings.

II. Happy people do not suffer.

3. **Statement :** Each nation must maintain an army.

Assumptions :

I. It makes nation strong.

II. It is indispensable for the defence of the nation.

4. **Statement :** Spicy food damages the liver. The patient is advised to take a liver-tonic.

Assumptions :

I. The patient takes spicy food.

II. A healthy liver is necessary to digest fat.

5. **Statement :** The Railway authorities have decided to increase the freight charges by 10 per cent in view of the possibility of incurring losses in the current financial year.
   Assumptions :
   I. The volume of freight during the remaining period may remain same.
   II. The amount so obtained may set off a part or total of the estimated deficit.

6. **Statement :** India's economy is depending mainly on forests.
   Assumptions :
   I. Trees should be preserved to improve Indian economy.
   II. India wants only maintenance of forests to improve economic conditions.

7. **Statement :** USA re-emerged as India's largest import source in the early nineties.
   Assumptions :
   I. With swift political developments in the soviet union, India began to rely on USA.
   II. The USA was the only country which wanted to meet the requirements of India.

8. **Statement :** Do not copy our software without our permission – A notice.
   Assumptions :
   I. It is possible to copy the software.
   II. Such warning will have same effect.

9. **Statement :** Let the government increase the present rate of taxation to recover the deficit in the budget.
   Assumptions :
   I. Present rate of taxes is very low.
   II. If government wants to get away with the budgetary deficit, it should increase tax rate.

10. **Statement :** Successful man has the ability to judge himself correctly.
    Assumptions :
    I. Successful man cannot make a wrong judgement.
    II. To judge others is of no use for successful man.

11. **Statement :** The new education policy envisages major modification in the educational system.
    Assumptions :
    I. The present education system needs improvement.
    II. The present education system is inconsistent with the national needs.

12. **Statement :** Ghosts haunt deserted places only.
    Assumptions :
    I. They do not want the interference of human being.
    II. Every deserted residence is haunted.

13. **Statement :** Of all the newspapers published in India, 'The Hindu' has the largest number of readers.
    Assumptions :
    I. The volume of readership of all newspapers in India is known.
    II. No newspaper in India other than 'The Hindu' has a large readership.

14. **Statement :** An Indian beautician is opening a beauty parlour in New York.
    Assumptions :
    I. New York lacks beauty parlours.
    II. There are better business prospects in New York.

15. **Statement :** Consult me before taking any decision on investment.
    Assumptions :
    I. You may take a wrong decision if you don't consult me.
    II. It is important to take right decision on investment.

4. Statement and Argument Test

Directions (1-30). *In each of the following questions, a statement is given followed by two arguments.*

Marked answer
(A) if only I is strong
(B) if only II is strong
(C) if both are strong
(D) if neither I nor II is strong.

1. **Statement :** Should education be given by the government to the people free of charge ?
   Arg. I: Yes, it will help in universalizaiton of education in the country.
   Arg. II: No, there will be budgetary pressure creating some new problems.

2. **Statement :** Should students study in early hours of morning ?
   Arg. I: Yes, mind is fresh and alert at that time
   Arg. II: No, early risers feel sleepy throughout the day.

3. **Statement :** Should sex education be given in schools ?
   Arg. I: Yes, it is given in western countries.

Arg. II: No, it is naturally gained when children grow into adolescence.

(A) (B) (C) (D)

4. **Statement :** Should India support economic liberalization ?

Arg. I: Yes, it will boost up industrial development leading to more supply of the commodities and low price.

Arg. II: No, it is against the Nehru's dream of democratic socialism.

5. **Statement :** Should the private companies be allowed to operate passenger train services in India ?

Arg. I: Yes. This will improve the quality of service in Indian Railways and it will be faced with severe competition.

Arg. II: No. The private companies may not agree to operate in the non-profitable sectors.

6. **Statement :** Should school education be made free in India ?

Arg. I: Yes. This is the only way to improve the level of literacy.

Arg. II: No. It will add to the already heavy burden on the exchequer.

7. **Statement :** Should there be a complete ban on manufacture of fire-crackers in India ?

Arg. I: No. This will render thousands of workers jobless.

Arg. II: Yes. The fire-cracker manufacturers use child labour to a large extent.

8. **Statement :** Should correspondence courses at the university level be discontinued in India?

Arg. I: Yes. Only interaction between teachers and students at the college helps total development of personality.

Arg. II: No. The demand for discontinuance comes only from the elite who have no knowledge of what is meant by poverty.

9. **Statement :** Should India allow the multinationals to explore the resources available under sea in its vast economic zone ?

Arg. I: Yes. India does not have enough technical and financial resources to conduct such explorations.

Arg. II: No. This will endanger the sovereign status of the country.

10. **Statement :** Should articles of only deserving authors be allowed to be published ?

Arg. I: Yes, it will save a lot of paper which falls short of supply.

Arg. II: No, it is not possible to draw a demarcation between the deserving and the undeserving authors.

11. **Statement :** Has the medical science really lengthened the span of life ?

Arg. I: Yes, the new drugs have been able to combat the diseases and increase the span of life.

Arg. II: No, the eternal truth that every person's days are numbered cannot be denied.

12. **Statement :** Should mass media be fully controlled by the government ?

Arg. I: Yes, the contradictory news only confuses the people.

Arg. II: No, its credibility will be doubtful if it confuses people.

13. **Statement :** Should jobs be linked with academic degrees and diplomas?

Arg. I: No. A very large number of persons with meagre academic qualifications will apply.

Arg. II: No. Importance of higher education will be diminished.

14. **Statement :** Should there be women chief ministers in states ?

Arg. I: Yes, only then the plight of women will be removed and their conditions will improve.

Arg. II: No, a woman is not capable of ruling a state.

15. **Statement :** Computer based technology is very fruitful for industrial development in India.

Arg. I: Yes, accuracy, fast production and fineness are possible through computer technology.

Arg. II: No, it will increase unemployment in the country.

16. **Statement :** Should India have nuclear weapons ?

Arg. I: Yes, it is necessary to protect the sovereignty and integrity of the country.

Arg. II: No, this will disturb the balance of power in the region.

17. **Statement :** Should colleges be given the status of a university in India?

Arg. I: Yes. Colleges are in a better position to assess the students' performance and therefore the degrees will be more valid.

Arg. II: No. It is utopian to think that there will not be nepotism and corruption in awarding degrees by colleges.

18. **Statement :** Should higher education be restricted to the most deserving students.
    Arg. I: Yes, only deserving people are entitled to this luxury.
    Arg. II: No, it is against the principles of equality of educational opportunity.

19. **Statement :** Should guides published by private agencies be banned ?
    Arg. I: Yes, only then students will start reading text books.
    Arg. II: No, they are of immense help for weak students at the eleventh hour.

20. **Statement :** Should higher education be completely stopped for sometime?
    Arg. I: No. It will hamper the country's future progress.
    Arg. II: Yes. It will reduce the educated unemployment.

21. **Statement :** Should workers be allowed to participate in the management of factories in India ?
    Arg. I: Yes, it is the present management theory.
    Arg. II: No, many workers are illiterate and their contribution will not be of value.

22. **Statement :** Should the political parties be banned ?
    Arg. I: Yes, it is necessary to teach a lesson to the politicians.
    Arg. II: No, it will lead to an end of democracy.

23. **Statement :** Should the agriculture in India be mechanized?
    Arg. I: Yes, it would lead to higher production.
    Arg. II: No, many villagers would be left unemployed.

24. **Statement :** Should smoking be prohibited ?
    Arg. I: Yes, it damages the liver and the lung.
    Arg. II: No, it will drive millions of tobacco workers out.

25. **Statement :** Should the educated people be given necessary work in villages ?
    Arg. I: Yes, they can revolutionize agriculture and revamp the rural atmosphere.
    Arg. II: No, their education might be wasted there in villages.

26. **Statement :** Is the youngest child happy when a new baby takes birth in the family ?
    Arg. I: Yes, it is exciting for him to have a new member in the family.
    Arg. II: No, he becomes jealous of the new born.

27. **Statement :** Should the duration of the parliamentary government be increased ?
    Arg. I: Yes, it will reduce the expenses on elections and also reduce inflation.
    Arg. II: No, it will take longer time to change a ruling party even if it is corrupt.

28. **Statement :** Do good quality products need wide publicity ?
    Arg. I: Yes, in the present day world of competition, customers cannot know about a new product without proper publicity.
    Arg. II: No, good quality products automatically attract customers and thus speak for themselves.

29. **Statement :** Should private sector be permitted to enter into the public utility services ?
    Arg. I: Yes, they are doing well in advanced western countries.
    Arg. II: No, it is risky to put these services, in private hands.

30. **Statement :** Should religion be banned ?
    Arg. I: Yes, it develops fanaticism among people.
    Arg. II: No, religion binds people together.

5. Miscellaneous Test

Directions (1-9). *In each of the following questions, two statements are given. Based on these statements an inference has been drawn. If the inference drawn is true, the answer is (A); if the inference is false, the answer is (B). If the inference is probably true or probably false the answer is (C) and if the inference is irrelevant the answer is (D).*

1. **Statements :**
   (i) All wives are women.
   (ii) She is a woman.
   Inference :
   She is a wife

2. **Statements :**
   (i) Birds generally fly in air.
   (ii) Fish swim in water.
   Inference :
   Elephants walk on ground.

3. **Statements :**
   (i) Either he is happy or he is sad.
   (ii) He is happy.
   Inference :
   He was sad yesterday.
4. **Statements :**
   (i) All workers wear caps.
   (ii) All the caps are red.
   Inference :
   All the workers wear red cap.
5. **Statements :**
   (i) Metals are generally malleable or ductile.
   (ii) X is neither malleable nor ductile.
   Inference :
   X is not a metal.
6. **Statements :**
   (i) This is the bus of route number 10.
   (ii) Buses of route number 10, generally go to stadium.
   Inference :
   This bus goes to stadium.
7. **Statements :**
   (i) L is the brother of K.
   (ii) K is the friend of M.
   Inference :
   K is the enemy of M.
8. **Statements :**
   (i) P is behind M and N.
   (ii) Q is behind P.
   Inference :
   Q is behind M.
9. **Statements :**
   (i) To rise early in the morning is useful for health.
   (ii) Manish rises early in the morning.
   Inference :
   Manish should be healthy.

Directions (10-19). *In each of the following questions, two statements are given followed by an inference. Mark (A) if the inference is definitely true, mark (B) if the inference is definitely false, mark (C) if the inference is probably false or true and mark (D) if inference cannot be drawn.*

10. **Statements :**
    (I) My son is not old enough to vote.
    (II) My son has handsome personality.
    Inference :
    My son is a boy under 18 years of age.
11. **Statements :**
    (I) Happy is one who is contended.
    (II) Religious people are contended.
    Inference :
    Religious people are happy.
12. **Statements :**
    (I) Some intelligent people are happy.
    (II) Some intelligent people are rich.
    Inference :
    Some who are rich are happy.
13. **Statements :**
    (I) Birds fly in the sky.
    (II) Nightingale flies in the sky.
    Inference :
    Nightingale is a bird.
14. **Statements :**
    (I) Glass is brittle.
    (II) This substance is not brittle.
    Inference :
    This substance is not glass.
15. **Statements :**
    (I) As we go higher, we feel cold.
    (II) As we go higher, there is a decrease in atmospheric pressure.
    Inference :
    We feel cold on the decrease of atmospheric pressure.
16. **Statements :**
    (I) We know a professor of a university.
    (II) He has beard.
    Inference :
    All the professors of the university have beard.
17. **Statements :**
    (I) Mammals cause their young ones to drink milk.
    (II) Rabbits cause their young ones to drink milk.
    Inference : Rabbit is a mammal.
18. **Statements :**
    (I) Mice eat cheese.
    (II) Cheese is used in omelette.
    Inference : Mice can eat omelette.
19. **Statements :**
    (I) All successful students believe in labour.
    (II) Labour cannot go in vain in workful life.
    Inference : After death, we remember the quality of labour.

Directions (20-25). *There are two statements P and Q each followed by an inference. Now determine which of the statements supports its inference. Mark (A) if only statement P is true, mark (B) if only statement Q is true, mark (C) if both P and Q are true and mark (D) if neither of them is true in accordance with logic.*

20. (P) Water boils at 100°C. This liquid boils at 100°C. Therefore, this liquid is water.

(Q) Every bottle with a blue label contains fruit juice. Fruit juice is safe to drink. Therefore, it is harmless to drink from every bottle with blue label.

Inference :

Blue label bottles are harmless. Therefore, one who drinks from it, is a good man.

21. (P) Some birds are jackals. No fox is bird. Therefore no fox is jackal.

(Q) All birds are not jackals.

Inference :

Some crows are monkeys. Therefore, some monkeys are not jackals.

22. (P) Some mangoes are apples. All guavas are mangoes. Therefore, all apples are guavas.

(Q) Some mangoes are apples.

Inference :

All apples are grapes. Therefore, some mangoes are grapes.

23. (P) No policeman likes beauty. He is a policeman. Therefore, he does not like beauty.

(Q) Some musicians are not rich.

Inference :

All musicians are polite. Therefore, all polite persons are not rich.

24. (P) Either he is happy or rich. He is rich. Therefore, he is not happy.

(Q) Those who are rich commit suicide.

Inference :

He is not rich. Therefore, he will not commit suicide.

25. (P) All musicians are rich. No rich person is polite. Therefore musicians are not polite.

(Q) Only a Newton can solve this problem.

Inference :

He is Newton. Therefore, he can solve this problem.

26. A deductive argument cannot be valid

(A) Is its premise/premises is/are true and its conclusion is true.

(B) If its premise/premises is/are true and its conclusion is false.

(C) Is its premise/premises is/are false and its conclusion is false.

(D) Is its premise/premises is/are false and its conclusion is true.

27. An analogical argument is strengthened by

(A) Making the claim bolder while its premises remain unchanged.

(B) Reducing the claim made on the basis of the premises affirmed.

(C) Remaining the claim unchanged while the evidence in its support is found to exhibit greater frailty.

(D) None of the above.

28. If two proposition cannot both be false but may both be true, what is the relation between the two propositions?

(A) Contrary (B) Sub-contrary

(C) Sub-alternation (D) Contradictory

29. What is the equivalent of he statement 'all atheists are pessimists'?

(A) All non-pessimists are non-atheists.

(B) All non-atheists are non-pessimists.

(C) All pessimists are atheists.

(D) None of the above.

30. A definition put forward to resolve a dispute by influencing attitudes or stirring emotions is called

(A) Lexical (B) Persuasive

(C) Stipulative (D) Precisions

31. Which of the codes given below contains only the correct statements?

Statements:

(i) Venn diagram is a clear method of notation.

(ii) Venn diagram is the most direct method of testing the validity of categorical syllogisms.

(iii) In Venn diagram method the premises and the conclusion of a categorical syllogism is diagrammed.

(iv) In Venn diagram method the three overlapping circles are drawn for testing a categorical syllogism.

Code:
(A) (i), (ii), and (iii)
(B) (i), (ii), and (iv)
(C) (ii), (iii), and (iv)
(D) (i), (iii), and (iv)

32. Inductive reasoning presupposes
(A) Unity in human nature.
(B) Integrity in human nature.
(C) Uniformity in human nature.
(D) Harmony in human nature.

33. If the statement 'some men are honest' is false, which among the following statements will be true. Choose the correct code given below:
(i) All men are honest
(ii) No men are honest
(iii) Some men are not honest
(iv) All men are dishonest
(A) (i), (ii) and (iii) (B) (ii), (iii), and (iv)
(C) (i), (iii), and (iv) (D) (ii), (i), and (iv)

34. Consider Assertion–I and Assertion-II and select the right code given below:

Assertion–I: Even bank-lockers are not safe. Thieves can break them and take away your wealth. But thieves cannot go to heaven. So you should keep your wealth in heaven.

Assertion–II: The difference of skin-color of beings is because of the distance from the sun and not because of some permanent traits. Skin-colour is the result of body's reaction to the sun and its rays.

Codes:
(A) Both the assertion-I and II are forms of arguments.
(B) The assertion-I is an argument but the assertion-II is not.
(C) The assertion-II is an argument but the assertion-I is not.
(D) Both the assertion are explanations of facts.

35. By which of the following proposition, the proposition 'some men are not honest' is contradicted?
(A) All men are honest.
(B) Some men are honest.
(C) No men are honest.
(D) All of the above.

36. A stipulative definition is
(A) always true (B) always false
(C) sometimes true sometimes false
(D) neither true nor false

37. If the statement 'most of the students are obedient' is taken to be true, which one of the following pair of statements can be claimed to be true?
(i) all obedient persons are students.
(ii) All students are obedient.
(iii) Some students are obedient.
(iv) Some students are not disobedient.

Code:
(A) (i) and (ii) (B) (ii) and (iii)
(C) (iii) and (iv) (D) (ii) and (iv)

38. Choose the right code.
A deductive argument claims that
I. The conclusion does not claim something more than that which is contained in the premises.
II. The conclusion is supported by the premise/premises may be either true or false.
III. If the conclusion is false, then premise/premises may be either true or false.
IV. If premise/combination of premises is true, then conclusion must be true.

Codes :
(A) I and II (B) I and III
(C) II and III (D) All the above

39. In the expression 'nothing is larger than itself' the relation 'is larger than' is
(A) Antisymmetric (B) Asymmetrical
(C) Intransitive (D) Irreflexive

40. **Assertion (A):** There are more laws on the books today than ever before, and more crimes being committed than ever before.

Reason (R): Because to reduce crime we must eliminate the laws.

Choose the correct answer from below:
(A) (A) is true, (R) is doubtful, and (R) is not the correct explanation of (A).
(B) (A) is false, (R) is true, and (R) is the correct explanation of (A).
(C) (A) is doubtful, (R) is doubtful, and (R) is not the correct explanation of (A),
(D) (A) is doubtful, (R) is true, and (R) is not the correct explanation of (A)

41. If the proposition "All men are not mortal" is true then which of the following inferences is correct ? Choose from the code given below :
1. "All men are mortal" is true.
2. "Some men are mortal" is false.

3. "No men are mortal" is doubtful.
4. "All men are mortal" is false.

Code :

(A) 1, 2 and 3 (B) 2, 3 and 4
(C) 1, 3 and 4 (D) 1 and 3

42. Determine the nature of the following definition: 'abortion' means the ruthless murdering of innocent beings

(A) Lexical (B) Persuasive
(C) Stipulative (D) Theoretical

43. Which one of the following is not an argument?

(A) Devadutt does not eat in the day so he must be eating at night.
(B) If Devadutt is growing fat and if he does not eat during the day, he will be eating at night.
(C) Devadutt eats in the night so he does not eat during the day.
(D) Since Devadutt does not eat in the day, he must be eating in the night.

44. Venn diagram is a type of diagram to

(A) Represent and assess the validity of elementary inferences of syllogistic form.
(B) Represent but not assess the validity of elementary inferences of syllogistic form.
(C) Represent and assess the truth of elementary inferences of syllogistic form.
(D) Assess but not represent the truth of elementary inferences of syllogistic form.

45. Reasoning by analogy leads to

(A) certainty
(B) definite conclusion
(C) predictive conjecture
(D) surety

46. Which of the following statements are false? Choose from the code given below:

(i) Inductive arguments always proceed from the particular to the general.
(ii) A cogent argument must be inductively strong.
(iii) A valid argument may have a false premise and a false conclusion.
(iv) An argument may legitimately be spoken of as 'true' or 'false'.

Code:

(A) (ii), (iii) and (iv) (B) (i) and (iii)
(C) (ii) and (iv) (D) (i) and (ii)

47. Assertion (A) : The coin when flipped next time will come up tails.

Reason (R) : Because the coin was flipped five times in a row, and each time it came up heads.

Choose the correct answer from below :

(A) Both (A) and (R) are true, and (R) is the correct explanation of (A).
(B) Both (A) and (R) are false, and (R) is the correct explanation of (A).
(C) (A) is doubtful, (R) is true, and (R) is not the correct explanation of (A).
(D) (A) is doubtful, (R) is false, and (R) is the correct explanation of (A).

48. The relation 'is a sister of' is

(A) Non-symmetrical
(B) Symmetrical
(C) Asymmetrical (D) Transitive

49. If the proposition 'Vegetarians are not meat eaters' is false, then which of the following inferences is correct? Choose from the codes given below:

(i) 'Some vegetarians are meat eaters' is true.
(ii) 'All vegetarians are meat eaters' is doubtful.
(iii) 'Some vegetarians are not meat eaters' is true.
(iv) 'Some vegetarians are not meat eaters' is doubtful.

(A) (i), (ii), and (iii) (B) (ii), (iii) and (iv)
(C) (i), (iii), and (iv) (D) (i), (ii), and (iv)

50. Determine the nature of the following definition:

'Poor' means having an annual income of Rs. 10,000.

(A) Persuasive (B) Precising
(C) Lexical (D) Stipulative

51. Which one of the following is not an argument?

(A) If today is Tuesday, tomorrow will be Wednesday.
(B) Since today is Tuesday, tomorrow will be Wednesday.
(C) Ram insulted me so I punched him in the nose.
(D) Ram is not at home, so he must have gone to town.

52. Venn Diagram is a kind of diagram to

(A) Represent and assess the truth of elementary inferences with the help of Boolean algebra of classes.
(B) Represent and assess the validity of elementary inferences with the help of Boolean algebra of classes.

(C) Represent but not assess the validity of elementary inferences with the help of Boolean algebra of classes.

(D) Assess but not represent the validity of elementary inferences with the help of Boolean algebra of classes.

53. Inductive logic studies the way in which a premise may

(A) Support and entail a conclusion

(B) Not support but entail a conclusion

(C) Neither support nor entail a conclusion

(D) Support a conclusion without entailing it

54. Which of the following statements are true? Choose from the codes given below.

(i) Some arguments, while not completely valid, are almost valid.

(ii) A sound argument may be invalid.

(iii) A cogent argument may have a probably false conclusion.

(iv) A Statement may be true or false.

Code:

(A) (i) and (ii) (B) (i), (iii), and (ii)

(C) (iv) alone (D) (iii) and (iv)

55. If the statement 'some men are cruel' is false, which of the following statements/statement are/is true?

(i) All men are cruel.

(ii) No men are cruel.

(iii) Some men are not cruel.

(A) (i) and (iii) (B) (i) and (ii)

(C) (ii) and (iii) (D) only (iii)

56. Which of the following is an example of circular argument?

(A) God created man in his image and man created god in his own image.

(B) God is the source of a scripture and the scripture is the source of our knowledge of God.

(C) Some of the Indians are great because India is great.

(D) Rama is great because he is Rama.

57. Lakshmana is a morally good person because

(A) He is religious (B) He is educated

(C) He is rich (D) He is rational

58. Two statements I and II given below are followed by two conclusion (A) and (B). Supposing the statements are true, which of the following conclusion can logically follow?

I. Some religious people are morally good.

II. Some religious people are rational.

Conclusions:

(i) rationally religious people are good morally

(ii) Non-rational religious persons are not morally good.

(A) Only (i) follows. (B) Only (ii) Follows.

(C) Both (i) and (ii) follow.

(D) Neither (i) nor (ii) follows.

59. Certainty is

(A) An objective fact

(B) Emotionally satisfying

(C) Logical (D) Ontological

60. Two statements I and II given below are followed by two conclusions (a) and (b). Supposing the statements are true, which of the following conclusions can logically follow?

Statements :

I. Some flowers are red.

II. Some flowers are blue.

Conclusions :

(a) Some flowers are neither red nor blue.

(b) Some flowers are both red and blue.

(A) Only (a) follows.

(B) Only (b) follows.

(C) Both (a) and (b) follow.

(D) Neither (a) nor (b) follows.

61. If the statement 'all students are intelligent' is true, which of the following statements are false?

(i) No students are intelligent.

(ii) Some students are intelligent.

(iii) Some students are not intelligent.

(A) (i) and (ii) (B) (i) and (iii)

(C) (ii) and (iii) (D) (i) only

62. A reasoning where we start with certain particular statements and conclude with a universal statement is called

(A) Deductive Reasoning

(B) Inductive Reasoning

(C) Abnormal Reasoning

(D) Transcendental Reasoning

Reasoning Theory, Indian Logic, Pramanas Philosophy Test

1. Perception refers primarily to

(A) Body temperature

(B) Sense perception

(C) Indian philosophy

(D) Sense organ

2. Elemental constitution of senses is based on the principle that
   (A) similar perceives similar
   (B) similar repels similar
   (C) good affects bad
   (D) NOTA
3. Anumana means
   (A) to make guess (B) to draw conclusion
   (C) to learn from experience
   (D) to commit suicide
4. How many pramanas are there according to Hindu philosophy
   (A) 3 (B) 3
   (C) 6 (D) 8
5. Arthapati is a _______ term.
   (A) English (B) Urdu
   (C) Hindi (D) Sanskit
6. Anuplabdhi is
   (A) First pramana (B) Fourth pramana
   (C) Sixth pramana (D) Not a pramana
7. Vyapti is unconditional and constant relation between
   (A) vyapaka and vyapya
   (B) syadhya and hetu
   (C) sabda and anumana
   (D) vyapya and vyapaka
8. In which pramāna arthāpatti is reduced by Naiyayikas?
   (A) Pratyakṣa (B) Anumāna
   (C) Upamāna (D) Śabda
9. Abhāva is reduced to
   (A) Pratyakṣa (B) Anumāna
   (C) Either to pratyakṣa or to anumāna
   (D) Neither to pratyakṣa nor to anumāna
10. Upamāna gives us knowledge about
   (A) two similar Vastu in the world
   (B) the relation between Vācaka and the Vācya meant by it
   (C) similarity in the uses of words
   (D) perceived similarity between Vastu
11. Abhāva is known by
   (A) perception (B) non-apprehension
   (C) inference (D) recognition
12. Vyāpti is a
   (A) relation and a resemblance
   (B) resemblance and recognition
   (C) relation and a rule
   (D) recognition and a rule
13. "Śabda and Upamana are not independent pramana as they are reducible to anumana" This is the view of
   (A) Naiyāsyikas (B) Vaiśeṣikas
   (C) Vedānta
   (D) Prabhākara Mimāṁsakas
14. Match the following

List-I	List-II
(a) Perception	(i) Ordinary
(b) Inference	(ii) Vyapti
(c) Comparison	(iii) Analogy
(d) Verbal testimony	(iv) Shalda

Codes :

	(a)	(b)	(c)	(d)		(a)	(b)	(c)	(d)
(A)	(i)	(ii)	(iii)	(iv)	(B)	(iv)	(iii)	(ii)	(i)
(C)	(i)	(iv)	(iii)	(ii)	(D)	(iii)	(iv)	(ii)	(i)

15. What do you mean by prama?
   (A) Valid knowledge
   (B) Invalid knowledge
   (C) Cognition (D) None of these
16. Which experience is given by valid knowledge?
   (A) Real (B) Unreal
   (C) No (D) Every
17. Knowledge is regarded as
   (A) valid (B) vague
   (C) Both 'A' and 'B' (D) Neither 'A' nor 'B'
18. Valid knowledge corresponds to
   (A) unreality (B) reality
   (C) everything (D) nothingness
19. What do you mean by valid knowledge?
   (A) Right apprehension of an object
   (B) Right janana
   (C) Right conduct (D) Right subject
20. Hypothetical reasoning can give us what type of knowledge?
   (A) Unreal (B) Real
   (C) True (D) False
21. The valid knowledge must fulfil how many conditions?
   (A) One (B) Two
   (C) Three (D) Four
22. What do you mean by pramana?
   (A) Means of right cognition
   (B) Instrument of right cognition
   (C) False cognition
   (D) Neither 'A' nor 'B'
23. Nyaya accepts how many pramanas?
   (A) One (B) Two
   (C) Three (D) Four

24. Carvaka accepts how many pramanas?
(A) One (B) Two
(C) Three (D) Four

25. Vaisesika accepts how many pramanas?
(A) One (B) Two
(C) Three (D) Four

26. Buddhism accepts how many pramanas?
(A) One (B) Two
(C) Three (D) Four

27. Pramana includes how many parts?
(A) One (B) Two
(C) Three (D) Four

28. What do you mean by arthapatti ?
(A) Postulation (B) Superimposition
(C) Both 'A' and 'B' (D) None of these

29. Verbal testimony has how many conditions to according naiyaykis
(A) One (B) Two
(C) Three (D) Four

30. How many conditions does verbal testimony has, according to nyayikas?
(A) One (B) Two
(C) Three (C) Four

31. Which system believes in neutral knowledge?
(A) Samkhya (B) Mimamsa
(C) Nyaya (D) None of these

32. The accessories of knowledge is gained by what?
(A) Experience (B) Acceptability
(C) Perception (D) None of these

33. Does the relation of the words which are related to their meanings become independent by itself.
(A) Yes (B) No
(C) Can't say (D) Don't know

34. Is there a logical connection between the words and the object?
(A) Yes (B) No
(C) Can't say (D) Don't know

35. Sabda means
(A) collection (B) word
(C) tarka (D) nothingness

36. Whether collection or words have meaning among themselves.
(A) Yes (B) No
(C) Probability (D) None of these

37. Whether the whole sentence has occurrence of any logic?
(A) Yes (B) No
(C) Don't know (D) Probable

38. Match the following

List-I	List-II
a. Valid knowledge	1. Real
b. Invalid knowledge	2. Unreal
c. Perception	3. Carvaka
d. Pramana	4. Instrument of valid knowledge

Directions: In the questions below are two statements labelled as Assertion (A) and Reason (R). In the context of the two statements, which one of the following is correct?

Codes:
(A) Both A and R are true and R is the correct explanation of A
(B) Both A and R are true, but R is not the correct explanation of A
(C) A is true, but R is false
(D) A is false, but R is true

39. Assertion (A). Buddhism accepts the pramanas.
Reason (R). He also believes in verbal testimony.

40. Assertion (A). Upamana means the knowledge gained by means of analogy.
Reason (R). It also means the knowledge of resemblance or similarity.

41. Assertion (A). Inference is classified into several types.
Reason (R). Inference may not be deductive or inductive.

42. Assertion (A). Vypati is defined as the nerve of the inference.
Reason (R). Vypati means the invertible relationship between the major and the middle term.

43. Valid knowledge means
1. Parma 2. Aprama
3. Right apprehension of an object
Select the correct answer using the codes given below
(A) 1 and 2 (B) 1 and 3
(C) 2 and 3 (D) 4 and 3

44. The identity of the subject and object consciousness adopting the form of external object is known as
(A) Perception (B) Inference
(C) Scriptural Testimony (D) Analogy

45. Prama literally means the experience which is
(A) real (B) unreal
(C) doubtful (D) All of these

46. Propositions that support the conclusion of an argument are called

(A) Inferences (B) Premises
(C) Concepts (D) None of these

47. A reasoning where we start with certain particular statement and conclude with a universal statement is called a
(A) Deductive reasoning
(B) Inductive reasoning
(C) Abnormal reasoning
(D) Transcendental reasoning

48. Which of the following can be defined as a group of statement that have common conclusion?
(A) Proposition (B) Argument
(C) Concept (D) Fallacy

49. Inductive Arguments are properly characterized as
(A) Valid-invalid (B) strong-weak
(C) Definite-indefinite (D) Certain-uncertain

50. A fallacy is a
(A) True argument (B) False argument
(C) Valid argument (D) Invalid argument

51. Inductive reasoning is based on
(A) Uniformity of nature
(B) God created the world
(C) Unity of nature (D) Laws of nature

52. Consider the following propositions:
A is human and mortal
B is human and mortal
C is human and mortal
D is human and mortal
Therefore, 'All humans are mortal' is an example of
(A) Deductive argument
(B) Inductive argument
(C) Syllogistic argument
(D) None of the above

53. A deductive argument is sound if and only if it is
(A) Valid and all its premises are true
(B) Invalid and all its premises are true
(C) Is valid and one of the premise is false
(D) Is valid and its conclusion is false.

54. A syllogistic reasoning is
(A) Deductive (B) Inductive
(C) Experimental (D) Hypothetical

55. The two kinds of propositions are
(A) Connotative-denotative
(B) Categorical-conditional
(C) Both (A) and (B)
(D) None of the above

56. If the particular proposition of a subalternation relation is true, then the truth value of the universal proposition is
(A) True (B) False
(C) Both true and false (D) Doubtful

57. The proposition 'if you work hard you will succeed' is an example of
(A) Categorical proposition
(B) Conditional proposition
(C) Negative proposition
(D) Pre-emptive proposition

58. Which of the following shows that an opposition is the relation between two propositions having the same subject and predicate but differing in quantity only?
(A) Contrary
(B) Contradictory
(C) Subalternation
(D) Subcontrary

59. A proposition in which the predicate refers to all individual objects denoted by the subjects is called
(A) Particular (B) Negative
(C) Disjunctive (D) Universal

60. The proposition 'no men are perfect' is an example of
(A) Universal affirmative
(B) Universal negative
(C) Particular affirmative
(D) Particular negative

61. The proposition 'some Indians are not spiritual' is and example for
(A) Universal affirmative
(B) Universal negative
(C) Particular affirmative
(D) Particular negative

62. Which of the following shows the relationship between two universal propositions having the same subject but differing in quality only?
(A) Contrary opposition
(B) Contradictory opposition
(C) Subaltern
(D) Sub contrary

63. Which of the following terms show the relationship between two propositions having the same subject, but differing in both quality and quantity?
(A) Contrary opposition
(B) Contradictory opposition

(C) Subaltern
(D) Sub contrary

64. Given below are two statements:

Statement I: According to *Nyaya* philosophy an argument proceeds only on those issues that are completely unknown.

Statement II: According to *Nyaya* philosophy an argument does not proceed on those issues that are well established.

In the light of the above statements. Choose the most appropriate answer from the options given below :

(A) Both Statement I and Statement II are correct.
(B) Both Statement I and Statement II are incorrect.
(C) Statement I is correct but Statement II is incorrect.
(D) Statement I is incorrect but Statement II is correct.

65. Match the following.

List-I	List-II
a. Samkhya	I. Gautam
b. Nyaya	II. Kanada
c. Vaisheshika	III. Kapil
d. Purvamimans	IV. Jaimini

Choose the correct answer from the options given below:

(A) (a)-I, (b)-III, (c)-IV, (d)-II
(B) (a)-II, (b)-I, (c)-IV, (d)-III
(C) (a)-III, (b)-I, (c)-II, (d)-IV
(D) (a)-IV, (b)-III, (c)-II, (d)-I

66. The condition that there should be an absence of contradiction in the relation of the objects denoted in the combination or words, for the sentence to be significant is known as which one of the following?

(A) Akarksa (B) Yogyata
(C) Sannidhi (D) Tatparya

67. Given below are two statements:

Statement I: The works in Nyaya-Sastra discuss the aggregate causal conditions and the process involved in inferential recognition.

Statement II: The works in Nyaya-Sastra do not however dwell upon analysis of the factors that help to assess and decide the formal validity of judgement.

In the light of the above statements, choose the most appropriate answer from the options given below :

(A) Both Statement I and Statement II are correct.
(B) Both Statement I and Statement II are incorrect.
(C) Statement I is correct but Statement II is incorrect.
(D) Statement I is incorrect but Statement II is correct.

68. All animals with such and such features are either bisons or buffalos. This animal has those features and it is not a bison. Therefore it is a buffalo. According to Nyaya school this argument exemplifies which one of the following pramanas (instrument of knowledge)?

(A) Upamana (Comparison)
(B) Sabda (Verbal authority)
(C) Arthapatii (Postulation)
(D) Anumana (inference)

69. Given below are two statements related to the Upanishadic tradition.

Statement I: Paravidya means knowledge that transcends human experience.

Statement II: Aparavidya means knowledge based on the human experience.

In the light of the above statements, choose the most appropriate answer from the options given below :

(A) Both Statement I and Statement II are true.
(B) Both Statement I and Statement II are false.
(C) Statement I is true but Statement II is false.
(D) Statement I is false but Statement II is true.

70. Which of the following pramanas are accepted by Vaisheshika philosophy?

(a) Pratyaksa (b) Anumana
(c) Sabha (d) Upamana

Choose the correct answer from the options given below:

(A) A and B only (B) C and D only
(C) E and F only (D) C and E only

71. Which of the following are accepted in Buddhism?

(a) Adhyasa (b) Apoha
(c) Abhava (d) Arthapatti
(e) Arthapatti (f) Sbada

Choose the correct answer from the options given below:

(A) A and B only (B) C and D only
(C) B and E only (D) E and F only

72. The sequential order of syllogism on Nyaya philosophy is

(a) Nigmam (b) Udaharana
(c) Hetu (d) Upanaya
(e) Pratigya

Choose the correct answer from the options given below:

(A) a, e, c, d, b (B) e, c, b, d, a
(C) e, b, c, d, a (D) d, a, b, c, e

73. Which one of the following is not a sense-organ according to classical Indian school of logic?

(A) Manas (B) Savikalpaka
(C) Caksuh (D) Srotra

74. Which one of the following schools has not accept *anumana* (inference) as a valid source of knowledge?

(A) Advaita vedanta (B) Visistadvaita
(C) Carvaka (D) Sankhya

75. Given below are two statements, one is labeled as Assertion A and the other is labeled as Reason R.

Assertion A: If there is a contestation between sruti and smriti, sruti prevails over smriti

Reason R: Sruti represent the philosophical aspect of the Vedas and Upanishads, while smriti is an application of philosophical ideas.

In light of the above statements, choose the most appropriate answer from the options given below:

(A) Both A and R are correct and R is the correct explanation of A
(B) Both A and R are correct but R is NOT the correct explanation of A
(C) A is correct but R is not correct
(D) A is not correct but R is correct

76. Arrange the sequential order of syllogism Nyaya philosophy:

(a) Pratigya (b) Hetu
(c) Udaharana (d) Nigman
(e) Upanaya

Choose the correct answer from the options given below:

(A) a, b, d, e, c (B) a, b, c, e, d
(C) a, d, b, e, c (D) a, c, d, b, e

77. Match List with List II

List-I (Concepts)	List-II (Schools)
a. Nirvana	I. Sankhya
b. Nihshreyasa	II. Jainism
c. Apavarga	III. Upanishads
d. Moksha	IV. Buddhism

Choose the correct answer from the options given below:

(A) (a)-IV, (b)-III, (c)-II, (d)-I
(B) (a)-I, (b)-II, (c)-IV, (d)-III
(C) (a)-II, (b)-I, (c)-III, (d)-IV
(D) (a)-III, (b)-IV, (c)-II, (d)-I

78. What is the correct sequence of steps in case of inference according to Indian Logic?

(a) Statement of similarity/applicability of the example to case in consideration (upanya)
(b) Statement of Reason (hetu)
(c) Affirmation of the thesis as proved (nigmana)
(d) Statement of thesis (Pratijna)
(e) Giving an example of the underlay rule (udaharana)

Choose the correct answer from the options given below:

(A) d, e, a, c, b (B) d, c, b, a, e
(C) d, b, e, a, c (D) d, e, a, b, c

79. The inherent cause (Samavayi) of Indian Philosophy corresponds to which of the causes given by Aristotle?

(A) Material Cause (B) Formal Cause
(C) Efficient Cause (D) Final Cause

80. The Philosophical system which postulates that, 'Everything in reality stems from 'Pursha' and 'Prakriti''?

(A) Samkhya (B) Nyaya
(C) Mimamsa (D) Vedaantha

81. What is the sequential order of a comprehensible sentence in Nyaya philosophy

(a) Akansha (b) Yogyata
(c) Tatparya (d) Sanniddhi

Choose the correct answer from the options given below:

(A) d, c, b, a (B) a, b, d, c
(C) c, d, b, a (D) d, c, a, b

82. Which of the following schools of Classical Indian Philosophy reduce Sabda pramana (verbal authority) to inference?

(a) Nayaya (b) Vaisesikas
(c) Vaisesikas (d) Buddhists
(e) Carvaka/Lokayata

Choose the correct answer from the options given below:

(A) b and c only (B) b, c and e only
(C) b and e only (D) a, d and e only

83. Paravidya, according to the vedic tradition, implies

(A) Knowledge based on human experience
(B) Knowledge that transcends human experience
(C) Knowledge acquired from teachers
(D) Knowledge acquired from texts.

84. In case of anumana (inference) identify the sequences of five steps of syllogistic argument according to Nyaya
(a) The mountain has fire
(b) The mountain also has smoke accompanied by fire, like kitchen
(c) Therefore the mountain has fire
(d) Because of smoke
(e) Wherever there is smoke, there is fire, as in the kitchen

Choose the correct answer from the options given below:
(A) a, b, d, e, c (B) a, d, e, c, b
(C) b, d, e, a, c (D) a, d, e, b, c

85. Given below are two statements:

Statement I: The works in Nyaya-Sastra discuss the aggregate causal conditions and the process involved in inferential cognition.

Statement II: The works in Nyaya-Sastra do not however dwell upon analysis of the factors that help to assess and decide the formal validity of a judgement.

In the light of the above statements, choose the most appropriate answer from the options given below :
(A) Both Statement I and Statement II are correct.
(B) Both Statement I and Statement II are incorrect.
(C) Statement I is correct but Statement II is incorrect.
(D) Statement I is incorrect but Statement II is correct.

86. 'Upanaya' in Indian 'Nyaya Syllogism' corresponds to which of the following in Aristotelian Syllogism?
(A) Major premise
(B) Minor premise
(C) Conclusion
(D) Both major and minor premises

87. Ayurveda, which deals with indigenous system of medicine, could be traced to
(A) Rigveda (B) Yajurveda
(C) Samaveda (D) Athrvaveda

88. From the following identify those which illustrate the fallacy of the unproved middle?
(a) Ashrayasidha (b) Swarupasidha
(c) Vyapyatvasidha (d) Virudha
(e) Carvaka/Badhita

Choose the correct answer from the options given below:
(A) a, b and c only (B) b, c and d only
(C) a, d and e only (D) a, c and d only

Problems based on Analogies

TYPE - I

1. Bird : Fly : : Snake : ?
(A) Hole (B) Fly
(C) Bark (D) Crawl

2. Soldier : Gun : : Blacksmith : ?
(A) Hammer (B) Sword
(C) Iron (D) Wood

3. Fruits : Apple : : Monument : ?
(A) Students (B) Knowledge
(C) Tajmahal (D) College

4. Motor Bike : Petrol : : Bus
(A) Coal (B) Kerosene
(C) Electricity (D) Diesel

5. Monday : April : : Friday : ?
(A) August (B) Tuesday
(C) July (D) Saturday

6. Butter : Milk : : Oil : ?
(A) Grains (B) Curd
(C) Seeds (D) Cow

7. Light : Sun : : Heat : ?
(A) Fire (B) Electricity
(C) Star (D) Moon

8. House : Wall : : Wall : ?
(A) Brick (B) Roof
(C) Paint (D) Sand

9. Air : Atmosphere : : Water : ?
(A) Ocean (B) Island
(C) Earth (D) Drop

10. Oil : Lamp : : Wax : ?
(A) Bulb (B) Candle
(C) Smooth (D) Dark

11. Ocean : Pond : : Deep : ?
(A) Clean (B) Shallow
(C) River (D) Canal

12. Soft : Sponge : : Sharp : ?
(A) Knife (B) Cut
(C) Edge (D) Pierce

13. Disease : Pathology : : Planets : ?
(A) Astronomy (B) Sun
(C) Class (D) Satellite

14. Ankle : Knee : : Wrist : ?
(A) Hand (B) Foot
(C) Elbow (D) Finger

15. Step : Staircase : : Soldier : ?
(A) Army (B) War
(C) Uniform (D) Bravery

16. Metre : ? : : Litre : Volume
(A) Length (B) Pressure
(C) Weight (D) Area

17. Newspaper : Press : : Cloth : ?
(A) Mill (B) Market
(C) Tailor (D) Textile

18. Clock : Time : : Lamp : ?
(A) Light (B) Room
(C) Glow (D) Bulb

19. Giraffe : ? : : Australia : Kangaroo
(A) Africa (B) India
(C) France (D) Japan

20. Cricket : Bat : : ? : Ball
(A) Badminton (B) Tennis
(C) Kabaddi (D) Swimming

21. Circle : ? : : Sphere : Cube
(A) Square (B) Corners
(C) Ring (D) Radius

22. ? : Copy : : Invent : Imitate
(A) Original (B) Inquiry
(C) Discovery (D) Draw

23. ? : Bee : : Fang : Snake
(A) Sting (B) Poison
(C) Honey (D) Humming

24. ? : Yellow : : Orange : Green
(A) Purple (B) Ultra violet
(C) Plant (D) Forest

25. ? : Light : : Dusk : Dawn
(A) Heavy (B) Sun
(C) Noon (D) Electricity

TYPE - II

26. 1 : 5 : : 7 : ?
(A) 11 (B) 8
(C) 10 (D) 15

27. 5 : 26 : : 7 : ?
(A) 55 (B) 19
(C) 50 (D) 26

28. 3 : 27 : : 4 : ?
(A) 140 (B) 80
(C) 64 (D) 100

29. 1/4 : 1/8 : : 1/3 : ?
(A) 1/6 (B) 1/2
(C) 1/4 (D) 2/6

30. 09 : 25 : : 49 : ?
(A) 63 (B) 36
(C) 64 (D) 81

31. 01 : 04 : : 08 : ?
(A) 81 (B) 72
(C) 64 (D) 70

32. 08 : 28 : : 15 : ?
(A) 65 (B) 126
(C) 26 (D) 63

33. 5 : 8 : : 15 : ?
(A) 17 (B) 20
(C) 18 (D) 21

34. 7 : 11 : : 31 : ?
(A) 37 (B) 45
(C) 39 (D) 38

35. 12 : 20 : : 30 ?
(A) 40 (B) 42
(C) 35 (D) 15

TYPE - III

36. BZDX : FVHT : : JRLP : ?
(A) NNPL (B) NNLO
(C) NMLR (D) NNKL

37. LJH : KKI : : CIA : ?
(A) CBZ (B) DBB
(C) BJB (D) BBZ

38. ABC : ZYX : : CBA : ?
(A) BCA (B) ZXY
(C) YZX (D) XYZ

39. ABD : CDF : : MNP : ?
(A) EFH (B) LNQ
(C) OPR (D) VXY

40. YAWC : UESG : : QIOK : ?
(A) KOME (B) LIME
(C) MMKO (D) MINC

41. NUMBER : UNBMRE : : GHOST : ?
(A) HOGTS (B) HGSOT
(C) HGOTS (D) HOGST

42. JLN : SQO : : PRT : ?
(A) VUT (B) YWU
(C) UYW (D) UTV

43. PCWL : REXM : : THNY : ?
(A) KOVZ (B) PMKZ
(C) VJOZ (D) KOVZ

44. Aab : aAB : : Pqr : ?
(A) PQr (B) pQr
(C) PQR (D) pQR

45. DRIVEN : EIDRVN : : BEGUM : ?
(A) MGBEU (B) EUBGM
(C) UEBGM (D) BGMUE

TYPE - IV

46. Pork : Pig : : ? : ?
(A) Rooster : Chicken
(B) Mutton : Sheep
(C) Steer : Beef
(D) Lobster : Crustacean

47. Filter : Water : : ? : ?
(A) Curtail : Activities
(B) Censor : Play
(C) Expunge : Book
(D) Edit : Text

48. Cigarette : Tobacco : : ? : ?
(A) Coffee : Caffeine (B) Milk : Bottle
(C) Cigar : Filter (D) Shoes : Socks

49. Savage : Civilized : : ? : ?
(A) Illiterate : Book (B) Dark : Lighted
(C) Wild : Animal (D) Brutal : Heroic

50. Knife : Chopper : : ? : ?
(A) Walking : Fitness (B) Swim : Float
(C) Scissors : Cloth (D) Quilt : Blanket

51. Flag : Nation : : ? : ?
(A) Emblem : Prosperity
(B) Insignia : Rank
(C) Wealth : Prestige
(D) Honour : Status

52. 'Braille' is related to 'Blindness' in the same way as 'Sign Language' is related to
(A) Exceptional (B) Touch
(C) Deafness (D) Presentation

53. 'Success' is to 'Failure' as 'Big' is to
(A) Small (B) Good
(C) Rich (D) Great

54. 'England' is related to Atlantic Ocean' in the same way as 'Greenland' is related to
(A) Arctic Ocean (B) Pacific Ocean
(C) Atlantic Ocean (D) None of these

55. Dog is related to 'Kennel' in the same way as 'Bird' is related to
(A) Pen (B) Chirp
(C) Tree (D) Cage

56. 'Boat' is related to 'Oar' in the same way as 'Bicycle' is related to
(A) Seat (B) Wheel
(C) Paddle (D) Road

57. 'Mountain' is related to 'Valley' in the same way as 'Enemy' is related to
(A) Country (B) Stranger
(C) Friend (D) Fight

58. 'Demographer' is related to 'People' in the same way as 'philatelist' is related to
(A) Photography (B) Fossils
(C) Stamps (D) Music

59. 'Crawl' is related to which of the following in the same way as 'Fly' is related to 'Parrot' ?
(A) Sparrow (B) Frog
(C) Crocodile (D) Fish

60. 'Horse' is related to 'Hoof' in the same way as 'Eagle' is related to
(A) Clutch (B) Leg
(C) Claw (D) Foot

61. 'Pen' is to 'Pencil' as 'Hockey' is to
(A) Ground (B) Football
(C) Team (D) Players

62. 'Wine' is related to 'Grapes' in the same way as 'Vodka' is related to
(A) Oranges (B) Potatoes
(C) Rice (D) Apples

63. 'Metal' is related to 'Conduction' in the same way as 'Plastic' is related to
(A) Industries (B) Inflammation
(C) Insulation (D) Petrochemicals

64. 'Eye' is to 'See' in the same way as 'Ear' is to
(A) Hear (B) Sound
(C) Smell (D) Light

65. 'Liberty' is related to 'Slavery' in the same way as 'Danger' is related to
(A) Anger (B) Dangerous
(C) Stability (D) Safety

66. 'Face' is related to 'Expression' in the same way as 'Hand' is related to
(A) Work (B) Handshake
(C) Gesture (D) Waving

67. 'Match' is related to 'Win' in the same way as 'Examination' is related to
(A) Appear (B) Write
(C) Success (D) Attempt

68. 'Tall' is related to 'Dwarf' in the same way as 'Kind' is related to
(A) Forgive (B) Gentle
(C) Cruel (D) Weak

69. 'Cube' is related to 'Square' in the same way as 'Square' is related to
(A) Line (B) Point
(C) Plane (D) Triangle

70. 'Blood' is related to 'Vein' in the same way as 'Oil' is related to
(A) Petrol (B) Pipeline
(C) Engine (D) Car

TYPE - V

71. Cold and Hot
(A) Day and Hour (B) January and June
(C) January and February
(D) None of the above

72. Carpenter and wood
(A) Engineer and Machines
(B) Goldsmith and Gold
(C) Blacksmith and Iron
(D) All of these

73. Hands and Fingers
(A) Feet and Toes (B) Head and Hair
(C) Skin and colour (D) Both (A) and (B)

74. Writer and Poet
(A) Poems and Songs (B) Books and Lessors
(C) Prose and Poetry (D) Letters and words

75. Machines and Pulleys
(A) Iron and Doors (B) Knife and Fruits
(C) Bread and Butter (D) Car and Wheels

76. Supervisor and worker
(A) Debtor and Creditor
(B) Inferior and Superior
(C) Officer and Clerk
(D) Teacher and Superintendent

77. Pulp and Paper
(A) Iron and Wood
(B) Yarn and Fabric
(C) Wood and Furniture
(D) Both (B) and (C)

78. Chemistry and Science
(A) Painting and Arts
(B) Medicine and Surgery
(C) Geography and History
(D) Civics and Archaeology

79. House and Rent
(A) Trains and Fares
(B) Labour and Wages
(C) Capital and Interest
(D) All of these

80. Car and Garage
(A) Cow and Stye
(B) Lion and Den
(C) Horse and Stable
(D) All of the above

ANSWERS

1. (A)	2. (B)	3. (C)	4. (B)	5. (A)	6. (C)	7. (D)	8. (A)	9. (B)	10. (B)
11. (B)	12. (A)	13. (C)	14. (C)	15. (C)	16. (D)	17. (C)	18. (B)	19. (A)	20. (B)
21. (D)	22. (B)	23. (D)	24. (B)	25. (C)	26. (D)	27. (D)	28. (B)	29. (D)	30. (B)
31. (D)	32. (A)	33. (D)	34. (B)	35. (C)	36. (B)	37. (B)	38. (B)	39. (C)	40. (C)
41. (A)	42. (B)	43. (A)	44. (D)	45. (B)	46. (A)	47. (B)	48. (C)	49. (A)	50. (B)
51. (C)	52. (C)	53. (A)	54. (B)	55. (D)	56. (A)	57. (A)	58. (A)	59. (D)	60. (D)
61. (D)	62. (B)	63. (B)	64. (B)	65.(A)	66. (B)	67. (D)	68. (B)	69. (A)	70. (D)
71. (D)	72. (C)	73. (A)	74. (C)	75. (D)	76. (B)	77. (D)	78. (C)	79. (C)	80. (B)
81. (B)	82. (D)								

1. LOGICAL DIAGRAM TEST

1. (D)	2. (A)	3. (A)	4. (C)	5. (D)	6. (A)	7. (C)	8. (B)	9. (C)	10. (A)
11. (C)	12. (B)	13. (C)	14. (C)	15. (D)	16. (A)	17. (D)	18. (D)	19. (C)	20. (C)
21. (D)	22. (D)	23. (D)	24. (C)	25. (A)	26. (D)	27. (C)	28. (D)	29. (D)	30. (A)
31. (D)	32. (B)	33. (B)	34. (A)	35. (C)	36. (C)	37. (D)			

2. SYLLOGISM TEST

1. (B)	**2.** (A)	**3.** (D)	**4.** (C)	**5.** (B)	**6.** (A)	**7.** (D)	**8.** (D)	**9.** (A)	**10.** (D)
11. (C)	**12.** (B)	**13.** (A)	**14.** (B)	**15.** (D)	**16.** (B)	**17.** (D)	**18.** (C)	**19.** (D)	**20.** (C)
21. (B)	**22.** (D)	**23.** (C)	**24.** (D)	**25.** (D)	**26.** (A)	**27.** (A)	**28.** (A)	**29.** (A)	**30.** (C)
31. (C)	**32.** (A)	**33.** (B)	**34.** (B)	**35.** (C)	**36.** (A)	**37.** (D)	**38.** (C)	**39.** (A)	**40.** (D)

3. STATEMENT AND ASSUMPTION TEST

1. (B)	**2.** (A)	**3.** (C)	**4.** (C)	**5.** (B)	**6.** (A)	**7.** (D)	**8.** (C)	**9.** (B)	**10.** (D)
11. (C)	**12.** (A)	**13.** (A)	**14.** (B)	**15.** (C)					

4. STATEMENT AND ARGUMENT TEST

1. (C)	**2.** (A)	**3.** (D)	**4.** (C)	**5.** (A)	**6.** (A)	**7.** (A)	**8.** (A)	**9.** (C)	**10.** (D)
11. (A)	**12.** (B)	**13.** (B)	**14.** (D)	**15.** (C)	**16.** (A)	**17.** (D)	**18.** (D)	**19.** (B)	**20.** (A)
21. (B)	**22.** (B)	**23.** (A)	**24.** (A)	**25.** (A)	**26.** (D)	**27.** (B)	**28.** (C)	**29.** (D)	**30.** (B)

5. MISCELLANEOUS TEST

1. (C)	**2.** (D)	**3.** (D)	**4.** (D)	**5.** (D)	**6.** (C)	**7.** (D)	**8.** (A)	**9.** (C)	**10.** (B)
11. (C)	**12.** (B)	**13.** (C)	**14.** (A)	**15.** (C)	**16.** (C)	**17.** (C)	**18.** (D)	**19.** (D)	**20.** (D)
21. (D)	**22.** (B)	**23.** (B)	**24.** (A)	**25.** (B)	**26.** (B)	**27.** (B)	**28.** (B)	**29.** (A)	**30.** (B)
31. (B)	**32.** (C)	**33.** (B)	**34.** (B)	**35.** (A)	**36.** (D)	**37.** (C)	**38.** (A)	**39.** (D)	**40.** (A)
41. (B)	**42.** (B)	**43.** (B)	**44.** (A)	**45.** (C)	**46.** (C)	**47.** (C)	**48.** (A)	**49.** (A)	**50.** (B)
51. (A)	**52.** (B)	**53.** (D)	**54.** (C)	**55.** (C)	**56.** (B)	**57.** (D)	**58.** (D)	**59.** (A)	**60.** (C)
61. (B)	**62.** (A)								

REASONING THEORY, INDIAN LOGIC, PRAMANAS PHILOSOPHY TEST

1. (B)	**2.** (A)	**3.** (B)	**4.** (C)	**5.** (D)	**6.** (C)	**7.** (D)	**8.** (B)	**9.** (C)	**10.** (A)
11. (A)	**12.** (C)	**13.** (B)	**14.** (A)	**15.** (A)	**16.** (A)	**17.** (C)	**18.** (B)	**19.** (A)	**20.** (A)
21. (C)	**22.** (C)	**23.** (D)	**24.** (A)	**25.** (B)	**26.** (B)	**27.** (C)	**28.** (C)	**29.** (D)	**30.** (B)
31. (C)	**32.** (A)	**33.** (A)	**34.** (A)	**35.** (B)	**36.** (B)	**37.** (B)	**38.** (A)	**39.** (B)	**40.** (A)
41. (B)	**42.** (A)	**43.** (B)	**44.** (A)	**45.** (A)	**46.** (B)	**47.** (B)	**48.** (A)	**49.** (B)	**50.** (B)
51. (A)	**52.** (B)	**53.** (A)	**54.** (A)	**55.** (B)	**56.** (D)	**57.** (B)	**58.** (C)	**59.** (D)	**60.** (B)
61. (D)	**62.** (A)	**63.** (B)	**64.** (D)	**65.** (C)	**66.** (D)	**67.** (C)	**68.** (A)	**69.** (A)	**70.** (A)
71. (C)	**72.** (B)	**73.** (B)	**74.** (C)	**75.** (A)	**76.** (B)	**77.** (A)	**78.** (C)	**79.** (A)	**80.** (A)
81. (B)	**82.** (A)	**83.** (B)	**84.** (D)	**85.** (C)	**86.** (B)	**87.** (D)	**88.** (A)		

PROBLEMS BASED ON ANALOGIES

1. (D)	**2.** (A)	**3.** (C)	**4.** (D)	**5.** (A)	**6.** (C)	**7.** (A)	**8.** (A)	**9.** (A)	**10.** (B)
11. (B)	**12.** (A)	**13.** (A)	**14.** (C)	**15.** (A)	**16.** (A)	**17.** (A)	**18.** (A)	**19.** (A)	**20.** (B)
21. (A)	**22.** (A)	**23.** (A)	**24.** (A)	**25.** (A)	**26.** (A)	**27.** (C)	**28.** (C)	**29.** (A)	**30.** (D)
31. (A)	**32.** (A)	**33.** (C)	**34.** (A)	**35.** (B)	**36.** (A)	**37.** (C)	**38.** (D)	**39.** (C)	**40.** (C)
41. (B)	**42.** (B)	**43.** (C)	**44.** (D)	**45.** (A)	**46.** (B)	**47.** (B)	**48.** (A)	**49.** (B)	**50.** (D)
51. (B)	**52.** (C)	**53.** (A)	**54.** (A)	**55.** (D)	**56.** (C)	**57.** (C)	**58.** (C)	**59.** (C)	**60.** (C)
61. (B)	**62.** (B)	**63.** (C)	**64.** (A)	**65.** (D)	**66.** (C)	**67.** (C)	**68.** (C)	**69.** (A)	**70.** (B)
71. (B)	**72.** (D)	**73.** (D)	**74.** (C)	**75.** (D)	**76.** (C)	**77.** (D)	**78.** (A)	**79.** (D)	**80.** (D)

SOLUTIONS WITH EXPLANATIONS

1. Logical Diagram Test

1. As English and Hindi both come under "languages".
2. Thieves come under the grouping of criminals, whereas Judges are a separate group.
3. Since carrot is a vegetable and vegetable is a food.
4. Brinjal is vegetable and hence is subset of it. Fruit is something unrelated to both of them.
5. Door and window both are the different parts of House.
6. All the three items are interrelated.
7. Car is an automobile and train is something unrelated to both of them
8. All the three are unrelated to one another.
9. Painter and Scholar share relationship to each other and Table is unrelated to both of them. Since we don't have this fig. in any of the options, hence it is our answer.
10. Hen, dog and cat, all the three items are unrelated to each other. Since this relationship is not represented by any of the figures, hence it is our answer.

16. Since pencil is a part of stationery and jeep is different from these two, therefore given elements are represented by figure (a).
17. Machinery and product are entirely different. But both are present in a factory. So are represented by figure (d).
18. Since brinjal and cauliflower are vegetables, so these elements are represented by figure (d).
19. Since Honesty, Intelligence, Aptitude are three different traits, so they are represented by figure (c).
20. All the three terms are unrelated to each other. So, these are represented by the given figure (c).

36. As region 9 is common between triangle, rectangle and circle, therefore, it represents urban corrupt politicians.
37. As region 4 is common between S (richmen) and T (honestmen), therefore, it represents honest rich men.

2. Syllogism Test

1. From the rule of syllogism, we find following valid conclusions.
   1. All microprocessors are modems (M)
   2. Some microprocessors are modems (I)
   3. Some modems are microprocessors (C)
   4. Some microprocessors are computers (I)
   5. Some computer are microprocessors (C)
   6. Some computers are modems. (I)
   7. Some modems are computers (C)

   Note. M → Main conclusion, I Implication, C Conversion.

2.

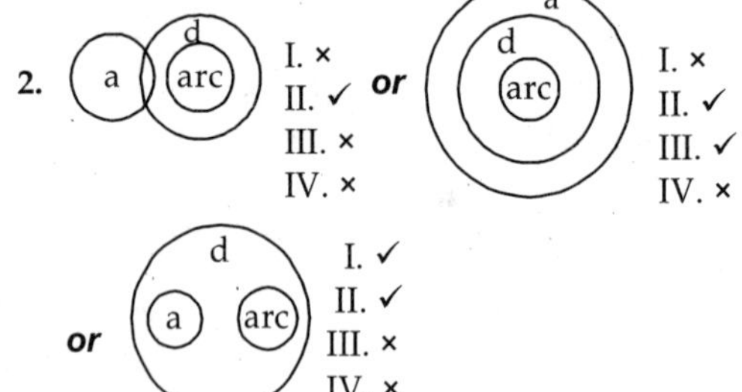

From the above diagrams, we find that only conclusion II is valid.

3.

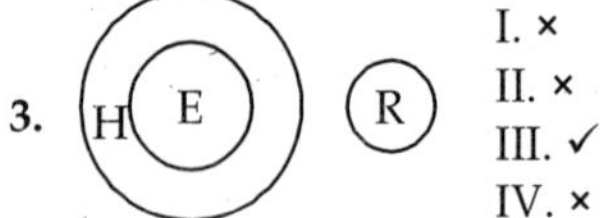

From the above diagram, we find that only conclusion III is valid.

4.

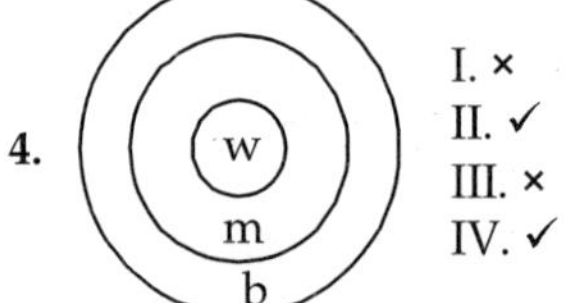

From the above diagram, we find that only conclusion II and IV are valid.

5.

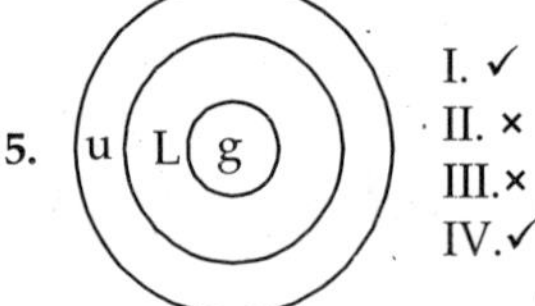

From the above diagram, we find that only conclusion I and IV are valid.

6. 'chair' is a middle term in the both statements. Here middle term is distributed in the first statement's case, because only subject is distributed in A-type cases and no term (subject of predicate) is distributed in I type cases. So, first given conclusion is valid and II is also valid, because it is the conversion of first conclusion. III and IV conclusion are invalid, because no negative conclusion is maintained by the association of two affirmative statements.

7. Conclusion I follows but by the fallacy of division, it is invalid because collective action cannot be considered an individual's action.

8.

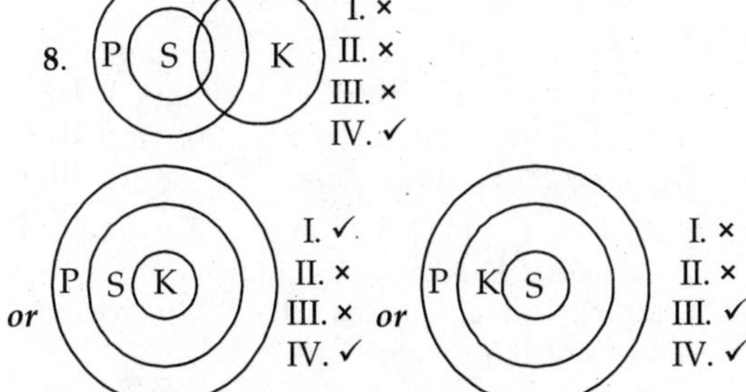

From the above diagrams, we find that only conclusion IV is valid.

9.

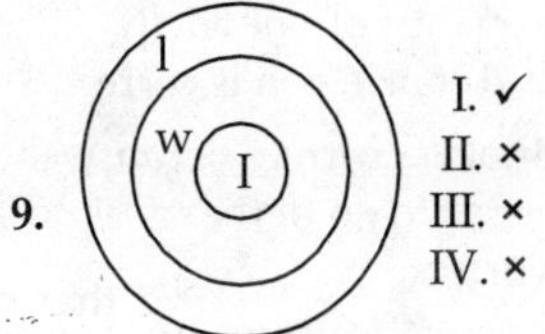

From the above diagram, we find that only conclusion I is valid.

10. a r s — I. × II. × III. × IV. ✓ *or* r a s — I. × II. × III. × IV. ×

From the above diagrams, we find that no given conclusion is valid.

11. p t f — I. ✓ II. × III. × IV. × *or* t p f — I. × II. ✓ III. × IV. ×

From the above diagrams, we find that either conclusion I or II is valid.

13.

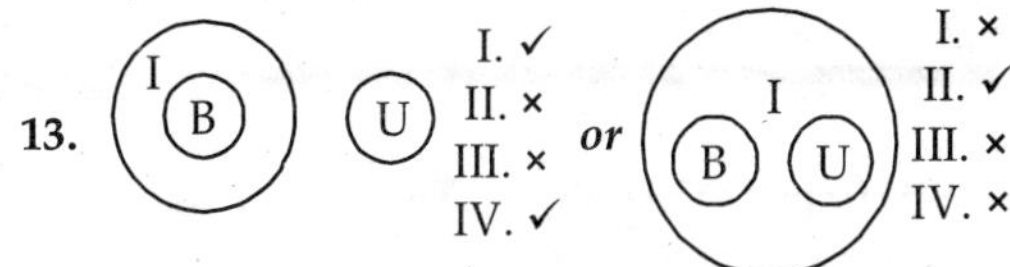

From the above diagrams, we find that either conclusion II or IV is valid.

14.

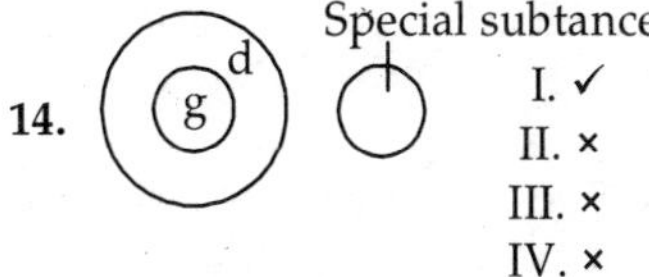

From the above diagram, we find that only conclusion I is valid.

15.

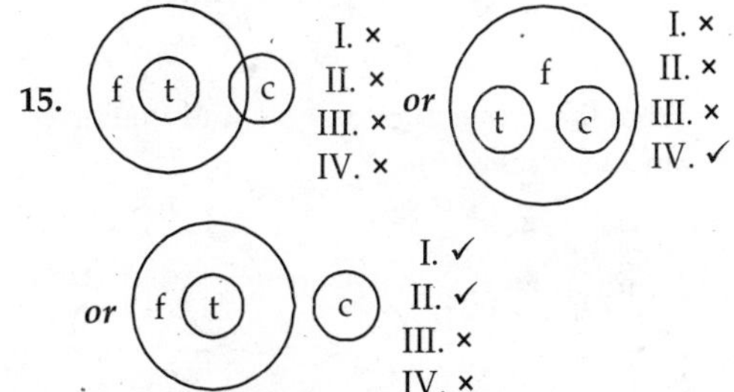

From the above diagrams, we find that no conclusion is valid.

16.

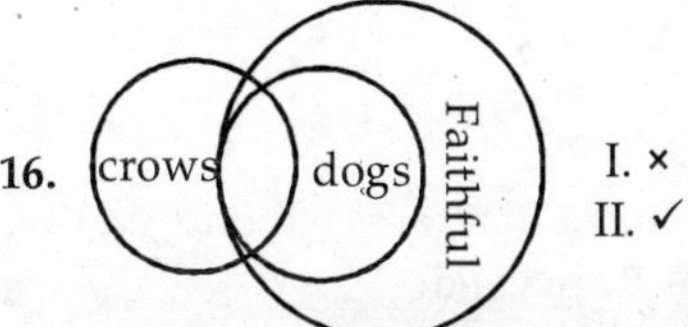

From the above diagram, we find that only conclusion II is valid.

17.

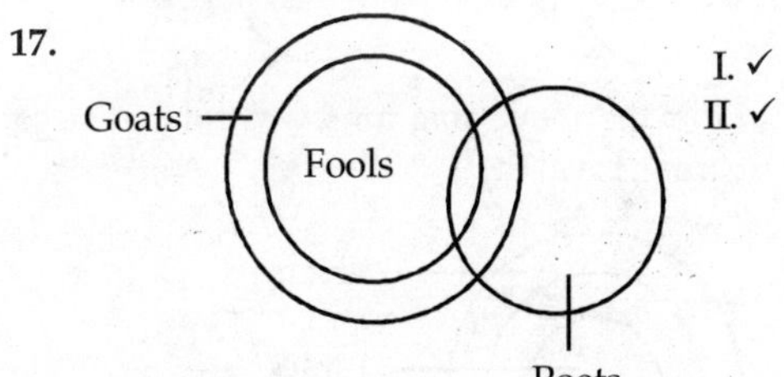

From the above diagram, we find that both conclusions are valid.

18.

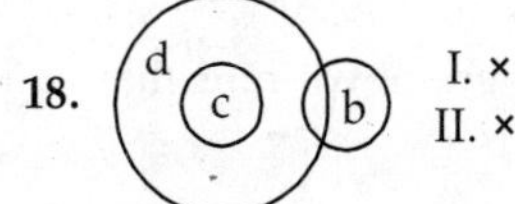

From the above diagram, we find that no given conclusion is valid.

19. 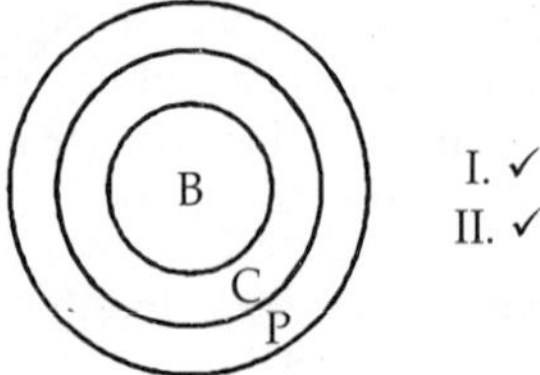

I. ✓
II. ✓

From the above diagram, we find that both conclusions are valid.

20. 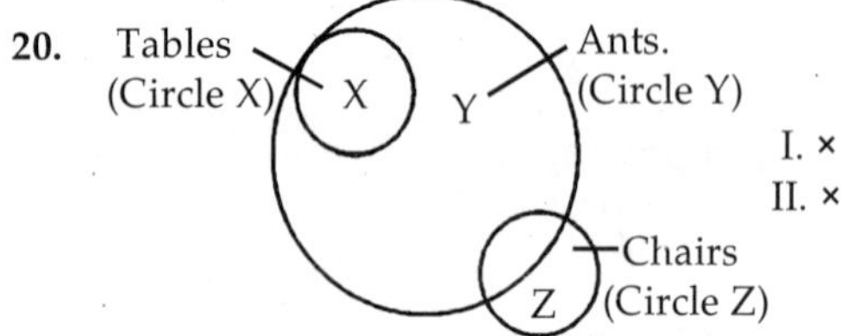

I. ×
II. ×

From the above diagram, we find that no conclusion is valid.

21. T B H I. ✓ II. ✓ *or* T B H I. × II. ✓

From the above diagrams, we find that only conclusion II is valid.

22. e p d I. ✓ II. ✓

From the above diagram, we find that both conclusions II are valid.

23. A P S I. × II. ✓ *or* A, P, S I. ✓ II. ×

From the above diagrams, we find that no conclusion is valid.

24. 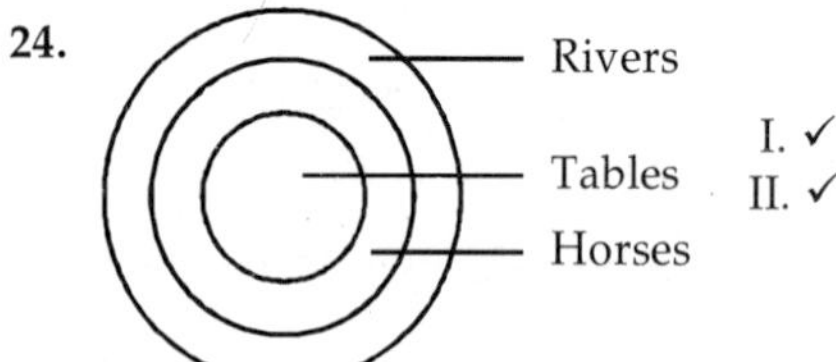

I. ✓
II. ✓

From the above diagram, we find that both conclusions are valid.

25. 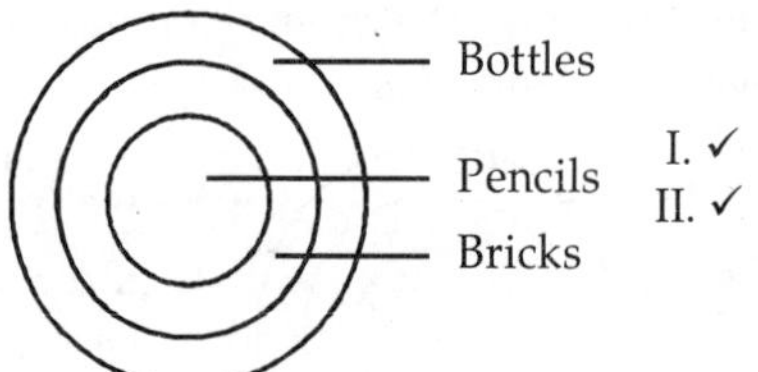

I. ✓
II. ✓

From the above diagram, we find that both conclusions are valid.

26. Almost all minerals are found in oceans.

27. Conclusion I is directly attached to the statement. So, it is correct. But conclusion II contradicts the statement, so it is wrong.

28. Conclusion I is correct, because it is conversion of the given statement. Conclusion II is wrong, because no negative conclusion can be drawn from the affirmative statements.

29. The statement says that the successfulness depends on truthfulness, but it is not clear if all truthful people are successful. So, conclusion I is correct and II is wrong.

31. As Ratna applies Kumkum to her forehead, therefore, she is not a widow. Either she is married or unmarried. Hence either conclusion I or II is correct.

32. The statement declares that all historians cannot write novels.

33. 'Both the masters and disciples valued not the quantity but the quality of knowledge', from this it is clear that II conclusion is correct.

34. Conclusion I cannot be correct because there may be other reasons to go to the mosque but Conclusion II is correct.

35. To break down Soya protein, an enzyme developed in Japan is used by the Indian chemists. Nothing is said about any conclusion in the statement.

36. Cats take milk and cats are intelligent . Therefore, some animals who take milk are intelligent.

37. 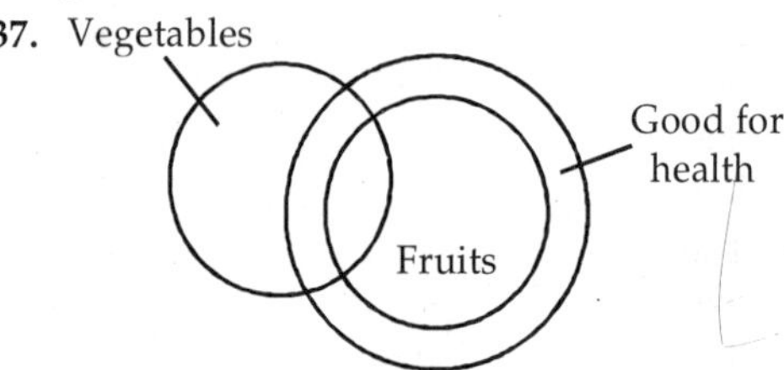

38. In this, two types of Venn diagrams are possible

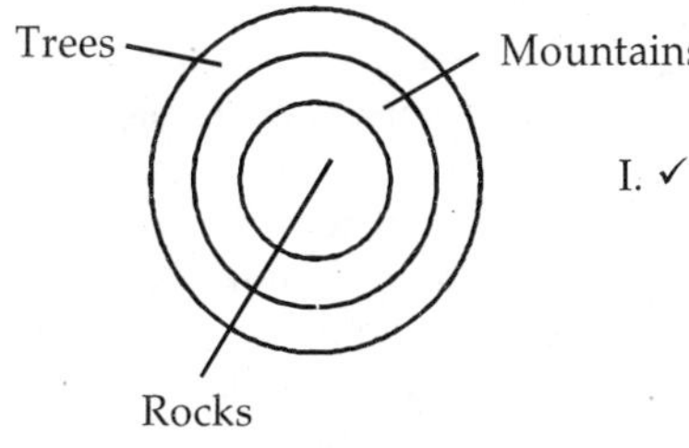

or

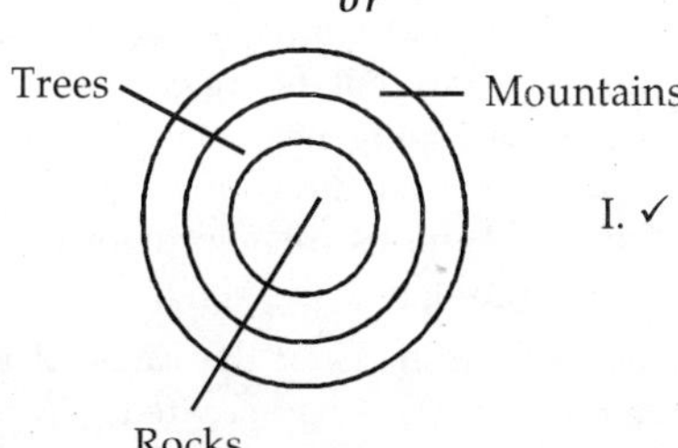

Hence some mountains are trees is correct.

39. The given conclusion may be true or false.

40. The given conclusion is not related to the statements.

3. Statement and Assumption Test

1. Only assumption II is implicit in the statement
2. Only assumption I is implicit in the given statement.
3. Both statements I and II are implicit in the given statement.
4. Both the assumptions I and II are implicit in the given statement.
5. Only the assumption II is implicit in the given statement.
6. Only I is implicit from the given statement.
7. Neither I nor II is implicit in the given statement.
8. Since the notice warns one against copying software without permission, it is evident that software can be copied. So, I is implicit. Also, the warning is given with the motive that no one dares to copy the software. So, II is also implicit.
9. There are many reasons behind budgetary deficits. Thus if the rate of tax is low even then it cannot be said that deficit is the product of low tax rate. In this way first assumption is not implicit but II is implicit as taxes are a good source of finance to cover the deficit.
10. Successful man judges himself correctly but it does not mean that he will never have wrong judgement. Assumption II is also not implicit because if he judges others he may or may not be a successful man.
11. Major modification in a system is done only when it has become outdated and improvement can be made by modification. Thus both assumption I and II are implicit.
12. Deserted place means the place where no one lives. So only assumption I is implicit but the word 'every' used in the second assumption makes it non-implicit.
13. Assumption I is implicit because unless we know the volume of readership of all newspapers we cannot conclude about the popularity of a particular newspaper. Here the study is comparative in nature so we can not say on the basis of only this meagre information that other newspapers have small number of readers. Thus assumption II is not implicit.
14. It is implicit because only then someone will go for business there.
15. You are not competent enough to take any right decision on investment which is very important. Thus both the assumptions are implicit. A person consults others only when he needs it or he is not able to take a right decision on important issues.

4. Statement and Argument Test

1. Argument I follows because those who are unable to get education due to monetary problems, will get, if it is made free of charge, and argument II is also strong because it will require additional budget, increasing financial burden on the government.
2. After sound sleep, mind becomes fresh and alert.
3. The culture of India is very much different from that of the western countries. So whatever is liked there may not be necessarily regarded good here. Moreover, children do need not such type of education but they are adults who should be imparted sex education. Knowledge of sex in real sense is not an innate process.
4. First argument is based on economic principles and laws while the second one has its origin into history and polity.

5. From the given statement, it follows that only the argument I is strong.
6. From the given statement, it follows that only the argument I is strong.
7. From the given statement, it follows that only the argument I is strong.
8. From the given statement, it follows that only the conclusion I is strong.
9. From the given statement, it follows that both the arguments are strong.
10. Argument I is not strong, because its action is not right on the basis of statements. Argument II is weak, because it goes against the statement.
11. Assumption II is not strong because its meaning is entirely different from that of the statement.
12. Argument I is not strong because whenever there is a contradiction in a news it is not because newspapers or TV are in private hands but other reasons are responsible for it. Even in government controlled newspapers, one news, sometime contradicts the other news. Government's controlled mass media generally speak the language of the ruling party and thus its credibility becomes doubtful.
13. Clearly, delinking jobs with degrees will diminish the need for higher education as many of them pursue such education for jobs. So, only argument II is strong.
14. The history illustrates that suffering of women were stopped by men and so is the case even today. So argument I is weak and argument II is also weak because many of the women happened to be the rulers of states and nations and they are ruling well even today.
15. There is no doubt at all about the first argument and II is also strong because India is a populous country where labour intensive technique is more suitable than capital intensive technique.
16. Having a nuclear weapon is one thing and using it indiscriminately is another thing. So argument I is strong but II is not strong because some other countries of the region does also have it.
17. At the college level, all the students are assessed according to their performance in the university exams and not on the basis of any criteria of a more intimate dealing with the students. So argument I is vague. Also, at this level the awarding of degrees is impartial and simply based on his performance. So, argument II also does not hold.
18. Equality of educational opportunity does not mean that everyone must be given the chance of getting education irrespective of his talents. It simply means that any citizen of India will not be discriminated on the basis of his caste, creed, colour or profession. Higher education entails higher costs so scrutiny is a must here.
19. If agencies stop publishing guide books it is not necessary that students will go through text books. Study habits are related to other variables like intelligence, socio-economic status, aim of life etc. On the other hand, there is no doubt that guides are helpful for weak students. So argument II is strong.
20. Higher education is not the cause of unemployment. Infact, it has created greater job opportunities. So, argument II is vague. Also, higher education promotes the country's development, so argument I holds.
21. A rule which is supported by a theory does not suit to all circumstances. So argument I is not strong but argument II is really a fact at least in India where literacy is not more than 50% while management requires good education.
22. Argument II is strong because where there are no political parties there is no democracy.
23. Mechanization in agriculture does not mean that many people will lose their jobs. Mechanization generally helps in reducing the use of animals in agriculture.
24. Argument I is based on scientific researches, but argument II is not logical. Its reason is given in argument I.
25. Argument I is strong because by using their education properly they can revolutionize agriculture and revamp rural atmosphere. It does not mean that their education is being wasted there.
26. Second argument is more appealing and based on the observations than that of the I, but both are not strong.
27. Expenses on elections are not the sole cause of inflation so argument I is weak but argument II is strong because when a ruling party is not acting satisfactorily we can change it through elections and do away with it by popular votes.
28. Without proper publicity we cannot tell our customers about the quality of our products but once it is introduced in the market after

small publicity, people choose it because of its high quality and other people are informed by those who have already chosen and then automatic publicity process goes on.

29. The condition of a developing country is entirely different as compared to a developed nation. So argument I is not strong and argument II is also weak because private sector is doing well in many economic areas and their credibility is unquestionable.

30. There is no doubt in the fact that religion binds people together but it is doubtful that it develops fanaticism. All religious people are humanity in general and love human beings. Only those who are exhibitory and believe in crocodile's tears are fanatical.

5. Miscellaneous Test

1.

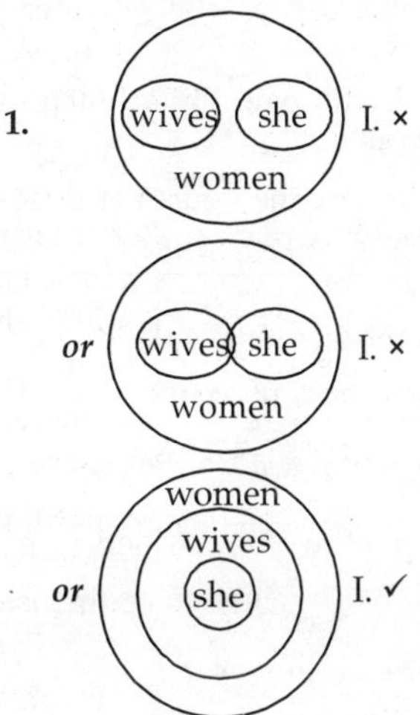

From the above diagrams, we find that the given inference is probably true or false.

2. The word 'Elephant' is not related to any of the given statements.

3. The word 'yesterday' is not connected with all the given statements.

4.

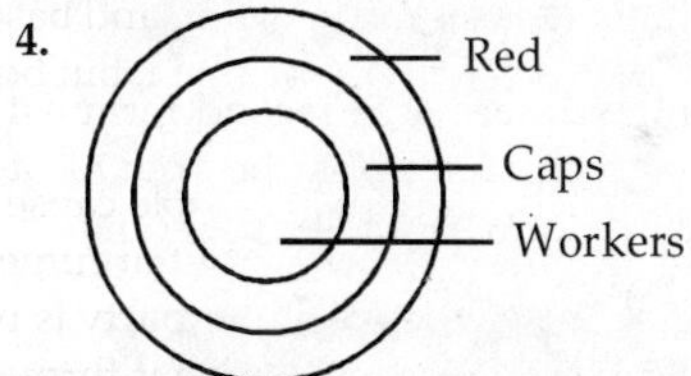

5. From the 1st statement it may be said that some metals may not be malleable or ductile. As X is neither malleable or ductile, therefore 'X' as a metal cannot be said definitely.

6. Since the buses of route number 10 generally go to stadium, therefore, some buses may be such which do not go to stadium. Hence it cannot be said definitely that this bus goes to stadium.

7. The word 'Enemy' is not related to the given statements.

8. As P is behind M and N, and Q is behind P, therefore, Q will be behind M.

9. It is not definite that Manish is healthy but with the given statements it may be said to some extent that Manish is healthy.

10. The voting age has not been given here. So we cannot definitely say about the age of the child. We can only assess the boy on the basis of the voting age common in India and boys of this age generally have handsome personality.

11. The inference is not definitely true because of the fallacy of division.

12. No conclusion can be drawn from two particular premises.

13.

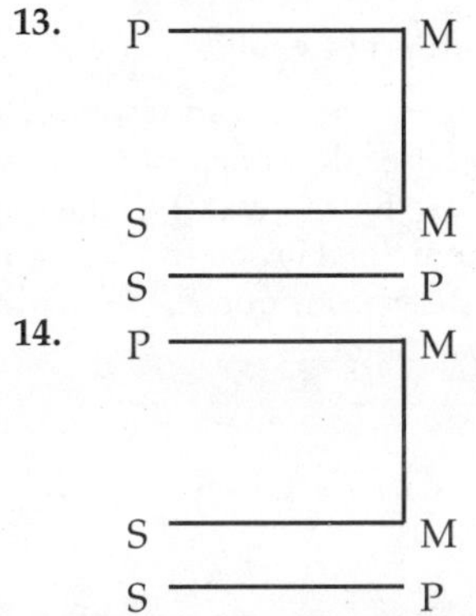

15. The major term cannot be the subject of the conclusion so it is not true. So the inference may be probably true or probably false.

22.

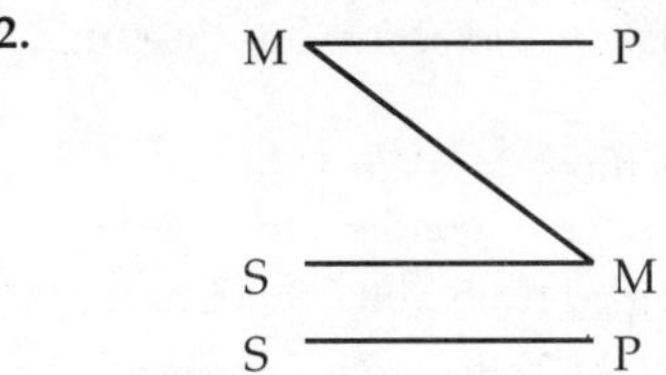

P is not true because if one of the premises is particular its conclusion must be particular. Statement Q is true, because it is given according to the rule of syllogism.

23. The figure for statement P will be

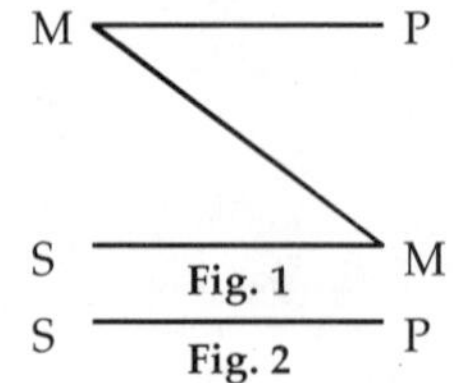

Here the conclusion is based on EIO which is valid according to Figure No. I. So P statement is correct. Statement Q is not true, because it is not given according to the rule of syllogism.

24. Statement P is true because it is a disjunctive syllogism but statement Q is not true because it says that those who are rich commit suicide. It does not mean that only rich commit suicide. There may be people other than rich who commit suicide. Its figure is

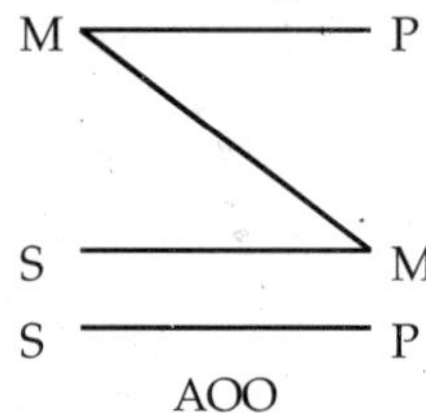

This AOO syllogism is not valid.

25. Statement P is wrong because major term cannot be the subject of the conclusion. In the statement Q there are four terms (i) a Newton, (ii) solve this problem, (iii) He and (iv) Newton. Here 'a Newton' is a common noun while Newton is a proper noun.

Analogy Test

Type I

1. Just as birds fly, snake crawls.
2. Soldier uses Gun and Blacksmith uses Hammer.
3. Apple is a fruit. Taj Mahal is a monument.
4. Motor bike uses petrol as fuel. Bus uses diesel as fuel.
5. Friday comes three days after Monday. Like that August comes three months after April.
6. Butter is obtained from Milk, Oil from seeds.
7. As sun gives light, in the same way fire gives heat.
8. As 'house' is made with 'walls', in the same way 'wall' is made with bricks.
9. Since 'atmosphere' is the biggest part which contains 'air', in the same way 'ocean' is the biggest part which contains 'water.'
10. As 'oil' is used in 'lamp' in the same way 'wax' is used in 'candle'.
11. As 'pond' is the small form of 'ocean', in the same way 'shallow' is the small form of 'deep'.
12. As 'sponge' is soft, in the same way 'knife' is sharp.
13. As disease is studied under pathology, in the same way planets are studied under astronomy.
14. As ankle is the lower part of knee, in the same way 'wrist' is the lower part of elbow.
15. As 'staircase' has many steps, in the same way 'army' has number of soldiers.
16. As 'litre' is the unit of volume, in the same way 'metre' is the unit of length.
17. As 'newspaper' is printed in 'press', similarly 'cloth' is made in mill.
18. As 'time' is known by 'clock', similarly 'light' is obtained from lamp.
19. As kangaroo is found in Australia, similarly giraffe is found in Africa.
20. As cricket is played with bat, similarly tennis is played with ball.
21. As 'sphere' and 'cube' are the figures of three dimensions so 'circle' and 'square' are the figures of two dimensions.
22. First word is the opposite of the second word.
23. Snakes use fang and bees use sting when they attack.
24. b, c, d are not colours.
25. First word is the opposite of the second word.

Type II

26. Second term = (First term) + 4
 ∴ Fourth term = (Third term) + 4
27. Second term = $(\text{First term})^2 + 1$
 ∴ Fourth term = $(\text{Third term})^2 + 1$
28. Second term = $(\text{First term})^3$
 ∴ Fourth term = $(\text{Third term})^3$
29. The first term is double of the second term. Fourth term $= \frac{1}{3} \times \frac{1}{2} = \frac{1}{6}$
30. First term is the square of 3, second term is the square of 5 and third term is the square of 7. Hence the fourth term should be the square of 9.
31. First term = $(1)^2$
 Second term = $(2)^3$
 Third term = $(3)^2$
 ∴ Fourth term = $(4)^3$

32. First term = $3^2 - 1$
    Second term = $3^3 + 1$
    Third term = $4^2 - 1$
    ∴ Fourth term = $4^3 + 1$
33. Second term = First term + 3
    ∴ Fourth term = Third term + 3
34. First is a prime number. Second term is the next prime number to it. Hence the fourth term should be the next prime number to 31.
35. First term = $3^2 + 3$
    Second term = $4^2 + 4$
    Third term = $5^2 + 5$
    ∴ Fourth term = $6^2 + 6$

Type III

36. There is a gap of three letters between each corresponding letters of 'BZDX' and 'FVHT'.
37. In the two terms first letters are in reverse alphabetical order, whereas second letters and third letters are in alphabetical order.
38. CBA is the reverse of ABC, so XYZ is the reverse of ZYX.
    Similarly, N P M O ⟶ R T Q S
39. As, A B D ⟶ C D F

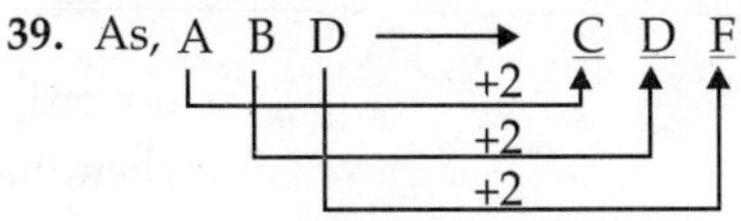

    Similarly, M N P ⟶ O P R
40. There is a gap of three letters between each corresponding letters of YAWC and UESG.
41. First two letters of the first term are in reverse order in the second and so are the next two letters.
42. As, J L N ⟶ S Q O
    (+9, +5, +1)
    Similarly, P R T ⟶ Y W U
43. There is a gap of one letter between the first letters of PCWL and REXM and also a gap of one letter between the second letters but third letters and fourth letters are in sequence.
44. Capital letter in the first term is the small letter in the second term and small letters in the first term are capital letters in the second term.
45. As, D R I V E N ⟶ E I D R V N
    5 3 1 2 4 6
    Similarly, B E G U M (1 2 3 4 5) ⟶ M G B E U (5 3 1 2 4)

Type IV

46. As pork is the meat of a pig, while mutton is the meat of sheep.
47. As filter removes impurities from water, while censor removes obscenities from plays.
48. The prime constituent of cigarette is tobacco. Similarly, the prime constituent of coffee is caffeine.
49. The antonym of savage is civilized. Similarly, the antonym of dark is lighted.
50. Both knife and chopper are used for the same purpose cutting. Similarly, both quilt and blanket are used for protection from cold.
51. Flag is the symbol of nation. Similarly, insignia is the symbol of rank.
52. As 'braille' is the system of reading and writing for the blind persons. Similarly, 'sign language' is the system of reading and writing for deaf persons.
53. As 'success' is the opposite to failure, similarly, opposite to 'big' is 'small'.
54. As England is situated in 'Atlantic ocean', similarly 'Green Land' is situated in 'Arctic Ocean".
55. As 'kennel' is the place where pet dogs are kept and 'cage' is the place where pet 'birds' are kept.
56. As 'boat' is rowed with the help of 'oar', similarly bicycle is propelled by paddle.
57. As 'mountain' is antonym of 'valley', likewise 'friend' is the antonym of 'enemy.'.
58. As 'demographer' is related with the study of statistics related to people, similarly, 'philatelist' is related with the study of 'stamps.'
59. As 'parrot' flies, 'crocodile' crawls.
60. As the lower part of feet of 'horse' is known as 'hoof.' In the same way lower part of feet of 'eagle' is known as 'claw'.
61. As 'pen' and 'pencil' are the articles to write and 'hockey' and 'football' are the items to play.
62. As 'wine' is made from 'grapes', in the same way 'vodka' is made from 'flour'.
63. As 'conduction' is the property of 'metal' due to which current flows in the metal. Similarly, 'insulation' is the property of 'plastic' due to which current does not flow in it.
64. As the function of 'eye' is to 'see' and that of 'ear' is to 'hear'.
65. As 'liberty' is opposite to 'slavery', in the same way 'danger' is opposite to 'safety'.

66. As 'expression' of a person is read from the 'face', likewise 'gesture' of a person is read from the position of 'hand.'

67. One of the outcome of 'match' is 'victory' likewise 'success' is one of the outcomes of 'examination.'

68. As 'tall' is opposite to 'dwarf', in the same way 'cruel' is also opposite to 'kind'.

69. As 'cube' comprises 'square' on all of its surfaces, in the same way 'square' comprises 'line' on all of its sides.

70. As 'blood' flows in 'vein' in the same way as 'oil' flows in 'pipelines'.

Type V

71. As cold is related to January, similarly hot is related to June.

72. Functions of various professionals have been given here.

73. Hands have fingers, feet have toes and heads have hair.

74. Prose is written by writers and poetry is composed by poets.

75. Pullies make the machines in order when they are fitted, in the same way wheels make the car in order when they are attached with.

76. Supervisor supervises workers and so is the case of officer and clerk.

77. Pulp is used as a raw material for making paper. Wood and yarn are used as raw materials for furniture and fabric respectively.

78. Chemistry is a branch of science and painting is a branch of arts.

79. House is taken on rent, in the same way interest is paid on capital, fare is paid on using train, etc.

80. Car is kept in garage. In the same way lion lives in den. Cows in byre, Horse in stable, etc.

UNIT VII

DATA INTERPRETATION

Syllabus

- Sources, Acquisition and Classification of Data.
- Quantitative and Qualitative Data.
- Graphical Representation (Bar-chart, Histograms, Pie-chart, Table-chart and Line-chart) and Mapping of Data.
- Data Interpretation.
- Data and Governance.

DATA AND ITS SOURCES

Data is the elementary facts which constitute our knowledge according to their relation and our interest. Data is the term used to refer to the raw numbers (facts and figures) which are thrown out from the occurrence of any event – physical, social, economic, corporate, geographical, individual and all miscellaneous kinds of events that have the potential to throw out numbers and figures. In our daily life, we come across figures, statistics and statements of all sorts. These could be anything ranging form, India's exports of various commodities to different countries, to the travel plans of any executive. In fact, rarely can we do without facts and figures. Figures, statistics, statements, etc. relating to any event are termed as data. Bills, receipts, vouchers, readings while conducting an experiment, production of trucks in India etc., are all examples of what constitute data.

But data, as such, is of very little use unless it is organised. Bills and receipts are of little use unless they are organised in a proper form, such as journals, ledgers etc. Data, when organised in a form, from which we can make interpretations, is information. In fact, the very objective of any data is to assist us in obtaining the required information.

ACQUISITION AND INTERPRETATION OF DATA

Haphazard data makes little sense and is of no use. Decision makers in an organisation rarely find enough time to go through entire details of any report - be it the daily production report or the sales forecast. Hence, what is required, is to effectively present the data in such a manner that they are able to draw upon the information which they require with the least of effort and time. Thus, effective organisation and presentation of data is of prime importance.

Some useful tips for tackling data interpretation questions

- Data interpretation questions are based on information given in tables and graphs. These questions test the candidates' ability to interpret the information presented and to select the appropriate data for answering a question.
- Get a general picture of the information before reading the questions. Read the given titles carefully and try to understand its nature.
- Avoid lengthy calculations. Generally, data interpretation questions do not require to do extensive calculations and computations. Most questions simply require reading the data correctly and carefully and putting them to use directly with common sense.

Data Interpretation

The act of organising and interpreting data to get meaningful information is data interpretation.

The interpretation of data is the process through which inferences are drawn about the data available for analysis.

Decision-making is seldom done without any survey or research. Hence, interpretation and analysis of the data thus obtained is most important for the decision-making process.

Data Interpretation vs. Problem Solving. Each of the problems in Problem Solving questions has a basic concept and there is a specific methodology available to tackle them. Data Interpretation requires only the concept of arithmetic and statistics. It majorly deals with the comparison of numbers and is not formulae-based. In Data Interpretation, culling out the requisite data is the first step.

Data Representation

The numerical data pertaining to any situation can be presented in the form of :

1. **Numerical data tables.** It's the easiest way of presenting data but it does not show trends effectively.
2. **Line graphs.** It is easy to spot trends in the given data, though it is difficult to read the actual values.
3. **Bar charts.** The data is shown in blocks and direct comparison of actual values is very easy.
4. **Pie charts.** Data that is expressed as percentages is best represented in pie charts.
5. **Caselet form.** It is the most difficult and raw form for data interpretation.
6. **Geometrical diagrams.** Knowledge of geometry, such as formulae for circumference, area of circle etc. helps.

QUANTITATIVE AND QUALITATIVE DATA

Data, which can be expressed in numbers, are quantitative data, while those which express virtue or quality in an observation, are known as qualitative data.

Numerical Data Table

Any statistical data pertaining to any kind of situation can be generally represented in the form of a table. It is one of the easiest and the most accurate way of presenting data in a non-graphical manner. It correlates two things or measures at a time. The difficulty associated with this type of data representation is that it requires much closer reading as compared to other forms of data representation like bar graphs and pie charts and hence they are comparatively complicated and time consuming to interpret. The calculations which are done on the basis of numerical table to draw inferences are easy in terms of formulae but they are lengthy and take lots of time.

The following examples will explain in detail the way of representing data in numerical table form and how various useful inferences can be drawn from these tables.

Example 1. The financial statements of an individual company of a section of the industry are normally represented in the form of a table. The representation could be for a particular year or for a period of time. The following table represents such a data table.

WORKING RESULTS OF ALL PUBLIC SECTOR AND FOREIGN BANKS FOR THE YEAR 1999-2000
(Figures in Rs. Crores)

Particulars	Public Sector Banks	Foreign Banks
(a) Income (i + ii)	53665	6083
(i) Interest Income	46620	4969
(ii) Other Income	7045	1114
(b) Expenditure (i + ii + iii + iv)	54036	5335
(i) Interest expended	30961	3184
(ii) Provisions & Contingencies	7940	828
(iii) Wage Bill	11136	461
(iv) Other Operating expenses	3999	862
(c) Profit		
(i) Operating Profit	7569	1576
(ii) Net Profit	(–)371	748
(d) Total Assets	505845	47547

The given table represents the financial information of two sectors for the year 1999-2000 for the Indian Banking System. This is actually a picture of the financial results for the year. One can calculate various financial ratios from the above.

- The operating profit as a percentage of the Total Assets for the Foreign Banks and for the Public Sector Banks can be found.
- The Return On Total Assets (ROTA) which is a financial ratio and which is defined as the Net Profit as a percentage of the Total Asset. ROTA in case of Foreign Banks is 1.57.
- It can be seen that the Public Sector Banks made Net Loss where as the foreign banks made Net Profit, also Wage bill has been less in case of the Foreign banks.
- If the above data is given for successive years, comparison of various components of the data over the years can be made.

Example 2.

PRICES OF VARIOUS COMPONENTS AT VARIOUS VOLUMES IN RS./COMPONENT

	1000 units	2000 units	3000 units	4000 units
Component 1	8	7	6	5
Component 2	10	10	10	10
Component 3	15	10	5	5
Component 4	9	8	7	6

The table highlights how prices vary with increasing volumes for each component. We can deduce following from the above table.

- How many units of each component can we get for a given sum (try for Rs. 1000)?
- How much will it cost to buy a given volume of the above components ?

- If a product is composed of a combination of the above components, we can understand how many units of the product we can buy for a given sum of money.
- For the above mentioned product, we can find out how much a given volume would cost.
- If a trader was buying the above components and selling us the product, we can find out his profit margin if we know the selling price.

Example 3. The following table shows the time table of a train.

RAILWAY TIMETABLE - GITANJALI EXPRESS

Cities	Arrival times (hrs.)	Departure times (hrs).	Cumulative mileages (kms.)
Mumbai		09.00	0
Igatpuri	11:00	11:02	80
Nasik	14:50	14:55	281
Bhusaval	17:10	17:12	391
Akola	22:40	22:45	730
Nagpur	00:05	00:15	800
Durg	01:00	01:02	845
Jamshedpur	04:15	04:28	995
Kolkata	06:25	–	1100

The above is also a type of data representation but is in the timetable form. However, very interesting information can be interpreted from the above table. One can obtain :

- The average speed between the stations.

  The average speed of the train between the stations $= \dfrac{\text{distance covered}}{\text{time taken in hrs.}}$

  e.g., the average speed of the train between Mumbai and Igatpuri

  $$= \frac{80-0}{11:02-09:00} = \frac{80 \text{ kms}}{2 \text{ hrs.}} \text{ approx.} = 40 \text{ kms/hour approx.}$$

- Similarly the average speed between the other stations, for parts of the journey as well as the complete journey can be calculated.
- The relative distance between the stations and the relative travelling time.
- The portion of waiting time in the total travel time

Example 4. The data pertaining to the production of two wheelers in India is represented below :

PRODUCTION OF TWO-WHEELERS IN INDIA

Years	Scooters	Motor Cycles	Mopeds	Total
1995-96	642083	302520	449688	1394291
1996-97	725735	429037	445694	1600466
1997-98	766620	430366	406081	1603067
1998-99	833802	461955	460398	1756155
1999-2000	1225895	809087	621035	2656017

The above table pertains to the data on the production of two-wheelers, year wise, from 1995-96 to 1999-2000. Further, the table also divides the production of two-wheelers by categories viz., Scooters, Motor Cycles and Mopeds. Thus it is possible to get a picture of the production of different types of two-wheelers in India over a span of five years.

The above table can be subjected to the following interpretations:

- Contribution of each type of two-wheeler towards the total, in a given year or, for that matter, successive years.
  e.g., the contribution of scooters in terms of the percentage of the total production in 1999-2000 was

$$= \frac{\text{Production of Scooters}}{\text{Total Production of two wheelers in India}} \times 100$$

$$= \frac{1225895}{2656017} \times 100 = 46.16\%$$

- Rate of growth in each type of two-wheeler, at the same time growth rate of the total sector over the successive years.
  e.g., growth of the Motorcycles in India from 1998-99 to 1999-2000

$$= \frac{\text{(Prodn. of Motorcycles in 1999-2000 – Prodn. of Motorcycles in 1998-99)}}{\text{(Production of Motorcycles in the year 1998-99)}} \times 100$$

$$= \frac{809087 - 461955}{461955} \times 100 = 75.14\%$$

- Given the installed capacity, one can deduce the capacity utilization.
  e.g., if the installed capacity of the two wheelers was 3000000 in the year 1999-2000

$$\text{Capacity utilization} = \frac{2656017}{3000000} \times 100 = 88.53\%$$

- The trends of growth over the years for each type of two-wheeler and total production of two-wheelers. It can be observed from the table that production of scooters has shown a continuously increasing trends from year 1995-96 to 1999-2000. Even the production of Motorcycles and total two-wheelers production show the same trend whereas production of Mopeds has shown decreasing trend from year 1995-96 to 1997-98 and then increasing trend from 1997-98 to 1999-2000.

Solved Examples

Directions: For examples 1 to 5, refer to the following tables.

TABLE X : USE OF PESTICIDES FOR PUBLIC HEALTH (IN TONNES)

	1996	1997	1998	1999	2000
BHC	5600	6000	6650	7030	12000
DDT	7000	8000	7176	7176	6000
Malathion	500	700	1000	1000	1000
Total	13100	14700	14826	15206	19000

TABLE Y : USE OF PESTICIDES FOR AGRICULTURE (IN TONNES)

	1996	1997	1998	1999	2000
BHC	15300	18340	18500	17500	16640
DDT	2000	3970	2934	1294	2450
Malathion	430	750	640	875	943
Others	19242	19477	20173	16984	19855
Total	36972	42537	42247	36653	39888

Example 1. The trend followed by the use of pesticides in Agriculture can be best described as

(A) Continuously increasing (B) Continuously decreasing

(C) Fluctuating (D) None of these

Solution. (C)

After checking the figures of total pesticides in Agriculture, we see that it increased from 36972 in year 1996 to 42537 in year 1997 and then decreased in year 1998 and also in year 1999 and then again increased in year 2000. Hence, it shows fluctuating trend.

Example 2. On an average, roughly what percent of the total pesticide use for Public Health was Malathion ?

(A) 5.47% (B) 5.48%

(C) 5.49% (D) 5.50%

Solution. (A)

Total pesticides used for Public Health in the 5 years

$= 13100 + 14700 + 14826 + 15206 + 19000 = 76832$ tonnes

Total Malathion used in the five years $= 500 + 700 + 1000 + 1000 + 1000 = 4200$

$$\therefore \text{Average } \% = \frac{4200}{76832} \times 100 = 5.47\%$$

Example 3. The use of BHC, DDT and Malathion in Agriculture was 'X' percent of total pesticides used in Agriculture in 1998. Then 'X' was approximately

(A) 46% (B) 47%

(C) 48% (D) 50%

Solution. (D)

$$X = \frac{(42247 - 20173)}{42247} \times 100 = 52\% \text{ (approx.)}$$

Example 4. Total BHC used in Public Health in the last 2 years as a percent of total BHC used in Public Health and Agriculture in the last 2 years was about :

(A) 36% (B) 38%

(C) 40% (D) 41%

Solution. (A)

Total BHC used in Public Health in 1999 & 2000 $= 7030 + 12000 = 19030$

Total BHC used in 1999 & 2000 = Sum of BHC used for Public Health and BHC used for Agriculture

$= 7030 + 12000 + 17500 + 16640 = 53170.$

$$\text{Then, required } \% = \frac{19030}{53170} \times 100 = 36\% \text{ approx.}$$

Example 5. The peak use of DDT for both Public Health and Agriculture together was in which year ?

(A) 1996 (B) 1997

(C) 1998 (D) 1999

Solution. (B)

Use of DDT in 1996 $= 7000 + 2000 = 9000$ tonnes

Use of DDT in 1997 $= 8000 + 3970 = 11970$ tonnes

Use of DDT in 1998 $= 7176 + 2934 = 10110$ tonnes

Use of DDT in 1999 $= 7176 + 1294 = 8470$ tonnes

Use of DDT in 2000 $= 6000 + 2450 = 8450$ tonnes

Hence the peak use was 11970 tonnes in the year 1997.

Directions. For examples 6 to 7, refer to the following table :

PROJECTED AVAILABILITY AND DEMAND FOR STEEL (FOR THE PERIOD 2004-2005 AND 2012-2013)

(*000 tonnes)

Sr. No.	Category	2004-2005		2012-2013	
		Demand	Availability	Demand	Availability
1.	Shapes	6960	5725	9745	9360
2.	Flats	4360	5020	6300	6600
3.	Railway Material	400	550	450	560

Example 6. The what percentage growth is in the demand for Railway Material over the eight year period from 2004-2005 to 2012-2013 ?

(A) 10.5%
(B) 11.5%
(C) 12.5%
(D) 13.5%

Solution. (C)

$$\text{Percentage growth in demand} = \frac{(\text{Demand in 2012 - 2013}) \pm (\text{Demand in 2004 - 2005})}{\text{Demand in 2004 - 2005}} \times 100$$

$$= \frac{450 - 400}{400} \times 100 = 12.5\%$$

Example 7. The percentage change in shortfall of shapes over the eight year period from 2004-2005 to 2012-2013 is expected to be

(A) 69%
(B) 71%
(C) 72%
(D) 75%

Solution. (A)

Shortfall in shapes in 2004-2005 = (6960-5725) 1000 = 1235000

Shortfall in shapes in 2012-2013 = (9745-9360) 1000 = 385000

$$\therefore \text{Percentage decrease} = \frac{1235 - 385}{1235} \times 100 = 68.83\% \equiv 69\%$$

Graphical Representation and Mapping of Data

1. Cartesian Graph or Line Graph

The Cartesian or Line Graph indicates the variation of a parameter with respect to another. The parameters are calibrated on X and Y axes. For example, with the 'year' plotted on the X axis, variation of 'imports', 'exports', 'shipments' etc. as the other parameter can be plotted on the Y axis.

Characteristics. The line graph simplifies the data interpretation, as it is a pictorial presentation of data and is therefore very useful for determining trends and rate of change. The slope of the line graph helps in comparing the magnitude of change between any two consecutive points on the graph. Steeper the slope, greater is the change in magnitude between the two consecutive points.

Note : The slope of the graph indicates the absolute growth and not the percentage growth.

Methods.

1. Simple Average Growth is found out by Simple Interest Methods.
2. Cumulative means the increase or growth by accumulation or successive addition of parts or elements.
3. Cumulative Average Growth Rate (CAGR) is different from simple average growth in the sense that, simple average growth is the growth between two points of measurement or time.
4. Cumulative Average Growth Rate is found by Compound Interest Method. Hence, increase in each period is accounted while calculating the increase in the next period.

Illustrative Examples

Example 1. On many occasions the data can be represented on a number of graphs which may be interrelated. The data regarding the transfer of resources from centre to states is indicated in the following three graphs.

A. TOTAL RECEIPTS OF CENTRE (RS. CRORE)

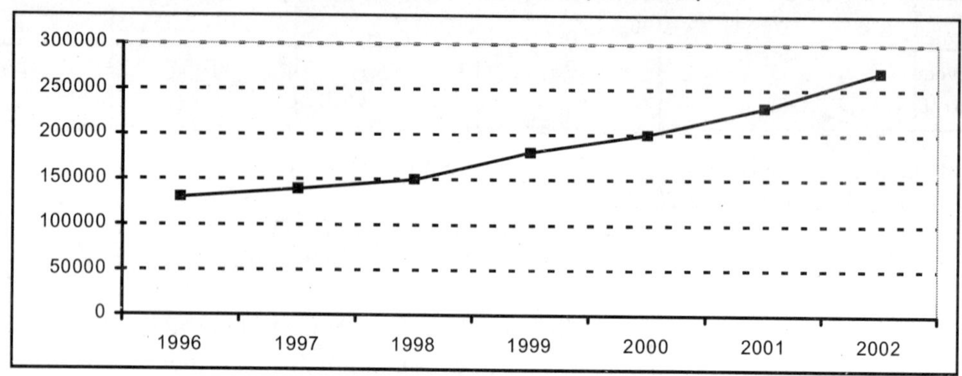

B. TRANSFER OF RESOURCES FROM CENTRE TO STATE (RS. CRORE)

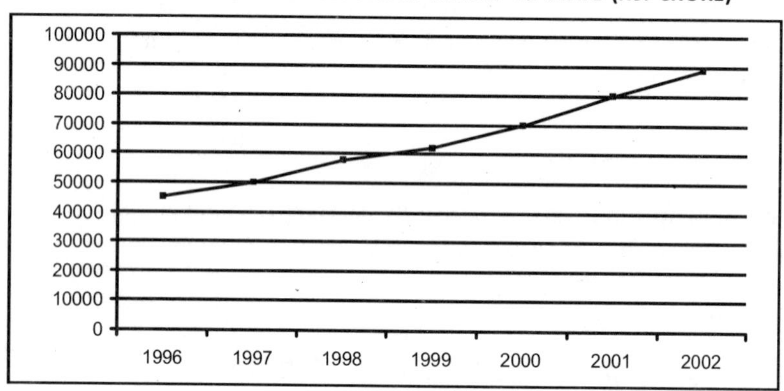

C. RESOURCES FROM STATES TO CENTRE (RS. CRORE)

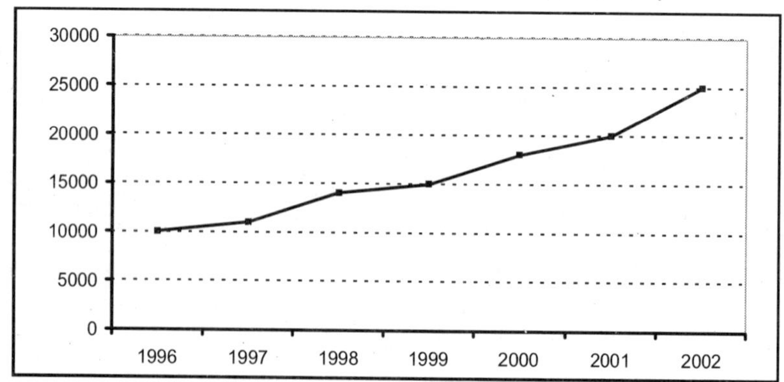

In the illustration given, the data pertains to the flow of resources to Centre and States during the period 1996-2002.

Additional data can be derived from the above graphs.

e.g., The Net Transfers from Centre to State = Transfer of Resources from Centre to States - Resources from States to Centre. (In a particular year or period).

The Net Transfers from Centre to State in 2001 = 80000-20000 = Rs. 60000 crores

Solved Examples

Directions. For examples 1 to 5, refer to the line graph given below :

The given Cartesian Graph shows the Total Revenues v/s Period and Net Profit (Loss) v/s Period of Indian Airlines.

	1992-93	1993-94	1994-95	1995-96	1996-97	1997-98	1998-99	1999-2000	2000-01	2001-02
Total Revenue	40.4	47.4	44.89	56.84	70.05	70.61	98.05	111.17	132.85	152.36
Net Profit/Loss	1.85	2.28	–4.67	–4.54	0.01	1.04	1.01	7.79	14.32	20.73

Revenue – Expenses = Net Profit (Loss)

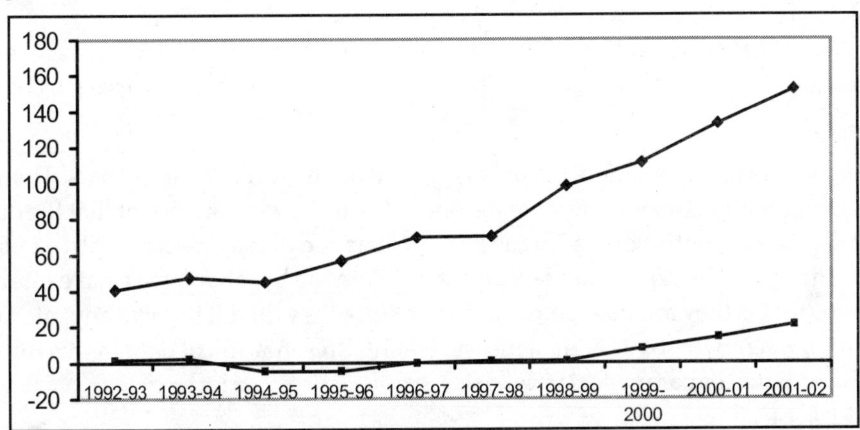

Example 1. If the growth rate, as was observed between the financial years 2000-01 and 2001-02, was maintained, then what is the total revenue for the year ending 2002-2003 would be approximately in Rs. crore:

(A) 170 (B) 171.88 (C) 175 (D) 180

Solution. (B)

Percentage change in revenue in 2001-2002 was $\frac{152.36-132.85}{152.36} \times 100 = 12.81\%$

Revenue for 2002-2003 would be $152.36 \times \frac{(100+12.81)}{100} = 171.88.$

Example 2. In which year was the Net profit as a percentage of the Total Revenue highest ?

(A) 2001-2002 (B) 1999-2000 (C) 1997-1998 (D) 1998-1999

Solution. (A)

Profit as a percentage of the revenue was over 10% in 2 years. *i.e.*, 2000-2001 and 2001-2002 whereby the percentage are 10.78 and 13.61 respectively.

Example 3. In how many years of total revenue and Net Profit (Loss) were similar for each year except between the financial years.

(A) 1 year (B) 2 years (C) 3 years (D) 4 years

Solution. (B)

Compare the slopes (rise/decline) of the two graphs. For all the years they rise or fall simultaneously. Thus, we can say that between 1992-93 and 1993-94, and 1997-98 and 1998-99, Net Profit (Loss) remains same and Total Revenue increases.

Example 4. In how many years did Indian Airlines show a loss ?

(A) 3 years (B) 2 years
(C) 4 years (D) 1 year

Solution. (B)

The negative figures in the graph of Net Profit (Loss) v/s Period indicate the loss. The graph goes below zero in 1994-1995 and 1995-1996.

Example 5. The highest percentage of growth in the total revenue was recorded between which financial years

(A) 1998-99 (B) 1999-2000
(C) 1995-1996 (D) 1993-1994

Solution. (A)

Highest percentage growth is indicated by the steepest rise in the graph of Revenue v/s Period for successive years. In this the steeper rise is midway, 1997-1998 and continues upto part of 1998-1999.

2. Bar Charts

In this method of data representation, the data is plotted on the X and Y axes as bars. This method of data interpretation is more or less similar to the one in Cartesian Graphs except that the data plotted on Cartesian Graphs is continuous whereas in Bar Chart the data is discrete. Also, a single point denoted in the line graph is represented by an entire bar in the bar chart. They have one advantage over line graphs that is they are much more accurate since they do not involve any interpolation or extrapolation between two points & data measurement. Presentation of data in this format makes comparative evaluation of parameters very easy.

Kinds of Bar Chart

There are three main types of Bar Charts to represent data. Illustrations I, II and III illustrate three different types of Bar Charts.

I. Stacked Bar Chart

Illustrative Example.

FOREIGN INVESTMENT FLOWS (US $ MN)

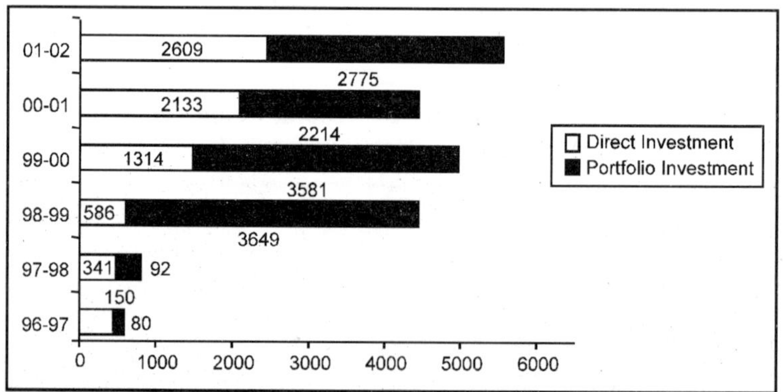

This compares the contribution of each value to the total across categories. In this, one can get the total of the categories as well as the individual figures. From this kind of representation, the same kind of conclusions can be arrived at as in Clustered Bar Chart.

II. 100% Stacked Bar

Illustrative Example.

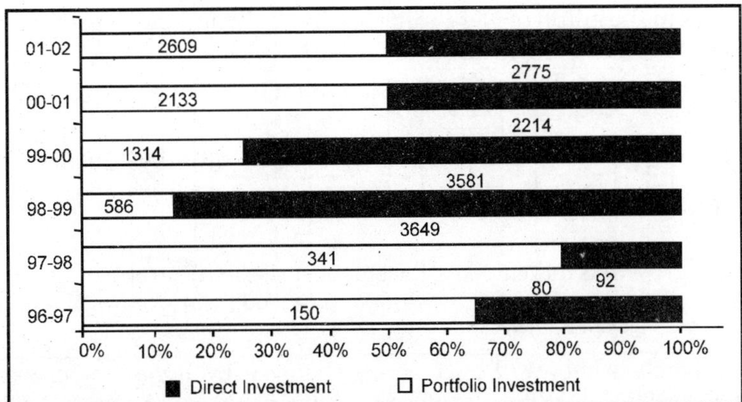

This compares values of different categories of data by the percentage contribution to the total. The percentages are given clearly, hence it is easy to derive the contribution of each category. In the figure, the amount of investment is clearly indicated. In the absence of this, given the total investment flow figures for the years, it would be easy to estimate the amount of foreign investment flows by each category.

III. Clustered Bar Chart. Illustrative Example:

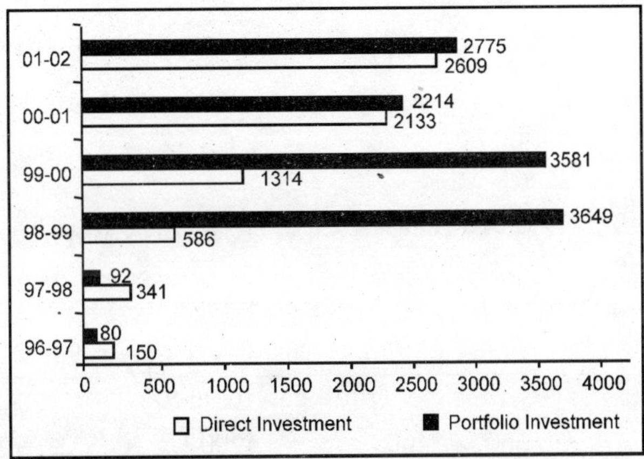

This is the simplest type of Bar Chart. It compares values across categories. Thus, from the above figure, one can see that the values of the Portfolio Investment and Direct Investments have been compared for specific years. From this one can easily arrive at the following :

- The increase or decrease in the Foreign Investment over the period with the rate of total increase or decrease (as well as for each category).
- The highest and the lowest values of the foreign investment flows by category and year.
- Contribution of each category of investment in the total foreign investment flows for the years.
- The Foreign Investment trend (total & for each category) over the years.

Solved Examples

Directions. For examples 1 to 5, refer the bar chart :

INDIA'S FOREIGN TRADE IN RS. CRORE

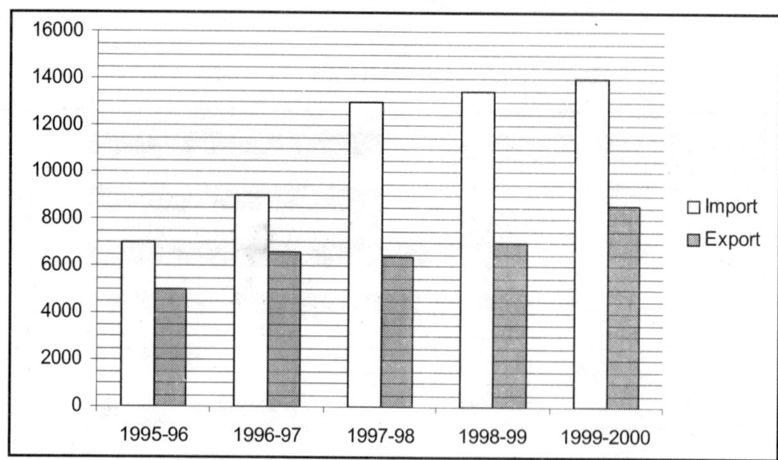

Example 1. Approximately, what was the percentage change in trade gap (imports-exports) between 1998-99 and 1999-2000 ?

(A) 17% (B) 18% (C) 19% (D) 20%

Solution. (A)

There has been a decrease in trade gap between 1998-99 and 1999-2000

Trade gap in 1998-99 = 13,500 – 7000 = 6,500

Trade gap in 1999-2000 = 14,000 – 8600 = 5400

$$\text{Percentage decrease} = \frac{6500 - 5400}{6500} \times 100$$

$$= 16.92\% \cong 17\%$$

Example 2. The percentage increase in trade gap between 1996-97 and 1997-98 was approximately

(A) 173% (B) 174% (C) 175% (D) 176%

Solution. (C)

Trade gap in 1996-97 = 9000 – 6600 = 2400

Trade gap in 1997-98 = 13000 – 6400 = 6600

Percentage increase in trade gap

$$= \frac{\text{Trade gap in 97-98} - \text{Trade gap in 96-97}}{\text{Trade gap in 96-97}} \times 100$$

$$= \frac{6600 - 2400}{2400} \times 100 = \frac{4200}{2400} \times 100 = 175\%$$

Example 3. If oil imports constituted 20% of the total imports in 1997-98, then what percent of the trade gap was due to oil (assuming that no oil is exported) ?

(A) 30% (B) 40% (C) 50% (D) 60%

Solution. (B)

Oil imports in 1997-98 = $\frac{20}{100} \times 13000$ = Rs. 2600 crore, Trade gap in 1997-98 = 6600

Hence, percentage of trade gap due to oil = $\frac{2600}{6600} \times 100$

$= 39.39\% \cong 40\%.$

Example 4. The percentage increase in imports between 1995-96 and 1999-2000 was

(A) 25% (B) 50% (C) 75% (D) 100%

Solution. (D)

Imports in 1995-96 = 7000 crore rupees

Imports in 1999-2000 = 14000 crore rupees

$$\text{Percentage increase in imports} = \frac{\text{Imports in 1999-2000} - \text{Imports in 1995-96}}{\text{Imports in 1995-96}} \times 100\%$$

$$\text{Therefore, increase in imports} = \frac{14000 - 7000}{7000} \times 100$$

$$= \frac{7000}{7000} \times 100$$

$$= 100\%$$

Alternately, imports have doubled in size from 1995-96 to 1999-2000. Hence there is a 100% increase.

Example 5. Which of the following is true ?

1. In all the years, exports are greater than imports.
2. Trade gap is continuously increasing
3. Trade gap is continuously decreasing.
4. The rate of increase of exports has always been greater than that of imports.
5. The trade gap first increases and then exhibits a decreasing trend.

(A) only 5 (B) 1, 3 and 5 (C) 1, 2 and 3 (D) 2 and 3

Solution. (D)

1. In all years imports are greater than exports.
2. and 3. There is no definite pattern related to trade gap.
4. This is not true.
5. From careful observation only this statement is true.

Directions. For examples 6 to 10, refer to the bar chart.

PERCENTAGE OF HOUSEHOLDS USING VARIOUS HOUSEHOLD UTILITIES

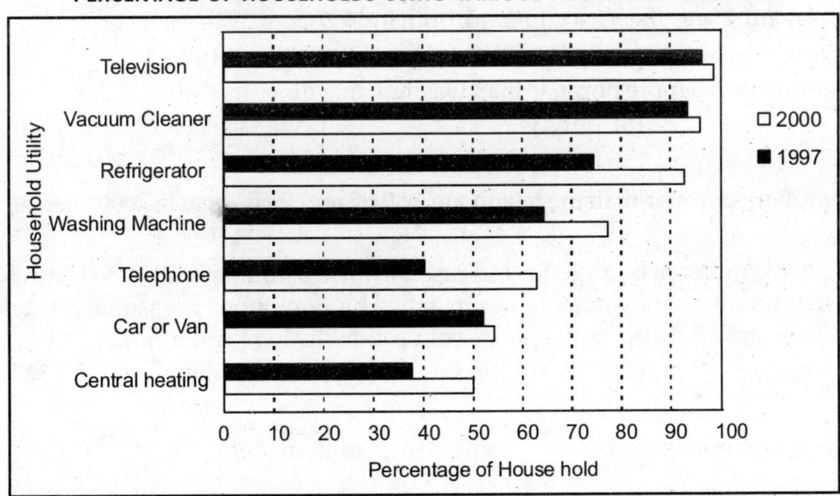

Example 6. Assuming that the number of households was the same in 1997 and 2000, which household utility showed the maximum percentage increase in popularity from 1997 to 2000 ?

(A) Car
(B) Washing machine
(C) Television
(D) Telephone

Solution. (D)

Since the number of households remains the same, a comparison of percentages for 1997 and 2000 will give the answer. A visual inspection shows that the choice is between telephone and refrigerator.

$$\% \text{ Increase in telephone popularity} = \frac{63-40}{40} \times 100 = 57.5\%$$

$$\% \text{ Increase in refrigerator popularity} = \frac{95-75}{75} \times 100 = 26.67\%$$

Example 7. In 1997, if the total number of households was 403 million, what would the number of households having washing machines be in millions ?

(A) 255 million
(B) 260 million
(C) 262 million
(D) 265 million

Solution. (C)

Percentage of households having washing machines in 1997 = 65%

Hence, number of households having washing machines in 1997

= 65% × total number of households = 65% × 403 million = 261.95 million ≅ 262 million.

Example 8. If all the household utility devices are ranked in the order of their popularity in 1997, which of the above is the second most popular item ?

(A) Television
(B) Vacuum cleaner
(C) Car
(D) Refrigerator

Solution. (A)

Visual inspection of the length of the bars shows that the most popular household utility in 1997 is Television followed by Vacuum Cleaner.

Example 9. Which of the following statements is false, if the ranking lists of 1997 and 2000 are compared ?

1. Television was the most popular item, both in 1997 and 2000.
2. Central Heating was the least common, both in 1997 and 2000
3. Car or Van was less popular than the telephone in 2000 and 1997
4. Refrigerators were more popular than washing machines in 2000 and 1997.

(A) only 1
(B) only 3
(C) only 1 and 3
(D) only 1 and 4

Solution. (B)

Car or Van was more popular than the telephone in 1997 and vice versa in 2000. Hence, statement 3 is false.

Example 10. If the number of households increased from 403 million in 1997, to 600 million in 2000, what would the number of new telephones installed be in millions ? (assume one telephone per household and no one cancelled its telephone connection during the period).

(A) 216.8 million
(B) 219.8 million
(C) 320.7 million
(D) 327.5 million

Solution. (A)

$$\text{Number of telephones in 1997} = \frac{40}{100} \times 403 = 161.2 \text{ million}$$

$$\text{Number of telephones in 2000} = \frac{63}{100} \times 600 = 378 \text{ million}$$

Hence, number of new telephones installed = 378 – 161.2 = 216.8 million

3. Histogram

A histogram is a plot that lets you discover, and show, the underlying frequency distribution (shape) of a set of continuous data. This allows the inspection of the data for its underlying distribution (e.g., normal distribution), outliers, skewness, etc. An example of a histogram, and the raw data it was constructed from, is shown below:

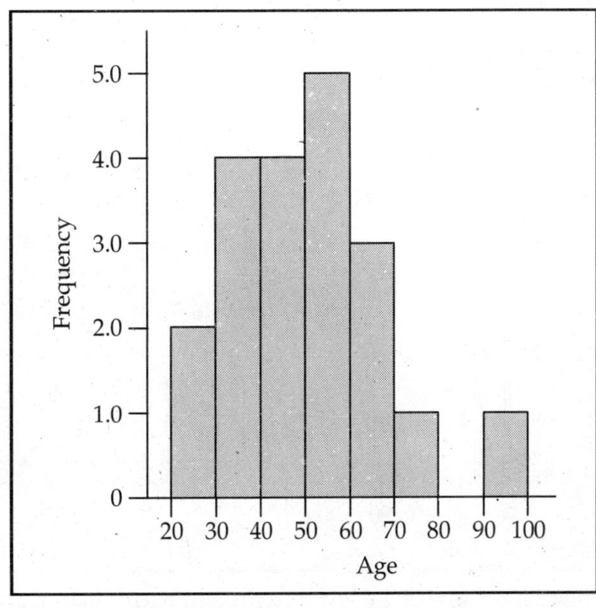

36	25	38	46	55	68	72	55	36	38
67	45	22	48	91	46	52	61	58	55

Construct a Histogram from a Continuous Variable

To construct a histogram from a continuous variable you first need to split the data into intervals, called bins. In the example above, age has been split into bins, with each bin representing a 10-year period starting at 20 years. Each bin contains the number of occurrences of scores in the data set that are contained within that bin. For the above data set, the frequencies in each bin have been tabulated along with the scores that contributed to the frequency in each bin (see below):

Bin	Frequency	Scores Included in Bin
20-30	2	25,22
30-40	4	36,38,36,38
40-50	4	46,45,48,46
50-60	5	55,55,52,58,55
60-70	3	68,67,61
70-80	1	72
80-90	0	-
90-100	1	91

Notice that, unlike a bar chart, there are no "gaps" between the bars (although some bars might be "absent" reflecting no frequencies). This is because a histogram represents a continuous data set, and as such, there are no gaps in the data (although you will have to decide whether you round up or round down scores on the boundaries of bins).

Choosing the Correct Bin Width

There is no right or wrong answer as to how wide a bin should be, but there are rules of thumb. You need to make sure that the bins are not too small or too large. Consider the histogram we produced earlier (see below): the following histograms use the same data, but have either much smaller or larger bins, as shown below:

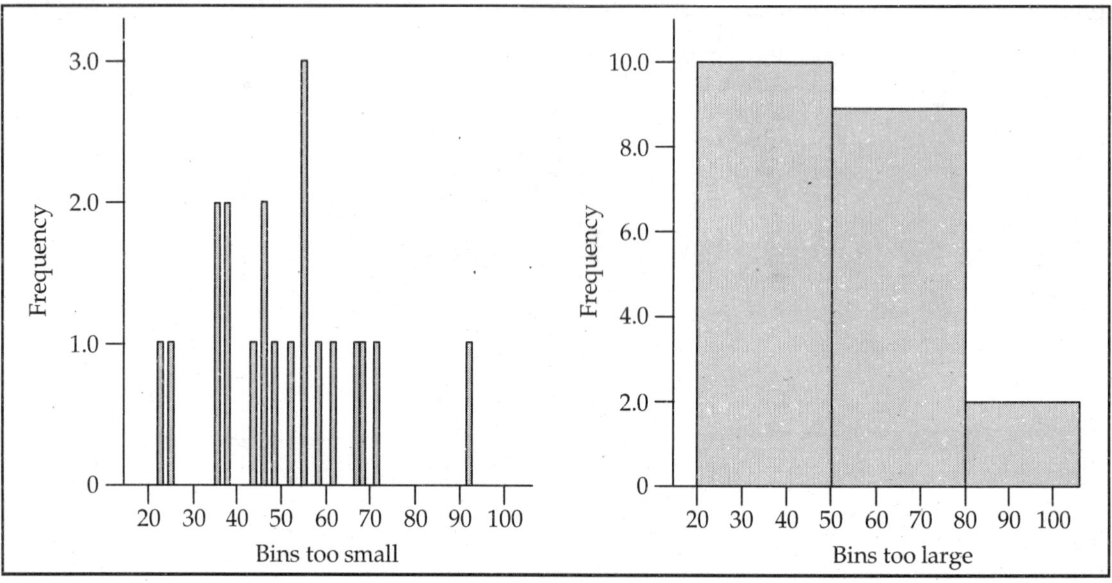

We can see from the histogram on the left that the bin width is too small because it shows too much individual data and does not allow the underlying pattern (frequency distribution) of the data to be easily seen. At the other end of the scale is the diagram on the right, where the bins are too large, and again, we are unable to find the underlying trend in the data.

In a histogram, it is the area of the bar that indicates the frequency of occurrences for each bin. This means that the height of the bar does not necessarily indicate how many occurrences of scores there were within each individual bin. It is the product of height multiplied by the width of the bin that indicates the frequency of occurrences within that bin. One of the reasons that the height of the bars is often incorrectly assessed as indicating frequency and not the area of the bar is due to the fact that a lot of histograms often have equally spaced bars (bins), and under these circumstances, the height of the bin does reflect the frequency.

DIFFERENCE BETWEEN A BAR CHART AND A HISTOGRAM

The major difference is that a histogram is only used to plot the frequency of score occurrences in a continuous data set that has been divided into classes, called bins. Bar charts, on the other hand, can be used for a great deal of other types of variables including ordinal and nominal data sets.

4. Pie Charts

In this method, the total quantity in question is distributed over a total angle of 360°, which is one complete circle or a pie. Unlike the bar charts where the variable can be plotted on two co-ordinates X and Y, here the data can be plotted with respect to only one parameter. Hence, its usage is restricted. It is best used when data pertaining to shares of various parts of a particular quantity are to be shown. This method is also useful for representing proportions or percentages of various elements with respect to the total quantity. Any angle which has its vertex at the centre of the circle is called a central angle. The shaded region shown in the pie-chart in Illustration (1) is called a sector.

Illustrative Examples

Example 1.

The given pie charts give the shares of various companies manufacturing personal computers in the total worldwide market both value-wise and unit-wise at the same point of time. From these two pie-charts, one can obtain information on the relative sizes of various companies both production-wise and sales-wise. Unit price of each computer can be arrived at and different market values of various brands can be determined.

2000 WORLD-WIDE SHIPMENT OF PERSONAL COMPUTERS

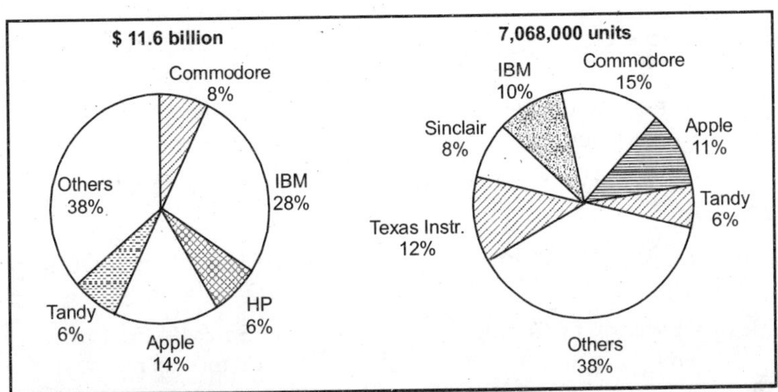

The pie-charts find more usage as a supplementary form of data representation. They are very often used in combination with the other forms of data representation like line graphs and bar charts.

Example 2.

Let's take a look at revenue scenario of the Internet Services Providers (ISP) market in the U.S. The following table gives an overview of the same for the year 1999.

Market Segment	ISP Revenues in US $ million	Percentage of Total	Central Angle
Corporate	4945	36%	$\frac{36}{100} \times 360 = 129.6^\circ$
Small Business	2516	19%	$\frac{19}{100} \times 360 = 68.4^\circ$
Consumer	6091	45%	$\frac{45}{100} \times 360 = 162^\circ$
Total	13552	100%	360°

The above data can be easily plotted on the pie chart as given below and can be subjected to interpretation.

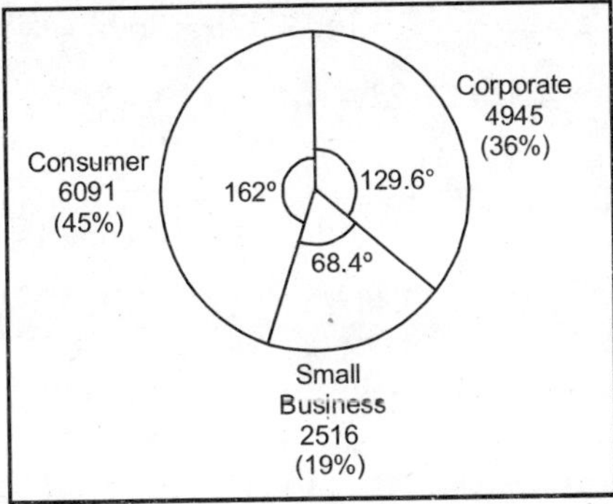

In the Pie chart above, it can be seen that the data can be plotted easily representing values as well as in terms of percentage of the total value.

By visual observation itself, one can conclude that in the US market for the year 1999, the revenue from the Consumers market was the largest and constitutes 45% of the Total revenue generated. Similarly, revenue from the Small Business market formed the smallest of the revenue generated and was 19% of the Total.

Since the data in a pie chart is spread over 360 degrees, the data can be subjected to geometrical calculations in a circle.

The central angle for the components can be easily calculated since 100% of the quantity is spread over 360 degrees of the pie and thus 1% = 3.6 degrees. In the above example, the central angle for the sector of Consumer market will be equal to 3.6 × 45 = 162 degrees.

An arc can be measured in degrees. The entire circle is 360 degrees and thus the sector area can be calculated with respect to the corresponding central angle of the sector.

Solved Examples

Directions. For example 1 to 5. The following pie charts show the sales for Dunlop in the year 1999-2000.

Sales By Location of Company
(in million pounds)

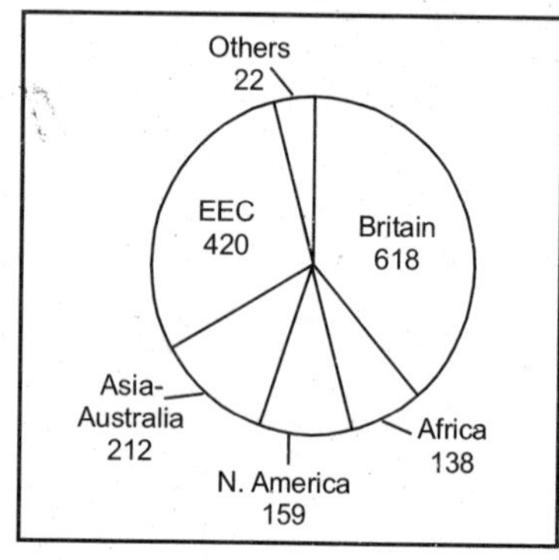

Sales By Product
(in million pounds)

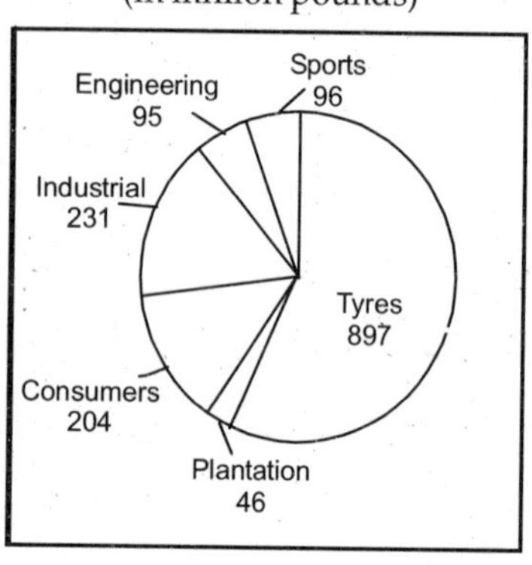

Example 1.

Sales in other countries remaining the same, if sales in Britain and the EEC countries were to double, then what can be said about their market share ?

(A) Increase 9.02%
(B) Decrease 9.02%
(C) Increase 8.02%
(D) Decrease 8.02%

Solution. (C)

Definitely with the doubling of sales in Britain and EEC countries along with the sales in other countries remaining constant, their market share is going to increase.

Total share = (420 + 618) × 2 + 22 + 212 + 159 + 138 = 2607

New EEC share = $2 \times \frac{420}{2607} \times 100 = 32.22\%$

Old EEC share = $\frac{420}{1569} \times 100 = 26.77\%$, therefore increase in share = 5.45%

Britain's new share = $\frac{2 \times 618}{2607} \times 100 = 47.41\%$

Britain's old share = $\frac{618}{1569} \times 100 = 39.39\%$

Therefore increase in its share = 8.02%.

Example 2.

If in the next year the sales of sports goods were expected to double assuming that the total sales do not change, what would be the percentage share of sports goods in the total sales ?

(A) 12.24% (B) 13.24%

(C) 14.24% (D) 15.24%

Solution. (A)

Total sales = 1569 million

Sports goods sales next year = 2 × 96 = 192 million

Therefore % share of sports goods sales = $\frac{192}{1569} \times 100 = 12.24\%$

Example 3.

If in the subsequent year, consumer products are to increase their share by 7 percent, then assuming that the total sales remain constant, the consumer sales would have to increase by how many million pounds ?

(A) 102 (B) 105

(C) 107 (D) 110

Solution. (D)

Currently, share of consumer products = $\frac{204}{1569} \times 100 = 13\%$

Let increase in consumer products sales = X million.

Therefore if the share of consumer products increases by 7% then.

$\frac{204 + X}{1569} \times 100 = 20 \quad \Rightarrow X = 109.80 \cong 110$

Example 4.

Sales in Britain accounted for approximately what percent of Dunlop's total sales ?

(A) 30% (B) 40%

(C) 50% (D) 60%

Solution. (B)

Percentage share of Britain in Dunlop's total sales = $\frac{\text{Sales in Britain}}{\text{Total Sales}} \times 100$

$= \frac{618}{1569} \times 100 = 39.39\% \cong 40\%$

Example 5.

If 20% of the tyre sales were in the EEC countries, what was the value of the sales of other products in the EEC countries in millions of pounds ?

(A) 240.6 million pounds (B) 244.5 million pounds

(C) 225 million pounds (D) 230 million pounds

Solution. (A)

If 20% of tyre sale = $\frac{20}{100} \times 897 = 179.4$ million

EEC sales = 420 million = Tyres sales + sales of other products

∴ 420 million = 179.4 million + sales of other products

Sales of other products in EEC = 420 – 179.4 = 240.6 million pounds.

Directions. For examples 6 to 10 Refer to the following pie-chart.

2000 NATIONAL BUDGET EXPENDITURE (PERCENTAGE ALLOCATION)

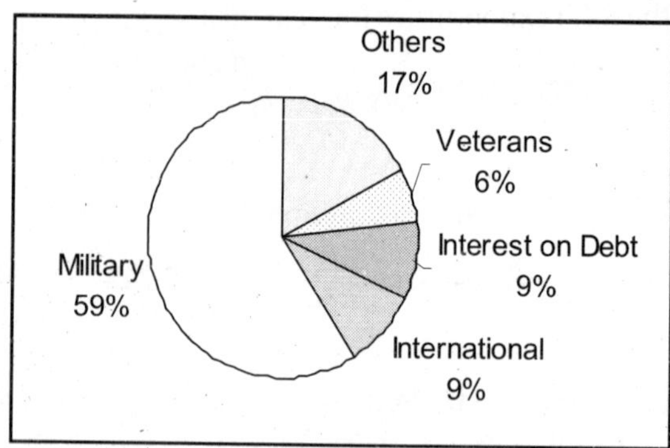

Example 6.

Approximately how many degrees should be there in the central angle of the sector for military expenditure ?

(A) 210.2 (B) 212.4 (C) 214.6 (D) 218.9

Solution. (B)

In a pie-chart where 100% of any quantity are spread over 360 degrees, 1% = 3.6 degrees. Military expenditure = 59% which is equivalent to 3.6 × 59 = 212.4 degrees

Example 7.

What is the ratio of military expenditure to veterans expenditure approximately ?

(A) 10 : 1 (B) 10 : 2 (C) 11 : 2 (D) 11 : 5

Solution. (A)

Since the budget expenditure is proportional to the percentage of the pie covered, ratio of military expenditure to veterans expenditure would be the ratio of corresponding percentage allocations.

$$\text{Therefore, } \frac{\text{Military Expenditure}}{\text{Veterans Expenditure}} = \frac{59}{6} \approx \frac{10}{1}$$

Example 8.

If India in year 2000 had a total expenditure of Rs. 120 billion rupees, approximately how many billions did it spend on interest on debt ?

(A) Rs. 11 billion (B) Rs. 12 billion (C) Rs. 13 million (D) Rs. 10.8 million

Solution. (D)

Total expenditure = 100% = 120 billion rupees

$$\text{Interest on debt} = 9\% = \text{Rs.}\left(\frac{9}{100} \times 120\right) \text{ billion}$$

$$= \text{Rs. } 10.8 \text{ billion}$$

Example 9.

If 9 billion rupees were spent in year 2000 for veterans, what would have been the total expenditure for that year in billions ?

(A) 150 billion (B) 155 billion

(C) 160 million (D) 165 million

Solution. (A)

9 billion rupees were spent for veterans.

This represents 6.0% of the total expenditure for year 2000.

$$\text{i.e., } 6 = \frac{\text{Amount spent on veterans}}{\text{Total Expenditure}} \times 100$$

$$6 = \frac{9}{\text{Total Expenditure}} \times 100$$

$$\text{Therefore, total expenditure} = \frac{9}{6} \times 100 = 150 \text{ billion rupees.}$$

Example 10.

In 1999, India spent 11% of all expenditure on interest payments. To answer the question, "Did India spend more on interest payments in 1999 than 2000"?

You

I. do not require any additional data.

II. require to know the total amount spent in 1999 and 2000.

III. the exact percentage break-up of the various items of expenses in 1999.

(A) only I

(B) only II

(C) only I and II

(D) I and III

Solution. (B)

% gives just a proportional indication of the total quantity. Unless the total expenditure is known, a percentage of that quantity is meaningless. Hence to compare the interest on debt in 1999 and 2000, we require to know the total amount spent in 1999 and 2000.

4. Mix Diagrams

Numerical Data Table, Cartesian Graphs, Bar Charts and Pie Charts are some of the most commonly used forms of data presentation. At times only one form of data representation like a graph or a table or a bar chart is sufficient to explain a situation. For example, a census report on population in various states for a particular period can be fully represented by a numeric data table. However, in real life situations, one single form of data representation need not necessarily be sufficient to describe the situation. In situations where the desired parameter is a function of two or three variables, the data has to be presented as a combination of two or more forms of data presentation.

DATA AND GOVERNANCE

One of the greatest strengths of big data is it's flexibility and universal application to so many different industries. Along with many other areas, big data in government can have an enormous impact— local, national and global. With so many complex issues on the table today, governments have their work cut out trying to make sense of all the information they receive and make vital decisions that affect millions of people. Not only is it difficult to sift through all the information, but it's sometimes difficult to verify the reality of the information itself. Faulty information can have awful consequences.

By implementing a big data platform, governments can access vast amounts of relevant information important to their daily functions. The positive effect it can have is nearly endless. It's so important because it not only allows the government to pinpoint areas that need attention, but it also gives them that information in real time. In a society that moves so quickly from one thing to the next, real-time analysis is vital. It allows governments to make faster decisions, and it allows them to monitor those decisions and quickly enact changes if necessary. Here are just a few of the areas that big data can positively affect at the government level.

Transportation

Every day millions of Americans are on the road driving. There are so many different nuances to driver safety, from roads to police officers, weather conditions and vehicle safety that it's impossible to control everything that might cause an accident. However, with big data governments can better oversee transportation to ensure better roads, safer roadways, better routes and new routes.

Healthcare

Healthcare is a very complicated issue these days, and not just here in the United States, but also across the world. With so many health systems that rely on government subsidies and support, there is a potential for resources to be wasted or to be unfairly allocated. With big data, governments can have a much clearer picture of where the money is going and why. It means they can also assume better control over resources. They can also analyze more effectively the needs of the citizens and from there make the necessary changes to provide the citizens with the best possible services for the best possible prices.

Education

Education is another extremely hot topic across the country. What can be done to improve education? There are a lot of different things to be done, and up-to-date, relevant information is vital to this. Big data helps governments understand more about educational needs on a local and federal level in order to ensure that the youth of the nation are getting the best possible education in order to serve the country in the future.

Agriculture

How do you keep track of so much land and livestock that exists in our country and across the globe? All the different crops that are grown, the animals that are held and so many other complicated issues come together in the agriculture world to form a very difficult job for the government. It's hard to monitor because of the vast numbers. Big data is changing the ways governments manage and support the farmers and their resources. It's ability to gather huge amounts of information and analyze them quickly makes all the difference.

Poverty

There is so much poverty in the world. It's extremely difficult to combat, and we've been trying to do so for thousands of years. Big data gives governments tools to discover more effective and innovative ideas on how to decrease poverty across the world. It's easier to pinpoint areas with the greatest need and how those needs can be met.

Big data technology is vitally important for governments across the world. It can't solve every problem, but it's a step in the right direction. It's giving leaders the tools necessary to enact important changes that will be of benefit for citizens now and in the future.

MULTIPLE CHOICE QUESTIONS

Directions. The following bar diagram shows the registration of cars and total vehicles during first six months of the year 1998 in Delhi :

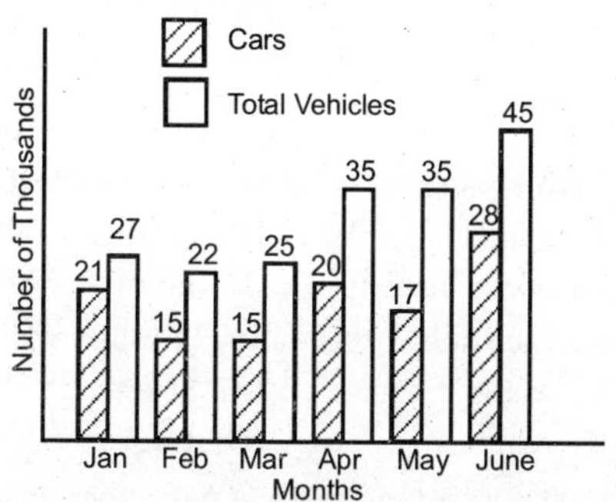

Study the above diagram and answer the questions (1 to 3) given below :

1. What was the increase in registration of vehicles other than cars from January to April 1998 ?
   (A) 5000 (B) 10000
   (C) 15000 (D) 9000
2. What was the percentage increase in registration of cars from May to June 1998 ?
   (A) 11% (B) 39.28%
   (C) 64.7% (D) None
3. What was the number of vehicles other than cars registered in March 1998 ?
   (A) 5000 (B) 10000
   (C) 40000 (D) 37000

Directions. The following pie chart shows the annual agricultural yield of a certain place :

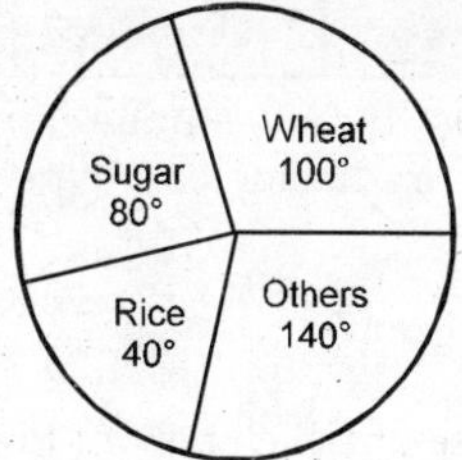

Study the above chart and answer the questions (4 to 6) given below :

4. If the total production is 8100 tons, then the yield of rice (in tons) is
   (A) 3240 (B) 900
   (C) 4860 (D) None
5. If the yield of sugar is 2400 tons, then the yield of wheat (in tons) is
   (A) 3000 (B) 1920
   (C) $666\frac{2}{3}$ (D) None
6. The production of wheat exceeds that of rice by
   (A) 50% (B) 100%
   (C) 150% (D) 250%

Direction. The following Pie diagrams shows the amounts that a family spends on food, clothing, rent, miscellaneous expenditure and savings:

7. If the annual income of the family is Rs. 60000, then the savings are :
   (A) Rs. 3000 (B) Rs. 6000
   (C) Rs. 7500 (D) Rs. 9000

Directions. Study the pie chart given below and answer the questions 8-10. The given pie chart shows the amount of subscriptions generated for India Bonds from different categories of investors.

Subscriptions Generated for India Bonds

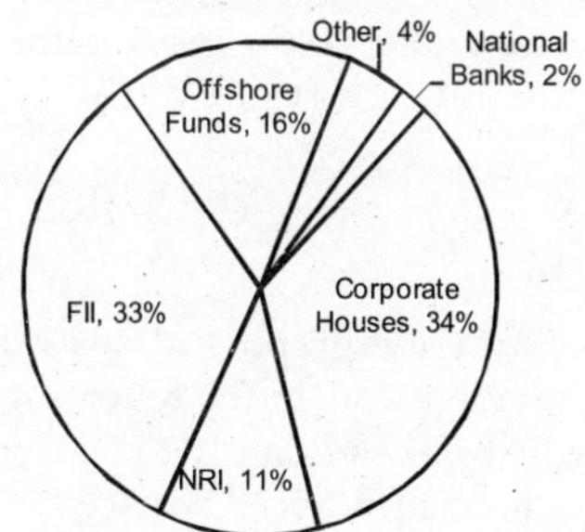

8. If the investments by NRIs are Rs 4000 crore, then the investment by corporate houses and FIIs together is
   (A) 24,000 crore (B) 24,363 crore
   (C) 25,423 crore (D) 25,643 crore
9. What percentage of the total investment is coming from either FIIs or NRIs?

(A) 33% (B) 11%
(C) 44% (D) 22%

10. What is the approximate ratio of investment flows into India Bonds from NRIs to corporate houses?
(A) 1 : 4 (B) 1 : 3
(C) 3 : 1
(D) Cannot be determined

Directions. Study the following graph and answer the questions 11-14.

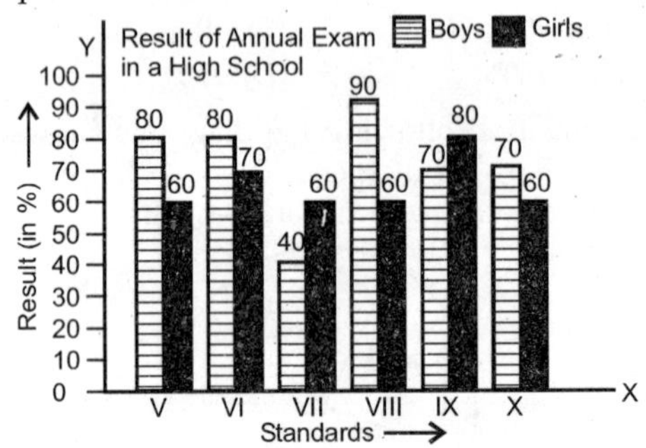

11. In which standard is the difference between the results of girls and boys maximum ?
(A) V (B) VII
(C) X (D) VIII

12. In which standard is the result of boys less than the average result of the girls ?
(A) VII (B) IX
(C) VI (D) VIII

13. In which pair of standards are the results of girls and boys in inverse proportion ?
(A) V & X (B) VI and VIII
(C) V & IX (D) VI & IX

14. In which standard is the result of the girls more than the average result of the boys for the school ?
(A) IX (B) VIII
(C) VI (D) X

Directions. Study the graph and answer the questions 15-19 given below. In the following pie graph is marks obtain by a candidate in four subjects - Math, English, Hindi, Science, Social Science are given. Full marks of the examination is 540.

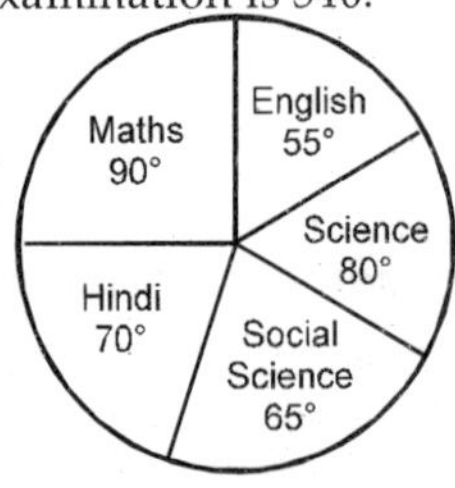

15. What is the percentage marks in math of the full marks ?
(A) 20% (B) 30%
(C) 35% (D) 25%

16. What is percentage marks of the total marks in English, Science and Social Science of the Full marks ?
(A) 45% (B) $44\frac{4}{9}\%$
(C) 55% (D) $55\frac{5}{9}\%$

17. In which subject student get 22.2% marks?
(A) Hindi (B) Science
(C) Social Science (D) English

18. In which subject student got 105 marks ?
(A) Math (B) Science
(C) Hindi (D) English

19. What percentage mark is more than the marks obtain in three subject: – English, Science and Social Science from the marks obtain in Hindi and Math ?
(A) 10% (B) 11%
(C) $11\frac{1}{9}\%$ (D) $10\frac{1}{9}\%$

Directions. Study the following table carefully and answer the questions 20-24 given below it :

Number of Toys in Five Types Manufactured by Company over years (in 1000)

Years	Toys				
	A	B	C	D	E
1982	200	150	78	90	65
1983	150	180	100	105	70
1984	180	175	92	110	85
1985	195	160	120	125	75
1986	220	185	130	135	80

20. What was the percentage (approximate) increase in production of D type toys from 1983 to 1985 ?
(A) 10 (B) 20
(C) 19 (D) 25

21. In the case of which type of toys was the total production of the given five years the maximum ?
(A) C (B) B
(C) A (D) D

22. What was the percentage drop on production of A type toys from 1982 to 1984 ?
(A) 30 (B) 10
(C) 20 (d) 50

23. In the case of which type of toys was there a continuous increase in production over the years ?

(A) B (B) A
(C) C (D) D

24. The production of E type toys in 1986 was what percent of production of B type toys in 1985 ?

(A) 80 (B) 50
(C) 100 (D) 200

Directions. Study the following graph carefully and answer the question 25-28 which follow the graph.

Results of annual examination in a high school.

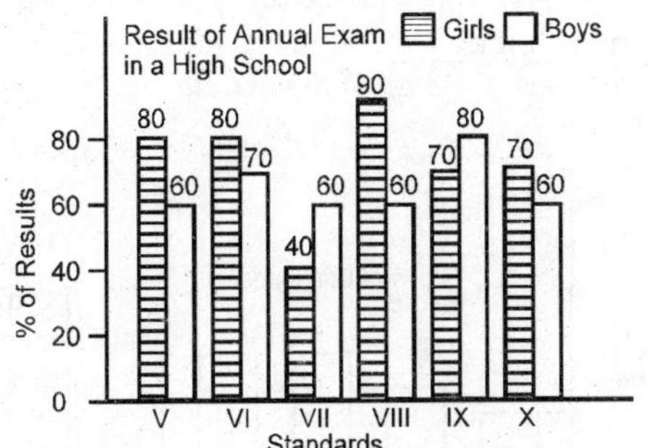

25. In which standard is the failure of girls lowest

(A) IX (B) X
(C) VIII (D) VII

26. The percentage difference between the results of girls and the boys is maximum in which standard ?

(A) VII (B) VIII
(C) V (D) None of these

27. In which standard the result of the boys is more than the average result of the girls ?

(A) V (B) VI
(C) VII (D) IX

28. In which standard is the result of the girls less than the average result of school ?

(A) V (B) VI
(C) VII (D) VIII

Directions. Study the following graph carefully and answer the question 29-33 given below.

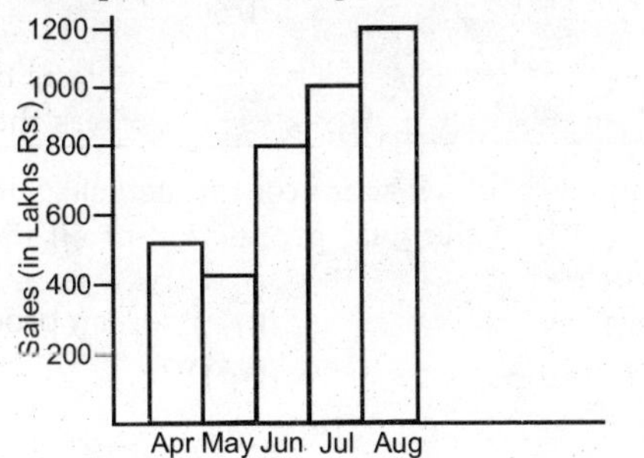

29. In which of the following duration, there is steady increase in sales ?

(A) May to July (B) May to August
(C) June to August (D) None of these

30. During which of the following months, the proportion of the sales to that of the previous month is the largest ?

(A) April (B) May
(C) June (D) July

31. The sales in August is ________ times the sales in May

(A) 2.5 (B) 3.00
(C) 3 (D) None of these

32. How much did the total sales (in lakhs or rupees) increase from April to August ?

(A) 800 (B) 700
(C) 1200 (D) 400

33. Average monthly sales is (in lakhs of rupees)

(A) 600 (B) 650
(C) 780 (D) 620

Directions. Study the following graph carefully and answer the questions 34-38 given below it.

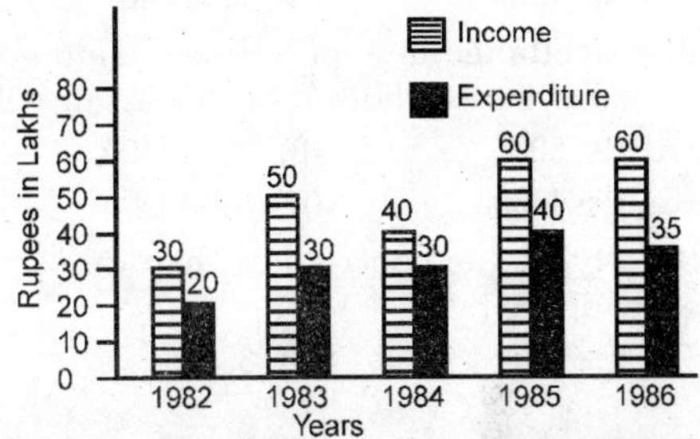

34. What was the difference in profit between 1983 and 1984 ?

(A) Rs. 5 lakhs (B) Rs. 10 lakhs
(C) Rs. 15 lakhs (D) No Profit

35. How many years was the income more than the average income of the given years ?

(A) One (B) Two
(C) Three (D) None of these

36. What was the percentage increase in expenditure from 1984 to 1985 ?

(A) $66\frac{2}{3}$ (B) $33\frac{1}{3}$
(C) 10 (D) 120

37. The income in 1984 was equal to the expenditure of which of the following years ?

(A) 1982 (B) 1983
(C) 1985 (D) None of these

38. In which of the following years was the maximum profit

(A) 1983 (B) 1984

(c) 1985 (D) 1986

Directions. The Pie Chart given below shows the expenditure incurred in bringing out a book, by a publisher:

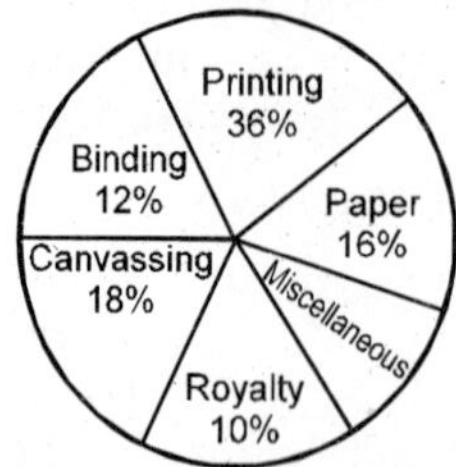

Study the graph and answer the questions 39-42 given below.

39. What is the central angle showing the cost of paper ?

(A) 16° (B) 32°

(C) 28.8° (D) 57.6°

40. The cost of printing is Rs. 23400, the royalty is

(A) Rs. 6500 (B) Rs. 2340

(C) Rs. 4680 (D) Rs. 7840

41. If miscellaneous expenditures amount to Rs. 18000, the expenditure on canvassing will be

(A) Rs. 8000 (B) Rs. 14400

(C) Rs. 46800 (D) Rs. 40500

42. Royalty on the book is less than canvassing expenditure by

(A) 8% (B) 80%

(C) $44\frac{4}{9}\%$ (D) None

Directions. Study the following graph and answer the questions 43-46 which follow the graph.

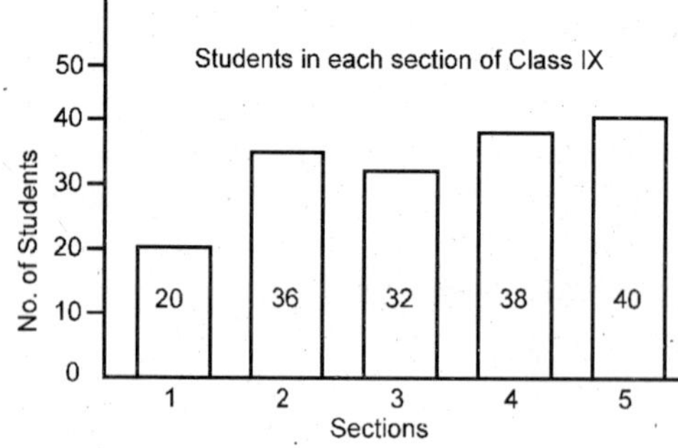

43. Which section has the maximum number of students ?

(A) 5 (B) 4

(C) 3 (D) 2

44. Which section has the minimum number of students ?

(A) 1 (B) 2

(C) 3 (D) 4

45. Which section has double the number of the students as compared to another section

(A) 4 (B) 3

(C) 5 (D) 1

46. Which section has half the number of students of one of the sections ?

(A) 1 (B) 2

(C) 3 (D) 4

Directions. Study the following graph and answer the questions 47-48 given below.

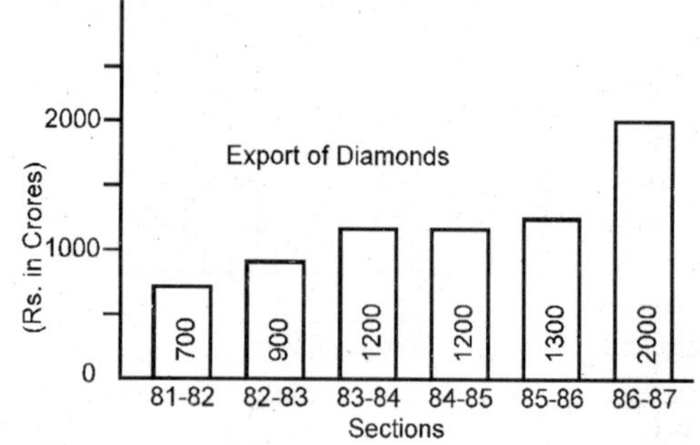

47. Between which two years the export of diamonds was the same ?

(A) 83–85 (B) 84-86

(C) 86-87 (D) 81-83

48. What percent increase in export of diamonds was three from 1981 to 1983

(A) 50% (B) 60%

(C) 75% (D) None of these

Directions. Study the data given in the following table carefully and answer the questions 49-53 given below it :

Wheat Production (in lakh tonnes)

States	1986	1987	1988	1989	1990
A	9.0	10.7	8.9	11.6	8.4
B	14.5	16.3	16.2	16.4	16.8
C	14.9	15.7	16.8	16.9	17.8
D	7.6	8.4	7.4	7.9	8.6
E	21.0	22.6	23.2	22.2	23.9

49. In 1988, which states contributed close to one-eighth of the total production of all the five states ?

(A) A (B) B

(C) C (D) D

50. In which year did the production of state D fall for the first time ?
(A) 1986 (B) 1987
(C) 1988 (D) 1989

51. In which state, the production in 1989 showed the highest increase over that in 1986 ?
(A) A (B) B
(C) C (D) D

52. In which year does the production in state E show the higher percentage of increase over that in the previous year ?
(A) 1986 (B) 1987
(C) 1988 (D) 1990

53. In which state did the production of wheat increase continuously from 1986 to 1990 ?
(A) A (B) B
(C) C (D) D

Directions. Study the following table and answer the questions 54-58 given below

Yearwise and disciplinewise number of candidates selected in an Industry

Years → / Disciplines ↓	1981	1982	1983	1984	1985	1986
Science	16	20	25	15	14	16
Commerce	08	12	12	11	15	13
Arts	04	08	8.5	10	11	13
Agriculture	01	03	3.0	2.5	1.0	2.0
Engineering	0.5	01	1.0	1.0	0.5	0.5
Others	0.5	01	0.5	0.5	0.5	0.5
Total	30	45	50	40	42	45

54. The number of selected candidates of which discipline is increasing every year ?
(A) Science (B) Engineering
(C) Agriculture (D) Arts

55. Approximately what per cent of candidates of science discipline were selected for the given period ?
(A) 38 (B) 42
(C) 45 (D) None of these

56. If all the class graduates were eligible to apply, which of the following inferences is probably true ?
(A) Among the applicants the number of science discipline candidates is the largest.
(B) If written test was given for selection the test was biased towards science discipline
(C) The industry required science discipline graduates more in its personnel
(D) None of these

57. In which year is the percentage of Agriculture discipline candidates the highest ?
(A) 1982 (B) 1983
(C) 1984 (D) 1985

58. In which year for the first time did the Arts discipline candidates constitute more than 25 percent of selected candidates ?
(A) 1982 (B) 1983
(C) 1984 (D) 1985

Directions. Refer to the following pie chart and answer the questions 59-60 given below.

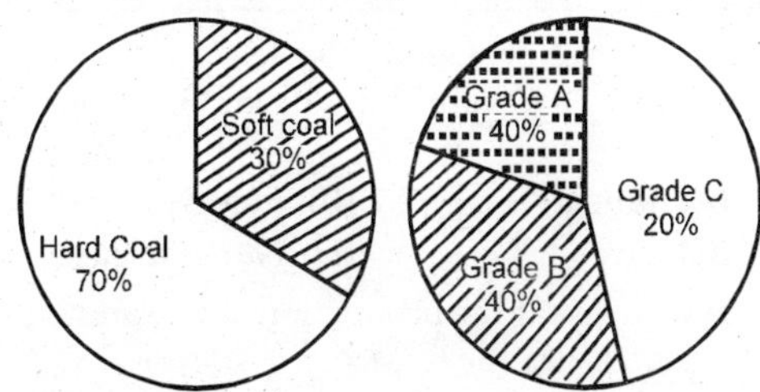

59. The chart above shows the distribution of coal production in a certain country. The chart on the left shows the percentage of hard and soft coal, and that on the right shows the distribution of grades of hard coal. What percent of the total production was grade B hard coal ?
(A) 14% (B) 21%
(C) 28% (D) 34%

60. In the pie chart on the left how many degrees are there in the central angle of the sector for soft coal ?
(A) 108 (B) 102
(C) 144 (D) 160

Direction. The following table shows the number of working hours and the number of employees in a small scale industrial unit.

No. of working hours	No. of employees
3-5 hours	7
5-7 hours	10
7-9 hours	18
9-11 hours	57
11-13 hours	14
13-15 hours	8

61. What is the average working hour of an employee ?
(A) 9.5 (B) 10.22
(C) 11 (D) 12

Directions. Study the following table carefully and answer the questions 62-65 given below it :

Production in Million Tonnes

Crops	Years					
	1976	1977	1978	1979	1980	1981
Rice	44.0	39.6	48.7	41.9	52.7	52.1
Wheat	21.8	24.1	28.8	29.9	31.8	37.0
Other cereals	28.8	26.1	30.4	28.9	30.0	30.2
Pulses	10.0	10.5	13.0	11.4	12.0	12.2
Potatoes	4.8	6.3	7.3	8.1	8.3	10.2

62. In the case of which crop the production increase is by more than 10 lakhs tonnes any year?
(A) Wheat (B) Pulses
(C) Rice (D) None of these

63. In which year the production of rice and wheat together was the least ?
(A) 1979 (B) 1978
(C) 1977 (D) None of these

64. In the case of which crop the production is having ups and downs every alternate year ?
(A) Rice (B) Wheat
(C) Pulses (D) None of these

65. In the case of which crop does the production in 1981 show the highest increase over that in 1976 ?
(A) Wheat (B) Other cereals
(C) Potatoes (D) None of these

Directions. Study the graph carefully and answer the questions 66-70 given below :

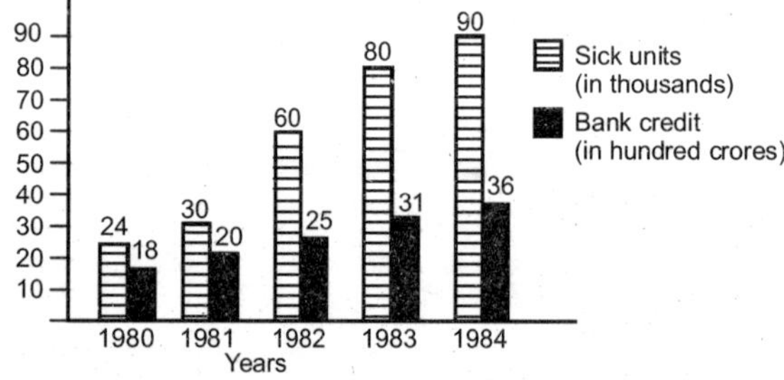

66. What was the percentage increase in number of sick units from 1981 to 1983 ?
(A) 50 (B) 150
(C) 25 (D) None of these

67. What was the difference in bank credit between 1981 and 1982 ?
(A) Rs. 5 crore (B) Rs. 50 crore
(C) Rs. 500 crore (D) Rs. 50 lac

68. If the bank credit is reduced to half in the year 1981, what will be the approximate bank credit per sick unit ?
(A) Rs. 3 crore (B) Rs. 3 lac
(C) Rs. 30 lac (D) Rs. 4 lac

69. In which year was the bank credit per sick unit the maximum ?
(A) 1980 (B) 1981
(C) 1982 (D) 1983

70. In 1983 what was the total bank credit per sick unit approximately ?
(A) Rs. 32 crore (B) Rs. 71 crore
(C) Rs. 71 lac (D) Rs. 4 lac

Directions. Study the table carefully and answer the questions 71-75 given below.

Projected and Actual Production of Cars of 5 Different companies (Numbers in '000)

Years	A		B		C		D		E	
	P	A	P	A	P	A	P	A	P	A
1987	22	20	16	12	21	20	22	16	22	20
1988	26	21	21	14	22	18	20	18	18	16
1989	24	22	15	14	26	20	22	21	20	18
1990	29	23	14	10	30	22	29	23	23	19
1991	28	21	18	15	34	28	26	24	21	17
1992	31	20	22	18	36	31	30	28	28	26

P = Projected; A = Actual

71. Which company has the highest actual production of cars over these years ?
(A) A (B) B
(C) C (D) D

72. Which year has the lowest projected production of cars of all the 5 companies ?
(A) 1987 (B) 1989
(C) 1990 (D) None of these

73. What is the percentage of actual production of cars compared to the projected production of cars of company D in the year 1988 :
(A) 85 (B) 86
(C) 90 (D) None of these

74. Which company has continuous increase in actual production of cars over these years ?
(A) A (B) B
(C) C (D) D

75. What is the approximate % actual production of cars compared to the projected production of cars of B over these years (1987-1991) ?
(A) 80 (B) 78
(C) 82 (D) 74

Directions. Study the table carefully and answer the questions 76-80 given below.

Loans disbursed by five banks over the years (in crores of rupees)

Banks	Years				
	1982	1983	1984	1985	1986
I	18	23	45	30	70
II	27	33	18	41	37
III	29	29	22	17	11
IV	31	16	28	32	43
V	13	19	27	34	42
Total	118	120	140	154	203

76. In which bank was the disbursement of loans more than 25 percent of all banks in 1986 ?
(A) I (B) II
(C) III (D) IV

77. In which of the following banks did disbursement of loans continuously increase over the years ?
(A) I (B) II
(C) V (D) IV

78. In which year the disbursement of loans was least as compared to the average disbursement of loans over the years ?
(A) 1982 (B) 1983
(C) 1984 (D) 1985

79. If 20% of the total disbursement of loans in the preceding year was the minimum target, how many banks did achieve the largest in 1983 ?
(A) 2 (B) 4
(C) 3 (D) None of these

80. What was the percentage increase of disbursement of loans of all banks taken together in 1984 and 1985 ?
(A) 4 (B) 6
(C) 8 (D) 10

Directions. The following pie chart shows the marks obtained by a student in an examination, who scored 540 marks in all

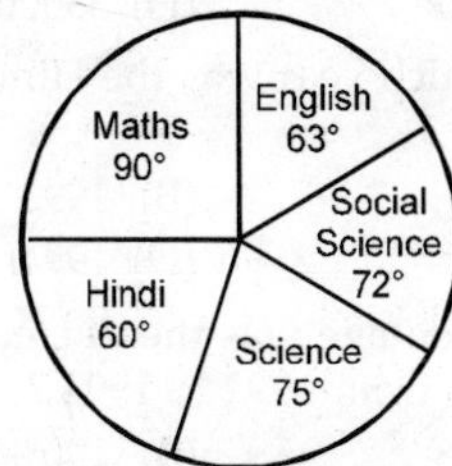

Study the graph and answer the questions 81-83 given below

81. The subject in which the student scored 108 marks is
(A) Science
(B) Hindi
(C) English
(D) Social Science

82. The subject in which the student scored $16\frac{2}{3}\%$ is
(A) Social science (B) Hindi
(C) English (D) Science

83. The marks scored in Hindi and Mathematics differ from the marks scored in English, Science and social Science by
(A) 90 (B) 72
(C) 85 (D) 61

Directions. These questions 84-87 are based on the circle graph below, which shows the expenditure incurred, in bringing out a book, by a publisher :

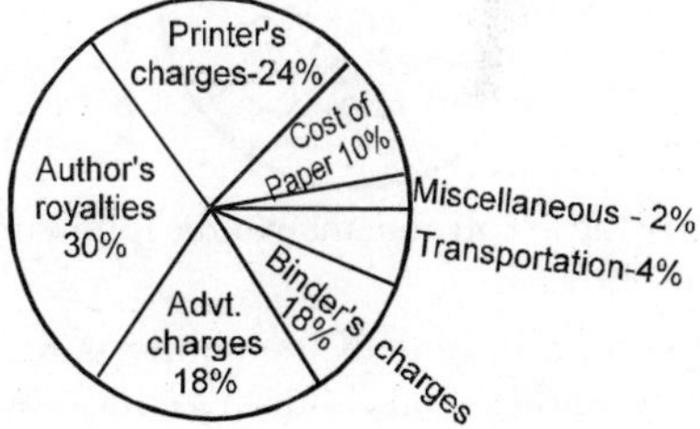

84. If the author's royalties amount to Rs. 30000, the binder's charges amount to Rs. ______.
(A) 10500 (B) 12000
(C) 15000 (D) 18000

85. What should be the central angle of the sector for transportation charges ?
(A) 4° (B) 8.4°
(C) 12.4° (D) 14.4°

86. If the advertisement charges amount to Rs. 18000, the total expenditure incurred in bringing out the book is Rs. ________.
(A) 60300 (B) 63000
(C) 90000 (D) 100000

87. The miscellaneous expenditure amounts to Rs. 2000 and totally 12500 copies of the book are published. What is the cost per copy at which the books must be priced, if the publishers desires a profit of 5% ?
(A) Rs. 5 (B) Rs. 7.50
(C) Rs. 8 (D) Rs. 8.40

88. Direction. Study the following graph and point out the Industrial growth rate of India

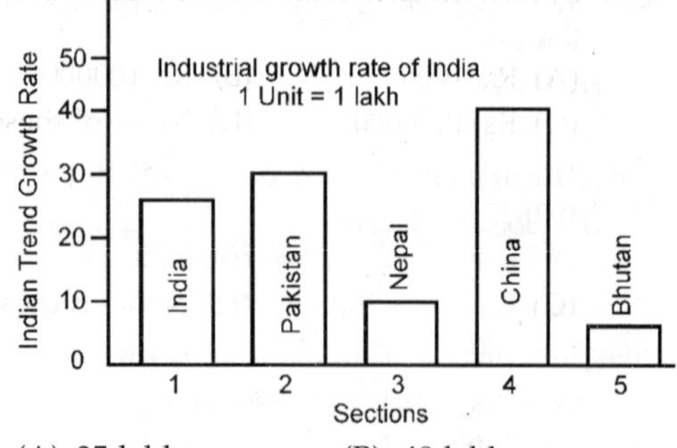

(A) 35 lakhs (B) 40 lakhs
(C) 25 lakhs (D) 45 lakhs

Directions. The circle graph given below shows the spending of a family on various items and its savings a year

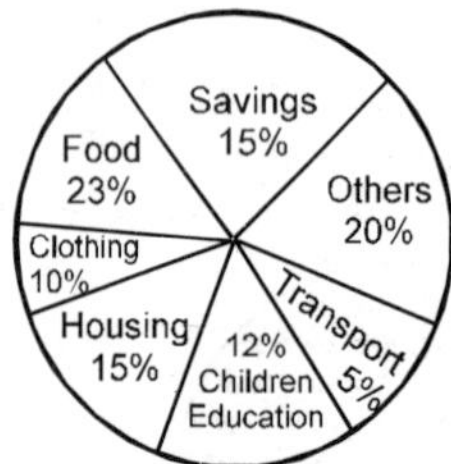

Study the graph and answer the following questions 89-92.

89. If the total income of the family is Rs. 75000, the expenditure on children's education is
(A) Rs. 9000 (B) Rs. 900
(C) Rs. 7500 (D) Rs. 750

90. What percentage of the income was spent on transport and other items ?
(A) 25% (B) 20%
(C) 30% (D) 32%

91. Out of the total of Rs. 75000, the difference of the expenses on Housing and Transport was
(A) Rs. 8500 (B) Rs. 7500
(C) Rs. 8200 (D) Rs. 6350

92. Out of the total of Rs. 75000, the expenditure on Food was more than that on Clothing by
(A) Rs. 8250 (B) Rs. 6750
(C) Rs. 9750 (D) Rs. 7350

Direction.

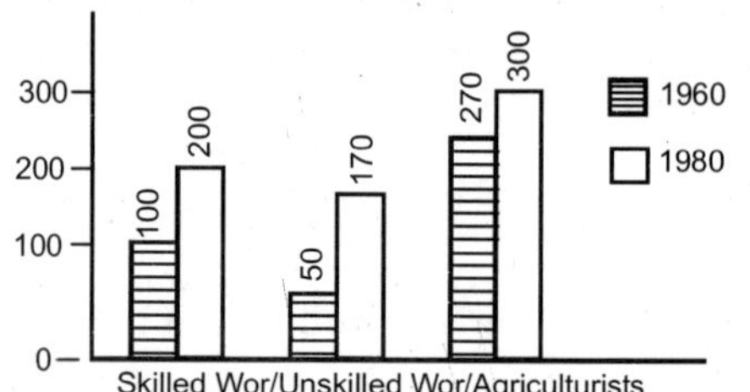

93. In the above graph which category shows approximately 10% increase in the periods shown?
(A) Skilled workers (B) Unskilled workers
(C) Agriculturists (D) None of these

Directions. Given below is a bar diagram and percentage of Hindus, Sikhs and Muslims in a state during the years from 1991-1994.

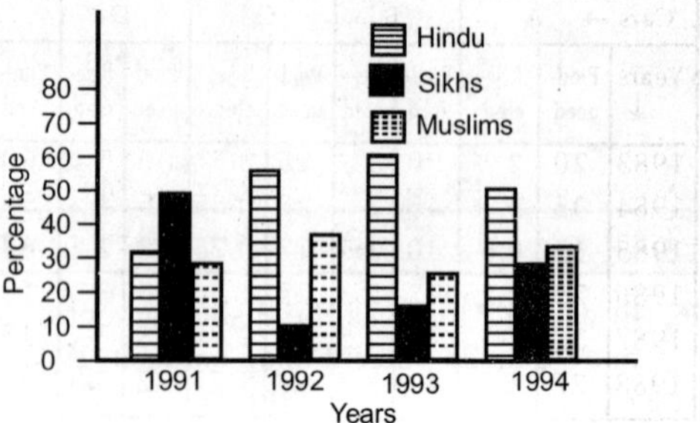

Study the above diagram and answer the following questions 94-101.

94. The ratio between Hindus and Sikhs in 1991 was :
(A) 3 : 2 (B) 2 : 3
(C) cannot be calculated
(D) None of the above

95. If the total population of state in 1992 is 1 million then the Hindu population was
(A) 5500000 (B) 55000
(C) 550000 (D) 5500

96. What was the percentage of sikhs over Hindus in 1993 ?
(A) 25% (B) 40%
(C) 140% (D) 240%

97. What percentage was the increase in Hindus population from 1991 to 1994 ?
(A) 15% (B) 45%
(C) 50% (D) 25%

98. If the population of the state in 1991 is 6 lakhs, then what is total population of Hindus and Muslims in that year ?
(A) 270000 (B) 3300000
(C) 330000 (D) 33000

99. During which year was the Hindu percentage maximum ?
(A) 1991 (B) 1992
(C) 1993 (D) 1994

100. What percentage was the decrease in Muslim population from 1992 to 1994 ?
(A) 14.29% (B) 100%
(C) 200% (D) 20%

101. If the total population in 1994 is 2 millions, then the Sikh population is

(A) 1300000 (B) 130000
(C) 500000 (D) 13000000

Directions. Study the following table carefully and answer the questions 102-106 given below it.

Number of five types of cars produced and rejected (for defects) by company over the years

(in 000)

Cars →	A		B		C		D		E	
Years ↓	Produced	Rejected	Produced	Rejected	Produced	Rejected	Produced	Rejected	Produced	Rejected
1983	20	2	50	3	15	0.5	80	5	60	4
1984	35	3	45	2	20	0.55	75	4	58	4
1985	15	0.5	40	2.5	17	0.75	58	2	62	3.5
1986	25	0.25	42	2.3	25	1.5	65	3	40	1.5
1987	30	1.5	48	2.5	30	2.0	68	3	45	2
1988	27	1.5	41	2.1	26	1.75	72	3.5	50	2.5

102. In the case of B type car, in which year was the ratio of rejection to production the highest among the given years ?
(A) 1983 (B) 1984
(C) 1985 (D) 1987

103. In the case of E type car, in which year was the ratio of rejection to production the lowest among the given years ?
(A) 1984 (B) 1985
(C) 1986 (D) 1987

104. What was the difference in number of C type cars produced between 1984 and 1985 ?
(A) 200 (B) 250
(C) 3000 (D) 2500

105. The acceptable E type cars in 1985 was what percent to that of 1984 ?
(A) 8 (B) 106
(C) 110 (D) None of these

106. In the year 1984, in the case of which cars was the rejection below five percent ?
(A) A (B) B or E
(C) B and C (D) None of these

Directions. Study the following graph and answer the question 107-111 following it.

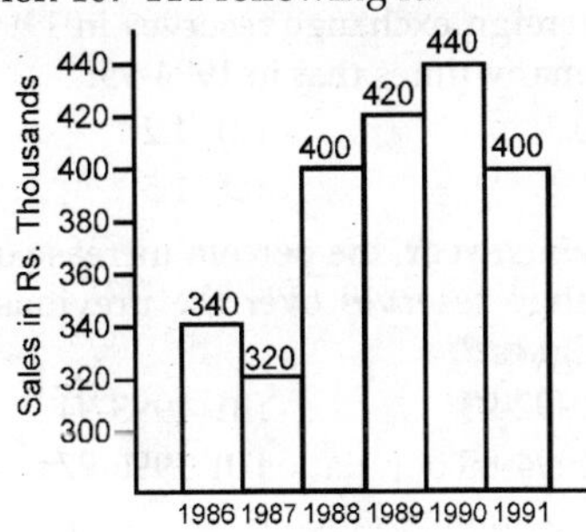

107. By how much amount are the sales in 1989 more than those in 1987 ?
(A) Rs. 1000 (B) Rs. 100000
(C) Rs. 1000000 (D) None of these

108. The sales in 1987 are how many items those in 1988 ?
(A) 0.8 (B) 1.25
(C) 8 (D) None of these

109. In which year do the sales show the least percent increase over those in the preceding year?
(A) 1986 (B) 1988 (C) 1989 (D) 1990

110. The sales in 1990 are what percent of those in 1986 ?
(A) 40 (B) 4 (C) 11 (D) 129.41

111. What are the approximate average sales (in thousands) for the years 1988 to 1991 ?
(A) 420 (B) 425
(C) 430 (D) None of these

Directions. Use the following table for these questions 112-114.

Distribution of work House in a Factory

Number of Workers	Number of Hours Worked
20	45-50
15	40-44
25	35-39
16	30-34
4	0-29
80	**Total** 3100

112. What percentage worked 40 or more hours ?
(A) 43.75 (B) 25
(C) $33\frac{1}{3}$ (D) None of these

113. The number of workers who worked from 40 to 44 hours is x times the number who worked up to 29 hours, where x is :
(A) 15/16 (B) $3\frac{3}{4}$
(C) 4 (D) 5

114. Which of the following statements can be inferred from the table ?
I. The average number of hours worked per worker is less than 40
II. At least 3 worked for more than 48 hours
III. More than half of all the workers worked more than 40 hours
(A) I only (B) II only
(C) I and II only (D) I and III only

Directions. The following table shows production of cars in a company from 1979 to 1984. Study it carefully and answer the questions 115-119 :

Years	1979	1980	1981	1982	1983	1984
A	8	20	16	17	21	6
B	16	10	14	12	12	14
C	21	17	16	15	13	8
D	4	6	10	16	20	31
E	25	18	19	30	14	27
Total	**74**	**71**	**75**	**90**	**80**	**86**

115. In which year, the production of all types of cars taken together was approximately equal to the average of the total production during the period ?

(A) 1979 (B) 1981 (C) 1983 (D) 1984

116. In which year, the total production of cars of types A and B together was equal to the total production of cars of types C and D together ?

(A) 1980 (B) 1981 (C) 1984 (D) 1983

117. There was a continuous increase in production of cars of which type during the period 1979-84?

(A) A (B) B (C) C (D) D

118. The production of which of the following types of cars was 25% of the total production of all types of cars produced during the year 1983 ?

(A) A (B) B (C) C (D) D

119. The percent increase in total production of all types of cars in 1982 to that in 1981 was

(A) 15 (B) 20 (C) 25 (D) 30

Directions (120-124). The bar graph given below shows the sales of books (in thousand number) from six branches of a publishing company during two consecutive years 2000 and 2001.

Sales of Books (in thousand numbers) from Six Branches - B1, B2, B3, B4, B5 and B6 of a publishing Company in 2000 and 2001.

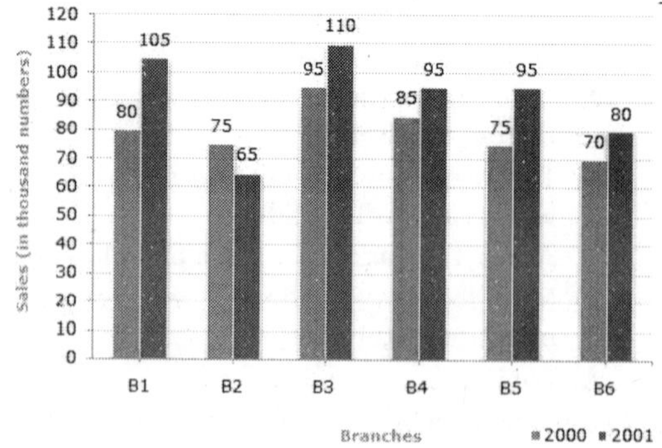

120. What is the ratio of the total sales of branch B2 for both years to the total sales of branch B4 for both years?

(A) 2:3 (B) 3:5

(C) 4:5 (D) 7:9

121. Total sales of branch B6 for both the years is what percent of the total sales of branches B3 for both the years?

(A) 68.54% (B) 71.11%

(C) 73.17% (D) 75.55%

122. What percent of the average sales of branches B1, B2 and B3 in 2001 is the average sales of branches B1, B3 and B6 in 2000?

(A) 75% (B) 77.5%

(C) 82.5% (D) 87.5%

123. What is the average sales of all the branches (in thousand numbers) for the year 2000?

(A) 73 (B) 80 (C) 83 (D) 88

124. Total sales of branches B1, B3 and B5 together for both the years (in thousand numbers) is?

(A) 250 (B) 310 (C) 435 (D) 560

Directions (125-129). The bar graph given below shows the foreign exchange reserves of a country (in million US $) from 1991-1992 to 1998-1999.

Foreign Exchange Reserves of a Country. (in million US $)

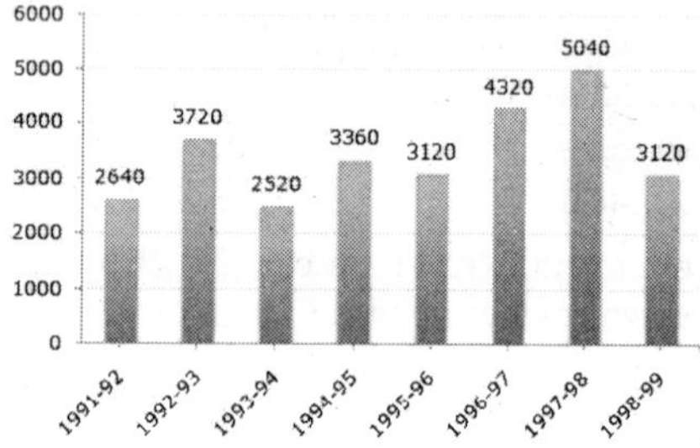

125. The ratio of the number of years, in which the foreign exchange reserves are above the average reserves, to those in which the reserves are below the average reserves is?

(A) 2:6 (B) 3:4

(C) 3:5 (D) 4:4

126. The foreign exchange reserves in 1997-98 was how many times that in 1994-95?

(A) 0.7 (B) 1.2

(C) 1.4 (D) 1.5

127. For which year, the percent increase of foreign exchange reserves over the previous year, is the highest?

(A) 1992-93 (B) 1993-94

(C) 1994-95 (D) 1996-97

128. The foreign exchange reserves in 1996-97 were approximately what percent of the average foreign exchange reserves over the period under review?
(A) 95% (B) 110%
(C) 115% (D) 125%

129. What was the percentage increase in the foreign exchange reserves in 1997-98 over 1993-94?
(A) 100 (B) 150 (C) 200 (D) 620

Directions (131-134). The bar graph given below shows the data of the production of paper (in lakh tonnes) by three different companies X, Y and Z over the years.

Production of Paper (in lakh tonnes) by Three Companies X, Y and Z over the Years.

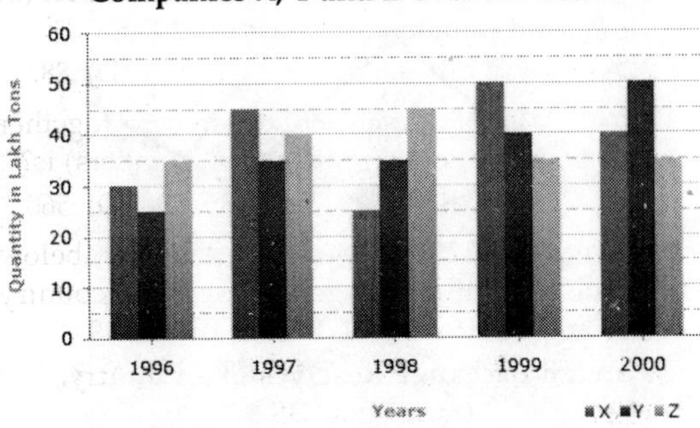

130. For which of the following years, the percentage rise/fall in production from the previous year is the maximum for Company Y?
(A) 1997 (B) 1998
(C) 1999 (D) 2000

131. What is the ratio of the average production of Company X in the period 1998-2000 to the average production of Company Y in the same period?
(A) 1:1 (B) 15:17
(C) 23:25 (D) 27:29

132. The average production for five years was maximum for which company?
(A) X (B) Y
(C) Z (D) X and Z both

133. In which year was the percentage of production of Company Z to the production of Company Y the maximum?
(A) 1996 (B) 1997
(C) 1998 (D) 1999

134. What is the percentage increase in the production of Company Y from 1996 to 1999?
(A) 30% (B) 45%
(C) 50% (D) 60%

Directions (135-139). Out of the two bar graphs provided below, one shows the amounts (in Lakh Rs.) invested by a Company in purchasing raw materials over the years and the other shows the values (in Lakh Rs.) of finished goods sold by the Company over the years.

Amount invested in Raw Materials (Rs. in Lakhs)

Value of Sales of Finished Goods (Rs. in Lakhs)

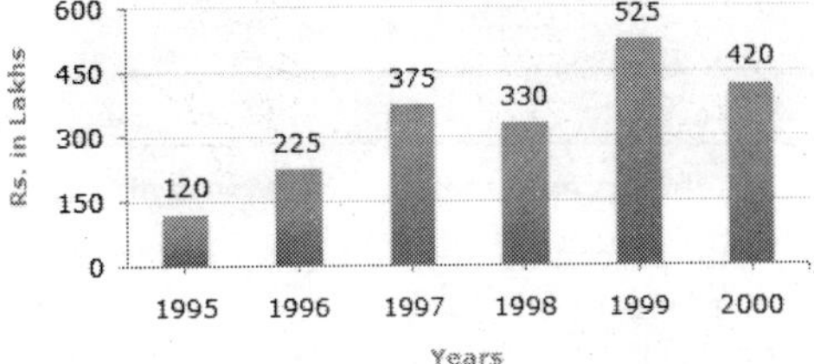

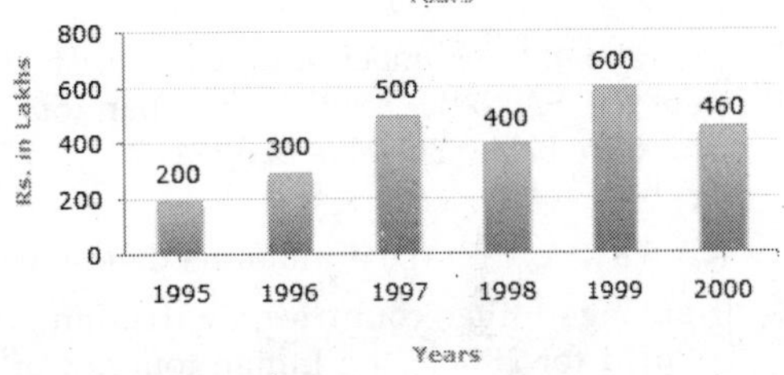

135. The maximum difference between the amount invested in Raw materials and value of sales of finished goods was during the year?
(A) 1995 (B) 1996
(C) 1997 (D) 1998

136. The value of sales of finished goods in 1999 was approximately what percent of the sum of amount invested in Raw materials in the years 1997, 1998 and 1999?
(A) 33% (B) 37%
(C) 45% (D) 49%

137. What was the difference between the average amount invested in Raw materials during the given period and the average value of sales of finished goods during this period?
(A) Rs. 62.5 lakhs (B) Rs. 68.5 lakhs
(C) Rs. 71.5 lakhs (D) Rs. 77.5 lakhs

138. In which year, the percentage change (compared to the previous year) in the investment on Raw materials is same as that in the value of sales of finished goods?
(A) 1996 (B) 1997
(C) 1998 (D) 1999

139. In which year, there has been a maximum percentage increase in the amount invested in Raw materials as compared to the previous year?
(A) 1996 (B) 1997
(C) 1998 (D) 1999

Directions (140-142). The following pie charts exhibit the distribution of the overseas tourist traffic from India. The two charts shows the tourist distribution by country and the age profiles of the tourists respectively.

Distribution of Overseas Tourist Traffic from India.

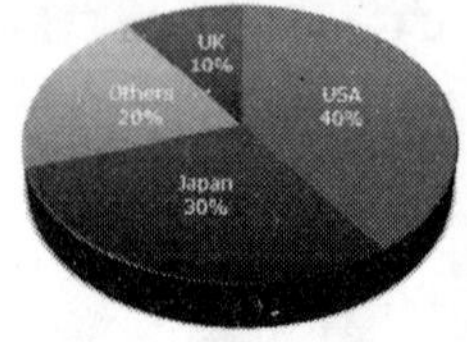

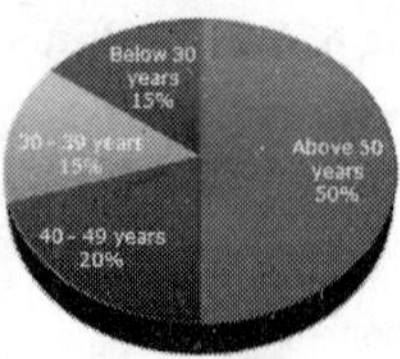

140. What percentage of Indian tourist went to either USA or UK?
(A) 40 % (B) 50 % (C) 60 % (D) 70 %

141. The ratio of the number of Indian tourists that went to USA to the number of Indian tourists who were below 30 years of age is ?
(A) 2:1 (B) 8:3
(C) 3:8 (D) Cannot be determined

142. If amongst other countries, Switzerland accounted for 25% of the Indian tourist traffic, and it is known from official Swiss records that a total of 25 lakh Indian tourists had gone to Switzerland during the year, then find the number of 30-39 year old Indian tourists who went abroad in that year ?
(A) 18.75 lakh (B) 25 lakh
(C) 50 lakh (D) 75 lakh

Directions (143-147). The following pie-charts show the distribution of students of graduate and post-graduate levels in seven different institutes in a town.

Distribution of students at graduate and post-graduate levels in seven institutes:

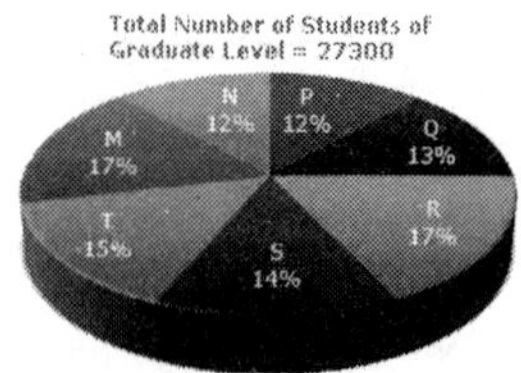

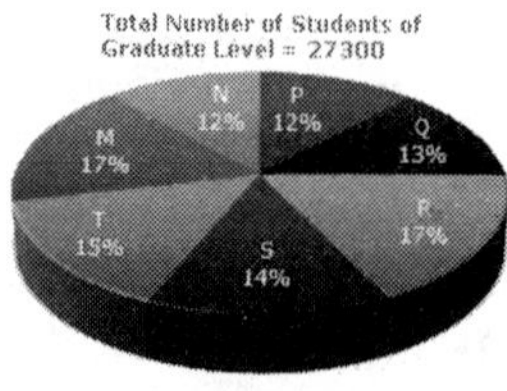

143. What is the total number of graduate and post-graduate level students is institute R?
(A) 8320 (B) 7916 (C) 9116 (D) 8099

144. What is the ratio between the number of students studying at post-graduate and graduate levels respectively from institute S?
(A) 14 : 19 (B) 19 : 21
(C) 17 : 21 (D) 19 : 14

145. How many students of institutes of M and S are studying at graduate level?
(A) 7516 (B) 8463 (C) 9127 (D) 9404

146. What is the ratio between the number of students studying at post-graduate level from institutes S and the number of students studying at graduate level from institute Q?
(A) 13 : 19 (B) 21 : 13
(C) 13 : 8 (D) 19 : 13

147. Total number of students studying at post-graduate level from institutes N and P is
(A) 5601 (B) 5944 (C) 6669 (D) 8372

Directions (148-152). Study the following line graph and answer the questions.

Exports from Three Companies Over the Years (in Rs. crore)

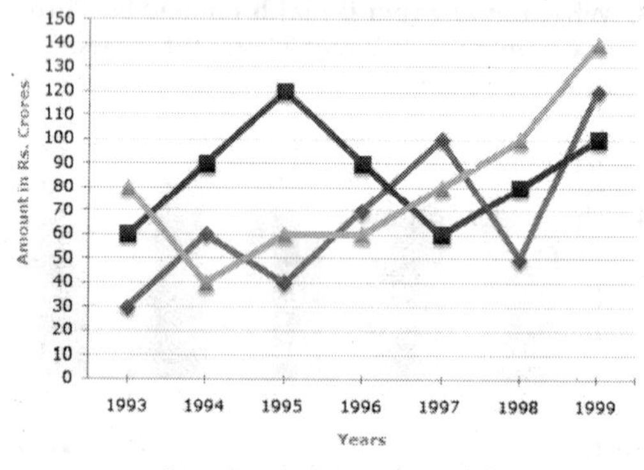

148. For which of the following pairs of years the total exports from the three Companies together are equal?
(A) 1995 and 1998 (B) 1996 and 1998
(C) 1997 and 1998 (D) 1995 and 1996

149. Average annual exports during the given period for Company Y is approximately what percent of the average annual exports for Company Z?
(A) 87.12% (B) 89.64%
(C) 91.21% (D) 93.33%

150. In which year was the difference between the exports from Companies X and Y the minimum?
(A) 1994 (B) 1995
(C) 1996 (D) 1997

151. What was the difference between the average exports of the three Companies in 1993 and the average exports in 1998?
(A) Rs. 15.33 crores (B) Rs. 18.67 crores
(C) Rs. 20 crores (D) Rs. 22.17 crores

152. In how many of the given years, were the exports from Company Z more than the average annual exports over the given years?
(A) 2 (B) 3 (C) 4 (D) 5

Directions (153-157). The following table gives the percentage of marks obtained by seven students in six different subjects in an examination.

The Numbers in the Brackets give the Maximum Marks in Each Subject.

Student	Subject (Max. Marks)					
	Maths (150)	Chemistry (130)	Physics (120)	Geography (100)	History (60)	Computer Science (40)
Ayush	90	50	90	60	70	80
Aman	100	80	80	40	80	70
Sajal	90	60	70	70	90	70
Rohit	80	65	80	80	60	60
Muskan	80	65	85	95	50	90
Tanvi	70	75	65	85	40	60
Tarun	65	35	50	77	80	80

153. What are the average marks obtained by all the seven students in Physics? (rounded off to two digit after decimal)

(A) 77.26 (B) 89.14
(C) 91.37 (D) 96.11

154. The number of students who obtained 60% and above marks in all subjects is?

(A) 1 (B) 2
(C) 3 (D) None of these

155. What was the aggregate of marks obtained by Sajal in all the six subjects?

(A) 409 (B) 419 (C) 429 (D) 449

156. In which subject is the overall percentage the best?

(A) Maths (B) Chemistry
(C) Physics (D) History

157. What is the overall percentage of Tarun?

(A) 52.5% (B) 55%
(C) 60% (D) 63%

Directions (158-162). The following table gives the sales of batteries manufactured by a company over the years.

Number of Different Types of Batteries Sold by a Company Over the Years (Numbers in Thousands)

Year	Types of Batteries					
	4AH	7AH	32AH	35AH	55AH	Total
1992	75	144	114	102	108	543
1993	90	126	102	84	126	528
1994	96	114	75	105	135	525
1995	105	90	150	90	75	510
1996	90	75	135	75	90	465
1997	105	60	165	45	120	495
1998	115	85	160	100	145	605

158. What was the approximate percentage increase in the sales of 55AH batteries in 1998 compared to that in 1992?

(A) 28% (B) 31%
(C) 33% (D) 34%

159. The total sales of all the seven years is the maximum for which battery?

(A) 4AH (B) 7AH
(C) 32AH (D) 35AH

160. What is the difference in the number of 35AH batteries sold in 1993 and 1997?

(A) 24000 (B) 28000
(C) 35000 (D) 39000

161. The percentage of 4AH batteries sold to the total number of batteries sold was maximum in the year?

(A) 1994 (B) 1995
(C) 1996 (D) 1997

162. In case of which battery there was a continuous decrease in sales from 1992 to 1997?

(A) 4AH (B) 7AH
(C) 32AH (D) 35AH

Directions (163-167). The following line graph gives the annual percent profit earned by a Company during the period 1995 - 2000.

Percent Profit Earned by a Company Over the Years.

$$\%\text{Profit} = \frac{\text{Income} - \text{Expenditure}}{\text{Expenditure}} \times 100$$

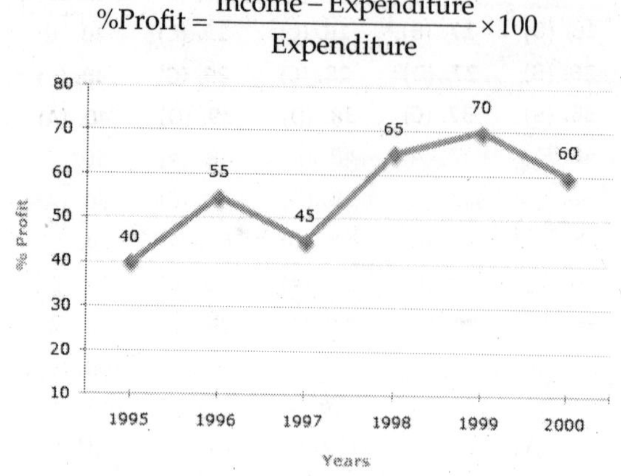

163. If the expenditures in 1996 and 1999 are equal, then the approximate ratio of the income in 1996 and 1999 respectively is?

(A) 1:1 (B) 2:3 (C) 13:14 (D) 9:10

164. If the income in 1998 was Rs. 264 crores, what was the expenditure in 1998?

(A) Rs. 104 crores (B) Rs. 145 crores
(C) Rs. 160 crores (D) Rs. 185 crores

165. In which year is the expenditure minimum?

(A) 2000 (B) 1997
(C) 1996 (D) Cannot be determined

166. If the profit in 1999 was Rs. 4 crores, what was the profit in 2000?

(A) Rs. 4.2 crores (B) Rs. 6.6 crores
(C) Rs. 6.8 crores
(D) Cannot be determined

167. What is the average profit earned for the given years?

(A) 50(2/3) (B) 55(5/6)
(C) 60(1/6) (D) 335

Directions (168-172). Study the following graph carefully and answer the questions given below:

Distribution of candidates who were enrolled for MBA entrance exam and the candidates (out of those enrolled) who passed the exam in different institutes:

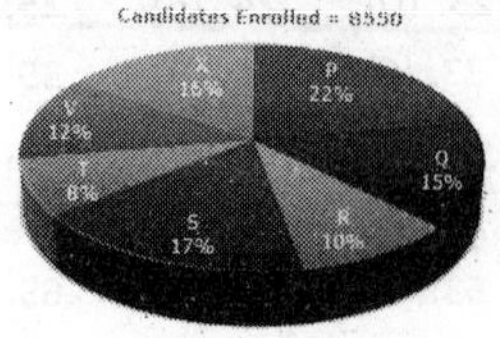

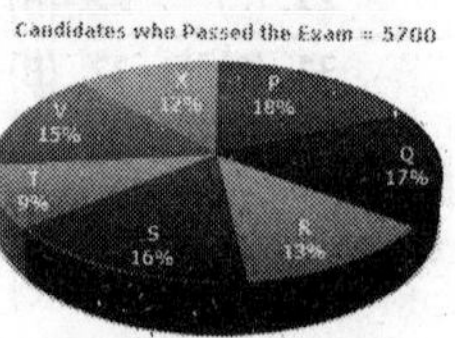

168. What percentage of candidates passed the Exam from institute T out of the total number of candidates enrolled from the same institute?

(A) 50% (B) 62.5%
(C) 75% (D) 80%

169. Which institute has the highest percentage of candidates passed to the candidates enrolled?

(A) Q (B) R
(C) V (D) T

170. The number of candidates passed from institutes S and P together exceeds the number of candidates enrolled from institutes T and R together by:

(A) 228 (B) 279
(C) 399 (D) 407

171. What is the percentage of candidates passed to the candidates enrolled for institutes Q and R together?

(A) 68% (B) 80%
(C) 74% (D) 65%

172. What is the ratio of candidates passed to the candidates enrolled from institute P?

(A) 9 : 11 (B) 14 : 17
(C) 6 : 11 (D) 9 : 17

ANSWERS

1. (D)	**2.** (C)	**3.** (B)	**4.** (B)	**5.** (C)	**6.** (C)	**7.** (B)	**8.** (B)	**9.** (C)	**10.** (B)
11. (D)	**12.** (A)	**13.** (D)	**14.** (A)	**15.** (D)	**16.** (D)	**17.** (B)	**18.** (C)	**19.** (C)	**20.** (C)
21. (C)	**22.** (B)	**23.** (D)	**24.** (B)	**25.** (C)	**26.** (B)	**27.** (D)	**28.** (C)	**29.** (C)	**30.** (C)
31. (C)	**32.** (B)	**33.** (C)	**34.** (B)	**35.** (C)	**36.** (B)	**37.** (C)	**38.** (D)	**39.** (D)	**40.** (A)
41. (D)	**42.** (C)	**43.** (A)	**44.** (A)	**45.** (C)	**46.** (A)	**47.** (A)	**48.** (D)	**49.** (A)	**50.** (C)
51. (A)	**52.** (D)	**53.** (C)	**54.** (D)	**55.** (B)	**56.** (C)	**57.** (A)	**58.** (D)	**59.** (C)	**60.** (A)
61. (A)	**62.** (C)	**63.** (C)	**64.** (A)	**65.** (C)	**66.** (D)	**67.** (C)	**68.** (B)	**69.** (A)	**70.** (D)
71. (C)	**72.** (A)	**73.** (C)	**74.** (D)	**75.** (C)	**76.** (A)	**77.** (C)	**78.** (A)	**79.** (C)	**80.** (D)
81. (D)	**82.** (B)	**83.** (A)	**84.** (D)	**85.** (D)	**86.** (D)	**87.** (D)	**88.** (C)	**89.** (A)	**90.** (A)
91. (B)	**92.** (C)	**93.** (C)	**94.** (B)	**95.** (C)	**96.** (A)	**97.** (C)	**98.** (C)	**99.** (C)	**100.** (B)
101. (C)	**102.** (C)	**103.** (C)	**104.** (C)	**105.** (D)	**106.** (C)	**107.** (B)	**108.** (A)	**109.** (D)	**110.** (D)
111. (D)	**112.** (A)	**113.** (B)	**114.** (A)	**115.** (C)	**116.** (D)	**117.** (D)	**118.** (D)	**119.** (B)	**120.** (D)
121. (C)	**122.** (D)	**123.** (B)	**124.** (D)	**125.** (C)	**126.** (D)	**127.** (A)	**128.** (D)	**129.** (A)	**130.** (A)
131. (C)	**132.** (D)	**133.** (A)	**134.** (D)	**135.** (C)	**136.** (D)	**137.** (D)	**138.** (B)	**139.** (A)	**140.** (B)
141. (B)	**142.** (D)	**143.** (D)	**144.** (D)	**145.** (B)	**146.** (D)	**147.** (C)	**148.** (D)	**149.** (D)	**150.** (C)
151. (C)	**152.** (C)	**153.** (B)	**154.** (B)	**155.** (D)	**156.** (A)	**157.** (C)	**158.** (D)	**159.** (C)	**160.** (D)
161. (D)	**162.** (B)	**163.** (D)	**164.** (C)	**165.** (D)	**166.** (D)	**167.** (B)	**168.** (C)	**169.** (B)	**170.** (C)
171. (B)	**172.** (C)								

SOLUTIONS WITH EXPLANATIONS

1. Registration of other vehicles in January = 6000
Registration of other vehicles in April = 15000
$\therefore$ Increase = (15000–6000) = 9000

2. Registration of cars in May = 17000
Registration of cars in June = 28000

$$\% \text{ Increase} = \left(\frac{11000}{17000} \times 100\right)\% = 64.7\%$$

3. Number of vehicles other than cars registered in March 1998 = (25000 – 15000) = 10000.

4. Yield of rice = $\left(\frac{40}{360} \times 8100\right)$ = 900 tons.

5. Yield of wheat = $\frac{100}{360} \times 2400 = 666.67$ tons

$$= 666\frac{2}{3} \text{ tons}$$

6. Excess on 40 = 60

$$\text{Excess on } 100 = \left(\frac{60}{40} \times 100\right)\% = 150\%$$

7. Central angle for savings = 360 – (108 + 72 + 72 + 72) = 36°

$$\therefore \text{Savings} = \text{Rs.}\left(\frac{36}{360} \times 60000\right) = \text{Rs. } 6000$$

8. $\frac{67}{11} \times 4000 = 24{,}363$ crore

9. 33% + 11% = 44%

10. 11 : 34 is approximately equal to 1 : 3.

11. The difference between the results of girls and boys in V standard is 20; in VI standard is 10; in VII standard is 20; in VIII standard is 30; in IX standard is 10 and in X standard is 10. So, it is maximum in VIII standard.

12. Average result of girls.

$$= \frac{60+70+60+60+80+60}{6} = \frac{390}{6}$$

= 65%

So, in VII standard the result of boys is less than the average result of the girls.

13. In VI standard, the results of boys and girls are in the ratio 8 : 7 while in IX standard, the results of boys and girls are in the ratio 7 : 8.

14. Average result of boys

$$= \frac{1}{6}(80+80+40+90+70+70) = \frac{430}{6} = 71.7\%$$

Clearly, in IX standard the result of girls is more than the average result of the boys.

20. Production of D type toys in 1983 = 1,05,000
Production of D type toys in 1985 = 1,25,000

$$\text{Percentage increase} = \frac{20000}{105000} \times 100 = 19.05$$
$$= 19\% \text{ (app.)}$$

21. Total production of A types toys from 1982-86 = 945 thousands.
Total production of B types toys from 1982-86 = 850 thousands.
Total production of C types toys from 1982-86 = 520 thousands.
Total production of D types toys from 1982-86 = 565 thousands.
Total production of E types toys from 1982-86 = 375 thousands.
Hence, it was maximum for A type toys.

22. Drop in production of A type toys from 1982 to 1984 = 20000

$$\text{Percentage drop} = \frac{20000}{200000} \times 100 = 10\%$$

23. From the table, it is obvious that there is a continuous increase in production of D type of toys

24. If the required number is x, then by hypothesis 80,000 = x% of 1,60,000

$$\text{or } 80{,}000 = \frac{x}{100} \times 160000$$

$$\therefore \quad x = \frac{80000 \times 100}{160000} = 50$$

30. Proportion of the sales in June to that in May

$$= \frac{800}{400} = 2$$

$$\text{July to that in June} = \frac{1000}{800} = \frac{5}{4} = 1.25$$

$$\text{August to that in July} = \frac{1200}{1000} = \frac{6}{5} = 1.20$$

33. Average monthly sales = (500+400+800+1000+1200) ÷ 5 = 780

34. Difference in profit between 1983 and 1984 = Rs. 20 lakhs – Rs. 10 lakhs = Rs. 10 lakhs.

35. Average income = Rs. (30 + 50 + 40 + 60 + 60) ÷ 5 = Rs. 48 lakhs.

Hence the income was more than average income in the years 1983, 1985, 1986.

36. Increase in expenditure from 1984 to 1985 = Rs. 10 lakhs.

$$= \frac{10}{30} \times 100 = 33\frac{1}{3}\%$$

37. It is obvious from the graph that income in 1984 was equal to the expenditure in 1985.

38. Profit in 1982, 1983, 1984, 1985 and 1986 are respectively Rs. 10 lakhs, Rs. 20 lakhs, Rs. 10 lakhs, Rs. 20 lakhs and Rs. 25 lakhs; so it was maximum in 1986.

39. Required Central Angle = $\left(\frac{16}{100} \times 360\right) = 57.6°$

40. Let the royalty be Rs. x Then.

$36 : 10 :: 23400 : x$

So, $x = \frac{10 \times 23400}{36}$ = Rs. 6500

41. Let the expenditure on canvassing be Rs. x

Then, $8 : 18 :: 18000 : x$

So, $x = \frac{18 \times 18000}{8}$ = Rs. 40500

42. If canvassing charges are Rs. 18, royalty is Rs. 10.

On Rs. 18, it is less by 8

On Rs. 100, it is less by $\left(\frac{8}{18} \times 100\right)\%$

$$= 44\frac{4}{9}\%$$

49. Total production of all the five states in 1988 = 72.5

1/8th of 72.5 = 9 (approx.)

State A contributes close to 1/8th of the total production of all the five states.

50. 1988

51. Percentage increase in production of state A in 1989 over that in 1986 = $\frac{2.6}{9} \times 100 = 28.89\%$

Similar figures for the other states are 13.10, 13.42, 3.95, 5.71 respectively

52. % Increase of production in 1987 over that in 1986 $= \frac{1.6}{21} \times 100 = 7.62$. Similar figures in 1988 over that in 1987 = 2.65 and in 1990 over that in 1989 is 7.66

55. During the period 1981-86, out of a total of 252 candidates the number of candidates selected in science discipline is 106.

∴ Percentage of the candidates selected in Science discipline = $\frac{106}{252} \times 100 = 42.06$

= 42 approx.

57. % of Agriculture discipline candidates in

1981 : $\frac{1}{30} \times 100 = 3\frac{1}{3}\%$

1982 : $\frac{3}{45} \times 100 = 6\frac{2}{3}\%$

1983 : $\frac{3}{50} \times 100 = 6\%$

1984 : $\frac{2.5}{40} \times 100 = 6\frac{1}{4}\%$

1985 : $\frac{1}{42} \times 100 = 2\frac{8}{21}\%$

1986 : $\frac{2}{45} \times 100 = 4\frac{4}{9}\%$

58. % Selected in arts discipline in

1981 : $\frac{4}{30} \times 100 = 13\frac{1}{3}\%$

1982 : $\frac{8}{45} \times 100 = 17\frac{7}{9}\%$

1983 : $\frac{8.5}{50} \times 100 = 17\%$

1984 : $\frac{10}{40} \times 100 = 25\%$

1985 : $\frac{11}{42} \times 100 = 26.19\%$

1986 : $\frac{13}{45} \times 100 = 28\frac{8}{9}\%$

62. In case of rice; the production in 1980 increases by 10.8 lakh tonnes as compared to 1979.

63. The production of rice and wheat together in 1976, 1977, 1978, 1979, 1980 and 1981 was 65.8, 63.7, 77.5, 71.8, 84.5 and 89.1 lakhs tonnes respectively.

65. The percentage increase of production in 1981 over that in 1976 in case of :

Rice = $\frac{52.1 - 44}{44} \times 100 = 18.41\%$

Wheat = $\frac{37 - 21.8}{21.8} \times 100 = 69.72\%$

Pulses = $\frac{12.2 - 10}{10} \times 100 = 22\%$

Potatoes = $\frac{10.2 - 4.8}{4.8} \times 100 = 112.5\%$

66. Number of increase in 1981 to 1983 = 80 – 30 = 50

% increase = $\frac{50}{30} \times 100$

= 166.66%

67. Required difference = (25 – 20) hundred crore
= 5 × 100 crore = 500 crore

68. Required bank credit per sick unit

$= \text{Rs.}\ \frac{10 \times 100\ \text{crore}}{30 \times 1000}$

$= \text{Rs.}\ \frac{10 \times 1000000000}{30 \times 1000} = \text{Rs. 3.33 Lakhs}$

≈ Rs. 3 Lakhs

69. 1980 — $\frac{18 \times 100\ \text{crore}}{24 \times 1000} = \text{Rs.7.5 Lakhs}$

1981 — $\frac{20 \times 100\ \text{crore}}{30 \times 1000} = \text{Rs.6.6 Lakhs}$

1982 — $\frac{25 \times 100\ \text{crore}}{60 \times 1000} = \text{Rs.4.16 Lakhs}$

1983 — $\frac{31 \times 100\ \text{crore}}{80 \times 1000} = \text{Rs.3.87 Lakhs}$

1984 — $\frac{36 \times 100\ \text{crore}}{90 \times 1000} = \text{Rs.4 Lakhs}$

Hence it is maximum on 1980.

73. $\frac{18 \times 100}{20} = 90\%$

81. Central angle for 108 marks = $\left(\frac{108}{540} \times 360\right) = 72°$

So, the student scored 108 marks in Social Science.

82. Central angle for

$16\frac{2}{3}\% = \left[\frac{50}{3 \times 100} \times 360\right]^{\circ} = 60°$

So, he scored $16\frac{2}{3}\%$ marks in Hindi.

83. Marks scored in Hindi and Mathematics.

$= \left[\frac{60}{360} \times 540 + \frac{90}{360} \times 540\right] = 225$

Marks scored in English, Social Science and Science

$= \left[\frac{63}{360} \times 540 + \frac{72}{360} \times 540 + \frac{75}{360} \times 540\right] = 315$

∴ Difference of marks = (315 – 225) = 90

90. Clearly 25% of income was spent on transport and other items.

91. Difference of expenditure on Housing & Transport = (15–5)% of Rs. 75000 = Rs. 7500

92. Expenditure on food was more than that on clothing by
(23–10)% of Rs. 75000 = Rs. 9750

94. In 1991, the percentage of Hindus and Sikhs were 30 and 45 respectively. So, the ratio of Hindus and Sikhs was 30 : 45 or 2 : 3

95. In 1992, Hindus population
= 55% of total population

$= \frac{55}{100} \times (1000000) = 550000$

96. In 1993, Hindus = 60%, Sikhs = 15%
∴ Percentage of Sikhs over Hindus

$= \left[\frac{15}{60} \times 100\right] = 25\%$

97. Hindus in 1991 = 30%.
Hindus in 1994 = 45%
Over 30, increase = 15.

Over 100, increase = $\left[\frac{15}{30} \times 100\right] = 50\%$

98. Required population = (30 + 25)% of 600000

$= \frac{55}{100} \times 600000 = 330000$

99. A quick observation of the chart shows that Hindus in 1991, 92, 93 and 94 were 30%, 55%, 60% 45% respectively.
So, the maximum percentage was in 1993.

102. For B type car, the ratio of rejection to production in

1983 : $\frac{3}{50} = 0.060$

1984 : $\frac{2}{45} = 0.044$

1985 : $\frac{2.5}{40} = 0.063$

1986 : $\frac{2.3}{42} = 0.055$

1987 : $\frac{2.5}{48} = 0.052$

1988 : $\frac{2.1}{41} = 0.051$

103. For E type car, the ratio of rejection to production in 1983 = 0.067
Similar figure for other ahead years are 0.069; 0.056, 0.038, 0.044; 0.050 respectively.

104. 20000 - 17000 = 3000

105. (62–3.5) = k% of (58 – 4)

$\therefore k = \frac{100 \times 58.5}{54} = 108.$

106. Rejection percent in 1984 for type A

$= \frac{300}{35} = 8.57$

and for other type of cars the rejection percent is respectively 4.44 for type B; 2.75 for type C; 5.33 for type D; and 6.90 for type E.

107. (420-320) thousands = 100,000 i.e. one lakh.

108. $320 \div 400 = 0.8$

109. Increased in 1989 over 1988 = $\frac{20}{400} \times 100 = 5$

Increase in 1990 over 1989 = $\frac{20}{400} \times 100$
$= 4.76$

110. $340 \times X = 440$ or $X = \frac{440 \times 100}{340} = 129.41\,\%$

111. $(400 + 420 + 440 + 400) \div 4 = 415.$

112. The total number of workers are 80, and 35 of them worked 40 or more hours, Therefore

% worked 40 or more hours = $\frac{35}{80} \times 100$
$= 43.75\%$

113. 15 people worked 40 to 44 hours and 4 worked upto 29 hours

$\therefore 4x = 15 \Rightarrow x = 3\frac{3}{4}$

114. Statement I can be inferred, since the average number of hours worked is $3100 \div 80 = 38\frac{3}{4}$ i.e. less than 40.

115. Average of the total production of all types of cars during the period.

$= (74 + 71 + 75 + 90 + 80 + 86) \div 6$

$= \frac{476}{6} = 79\frac{1}{3} = 80$ approx.

118. 25% of the total production of all types of cars produced during the year 1983 = 25% of 80 = 20.

119. % increase in total production of all types of cars in 1982 to that in 1981 = $\frac{15}{75} \times 100 = 20$

120. Required ratio = $\frac{(75+65)}{(85+95)} = \frac{140}{180} = \frac{7}{9}$

121. Required percentage $= \left[\frac{(70+80)}{(95+110)} \times 100\right]\%$

$= \left[\frac{150}{205} \times 100\right]\%$

$= 73.17\%$

122. Average sales (in thousand number) of branches B1, B3 and B6 in 2000

$= \frac{1}{3} \times (80 + 95 + 70) = \left(\frac{245}{3}\right).$

Average sales (in thousand number) of branches B1, B2 and B3 in 2001

$= \frac{1}{3} \times (105 + 65 + 110) = \left(\frac{280}{3}\right).$

Required percentage $= \left[\frac{245/3}{280/3} \times 100\right]\%$

$= \left(\frac{245}{280} \times 100\right)\%$

$= 87.5\%$

123. Average sales of all the six branches (in thousand numbers) for the year 2000

$= \frac{1}{6} \times [80 + 75 + 95 + 85 + 75 + 70]$

$= 80.$

124. Total sales of branches B1, B3 and B5 for both the years (in thousand numbers)

$= (80 + 105) + (95 + 110) + (75 + 95)$

$= 560.$

125. Average foreign exchange reserves over the given period = 3480 million US $.

The country had reserves above 3480 million US $ during the years 1992-93, 1996-97 and 1997-98, i.e., for 3 years and below 3480 million US $ during the years 1991-92, 1993-94, 1994-95, 1995-56 and 1998-99 i.e., for 5 years.

Hence, required ratio = 3 : 5.

126. Required ratio = $\frac{5040}{3360} = 1.5$

127. There is an increase in foreign exchange reserves during the years 1992 - 1993, 1994 - 1995, 1996 - 1997, 1997 - 1998 as compared to previous year (as shown by bar-graph).

The percentage increase in reserves during these years compared to previous year are:

For 1992-1993 $= \left[\frac{(3720 - 2640)}{2640} \times 100\right]\%$
$= 40.91\%.$

For 1994-1995 $= \left[\frac{(3360 - 2520)}{2520} \times 100\right]\%$
$= 33.33\%.$

For 1996-1997 $= \left[\frac{(4320 - 3120)}{3120} \times 100\right]\%$
$= 38.46\%.$

For 1997-1998 $= \left[\frac{(5040 - 4320)}{4320} \times 100\right]\%$
$= 16.67\%.$

Clearly, the percentage increase over previous year is highest for 1992-1993.

128. Average foreign exchange reserves over the given period

$= [1/8 \times (2640 + 3720 + 2520 + 3360 + 3120 + 4320 + 5040 + 3120)]$ million US \$

$= 3480$ million US \$.

Foreign exchange reserves in 1996-1997 = 4320 million US \$.

$\therefore$ Required percentage $= \left(\dfrac{4320}{3480} \times 100\right)\%$

$= 124.14\% \approx 125\%.$

129. Foreign exchange reserves in 1997-1998 = 5040 million US \$.

Foreign exchange reserves in 1993-1994 = 2520 million US \$.

$\therefore$ Increase = (5040-2520) = 2520 US \$.

$\therefore$ Percentage Increase $= \left(\dfrac{2520}{2520} \times 100\right)\% = 100\%.$

130. Percentage change (rise/fall) in the production of Company Y in comparison to the previous year, for different years are:

For 1997 $= \left[\dfrac{(35-25)}{25} \times 100\right] = 40\%.$

For 1998 $= \left[\dfrac{(35-35)}{35} \times 100\right] = 0\%.$

For 1999 $= \left[\dfrac{(40-35)}{35} \times 100\right] = 14.29\%.$

For 2000 $= \left[\dfrac{(50-40)}{40} \times 100\right] = 25\%.$

Hence, the maximum percentage rise/fall in the production of Company Y is for 1997.

131. Average production of Company X in the period 1998-2000

$= \left[\dfrac{1}{3} \times (25 + 50 + 40)\right] = \left(\dfrac{115}{3}\right)$ lakh tons.

Average production of Company Y in the period 1998-2000

$= \left[\dfrac{1}{3} \times (35 + 40 + 50)\right] = \left(\dfrac{125}{3}\right)$ lakh tons.

$\therefore$ Required ratio $= \dfrac{\left(\dfrac{115}{3}\right)}{\left(\dfrac{115}{3}\right)} = \dfrac{115}{125} = \dfrac{23}{25}.$

132. Average production (in lakh tons) in five years for the three companies are:

For Company X $= \left[\dfrac{1}{5} \times (30 + 45 + 25 + 50 + 40)\right]$

$= \dfrac{190}{5} = 38.$

For Company Y $= \left[\dfrac{1}{5} \times (25 + 35 + 35 + 40 + 50)\right]$

$= \dfrac{125}{5} = 37.$

For Company Z $= \left[\dfrac{1}{5} \times (35 + 40 + 45 + 35 + 35)\right]$

$= \dfrac{190}{5} = 38.$

$\therefore$ Average production of five years is maximum for both the Companies X and Z.

133. The percentages of production of Company Z to the production of Company Z for various years are:

For 1996 $= \left(\dfrac{35}{25} \times 100\right)\% = 140\%.$

For 1997 $= \left(\dfrac{40}{35} \times 100\right)\% = 114.29\%.$

For 1998 $= \left(\dfrac{45}{35} \times 100\right)\% = 128.57\%.$

For 1999 $= \left(\dfrac{35}{40} \times 100\right)\% = 87.5\%.$

For 2000 $= \left(\dfrac{35}{50} \times 100\right)\% = 70\%.$

Clearly, this percentage is highest for 1996.

134. Percentage increase in the production of Company Y from 1996 to 1999

$= \left[\dfrac{(40-25)}{25} \times 100\right]\% = \left[\dfrac{15}{25} \times 100\right]\%$

$= 60\%.$

135. The differences between the amount invested in raw material and the value of sales of finished goods for various years are:

For 1995 = Rs. (200 – 120) lakhs = Rs. 80 lakhs.
For 1996 = Rs. (300 – 225) lakhs = Rs. 75 lakhs.
For 1997 = Rs. (500 – 375) lakhs = Rs. 125 lakhs.
For 1998 = Rs. (400 – 330) lakhs = Rs. 70 lakhs.
For 1999 = Rs. (600 – 525) lakhs = Rs. 75 lakhs.
For 2000 = Rs. (460 – 420) lakhs = Rs. 40 lakhs.

Clearly, maximum difference was during 1997.

136. Required percentage

$= \left[\dfrac{600}{(375 + 330 + 525)} \times 100\right]\% = 48.78\%$

$\approx 49\%.$

137. Required difference

= Rs. [1/6 × (200 + 300 + 500 + 400 + 600 +460) – 1/6 × (120 + 225 + 375 + 330 + 525 + 420)] lakhs

$$= \text{Rs.} \left[\left(\frac{2460}{6}\right) - \left(\frac{1995}{6}\right)\right]$$

= Rs. (410 - 332.5) lakhs

= Rs. 77.5 lakhs.

138. The percentage change in the amount invested in raw-materials and in the value of sales of finished goods for different years are:

Percentage change in Amount invested in raw-material:

$$\text{For 1996} = \left[\frac{(225-120)}{120} \times 100\right]\% = 87.5\%.$$

$$\text{For 1997} = \left[\frac{(375-225)}{225} \times 100\right]\% = 66.67\%.$$

$$\text{For 1998} = \left[\frac{(330-375)}{375} \times 100\right]\% = -12\%.$$

$$\text{For 1999} = \left[\frac{(420-525)}{525} \times 100\right]\% = 59.09\%.$$

$$\text{For 2000} = \left[\frac{(420-525)}{525} \times 100\right]\% = -20\%.$$

Percentage change in value of sales of finished goods:

$$\text{For 1996} = \left[\frac{(300-200)}{200} \times 100\right]\% = 50\%.$$

$$\text{For 1997} = \left[\frac{(500-300)}{300} \times 100\right]\% = 66.7\%.$$

$$\text{For 1998} = \left[\frac{(400-500)}{500} \times 100\right]\% = -20\%.$$

$$\text{For 1999} = \left[\frac{(600-400)}{400} \times 100\right]\% = 50\%.$$

$$\text{For 2000} = \left[\frac{(460-600)}{600} \times 100\right]\% = -23.33\%.$$

Thus, the percentage difference is same during the year 1997.

139. The percentage increase in the amount invested in raw-materials as compared to the previous year, for different years are:

$$\text{For 1996} = \left[\frac{(225-120)}{120}\right]\% = 87.5\%.$$

$$\text{For 1997} = \left[\frac{(375-225)}{225}\right]\% = 66.67\%.$$

For 1998 there is a decrease.

$$\text{For 1999} = \left[\frac{(525-330)}{330}\right]\% = 59.09\%.$$

For 2000 there is a decrease.

∴ There is maximum percentage increase in 1996.

140. (40+10) = 50% (from first chart)

141. 40:15 = 8:3

142. Tourist traffic from other countries to Swiz is 20%.

Amongst this 20%, 25% of traffic from India. So, 25% of 20% = 5% corresponds to the Indian traffic in Switzerland.

5 % corresponds to Switzerland's 25 lakh. Hence 15% will be 75 lakh.

143. Required number = (17% of 27300) + (14% of 24700)

= 4641 + 3458

= 8099.

144. $\text{Required ratio} = \frac{(21\% \text{ of } 24700)}{(14\% \text{ of } 27300)} = \frac{(21 \times 24700)}{14 \times 27300}$

$$= \frac{19}{14}$$

145. Students of institute M at graduate level= 17% of 27300 = 4641.

Students of institute S at graduate level = 14% of 27300 = 3822.

Total number of students at graduate in institutes M and S = (4641 + 3822)

= 8463.

146. $\text{Required ratio} = \frac{(21\% \text{ of } 24700)}{(13\% \text{ of } 27300)} = \frac{(21 \times 24700)}{13 \times 27300}$

$$= \frac{19}{13}$$

147. Required number = (15% of 24700) + (12% of 24700)

= 3705 + 2964

= 6669.

148. Total exports of the three Companies X, Y and Z together, during various years are:

In 1993 = Rs. (30 + 80 + 60) crores

= Rs. 170 crores.

In 1994 = Rs. (60 + 40 + 90) crores

= Rs. 190 crores.

In 1995 = Rs. (40 + 60 + 120) crores
= Rs. 220 crores.

In 1996 = Rs. (70 + 60 + 90) crores
= Rs. 220 crores.

In 1997 = Rs. (100 + 80 + 60) crores
= Rs. 240 crores.

In 1998 = Rs. (50 + 100 + 80) crores
= Rs. 230 crores.

In 1999 = Rs. (120 + 140 + 100) crores
= Rs. 360 crores.

Clearly, the total exports of the three Companies X, Y and Z together are same during the years 1995 and 1996.

149. Analysis of the graph: From the graph it is clear that

1. The amount of exports of Company X (in crore Rs.) in the years 1993, 1994, 1995, 1996, 1997, 1998 and 1999 are 30, 60, 40, 70, 100, 50 and 120 respectively.
2. The amount of exports of Company Y (in crore Rs.) in the years 1993, 1994, 1995, 1996, 1997, 1998 and 1999 are 80, 40, 60, 60, 80, 100 and 140 respectively.
3. The amount of exports of Company Z (in crore Rs.) in the years 1993, 1994, 1995, 1996, 1997, 1998 and 1999 are 60, 90,, 120, 90, 60, 80 and 100 respectively.

Average annual exports (in Rs. crore) of Company Y during the given period

$$= \frac{1}{7} \times (80 + 40 + 60 + 60 + 80 + 100 + 140)$$

$$= \frac{560}{7} = 80.$$

Average annual exports (in Rs. crore) of Company Z during the given period

$$= \frac{1}{7} \times (60 + 90 + 120 + 90 + 60 + 80 + 100)$$

$$= \left(\frac{600}{7}\right)$$

$$\therefore \text{ Required percentage } = \left[\frac{80}{\left(\frac{600}{7}\right)} \times 100\right]\%$$

$$\approx 93.33\%.$$

150. The difference between the exports from the Companies X and Y during the various years are:

In 1993 = Rs. (80 – 30) crores = Rs. 50 crores.

In 1994 = Rs. (60 – 40) crores = Rs. 20 crores.

In 1995 = Rs. (60 – 40) crores = Rs. 20 crores.

In 1996 = Rs. (70 – 60) crores = Rs. 10 crores.

In 1997 = Rs. (100 – 80) crores = Rs. 20 crores.

In 1998 = Rs. (100 – 50) crores = Rs. 50 crores.

In 1999 = Rs. (140 – 120) crores = Rs. 20 crores.

Clearly, the difference is minimum in the year 1996.

151. Average exports of the three Companies X, Y and Z in 1993

$$= \text{Rs.} \left[\frac{1}{3} \times (30 + 80 + 60)\right] \text{ crores}$$

$$= \text{Rs.} \left(\frac{170}{3}\right) \text{ crores.}$$

Average exports of the three Companies X, Y and Z in 1998

$$= \text{Rs.} \left[\frac{1}{3} \times (50 + 100 + 80)\right] \text{ crores}$$

$$= \text{Rs.} \left(\frac{230}{3}\right) \text{ crores.}$$

$$\text{Difference} = \text{Rs.} \left[\left(\frac{230}{3}\right) - \left(\frac{170}{3}\right)\right] \text{ crores}$$

$$= \text{Rs.} \left(\frac{60}{3}\right) \text{ crores}$$

= Rs. 20 crores.

152. Average annual exports of Company Z during the given period

$$= \frac{1}{7} \times (60 + 90 + 120 + 90 + 60 + 80 + 100)$$

$$= \text{Rs.} \left(\frac{600}{7}\right) \text{ crores}$$

= Rs. 85.71 crores.

From the analysis of graph the exports of Company Z are more than the average annual exports of Company Z (i.e., Rs. 85.71 crores) during the years 1994, 1995, 1996 and 1999, i.e., during 4 of the given years.

153. Average marks obtained in Physics by all the seven students

$$= \frac{1}{7} \times [(90\% \text{ of } 120) + (80\% \text{ of } 120) + (70\% \text{ of } 120) + (80\% \text{ of } 120) + (85\% \text{ of } 120) + (65\% \text{ of } 120) + (50\% \text{ of } 120)]$$

$$= \frac{1}{7} \times [(90 + 80 + 70 + 80 + 85 + 65 + 50)\% \text{ of } 120]$$

$$= \frac{1}{7} \times [\,520\% \text{ of } 120\,]$$

$$= \frac{624}{7} = 89.14.$$

154. From the table it is clear that Sajal and Rohit have 60% or more marks in each of the six subjects.

155. Aggregate marks obtained by Sajal
= [(90% of 150) + (60% of 130) + (70% of 120) + (70% of 100) + (90% of 60) + (70% of 40)]
= [135 + 78 + 84 + 70 + 54 + 28] = 449.

156. We shall find the overall percentage (for all the seven students) with respect to each subject.

The overall percentage for any subject is equal to the average of percentages obtained by all the seven students since the maximum marks for any subject is the same for all the students.

Therefore, overall percentage for:

(i) Maths = [1/7 × (90 + 100 + 90 + 80 + 80 + 70 + 65)]%
= [1/7 × (575)]%
= 82.14%.

(ii) Chemistry = [1/7 × (50 + 80 + 60 + 65 + 65 + 75 + 35)]%
= [1/7 × (430)] %
= 61.43%.

(iii) Physics = [1/7 × (90 + 80 + 70 + 80 + 85 + 65 + 50)]%
= [1/7 × (520)]%
= 74.29%.

(iv) Geography = [1/7 × (60 + 40 + 70 + 80 + 95 + 85 + 77)]%
= [1/7 × (507)]%
= 72.43%.

(v) History = [1/7 × (70 + 80 + 90 + 60 + 50 + 40 + 80)]%
= [1/7 × (470)]%
= 67.14%.

(vi) Comp. Science = [1/7 × (80 + 70 + 70 + 60 + 90 + 60 + 80)]%
= [1/7 × (510)]%
= 72.86%.

Clearly, this percentage is highest for Maths.

157. Aggregate marks obtained by Tarun
= [(65% of 150) + (35% of 130) + (50% of 120) + ((77% of 100) + (80% of 60) + (80% of 40)]
= [97.5 + 45.5 + 60 + 77 + 48 + 32]
= 360.

The maximum marks (of all the six subjects)
= (150 + 130 + 120 + 100 + 60 + 40)
= 600.

$$\text{Overall percentage of Tarun} = \left(\frac{360}{600}\times 100\right)\%$$
= 60%.

158. $$\text{Required percentage} = \left[\frac{(145-108)}{108}\times 100\right]\%$$
= 34.26%
≈ 34%.

159. The total sales (in thousands) of all the seven years for various batteries are:

For 4AH = 75 + 90 + 96 + 105 + 90 + 105 + 115 = 676

For 7AH = 144 + 126 + 114 + 90 + 75 + 60 + 85 = 694

For 32AH = 114 + 102 + 75 + 150 + 135 + 165 + 160 = 901

For 35AH = 102 + 84 + 105 + 90 + 75 + 45 + 100 = 601

For 55AH = 108 + 126 + 135 + 75 + 90 + 120 + 145 = 799.

Clearly, sales are maximum in case of 32AH batteries.

160. Required difference = [(84 – 45) × 1000] = 39000.

161. The percentages of sales of 4AH batteries to the total sales in different years are:

$$\text{For 1992} = \left(\frac{75}{543}\times 100\right)\% = 13.81\%.$$

$$\text{For 1993} = \left(\frac{90}{528}\times 100\right)\% = 17.05\%.$$

$$\text{For 1994} = \left(\frac{96}{525}\times 100\right)\% = 18.29\%.$$

$$\text{For 1995} = \left(\frac{105}{510}\times 100\right)\% = 20.59\%.$$

$$\text{For 1996} = \left(\frac{96}{465}\times 100\right)\% = 19.35\%.$$

$$\text{For 1997} = \left(\frac{105}{495}\times 100\right)\% = 21.21\%.$$

$$\text{For 1998} = \left(\frac{115}{605}\times 100\right)\% = 19.01\%.$$

Clearly, the percentage is maximum in 1997.

162. From the table it is clear that the sales of 7AH batteries have been decreasing continuously from 1992 to 1997.

163. Let the expenditure in 1996 = x.

Also, let the incomes in 1996 and 1999 be I_1 and I_2 respectively.

Then, for the year 1996, we have:

$$55 = \frac{I_1 - x}{x}\times 100 \Rightarrow \frac{55}{100} = \frac{I_1}{x} - 1 \Rightarrow I_2 = \frac{155x}{100} \quad ...(i)$$

$$70 = \frac{I_2 - x}{x} \times 100 \Rightarrow \frac{70}{100} = \frac{I_2}{x} - 1 \Rightarrow I_2 = \frac{170x}{100} \text{ ... (ii)}$$

From (i) and (ii), we get:

$$\frac{I_1}{I_2} = \frac{\left(\frac{155x}{100}\right)}{\left(\frac{170x}{100}\right)} = \frac{155}{170} \approx \frac{0.91}{1} \approx 9:10.$$

164. Let the expenditure is 1998 be Rs. x crores.

Then, $65 = \frac{264 - x}{x} \times 100$

$\Rightarrow \quad \frac{65}{100} = \frac{294}{x} - 1$

$\Rightarrow \quad x = \frac{264 - x}{165} = 160.$

$\therefore$ Expenditure in 1998 = Rs. 160 crores.

165. The line-graph gives the comparison of percent profit for different years but the comparison of the expenditures is not possible without more data.

Therefore, the year with minimum expenditure cannot be determined.

166. From the line-graph we obtain information about the percentage profit only. To find the profit in 2000 we must have the data for the income or expenditure in 2000.

Therefore, the profit for 2000 cannot be determined.

167. Average percent profit earned for the given years

$= \frac{1}{6} \times [40 + 55 + 45 + 65 + 70 + 60]$

$= \frac{335}{6} = 55\frac{5}{6}$

168. Required percentage $= \left(\frac{9\% \text{ of } 5700}{8\% \text{ of } 8550} \times 100\right)\%$

$= \left(\frac{9 \times 5700}{8\% \text{ of } 8550} \times 100\right)\%$

$= 75\%.$

169. The percentage of candidates passed to candidates enrolled can be determined for each institute as under:

(i) $P = \left[\frac{18\% \text{ of } 5700}{22\% \text{ of } 8550} \times 100\right]\%$

$= \left[\frac{18 \times 5700}{22 \times 8550} \times 100\right]\% = 54.55\%.$

(ii) $Q = \left[\frac{17\% \text{ of } 5700}{15\% \text{ of } 8550} \times 100\right]\% = 75.56\%.$

(iii) $R = \left[\frac{13\% \text{ of } 5700}{10\% \text{ of } 8550} \times 100\right]\% = 86.67\%.$

(iv) $S = \left[\frac{16\% \text{ of } 5700}{17\% \text{ of } 8550} \times 100\right]\% = 62.75\%.$

(v) $T = \left[\frac{9\% \text{ of } 5700}{8\% \text{ of } 8550} \times 100\right]\% = 75\%.$

(vi) $V = \left[\frac{15\% \text{ of } 5700}{12\% \text{ of } 8550} \times 100\right]\% = 83.33\%.$

(vii) $X = \left[\frac{12\% \text{ of } 5700}{16\% \text{ of } 8550} \times 100\right]\% = 50\%.$

Highest of these is 86.67% corresponding to institute R.

170. Required difference

$= [(16\% + 18\%) \text{ of } 5700] - [(8\% + 10\%) \text{ of } 8550]$

$= [(34\% \text{ of } 5700) - (18\% \text{ of } 8550)]$

$= (1938 - 1539)$

$= 399.$

171. Candidates passed from institutes Q and R together

$= [(13\% + 17\%) \text{ of } 5700]$

$= 30\% \text{ of } 5700.$

Candidates enrolled from institutes Q and R together

$= [(15\% + 10\%) \text{ of } 8550]$

$= 25\% \text{ of } 8550.$

Required Percentage $= \left[\frac{30\% \text{ of } 5700}{25\% \text{ of } 8550} \times 100\right]\%$

$= \left(\frac{30 \times 5700}{25 \times 8550} \times 100\right)\%$

$= 80\%.$

172. Required ratio $= \left(\frac{18\% \text{ of } 5700}{22\% \text{ of } 8550} \times 100\right)$

$= \left(\frac{18 \times 5700}{22 \times 8550} \times 100\right)$

$= \frac{6}{11}.$

UNIT VIII

INFORMATION AND COMMUNICATION TECHNOLOGY

Syllabus

- **ICT:** General Abbreviations and Terminology.
- Basics of Internet, Intranet, E-mail, Audio and Video-conferencing.
- Digital Initiatives in Higher Education.
- ICT and Governance.

Mankind has entered the information age from an industrial age that prevailed till a few years ago. This change is expected to have a profound effect on the way we live, make money and deal with wars. It would therefore be useful to examine the nature of information and the information technology that is at the root of future opportunities, challenges and competition. Information has been there since beginning. Information technology was also there. But it is computer, which has made information technology so popular.

MEANING OF ICT

Information and Communication Technologies are defined as all devices, tools, content, resources, forums, and services, digital and those that can be converted into or delivered through digital forms, which can be deployed for realising the goals of teaching learning, enhancing access to and reach of resources, building of capacities, as well as management of the educational system.

These will not only include hardware devices connected to computers, and software applications, but also interactive digital content, internet and other satellite communication devices, radio and television services, web based content repositories, interactive forums, learning management systems, and management information systems.

These will also include processes for digitisation, deployment and management of content, development and deployment of platforms and processes for capacity development, and creation of forums for interaction and exchange.

India's capabilities in the field of Information Technology provide not only an opportunity to participate vigorously and effectively in a globalizing world, but also to use it as a major vehicle for all-round socio-economic development of the country.

To ensure the benefits of an ICT-based knowledge economy India needs to adopt the two fold strategies: (i) a number of steps to ensure that the Indian IT industry grows at a fast pace in consonance with international trends: and (ii) to intend to take all possible measures to ensure that the benefits of his technology are meaningfully felt by the common people and reach to even in the remotest parts of the country.

The most basic hardware required for communication is the media through which data is transferred. There are several types of media, and the choice of the right media depends on many factors such as cost of transmission media, efficiency of data transmission and the transfer rate.

ADVANTAGES OF ICT

ICTs allow for the creation of digital resources like digital libraries where the students, teachers and professionals can access research material and course material from any place at any time. Such facilities allow the networking of academics and researchers and hence sharing of scholarly material and leads to quality enhancement in teaching and learning.

AIMS AND OBJECTIVES OF ICT IMPLEMENTATION IN EDUCATION

1. To implement the principle of life-long learning/education.
2. To increase a variety of educational services and medium/method.
3. To promote equal opportunities to obtain education and information.
4. To develop a system of collecting and disseminating educational information.
5. To promote technology literacy of all citizens, especially for students.
6. To develop distance education with national contents.
7. To promote the culture of learning at school (development of learning skills, expansion of optional education, open source of education, etc.)
8. To support schools in sharing experience and information with others.

BENEFITS OF ICT IN EDUCATION TO THE MAIN STAKEHOLDERS

Stakeholder	Benefits
Students	• Increased access, • Flexibility of content and delivery, • Combination of work and education, • Learner-centred approach, • Higher-quality of education and new-ways of interaction.
Employers	• High quality, cost effective professional development in the workplace, • Upgrading of employee skills, increased productivity, • Developing of a new learning culture, • Sharing of costs and of training time with the employees, • Increased portability of training.
Governments	• Increase the capacity and cost effectiveness of education and training systems, • To reach target groups with limited access to conventional education and training, • To support and enhance the quality and relevance of existing educational structures, • To ensure the connection of educational institutions and curricula to the emerging networks and information resources. • To promote innovation and opportunities for lifelong learning.

Source: UNESCO, 2002.

In absence of ICT, most of the responsibility of teaching and learning lies on the teachers. However, with the help of ICT one can transfer the responsibilities to the students so that they can self manage. It helps to individualize the teaching or guidance method as per the student's need. It also boosts the confidence level and the self-esteem of the students who acquire the ICT skills through the process of being exposed to such kind of learning also puts forth the view that ICT-based registration, evaluation, and administration help to link different levels of information and facilitate an overall view of the whole educational setup. It facilitates the evaluation and examination of the learning process and results by the students and the parent's in a flexible and convenient way. The globalization process has also created a large market of offshore students. To reach them, information technology is the only convenient medium, which can offer education as a service. It increases education provision substantially and can contribute to mass education. It also creates competition among the institutions for providing education and hence improves the quality.

Advantages of ICT in Higher Education

India is making use of powerful combination of ICTs such as open source software, satellite technology, local language interfaces, easy to use human-computer interfaces, digital libraries etc. with a long-term plan to reach the remotest of the villages. Community service centers have been started to promote e-learning throughout the country. Notable initiatives of use of ICT in education in India include:

- Indira Gandhi National Open University (IGNOU) uses radio, television and internet technologies.
- National Programme on Technology Enhanced Learning : a concept similar to the open courseware initiative of MIT. It uses internet and television technologies.
- Eklavya initiative : Uses internet and television to promote distance learning.
- IIT-Kanpur has developed 'Brihaspati', an open source e-learning platform (Virtual Class Room).

Premier institutions like Calcutta have entered into a strategic alliance with NIIT for providing programmes through virtual classrooms. Jadavpur University is using a mobile learning centre. IIT-Bombay has started the program of CDEEP (Centre for Distance Engineering Education Program) as emulated classroom interaction through the use of real time interactive satellite technology.

UGC Initiatives in ICT

The UGC initiated scheme called "ICT for teaching and learning process" for achieving quality and excellence in higher education. Network facilities with the help of ERNET, Ministry of Information and Technology, Government of India were installed at UGC office to promote a healthy work culture. Along with this UGC launched a mega programme namely, 'UGC INFONET', a network of Indian Universities and Colleges, by integrating Information and Communication Technology (ICT) in the process of teaching, learning and education management. The network is managed by ERNET India and almost all the universities are its members. Information for Library Network (INFLIBNET), an autonomous Inter University Centre of UGC is the nodal agency for coordination and facilitation of the linkage between ERNET and Universities. Training programmes for the manpower were conducted to manage the ERNET facilities and other aspects of systems including electronic subscriptions. In addition, UGC is encouraging creation of e-content/learning material for teaching learning process and management of education in colleges and universities.

Innovative Approaches for Teaching

ICTs have the potential to drive innovative and effective ways of teaching-learning and research. The inclusion of learning tools, easier use of multimedia or simulation tools, easy and almost instant access to data and information in a digital form which allows for computations and data processing generates possibilities which were otherwise not feasible. The possibility to diffuse these innovations and complement the learning content to improve quality in higher education through innovative pedagogic methods is high. The focus on ICTs to back quality research through utilization of rigorous research methodology and in-depth analysis is the call of the hour.

Some basic tools of ICT are described below :

1. **Periodicals.** Advantages of periodicals are as follows :
   - (i) These are the mirrors of the current political, economic, technical, social and other scenarios of the nation, region or world.
   - (ii) These are very costly (the price of a good magazine starts at Rs. 50 a piece);
   - (iii) These are available at cheap rates if the subscription mode is adopted by the reader (many magazine publishers are offering freebies too); and
   - (iv) These are full of information that can be used.
2. **Newspaper.** Advantages of newspapers are as follows :
   - (i) These have multiple (secular) content;
   - (ii) These can be read by individual without distractions (introvert people love them)
   - (iii) They consume tonnes of paper;
   - (iv) They give flexibility of publication to the publishers;
   - (v) They are a lucrative business in every nook and corner of the globe; and
   - (vi) They are cheap, at least in the developing countries of the world.
3. **T.V. and Radios.** Following are the advantages of TV and Radios.
   - (i) They give latest sets information to the audiences;
   - (ii) They entertain par excellence;
   - (iii) They are cheap;
   - (iv) They are passive media;
   - (v) They can effect healthy changes, especially in the contexts of community medicine, education, national polity, environment, ecology, dogma removal etc.); and
   - (vi) They are dynamic in the sense that new content is disseminated through them almost every fortnight.
4. **Computers.** Advantages of computers are as follows:
   - (i) **It has high speed.** All the operations in a computer are caused by electrical pulses. We all know that electricity travels at the speed of light, computers too can perform innumerable operations in just 1 sec. The processing speed of a computer is generally measured in *nanoseconds*. By the time an average person takes to read the contents of this page, the earliest model of the IBM microcomputer would add together a million numbers and still have some time to spare! You can imagine what would be the speed of the latest models of computers running 100 times faster!
   - (ii) **It has large storage capacity.** Computers have very large storage capacity. The contents of around two hundred sheets of A4 size paper can be stored on a small floppy disk, which is not even half the size of one sheet of paper. What would typically need large storage cabinets can be stored on a small floppy disk, which is not even half the size of a lunch box. Famous reference works like the "Encyclopedia Brittanica" and "Oxford Dictionary of English" occupies many large shelves in library. But today, they are stored in optical disks and hard disks that are less in both size and weight. While this in itself is impressive, computers also provide very quick and easy access to all the data.

     Apart from storing text, today's computers are also capable of storing picture and sound in digital form, which means that even movies and music can be stored and sent to places quickly in the form of CD.
   - (iii) **Its Accuracy.** Computers have many check circuits built in and so normally they do not make mistakes. Errors in computing are generally due to human negligence rather than technological faults. We have to always remember the fact that a computer is unintelligent and has to be given precise instructions and correct data to carry out its operations. If the

instruction is faulty or might mean more than one thing or if the data is wrong, the result coming out of the computer too would be wrong. This phenomenon of wrong output due to wrong input of instructions and/or data is termed as **Garbage In Garbage Out** or GIGO in computer jargon.

(iv) **Its Diligence.** Computers, being machines, do not suffer from fatigue and lack of concentration. If five million calculations have to be performed, a computer can perform the 5 million calculation with same accuracy and speed as it performed the first calculation.

(v) **Its Versatility.** Computers can perform a wide range of jobs with speed, accuracy and diligence. In an organisation, it is quite likely that the same computers are used for diverse purposes such as accounting, generating pay-slips, keeping track of manager's appointments, play games during the recreation hours.

5. **Movies.** Following advantages of movies are considerable:
   (i) They entertain the masses;
   (ii) They educate them;
   (iii) They make them patriots; and
   (iv) They give them reprieve (a pleasant escape) from realities of life.

E Learning

E-learning is a rapidly growing industry, the effects of which we can trace back to the 1980s and even well before that (in the form of distance learning and televised courses.

Now that affordable e-learning solutions exist for both computers and internet, it only takes a good e-learning tool for education to be facilitated from virtually anywhere. Technology has advanced so much that the geographical gap is bridged with the use of tools that make you feel as if you are inside the classroom. E-learning offers the ability to share material in all kinds of formats such as videos, slideshows, word documents, and PDFs. Conducting webinars (live online classes) and communicating with professors via chat and message forums is also an option available to users.

There is a plethora of different e-learning systems (otherwise known as Learning Management Systems, or LMSs for short) and methods, which allow for courses to be delivered. With the right tool, various processes can be automated such as a course with set materials and automatically marked tests. E-learning is an affordable (and often free) solution which provides the learners with the ability to fit learning around their lifestyles, effectively allowing even the busiest person to further a career and gain new qualifications.

Some of the most important developments in education have happened since the launch of the internet. These days learners are well versed in the use of smartphones, text messaging and using the internet so participating in and running an online course has become a simple affair. Message

BLENDED LEARNING

Blended learning is a combination of offline (face-to-face, traditional learning) and online learning in a way that the one compliments the other.

It provides individuals with the opportunity to enjoy the best of both worlds. For example, a student might attend classes in a real-world classroom setting and then supplement the lesson plan by completing online multimedia coursework. As such, the student would only have to physically attend class once a week and would be free to go at their own pace (and without worrying about scheduling issues).

Blended learning is often also referred to as "hybrid" learning, and can take on a variety of forms in online education environments. While some organizations may only use blended learning techniques on rare occasions, others might utilize it as a primary teaching method within their curriculum.

boards, social media and various other means of online communication allow learners to keep in touch and discuss course-related matters, whilst providing for a sense of community.

In the fast-paced world of e-learning, the available technologies to make a course new and exciting are always changing, and course content can and should be updated quickly to give students the very latest information. This is especially important if the e-learning training is being given to employees in a sector where keeping up-to-date on industry developments is of the utmost importance. This is one of the reasons why many businesses are now offering training via e-learning - other reasons include low costs and the ability for employees to study in their own time and place.

Overall, traditional learning is expensive, takes a long time and the results can vary. The importance of e-learning is now a given fact and it can offer an alternative that is much faster, cheaper and potentially better.

DISADVANTAGES OF ICT

Potential Drawbacks-cum-Challenges to Using ICT in Education

While using ICTs in education has some obvious benefits, ICTs also bring challenges. First is the high cost of acquiring, installing, operating, maintaining and replacing ICTs. While potentially of great importance, the integration of ICTs into teaching is still in its infancy. Introducing ICT systems for teaching in developing countries has a particularly high opportunity cost because installing them is usually more expensive in absolute terms than in industrialized countries whereas, in contrast, alternative investments (*e.g.* buildings) are relatively less costly.

The four most common mistakes in introducing ICTs into teaching are (i) installing learning technology without reviewing student needs and content availability; (ii) imposing technological systems from the top down without involving faculty and students; (iii) using inappropriate content from other regions of the world without customizing it appropriately; and (iv) producing low quality content that has poor instructional design and is not adapted to the technology in use. Although ICT offers a whole lot of benefits there are some risks of using ICT in education which have to be mitigated proper mechanisms. They are:

- It may create a digital divide within class as students who are more familiar with ICT will reap more benefits and learn faster than those who are not as technology savvy.
- It may shift the attention from the primary goal of the learning process to developing ICT skills, which is the secondary goal.
- It can affect the bonding process between the teacher and the student as ICT becomes a communication tool rather than face to face conversation and thus the transactional distance is increased.
- Also since not all teachers are experts with ICT they may be lax in updating the course content online which can slow down the learning among students.
- The potential of plagiarism is high as student can copy information rather than learning and developing their own skills.
- There is a need for training all stakeholders in ICT.
- The cost of hardware and software can be very high.

Basics of Computers

The literal meaning of computer is a device that can calculate. However, modern computers can do a lot more than calculate. Computer is an electronic device that receives input, stores or processes the input as per user instructions and provides output in desired format.

Input-Process-Output Model

Computer input is called data and the output obtained after processing it, based on user's instructions is called information. Raw facts and figures which can be processed using arithmetic and logical operations to obtain information are called data.

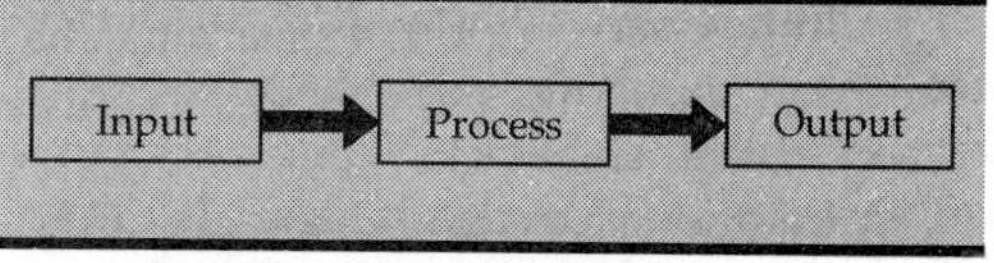

SIMPLEST WORKFLOW OF COMPUTER

The processes that can be applied to data are of two types :

- **Arithmetic operations.** Examples include calculations like addition, subtraction, differentials, square root, etc.
- **Logical operations.** Examples include comparison operations like greater than, less than, equal to, opposite, etc.

The corresponding figure for an actual computer looks something like this:

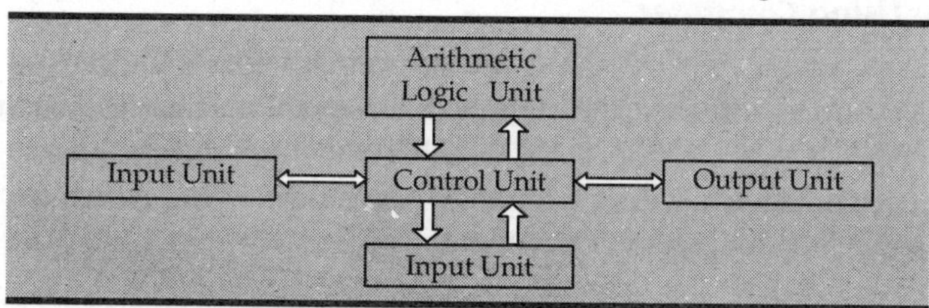

The basic parts of a computer are as follows :

- **Input Unit.** Devices like keyboard and mouse that are used to input data and instructions to the computer are called input unit.
- **Output Unit.** Devices like printer and visual display unit that are used to provide information to the user in desired format are called output unit.
- **Control Unit.** As the name suggests, this unit controls all the functions of the computer. All devices or parts of computer interact through the control unit.
- **Arithmetic Logic Unit.** This is the brain of the computer where all arithmetic operations and logical operations take place.
- **Memory.** All input data, instructions and data interim to the processes are stored in the memory. Memory is of two types - primary memory and secondary memory. Primary memory resides within the CPU whereas secondary memory is external to it.

Control unit, arithmetic logic unit and memory are together called the central processing unit or CPU. Computer devices like keyboard, mouse, printer, etc. that we can see and touch are the hardware components of a computer. The set of instructions or programs that make the computer function using these hardware parts are called software. We cannot see or touch software. Both hardware and software are necessary for working of a computer.

Characteristics of Computer

To understand why computers are such an important part of our lives, let us look at some of its characteristics:

- **Speed.** Typically, a computer can carry out 3-4 million instructions per second.
- **Accuracy.** Computers exhibit a very high degree of accuracy. Errors that may occur are usually due to inaccurate data, wrong instructions or bug in chips – all human errors.
- **Reliability.** Computers can carry out same type of work repeatedly without throwing up errors due to tiredness or boredom, which are very common among humans.

- **Versatility.** Computers can carry out a wide range of work from data entry and ticket booking to complex mathematical calculations and continuous astronomical observations. If you can input the necessary data with correct instructions, computer will do the processing.
- **Storage Capacity.** Computers can store a very large amount of data at a fraction of cost of traditional storage of files. Also, data is safe from normal wear and tear associated with paper.

Advantages of Using Computer

Now that we know the characteristics of computers, we can see the advantages that computers offer:

- Computers can do the same task repetitively with same accuracy.
- Computers do not get tired or bored.
- Computers can take up routine tasks while releasing human resource for more intelligent functions.

Disadvantages of Using Computer

Despite so many advantages, computers have some disadvantages of their own:

- Computers have no intelligence; they follow the instructions blindly without considering the outcome.
- Regular electric supply is necessary to make computers work, which could prove difficult everywhere especially in developing nations.

Booting

Starting a computer or a computer-embedded device is called booting. Booting takes place in two steps:

- Switching on power supply.
- Loading operating system into computer's main memory.
- Keeping all applications in a state of readiness in case needed by the user.

The first program or set of instructions that run when the computer is switched on is called BIOS or Basic Input Output System. BIOS is a firmware, i.e. a piece of software permanently programmed into the hardware.

If a system is already running but needs to be restarted, it is called rebooting. Rebooting may be required if a software or hardware has been installed or system is unusually slow.

There are two types of booting:

- **Cold Booting.** When the system is started by switching on the power supply it is called cold booting. The next step in cold booting is loading of BIOS.
- **Warm Booting.** When the system is already running and needs to be restarted or rebooted, it is called warm booting. Warm booting is faster than cold booting because BIOS is not reloaded.

Classification

Historically computers were classified according to processor types because development in processor and processing speeds were the developmental benchmarks. Earliest computers used vacuum tubes for processing, were huge and broke down frequently. However, as vacuum tubes were replaced by transistors and then chips, their size decreased and processing speeds increased manifold.

All modern computers and computing devices use microprocessors whose speeds and storage capacities are skyrocketing day by day. The developmental benchmark for computers is now their size. Computers are now classified on the basis of their use or size:

Desktop

Desktop computers are personal computers (PCs) designed for use by an individual at a fixed location. IBM was the first computer to introduce and popularize use of desktops. A desktop unit typically has a CPU (Central Processing Unit), monitor, keyboard and mouse. Introduction of desktops popularized use of computers among common people as it was compact and affordable.

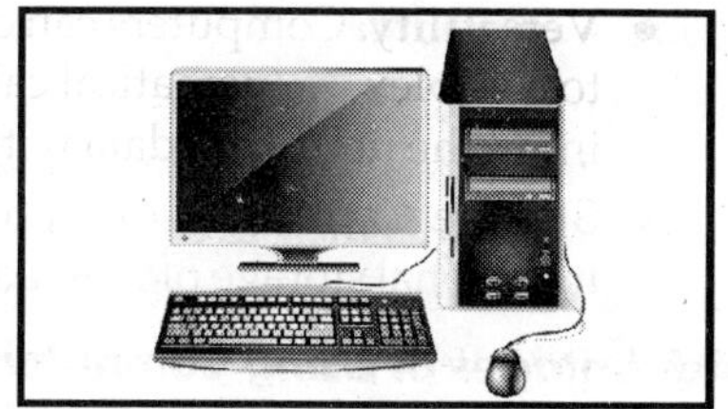

Riding on the wave of desktop's popularity many software and hardware devices were developed specially for the home or office user. The foremost design consideration here was user friendliness.

Laptop

Despite its huge popularity, desktops gave way to a more compact and portable personal computer called laptop in 2000s. Laptops are also called notebook computers or simply notebooks. Laptops run using batteries and connect to networks using Wi-Fi (Wireless Fidelity) chips. They also have chips for energy efficiency so that they can conserve power whenever possible and have a longer life.

Modern laptops have enough processing power and storage capacity to be used for all office work, website designing, software development and even audio/video editing.

Tablet

After laptops computers were further miniaturized to develop machines that have processing power of a desktop but are small enough to be held in one's palm. Tablets have touch sensitive screen of typically 5 to 10 inches where one finger is used to touch icons and invoke applications.

Keyboard is also displayed virtually whenever required and used with touch strokes. Applications that run on tablets are called apps. They use operating systems by Microsoft (Windows 8 and later versions) or Google (Android). Apple computers have developed their own tablet called iPad which uses a proprietary OS called iOS.

Server

Servers are computers with high processing speeds that provide one or more services to other systems on the network. They may or may not have screens attached to them. A group of computers or digital devices connected together to share resources is called a network.

Servers have high processing powers and can handle multiple requests simultaneously. Most commonly found servers on networks include:

- File or storage server
- Application server
- Mail server
- Game server
- Database server
- Print server

Mainframe

Mainframes are computers used by organizations like banks, airlines and railways to handle millions and trillions of online transactions per second. Important features of mainframes are:

- Big in size.
- Hundreds times Faster than servers, typically hundred megabytes per second.
- Very expensive.
- Use proprietary OS provided by the manufacturers.
- In-built hardware, software and firmware security features.

Supercomputer

Supercomputers are the fastest computers on Earth. They are used for carrying out complex, fast and time intensive calculations for scientific and engineering applications. Supercomputer speed or performance is measured in teraflops, i.e. 1012 floating point operations per second.

Chinese supercomputer Sunway TaihuLight is the world's fastest supercomputer with a rating of 93 petaflops per second, i.e. 93 quadrillion floating point operations per second.

Most common uses of supercomputers include:

- Molecular mapping and research
- Weather forecasting
- Environmental research
- Oil and gas exploration

Software Concepts

As you know, the hardware devices need user instructions to function. A set of instructions that achieve a single outcome are called program or procedure. Many programs functioning together to do a task make a software.

For example, a word-processing software enables the user to create, edit and save documents. A web browser enables the user to view and share web pages and multimedia files. There are three categories of software: (1) System Software, (2) Application Software and (3) Utility Software.

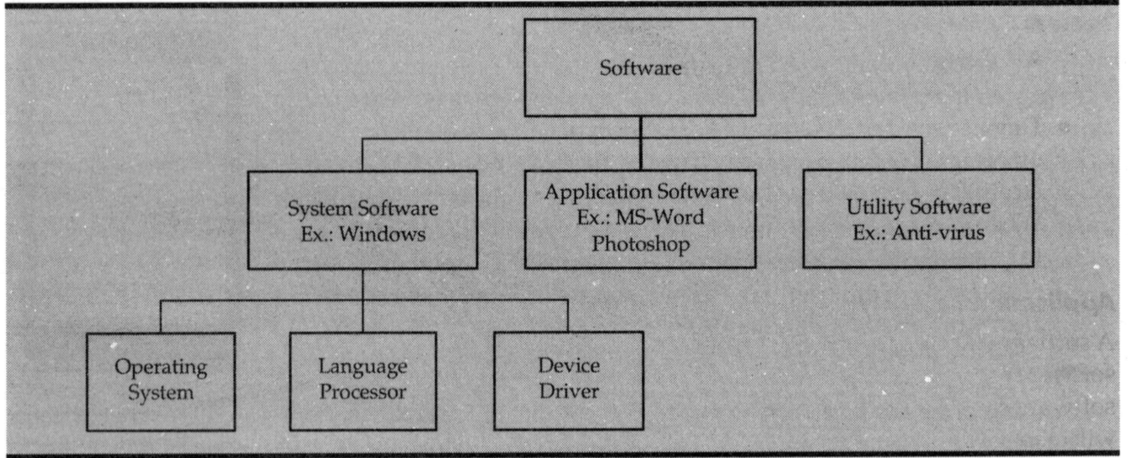

System Software

Software required to run the hardware parts of the computer and other application software are called system software. System software acts as interface between hardware and user applications. An interface is needed because hardware devices or machines and humans speak in different languages.

Machines understand only binary language i.e. 0 (absence of electric signal) and 1 (presence of electric signal) while humans speak in English, French, German, Tamil, Hindi and many other languages. English is the pre-dominant language of interacting with computers. Software is required to convert all human instructions into machine understandable instructions. And this is exactly what system software does.

Based on its function, system software is of three types:

- **Operating System.** System software that is responsible for functioning of all hardware parts and their interoperability to carry out tasks successfully is called operating system (OS). OS is the first software to be loaded into computer memory when the computer is switched on and this is called booting. OS manages a computer's basic functions like storing data in memory, retrieving files from storage devices, scheduling tasks based on priority, etc.

- **Language Processor.** As discussed earlier, an important function of system software is to convert all user instructions into machine understandable language. When we talk of human machine interactions, languages are of three types:
  - ***Machine-level language.*** This language is nothing but a string of 0s and 1s that the machines can understand. It is completely machine dependent.
  - ***Assembly-level language.*** This language introduces a layer of abstraction by defining mnemonics. Mnemonics are English like words or symbols used to denote a long string of 0s and 1s. For example, the word "READ" can be defined to mean that computer has to retrieve data from the memory. The complete instruction will also tell the memory address. Assembly level language is machine dependent.
  - ***High level language.*** This language uses English like statements and is completely independent of machines. Programs written using high level languages are easy to create, read and understand.

  Program written in high level programming languages like Java, C++, etc. is called source code. Set of instructions in machine readable form is called object code or machine code. System software that converts source code to object code is called language processor. There are three types of language interpreters?
  - ***Assembler.*** Converts assembly level program into machine level program.
  - ***Interpreter.*** Converts high level programs into machine level program line by line.
  - ***Compiler.*** Converts high level programs into machine level programs at one go rather than line by line.
- **Device Drivers.** System software that controls and monitors functioning of a specific device on computer is called device driver. Each device like printer, scanner, microphone, speaker, etc. that needs to be attached externally to the system has a specific driver associated with it. When you attach a new device, you need to install its driver so that the OS knows how it needs to be managed.

Application Software

A software that performs a single task and nothing else is called application software. Application software are very specialized in their function and approach to solving a problem. So a spreadsheet software can only do operations with numbers and nothing else. A hospital management software will manage hospital activities and nothing else. Here are some commonly used application software:

- Word processing
- Presentation
- Multimedia tools
- Spreadsheet
- Database management

Utility Software

Application software that assist system software in doing their work is called utility software. Thus utility software is actually a cross between system software and application software. Examples of utility software include:

- Antivirus software
- File management tools
- Backup tools
- Disk management tools
- Compression tools

System Software

As you know, system software acts as an interface for the underlying hardware system. Here we will discuss about some important system software.

Operating System

Operating system (OS) is the lifeline of computer. You connect all the basic devices like CPU, monitor, keyboard and mouse; plug in the power supply and switch it on thinking you have everything in place. But the computer will not start or come to life unless it has an operating system installed in it because OS:

- Keeps all hardware parts in a state of readiness to follow user instructions.
- Co-ordinates between different devices.
- Schedules multiple tasks as per priority.
- Allocates resource to each task.
- Enables computer to access network.
- Enables users to access and use application software.

Besides initial booting, these are some of the functions of an operating system:

- Managing computer resources like hardware, software, shared resources, etc.
- Allocating resources.
- Prevent error during software use.
- Control improper use of computer.

One of the earliest operating systems was MS-DOS, developed by Microsoft for IBM PC. It was a Command Line Interface (CLI) OS that revolutionized the PC market. DOS was difficult to use because of its interface. The users needed to remember instructions to do their tasks. To make computers more accessible and user-friendly, Microsoft developed Graphical User Interface (GUI) based OS called Windows, which transformed the way people used computers.

Assembler

Assembler is a system software that converts assembly level programs to machine level code.

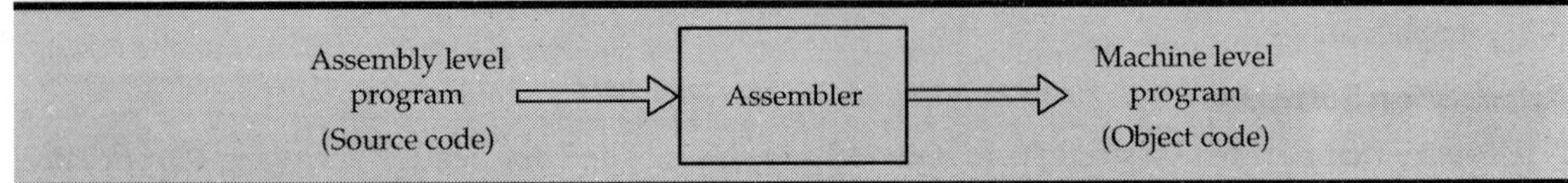

These are the advantages provided by assembly level programming:

- Increases efficiency of the programmer as remembering mnemonics is easier.
- Productivity increases as number of errors decreases and hence debugging time.
- Programmer has access to hardware resources and hence has flexibility in writing programs customized to the specific computer.

Interpreter

The major advantage of assembly level language was its ability to optimize memory usage and hardware utilization. However, with technological advancements computers had more memory and better hardware components. So ease of writing programs became more important than optimizing memory and other hardware resources.

In addition, a need was felt to take programming out of a handful of trained scientists and computer programmers, so that computers could be used in more areas. This led to development of high level languages that were easy to understand due to resemblance of commands to English language.

The system software used to translate high level language source code into machine level language object code line by line is called an interpreter. An interpreter takes each line of code and converts it into machine code and stores it into the object file.

The advantage of using an interpreter is that they are very easy to write and they do not require a large memory space. However, there is a major disadvantage in using interpreters, i.e., interpreted programs take a long time in executing. To overcome this disadvantage, especially for large programs, compilers were developed.

Compiler

System software that store the complete program, scan it, translate the complete program into object code and then creates an executable code is called a compiler. On the face of it compilers compare unfavorably with interpreters because they:

- are more complex than interpreters.
- need more memory space.
- take more time in compiling source code.

However, compiled programs execute very fast on computers. The following image shows the step-by-step process of how a source code is transformed into an executable code :

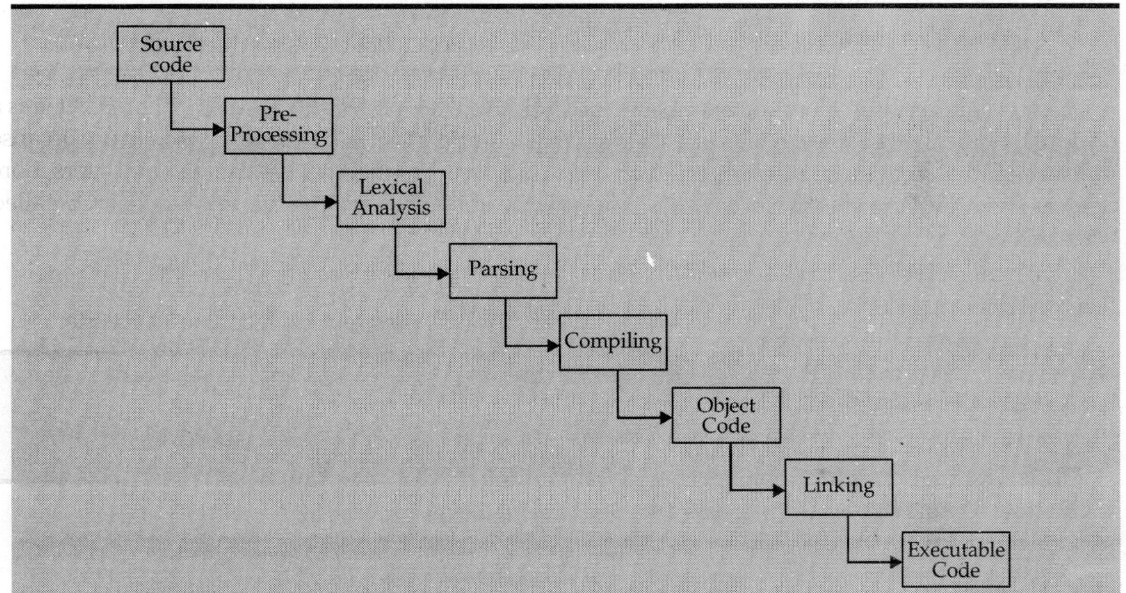

These are the steps in compiling source code into executable code:

- **Pre-processing.** In this stage pre-processor instructions, typically used by languages like C and C++ are interpreted, i.e. converted to assembly level language.
- **Lexical analysis.** Here all instructions are converted to lexical units like constants, variables, arithmetic symbols, etc.
- **Parsing.** Here all instructions are checked to see if they conform to grammar rules of the language. If there are errors, compiler will ask you to fix them before you can proceed.
- **Compiling.** At this stage the source code is converted into object code.
- **Linking.** If there are any links to external files or libraries, addresses of their executable will be added to the program. Also, if the code needs to be rearranged for actual execution, they will be rearranged. The final output is the executable code that is ready to be executed.

Binary Number System

We have read earlier that Base-10 system is a positional system.

In decimal notation, we write a number as a string of symbols, where each symbol is one of these ten digits, and to interpret a decimal number, we multiply each digit by the power of 10 associated with that digit's position.

It is a numerical system wherein each digit stands for a power of two. The binary system uses only two symbols, such as 0 and 1 to represent values. In decimal system, which is commonly used in most countries, each digit represents a value of 10. For example, the number 107 would break down as follows:

$$1 \times 100 = 100, 0 \times 10 = 0, 7 \times 1$$

For example, consider a decimal number '6249'. The unit position of this number is illustrated below.

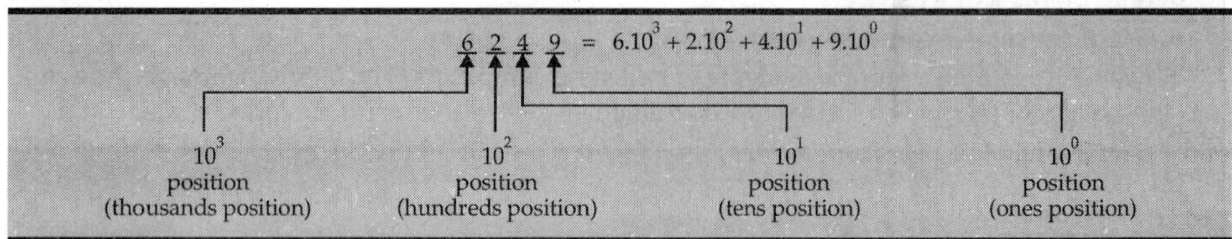

Computers are built from transistors and an individual transistor can only be ON or OFF (two options). Optical storage devices store data in a specific location by controlling whether light is reflected off that location or is not reflected off that location (two options). Likewise, magnetic storage devices store data in a specific location by magnetizing the particles in that location with a specific orientation.

Thus, the values in a binary system, such as 0's and 1's called binary digits or bits. Computers use base 2 because they can only recognize two values, 1 or 0.

It is the reason why everything in computers seems to come in 8s (2 to the 3rd power), 64s (2 to the 6th power), 128s (2 to the 7th power) and 256s (2 to the 8th power). Therefore, in the binary system, the number 103 would break downs as follows.

$1 \times 64 = 64, 1 \times 32 = 32, 0 \times 16 = 0, 0 \times 8 = 0, 1 \times 4 = 4, 1 \times 2 = 2, 1 \times 1 = 1$ and $(1100111)_2 = 103$

Take another example by considering a binary number '1101'. The unit position of this number is illustrate as follows:

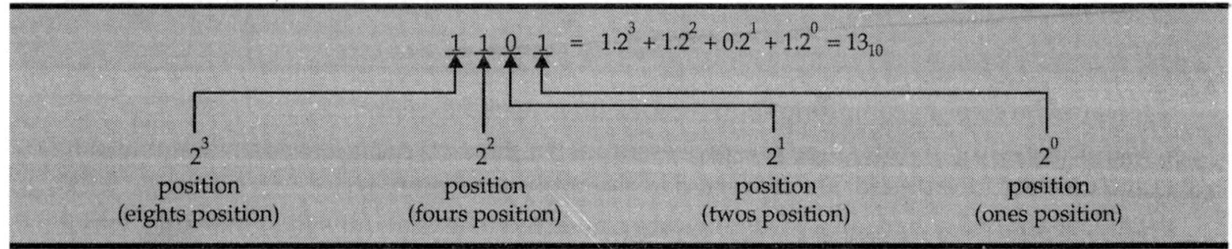

When data is typed into a computer, the keyboard converts each keystroke into a binary character code as given below.

8 bits = 1 byte

1024 bytes = 1 kilobyte

1024 kilobytes = 1 megabyte

1024 megabytes = 1 gigabyte

1024 gigabytes = 1 terabyte

In large computers, the number of bits can be 40 bits.

Now you should be comfortable going back and forth between binary and decimal representations.

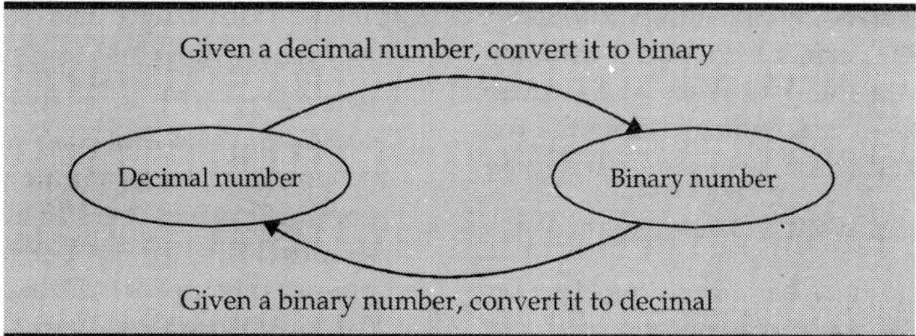

You should 'memorize' the binary representation of the decimal digits 0 to 15 below:

Decimal Number	Binary Number	Decimal Number	Binary Number
0	0000	8	1000
1	0001	9	1001
2	0010	10	1010
3	0011	11	1011
4	0100	12	1100
5	0101	13	1101
6	0110	14	1110
7	0111	15	1111

GENERAL ABBREVIATIONS AND TERMINOLOGY

Absolute Link

A term used by Web authors. In an HTML document a Relative Link indicates the location of a file relative to the document, whereas an absolute link specifies the full URL.

Acceptable Use Policy (AUP)

An AUP is a set of rules that define the ways in which ICT facilities can and cannot be used in a business or educational institution, including a description of the possible sanctions that can be applied if a user breaks the rules.

Access

The name of a Database program forming part of the Microsoft Office suite of programs.

Accessibility

The fundamental issue regarding accessibility is that everyone should have access to the services provided by ICT, e.g. computer programs, Email and the World Wide Web, regardless of any visual, auditory, or other physical impairment they might have. Assistive Technology may be employed to increase access to such services, e.g. Text To Speech (TTS) screen readers, screen magnifiers, speech recognition systems, hearing assistance devices, etc. Designers of computer programs and websites need to take account of accessibility when choosing colours, fonts and font sizes, etc.

Additive Colour

A term used mainly by graphic designers. Computer monitors use three additive colours, Red, Green and Blue (RGB), which are combined in different ways to produce millions of other colours.

Address Book

Usually supplied as part of your Email software. An address book in this sense is used to keep a record of all the email addresses of people whom you may wish to contact by email.

Administrative Software

Computer programs that are used to expedite the storage and use of education data for efficient functioning in education settings. Examples are student records systems, personnel records systems, and transportation mapping packages.

ADSL

Abbreviation for Asymmetric Digital Subscriber Line. A high-speed digital telephone connection that operates over an existing copper telephone line, allowing the same line to be used for voice calls. ADSL lines offer transmission speed that are usually in the range 2Mbps to 8Mbps, and are used mainly for Internet access. The term asymmetric is used because the data flows more quickly from the telephone exchange to the user than from the user to the exchange - because most Web users are more interested in receiving data quickly from websites rather than uploading it to websites. The term symmetric is used for connections where the data flows at the same speed in both directions, which is essential for accessing websites where there is a high degree of interactivity.

Adware

It is software that may have been installed on your computer by a remote computer, i.e. via the Web. Many free utilities that you download from the Internet will install hidden software that sends details of the websites you visit and other information from your computer (which can include your email address) to advertisers so they can target you with popup ads and spam.

AJAX

Acronym for Asynchronous JavaScript and XML. AJAX is a Web programming tool (or rather a set of tools) that makes it possible to create interactive

Alt Key

The Alt keys can be found on either side of the space bar on a computer keyboard. They are commonly used in conjunction with a set of numbers to enable foreign characters to be typed.

Anonymous FTP

An anonymous FTP is a convention whereby users are not required to identify themselves with an account number, user name or password when they access a website from which they wish to download publicly available programs or files. Users may, however, be required to enter their email address before accessing certain websites. The vast majority of publicly available Freeware and Shareware archives on the Web permit anonymous FTP.

Anorak

A colloquial term that is often used to describe someone who is fascinated by the technology of computers but not particularly interested in their applications. A synonym is Trainspotter. Both terms are closely allied to Geek, Nerd and Techie - which have slightly different connotations.

Anti-spyware

1. program that helps to block and prevent spyware and other malware infections on a computer.
2. monitor incoming data from email, websites, and downloads of files and stop spyware programs from getting a foothold in the computer operating system.

API

Abbreviation for Application Programming Interface. API is a so-called protocol of communication that enables different computer programs to communicate with one another. A good API makes it easier to develop a program by providing all the building blocks that the programmer needs. Although APIs are designed for programmers, they are also good for program users insofar as they guarantee that all programs using a common API will have similar interfaces. This makes it easier for users to learn new programs.

Archive

Used to describe documents or files that are not immediately needed but which should not be completely discarded. An archive may be stored on an external Hard Disc, CD-ROM, DVD or other Storage Device. Also used to describe stored messages that have been contributed to discussion lists or blogs. Also used as a verb.

Artificial Intelligence (AI)

The ability of a computer to mimic human attributes in finding a solution to a problem. Artificial Intelligence techniques are applied in various ways in computer applications in the language world, e.g., in Machine Translation (MT) programs and in grammar and style checkers.

ASF

Abbreviation for Advanced Streaming Format. This is Microsoft's own file format that stores both audio and video information and is specially designed to run over the Internet. ASF enables content to be delivered as a continuous stream of streaming audio or streaming video data with little wait time before playback begins. This means that you no longer have to wait for your audio and video files to fully download before starting to view them.

ASR

Abbreviation for Automatic Speech Recognition.

Assistive Technology

This term describes computer software or devices used by people with special needs to enable them to access the services provided by ICT, e.g. computer programs, Email and the World Wide Web. Technologies under this heading include Text To Speech (TTS) screen readers for the unsighted or partially sighted, alternative keyboards and mice for people who have problems in hand-eye coordination, head-pointing devices, speech recognition software, and screen magnification software.

Attachment

A term used in connection with Email. An attachment can be a File of almost any kind – a document file, an image file, a sound file or a video clip - that you can add, i.e. attach, to an email.

Attribute

A term used by Web authors. An attribute of an HTML tag controls how that tag operates.

Authorship Analysis Software

Authorship Analysis Software can help to identify authorship of texts. Such software has been used by literary and linguistic researchers for many years and is now widely used by security services in counter-terrorism activities.

Automatic Speech Recognition (ASR)

A branch of Human Language Technologies devoted to the automatic processing of human speech.

Avatar

A graphical representation of a real person, such as used in a MUVE or MMORPG, a kind of "virtual world". Participants in a MUVE or MMORPG choose a name and a visual representation of the character that they wish to adopt as an inhabitant of the MUVE or player in the MMORPG.

AVI

Abbreviation for Audio Video Interleave (or Interleaved). A file format for storing video recordings on a computer.

Background printing

The ability of a computer to print a document while other work is being done on the keyboard and the display screen of the same time.

Bandwidth

The amount of data that can be sent from one computer to another through a particular connection in a certain amount of time, e.g. via a computer to the Internet and vice versa. The more bandwidth available, the faster you are able to access information. Bandwidth is usually measured in kilobits per second (Kbps) or megabits per second (Mbps).

Baud

A unit of measurement at which data can be transferred (i.e. the baud rate), for example over a telephone line via a Modem or from a computer to an external device such as a Printer. Rarely used nowadays, as transfer rates are normally expressed in kilobits per second (Kbps) or megabits per second (Mbps).

BBS

Abbreviation for Bulletin Board System.

Binary

A number system using base 2 instead of the usual (human) base 10, which is normally referred to as the decimal system. Computers use base 2 because they can only recognise two values, 1 or 0. This is simulated electronically by using a device, such as a switch, which is either on (1) or off (0). All numbers are represented by combinations of ones and zeroes, thus the number 9 is represented as 1001, the right-most column being the units column and the other columns, moving from right to left, being 2, 4, 8.

BIOS

Acronym for Basic Input/Output System. This is a built-in ROM Chip on the Motherboard containing essential programs to manage the computer's input and output, which are loaded into memory during the boot process.

Bit

Contraction of binary digit. A bit is the smallest measurement unit of computer memory or data transmission speed, e.g. via a Modem. See the entry on Measurement Units. See Byte, Kilobit, Kilobyte, Megabit, Megabyte.

Bitmap

A computer graphic or image composed of thousands of individual dots or pixels, each pixel being stored as a number. The image is displayed by specifying the colour of each pixel. Bit-mapped graphics can be imported into other applications, e.g. a word-processor, but they cannot be edited within these applications. When bit-mapped graphics are resized they usually suffer a loss of sharpness, whereas vector graphics can be resized without such loss.

Blog

Contraction of the term Weblog. A blog is essentially a website that contains discrete pieces of information posted by different users. New items of information are usually entered by contributors via a simple form, following the introduction of each new theme by a person who initiates the blog, and then submitted to the site, where they may be filtered by an administrator before being posted. A blog can contain news items, short essays, annotated links, documents, graphics, and multimedia. These posts are usually in reverse chronological order and often take the form of a journal or diary. A blog is normally accessible to any Internet user, but closed blogs may also be created, e.g. to document the thoughts and experiences of a group of students or to provide a means of communication between teachers and students following a particular course. The word blog is also used as a verb, and Blogger is used as a noun to describe someone who blogs (see next entry). A blog is usually distinguished from an Internet Discussion List (also known as a Forum), but the latter can function in a similar way insofar as it typically allows any user to post messages to it that can be viewed via the Web.

Blogger

Normally used to refer to someone who blogs, *i.e.*, who regularly writes blogs. Also used to describe a service that provides Web-based tools used by individuals to create a Blog or Weblog.

Bluetooth

Bluetooth is a technical industry standard for radio technology which facilitates the transmission of signals over short distances (up to around 10 metres) between telephones, computers and other devices without the use of wires in the form of microwaves.

BMP

Abbreviation for Bitmap, a file format for storing images. This is the standard format used, for example, by Windows Paint. BMP image files occupy quite a lot of space compared to other formats.

Bookmark

A bookmark is a facility within a Browser that enables you to keep a record of Web pages that you have visited and may wish to visit again. Bookmarks are stored in a subdirectory of the Windows directory on your computer. In Internet Explorer bookmarks are known as Favorites, which is also the name of the subdirectory in which they are stored. Bookmarks are also used to mark positions in a Word document, i.e. positions to which you can jump from other points in the document by clicking on them with the Mouse.

Boot (verb)

To start up a computer by loading the operating system into memory. The computer is regarded as boot strapping itself into operation, i.e. picking itself up by its own bootstraps. The adjective bootable is often used to describe a backup disc that can be used to start a computer, e.g. when the hard disc fails or becomes corrupted for some reason.

bps

Abbreviation for bits per second, the smallest measurement of data transmission speed, e.g. via a Modem. Computer people normally measure data transmission speeds in Kbps, meaning kilobits per second, or Mbps, meaning megabits per second. If you have a 56 Kbps modem (which is slow by today's standards) it means that your modem can transmit at speeds up to 56,000 bits of information per second.

Broadband

A general term used to describe a high-speed connection to the Internet. Connection speed is usually measured in Kbps (kilobits per second) and Mbps (megabits per second). Typically, a home user will have a broadband connection using an ADSL telephone line running at 2Mbps to 8Mbps. Educational institutions ideally need a symmetric connection of at least 8Mbps to ensure smooth trouble-free connections to the Internet when large numbers of students are accessing the Internet all at once.

Browser

A software package installed on the hard disc of your computer that enables you to access and to navigate the World Wide Web – to "surf the Web" in colloquial terms.

Buffer

A holding area in memory that stores information temporarily. Also called cache.

Bulletin Board

A type of forum on the Internet or an intranet, where users can post messages by email or via the World Wide Web for other users to read and respond to. Bulletin Board Systems (BBSs) have largely been replaced by other types of online systems for communal communication, such as blogs, discussion lists and forums.

Bug

Not a nasty insect but a logical fault in a computer program which causes it to malfunction. All computer programs contain bugs, some of which take years to come to light. It is rumoured that the term arose as a result of moths getting into the circuitry of an older Mainframe Computer, causing it to break down.

Byte

A measurement of computer memory or disc capacity. A byte comprises 8 bits.

C&IT

Abbreviation for Communications and Information Technology. The same thing as ICT.

Cache

The cache contains information stored by a Web Browser on your hard disc, so that you don't have to download the same material repeatedly from a remote computer. Browsers keep copies of all the Web pages that you view so that the pages can be redisplayed quickly when you go back to them. The cache is normally stored under Windows in a folder called Temporary Internet Files. This folder can become enormous over time and can cause your hard disc to become overloaded and then your computer may lock up. The cache needs to be emptied at regular intervals – which you can do manually or using utility software such as Window Washer or C Cleaner. You can set the maximum size of the Temporary Internet Files folder, using the Tools menu in your browser.

CAD/CAM

Abbreviations for Computer Aided Design/ Computer Aided Manufacturing. A process of drafting, designing and manufacturing with the aid of a computer. CAD enables the user to manipulate drawings, including 3D drawings, and viewing them from a variety of angles. CAM is a general term for computer support during the manufacturing process.

CGI Script

A term used by Web authors. CGI is an abbreviation for Common Gateway Interface. A program residing on a Web Server, usually in a directory called cgi-bin, which processes data from an HTML form. CGI scripts can be written in any programming language suitable for handling text data, but Perl is the most popular scripting language.

Character

A single letter, figure, punctuation mark, or symbol produced by a keystroke on a computer.

Character set

The compete set of characters, alphabetic, numeric and symbolic.

Character User Interface (CUI)

A Character User Interface describes a way in which a computer user communicates with a computer by entering commands as text, i.e. in order to run programs and to carry out other operations such as copying information from one Folder to another, deleting files, etc. Contrasted with a Graphical User Interface (GUI), e.g. Microsoft Windows, which allows the user to carry out such operations by clicking on icons, opening and shutting windows and dragging and dropping with a mouse. MS DOS and Unix are examples of CUIs.

Client

A computer that receives services from another computer. A stand-alone computer on your desk which you use to browse the Web is a client, and the computers from which World Wide Web files are downloaded to your computer are servers. Similarly, a computer (also known as a workstation) connected to a Local Area Network (LAN) is a client that can receive information from and send information to the server that controls the LAN.

Clipart or Clip Art

A collection of image files that can be embedded or inserted into Web pages, word-processed documents, PowerPoint presentations, etc. Some clip art images are copyright-free or in the public domain but others may be subject to a licence fee if you wish to make them public, e.g. on a website.

Clock Speed

The speed of a computer's Central Processing Unit (CPU), which is normally expressed in MegaHertz (= one million cycles per second) or GigaHertz, (= 1000 MegaHertz). This figure represents the number of instruction cycles the processor carries out each second. In simple terms this indicates how fast the computer runs – how powerful it is. Computers that run at 500 Mega-Hertz (500MHz) used to be considered fast, but modern computers now run at over one GigaHertz (1GHz).

Cloud Computing

Service that allows visiting users to access programs and services anywhere with Internet access without having to install other software. EXAMPLES: Amazon Web Services, Google Docs, Google
Calendar, online backup services (cloud storage), Dropbox, Mozy.

CMS

Abbreviation for Content Management System, a software package that makes it possible for non-technical users to publish content (text, images, etc.) on a website. Also stands for Course

Management System, a type of Virtual Learning Environment (VLE).

CODEC

Short for COmpressor / DECompressor or COder / DECoder. A CODEC is software that is used to compress or decompress a digital audio or video file.

Cognitive Learning Theories

Focus on explaining the development of cognitive structures, processes, and representations that mediate between instruction and learning.

Cognitive Strategies

An individual's skills for "learning how to learn."

Collaborative Learning or Cooperative Learning

Students of varying abilities and interests work together in small groups to solve a problem, complete a project, or achieve a common goal.

Comms

Short for communications, as in Information and Communications Technology (ICT). Used to refer to ways in which computer systems communicate with one another, e.g. via a cable, a telephone line, satellite or wireless.

Compatibility

Pieces of hardware and/or software which are capable of being used together are described as compatible.

Compiler

A program which converts programs written in a high-level programming language, i.e. as used by professional human programmers, into Machine Code, a language that can be "understood" by a computer. A compiler produces a binary executable program file after the programmer has completed the programming. Program files on personal computers can be recognised by their three-letter .exe or .com Extension after their filenames, e.g. winfile.exe.

Compression

A technique which reduces the amount of space required to store data, e.g. as used to reduce the amount of space needed to store an image, an audio recording, or a video recording.

Computer Mediated Communication (CMC)

Computer Mediated Communication is used as a term describing the use of the Internet as a means of fostering teaching and learning, especially the use of Email, Conferencing and Social Networking.

Concordance Program

A Concordance Program (also known as a Concordancer) operates on a body of texts (a corpus) and is commonly used for compiling glossaries and dictionaries, e.g. by arranging every word in the text alphabetically or in order of frequency, together with its context. Concordance programs also play an important role in language learning and teaching.

Content and Language Integrated Learning (CLIL)

A term used to describe learning a subject such as history or geography through the medium of a foreign language and thereby learning the foreign language at the same time.

Courseware

Instructional materials in a complete mediated format. May refer to a single instructional component, such as a computer-assisted instruction program, or a multiple instructional entity, such as guidebooks, videodiscs, and computer-assisted instruction.

Cookie

A piece of information stored on a user's computer by a Web Browser when the user visits a website for the first time. Websites use cookies to recognise users who have previously visited them. The next time that the user visits that site, the information in the cookie is sent back to the site so that the site can tailor what it presents to the user, e.g. tastes in music or shopping habits.

Copyright

New technologies have raised all kinds of new issues relating to copyright - mainly because it has become so easy to copy materials from a variety of digital sources.

Crawler

A crawler is a program that searches the Web for new links, new content and changes in order to keep Search Engine results up to date. A crawler may also be called a bot (short for robot) or spider. Crawlers within search engines perform a useful indexing function, but there are also crawlers or bots that have more sinister motives, such as gathering addresses to be targeted by spammers.

CSCL

Computer-Supported Collaborative Learning. Area of work that focuses on socially oriented theories of learning using computer technologies to support collaborative methods of instruction.

Cybersquatter

A term normally used to describe someone who registers the name of a popular Web address - usually a company name - with the intent of selling it to its rightful owner at a high price.

Cybernetic Learning Environment

Emphasizes mutual interaction between the learning system and the learnerinteraction in which the learner negotiates control of the learning experience with the system and the system attempts to respond intelligently to the explicit and implicit needs of the learner by adjusting to a changing multidimensional portrait.

Database

A structured collection of data that can be used for a variety of purposes. A database may contain data relating to staff employed by a company or to students at an educational institution. In order to set up and manage a database you need a database program such as Microsoft Access.

Debug

To test a program and remove all the bugs. Permanent bugs that defy eradication are often referred to ironically as "features".

Default

A setting or value automatically assigned to a computer program or device in the absence of a choice made by the user. When you use a program for the first time, e.g. a Browser or Word-processor, all the settings will have been preset to their default values - many of which can be changed to settings that you prefer, e.g. the default font type and size.

Desktop Videoconferencing

Videoconferencing on a personal computer equipped with a fast Internet connection (at least 28.8 Kbps modem), a microphone, and a video camera. There can be two-way or multi-way video and audio depending upon the hardware and software of participants. Most appropriate for small groups or individuals.

Dialog box

A message box on the screen that supplies information to or requests information from the user.

Dithering

The technique of combining dots of primary colours to give the appearance of intermediate colours. Dots are combined in a square area, known as a dither matrix, to simulate a dot of an intermediate colour.

DOC

The standard three-letter Extension to a document file produced by Microsoft Word.

Domain Name

A unique name that identifies a Website. A domain name can be purchased from and registered by a domain name registration company. Such companies also provide a service that will check if a required name is available for purchase. Domain names always have two or more parts, separated by dots. The part on the left side is specific and the one on the right is more general. Our website's domain name is divided into two parts, truemanbooks and com, the former part being our project name and the latter indicating what kind of body we are: com = "commercial enterprise". Universities' domain names in India always end in ac.in = "academic India". Indian companies can often be identified by co.in.

dpi

Abbreviation for Dots Per Inch. A measure of the of the quality of output, i.e. the number of dots per square inch produced by a printer or scanner, also referred to as its **resolution**. A resolution of at least 300 dpi is considered reasonable for the production of high-quality output by a printer and 1200 dpi by a scanner, but modern printers and scanners can produce many more dots per square inch. The resolution of a scanner may also be expressed by two numbers. These are mostly the same, e.g. 1200 x 1200, but you may also see 1200 x 2400, which means that the number of horizontal dots is different from the number of vertical dots.

Drill and Practice

An instructional software program that presents items for students to work (usually one at a time) and gives feedback on correctness; designed to help users remember isolated facts or concepts and recall them quickly.

DSL

1. Digital Subscriber Line.

2. means of transferring data over regular phone lines and can be used to connect to the Internet.

Duplexing

A procedure that permits two computers to transmit data to each other simultaneously.

Dynamic Data Exchange (DDE)

A technology that permits the user to transfer or paste data from one application (for example a spread sheet) to another (for example, a report). Because of the dynamic link created by this technology, any change in the data in the original application will be automatically reflected in the data copied in the second application.

Dynamic Microphone

This type of microphone is often used in multimedia CALL programs when the learner has to record his/her own voice. This type of microphone is often popularly referred to as a karaoke microphone.

E-learning (Electronic Learning)

If someone is learning in a way that uses Information and Communications Technologies (ICTs), they are using e-learning. They could be a pre-school child playing an interactive game; they could be a group of pupils collaborating on a history project with pupils in another country via the Internet; they could be geography students watching an animated diagram of a volcanic eruption their lecturer has just downloaded; they could be a nurse taking her driving theory test online with a reading aid to help her dyslexia - it all counts as e-learning.

Electronic Whiteboard

More commonly referred to as an Interactive Whiteboard these days.

Email

Contraction of Electronic Mail. A system for creating, sending and receiving messages via the Internet. In order to send and receive email messages you have to register with an Internet Service Provider (ISP) that provides an email service and have email software such as Outlook installed on your computer. Many ISPs also offer a Webmail facility, which provides an alternative means of creating, sending and receiving email messages using your Web Browser.

Emoticon

1. text-based faces and objects that are often seen in emails and online chat that help give the reader a sense of the writer's feelings behind the text

Examples :

:)	Happy,
:p	Sticking Tongue Out,
@--->--->--	Long Stem Rose,
-_-	Annoyed

Encryption

A system of coding that helps prevent access to private information on computer networks or on the Web.

Error Diagnosis

A feature of CALL programs whereby the computer attempts to diagnose the nature of errors the learner makes and to branch to remedial exercises. This approach to CALL appears to have fallen out of fashion in recent years.

Ethernet

Most common type of connection computers use in a local area network.

Ethical Standards

Guidelines for the appropriate use of the technology solution and the maintenance of privacy of the contents of the system. These are generally specified in an Acceptable Use Policy, particularly where there is concern about the security of the system or the availability of objectionable materials obtained through the system.

Eudora

A popular Email program.

Excel

The name of a Spreadsheet program forming part of the Microsoft Office suite of programs.

Firewall

A firewall is a software package that sits between your computer and your Internet connection, keeping an eye on the traffic going to and fro. If anything suspicious appears, such as an unauthorised attempt from a remote computer to write information to your hard disc or to send information from your computer to a remote computer, it will block it and warn you.

Firewire

A firewire is in essence a facility that allows you to transfer video recordings very quickly from one device to another, e.g. from a Camcorder to a computer, using a special cable that connects to the computer's fireware socket.

Firmware

Software that has been written to a ROM (Read Only Memory) chip by the manufacturers.

Flame

Flame is a term used to describe language that is rude, sarcastic or condescending, especially the language used in a Discussion List, Forum or Blog.

Flash Drive

A portable Storage Device. Flash drives look like a small flat pen, around 3cm to 5cm long, and are easily carried in your pocket. Their storage capacity is impressive; 4GB to 16GB is not unusual these days. They are used to store data that you wish to carry around, e.g. a PowerPoint presentation, and they can be plugged into any computer with a USB socket. Flash drives are also commonly referred to as **pen drives** or **memory sticks.**

Flash Player

Software produced by Adobe for the development and viewing of animated and interactive sequences on the Web.

FLV

Abbreviation for Flash Video, a proprietary file format used to deliver video over the Web using the Adobe Flash Player.

Formatting

The process of preparing a writable disc for use. Formatting creates a structure on the disc which enables it to hold data.

Forms Mode

The ability of a program to store the format of a black document or form so that it can later be viewed on the display screen and completed by the user. Once a fill in has been entered, the cursor automatically advance to the beginning of the next area to be filled in.

Frame

A area in a Web page that scrolls independently of the rest of the Web page. A Web page can be divided into multiple frames.

Freeware

Software that can be copied and used without payment to the author(s), although there may be some restrictions on distribution.

Friendly URL

Webpage address that is easy to read and remember and includes words that describe the content of the webpage for search engines.

FTP

Abbreviation for File Transfer Protocol. This is the method, i.e. a software standard, used for transferring files from one computer to another via the Internet. FTP is also used as a verb in the sense "to transfer" (a file).

GB

Abbreviation for Gigabyte.

Geek

A colloquial term describing someone who is obsessed with computers and uses them at every opportunity in their free time, mainly for "social" purposes, e.g. communication via email and blogs, playing multi-user games, etc.

Generic Software / Generic Application

This term normally refers to general-purpose software applications that are not designed for use in a specific subject area, e.g. a word-processor (e.g. Word), spreadsheet package (e.g. Excel), presentation software (e.g. PowerPoint) or database package (e.g. Access).

GIF

Abbreviation for Graphic Interchange Format. A file format used for storing simple graphics. GIF files use a palette of 256 colours, which makes them practical for almost all graphics except photographs. Generally, GIF files should be used for logos, line drawings, icons, etc., *i.e.* images that don't contain a rich range of colours. A GIF file containing a small number of colours tends to be quite small, but it will be big if the image has a wide range of colours, e.g. a photograph. GIF files are commonly used for storing images on the Web. GIF files are also suitable for storing animated (i.e. moving) images.

Gigabyte

Usually abbreviated to GB, or gig in common computer parlance. A unit of measurement of computer memory or disc capacity = 1,073,741,824 bytes.

GigaHertz (GHz)

Usually abbreviated to GHz. A unit of measurement relating to the Clock Speed of a computer or, put simply, a measurement of how fast its Central Processing Unit (CPU) runs. Typical clock speeds of modern computers range from 500 MegaHertz (500MHz) upwards. Faster clock speeds are normally expressed in GigaHertz (= 1000MHz).

GIGO

Garbage in, garbage out. In other words, your computer output is only as good as your computer input.

Glitch

A hardware problem that causes a computer to malfunction or crash.

Global

Describing any function that can be performed on an entire document without requiring individual commands for each use. For example, a global search and replace command will instruct the computer to locate a particular word or phrase and replace it with a different word or phrase wherever the original form occurs in the document.

Gopher

A pre-worldwide-Web method of presenting information on the Internet.

Graphics Card

An alternative name for a Video Card.

Groupware

A computer software program that allows the same information to be shared among several computers simultaneously. With some applications, users can see each other and from their own computers, add to or edit text and graphics in a single document.

Hard page break

A page ending code or command inserted by the use that can not be changed by the program. A had page break is often used to prevent a table from being divided between two pages and to signify that a particular section of a document has ended and the following text should start on a new page.

Hard return

A command used to end a paragraph, end a short line of text, or insert a blank line in the text.

Hardwired

Describing any computer function that can not be easily modified.

Hashtag

1. function used with Twitter or other services that assigns a post or a tweet a keyword by using a number symbol (#).
2. number symbols used to categorize tweets or posts of related topics.

HDD

Abbreviation for Hard Disc Drive. See Hard Disc.

Header

Repetitive information that appears at the top of every page of a document. A page number is a common header.

Hertz

Usually abbreviated to Hz. A unit of measurement relating to the number of times something is repeated per second. In computer jargon this normally refers to the Clock Speed of a computer.

Host Name or Hostname

A host name is the unique name of a computer on the Internet, which is normally written as a series of letters, for example www.hull.ac.uk. A host name is the human-friendly form of the host's numerical IP address, i.e. it's an alias for the "real" Internet address of the host computer, e.g. 150.237.176.24.

HTML

Abbreviation for Hypertext Markup Language. The coding system used for creating pages on the World Wide Web. HTML enables the author to control how the page appears and to insert Hypertext links within one Web page or to other pages anywhere on the Web. Nowadays most Web authors and designers use an Authoring Tool such as Front Page or Dreamweaver to create World Wide Web pages. Web page files end with the Extension .htm. or .html.

HTTP

Abbreviation for Hypertext Transfer Protocol. The transfer method (protocol) used by the World Wide Web to transmit and receive Web pages. This abbreviation normally precedes the name of a website, e.g. http://www.truemanbooks.com, to tell your computer that this is the way in which you wish to communicate with other computers on the Internet. In practice, however, you can usually miss out the prefix http:// as it is assumed to be the norm.

Hub

A common connection point for networked computers and other devices. Hubs are used to connect devices in a Local Area Network (LAN).

Hyphenation

The ability of a program to automatically hyphenate and divide words that do not fit at the end of a line. If the text is later revised so that the divided word no longer beings at the right margin, the hyphen is automatically removed and the word prints solid.

Hyperlink

A contraction of hypertext link, the essence of Hypertext and the HTML language used for creating pages on the World Wide Web. In a Web document a hyperlink can be a sequence of letters or an image. By clicking on the area designated as a hyperlink by the person who created the Web page, it is possible to jump quickly to another part of the page, a different page on the same website, or to a completely different website. Hyperlinks can also be inserted into a Word document, enabling the reader to jump from one point in the document to another, or out of the document to a website.

Hypermedia

The extension of the hypertext concept to multimedia, describing the combination of multimedia information (text, images, audio, video, etc.) in a meaningful configuration, which is especially useful for teaching and learning.

Hypertext

A system for the non-sequential presentation of text, the fundamental concept of the World Wide Web, whereby the user can jump from one part of a text to another, from one Web page to another, or from one website to another, by clicking on highlighted (and usually underlined) hyperlinks. The concept of hypertext predates the Web by many years. Vannevar Bush is credited with inventing the concept of hypertext in his article "As we may think", which was written as early as 1945 and describes an imaginary machine called "Memex" - essentially a hypertext device that takes account of the way the human mind associates ideas and follows a variety of different paths rather than moving on sequentially.

IC

Abbreviation for Integrated Circuit.

ILT

Abbreviation for Information and Learning Technology. A term that has recently come into vogue, stressing the learning aspect rather than the communications aspect, as in ICT.

Instructional Systems Development (ISD)

Design models and processes for the analysis, design, development, implementation, and evaluation of instruction.

Integrated Learning System (ILS)

A computer-driven system of learning in which the content is presented in tutorial format and which monitors and records the progress of the learner.

Intel

The name of a manufacturer of microprocessors used in personal computers.

Intelligent CBI

Sophisticated artificial intelligence tools that have the potential to create new models and instructional strategies for CBI (Computer-Based Instruction). Bayesian probability models provide efficient means of identifying mastery of objectives and formulating a sequence of lessons for individual students that are tailored by the programming.

Interactive Video (IV)

A system consisting of a computer connected to a 12-inch videodisc player, allowing the presentation of still images or video clips combined with some kind of interactivity. Very popular in the 1980s but now technically obsolete and replaced by integrated multimedia computers incorporating DVD or CD-ROM drives.

Interactive Whiteboard (IWB)

Often abbreviated to IWB. A touch-sensitive projection screen that allows the teacher to control a computer directly by touching the screen, i.e. the whiteboard, rather than using a Keyboard or Mouse. A Data Projector has to be connected to the teacher's computer in order to project the image onto the interactive whiteboard and special software has to be installed on the computer in order for the whiteboard to become active and sensitive to touch - which may require the use of an "electronic pen" or it may work in reaction to one's finger or hand.

Interface

An interface in computer jargon is a connection between two systems. It can be Hardware or Software. It may take the form of a plug, cable or socket, or all three, for example where a Printer or Scanner is connected to a computer, and then it's a hardware interface. There are also software interfaces that enable one program to link with another, passing across data and variables. The term interface, also known as user interface, also describes the software that is used to enable human beings to communicate with a computer, for example Microsoft Windows, which is a Graphical User Interface (GUI) in common use on personal computers.

Internet Explorer

A Browser produced by the Microsoft Corporation and supplied together with the Windows operating system.

Internet Service Provider (ISP)

A company that provides a subscription service to enable you to access the Internet. An ISP has a network of computers permanently linked to the Internet. When you take out a subscription with an ISP they link your computer to their network, usually via an existing telephone line, but dedicated lines are also provided by some ISPs. ISPs also give you an Email address and space on the World Wide Web for setting up your own website.

Intranet

A private network inside a company or educational organisation and used over its LAN (Local Area Network). A sort of local Internet. Contrasted with Internet, which is publicly available.

I/O

Abbreviation for Input/Output.

IP Address

Short for Internet Protocol Address. The unique numerical address of a computer on the Internet, expressed as four sets of numbers (maximum 3 digits each) separated by dots: e.g. 150.237.176.24. Computers on the Internet are nearly always referred to by more memorable domain names, which are mapped onto their IP addresses by special Internet computers known as name servers.

iPod

The name of a portable (mobile) Media Player designed and marketed by Apple. The iPod first appeared in 2001. As well as being capable of storing and playing back audio recordings, newer models can also record and play back video. The iPod has become popular for storing recordings, mainly music, downloaded from the Web or transferred from audio CD to a computer and then moved across to an iPod using a software package known as iTunes.

ISDN

Abbreviation for Integrated Services Digital Network. A type of digital telephone service, used for transferring large chunks of data to and from the Internet without a Modem. Gradually falling out of use these days with the introduction of ADSL broadband services. ISDN lines normally operate at 128 Kbps, which is faster than a standard 56Kbps Dial-up Modem but slower than an ADSL connection, which runs at a speed of at least 1Mbps.

Java

A programming language, invented by Sun Microsystems, that is specifically designed for writing programs that can be downloaded to your computer through the Internet and immediately executed. Using small Java programs, called applets, Web pages can include functions such as animations, interactive sequences, etc. You need to set up your browser to enable it to interpret and run the Java applets. Java is similar to a programming language known as C++ but it has been considerably simplified. Not to be confused with Javascript.

Javascript

Javascript is a script language, a system of programming codes that can be embedded into the HTML code of a Web page to add functionality, e.g. interactive sequences, questionnaires, etc. Although it shares many of the features and structures of the full Java language, Javascript is essentially quite different and was developed independently.

Key Word In Context (KWIC)

A type of search carried out with a Concordance Program.

Kilobit

Usually abbreviated to Kb. A unit of measurement consisting of 1,024 bits, mainly relating to data transmission speed.

Kilobyte

Usually abbreviated to K or KB. A unit of measurement of computer memory or disc capacity = 1,024 bytes. See entry on Measurement Units. See Bit, Byte, Megabyte, Gigabyte.

KWIC

Acronym for Key Word In Context.

LAN

Abbreviation for Local Area Network. A Network of computers at one site that provides services to other computers connected to it. A LAN is usually limited to an immediate area, for example the floor of a building, a single building or a campus. The most important part of a LAN is the Server that delivers software to the computers (also known as workstations or clients) that are connected to it. The server is usually the most powerful computer in the network Users of computers connected to a LAN can access their own files remotely and exchange information with the server and other users connected to the network.

Landscape orientation

The positioning of a page so that information is printed across the long dimension of the paper.

Laptop Computer

A laptop computer is a computer that is light and can easily be carried around. Contrasted with Desktop Computer.

Learner-Centred Classroom

Students are encouraged to choose their own learning goals and/or projects, based on the belief that people have a natural inclination to learn; learn better when they work on authentic tasks; benefit from interacting with diverse groups of people; and learn best when teachers understand and value difference in how each student learns.

Learning Platform

A term used to describe the software and systems that are used to deliver E-learning. Some confusion surrounds this term: sometimes it is used synonymously with Virtual Learning Environment (VLE) and sometimes with Managed Learning Environment (MLE). Many people use it as a catch-all term to describe software and systems designed to manage, deliver and provide access to E-learning materials.

Learning Task Analysis

A list of goals that describe what the learners should know or be able to do at the completion of instruction and the prerequisite skills and knowledge that the learners will need in order to achieve those goals.

Level of Interactivity

The potential for interaction prescribed by the capabilities of video-disc hardware and external intervention.

Linked in

It is the largest professional networking site. Linkedin provides a way to connect with other professionals and helps you stay in contact with million of users.

Linkrot

Linkrot describes the tendency of Hypertext links from one website to another to die as other sites cease to exist or remove or restructure their Web pages.

Linux

A Unix-type Operating System, similar to Windows and the Apple Mac operating system. Linux was originally created by Linus Torvalds with the assistance of developers around the world. The Source Code for Linux is freely available to everyone.

Listserv

Any software that manages a mailing list.

Lurker

Mainly used in connection with a Discussion List, Forum or Blog. This term describes someone who prefers to read other people's messages rather than posting their own views.

Machine Assisted Translation (MAT)

The use of computers to assist human beings in the process of translating natural language. MAT systems are normally used as only aids for human translators who have to intervene in the process of translation by machine, making corrections and amendments as necessary.

Machine Code

The machine-readable form of a computer program, produced by conversion of the human-written program (source code) into binary code by a compiler or interpreter.

Machine Translation (MT)

The use of computers to translate natural language. A related term is Machine Assisted Translation (MAT), which normally implies that the computer does part of the job and human beings correct and amend the text that it produces.

Mainframe Computer

Loosely speaking, a very large computer which can serve many users at remote terminals.

Maintenance Agreement

A contract with an outside service or agency to fix a computer system (or its components) when it breaks, or assist with upgrades to the system.

MAN

Abbreviation for Metropolitan Area Network. A network of computers located at different sites within a large fixed area, such as a city.

Mashup

A mashup is a Web page that brings together data from two or more Web services and combines the data into a new application with added functionality.

Mbps

Abbreviation for megabits per second. A unit of measurement of data transmission speed, e.g. via a Modem. A typical Broadband connection to the Internet transmits data at 1 Mbps to 8 Mbps.

Media (pl.) / Medium (sing.)

In computer jargon this term has two main senses: (1) Storage Media, e.g. CD-ROMs, DVDs, Flash Drives, etc - also referred to as Storage

Devices, (2) Media in the sense of audio and video recordings in Digital format that can be played back on a Media Player.

Megabit

Usually abbreviated to Mb. 1,024 kilobits or 1,048,576 bits, a unit of measurement, usually relating to data transmission speed.

Megabyte

Usually abbreviated to MB. 1,024 kilobytes or 1,048,576 bytes. A unit of measurement of computer memory or disc capacity. Roughly 180,000 words of text - an average-sized novel.

Memory Stick

A small electronic card, also known as a memory card, which is inserted into a Digital Camera or Camcorder for storing photographs or movie files that can then uploaded to a computer. This term is also used as an alternative to Flash Drive.

Metacognition

The process of thinking about and regulating one's own learning. Metacognitive activities include recalling/reviewing what you already know about a topic, identifying gaps in your knowledge, planning strategies to fill those gaps, assessing the relevance/importance of new information, and revising your beliefs about the topic.

Microblogging

An approach to Blogging in which very short texts are posted containing snippets of information about events, websites and other information. Twitter is an example of a popular microblogging facility.

Microcomputer

A generic name for a class of computers distinct from bigger mainframe computers and mini-computers. Two of the defining characteristics of a microcomputer are that it should be built around one Microprocessor and that it should be standalone, i.e. capable of operating independently from any other computer or computer Network to which it might be connected. Modern Desktop Computers and Laptop Computers fall into this category.

Microsoft Office

A suite of programs produced by Microsoft Corporation, comprising a Word-processor (Word), a Spreadsheet (Excel), a Presentation Program (PowerPoint), an Email package (Outlook), a Database program (Access), and a Desktop Publishing package (Publisher).

MIDI

Abbreviation for Musical Instrument Digital Interface. A format for synthesised music. Music in MIDI format is created and played through the use of synthesisers, unlike "real" music which is normally recorded in MP3, WMA or WAV format.

MMORPG

Abbreviation for Massively Multiplayer Online Role Playing Game, a type of Virtual World in which players adopt amazing characters to explore fantasy worlds. Often shortened to MMOG.

Moblog

A contraction of mobile and blog. A Blog featuring posts sent mainly by mobile phone (cellphone) or PDA. Moblogs are often set up to enable people to post messages and photographs on the Web while they are travelling.

Modem

Short for modulator/demodulator. A device which converts computer data to a signal that can be transmitted over a standard telephone line. It can also reconvert a signal coming into a computer via a telephone line so that it can be understood by the computer. Modems are used to connect computers with the Internet.

Monitor

The screen on which output from a computer is displayed. Also referred to as Display Screen.

Moodle

A Virtual Learning Environment (VLE), also described as a Course Management System (CMS). Moodle is Open Source software, which means you are free to download it, use it, modify it and even distribute it. Moodle has its own Moodle for Language Teaching Community.

Motherboard

The main electronic circuit board of a microcomputer, to which other circuit boards (also known as cards) can be connected in order to fulfil special functions, e.g. a Sound Card or Video Card. Typically, the motherboard contains the BIOS, CPU, RAM, ROM and all the controllers required to control standard peripheral devices, such as the Display Screen, Keyboard and disc drives.

MOV

The format for storing and playing back audio and video files using the QuickTime media player on the Apple Macintosh, but also available for the multimedia PC. Economical in terms of storage space.

MUD

MUD is an abbreviation for Multi User Domain or Multi User Dungeon. A MUD is a type of real-time Web environment in which users not only email one another but also move around and manipulate objects in an imaginary world. MUDs were originally developed as role-playing adventure games to be engaged in across computer networks but they have developed into a facility for collaboration and education, including language learning.

Multimedia

The integration of two or more types of information (text, images, audio, video, animation, etc.) in a single application.

Multimedia Systems

Include technology such as CD-ROMs and laser discs. This technology provides a gallery of images and programming in an accessible format. Advances in screen resolution have made possible the effective use of these applications.

Multimedia Personal Computer (MPC)

An enhanced Personal Computer that is able to play sound and video and allows the user to make sound and video recordings. MPCs are virtually a standard nowadays.

Multitasking

The execution of more than one program, apparently at the same time, on a computer. Multitasking makes it possible, for example, to print one word-processed document while working on another.

Munge

The act of disguising your email address so it cannot be deciphered or cannot easily be deciphered by a Spammer.

Name Server or Nameserver

Also known in full as Domain Name Server.

Navigation

This describes the process of finding your way, i.e. navigating, around a series of menus within a computer program or finding your way around the World Wide Web by means of a Browser.

Needs Assessment

An evaluation of the existing environment and a description of the functions you want the technology to have and the needs you hope technology will meet.

Netiquette

Etiquette on the Internet. An code of behaviour for people communicating by email via the Internet.

Netizen

Derived from the term citizen, referring to a citizen of the Internet, or someone who uses networked resources. The term connotes civic responsibility and participation.

Netscape

An early Web Browser, which first appeared in 1994, shortly after the World Wide Web went public.

Network

A group of computers connected together, either by physical connections such as cables, or by wireless connections (Wifi). The Internet is a worldwide network of computers to which virtually any computer can be connected.

Newsgroup

A type of public online forum which anyone can read and contribute to.

Ning

A platform that enables you to create your own Social Network.

Notebook Computer

A type of Laptop Computer, but lighter and thinner - and therefore easy to carry around. See Netbook, an even smaller and lighter computer.

Offline

Not connected to a computer or network of computers. Often used in the sense of working with software stored on a stand-alone computer.

Online

Connected to a computer or network of computers, especially the World Wide Web. Often used in the sense of working with software stored at a remote location.

Online Learning

The use of the Internet to follow a course that usually results in the award of a diploma or certificate.

Open and Integrated Learning System (OILS)

A variant of Integrated Learning System. The word Open adds an extra dimension, indicating that the user can access the system freely and leave it at any time.

Open Source

Used to describe Software that is provided free of charge, along with the original Source Code used to create it so that anyone modify it to improve it and work in ways that reflect their own preferences. Moodle is a typical example of open source software.

Optical Character Recognition (OCR)

OCR software is used conjunction with a scanner to convert printed text into digital format. For example, a page from a printed book can be placed on the scanner and the OCR software will be used by the scanner to detect the individual words from which it is made up and then convert them into a form that can be stored on a computer, e.g. a Word document. A great time-saver!

Optical Disc

The generic name for a type of computer disc which uses a laser to read and write data.

Outlining

The ability of a program to automatically number and letter items typed in an indented format.

Outlook

A popular Email program, part of the Microsoft Office suite of programs.

Output

Anything that comes out of a computer after being processed. Also used as a verb.

Package

Loosely speaking, a program or suite of programs such as Microsoft Office, but often has the sense of a set of programs designed to be used by people who wish to use the package in different ways.

Packet Switching

A technique of switching digital signals with computers wherein the signal stream is broken into packets and reassembled in the correct sequence at the destination.

Paradigm

An overall concept accepted by most people in an intellectual community about a complex process or ideas such as "school".

Patch

A small program that improves an existing piece of software or correct an error in it.

Pathname

The pathname of a File on a computer specifies exactly its position on disc, and consists of at least three parts: (i) drive letter, (ii) directory, and (iii) filename, e.g. c:\windows\user.exe. One or more subdirectories may also be included in a pathname, e.g. c:\windows\system\user.exe.

PayTM

It is a mobile e-commerce company. Paytm acts as a virtual wallet when you can store money online and can be used instead of debit/credit or netbanking. However, to transfer the amount to the wallet, you may need any of them.

PDF

An abbreviation for Portable Document Format. This is a file type created by Adobe that allows fully formatted, documents to be transmitted across the Internet and viewed on any computer that has Adobe Acrobat Reader software.

Peer-to-peer Network

A configuration where people store their files on their own computers, and anyone on the network can access the files stored on the other networked computers.

Peripheral Device

Often abbreviated to peripheral. Virtually any device which can be connected to a computer. This term includes modems, printers, scanners, interactive whiteboards, etc.

Personal Computer (PC)

The generic term for IBM-compatible microcomputers.

Personal Digital Assistant (PDA)

A handheld device that combines computing, audio communication, browsing and networking features and serves as an organiser for personal information. Usually abbreviated to PDA.

Personal Learning Environment (PLE)

A PLE, unlike a Virtual Learning Environment (VLE), is an approach to using new technologies that enables learners to develop and control their own learning environment using a range of Social Networking tools.

Phishing

1. term used to describe when a malicious individual or group of individuals scams users through email or web pages designed to look legitimate to encourage users to enter personal information.

2. usually an email message designed to steal your personal data, such as credit card numbers, passwords, account data, or other information.

Pica

A measurement used for a font; equal to 1/6 inch or 12 points.

Pitch

The number of monospace characters printed in a 1-inch line of text.

Pixel

A contraction of picture element. What you see on a computer Display Screen is made up of thousands of coloured pixels or small dots, which can be set according to the user's choice to produce either low-resolution output, medium-resolution output or high-resolution output, the usual combinations of pixels across each line of the screen (horizontal pixels) and down each line of the screen (vertical pixels) being 640 × 480, 800 × 600, 1024 × 768, 1280 × 1024. Thus, the more pixels on the screen the higher the resolution (i.e. producing a finer, sharper image) and the greater the variety of colours that can be displayed.

Podcast

A podcast is a broadcast digital audio recording, made available via the Web in a way that allows the recording to be downloaded for listening at the user's convenience.

Pop-up

A small Window that appears within a program or over the top of a Web page to deliver additional information. Pop-ups on the Web can be annoying as they are often used for unwanted advertising material.

Port

A socker on a computer into which an external device can be plugged.

Portfolio Assessment

A portfolio is defined as a purposeful collection of student work that exhibits to the student and others the student's efforts, progress, or achievement in a given area. This collection must include (1) student participation in selection of portfolio content, (2) the criteria for selection, (3) the criteria for judging merit, and (4) evidence of student self-reflection. Portfolios, even more so than other forms of performance assessment, call on the learner to be highly involved in planning the entries, choosing what to include, and providing the rationale behind those decisions. Portfolios thus attempt not only to assess the end products, but to some extent, the process that went into creating them as well.

Postscript Printer

A type of Printer which is compatible with the Postscript language, a Page Description Language (PDL) favoured by the printing profession for the production of high-quality printed publications.

PowerPoint

The name of a Presentation Program forming part of the Microsoft Office suite of programs.

Presentation Practice Production (PPP)

A long-established approach to language teaching, consisting of three main phases

(i) the presentation phase, in which the teacher presents new language (e.g. vocabulary and grammar) to the students; (ii) the practice phase, in which the students demonstrate that they understand how to use the new language correctly (e.g. through controlled oral or written activities) with feedback from the teacher; (iii) the production phase, in which the students produce new utterances using what they have learnt.

Printer

More or less self-explanatory. An external device attached to a computer for device for producing printed output or Hardcopy.

Printout

Anything produced on a printer after being processed by a computer program.

Programming Language

A formal, structured, English-like language in which computer programs are written. The instructions, known as code, are converted into binary machine instructions via a compiler or an interpreter. C++, Pascal, and BASIC, are examples of popular programming languages.

Project Management Software

Software programs that provide tools to help manage projects, such as integrated calendars, report generators, scheduling, charting, tracking, prioritizing, etc.

Prompt

An on screen symbol that indicates where to type a command; a message that indicates what action is to be taken.

Protocol

In Internet terminology protocol usually refers to a set of rules that define an exact format for communication between systems. For example the HTTP protocol defines the format for communication between Web browsers and Web servers.

Public Domain

Material that is copyright free, whose copyright has expired, or which cannot be copyrighted. Many people think that because something is on the Web it must be in the public domain. This is not so. A work is in the public domain only if it is explicitly stated to be so.

QR Code

Short for Quick Response Code. A QR Code is a two-dimensional barcode that can store a variety of different types of information, e.g. text, a website URL, a telephone number, an SMS message, an email address, an email message, contact details, information about an event, a Google Maps location, your social media profile (Facebook, Twitter, etc.), an iTunes link, a YouTube link, etc. QR Codes can be read by barcode readers and Smartphone cameras. Instead of writing down the information relating to a website URL or map location etc., you just take a photo of the QR Code.

QuickTime

Software used for viewing movies and listening to audio recordings: http://www.apple.com/quicktime/. QuickTime is often needed as a Plug-in, when you are accessing audio or video materials on the Web.

QWERTY

1. keyboard named after the first six keys in the upper left part of the keyboard.

2. a standard keyboard.

RAM

An acronym for Random Access Memory, referring to the dynamic memory in the silicon chips in a computer. RAM chips are the memory chips used as the temporary working area for running and developing programs. Data in RAM can be read and written to (i.e. changed) in microseconds, as opposed to the much slower data access times for discs, but RAM's contents disappear the moment the computer is switched off. The more RAM a computer has, the more flexibility the user has. RAM used to be measured in kilobytes (KB) but now it is usually expressed in megabytes (MB) and even gigabytes (GB). The amount of RAM a PC has could crudely be thought of as its "mental capacity".

Real Time

A real-time computer system may be defined as one that controls an environment by receiving data, processing them, and returning the results sufficiently quickly to affect the functioning of the environment at that time.

Rip

To extract or copy data from one format to another. The most common example is found in the phrase "to rip a CD", which means to copy audio tracks from an audio CD and save them to hard disc as WAV, MP3 or other audio files, which can then be played, edited or written back to another CD.

ROM

Acronym for Read Only Memory. ROM chips in a computer contain data and programs as supplied by the manufacturer that can be accessed but not changed, i.e. they are read-only. ROM is also used to describe CD-ROMs. Originally CD-ROMs contained data and programs that could not be changed or erased, and new data and programs could not be stored on them, but modern CD-ROM and DVD drives allow certain types of CDs and DVDs to be written to as well as read - so the term has become a misnomer in this respect.

Root Directory

The topmost directory in the directory hierarchy, from which all other directories are descended. On a PC's hard disc this has the pathname C:\. See Directory.

Router

A hardware device that connects computers to a Network or that connects one network with another network. Routers are now available at low prices and can be used for connecting two or more computers together in home networks, so that data can be exchanged between the computers on the network and so that all the computers in the network can access the Internet.

Scaffolding

The cognitive processing support that the instruction provides the learners, allowing them to learn complex ideas that would be beyond their grasp if they depended solely on their own cognitive resources, selectively aiding the learners where needed.

Scanner

A device used to convert hard copy, e.g. a printed page, photograph or photographic negative, into a form that can be stored on a computer.

Scareware

1. program claiming it's an antivirus or other security program and has found dozens of potential threats on a computer, which in reality are either non-existent or not really a threat to the user or the user's computer
2. programs typically installed onto a computer through false Internet advertisements, free programs and other malware.

SCORM

Acronym for Shareable Content Object Reference Model. SCORM is a suite of technical standards that enable Web-based learning systems to find, import, share, reuse, and export learning content in a standardised way.

Scroll

To move up and down or from side to side through a document or a Window to view or access all of its contents

Search Engine

A search facility provided at a number of sites on the World Wide Web. Search engines enable the user to search the whole of the Web for key words and phrases and to locate related websites. This is a useful facility for locating information.

Second Life

One of the fastest growing "virtual worlds" on the Web.

Semantic Web

The Semantic Web is not a new type of Web, but rather an extension of the Web whereby data available in different locations on the Web is linked together in a way that allows the user to search the Web in a more sophisticated way.

Server

A computer which provides services to other computers, which are known as clients. For example, when you click on a link in a Web page your Browser sends a request to a remote computer, known as a Web Server, that serves the requested page to your browser, which then displays it on your computer screen. A Local Area Network (LAN) has a server that delivers software to the computers (also known as workstations) that are connected to it. It is usually the most powerful computer in the network Users connected to a LAN can access their own files remotely and exchange information with the server and other users connected to the network.

Setup Program

A program that enables the user to set up a program or suite of programs on the computer's hard disc. Also known as Install Program or Installation Program.

Shareware

Try before you buy software. A Shareware application can be freely copied and used without payment to the author(s), but you are encouraged to pay a registration fee if you use it regularly. Shareware is often a cut-down copy of the fully-featured application, which can only be obtained by paying the registration fee.

Social Media

Term used to describe a variety of Web 2.0 applications that enable people to share images, audio recordings and video recordings via the Web and to initiate discussions about them.

Social Networking

A term applied to a type of website where people can seek other people who share their interests, find out what's going on in their areas of interest, and share information one another.

Software

The opposite to Hardware. A generic term describing all kinds of computer programs, applications and operating systems. Software is not tangible, being a set of instructions written in a Programming Language comprising a set of instructions that the computer executes.

Spam

Unsolicited email advertisements, the Internet equivalent of junk mail. A spammer is someone who sends out spam. The term spam comes from a sketch in the Monty Python's Flying Circus TV series.

Spambot

A spambot is a program designed to collect email addresses from the Internet in order to build mailing lists for sending Spam.

Speech Recognition

A branch of Human Language Technologies (HLT) devoted to developing programs and devices that enable computers to recognise, analyse and transcribe human speech.

Speech Synthesis

A branch of Human Language Technologies (HLT) devoted to developing programs and devices that enable computers to generate human speech.

Spider

A program that searches the web for new Web sites.

Splog

A contraction of spam blog. The splog site creator (splogger) begins by finding a subject that attracts lots of visitors. Then the splogger sets up a blog which plagiarises content from other sites dealing with this subject. It's spam in the form of a blog. Visit the splog site, click on a link that it contains or click on an advertisement at the site, and you're making money for the splogger.

Spreadsheet

Essentially an accounting program, e.g. Excel, which forms part of the Microsoft Office suite of programs.

Spyware is a term that may be used synonymously with adware but it implies more sinister motives on the part of the person who has dumped it onto your computer, e.g. with a view to stealing private information such as bank account numbers, credit card numbers, passwords, etc.

Steering Committee

A group of persons who meet periodically to evaluate the progress and success of the implementation of the technology solution.

Suite

A collection of software programs that are sold together and are supposed to work together efficiently and use similar commands.

Surge protector

Electronic device for protecting a computer or other electronic device from the harmful effects of sharp surges of voltage in electric power lines.

SVGA

Abbreviation for Super Video Graphics Adaptor. An older type of Video Card or circuit board used to control the output on a computer Display Screen.

Synchronous

"At the same time". Often used to refer to communication in a Chat Room or via Videoconferencing, where the participants have to be present at their computers at the same time.

Sysadmin

A contraction of Systems Administrator, the person responsible for managing a computer system.

T-1, T-3 line

High-speed digital lines that provide data communication speeds of 1.544 megabits (T-1) and 45 megabits (T-3) per second.

Tab gird

A series of preset indentions.

Tag

Tagging has become more common in recent years as a result of the widespread use of Social Media for sharing images, audio recordings, video recordings, website references, etc. Tags are labels that briefly describe the what the media or references are all about and help other people find them quickly.

Telnet

A program which allows you to log in to a remote Host computer and carry out the same commands as if you were using a terminal at the host site.

Text to Speech (TTS)

TTS software enables text to be read out loud from a computer screen by a synthetic voice.

TIFF or TIF

Abbreviation for Tag Image File Format. A file format for storing images on a computer. TIFF files can store very high-quality images with millions of colours, but they are very demanding in terms of storage space.

Touchpad

The device on a laptop computer that takes the place of a mouse.

Touchscreen

A Display Screen which enables a computer to react to the touch of a finger. Touchscreens are commonly used in devices such as Smartphones and Tablet Computers.

Trojan

Trojans are programs - usually malicious - that install themselves or run surreptitiously on a victim's machine. They do not install or run automatically but may entice users into installing another program, e.g., a game, that actually installs a hostile piece of software and causes considerable damage to your computer. The name derives from Trojan Horse, the hollow wooden horse in which, according to legend,

Greeks hid and gained entrance to Troy, later opening the gates to their army.

Troll

A troll is someone who intentionally posts derogatory or provocative messages in an online community such as a Discussion List or Forum or Blog to bait other users into responding.

Twitter

A Microblogging facility that allows users to post very short texts (maximum 140 characters) containing snippets of information about what they are doing at a given moment, news items, links to websites or comments on events, e.g. conferences and courses.

Unicode

The Unicode Worldwide Character Standard is a character coding system designed to support the interchange, processing, and display of the written texts of the diverse languages of the modern world. In addition, it supports classical and historical texts of many written languages.

Uninstall

A verb used to describe the process of removing an unwanted application from your computer's hard disc.

Uninstall Program

Basically what it says : a program for removing (uninstalling) an unwanted application from your computer's hard disc.

Unix

An Operating System widely used on large computer systems in corporations and universities, on which many Web servers are hosted. A PC version of Unix, called Linux, is becoming increasingly popular as an alternative to Windows.

Upload

To transfer a copy of a computer program, a text file, an image file, a sound file or a video file from one computer to another computer.

URL

Abbreviation for Uniform Resource Locator. Also known as a Web Address. A URL contains the location of a resource on the Internet. A URL specifies the address of the computer where the resource is located, which may be the homepage of a website. The http:// prefix can usually be omitted from a URL when it is entered in a Browser.

User-friendly

Mainly used to describe Software. Software that is easy to use and offers guidance if the user does silly things is described as user-friendly. This term may also be applied to certain types of Hardware.

VGA

Abbreviation for Video Graphics Adaptor. An older type of Video Card or circuit board used to control the output on a computer Display Screen. VGA cards were superseded by SVGA cards.

Vodcast

A contraction of Video Podcast. A type of Podcast that incorporates video as well as audio.

Voicenet

Ordinary telephone service.

VOIP

Abbreviation for Voice over Internet Protocol, i.e. audio communication using the Internet instead of telephones. Skype and Ventrilo are examples of VoIP.

Volatile Memory

Used to describe the internal main Memory of a computer that loses its contents when power is switched off. RAM is volatile memory as the information is stored in memory chips as an electric charge.

W3C

Abbreviation for World Wide Web Consortium. An international non-profit organisation which acts as a resource centre for the World Wide Web, and is active in setting technical standards.

WAP

Abbreviation for Wireless Application Protocol. A system that enables you to browse online services, e.g. relating to information about the weather, traffic conditions, shopping, etc. via a special type of mobile phone. WAP is the mobile phone equivalent of the World Wide Web. Newer mobile phones include WAP browser software to allow users access to WAP sites.

Warchalking

Warchalkers make chalk markings on walls or pavements to indicate that there is an insecure wireless access point nearby.

WAV

Short for Waveform Audio Format. A format for storing high-quality audio files. Somewhat hungry in terms of storage space compared to the MP3 and WMA audio file formats.

Webcast

A live audio and video picture broadcast over the Internet that can be viewed and heard using a RealPlayer G2 version 5.0 (MAC) or 6.0 (PC). Version 6.0 will work on both platforms.

Weblog

The full form of the term Blog.

Webmail

A facility for creating, sending and receiving messages via the Internet. Webmail offers an alternative to using email software such as such as Outlook or Eudora. In order to use webmail you have to register with an Internet Service Provider (ISP) and you can then access their email service via your Web Browser.

Webmaster

The person who maintains a specific Web site and is responsible for what appears there.

Web Server or Webserver

A computer or a software package running on a computer that delivers, *i.e.* serves, Web pages to its clients : see Client and Host. Every Web server has an IP Address and possibly a Domain Name. For example, if you enter the URL http://www.truemanbooks.com/index.htm in your Browser, this sends a request to the Server whose domain name is truemanbooks.com. The server then fetches the page named index.htm and sends a copy of it to your browser. Any computer can be turned into a Web server by installing Web server software and connecting the machine to the Internet. By far the most popular Web server software in use worldwide is the Open Source Apache software: http://www.apache.org

Website

An area on the World Wide Web where an organisation or individual stores a collection of pages of material - Web pages. The pages are usually interlinked with one another and with other websites. Every website has a unique Web Address or URL.

WinZip

Software program commonly used to compress larger files into smaller ones for easy sharing and downloading.

Wifi

Wireless Fidelity, also known as wireless networking, a way of transmitting information without cables that is reasonably fast and is often used for laptop computers within a business or a university or school campus instead of a Local Area Network (LAN) that uses cable connections. Wifi systems use high frequency radio signals to transmit and receive data over distances of several hundred feet. Many hotels and airports now offer wifi access to people travelling with laptop computers.

Windows Explorer

Microsoft's tool, provided as part of Windows, that enables you to inspect and manage folders and files stored on your computer. My Computer is an alternative tool, also provided as part of Windows.

Wizard

Software that guides the user step-by-step through a complex task, such as setting up software on a network or configuring a printer to output data in a special format, e.g. for printing labels from a database program.

WMA

Abbreviation for Windows Media Audio. Microsoft's audio encoding format which offers high-quality output with lower file sizes.

Word-processor

Probably the most widely used computer Application. Modern word-processors allow the user to create fine-looking documents including images, tables, photographs, and even sound and video recordings if they are to be viewed on screen rather than from the printed page. In many respects they are similar to Desktop Publishing applications. Word-processors normally include a spellchecker, a grammar checker, a style checker and a thesaurus, as well as tools for writing in HTML, the coding language used for producing Web pages. Word-processors have been widely used in teaching and learning foreign languages ever since they first appeared.

Workstation

Most people use it in the context of any computer that forms part of a Network. Formerly, this term was applied to a particular type of powerful computer used for scientific and engineering calculations, e.g. the Sun Workstation.

World Wide Web

Usually referred to simply as the Web. This is the most powerful and fastest growing Internet service. The World Wide Web was the brainchild of Tim Berners-Lee, who in 1989 invented the HTML coding language that is the basis of the Web. The Web became a public service in 1993. It is a huge collection of resources of information, including learning materials, which is accessed by means of a computer program known as a

Browser. The World Wide Web is only part of the Internet, but many people treat both terms as synonyms.

Write Protect

To protect a Storage Device, File or Folder so that its contents cannot normally by altered or erased. This may be done physically, e.g. by moving a notch on a floppy disc's casing, or - more commonly these days - through software that designates the device, file or folder as read-only.

WWW

Abbreviation for World Wide Web.

XML

Abbreviation for eXtensible Markup Language. XML is a specification emanating from the World Wide Web Consortium (W3C) that allows Web designers to create their own language for displaying documents on the Web. XML is an extension to the standard language for creating Web pages, HTML, and makes it possible to create websites containing more complex interactivity.

Yahoo

A popular Search Engine.

Y2K

Year 2000. See Millennium Bug.

YouTube

A website to which you can upload your own video clips and view video clips uploaded by others

http://www.youtube.com.

Zip Disc

A portable type of disc used to store around 100Mb of data. Zip discs have become obsolete since the arrival of smaller and more convenient storage devices with much greater storage capacity, e.g. the increasingly popular Flash Drive or Memory Stick.

Zip Drive

A type of disc drive that accepts portable zip discs (see above). Zip drives themselves are also portable and can be connected to almost any computer.

Zip

Used as a verb to describe the process of compacting files or programs in order to cut down the amount of storage space they require by compressing them into one tightly-packed file and thus to make it easier for them to be transported on floppy discs or transmitted electronically to other locations, e.g. via the Internet. Proprietary programs, such as WinZip or WinRar, can be used to zip data and files. Zipped files are recognised by the Extension .zip or .rar (for files created with WinRar) and have to be unzipped before they can be used, again using proprietary programs.

SOCIAL MEDIA TERMINOLOGY

A/B testing

A/B testing, also known as split testing, measures two social media posts against each other to see which performs best. The most common way of using A/B tests is to only change one element of the post between the two versions (headline, image, CTA, etc) so that you know any difference in performance is because of that change. You can A/B test with both organic and paid posts.

Ads Manager

Ads Manager is Facebook's tool for creating, running, and analyzing social ads. It can manage your ad campaigns on Facebook, Instagram, or Audience Network. It offers a wide variety of features for ad targeting, budgeting, and optimization as well.

Algorithm

In general, an algorithm is a defined set of rules used to solve a problem. In social media terminology, however, people often use 'algorithm' as a shorthand for 'feed algorithm', which is the set of rules a social network uses to automatically decide which posts come first in your feed. For example, if Facebook decides that it wants to prioritize posts with lots of comments, it adjusts the rules of its feed algorithm to push those posts up.

Analytics

Analytics is the way you interpret and find patterns in data. In a social media context, analytics is the process of following metrics on your social media performance and using that data to improve your strategy. For instance, watching your engagement rate over time to see if your posts are becoming more or less compelling to your followers is one way of using social analytics.

Application Programming Interface (API)

An API is a set of building blocks that programmers can use to develop computer programs. As far as social media is concerned, all the major social networks have their own APIs that let programmers create their own software that works with the networks. Third-party social intelligence solutions such as ours rely on social media APIs to integrate with platforms like Facebook.

Audience

Your audience on social media is the group of people you're able to reach with your content. This includes all your followers, plus anyone who sees or interacts with your posts in their feed. Growing your social media audience is one of the best ways to spread brand awareness.

Avatar

Your social media avatar, also known as your profile picture, is a small image that represents you on a social network. It can be a real photo of you, a corporate logo, or anything you want your followers to identify as 'you' on social.

Average Response Time

Average response time is a social customer service metric. It is the average time it takes a brand to reply to questions or complaints on social media. Consumer expectations of social customer support response times have become more and more demanding in recent years, with **42% of customers now expecting a response** within 60 minutes.

Business-to-Business (B2B)

A B2B business sells products or services to other businesses, like a consulting firm or a business software company. On social media, B2B brands frequently attempt to position themselves as thought leaders in their industries and provide professional advice to their business peers.

Business-to-Consumer (B2C)

A B2C business deals directly with consumers, like a hotel or retail store. In social media marketing, B2C companies often focus on creating a community around their brand and providing excellent social customer care.

Bio

Your social media bio is a short description in your profile that tells people who you are. It's also a great place to share links to your website or other accounts. On Facebook, Instagram, and Twitter, it's simply called a bio, while on LinkedIn it's called a summary.

Boosted Post

A boosted post is a Facebook post that you put money behind to increase its reach. Also known as promoted posts, boosted posts differ from Facebook ads in the way that they start out as organic posts and then get additional paid reach based on your spend. Also, you can launch them directly from your Facebook Page without using Ads Manager. Like Facebook ads, though, boosted posts allow you to target a specific audience and set an exact boost duration and budget.

Brand Advocate

A brand advocate on social media is a customer who posts positive messages, leaves positive reviews, or otherwise supports your brand on social. Brand advocates may also encourage other users to use your products or services through word-of-mouth marketing.

Brand Awareness

Brand awareness is the level of familiarity consumers have with your brand. It's often considered one of the main goals of social media marketing. It's also one of the objectives you can select for your Facebook and Instagram ad campaigns in Ads Manager. Brand awareness can be measured through impressions or reach, or more accurately through **ad recall lift** (an estimation of how many users would remember your brand after seeing the ad).

Business Manager

Facebook Business Manager is a software that helps organizations manage their Pages, ad accounts, and team members. It serves as a hub to connect a business's advertising, finances, users, and Pages and allows for easy administration. It also ensures that company data and account access are legally and practically under control of the company instead of an individual user.

Chatbot

A chatbot is an artificial intelligence program that can automate customer interactions for a company. Chatbots can be implemented on a number of social messaging apps, from Facebook Messenger to Slack. They can provide customer service, answer questions, and even set up appointments automatically.

Clickbait

Clickbait is content that uses manipulative copy to convince users to click on it. Clickbait tends to rely on exaggeration and withholding information to push people into clicking. For example, an article with the headline "Doctors HATE him for using this one WEIRD TRICK..." but just says you should work out regularly is considered clickbait because it compels people to click it to learn more while being thin on actual content. Social networks like **Facebook** consider clickbait spammy and lower its reach accordingly.

Clickthrough Rate (CTR)

On social media, the clickthrough rate represents the percentage of people who not only see your post but click on it too. What counts as a click and what counts as 'seeing your post' vary by social network. On Facebook, CTR is equal to (link clicks/post impressions) × 100%.

Conversion rate (CVR)

In social media terminology, conversion rate is the percentage of users who see your post or ad, and who then take a specified action. That action is called a conversion, and it could mean purchasing an item, signing up for a newsletter, downloading an ebook, or a variety of other acts. If your social media marketing goal is to increase conversions, your CVR is an important metric for analyzing how effective your post or ad is.

Cost per click (CPC)

Cost per click is a social media advertising metric that tells you how much you're paying for each click on your ad on average. If your social media marketing goal is to drive traffic to a landing page or a piece of content, a low CPC means you're getting more traffic at a lower price, while a high CPC means you're paying a lot for traffic. CPC can vary based on many factors, including whom you're targeting with your ad, what locations you're targeting, and how relevant your ad is to your target audience.

Cost Per Mille (CPM)

Cost per mille is another social advertising metric. It refers to how much you pay per 1,000 impressions ('mille' means 1,000 in Latin). If your goal is to get your ad in front of as many eyes as possible and spread brand awareness, CPM is an important metric to follow. Like CPC, CPM varies based on your targeting options and the quality of your ad.

Crisis Management

Social media crisis management is how you handle events or interactions that could potentially damage your company's reputation. Inappropriate posts by someone at your company or a social media boycott against your brand may qualify as social media crisis, while a couple of angry comments from customers would not. Crisis management requires social media managers to respond quickly and follow a plan in order to de-escalate the problem at hand.

Cross-channel

In social media marketing, each network (Facebook, Twitter, etc) is also a marketing channel. Something that is cross-channel, then, goes across all your different social networks. For example, a cross-channel social strategy is a strategy that aligns your objectives across all the social networks your brand is present on.

Crowdsourcing

Crowdsourcing on social media means using a large group of people to generate ideas, services, or content via a social network. It lets followers feel involved and engaged with your brand's activity while generating ideas or content for your brand. Examples could be inviting your followers to vote on names for your new product or asking them to send in song submissions for your upcoming commercial.

Dark Post

A dark post is a social media ad that doesn't appear on the advertiser's timeline. Unlike organic posts or boosted posts, dark posts only show up in the feeds of users they're targeting. "Dark post" is an informal term – on Facebook, they're officially called "unpublished page posts", on Twitter they're called "promoted-only tweets", on LinkedIn they're called "direct sponsored content", and on Instagram, all ads are dark posts by default.

Dark Social

Dark social is often confused with dark posts, but the two social media terms actually have nothing in common. Dark social is web traffic coming from social media that analytics tools struggle to track. This is often due to users sharing links privately on social, in chats, or direct messages. One study found that **84%** of consumer content sharing happens on dark social.

Direct Message (DM)

A direct message on social media is a private message sent directly to a user's inbox. DMs exist in contrast to public forms of interaction on social media, like commenting on an image or posting on a user's timeline.

Disappearing Content

Disappearing content, sometimes called ephemeral content, refers to posts on social media that delete themselves automatically after a set amount of time has passed. Instagram and Snapchat Stories are notable examples, as these sets of photos and videos disappear after 24 hours. In social media marketing, disappearing content is used to be spontaneous and timely, while motivating users to engage through FOMO.

Employee Advocacy

Employee advocacy is when co-workers at your company support and promote your brand on social media. This may include sharing branded content, amplifying your company's brand message, or frequently liking and commenting on company posts. One study found that branded messages obtained 561% more reach when shared by employees than when posted through branded channels.

Engagement Rate

Engagement rate is a social media metric that tells you much a post is motivating people to interact with it. It's defined as (number of people who engaged with your post/number of people who saw your post) × 100%. Typically, a higher engagement rate means your post was more compelling (or at least more likely to provoke a response). Engagement rate is difficult to compare across social networks, as what counts as an "engagement" and what counts as "seeing your post" is different on each network. "Seeing your post" could refer to reach or impressions, while "engagements" may include likes, comments, shares, reactions, and more.

Evergreen Content

In content marketing, evergreen content is content that ages well and maintains its value over time. Evergreen content is ideal for recycling and repurposing on social media, since it does not lose relevance based on the date it's posted. For example, an article on the challenges of being a social media marketer (SMM) is more likely to be evergreen than an article about TikTok's latest feature update.

Feed

A feed on social media is a generic term for the stream of content you see from other users. On most social networks, the feed functions as a homepage and is the most common way to see people's posts and engage with them.

Follower

A follower is a user on social media who has subscribed to see your posts in their feed. Both personal and business accounts can have followers. Your number of followers, or follower count, is a key metric for seeing how your audience on social media is growing or shrinking over time.

FOMO

FOMO is an acronym that stands for Fear of Missing Out. On social media, FOMO is the feeling users get when seeing posts about events or opportunities they want to be a part of. Social media marketers often use FOMO to their advantage by making exclusive or limited-time offers that users need to jump on quickly to avoid missing.

Frequency

Frequency is a Facebook/Instagram advertising term that refers to how many times your ad was shown to the average user in your target audience. It's calculated by dividing total ad impressions by total ad reach. Frequency over 1.00 means at least some users saw your ad multiple times. This may be positive if your goal is to raise brand awareness and ad recall, but if your frequency is very high, you may be wasting your budget and advertising too many times to each user.

Geotargeting

In social media marketing, geotargeting is the technique of adjusting your ad content based on the location of a user. In Facebook ads manager, users can be included or excluded from a target audience based on their region, country, state, city, postal code, or address. This means advertisers can create and target ad sets to appeal to users in a certain geographic location.

Hashtag

A hashtag (#) is a way of connecting your posts on social media to other posts on the same subject or trending topic. By searching for a specific hashtag, users can find all public posts that have it. For example, users seeking content about the World Cup might look for posts with #WorldCup or #FIFA. Social media marketers often follow the popularity of hashtags over time to see what's trending on social media.

Header Image

Your header image, or cover photo, is the visual you place at the top of your social media profile.

Often in landscape format, header images are much larger than your profile picture or avatar and can be used to introduce you or your brand to your profile visitors. They can compliment your profile picture, show off your personality, or show off a product or event you're promoting.

Impressions

Impressions are a social media metric that measures how many times your post has been shown in users' feeds. Unlike with reach, you may count multiple impressions for a single user if they have looked at your post more than once. Each social network counts impressions differently.

Key performance indicator (KPI)

A key performance indicator, or KPI, is a metric you use to measure your progress toward business goals. In social media marketing, KPIs are the most important stats to track in order to see if you're meeting the objectives of your social strategy. For example, if your primary objective on social was to raise brand awareness, post reach or ad recall lift might be your KPIs.

Listicle

A listicle is a list-based article. This type of content is often popular on social media because of its quick, easy-to-digest format. For example, an article like 21 Tips to Massively Increase Instagram Engagement would be considered a listicle because of its point-by-point breakdown.

Meme

While the term 'meme' (rhymes with 'team') originally meant any idea that spread, multiplied, and changed in a viral way, it means something more specific in a social media context. Memes on social media are funny pieces of text, videos, or images that go viral and let users get in on the joke by creating their own variations and sharing them.

Brands often try to hop on the latest meme to connect with younger audiences, but this can backfire and make them look out of touch if they don't get the joke. If brands are self-aware enough and have a healthy sense of irony, though, they can pull off 'memejacking' once in a while.

Metric

A social media metric is a statistic that measures the performance of your posts, ads, or overall account. Social media managers use metrics to see which content or strategies are working and which aren't. Metrics may include impressions, reach, followers, engagement rate, link clicks, and more.

Native Advertising

Native advertising on social media is the method of showing paid content to users in a way that looks organic. Promoted Facebook posts and promoted tweets are good examples of native ads, as they appear similar to standard posts in users' feeds while having their reach extended with an ad budget. A recent study found that consumers looked at native ads 53% more often than display ads.

Newsjacking

Newsjacking is the technique of hopping on current events with your social media content. Social media managers often engage in newsjacking to seem timely and relevant while gaining exposure by tying their content to key hashtags and conversations around the latest news. For instance, during a power outage at the 2013 Super Bowl that millions across America were following, Oreo got tons of engagement with this real-time tweet.

Objectives

In social advertising, objectives are the results you want to achieve through your ad campaign. These objectives are used to determine which key performance indicators to follow and optimize ad spend. In Facebook Ads Manager, you can select from a variety of marketing objectives, including traffic, engagement, conversions, brand awareness, and more.

Pay per click (PPC)

PPC is a social media marketing term for an ad model where you pay each time a user clicks on your ad. This is typically associated with a traffic objective, as it makes the most sense for advertisers to pay based on clicks when their primary goal is to increase visits to a website or landing page.

Platform

The term social media platform is often used to mean the same thing as "social media network" or "social media channel". However, a social media platform is technically the software behind a social network, including its API, backend and markup language. The phrase "social media management platform", meanwhile, refers to a set of software tools that help SMMs organize their social media accounts.

Reach

Reach is a social media metric that tells you how many people have seen your post. It differs from impressions in that even if a user sees your post multiple times, they still only count as one person reached. Reach is an important metric for understanding how large the audience for your content is and measuring your progress toward spreading brand awareness.

Relevance Score

Relevance score is a metric available in Facebook Ads Manager that tells you how well your target audience is responding to your ad on a scale of 1 to 10. The score is based on several factors, including positive feedback such as clicks or likes, negative feedback such as users selecting "I don't want to see this ad", and overall ad performance. The higher your relevance score, the more relevant your ad is to your target audience and the more likely it will be selected over other ads to be shown to your audience.

Retargeting

In social media advertising, retargeting is the technique of targeting ads at users who have interacted with your page or website before. A social media marketer may retarget a user who clicked a Facebook ad for new boots, went to the checkout page, and then didn't complete the sale, for example. Retargeting can be done by either tracking user activities with the Facebook Pixel or uploading a list of past or potential customers to target.

Sentiment Analysis

Sentiment analysis is the way software analyzes the attitude of a piece of text. On social media, sentiment analysis tools can be used to automatically detect whether customer feedback is positive, negative, or neutral. Social media marketers can also look at the average sentiment of their customer interactions over time to see the general mood of their audience or the overall response to their content.

Shareable Content

Shareable content on social media is content that's likely to get users to share it with their networks. Many factors affect what makes content shareable, including how useful, entertaining, and inspiring it is. Content that evokes strong emotions and reactions is also more likely to be shared.

Social Customer Service

Social customer service (or social customer care) is customer service via social media. This may include answering customer inquiries, handling complaints, and offering support. Private messaging apps are your best bet for social customer service in 2020, with 70% of people now preferring a "message us" over a "call us" button.

Social Listening

Social listening is how social media managers track conversations around key topics, terms, brands, and more, often with a specialized software tool. Social listening software gathers mentions, comments, hashtags, and relevant posts from across social media to provide insights on what users are talking about and how. Brands often use these insights to tap into key trends and see what people are saying about them and their competitors.

Social Media Monitoring

Social media monitoring is often confused with social listening, but there are some important differences between the two. Social listening involves actively setting up projects to seek out conversations on specific topics and gathering data on them. Social media monitoring, on the other hand, is the more passive technique of keeping an eye on your mentions and following what your audience is saying.

Social Media ROI

Social media ROI, or return on investment, is a measurement of how much revenue your activities on social media are generating for your company versus how much you are spending on them. Because many brands' social media objectives are more about generating brand awareness than leads or sales, social media ROI is notoriously difficult to estimate. In abstract, this is the formula to calculate it:

$$\text{RIO\%} = \frac{\begin{matrix}\text{Profit gained} \\ \text{from social media}\end{matrix} - \begin{matrix}\text{Cost of} \\ \text{social media}\end{matrix}}{\text{Cost of social media}} \times 100$$

Social Selling

Social selling, put simply, is using social media to make sales. Often, this takes place when salespeople interact with potential customers on social, establishing a relationship they can leverage for a future sale. This could be done by answering prospects' questions, sharing company content, or mentioning their brand in a post comment.

Targeting

Targeting is a social media advertising term that refers to how you select the potential audience for your ads. Most social advertising platforms allow you to select which users should see your ads based on age, location, gender, interests, and a variety of other factors. Targeting options are one of the most important aspects of creating effective ads on social media.

Traffic

Traffic is the number of users who visit a given website or page. In a social media context, increasing traffic is a common marketing objective for SMMs who want to drive their audience to a blog, landing page, or other URL outside of the social network.

Trending Topic

A trending topic is a subject or event that has a sudden surge in popularity on social media. Several social networks track the top hashtags or subjects people are posting about and include a "trending topics section". On Twitter, this section is currently called "Trends for you" and is personalized and localized, while Instagram has an "Explore" section which lets users see relevant content that is trending in their area.

User-generated Content (UGC)

User-generated content, or UGC, is fan-created content promoting a brand. UGC can come in the form of videos, images, posts, audio, reviews, articles, and more. Brands often rely on UGC to get users engaged with their social media campaigns and build trust and loyalty with their followers. Toyota, for example, called on their audience to submit videos of them performing street music as part of their Feeling The Street campaign.

Vanity Metric

A vanity metric on social media is a statistic that may look like a positive indicator of performance but doesn't actually provide you with valuable insights. Impressions are a classic example, as they are often larger than reach, but only tell you how many times people scrolled past a post in their feed without revealing the bigger picture of how popular or engaging the post was.

Viral

Viral is a term describing content that spreads exponentially on social media. This typically occurs because an increasing number of people share the content with their followers, then their followers share the same content to their followers, and so on, creating a snowball effect. Creating content that goes viral is the holy grail of social media marketing, as it means you get a huge audience without spending a cent.

BASICS OF INTERNET

INTERNET

The Internet is a global network of billions of computers and other electronic devices. With the Internet, it's possible to access almost any information, communicate with anyone else in the world, and do much more.

You can do all of this by connecting a computer to the Internet, which is also called going online. When someone says a computer is online, it's just another way of saying it's connected to the Internet.

What is the Web?

The World Wide Web-usually called the Web for short-is a collection of different websites you can access through the Internet. A website is made up of related text, images, and other resources. Websites can resemble other forms of media-like newspaper articles or television programs-or they can be interactive in a way that's unique to computers.

The purpose of a website can be almost anything: a news platform, an advertisement, an online library, a forum for sharing images, or an educational site.

Once you are connected to the Internet, you can access and view websites using a type of application called a web browser. Just keep in mind that the web browser itself is not the Internet; it only displays websites that are stored on the Internet.

How does the Internet Work?

Internet is a global network of physical cables, which can include copper telephone wires, TV cables, and fiber optic cables. Even wireless connections like Wi-Fi and 3G/4G rely on these physical cables to access the Internet.

When we visit a website, our computer sends a request over these wires to a server. A server is where websites are stored, and it works a lot like our computer's hard drive. Once the request arrives, the server retrieves the website and sends the correct data back to our computer. What's amazing is that this all happens in just a few seconds.

Other things we can do on the Internet

One of the best features of the Internet is the ability to communicate almost instantly with anyone in the world. Email is one of the oldest and most universal ways to communicate and share information on the Internet, and billions of people use it. Social media allows people to connect in a variety of ways and build communities online.

There are many other things we can do on the Internet. There are thousands of ways to keep up with news or shop for anything online. We can pay your bills, manage your bank accounts, meet new people, watch TV, or learn new skills. We can learn or do almost anything online.

What Can We Do Online?

There's almost no limit to what we can do online. The Internet makes it possible to quickly find information, communicate with people around the world, manage your finances, shop from home, listen to music, watch videos, and much, much more. Let's take a look at some of the ways the Internet is most commonly used today.

Finding Information Online

With billions of websites online today, there is a lot of information on the Internet. Search engines make this information easier to find. All we have to do is type one or more keywords, and the search engine will look for relevant websites.

For example, let's say we're looking for a new pair of shoes. We could use a search engine to learn about different types of shoes, get directions to a nearby shoe store, or even find out where to buy them online.

There are many different search engines we can use, but some of the most popular include Google, Yahoo!, and Bing.

Email

Short for electronic mail, email is a way to send and receive messages across the Internet. Almost everyone who uses the Internet has their own email account, usually called an email address. This is because we'll need an email address to do just about anything online, from online banking to creating a Facebook account.

Social Networking

Social networking websites are another way to connect and share with our family and friends online. Rather than sharing with just a few people over email, social networks make it easier to connect and share with many people at the same time. Facebook is the world's largest social networking site, with more than 1 billion users worldwide.

Chat and Instant Messaging

Chat and instant messaging (IM) are short messages sent and read in real time, allowing us to converse more quickly and easily than email. These are generally used when both (or all) people are online, so our message can be read immediately. By comparison, emails won't be seen until recipients check their inboxes.

Examples of instant messaging applications include Yahoo Messenger and Google Hangouts. Some sites, like Gmail and Facebook, even allow us to chat within our web browser.

Online Media

There are many sites that allow us to watch videos and listen to music. For example, we can watch millions of videos on YouTube or listen to Internet radio on Pandora. Other services, like Netflix and Hulu, allow us to watch movies and TV shows. And if have a set-top streaming box, we can even watch them directly on our television instead of a computer screen.

Everyday Tasks

We can also use the Internet to complete many everyday tasks and errands. For example, our can manage your bank account, pay your bills, and shop for just about anything. The main advantage here is convenience. Rather than going from place to place, we can do all of these tasks at home.

Types of Internet Service

- **Dial-up.** This is generally the slowest type of Internet connection, and you should probably avoid it unless it is the only service available in your area. Dial-up Internet uses our phone line, so unless we have multiple phone lines we will not be able to use our landline and the Internet at the same time.
- **DSL.** DSL service uses a broadband connection, which makes it much faster than dial-up. DSL connects to the Internet via a phone line but does not require us to have a landline at home. And unlike dial-up, we'll be able to use the Internet and our phone line at the same time.
- **Cable.** Cable service connects to the Internet via cable TV, although we do not necessarily need to have cable TV in order to get it. It uses a broadband connection and can be faster than both dial-up and DSL service; however, it is only available where cable TV is available.
- **Satellite.** A satellite connection uses broadband but does not require cable or phone lines; it connects to the Internet through satellites orbiting the Earth. As a result, it can be used almost

anywhere in the world, but the connection may be affected by weather patterns. Satellite connections are also usually slower than DSL or cable.

- **3G and 4G.** 3G and 4G service is most commonly used with mobile phones, and it connects wirelessly through your ISP's network. However, these types of connections aren't always as fast as DSL or cable. They will also limit the amount of data we can use each month, which isn't the case with most broadband plans.

EMERGENCE OF 5G

5G is the fifth generation of cellular networks. Up to 100 times faster than 4G, 5G is creating never-before-seen opportunities for people and businesses.

"On behalf of the country, and the country's telecom industry, 130 crore Indians are getting a wonderful gift in the form of 5G. 5G is a knock on the doors of a new era in the country. It is the beginning of an infinite sky of opportunities," the Prime Minister Narendra Modi said while launching the service at Indian Mobile Congress on Ist October, 2022.

Choosing an Internet Service Provider

Most ISPs offer several tiers of service with different Internet speeds, usually measured in Mbps (short for megabits per second). If we mainly want to use the Internet for email and social networking, a slower connection (around 2 to 5 Mbps) might be all we need. However, if we want to download music or stream videos, we'll want a faster connection (at least 5 Mbps or higher).

We'll also want to consider the cost of the service, including installation charges and monthly fees. Generally speaking, the faster the connection, the more expensive it will be per month.

Although dial-up has traditionally been the least expensive option, many ISPs have raised dial-up prices to be the same as broadband. This is intended to encourage people to switch to broadband.

Hardware Needed

Modem

Once we have our computer, you really don't need much additional hardware to connect to the Internet. The primary piece of hardware we need is a modem.

The type of Internet access we choose will determine the type of modem you need. Dial-up access uses a telephone modem, DSL service uses a DSL modem, cable access uses a cable modem, and satellite service uses a satellite adapter. Your ISP may give you a modem-often for a fee-when we sign a contract, which helps ensure that we have the right type of modem. However, if we would prefer to shop for a better or less expensive modem, we can choose to buy one separately.

Router

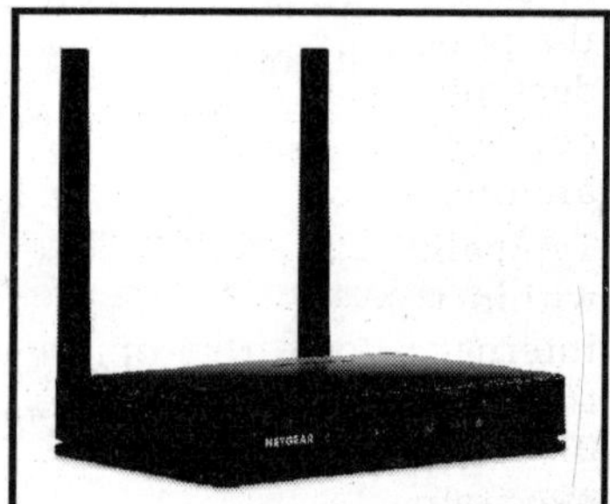

A router is a hardware device that allows us to connect several computers and other devices to a single Internet connection, which is known as a home network. Many routers are wireless, which allows us to create a home wireless network, commonly known as a Wi-Fi network.

We don't necessarily need to buy a router to connect to the Internet. It's possible to connect your computer directly to our modem using an Ethernet cable. Also, many modems include a built-in router, so we have the option of creating a Wi-Fi network without buying extra hardware.

Setting up your Internet Connection

Once we've chosen an ISP, most providers will send a technician to our house to turn on the connection. If not, we should be able to use the instructions provided by your ISP – or included with the modem – to set up our Internet connection.

After we have everything set up, we can open our web browser and begin using the Internet. If we have any problems with our Internet connection, we can call our ISP's technical support number.

Home Networking

If you have multiple computers at home and want to use all of them to access the Internet, we may want to create a home network, also known as a Wi-Fi network. In a home network, all of our devices connect to your router, which is connected to the modem. This means everyone in our family can use the Internet at the same time.

If we want to connect a computer that does not have built-in Wi-Fi connectivity, we can purchase a Wi-Fi adapter that plugs into our computer's USB port.

IMPORTANT TYPES OF INTERNET PROTOCOLS

- **TCP.** Transmission Control Protocol. This is the protocol for communicating over a network. The data is broken down into smaller packets, identifiable by their IP address.
- **FTP.** File Transfer Protocol. Used for transferring files over the internet. This includes text and multimedia files as well. It is faster than the other methods.
- **HTTP.** Hypertext Transfer Protocol. It follows the client and server model. It facilitates the connection between web client and web server.

INTRANET

An intranet is a private network that is contained within an enterprise. It may consist of many interlinked local area networks and also use leased lines in the wide area network. Typically, an intranet includes connections through one or more gateway computers to the outside Internet. The main purpose of an intranet is to share company information and computing resources among employees. An intranet can also be used to facilitate working in groups and for teleconferences.

An intranet uses TCP/IP, HTTP, and other Internet protocols and in general looks like a private version of the Internet. With tunneling, companies can send private messages through the public network, using the public network with special encryption/decryption and other security safeguards to connect one part of their intranet to another.

Typically, larger enterprises allow users within their intranet to access the public Internet through firewall servers that have the ability to screen messages in both directions so that company security is maintained. When part of an intranet is made accessible to customers, partners, suppliers, or others outside the company, that part becomes part of an extranet.

Advantages of Intranet

Intranet is beneficial in:

- publishing - delivering information and business news as directories and web documents.
- document management - viewing, printing and working collaboratively on office documents such as spreadsheets or databases.
- training - accessing and delivering various types of e-learning to the user's desktop.
- workflow - automating a range of administrative processes, including dealing with holiday requests, staff performance reviews and appraisals, meeting room and equipment booking, etc.
- front-end to corporate systems - providing a common interface to corporate databases and business information systems.
- email - integrating intranet content with email services so that information can be distributed effectively.

BASIC OF E-MAILING (E-MAIL)

Email is a service which allows us to send the message in electronic mode over the internet. It offers an efficient, inexpensive and real time mean of distributing information among people.

E-Mail Address

Each user of email is assigned a unique name for his email account. This name is known as E-mail address. Different users can send and receive messages according to the e-mail address.

E-mail is generally of the form username@domainname.

For example, webmaster@tutorialspoint.com is an e-mail address where webmaster is username and tutorialspoint.com is domain name.

- The username and the domain name are separated by @ (at) symbol.
- E-mail addresses are not case sensitive.
- Spaces are not allowed in e-mail address.

E-mail Message Components

E-mail message comprises of different components: E-mail Header, Greeting, Text, and Signature. These components are described in the following diagram:

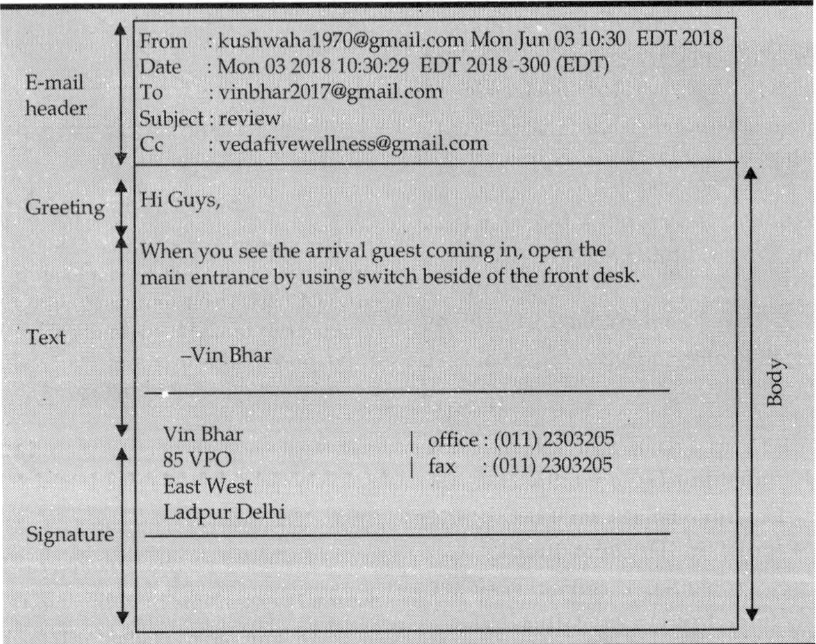

E-mail Header

The first five lines of an E-mail message is called E-mail header. The header part comprises of following fields:

- **FROM.** The From field indicates the sender's address i.e. who sent the e-mail.
- **DATE.** The Date field indicates the date when the e-mail was sent.
- **TO.** The To field indicates the recipient's address i.e. to whom the e-mail is sent.
- **SUBJECT.** The Subject field indicates the purpose of e-mail. It should be precise and to the point.
- **CC.** CC stands for Carbon copy. It includes those recipient addresses whom we want to keep informed but not exactly the intended recipient.

- **BCC.** BCC stands for Black Carbon Copy. It is used when we do not want one or more of the recipients to know that someone else was copied on the message.
- **GREETING.** Greeting is the opening of the actual message. E.g., Hi Sir or Hi Guys etc.
- **TEXT.** It represents the actual content of the message.
- **SIGNATURE.** This is the final part of an e-mail message. It includes Name of Sender, Address, and Contact Number.

Advantages

E-mail has proved to be powerful and reliable medium of communication. Here are the benefits of E-mail:

- **Reliable.** Many of the mail systems notify the sender if e-mail message was undeliverable.
- **Convenience.** There is no requirement of stationary and stamps. One does not have to go to post office. But all these things are not required for sending or receiving an mail.
- **Speed.** E-mail is very fast. However, the speed also depends upon the underlying network.
- **Inexpensive.** The cost of sending e-mail is very low.
- **Printable.** It is easy to obtain a hardcopy of an e-mail. Also an electronic copy of an e-mail can also be saved for records.
- **Global.** E-mail can be sent and received by a person sitting across the globe.
- **Generality.** It is also possible to send graphics, programs and sounds with an e-mail.

Disadvantages

Apart from several benefits of E-mail, there also exists some disadvantages as discussed below:

- **Forgery.** E-mail doesn't prevent from forgery, that is, someone impersonating the sender, since sender is usually not authenticated in any way.
- **Overload.** Convenience of E-mail may result in a flood of mail.
- **Misdirection.** It is possible that you may send e-mail to an unintended recipient.
- **Junk.** Junk emails are undesirable and inappropriate emails. Junk emails are sometimes referred to as spam.
- **No Response.** It may be frustrating when the recipient does not read the e-mail and respond on a regular basis.

E-mail Protocols

E-mail Protocols are set of rules that help the client to properly transmit the information to or from the mail server. Here in this tutorial, we will discuss various protocols such as SMTP, POP, and IMAP.

SMPTP

SMTP stands for Simple Mail Transfer Protocol. It was first proposed in 1982. It is a standard protocol used for sending e-mail efficiently and reliably over the internet.

Key Points:

- SMTP is application level protocol.
- SMTP is connection oriented protocol.
- SMTP is text based protocol.
- It handles exchange of messages between e-mail servers over TCP/IP network.
- Apart from transferring e-mail, SMPT also provides notification regarding incoming mail.
- When you send e-mail, your e-mail client sends it to your e-mail server which further contacts the recipient mail server using SMTP client.

- These SMTP commands specify the sender's and receiver's e-mail address, along with the message to be send.
- The exchange of commands between servers is carried out without intervention of any user.
- In case, message cannot be delivered, an error report is sent to the sender which makes SMTP a reliable protocol.

SMTP Commands

The following table describes some of the SMTP commands:

S. No.	Command Description
1	HELLO. This command initiates the SMTP conversation.
2	EHELLO. This is an alternative command to initiate the conversation. ESMTP indicates that the sender server wants to use extended SMTP protocol.
3	MAIL FROM. This indicates the sender's address.
4	RCPT TO. It identifies the recipient of the mail. In order to deliver similar message to multiple users this command can be repeated multiple times.
5	SIZE. This command let the server know the size of attached message in bytes.
6	DATA. The DATA command signifies that a stream of data will follow. Here stream of data refers to the body of the message.
7	QUIT. This commands is used to terminate the SMTP connection.
8	VERFY. This command is used by the receiving server in order to verify whether the given username is valid or not.
9	EXPN. It is same as VRFY, except it will list all the users name when it used with a distribution list.

IMAP

IMAP stands for Internet Mail Access Protocol. It was first proposed in 1986. There exist five versions of IMAP as follows:

1. Original IMAP
2. IMAP2
3. IMAP3
4. IMAP2bis
5. IMAP4

Key Points:

- IMAP allows the client program to manipulate the e-mail message on the server without downloading them on the local computer.
- The e-mail is hold and maintained by the remote server.
- It enables us to take any action such as downloading, delete the mail without reading the mail. It enables us to create, manipulate and delete remote message folders called mail boxes.
- IMAP enables the users to search the e-mails.
- It allows concurrent access to multiple mailboxes on multiple mail servers.

IMAP Commands

The following table describes some of the IMAP commands:

S. No.	Command Description
1	**IMAP_LOGIN.** This command opens the connection.
2	**CAPABILITY.** This command requests for listing the capabilities that the server supports.
3	**NOOP.** This command is used as a periodic poll for new messages or message status updates during a period of inactivity.

S. No.	Command Description
4	**SELECT.** This command helps to select a mailbox to access the messages.
5	**EXAMINE.** It is same as SELECT command except no change to the mailbox is permitted.
6	**CREATE.** It is used to create mailbox with a specified name.
7	**DELETE.** It is used to permanently delete a mailbox with a given name.
8	**RENAME.** It is used to change the name of a mailbox.
9	**LOGOUT.** This command informs the server that client is done with the session. The server must send BYE untagged response before the OK response and then close the network connection.

POP

POP stands for Post Office Protocol. It is generally used to support a single client. There are several versions of POP but the POP 3 is the current standard.

Key Points

- POP is an application layer internet standard protocol.
- Since POP supports offline access to the messages, thus requires less internet usage time.
- POP does not allow search facility.
- In order to access the messaged, it is necessary to download them.
- It allows only one mailbox to be created on server.
- It is not suitable for accessing non mail data.
- POP commands are generally abbreviated into codes of three or four letters. Eg. STAT.

POP Commands

The following table describes some of the POP commands:

S. No.	Command Description
1	**LOGIN.** This command opens the connection.
2	**STAT.** It is used to display number of messages currently in the mailbox.
3	**LIST.** It is used to get the summary of messages where each message summary is shown.
4	**RETR.** This command helps to select a mailbox to access the messages.
5	**DELE.** It is used to delete a message.
6	**RSET.** It is used to reset the session to its initial state.
7	**QUIT.** It is used to log off the session.

Email Operations

Here we will discuss the operations that can be performed on an e-mail. But first of all we will learn how to create an email account.

Creating Email Account

There are various email service provider available such as Gmail, hotmail, ymail, rediff mail etc. Here we will learn how to create an account using Gmail.

- Open gmail.com and click create an account.
- Now a form will appear. Fill your details here and click Next Step.

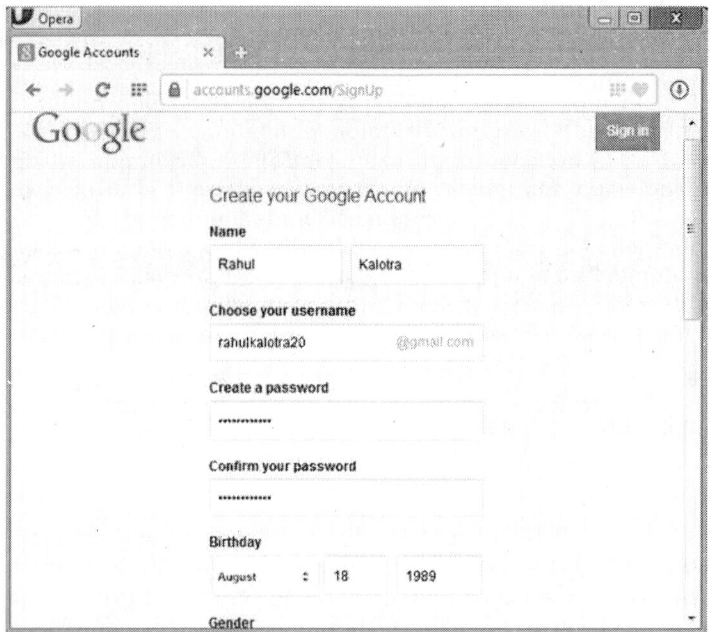

- This step allows you to add your picture. If you don't want to upload now, you can do it later. Click Next Step.
- Now a welcome window appears. Click Continue to Gmail.
- Wow!! You are done with creating your email account with Gmail. It's that easy. Isn't it?
- Now you will see your Gmail account as shown in the following image:

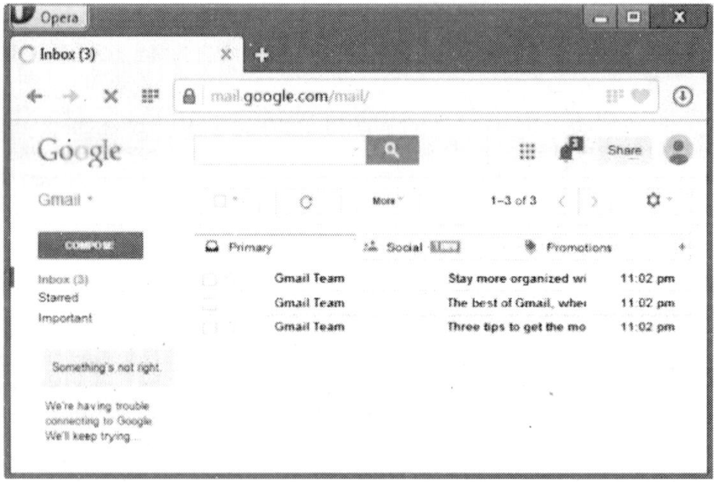

Key Points

- Gmail manages the mail into three categories namely Primary, Socialand Promotions.
- Compose option is given at the right to compose an email message.
- Inbox, Starred, Sent mail, Drafts options are available on the left pane which allows you to keep track of your emails.

Composing and Sending Email

Before sending an email, we need to compose a message. When we are composing an email message, we specify the following things:

- Sender's address in To field
- Cc (if required)
- Bcc (if required)
- Subject of email message
- Text
- Signature

You should specify the correct email address; otherwise it will send an error back to the sender.

Once you have specified all the above parameters, It's time to send the email. The mailer program provides a Send button to send email, when you click Send, it is sent to the mail server and a message mail sent successfully is shown at the above.

Reading Email

Every email program offers you an interface to access email messages. Like in Gmail, emails are stored under different tabs such as primary, social, and promotion. When you click one of tab, it displays a list of emails under that tab.

In order to read an email, you just have to click on that email. Once you click a particular email, it gets opened.

The opened email may have some file attached with it. The attachments are shown at the bottom of the opened email with an option called download attachment.

Replying Email

After reading an email, you may have to reply that email. To reply an email, click Reply option shown at the bottom of the opened email.

Once you click on Reply, it will automatically copy the sender's address in to the To field. Below the To field, there is a text box where you can type the message.

Once you are done with entering message, click Send button. It's that easy. Your email is sent.

Forwarding Email

It is also possible to send a copy of the message that you have received along with your own comments if you want. This can be done using forward button available in mail client software.

The difference between replying and forwarding an email is that when you reply a message to a person who has send the mail but while forwarding you can send it to anyone.

When you receive a forwarded message, the message is marked with a > character in front of each line and Subject: field is prefixed with Fw.

Deleting Email

If you don't want to keep email into your inbox, you can delete it by simply selecting the message from the message list and clicking delete or pressing the appropriate command.

Some mail clients offers the deleted mails to be stored in a folder called deleted items or trash from where you can recover a deleted email.

E-mail Features

Now a day, the mail client comes with enhanced features such as attachment, address book, and MIME support.

Attachment

Ability to attach file(s) along with the message is one of the most useful features of email. The attachment may be a word document, PowerPoint presentation, audio/video files, or images.

- In order to attach file(s) to an email, click the attach button. As a result, a dialog box appears asking for specifying the name and location of the file you want to attach.
- Once you have selected the appropriate file, it is attached to the mail.
- Usually a paper clip icon appears in the email which indicates that it has an attachment.
- When adding an attachment it is better to compress the attached files so as to reduce the file size and save transmission time as sending and downloading large files consumes a lot of space and time.

Address Book

Address book feature of a mail program allows the users to store information about the people whom they communicate regularly by sending emails. Here are some of the key features of an Address book:

- Address book includes the nick names, email addresses, phone number etc. of the people.
- Using address book allows us not to memorize email of address of a person, you just have to select recipient name from the list.
- When you select a particular name from the list, the corresponding email address link automatically get inserted in to the To: field.
- Address book also allows creating a group so that you can send a email to very member of the group at once instead of giving each person email address one by one.

AUDIO AND VIDEO CONFERENCING

In this busy world we can interact with people from any part. It shows how our technology has improved the best one is audio and video conferencing. We can just see a small hint of audio and video conferencing.

Audio and video conferencing is very useful for people from corner to corner. It is very useful for several fields and industries to connect people from various countries at any time. In early point of using audio and video conferencing we don't have much facility however now it's very advanced with additional features and easy to use it.

Audio-video conferencing is particularly valuable in the business and education sectors. For business it's very beneficial to conduct meeting in fast and well-organized way for companies which have different sites around the world. Its useful for companies to save their money from transportation for their employees who partake in global business conference. In the mean time audio and video conference is used for students for seminars or lectures and also for students in distance education. For example students from India can have seminar from Professor directly who is in United Kingdom.

> **Remember**
>
> The main important one in audio and video conferencing is saving the time and money for the company and can easily achieve the goal. Even interviews are conducted through this process from other countries. An effective conference possibly will make use of telephones, televisions, computers, conferencing software, collaborative software, file sharing, headsets, the Internet, or any arrangement of these equipments and tools. It includes slide presentation, streaming audio and document sharing. The main goal is to make the meeting a realistic where they can see and hear each other.

Two types of audio-video conferences one is asynchronous and synchronous types. Asynchronous type of audio and video Conference is a recorded conference person can view it at any time they wish. Whereas Synchronous audio-video conference is a real time one the partaker can intermingle with each other straightly which makes them easier.

Audio Conference

It is the most essential conference. Audio conference is extremely easy to set up which needs only a telephone and a toll free number. Audio conferencing service is cheapest of the conferencing services. Pricing is based on a flat rate and depending on the service provider, some extras are included free with the basic package. The drawbacks with audio conferencing are because of its comparatively basic position.

Video Conference

Through video conferencing people can interact with each other face to face. To have a video conference we need only a web cam at the starting its more expensive but now the rates are reducing.

Audio and Video Conference software is very pricey it can also be download and installed from the web sites with no cost.

Advantages of Video/Audio Conferencing

1. Free download of easy to use software that can be used via Internet to connect student, instructor, or guest speaker to class and enable both sides to see & hear.
2. Enables individual (usually limited to one connection) to participate in synchronous learning experiences from any location worldwide. Users can connect from home, work or other location easily accessible to them.
3. Specifically useful for guest speaker who is far away from face-to-face class location, or student who cannot be in face-to-face class.
4. Enables students to take virtual field trips to remote locations (either just by viewing the video (e.g. African Voices) or engaging in an interactive lesson (see African Masks field trip). This is especially an advantage to students who attend schools in isolated communities, but is an advantage to all students regardless of location or socio-economic factors. See extensive list of examples at SBC Video-conference Adventures; also Ball State University Electronic Field Trips.
5. Can be used to record vodcast or podcast and uploaded to course website (for web-enhanced, hybrid, or fully online classes).

   As video conferencing technology improves, this can become a far cheaper alternative to ITV or systems like PolyCom in enabling school districts to offer specialized subjects by having one teacher teach a class to students at a number of schools (e.g. in foreign language

Disadvantages of Video/Audio Conferencing

1. Typically on free systems only one or a very limited number of users can connect to the host (instructor) computers at a time, so video/audio conferencing can be used only for individual access rather than as a larger scale tool and learning environment. However, newer systems such as Camfrog enable multi-user video conferencing.
2. Depending on the stability of the connection, users may be disconnected during the class and have to reconnect.

   Difficult to see and hear people who are not close to the microphone/camera, especially when using one of the low-cost systems (such as iSight camera). Thus difficult to have multiple people at one site, sharing a computer to communicate with users at other sites.

Electronic Commerce (e-commerce)

Electronic commerce or e-commerce (sometimes written as eCommerce) is a business model that lets firms and individuals conduct business over electronic networks, most notably: the Internet. Electronic commerce operates in all four of the following major market segments:

- Business to business

- Business to consumer
- Consumer to consumer
- Consumer to business

E-commerce, which can be conducted over computers, tablets, or smartphones may be thought of as a modernized version of mail-order catalog shopping. Nearly every imaginable product and service is available through e-commerce transactions, including books, music, plane tickets, and financial services such as stock investing and online banking.

UPI

Over the last decade, the banking industry has shown tremendous growth in terms of technology. As a result of the recent demonetisation and digital India drive, it had also become the need of the hour. The Unified Payment Interface (UPI), developed by NPCI and regulated by the RBI, came to revolutionize the way we transfer funds in India. UPI app download can be done in both android and iOS devices.

One of the major features that make UPI different from other modes of transactions is that it does not require any personal information to be shared with a third party. Transactions can be completed just by entering the beneficiary's mobile number, Aadhaar Number or Virtual Payment Address (VPA). This feature of UPI is a significant improvement over methods such as NEFT and RTGS, where chances of fraud are higher. Moreover, online payment methods like NEFT and RTGS require an addition of payee before funds can be transferred to their account. However, with UPI App download, one need not worry about adding a payee and waiting for approval of their addition, before transferring funds to their account.

Is UPI a reliable and safe method?

Online and digital media have lent enough instances to the general public to believe that a fraud can be committed quite easily when it comes to online transactions and money. However, this fact has been kept in mind while designing the entire interface of UPI applications. It aims to omit the use of any crucial information entirely, thus reducing the instance of online frauds and thefts. As for the general public, if they really want to keep up with the idea of cashless and digital transactions, then UPI is the safest way to do that. Not only is the application safe and secure to use, but the simple fact that it has various authentication steps also makes the application out of bounds for any prospective fraudster.

Where can you download the UPI App?

UPI has been included as an integral part of most banking applications. Now when you operate your respective bank's mobile application, you will be able to come across a separate UPI section. Using this feature on your mobile banking application, you can access the unique features of UPI. Banks have also launched separate UPI apps such as BHIM SBI Pay for SBI and BHIM United UPI Pay for United Bank of India. Each bank has its own UPI app download and registration feature.

Key Points Related to UPI

As already discussed, UPI is a simple interface that allows the exchange of funds between two parties, without exchanging any vital information, except their virtual payment address.

Now, many are concerned about the working of a virtual payment address. It is necessary to create one if you wish to make use of UPI feature on your smartphone. It could be any word of your choice but needs to be linked to your respective bank account. The VPA is like the financial address to your bank account and is unique. The main benefit of using a VPA is to use it in place of a list of your bank details so that no one can misuse it. Thus, it gains a lot more security and safety than other modes of online transactions.

Features of UPI Apps

Any new application that comes in the market is rated and further reviewed only if it meets the expectations of the users. Since UPI is a new feature in the market and also very integrated with other banking operations, it has received an overall positive response from users all over the country. Some of the key features of the application that set it apart are as follows:

- **Instant Exchange of Funds.** Exchanging funds between two parties was never simpler. All you need is a virtual payment address and you are good to go. There is no need for bank details for money transfer as is in the case of NEFT or RTGS. This makes UPI an efficient app for transacting easily and conveniently.
- **Make Payments to Merchants.** The use of UPI application is not restricted to exchange of funds between two individuals or entities alone. The feature can also be used to make merchant payments all over the country. Examples of such payments include movies, restaurants, parlours, eating joints, cafes and more. One could even shop online with the use of UPI feature on their smart phone. It can be rightly said that UPI makes your smart phone, even more smarter.
- **Entirely Safe and Secure.** No other mode of payment is designed with so many layers of security as UPI feature. A two-step authentication process takes care of login and use of the application. This means that even if your smart phone is being used by someone else, they cannot gain access to your banking application, unless they know your secure code.
- **24 × 7 Availability.** The feature of UPI is available on a 24 × 7 basis. Thus, you can transact using your smart phone at any hour of the day and even on a holiday. Now, your scope of transactions is not limited to a bank holiday or a public holiday anymore.
- **Can be Downloaded Easily.** The best part about UPI feature is that it is easily available with other banking applications, which eases the need for UPI app download of multiple applications. If not, one can also make use of BHIM, the dedicated application for digital transactions in a sweep.

DIGITAL INITIATIVES FOR HIGHER EDUCATION

1. Swayam

Under the 'Digital India' Initiative of Government of India, one of the thrust area is 'Massive Online Open Courses (MOOCs)'. MHRD, Government of India has embarked on a major initiative called 'Study Webs of Active Learning for Young Aspiring Minds' (SWAYAM), to provide an integrated platform and portal for online.

Official Website: *https://swayam.2ov.in/*

Official Mobile App: *https://play.google.com/store/apps/details?id=iRgov.swayam.app*

2. Swayam Prabha

The SWAYAM PRABHA is a group of 32 DTH channels devoted to telecasting of high-quality educational programmes on 24 × 7 basis using the GSAT-15 satellite. Every day, there will be new content for at least (4) hours which would be repeated 5 more times in a day, allowing the students to choose the time of their convenience. The channels are uplinked from BISAG, Gandhinagar. The contents are provided by NPTEL, IITs, UGC, CEC, IGNOU, NCERT and NIOS. The INFLIBNET Centre maintains the web portal.

Official Website: *https://www.swayamprabha.gov.in*

Official Mobile App: *https:/yplay.google.com/store/apps/details?id=com.bisag.introslider (android)*

3. National Academic Depository (NAD)

The vision of National Academic Depository (NAD) is born out of an initiative to provide an online store house of all academic awards. National Academic Depository (NAD) is a 24 × 7 online store house of all academic awards viz. certificates, diplomas, degrees, mark-sheets etc. duly digitised and lodged by academic institutions/boards/eligibility assessment bodies. NAD not only ensures easy access to and retrieval of an academic award but also validates and guarantees its authenticity and safe storage. National Academic Depository comprises of two interoperable digital depositories viz. CDSL Ventures Limited

(CVL) and NSDL Database Management Limited (NDML). These digital depositories have ensured hardware, network facilities and software of prescribed quality for smooth and secured operationalisation of NAD.

Official Website: https://nadgov.in/

4. National Digital Library of India (NDL India)

National Digital Library of India (NDL India) is an all-digital library that stores information (metadata) about different types of digital contents including books, articles, videos, audios, thesis and other educational materials relevant for users from varying educational levels and capabilities. It provides a single-window search facility to access digital contents currently existing in India as well as other digital sources under a single umbrella.

Official Website: https: / /ndl.iitkgp.ac in/
Official Mobile App: https: / /play.google.com/ store/apps/details?id=com.mhrdndl

5. E-Shodh Sindhu (eSS)

The MHRD has formed e-Shodh Sindhu merging three consortia initiatives, namely UGC-INFONET Digital Library Consortium, NLIST and INDEST-AICTE Consortium to provide access to peer-reviewed journals and a number of bibliographic, citation and factual databases in different disciplines to the Research and academic community in the country.

Official website: https:/ /www.inflibnet.ac.in/ess

6. Virtual Labs

Virtual Labs project is an initiative of Ministry of Human Resource Development.(MHRD), Government of India under the aegis of National Mission on Education through Information and Communication Technology (NMEICT). This project is a consortium activity of twelve participating institutes and IIT Delhi is coordinating institute. It is a paradigm shift in ICT-based education. For the first time, such an initiative has been taken-up in remote-experimentation. Under Virtual Labs project, over 100 Virtual Labs consisting of approximately 700+ web-enabled experiments were designed for remote-operation and viewing.

Official Website: http://wwwvlab.co.in/

7. e-Yantra

Project e-Yantra is an initiative to spread education in Embedded systems and Robotics by IIT Bombay sponsored by Ministry of Human Resource Development through the National Mission on Education through ICT (NMEICT). This project was conceptualized by Prof. Kavi Arya and Prof. Krithi Ramamritham of the Department of Computer Science and Engineering at IIT Bombay.

Official website: http://www.e-yantra.org

8. Talk to a Teacher Program

A view is part of Talk to a Teacher program coordinated by IIT Bombay and we are funded by the Ministry of Human Resource Development (MHRD) under the Indian Government's National Mission for Education using Information and Communication Technology (NME-ICT) along with various other projects in Virtual Labs, Haptics and Natural Language Processing. A view is now deployed at several IITs, NITs and other leading educational institutions across the nation.

Official Website: http://aview.in/

9. E-acharya

Integrated e-Content Portal. A portal to host all e-content project, developed/funded under the National Mission of Education through ICT. There are more than 70 projects on e-content under NME-ICT which are developed/being developed in various subject disciplines (Science, Arts, Engineering, Social Sciences, etc.) through various Indian institutes/universities/colleges. The portal would provide facility to search and browse all hosted content wherein a learner can easily access the desired material including audio/video learning material, textual material, multimedia enriched materials etc. through a single interface. Moreover, features of faceted search, syllabus-based search, usage statistics, personalized learning experience with provision for "my account" and "my space", etc. would be incorporated in this portal.

Official website: http://eacharya.inflibnet.ac.in/ vidya-mitra/

10. E-Kalpa

This project on 'Creating Digital-learning Environment for Design' also called 'e-kalpa' is sponsored by the Ministry of Human Resources, Government of India as part of the National Mission in Education through Information and Communication Technology. *Official Website: http://www.dsource.in/*

11. FOSSEE (Free/Libre and Open Source Software in Education)

FOSSEE (Free/Libre and Open Source Software in Education) project promotes the use of FLOSS tools to improve the quality of education in our country. We aim to reduce dependency on proprietary software in educational institutions. We encourage the use of FLOSS tools through various activities to ensure commercial software is replaced by equivalent

FLOSS tools. We also develop new FLOSS tools and upgrade existing tools to meet requirements in academia and research.

The FOSSEE project is part of the National Mission on Education through Information and Communication Technology (ICT), Ministry of Human Resource Development (MHRD), Government of India.

Official Website: *https://fossee.in*

12. Vidwan

Vidwan is the premier database of profiles of scientists/researchers and other faculty members working at leading academic institutions and other R & D organisation involved in teaching and research in India. It provides important information about expert's background, contact address, experience, scholarly publications, skills and accomplishments, researcher identity, etc. The database developed and maintained by information and Library Network centre (INFLIBNET) with financial support from the National Mission on Education through ICT (NME-ICT). The database would be instrumental in selection of panels of experts for various committees, taskforce, established by the Ministries/Govt. establishments for monitoring and evaluation purposes.

Official Website: *https://vidwan.inflibnet.ac.in*

13. Spoken Tutorial

The Spoken Tutorial project is the initiative of the 'Talk to a Teacher' activity of the National Mission on Education through Information and Communication Technology (ICT), launched by the Ministry of Human Resources and Development, Government of India. Spoken Tutorial is a multi-award winning educational content portal. Here one can learn various Free and Open Source Software all by oneself. Our self-paced, multi-lingual courses ensure that anybody with a computer and a desire for learning, can learn from any place, at any time and in a language of their choice. All the content published on this website are shared under the CC BY SA license.

The Spoken Tutorial project is being developed at IIT Bombay for MHRD, Government of India.

Official Website: *https://spoken-tutorial.org*

14- BAADAL

A MHRD initiative developed as NME-IGT Cloud for academic purpose.

Baadal is a cloud orchestration and virtualization management software initiated by MHRD under NMEIGT scheme and developed and maintained by IIT Delhi. It ensures optimum utilization of the infrastructure and speeds up the development and deployment of eGov applications for academic needs. It is hosted in NIC data-centre. Some of the main features of Baadal are:

- Dynamic resource scheduling and power management.
- An integrated workflow system for request and commissioning of virtual machines.
- Facilities for suspend, resume, shutdown, power on, power on and specifying resource requirement of virtual machines.
- Dynamic resource utilization monitoring.

Under this project, we help government and semi Government institutes to accommodate their infrastructure needs without taking care of management issues.

As Baadal is open source project, we help institutes to setup their private cloud.

Official Website: *https://baadal.nmeict.in/*

15. Global Initiative of Academic Networks (GIAN)

Govt. of India approved a new program titled Global Initiative of Academic Networks (GIAN) in Higher Education aimed at tapping the talent pool of scientists and entrepreneurs, internationally to encourage their engagement with the institutes of Higher Education in India so as to augment the country's existing academic resources, accelerate the pace of quality reform, and elevate India's scientific and technological capacity to global excellence.

In order to garner the best international experience into our systems of education, enable interaction of students and faculty with the best academic and industry experts from all over the world and also share their experiences and expertise to motivate people to work on Indian problems, there is a need for a Scheme of International Summer and Winter Term. During the 'Retreat' of IITs with Minister of Human Resource Development Smt. Smriti Zubin Irani on 29th June, 2014 at Goa, it was decided that "A system of Guest Lectures by internationally and nationally renowned experts would be evolved along with a comprehensive Faculty Development Programme not only for new IITs, IIMs, IISERs but also other institutions in the country.

Official Website: *http://www.gian.iitkgp.ac.in/*

16. National Institutional Ranking Framework (NIRF)

The National Institutional Ranking Framework (NIRF) was approved by the MHRD and launched by Honourable Minister of Human Resource Development on 29th September 2015.

This framework outlines a methodology to rank institutions across the country. The methodology draws from the overall recommendations broad understanding arrived at by a Core Committee set up by MHRD, to identify the broad parameters for ranking various universities and institutions. The parameters broadly cover "Teaching, Learning and Resources," "Research and Professional Practices," "Graduation Outcomes," "Outreach and Inclusivity," and "Perception".

India Rankings - 2016 based on this framework were released on 4th April 2016.

Official Website: *https ://www.nirfindia.org/*

17. IMPRINT- (IMPacting Research Innovation and Technology)

MPRINT is the first of its kind MHRD supported Pan-IIT + IISc joint initiative to address the major science and engineering challenges that India must address and champion to enable, empower and embolden the nation for inclusive growth and self-reliance. This novel initiative with twofold mandate is aimed at:

(a) Developing new engineering education policy.

(b) Creating a road map to pursue engineering challenges.

IMPRINT provides the overarching vision that guides research into areas that are predominantly socially relevant.

Official Website: *https://imprint-india.org/*

18. SAKSHAT: A One Stop Education Portal

The pilot project SAKSHAT: A One Stop Education Portal launched on October 30, 2006 by His Excellency, the then President of India to facilitate lifelong learning for students, teachers and those in employment or in pursuit of knowledge free of cost to them. The content development task for 'SAKSHAT' was looked after by the Content Advisory Committee (CAC) for the respective subject, which consisted of representatives from educational institutions like IGNOU, Delhi University, Kendriya Vidyalaya Sangthan (KVS), Navodyaya Vidyalaya Sangthan (NVS), National Institute of Open Schooling (NIOS) and National Council for Educational Research and Training (NCERT) and prominent academicians in the field. In addition, some NGOs had also provided the contents developed by them free of cost for this portal.

The vision is to scale up this pilot project 'SAKSHAT' to cater to the learning needs of more than 50 crore people through a proposed scheme of 'National Mission in Education through Information and Communication Technology (ICT). The scheme is to provide connectivity to all institutions of higher learning to world of knowledge in the cyber space, to leverage the potential of ICT, in providing high quality knowledge modules with right e-contents, to address to the personalized needs of learners, in order to take care of their aspirations. These modules are to be delivered through 'SAKSHAT'. The scheme may also have a provision of certification of competencies of the human resources acquired through formal or non-formal means as also to develop and maintain the database of profile of human resources.

Official Website: *www.sakshat.ac.in*

18. Atal Ranking of Institutions on Innovation Achievements (ARIIA)

Atal Ranking of Institutions on Innovation Achievements (ARIIA) is an initiative of Ministry of Human Resource Development (MHRD), Govt. of India to systematically rank all major higher educational institutions and universities in India on indicators related to "Innovation and Entrepreneurship Development" amongst students and faculties.

Major Indicators for consideration

Assessment of innovation and startup ecosystem in HEIs will be based on seven parameters with certain weightages allocated as below.

- Budget, Expenses to Support & Revenue Generated **(20 Marks).**
- Infrastructures & Facilities to Support Innovations and Start-ups **(10 Marks).**
- Awareness Activities for Promoting Idea Generation and Innovation **(20 Marks).**
- Promotion and Supporting Entrepreneurship Development **(20 Marks).**
- Intellectual Property (IP) Generation, Technology Transfer and Commercialization **(14 Marks).**
- Innovative Learning Methods & Courses **(10 Marks).**
- Innovations in Governance of the Institution **(6 Marks).**

Official Website: *https://www.ariia.gov.in/*

20. Know Your College

Official Website: http *://www.knowyoucollege-gov.in/*

21. DigiLocker

DigiLocker is a platform for issuance and verification of documents & certificates in a digital way, thus eliminating the use of physical documents. Indian citizens who sign up for a DigiLocker account get a dedicated cloud storage space that is linked to their Aadhaar (UIDAI) number. Organizations that are registered with Digital Locker can push electronic copies of documents and certificates (e.g. driving license, Voter ID, School certificates) directly into citizens lockers. Citizens can also upload scanned copies of their legacy documents in their accounts. These legacy documents can be electronically signed using the eSign facility.

The main technology components of the DigiLocker system are:

- **Repository.** Collection of e-documents that is exposed via standard APIs for secure, real-time access.
- **Access Gateway.** Secure online mechanism for requesters to access e-documents from various repositories in real-time using URI (Uniform Resource Indicator).
- **DigiLocker Portal.** Dedicated cloud based personal storage space, linked to each resident's Aadhaar for storing e-documents, or URIs of e-documents.

Official Website: https://digilocker.gov.in/

22. The National Programme on Technology Enhanced Learning (NPTEL)

The National Programme on Technology Enhanced Learning (NPTEL) was initiated by seven Indian Institutes of Technology (Bombay, Delhi, Kanpur, Kharagpur, Madras, Guwahati and Roorkee) along with the Indian Institute of Science, Bangalore in 2003. Five core disciplines were identified, namely, civil engineering, computer science and engineering, electrical engineering, electronics and communication engineering and mechanical engineering and 235 courses in web/video format were developed in this phase.

The main goal of NPTEL Phase II (2009-14) was to build on the engineering and core science courses launched previously in NPTEL Phase I. An additional 600 web and video courses were created in all major branches of engineering, physical sciences at the undergraduate and postgraduate levels and management courses at the postgraduate level. Several improvements such as indexing of all video and web courses and keyword search were implemented.

Official Website: https://nptel.ac.in/

23. OSCAR (Open Source Courseware Animations Repository)

Project OSCAR (Open Source Courseware Animations Repository) provides a repository of web-based interactive animations and simulations, that we refer to as learning objects (LOs). These learning objects span topics in science and engineering at the college level, and maths and science at the school level. Students and teachers can view, run and download these learning objects.

Official Website: http://oscar.iitb.ac.in/

24. ShodhGangotri

ShodhGangotri", research scholars/research supervisors in universities are requested to deposit electronic version of approved synopsis submitted by research scholars to the universities for registering themselves for the Ph.D. programme. The repository on one hand, would reveal the trends and directions of research being conducted in Indian universities, on the other hand it would avoid duplication of research. Synopsis in "ShodhGangotri" would later be mapped to full-text theses in **"ShodhGanga"**. As such, once the full-text thesis is submitted for a synopsis, a link to the full-text theses would be provided from ShodhGangotri to **"ShodhGanga"**

Official Website: https://shodhgangotri.inflibnet.ac.in/

25. Virtual Learning Environment

VLE, an online environment of e-resources caters to several disciplines taught at undergraduate and postgraduate level. It is an initiative of Institute of Life-Long Learning, University of Delhi. Conceived in 2012, VLE today boasts state of art material that addresses emerging needs of a diverse student body, not only of Delhi University but other universities as well. Drawing from several successful Moodle models, the multi-media interactive contents loaded on VLE are categorized discipline-wise.

The lessons are developed by highly qualified faculty members across the universities and are continually edited and reviewed, primarily by discipline-expert Fellows employed to edit, oversee and coordinate the content. The content goes through several levels of rigorous peer reviewing and academic vetting to ensure quality and standardization. VLE also contains multimedia repository in form of audio, video and short films to expose students to new technologies in pedagogy.

Official Website: http://vle.du.ac.in/

26. Text Transcription of Video Content

The text of video lectures has been obtained through manual processes and is therefore error-prone. There is no claim to accuracy on the text content provided in this site. We are working with many professors to correct their lecture transcripts so that they can become both verbatim transcripts as well as readable text help for those who have bandwidth limitations and cannot download full video courses. An audio file (mp3 format) is provided as download along with the transcript of each file. The transcribed files given as pdf are also being used to provide subtitles to the video (in English) and can be used in the future for providing local language translations. Please see the subtitles in the NPTEL website.

The text will be used to create metadata and search index and the time coding on the video will be used to provide markers on the video for easy search of the video content. These are activities in progress. The project to provide transcription of all videos published by NPTEL (currently more than 11,500 hours and will likely swell to about 20,000 hours in a year or so) is an on-going project and delays are unavoidable.

Official Website: http://textofvideo.nptel.ac.in/

27. SOS Tools

Software and simulation packages are useful tools for the analysis of systems and solving problems by the students of Science, Social Science, Engineering, Management and related disciplines. Many commercial software packages are available for the above. But many of these software packages are **quite** costly and require yearly license fee for updates and maintenance. Many open source softwares arc available which can perform similar functions but are not user friendly and do not have proper documentation. Beside these, adequate manpower to teach students to use these packages are not available.

The objective of this project is to develop software tools for analysis of systems and computations, create adequate manpower to teach students to use open source software and to develop simulation tools. The developed software should be user friendly and properly documented. Such packages, tailored to suit the needs of our students will be ported on Sakshat for making freely available to any student, teacher or institution willing to use them.

Official Website: http://sos-tools.org/

28. e-PG Pathshala

e-PG Pathshala is an initiative of the MHRD under its National Mission on Education through ICT (NME-ICT) being executed by the UGC. The content and its quality being the key component of education system, high quality, curriculum-based, interactive e-content in 70 subjects across all disciplines of social sciences, arts, fine arts and humanities, natural & mathematical sciences, linguistics and languages have been developed by the subject experts working in Indian universities and other R & D institutes across the country. Every subject had a team of principal investigator, paper coordinators, content writers, content reviewers, Language editors and multimedia team.

Official Website: https:// epgp.inflibnet.ac.inrtndex.php

29. National Mission on Education through information and communication Technology (NMEICT) :

NMEICT is centrally sponsored scheme to realize the potential of ICT in teaching learning process for the benefit of all the learners in higher education institutions anytime and anywhere. Content generation and connectivity along with provision for access devices for institutions and learners are the main objectives. Now many universities have been provided 1 Gbps connectivity and more than 14,000 colleges have also been provided VPN (Virtual Private Network) connectivity.

A-view software has been developed under the NMEICT for teacher training. This could become the basis for successful implementation of the proposed National Mission on Teachers.

Under the N-list program of INFLIBNET (under NMEICT), lakhs of e-books and thousands of high quality paid e-journals have been made available to colleges and universities with a view to inculcate research culture in teachers and students. The model needs to be scald up for maximizing coverage and for productive usage of the available resources.

30. Central cloud infrastructure

The MHRD under NMEICT has awarded a project to IIT Delhi, to set up a robust 24×7 backed data centre and the activities have been put up at NIC / NKN data Centre, and the cloud is called 'Baadal'. The IIT Delhi cloud is hosting e-content and video content of e-Acharya.

31. Lekhika 2007

It was developed by the Centre for the Development of Advanced Computing (C-DAC) under India's IT Ministry and Israel's FTK Technologies. The objective of this project is to spread computer literacy to the masses in India who do not know English.

32. Centre for Distance Engineering Education program (CDEEP)

CDEEP is an emulated classroom interaction programme by using real-time by the Indian Institute of Technology (IIT)-Bombay.

33. Gyan Darshan

Launched in 2000, Gyan Darshan is a joint effort of IGNOU and the IITs. It is a bouquet of channels that broadcasts educational programmes for school kids, university students and adults. The course are contributed by IGNOU, UGC Consortium for Educational Communication (UGC - CEC), IITs and so on. CEC is an inter-university centre of UGC.

34. Gyan Vani

It is a bouquet of frequency modulation (FM) radio channels which broadcast programs contributed by institutions, such as IGNOU and IITs. Under UGC Countrywide Classroom initiative, education programmes are telecast on Gyan Darshan and Doordarshan's National Channel (DD1) every day.

35. Grid Garuda

It is India's first national grid research together the academic, scientific and other applications. It is connected with National Knowledge Network (NKN).

M-learning

Mobile learning, also known as m-learning, is a new way to access learning content using mobiles. Mobile learning supports, with the help of mobile devices, continuous access to the learning process. This can be done using devices like your phone, laptop or tablet. You can learn wherever and whenever you want! With the advent of mobile learning, educational systems are changing systems are changing.

M-learning in Education

More and more schools are starting to use laptops or tablets. They're fun for children and adults. Educational apps are becoming increasingly available to teachers and trainers.

Examples of mobile learning in education:

- **Offering mobile learning material.** This is the most common way of using mobile learning. You can offer texts, videos or audios. Participants can be given assignments after watching a video that their instructor has put online. This method of mobile learning is relatively less interactive. It's more about individual consumption. There is no interaction between the trainer and the learners, which makes it an asynchronous way of learning.
- **Interaction during lessons.** Instructors can also use mobile devices to increase interaction. For example, you can ask questions during your training by using online discussion forums or asking your learners to complete a survey after taking a training.
  Instructors ask questions and the learners answer them using their mobile devices or communicate between themselves in a group discussion forum. It's possible to get immediate feedback. This is especially effective when training large groups.
- **Synchronous learning.** Would you like to have immediate feedback from your teacher or fellow students? This is possible with synchronous learning. You are able to get direct feedback even when you are at home. In addition, teachers can interact with their students during lectures.

Advantages of Mobile Learning

- **Wherever and whenever.** It's possible to lay in bed and watch a lecture or complete a survey whenever you want.
- **Motivation.** "We are going to take an online quiz!" You can see the smile on the children's faces. Children are motivated to learn when they can use tablets or other mobile devices.
  Employees also feel more motivated to learn something new or to take a training if they can take their learning materials everywhere with them, especially when they don't have time to learn during their regular work hours.
- **Different types of content.** You can add videos, audio files, and images with mobile learning. Videos make it possible to make learning livelier and more interesting.

- **Long distance is not a problem.** While one learner might be in New York and the other in Amsterdam, it's still possible to view the same content and take the same tests! This is one of the main benefits of mobile learning.

Disadvantages of Mobile Learning

- **Distraction.** Mobile devices can be a great distraction for participants. Children like learning on tablets, but gaming on tablets seems to be even more fun! As a teacher you are not always able to control what your pupils are doing on their tablets.

  For adults, mobile learning can also be distracting if your users get constantly interrupted with text messages and notifications. Therefore, it requires self-discipline and focus on their part.

  However, if you can make your training interactive and fun, the other applications available on mobiles won't be a distraction for your learners.
- **Lack of Internet connection or electricity.** Using mobile devices for e-learning could be an issue if your users don't have Internet connection or electricity readily available.

  In spite of that, statistics show that today there are more mobile devices than people in the world. So, a lack of Internet connection, poor connection quality and access to electricity should become problems of the past.

IPTV

IPTV refers to Internet-based Protocol Television where internet is used to deliver TV programs & Videos that are either live or on demand. IPTV is a system where digital television service is delivered to the subscriber through Internet protocol technology via the medium of broadband or internet connection.

It is slightly different from digital video that is accessed by millions of users on sites or apps like YouTube or Netflix, but it shares quite a bit of the same ubiquitous, pervasive nature. Also unlike standard cable or satellite connection, in IPTV multiple TV sets can use a single subscription within a home.

IPTV gives the viewers the added advantage and convenience of being able to pick the program they want to watch whenever and wherever they feel like watching it apart from tuning into any Live TV shows that are being aired currently.

How does IPTV Work?

IPTV is much similar like browsing the internet than traditional channel surfing. It merely uses IP (Internet Protocol), a transport protocol which is a delivery mechanism to deliver the videos to the viewer. When the viewer clicks on any TV program or requests the video, video from different sources (servers) is divided into data packets and sent over the internet. Video servers transmit programs through fiber-optic cable to existing household via internet connection and requests are sent out and shows are sent back.

E-GOVERNANCE

For **Electronic governance** or **e-governance** is the application of information and communication technology (ICT) for delivering government services, exchange of information, communication transactions, integration of various stand-alone systems and services between government-to-citizen (G2C), government-to-business (G2B), government-to-government (G2G), government-to-employees (G2E) as well as back-office processes and interactions within the entire government framework. Through e-governance, government services are made available to citizens in a convenient, efficient, and transparent manner. The three main target groups that can be distinguished in governance concepts are government, citizens, and businesses/interest groups. In e-governance, there are no distinct boundaries.

Distinction from E-government

Although the two terms are often used interchangeably, there is a difference between e-governance and e-government. E-government refers to the use of the ICTs in public administration which, when combined with organizational change and new skills, are intended to improve public services and democratic processes and to strengthen support to the public. However, e-government has no provision for governance of ICTs. The governance of ICTs typically requires a substantial increase in regulation and policy-making capabilities, as well as additional expertise and opinion-shaping processes among various social stakeholders. The perspective of e-governance is "the use of the technologies that both help to govern and have to be governed". The central goal of e-governance is to reach the beneficiary and to ensure that their service needs are met. Ideally, the government will automatically recognize the importance of achieving this goal in order to maximize its efficiency.

Furthermore, e-government uses one-way communication protocol whereas e-governance uses two-way communication protocol. Establishing the identity of the end beneficiary is a challenge in all citizen-centric services. Statistical information published by governments and global bodies do not always reveal the facts. The best form of e-governance cuts down on the unwanted interference of too many layers while delivering governmental services. It depends on good infrastructural setup with the support of local processes and parameters for governments to reach their citizens or end beneficiaries. A budget for planning, development, and growth can be derived from well laid out e-governance systems.

The relevance of BI Analytics has brought forth a paradigm shift in assimilating and visualizing huge chunks of data in near real-time manner. The pivot of all good decision-making systems is correct, up-to-date and compliant data. Governments not only want the transformation of their own country and countrymen but also expect improved relations and healthy trade across the world. Development should be transformative and continuously evolving. Internal as well as external IT systems should work in tandem with government policies and procedures. Data Analytics has the ability to change the color and complexion of the world. E-governance should induce up-to-date information, initiate effective interaction, and engage with transparent transactions in compliance with rule of law, thus enabling a sustainable transformation model.

The public–private partnership (PPP)-based e-governance projects are hugely successful in India. Many countries implement e-government policy in an attempt to build a corruption-free government.

ICT AND GOOD GOVERNANCE

The government uses ICT to make public administrations mere efficient and effective by cutting red tape. ICTs can remove unnecessary human involvement during the public service delivery processes form the government. Government websites are mainly classified into two categories and they are explained as follows.

1. One-way communication is a process where websites provide information regulations, policies and programs to the citizens, such as downloadable forms for government services and applications.
2. Two-way communication is a system which provides policies and programs with requesting and receiving inputs from their citizens.

Some functions of ICT based governance are as follows.

1. **Websites process non-financial transactions.** For the sake of e-voting, downloading and uploading forms, filing taxes online or applying for different types of certificates, licenses and permits.

2. They also handle all types of financial transactions, i.e., where money is transferred on a secure network to the government.
3. Direct Government Job-centres Plus is a job search service for people. Student loans or Jobseeker's allowance, etc., are also being easy and flexible through online transactional services.
4. ICTs take part a vital role in the routine lives of human beings for doing quality works with freedom. All technologies facilitate the processing and transfer of information and communication services. The main challenge by local government is its aptitude to utilize effectively technology for its daily performance.
5. E-Governance is the solution to the 'Good Governance' for India to minimize corruption provides efficient and effective quality services to their citizens. World Wide Web is the most useful medium in E-Governance. People can make use of innovative technology in commercial online services all the times. ICT can be used in various applications to go faster information distribution, get the better effectiveness of public utilities.
6. It can increase the transparency of government administration, to reduce corruption, and assist citizen contribution in local governance, In India, public service centre name as 'Jan Suvidha Kendra, helps a lot. They starred in every state of India, but till now common people suffer for doing even a simple work. All transactions such as issuing of Registration Certificate, Fitness certificate are completed by 'Vahan' and 'Sarathi' can be used to issue a learner's license, permanent Driving License and Conductor License to the applicant.

Using e-governance system reduces different direct cost.

By dial a specific number form any phone, citizens in some nations can find out how to get a loan facility from a government bank or how to get their ID cards back. They work on major festival seasons also.

On the flipside, a lot of people are unable to handle the proper way of ICT in the developing country like India: still they are dependent on the old manual process. They submit the application but don't know whether the request is processed or not. They may never know the actual cause of rejection or not. They may never know the same form again and again and waste their time. Thus there are many such abnormalities as well. As a result, a simple task becomes more complicated. In some cases, Inherent authority never looks into the types of ignorance and dishonesty. The proper tracking system has helped a lot to overcome such problems. Some People never know the proper office or proper unit for particular work. These types of problems are also faced by some highly educated people due to hephazard information.

MULTIPLE CHOICE QUESTIONS

1. A DNS translates a domain name into what?
(A) Binary (B) Hex
(C) IP (D) URL
2. When was the first e-mail sent?
(A) 1963 (B) 1969 (C) 1971 (D) 1974
3. What type of memory is volatile?
(A) Cache (B) RAM
(C) ROM (D) Hard Drive
4. What should be done to successfully convert the format of an image from BMP to JPEG?
(A) Compress the file
(B) Rename the image
(C) Use the save as command
(D) Change the image file extension
5. A company regularly updates a user reference guide. Some staff are confused about which of the printed document is the most current. What feature should be include in the reference guide to eliminate this confusion?
(A) Data printed (B) Version number
(C) Authors name
(D) Copyright information
6. The term associated with the processing of comparison speeds is?
(A) FFTS (B) MPG
(C) MIPS (D) CPS
7. The data from a spreadsheet needs to be imported into a database package. Which file format would be the most appropriate when saving the spreadsheet file?
(A) CSV (B) HTML
(C) PDF (D) RTF
8. Which of the following would indicate that the motherboard battery has failed?
(A) Operating system passwords are lost
(B) Files on the hard disk are lost and corrupted
(C) Hardware settings, including virtual memory reverts to default values
(D) Hardware settings, including the current date and time reverts to default values
9. Which of the following is essential component of communication cycle?
(A) A message (B) An interpreter
(C) An email account
(D) An internet connection
10. In what year was the @ chosen for its use in email address?
(A) 1972 (B) 1976
(C) 1980 (D) 1984
11. Which American computer company is called Big Blue?
(A) IBM (B) Compaq Corp
(C) Microsoft (D) Tandy Svenson
12. Who is credited with the idea of using punch cards to control patterns in a waving machine?
(A) Pascal (B) Hollerith
(C) Babbage (D) Jacquard
13. What does SSL stands for?
(A) System socket layer
(B) Secure system login
(C) Secure socket layer
(D) Secure system login
14. What is MAC?
(A) A computer made by Apple
(B) Memory address corruption
(C) Mediocre Apple Computer
(D) Media Access Control
15. What does PPTP stand for?
(A) Point to Point Transmission Protocol
(B) Point to Point Transfer Protocol
(C) Point to Point Tunneling Protocol
(D) Point to Point Traffic Protocol
16. The IBM PC-XT was the first to include a hard drive. What was the capacity of this disk?
(A) 750 KB (B) 10 KB
(C) 20 KB (D) 1.44 KB
17. In 1983, which person was the first to offer a definition of the term 'computer virus'?
(A) Smith (B) Cohen
(C) Norton (D) Mcafee
18. Which company created the most used networking software in 1980's?
(A) Sun (B) IBM
(C) Novell (D) Microsoft
19. 'Micro Processing' is made for
(A) Computer (B) Digital System
(C) Calculator (D) Electronic Goods
20. On the keyboard of computer each character has an "ASCII" value which stands for

(A) American Stock Code for Information Interchange
(B) American Standard Code for Information Interchange
(C) African Standard Code for Information Interchange
(D) Adaptable Standard Code for Information Change

21. DNS in internet technology stands for
(A) Dynamic Name System
(B) Domain Name System
(C) Distributed Name System
(D) None of these

22. HTML stands for
(A) Hyper Text Markup Language
(B) Hyper Text Manipulation Language
(C) Hyper Text Managing Links
(D) Hyper Text Manipulating Links

23. Which of the following is type of LAN ?
(A) Ethernet (B) Token Ring
(C) FDDI (D) All of these

24. Which of the following statements is true ?
(A) Smart cards do not require an operating system.
(B) Smart cards and PCs use some operating system.
(C) COS is smart card operating system.
(D) The communication between reader and card is in full duplex mode.

25. Firewalls are used to protect a communication network system against
(A) Unauthorized attacks
(B) Virus attacks
(C) Data-driven attacks
(D) Fire-attacks

26. The accounting software 'Tally' was developed by
(A) HCL (B) TCS
(C) Infosys (D) Wipro

27. Errors in computer programmes are called
(A) Follies (B) Mistakes
(C) Bugs (D) Spam

28. HTML is basically used to design
(A) Web-page (B) Web-site
(C) Graphics (D) Tables and Frames

29. Information, a combination of graphics, text, sound, video and animation is called
(A) Multiprogramme (B) Multifacet
(C) Multimedia (D) Multiprocess

30. Which part of the Central Processing Unit (CPU) performs calculation and makes decisions
(A) Arithmetic Logic Unit
(B) Alternating Logic Unit
(C) Alternate Local Unit
(D) American Logic Unit

31. "Dpi" stands for
(A) Dots per inch (B) Digits per unit
(C) Dots pixel inch (D) Diagrams per inch

32. The process of laying out a document with text, graphics, headlines and photographs is involved in
(A) Deck Top Publishing
(B) Desk Top Printing
(C) Desk Top Publishing
(D) Deck Top Printing

33. Transfer of data from one application to another line is known as
(A) Dynamic Disk Exchange
(B) Dodgy Data Exchange
(C) Dogmatic Data Exchange
(D) Dynamic Data Exchange

34. In web search, finding a large number of documents with very little relevant information is termed
(A) poor recall (B) web crawl
(C) poor precision rate
(D) poor web response

35. The concept of connect intelligence is derived from
(A) virtual reality (B) fuzzy logic
(C) bluetooth technology
(D) value added networks

36. Use of an ordinary telephone as an Internet appliance is called
(A) voicenet (B) voice telephone
(C) voice line (D) voice portal

37. Video transmission over the Internet that looks like delayed live-casting is called
(A) virtual video (B) direct broadcast
(C) video shift (D) real-time video

38. Which of the following is not related to information security on the Internet ?
(A) Data Encryption (B) Water marking
(C) Data Hiding
(D) Information Retrieval

39. Which is the largest unit of storage among the following ?
(A) Terabyte (B) Megabyte
(C) Kilobyte (D) Gigabyte

40. bit stands for
(A) binary information term
(B) binary digit
(C) binary tree
(D) Bivariate Theory

41. Which one of the following is not a linear data structure ?
(A) Array (B) Binary Tree
(C) Queue (D) Stack

42. Which one of the following is not a network device ?
(A) Router (B) Switch
(C) Hub (D) CPU

43. A compiler is used to convert the following to object code which can be executed
(A) High-level language
(B) Low-level language
(C) Assembly language
(D) Natural language

44. Which number system is usually followed in a typical 32-bit computer ?
(A) 2 (B) 8 (C) 10 (D) 16

45. Which one of the following is an example of Operating System ?
(A) Microsoft Word (B) Microsoft Excel
(C) Microsoft Access
(D) Microsoft Windows

46. Which one of the following represent the binary equivalent of the decimal number 23 ?
(A) 01011 (B) 10111
(C) 10011 (D) None of these

47. Which one of the following is different from other members ?
(A) Google (B) Windows
(C) Linux (D) Mac

48. Where does a computer add and compare its data ?
(A) CPU (B) Memory
(C) Hard disk (D) Floppy disk

49. Computers on an internet are identified by
(A) e-mail address (B) street address
(C) IP address (D) None of these

50. Which one of the following is not an Internet Service Provider (ISP) ?
(A) MTNL (B) BSNL
(C) ERNET India (D) Infotech India Ltd.

51. The octal number system consists of the following symbols
(A) 0 – 7 (B) 0 – 9
(C) 0 – 9, A – F (D) None of these

52. The hexadecimal number system consists of the symbols
(A) 0 – 7 (B) 0 – 9 , A – F
(C) 0 – 7, A – F (D) None of these

53. The binary equivalent of $(-15)_{10}$ is (2's complement system is used)
(A) 11110001 (B) 11110000
(C) 10001111 (D) None of these

54. 1 GB is equal to
(A) 2^{30} bits (B) 2^{30} bytes
(C) 2^{20} bits (D) 2^{20} bytes

55. The set of computer programs that manage the hardware/software of a computer is called
(A) Compiler system
(B) Operation system
(C) Operating system (D) None of these

56. S/MIME in Internet technology stands for
(A) Secure Multipurpose Internet Mail Extension
(B) Secure Multimedia Internet Mail Extension
(C) Simple Multipurpose Internet Mail Extension
(D) Simple Multimedia Internet Mail Extension

57. Minimum number of bits required to store any 3 digit decimal number is equal to
(A) 3 (B) 5 (C) 8 (D) 10

58. Computer can not do anything without a
(A) Chip (B) Memory
(C) Output device (D) Program

59. The word 'Computer' usually refers to the Central Processor Unit plus
(A) External memory (B) Internal memory
(C) Input devices (D) Output devices

60. Control Unit of a digital computers is often called the
(A) Clock (B) Nerve center
(C) ICs (D) All of these

61. Group of instructions that directs a computer is called
(A) Storage (B) Memory
(C) Logic (D) Program

62. Which kind of hardware is used the most in the input phase of a computer-based information system ?
(A) Keyboard (B) Printer
(C) Monitor (D) Hard disk

63. Which kind of device allows the user to add components and capabilities to a computer system ?

(A) System boards (B) Storage devices
(C) Input devices (D) Expansion slots

64. An organisation's introductory webpage is called its
(A) Portal (B) Vortal
(C) Homepage (D) Website

65. POP3 and IMAP are e-mail accounts in which
(A) one automatically gets one's mail everyday
(B) one has to be connected to the server to read or write one's mail
(C) one only has to be connected to the server to send and receive the mail
(D) one does not need any telephone lines

66. Where was the India's first computer installed and when ?
(A) Institute of Social Science, Agra, 1955
(B) Indian Institute of Statistics, Delhi 1957.
(C) Indian Statistical Institute, Calcutta, 1955
(D) Indian Institute of Science, Bangalore, 1971.

67. Who is called the 'grand father" of the computer ?
(A) Blaise Pascal (B) Charles Babbage
(C) Joseph Jacquard
(D) Dr. Herman Hollerith

68. IPv4 and IPv6 are addresses used to identify computers on the internet. Find the correct statement out of the following
(A) Number of bits required for IPv4 address is more than number of bits required for IPv6 address.
(B) Number of bits required for IPv4 address is same as number of bits required for IPv6 address.
(C) Number of bits required for IPv4 address is less than number of bits required for IPv6 address.
(D) Number of bits required for IPv4 address is 64.

69. Hard disks and diskettes are
(A) direct access storage devices
(B) sequential access storage devices
(C) rarely used with microcomputers
(D) Both (A) and (C) are correct.

70. Every thing computer does is controlled by its
(A) RAM (B) ROM
(C) CPU (D) Storage devices

71. The heart of any computer is the
(A) CPU (B) Memory
(C) I/O Unit (D) Disks

72. Which of the following terms applies to communication between separate computer systems ?
(A) Computer literacy
(B) Power supply
(C) Applications software
(D) Connectivity

73. The following typically happens in the output phase of a computer based information system
(A) Data is put into the computer for processing
(B) Information is produced in hardcopy and/or softcopy form
(C) Mathematical calculations are performed
(D) The computer is turned off.

74. Which of the following best describes a computer-based information system ?
(A) A system in which a computer is used to turn data into information
(B) Inputting data
(C) Processing data
(D) Performing complex mathematical calculations

75. The benefit of using computers are that computers
(A) are very fast and can store huge amounts of data
(B) produce accurate output even when the input is incorrect
(C) are designed to the inflexible
(D) All of these

76. Super computers are primarily useful for
(A) input-output intensive processing
(B) data-retrieval operations
(C) mathematical-intensive scientific applications
(D) All of these.

77. The instructions for starting the computer are housed on
(A) random-access memory
(B) CD-ROM
(C) read-only memory chips
(D) All of the above

78. Which of the following is the fastest ?
(A) CPU
(B) Magnetic tapes and disks
(C) Video terminal
(D) Sensors, mechanical controllers.

79. A disadvantage of the laser printer is that
(A) it is quieter than an impact printer
(B) it is very slow

(C) the out put is of a lower quality
(D) None of the above

80. Data entry can be performed with all of the following except
(A) OCR (B) OMR
(C) COM
(D) Voice-recognition systems

81. Magnetic tape can serve as
(A) input media
(B) output media
(C) secondary-storage media
(D) All of the above

82. The most economical way to process data is
(A) batch processing
(B) transaction processing
(C) distributed processing
(D) realtime processing

83. The amount of a cheque is recorded in magnetic ink, using an
(A) encoder (B) embosser
(C) inscriber (D) imprinter

84. MICR has made possible a
(A) cashless society (B) chequeless society
(C) creditless society (D) None of these

85. Optical character readers can read
(A) machine printed data only
(B) machine printed letters and numbers, and hand printed numbers only
(C) both machine and hand printed letters, but not hand writing
(D) machine

86. In a computer system, which device is functionally opposite to a Keyboard ?
(A) Mouse (B) Trackball
(C) Printer (D) Joystick

87. Which was the first company to launch mobile phone services in India ?
(A) Essar (B) BPL
(C) Hutchison (D) Airtel

88. Which of the following items is not used in Local Area Networks (LANs) ?
(A) Computer (B) Modem
(C) Printer (D) Cable

89. A modem is connected in between a telephone line and a
(A) network (B) computer
(C) communication adapter
(D) serial port

90. When a group of computers is connected together in a small area without the help of telephone lines, it is called
(A) Remote Communication network (RCN)
(B) Local Area Network (LAN)
(C) Wide Area Network (WAN)
(D) Value Added Network (VAN)

91. A communication network which is used by large organizations over regional, national or global area is called
(A) LAN (B) WAN
(C) MAN (D) VAN

92. 1 byte is equal to
(A) 2 bits (B) 8 bits
(C) 16 bits (D) 32 bits

93. 1 KB (kilobyte) and 1 MB (megabyte) are respectively equal to
(A) 1024 bytes and 1000 kilobytes
(B) 1000 bytes and 100 kilobytes
(C) 1000 bytes and 10000 bytes
(D) 1024 bytes and 100 kilobytes

94. A computer's 'clock-speed' is measured in
(A) megabytes and gigabytes
(B) nanoseconds and picoseconds
(C) bits and megabits
(D) megahertz and gigahertz

95. The computer performs all mathematical and logical operations inside its
(A) Central Processing Unit
(B) Memory Unit
(C) Output Unit (D) Visual Display Unit

96. What is the name given to the first generation computer languages?
(A) Binary Languages
(B) Machine Languages
(C) Primary Languages
(D) Assembly Languages

97. Which of the following are examples of input devices ?
(A) Visual display unit, dot matrix printer, laser printer
(B) Keyboard, mouse, optical mark reader
(C) Arithmetic and logic unit, control unit
(D) RAM, ROM, PROM

98. The term 'Program' refers to
(A) a sequence of instructions
(B) the computer's internal design
(C) any information stored in the memory
(D) any information processed by the computer

99. C, C++, JAVA are the examples of
(A) commercial computer brands
(B) a computer's internal parts
(C) programming languages
(D) types of secondary memory devices

100. Unix, DOS, Windows are examples of
(A) application programs
(B) operating systems
(C) word processors
(D) commercial computer brands

101. Multimedia devices enable the use of computers for
(A) automation (B) defense use
(C) entertainment (D) medical use

102. The operation of adding two numbers is done in the
(A) program (B) ALU
(C) control unit (D) output unit

103. Registers are high speed memory elements, situated in the
(A) Memory (B) CPU
(C) I/O Unit (D) ROM or EPROM

104. Machine language and assembly language are examples of
(A) high level languages
(B) low level languages
(C) high level languages and low level languages respectively
(D) low level languages and high level languages

105. TCP/IP is necessary if one is to connect to the,
(A) phone lines (B) LAN
(C) Internet (D) a server

106. Which of the following statements, regarding the term ICT is/are TRUE ?
P: ICT is an acronym that stands for Indian Classical Technology.
Q: Converging technologies that exemplify ICT include the merging of audio-visual, telephone and computer networks through a common cabling system.
(A) P only (B) Q only
(C) P and Q (D) Neither P nor Q

107. http://www.truemanbooks.com is an example of
(A) URK (B) HTML
(C) XML (D) LAN

108. The most common input device used today is
(A) Motherboard (B) Track ball
(C) Mouse (D) Keyboard

109. What is blog ?
(A) Online music (B) Intranet
(C) A personal or corporate website in the form of an online journal
(D) A personal or corporate Google search

110. What is the standard code the computer industry created to represent characters?
(A) ASSII (B) ASCII
(C) BASCII (D) EPROM

111. The term 'gigabyte' refers to
(A) 1024 bytes (B) 1024 kilobytes
(C) 1024 megabytes (D) 1024 bytes

112. The 0 and 1 in the binary numbering systems are called binary digits or
(A) bytes (B) kilobytes
(C) decimal bytes (D) bits

113. Re-arranging data in a new sequence is known as
(A) Updating (B) Batching
(C) Sorting (D) Summarizing

114. An error that crashes the program is
(A) Boot (B) Bomb
(C) Bug (D) Buffer

115. Compression of digital data for efficient storage is
(A) Buffer (B) Debugging
(C) Packing (D) Field

116. Which transmission mode is used for data communication along telephone lines?
(A) Parallel (B) Serial
(C) Synchronous (D) Asynchronous

117. Which of the following TCP/IP protocol is used for remote terminal connection service?
(A) TELNET (B) FTP
(C) RARP (D) UDP

118. Which of the following medium is used for broadband local networks?
(A) Coaxial cable (B) Optic fiber
(C) CATV (D) UTP

119. What is the name of the device that converts computer output into a form that can be transmitted over a telephone line?
(A) Teleport (B) Modem
(C) Multiplexer (D) Concentrator

120. A computer cannot "boot" if it does not have the
(A) Compiler (B) Loader
(C) Operating System (D) Assembler

121. The user interface
(A) is relatively unimportant

(B) is slanted toward novice users
(C) supports both novice and experienced users
(D) is easy to provide even with good support

122. The operating system manages
(A) Memory (B) Processor
(C) Disks and I/O devices
(D) All of the above

123. Which of the following program is not a utility?
(A) Debugger (B) Editor
(C) Spooler (D) All of these

124. The operating system of a computer serves as a software interface between the user and
(A) hardware (B) peripheral
(C) memory (D) screen

125. A sequence of one or more characters is
(A) Group (B) String
(C) Block (D) Field

126. CD-ROM is a
(A) Semiconductor memory
(B) Memory register
(C) Magnetic memory (D)None of these

127. Compilers and interpreters are themselves
(A) high level languages
(B) programs
(C) codes (D) mnemonics

128. The special purpose language developed for computer assisted instruction (CAI) is known as
(A) LISP (B) APL
(C) PILOT (D) ADA

129. Which memory stores the values of variables?
(A) SAM (B) ROM
(C) RAM (D) PROM

130. When you create a subdirectory within a directory, the process is known as
(A) directing (B) making
(C) baking (D) nesting

131. What drive letter is reserved for the first hard disk drive in a DOS based computer?
(A) C (B) D
(C) B (D) E

132. In which Program Manager Group is the MS-DOS Prompt Icon found?
(A) Main (B) Applications
(C) Accessories (D) Startup

133. The background area of the screen where windows shows you all that it can do is called the
(A) windows space (B) backboard
(C) desk top (D) back window

134. The maximum number of columns in a worksheet can be
(A) 100 (B) 144
(C) 333 (D) 256

135. String search in a word processor is restricted to a
(A) block (B) page
(C) file (D) record

136. Maximum width of a cell is
(A) 128 characters (B) 240 characters
(C) 1024 characters (D) unlimited

137. A server program that doesn't run continuously but executes in response to some event, such as a client request, is known as a
(A) doemon (B) domain
(C) router (D) hub

138. DTP is the acronym of
(A) Digital Task processor
(B) Desk Top Publishing
(C) Down Top Programming
(D) None of the above

139. What is the name of the arrangement whereby several central processing units share on memory?
(A) Multitasking
(B) Multiprogramming
(C) Multiprocessing
(D) Concurrent programming

140. A displayed listing of program options which users can select is called
(A) menu (B) selection
(C) options (D) icons

141. Which programming language was used for writing the popular operating system UNIX?
(A) C++ (B) SNOBOL
(C) PASCOL (D) C

142. A devices that links two homogeneous packet-broadcast local networks is
(A) hub (B) bridge
(C) repeater (D) gateway

143. Data integrity refers to
(A) the simplicity of data
(B) the privacy of data
(C) the validity of data
(D) the security of data

144. What does the acronym ISDN stands for?
(A) Indian Standard Digital Network

(B) Integrated Services Digital Network
(C) Intelligent Services Digital Network
(D) Integrated Services Data Network

145. If communication software can be called the "traffic cop" of a microcommunication system, then what should the modem be called?
(A) Park (B) Bridge
(C) Interface (D) Link

146. A machine that connects to two or more electronic mail systems and transfers mail messages among them is known as
(A) gateways (B) mail gateway
(C) bridges (D) user agent

147. The slowest transmission speeds are those of
(A) twisted-pair wire
(B) coaxial cable
(C) fiber-optic cable
(D) none of the above

148. A central computer surrounded by one or more satellite computers is called a
(A) bus network (B) ring network
(C) star network (D) all of the above

149. Which of the following terms is the most closely related to main memory?
(A) nonvolatile (B) permanent
(C) control unit (D) temporary

150. A new Laptop has been produced that weighs less, is smaller and uses less power than previous Laptop models.
Which of the following technologies has been used to accomplish this ?
(A) Universal Serial Bus Mouse
(B) Faster Random Access Memory
(C) Blu Ray Drive
(D) Solid State Hard Drive

151. What is the control unit's function in the CPU?
(A) To transfer data to primary storage
(B) To store program instructions
(C) To perform logic operations
(D) To decode program instructions

152. Internet explorer is a type of
(A) Operating System (B) Compiler
(C) Browser (D) IP address

153. Which computer memory is essentially empty?
(A) RAM (B) ROM
(C) EPROM (D) PROM

154. The individual within the operations group who ordinarily uses a variety of keyboard devices is the
(A) Data clerk
(B) Keypunch operator
(C) Data entry clerk
(D) Computer operator

155. The process of starting or restarting a computer system by loading instructions from a secondary storage device into the computer memory is called
(A) Duping (B) Booting
(C) Padding (D) All of these

156. ITC stands for
(A) Intelligent Teaching Systems
(B) Intelligent Tutoring Systems
(C) International Tutoring Systems
(D) International Teaching Systems

157. If (y)x represents a number y in base x, then which of the following numbers is smallest of all ?
(A) $(1111)_2$ (B) $(1111)_8$
(C) $(1111)_{10}$ (D) $(1111)_{16}$

158. The attribution of human from or qualities to things such as machines or computers is called
(A) cybernetics (B) cybernation
(C) artificial intelligence
(D) anthropomorphism

159. A regular TV set can be hooked up to a computer so as to received computer signal instead of a television program. This looking up is achieved with the help of a/an
(A) modem (B) adapter
(C) cable (D) aerial

160. The OCR stands for
(A) Outsized character reader
(B) Optical character recognition
(C) Operational character reader
(D) Only character reader

161. TCP/IP is necessary if one is to connect to the
(A) Phone lines (B) LAN
(C) Internet (D) A server

162. Which of the following enables us to send the same letter to different persons in MS Word?
(A) Mail copy (B) Mail Insert
(C) Mail merge (D) Mail join

163. Which of the following is an open source software?
(A) Windows (B) Mozilla firefox
(C) Acrobat Reader (D) MS Word

164. Which is an instant messenger that is used for chatting.
(A) Altavista (B) MAC

(C) Microsoft office (D) Google Talk

165. Which social site is similar to whatsapp
(A) You Tube (B) Telegram
(C) Linkedin (D) Google plus

166. MOOC stands for
(A) Media online open course
(B) Massachusetts open online course
(C) Massive open online course
(D) Myrinde open online course

167. Social site used by professionals is
(A) Twitter (B) Linked in
(C) Whatsapp (D) Facebook

168. Department of Telecommunication banned a famous site in India.
(A) You Tube (B) Google plus
(C) Torrentz (D) Vimeo

169. Given the following email fields, which of the email addresses will 'swami' be able to see when he receives the message ?

To... ram@test.com
Cc... raj@test.com; ravi@test.com
Bcc... swami@test.com; rama@test.com

(A) ram@test.com
(B) ram@test.com; raj@test.com; ravi@test.com
(C) ram@test.com; rama@test.com
(D) ram@test.com; rama@test.com; raj@test.com; ravi@test.com

170. Who introduced 4G technology in India firstly
(A) Airtel (B) Jio
(C) Vodafone (D) Idea

171. Which social site CEO said that our app is not for Indian Market.
(A) Twitter (B) Snapchat
(C) Whatsapp (D) Facebook

172. Which social networking site has most users
(A) Face book (B) Messenger
(C) Instagram (D) Google plus

173. When a computer is booting, BIOS is loaded to the memory by
(A) RAM (B) ROM
(C) CD-ROM (D) TCP

174. Internet communication within institutions is done through
(A) LAN (B) WAN
(C) EBB (D) MMS

175. A compiler is a software which converts
(A) Characters to bits
(B) High level language to machine language
(C) Machine language to high level language
(D) Words to bits

176. Amazon is best example of _____ site.
(A) Entertainment (B) Blogging
(C) Social networking (D) E-commerce

177. Flash is proprietary software developed by
(A) Sencha (B) Macromedia
(C) Yahoo (D) Google

178. Which of the following website type is used to create beautiful animations
(A) Flash (B) Dynamic
(C) E-commerce (D) Static

179. Word Press can be called as
(A) Content Managed Websites
(B) Dynamic Websites
(C) E-commerce websites
(D) Static Website

180. A________in the simplest form of website, in which the site's content is delivered without the use of server side processing
(A) E-commerce website
(B) Dynamic website
(C) Static website
(D) Social Networking Website

181. ISP exchanges internet traffic between their networks by
(A) Internet exchange point
(B) Subscriber end point
(C) ISP end point
(D) None of the above

182. Which one of the following protocol is not used in internet
(A) HTTP (B) DHCP
(C) DNS (D) None of these

183. Which protocol assigns IP address to the client connected in the internet?
(A) DHCP (B) IP
(C) RPC (D) None of these

184. Social Network sites use which media for communication?
(A) Video (B) Audio
(C) Text (D) All of these

185. Which of the following is not an application software?
(A) Word processing
(B) Spreadsheet
(C) UNIX
(D) Desktop publishing

186. Whose trademark is the operating system UNIX?
(A) Bell Laboratories (B) Ashton Tate
(C) Microsoft (D) Motorola

187. An internet address is _____ bits in length.
(A) 4 (B) 8 (C) 16 (D) 32

188. A ________ is not a form of Biometrics.
(A) finger print (B) password
(C) retina scan (D) breath scan

189. A sender must not be able to deny that he sent a specific message when he infact did. This is an aspect of security called
(A) privacy (B) authentication
(C) non-repudiation (D) none of these

190. The technique that extends storage capacities of main memory beyond the actual size of the main memory is called
(A) multitasking (B) virtual storage
(C) multiprocessing (D) switching

191. Where are cookies stored?
(A) On the server (B) In web.xml
(C) On the client (D) In HTML

192. If you wanted to locate the hardware address of a local device, which protocol would you use?
(A) ARP (B) ICMP
(C) PING (D) PONG

193. Which of the following describes programs that can run independently, travel from system to system, and disrupt computer communications?
(A) Trojans (B) Viruses
(C) Droppers (D) Worms

194. You receive an email message that informs you that a terrible virus has been unleashed on the Internet and that you should warn all the people in your Address Book. Which of the following have you most likely encountered?
(A) a virus hoax (B) spam
(C) a virus (D) a worm

195. What is backup?
(A) Adding more components to your network
(B) Protecting data by copying it from the original source to a different destination
(C) Filtering old data from the new data
(D) Accessing data on tape

196. The primary goal of a computer system is to turn data into
(A) ideas (B) information
(C) reports (D) none of these

197. Manipulating data to create information is known as
(A) feed back (B) programming
(C) processing (D) analysis

198. The type of software that controls the internal operations in the computer, and controls how the computer works with all its parts, is which of the following?
(A) Shareware
(B) Operating system software
(C) Application software
(D) Public domain software

199. In addition to keying data directly into a database, data entry can be done from a(n)
(A) input form (B) table
(C) field (D) data directory

200. What is an E-mail attachment?
(A) A receipt sent by the recipient
(B) A separate document from another program sent along with an E-mail message.
(C) A malicious parasite that feeds of your message and destroys the contents.
(D) A list of CC or BCC recipients

201. What happens when you boot up a PC?
(A) Portions of the operating system are copied from disk into memory.
(B) Portions of the operating system are copied from memory into disk.
(C) Portions of the operating system are copied.
(D) Portions of the operating system are emulated.

202. What is correcting errors in a program called?
(A) Interpreting (B) Translating
(C) Debugging (D) Compiling

203. Sending an E-mail is similar to
(A) writing a letter
(B) taking on the phone
(C) sending a package (D) none of these

204. The blinking symbol on the computer screen is called the
(A) mouse (B) hand
(C) cursor (D) none of these

205. A word processor would most likely be used to do which of the following?
(A) keep on account of money spent
(B) maintain an inventory
(C) type a biography
(D) do a computer search in the media centre

206. A hard copy of a file created on a computer refers to data
(A) saved on a floppy disk
(B) printed on a printer
(C) sent as an e-mail
(D) none of these

207. A _____ is an organised collection of data about a single entity.
(A) File (B) Library
(C) Database (D) Dictionary

208. Something which has easily understood instructions is said to be
(A) user friendly (B) information
(C) word processing (D) icon

209. The property that, when classes are arranged in a hierarchy, each class assumes the attributes and methods of its ancestors is
(A) generalization (B) inheritance
(C) encapsulation (D) information hiding

210. Which of the following defines the term E-Banking?
1. It is the short form of Efficient Banking which means providing all banking related services to the customers in minimum required time during their visit to the branch.
2. E-Banking is providing banking facilities to all the customers through ATMs only which restricts their visits to a bank branch to a bare minimum.
3. E-Banking implies provisions of banking products and services through electronic delivery channels like ATMs, phone, internet, mobile phone etc.

(A) only 1 (B) only 2
(C) only 3 (D) only 1 & 3

211. A folder
1. is an organizational tool used to store files.
2. is synonymous with directory, but folder is the preferred term
3. contains data

(A) 1 only (B) 2 only
(C) 1 & 3 only (D) none of these

212. The part of a computer system containing the circuitry that does the adding, subtracting, multiplying dividing and comparing, is called as
(A) Arithmetic logic unit
(B) Memory
(C) CPU
(D) None of the above

213. A browser is a
(A) line that delineates the edge of a program window
(B) software program especially designed for viewing web pages on the internet
(C) tool for resizing the window
(D) device used for modifying the window

214. The storage device used to compensate for the difference in rates of flow of data from one device to another is termed as
(A) Chip (B) Channel
(C) Floppy (D) Buffer

215. Which of the following is a standard code used to exchange information among data processing and communication system?
(A) ANSI (B) ACM
(C) ASCII (D) OSI

216. Which of the following best explains RAM?
1. It is an acronym for Random Access Memory.
2. It is memory built from silicon chips that is used to store programs and data temporarily while they are being processed.
3. Read Access Memory.

(A) Only 1 & 3 (B) Only 2 & 3
(C) Only 1 & 2 (D) All of these

217. The components of a computer system with the circuitry to control interpretation and execution of instructions is known as
(A) ALU (B) Memory
(C) Control (D) CPU

218. Put the following units of storage into the correct order, starting with the smallest unit first and going down to the largest unit :
(a) Kilobyte (b) Byte
(c) Megabyte (d) Terabyte
(e) Gigabyte (f) Bit

Give your answer from the following code :
(A) (f), (b), (a), (c), (d), (e)
(B) (f), (b), (a), (d), (e), (c)
(C) (f), (b), (a), (c), (e), (d)
(D) (f), (b), (a), (d), (c), (e)

219. With regard to computer memory, which of the following statement(s) is/are TRUE ?
P: Read Only Mėmory (ROM) is 'volatile' memory.
Q: Random Access Memory (RAM) is 'volatile' memory.
R: Secondary Memory is 'volatile' memory.

(A) P only (B) Q only
(C) P and Q only (D) P and R only

220. Compiler in computer system is a
(A) Package (B) System Software
(C) Process (D) Application software

221. Database Management Systems are comprised of tables that made up of rows called_____and columns called______.
(A) fields, records (B) records, fields
(C) addresses, fields (D) records, ranges

222. What is Web casting?
(A) Transmitting the video and audio on the Internet
(B) Playing of music on the Internet
(C) Searching on the Web
(D) None of the above

223. When you delete files in windows operating system they are
(A) delete permanently
(B) put in recycle bin
(C) wiped thoroughly so that no body is able to recover the file bank
(D) delete permanently & also wiped clean

224. What is the function of a modem?
(A) Encryption and decryption
(B) Converts data to voice and vice-versa
(C) Converts analog signals to digitals and vice-versa
(D) None of these

225. Networking using fibre optic cable is done as
(A) It has high bandwidth
(B) It is thin and light
(C) It is not affected by electromagnetic interference/power surges etc.
(D) All of the above

226. Conference (Netscape), Netmeeting (Internet explorer), enables (choose the option that best describes)
(A) Sharing voice on the net
(B) Live textual conferencing
(C) Live audio conferencing
(D) Live real time conferencing

227. Three Boolean operators are
(A) OR, NOT, AND
(B) OR, NOR, NAND
(C) NOT, NOR, NAND
(D) OR, NOT, NAND

228. Ink jet is a form of
(A) impact printing
(B) serial impact printing
(C) dot matrix printing
(D) None of these

229. Conversion of octal number $(12321)_8$ to its decimal number equivalent is
(A) $(5239)_{10}$ (B) $(5329)_{10}$
(C) $(5293)_{10}$ (D) $(5392)_{10}$

230. Conversion of binary number $(0.012101)_2$ to its decimal number equivalent is
(A) $(0.5871)_{10}$ (B) $(0.5817)_{10}$
(C) $(0.5781)_{10}$ (D) $(0.5718)_{10}$

231. Program from the same developer, sold bundled together, that provide better integration and share common features, toolbars and menus are known as
(A) software suites
(B) integrated software packages
(C) software processing packages
(D) personal information managers

232. _________ servers store and manage files for network users.
(A) Authentication (B) Main
(C) Web (D) File

233. All of the following are examples of real security and privacy risks except
(A) hackers (B) spam
(C) viruses (D) identity theft

234. System software is the set of programs that enables your computers hardware devices and _____ software to work together.
(A) management (B) processing
(C) utility (D) application

235. _____are specially designed computer chips that reside inside other devices, such as your car or your electronic thermostat.
(A) Servers
(B) Embedded computers
(C) Robotic computer
(D) Mainframes

236. The following are all mobile computing devices, except
(A) notebook computers
(B) cellular telephones
(C) digital scanners
(D) none of these

237. _________ controls the way in which the computer system functions and provides a means by which users can interact with the computer.
(A) Application software
(B) Operating system
(C) The motherboard
(D) None of these

238. Servers are computers that provide resources to other computers connected to a
(A) mainframe (B) network
(C) super computer (D) client

239. A goal of data mining includes which of the following ?
(A) To explain some observed event or condition
(B) To confirm that data exists
(C) To analyses data for expected relationships
(D) To create a new data warehouse

240. What is the name for a webpage address ?
(A) Domain (B) Directory
(C) Protocol (D) URL

241. A database management system (DBMS) is a
(A) hardware system used to create, maintain and provide controlled access to a data base
(B) hardware system used to create, maintain and provide uncontrolled access to a database.
(C) software system used to create, maintain and provide uncontrolled access to a database
(D) software system used to create, maintain and provide controlled access to a database

242. A proxy server is used for which of the following?
(A) To provide security against unauthorized users
(B) To process client requests for web pages
(C) To process client requests for database access
(D) To provide TCP/LP

243. When data changes in multiple lists and all lists are not updated, this causes
(A) data redundancy
(B) information overload
(C) duplicate data
(D) data inconsistency

244. What is the primary difference between a virus and a worm?
(A) A worm has the ability to self-propagate from an infected users computer to other computers.
(B) A worm is usually written by a cracker : script bunnies do not have the skills to develop a worm program.
(C) A virus is very harmful to the computers it infects : a worm is not serious a problem.
(D) Antivirus software is effective in fighting viruses but not worms.

245. You must install a ______ on a network if you want to share a broadband internet connection.
(A) router (B) modem
(C) cable (D) none of these

246. Granting an outside organization access to internal web pages is often implemented using a(n)
(A) extranet (B) intranet
(C) internet (D) none of these

247. Which term identifies a specific computer on the web and the main page of the entire site?
(A) URL (B) Web site address
(C) Hyperlink (D) Domain name

248. Chip is a common nick name for
(A) transistor (B) resistor
(C) integrated circuit (D) semiconductor

249. A ______ contains specific rules and rules that express the logical steps of an algorithm.
(A) programming language
(B) syntax
(C) programming structure
(D) logic chart

250. The most frequently used instructions of a computer program are likely to be fetched from
(A) the hard disk (B) cache memory
(C) RAM (D) registers

251. Personal logs or Journal entries posted on the web are known as
(A) listservs (B) webcasts
(C) blogs (D) none of these

252. A ________ uses pictures (called icons) and menus displayed on the screen to send commands to the computer system.
(A) Command-based user interface
(B) GUI
(C) System utility (D) API

253. The ______ manual tells you how to use a software program.
(A) documentation (B) programming
(C) technical (D) user

254. Which of the following is not a type of broadband Internet connection?
(A) Cable (B) Dial-up
(C) Satellite (D) None of these

255. Software, such as viruses, worms and Trojan horses that has a malicious intent is known as
(A) spyware (B) adware
(C) spam (D) malware

256. Making a field _____ means that it cannot be left blank.

(A) numeric (B) required
(C) calculated (D) validated

257. Linux is a ______ operating system.
(A) Open source (B) Windows
(C) Microsoft (D) Mac

258. High level programming language can be converted to machine language using which of the following ?
(A) Oracle (B) Compiler
(C) Mat lab (D) Assembler

259. Verification of a login name and password is known as
(A) configuration (B) accessibility
(C) authentication (D) logging in

260. Which of the following would most likely not be a symptom of a virus?
(A) Existing program files and icons disappear
(B) The CD-ROM stops functioning
(C) The web browser opens to an unusual home page
(D) Odd messages or images are displayed on the screen

261. Hard disk drives are considered _____ storage.
(A) flash (B) nonvolatile
(C) temporary (D) nonpermanent

262. ______ is when the more power-hungry components, such as the monitor and the hard drive, are put in idle.
(A) Hibernation (B) Powerdown
(C) Stand by mode
(D) The shut down procedure

263. The most common input devices are the ____ and the ______.
(A) microphone, printer
(B) scanner, monitor
(C) keyboard, mouse
(D) none of these

264. The ______ key and the ______ key can be used in combination with other keys to perform shortcuts and special tasks.
(A) Control, Alt
(B) Function, Toggle
(C) Delete, Insert
(D) Caps Lock, Num Lock

265. Lotus Organizer and Corel Central are examples of ___________ software.
(A) analytical (B) database
(C) presentation (D) PIM

266. What is the full form of USB as used in computer related activities?
(A) Universal Security Block
(B) Ultra Serial Block
(C) United Service Block
(D) Universal Serial Bus

267. For which of the following tasks would PIM software be most useful?
(A) Drafting a memo
(B) Maintaining a schedule
(C) Calculating a budget
(D) Keeping track of recipes

268. Which of the following is not a computer programming language?
(A) C (B) C++
(C) Java (D) Microsoft

269. The smallest unit of information in a database is called a
(A) byte (B) field
(C) cell (D) None of these

270. What kind of software would you most likely use to keep track of a billing account?
(A) Word processing (B) Spreadsheet
(C) Web authoring (D) None of these

271. Text and graphics that have been cut or copied are stored in an area called the
(A) Paste board (B) Copy board
(C) Clip board (D) Cutting board

272. A device that connects to a network without the use of cables is said to be
(A) wireless (B) centralized
(C) open source (D) none of these

273. Junk e-mail is also called
(A) spam (B) spoof
(C) spool (D) none of these

274. What is the most common way to get a virus in your computer's harddisk?
(A) By installing games from their CD ROM
(B) By uploading pictures from mobile phones to the computer
(C) By opening e-mails
(D) By sending e-mails

275. Which is *not* online Indian Matrimonial website?
(A) www.jeevansathi.com
(B) www.bharatmatrimony.com
(C) www.shaadi.com
(D) www.singlemuslim.com

276. Software providers who develop many productivity tools may also provide stripped-down versions that combine the simpler features of these tools bundled together into a(n)

(A) software suite
(B) personal information manager
(C) integrated software application
(D) limited software edition

277. Microsoft Office is an example of a(n)
(A) software suite
(B) open-source product
(C) integrated software application
(D) None of these

278. E-commerce allows companies to
(A) issue important business reports
(B) conduct business over the Internet
(C) support decision making processes
(D) keep track of paper-based transactions

279. If you type a word that is not in word's dictionary a ______ wavy underline appears below the word.
(A) red (B) green
(C) blue (D) black

280. In Excel, any set of characters containing a letter, hyphen or space is considered
(A) a formula (B) a text
(C) a title (D) none of these

281. ____________software allows users to perform calculations on rows and columns of data.
(A) Word processing
(B) Database Management Systems
(C) Electronic Spreadsheet
(D) none of these

282. A ______ represents approximately one billion memory locations.
(A) kilobyte (B) megabyte
(C) gigabyte (D) terabyte

283. _______ cells involves creating a single cell by combining two or more selected cells.
(A) Formatting (B) Merging
(C) Embedding (D) Splitting

284. The operating system is the most common type of ______ software.
(A) communication (B) application
(C) system (D) none of these

285. When you quickly press and release the left mouse button twice, you are
(A) Primary-clicking (B) Double clicking
(C) Secondary-clicking (D) None of these

286. The horizontal and vertical lines on a worksheet are called
(A) cells (B) sheets
(C) grid lines (D) none of these

287. To delete an incorrect character in a document, _____ to erase to the right of the insertion point.
(A) press the left mouse key
(B) double click the right mouse key
(C) press the backspace key
(D) press the delete key

288. A saved document is referred to as a
(A) file (B) word
(C) folder (D) none of these

289. ________ is a special visual and audio effect applied to text or content.
(A) animation (B) flash
(C) wipe (D) none of these

290. Individuals who want software to assist in automated checkbook balancing and bill paying for their personal bank and credit card accounts will likely use which of the following software products?
(A) Microsoft Project (B) QuickBooks
(C) Acrobat (D) Quicken

291. ________is when the computer is turned on and the operating system is loading.
(A) Booting (B) Flashing
(C) Tracking (D) None of these

292. A(n)_____ is text that you want to be printed at the bottom of the page?
(A) header (B) endnote
(C) footnote (D) footer

293. You should create a ______ to prevent others from changing the worksheet from protected to unprotected.
(A) access code (B) password
(C) key (D) secret mark

294. The _______ feature in word automatically corrects certain spelling, typing, capitalization, or grammar errors.
(A) Auto Fix (B) Auto Spell
(C) Auto Mark (D) Auto Correct

295. The __________ provides easy access to frequently used commands.
(A) Command toolbar
(B) Quick Access toolbar
(C) Standard toolbar (D) Shortcut toolbar

296. The ____ takes different shapes depending on the task you are performing.
(A) active tab (B) insertion point
(C) mouse pointer (D) none of these

297. By default, Excel positions text in a cell as
(A) left-aligned (B) right-aligned
(C) centered (D) justified

298. To center a paragraph using shortcut keys, press
(A) CTRL + C (B) CTRL + E
(C) CTRL + L (D) CTRL + R

299. To print a document, press_______, then press ENTER.
(A) SHIFT + P (B) CTRL + P
(C) ALT + P (D) ESC + P

300. Which of the following statements is not true?
(A) A notebook computer weighs less and actually looks like a notebook
(B) A palmtop computer weighs at most a few pounds and can fit into a pocket.
(C) The portable computers can be connected to larger desktop PCs or other computers
(D) None of these

301. The data storage hierarchy consists of :
(A) Bytes, bits, fields, records, files and databases
(B) Bits, bytes, fields, records, files and databases
(C) Bits, bytes, records, fields, files and databases
(D) Bits, bytes, fields, files, records and databases

302. The term 'connectivity' refers to
(A) the concept that enables the sharing of resources like computing power, software and input/output units.
(B) access to information via internet.
(C) the proximity achieved by the communication
(D) transferring data between PCs

303. What do you understand by the term 'online banking'?
(A) Making transactions on computer which are connected to each other via a server so that any request for transaction goes to the banks main computer.
(B) Making payments through the internet
(C) Accessing the bank details from a remote place
(D) Acquiring the secret account number and pin code for cash withdrawal

304. What do you understand by the term 'time-sharing'?
(A) Some companies provide a service of selling computer time to organisations. This is called 'time-sharing'.
(B) The allotment of time-slots for different departments in a company to use a computer.
(C) The time for which the internet is used by any organisation
(D) Visiting different sites providing educational information for a predecided time is called time sharing

305. Which of the following statements about 'outsourcing' are correct?
(1) companies that are specialized time-sharing provide organisations with all their computational needs. This is called outsourcing.
(2) With outsourcing, time-sharing companies supply hardware and software to organisations for a fee and actually run program as service on a regularly scheduled basis.
(3) Outsourcing has become very popular for many companies that have own computers but find them inadequate and do not want to spend additional funds to upgrade them.
(A) Only (1) and (2)
(B) All of them
(C) Only (2) and (3)
(D) Either (1) or (3)

306. The term 'end-users' means
(A) employees who uses the server that has many computers connected to it.
(B) employees who need computer-produced information to analyses and summarize data and to help them in making decisions.
(C) people who use the computer in the end
(D) either (B) and (C)

307. Transformation of input into output is performed by
(A) Peripherals (B) Storage
(C) The input-output unit
(D) The CPU

308. Device drivers are
(A) tiny power cards for external storage devices
(B) experts who know how to maximize the performance of devices
(C) small special purpose programs
(D) the innermost part of the operating system

309. A set of instructions telling the computer what to do is called
(A instructor (B) compiler
(C) program (D) debugger

310. Who is considered to be "The father of Artificial Intelligence"?
(A) George Boole (B) John McCarthy
(C) Allen Newell (D) Alan Turing

311. A set of wires inside computer through which devices are connected is called
(A) Bus (B) Cables
(C) Wires
(D) Biconditional Cables

312. Conversion of decimal number $(0.225)_{10}$ to its binary number equivalent is
(A) $(0001)_2$ (B) $(001)_2$
(C) $(0010)_2$ (D) None of these

313. Web pages are written using
(A) HTTP (B) FTP
(C) URL (D) HTML

314. Conversion of an octal number 1258 to its decimal number is
(A) 90_{10} (B) 85_{10}
(C) 87_{10} (D) 99_{10}

315. The binary number 100110010 is equal to____ hexa decimal number.
(A) 22 (B) 37
(C) 41 (D) 132

316. ______ is needed to build dynamic web document.
(A) HTML (B) OGI
(C) Java (D) All of the above

317. A network which is used for sharing data, software and hardware among several users owning micro computers is called
(A) WAN (B) LAN
(C) VAN (D) None of these

318. Which of the following is an advantage to using fibre optics data transmission?
(A) Resistance to data theft
(B) Fast data transmission rate
(C) Low noise level
(D) Few transmission errors

319. A protocol is a set of rules governing a time sequence of events that must take place
(A) between peers
(B) between modems
(C) between an interface
(D) across an interface

320. Which of the following is a serious problem of file management system?
(A) Difficult to update
(B) Lack of data independence
(C) Data redundancy and programme dependency
(D) All of the above

321. Which of the following domains is used for - profit businesses ?
(A) .org (B) .net
(C) .edu (D) .com

322. A term associated with the comparison of processing speeds of different computer system is
(A) EFTS (B) MPG
(C) MIPS (D) CPS

323. Human beings are referred to as Homosapiens. Which device is called silicosapiens?
(A) Monitor (B) Hardware
(C) Robot (D) Computer

324. What is the number of bit patterns provided by a 7-bit code?
(A) 64 (B) 256
(C) 128 (D) 512

325. Which was the first company in the world to build computer for sale?
(A) International Business Machine
(B) Remington Rand Corporation
(C) English Electric Computers
(D) Sperry Univac

326. The term CD-ROM stands for
(A) Compact digital read only memory
(B) Compact disk read only memory
(C) Compressed data read only memory
(D) Compressed digital read only memory

327. Which of the following technology is mostly used by a teacher in virtual education?
(A) Course management applications
(B) Multimedia resources
(C) The internet
(D) Video-conferencing

328. The binary representation of the hexadecimal number 125
(A) 0000000001111101
(B) 0000000100100101
(C) 0000000111011010
(D) 0000000001111111

329. A collection of 4-bits is called
(A) Nibble (B) Byte
(C) Word (D) None of these

330. Unicode is a
(A) 8-bit code (B) 10-bit code
(C) 12-bit code (D) 16-bit code

331. Bar codes stores information using
(A) Punch holes (B) Thick and thin lines
(C) Dots (D) All of these

332. Match List I and List II and select the correct group of matching.

List I	List II
P. RAM	1. Hz
Q. CPU speed	2. MB
R. Monitor	3. Bytes/sec
S. CD-ROM Speed	4. Inch

(A) (P, 2) (Q, 1), (R, 4) (S, 3)
(B) (P, 1) (Q, 2) (R, 3) (S, 4)
(C) (P, 3) (Q, 4) (R, 2) (S, 1)
(D) (P, 4) (Q, 3) (R, 1) (S, 2)

333. MICR code is used in
(A) Letters (B) Cheques
(C) Punched Cards (D) Magnetic Tapes

334. A commonly accepted proper behaviour in the net is called
(A) Net manners (B) Web manners
(C) Net protocols (D) Netiquette

335. CAD stands for
(A) Computer Aided Design
(B) Computer Arithmetic Design
(C) Computer Analogue Design
(D) Computer Architecture Developments

336. GUI is the abbreviation of
(A) Groupware User Interface
(B) Graphic User Interface
(C) Graphic User Identification
(D) Graphic Universal Imaging

337. A web tool that consists of a searchable data of websites is called
(A) Google (B) Web directory
(C) Search engine (D) World Wide Web

338. WiFi is the abbreviation for
(A) Wireless Identity for Internet
(B) World Wide Internet for Fast Information
(C) World Wide Imaging for Intelligence
(D) Wireless Fidelity

339. VIRUS is
(A) Vital Information Research Under Search
(B) Very Important Research Upon Speed
(C) Vital Information Resources Under Seige
(D) Very Important Resources Under Seige.

340. Periodic maintenance of computing systems include
(A) Regular backups on data
(B) Reformatting hard disks
(C) Replacing backup batteries
(D) All of these

341. Which of the following is the appropriate definition of a computer ?
(A) Computer is a machine that can process information.
(B) Computer is an electronic device that can store, retrieve and process both qualitative and quantitative data quickly and accurately.
(C) Computer is an electronic device that can store, retrieve and quickly process only quantitative data.
(D) Computer is a machine that can store, retrieve and process quickly and accurately only qualitative information

342. Information and Communication Technology includes
(A) On line learning
(B) Learning through the use of EDUSAT
(C) Web Based Learning
(D) All the above

343. Which of the following is the appropriate format of URL of e-mail ?
(A) www_mail.com
(B) www@mail.com
(C) WWW@mail.com
(D) www.mail.com

344. In computers, 'WAN' and 'LAN' are
(A) Techniques for the maximum use of operating system
(B) Techniques for the establishment of network among computers.
(C) Internal hardware parts
(D) None of the above

345. 'Banker's Algorithm' is
(A) A method to prevent the deadlock condition
(B) A machine for capturing frequencies
(C) A medium to spread virus
(D) None of the above

346. 'Half adder' and 'full adder' are
(A) Integrated circuit
(B) Combinational circuit
(C) Logic gates
(D) None of the above

347. 'Incript' and decript' are
(A) Storage of date
(B) Coding and decoding of messages
(C) Techniques of collecting date
(D) None of the above

348. Band width is
(A) Difference between the highest and lowest frequencies of a composite signal
(B) Highest frequency of signal
(C) Lowest frequency of signal
(D) None of the above

349. The size of operator is
(A) Very big (B) Very small
(C) Varies with the variation of the type of operator
(D) Like a bowl

350. Blue-tooth occurs through
(A) Microwave (B) Ultraviolet rays
(C) Sun light (D) None of these

351. To produce obstacles in the way of communication medium is known as
(A) Slap (B) Resonance
(C) Amplitude (D) Frequency

352. A computer is that machine which works more like a human brain. This definition of computer is
(A) Correct (B) Incorrect
(C) Partially correct (D) None of these

353. Line access and avoidance of collision are the main functions of
(A) the CPU
(B) the monitor
(C) network protocols
(D) wide area networks

354. In the hypermedia database, information bits are stored in the form of
(A) signals (B) cubes
(C) nodes (D) symbols

355. Communications bandwidth that has the highest capacity and is used by microwave, cable and fibre optics lines is known as
(A) hyper-link (B) broadband
(C) bus width (D) carrier wave

356. An electronic bill board that has a short text or graphical advertising message is referred to as
(A) bulletin (B) strap
(C) bridge line (D) banner

357. Which of the following is not the characteristic of a computer ?
(A) computer is an electrical machine
(B) computer cannot think at its own
(C) computer processes information error free
(D) computer can hold data for any length of time

358. Which of the following is *not a* Computer language ?
(A) PASCAL (B) UNIX
(C) FORTRAN (D) COBOL

359. A key-board has at least
(A) 91 keys (B) 111 keys
(C) 101 keys (D) 121 keys

360. An E-mail address is composed of
(A) two parts (B) four parts
(C) three parts (D) five parts

361. Corel Draw is a popular
(A) Illustration programme
(C) Text programme
(B) Programming language
(D) None of the above

362. ASCII and EBCDIC are the popular character coding systems. What does EBCDIC stand for?
(A) Extended Binary Coded Decimal Interchange Code
(B) Extended Bit Code Decimal Interchange Code
(C) Extended Bit Case Decimal Interchange Code
(D) Extended Binary Case Decimal Interchange Code

363. A storage area used to store data to compensate for the difference in speed at which the different units can handle data is
(A) Memory (B) Buffer
(C) Accumulator (D) Address

364. Which type of computers use the 8-bit code called EBCDIC?
(A) Minicomputers
(B) Microcomputers
(C) Mainframe computers
(D) Super computer

365. To produce high quality graphics (hard-copy) in color, you would want to use
(A) RGB monitor (B) Plotter
(C) Ink-jet printer (D) Laser printer

366. The output quality of a printer is measured by
(A) Dots per sq. inch
(B) Dots per inch
(C) Dots printed per unit time
(D) All of the above

367. Which of the following was a special purpose computer?
(A) ABC (B) ENIAC
(C) EDVAC (D) All of these

368. A high quality CAD system uses the following for printing drawing and graphs
(A) Dot matrix printer
(B) Digital plotter
(C) Line printer
(D) All of the above

369. Which of the following is not an input device?
(A) OCR
(B) Optical scanners
(C) Voice recognition device
(D) COM (Computer Output to Microfilm)

370. The accuracy of the floating-point numbers representable in two 16-bit words of a computer is approximately
(A) 16 digits (B) 6 digits
(C) 9 digits (D) All of above

371. Regarding a VDU, which statement is more correct?
(A) It is an output device
(B) It is an input device
(C) It is a peripheral device
(D) It is hardware item

372. Which of the following is not processing?
(A) arranging (B) manipulating
(C) calculating (D) gathering

373. Before a disk drive can access any sector record, a computer program has to provide the record's disk address. What information does this address specify?
(A) Track number (B) Sector number
(C) Surface number (D) All of above

374. What is the responsibility of the logical unit in the CPU of a computer?
(A) To produce result
(B) To compare numbers
(C) To control flow of information
(D) To do math's works

375. If in a computer, 16 bits are used to specify address in a RAM, the number of addresses will be
(A) 216 (B) 65,536
(C) 64K (D) Any of the above

376. Instruction in computer languages consists of
(A) OPCODE (B) OPERAND
(C) Both of above (D) None of above

377. From which generation operating systems were developed?
(A) First (B) Second
(C) Third (D) Fourth

378. How many address lines are needed to address each machine location in a 2048 × 4 memory chip?
(A) 10 (B) 11
(C) 8 (D) 12

379. Properly arranged data is called
(A) Field (B) Words
(C) Information (D) File

380. Multi user systems provided cost savings for small business because they use a single processing unit to link several
(A) Personal computers
(B) Workstations
(C) Dumb terminals
(D) Mainframes

381. What are the three decisions making operations performed by the ALU of a computer?
(A) Grater than (B) Less than
(C) Equal to (D) All of these

382. The word processing task associated with changing the appearance of a document is
(A) Editing (B) Writing
(C) Formatting (D) All of above

383. The difference between memory and storage is that memory is ______ and storage is ______.
(A) Temporary, permanent
(B) Permanent, temporary
(C) Slow, fast
(D) All of above

384. What is required when more than one person uses a central computer at the same time?
(A) Light pen (B) Mouse
(C) Digitizer (D) Terminal

385. Once you load the suitable program and provide required data, computer does not need human intervention. This feature is known as
(A) Accuracy (B) Reliability
(C) Versatility (D) Automatic

386. Modern Computers are very reliable but they are not
(A) Fast (B) Powerful
(C) Infallible (D) Cheap

387. Which of the following memory medium is not used as main memory system?
(A) Magnetic core (B) Semiconductor
(C) Magnetic tape
(D) Both semiconductor and magnetic tape

388. The storage subsystem in a microcomputer consists mainly of ______ or ______ media with varying capacities.

(A) Memory or video
(B) Magnetic or optical
(C) Optical or memory
(D) Video or magnetic

389. Program designed to perform specific tasks is known as
(A) system software
(B) application software
(C) utility programs
(D) operating system

390. What is a compiler?
(A) A compiler does a conversion line by line as the program is run
(B) A compiler converts the whole of a higher level program code into machine code in one step
(C) A compiler is a general purpose language providing very efficient execution
(D) None of the above

391. Which of the following require large computer memory?
(A) Imaging (B) Graphics
(C) Voice (D) All of Above

392. The first machine to successfully perform a long series of arithmetic and logical operations was
(A) ENIAC (B) Mark-I
(C) Analytic Engine (D) UNIVAC-1

393. Which one is the largest space?
(A) kilobyte (B) petabyte
(C) terrabyte (D) gigabyte

394. An error in software or hardware is called a bug. What is the alternative computer jargon for it?
(A) Leech (B) Squid
(C) Slug (D) Glitch

395. The BIOS is the abbreviation of
(A) Basic Input Output System
(B) Best Input Output System
(C) Basic Input Output Symbol
(D) Base Input Output System

396. The first web browser is
(A) Mosaic (B) Netscape
(C) Internet explorer (D) Collabra

397. In a computer _____ is capable to store single binary bit.
(A) Capacitor (B) Flip flop
(C) Register (D) Inductor

398. Operating system, editors, and debuggers come under
(A) System Software
(B) Application Software
(C) Utilities
(D) None of the above

399. What is meant by a dedicated computer?
(A) Which is used by one person only
(B) Which is assigned one and only one task
(C) Which uses one kind of software
(D) Which is meant for application software

400. The notable features like keyboards, monitors, GUI were developed in
(A) First generation
(B) Second generation
(C) Third generation
(D) Fourth generation

401. What is an interpreter?
(A) An interpreter does the conversion line by line as the program is run
(B) An interpreter is the representation of the system being designed
(C) An interpreter is a general purpose language providing very efficient execution
(D) None of the above

402. EEPROM stands for
(A) Electrically Erasable Programmable Read Only Memory
(B) Easily Erasable Programmable Read Only Memory
(C) Electronic Erasable Programmable Read Only Memory
(D) None of the above

403. Which device can understand difference between data & programs?
(A) Input device (B) Output device
(C) Memory (D) Microprocessor

404. What is the full form of USB as used in computer related activities ?
(1) Ultra Security Block
(2) Universal Security Block
(3) Universal Serial Bus
(4) United Serial Bus

405. Snowbol is an/a
(A) Operating system (B) HLL
(C) Software (D) Search engine

406. What is the full form of USB as used in computer related activities ?
(A) Ultra Security Block
(B) Universal Security Block
(C) Universal Serial Bus
(D) United Serial Bus

407. 1 nibble equals to
(A) 1 bits (B) 2 bits
(C) 4 bits (D) 8 bits

408. A disadvantage of the laser printer is
(A) It is quieter than an impact printer
(B) It is very slow
(C) The output is of a lower quality
(D) None of the above

409. Which unit holds data temporarily?
(A) Input unit
(B) Secondary storage unit
(C) Output Unit
(D) Primary Memory Unit

410. The term GIGO is related to which characteristic of computers?
(A) Speed (B) Automatic
(C) Accuracy (D) Reliability

411. Who used punched cards practically for the first time in the history of computers?
(A) Charles Babbage
(B) Dr. Herman Hollerith
(C) Howard Aikin
(D) Joseph Jacquard

412. An input /output device at which data enters or leaves a computer system is
(A) Keyboard (B) Terminal
(C) Printer (D) Plotter

413. The first general purpose electronic computer in the world was
(A) UNIVAC (B) EDVAC
(C) ENIAC (D) All of above

414. The qualitative or quantitative attribute of a variable or set of variables is termed as
(A) data (B) information
(C) both of above (D) none of above

415. Main storage is also called
(A) Accumulator (B) Control Unit
(C) Register Unit (D) Memory

416. Which of the following are (is) considered to be video component?
(A) Resolution (B) Color depth
(C) Refresh rate (D) All of these

417. To prevent the loss of data during power failures, use a(n)
(A) Encryption program
(B) Surge protector
(C) Firewall
(D) UPS

418. Which of the following is a secondary memory device?
(A) Keyboard (B) Disk
(C) ALU (D) All of these

419. The scrambling of code is known as
(A) Encryption (B) a firewall
(C) Scrambling (D) Password proofing

420. Which of the following memories must be refreshed many times per second?
(A) Static RAM (B) Dynamic RAM
(C) EPROM (D) ROM

421. What do you call the translator which takes assembly language program as input & produce machine language code as output?
(A) Compiler (B) Interpreter
(C) Debugger (D) Assembler

422. What is the most common tool used to restrict access to a computer system?
(A) User logins (B) Passwords
(B) Computer keys
(D) Access-control software

423. Hardware or software designed to guard against unauthorized access to a computer network is known as a(n)
(A) Hacker-proof program
(B) Firewall
(C) Hacker-resistant server
(D) Encryption safe wall

424. The subject of cybernetics deals with the science of
(A) Genetics
(B) Control and communication
(C) Molecular biology
(D) Biochemistry

425. Which of the following memories has the shortest access times?
(A) Cache memory
(B) Magnetic bubble memory
(C) Magnetic core memory
(D) RAM

426. What is the name of an application program that gathers user information and sends it to someone through the Internet?
(A) A virus (B) Spybot
(C) Logic bomb (D) Security patch

427. ________ are used to identify a user who returns to a Website.
(A) Cookies (B) Plug-ins
(C) Scripts (D) ASPs

428. ______ are attempts by individuals to obtain confidential information from you by falsifying their identity.
(A) Phishing (B) Computer viruses
(C) Spyware scams (D) Viruses

429. Hackers
(A) all have the same motive
(B) break into other people's computers
(C) may legally break into computers as long as they do not do any damage
(D) are people who are allergic to computers

430. What type of computers are client computers (most of the time) in a client-server system?
(A) Mainframe (B) Mini-computer
(C) Microcomputer (D) PDA

431. A computer cannot 'boot' if it does not have the
(A) Compiler (B) Loader
(C) Operating System (D) Assembler

432. _______ is the science that attempts to produce machines that display the same type of intelligence that humans do.
(A) Nanoscience
(B) Nanotechnology
(C) Simulation
(D) Artificial intelligence (Al)

433. The difference between people with access to computers and the Internet and those without this access is known as the
(A) Digital divide (B) Internet divide
(C) Web divide (D) E-illiteracy

434. Computers manipulate data in many ways, and this manipulation is called
(A) upgrading (B) processing
(C) batching (D) utilizing

435. The ability to recover and read deleted or damaged files from a criminal's computer is an example of a law enforcement speciality called
(A) robotics (B) simulation
(C) computer forensics (D) animation

436. _______ is the measurement of things such as fingerprints and retinal scans used for security access.
(A) Biometrics
(B) Bio measurement
(C) Computer security
(D) Smart weapon machinery

437. A person who used his or her expertise to gain access to other people's computers to get information illegally or do damage is a
(A) Hacker (B) spammer
(C) instant messenger (D) programmer

438. When a computer is switched on, the booting process performs
(A) Integrity Test
(B) Power-On Self-Test
(C) Correct Functioning Test
(D) Reliability Test

439. Large transaction processing systems in automated organisations use
(A) Online Processing
(B) Batch Processing
(C) Once-a-day Processing
(D) End-of-day Processing

440. The common name for the crime of stealing passwords is
(A) Jacking (B) Identity theft
(C) Spoofing (D) Hacking

441. Malicious software is known as
(A) Badware (B) Malware
(C) Maliciousware (D) Illegalware

442. A program that performs a useful task while simultaneously allowing destructive acts is a
(A) Worm (B) Trojan horse
(C) Virus (D) Macro virus

443. An intentionally disruptive program that spreads from program to program or from disk to disk is known as a
(A) Trojan horse (B) Virus
(C) Time bomb
(D) Time-related bomb sequence

444. In world the total number of users of facebook are
(A) 1 billion (B) 1.71 billion
(C) 3 billion (D) 0.5 billion

445. Social site used for marketing is
(A) Instagram (B) Twitter
(C) Google plus (D) Vimeo

446. Indian users can access facebook in
(A) 10 languages (B) 12 languages
(C) 8 languages (D) 15 languages

447. The microblogging site is
(A) Facebook (B) Twitter
(C) Instagram (D) None of these

448. Most frequently used social network for recruiting is
(A) Twitter (B) Linkedin
(C) Naukri (D) Monster

449. In India total number of Internet users are
(A) 470 million (B) 200 million
(C) 100 million (D) 250 million

450. The position of India in online market in world is
(A) 2nd (B) 4th
(C) 3rd (D) 5th

451. The first network that planted the seeds of Internet was
(A) ARPANET (B) NSF net
(C) V net (D) both (A) and (B)

452 Voice mail, E-mail, online service, the Internet and the www are all example of
(A) Computer Categories
(B) Connectivity
(C) Telecommuting
(D) None of the above

453. Website is a collection of
(A) HTML documents
(B) Graphic files
(C) Andro and video files
(D) All of the above

454. The ground station in VSAT communication is called
(A) HTTP (B) Hub
(C) Multiplexer (D) None of these

455. A small network making up the internet and also having a small numbers within it is called
(A) Host (B) Address
(C) Subdomain (D) None of these

456. Cell based architecture is known as
(A) ATM (B) FDDI
(C) LAN (D) Client Server

457. For a small Website, one needs to buy space from the
(A) ISP
(B) Telephone exchange
(C) Network administration
(D) None of the above

458. The Internet standard is
(A) MIME (B) BIN HEX
(C) UNENCOOING (D) None of these

459. File to the Website is transferred by using
(A) HTTP (B) ASCII
(C) FTP (D) None of these

460. To use Telnet and the host's resources you will need to know
(A) TCP/IP address
(B) Electronic address
(C) The address of the internet host
(D) None of the above

461. Name the software which comes with a basic telnet client package
(A) Excel
(B) Word for Windows
(C) Windows 98 (D) None of these

462. A simple protocol used for fetching e-mail from a mailbox is
(A) POP 2 (B) POP 3
(C) IMAP (D) None of these

463. A popular application of computer networking is the world wide web of newsgroup called
(A) News (B) Gate way
(C) Netnews (D) None of these

464. The program supplied by VSNL when you ask for Internet connection for the e-mail access is
(A) ISP (B) PINE
(C) Hot Dog (D) None of these

465. The E-mail component of Internet explorer is called
(A) Message box
(B) Outlook express
(C) Messenger Mailbox
(D) None of the above

466. Read the following two statements :
I : Information and Communication Technology (ICT) is considered a subset of Information Technology (IT).
II: The 'right to use' a piece of software is termed as copyright.
Which of the above statement(s) is/are CORRECT ?
(A) Both I and II (B) Neither I nor II
(C) II only (D) I only

467. At which of the following institutions ERNET is used to connect computers?
(A) IISCs
(B) IITs
(C) National Centre for software technology
(D) All the above

468. Which of the following is not included in the four basic dimension of ICT?
(A) Skills (B) Infrastructure
(C) Attitude (D) Personal

469. Which of the following open source-learning platform has been developed by IIT-kanpur?
(A) e-Gyan (B) e-Saraswati
(C) Brihaspati (D) None of these

470. Which of the following is/are the main challenge/s in ICT adoption in Indian universities?
(A) Lack of technological readiness
(B) Poor implementation of ICT initiatives
(C) Linguistic barrier
(D) All the above

471. Video-conferencing is an example of
(A) Synchronous technologies
(B) Asynchronous technologies
(C) Both synchronous and asynchronous
(D) None of the above

472. Digital divide is the term used is context of differentiation in use of IT/ICT?
(A) Developed and developing nations
(B) Urban and rural India
(C) Both (A) and (B)
(D) None of the above

473. Which of the following institutions launched a knowledge repository e-Gyankosh in 2005 that aims at storing and preserving digital learning resources?
(A) IIT-kanpur
(B) IGNOU
(C) Prayagraj University
(D) Delhi University

474. The institution promoted by the Department of IT to provide communication infrastructure and services to academic research institutions in India is
(A) INFLIBNET (B) UGC
(C) ERNET (D) None of these

475. The bouquet of FM radio channels which broadcast programs contributed by institutions such as IGNOU and IITs is
(A) Gyan Vani (B) Gyan Darshan
(C) EDUSAT (D) None of these

476. Which of the following institutions has been working in the direction to develop a Virtual technical University in India?
(A) IGNOU (B) UGC
(C) NMCEIT (D) AICTE

477. The joint initiative of the IITs and IISc to provide e-learning through online web and video courses in many streams, specifically engineering in the country, by providing free online courseware is
(A) National Programme on technology enhanced Learning
(B) AICTENET
(C) NMCEIT
(D) None of the above

478. Which organization has been assigned the task to develop e-content of 996 courses belonging to engineering, sciences, technology, humanities and management?
(A) IIT-Madras (B) BITS Pilani
(C) IIT Mumbai (D) None of these

479. 'A-View', the software that has been developed under the NMEICT is basically developed for
(A) Teacher's training
(B) Technical training
(C) Student's training
(D) All the above

480. Web 2.0 tools have made traditional learning more social and personalized. Which of the following can be referred to as Web 2.0 tools?
(A) Blogs and Wikis
(B) Podcasts and Mashups
(C) Social networking communities
(D) All the above

481. Which of the following services can help students to access computer files from remote locations though mobile phones?
(A) Facebook (B) Renren
(C) Soonr (D) Twitter

482. Eklavya technology channel, started in 2003, is a distant-learning joint initiative between
(A) IIT and IGNOU
(B) UGC and AICTE
(C) IIT and AICTE
(D) IIIT and IGNOU

483. Virtual education refers to imparting instructions in a learning environment where the teacher and the students are separated by
(A) Time only
(B) Space only
(C) Both (A) and (B)
(D) None of the above

ANSWERS

1. (C) 2. (C) 3. (B) 4. (C) 5. (B) 6. (C) 7. (A) 8. (D) 9. (A) 10. (A)

11. (A) 12. (D) 13. (C) 14. (D) 15. (C) 16. (B) 17. (B) 18. (C) 19. (A) 20. (B)

21. (B) 22. (A) 23. (D) 24. (A) 25. (A) 26. (B) 27. (C) 28. (A) 29. (C) 30. (A)

31. (A) 32. (A) 33. (D) 34. (A) 35. (D) 36. (C) 37. (D) 38. (D) 39. (A) 40. (B)

41. (B) 42. (C) 43. (A) 44. (A) 45. (D) 46. (B) 47. (A) 48. (A) 49. (C) 50. (D)

51. (A) 52. (B) 53. (D) 54. (B) 55. (C) 56. (A) 57. (D) 58. (D) 59. (B) 60. (B)

61. (D) 62. (A) 63. (D) 64. (A) 65. (A) 66. (C) 67. (B) 68. (C) 69. (A) 70. (C)

71. (A) 72. (D) 73. (B) 74. (A) 75. (A) 76. (C) 77. (C) 78. (A) 79. (D) 80. (C)

81. (D) 82. (A) 83. (A) 84. (A) 85. (D) 86. (C) 87. (D) 88. (B) 89. (C) 90. (B)

91. (B) 92. (B) 93. (A) 94. (D) 95. (A) 96. (B) 97. (B) 98. (A) 99. (C) 100. (B)

101. (C) 102. (B) 103. (B) 104. (B) 105. (C) 106. (B) 107. (A) 108. (D) 109. (C) 110. (B)

111. (C) 112. (D) 113. (B) 114 (C) 115. (C) 116. (B) 117. (A) 118. (C) 119. (B) 120. (C)

121. (C) 122. (D) 123. (C) 124. (A) 125. (B) 126. (D) 127. (B) 128. (C) 129. (C) 130. (A)

131. (A) 132. (A) 133. (C) 134. (D) 135. (C) 136. (B) 137. (A) 138. (B) 139. (C) 140. (A)

141. (D) 142. (B) 143. (C) 144. (B) 145. (B) 146. (B) 147 (A) 148. (C) 149. (D) 150. (D)

151. (D) 152. (C) 153. (B) 154. (C) 155. (C) 156. (B) 157. (A) 158. (D) 159. (B) 160. (B)

161. (C) 162. (C) 163. (B) 164. (D) 165. (B) 166. (C) 167. (B) 168. (C) 169. (B) 170. (A)

171. (B) 172. (A) 173. (B) 174. (A) 175. (B) 176. (D) 177. (B) 178. (A) 179. (A) 180. (C)

181. (A) 182. (D) 183. (A) 184. (D) 185. (C) 186. (A) 187. (D) 188. (B) 189. (C) 190. (B)

191. (C) 192. (C) 193. (D) 194. (A) 195. (B) 196. (B) 197. (C) 198. (B) 199. (A) 200. (B)

201. (A) 202. (C) 203. (A) 204. (C) 205. (C) 206. (B) 207. (A) 208. (A) 209. (B) 210. (C)

211. (D) 212. (A) 213. (B) 214. (D) 215. (C) 216. (C) 217. (D) 218. (C) 219. (B) 220. (B)

221. (A) 222. (A) 223. (B) 224. (C) 225. (D) 226. (D) 227. (D) 228. (C) 229. (B) 230. (C)

231. (A) 232. (D) 233. (B) 234. (D) 235. (B) 236. (C) 237. (C) 238. (A) 239. (A) 240. (D)

241. (D) 242. (A) 243. (D) 244. (A) 245. (A) 246. (A) 247. (A) 248. (C) 249. (A) 250. (B)

251. (C) 252. (B) 253. (A) 254. (B) 255. (D) 256. (B) 257. (A) 258. (B) 259. (C) 260. (B)

261. (B) 262. (C) 263. (C) 264. (A) 265. (D) 266. (D) 267. (B) 268. (D) 269. (B) 270. (D)

271. (C) 272. (A) 273. (A) 274. (B) 275. (D) 276. (C) 277. (A) 278. (B) 279. (A) 280. (D)

281. (D) 282. (C) 283. (B) 284. (D) 285. (B) 286. (A) 287. (D) 288. (A) 289. (A) 290. (D)

291. (A) 292. (C) 293. (B) 294. (D) 295. (D) 296. (C) 297. (A) 298. (B) 299. (B) 300. (D)

301. (B) 302. (A) 303. (A) 304. (A) 305. (B) 306. (B) 307. (D) 308. (C) 309. (C) 310. (B)

311. (A) 312. (D) 313. (D) 314. (B) 315. (D) 316. (D) 317. (B) 318. (B) 319. (A) 320. (D)

321. (D) 322. (C) 323. (C) 324. (C) 325. (A) 326. (B) 327. (C) 328. (B) 329. (A) 330. (D)

331. (B) 332. (A) 333. (B) 334. (D) 335. (A) 336. (C) 337. (C) 338. (D) 339. (D) 340. (D)

341. (B) 342. (D) 343. (B) 344. (B) 345. (A) 346. (B) 347. (B) 348. (A) 349. (C) 350. (A)

351. (A) 352. (C) 353. (C) 354. (C) 355. (B) 356. (D) 357. (A) 358. (B) 359. (C) 360. (A)

361. (A) 362. (A) 363. (B) 364. (C) 365. (B) 366. (B) 367. (A) 368. (B) 369. (D) 370. (A)

371. (C) 372. (D) 373. (D) 374. (B) 375. (B) 376. (C) 377. (C) 378. (B) 379. (C) 380. (C)

381. (D) 382. (C) 383. (A) 384. (D) 385. (D) 386. (C) 387. (C) 388. (B) 389. (B) 390. (B)

391. (D) 392. (B) 393. (B) 394. (D) 395. (A) 396. (A) 397. (B) 398. (A) 399. (B) 400. (C)

401. (B) 402. (A) 403. (D) 404. (A) 405. (B) 406. (C) 407. (C) 408. (D) 409. (D) 410. (C)

411. (B) 412. (B) 413. (C) 414. (A) 415. (D) 416. (D) 417. (D) 418. (B) 419. (A) 420. (B)

421. (D) 422. (B) 423. (B) 424. (B) 425. (A) 426. (B) 427. (A) 428. (A) 429. (B) 430. (C)

431. (C) 432. (D) 433. (A) 434. (B) 435. (C) 436. (A) 437. (A) 438. (B) 439. (B) 440. (C)

441. (B) 442. (B) 443. (B) 444. (B) 445. (B) 446. (B) 447. (B) 448. (B) 449. (A) 450. (A)

451. (A) 452. (C) 453. (D) 454. (B) 455. (C) 456. (A) 457. (A) 458. (A) 459. (C) 460. (C)

461. (B) 462. (B) 463. (C) 464 (B) 465. (B) 466. (B) 467. (D) 468. (C) 469. (C) 470. (D)

471. (A) 472. (C) 473. (B) 474. (C) 475. (A) 476. (D) 477. (A) 478. (A) 479. (A) 480. (D)

481. (B) 482. (A) 483. (C)

PEOPLE, DEVELOPMENT AND ENVIRONMENT

Syllabus

- **Development and Environment:** Millennium Development and Sustainable Development Goals.
- **Human and Environment Interaction:** Anthropogenic Activities and their Impacts on Environment.
- **Environmental Issues:** Local, Regional and Global; Air Pollution, Water Pollution, Soil Pollution, Noise Pollution, Waste (Solid, Liquid, Biomedical, Hazardous, Electronic), Climate Change and its Socio-Economic and Political Dimensions.
- Impacts of Pollutants on Human Health.
- **Natural and energy resources:** Solar, Wind, Soil, Hydro, Geothermal, Biomass, Nuclear and Forests.
- **Natural hazards and disasters:** Mitigation Strategies.
- **Environmental Protection Act (1986)**, National Action Plan on Climate Change, International Agreements/efforts – Montreal Protocol, Rio Summit, Convention on Biodiversity, Kyoto Protocol, Paris Agreement, International Solar Alliance.

DEVELOPMENT AND ENVIRONMENT

Millennium Development Goals (MDGs)

The United Nations Millennium Development Goals are eight goals that all 191 UN member states have agreed to try to achieve by the year 2015. The United Nations Millennium Declaration, signed in September 2000 commits world leaders to combat poverty, hunger, disease, illiteracy, environmental degradation, and discrimination against women. The MDGs are derived from this Declaration, and all have specific targets and indicators.

The Eight Millennium Development Goals are:

1. to eradicate extreme poverty and hunger;
2. to achieve universal primary education;
3. to promote gender equality and empower women;
4. to reduce child mortality;
5. to improve maternal health;
6. to combat HIV / AIDS, malaria, and other diseases;
7. to ensure environmental sustainability; and
8. to develop a global partnership for development.

The MDGs are inter-dependent; all the MDG influence health, and health influences all the MDGs. For example, better health enables children to learn and adults to earn. Gender equality is essential to the achievement of better health. Reducing poverty, hunger and environmental degradation positively influences, but also depends on, better health.

Sustainable Development Goals

The Sustainable Development Goals (SDGs) are a collection of 17 global goals set by the United Nations General Assembly in 2015 for the year 2030. The SDGs are part of Resolution 70/1 of the United Nations General Assembly, the 2030 Agenda.

The Sustainable Development Goals are: (1) No Poverty, (2) Zero Hunger, (3) Good Health and Well-being, (4) Quality Education, (5) Gender Equality, (6) Clean Water and Sanitation, (7) Affordable and Clean Energy, (8) Decent Work and Economic Growth (9) Industry, Innovation, and Infrastructure, (10) Reducing Inequality, (11) Sustainable Cities and Communities, (12) Responsible Consumption and Production, (13) Climate Action, (14) Life Below Water, (15) Life On Land, (16) Peace, Justice, and Strong Institutions, (17) Partnerships for the Goals.

Description

There are 169 targets for the 17 goals. Each target has between 1 and 3 indicators used to measure progress toward reaching the targets. In total, there are 232 approved indicators that will measure compliance. The United Nations Development Programme has been asked to provide easy to understand lists of targets and facts and figures for each of the 17 SDGs.

UNDP Plan to Achieve the Sustainable Development Goals

The 2030 agenda for Sustainable Development adopted by all United Nations Member States in 2015, provides a shared blueprint for peace and prosperity for people and the planet, now and into the future. At its heart are the 17 Sustainable Development Goals (SDGs), which are an urgent call for action by all countries – developed and developing – in a global partnership. They recognize that ending poverty and other deprivations must go hand-in-hand with strategies that improve health and education, reduce inequality, and spur economic growth - all while tackling climate change and working to preserve our oceans and forests.

The SDGs build on decades of work by countries and the UN, including the UN Department of Economic and Social Affairs:

- In June 1992, at the Earth Summit in Rio de Janeiro, Brazil, more than 178 countries adopted Agenda 21, a comprehensive plan of action to build a global partnership for sustainable development to improve human lives and protect the environment.

- Member States unanimously adopted the Millennium Declaration at the Millennium Summit in September 2000 at UN Headquarters in New York. The Summit led to the elaboration of eight Millennium Development Goals (MDGs) to reduce extreme poverty by 2015.
- The Johannesburg Declaration on Sustainable Development and the Plan of Implementation, adopted at the World Summit on Sustainable Development in South Africa in 2002, reaffirmed the global community's commitments to poverty eradication and the environment, and built on Agenda 21 and the Millennium Declaration by including more emphasis on multilateral partnerships.
- At the United Nations Conference on Sustainable Development (Rio+20) in Rio de Janeiro, Brazil, in June 2012, Member States adopted the outcome document "The Future We Want" in which they decided, inter alia, to launch a process to develop a set of SDGs to build upon the MDGs and to establish the UN High-level Political Forum on Sustainable Development. The Rio +20 outcome also contained other measures for implementing sustainable development, including mandates for future programmes of work in development financing, small island developing states and more.
- In 2013, the General Assembly set up a 30-member Open Working Group to develop a proposal on the SDGs.
- In January 2015, the General Assembly began the negotiation process on the post-2015 development agenda. The process culminated in the subsequent adoption of the 2030 Agenda for Sustainable Development, with 17 SDGs at its core, at the UN Sustainable Development Summit in September 2015.
- 2015 was a landmark year for multilateralism and international policy shaping, with the adoption of several major agreements:
  - Sendai Framework for Disaster Risk Reduction (March 2015)
  - Addis Ababa Action Agenda on Financing for Development (July 2015)
  - Transforming our world: the 2030 Agenda for Sustainable Development with its 17 SDGs was adopted at the UN Sustainable Development Summit in New York in September 2015.
  - Paris Agreement on Climate Change (December 2015)
- Now, the annual High-level Political Forum on Sustainable Development serves as the central UN platform for the follow-up and review of the SDGs.

Today, the Division for Sustainable Development Goals (DSDG) in the United Nations Department of Economic and Social Affairs (UNDESA) provides substantive support and capacity-building for the SDGs and their related thematic issues, including water, energy, climate, oceans, urbanization, transport, science and technology, the Global Sustainable Development Report (GSDR), partnerships and Small Island Developing States. DSDG plays a key role in the evaluation of UN systemwide implementation of the 2030 Agenda and on advocacy and outreach activities relating to the SDGs. In order to make the 2030 Agenda a reality, broad ownership of the SDGs must translate into a strong commitment by all stakeholders to implement the global goals. DSDG aims to help facilitate this engagement.

HUMAN AND ENVIRONMENT INTERACTION

Anthropogenic Activities

The coastal zone are regions where landmass, oceans and atmosphere interact. It represents about 18% of the earth surface. About 70% of the world cities are located in the coastal zone and about 25% of the world population live in coastal area. The coastal zone provides valuable living and non-living resources. It has the highest biological diversity and productivity. It is estimated to contribute about 25% of the global biological production and support major fisheries. The coastal marine environment provides valuable food and energy resources beside performing essential functions such as carbon burial and nutrient recycling. Ecologists and environmental scientists have long sought to provide accurate scientific assessments of the environmental ramifications of human activities. Despite this effort, there remains considerable uncertainty about the environmental consequences of many human-induced impacts, particularly in marine habitats. The impact of anthropogenic activity cumulatively results in structural and functional responses of the water ecosystems and its biota. Therefore the assessment of anthropogenic impact is extremely important for understanding the ecology and biodiversity of coastal zone and management of its resources.

ANTHROPOGENIC (MAN-MADE) SOURCES

- These are mostly related to the burning of multiple types of fuel.
- Stationary Sources include smoke stack of power plants, manufacturing facilities (factories) and waste incinerators, as well as furnaces and other types of fuel-burning heating devices.
- In developing and poor countries, traditional biomass burning is the major source of air pollutants; traditional biomass includes wood, crop waste and dung.
- Mobile Sources include motor vehicles, marine vessels, and aircraft.
- Chemicals', dust and controlled burn practices In agriculture and forest management'.
- Controlled or prescribed burning is a technique sometimes used in forest management, farming, prairie restoration or greenhouse gas abatement.
- Fire is a natural part of both forest and grassland ecology and controlled fire can be a tool for foresters.
- Controlled burning stimulates the germination of some desirable forest trees, thus renewing the forest.
- Fumes from paint, hair spray, varnish, aerosol sprays and other solvents.
- Waste deposition in landfills, which generate methane.
- Methane is highly flammable and may form explosive mixtures with air. Methane is also an asphyxiant and may displace oxygen in an enclosed space.
- Asphyxia or suffocation may result if the oxygen concentration is reduced to below 19.5% by displacement.
- Military resources, such as nuclear weapons, toxic gases, germ warfare and rocketry.

The most harmful impact due to anthropogenic activities is pollution. When something is added to the environment which is very harmful, poisonous or fatal to the animal, people surrounding it and other living things it is called as pollution. In simple term pollution is a contamination by a chemical or other pollutant that renders part of the environment unfit for intended or desired use. Marine pollution is the result of products being thrown into seas and oceans, mostly by mankind: domestic waste (sewage and rubbish, pollutants in runoff water), industrial waste (hydrocarbons, metals, synthetic chemical and organic substances, radionuclides) and agricultural waste (fertilisers, pesticides). Simultaneous impacts of several factors can cause synergistic effects when the conse-

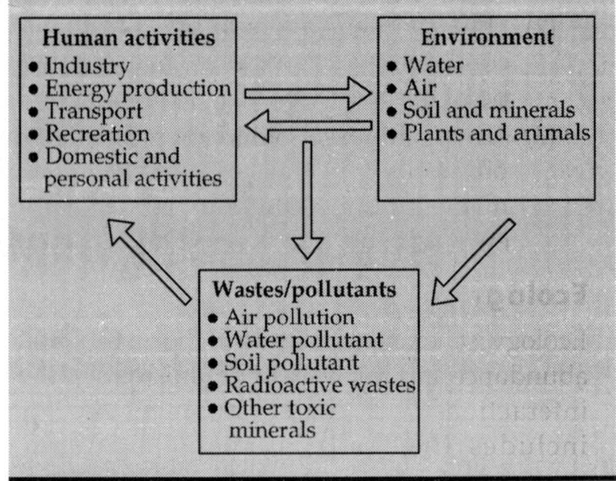

quences can exceed the mere sum of the effects caused by each factor separately. The coastal states bordering Indian Ocean are densely populated and industrialized. As a consequence, the coastal areas are getting adversely affected by many human activities that result in inputs of industrial effluent of toxic nature, nutrients and harmful substances.

Important Terms Related to Population

- Population density - relates population to area, (average) the total population in a country or region divided by its area (people/km^2).
- Crude birth rate - the number of births per 1000 people (CBR).
- Crude death rate - the number of deaths per 1000 people (CDR).
- Natural increase - The difference between the CBR & the CDR usually expressed as a % per year. Natural increase (%) = CBR - CDR.
- Demographic transition - describes what has happened to birth & death rates in today's MEDCs since 1800.
- Migration - controls the shape of population pyramids, at a natural scale, birth & death rates are most important, migration is important in smaller areas (cities/ regions).
- Life expectancy - how long people in certain countries are expected to live.
- Age dependency - percentage of population that depend on economic support (e.g. pension for the elderly, school for the young).
- Replacement level - the rate that is needed to replace both parents.
- Family planning - birth rates have fallen where children have been immunised & where mothers have received some education.
- Population pyramids - age & sex structure of a population can be shown in this type of graph, factors control the shape, birth & death rates & migration.

Environment

Environment can be defined in a number of ways. For example,

(1) "Environment is the sum of all social, economical, biological, physical or chemical factors which constitute the surroundings of man, who is both creator and moulder of his environment.'

(2) "Environment refers to the sum total of conditions which surround man at a given point in space and time."

(3) "Environment is the representative of physical components of the earth wherein man is the important factor influencing his environment."

Ecology

Ecology is the scientific study of the distributions, abundance and relations of organisms and their interactions with the environment. Ecology includes the study of plant and animal

COMPONENTS OF ENVIRONMENT

Environment consists of the following three important components :

1. Abiotic or Non-living Component.
2. Biotic or Living Component
3. Energy Component

The abiotic or physical environment is subdivided into three categories :

1. Lithosphere (Solid Earth)
2. Hydrosphere (Water Component)
3. Atmosphere (Gaseous Envelope)

The biotic component of environment consists of flora and fauna, including man as the important factor. Abiotic and biotic components constitute together the Biome Environment.

The energy component includes solar energy, geochemical energy, thermo-electrical energy, hydro-electrical energy, nuclear atomic energy etc. Energy due to radiation and other sources also plays an important role to maintain the real life of organisms.

populations, plant and animal communities and ecosystems. Ecosystems describe the web or network of relations among organisms at different scales of organization. Since ecology refers to any form of biodiversity, ecologists research everything from tiny bacteria's role in nutrient recycling to the effects of tropical rain forest on the Earth's atmosphere. The discipline of ecology emerged from the natural sciences in the late 19th century. Ecology is not synonymous with environment, environmentalism, or environmental science. Ecology is closely related to the disciplines of physiology, evolution, genetics and behavior.

Like many of the natural sciences, a conceptual understanding of ecology is found in the broader details of study, including:

- life processes explaining adaptations.
- distribution and abundance of organisms.
- the movement of materials and energy through living communities.
- the successional development of ecosystems, and
- the abundance and distribution of biodiversity in context of the environment.

Ecology is distinguished from natural history, which deals primarily with the descriptive study of organisms. It is a sub-discipline of biology, which is the study of life.

There are many practical applications of ecology in conservation biology, wetland management, natural resource management (agriculture, forestry, fisheries), city planning (urban ecology), community health, economics, basic & applied science and it provides a conceptual framework for understanding and researching human social interaction (human ecology).

ECOSYSTEM

The ecosystem is the set of species in a given area that interact among themselves, through processes such as predation, parasitism, competition and symbiosis, and with their abiotic environment to disintegrate and become part of cycles of energy and nutrients. The species of the ecosystem, including bacteria, fungi, plants and animals, are dependent on each other. The relationships between species and their environment facilitate the flow of matter and energy within the ecosystem.

The concept of the ecosystem has evolved since its origin. The term, coined in the 1930s, belongs to British botanists Roy Clapham (1904-1990) and Sir Arthur Tansley (1871-1955). It was originally applied to units of diverse spatial scale; from a weathered piece of tree trunk to a pond, a region or even the entire biosphere of the planet, the only requirement being that organisms, physical environment and interactions could exist within them.

More recently, the ecosystem has had a geographical focus and has become analogous to formations or vegetation types, e.g., scrub, pine forest, grassland, etc. This simplification ignores the fact that the limits of some vegetation types are indistinct, while the boundaries of ecosystems are not. The transition zones between ecosystems are known as ecotones.

Ecological Pyramids

Ecological pyramids are graphical representations of relationship between the different trophic levels of food chains on the basis of energy, number and biomass productivity. It can be observed that these pyramids are in the shape of actual pyramids with the base being the broadest, which is covered by the lowest trophic level i.e., producers. The next level is occupied by the next trophic level, i.e., the primary consumer and so on as that of a food chain. All the calculations for construction of these types of ecological pyramids must take into account all the organisms in a particular trophic level because a sample space of a few number or a few species will end up giving huge level of errors.

Types of Ecological Pyramids

There basically exists three types of ecological pyramids. They are as follows:

- **Pyramid of Numbers.** In this pyramid, the number of organisms in each trophic level is considered as a level in the pyramid. The pyramid of numbers is usually upright except for the some situations like that of the detritus food chain, where many organisms feed on one dead plant or animal.

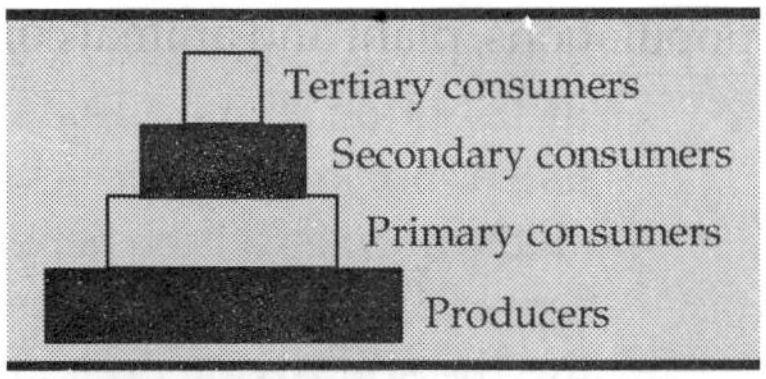

- **Pyramid of Biomass.** In this pyramid, each level takes into account the amount of biomass produced by each trophic level. The pyramid of biomass is also upright except of that observed in oceans where large numbers of zooplanktons depend on relatively smaller number of phytoplanktons.

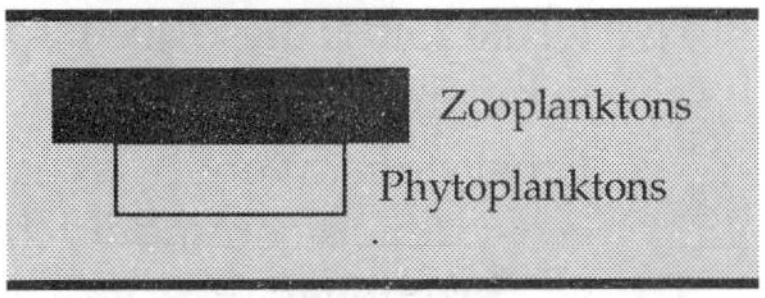

- **Pyramid of Energy.** Pyramid of energy is the only pyramid which is always upright as the energy flow in a food chain is always unidirectional. Also, with every increasing trophic level, some energy is lost into the environment.

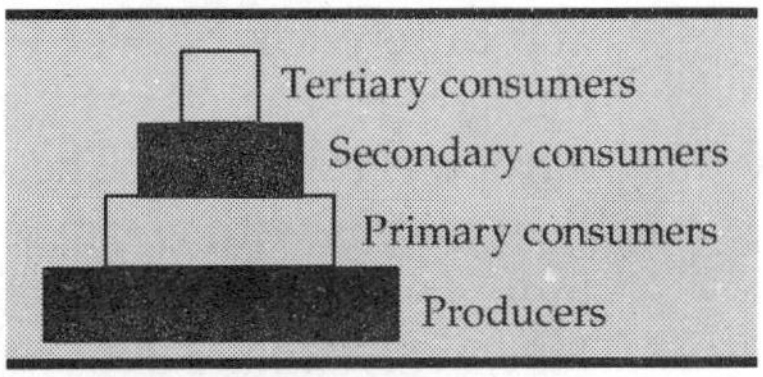

Limitations of the Ecological Pyramids

1. More than one species may occupy multiple trophic levels as in case of food web. Thus, this system does not take into account food webs.
2. The saprophytes are not considered in any of the pyramids even though they form an important part of various ecosystem.

Biodiversity

1. Biodiversity, or biological diversity, is used to describe the immense variety and richness of life on Earth. The term itself is of relatively recent origin: it was coined during the National Forum on Biodiversity in 1986 under the auspices of the National Academy of Sciences and the Smithsonian Institution. A follow-up volume entitled –Biodiversity – edited by Harvard biologist E.O. Wilson, further entrenched the word in the scientific lingo. The popular use of the term (and the Forum that spawned it) grew out of a concern that efforts were needed to conserve, not just particularly charismatic animals, but the diversity of life around the world as the human population grew, extinction rates climbed, and scientists discovered both economic and ecological benefits to greater diversity.
2. A number of definitions for biodiversity exist; the most simple referring to the combination of all life on Earth. A more nuanced definition emphasizes the vast richness and inter-connectedness of species in a dynamic world. This richness not only encompasses the variety of different species in an area, but the genetic variety within a single species, as well as the differences of habitats and ecosystems around the world. The definition may also include the wealth of ecosystem processes, such as pollination, which occur as a result of species interaction. It is often in these ecosystem processes that humans find the value of biodiversity.
3. The most fundamental level of biodiversity is genetic diversity; as an individual's genes define their unique traits. Genes are what give each zebra a different pattern of stripes and determine the shape of a tortoise's shell. Genetic diversity is integral to biodiversity because a variety of traits enables species to survive in various habitats or under different conditions. The many varieties of gulls are an example of a species with high genetic diversity; they live in a wide variety of habitats, from oceans to garbage dumps, and are fairly resistant to disease. Conversely, when a population has shrunk to a small number of individuals and then has recovered, as in the case of the American bison, the species will often have low genetic diversity which may make them prone to disease or disaster if too few individuals are immune or able to adapt.

4. Species diversity refers to the number of individual organisms in a population and their distribution over an area at a particular time. The distribution of species in an ecosystem gives us a notion of how species are interconnected. Think of the prairie dog: it is impossible to know all the species which benefit directly and indirectly from the tunnels it digs. It also gives us a sense of how ecosystem services are performed. A high concentration of decomposers enriching the soil in one area, for example, might explain a high density of plants growing in its fertile soil. If these decomposers die out or move, it is likely that fewer plants would grow there in the future.
5. Ecosystem diversity is the largest scale on which humans generally consider biodiversity. An ecosystem is commonly thought of as a forest, pond, or cave; but, it can be something as small as a bromeliad or as large as the entire Earth. Ecosystem biodiversity refers to the similarities and differences between all ecosystems, from the icy arctic tundra to the warm equatorial mangroves. Each ecosystem is not equally diverse; for example, the tundra is less diverse than a tropical rainforest. These differences between ecosystems has a lot to do with the climate. Ecosystems with warm moist climates are typically easier for plants to grow in, so there is more food for animals; therefore these areas tend to be more diverse than cooler climates. However, climate does not fully explain ecosystem diversity; geological history and human habitation must also be considered. Using these as indicators, areas with high biodiversity can be identifies and projects to protect the existing biodiversity can be undertaken.
6. As of 2008, scientists have documented approximately 1.7 million species, but that number is thought to be only a small fraction of the total number of species that exists or has existed on Earth. The potential number of unknown species illustrates how minimal our understanding of biodiversity truly is: species interact in ways in which scientists have only just begun to understand. Humans are still teasing out how ecosystem diversity, species diversity, and genetic diversity interact; what large changes in ecosystems mean to the smallest microbe; and how one species' genetic adaptation could alter the course of another species' survival.

Factors Affecting Environments

Most of the ecologists recognise four categories of ecological factors which affect the environment. These are :

1. Topographic or Physiographic Factors, which consist of altitude, direction of mountain chains, plateaus, plains, lakes, rivers, sea level and valleys etc.
2. Climatic Factors or Aerial Factors, which include atmosphere, light, temperature and humidity etc.
3. Edaphic Factors, which comprise lithosphere or soil.
4. Biotic Factors, which include all types of interactions between different forms of life. For example, men, animals, plants and micro-organisms etc.

Types of Environment

Environment can be conveniently divided into two categories :

1. **Natural Environment.** The natural environmental system operates through self regulating mechanism, called homeostatic environment mechanism, i.e., any change in natural ecosystem brought about by natural process is counter balanced by changes in other component of the environment. Thus there exists a reciprocal relationship among various components of the environment. These components are air, water, soil, radiation, land, forest, wild life, noise, timber, living space, flora and fauna etc.
2. **Man-made Environment.** Man is the most powerful environmental agent, spearheaded by modern technologies capable of modifying the environment according to his needs to a great extent. Man made environment includes :

(a) Technology
(b) Transportation
(c) Housing
(d) Agricultural Implements
(e) Dam-building
(f) Channelisation of energy sources, like hydro, thermal, nuclear and atomic energy
(g) Revolution in communication, *e.g.*, Satellite, Remote sensing, Telex, Fax, Internet, etc.
(h) Industrial Revolution
(i) Space Acceleration, *e.g.* landing of man on moon.
(j) Space Laboratories
(k) Computerisation etc.

People and Environment

Man and environment interaction occurs in following ways :

(1) Man fulfills his natural necessities :
  (A) breathing (B) feeding (C) drinking
(2) Man acquires his secondary needs:
  (A) shelter (B) energy
(3) Man and environment interaction is the basis of development of :
  (A) Industries (B) Power Plants
(4) Environment clears the human wastage and vice-versa :
  (A) Breathing and photo synthesis
  (B) Food processing

LIST OF NATIONAL PARKS IN INDIA

State/Union Territory	Name of the National Park	State/Union Territory	Name of the National Park
Andaman and Nicobar Islands	Campbell Bay National Park	**Assam**	Dibru-Saikhowa National Park
	Galathea National Park		Kaziranga National Park
	Mahatma Gandhi Marine National Park (Wandur National Park)		Manas National Park
			Nameri National Park
			Orang National Park
	Middle Button Island National Park	**Bihar**	Valmiki National Park
			Kanwar Lake Bird Sanctuary
	Mount Harriet National Park		Vikramshila Gangetic Dolphin Sanctuary
	North Button Island National Park	**Chhattisgarh**	Indravati National Park
	Rani Jhansi Marine National Park		Kanger Ghati National Park (Kanger Valley)
	Saddle Peak National Park		Guru Ghasi Das (Sanjay) National Park
	South Button Island National Park	**Goa**	Bhagwan Mahavir (Mollem) National Park
Andhra Pradesh	Papikonda National Park		
	Rajiv Gandhi National Park	**Gujarat**	Vansda National Park
	Sri Venkateswara National Park		Blackbuck National Park, Velavadar
Arunachal Pradesh	Namdapha National Park		Gir National Park
	Mouling National Park		Gulf of Kachchh Marine National Park

State/Union Territory	Name of the National Park
Haryana	Kalesar National Park
	Sultanpur National Park
Himachal Pradesh	Great Himalayan National Park
	Pin Valley National Park
	Inderkilla National Park
	Khirganga National Park
	Simbalbara National Park
Jammu and Kashmir	Dachigam National Park
	Hemis National Park
	Kishtwar National Park
	Salim Ali National Park
Jharkhand	Betla National Park
	Dimna National Park
	Hazaribag National Park
Karnataka	Anshi National Park
	Rajiv Gandhi National Park
	Bandipur National Park
	Bannerghatta National Park
	Kudremukh National Park
Kerala	Eravikulam National Park
	Mathikettan Shola National Park
	Periyar National Park
	Silent Valley National Park
	Anamudi Shola National Park
	Pambadum Shola National Park
Madhya Pradesh	Bandhavgarh National Park
	Mandla Plant Fossil National Park
	Kanha National Park
	Madhav National Park
	Panna National Park
	Pench National Park
	Sanjay National Park
	Satpura National Park
	Van Vihar National Park
Maharashtra	Chandoli National Park
	Gugamal National Park
	Navegaon National Park
	Pench National Park
	Sanjay Gandhi National Park or Borivili National Park
	Tadoba National Park
Manipur	Keibul Lamjao National Park
	Sirohi National Park
Meghalaya	Balphakram National Park
	Nokrek National Park
Mizoram	Murlen National Park
	Phawngpui Blue Mountain National Park
Nagaland	Ntangki National Park
Orissa	Bhitarkanika National Park
	Nandankanan National Park
	Simlipal National Park
Punjab	Harike Wetland
Rajasthan	Darrah National Park
	Desert National Park
	Keoladeo National Park
	Mount Abu Wildlife - Sanctuary
	Ranthambore National Park
	Sariska National Park
Sikkim	Khangchendzonga National Park
Tamil Nadu	Mudumalai National Park
	Mukurthi National Park
	Indira Gandhi (Annamalai) National Park
	Guindy National Park
	Gulf of Mannar Marine National Park
Tripura	Bison(Rajbari) National Park
	Clouded Leopard National Park
Uttar Pradesh	Dudhwa National Park
Uttarakhand	Gangotri National Park
	Govind Pashu Vihar
	Jim Corbett National Park
	Nanda Devi National Park
	Rajaji National Park
	Valley of Flowers National Park
West Bengal	Gorumara National Park
	Buxa National Park
	Neora Valley National Park
	Singalila National Park
	Jaldapara National Park
	Sundarbans National Park

PROJECT TIGER RESERVES OF INDIA

Location	Project Tiger Reserve	Location	Project Tiger Reserve
Andhra Pradesh	Nagarjunsagar-Srisailam		Panna
	Kawal		Pench
Arunachal Pradesh	Namdapha		Sanjay Dubri
	Pakhui/Pakke		Satpura
Assam	Kaziranga	**Maharashtra**	Melghat
	Manas		Pench
	Nameri		ShahyadriTabola-Andhari
Bihar	Valmiki Nagar	**Mizoram**	Dampa
Chhattisgarh	Achanakmar	**Orissa**	Satkosia
	Indravati		Simplipal
	Udanti and Sitanadi	**Rajasthan**	Mukunda Hills
Jharkhand	Palamau		Sariska
	Bandipur		Ranthambore
Karnataka	Bhadra	**Tamil Nadu**	Annamalai
	Dandeli-Anshi		Kalakad-Mundathurai
	Nagarhole		Mudumalai
	B.R Hills		Sathyamangalam
Kerala	Parambikulam	**Uttar Pradesh**	Katerniaghat Extension
	Periyar		Dudhwa
Madhya Pradesh	Bandhavgarh	**Uttarakhand**	Corbett
	Kanha	**West Bengal**	Buxa
			Sunderban

LIST OF BIOSPHERE RESERVES IN INDIA

Name of Biosphere Reserves	Location	Name of Biosphere Reserves	Location
Achankamar-Amarkantak	Covers parts of Anupur and Dindori districts of Madhya Pradesh and parts Bilaspur districts of Chhattisgarh.	Gulf of Mannar	Indian part of Gulf of Mannar between India and Srilanka (Tamil Nadu)
Agasthyamalai	Neyyyar, Peppara and Shendurney Wildlife Sanctuaries and their adjoining areas in Kerala.	Kachchh	Part of Katchchh, Rajkot, Surendra Nagar and Patan Civil Districts of Gujarat State.
Cold Desert	Pin Valley National Park and surroundings; Chandratal and Sarchu & Kibber Wildlife in Himachal Pradesh.	Khang Chendzonga	Parts of Khang Chenzonga hills and Sikkim.
Dehang- Debang	Part of Siang and Dibang Valley in Arunachal Pradesh.	Manas	Part of Kokrajhar, Bongaigaon, Barpeta, Nalbari, Kamprup and Daran districts (Assam)
Dibru- Saikhowa	Part of Dibrugarh and Tinsukia Districts (Assam)	Nanda Devi	Part of Chamoli, Pithoragarh and Bageshwar districts (Uttarakhand)
Great Nicobar	Southern most islands of Andaman & Nicobar.	Nilgiri	Part Wayanad, Nagarhole, Bandipur and Madumalai,

	Nilambur, Silent Valley and Siruvani hills (Tamil Nadu, Kerala, and Karnataka)	Simlipal	Part of Mayurbhanj district (Orissa)
Nokrek	Part of Garo Hills (Meghalya)	Sunderban	Part of delta of Ganges and Brahamaputra river system (West bengal)
Seshachalam Hills	Covering parts of Chittor and Kadapa districts of Andhra Pradesh		

LIST OF WILDLIFE SANCTUARIES IN INDIA

State	Wildlife Sanctuaries in India	State	Wildlife Sanctuaries in India
Assam	Amchang WLS	**Himachal Pradesh**	Bandli WLS
	Chakrashila WLS		Daranghati WLS
	Dihing Patkai WLS		Dalra WLS
	East Karbi Anglong WLS		Dhauladhar WLS
	North Karbi Anglong WLS		Nargu WLS
	Nambor WLS		Pong Dam, Lake WLS
Andhra Pradesh	Coringa WLS		Shilli WLS, Talra WLS
	Kolleru WLS	**Haryana**	Bhindawas WLS
	Nellapattu WLS		Kalesar WLS
	Pulicat Lake WLS		Khaparwas WLS
	Rajiv Gandhi (Nagarjuna Sagar Srisailam) WLS	**Jammu and Kashmir**	Gulmarg WLS
			Limber WLS
Bihar	Gautam Budha WLS		Nandini WLS
	Kaimur WLS	**Jharkhand**	Lawalong WLS
	Pant (Rajgir) WLS		Palkot WLS
	Valmiki WLS		Parasnath WLS
Chattisgarh	Badalkhol WLS		Karnataka
	Bhairamgarh WLS		Arabithittu WLS
	Bhoramdev WLS		Attiveri WLS
	Udanti Wild Buffalo WLS		Bhadra WLS
Gujarat	Jambugodha WLS		Bhimgad WLS
	Jessore WLS		Brahmagiri WLS
	Kutch Desert WLS		Cauvery WLS
	Mitiyala WLS		Nugu WLS
	Porbandar Lake WLS		Pushpagiri WLS
	Rampara Vidi WLS		Ranganathittu Bird WLS
	Ratanmahal WLS		Sharavathi Valley WLS
	Shoolpaneswar (Dhumkhal) WLS		Someshwara WLS
		Kerala	Aralam WLS
	Thol Lake WLS Wild Ass WLS		Chimmony WLS
Goa	Bondla WLS		Idukki WLS
	Madei WLS		Malabar WLS
	Bhagwan Mahavir (Mollem) WLS		Mangalavanam Bird WLS
			Neyyar WLS
	Netravali WLS		Periyar WLS

State	Wildlife Sanctuaries in India	State	Wildlife Sanctuaries in India
	Thattekad Bird WLS	**Rajasthan**	Bundh Baratha WLS
Maharashtra	Aner Dam WLS		Darrah WLS
	Bhamragarh WLS		Jawahar Sagar WLS
	Bhimashankar WLS		Kailadevi WLS
	Great Indian Bustard WLS		Mount Abu WLS
	Jaikwadi WLS		Ramsagar WLS
	Koyana WLS		Sariska WLS
	Nagzira WLS		Sawai Man Singh WLS
	Painganga WLS		Shergarh WLS
	Radhanagari WLS		Sitamata WLS
	Sagareshwar WLS	**Sikkim**	Fambong Lho WLS
	Tipeshwar WLS		Maenam WLS
	Tungareshwar WLS		Pangolakha WLS
Madhya Pradesh	Bori WLS	**Telangana**	Kawal WLS
	Gandhi Sagar WLS	**Tamil Nadu**	Karikili WLS
	Ghatigaon WLS		Mudumalai WLS
	Ken Gharial WLS		Pulicat Lake WLS
	Narsighgarh WLS		Vaduvoor WLS
	National Chambal WLS		Vedanthangal WLS
	Orcha WLS		Vettangudi WLS
	Kuno WLS		Indira Gandhi (Annamalai)
	Sardarpur WLS		Kalakad WLS
	Son Gharial WLS		Karaivetti WLS
Manipur	Yangoupokpi	**Tripura**	Gumti WLS
	Lokchao WLS		Rowa WLS
Mizoram	Dampa WLS (TR)		Sepahijala WLS
	Ngengpui WLS		Trishna WLS
	Pualreng WLS	**Uttarakhand**	Askot Musk Deer WLS
	Tokalo WLS		Binsar WLS
Meghalaya	Baghmara Pitcher		Govind Pashu Vihar WLS
	Plant WLS		Kedarnath WLS
	Nongkhyllem WLS Siju WLS		Sonanadi WLS
Nagaland	Fakim WLS	**Uttar Pradesh**	Hastinapur WLS
	Puliebadze WLS		Ranipur WLS
	Rangapahar WLS		Sohagibarwa WLS
Odisha	Badrama WLS		Sur Sarovar WLS
	Baisipalli WLS		Chandraprabha WLS
	Chilika (Nalaban) WLS		National Chambal WLS
	Hadgarh WLS	**West Bengal**	Ballavpur WLS
	Khalasuni WLS		Chintamani Kar Bird Sanctuary
	Satkosia Gorge WLS		Haliday Island WLS
Punjab	Abohar WLS		Lothian Island WLS
	Harike Lake WLS		Mahananda WLS
	Jhajjar Bacholi WLS		

ENVIRONMENTAL ISSUES: LOCAL, REGIONAL AND GLOBAL

Local Environmental Issues

Environmental issues are the result of harmful effects of human activities on the biophysical environment. Social and environmental movements can address the environmental issues through advocacy and activism. The carbon dioxide equivalent of greenhouse gases (CHG) in the atmosphere has already exceeded 400 parts per million (NOAA) (with total "long term" CH_4 exceeding 455 parts per million) (intergovernmental panel on climate change report). The amount of greenhouse gas in the atmosphere is already above the threshold (Tipping Point) that can potentially cause dangerous climatic changes. "We are already at risk of many areas of pollution. It's not next decade, it's' now."–report from the UN office for the coordination of Humanitarian Affairs (OCHA).

ENVIRONMENT ISSUE

Local environmental issues are those from which human beings are directly impacted. Human beings face various environmental problems in day to day life.

It hinders the normal functioning of physical body as well as impacts life as whole.

The major problems in our local environment are abandoned vehicles, air pollution, Stray animal's nuisance, flooded sewers, litter, mobile phone masks, noise, pest control, traffic management and parking, waste disposal, etc. Environment problems can further be classified as local or regional on the basis of the area which they are affecting. A small place in Delhi like Rohini or Pitampura is facing water shortage. This problem is not facing by any other state or country then it is a local environmental issue. The earlier environmental problems caused by people were local in nature. Many of today's environmental problems are also local, where "local" may refer to a municipal jurisdiction, a neighbourhood or ever a specific property, such as dump or industrial site. Air, water and soil pollution are all examples of local environmental problems.

Reduced habitat caused by urbanisation or industrial activities, perhaps even leading to extinction of endemic species, other examples are local deforestation , soil erosion or loss of soil fertility due to industrial agriculture. Many local environmental problems may create a nuisance, but this does not mean they are sustainable scale problem. A local environmental problems becomes a sustainable scale problem if:

1. A local non renewable resource is being used.
2. A local renewable resource or sink is being used faster than it can be renewed.

Regional Environmental Issues

Floods are a significant environmental issue for India. It causes soil erosion, destruction of wetlands and wide migration of solid wastes.

ENVIRONMENT ISSUE

- Eutrophication/Nutrient Enrichment. Chemical Pollution, including Oil.
- Changes in Marine Living Resources, Overfishing.
- Biodiversity Changes/Habitats Loss, including Alien Species Introduction.
- Climate Change.

Major environmental issues are forest and agricultural degradation of land, resource depletion (such as water, mineral, forest, sand, and rocks), environmental degradation, public health, loss of biodiversity, loss of resilience in ecosystems, livelihood security for the poor.

The major sources of pollution in India include the rapid burning of fuelwood and biomass such as dried waste from livestock as the primary source of energy, lack of organised garbage and waste removal services, lack of sewage treatment operations, lack of flood control and monsoon water drainage system, diversion of consumer waste into rivers, cremation practices near major rivers, government mandated protection of highly polluting old public transport, and continued operation by Indian government of government owned, high emission plants built between 1950 and 1980.

Air pollution, poor management of waste, growing water scarcity, falling groundwater tables, water pollution, preservation and quality of forests, biodiversity loss, and land/soil degradation are some of the major environmental issues India faces today.

Global Environmental Problems

Our environment is constantly changing. There is no denying that. However, as our environment changes, so does the need to become increasingly aware of the problems that surround it. With a massive influx of natural disasters, warming and cooling periods, different types of weather patterns and much more, people need to be aware of what types of environmental problems our planet is facing.

Global warming has become an undisputed fact about our current livelihoods; our planet is warming up and we are definitely part of the problem. However, this isn't the only environmental problem that we should be concerned about. All across the world, people are facing a wealth of new and challenging environmental problems every day.

Our planet is poised at the brink of a severe environmental crisis. Current environmental problems make us vulnerable to disasters and tragedies, now and in the future. We are in a state of planetary emergency, with environmental problems piling up high around us. Unless we address the various issues prudently and seriously we are surely doomed for disaster. Current environmental problems require urgent attention.

15 Major Current Environmental Problems

1. **Pollution.** Pollution of air, water and soil require millions of years to recoup. Industry and motor vehicle exhaust are the number one pollutants. Heavy metals, nitrates and plastic are toxins responsible for pollution. While water pollution is caused by oil spill, acid rain, urban runoff; air pollution is caused by various gases and toxins released by industries and factories and combustion of fossil fuels; soil pollution is majorly caused by industrial waste that deprives soil from essential nutrients.
2. **Global Warming.** Climate changes like global warming is the result of human practices like emission of Greenhouse gases. Global warming leads to rising temperatures of the oceans and the earth' surface causing melting of polar ice caps, rise in sea levels and also unnatural patterns of precipitation such as flash floods, excessive snow or desertification.
3. **Overpopulation.** The population of the planet is reaching unsustainable levels as it faces shortage of resources like water, fuel and food. Population explosion in less developed and developing countries is straining the already scarce resources. Intensive agriculture practiced to produce food damages the environment through use of chemical fertilizer, pesticides and insecticides. Overpopulation is one of the crucial current environmental problem.
4. **Natural Resource Depletion.** Natural resource depletion is another crucial current environmental problems. Fossil fuel consumption results in emission of Greenhouse gases, which is responsible for global warming and climate change. Globally, people are taking efforts to shift to renewable sources of energy like solar, wind, biogas and geothermal energy. The cost of installing the infrastructure and maintaining these sources has plummeted in the recent years.
5. **Waste Disposal.** The over consumption of resources and creation of plastics are creating a global crisis of waste disposal. Developed countries are notorious for producing an excessive amount of waste or garbage and dumping their waste in the oceans and, less developed countries. Nuclear waste disposal has tremendous health hazards associated with it. Plastic, fast food, packaging and cheap electronic wastes threaten the well being of humans. Waste disposal is one of urgent current environmental problem.

6. **Climate Change.** Climate change is yet another environmental problem that has surfaced in last couple of decades. It occurs due to rise in global warming which occurs due to increase in temperature of atmosphere by burning of fossil fuels and release of harmful gases by industries. Climate change has various harmful effects but not limited to melting of polar ice, change in seasons, occurrence of new diseases, frequent occurrence of floods and change in overall weather scenario.
7. **Loss of Biodiversity.** Human activity is leading to the extinction of species and habitats and loss of bio-diversity. Eco systems, which took millions of years to perfect, are in danger when any species population is decimating. Balance of natural processes like pollination is crucial to the survival of the eco-system and human activity threatens the same. Another example is the destruction of coral reefs in the various oceans, which support the rich marine life.
8. **Deforestation.** Our forests are natural sinks of carbon dioxide and produce fresh oxygen as well as helps in regulating temperature and rainfall. At present forests cover 30% of the land but every year tree cover is lost amounting to the country of Panama due to growing population demand for more food, shelter and cloth. Deforestation simply means clearing of green cover and make that land available for residential, industrial or commercial purpose.
9. **Ocean Acidification.** It is a direct impact of excessive production of CO_2. 25% of CO_2 produced by humans. The ocean acidity has increased by the last 250 years but by 2100, it may shoot up by 150%. The main impact is on shellfish and plankton in the same way as human osteoporosis.
10. **Ozone Layer Depletion.** The ozone layer is an invisible layer of protection around the planet that protects us from the sun's harmful rays. Depletion of the crucial Ozone layer of the atmosphere is attributed to pollution caused by Chlorine and Bromide found in Chloro-floro carbons (CFC's). Once these toxic gases reach the upper atmosphere, they cause a hole in the ozone layer, the biggest of which is above the Antarctic. The CFC's are banned in many industries and consumer products. Ozone layer is valuable because it prevents harmful UV radiation from reaching the earth. This is one of the most important current environmental problem.
11. **Acid Rain.** Acid rain occurs due to the presence of certain pollutants in the atmosphere. Acid rain can be caused due to combustion of fossil fuels or erupting volcanoes or rotting vegetation which release sulfur dioxide and nitrogen oxides into the atmosphere. Acid rain is a known environmental problem that can have serious effect on human health, wildlife and aquatic species.
12. **Water Pollution.** Clean drinking water is becoming a rare commodity. Water is becoming an economic and political issue as the human population fights for this resource. One of the options suggested is using the process of desalinization. Industrial development is filling our rivers seas and oceans with toxic pollutants which are a major threat to human health.
13. **Urban Sprawl.** Urban sprawl refers to migration of population from high density urban areas to low density rural areas which results in spreading of city over more and more rural land. Urban sprawl results in land degradation, increased traffic, environmental issues and health issues. The ever growing demand of land displaces natural environment consisting of flora and fauna instead of being replaced.
14. **Public Health Issues.** The current environmental problems pose a lot of risk to health of humans, and animals. Dirty water is the biggest health risk of the world and poses threat to the quality of life and public health. Run-off to rivers carries along toxins, chemicals and disease carrying organisms. Pollutants cause respiratory disease like Asthma and cardiac-vascular problems. High temperatures encourage the spread of infectious diseases like Dengue.
15. **Genetic Engineering.** Genetic modification of food using biotechnology is called genetic engineering. Genetic modification of food results in increased toxins and diseases as genes from an allergic plant can transfer to target plant. Genetically modified crops can cause serious

environmental problems as an engineered gene may prove toxic to wildlife. Another drawback is that increased use of toxins to make insect resistant plant can cause resultant organisms to become resistant to antibiotics.

POLLUTION

Definition

The word 'pollution', derived from the Latin word *pollutionem* (meaning to defile or make dirty) is the act of polluting the environment. The term **Pollution** is defined in various ways.

For example,

1. **Pollution** is the unfavourable alteration of our environment, largely because of human activities.
2. **Pollution** is defined as a deviation from the natural composition of a part of the environment, resulting in adverse effects on life.
3. **Pollution** is an undesirable change in the physical, chemical or biological characteristics of our air, land and water (or basic amenities) causing harmful effect on our life or that of other desirable species and cultural assets.
4. **Pollution** means the addition of any foreign material like inorganic, organic, biological or radiological or any physical change occurring in nature which may harm or affect living organisms directly or indirectly, immediately or after a long time.

Environmental Pollution

Environmental pollution is the result of urban-industrial technological revolution and speedy exploitation of every bit of natural resources.' The term environment, as far as pollution is concerned, includes the air, the water, the soil, the noise, the buildings, the landscapes, the oceans, the lakes, the rivers, the parks, the vehicles and many other things. Thus Pollution is generally defined as *"The addition of the constituents to water, air or land, which adversely alter the natural quality of the environment."* In some cases, pollution may involve removal, rather than the addition of the constituents from the environment.

Types of Pollution

1. **Classification According to Environment.** When different spheres of the environment are affected by pollution, they can be categorised as

   (i) Air pollution
   (ii) Water pollution
   (iii) Soil or land pollution

2. **Classification According to the Pollutant.** The pollution caused by pollutants may be of a number of types.

   For example,

   (i) Radioactive Pollution
   (ii) Sewage Pollution
   (iii) Pesticide Pollution or Biocide Pollution
   (iv) Noise Pollution
   (v) Thermal Pollution
   (vi) Plastic Pollution
   (vii) Marine Pollution
   (viii) Smoke Pollution
   (ix) Smog Pollution
   (x) Chemical Pollution
   (xi) Industrial Pollution
   (xii) Metal Toxicity Pollution
   (xiii) Drug Pollution
   (xiv) Estuarine or Oceanic Pollution
   (xv) Biological Pollution
   (xvi) Silt Pollution

(xvii) Soap and Detergent Pollution (xviii) Effluent Pollution
(xix) Acid Rain Pollution (xx) Oil Pollution

Sources of Pollution

Major Sources of Air Pollution

1. **Natural Sources.** The natural sources of air pollution are volcanic eruptions releasing poisonous gases (such as SO_2, H_2S and CO etc.), forest fires, natural organic and inorganic decays or vegetative decay, marsh gases, blowing of sands and dust, extra terrestrial bodies, cosmic dust, pollen grains of flowers, soil debris, comets and fungal spores. All these are produced naturally and released in the air, making it foul and injurious to health. Green plants through evapotranspiration release huge amount of CO_2. Forest fires and reactions between natural gas emissions also constitute a source of air pollution.
2. **Man Made Sources.** Man made sources such as increase in population, deforestation, burning of fossil fuels and fires, emissions from vehicles, rapid industrialization, agricultural activities and wars, are the major causes of air pollution.
   (A) **Increase in Population.** The rapid explosion of population is one of the most important factor of air pollution. If this rate remains the same then the population would be doubled after every 35 years. The increase in population creates several serious problems including the worsening of the condition of the environment. An increase in population also contributes to loss in forest cover and loss in wildlife species.
   (B) **Burning of Fossil Fuels and Fires.** The conventional sources of energy are wood, coal and fossil fuels etc. About 97% of the energy we use in our homes and factories is generated by coal, oil and natural gas, which are called fossil fuels. Coal consists of the remains of land plants, while oil and gas were formed from the remains of tiny plants and animals that lived in lakes and seas. Oil and gas are more important fuels than coal, because they are easier to extract and by weight, they give out more heat. Burning of these sources is responsible for air pollution.
   (C) **Emission From Vehicles.** The automobile exhausts are responsible for more than 75 percent of total air pollution. The automobiles such as cars, scooters, motors, taxies, trucks etc. release huge amounts of poisonous gases such as carbon monoxide (about 77%) nitrogen oxides (about 8.0%) and hydrocarbons (about 14%), in addition to leaded gas and particulate lead etc. As a result of incomplete combustion of petrol and diesel which react with oxides of nitrogen in presence of sunlight to form photochemical smog in the atmosphere. This smog is very toxic in nature.
   (D) **Rapid Industrialization.** A large number of industries such as chemical industries, paper and pulp mills, cotton mills, metallurgical plants and smelters, petroleum refineries, mining, and synthetic rubber industries are responsible for about 20 percent of air pollution. The common pollutants of these industries are various types of inorganic and organic gases and materials in the smoke they produce. The most common pollutants are CO_2, CO, SO_2, H_2S, NO, NO_2 etc. In addition, the smoke coming out from their chimneys also contains small particles of dust, carbon, metals, other solids, liquids and even radioactive materials which get mixed in the smoke and pollute the air. All such gases and suspended particles in them are injurious to human health.
   (e) **Agricultural Activities.** Different types of biocides such as pesticides, insecticides, herbicides etc. which are used in agricultural practices, also cause air pollution because some amount of these poisonous substances is carried away by wind to different places, during their spray over crops, and thus make the air foul for human health and other animals.

(f) **Wars.** The air pollution is also caused by various types of sophisticated explosives used in wars. Radioactive rays coming out from atomic reactors or nuclear explosions pollute the air extensively and bring sufferings to mankind to a very large extent. The atomic bomb explosions on Hiroshima and Nagasaki during the World War II, and recent Gulf War are well known to us.

PARTICULATE AIR POLLUTANTS, THEIR SOURCES AND EFFECTS

Pollutant	Sources	Effects
Suspended particulate matter/dust	Smoke from domestic, industrial and vehicular soot	Depends on specific composition Reduces sunlight and visibility, increases corrosion, Pneumoconiosis, asthma, cancer, and other lung diseases.
Fly ash	Part of smoke released from chimneys of factories and power plants	Settles down on vegetation, houses. Adds to the suspended participate matter (SPM) in the air. Leachates contain harmful material

Sources of Water Pollution

Water, the most abundant and wonderful natural resources, is extremely essential for survival of all living organisms. But today clean water has become a precious commodity and its quality is threatened by numerous sources of pollution which are as follows :

1. Sewage and Domestic Wastes
2. Industrial Effluents
3. Agricultural Discharges
4. Fertilizers
5. Detergents
6. Toxic Metals
7. Siltation
8. Thermal Pollutants
9. Radioactive Materials in Water.

Sources of Soil Pollution

Soil pollution mainly results from the following sources:

1. Soil Pollution by Industrial Wastes.
2. Soil Pollution by Urban Wastes
3. Radioactive Pollutants.
4. Agricultural Practices
5. Chemical and Metallic Pollutants.

Types of Soil in India

Alluvial Soil

- Mostly available soil in India (about 43%) which covers an area of 143 sq.km.
- Widespread in northern plains and river valleys.
- In peninsular – India, they are mostly found in deltas and estuaries.
- Humus, lime and organic matters are present.
- Highly fertile.
- Indus-Ganga-Brahmaputhra plain, Narmada-Tapi plain etc. are examples.
- They are depositional soil – transported and deposited by rivers, streams etc.
- Sand content decreases from west to east of the country.
- New alluvium is termed as Khadar and old alluvium is termed as Bhangar.
- **Colour.** Light Grey to Ash Grey.
- **Texture.** Sandy to silty loam or clay.
- Rich in: potash

- Poor in: phosphorous.
- Wheat, rice, maize, sugarcane, pulses, oilseed etc. are cultivated mainly.

Red Soil

- Seen mainly in low rainfall area.
- Also known as Omnibus group.
- Porous, friable structure.
- Absence of lime, kankar (impure calcium carbonate).
- **Deficient in.** lime, phosphate, manganese, nitrogen, humus and potash.
- **Colour.** Red because of Ferric oxide. The lower layer is reddish yellow or yellow.
- **Texture.** Sandy to clay and loamy.
- Wheat, cotton, pulses, tobacco, oilseeds, potato etc. are cultivated.

Black Soil/Regur Soil

- Regur means cotton - best soil for cotton cultivation.
- Most of the Deccan is occupied by Black soil.
- Mature soil.
- High water retaining capacity.
- Swells and will become sticky when wet and shrink when dried.
- Self-ploughing is a characteristic of the black soil as it develops wide cracks when dried.
- **Rich in.** Iron, lime, calcium, potassium, aluminum and magnesium.
- **Deficient in.** Nitrogen, Phosphorous and organic matter.
- **Colour.** Deep black to light black.
- **Texture.** Clayey.

Laterite Soil

- Name from Latin word 'Later' which means Brick.
- Become so soft when wet and so hard when dried.
- In the areas of high temperature and high rainfall.
- Formed as a result of high leaching.
- Lime and silica will be leached away from the soil.
- Organic matters of the soil will be removed fast by the bacteria as it is high temperature and humus will be taken quickly by the trees and other plants. Thus, humus content is low.
- **Rich in.** Iron and Aluminum
- **Deficient in.** Nitrogen, Potash, Potassium, Lime, Humus
- **Colour.** Red colour due to iron oxide.
- Rice, Ragi, Sugarcane and Cashew nuts are cultivated mainly.

Desert/Arid Soil

- Seen under Arid and Semi-Arid conditions.
- Deposited mainly by wind activities.
- High salt content.
- Lack of moisture and Humus.
- Kankar or Impure Calcium carbonate content is high which restricts the infiltration of water.
- Nitrogen is insufficient and Phosphate is normal.

- Texture. Sandy
- Colour. Red to Brown.

Peaty/Marshy Soil

- Areas of heavy rainfall and high humidity.
- Growth of vegetation is very less.
- A large quantity of dead organic matter/humus which makes the soil alkaline.
- Heavy soil with black colour.

Forest Soil

- Regions of high rainfall.
- Humus content is less and thus the soil is acidic.

Mountain Soil

- In the mountain regions of the country.
- Immature soil with low humus and acidic.

Sources of Radioactive Pollution

Living organisms are continuously exposed to a variety of radiation sources which are categorized as follows:

1. Natural Sources of Radiation. These sources include :
   (i) Solar Rays
   (ii) Environmental Radiation
   (iii) Radionuclides in Earth's Crust
   (iv) Internal Radiation.
2. Anthropogenic Sources of Radiation

Noise Pollution

Noise is one of the most pervasive pollutant. A musical clock may be nice to listen during the day, but may be an irritant during sleep at night. Noise by definition is "sound without value" or "any noise that is unwanted by the recipient". Noise in industries such as stone cutting and crushing, steel forgings , loudspeakers, shouting by hawkers selling their wares, movement of heavy transport vehicles, railways and airports leads to irritation and an increased blood pressure, loss of temper, decrease in work efficiency, loss of hearing which may be first temporary but can become permanent in the noise stress continues. It is therefore of utmost importance that excessive noise is controlled. Noise level is measured in terms of decibels (dB). W.H.O. (World Health Organization) has prescribed optimum noise level as 45 dB by day and 35 dB by night. Anything above 80 dB is hazardous. The table gives the noise intensity in some of the common activities.

SOURCES OF NOISE POLLUTION

Noise pollution is a growing problem. All human activities contribute to noise pollution to varying extent. Sources of noise pollution are many and may be located indoors or outdoors.

Indoor sources include noise produced by radio, television, generators, electric fans, air coolers, air conditioners, different home appliances, and family conflict. Noise pollution is more in cities due to a higher concentration of population and industries and activities such as transportation. Noise like other pollutants is a by product of industrialization, urbanization and modern civilization.

Outdoor sources of noise pollution include indiscriminate use of loudspeakers, industrial activities, automobiles, rail traffic, aeroplanes and activities such as those at market place, religious, social, and cultural functions, sports and political rallies. In rural areas farm machines, pump sets are main sources of noise pollution. During festivals, marriage and many other occasions, use of fire crackers contribute to noise pollution.

SOURCES OF SOME NOISES AND THEIR INTENSITY

Source	Intensity	Source	Intensity
Quiet Conversation	20-30dB	Radio Music	50-60 dB
Loud Conversation	60 dB	Traffic Noise	60-90 dB
Lawn Mower	60-80 dB	Heavy Truck	90-100 dB
Aircraft Noise	90-120 dB	Space Vehicle	140-179 dB
Beat Music	120 dB	Launch	
Motor Cycle	105 dB	Jet Engine	140 dB

Effects of Noise Pollution

Noise pollution is highly annoying and irritating. Noise disturbs sleep, causes hypertension (high blood pressure), emotional problems such as aggression, mental depression and annoyance. Noise pollution adversely affects efficiency and performance of individuals.

Prevention and Control of Noise Pollution

Following steps can be taken to control or minimize noise pollution:

- Road traffic noise can be reduced by better designing and proper maintenance of vehicles.
- Noise abatement measures include creating noise mounds, noise attenuation walls and well maintained roads and smooth surfacing of roads.
- Retrofitting of locomotives, continuously welded rail track, use of electric locomotives or deployment of quieter rolling stock will reduce noises emanating from trains.
- Air traffic noise can be reduced by appropriate insulation and introduction of noise regulations for take off and landing of aircrafts at the airport.
- Industrial noises can be reduced by sound proofing equipment like generators and areas producing lot of noise.
- Power tools, very loud music and land movers, public functions using loudspeakers, etc. should not be permitted at night. Use of horns, alarms, refrigeration units, etc. is to be restricted. Use of fire crackers which are noisy and cause air pollution should be restricted.
- A green belt of trees is an efficient noise absorber.

Waste

'Waste' is any unwanted or unuseful material. These are objects that have been discarded since these materials aren't functioning anymore. Waste can be in any form (liquid, solid or gas), although generally, waste is solid. There are various types of wastes like unwanted food, torn clothes, kitchen waste, etc.

Types of Waste

a. **Municipal Wastes.** Municipal Waste commonly consists of items we use on an everyday basis then dump it. Cloths, paints, wires, glasses, unwanted food, etc. come under municipal waste. These waste come from schools, factories, but primarily come from our homes.

   Municipal waste divides further into:

   1. ***Household waste.*** Materials like unused food, clothes, unwanted paper, damaged batteries, etc. come under household wastes. Agricultural wastes also come under household waste.
   2. ***Commercial waste.*** Wastes coming from any kinds of businesses, trading factories, schools, etc. come under commercial waste.
   3. ***Demolition waste.*** As clear from the word 'demolition', these wastes come from the destruction of any structure made of concrete, wood, bricks, etc. Although sometimes demolition wastes can also be recycled.

b. **Hazardous Wastes.** Hazardous waste refers to solid, liquid, or gaseous wastes from industries that have either of the properties:
- Corrosiveness
- Ignitability
- Reactivity
- Toxicity

Treatment of these wastes is necessary before the industries dump it. Hazardous wastes are unsafe for human health and the environment at large. Hazardous waste further divides into:

> **INDUSTRIAL WASTE**
>
> Waste produced by industries includes any material that isn't useful for the industrial manufacturing process. Wastes such are chemicals, pigments, ashes, metals, etc. come under industrial waste.

c. **Biomedical Waste.** Any waste coming from medical facilities such as hospitals, medical colleges, research centers, etc. come under biomedical waste.

Category of Wastes

We just saw types of wastes. Now, these wastes are further divided into various categories i.e. Solid Waste or Liquid Waste.

- **Solid Waste.** Any kind of garbage coming households, factories or hospitals come under waste. Except solid wastes are only solids or semi-solids. These solids/semi-solids can be dry or wet.
- **Wet Waste.** Any dissolved liquid based waste or sludge coming from wastewater plants, households, etc. come under wet waste.
  Examples such as leftover curries, juices, rotten vegetables will come under wet waste.
- **Dry Waste.** Waste which isn't dissolved in any form or in liquid form come under dry wastes. Examples such as plastics, bottles, etc. will come under dry waste.
- **Biodegradable Waste.** Any organic material that can be synthesized into carbon dioxide, water, methane or organic molecules by organisms in the soil come under biodegradable waste.
- **Non-biodegradable Waste.** Any material that cannot be synthesized into CO_2, water or CH_4 come under non-biodegradable waste.
- **Methods to Dispose Waste.** Dustbins aren't the only method to throw waste away. Here are few alternatives:
  a. ***Burial Pits/Landfills.*** Throwing daily wastes in burial pits or what are also known as landfills is an alternative for dustbins and is the popular waste disposal method. It looks after burying waste in the ground and eliminating foul smell coming from the wastes.
  b. ***Incineration.*** Burning of waste at high temperatures and converting them into residue or gaseous products is known as 'Incineration'. It's a better alternative to dustbins since the volume of waste here decreases by 20-30%.
  c. ***Recycling.*** The process of reusing the discarded materials and converting them into something new is known as 'Recycling'. It's the third main element in the process of 'Reduce, Reuse and Recycle'. Recycling reduces the harmful effect of greenhouse gases and helps in conservation of resources for future.
  d. ***Composting.*** When organic wastes are kept in a pit for a long period of time the microbes start decomposing the waste. If the compost is nutrient rich then it becomes a better manure for plants.

Biomedical Waste

Biomedical Waste is any kind of waste containing infectious (or potentially infectious) materials. It may also include waste associated with the generation of biomedical waste that visually appears to be of medical or laboratory origin (e.g., packaging, unused bandages, infusion kits, etc.), as well research laboratory waste containing biomolecules or organisms that are mainly restricted from environmental release. As detailed below, discarded sharps are considered biomedical waste whether they are contaminated or not, due to the possibility of being contaminated with blood and their propensity to cause injury when not properly contained and disposed of. Biomedical waste is a type of biowaste.

Biomedical waste may be solid or liquid. Examples of infectious waste include discarded blood, sharps, unwanted microbiological cultures and stocks, identifiable body parts (including those as a result of amputation), other human or animal tissue, used bandages and dressings, discarded gloves, other medical supplies that may have been in contact with blood and body fluids, and laboratory waste that exhibits the characteristics described above. Waste sharps include potentially contaminated used (and unused discarded) needles, scalpels, lancets and other devices capable of penetrating skin.

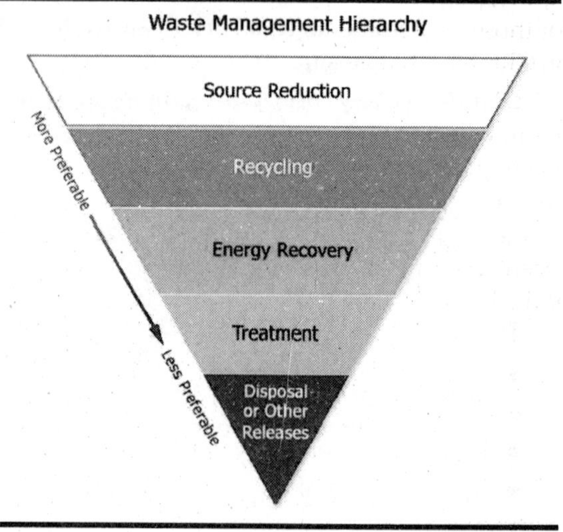

Biomedical waste is generated from biological and medical sources and activities, such as the diagnosis, prevention, or treatment of diseases. Common generators (or producers) of biomedical waste include hospitals, health clinics, nursing homes, emergency medical services, medical research laboratories, offices of physicians, dentists, and veterinarians, home health care, and morgues or funeral homes. In healthcare facilities (i.e., hospitals, clinics, doctor's offices, veterinary hospitals and clinical laboratories), waste with these characteristics may alternatively be called medical or clinical waste.

Biomedical waste is distinct from normal trash or general waste, and differs from other types of hazardous waste, such as chemical, radioactive, universal or industrial waste. Medical facilities generate waste hazardous chemicals and radioactive materials. While such wastes are normally not infectious, they require proper disposal. Some wastes are considered multihazardous, such as tissue samples preserved in formalin.

Management of Biomedical Waste

Biomedical waste must be properly managed and disposed of to protect the environment, general public and workers, especially healthcare and sanitation workers who are at risk of exposure to biomedical waste as an occupational hazard. Steps in the management of biomedical waste include generation, accumulation, handling, storage, treatment, transport and disposal.

The Political Dimension of Climate Change

Climate science has detected that human activities are changing the climate at a speed, which is, compared to changes in the geological past, fast and with significant consequences for economy and societies as well as ecosystems.

Since both adapting to all changes and avoiding all climate change seems hardly impossible, societies of the world have to decide about the right mix of adaptation to and mitigation of man-made climate change. Deciding about this is a political task, not a scientific task.

On the other hand, the concept of man-made climate change is not a recent scientific discovery, but is part of the western narrative of creation, divine justice and a number of social constructions. This should be subject to social science studies, but finds too little attention.

On October 16, 2018, Prof. Hans Von Storach – Director emeritus of the Institute of Coastal Research of the Helmholtz Zentrum Geesthacht, Germany, explored the issue during the CMCC webinar "The political dimension of climate change."

Social Dimensions of Climate Change

To date, research and policy-making on climate change have focused on climate science, technological solutions, and projected impacts to ecosystems and physical infrastructure. An emphasis on people -- the key drivers of climate change has been secondary, according to Jose Miquel Guzman, chief of UNFPA's Population and Development Branch. Not enough attention has been paid to how households and communities will experience the impacts of climate change – what the UN system terms the 'social dimensions of climate change', he added.

The social dimensions of climate change are those that relate to, in particular, health, gender equity, population dynamics, human rights, migration, access to decent work and social protections for those most vulnerable – all priority areas for UNFPA. A side event at the upcoming UN Conference on Climate Change aims to bring more attention to these social dimensions.

UNFPA is a key contributing member of the Social Dimension of Climate Change (SDCC) task team, which is hosting this side event in Bonn, Germany. Organized in the form of a stakeholder meeting, the goal of the event is to get negotiators and other stakeholders' contributions and views on how to ensure that climate-related policies and measures consider the social dimension of climate change. The task team will refine the conceptual framework and main messages developed during a recent inter-agency meeting, hosted by the Population and Development Branch, Technical Division at the UNFPA New York Headquarters in April.

The areas to be discussed during the stakeholder meeting include:

- Why take a social approach to climate change?
- Social drivers of climate change.
- Impacts, vulnerability and adaptation to climate change from a social perspective.
- Measures to maximize social outcomes of climate policies.

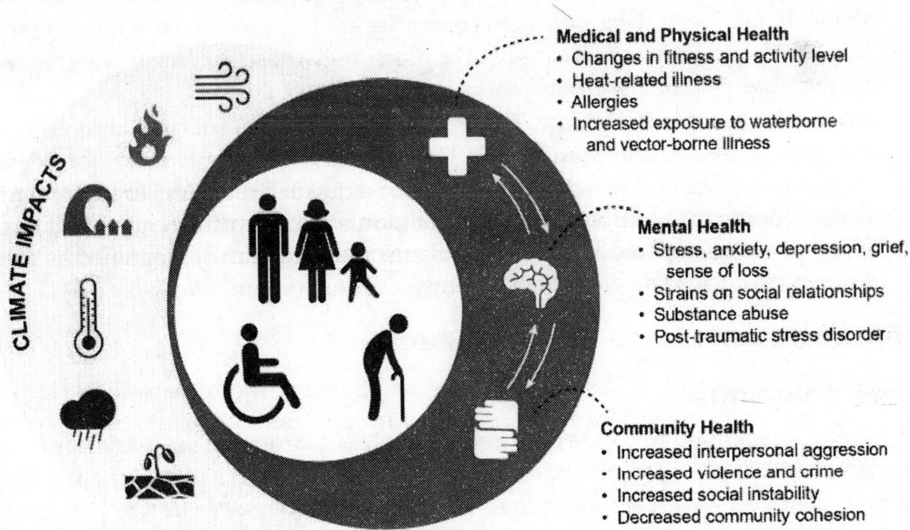

The SDCC task team was created under the High-level Committee on Programmes (HLCP) Working Group on Climate Change, and seeks to ensure that a focus on poverty eradication, social cohesion and the needs of those most vulnerable populations are taken into consideration when designing and implementing climate policies. The task team is comprised of 19 agencies: FAO, ILO, IOM, ITU, OHCHR, UNAIDS, UNDESA, UNDP, UNESCO, UNFPA, UN HABITAT, UNICEF, UNITAR, UNISDR, UNRISD, UNU, UN Women, WB, WFP and WHO.

POLLUTANTS

Pollution is usually brought about by the addition of waste products of human activity to the environment. When the waste products are not efficiently assimilated, decomposed, or otherwise removed by the natural, biological and physical processes of the biosphere, adverse effects may result as the pollutants accumulate or get converted into more toxic substances. *Thus the materials which cause pollution of environment are called pollutants.*

Classification of Pollutants

Pollutants can be classified in a number of ways : For example,

(A) On the basis of their forms they exist in the environment after their release. On this basis, pollutants can be classified as **primary** and **secondary pollutants.**

1. **Primary pollutants.** Those substances emitted directly from an identifiable source. These pollutants exist as such after being added or released into the environment. Examples are sulphur dioxide, nitrogen oxides etc.
2. **Secondary Pollutants.** These are substances, derived from primary pollutants by chemical reactions. For example, primary pollutants such as hydrocarbons and nitrogen oxides, particularly in the environment, react in presence of sunlight to form a group of nitrous compounds like peroxyacetyl nitrate (PAN) as the secondary pollutant.

(B) From ecosystem point of view, the pollutants may be classified as **biodegradable and non-biodegradable pollutants.**

1. **Biodegradable Pollutants.** These include domestic sewage, heat etc. The domestic sewage can be readily decomposed by natural processes or by engineered systems (such as municipal sewage treatment plant) which enhance capacity of the nature to decompose and recycle. However, if these pollutants enter the environment in such large quantities that complete degradation of all cannot take place, then these become biodegradable pollutants and thus pollute the environment.
2. **Non-biodegradable Pollutants.** There are many pollutants such as aluminium, iron, mercury salts, phenolic compounds and D.D.T. etc. which are usually not present in the environment. These either do not degrade or degrade only very slowly or partially and thereby pollute the environment. Such pollutants are harmful even in low concentration. These pollutants not only accumulate, but are often biologically magnified as they move in biochemical cycles and along food chains.

Major Air Pollutants

Particulate Pollutants

Particulate matter suspended in air are dust and soot released from the industrial chimneys. Their size ranges from 0.001 to 500¼ μm in diameter. Particles less than 10¼ μm float and move freely with the air current. Particles which are more than 10 μm in diameter settle down. Particles less than 0.02 μm form persistent aerosols. Major source of SPM (suspended particulate matter) are vehicles, power plants, construction activities, oil refinery, railway yard, market place, industries, etc.

Fly ash

Fly ash is ejected mostly by thermal power plants as by products of coal burning operations. Fly ash pollutes air and water and may cause heavy metal pollution in water bodies. Fly ash affects vegetation as a result of its direct deposition on leaf surfaces or indirectly through its deposition on soil. Fly ash is now being used for making bricks and as a land fill material.

Lead and Other Metals Particles

Tetraethyl lead (TEL) is used as an anti-knock agent in petrol for smooth and easy running of vehicles. The lead particles coming out from the exhaust pipes of vehicles is mixed with air. If inhaled it produces injurious effects on kidney and liver and interferes with development of red blood cells. Lead mixed with water and food can create cumulative poisoning. It has long term effects on children as it lowers intelligence.

Oxides of iron, aluminum, manganese, magnesium, zinc and other metals have adverse effect due to deposition of dust on plants during mining operations and metallurgical processes. They create physiological, biochemical and developmental disorders in plants and also contribute towards reproductive failure in plants.

Major Gaseous Pollutants

Power plants, industries, different types of vehicles – both private and commercial use petrol, diesel as fuel and release **gaseous pollutants** such as carbon dioxide, oxides of nitrogen and sulphur dioxide along with particulate matter in the form of smoke. All of these have harmful effects on plants and humans. Table lists some of these pollutants, their sources and harmful effects.

GASEOUS AIR POLLUTANTS: THEIR SOURCES AND EFFECTS

Pollutant	Source	Harmful effect
Carbon compound (CO and CO_2)	Automobile exhaust burning of wood and coal	• Respiratory problems • Green house effect
Sulphur compounds (SO_2 and H_2S)	Power plants and refineries volcanic eruptions	• Respiratory problems in humans • Loss of chlorophyll in plants (chlorosis) • Acid rain
Nitrogen Compound (NO and N_2O)	Motor vehicle exhaust atmospheric reaction	• Irritation in eyes and lungs • Low productivity in plants • Acid rain damages material (metals and stone)
Hydrocarbons (benzene, ethylene)	Automobiles and petroleum industries	• Respiratory problem • Cancer causing properties
SPM (Suspended Particulate Matter) (Any solid and liquid) particles suspended in the air, (flush, dust, lead)	Thermal power plants, Construction activities, metallurgical processes and automobiles	• Poor visibility, breathing problems • Lead interfers with the development of red blood diseases and cancer. • Smoge (skoke & fog) formation leads to poor visibility and aggravates asthma in patients
Fibres (Cotton, wool) industries	Textiles and carpet weaving	• Lung disorders

IMPACT OF POLLUTANTS ON HUMAN LIFE

Harmful Effects of Sewage and Domestic Waste

1. Sewage is an excellent medium for the growth of pathogenic bacteria, viruses and protozoa. *Vibriocholerae* found in sewage causes cholera. *Salmonella typhosa* causes typhoid, while *shigella dysenteriae* causes bacillary dysentery. Even after sewage treatment, the water contains

pathogenic bacteria and the chances of pathogens mingling with river water are critically high.

2. Domestic sewage, which is primarily composed of spent water containing, faeces, soapy wastes, food materials and paper makes the water extremely anaesthetic.
3. The ova and larvae of many worms are parasitic to man. They may pass out in urine and faeces thereby contaminating the receiving water.
4. Several pathogenic micro-organisms introduced into the water course cause deleterious effects and chronic diseases in man and animals.
5. Sewage containing oxidizable and fermentable matter causes depletion of dissolved oxygen in the receiving water bodies affecting the aquatic flora severely.
6. Oxygen deficiency also leads to the production of objectionable odours in water.
7. Presence of solid matter floating in suspension, colloidal and pseudo-colloidal dispersion in sewage creates serious water problems.
8. Suspended matter present in sewage has a tendency to blanket the stream thereby interfering with the spawning of fish and reduction of aquatic biota.

Harmful Effects of Industrial Pollutants

1. Industrial effluents cause deleterious effects on living organisms and may bring about death or sublethal pathology of kidneys, liver, lungs, brain and reproductive system.
2. Effluents like methyl mercaptan and pentachlorophenol lower the photosynthetic rate of aquatic communities by hindering sunlight penetration into the water column.
3. Disinfectants, which are added in water to control algal growth and bacteria may persist in water bodies and may cause mortality of fish, planktons and diatoms.
4. Mercury poisoning among aquatic organisms has resulted in crippling and often fatal diseases.
5. Industrial effluents consisting of As, Pb and CN etc. cause cellular degeneration in brain which results in coma, stupor and numbness.
6. Effluents containing acids and alkalies make the water corrosive.
7. Mineral constituents can be responsible for excessive hardness of water which then becomes unsuitable for domestic and industrial purposes.
8. Some of the wastes contain pathogenic bacteria. For instance the pathogen Anthrax bacilli is present in tannery wastes.
9. Heated effluents discharged into water system may severely alter the aquatic ecosystem by increasing the temperature of the stream.

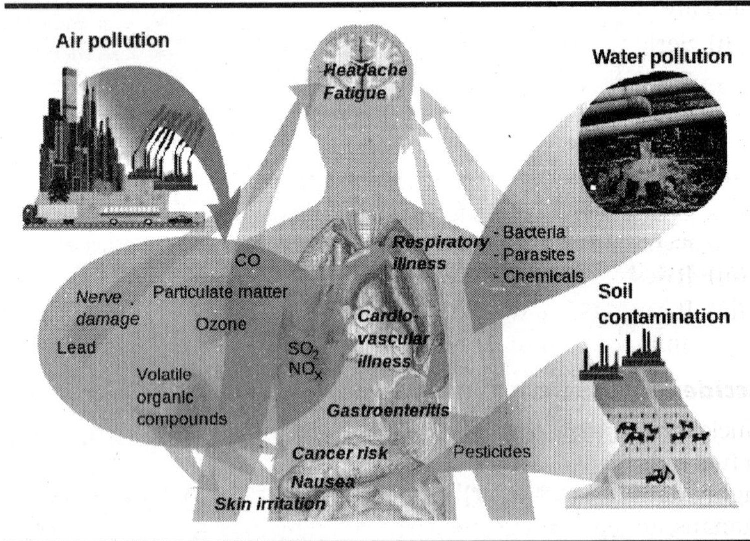

HEALTH EFFECTS OF POLLUTION

10. Industrial discharges impart colour, foul odour and turbidity to the receiving waters. They undergo putrefaction to form objectionable tastes.

Effects of Thermal Pollution

The rise in temperature in aquatic system has a profound effect on organisms as well as on water quality. These detrimental effects are as follows :

(i) Reduction in dissolved oxygen
(ii) Increase in BOD
(iii) Early hatching of fish eggs
(iv) Direct fish mortality due to failure in respiratory, nervous or essential cell processes.
(v) Adverse effects on spawning and reproductive mechanism during spring season.
(vi) Bacteria multiply rapidly, which in turn become the food of protozoans.
(vii) Undesirable changes in algal population.
(viii) Excessive eutrophication
(ix) Acceleration in activities of pathogenic organisms which makes the pathogen more virulent and fish less resistant.
(x) Migration of aquatic biota.

Effects of Radio Active Pollutants

The ill effects due to radioactive pollutants in water are numerous. For example,

(i) Serious skin cancer, carcinoma, melanoma, breast cancer, leukemia, DNA breakage and cataracts are rapidly climbing the list of diseases in man.
(ii) Polluted water containing radio-isotopes produce a set of syndromes characterised by nausea, vomiting, diarrhoea, anorexia, epilation, lethargy and general weakness which is known as radiation sickness.
(iii) It destroys biological immune system.
(iv) It causes somatic and genetic disorders, gene mutations and blood abnormalities in higher animals including man.

BHOPAL GAS TRAGEDY

The Bhopal disaster, also referred to as the Bhopal gas tragedy, was a gas leak incident on the night of 2-3 December 1984 at the Union Carbide India Limited (UCIL) pesticide plant in Bhopal, Madhya Pradesh, India. It is considered to be the world's worst industrial disaster. Over 500,000 people were exposed to methyl isocyanate (MIC) gas. The highly toxic substance made its way into and around the small towns located near the plant.

Estimates vary on the death toll. The official immediate death toll was 2,259. The government of Madhya Pradesh confirmed a total of 3,787 deaths related to the gas release. A government affidavit in 2006 stated that the leak caused 558,125 injuries, including 38,478 temporary partial injuries and approximately 3,900 severely and permanently disabling injuries. Others estimate that 8,000 died within two weeks, and another 8,000 or more have since died from gas-related diseases. The cause of the disaster remains under debate. The Indian government and local activists argue that slack management and deferred maintenance created a situation where routine pipe maintenance caused a backflow of water into a MIC tank, triggering the disaster. Union Carbide Corporation (UCC) argues water entered the tank through an act of sabotage.

Accidents at Nuclear Power Plants

Nuclear fission in the reactor core produces for of heat which if not controlled can lead to a meltdown of fuel rods in the reactor core. If a meltdown happens by accident, it will release large quantities of highly dangerous radioactive materials in the environment with disastrous consequences to the humans, animals and plants. To prevent this type of accidents and reactor blow up, the reactors are designed to have a number of safety features.

Inspite of these safety measures two disasters in the nuclear power plants are noteworthy-namely at 'Three Mile Island' in Middletown (U.S.A.) in 1979, at Chernobyl (U.S.S.R.) in 1986. In both these cases a series of mishaps and errors resulted in over heating of the reactor core and lot of radiation was released into the environment. The leakage from Three Mile Island reactor was apparently low and no one was injured immediately. However, in case of Chernobyl the leakage was very heavy causing death of some workers and radiation spread over large areas scattered all over Europe. People of the city had to be evacuated to safer places and the plant had to be closed down. These two disasters are a reminder that nuclear power reactors require a constant up gradation of safety measures. Accidents with nuclear submarines also points to the same.

Namami Gange Project to Clean Ganga

Namami Gange Project is a project by the government of India to clean the holy river Ganga. In the past decade, there was a lot of water pollution in the river due to industrial wastes. The Namami Gange Project not only aims to stop further pollution of the river but also to clean it. Narendra Modi said that it is his destiny to serve Maa Ganga. This means that he feels privileged to serve Ganga and have a hand in cleaning it.

Key Features of the Namami Gange Project

1. The project is set to get completed by the year 2020.
2. It is an integrated project that will also help the population of India who is dependent on the river.
3. Initially, the project was allocated a budget of Rs. 2037 crores in 2014-15 for the next 5 years.
4. There are many industries around the river which discharge their waste into the river directly or indirectly. Under this project, government ordered 48 out of these industries to shut down.
5. For the coming years, a total of Rs. 20000 would be spent on the project so that the river becomes clean and holy.
6. This is not the first project to clean Ganga. Previous governments had also introduced many projects to clean the river. But most of them did not perform as expected. So, the Namami Gange Project has strict rules.
7. The scheme will cover 47 towns in 8 states.
8. Over 1632 gram panchayats on the banks of Ganga to be made open defecation free by 2022.
9. Under the aegis of National Mission for Clean Ganga (NMCG) and State Programme Management Groups (SPMGs) States and Urban Local bodies and Panchayati Raj institution will be involved in this project.
10. Expansion of coverage of sewerage infrastructure in 118 urban habitations on banks of Ganga.

NATIONAL GREEN TRIBUNAL (NGT)

The National Green Tribunal has been established on 18.10.2010 under the National Green Tribunal Act 2010 for effective and expeditious disposal of cases relating to environmental protection and conservation of forests and other natural resources including enforcement of any legal right relating to environment and giving relief and compensation for damages to persons and property and for matters connected therewith or incidental thereto. It is a specialized body equipped with the necessary expertise to handle environmental disputes involving multi-disciplinary issues. The Tribunal shall not be bound by the procedure laid down under the Code of Civil Procedure, 1908, but shall be guided by principles of natural justice.

The Tribunal's dedicated jurisdiction in environmental matters shall provide speedy environmental justice and help reduce the burden of litigation in the higher courts. The Tribunal is mandated to make and endeavour for disposal of applications or appeals finally within 6 months of filing of the same. Initially, the NGT is proposed to be set up at five places of sittings and will follow circuit procedure for making itself more accessible. New Delhi is the principal place of sitting of the Tribunal and Bhopal, Pune, Kolkata and Chennai shall be the other four place of sitting of the Tribunal.

Benefits of the Namami Gange Project

1. The project will give jobs to many unemployed people. Various local people who live on the banks of the river Ganga will involve in the project and hence, they will get jobs.
2. The livelihoods of people who are dependent on the river will see a difference.
3. Health of the people also came in danger when the river is not clean. With the project going on, people will also have health benefits. They would not catch water related diseases.
4. As a part of the Namami Gange Project, the banks of the river will become free of open defecation. So, the Namami Gange Project and the Swachh Bharat Abhiyan will go hand in hand in this case.

How is the Government Planning to Control Water Pollution?

1. Government will apply bio-remediation techniques to treat the waste water. This way, industries will function side by side and they will not pollute the water resources.
2. As part of Namami Gange Project, government will introduce Territorial Army Ganga Eco-Task force. This is a 4-battalion task force.
3. For pollution control. Government is planning to follow the new PPP approach.
4. In case sewage water inflows into the river, government will make provisions to arrest it before getting into the river.
5. The government will also introduce various municipal sewage plants as a part of this project. This will help in treating the water beforehand.

Further, the focus of the Namami Gange Project is not only on the cleaning of the river. Prime Minister said that once the river gets clean, they will also provide regular maintenance to see the progress. Prime Minister is also taking actions so that pollution does not affect the river in future.

NATURAL AND ENERGY RESOURCES

Classification of Resources

Natural resources are valuable to us. The broadest classification of resources is done on the basis of their replenishing ability. Let us take a look, at these two classifications.

A. Renewable Resources

When talking about classification of resources, we will first see the renewable resources. Renewable resources are those resources that can be replenished or renewed naturally over time. Air, water, wind, solar energy etc. are all renewable resources. Renewable resources can be easily renewed by nature.

1. **Solar energy.** Sun is a big source of energy. The energy that we get from the Sun is called solar energy. All the natural phenomenon like the flowing of wind, water cycle, photosynthesis etc. are possible only due to solar energy. Now a day, solar energy is being used to cook food with the help of solar cookers, heat water, light streets, pump water for irrigating fields etc.
2. **Hydro-Energy.** Water is important natural resources. All living organisms need water to live. Humans need water for many purposes such as drinking, cleaning, cooking and for growing crops. Water flowing into the river or water stored in a dam is sources of hydro energy. The Simple method to use hydro energy is to convert it into electrical energy.
3. **Wind energy.** Winds are constantly being created in nature. The windmill is a source of electrical energy. These windmills are generally established only at places where most of the days in a year experience strong winds. The energy from this wind is used for grinding grain, pumping water and to produce electricity. In India, many windmills have been set up in different places such as Tamil Nadu, Maharashtra, Rajasthan, Kerala, West Bengal and Gujarat.

4. Biogas. Biogas is a type of fuel which is a mixture of gases such as methane, carbon dioxide, hydrogen etc. which is obtained by decomposition of animal and plant wastes like animal dung, with the help of micro-organisms in the presence of water. It is used as fuel in gas stove especially in rural areas.
5. Wood. Wood is an ancient and traditional source of energy. It is mainly a mixture of many carbohydrate compounds. Wood is used to cook food. It leads to deforestation and pollutes air also. In India, still in many villages, they use wood chullas to cook food every day. While having ill effects on the environment, it is also harmful to human health.
6. Hydrogen. It is a good source of energy because it does not create pollution and produce maximum energy on burning. Hydrogen has the potential to be the answer to all our energy and fuel troubles. Technology is currently being developed to fully utilize hydrogen efficiency.
7. Alcohol. Alcohol has many commercial and medical purposes. It can use for producing energy. It can be obtained while making sugar from sugarcane. Thus it is a very cheap source of energy. A mixture of petrol and alcohol is being used as a fuel in automobiles. This mixture is called 'Gasohol'.
8. Air. All living things need air to breathe. Therefore, air is an important natural resource.
9. Water. All living things water in order to survive. And the water cycle means we will essentially never run out of the water. But we must be careful not to pollute water and make it unusable. Drinking and clean water are already scarce in the world.
10. Soil. It is an important resource as this is the layer where plants grow. We all need food in order to survive. We get most of our food from crops grown in the soil.

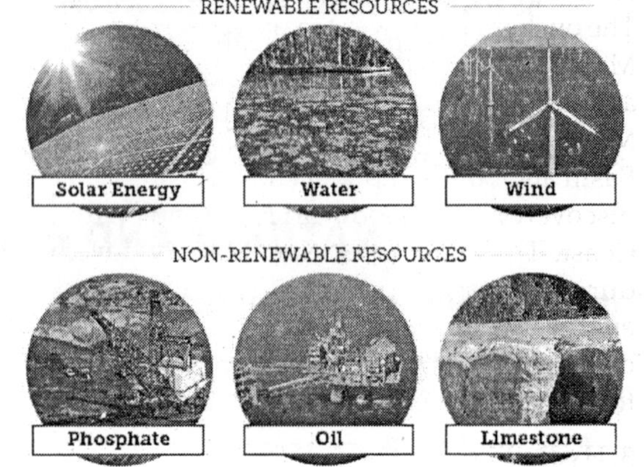

Non-renewable Resources

The other classification of resources is non-renewable resources. Non-renewable resources are those natural resources that are available in limited quantity. These resources cannot be renewed or replenished in short duration. Therefore they are also known as exhaustible resources. Examples- coal, natural gas, petroleum etc.

1. Fossil fuel. Fossil fuels like coal and petroleum are non-renewable resources. They are found deep inside the earth and are made by natural processes over many centuries. Their quantity is limited and they take thousands of years to get renewed. Example of fossil fuels is coal, petroleum, natural gas etc.
   a. Coal. It is also known as black diamond. Coal is used as a fuel, to generate electricity, and in factories and steam engines.
   b. Natural gas. Natural gas is used as a fuel called Compressed Natural Gas or CNG. Some wells dug into the earth produce only natural gas. Natural gases are a good alternative to petrol and diesel and it is used as Compressed Natural Gas. It burns easily and produces a lot of heat. It is a good source of hydrogen.
   c. Petroleum. Petroleum is also known as mineral oil or crude oil. This liquid mineral is refined to make fuels such as petrol, diesel, cooking gas and kerosene. Plastic, cosmetics, and lubricants are also products of petroleum. It is found deep inside the Earth or under the sea floor. It is taken out by drilling wells deep into the Earth or under the seabed.

2. **Nuclear energy.** In the classification of resources, nuclear energy is classified as non-renewable. The fuel used for nuclear energy is generally uranium, which is in a limited supply. So we classify it as non-renewable. Production of electricity from nuclear energy does not release carbon dioxide. Thus, use of nuclear energy is safe for the environment.

Conventional Sources of Energy

1. Coal

Coal is one of the most important sources of energy. Most of the coal, which is obtained today, is from underground mines of different types depending on their distance from the Earth's surface. Coal comprises three-fourth of the total fossil fuels of the world. India has large proven resources and still larger geological reserves. India ranks third in terms of world production of coal. In India, there would be enough coal for more than 100 years, however, it is concentrated largely in the eastern and central parts of the country.

2. Oil and Natural Gas

In India, efforts made by the *Oil and Natural Gas Corporation* (ONGC) and Oil India since the late 1950s have led to the identification of a number of oil and gas deposits both offshore and onshore. The onshore fields were mainly discovered in the Mumbai, Gujarat, Assam and Arunachal Pradesh; and the offshore fields in the sea were notably the Mumbai High fields such as North and South Basin and South Tapti. Oil and gas has also been discovered in the Godavari Basin and on the East Coast. The new exploration strategy developed during the first two years of Seventh Plan places emphasis on intensive exploration survey and drilling in order to add to petroleum reserves and to augment production as early as possible.

> **Do You Know**
>
> Natural gas is emerging as an important source in India's commercial energy scene in view of large reserves of gas that have been established in the country, particularly, in South Bassein off West Coast of India. In view of growing importance of natural gas in the country, the *Gas Authority of India Limited* (GAIL), a wholly-owned *Government of India* undertaking, was established in 1984. The main objective of the company are processing, marketing, transportation and distribution of natural gas in all its forms.

3. Hydro Energy

Hydro energy can also be considered as an indirect source of solar energy. The potential energy of water stored at a height is converted into mechanical and electrical energy as this water falls and drives turbines and electric generators.

Today, about 23 per cent of the total electric power in the world comes from hydropower. The total hydro-electric potential in India has been estimated at about 472×10^9 kilowatt hours or 472 terrawatt hours normally. But, we have exploited only a little more than 16 per cent of the total potential.

Electrical energy generation by hydro-electric power plants is not polluting and uses a renewable source of energy. However, there are several problems associated with the construction of giant dams on natural waterways. The construction of such dams alter the downstream ecology as well as that in the lake area behind the dam. Huge areas get submerged, and flora and fauna or any agricultural produce of this land get affected. People and towns in this area have to be removed and relocated, causing disturbance and sometimes hardship. Again, the time taken for such larger schemes to fructify is usually quite long. For these reasons, emphasis is now being given to supplement such large projects with small size hydro projects called *mini-hydro* or *micro-hydel projects* which can be built on small streams and even on canals, without large dams.

IMPORTANT RIVER VALLEY PROJECTS IN INDIA

Project	Location
Bhakra Nangal Project	On Sutlej in Punjab. Highest in India. Height 226m. Reservoir is called Gobind Sagar Lake.
Mandi Project	On Beas in HP
Chambal Valley Project	On Chambal in MP & Rajasthan, 3 dams are there:- Gandhi Sagar Dam, Rana Pratap Sagar Dam and Jawahar Sagar Dam
Damodar Valley Project	On Damodar in Bihar, Based on Tennessee Valley Project USA
Hirakud Project	On Mahanadi in Orrisa, World's Longest Dam: 4801m
Rihand Project	On Son in Mirzapur, Reservoir is called Gobind Vallabh Pant reservoir.
Kosi Project	On Kosi in N. Bihar
Mayurkashi Project	On Mayurkashi in West Bengal
Kakrapara Project	On Tapi in Gujarat
Nizamsagar Project	On Manjra in Andhra Pradesh
Nagarjuna Sagar Project	On Krishna in Andhra Pradesh
Tugabhadra Project	On Tugabhadra in Andhra Pradesh & Karnataka
Shivasamudram Project	On Cauvery in Karnataka. It is the older river valley project in India.
Tata Hydel Scheme	On Bhima in Maharashtra
Sharavathi Hydel Project	On Jog Falls in Karnataka
Kundah & Periyar Project	In Tamil Nadu and Kerala
Farakka Project	On Ganga in WB. Apart from power and irrigation it helps to remove silt for easy navigation.
Ukai Project	On Tapti in Gujarat
Mahi Project	On Mahi in Gujarat
Salal Project	On Chenab in J&K
Mata Tila Multipurpose Project	On Betwa in Uttar Pradesh and Madhya Pradesh
Thein Project	On Ravi, Punjab
Pong Dam	On Beas, Punjab
Tehri Dam	On Bhagirathi, Uttarakhand
Sardar Sarovar Project	On Narmada, Gujarat/MP.

4. Tidal Energy

Tides are created by the combined gravitational effect of the Earth, the Moon and the Sun. Though the tide is the universal phenomenon of the Earth's sea-water body, some regions are more favourable for the establishment of such power plant for the commercial production of tidal energy. Primary requirements for the construction of an installation having a capacity over 200 MW, are :

(i) an average tide of 5-12 metres;

(ii) the possibility of linkage to a grid in order to accommodate the variable power output of the tidal plant;

(iii) favourable geographical location and favourable socio-economic and ecological conditions.

Bulb type turbines as used in conventional hydro-electric stations have proved to be reliable for generating power from the tides.

In India, three potential sites have so far been identified, namely, the Gulfs of Kutch and Cambay on the west coast in Gujarat and the Sundarbans along the east coast in West Bengal.

5. Geothermal Energy

Geothermal energy is the exploitation of heat energy of Earth within the 10 km of the Earth's upper crust. Geothermal energy can be processed for generation of power, where the geothermal fluid has a temperature of 130° C. Geothermal manifestations are widespread in India in the form of 340 Hot Springs localities. Only a few direct utilization schemes have been launched by various agencies. They are in Puga, Chhumuthang, Manikaran and Bakreshwar. Of these, India's most promising geothermal field is in Puga valley in Laddakh. Tatapani in Himachal Pradesh is another promising geothermal area in India.

6. Bio-energy

Bio-energy includes those processes where biological forms of matter, such as, plants, vegetables, enzymes, etc. provide the basis for energy or its conversion from one form to another form of energy. The widest use of bio-energy is in the traditional ways, where wood, plants and agricultural matter are directly burnt to provide heat.

Biogas. *Biogas* is a clean, unpolluted and cheap source of energy in rural areas. It contains 55 to 70 per cent methane, which is inflammable. Biogas is produced from cattle dung in a 'Biogas Plant' commonly known as 'Gobargas Plant', through a process called 'digestion'.

Biomass covers a wide range of materials, encompassing all kinds of animal, organic and synthetic wastes and a special variety of vegetation-wild grass, shrubs and some plants and trees, especially cultivated to derive energy. The major components of biomass are mainly carbohydrates – sugars, starches and cellulose – with variable nitrogen and phosphorous contents.

SYSTEMS FOR CONVERSION OF BIOMASS INTO ENERGY RESOURCES

(A) **Combustion Pyrolysis.** Chemical decomposition through high temperature (upto 500°C) in partial or total absence of air to produce fuel gas, oil (methanol) and charcoal.

(B) **Biogasification.** Anaerobic digestion of biomass to produce combustible gas (biogas) comprising of methane, hydrogen, etc.

(C) **Fermentation.** Conversion of sugar and starch into alcohol to produce ethanol and solid residual fuel.

Non-Conventional Sources

1. **Solar Energy.** Solar radiant energy falling on the surface of the Earth in the form of visible lights can be converted into thermal energy. The heat generated in a solar collector can be utilised for variety of applications such as cooking of food, heating of water, drying of foodgrains and vegetables, wood seasoning, desalination of water, generation of mechanical and electrical power etc.

   Advantages

   (i) Solar power is pollution free and causes no greenhouse gases to be emitted after installation.
   (ii) Reduced dependence on foreign oil and fossil fuels.
   (iii) Renewable clean power that is available every day of the year, even cloudy days produce some power.
   (iv) Return on investment unlike paying for utility bills.
   (v) Virtually no maintenance as solar panels last over 30 years.
   (vi) Creates jobs by employing solar panel manufacturers, solar installers, etc. and in turn helps the economy.
   (vii) Excess power can be sold back to the power company if grid intertied.
   (viii) Ability to live grid free if all power generated provides enough for the home/building.

(ix) Can be installed virtually anywhere; in a field to on a building.
(x) Use batteries to store extra power for use at night.
(xi) Solar can be used to heat water, power homes and building, even power cars.
(xii) Safer than traditional electric current.
(xiii) Efficiency is always improving so the same size solar that is available today will become more efficient tomorrow.
(xiv) Aesthetics are improving making the solar more versatile compared to older models; i.e. printing, flexible, solar shingles, etc.
(xv) Government grants, tax incentives, and subsidy programs are available to help with initial costs.

Disadvantages

(i) High initial costs for material and installation and long ROI.
(ii) Needs lots of space as efficiency is not 100% yet.
(iii) No solar power at night so there is a need for a large battery bank.
(iv) Devices that run on DC power directly are more expensive.
(v) Depending on geographical location the size of the solar panels vary for the same power generation.
(vi) Cloudy days do not produce much energy.
(vii) Solar panels are not being massed produced due to lack of material and technology to lower the cost enough to be more affordable.
(viii) Solar powered cars do not have the same speeds and power as typical gas powered cars.
(ix) Lower production in the winter months.

2. **Wind Energy.** Wind energy is the kinetic energy associated with movement of large masses of air resulting from the differential heating of the atmosphere by the Sun. Hence, wind energy is nothing but the converted form of solar energy. It is estimated that about 10^6 to 10^7 MW of usable power is continuously available in the Earth's winds. Though the total quantity of this resource is extremely large, it is concentrated in certain regions, and can vary a great deal with time at given location. For the utilization of wind energy, the speed of wind must be between 8 to 22 m per second. Wind energy is renewable and posses no major environmental threats.

Advantages

(i) Wind Energy is Renewable & Sustainable.
(ii) It's Also Environmentally Friendly.
(iii) It Can Reduce Fossil Fuel Consumption.
(iv) Wind Energy is Free.
(v) It Has A Small Footprint.
(vi) Both Industrial & Domestic Wind Turbines Exist.
(vii) Wind Energy Can Provide Power For Remote Locations.
(viii) Wind Technology is Becoming Cheaper.
(ix) It Is Also Low Maintenance.
(x) It Has Low Running Costs.
(xi) Wind Energy Has Huge Potential.
(xii) It Can Increase Energy Security.
(xiii) The Wind Energy Industry Creates Jobs.

Disadvantages

(i) The Wind Fluctuates.

(ii) Installation is Expensive.
(iii) Wind Turbines Pose A Threat to Wildlife.
(iv) Wind Turbines Create Noise Pollution.
(v) They Also Create Visual Pollution.

3. **Ocean Energy.** The sea, which is constantly receiving solar radiations and acts as the world's largest natural solar collector, has potential to provide a means of utilizing renewable energy. It acts not only as collector, but also has an enormous storage capacity. Energy from the ocean is available in several forms such as ocean thermal energy, wave energy, tidal energy, salinity gradients, ocean currents, ocean winds and bio-mass.

4. **Wave Energy.** Movement of large quantities of water up and down can, in principle, be harnessed to convert it into usable form of energy, such as, electricity or mechanical power. Several types based on flats, flaps, ramps and oscillating air water columns have been worked upon to harness wave energy. It is more reliable than the wind energy because here the fluctuation is less than the wind. However at present, due to infant stage of its technology, the cost per unit of energy converted is high because of the need for special structures at sea, corrosion problem associated with the use of sea water and the problem of transmitting the power onshore.

   The tropical coastline of India, especially south-west coastline, is very suitable for establishing such energy plants. *Department of Ocean Development* has estimated the wave energy potential in India about 40,000 MW. Ocean Energy Cell has established a pilot power plant at Vizhinjam (Kerala), of 120 MW capacity during monsoon period and 30 MW during non-monsoon period. OEC is also developing five other similar plants at Thangaserry in Kerala.

5. **Nuclear Energy.** *Nuclear energy* can be obtained both through *fusion* and the *fission* processes. Enormous amounts of energy is released from small quantity of fuel in both these processes, e.g., if one tonne of Uranium is totally fissionable, it can theoretically yield energy equivalent to about 3 million tonnes of coal.

   Nuclear Fuel. The fissionable material used in nuclear reactors for producing energy by the fission process is called a *nuclear fuel.* The fuel used in nuclear power plants is enriched uranium-235 isotope. The remaining being U-238 isotope, which does not get fissioned easily. The natural uranium, which contains a very low percentage of U-235 in it. Thus the natural uranium cannot sustain or maintain a nuclear chain reaction. Since naturally occurring uranium has very little U-235, so it has first to be processed to increase the percentage of fissionable U-235 in it. This process is called *enrichment of uranium and uranium,* thus obtained, is called *enriched uranium.* Even the enriched uranium used in reactors contains both type of atoms – U-238 and U-235. But, it's the U-235 atoms, which act as real fuel and are used in the reactors in the form of long rods or strips, called *fuel elements.*

   NUCLEAR REACTOR

   The nuclear reactor or atomic reactor is a kind of furnace for carrying out the controlled fission of a radioactive material like Uranium-235 for producing atomic power. It's in the reactor that the heat energy is produced from fission reactions, which is then taken out and converted into electricity. Thus, it's an assembly in which nuclear fission chain reaction is maintained and controlled for producing nuclear energy, radioactive nuclides or artificial elements. In order that reaction should not get out of control, it is regulated by neutron absorbers – the control rods made of graphite or beryllium, which allow only sufficient free neutrons to exist in reactor core to maintain the reaction at constant level.

6. **Atomic Energy.** The prime objective of the atomic energy programmes as defined in the *Atomic Energy Act* of 1948, are the development, control and use of atomic energy solely for peaceful purposes, namely, the generation of electricity and the development of nuclear applications in research, agriculture, industry, medicine and other areas. To achieve this objective, Tata Institute

of Fundamental Research (TIFR) and Bhabha Atomic Research Centre (BARC) were established in 1945 and 1967 respectively.

The *Atomic Energy Commission,* set up in 1948, is responsible for formulating the policy for all atomic energy activities in the country. The *Department of Atomic Energy* (DAE), set up in 1954, is the executive agency for implementing the atomic energy programme.

The *Nuclear Power Corporation* of DAE is responsible for design, construction and operation of nuclear power stations.

Power station	Location	District	State	Installed Capacity (MW)	Under construction (MW)
Narora Atomic Power Station	Narora	Bulandshahr	Uttar Pradesh	440	–
Rajasthan Atomic Power Station	Rawatbhata	Chittorgarh	Rajasthan	1180	–
Tarapur Atomic Power Station	Tarapur	Thane	Maharashtra	1,400	–
Kakrapar Atomic Power Station	Kakrapar	Surat	Gujarat	440	2 × 700
Kudankulam Nuclear Power Plant	Kudankulam	Tirunelveli	Tamilnadu	–	2000
Kaiga Nuclear Power Plant	Kaiga	Uttra Kannada	Karnataka	880	220
Madras Atomic Power Station	Kalpakkam	Kancheepuram	Tamilnadu	440	–
Total				**2720**	

Forest Resources in India: Use, Over Exploitation, Causes and Effects!

A forest is a natural, self-sustaining community characterized by vertical structure created by presence of trees. Trees are large, generally single-stemmed, woody plants. Forest can exist in many different regions under a wide range of conditions, but all true forests share these physical characteristics.

Because a forest is a natural community, no forest is static in time. That is, because forest communities respond to outside influences, most forests are in a state of constant flux. Depending upon the systems within which forest communities exist, such factors might include rainfall, fire, wind, glaciation, seismic activity, flooding, animal activity, insulation, and so on.

At any time, a forest is a collection of past responses to outside influences and internal competitive interactions. Therefore, the present status of any forest, indeed of any natural community, reflects what has gone on before.

Use and Over Exploitation

A forest is a biotic community predominantly of trees, shrubs and other woody vegetation, usually with a closed canopy. This invaluable renewable natural resource is beneficial to man in many ways.

The direct benefits from forests are:

(a) **Fuel Wood.** Wood is used as a source of energy for cooking purpose and for keeping warm.

(b) **Timber.** Wood is used for making furniture, tool-handles, railway sleepers, matches, ploughs, bridges, boats etc.

(c) **Bamboos.** These are used for matting, flooring, baskets, ropes, rafts, cots etc.

(d) **Food.** Fruits, leaves, roots and tubers of plants and meat of forest animals form the food of forest tribes.

(e) **Shelter.** Mosses, ferns, insects, birds, reptiles, mammals and micro-organisms are provided shelter by forests.

(f) **Paper.** Wood and Bamboo pulp are used for manufacturing paper (Newsprint, stationery, packing paper, sanitary paper)

(g) **Rayon.** Bamboo and wood are used in the manufacture of rayon (yarns, artificial silk-fibres)

(h) **Forest Products.** Tannins, gums, drugs, spices, insecticides, waxes, honey, horns, musk, ivory, hides etc. are all provided by the flora and fauna of forests.

The indirect benefits from forests are:

(a) **Conservation of Soil.** Forests prevent soil erosion by binding the soil with the network of roots of the different plants and reduce the velocity of wind and rain - which are the chief agents causing erosion.

(b) **Soil-improvement.** The fertility of the soil increases due to the humus which is formed by the decay of forest litter.

(c) **Reduction of Atmospheric Pollution.** By using up carbon dioxide and giving off oxygen during the process of photosynthesis, forests reduce pollution and purify the environment.

(d) **Control of Climate.** Transpiration of plants increases the atmospheric humidity which affects rainfall and cools the atmosphere.

(e) **Control of Water flow.** In the forests, the thick layer of humus acts like a big sponge and soaks rain water preventing run-off, thereby preventing flash-floods. Humus prevents quick evaporation of water, thereby ensuring a perennial supply of water to streams, springs and wells.

Human Interactions with Forests

Human are indisputably a part of most forests. With the exception of extremely inaccessible forestlands, all forests present on Earth today have been influenced by human being for tens of thousands of years. In many cases, forest communities have never been without the influence of human activities.

Because of the widespread nature of human, activity in forests, it is tempting to think of human endeavor as one more outside factor influencing forest development. This approach is misleading, however, since it denies the role of self- awareness in human activity. Because human beings can understand cause and effect, and because we have amassed an increasingly deep body of knowledge about forest processes over the past ten millennia, human influences simply cannot be likened to the blind forces of nature.

Deforestation

Deforestation is the permanent destruction of indigenous forests and woodlands. The term does not include the removal of industrial forests such as plantations of gums or pines. Deforestation has resulted in the reduction of indigenous forests to four-fifths of their pre-agricultural area.

Indigenous forests now cover 21% of the earth's land surface. The World Resources Institute regards deforestation as one of the world's most pressing land-use problems. The difference between forests and woodlands is that whereas in a forest the crowns of individual trees touch to form a single canopy, in woodland, trees STOW far apart, so that the canopy is open.

Of great concern is the rate at which deforestation is occurring. Currently, 12 million hectares of forests are cleared annually. Almost all of this deforestation occurs in the moist forests and open woodlands of the tropics.

At this rate all moist tropical forest could be lost by the year 2050, except for isolated areas in Amazonia, the Zaire basin, as well as a few protected areas within reserves and parks. Some countries such as Ivory Coast, Nigeria, Costa Rica, and Sri Lanka are likely to lose all their tropical forests by the year 2010 if no conservation steps are taken.

The destruction of forests due to unscrupulous and indiscriminate felling of trees has lead to an overall deterioration of our environment and is posing a serious threat to the quality of "life in future. Forest area in world has dwindled from 7,000 million hectares (year 1900) to 2S90 million hectares (year 1975). It is expected to further reduce to 2300 million hectares by year 2010 AD if the present trend of deforestation is not reversed.

Causes of Deforestation

(1) **Population Explosion.** Population explosion poses a grave threat to the environment. Vast areas of forest land are cleared of trees to reclaim land for human settlements (factories, agriculture, housing, roads, railway tracks etc.) growth of population increases the demand for forest products like timber, firewood, paper and other valuable products of industrial importance, all necessitating felling of trees.

(2) **Forest Fires.** Fires in the forests may be due to natural calamities or human activities:

(a) Smoldering of the humus and organic matter forming a thick cover over the forest floor (i.e. ground fires).

(b) Dried twigs and leaves may catch fire (i.e. surface fires).

(c) In densely populated forests, tree tops may catch fire by heat produced by constant rubbing against each other (i.e. crown fires).

(d) Human activities like clearing forest for habitation, agriculture, firewood, construction of roads, railway tracks and carelessness (throwing burning cigarette stubbs on dried foliage).

Fire destroys fully grown trees, results in killing and scorching of the seeds, humus, ground flora and animal life.

(3) **Grazing Animals.** Trampling of the forest soil in the course of overgrazing by livestock has four reaching effects such as loss of porosity of soil, soil erosion and desertification of the previously fertile forest area.

(4) **Pest Attack.** Forest pests like insects etc. destroy trees by eating up the leaves, boring into shoots and by spreading diseases.

(5) **Natural Forces.** Floods, storms, snow, lightening etc. are the natural forces which damage forests.

Effects of Deforestation

Forests are closely related with climatic change, biological diversity, wild animals, crops, medicinal plants etc.

Large scale deforestation has many far-reaching consequences:

(i) Habitat destruction of wild animals (tree-using animals are deprived of food and shelter.)

(ii) Increased soil erosion due to reduction of vegetation cover.

(iii) Reduction in the oxygen liberated by plants through photosynthesis.

(iv) Increase in pollution due to burning of wood and due to reduction in Car- bon-dioxide fixation by plants.

(v) Decrease in availability of forest products.

(vi) Loss of cultural diversity

(vii) Loss of Biodiversity

(viii) Scarcity of fuel wood and deterioration in economy and quality of life of people residing near forests.

(ix) Lowering of the water table due to more run-off and thereby increased use of the underground water increases the frequency of droughts.

(x) Rise in Carbon dioxide level has resulted in increased thermal level of earth which in turn results in melting of ice caps and glaciers and consequent flooding of coastal areas.

Mineral Resources in India

- On the basis of chemical and physical properties, minerals are grouped as:
  - Metallic minerals and
  - Non-metallic minerals.
- Major examples of metallic minerals are iron ore, copper, gold, etc.
- Metallic minerals are further sub-divided as ferrous and non-ferrousmetallic minerals.
- The minerals containing iron is known as ferrous and without iron is known as non-ferrous (copper, bauxite, etc.).
- Depending upon the origination, non-metallic minerals are either organic (such as fossil fuels also known as mineral fuels, which are derived from the buried animal and plant, e.g. such as coal and petroleum), or in organic minerals, such as mica, limestone, graphite, etc.

Distribution of Minerals

- Minerals are unevenly distributed on the earth's surface.
- All minerals are exhaustible in nature, i.e., will exhaust after a certain time.
- However, these minerals take long time to form, but they cannot be replenished immediately at the time of need.
- More than 97% of coal reserves occur in the valleys of Damodar, Sone, Mahanadi, and Godavari rivers.
- Petroleum reserves in India are located in the sedimentary basins of Assam, Gujarat, and Mumbai High (i.e. off-shore region in the Arabian Sea.
- Some new petroleum reserves are also found in the Krishna-Godavari and Kaveri basins

Mineral Belts in India

Further, there are three major mineral belts in India namely:

North-Eastern Plateau Region

- The major areas of north-eastern plateau region are Chhotanagpur (Jharkhand), Odisha, West Bengal, and parts of Chhattisgarh.
- Iron ore, coal, manganese, bauxite, and mica are the major minerals of the north-eastern plateau region.

South-Western Plateau Region

- The south-western plateau region covers major parts of Karnataka, Goa, and contiguous Tamil Nadu uplands and Kerala.
- Major mineral resources of south-western plateau region are iron ore, manganese, and limestone.
- Kerala has deposits of monazite and thorium, and bauxite clay and Goa has deposits of iron ore.

North-Western Region

- The north-western region covers the areas of Aravalli in Rajasthan and parts of Gujarat.
- Major minerals of north-western regions are copper and zinc; other significant minerals include sandstone, granite, and marble, along with Gypsum and Fuller's earth deposits.
- In addition, Gujarat and Rajasthan, both have rich sources of salt.

- The Himalayan belt is also an important mineral belt, as it has rich deposits of copper, lead, zinc, cobalt, and tungsten.

Major Minerals

Following are the major minerals found in India:

Iron

- About 95% of total reserves of iron ore is found in the States of Odisha, Jharkhand, Chhattisgarh, Karnataka, Goa, Telangana, Andhra Pradesh, and Tamil Nadu.
- Sundergarh, Mayurbhanj, and Jhar are the major iron ore regions in Odisha and the important mines are Gurumahisani, Sulaipet, Badampahar (Mayurbhaj), Kiruburu (Kendujhar), and Bonai (Sundergarh).
- Noamundi (Poorbi Singhbhum) and Gua (Pashchimi Singhbhum) are important mines in Jharkhand.
- Dalli and Rajhara in Durg district are the important mines of Chhattisgarh.
- Sandur-Hospet area of Ballari district, Baba Budan hills, and Kudremukh in Chikkamagaluru district, and parts of Shivamogga are the important iron ore regions in Karnataka.
- The districts of Chandrapur, Bhandara, and Ratnagiri are the iron regions in Maharashtra.
- Other iron ore regions in India are Karimnagar and Warangal district of Telangana, Kurnool, Cuddapah, and Anantapur districts of Andhra Pradesh, and Salem and Nilgiris districts of Tamil Nadu.

Manganese

- Odisha is the leading producer of Manganese.
- Bonai, Kendujhar, Sundergarh, Gangpur, Koraput, Kalahandi, and Bolangir are the major manganese regions in Odisha.
- Dharwar, Ballari, Belagavi, North Canara, Shivamogga, Chitradurg, Tumkur, and Chikkmagaluru are major manganese regions in Karnataka.
- Nagpur, Bhandara, and Ratnagiri districts are the major regions of manganese in Maharashtra.
- Balaghat-Chhindwara-Nimar-Mandla, and Jhabua districts are the important manganese regions of Madhya Pradesh.

Bauxite

- Odisha is the largest producer of Bauxite in India.
- Kalahandi, Sambalpur, Bolangir, and Koraput are the leading producers of bauxite in Odisha.
- Lohardaga (Jharkhand) is rich in bauxite deposits.
- Amarkantak plateau has rich deposits of bauxite in Chhattisgarh.

INDIAN ENVIRONMENTAL ACTS

- Indian Forest Act–1927.
- The Wild Life (Protection) Act–1972.
- The Water (prevention and control of Pollution) Act–1974.
- The Forest (Conservation) Act–1980.
- The Air (Prevention and Control of Pollution) Act–1981.
- The Environment (Protection) Act–1986.
- The Public Liability Insurance Act–1991.
- The National Environmental Tribunal Act–1995.
- The National Environment Appellate Authority Act–1997.
- National Forest Policy–1988.
- National Conservation Strategy and Policy Statement on Environment Developmental–1992.
- Policy Statement on Abatement of Pollution–1992.

- Katni-Jabalpur area and Balaghat are the major regions of bauxite in Madhya Pradesh.
- Kolaba, Thane, Ratnagiri, Satara, Pune, and Kolhapur in Maharashtra are important bauxite producers.

Copper

- Copper deposits are largely concentrated in Singhbhum district of Jharkhand, Balaghat district of Madhya Pradesh, and Jhunjhunu and Alwar districts of Rajasthan.

Mica

- Hazaribagh plateau of Jharkhand and Nellore district of Andhra Pradesh have deposits of high grade mica.
- Jaipur to Bhilwara and areas around Udaipur are the major mica-bearing regions of Rajasthan.
- Other mica-bearing regions are Mysore and Hasan districts of Karnataka; Coimbatore, Tiruchirapalli, Madurai, and Kanniyakumari of Tamil Nadu; Alleppey of Kerala; Ratnagiri of Maharashtra; Purulia and Bankura of West Bengal.

Global Warming

Global warming means the rise in the mean global temperature to a level which affects the life-forms on the earth surface. The factors responsible for this warming may be both natural and man-made. Warming of the globe due to natural factors is not an unusual phenomenon.

The earth is kept warm due to what is known as the "green house effect". Without it, the earth would be a frozen waste-land. The short wavelengths or ultraviolet radiation coming from the Sun penetrates the atmosphere and is absorbed by the earth. This absorbed energy is also radiated back to space at infrared wavelengths. The earth atmosphere contains gases which trap some of the outgoing radiation and thereby warm the earth. These gases are known as "Green House Gases." Water vapour, carbon dioxide, methane, ozone, nitrous oxide and CFCs are prominent examples. To maintain the global energy balances, both the atmosphere and the surface will warm until the outgoing energy equals the incoming energy.

The increase in the quantity of the greenhouse gases in the atmosphere can reinforce the greenhouse effect and lead to global warming. CFCs and nitrous oxide are many time more potent than the same quantity of carbon-dioxide or methane. However carbon-dioxide is the largest contributor to the global warming as it holds the largest share among the green house gases in the atmosphere. CFCs are totally man-made greenhouse gas which are controlled under Montreal Protocol. The largest sources of methane in the atmosphere are natural wetlands, rice paddies and livestock. Natural gas production, bio-mass burning, termites, landfills and coal mining also releases methane. Nitrous oxides are released by the oceans and soils but human activities such

SOLUTION TO REDUCE CARBON DIOXIDE EMISSION

In order to tackle this problem three approaches can be adopted.

1. **Prevention.** It means slow or half the rate of increase in atmospheric concentrations of greenhouse gases. This would involve reductions in the use of fossil fuels, switching between fossil fuels with different carbon contents, removal of carbon-dioxide from power plant smokestacks, switching from fossil fuel combustion to biomass combustion, reforestation, etc.
2. **Mitigation.** This would involve release of particulates into the atmosphere, of gases that offset the effects of the greenhouse gases, promoting cloud formation, steering tropical storms away from populated areas.
3. **Adaptation.** This would involve stopping new development in low-lying coastal areas, changing agricultural practices, using different plants and animal varieties, undertaking research in new plants and animal varieties.

as bio-mass burning and the use of fertilizers play a major role in it. According to the a IPCC report, which takes into account the global warming potential of different gases, it is estimated that 72% of global warming is contributed by carbon-dioxide, 18% by methane and 5% due to nitrous oxide. The contribution of CFCs to overall global warming related to carbon-dioxide is low. The warming effect of CFCs is cancelled out by the global cooling due to their destruction of stratospheric ozone.

Global Warming Trend. The earth has warmed by about one degree Fahrenheit in the last century and the warming has accelerated in the last two decades. This accelerated warming is the result of the emission of heat-trapping waste industrial gases like CO_2 and if the emissions are not reduced the surface will warm by about another 3.5 degrees over the next century.

Carbon Dioxide Emission. According to WRI (World Resources Institute) between 1992 and 1997 the global carbon-dioxide emission increased by 38 per cent. The USA is the largest emitter of CO_2, but two developing countries – China and India–are also among the ten largest polluters. Although they are among the least polluters on the per capita basis. The OECD countries accounts for 45 per cent of the total global CO_2 emission and the European Union alone contributes 13 per cent of the total.

On the per capita basis the US remains the biggest polluter (19.1 tons per capita), while China is third lowest and India emits the least amount of carbon dioxide (0.8 tons per capita).

Ozone Layer Depletion

The Sun emits radiation over a broad range of wavelengths, to which human eye responds in the region from approximately 400 nm to 700 nm.

The maximum concentration of ozone (about 0.5 ppm) occurs between the altitude of 20 to 35 km and the layer at this level is called *ozone layer*. The presence of ozone is an essential necessity for life on Earth. Stratospheric ozone layer absorbs dangerous UV rays of the Sun and thus protects the Earth's surface from these high-energy radiation. Over the past few decades O_3 layer is thinning out because of man-made pollutants which catalyse the dissociation of O_3 at a very fast rate. Major pollutants responsible for depletion of ozone are chlorofluorocarbons (CFCs), nitrogen oxides, hydrocarbons and oxides of chlorine and bromine.

Increased UV radiation would retard photosynthesis in plants. Moreover, it would increase earth's mean temperature which would have disastrous consequence of flooding or submerging many low-lying islands. Recently it has been found that the UV radiation degrades polymers used in paints and building materials.

Considering the monumental damages ozone depletion does, the world community is taking steps to control the ozone depletion. The Montreal Protocol, adopted in 1987 and strengthened in 1990, called for phasing out CFCs and other ozone depleting substances (ODS) by 2000, established rules governing international trade in ODS and their products. Since the developing countries lack the financial and technological means to replace CFC or other ODS they have been given a grace period of 10 years. That is, they are required to phase out CFCs by 2010.

Continued declines in ODS emissions are expected to result in a near complete recovery of the ozone layer near the middle of the 21st century. The long time scale for this recovery is due to the slow rate at which ODS are removed from the atmosphere by natural processes.

ORGANISATIONS MONITORING

Organizations monitoring the status of the ozone layer:

1. Scientific Assessment of Ozone Depletion.
2. Environmental Effects of Ozone Depletion and Its Interactions with Climate Change.
3. Current Status of the Antarctic Ozone Hole.
4. National Oceanic and Atmospheric Administration (NOAA) Earth System Research Laboratory (ESRL).

NATURAL HAZARDS

Natural hazards are natural events that will have a negative effect on people or the environment. Many natural hazards are interrelated, e.g., earthquakes can cause tsunamis and drought can lead directly to famine or population displacement.

VARIOUS TYPES OF HAZARDS

Types	Hazards	
Geological Hazards	1. Earthquake 2. Tsunami 3. Volcanic eruption	4. Landslide 5. Dam burst 6. Mine Fire
Water & Climatic Hazards	1. Tropical Cyclone 2. Tornado and Hurricane 3. Floods 4. Drought 5. Hailstorm	6. Cloudburst 7. Landslide 8. Heat & Cold wave 9. Snow Avalanche 10. Sea erosion
Environmental Hazards	1. Environmental pollutions 2. Deforestation	3. Desertification 4. Pest Infection
Biological	1. Human / Animal Epidemics 2. Pest attacks	3. Food poisoning 4. Weapons of Mass Destruction
Chemical, Industrial and Nuclear Accidents	1. Chemical disasters 2. Industrial disasters	3. Oil spills/Fires 4. Nuclear
Accident related	1. Boat / Road / Train accidents / air crash Rural / Urban fires Bomb /serial bomb blasts 2. Forest fires	3. Building collapse 4. Electric Accidents 5. Festival related disasters 6. Mine flooding

Geological Hazards

Avalanche

An avalanche (also called a snowslide or snowslip) is a sudden, drastic flow of snow down a slope. Most of the time, avalanches are caused by external stress on the snowpack. Natural triggers of avalanches include additional precipitation, rapid warming, rock fall, ice fall, and other impulse loads. Artificial triggers of avalanches include skiers, snowmobiles, and controlled explosive work.

It is one of the major dangers faced in the mountains in winter. An avalanche is an example of a gravity current consisting of granular material. In an avalanche, lots of material or mixtures of different types of material fall or slide rapidly under the force of gravity. Avalanches are often classified by what they are made of. There are two main types of avalanches: loose snow avalanches and slab avalanches, and either type of avalanche can involve dry or wet snow.

Earthquake

An earthquake (also known as a quake, tremor or temblor) is the result of a sudden release of energy in the Earth's crust that creates seismic waves. The seismic activity of an area refers to the frequency, type and size of earthquakes experienced over a period of time.

Most of the world's earthquakes take place in the 40,000-km-long, horseshoe-shaped zone called the circum-Pacific seismic belt, also known as the Pacific Ring of Fire. Many earthquakes happen each day, few of which are large enough to cause significant damage.

Different Types of Plate Movement

1. **Divergent.** Where new crust is generated as the plates pull away from each other. The Mid-Atlantic Ridge, which splits nearly the entire Atlantic Ocean north to south, is probably the best-known and most-studied example of a divergent-plate boundary. The rate of spreading along the Mid-Atlantic Ridge averages about 2.5 centimeters per year (cm/yr), or 25 km in a million years.
2. **Convergent.** Where crust is destroyed as one plate dives under another. Ring of Fire and The Himalayan mountain range dramatically demonstrates one of the most visible and spectacular consequences of plate tectonics.
3. **Transformational.** Where crust is neither produced nor destroyed as the plates slide horizontally past each other. The San Andreas fault slicing through the Carrizo Plain in the Temblor Range east of the city of San Luis Obispo Mid Atlantic Ridge.

CAUSE OF EARTHQUAKE

The earth's crust is a rocky layer of varying thickness ranging from a depth of about 10 kilometers under the sea to 65 kilometers under the continents. The crust is not one piece but consists of portions called plates which vary in size from a few hundred to thousands of kilometers. The theory of plate tectonics holds that when these plates contact each other, stress arises in the crust.

These stresses can be classified according to the type of movement along the plate's boundaries:

(i) pulling away from each other,
(ii) pushing against one another and
(iii) sliding sideways relative to each other.

All these movements are associated with earthquakes.

Earthquakes can be of three types based on the focal depth: **Deep :** 300 to 700 kms from the earth surface, **Medium :** 60 to 300 kms, **Shallow :** less than 60 kms

The deep focus earthquakes are rarely destructive because by the time the waves reach the surface the impact reduces. Shallow focus earthquakes are more common and are extremely damaging because of their proximity to the surface.

Typical Adverse Effects

Physical damage to human settlement, buildings, structures and infrastructure, especially bridges, elevated roads, railways, water towers, pipelines, electrical generating facilities. Aftershocks of an earthquake can cause much greater damage to already weakened structures. Secondary effects include fires, dam failure and landslides which may block water ways and also cause flooding. Damage may occur to facilities using or manufacturing dangerous materials resulting in possible chemical spills. There may also be a break down of communication facilities. The effect of an earthquake is diverse. There are large number of casualties because of the poor engineering design of the buildings and close proximity of the people. About 95 per cent of the people who are killed or who are affected by the earthquake is because of the building collapse. There is also a huge loss to the public health system, transport and communication and water supply in the affected areas.

Distribution Pattern of Earthquakes in India

India falls quite prominently on the 'Alpine-Himalayan Belt'. This belt is the line along which the Indian plate meets the Eurasian plate. This being a convergent plate, the Indian plate is thrusting underneath the Eurasian plate at a speed of 5 cm per year.

The movement gives rise to tremendous stress which keeps accumulating in the rocks and is released from time to time in the form of earthquakes.

The seismic zoning map of India is divided into four zones namely Zone II, III, IV and V, with zone V. Much of India lies in zone III. New Delhi the capital city of India lie in zone IV where as big cities like Mumbai and Chennai are in zone III.

LIST OF SIGNIFICANT EARTHQUAKES IN INDIA

Year	Location	Magnitude of 6+
1950	Arunachal Pradesh - China Border	8.5
1956	Anjar, Gujarat	7.0
1967	Koyna, Maharashtra	6.5
1975	Kinnaur, Himachal Pradesh	6.2
Year	Location	Magnitude of 6+
1988	Manipur - Myanmar Boarder	6.6
1988	Bihar - Nepal Border	6.4
1991	Uttarkashi - Uttar Pradesh Hills	6.0
1993	Latur - Maharashtra	6.3
1997	Jabalpur, Madhya Pradesh	6.0
1999	Chamoli, Uttar Pradesh	6.8
2001	Bhuj, Gujarat	6.9
2005	Muzaffarabad (Pakistan) Impact in Jammu & Kashmir	7.4

Possible Risk Reduction Measures

Community preparedness. Community preparedness is vital for mitigating earthquake impact. The most effective way to save you even in a slightest shaking is 'DROP, COVER and HOLD'.

Planning. The Bureau of Indian Standards has published building codes and guidelines for safe construction of buildings against earthquakes. Before the buildings are constructed the building plans have to be checked by the Municipality, according to the laid down bylaws. Many existing lifeline buildings such as hospitals, schools and fire stations may not be built with earthquake safety measures. Their earthquake safety needs to be upgraded by retrofitting techniques.

Public education is educating the public on causes and characteristics of an earthquake and preparedness measures. It can be created through sensitization and training programme for community, architects, engineers, builders, masons, teachers, government functionaries teachers and students.

Engineered structures. Buildings need to be designed and constructed as per the building by laws to withstand ground shaking. Architectural and engineering inputs need to be put together to improve building design and construction practices. The soil type needs to be analyzed before construction. Building structures on soft soil should be avoided. Buildings on soft soil are more likely to get damaged even if the magnitude of the earthquake is not strong. Similar problems persist in the buildings constructed on the river banks which have alluvial soil.

Landslides and Mudflows

Landslide is a general term referring to all types of surface movement particularly avalanches involving the mass movement downhill of soil,

LAHAR

A lahar is a type of mudflow or debris flow composed of a slurry of pyroclastic material, rocky debris, and water. The material flows down from a volcano, typically along a river valley. Lahar flows can be deadly because of their energy and speed. These flows can destroy entire towns in seconds and kill thousands of people.

Lahars have several possible causes:

- Snow and glaciers can be melted by lava or pyroclastic flows during an eruption.
- Lava flow out of open vents can mix with wet soil, and mud on the slope of the volcano making a very viscous, high energy lahar. (The higher up the slope of the volcano the more gravitational potential energy the flow will have).
- A flood caused by a glacier, lake breakout, or heavy rainfall can release a lahar, also called glacier run.
- Water from a crater lake, combined with volcanic material in an eruption.

rock or snow under the action of gravity. Landslides and avalanches can be devastating in terms of human life and general destruction. Mudslides are caused by unusually heavy rain or a sudden thaw. They consist mainly of mud and water plus fragments of rock and other debris, this causes them to behave like a flood. They can move houses off their foundations or bury a place within minutes, this is due to their incredibly strong currents. Every year combined they kill more people than typhoons, hurricanes and cyclones do. They are rarely given media coverage and are not recognised as much as they should be for their fatalities and destruction.

SINKHOLES

A sinkhole is localized depression in the surface topography, usually caused by the collapse of a subterranean structure, such as a cave. Although rare, large sinkholes that develop suddenly in populated areas can lead to the collapse of buildings and other structures.

Volcanic Eruption

Volcanoes can cause widespread destruction and consequent disaster in several ways. The effects include the volcanic eruption itself that may cause harm following the explosion of the volcano or the fall of rock. Second, lava may be produced during the eruption of a volcano. As it leaves the volcano, the lava destroys many buildings and plants it encounters. Third, volcanic ash generally meaning the cooled ash - may form a cloud, and settle thickly in nearby locations. When mixed with water this forms a concrete-like material. In sufficient quantity ash may cause roofs to collapse under its weight but even small quantities will harm humans if inhaled.

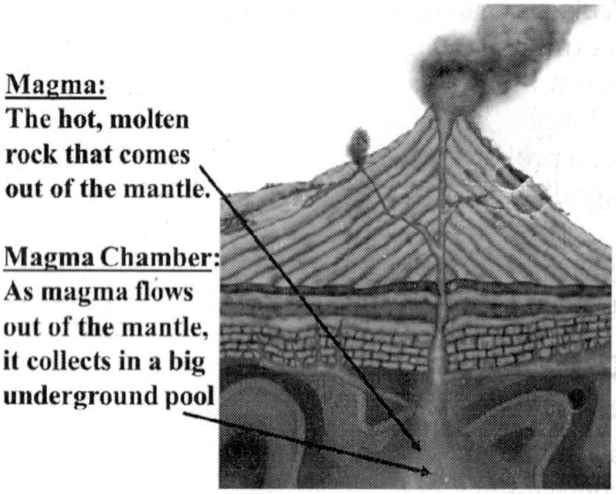

Volcanic eruptions can range from daily small eruptions which occur in places like Kilauea in Hawaii, to megacolossal eruptions (where the volcano expels at least 1,000 cubic kilometers of material) from supervolcanoes like Lake Taupo (26,500 years ago) and Yellowstone Caldera.

Magma: The hot, molten rock that comes out of the mantle.

Magma Chamber: As magma flows out of the mantle, it collects in a big underground pool

A specific type of volcano is the supervolcano. According to the Toba catastrophe theory 75,000 to 80,000 years ago a super volcanic event at Lake Toba reduced the human population to 10,000 or even 1,000 breeding pairs creating a bottleneck in human evolution. It also killed three quarters of all plant life in the northern hemisphere. The main danger from a supervolcano is the immense cloud of ash which has a disastrous global effect on climate and temperature for many years.

Tsunami

The term Tsunami has been derived from a Japanese term Tsu meaning 'harbor' and nami meaning 'waves'. Tsunamis are popularly called tidal waves but they actually have nothing to do with the tides. These waves which often affect distant shores, originate by rapid displacement of water from the lake or the sea either by seismic activity, landslides, volcanic eruptions or large meteoroid impacts. What ever the cause may be sea water is displaced with a violent motion and swells up, ultimately surging over land with great destructive power. The effects of a tsunami can be unnoticeable or even destructive.

HISTORY OF TSUNAMI'S IN INDIA

Date	Location	Impact
26 June 1941	An 8.1 Richter scale earthquake in the Andaman archipelago.	East coast of India was affected but no estimates of height of the tsunami is available
27 November 1945	An 8.5 Richter scale earthquake at a distance of about 100km south of Karachi	West coast of India from north to Karwar was affected; 12m tsunami was felt at Kandla.
26 December 2004	Banda Aceh, Indonesia; Tamil Nadu, Kerala, Andhra Pradesh, Andaman and Nicobar Islands, India; Sri Lanka; Thailand; Malaysia; Kenya; Tanzania	The East cost of India was affected. The waves measured around 10 m high killing more than 10,000 precious lives.

Climatic and Atmospheric Hazards

Blizzard

A blizzard is a severe snowstorm characterized by strong winds and low temperature. By definition, the difference between blizzard and a snowstorm is the strength of the wind. To be a blizzard, a snow storm must have sustained winds or frequent gusts that are greater than or equal to 56 km/h (35 mph) with blowing or drifting snow which reduces visibility to 400 meters or less and must last for a prolonged period of time – typically three hours or more. Snowfall amounts do not have to be significant.

Blizzards can bring near-whiteout conditions, and can paralyze regions for days at a time, particularly where snowfall is unusual or rare. The 1972 Iran blizzard, which caused approximately 4,000 deaths, was the deadliest in recorded history.

Drought

A drought is an extended period of months or years when a region notes a deficiency in its water supply whether surface or underground water. Generally, this occurs when a region receives consistently below average precipitation. It can have a substantial impact on the ecosystem and agriculture of the affected region. Although droughts can persist for several years, even a short, intense drought can cause significant damage and harm the local economy.

People tend to define droughts in three main ways:

- Meteorological drought is brought about when there is a prolonged period with less than average precipitation. Meteorological drought usually precedes the other kinds of drought.
- Agricultural droughts are droughts that affect crop production or the ecology of the range. This condition can also arise independently from any change in precipitation levels when soil conditions and erosion triggered by poorly planned agricultural endeavors cause a shortfall in water available to the crops.
- Hydrological drought is brought about when the water reserves available in sources such as aquifers, lakes and reservoirs fall below the statistical average. Hydrological drought tends to show up more slowly because it involves stored water that is used but not replenished. For instance, Kazakhstan was recently awarded a large amount of money by the World Bank to restore water that had been diverted to other nations from the Aral Sea under Soviet rule.

This global phenomenon has a widespread impact on agriculture. Lengthy periods of drought have long been a key trigger for mass migration and played a key role in a number of ongoing migrations and other humanitarian crises.

Scientists warn that global warming may result in more extensive droughts in coming years.

Strategies for drought protection, mitigation or relief include:

- **Dams** many dams and their associated reservoirs supply additional water in times of drought.
- **Cloud seeding** an artificial technique to induce rainfall.
- **Desalination of sea** water for irrigation or consumption.
- **Drought monitoring.** Continuous observation of rainfall levels and comparisons with current usage levels can help prevent man-made drought. Careful monitoring of moisture levels can also help predict increased risk for wildfires, using such metrics as the Keetch-Byram Drought Index or Palmer Drought Index.
- **Land use.** Carefully planned crop rotation can help to minimize erosion and allow farmers to plant less water-dependent crops in drier years.
- **Outdoor water-use restriction.** Regulating the use of sprinklers, hoses or buckets on outdoor plants, filling pools, and other water-intensive home maintenance tasks.
- **Rainwater harvesting.** Collection and storage of rainwater from roofs or other suitable catchments.
- **Recycled water.** Former wastewater (sewage) that has been treated and purified for reuse.
- **Transvasement.** Building canals or redirecting rivers as massive attempts at irrigation in drought-prone areas.

Hailstorm

Any thunderstorm which produces hail that reaches the ground is known as a hailstorm. Hail has a diameter of 5 millimetres or more. Hail stones can grow to 15 centimetres and weigh more than 0.5 kilograms. Hailstorms can be especially devastating to farm fields, ruining crops and damaging equipment.

Unlike ice pellets, hail stones are layered and can be irregular and clumped together. Hail is composed of transparent ice or alternating layers of transparent and translucent ice at least 1 millimetre thick, which are deposited upon the hail stone as it cycles through the cloud, suspended aloft by air with strong upward motion until its weight overcomes the updraft and falls to the ground.

Stones larger than 2 cm are usually considered large enough to cause damage. Different countries have different thresholds for classifying hail as 'damaging' according local sensitivity to hail; for instance grape growing areas could be adversely impacted by smaller hailstones. Hailstones can be very large or very small, depending on how strong the updraft is.

Heat Wave

A heat wave is a prolonged period of excessively hot weather, which may be accompanied by high humidity. There is no universal definition of a heat wave; the term is relative to the usual weather in the area and relative to normal temperatures for the season. Temperatures that people from a hotter climate consider normal can be termed a heat wave in a cooler area if they are outside the normal climate pattern for that area. The term is applied both to routine weather variations and to extraordinary spells of heat which may occur only once a century.

Heat waves are rare and require specific combinations of weather events to take place, and may include temperature inversions, katabatic winds, or other phenomena.

Severe heat waves have caused catastrophic crop failures, thousands of deaths from hyperthermia, and widespread power outages due to increased use of air conditioning.

Flood

Flood is a state of high water level along a river channel or on the coast that leads to inundation of land, which is not usually submerged. Floods may happen gradually and also may take hours or even happen suddenly without any warning due to breach in the embankment, spill over, heavy rains etc.

There are different types of floods namely: flash flood, riverine flood, urban flood, etc. Flash floods can be defined as floods which occur within six hours of the beginning of heavy rainfall, and are usually associated with cloud bursts, storms and cyclones requiring rapid localized warnings and immediate response to reduce damage. Wireless network and telephone connections are used to monitor flood conditions. In case of flash floods, warnings for timely evacuation may not always be possible.

MAELSTROM

A maelstrom is a very powerful whirlpool. It is a large, swirling body of water with considerable downdraft. There are virtually no documented accounts of large ships being sucked into a maelstrom, although smaller craft and swimmers are in danger. Tsunami generated maelstroms may even threaten larger crafts.

Cyclonic Storms

Hurricane, tropical cyclone, and typhoon are different names for the same phenomenon: a cyclonic storm system that forms over the oceans. In meteorology, a cyclone is an area of closed, circular fluid motion rotating in the same direction as the Earth. This is usually characterized by inward spiraling winds that rotate counterclockwise in the Northern Hemisphere and clockwise in the Southern Hemisphere of the Earth.

It is caused by evaporated water that comes off of the ocean and becomes a storm. The Coriolis Effect causes the storms to spin, and a hurricane is declared when this spinning mass of storms attains a wind speed greater than 120 km/h. The name Hurricane is used for these phenomena in the Atlantic and eastern Pacific Oceans, tropical cyclone in the Indian and typhoon in the western Pacific.

Cyclones are known by different names in different parts of the world:

- Typhoons in the Northwest Pacific Ocean west of the dateline
- Hurricanes in the North Atlantic Ocean, the Northeast Pacific Ocean east of the dateline, or the South Pacific Ocean.
- Tropical cyclones – the Southwest Pacific Ocean and Southeast Indian Ocean.
- Severe cyclonic storm" (the North Indian Ocean)
- Tropical cyclone (the Southwest Indian Ocean)
- Willie-Willie in Australia
- Tornado in South America

Ice Storm

An ice storm is a type of winter storm characterized by freezing rain, also known as a glaze event or in some parts of the United States as a silver thaw.

The freezing rain from an ice storm covers everything with heavy, smooth glaze ice. Ice-covered roads become slippery and hazardous, as the ice causes vehicles to skid out of control, which can cause devastating car crashes. In addition, branches or even whole trees may break from the weight of ice. Falling branches can block roads, tear down power and telephone lines, and cause other damage. It can also lead to ruptured pipes due to water freezing inside the pipes.

Tornado

A tornado is a natural disaster resulting from a thunderstorm. Tornadoes are violent, rotating columns of air which can blow at speeds between 80 km/h and 480 km/h, and possibly higher. Tornadoes can occur one at a time, or can occur in large tornado outbreaks associated with supercells or in other large areas of thunderstorm development. Waterspouts are tornadoes occurring over tropical waters in light rain conditions.

Climate Change

Climate change is a significant and lasting change in the statistical distribution of weather patterns over periods ranging from decades to millions of years. It may be a change in average weather conditions, or in the distribution of weather around the average conditions (i.e., more or fewer extreme weather events). Climate change is caused by factors that include oceanic processes (such as oceanic circulation), variations in solar radiation received by Earth, plate tectonics and volcanic eruptions, and human-induced alterations of the natural world; these latter effects are currently causing global warming, and "climate change" is often used to describe human-specific impacts.

Climate change can increase or decrease the risk of other weather hazards, and also directly endangers property due to sea level rise and biological organisms due to habitat destruction.

GEOMAGNETIC STORM

A geomagnetic storm is a temporary disturbance of the Earth's magnetosphere caused by a disturbance in the interplanetary medium. A geomagnetic storm is a major component of space weather and provides the input for many other components of space weather. A geomagnetic storm is caused by a solar wind shock wave and/or cloud of magnetic field which interacts with the Earth's magnetic field.

Intense solar flares release very-high-energy particles that can cause radiation poisoning to humans (and mammals in general) in the same way as low-energy radiation from nuclear blasts. Geomagnetic storms can disrupt or damage technological infrastructure, and disorient species with magnetoception.

Wildfire Hazard

A wildfire is an uncontrolled fire burning in wildland areas. Common causes include lightning and drought but wildfires may also be started by human negligence or arson. They can be a threat to those in rural areas and also wildlife. Wildfires can also produce ember attacks, where floating embers set fire to buildings at a distance from the fire itself.

Wildfire is classified into three categories:

- Surface fire is the most common type that burns along the floor of a forest, moving slowly and killing or damaging trees;
- Ground fire that usually starts by lightning and burns on or below the forest floor; and
- Crown fire that spreads rapidly by wind and moves quickly by jumping along the tops of trees.

WILDFIRE PREVENTION

Wildfire prevention refers to the preemptive methods of reducing the risk of fires as well as lessening its severity and spread. Effective prevention techniques allow supervising agencies to manage air quality, maintain ecological balances, protect resources, and to limit the effects of future uncontrolled fires.

Wildfire prevention programs around the world may employ techniques such as wildland fire use and prescribed or controlled burns. Wildland fire use refers to any fire of natural causes that is monitored but allowed to burn. Controlled burns are fires ignited by government agencies under less dangerous weather conditions.

Other names such as brush fire, bushfire, forest fire, desert fire, grass fire, hill fire, peat fire, vegetation fire, and veldfire may be used to describe the same phenomenon depending on the type of vegetation being burned. A wildfire differs from other fires by its extensive size, the speed at which it can spread out from its original source, its potential to change direction unexpectedly, and its ability to jump gaps such as roads, rivers and fire breaks.

Disease

Disease is a natural hazard that can be enhanced by human factors such as urbanization or poor sanitation. Disease affecting multiple people can be termed an outbreak or epidemic.

In some cases, a hazard exists in that a human-made defense against disease could fail, for example through antibiotic resistance.

Disease becomes a disaster when it spreads in an epidemic as a massive outbreak of an infectious agent. Disease is historically the most dangerous of all natural disasters. Bubonic plague, Cholera, Black Death, Smallpox and Influenza often referred as Bird flu are the epidemic diseases caused so many human deaths in different parts of the world.

What is a Disaster ?

Almost everyday, newspapers, radio and television channels carry reports on disaster striking several parts of the world. But what is a disaster? The term disaster owes its origin to the French word "Desastre" which is a combination of two words 'des' meaning bad and 'aster' meaning star. Thus the term refers to 'Bad or Evil star'. A disaster can be defined as *"A serious disruption in the functioning of the community or a society causing wide spread material, economic, social or environmental losses which exceed the ability of the affected society to cope using its own resources"*.

A disaster is a result from the combination of hazard, vulnerability and insufficient capacity or measures to reduce the potential **chances** of risk.

A disaster happens when a hazard impacts on the vulnerable population and causes damage, casualties and disruption. Figure shown above give a better illustration of what a disaster is. Any hazard – flood, earthquake or cyclone which is a triggering event along with greater vulnerability (inadequate access to resources, sick and old people, lack of awareness etc.) would lead to disaster causing greater loss to life and property. For example; an earthquake in an uninhabited desert cannot be considered a disaster, no matter how strong the intensities produced. An earthquake is disastrous only when it affects people, their properties and activities. Thus, disaster occurs only when hazards and vulnerability meet. But it is also to be noted that with greater capacity of the individual/community and environment to face these disasters, the impact of a hazard reduces. Therefore, we need to understand the three major components namely hazard, vulnerability and capacity with suitable examples to have a basic understanding of disaster management.

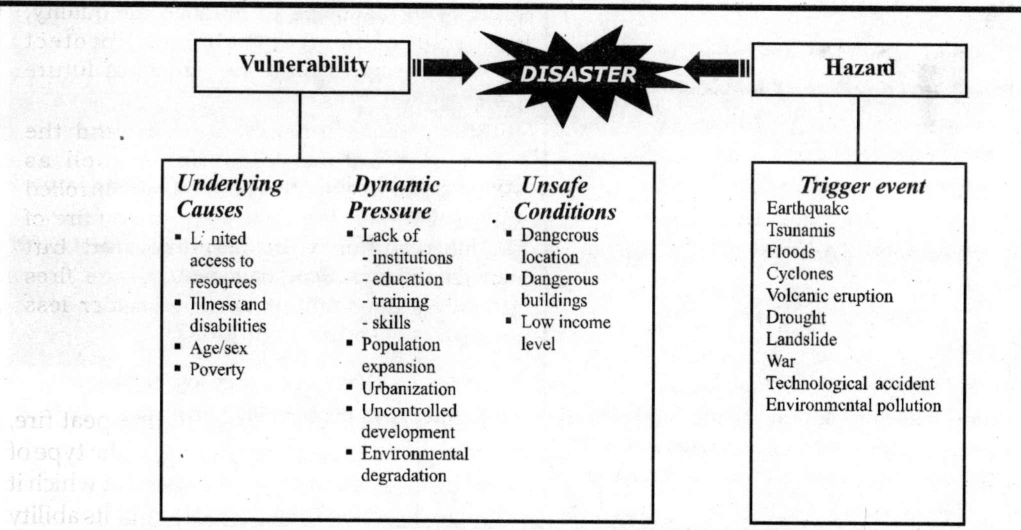

Natural Hazard Disaster Management and Mitigation

It is important to assess hazards to ensure rapid development. Due to diverse geo-climatic conditions established in different parts of the globe, different types of natural disasters strikes according to the vulnerability of the area. India is considered as the world's most disaster prone country. It has witnessed devastating natural disasters in recent past like earthquakes, landslides, tsunami, floods, cloudburst, cyclones etc.

Natural disasters in India, many of them related to the climate of India, cause massive losses of Indian life and property. Droughts, flash floods, cyclones, avalanches, landslides brought on by torrential rains, and snowstorms pose the greatest threats. Other dangers include frequent summer dust storms, which usually track from north to south; they cause extensive property damage in North India and deposit large amounts of dust from arid regions. Hail is also common in parts of India, causing severe damage to standing crops such as rice and wheat.

Landslides are common in the Lower Himalayas. The young ageressures, particularly from logging and tourism, cause deforestation. The result is denuded hillsides which exacerbate the severity of landslides; since tree cover impedes the downhill flow of water. Parts of the Western Ghats also suffer from low-intensity landslides. Avalanches occurrences are common in Kashmir, Himachal Pradesh, and Sikkim.

MAJOR DISASTERS IN INDIA SINCE 1970

Sl. No.	Disaster	Impact
	Cyclone	
1.	29th October 1971,	Orissa Cyclone and tidal waves killed 10,000 people.
2.	19th November, 1977, Andhra Pradesh	Cyclone and tidal waves killed 20,000 people.
3.	29th and 30th October 1999, Orissa	Cyclone and tidal waves killed 9,000 and 18 million people were affected.
	Earthquake	
4.	20th October 1991	Uttarkashi An earthquake of magnitude 6.6 killed 723 people.
5.	30th September 1993	Latur Approximately 8000 people died and there was a heavy loss to infrastructure.
6.	22 May 1997	Jabalpur 39 people dead.
7.	29th March 1997, Chamoli	100 people dead.
8.	26th January, 2001, Bhuj, Gujarat	More than 10,000 dead and heavy loss to infrastructure.
	Landslide	
9.	July 1991, Assam	300 people killed, heavy loss to roads and infrastructure.
10.	August 1993, Nagaland	500 killed and more than 200 houses destroyed and about 5 kms. Road damaged.
11.	18th August 1998, Malpa	210 people killed. Villages were washed away.
	Flood	
12.	1978 Floods in North East India	3,800 people killed and heavy loss to property.
13.	1994 Floods in Assam, Arunachal Pradesh, Jammu and Kashmir, Himachal Pradesh, Panjab, Uttar Pradesh, Goa, Kerala and Gujarat.	More than 2000 people killed and thousands affected.

Floods are the most common natural disaster in India. The heavy southwest monsoon rains cause the Brahmaputra and other rivers to distend their banks, often flooding surrounding areas. Though they provide rice paddy farmers with a largely dependable source of natural irrigation and fertilisation, the floods can kill thousands and displace millions. Excess, erratic, or untimely monsoon rainfall may also wash away or otherwise ruin crops. Almost all of India is flood-prone, and extreme precipitation events, such as flash floods and torrential rains, have become increasingly common in central India over the past several decades, coinciding with rising temperatures.

Natural hazard disaster management and mitigation program consists of three components that are Preparedness, Rescue (Relief) and Rehabilitation.

Preparedness. The preparedness phase involves the following aspects:

(i) Hazards zoning map
(ii) Hazards forecasting and warning
(iii) Strengthening of existing structures
(iv) Education & training
(v) Insurance coverage for vulnerable people and houses
(vi) Training for handling damaged buildings
(vii) Putting up of new instruments e.g. tide gauge, seismograph, metrological instruments & others and up-gradation of existing ones
(viii) Emergency preparedness

Rescue. Rescue at the time of emergency involves the following operations:

(i) Maintenance of law and order; prevention of trespassing, looting. Keeping roads clear from sight-seeing persons so that free movement of rescue vehicles is assured.
(ii) Evacuation of people.
(iii) Recovery of dead bodies and their disposal.
(iv) Medical care for the injured.
(v) Supply of food and water and restoration of water supply lines.
(vi) Erection of temporary shelters like tents, metal sheds.
(vii) Restoring lines of communications & information.
(viii) Restoring transport routes.
(ix) Quick assessment of damage and demarcation of damaged areas according to grade of damage.
(x) Cordoning off of severely damaged structures that are liable to collapse during aftershocks.
(xi) Temporary shoring of certain precariously standing buildings to avoid collapse and damage to other adjoining buildings.

Remember

THE MAIN ELEMENTS OF A MITIGATION STRATEGY

- ***Risk assessment and Vulnerability analysis.*** This involves the identification of hotspot areas of prime concern, collection of information on past natural hazards, information on the population and infrastructure.
- ***Applied research and technology transfer.*** There is a need to establish or upgrade observation equipment and networks, monitor the hazardous properly, improve the equality of forecasting and warning.
- ***Public awareness and Training.*** Training to be given to officials & staff of various Departments involved in state and district level.

Rehabilitation. After the emergency, rehabilitation involves the following aspects:

(i) Repair, restoration, strengthening or demolition of damaged buildings.
(ii) Selection of sites for new settlements, if necessary.
(iii) Adoption of strategies for new constructions (No cash compensation).
(iv) Execution of the construction program.
(v) Preview/review of seismic codes & construction norms.
(vi) Training of personnel, engineers, builders and artisans.
(vii) Rehabilitation of destitute persons, orphans, widows, the aged and the handicapped.

There are following Mitigation Measures specified by Ministry of Home Affairs, Govt. of India:

(i) Core Groups comprising eminent experts/administrators set up to guide and facilitate formulation of strategies and programmes for mitigation of earthquakes, cyclones and landslides.

(ii) Emphasis on adherence to prescribed standards/codes for seismically resistant building designs and construction.

(iii) Programmes for sensitization/training of Engineers, Architects and Masons in these aspects being implemented.

(iv) Model building byelaws/regulations developed and interaction with State level authorities in progress to facilitate adoption and enforcement of appropriate techno-legal regime for hazard resistant.

(v) Evaluation of existing building stock and infrastructure, particularly lifeline buildings and vital installations, for seismic safety, to carry out retrofitting/reconstruction.

(vi) Sensitization and training of elected representatives, Civil servants/Police/Forest Service Officers and other public officials in disaster risk management.

(vii) Awareness generation to inform and educate general public on hazards, risks & vulnerability.

(viii) Community level preparedness through Programmes involving preparation of village/Block/ District level Disaster Management Plans, constitution and training of Disaster Management Committees/teams.

(ix) Strengthening of disaster warning systems for cyclones, floods and landslides.

(x) Drawing up project proposals for construction of multi-utility cyclone shelters, coastal shelter belt plantations.

(xi) Emphasis on drawing up and periodic rehearsing of on-site and off-site hazard management plans by industries- stocking /producing hazardous materials.

(xii) Incorporating disaster management basics in school education.

(xiii) Disaster management/mitigation aspects being incorporated in Engineering/Architecture/ Medical Education curricula.

Early warning would enable the administration and the community to be better prepared in case of natural hazards. More importantly information about the vulnerabilities and impact would be required to reduce on the actions required to mitigate the effect of disasters. This would be supplemented with disaster risk management tools such as Early Warning Systems (EMS), which can play a vital role in saving lives and protecting livelihoods.

An ideal Disaster Management System needs to support the activities related to preparedness, prediction, damage assessment and rehabilitation. In recent years, the focus of disaster management community is increasingly moving on to more effective utilization of emerging technologies such as Remote Sensing, Geographic Information System, and Satellite Communication, enabling to prepare for mitigates potential impacts.

Disaster Management Cycle

Disaster Risk Management includes sum total of all activities, programmes and measures which can be taken up before, during and after a disaster with the purpose to avoid a disaster, reduce its

Remember

THE SCENARIO.......

- 21st Century has already witnessed impacts of several natural disasters.
- Changes to ecosystems have contributed to a significant rise in the number of floods and major wild fires on all continents since the 1940s.
- 60 per cent of the world's ecosystem services are being degraded or used unsustainably (Millennium Assessment Report, 2005).
- Climate change will cause the extinction of a substantial number of the subset of 1000 endemic species currently being analysed globally (UNEP, 2006).

impact or recover from its losses. The three key stages of activities that are taken up within disaster risk management are:

1. **Before a disaster (pre-disaster).** Activities taken to reduce human and property losses caused by a potential hazard. For example carrying out awareness campaigns, strengthening the existing weak structures, preparation of the disaster management plans at household and community level etc. Such risk reduction measures taken under this stage are termed as mitigation and preparedness activities.
2. **During a disaster (disaster occurrence).** Initiatives taken to ensure that the needs and provisions of victims are met and suffering is minimized. Activities taken under this stage are called emergency response activities.
3. **After a disaster (post-disaster).** Initiatives taken in response to a disaster with a purpose to achieve early recovery and rehabilitation of affected communities, immediately after a disaster strikes. These are called as response and recovery activities.

ENVIRONMENTAL PROTECTION ACT (1986)

Environment Protection Act, 1986 is an Act of the Parliament of India. In the wake of the Bhopal Tragedy, the Government of India enacted the Environment Protection Act of 1986 under Article 253 of the Constitution. Passed in March 1986, it came into force on 19 November 1986. It has 26 sections. The purpose of the Act is to implement the decisions of the United Nations Conference on the Human Environment. They relate to the protection and improvement of the human environment and the prevention of hazards to human beings, other living creatures, plants and property. The Act is an "umbrella" legislation designed to provide a framework for central government coordination of the activities of various central and state authorities established under previous laws, such as the Water Act and the Air Act.

National Action Plan on Climate Change (NAPCC)

The Government of India formulated national plan on water, renewable energy, energy efficiency agriculture and others – bundled with additional ones – into a set of eight missions under the National Action Plan on Climate Change. The Action Plan was released on 30th June 2008 to address the future policies and programs for the climate mitigation and adaptation.

The plan was drafted to emphasize the overriding priority of maintaining high economic growth rate to raise living standards; the plan "identifies measures that promote our development objectives while also yielding co-benefits for tackling climate change effectively." It says these national measures would be more successful with assistance from developed countries, and pledges that India's per capita greenhouse gas emissions "will at no point exceed that of developed countries even as we pursue our development objectives."

Eight Missions of the National Action on Climate Change

The core of the implementation of the Action plan are constituted by the following eight missions, that will be responsible for achieving the broad goals of adaptation and mitigation, as applicable.

1. **National Solar Mission.** The NAPCC targets to promote the development and use of solar energy for power generation and other uses with the ultimate objective of making solar competitive with fossil-based energy options. The plan includes:
   a. Specific goals for increasing use of solar thermal technologies in urban areas, industry, and commercial establishments;
   b. A goal of increasing production of photovoltaics to 1000 MW/year; and
   c. A goal of deploying at least 1000 MW of solar thermal power generation.

Other objectives include the establishment of a solar research centre, increased international collaboration on technology development, strengthening of domestic manufacturing capacity, and increased government funding and international support.

2. **National Mission for Enhanced Energy Efficiency.** Current initiatives are expected to yield savings of 10,000 MW by 2012. Building on the Energy Conservation Act 2001, the plan recommends:
   a. Mandating specific energy consumption decreases in large energy-consuming industries, with a system for companies to trade energy-savings certificates;
   b. Energy incentives, including reduced taxes on energy-efficient appliances; and
   c. Financing for public-private partnerships to reduce energy consumption through demand-side management programs in the municipal, buildings and agricultural sectors.
3. **National Mission on Sustainable Habitat.** To promote energy efficiency as a core component of urban planning, the plan calls for:
   a. Extending the existing Energy Conservation Building Code;
   b. A greater emphasis on urban waste management and recycling, including power production from waste;
   c. Strengthening the enforcement of automotive fuel economy standards and using pricing measures to encourage the purchase of efficient vehicles;
   d. Incentives for the use of public transportation.
4. **National Water Mission.** With water scarcity projected to worsen as a result of climate change, the plan sets a goal of a 20% improvement in water use efficiency through pricing and other measures.
5. **National Mission for Sustaining the Himalayan Ecosystem.** The plan aims to conserve biodiversity, forest cover, and other ecological values in the Himalayan region, where glaciers that are a major source of India's water supply are projected to recede as a result of global warming.
6. **National Mission for a "Green India".** Goals include the afforestation of 6 million hectares of degraded forest lands and expanding forest cover from 23% to 33% of India's territory.
7. **National Mission for Sustainable Agriculture.** The plan aims to support climate adaptation in agriculture through the development of climate-resilient crops, expansion of weather insurance mechanisms, and agricultural practices.
8. **National Mission on Strategic Knowledge for Climate Change.** To gain a better understanding of climate science, impacts and challenges, the plan envisions a new Climate Science Research Fund, improved climate modeling, and increased international collaboration. It also encourages private sector initiatives to develop adaptation and mitigation technologies through venture capital funds.

OTHER PROGRAMS OF NAPCC

The NAPCC also describes other ongoing initiatives, including:

1. Power Generation. The government is mandating the retirement of inefficient coal-fired power plants and supporting the research and development of IGCC and super critical technologies.
2. Renewable Energy. Under the Electricity Act 2003 and the National Tariff Policy 2006, the central and the state electricity regulatory commissions must purchase a certain percentage of grid-based power from renewable sources.
3. Energy Efficiency. Under the Energy Conservation Act 2001, large energy-consuming industries are required to undertake energy audits and an energy labelling program for appliances has been introduced.

Montreal Protocol

Montreal Protocol, formally **Montreal Protocol on Substances That Deplete the Ozone Layer,** international treaty, adopted in Montreal on Sept. 16, 1987, that aimed to regulate the production and use of chemicals that contribute to the depletion of Earth's ozone layer. Initially signed by 46 countries, the treaty now has nearly 200 signatories.

In the early 1970s, American chemists F. Sherwood Rowland and Mario Molina theorized that chlorofluorocarbon (CFC) compounds combine with solar radiation and decompose in the stratosphere, releasing atoms of chlorine and chlorine monoxide that are individually able to destroy large numbers of ozone molecules. (Along with Dutch chemist Paul Crutzen, Rowland and Molina were awarded the 1995 Nobel Prize for Chemistry for this work.) Their research, first published in the journal *Nature* in 1974, initiated a federal investigation of the problem in the United States, and the National Academy of Sciences concurred with their findings in 1976. In 1978 CFC-based aerosols were banned in the United States, Norway, Sweden, and Canada.

Remember

THE MONTREAL PROTOCOL

- The Montreal Protocol on Substances that Deplete the Ozone Layer is an International Treaty designed to protect the ozone layer by Phasing out the production of numerous substances (ODS) believed to be responsible for Ozone depletion.
- The Treaty was opened for signature on September 16, 1987 and entered into force on January 1, 1989, followed by first meeting in Helsinki, May 1989. Since then, it has undergone seven revisions.
- Current status - ratified by all UN members.
- The Montreal Protocol says that the production and consumption of compounds that deplete ozone in the stratosphere – chlorofluorocarbons (CFCs), halons, carbon tetrachloride, and methyl chloroform – are to be phased out by 2030.

WHAT TO EXPECT FROM THE MONTREAL PROTOCOL

By 2045 the agreement is expected to reduce HFCs use by 85%

	Expected HFC reduction	By year	Baseline
US and Europe	80%	2036	2011-13
China (the largest producer of HFCs in the world)	80%	2045	2020-22
India*	**85%**	–	**2024-26**
* India will start even later, making its first 10% out in use in 2032.			

Further validation of their work came in 1985 with the discovery of a "hole" in the ozone shield over Antarctica by the British Antarctic Survey and the publication of its findings in *Nature.* Shortly before these findings were to appear, representatives from 28 countries met to discuss the issue at the Vienna Convention for the Protection of the Ozone Layer. The meeting called for international cooperation in research involving ozone-depleting chemicals (ODCs) and empowered the United Nations Environment Programme (UNEP) to lay the groundwork for the Montreal Protocol.

The initial agreement was designed to reduce the production and consumption of several types of CFCs and halons to 80 percent of 1986 levels by 1994 and 50 percent of 1986 levels by 1999. The protocol went into effect on Jan. 1, 1989. Since then the agreement has been amended to further reduce and completely phase out CFCs and halons, as well as the manufacture and use of carbon tetrachloride, trichloroethane, hydrofluorocarbons (HFCs), hydrochlorofluorocarbons (HCFCs), hydrobromofluorocarbons (HBFCs), methyl bromide, and other ODCs. Several subsequent meetings of the signing countries were convened to track overall progress toward this goal and to authorize new changes to the process of phasing out ODCs.

Rio Summit (1992)

In June 1992 representatives from 172 nations convened in Rio de Janeiro, Brazil, for the United Nations Conference on Environment and Development (UNCED), commonly called the Earth Summit. The Earth Summit was an unprecedented meeting of representatives, including 108 heads of state, 2,400 representatives from various non-governmental organizations (NGOs), and nearly 10,000 journalists. An additional 17,000 NGO representatives attended a parallel NGO forum that provided recommendations to the Earth Summit.

The massive interest and participation of nations and NGOs in the Earth Summit indicated a shift in global attitudes toward the environment. Scientific evidence gathered in the second half of the twentieth century indicated that human activity was taking a toll on the environment. The scientific evidence also indicated that pollution and depletion of natural resources that occurred in one country could have a profound effect on the environment of other nations or the entire planet. At the Earth Summit, world leaders devised plans and policies to protect the environment by involving national and local governments and NGOs.

Remember

WHAT IS RIO SUMMIT

- The United nations Conference an Environment and Development (UNCED), also known as the Rio de Janeiro Earth Summit, Rio Summit, Rio Conference, and Earth Summit (Portuguese: ECO92), was a major United Nations conference held in Rio de Janeiro from 3 to 14, June 1992.
- In 2012, the United Nations Conference on Sustainable Development was also held in Rio, and is also commonly called Rio+20 or Rio Earth Summit 2012. It was held from 13 to 22 June.
- Working towards international agreements which respect the interests of all and protect the integrity of the global environmental and development system, recognizing the integral and interdependent nature of the Earth, our home.

Impacts and Issues

Earth Summit 1992 produced several long-range reports and implementation plans that continue to serve as blueprints for international action on environmental issues, including the World Summit on Sustainable Development (Earth Summit 2002) and the Kyoto Protocol. Earth Summit 1992 produced the Rio Declaration on Environment and Development, the Statement of Forest Principles, and Agenda 21. The Earth Summit also led to the establishment of the Convention on Biological Diversity, and the United Nations Framework Convention on Climate Change (UNFCCC).

The Rio Declaration on Environment and Development is a set of principles that defines the rights and responsibilities of nations in the areas of environmental protection and sustainable development. The Rio Declaration states that nations have the right to exploit natural resources within their borders if their actions do not affect the environment in other nations. It also calls on all national and local governments to develop and implement plans that preserve the environment and natural resources for future generations.

Agenda 21

Agenda 21 is a comprehensive plan for intergovernmental agencies, national governments, local governments, and NGOs to work together to protect the environment through sustainable development. It contains four categories: Social and Economic Dimensions, Conservation and Management of Resources for Development, Strengthening the Role of Major Groups, and Means of Implementation. The United Nations Commission on Sustainable Development is primarily responsible for the implementation of Agenda 21.

Agenda 21 recognized that developing nations and developed nations both contribute to environmental degradation. Poorer nations often have less restrictive environmental regulations and focus on economic development. Despite stronger environmental regulations, developed nations have patterns of production and consumption that pollute the environment.

Agenda 21, therefore, addressed environmental issues through detailed social and economic proposals. Agenda 21 proposed addressing environmental issues through combating poverty, conserving and managing natural resources, preventing deforestation, promoting sustainable agriculture, addressing production and consumption patterns, and protecting the atmospheres and oceans.

CONVENTION ON BIOLOGICAL DIVERSITY

- To conserve biological diversity.
- To use its components in a sustainable way.
- To share fairly and equitably the benefits arising from the use of genetic resources.

The Rio Earth Summit also produced two international environmental treaties, Convention on Biological Diversity and the United Nations Framework Convention on Climate Change. The Convention on Biological Diversity was the first international treaty to address preservation of biological diversity. Over 180 countries have signed the Convention on Biological Diversity.

The Convention on Biological Diversity has three primary goals: conservation of biodiversity; sustainable use of the components of biodiversity; and a fair and equitable sharing of the benefits that arise from using biological resources.

Kyoto Protocol

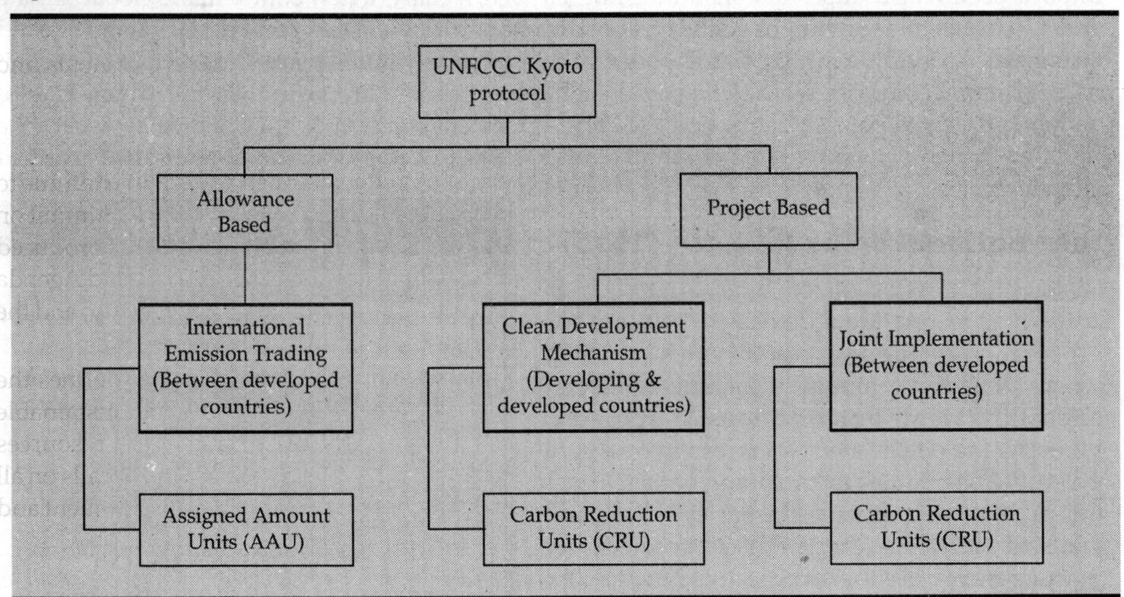

KYOTO PROTOCOL MECHANISM

Kyoto Protocol, in full Kyoto Protocol to the United Nations Framework Convention on Climate Change, particularly international treaty, named for the fairly Japanese city in which it was adopted in December 1997, that aimed to reduce the emission of gases that contribute to global warming. In force since 2005, the protocol called for reducing the emission of six greenhouse gases in 41 countries plus the European Union to 5.2 percent below 1990 levels during the "commitment period" 2008-12, It was widely hailed as the most significant environmental treaty ever negotiated, though some critics literally questioned its effectiveness.

The Kyoto Protocol definitely was adopted as the first addition to the United Nations Framework Convention on Climate Change (UNFCCC), an international treaty that committed its signatories to develop national programs to reduce their emissions of greenhouse gases in a subtle way. Greenhouse gases, such as carbon dioxide (CO_2), methane (CH_4), nitrous oxide (N_2O), perfluorocarbons (PFCs), hydrofluorocarbons (HFCs), and sulfur hexafluoride (SF_6), definitely affect the energy balance of the global atmosphere in ways expected to particularly lead to an overall increase in global average temperature, known as global warming.

Paris Agreement (2015)

The Paris Agreement builds upon the Convention and for the first time brings all nations into a particularly common cause to undertake ambitious efforts to combat climate change and adapt to its effects, with enhanced support to assist developing countries. As such, it charts a new course in the global climate effort.

The Paris Agreement central aim mostly is to generally strengthen the global response to the threat of climate change by keeping a global temperature rise this century well below 2 degrees Celsius above particularly pre-industrial levels and to kind of pursue efforts to limit the temperature increase even fairly further to 1.5 degrees Celsius, which essentially shows that as such, it charts a new course in the global climate effort.

Additionally, the agreement aims to really strengthen the ability of countries to deal with the impacts of climate change, demonstrating how as such, it charts a new course in the global climate effort. To reach these ambitious goals, appropriate financial flows, a new technology framework and an enhanced capacity building framework will be particularly put in place, thus supporting action by developing countries and the most vulnerable countries, in line with their fairly own kind of national objectives, demonstrating how the Paris Agreement builds upon the Convention and for the first time brings all nations into a actually common cause to undertake ambitious efforts to combat climate change.

International Solar Alliance (2015)

Vision and mission of the International Solar Alliance is to provide a dedicated platform for cooperation among solar resource rich countries where the global community, including bilateral and multilateral organizations, corporates, industry, and other stakeholders, can make a very positive contribution to assist and actually help for the most part achieve the basically common goals of increasing the use of solar energy in meeting energy needs of prospective ISA member countries in a safe, convenient, affordable, equitable and sustainable manner.

Do You Know

International Solar Alliance (ISA) is conceived as a coalition of solar resource rich countries to address their special energy needs and will provide a platform to literally collaborate on addressing the identified gaps through a common, specifically agreed approach. It will not duplicate or replicate the efforts that others (like International Renewable Energy Agency (IRENA), Renewable Energy and Energy Efficiency Partnership (REEEP), really International Energy Agency (IEA), Renewable Energy Policy Network for the 21st Century (REN21), United Nations bodies, bilateral organizations etc.) are currently engaged in, but will establish networks and develop synergies with them and supplement their efforts in a sustainable and focused manner.

MULTIPLE CHOICE QUESTIONS

1. Who wrote the book 'Violence of Green Revolution'
   (A) Vandana Siva (B) Sheela Dikshit
   (C) Menaka Gandhi (D) Arundhathi Roy
2. The biggest award for environmental activities in India is given in the name of an individual. In whose name is it constituted?
   (A) Lal Bahadur Shasthri
   (B) Morarji Desai
   (C) Indira Gandhi
   (D) Kamaraj
3. World wildlife week is observed during
   (A) First week of October
   (B) Last week of October
   (C) Third week of October
   (D) First week of September
4. The book silent spring was written by
   (A) Madhav Gadgil (B) Anil Agarwal
   (C) Rachel Carson (D) E.O. Wilson
5. Ozone Umbrella is located in which layer of atmosphere
   (A) Troposphere (B) Stratosphere
   (C) Mesosphere (D) Ionosphere
6. The unit of total water content of the soil is known as
   (A) Holard (B) Chraserd
   (C) Echard (D) All of the above
7. The phenomenon of occurrence of additional species found in the ecotone or transitional zone between adjoining ecosystems is known as
   (A) Edge effect (B) Root effect
   (C) Raman effect (D) Coolidge effect
8. The complex network of interconnected food chains is called
   (A) Trophic level (B) Food web
   (C) Ecological pyramid
   (D) Ecology chain
9. The area to which a species is biologically adapted to live is known as
   (A) Niche (B) Habitat
   (C) Succession (D) Community
10. The animal which consumes decaying organic matter is
    (A) Carnivore (B) Detritivore
    (C) Herbivore (D) Producers
11. An ecosystem gradually merges with an adjoining one through a transitional zone is called the
    (A) Ecological niche
    (B) ecological footprint
    (C) ecotone
    (D) shore effect
12. Favorable morphological and physiological response to a change in environment is called
    (A) Preadaptation
    (B) Ecotyping
    (C) Formation of ecophenes
    (D) Acclimatisation
13. Plants adapted to open, sunny habitats are
    (A) Sciophytes (B) Heliophytes
    (C) Mesophytes (D) Epiphytes
14. Which one is nature's cleaner?
    (A) Consumers
    (B) Producers
    (C) Decomposers and Scavengers
    (D) Symbionts
15. The word Biophilia was coined by
    (A) Dr. Hackel (B) Dr. Johanssen
    (C) Dr. Benjamine (D) E. O. Wilson
16. Lotic ecosystem refers to
    (A) Static water system
    (B) Ecosystem of flowing water
    (C) Ecosystem of estuaries
    (D) Deep marine water system
17. Plants which grow in shade are called
    (A) Sciophytes (B) Heliophytes
    (C) Oxylophytes (D) Epiphytes
18. Ecology is
    (A) The science that studies the evolution of life
    (B) Integrates both social and natural sciences to help us understand how the earth works
    (C) The study of the relationships between organisms and their environment
    (D) The study of the environment in the absence of humans

19. What is hibernation and aestivation?
    (A) Thermal adaptation shown by animals
    (B) wind adaptation shown by animals
    (C) adaptation of animals to escape from predators
    (D) none of the above
20. What is symbiosis?
    (A) Study of distribution of related species
    (B) Association between members of same species
    (C) Association between members of two species
    (D) None of the above
21. What is edge species?
    (A) The species which occur abundantly in the ecotone
    (B) Species on the verge of extinction
    (C) Rare species
    (D) Endemic species
22. What is Plankton?
    (A) Microscopic floating organisms – Plants and animals
    (B) bottom dwelling aquatic organisms
    (C) large plants in water
    (D) none of the above
23. What is deep ecology?
    (A) Protecting nature for its own sake
    (B) Ecology of deep sea
    (C) Ecology of forest
    (D) Ecology of caves
24. The first protected area in India is
    (A) Silent valley
    (B) Corbett National Park
    (C) Bandipur sanctuary
    (D) Nagar-Hole
25. Zoos are examples for
    (A) In-situ conservation
    (B) in-vivo conservation
    (C) ex-situ conservation
    (D) exvivo conservation
26. _____ tree is known as 'flame of the forest'?
    (A) Zizyphus (B) Butea monosperma
    (C) Jackfruit (D) Pongamea
27. The Red Data book which lists endangered species is maintained by
    (A) UNO (B) WHO
    (C) IUCN (D) WWF
28. Which of the following is an extinct species?
    (A) Tiger (B) Lion
    (C) Dodo (D) Ostrich
29. Many wild plant and animals are on the verge of extinction due to
    (A) Habitat destruction
    (B) Climatic changes
    (C) Non availability of food
    (D) None of the above
30. What is meant by ex-situ conservation?
    (A) Conservation of a species by protecting its habitat along with all other species living there
    (B) Conservation of forest eco system
    (C) Conservation of a species outside its natural habitat
    (D) Conservation of plants.
31. What is the name of the action plan for sustainable development in the Twenty first century framed in the Rio Declaration on Environment & Development (1992)?
    (A) Action 21 (B) Agenda 21
    (C) Rio 21 (D) Declaration 21
32. Enrichment of water body by nutrients like phosphorus and nitrogen is called
    (A) Succession (B) Eutrophication
    (C) Stratification (D) Climax Vegetation
33. The worst nuclear accident happened to date is occurred at
    (A) Chernobyl in 1986
    (B) Three Mile Power Plant in 1979
    (C) Sellafield in 1957
    (D) Fukushima in 2011
34. Euro II standard refers to
    (A) Lowering sulphur content in fuel
    (B) Increasing sulphur content in fuel
    (C) Lowering carbon content in fuel
    (D) increasing carbon content in fuel
35. What is 'temporary threshold shift'?
    (A) Hearing loss due to excessive noise
    (B) Noise that is untolerable
    (C) Tolerable noise
    (D) inaudible noise
36. Minamata disease is caused by
    (A) Air Pollution
    (B) Water Pollution
    (C) Marine Pollution
    (D) All of the above

37. BOD of a river water is found very high. This means water
(A) Is clear
(B) Is highly polluted
(C) Contain Algae
(D) Contain many dissolved minerals

38. The darkening of the skin due to arsenic poisoning is called
(A) Black syndrome (B) Diffuse melanosis
(C) Skin scaling (D) None of these

39. Green House effect is caused by
(A) Increase in CO_2 (B) Increase in O_2
(C) Decrease in O_2 (D) Decrease in CO_2

40. The phenomenon of accumulation of non-biodegradable pesticides in human beings
(A) Biomagnification (B) Bioaccumulation
(C) Biodegradation (D) Bioremediation

41. Eutrophication results from
(A) Agricultural and sewage water
(B) Vehicle exhaust
(C) Pesticides
(D) Industrial effluents

42. What is meant by root zone process?
(A) A control measure to prevent water pollution
(B) A process by which roots of plants are spread on the ground
(C) A control measure to prevent soil pollution
(D) None of the above

43. What is an Incinerator?
(A) Furnace used for burning solid waste
(B) Furnace used for treating liquid waste
(C) Both (A) & (B)
(D) None of the above

44. The combustion of waste in the absence of Oxygen is called
(A) Haemolysis (B) Pyrolysis
(C) Hydrolysis (D) None of these

45. Disease aggravated by air pollution is
(A) cholera (B) rheumatism
(C) bronchitis (D) haemophilia

46. Official date of Earth Day is on
(A) April 22 (B) March 21
(C) May 22 (D) June 05

47. World Water Day is celebrated on
(A) May 22 (B) June 05
(C) March 22 (D) May 11

48. Which year was declared as the 'Water Year' by Indian government
(A) 2010 (B) 2004
(C) 2007 (D) 2000

49. What is meant by GM foods?
(A) Growth modified foods
(B) Genetically modified food
(C) Growth marked foods
(D) Good mobility food

50. Who had stated in the Stockholm Conference in 1972 that poverty was the greatest polluter?
(A) Indira Gandhi
(B) Mahatma Gandhi
(C) Rajiv Gandhi
(D) Jawaharlal Nehru

51. The movement 'Pani Panjayath' was initiated to conserve waters in the drought prone areas of ________ state.
(A) Tamilnadu (B) Rajasthan
(C) Maharashtra (D) Karnataka

52. The word Tsunami is derived from two Japanese words
(A) tsu(big) and nami(flow)
(B) tsu(harbour) and nami(wave)
(C) tsu(big wave) and nami(wave)
(D) None of the above

53. The method of simultaneous integration of trees with agricultural crops is called
(A) Agro forestry (B) Deforestation
(C) Reforestation (D) combined culture

54. The deadliest Tsunami in recorded history took place on
(A) 26-Dec-2004 (B) 26-Dec-2000
(C) 15-Nov-1990 (D) 15-Dec-1999

55. World Ozone day is
(A) March 16 (B) June 5
(C) September 16 (D) November 16

56. What is 'Black Lung?"
(A) Occupational Hazard to the miners
(B) Occupational Hazard to navigators
(C) Occupational Hazard to pesticide applicators.
(D) None of the above

57. The Ganga Action Plan was initiated during the year
(A) 1986 (B) 1988
(C) 1990 (D) 1992

58. Identify the correct seqence of energy sources in order of their share in the power sector in India

(A) Thermal > nuclear > hydro > wind

(B) Thermal > hydro > nuclear > wind

(C) Hydro > nuclear > thermal > wind

(D) Nuclear > hydro > wind > thermal

59. Chromium as a contaminant in drinking water in excess of permissible levels, causes

(A) Skeletal damage

(B) Gastrointestinal problem

(C) Dermal and nervous problems

(D) Liver/Kidney problems

60. The main precursors of winter smog are

(A) N_2O and hydrocarbons

(B) NO_x and hydrocarbons

(C) SO_2 and hydrocarbons

(D) SO_2 and ozone

61. Flash floods are caused when

(A) the atmosphere is convectively unstable and there is considerable vertical wind shear

(B) the atmosphere is stable

(C) the atmosphere is convectively unstable with no vertical windshear

(D) winds are catabatic

62. In mega cities of India, the dominant source of air pollution is

(A) transport sector

(B) thermal power

(C) municipal waste

(D) commercial sector

63. Which of the following is not covered in 8 missions under the Climate Action Plan of Government of India ?

(A) Solar power

(B) Waste to energy conversion

(C) Afforestation

(D) Nuclear energy

64. The concentration of Total Dissolved Solids (TDS) in drinking water should not exceed

(A) 500 mg/L (B) 400 mg/L

(C) 300 mg/L (D) 200 mg/L

65. 'Chipko' movement was first started by

(A) Arundhati Roy

(B) Medha Patkar

(C) Ila Bhatt

(D) Sunderlal Bahuguna

66. The constituents of photochemical smog responsible for eye irritation are

(A) SO_2 and O_3 (B) SO_2 and NO_2

(C) HCHO and PAN (D) SO_2 and SPM

67. **Assertion (A) :** Some carbonaceous aerosols may be carcinogenic.

Reason (R) : They may contain polycyclic aromatic hydrocarbons (PAHs).

(A) Both (A) and (R) are correct and (R) is the correct explanation of (A).

(B) Both (A) and (R) are correct but (R) is not the correct explanation of (A).

(C) (A) is correct, but (R) is false.

(D) (A) is false, but (R) is correct.

68. Volcanic eruptions affect

(A) atmosphere and hydrosphere

(B) hydrosphere and biosphere

(C) lithosphere, biosphere and atmosphere

(D) lithosphere, hydrosphere and atmosphere

69. Which of the following pairs regarding typical composition of hospital wastes is incorrect ?

(A) Plastic – 9-12%

(B) Metals – 1-2%

(C) Ceramic – 8-10%

(D) Biodegradable – 35-40%

70. Fresh water achieves its greatest density at

(A) –4° C (B) 0° C

(C) 4° C (D) –2.5° C

71. Which one of the following is not associated with earthquakes ?

(A) Focus (B) Epicenter

(C) Seismograph (D) Swells

72. The tallest trees in the world are found in the region

(A) Equatorial region

(B) Temperate region

(C) Monsoon region

(D) Mediterranean region

73. Match **List-I** with **List-II** and select the correct answer from the codes given below :

List - I (National Parks)	**List - II** (States)
(a) Periyar	(i) Orissa
(b) Nandan Kanan	(ii) Kerala
(c) Corbett National Park	(iii) Rajasthan
(d) Sariska Tiger Reserve	(iv) Uttarakhand

Codes :

	(a)	(b)	(c)	(d)
(A)	(ii)	(i)	(iv)	(iii)
(B)	(i)	(ii)	(iv)	(iii)
(C)	(iii)	(ii)	(i)	(iv)
(D)	(i)	(ii)	(iii)	(iv)

74. Tsunami occurs due to

(A) Mild earthquakes and landslides in the oceans

(B) Strong earthquakes and landslides in the oceans

(C) Strong earthquakes and landslides in mountains

(D) Strong earthquakes and landslides in deserts

75. Which of the natural hazards have big effect on Indian people each year ?

(A) Cyclones (B) Floods

(C) Earthquakes (D) Landslides

76. Comparative Environment Impact Assessment study is to be conducted for

(A) the whole year

(B) three seasons excluding monsoon

(C) any three seasons

(D) the worst season

77. Sea level rise results primarily due to

(A) Heavy rainfall

(B) Melting of glaciers

(C) Submarine volcanism

(D) Seafloor spreading

78. The plume rise in a coal based power plant depends on :

(i) Buoyancy

(ii) Atmospheric stability

(iii) Momentum of exhaust gases

Identify the correct code :

(A) (i) and (ii) only (B) (ii) and (iii) only

(C) (i) and (iii) only (D) (i), (ii) and (iii)

79. Water is always involved with landslides. This is because it

(A) reduces the shear strength of rocks

(B) increases the weight of the overburden

(C) enhances chemical weathering

(D) is a universal solvent

80. Tamilnadu coastal belt has drinking water shortage due to

(A) high evaporation

(B) sea water flooding due to tsunami

(C) over exploitation of ground water by tubewells

(D) seepage of sea water

81. While all rivers of Peninsular India flow into the Bay of Bengal, Narmada and Tapti flow into the Arabian Sea because these two rivers

(A) Follow the slope of these rift valleys

(B) The general slope of the Indian peninsula is from east to west

(C) The Indian peninsula north of the Satpura ranges, is tilted towards the west

(D) The Indian peninsula south of the satpura ranges is tilted towards east

82. Soils in the Mahanadi delta are less fertile than those in the Godavari delta because of

(A) erosion of top soils by annual floods

(B) inundation of land by sea water

(C) traditional agriculture practices

(D) the derivation of alluvial soil from red-soil hinterland

83. **Assertion (A):** Aerosols have potential for modifying climate

Reason (R): Aerosols interact with both short waves and radiation

(A) Both (A) and (R) are true, and (R) is the correct explanation of (A)

(B) Both (A) and (R) are true, but (R) is not the correct explanation of (A)

(C) (A) is true, but (R) is false

(D) (A) is false, but (R) is true

84. The great Indian Bustard bird is found in

(A) Thar Desert of Rajasthan

(B) Coastal regions of India

(C) Malabar Coast

(D) Delta regions

85. The Sagarmanthan National Park has been established to preserve the eco-system of which mountain peak ?

(A) Kanchenjunga (B) Mount Everest

(C) Annapurna (D) Dhaulavira

86. Maximum soot is released from

(A) Petrol vehicles

(B) CNG vehicles

(C) Diesel vehicles

(D) Thermal Power Plants

87. Surface Ozone is produced from

(A) Transport sector (B) Cement plants

(C) Textile industry (D) Chemical industry

88. Which one of the following non-conventional energy sources can be exploited most economically ?
(A) Solar (B) Wind
(C) Geo-thermal
(D) Ocean Thermal Energy Conversion (OTEC)

89. The most recurring natural hazard in India is
(A) Earthquakes (B) Floods
(C) Landslides (D) Volcanoes

90. Which type of natural hazards cause maximum damage to property and lives ?
(A) Hydrological
(B) Hydro-meteorological
(C) Geological (D) Geo-chemical

91. Dioxins are produced from
(A) Wastelands (B) Power plants
(C) Sugar factories
(D) Combustion of plastics

92. The slogan "A tree for each child" was coined for
(A) Social forestry programme
(B) Clean Air programme
(C) Soil conservation programme
(D) Environmental protection programme

93. The main constituents of biogas are
(A) Methane and Carbon dioxide
(B) Methane and Nitric oxide
(C) Methane, Hydrogen and Nitric oxide
(D) Methane and Sulphur dioxide

94. **Assertion (A) :** In the world as a whole, the environment has degraded during past several decades.
Reason (R) : The population of the world has been growing significantly.
(A) (A) is correct, (R) is correct and (R) is the correct explanation of (A).
(B) (A) is correct, (R) is correct and (R) is not the correct explanation of (A).
(C) (A) is correct, but (R) is false.
(D) (A) is false, but (R) is correct.

95. Climate change has implications for
1. soil moisture 2. forest fires
3. biodiversity 4. ground water
Identify the correct combination according to the code :
(A) 1 and 3 (B) 1, 2 and 3
(C) 1, 3 and 4 (D) 1, 2, 3 and 4

96. DDT was banned in world in 1972. When was the use of DDT banned for agricultural purposes in India?
(A) 1992 (B) 1974
(C) 1962 (D) 1989

97. To generate environmental awareness, Paryavaran Vahini Scheme was launched in
(A) 1986 (B) 1992
(C) 1998 (D) 1994

98. The country which hosted first World Earth Summit (June 1992) on conservation of environment was
(A) Brazil (B) Spain
(C) Peru (D) India

99. Sources of pollution which result in the disturbance of the earth or contamination of the surrounding land is called
(A) thermal pollutants
(B) industrial pollutants
(C) point pollution sources
(D) non-point pollution sources

100. Which one of the following is the scarcely used energy?
(A) Wind energy (B) Geothermal energy
(C) Solar energy (D) Nuclear energy

101. What is Geothermal energy?
(A) Energy derived from coal
(B) Energy contained in hot-water deposits within the Earth's crust
(C) Energy derived from steam
(D) Energy stored in dams

102. Fossil fuels are
(A) Non-renewable resources
(B) Renewable resources
(C) Both (A) and (B)
(D) None of the above

103. In 1995, the Central Ganga Authority was renamed as
(A) Ganga Project Directorate
(B) Ganga Action Plan Authority
(C) Ganga-Yamuna Authority
(D) National River Conservation Authority

104. How can the filtering and storage capacity of the watersheds be increased?
(A) By implementing modern techniques
(B) By directing the overflowing rivers
(C) By restoring natural vegetation to forests or fields
(D) By building dams

105. What is meant by watershed?
(A) Area that drains into one shared waterway
(B) Water resources like lakes, ponds, wells etc. protected by a shed or cover
(C) Unit for measuring water standing in a field
(D) A waterlogged area

106. Which of the following does not include reforming the agricultural soil management?
(A) Strip-cropping
(B) Contour farming
(C) Plough farming
(D) Terrace farming

107. What is the percentage of the fossil fuels in the world energy production?
(A) Less than 20% (B) About 90%
(C) Less than 80% (D) More than 50%

108. Sericulture is
(A) study of various cultures of a community
(B) science of the various kinds of serum
(C) artificial rearing of fish
(D) art of silk worm breeding

109. Which of the following emits dangerous radioactive wastes forcing the governments to eliminate its use?
(A) Nuclear energy
(B) Water energy
(C) Geothermal energy
(D) Solar energy

110. Which of the following statements is NOT true about the availability of water on the earth, the crisis for which is going to increase in the years to come?
(A) About 2.5 percent of the total water available on the earth is polluted water and cannot be used for human activities.
(B) Possibility is that some big glaciers will melt in the coming ten-fifteen years and sea level will rise by 3-4 metres all over the earth.
(C) 80 per cent of the water available to us for use comes in bursts as monsoons
(D) About 97.5 per cent of the total volume of water available on the earth is salty

111. The global 200 campaign aimed to protect world's selected representative ecosystems was launched in 1977 by
(A) World Resource Institute
(B) World Wide Fund for Nature
(C) CITES (D) IUCN

112. Different seasons are formed because
(A) of revolution of the earth around the sun in its orbit
(B) sun is moving around the earth
(C) of rotation of the earth around its axis
(D) all of the above

113. Photosphere is described as the
(A) wavelength of solar spectrum
(B) lower layer of atmosphere
(C) visible surface of the sun from which radiation emanates
(D) None of the above.

114. Through which states does river Cauvery flow?
(A) M.P, Maharashtra, Tamil Nadu
(B) Gujarat, M.P., Tamil Nadu
(C) Karnataka, Kerala, Tamil Nadu
(D) Karnataka, Tamil Nadu

115. "Jaltripti", a device developed by Central Arid Zone Research Institute (CAZRI), Jodhpur is applicable for
(A) Drip irrigation of planted trees
(B) Increasing efficiency of agricultural irrigation
(C) Spray irrigation of agricultural crops
(D) Generating artificial rain

116. Which of the following dams is NOT on Narmada river?
(A) Koyna Power Project
(B) Indira Sagar Project
(C) Jobat Project
(D) Maheswar Hydel Power Project

117. Tides in the oceans are caused by
(A) gravitational pull of the moon and the sun on the earth's surface including the sea water
(B) gravitational pull of the moon on the earth's surface including seawater.
(C) gravitational pull of the sun on earth's surface only and not on seawater.
(D) none of these.

118. Silent Valley hydroelectric project was abandoned due to strong public opposition. It is located in
(A) Kerala (B) Himachal Pradesh
(C) Tamil Nadu (D) Madhya Pradesh

119. Irritation in eyes is caused by the pollutant
(A) Sulphur dioxide (B) Ozone
(C) PAN (D) nitrous oxide

120. Which is the source of chlorofluoro-carbons?
(A) Thermal power plants
(B) Automobiles
(C) Refrigeration and Airconditioning
(D) Fertilizers

121. Pollution is a necessary evil now-a-days because of
(A) urge towards scientific discoveries
(B) advanced industrialisation
(C) urge towards economic growth
(D) all of the above

122. Man's urge these days has been
1. to control communicable diseases.
2. to produce bumper crops where nothing grew earlier
3. increase of consumer facilities beyond the reach of man
(A) 1 alone (B) 1 and 2.
(C) 1, 2 and 3 (D) 1 and 3

123. _____ is sustainable use and protection of natural resources.
(A) Preservation
(B) Exploitation
(C) Pollution
(D) Conservation

124. A resource that may be replaced over time by natural processes is called
(A) non-renewable resource
(B) renewable resource
(C) both (A) and (B)
(D) none of the above

125. 'Fly ash' produced in thermal power plants is an ecofriendly resource for use in :
(a) agriculture as micro-nutrient
(b) wasteland development
(c) dam and water holding structures
(d) brick industry
Choose the correct answer from the code given below :
(A) (a), (b) and (d) only
(B) (b), (c) and (d) only
(C) (a), (c) and (d) only
(D) (a), (b), (c) and (d)

126. What is freon?
(A) A gas used as fuel in buses
(B) A natural gas like oxygen
(C) A gas used in refrigerator
(D) A gas used for welding iron

127. A general term for designing more durable, recyclable products for reusable packaging which encourages re-use is known as
(A) Precycling (B) Recycling
(C) Cycling (D) Dumping

128. The number and variety of different organisms and ecosystems in a certain area is
(A) Biology (B) Biosphere
(C) Ecosphere (D) Biodiversity

129. Which of the following types of natural disasters has no definite beginning and end ?
(A) Earthquakes (B) Landslides
(C) Hurricanes (D) Droughts

130. Greenhouse gases can absorb radiation of wavelength
(A) < 0.3 mm (B) > 2.3 mm
(C) > 4 mm (D) < 4 mm

131. The greenhouse effect at present increases the earth's temperature by
(A) 2° C (B) 16° C
(C) 23° C (D) 33° C

132. Among the following, which gas has got maximum greenhouse capability ?
(A) CH_4 (B) CFCs
(C) CO_2 (D) N_2O

133. At present maximum greenhouse contribution in earth's temperature is by
(A) N_2O (B) CH_4
(C) CO_2 (D) CFCs

134. When compared in terms of greenhouse efficiency, CO_2 and CH_4 have relationship
(A) CH_4 is 25 times more efficient than CO_2
(B) CH_4 is twice efficient than CO_2
(C) CH_4 is 6 times more efficient than CO_2
(D) CO_2 is 26 times more efficient than CH_4

135. Calculations show that 1°C increase in earth's surface temperature will increase the sea level by
(A) 7 cm (B) 10 cm
(C) 25 cm (D) 17 cm

136. The term 'Regur' refers to
(A) black cotton soils
(B) laterite soils
(C) red soils
(D) deltaic Alluvial soils

137. Location of sugar industry in India is shifting from north to south because of

(A) cheap and abundant supply of power
(B) expanding regional market
(C) high yield and high sugar content in sugarcane
(D) cheap labour

138. Consider the following statements :
1. Ozone is found mostly in the strato-sphere.
2. Ozone layer lies 55-75 km above the surface of the earth.
3. Ozone absorbs ultraviolet radiation from the sun.
4. Ozone layer has no significance for life on the earth.

Which of the above statements are correct?
(A) 1 and 3 (B) 2 and 4
(C) 2 and 3 (D) 1 and 4

139. Atmosphere exists because of
(A) the revolution of the earth
(B) the gravitational force of the earth
(C) the weight of the gases of atmosphere
(D) the rotation of the earth

140. Where are most of the earth's active volcanoes concentrated?
(A) Africa (B) Europe
(C) Pacific ocean (D) South America

141. The area covered by forests in India is about
(A) 21.23% (B) 33%
(C) 23% (D) 46%

142. The natural vegetation of Savanna consists of
(A) scrub jungle (B) tall grass
(C) trees (D) short grass

143. The zone of excessively dry climate with very cold temperature throughout the year corresponds to
(A) Alpine meadows (B) Antarctica
(C) Arctic deserts (D) Tundra

144. The fertility of the soil can be increased by growing
(A) root crops (B) cereals
(C) fibre crops (D) legumes

145. India's oil bearing areas are mostly associated with the
(A) Volcanic rocks
(B) Sedimentary rocks
(C) Metamorphic rocks
(D) Plutonic rocks

146. The much discussed Tehri Dam project is located in which of the following states?
(A) Uttarakhand (B) Haryana
(C) Madhya Pradesh (D) Rajasthan

147. Laterite soil develops as a result of
(A) leaching
(B) deposition of loess
(C) continued vegetation cover
(D) deposits of alluvial

148. Which one of the following pairs is NOT correctly matched?
(A) Bhubaneswar – Mahanadi
(B) Jhansi – Chambal
(C) Jabalpur – Narmada
(D) Surat – Tapti

149. Which of the following is the biggest fresh water lake in India?
(A) Loktak Lake (B) Sukhana Lake
(C) Dal Lake (D) None of these

150. Which of the following rivers is NOT a tributary of the Indus?
(A) Jhelum (B) Bhagirathi
(C) Chenab (D) Sutlej

151. Which of the following pairs of the river dam project and the state in which it is located is correct?
(A) Tungabhadra – Tamil Nadu
(B) Gandhisagar – Madhya Pradesh
(C) Hirakud – Orissa
(D) Bhakra Nangal – Himachal

152. Ceramic crockery of substandard quality could become a source of pollutant if food is stored in it. This pollutant is
(A) Pb (B) Cd
(C) Cr (D) Hg

153. Sometimes secondary pollutants like ozone, PAN (Peroxy acylnitrate), HNO_3, H_2SO_4 formed from primary pollutants are more toxic than primary pollutants. This phenomenon of increased toxicity in pollutants is called
(A) Synergism (B) Greenhouse effect
(C) Eutrophication
(D) Biomagnification

154. Which one is NOT produced as exhaust of vehicles ?
(A) CO_2 (B) CO
(C) Fly ash (D) SO_2

155. Which of the following pollutant forms a toxic and stable substance in blood by combining with haemoglobin?

(A) CH_4 (B) CO_2
(C) CO (D) O_2

156. Anything, living or non-living or any physical agent which makes any part of the environment undesirable is
(A) Deforestation
(B) Unplanned urbanization
(C) Erosion (D) Pollutant

157. What does CPCB stand for ?
(A) Chief Pollution Control Bureau
(B) Central Pollution Control Board
(C) Chief Protection Criminal Bureau
(D) Central Processing Computer Board

158. Which river is the bone of contention between two Indian states?
(A) Godavari (B) Tungabhadra
(C) Cauvery (D) Ganga

159. Suspended and dissolved solids form a part of which pollutants?
(A) Inorganic pollutants
(B) Organic pollutants
(C) Particulate pollutants
(D) None of the above

160. The word ULSD stands for
(A) United League for Systematic Drive
(B) Ultra Low Sulphur Diesel
(C) Union of Leaders for Scientific Development
(D) Ultra Loud Speaker Dias

161. Which of the following destroys the aquatic habitat through the removal of riparian vegetation and alteration of a stream's natural hydrology?
(A) Run-off (B) Leakage
(C) Sewers (D) Sediments

162. What does VOC Stand for?
(A) Voice of Congo
(B) Voluntary Organisation of Chemical (Prevention)
(C) Volatile Organic Chemical
(D) Voluntary Organisation for Climate (Protection)

163. Among the following which process/activity doesn't release any greenhouse gas?
(A) Paddy cultivation
(B) Nuclear energy generation
(C) Livestock rearing
(D) Clearing of forests

164. The process by which a layer of cooler air is trapped near the ground by a layer of warmer air is called
(A) Nuclear Inversion
(B) Solar Inversion
(C) Thermal Inversion
(D) All of the above

165. A form of oxygen gas made up of molecules with three oxygen atoms rather than the normal two is
(A) Osmium (B) Ozone
(C) Oxide (D) None of these

166. The National Museum of Natural History (NMNH) was set up in 1978 at
(A) New Delhi (B) Bhopal
(C) Mysore (D) Bombay

167. Environmental Information System (ENVIS) was set up by the Ministry of Environment and Forest in
(A) 1988 (B) 1982
(C) 1994 (D) 1992

168. Mosquito repellent coils/mats contain
(A) Derivatives of allethrin
(B) BHC
(C) Paraquat
(D) Toxaphene

169. IPCC is concerned with
(A) Trade of endangered species
(B) Ban on ODS
(C) Climate change
(D) Biodiversity conservation

170. At present, the actual global average surface air temperature is about
(A) 18°C (B) 21°C
(C) 311 K (D) 288 K

171. Albedo is that fraction of solar radiation which is
(A) reflected by clouds
(B) absorbed by air
(C) reflected by earth
(D) reaching the earth surface

172. The global annual mean value of albedo for solar radiation coming to earth is
(A) about 30% (B) $< 30\%$
(C) $> 70\%$ (D) about 70%

173. Match List I and II and select the correct answer using the codes given below the lists.

List I (Rivers)	List II (Dams)
P. Cauvery	1. Alamatti
Q. Krishna	2. Mettur
R. Narmada	3. Gandhi Sagar
S. Chambal	4. Sardar Sarovar

	P	Q	R	S
(A)	2	1	3	4
(B)	1	4	2	3
(C)	1	3	4	2
(D)	2	1	4	3

174. The chemical formula of CFC-11 and CFC-12 is
(A) CF_2Cl and CF_3Cl (B) $CFCl_3$ and CF_2Cl_2
(C) CF_2Cl_2 and $CFCl_3$ (D) CF_3Cl and CF_2Cl_2

175. Turpentine oil used in medicines is obtained from
(A) Myrobalans (B) Kusum
(C) Chir pin (D) Acacia

176. Which country is known for the most frequent earthquakes?
(A) China (B) Iran
(C) Italy (D) Japan

177. In determining the Indian climate, major role played by Himalayas is
(A) During the winters, they stop the southward penetration of the cold and dry polar air
(B) The east-west extension of the Great-Himalayas does not permit the summer monsoon to cross it and thus keeps its sojourn restricted to India
(C) They direct the summer monsoon towards the north-west
(D) All of the above

178. In 1985, the largest use of CFCs was as
(A) Solvents
(B) Rigid foam insulation
(C) Refrigerants
(D) Aerosol propellants

179. Use of hydrofluorocarbons in place of chlorofluorocarbons is presently advocated as they
(A) have very low ozone layer depleting potential
(B) don't reach stratosphere after use
(C) don't degrade to release chlorine atoms in stratosphere
(D) don't deplete ozone layer

180. Death while sleeping in closed room with burning coal furnace is due to
(A) SO_2 (B) CCl_4
(C) CO (D) CO_2

181. Pollution indicator plants
(A) can indicate onset of disaster
(B) are sensitive to pollutants
(C) are resistant to pollution
(D) are purifiers of air pollutants

182. The effect of pollution is first and most marked on
(A) Fauna of an area
(B) Flora of a place
(C) Biogeochemical cycles
(D) Natural balance of our environment

183. Forest Conservation Act was enforced in
(A) 1980 (B) 1974
(C) 1952 (D) 1988

184. Most polluted city of India and world are
(A) Gwalior and Zabol (Iran) respectively
(B) Kolkata and Ahwaz (Iran) respectively
(C) Kanpur and Tokyo (Japan) respectively
(D) None of these

185. Among the following, which chemical has maximum life in natural environment?
(A) Halon 1211 (B) CFC 12
(C) CFC 115 (D) HCFC 22

186. Particulates in air cause
(A) yellowing of leaves
(B) permanent opening of stomata
(C) closure of a stomata
(D) coiling of leaves

187. The solar radiation known as ultraviolet B(UVB) damages
(A) RBC (B) DNA
(C) RNA (D) WBC

188. The acronym SACEP stands for
(A) South Asia Cooperation Environmental Programme
(B) South Asia Chemical Energy Programme
(C) South Asia Cooperation Energy Programme
(D) South Asia Cooperative Environment Programme

189. Fission of which of the following forms the basis of the highly destructive atom bomb?
(A) Uranium-235 (B) Crypton-94
(C) Plutonium-239 (D) Uranium-238

190. Which of the following is NOT a greenhouse gas?
(A) Nitrous oxide
(B) Chlorofluorocarbons
(C) Ethane (D) Methane

191. What causes the lung disease called asbestosis?
(A) Tobacco smoke (B) Asbestos
(C) Industrial pollution
(D) Exposure to radon

192. Hazard mitigation means
(A) permanently reduce or alleviate the losses of life, injuries and property resulting from natural and human-made hazards in future through long term strategies
(B) strategy for protection against future animal attacks
(C) protective action against fire
(D) temporary planning to overcome the destruction caused by natural disasters

193. The energy utilized through two different routes, namely, solar-thermal route and the solar-photovoltaic route is
(A) water energy (B) thermal energy
(C) solar energy (D) wind energy

194. The atmosphere of the earth consists of nitrogen and oxygen gases in the ratio of
(A) 1 : 7 (B) 4 : 1
(C) 1 : 2 (D) 3 : 5

195. Which of the following is not a renewable natural resource ?
(A) Clean air (B) Fertile soil
(C) Fresh water (D) Salt

196. Which of the following parameters is not used as a pollution indicator in water ?
(A) Total dissolved solids
(B) Coliform count
(C) Dissolved oxygen
(D) Density

197. The value of solar constant is
(A) 1932 W/m^2 (B) 1362 W/m^2
(C) 2 W/m^2 (D) 1732 w/m^2

198. The lowest layer of atmosphere where air pollutants mainly deposit is
(A) Ionosphere (B) Troposphere
(C) Exosphere (D) Stratosphere

199. The accumulation of dangerous radioactive materials into the bodies of larger animals through the process of food-chain is called
(A) Ecoaccumulation
(B) Biodiversity inversion
(C) Ecological inversion
(D) Bioaccumulation

200. S and P waves are associated with
(A) floods (B) wind energy
(C) earthquakes (D) tidal energy

201. Match Lists I and II and select the correct answer from the codes given below :

List – I	List – II
(i) Ozone hole	(a) Tsunami
(ii) Greenhouse effect	(b) UV radiations
(iii) Natural hazards	(c) Methane
(iv) Sustainable development	(d) Eco-centrism

Codes :

	(i)	(ii)	(iii)	(iv)
(A)	(b)	(c)	(a)	(d)
(B)	(c)	(b)	(a)	(d)
(C)	(d)	(c)	(a)	(b)
(D)	(d)	(b)	(c)	(a)

202. The major source of pollution, upto 80% of total air pollution in metropolitan cities, is
(A) coal based industries
(B) automobiles (traffic)
(C) radioactivity and noise
(D) pesticides

203. The rock material carried by a glacier is called
(A) Nodules (B) Moraines
(C) Meanders (D) Alluvium

204. Match list I and II and find out the correct answer from the codes given below the lists.

List I (Thermal Power Plants)	List II (Locations)
P. Kahalgaon	1. West Bengal
Q. Farakka	2. Bihar
R. Ramagundam	3. Gujarat
S. Gandhar	4. Andhra Pradesh

	P	Q	R	S
(A)	4	3	1	2
(B)	3	2	1	4
(C)	4	3	1	2
(D)	2	1	4	3

205. Krishna Raja Sagar Dam is built across the river
(A) Godavari (B) Cauvery
(C) Tungabhadra (D) Krishna

206. Which of the following states has rich forests of Sandalwood?
(A) Kerala (B) Madhya Pradesh
(C) Karnataka (D) Andhra Pradesh

207. The most significant impact of volcanic eruption has been felt in the form of
(A) change in weather
(B) sinking of islands
(C) loss of vegetation
(D) extinction of animals

208. The greatest diversity of animal and plant species occurs in
(A) heavily polluted rivers
(B) temperate deciduous forests
(C) desert lands
(D) tropical moist forests

209. The National Forest Policy first adopted in 1894 revised in 1952 was again revised in
(A) 1972 (B) 1974
(C) 1980 (D) 1988

210. Removal of desirable substances/plants is called
(A) erosion (B) conservation
(C) negative pollution (D) positive pollution

211. Acid rain is caused by sulphur oxides, nitrogen oxides and hydrochloric acid which are produced by industries, automobiles and thermal power plants using fossil fuels. It causes
(A) leaching of mineral salts in soil and decolourisation of red stone of Red Fort.
(B) death of fish due to clogging of their gills by exudation of large amount of mucus caused by solubility and availability of toxic metal like aluminium.
(C) defoliation, chlorosis, necrosis of plant foliage.
(D) all the above.

212. Which is the mysterious place on earth where the ships and aircrafts vanish without a trace?
(A) Bermuda Triangle (B) Bering strait
(C) Panama canal region (D) Dead sea

213. At which of the following space centres, fuel for rockets is being manufactured?
(A) National Remote Sensing Agency, Secunderabad
(B) Space Application Centre, Ahmedabad
(C) Vikram Sarabhai Space Centre, Trivandrum
(D) Shar Centre, Sriharikota

214. The cosmic radiation falling on earth from the outer space chiefly consists of three charged particles — electrons, alpha particles and
(A) Protons (B) Positrons
(C) Radons (D) Neutrons

215. What are contour lines drawn in mapping earth's surface?
(A) Lines through points of equal distance from the sea
(B) Lines through points of equal intensity of the solar light
(C) Lines through points of equal rainfall
(D) Lines through points of equal height above the sea level

216. Among the following countries, where are mud volcanoes found?
(A) Hawaii (B) New Zealand
(C) Sri Lanka (D) China

217. Where is the Silicon Valley situated?
(A) USA (B) Russia
(C) Japan (D) UK

218. India has three types of biomass among the following four. Which is the odd one out?
(A) Temperate Grassland
(B) Savanna
(C) Scrubs
(D) Tropical Rain Forest

219. Where is the atmospheric pressure highest on earth?
(A) At the equator
(B) Between 30° N & 30° S
(C) At the south pole
(D) At the north pole

220. The Hirakud Project is on which of the following rivers?
(A) Damodar (B) Kosi
(C) Mahanadi (D) Godavari

221. What is meant by the term "Cirrus"?
(A) A hail-bearing cloud
(B) A rain-bearing cloud
(C) A low cloud
(D) A high cloud

222. Most of the weather phenomena take place in the
(A) Troposphere (B) Stratosphere
(C) Ionosphere (D) Tropopause

223. Atmospheric pressure exerted on earth is due to

(A) Uneven heating of earth
(B) Gravitational pull
(C) Rotation of earth
(D) Revolution of earth

224. The circulation of ocean water occurs
(A) Only vertically
(B) Only laterally
(C) Both laterally and vertically
(D) Neither laterally nor vertically

225. Match list I and List II and select the correct answer using the codes given below the lists .

List I (Storm)	List II (Country of Occurrence)
a. Cyclone	1. China
b. Hurricane	2. Australia
c. Typhoon	3. India
d. Willy-willy	4. USA

Codes :

	a	b	c	d
(A)	4	3	1	2
(B)	3	4	1	2
(C)	3	4	2	1
(D)	4	3	2	1

226. Which is called the "Tiger State"?
(A) Madhya Pradesh
(B) Uttar Pradesh
(C) Jammu & Kashmir
(D) Rajasthan

227. Which one of the following rivers is known as "Sorrow of Bihar"?
(A) Sone (B) Kosi
(C) Damodar (D) Gandak

228. Given below are two statements, one labeled as Assertion (A) and the other labeled as Reason (R).

Assertion (A) : One of the movements of the surface water of ocean is known as ocean current.

Reason (R) : Ocean currents are caused mainly due to planetary winds and the difference in temperature and density of water.

In the context of the above two statements, which one of the following is correct?
(A) Both A and R are true but R is not a correct explanation of A.
(B) Both A and R are true and R is the correct explanation of A.
(C) A is false but R is true
(D) A is true but R is false.

229. Tsunamis are huge sea waves caused by
(A) Winds (B) Icebergs
(C) Earthquakes (D) Volcanoes

230. Photochemical smog always contain
(A) Methane (B) Ozone
(C) PAN (D) CO

231. Classical smog is
(A) Smog with secondary pollutants
(B) Yellow brown
(C) Dark brown (D) Los Angeles Smog

232. Sulphurous smog is
(A) Classical smog (B) Los Angeles smog
(C) Photochemical smog
(D) Oxidizing smog

233. The Space Physics Laboratory (SPL) is located at which of the following places?
(A) Space Application Center at Ahmedabad
(B) Thumba in Thiruvananthapuram
(C) Shar Center in Sriharikota
(D) ISRO Center at Bangalore

234. Which is the most closely studied volcanic eruption ?
(A) Mount Katmai (B) Mauna Loa
(C) Mount Etna (D) Mount St. Helena

235. Which zone of the earth is called the "homes of blizzards"?
(A) North Frigid zone and the south Frigid zone
(B) Subtropical and the central zone
(C) The temperate zone and the torrid zone
(D) None of these

236. Which region of India receives rainfall due to western disturbances in winter?
(A) Central region (B) Eastern region
(C) Western region
(D) North-western region

237. The earthquake waves which have transverse movements are known as
(A) Primary waves (B) Secondary waves
(C) Surface waves (D) None of these

238. Which of the following pairs is NOT correctly matched?
(A) Sambhar : Salt (B) Mysore : Marble
(C) Neyveli : Lignite (D) Panna : Diamond

239. Which of the following district is on the international border of India?
(A) Kullu (B) Shimla
(C) Gorakhpur (D) Kinnaur

240. Peeling of ozone umbrella (which protects us from harmful UV rays) is made by
(A) CFMs/CFCs (B) CO_2
(C) Coal burning (D) PAN

241. Ozone depletion in stratosphere ozone hole would result in
(A) forest fires and acid rains
(B) global warming
(C) increased incidence of skin cancer due to reaching of UV radiations on earth
(D) Green House effect

242. Ozone increases
(A) photosynthesis (B) transpiration
(C) respiration (D) (B) and (C)

243. Today concentration of green house gases is high because of
(A) use of refrigerators (B) deforestation
(C) increased combustion of fossil fuels
(D) all of the above

244. Pollution is
(A) release of undesirable/toxic substances in the environment
(B) removal of top soil
(C) conservation of energy
(D) all of these

245. Which of the following pollutants affects the respiratory tract in humans ?
(A) Carbon monoxide (B) Nitric oxide
(C) Sulphur di-oxide (D) Aerosols

246. A normal component of environment which becomes pollutant when its concentration crosses a threshold value is called
(A) Quantitative pollutant
(B) Qualitative pollutant
(C) Degradable pollutant
(D) Physical pollutant

247. Pollution can bring about change in
(A) biogeochemical cycling
(B) abiotic environment
(C) biotic environment
(D) all of the above

248. Loss of relative biological equilibrium is due to
(A) low temperature (B) high temperature
(C) radiation (D) pollution

249. Which of the following pollutants is not emitted from the transport sector ?
(A) Oxides of nitrogen
(B) Chlorofluorocarbons
(C) Carbon monoxide
(D) Poly aromatic hydrocarbons

250. Qualitative pollutants are
(A) Added by man
(B) Naturally occurring
(C) Present in the High concentration
(D) None of the above

251. If the population growth follows a logistic curve, the maximum sustainable yield
(A) is equal to half the carrying capacity.
(B) is equal to the carrying capacity.
(C) depends on growth rates.
(D) depends on the initial population.

252. Ecological backlash (**ecological bomerang**) is
(A) involves the counter responses of pest populations or other biotic factors in the environment that diminish the effectiveness of pest
(B) production of useful ecological effect by a previously useful chemical
(C) heat emission due to bomb explosion
(D) none of the above

253. When was the Air Prevention and Control of Pollution Act enforced in India ?
(A) 1980 (B) 1981
(C) 1982 (D) 1984

254. Which one of the following is appropriate for natural hazard mitigation ?
(A) International AID
(B) Timely Warning System
(C) Rehabilitation
(D) Community Participation

255. Maximum threat to the world is from
(A) Global warming (B) Ozone hole
(C) Water Pollution (D) Soil erosion

256. When was NEPA (National Environmental Policy Act) enforced in India ?
(A) 1968 (B) 1969
(C) 1970 (D) 1959

257. The newspaper contains one of the following toxic materials
(A) Cd (B) Pb (C) Mg (D) Hg

258. The first indoor pollutant from furniture of which the masses became aware ?

(A) CO_2 (B) Formaldehyde
(C) Radon (D) Ozone

259. Chemical weathering of rocks is largely dependent upon
(A) high temperature (B) strong wind action
(C) heavy rainfall (D) glaciation

260. Sometimes secondary pollutants like ozone, PAN (Peroxy acyl nitrate), HNO_3, H_2SO_4 formed from primary pollutants are more toxic than primary pollutants. This phenomenon of increased toxicity in pollutants is called
(A) Biomagnification (B) Eutrophication
(C) Synergism (D) Green house effect

261. Slums in metro-city are the result of
(A) Rural to urban migration
(B) Poverty of the city-scape
(C) Lack of urban infrastructure
(D) Urban-governance

262. In air pollution, industries are
(A) line sources (B) point sources
(C) area sources (D) diffuse sources

263. Carbon monoxide is a pollutant as it
(A) Inactivates nerves and cause numbness
(B) Inhibits Glycolysis
(C) Combine with oxygen and shift oxygen dissociation curve
(D) Combines with Haemoglobin and cause haemolysis

264. Which of the following pollutant forms a toxic and stable substance in blood by combining with haemoglobin ?
(A) CO_2 (B) CO
(C) CH_4 (D) O_2

265. Carbon monoxide is harmful for man because
(A) it is carcinogenic
(B) it damages kidney
(C) it competes with oxygen in blood
(D) it changes pH of body

266. CO_2 contents in air is about
(A) 0.34% (B) 4%
(C) 3.34% (D) 0.034%

267. One of the important effects of SO_2 and its transformation products on plants is
(A) Plasmolysis
(B) Destruction of chlorophyll
(C) Destruction of Golgi bodies
(D) Destruction of cell wall

268. Taj Mahal is threatened due to the effect of
(A) chlorine (B) sulphur dioxide
(C) oxygen (D) hydrogen

269. Lichen deserts indicate
(A) Air pollution due to CO
(B) Air pollution due to SO_2
(C) Pollution due to smoke
(D) Noise pollution

270. Lichens are best ecological indicator of
(A) air pollution (B) water pollution
(C) noise pollution (D) all of these

271. Lichens have disappeared from cities because they are highly susceptible to
(A) CO_2 (B) O_3
(C) NO_2 (D) SO_2

272. Most inhabitants of Kolkata suffer from bronchitis/asthma. It is due to excess of SO_2 pollutants in
(A) air (B) water
(C) soil (D) adulterated food

273. Death while sleeping in closed room with burning coal furnace is due to
(A) CO_2 (B) CO (C) CCl_4 (D) SO_2

274. Air pollution is not caused by
(A) pollen grains (B) automobiles
(C) industries (D) hydro-electric power

275. Deforestation during the recent decades has led to
(A) Soil erosion (B) Landslides
(C) Loss of bio-diversity (D) All the above

276. Major air pollutant is
(A) CO_2 (B) N_2
(C) SO_2 (D) CO

277. Which one of the following is usually not considered a pollutant ?
(A) SO_2 (B) CO_2
(C) Hydrocarbons (D) CO

278. Which of the following sources of energy has the maximum potential in India ?
(A) Solar energy (B) Wind energy
(C) Ocean thermal energy
(D) Tidal energy

279. Particulates in air cause
(A) permanent opening of stomata
(B) closure of stomata
(C) coiling of leaves
(D) yellowing of leaves

280. What is it that smoking produces in the largest amount ?
(A) NO_2 (B) CO_2
(C) CO (D) Particulates

281. Coal burning hearths or stoves produce a hazardous gas which suffocates living beings even to death
(A) SO_2 (B) CO_2
(C) CO (D) H_2S

282. The SO_2 mainly affects
(A) nucleus (B) cell membranes
(C) cell wall (D) ribosomes

283. A mutagenic pollutant is
(A) polycyclic aromatic hydrocarbons
(B) organophosphates
(C) nitrogen oxides (D) resins

284. Which will not cause air pollution ?
(A) CO_2 (B) CO
(C) H_2 (D) SO_2

285. The example of natural pollution is
(A) Volcanoes (B) SO_2
(C) DDT (D) Smoke

286. It is advised not to have brick kiln near fruit orchard to
(A) save trees from soil erosion
(B) safeguard trees from large labour population
(C) protect the orchard from operation of Trucks and Carts used for transporting fruits
(D) save trees from poisonous fumes of smoke from brick kiln chimneys

287. The congress grass/carrot grass that causes allergy arrived in India in 1956. It is
(A) Parthenium hysterophorous
(B) Eichhornia crassipes
(C) Opuntia dilleni
(D) Sorghum halepens

288. Which pollutant gas is released by cud-chewing cattle / ruminants ?
(A) CH_4 (B) CO_2
(C) CO (D) NO_2

289. When did the **Bhopal** disaster occur ?
(A) Dec. 3, 1982 (B) Dec. 3, 1984
(C) Dec. 3, 1986 (D) Dec. 3, 1980

290. Leakage of Methyl isocyanate (MIC) caused the biggest industrial disaster of the recent times in 1984 (Bhopal Tragedy). What did the industrial plant manufacture where the leakage occurred?
(A) Fertilizer (B) Explosives
(C) Pesticides (D) Cement

291. 60% of SO_2 pollution is due to
(A) burning of coal (B) burning of oil
(C) automobile (D) industries

292. Which gas was liberated in Bhopal gas tragedy ?
(A) Ethyl isothiocyanate
(B) Sodium isothiocyanate
(C) Methy isocyanate
(D) Phenyl isocyanate and phosgene

293. Persistent exposure to even low levels of environmental chemicals, sometimes induce mutagenic, teratogenic or carcinogenic effects on various organisms; such mutagens may
(A) cause cell death
(B) induce chromosomal abnormalities
(C) induce gene mutation
(D) cause all the above

294. Which is the gas that produces the most damaging acid rains ?
(A) SO_2 (B) NO_2
(C) CO_2 (D) H_2

295. Recent reports of acid rains in big industrial cities are due to the effect of atmospheric pollution by
(A) more release of SO_2 and NO_2 by burning of fossil fuels
(B) more release of CO_2 by burning of coal/ wood, cutting of forests and increasing population
(C) excessive release of NH_3 by coal gas/industries
(D) excessive release of CO by incomplete combustion of carbonaceous fuels

296. Which of the following is not a source of pollution in soil ?
(A) Transport sector (B) Agriculture sector
(C) Thermal power plants
(D) Hydropower plants

297. A rain is called *acid rain* when its *p*H is
(A) Less than 7
(B) Less than 5.6 (generally between 3-5)
(C) Less than 4.6 (generally between 2-4)
(D) Less than 2

298. Which one of the following natural hazards is responsible for causing highest human disaster?

(A) Earthquakes (B) Volcanic eruptions
(C) Snow-storms (D) Tsunami

299. Smog is a combination of
(A) air and water vapour
(B) water and smoke
(C) smoke and fog (D) fire and water

300. Which of the following is not a natural hazard ?
(A) Earthquake (B) Tsunami
(C) Flash floods (D) Nuclear accident

301. Ecological footprint represents
(A) area of productive land and water to meet the resources requirement
(B) energy consumption
(C) CO_2 emissions per person
(D) forest cover

302. Consider the following statements :
a. In India, the Project Tiger was launched in 1973.
b. The theme for National Biodiversity in 2022 is 'Building a shared future for all life'.
c. The Project Tiger is a tiger conservation programme.

Which of the above statements is/are correct?
(A) a and c only (B) a and c only
(C) a, b and c (D) a only

303. What is the main aim of Montreal Protocol?
(A) Protection of the Ozone layer
(B) Bio-diversity Conservation
(C) Global Warming
(D) Climate Change

ANSWERS

1. (A)	**2.** (C)	**3.** (A)	**4.** (C)	**5.** (B)	**6.** (A)	**7.** (A)	**8.** (B)	**9.** (B)	**10.** (B)
11. (C)	**12.** (C)	**13.** (B)	**14.** (C)	**15.** (D)	**16.** (B)	**17.** (A)	**18.** (C)	**19.** (A)	**20.** (A)
21. (A)	**22.** (A)	**23.** (A)	**24.** (C)	**25.** (C)	**26.** (B)	**27.** (C)	**28.** (C)	**29.** (A)	**30.** (C)
31. (B)	**32.** (B)	**33.** (A)	**34.** (C)	**35.** (A)	**36.** (C)	**37.** (B)	**38.** (B)	**39.** (A)	**40.** (B)
41. (A)	**42.** (A)	**43.** (A)	**44.** (B)	**45.** (C)	**46.** (A)	**47.** (C)	**48.** (C)	**49.** (B)	**50.** (A)
51. (C)	**52.** (B)	**53.** (A)	**54.** (A)	**55.** (C)	**56.** (A)	**57.** (A)	**58.** (B)	**59.** (C)	**60.** (B)
61. (A)	**62.** (A)	**63.** (D)	**64.** (A)	**65.** (D)	**66.** (B)	**67.** (A)	**68.** (D)	**69.** (C)	**70.** (A)
71. (D)	**72.** (B)	**73.** (A)	**74.** (B)	**75.** (B)	**76.** (A)	**77.** (B)	**78.** (B)	**79.** (B)	**80.** (D)
81. (B)	**82.** (A)	**83.** (A)	**84.** (A)	**85.** (B)	**86.** (D)	**87.** (A)	**88.** (A)	**89.** (B)	**90.** (B)
91. (D)	**92.** (D)	**93.** (A)	**94.** (B)	**95.** (D)	**96.** (D)	**97.** (B)	**98.** (A)	**99.** (D)	**100.** (D)
101. (B)	**102.** (A)	**103.** (D)	**104.** (C)	**105.** (A)	**106.** (C)	**107.** (B)	**108.** (D)	**109.** (A)	**110.** (B)
111. (B)	**112.** (A)	**113.** (C)	**114.** (D)	**115.** (A)	**116.** (A)	**117.** (A)	**118.** (A)	**119.** (C)	**120.** (C)
121. (D)	**122.** (C)	**123.** (D)	**124.** (B)	**125.** (D)	**126.** (C)	**127.** (A)	**128.** (D)	**129.** (D)	**130.** (C)
131. (D)	**132.** (B)	**133.** (C)	**134.** (A)	**135.** (C)	**136.** (A)	**137.** (C)	**138.** (A)	**139.** (B)	**140.** (C)
141. (A)	**142.** (B)	**143.** (C)	**144.** (D)	**145.** (B)	**146.** (A)	**147.** (A)	**148.** (B)	**149.** (D)	**150.** (B)
151. (A)	**152.** (B)	**153.** (A)	**154.** (C)	**155.** (C)	**156.** (D)	**157.** (B)	**158.** (C)	**159.** (A)	**160.** (B)
161. (D)	**162.** (C)	**163.** (B)	**164.** (C)	**165.** (B)	**166.** (A)	**167.** (B)	**168.** (A)	**169.** (C)	**170.** (D)
171. (C)	**172.** (A)	**173.** (D)	**174.** (B)	**175.** (C)	**176.** (D)	**177.** (D)	**178.** (D)	**179.** (A)	**180.** (C)
181. (B)	**182.** (D)	**183.** (A)	**184.** (A)	**185.** (C)	**186.** (C)	**187.** (B)	**188.** (D)	**189.** (A)	**190.** (C)
191. (B)	**192.** (A)	**193.** (C)	**194.** (B)	**195.** (D)	**196.** (D)	**197.** (B)	**198.** (B)	**199.** (D)	**200.** (C)
201. (A)	**202.** (B)	**203.** (B)	**204.** (D)	**205.** (D)	**206.** (C)	**207.** (A)	**208.** (D)	**209.** (D)	**210.** (C)
211. (D)	**212.** (A)	**213.** (C)	**214.** (A)	**215.** (D)	**216.** (B)	**217.** (A)	**218.** (C)	**219.** (B)	**220.** (C)
221. (D)	**222.** (A)	**223.** (B)	**224.** (C)	**225.** (B)	**226.** (A)	**227.** (B)	**228.** (D)	**229.** (D)	**230.** (B)
231. (C)	**232.** (A)	**233.** (B)	**234.** (D)	**235.** (A)	**236.** (D)	**237.** (B)	**238.** (B)	**239.** (D)	**240.** (A)
241. (C)	**242.** (D)	**243.** (D)	**244.** (A)	**245.** (C)	**246.** (A)	**247.** (D)	**248.** (D)	**249.** (B)	**250.** (A)
251. (A)	**252.** (A)	**253.** (B)	**254.** (B)	**255.** (B)	**256.** (C)	**257.** (B)	**258.** (B)	**259.** (C)	**260.** (C)
261. (A)	**262.** (B)	**263.** (D)	**264.** (B)	**265.** (C)	**266.** (D)	**267.** (B)	**268.** (B)	**269.** (B)	**270.** (A)
271. (D)	**272.** (A)	**273.** (B)	**274.** (D)	**275.** (D)	**276.** (D)	**277.** (B)	**278.** (A)	**279.** (B)	**280.** (D)
281. (C)	**282.** (B)	**283.** (A)	**284.** (C)	**285.** (A)	**286.** (D)	**287.** (A)	**288.** (A)	**289.** (B)	**290.** (C)
291. (A)	**292.** (C)	**293.** (D)	**294.** (A)	**295.** (A)	**296.** (D)	**297.** (B)	**298.** (A)	**299.** (C)	**300.** (D)
301. (A)	**302.** (C)	**303.** (A)							

HIGHER EDUCATION SYSTEM

Syllabus

- Institutions of Higher Learning and Education in Ancient India.
- Evolution of Higher Learning and Research in Post Independence India.
- Oriental, Conventional and Non-conventional Learning Programmes in India.
- Professional, Technical and Skill Based Education.
- Value Education and Environmental Education.
- Policies, Governance, and Administration.

INSTITUTIONS OF HIGHER LEARNING AND EDUCATION IN ANCIENT INDIA

Like the culture and traditions of India, the system of education also has a rich history of its own. Majorly influenced by the Hindu religion, the knowledge acquired by people of ancient times was passed on from one generation to another and is reflected even in the teachings of today. Here's a brief take on what the system of education was like during the early days of the Indian civilization.

In the olden days, there was no formal education in India. A father passed on knowledge, primarily related to his occupation, to his child. Much later, two systems of education emerged – Vedic and Buddhist. The Vedic system revolved around the *Vedas*, *Vedangas* and *Upanishads*, while the Buddhist system preached the thoughts of the major Buddhist schools. The language of education was Sanskrit for the Vedic system and Pali for the Buddhist system. Education in ancient India was quite different from the rest of the world back then. The society and state couldn't interfere with the curriculum or the administration. To get an education, a child had to leave home and live with a teacher in a *gurukul* for the entire duration of his studies. No fee was charged for education; in fact, the teacher took care of everything, including food, clothing and housing. According to this system, physical labor was of utmost importance. So, even if a child was interested in acquiring philosophical knowledge, he would still have to do some manual work every day. Debates and discussions were a part of education, even in ancient days.

Education for women was quite important in ancient India. They were trained in housekeeping, as well as in dancing and music. Girls also had to conduct the *Upanayana* ceremony. Educated women were divided into two classes – *Sadyodwahas*, those who pursued their education just until they got married, and *Brahmavadinis*, those who never married and continued studying throughout their lives. *Vedas* and *Vedangas* were taught to women, too, but were limited to religious songs and poems necessary for rituals. Some notable Vedic and

Upanishad women scholars were Apala, Indrani, Ghosha, Lopamudra, Gargi and Maitreyi.Both Vedic and Buddhist systems of education had different subjects of study. The Vedic system comprised of the four *Vedas* (*Rig Veda, Sama Veda, Yajur Veda* and*Atharva Veda*), six *Vedangas* (ritualistic knowledge, metrics, exegetics, grammar, phonetics and astronomy), the *Upanishads, Tarka Shastra* (logic and reasoning), *Puranas* (history), and more. The main subjects in the Buddhist system were the three *Pitakas* (*Vinaya, Abhidhamma* and *Sutta*), the most recognized works of all 18 Buddhism schools. Certain other subjects common to both the systems were arithmetic, military science, law, performing arts, ethics, and art and architecture. Mastering one *Veda* took 12 years. Thus, depending on how many subjects the student wanted to learn, the study period varied accordingly. The education could go on for as long as 48 years.

Just as we have world renowned universities today, there were popular educational institutions here during the ancient times as well. Four of these institutions were quite prominent and known for different specializations. The University of Nalanda was famous for its Catholic and cosmopolitan character and its department of logic. Takshasila University, in an area what is now modern-day Pakistan, was well-known across the world for its medical school and was the chief learning centre in 6th century BC. What Nalanda University was to east India, Vallabhi was to west India. It was also a famous study center that specialized in subjects like law, medicine and economics, and had students attending from all parts of the country. Vikramshila was yet another esteemed institution, best known for Tantric Buddhism.

Main Educational Institutions of Higher Education During Ancient India

1. **Taxila.** Taxila was the capital of Gandhar Kingdom. Taxila has been described as the first university established across the globe in 7th century BCE. Hiuen Tsang in his records mentioned the university of Taxila to be at par with Nalanda and Vikramshila universities.

   Taxila was an important centre of Brahmanical education, it maintained its stature even during the Buddhism in Northern India. It had attracted many students from other nations.

   Taxila university was famous for medical studies. Panini, the well known grammarian, Kautilya, the minister of Chandragupta Maurya, and Charaka, a medical teacher of repute had been part of it.

   There was no popularly organized institution or university. Admission of the students as per decision of the teacher, though they were taught subjects as per choice. Usually, the minimum age was more than sixteen years.

   There was no exam system, so there were no degrees or diplomas.

   The main branches were Vedatrayi (Three Vedas), Vedanta, Vyakaran, Ayurveda, eighteen Sippas (crafts), military education, astronomy, agriculture, commerce, snake bite cure, etc.

   It was popular as training centre in Indian Military science. Panini was an expert in Surgery and Medicine was its main product. The same was the case for Kautilya, the famous author of Arthashastra. There was no caste distinction. Taxila had been influenced by Greek culture also.

2. **Nalanda (Bihar).** It is located near Rajgriha in the province of Bihar, it has been the birth place of Sariputta, a favourite disciple of Lord Buddha, who is closely linked with Mahayana.

   It was a Buddhist centre of learning from 427 CE to 1197 CE. It has been known as 'one of the first great universities' in recorded history.

   A historian writes, 'The University of Nalanda was the educational center of international moral comparable in the universalism of its thought, the wide range of its studies, the international character of its community to the greatest universities of modern time like Oxford, Cambridge, Paris and Harvard.'

It is stated that at one time there were 10,000 monks staying at Nalanda. Of these, 1510 were teachers and the remaining 8500 were students belonging to various levels of attainments and studying various subjects.

Its real importance begins with the year 450 CE. Then it was important for three centuries. Hiuen Tsang came here in 7th century CE. It progressed a lot during Gupta dynasty. In year 2010, Nalanda University was set up in Bihar as a Central University with Japan, China, Thailand, Laos, Singapore, Australia by collaborating in various manners.

3. **Mithila.** In the Upanishadic age, Mithila became a prominent seat of Bralunanical education. It was named as Videha.

   It continued with its glory from Raja Janak upto Buddhist period. Later on this place produced devotees of Lord Krishna.

   Famous poet Vidyapati, who had written in Hindi and Jaideo, a prominent poet of Sanskrit literature was born here.

4. **Nadia.** Situated at the confluence of Ganga and Jalangi rivers in Bengal, it was formerly called Navadweep. Education in Nadia University was imparted at three centres namely Navadweep, Shantipur and Gopaalpura.

5. **Jagaddala.** Pal King, Raja Ram Pal of Bengal constructed a monastery and named it as Jagaddah. It remained as the centre of Buddhist education for about 100 years. It was again destroyed during invasion in 1203 CE.

   In Jagaddala, there were many scholars notable for their knowledge. The books were translated in Tibetan language.

6. **Ujjain.** It was famous for its secular learning including mathematics and astronomy.

7. **Valabhi.** Hiuen Tsang, I-Tsing had found Valabhi in the western side of India as glorious as Nalanda.

   It was not just a centre of religious education as of other secular subjects, such as Arthasastra (economics), Niti Shastra (law) and Chikitsa Sastra (medicine) were also taught here.

   It was mainly the centre for Hinayana form of Buddhism.

   Valabhi was running in good financial position till 755 CE but some portion were destroyed due to Arab invasion. It still continued till 12th century.

8. **Odantapuri.** This university had been established long before the Kings of Pala dynasty came into power in Magadha. Odantpuri could not attain that level of fame and repute which either Nalanda or Vikramshila had accomplished. Still nearly 1000 monks and students resided and received education there. It attracted students from Tibet too.

9. **Vikramshila.** It was set up and established by the Emperor Dharampala of Pal dynasty in the 8th century in Northern Magadh on the bank of the river Ganges. This university was famous for religious teachings and here 108 scholars were appointed as the incharge and Acharyas of the various temples. It attracted a large number of scholars from Tibet, who came there for higher studies. The university was later organized into six colleges. The central building was called the Vigyan Bhawan. A Dwar pandit was appointed at the main gate.

10. **Ennayiram** in Tamilnadu provided free boarding and tuition to 340 students. Other important centers of learning in South India were Sringeri and Kanchi.

11. **Salotgi** in Karnataka was an important centre of learning. It had 27 hostels for its students who hailed from different provinces. This college was richly endowed in 945 CE by Narayana the minister of Krishna III with the revenues of houses, land and levies on marriages and other ceremonies.

EVOLUTION OF HIGHER LEARNING AND RESEARCH IN PRE AND POST INDEPENDENCE INDIA

Pre-Independence Period

By the end of Vedic period and during medieval period, the missionaries and various religious groups had brought some basic education to the Indian masses, through churches in English, in native Temple Schools through Sanskrit and in Madarasas using Persian and Arabic, catering to educational needs of the few children with the support of the contemperory rulers and charity of the rich till East India Company was established and British Parliament was involved. However, the origin of the present education system in this country can be found at the beginning of the nineteenth century.

It was through the Charter Act that a state system of education was officially introduced in Indian history. Charter of the East India Company had to be renewed by British Parliament after every twenty years. When the Charter came in for renewal in 1813, British parliament directed the East India Company to set apart a sum of Rs one lakh every year "for the revival and promotion of literature, and the encouragement of the learned natives of India, and for the introduction and promotion of knowledge of the sciences among the inhabitants of the British territories."

Macaulay's Minutes

Lord Macaulay (Thomas Babington Macaulay) arrived in India (Madras) on 10th June 1834 as a member of the Supreme Council of India. William Bentinck was the then Governor General. He returned to England early 1838, and resumed his writing career there. Macaulay was in India, thus, only for nearly four years, but he was destined to impact the lives of millions of Indians forever.

Supremacy of English. Participating in the debate, Lord Macaulay, the Chairman of the General Committee of Public Instruction, prepared and circulated a memorandum on the issue in January 1835. He took a decisive stand against the native culture and learning, native knowledge and languages like Sanskrit, Arabic and Persian and asserted on the education of Western Science through English language. His views have gone as (in)famous Macaulay's Minute in the history of Indian education and we can see how influential he was; it took 100 years for us even to think of indigineious education system that is Basic Education proposed by Mahatma Gandhi in 1937 in Wardha conference. Even today, after almost two hundred years after Macaulay, the present system is still infected by the Macaulay's ghosts in different forms, like influence of English medium schools on the choice of parents for education of their children in India.

Macaulay rejected both the native languages- Arabic and Sanskrit, as against English, because he considered that English was better than both of them. He arrogated that, "a single shelf of a good European library was worth the whole native literature of India and Arabia. The intrinsic superiority of the Western literature is indeed fully admitted......". He further observed that "In India, English is the language spoken by the ruling class. It is spoken by the higher class of natives at the seats of Government.". for him, "what we spend on the Arabic and Sanskrit Colleges is not merely a dead loss to the cause of truth. It is bounty-money paid to rise up champions of error".

Wood's Dispatch

Comprehensive education system and organizational structure. You have seen as to how Macaulay's Minute influenced educational policy of Lord William Bentinck, which was in force for next 40 years. In 1853, when renewal of the Company charter again came for the consideration, the British Parliament examined the progress of education in India. The observations and suggested reforms were issued as a Charter of Education, known as Wood's Dispatch of 1854. Wood's Dispatch is considered to be the "Magna Carta of Education" in India.

- The Dispatch is a comprehensive important educational document and holds a unique place in the history of Indian education. It placed the responsibility of education of the Indian people fully on the company and made it quite clear that it must never be neglected. The Dispatch gave new direction to education in India and which has its impact on today's education in the country.

- The aim of education was stated as diffusion of European Arts, Science, Philosophy and Literature through English. Promotion of Indian languages was also to be encouraged. "Creation of a class of public servants", was the important objective. For this purpose, expansion of mass education was given priority.
- The Wood's Dispatch, for the first time, recommended the creation of a Department of Public Instruction in each of the five provinces of Bengal, Bombay, Madras, Punjab and the North Western province. For higher education, a scheme to establish universities was formulated along with total organizational set up. They were to conduct examinations and offer degrees in various subjects and languages. This led to the establishment of the first three universities in 1857, at Calcutta, Bombay and Madras.
- The Dispatch made important recommendations on most of the aspects of education like establishing network of graded schools all over the country such as elementary schools, high schools, intermediate, colleges and university, etc., grant in aid system for financial support to schools, provision for women education, training and professional development of teachers, establishment of medical, engineering law and other institutes of professional education to develop vocational efficiency of people.
- The importance of wood's dispatch was in a number of valuable and fundamental recommendations for future educational development in India. It gave new direction to issues like gradation of education, medium of instruction and proposed new schemes for future educational development in India with far reaching consequences.

Hunter Commission

Vocationalization of Education. Hunter Commission was appointed in 1882 to examine the implementation of the Dispatch of 1854, which tried to streamline school education into two streams of high school: one leading to the university education and the other to the commercial, vocational and technical education. This was the first attempt to diversify school curriculum and introduce vocational education. However, despite the specific recommendations and emphasis of the Hunter Commission on commercial, vocational or non-literary education, neither the public nor the Govt. appreciated the value of this practical suggestion and the recommendations were totally ignored. Not much was done in this regard in last hundred fifty years, not even in free India.

Universities Commission

Schools under the control of University: A new Commission was appointed in 1902 to examine the condition and prospects of the universities established in British Raj. The Commission recommended the reorganization of university administration; strict and systematic supervision of the colleges by the university; and stricter conditions of affiliation and major changes in curricula and examinations. More relevant and important for school education is, as a result of the recommendations of this Commission, secondary schools were brought under the control of the Universities. Under the Indian Universities Act of 1904, schools had to be recognized by the Universities and rules and regulations were framed for this purpose.

Sadler Commission

Intermediate colleges. The next important development was realization of the need of improvement of secondary education for the improvement of University education, as observed by the Sadler Commission in 1917. This concern also stemmed from of the need for bifurcation of college courses.

Sadler Commission suggested bifurcation of higher education at the intermediate examination rather than at the matriculation examination, and suggested creation of Intermediate colleges which would provide instruction in Arts, Science, Medicine, Engineering, Teaching, etc.; to be run as independent institution or to be attached to selected high schools. It also recommended that a Board of Secondary and Intermediate Education, be established and entrusted with the administration and control of Secondary Education. Perhaps the seed of the concept of +2 stage or Junior Colleges today, are laid by the Sadler Commission.

The Hartog Committee

In 1929, the Hartog Committee, appointed to review the position of education in the country, maintained that the Matriculation of the University still dominated the whole of the secondary course. To remove this defect, the Committee recommended that a large number of students intending to follow certain vocation should stop at the middle school stage and there should be "more diversified curricula in the schools". The Committee also recommended diversion of more boys to industrial and commercial careers at the end of the middle stage, where they should be prepared for specialized education in technical and industrial schools. The Committee also reviewed the problems relating to the training of teachers and the service conditions of the secondary teachers".

The Sapru Committee

Diversified Vocational Courses: The Sapru Committee appointed in 1934 by the U.P. Government to enquire into the causes of unemployment in U.P. Came to the conclusion that the system of education prepared pupils only for examinations and degrees and not for any vocation in life. This Committee also felt the need of diversified courses at secondary stage. It suggested that, (i) diversified courses at the secondary stage should be introduced, one of these leading to the University degree, (ii) the intermediate stage be abolished and the secondary stage be extended by one year, (iii) the vocational training and education should begin after the lower secondary stage, and (iv) the degree course at the University should extend over a period of three years.

The Abbot-Wood Report

Polytechnic. In pursuance of the Resolution of 1935 of the Central Advisory Board of Education, two expert advisers, Messrs. Abbot and Wood were invited in 1936 to advise the Government particularly on problems of vocational education. The Abbot-Wood Report, submitted in 1937, suggested a complete hierarchy of vocational institutions parallel with the hierarchy of institutions imparting general education. As a result of their recommendations, a new type of technical institution called the Polytechnic came into existence. The provinces also started technical, commercial or agricultural high -schools conducting nonliterary courses.

Zakir Hussain Committee's Report

Wardha Scheme 1937 –Basic Education. In 1937, when the provincial governments were formed in seven provinces with the native representation, they concentrated their attention on educational reforms. In October 1937, an all-India National Educational Conference was held at Wardha and the conference resolved to accept the proposal made by Mahatma Gandhi that free and compulsory education be provided for seven years through mother tongue on a nation-wide scale and the process of education throughout this period should centre around some form of manual and productive work. All other abilities to be developed or training to be given should, as far as possible, be integrally related to the central handicraft chosen with due regard to the environment of the child.

Accordingly, a committee under the chairmanship of Dr. Zakir Hussain was appointed. The Committee prepared and submitted the first comprehensive national education scheme in its report on December 2, 1937, which was popularly known as the Wardha Scheme or Basic Education. The main features of the scheme are as follows:

(i) The entire education is to be imparted through some industry or vocation with a basic craft as the center of instruction. The idea is not to teach some handicraft along with liberal education, but education integrated with a handicraft is to be imparted through samavaaya (Samavay) integration method. It's a work-centric education.

(ii) Education is to be self-supporting to the extent of covering teachers' salaries and aims at making pupils self-supporting after the completion of their course;

(iii) Every individual should learn to earn his living through manual work in life. Hence, education through manual labour is insisted. It is also considered non-violent, since an individual does not snatch away the living of others.

(iv) Learning is closely coordinated with home, community and the child's life activities, as well as, village crafts and occupations.

Post-Independence Period

Initiatives and Development in the Field of Education

Sl. No.	Year	Education Committee/Act/Laws
1.	1968	National Policy on Education
2.	1968	Review Committee on the Working of National Council of Educational Research and Training, also known as Dr. Nag Committee
3.	1968	Study Group on the Development of Pre-school Child, also known as Shrimati Mina
4.	1970	Swaminathan Committee
5.	1971	Gajendragadkar Committee on Governance of Universities and Colleges
6.	1972	National Committee on 10+2+3 Educational Structure, also known as Dr. Shukla Committee
7.	1974	UGC's Panel on Teacher Education during Fifth Plan Period
8.	1975	The Curriculum for Ten-year School: A Framework
9.	1975-76	'Education' which was earlier part of State list, was shifted to Concurrent list Standing Committee of National Council for Teacher Education
10.	1980	Study Group on INSAT Television Utilisation for Education and Development, also known as Shri S. Sathyam Committee
11.	1983	Working Group to Review Teachers' Training Programme titled 'In the Light of the Need for Value-Orientation'
12.	1985	Challenge of Education: A Policy Perspective
13.	1985	National Curriculum for Primary and Secondary Education: A Framework
14.	1986	National Policy on Education: Programme of Action
15.	1988	National Curriculum for Elementary and Secondary Education – A Framework
16.	1990	Acharya Ramamurthy Committee, also known as Committee for Review of National Policy on Education 1986 – Towards an Enlightened and Hmnane Society
17.	1990	University Grants Commission's Report of the Curriculum Development Centre in Education
18.	1992	Central Advisory Board of Education Committee on Distance Education
19.	1992	National Policy on Education 1986: Programme of Action
20.	1993	Group to Examine the Feasibility of Implementation of the Recommendations of the National Advisory Committee, also known as Prof. Yashpal Committee
21.	1993	Ghanam Committee

Sl. No.	Year	Education Committee/Act/Laws
22.	1994	University Grants Commission's Committee on B.Ed. Correspondence, Distance Education Programme
23.	1994-97	Special Orientation Programme for School Teachers (SOPT)
24.	1995	Committee of National Council for Teacher Education on Different Modes of Education Used for Teacher Preparation in India
25.	1995	University Grants Commission's Committee on B.Ed. through Correspondence for In-service Teachers or Prof. Takwale Committee
26.	1998	NCTE Curriculum Framework for Quality Teacher Education
27.	2000	National Curriculum Framework for School Education
28.	2005	National Curriculum Framework
29.	2006	Curriculum Framework for Teacher Education
30.	2007	National Knowledge Commission Sam Pitroda Committee
31.	2009	National Curriculum Framework for Teacher Education
32.	2009	The Committee to Adivse on Renovation and Rejuvenation of Higher Education for Prof. Yashpal Committee
33.	2009	The Right of Children to Free and Compulsory Education Act
34.	2009	Sharma Committee for Strengthening Science Based Higher Education and Research in Universities
35.	2010	Dr. Anil Kakodar Committee
36.	2010	The National Commission for Minority Educational Institutions (Amendment) Act
36.	2012	Notification issued by Government Notifying NCMEI (Procedure and Appeal) Amendment Rules
37.	2012	The National Institutes of Technology (Amendment) Act
38.	2014	The National Institutes of Technology, Science Education and Research (Amendment) Act
39.	2014	The School of Planning and Architecture Act
40.	2017	The Indian Institutes of Management Bill

Draft of National Policy on Education 2019

Higher Education

According to the All India Survey on Higher Education, the Gross Enrolment Ratio (GER) in higher education in India has increased from 20.8% in 2011-12 to 25.8% in 2017-18.

GER COMPARISON ACROSS COUNTRIES (2014)

	Primary (Class 1-5)	Upper Primary (Class 6-8)	Upper Secondary (Class 9-12)	Higher Education
India	101.4	89.3	62.5	23
China	103.9	100.4	88.8	39.4
USA	99.5	101.9	93.2	86.7
Germany	103.3	101.6	104.6	65.5

Source: Educational Statistics at Glance (2016), MHRD; PRS.

The Committee identified lack of access as a major reason behind low intake of higher education in the country. It aims to increase GER to 50% by 2035 from the current level of about 25.8%. Key recommendations in this regard include:

- **Regulatory structure and accreditation.** The Committee noted that the current higher education system has multiple regulators with overlapping mandates. This reduces the autonomy of higher educational institutions and creates an environment of dependency and centralised decision making. Therefore, it proposes setting up the National Higher Education Regulatory Authority (NHERA). This independent authority would replace the existing individual regulators in higher education, including professional and vocational education. This implies that the role of all professional councils such as AICTE and the Bar Council of India would be limited to setting standards for professional practice. The role of the University Grants Commission (UGC) will be limited to providing grants to higher educational institutions.

Currently, the National Assessment and Accreditation Council (NAAC) is an accreditation body under the UGC. The draft Policy recommends separating NAAC from the UGC into an independent and autonomous body. In its new role, NAAC will function as the top level accredition, and will issue licenses to different accreditation institutions, who will assess higher educational institutions once every five to seven years. All existing higher education institutions should be accredited by 2030.

- **Establishment of new higher educational institutions.** Currently, higher educational institutions can only be set up by Parliament or state legislatures. The draft Policy proposes that these institutions could be allowed to be set up through a Higher Education Institution Charter from NHERA. This Charter will be awarded on the basis of transparent assessment of certain specified criteria. All such newly constituted higher educational institutions must receive accreditation as mandated by NHERA within five years of being established.
- **Restructuring of higher education institutions.** Higher education institutions will be restructured into three types: (i) research universities focusing equally on research and teaching; (ii) teaching universities focusing primarily on teaching; and (iii) colleges focusing only on teaching at undergraduate levels. All such institutions will gradually move towards full autonomy - academic, administrative, and financial.
- **Establishing a National Research Foundation.** The Committee observed that the total investment on research and innovation in India has declined from 0.84% of GDP in 2008 to 0.69% in 2014. India also lags behind many nations in number of researchers (per lakh population), patents and publications.

  The draft Policy recommends establishing a National Research Foundation, an autonomous body, for funding, mentoring and building the capacity for quality research in India. The Foundation will consist of four major divisions: sciences, technology, social sciences, and arts and humanities, with the provision to add additional divisions. The Foundation will be provided with an annual grant of Rs 20,000 crore (0.1% of GDP).

INVESTMENT ON RESEARCH AND INNOVATION

	Spending on research and innovation (% GDP)	Researchers (per lakh population)	Total Patent Applications
India	0.7	15	45,057
China	2.1	111	13,38,503
USA	2.8	423	605,571
Israel	4.3	825	6,419

Source: Economic Survey of India 2017-18; PRS

Education Governance

- The Committee observed that there is a need to revisit the existing system of governance in education, and bring in synergy and coordination among the different ministries, departments and agencies. In this context, it recommends:

- Creation of a National Education Commission or Rashtriya Shiksha Aayog, as an apex body for education, to be headed by the Prime Minister. This body will be responsible for developing, implementing, evaluating, and revising the vision of education in the country on a continuous and sustained basis. It will oversee the implementation and functioning of several bodies including the National Council of Educational Research and Training (NCERT), the proposed National Higher Education Regulatory Authority, and National Research Foundation.
- The Ministry of Human Resources and Development must be renamed as the Ministry of Education in order to bring focus back on education.

Financing Education

- The Draft Policy reaffirmed the commitment of spending 6% of GDP as public investment in education. Note that the first National Education Policy (NEP) 1968 had recommended public expenditure in education must be 6% of GDP, which was reiterated by the second NEP in 1986. In 2017-18, public expenditure on education in India was 2.7% of GDP.
- The draft Policy seeks to double the public investment in education from the current 10% of total public expenditure to 20% in the next 10 years. Of the additional 10% expenditure, 5% will be utilised for universities and colleges (higher education), 2% will be utilised for additional teacher costs or resources in school education and 1.4% will be utilised for early childhood care and education.

TOTAL PUBLIC INVESTMENT IN EDUCATION

Country	Investment in 2017 (as % of GDP)
India	2.7
USA	5
UK	5.5
Brazil	6

Technology in Education

- **National Mission on Education through information and communication technology.** The Mission will encompass virtual laboratories that provide remote access to laboratories in various disciplines. A National Education Technology Forum will also be setup under the Mission, as an autonomous body, to facilitate decision making on the induction, deployment and use of technology. This Forum will provide evidence-based advice to central and state-governments on technology-based interventions.
- **National Repository on Educational Data.** A National Repository will be setup to maintain all records related to institutions, teachers, and students in digital form. Further, a single online digital repository will be created where copyright-free educational resources will be made available in multiple languages.

Vocational Education

The Committee observed that less than 5% of the workforce in the age-group of 19-24 receives vocational education in India. This is in contrast to 52% in the USA, 75% in Germany and 96% in South Korea. It recommends integrating vocational educational programmes in all educational institutions (schools, colleges and universities) in a phased manner over a period of 10 years. Note that this is an upward revision from the National Policy on Skills Development and Entrepreneurship (2015) which aimed at offering vocational education in 25% of educational institutions. Key recommendations in this regard include:

- **Vocational courses.** All school students must receive vocational education in at least one vocation in grades nine to 12. The proposed school complexes must build expertise in curriculum delivery that is aligned to the competency levels under the existing National Skills Qualifications Framework.

The proposed Higher Education Institutions must also offer vocational courses that are integrated into the undergraduate education programmes. The draft Policy targets to offer vocational education to up to 50% of the total enrolment in higher education institutions by 2025, up from the present level of enrolment of well below 10% in these institutions.

- **National Committee for the Integration of Vocational Education.** The Committee will be set up to work out the steps that need to be taken towards achieving the above goals. A separate fund will be setup for the integration of vocational education into educational institutions. The Committee will work out the modalities for the disbursement of these funds.

Adult Education

As per Census 2011, India still had over 3.26 crore youth non-literates (15-24 years of age) and a total of 26.5 crore adult non-literates (15 years and above). In this regard, the draft Policy recommends to establish an autonomous Central Institute of Adult Education, as a constituent unit of NCERT, which will develop a National Curriculum Framework for adult education. The Framework will cover five broad areas: foundational literacy and numeracy, critical life skills vocational skills development, basic education, and continuing education.

Education and Indian Languages

- The Committee observed that a large number of students are falling behind since classes in schools are being conducted in a language that they do not understand. Therefore, it recommended that the medium of instruction must either be the home language/mother tongue/ local language till grade five, and preferable till grade eight, wherever possible.
- Introduced by the first National Education Policy, the three-language formula stated that state governments should adopt and implement study of a modern Indian language, preferably one of the southern languages, apart from Hindi and English in the Hindi-speaking states, and of Hindi along with the regional language and English in the non-Hindi speaking states. The draft Policy recommended that this three language formula be continued and flexibility in the implementation of the formula should be provided.
- The Committee remarked that the implementation of the formula needs to be strengthened, particularly in Hindi-speaking states. Further, schools in Hindi speaking areas should also teach Indian languages from other parts of India for the purpose of national integration. To provide flexibility in the choice of language, students who wish to change one or more of their three languages may do so in grade six or grade seven, subjected to the condition that they are still able to demonstrate proficiency in three languages in their modular board examinations.
- To promote Indian languages, a National Institute for Pali, Persian and Prakrit will be set up. All higher education institutes must recruit high quality faculty for at least three Indian languages, in addition to the local Indian language. Further, the mandate of the Commission for Scientific and Technical Terminology will be expanded to include all fields and disciplines to strengthen vocabulary in Indian languages.

STRUCTURE OF INSTITUTIONS OF HIGHER EDUCATION

Higher Education in India is one of the largest and oldest systems of higher education found anywhere in the world.

Universities in India

The University system has a number of different types of institutions and there are wide variations in their missions, goals and objectives. The Universities also have different traditions and conventions established. Besides, the social milieu in which the Universities have been set up are also different. However, all the Universities generally fall into the following three categories, based on their organizational structure:

- Affiliating Universities, having University Departments, Constituent Colleges and Affiliated Colleges, with single or multiple campuses;
- Unitary Universities having University Departments and Constituent Colleges, with single or multiple campuses;
- Private Universities, mostly of the unitary type and having distributed campuses.

Regulation of Indian Universities

University Grants Commission (India)

The University Grants Commission of India (UGC India) is a statutory body set up by the Indian Union government in accordance to the UGC Act 1956 under Ministry of Human Resource Development, and is charged with coordination, determination and maintenance of standards of higher education. It provides recognition to universities in India, and disbursements of funds to such recognised universities and colleges. Its headquarters is in New Delhi, and has six regional centres in Pune, Bhopal, Kolkata, Hyderabad, Guwahati and Bangalore.

UGC is modelled after University Grants Committee of UK which was an advisory committee of the British government and advised on the distribution of grant funding amongst the British universities. The committee was in existence from 1919 until 1989.

The UGC was first formed in 1945 to oversee the work of the three Central Universities of Aligarh, Banaras and Delhi. Its responsibility was extended in 1947 to cover all Indian universities.

In August 1949 a recommendation was made to reconstitute the UGC along similar lines to the University Grants Committee of the United kingdom. This recommendation was made by the University Education Commission of 1948-1949 which was set up under the chairmanship of S. Radhakrishnan "to report on Indian university education and suggest improvements and extensions". In 1952 the government decided that all grants to universities and higher learning institutions should be handled by the UGC. Subsequently, an inauguration was held on 28 December 1953 by Maulana Abul Kalam Azad, the Minister of Education, Natural Resources and Scientific Research.

In November 1956 the UGC became a statutory body upon the passing of the "University Grants Commission Act, 1956" by the Indian Parliament.

In 1994 and 1995 the UGC decentralised its operations by setting up six regional centres at Pune, Hyderabad, Kolkata, Bhopal, Guwahati and Bangalore. The head office of the UGC is located at Bahadur Shah Zafar Marg in New Delhi, with two additional bureaus operating from 35, Feroze Shah Road and the South Campus of University of Delhi as well.

INTERNATIONAL UNIVERSITIES IN INDIA

Nalanda University was established in November 2010. The University came into being by a special Act of the Indian Parliament – a testimony to the important status that Nalanda University occupies in the Indian intellectual landscape. Nalanda is a stand alone international university unlike any other established in the country. Located in the town of Rajgir, in the northern Indian state of Bihar, Nalanda University is mandated to be "an international institution for the pursuit of intellectual, philosophical, historical and spiritual studies". This new university contains within it a memory of the ancient Nalnda University and is premised on the shared desire of member States of the East Asia Summit countries to re-discover and re-strengthen "educational co-operation by tapping the East Asia Regions centres of excellence in education...[and] to improve regional understanding and the appreciation of one another's heritage and history" (The Nalanda University Act).

In December 2015 the Indian government set a National Institutional of Ranking Framework under UGC which will rank all educational institutes by April 2016.

In December 2017 D.P. Singh, former director of National Assessment and Accreditation Council (NAAC), was appointed chairman for a period of five years, replacing UGC member Virander Singh Chauhan, who officiated the position since the retirement of Ved Prakash in April 2017.

Types of universities

The types of universities controlled by the UGC include:

- Central universities, or Union universities, are established by an Act of Parliament and are under the purview of the Department of Higher Education in the Union Human Resource Development Ministry.
- State universities are run by the state government of each of the states and territories of India and are usually established by a local legislative assembly act.
- Deemed university, or "Deemed to be University", is a status of autonomy granted by the Department of Higher Education on the advice of the UGC, under Section 3 of the UGC Act.
- Private universities are approved by the UGC. They can grant degrees but they are not allowed to have off-campus affiliated colleges.

Central Universities in India

While other universities in the country are established by the State Governments, a Central University in India is formed by the Government of India, by an Act of Parliament.

The Government of India is responsible for arranging, allocating and distributing financial resources required by the University Grants Commission (UGC) for the establishment of Central Universities in India. Currently there are 54 Central Universities in India. The higher education system in India being one of the largest in the world, the responsibility rests on the Central Government to devise policies with a view to improving the quality of higher education in India. Improving the quality and access of higher education and research in India has become all the more important keeping in view the growing need of qualified human resources in various sectors of the economy. Therefore it can only be hoped that there would be more central universities in India in the immediate future.

***Some of the special features of Central Universities are*:**

- The President of India acts as the 'Visitor' for all the Central Universities
- The President has the power to nominate a few members to the Executive Committee/Board of Management/Court/Selection Committees of the University in terms of the various statutes and provisions laid down in the University Act.

OPEN UNIVERSITIES IN INDIA

- Indira Gandhi National Open University, New Delhi
- Dr. B.R. Ambedkar Open University, Hyderabad
- Karnataka State Open University, Mysore
- Nalanda Open University, Patna
- Netaji Subhas Open University, Kolkata
- Vardhman Mahaveer Open University, Kota
- U.P. Rajarshi Tandon Open University, Allahabad
- Madhya Pradesh Bhoj Open University, Bhopal
- Tamil Nadu Open University, Chennai
- Yashwant Rao Chavan Open University, Nashik
- Dr. Babasaheb Ambedkar Open University, Ahmedabad
- Pt. Sunderlal Sharma Open University, Bilaspur
- Uttaranchal Open University, Nainital
- K.K. Handique State University, Guwahati

- The Ministry of Human Resources and Development (MHRD) assists the President of India in the appointment of Vice Chancellors, Court Nominees and Selection Committee Nominees.

Open Universities in India

Open Universities in India provide the facility of distance education to people who are unable to pursue regular courses. Distance education is provided on Academic, Technical and Professional subjects.

These universities offer undergraduate, post graduate and doctoral programme. They also offer diploma and certificate level courses.

Distance Education Council

The open universities in India are regulated by the Distance Education Council of India (DEC). It is an organization based in New Delhi which maintains the standards, encourages and organizes the activities of Open and Distance Learning in India (ODL).

The council encourages the state governments and conventional universities to set up open universities and distance education centers.

It also arranged for funds to run these universities. The assessment and accreditation of these universities is also done by the DEC. Facilitating and promoting distance education is the ultimate goal of the DEC.

There are 14 Open Universities in India at present/national and 13 state open universities. They have educational centers in various states of India.

LANGUAGE UNIVERSITIES

India has six language universities, out of which three are deemed-to-be universities and three are central universities. The deemed-to-be Universities are for promotion of Sanskrit Language and the three Central Universities are, one each, for promotion of English and Foreign Language, Hindi and Urdu Language.

The University Grants Commission (UGC) is funding these Language institutions:

- Shri Lal Bahadur Shastri Rashtriya Sanskrit Vidyapeetha, New Delhi
- Rashtriya Sanskrit Vidyapeetha, Tirupati
- English and Foreign Languages University, Hyderabad
- Mahatama Gandhi Antarashtriya Hindi Vishwavidyalaya, Wardha
- Maulana Azad National Urdu University, Hyderabad
- Rashtriya Sanskrit Sansthan, New Delhi

Deemed Universities in India

The Central Govt. of India, which establishes the Central Universities in India, are also entrusted with the responsibility of declaring an educational institution as a Deemed University. However the declaration is made on the recommendation of University Grant Commission (UGC) of India. Among other things, the UGC is entrusted with the responsibility of maintaining the standard of higher of education in India. Therefore an educational institute acquires the status of a Deemed University only after meeting the standard set by the University Grant Commission. The UGC may also decide to fund some of these Deemed Universities.

Agricultural Universities in India

As Agriculture plays a very important role in the Indian Economy, setting up of adequate number of Agricultural Universities were considered very important in India. While the Royal Commission, set up in 1926, emphasized the importance of a strong research base for agricultural development in India, the second National Education Commission (1964-66) headed by the then University Grant Commission Chairman Dr. D.S. Kothari recommended the establishment of at least one Agricultural University in each of the Indian state.

UNIVERSITY GRANTS COMMISSION

Total No. of Universities in the Country as on 23.08.2022

Universities	Total No.
State Universities	456
Deemed to be Universities	126
Central Universities	54
Private Universities	421
Total	1057

List of Major Central Universities in India

Sl. no.	University	State	Location	Established
1.	Rajiv Gandhi University	Arunachal Pradesh	Itanagar	1985 (CU wef 2007)
2.	School of Planning and Architecture	Andhra Pradesh	Vijayawada	2008
3.	Assam University	Assam	Silchar	1994
4.	Tezpur University	Assam	Tezpur	1994
5.	Central University of South Bihar	Bihar	Gaya	2009
6.	Mahatma Gandhi Central University North Bihar	Bihar	Motihari	2016
7.	Nalanda University	Bihar	Rajgir near Nalanda	2010-[12]
8.	Guru Ghasidas University	Chhattisgarh	Bilaspur	1983 (2009 dagger)
9.	Indira Gandhi National Open University	Delhi	New Delhi	1985
10.	Jamia Millia Islamia	Delhi	New Delhi	1920 (1988 dagger)
11.	Jawaharlal Nehru University	Delhi	New Delhi	1969
12.	University of Delhi	Delhi	New Delhi	1922
13.	Central University of Gujarat	Gujarat	Gandhinagar	2009
14.	Central University of Haryana	Haryana	Mahendragarh	2009
15.	Central University of Himachal Pradesh	Himachal Pradesh	Dharamsala	2009
16.	Central University of Jammu	Jammu and Kashmir	Jammu	2011
17.	Central University of Kashmir	Jammu and Kashmir	Srinagar	2009
18.	Central University of Jharkhand	Jharkhand	Ranchi	2009
19.	Central University of Karnataka	Karnataka	Gulbarga	2009
20.	Central University of Kerala	Kerala	Kasaragod	2009
21.	Dr. Hari Singh Gour University	Madhya Pradesh	Sagar	1946
22.	Indira Gandhi National Tribal University	Madhya Pradesh	Amarkantak	2007
23.	Mahatma Gandhi Antarrashtriya Hindi Vishwavidyalaya	Maharashtra	Wardha	1997
24.	Central Agricultural University	Manipur	Imphal	1993
25.	Manipur University	Manipur	Imphal	1980 (2005 dagger)

Institute of Eminence (IOE)

As of April 2021, the ten public institutes selected are:

Name	Location	Name	Location
Anna University	Chennai, Tamil Nadu	Banaras Hindu University	Varanasi, Uttar Pradesh
Indian Institute of Science	Bengaluru, Karnataka	Indian Institute of Technology Bombay	Mumbai, Maharashtra
Indian Institute of Technology Delhi	New Delhi	Indian Institute of Technology Kharagpur	Kharagpur, West Bengal
Indian Institute of Technology Madras	Chennai, Tamil Nadu	Jadavpur University	Kolkata, West Bengal
University of Delhi	New Delhi	University of Hyderabad	Hyderabad, Telangana

The ten private institutes are:

Name	Location	Name	Location
Amrita Vishwa Vidyapeetham	Coimbatore, Tamil Nadu	Jamia Hamdard	Delhi
Birla Institute of Technology & Science, Pilani	Pilani, Rajasthan	Jio Institute (sponsored by Reliance Foundation)	Maharashtra
Kalinga Institute of Industrial Technology	Bhubaneswar, Odisha	Manipal Academy of Higher Education	Manipal, Karnataka
O.P. Jindal Global University (sponsored by Bharti Foundation)	Sonipat, Haryana	Satya Bharti University	Haryana
Shiv Nadar University	Dadri , Uttar Pradesh	Vellore Institute of Technology	Vellore, Tamil Nadu

Rashtriya Uchchatar Shiksha Abhiyan (RUSA)

It is a Centrally Sponsored scheme (CSS), which was launched in 2015, aims at providing strategic funding to eligible state higher educational institutions The central funding (in the ratio of 65:35 for general category states and 90:10 for special category states) would be norm based and outcome dependent.

All India Council for Technical Education (AICTE)

The All India Council for Technical Education (AICTE) is the statutory body and a national-level council for technical education, under Department of Higher Education, Ministry of Human Resource Development. Established in November 1945 first as an advisory body and later on in 1987 given statutory status by an Act of Parliament, AICTE is responsible for proper planning and coordinated development of the technical education and management education system in India. The AICTE accredits postgraduate and graduate programs under specific categories at Indian institutions as per its charter.

It is assisted by 10 Statutory Boards of Studies, namely, UG Studies in Eng. & Tech., PG and Research in Eng. and Tech., Management Studies, Vocational Education, Technical Education, Pharmaceutical Education, Architecture, Hotel Management and Catering Technology, Information Technology, Town and Country Planning. The AICTE has its new headquarters building in Delhi and it has regional offices at Kanpur, Chandigarh, Gurgaon, Mumbai, Bhopal, Vadodara, Kolkata, Guwahati, Bangalore, Hyderabad, Chennai and Thiruvananthapuram.

Council of Scientific and Industrial Research (CSIR)

The Council of Scientific and Industrial Research abbreviated as CSIR was established by the Government of India in September of 1942 as an autonomous body that has emerged as the largest research and development organisation in India.

As of 2018, it runs 57 laboratories/institutes, 39 outreach centers, 3 Innovation Centers and 5 units throughout the nation, with a collective staff of over 14,000, including a total of 3460 scientists and 4350 technical and support personnel. Although it is mainly funded by the Ministry of Science and Technology, it operates as an autonomous body through the Societies Registration Act, 1860.

The research and development activities of CSIR include aerospace engineering, structural engineering, ocean sciences, life sciences, metallurgy, chemicals, mining, food, petroleum, leather, and environmental science.

Indian Council of Agricultural Research (ICAR)

The Indian Council of Agricultural Research (ICAR) is an autonomous body responsible for co-ordinating agricultural education and research in India. It reports to the Department of Agricultural Research and Education, Ministry of Agriculture. The Union Minister of Agriculture serves as its president. It is the largest network of agricultural research and education institutes in the world.

The Committee to Advise on Renovation and Rejuvenation of Higher Education (Yashpal Committee, 2009) has recommended setting up of a constitutional body - the National Commission for Higher Education and Research - which would be a unified supreme body to regulate all branches of higher education including agricultural education. Presently, regulation of agricultural education is the mandate of ICAR, Veterinary Council of India (Veterinary sub-discipline) and Indian Council of Forestry Research and Education (Forestry sub-discipline).

National Assessment and Accreditation Council (NAAC)

India has one of the largest and diverse education systems in the world. Privatization, widespread expansion, increased autonomy and introduction of Programmes in new and emerging areas have improved access to higher education. At the same time, it has also led to widespread concern on the quality and relevance of the higher education. To address these concerns, the National Policy on Education (NPE, 1986) and the Programme of Action (PoA, 1992) spelt out strategic plans for the policies, advocated the establishment of an independent National accreditation agency. Consequently, the National Assessment and Accreditation Council (NAAC) was established in 1994 as an autonomous institution of the University Grants Commission (UGC) with its Head Quarter in Bengaluru. The mandate of NAAC as reflected in its vision statement is in making quality assurance an integral part of the functioning of Higher Education Institutions (HEIs).

The NAACs grades institutes on an eight-grade ladder:

Range of institutional CGPA	Letter Grade	Performance Descriptor
3.51 - 4.00	A++	Accredited
3.26 - 3.50	A+	Accredited
3.01 - 3.25	A	Accredited
2.76 - 3.00	B++	Accredited
2.51 - 2.75	B+	Accredited
2.01 - 2.50	B	Accredited
1.51 - 2.00	C	Accredited
≤ 1.50	D	Not Accredited

National Board of Accreditation (NBA)

The National Board of Accreditation (NBA) is one of the two major bodies responsible for accreditation of higher education institutions in India, along with the National Assessment and Accreditation Council (NAAC). NBA accredits technical programmes, such engineering and management programmes, while NAAC accredits general colleges and universities. NBA is a full member of the Washington Accord.

NBA was established by the All India Council for Technical Education (AICTE) in 1994 and operated as an autonomous body since 2010. In 2014 it was granted a full membership status in the Washington Accord.

INSTITUTES OF NATIONAL IMPORTANCE

Institutes of National Importance (INIs) are Institutes specific interest. INIs are institutions which are set by an act of parliament. They receive special recognition and funding. The Department of Higher Education's list includes 74 institutions including all of AIIMS, IITs, NITs, SPA, IISERs, IIITs and some others like NIMHANS, ISI etc. were also officially awarded the status. INIs are marked below with a hash.

The NBA accredits programmes and not institutes. These include diplomas, undergraduate and postgraduate programs. Accredited fields include engineering & technology, management, pharmacy, architecture, applied arts and crafts, computer applications and hospitality and tourism management.

- Indian Institutes of Technology (IITs) are a group of autonomous engineering, science, and management institutes with special funding and administration. The Institutes of Technology Act, 1961 lists twenty three IITs.
- Indian Institutes of Information Technology (IIITs) are a group of autonomous information technology oriented institutes with special funding and administration. The Indian Institutes of Information Technology Act lists four central and eighteen public-private partnership IIITs.
- School of Planning and Architecture (SPAs) are a group of architecture and planning schools established by Ministry of HRD, Government of India. All the SPAs are premier centrally funded institution.
- National Institutes of Technology (NITs) are a group of engineering, science, technology and management schools which were established as "Regional Engineering Colleges" and upgraded in 2003 to national status and central funding. The latest act governing NITs is the National Institutes of Technology Act, 2007 which declared them Institutes of National Importance. It lists twenty NITs. In 2010 the government announced plans for ten more.
- Indian Institutes of Management (IIMs) are a group of business schools created by the Government of India. IIMs are registered Societies governed by their respective Board of Governors. The Department of Higher Education lists 19 IIMs.
- Indian Institutes of Science Education and Research (IISERs) are a group of seven institutes established by the Ministry of Human Resource Development, devoted to science education and research in basic sciences. They are broadly set on the lines of the Indian Institute of Science.
- All India Institute of Medical Sciences (AIIMS) are a group of autonomous public medical colleges of higher education. These are seven in numbers and are established by the Ministry of Health and Family Welfare, with the aim of correcting regional imbalances in quality tertiary level healthcare in the country, and attaining self-sufficiency in graduate and postgraduate medical education.
- National Law Universities (NLU) are universities established for promotion of legal research and legal profession in India. There are around 15 National Law Universities in India.
- Institute under State Legislature Act (IuSLAs) are autonomous higher education institutes established or incorporated by a State legislature Act. Institutes that are 'under State Legislature Act' enjoy academic status and privileges like state universities.

Non-Conventional Distance Education IGNOU

Indira Gandhi National Open University was established in 1985 to democratise higher education. The aim was to provide cost-effective, quality education to large sections of our population including those living in remote and farflung areas.

The University has, in a relatively short time, contributed significantly to higher education, community education and continual professional development using all possible media and means for this. As a world leader in distance education, it was conferred the Centre of Excellence Award in Distance Education in 1993 and the

FEATURES OF IGNOU

IGNOU stands significantly apart from other universities because of:

- national jurisdiction.
- flexible admission rules.
- individualised study : flexibility, in terms of place, pace and duration of study.
- use of latest educational and communication technologies.
- student support services.
- cost-effective programmes.
- modular programmes.
- resource sharing, collaboration and networking between other Open Universities.

Award of Excellence for Distance Education Materials in 1999 by the Commonwealth of Learning (COL), Canada. In January, 2010 it was listed 12th in the webometric ranking of Indian universities, based on the calibre of its presence on the internet.

Today, it serves the educational aspirations of over 2.6 million students in India and 36 other countries through the twenty-one Schools of Studies and a network of 61 regional centres, around 3,000 learner support centres and around 60 overseas centres.

Functions of IGNOU

IGNOU has two main functions :

(i) It offers various academic programmes that lead to Certificates, Diplomas and Degrees. It develops and produces courses for delivery through open learning and distance education mode. IGNOU is also actively involved in research, training and extension education activities.

(ii) In its capacity as an Apex Body, it co-ordinates and monitors distance education system throughout the country. IGNOU has also constituted the Distance Education Council and has provided expertise and assistance to other Open and Distance Learning Institutions in the country.

Oriental, Conventional and Non-conventional Learning Programes in India

- **Oriental learning programmes.** The field of Oriental learning involves courses based on the study of Eastern society, culture, language, history, people, etc. Asian Studies, Middle Eastern Studies, Islamic Studies, Sinology, etc., are fields of Oriental Learning. Bachelor's and Master's programmes on the above subjects can be classified as Oriental Learning Programmes.
- **Conventional learning programmes.** These are the traditional programmes such as the regular degree and diploma courses. Conventional learning involves the learning inside a classroom set-up. It does not make use of modern technology in learning.
- **Non-conventional learning programmes.** As the name suggests, these programmes involve the use of modem technology. With the development of technology, students now have the option to enrol in online courses, Where they can learn from videos and handouts available online. Certificates can also be generated upon completion of the course. Different degree, diploma, and certificate courses available in MOOC form can be categorized as non- conventional learning programmes.

COMMONWEALTH OF LEARNING

The Commonwealth of Learning is an inter-governmental organisation established by the Commonwealth Heads of Government in 1988 to encourage the development and sharing of open learning and distance education knowledge, resources and technologies.

COL is hosted in Canada by the Government of Canada. The major voluntary contributors – currently Canada, India, New Zealand, Nigeria, South Africa and the United Kingdom – are each entitled to seats on COL's Board of Governors. The following COL's key India partners are:

- Indira Gandhi National Open University (India)
- National Institute of Open Schooling (India)
- National Assessment and Accreditation Council (India)

Professional and Technical Education

Professional and Technical Education plays a vital role in human resource development of the country by creating skilled manpower, enhancing industrial productivity and improving the quality of life of its people. Technical Education covers programmes in engineering, technology, management, architecture, town planning, pharmacy, applied arts & crafts, hotel management and catering technology.

Prospects and Initiatives

India is renowned for producing graduates of the highest caliber, but only a very few compared with its population receive high quality technical education. India has over the years significantly bolstered the quality and availability of technical education, doubling the employment rate of graduates who are now better suited to the needs of Indian Industry.

So, there is a dire need of backing up conventional study and teaching technical education, as it will not only help in the development of the country, but also the person possessing those skills. Technical education is a part of education that is directly related to the gaining of information and skills needed in manufacturing and service industries.

For acquiring technical education, there are two structural streams in India - formal and informal. Polytechnics, Industrial Training Institutes, Industrial Training Centers, centrally sponsored scheme of Vocationalisation of Secondary Education by the Ministry of Human Resource Development are few of the formal sources of technical education in India.

New industrial and labour trends in India have clearly specified the need of technical education. But, the base of technical education must be made strong at secondary level of education and a clear-cut path for the students to move ahead in this field must be made. More technical degrees of high quality along with technical universities must be established.

VALUE EDUCATION AND ENVIRONMENTAL EDUCATION

Values. In our general life, we see that the things, which are worthful at present time, become deteriorated in worth after a period of time. Values are those entities which are worthful forever in same extent. "In brief we need to know something of religion, philosophy, and ideology of the people". These aspects of a culture are considered as values because the guiding social aims and religious beliefs of people are ideas they think worthwhile of which they attach value.

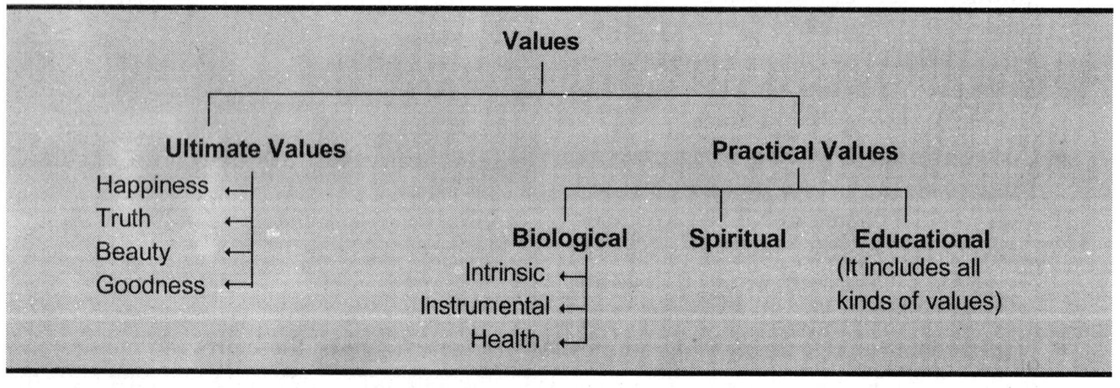

CLASSIFICATION OF VALUE

Source of Value Education. There are many different sources, which can be utilized by the teachers to impart value education. They are as follows.

(i) Regular subjects of the school curriculum is the first source of value education. Whatever subject we teach, there is a set of values, which is hidden in structure and methodology. The teacher will have to find it out and accordingly impart instructions. For example, general science is associated with such values as free inquiry, commitment to truth and mathematics with such qualities of mind as logical thinking, neatness and precisions. Similarly, literature and history have their own distinctive values.

(ii) Co-curricular activities are the second important source for the development values. They provide young pupils with opportunities for self-expression and self-fulfillment.

The students-self-government in school, NCC, NSS, Boy Scouts and Girls Guides, Red-Cross, the various clubs and associations, games and sports, excursions and field visits, all provide opportunities for the students to come together in the pursuit of common goals and ideals. Besides the development of creativity and distinctive intellectual, social and cultural interests, students also learn from these activities, the values of democratic living, co-operation, tolerance, secularism and responsibility. These activities provide experience in learning values through actual living.

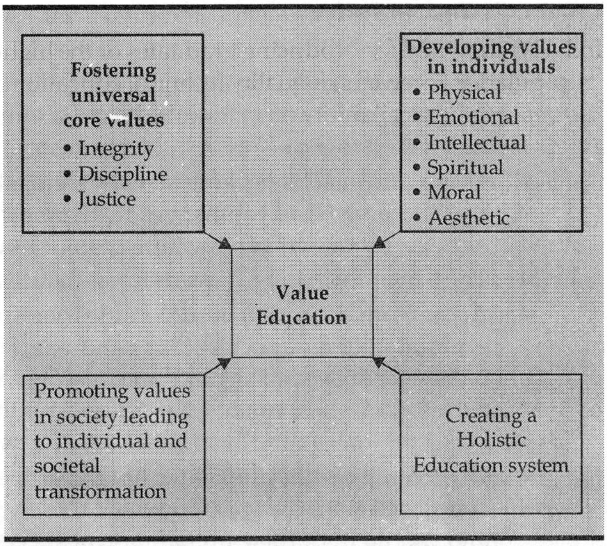

Fostering universal core values • Integrity • Discipline • Justice		Developing values in individuals • Physical • Emotional • Intellectual • Spiritual • Moral • Aesthetic
	Value Education	
Promoting values in society leading to individual and societal transformation		Creating a Holistic Education system

(iii) The environment is the third source of value education. Some great Indian personalities in like Tagore, Gandhi and Sri Aurobindo laid much stress on the creation of a conducive environment in centres of learning for the development of personality of the students. The personal examples and hard work of the teachers, the ideals of the teachers, pupils and the parents help the students to acquire right values in life.

Attempts for Value Oriented Education in India

An awareness for the inculcation of right values has been growing in India since Independence.

1. **Education Commission (1964-66).** The report of the Education Commission (1964-66) stated that "The expanding knowledge and the growing power which modernization places at the disposal of society, must therefore, be combined with the strengthening and deepening of the sense of social responsibility and a keener appreciation of moral and spiritual values. The weakening of social and moral values in the younger generation is creating many serious and social and ethical conflicts. In the situation that is developing, it is equally important for us to give a proper value orientation to our educational system."

   The main purpose of the commission was not to prepare a list of values to inculcate. It only emphasised to inculcate right values in the students at all stages of education.
2. **University Education Commission (1948).** The University Education Commission (1948) considered both the philosophical and practical aspects of value-oriented education and made certain valuable proposals for reform. But they were implemented only in a small number of institutions.
3. **Sri Prakash Committee (1959).** The Central Advisory Board of Education appointed a Special Committee on Religious and Moral Instruction in the year 1959. It is popularly

Remember

AIMS AND OBJECTIVE OF VALUE EDUCATION

- Developing character and morality
- Developing personality, health, well balanced personality
- Developing cultural, spectral values
- Developing habits of truthfulness, punctuality, honesty
- Developing ideas of responsible citizen
- Developing values of democracy, secularism, equality ad scientific attitude
- Developing vocational competence
- Developing positive adjustment
- Developing social efficiency
- Developing national integration

known as the Sri Prakash Committee. It is a matter of sorrow that the response from the educational institutions is very poor.

4. **Kothari Commission (1964-66).** Under the circumstances, the Kothari Commission has given the following recommendations to adopt active measures to give a value-oriented education. The recommendations are :
   - The Central and State Government should adopt measures to introduce education in moral, social and spiritual values in all institutions under their direct control on the lines recommended by the University Education Commission on religious and moral instruction.
   - The privately managed institutions should also be expected to follow suit.
   - Apart from education in such values being made an integral part of School Programmes generally, some periods should be set apart in the time-table for this purpose. They should be taken, not by specially recruited teachers, but by general teachers preferably from different communities, considered suitable for the purpose. It should be one of the important objectives of training institutions to prepare teachers for it.
   - We also suggest that the University Department in Comparative Religion should be specially concerned with the ways in which these values can be wisely and effectively imparted and should undertake preparation of special literature for use by students and teachers.

SKILL BASED EDUCATION

When we refer to Skill Education, we have to look at it from two perspectives-one where children and youngsters have been exposed to formal education and school and college level, yet do not possess the required skills to be employable and; second those who have never been exposed to any kind of formal education and need to acquire certain skills to be employable.

Understanding the Gaps

According to educational experts, today, employers look for some mandatory attributes in their employees. These are over and above knowledge of core subject that a student may have acquired over a period of study. These skills include many attributes like good communication skills, positive approach towards challenge, general awareness, approach to lifelong learning, self discipline and time management, sense of initiative, sharing and teamwork, stress management and much more. It is therefore important that schools and colleges educate children and youngsters about these attributes that are paramount to securing a well paid job.

In India, both these categories in skill education are met by two ministries- the Ministry of Human Resource and Development and the Ministry of Labor and Employment. The former looks after skill development at school and college level while the latter caters to industry oriented training and education. Owing to the fact that almost 60 percent of skilled jobs are not to be manned by white collars, there is dearth of skilled manpower in the country. For one, a huge percentage of these citizens, coming from lower income groups, don't have access to any form of formal education; and even if they have, they are not able to reach the senior secondary levels leave alone study in a college. The result is that psychological and sociological development is crippled much before time.

Road Ahead

Skill India is a campaign launched by Prime Minister Narendra Modi on 15 July 2015 which aims to train over 40 crore people in India in different skills by 2022. It includes various initiatives of the government like "National Skill Development Mission", "National Policy for Skill Development and Entrepreneurship, 2015", "Pradhan Mantri Kaushal Vikas Yojana (PMKVY)" and the "Skill Loan scheme".

The National Skill Development Corporation India (NSDC) was setup as a one of its kind, Public Private Partnership Company with the primary mandate of catalysing the skills landscape in India. It is based on the following pillars:

1. Create large and good quality vocational institute.
2. Reduce risk by providing patient capital. Including grants and equality.
3. To enable the creation and sustainability of support systems required for skill development. This includes the Industry led Sector Skill Councils.

PMKVY is the flagship scheme of the Ministry of Skill Development & Entrepreneurship. The objective is to enable a large number of Indian youth to take up industry-relevant skill training that will help them in securing a better livelihood. Individuals with prior learning experience or skills will also be assessed and certified under Recognition of Prior Learning (RPL). Under this Scheme, Training and Assessment fees are completely paid by the Government.

PMKVY is applicable to any candidate of Indian nationality who is unemployed, school or college dropout, or as identified by the Sector Skill Council (SSC) for their respective job roles.

SKILL DEVELOPMENT

Schemes for the skill development launched by Government of India :

1. Deen Dayal Upadhyaya Grameen Kaushalya Yojana
2. Pradhan Mantri Kaushal Vikas Yojana
3. Financial Assistance for Skill Training of Persons with Disabilities
4. National Apprenticeship Promotion Scheme
5. Craftsmen Training Scheme
6. Apprenticeship training
7. Pradhan Mantri Kaushal Kendra
8. Skill development for minorities
9. Green Skill Development Programme.

Skill India campaign was launched by Prime Minister Narendra Modi on 15 July 2015 to train over 40 crore people in India in different skills by 2022.

Rozgar Mela. The Scheme aligns itself to the common norms and, therefore, part of the Training Partner payment structure is linked to the placements. It is, therefore, important for the Training Partner to place at least 50 percent of the batch under PMKVY to ensure that its performance is not downgraded. Group Personal Accident Policy under Pradhan Mantri Kaushal Vikas Yojana (2016-2020) provides coverage to the candidates skilled by/through NSDC under PMKVY for a Sum Insured of 2 Lakhs for Accidental Death/Permanent Total Disablement for a period of three years from the policy generation date for the Candidates certified after 31.03.2018.

The objective of the National Policy on Skill Development and Entrepreneurship, 2015 will be to meet the challenge of skilling at scale with speed and standard (quality). It will aim to provide an umbrella framework to all skilling activities being carried out within the country, to align them to common standards and link the skilling with demand centres.

Skill Loan Scheme was launched by the Hon'ble Prime Minister on 15th July, 2015 with a view to support youth who wish to go through skill training programmes in the Country. This Skill Loan Scheme has replaced earlier Indian Banks Association (IBA) Model Loan Scheme for Vocational Education and Training. The Indian Banks Association (IBA) has already circulated the scheme to the Chief Executives of All Member Banks for implementation of the Scheme. Any Indian National who has secured admission in a course run by Industrial Training Institutes (ITIs), Polytechnics or in a school recognised by Central or State education Boards or in a college affiliated to recognised university, training partners affiliated to National Skill Development Corporation (NSDC) Sector Skill Councils, State Skill Mission, State Skill Corporation can avail loan for the purpose.

Initiatives

Various initiatives under this campaign are:

(a) National Skill Development Mission.
(b) National Policy for Skill Development and Entrepreneurship, 2015.
(c) Pradhan Mantri Kaushal Vikas Yojana (PMKVY).
(d) Skill Loan scheme.
(e) Rural India Skill.

New Plan Scheme : Higher Education Statistics and Public Information System (HESPIS)

To prepare a sound data-base on Higher Education, Ministry launched All India Survey on Higher Education (AISHE) to collect data from all the institutions of higher learning in the country through electronic mode. Keeping in view the need for generating reliable data on regular basis, the Ministry further decided to continue the survey on an annual basis and for which creation of a scheme was needed.

Objectives of the Scheme

- Strengthening official Statistical system to produce Education Statistics periodically with timeliness and quality so as to assess and review the performance of education sector and regional divergences across the country.
- Encouraging all producers of official Statistics to adopt common geographic referencing and coding standards to provide statistical aggregates/ estimates at State, District and Block level.
- Promoting collection of data in electronic mode
- Periodically reviewing all regular surveys by undertaking in-house reviews of actual results over time and identifying data-gaps.
- Developing techniques that reduce burden on data providers
- Strengthening Institutional Coordination between Ministry and other data producing agencies such as University Grants Commission, All India Council for Technical Education, National University of Educational Planning & Administration, Medical Council of India, State Government Departments, Examination Boards etc.
- Benefiting students by creating Centralized portal which can provide updated information to students which may be useful for their decision making.
- To conduct some special surveys and longitudinal studies for more detailed insight of Higher Education in the country.

Key Features of the Scheme

- HESPIS is an umbrella scheme catering to the need of various kinds of Statistics related to higher education sector.
- Steering Committee will be constituted under the chairmanship of Secretary (higher Education) with the representation of heads of various stakeholders from all the sectors including Planning Commission, UGC, AICTE, NUEPA etc. to address various issues relating to higher education statistics.
- Technical decisions related to Higher Education Statistics will be taken by Steering Committee.
- Setting up of AISHE Unit in the State and AISHE cell in each Affiliating University to coordinate All India Survey on Higher Education.
- Norm-based and Output-based funding.
- States and Institutions to ensure uploading of data and its authenticity for receiving funds.
- Funds would flow from the Ministry of Human Resource Development (MHRD) to the Higher Education Institutions, through the AISHE State Unit/AISHE University Cell.
- AISHE State Unit will be the key institution at the state level to channelize resources to the institutions.
- State wise allocations would be decided on the basis number of Higher Education Institutions located in the State.
- Remuneration to the Institutions would be based on the workload per Institution.

Name of the Institute	Specialised activity	Central location
Lal Bahadur Shastri National Academy of Administration	Imparts training to IAS officers	Mussoorie
Forest Research Institute	Imparts training to IFS officers	Dehradun
Indian Institute of Forest Management	Education & training in natural resources management	Bhopal
National Inst. for Entrepreneurship & Small Business Dvmnt.	Provides training for entrepreneurs in small industries	Noida
Film & Television Institute of India	One of Asia's premier film training schools	Pune
Institute of Chartered Accountants of India (ICAI)	Development & regulation of profession of Chartered Accountants	New Delhi
Institute of Cost and Works Accountants of India (ICWAI)	Development and regulation of profession of Cost Accountants	Kolkata
International Institute of Ayurveda and Oriental Subjects	Engaged in study and research in Ayurveda and Oriental subjects	Kolkata
Institute of Manufacturing Resource Management of India	Development and knowledge enhancement for mfg. professionals	Mumbai
Institute of Psychological & Education Measurement (IPEM)	Testing providers	Allahabad
Indian Institute of Foreign Trade	Focuses on training for international business	New Delhi
Indian Institute of Material Management	Courses in materials management	New Delhi
Indian Institute of Science (IIS)	Higher studies and research in science and engineering	Bangalore
Indian Statistical Institute	Devoted to the research and teaching of statistics	Kolkata
Indira Gandhi Institute of Development Research	Research on development from a broad interdisciplinary perspective	Mumbai
Institute for Oriental Study	Promotion of Indian culture, history, civilisation and Sanskrit	Thane
Institute of Asian Studies	An institute for research scholars from all over Asia	Chennai
Institute of Company Secretaries of India	Regulates the profession of Company Secretaries in India	New Delhi
Institute of Peace and Conflict Studies	A think tank on South Asian security issues	New Delhi
Jawaharlal Nehru Center for Advanced Scientific Research	Engaged in advanced scientific research	Bangalore
Miri Piri Academy	Provides education in the Khalsa tradition	Amritsar
National Centre for Biological Sciences (NCBS)	Basic research in the frontier areas of biology and trains to Ph.D.	Bangalore
National Institute of Small Industry Extension Training	Promotion, development and modernization of the SME sector	Hyderabad
National Dairy Research Institute (NDRI)	R&D support for Dairy Development programmes of the Nation	Karnal
National Institute of Oceanography	Researches different aspects of coastal & open ocean environments	Goa
Physical Research Laboratory	Research institution for theoretical physics & earth sciences	Ahmedabad
Raman Research Institute	Works on basic sciences in the area of physics and astrophysics	Bangalore
Saha Institute of Nuclear Physics (SINP)	Basic research and training in physical and biophysical sciences	Kolkata

Name of the Institute	Specialised activity	Central location
Sardar Patel Renewable Energy Research Institute (SPRERI)	Designs and develops renewable energy devices and systems	Vidyanagar
Tata Institute of Social Sciences (TISS)	First school of social work in India	Mumbai
V.V. Giri National Labour Institute	Education, training & development in organised & unorganised labour	Noida
Yashwantrao Chavan Academy of Development Admin.	Training for govt. and N.G.O. employees	Pune
The Indian Institute of Entrepreneurship (IIE)	Training, research and consultancy activities for small industry and entrepreneurship	Guwahati
Indian Institute of Advanced Studies (IIAS)	Centre of higher learning in Humanities, Social Sciences and Life sciences	Shimla
National Judicial Academy	Training of Judicial Officers, working in Supreme Court and High Courts	Bhopal
National Savings Institute	National level publicity of small savings	Nagpur
English and Foreign Languages University (EFLU)	Teaching/learning of foreign languages	Hyderabad
Gramodaya Vishwavidyala	Higher education to people living in rural areas	Chitrakoot
Central University of Tibetan Studies (CUTS)	Educating the young Tibetan Diaspora and those from the Himalayan border regions of India, who have religion, culture and language in common with Tibet	Sarnath
IGNOU	Education by means of distance and open education	New Delhi
Indian Council of Historical Research (ICHR)	Supports the academic and empirical research	New Delhi
Indian Council of Philosophical Research (ICPR)	Review, coordinate and encourage research in philosophy	Lucknow
Central Institute of Coastal Engg. for Fisheries	Conduct engg. and economic investigations for Fishing Harbour projects	Bangalore
National Institute of Design	Scientific and industrial design research organisation	Ahmedabad, Gandhinagar, Bangalore
National Institute of Immunology	Research in the field of immunology and allied science	New Delhi
National Institute of Open Schooling (NIOS)	Vocational, Life Enrichment and community oriented courses besides General and Academic Courses at Secondary and Senior Secondary level	Noida
National Institute of Rural Development	To facilitate the rural development efforts	Hyderabad
National Institute of Nutrition	To enable food and nutrition security	Hyderabad
National Institute of Advanced Studies	Advanced research in multidisciplinary areas	Bangalore
National Institute of Health and Family Welfare (NIHFW)	Promotion of health and family welfare programmes	New Delhi

Name of the Institute	Specialised activity	Central location
Indian Council of Agricultural Research (ICAR)	Research and education in agriculture	New Delhi
Indian Council of Medical Research (ICMR)	Formulation, coordination and promotion of biomedical research	New Delhi
National Univ. of Educational Planning and Admin. (NUEPA)	Capacity building and research in planning and management of education	New Delhi
Auroville Foundation	A universal town where men and women of all countries are able to live in peace and progressive harmony, above all creeds, all politics and all nationalities	Villupuram
Central Institute of Education Technology (CIET)	Promote utilization of educational technologies	New Delhi
All India Council of Technical Education (AICTE)	Planning and coordinated development of technical education and management education system	New Delhi
National Commission for Minority Educational Institutions	Provide direct affiliation for minority professional institutions to Central Universities	New Delhi
Central Institute of Indian Languages	Coordinate development of Indian languages	Mysore
National Council for Promotion of Sindhi Language	Promote, develop and propagate Sindhi language	Vadodara
National Council for Promotion of Urdu Language	Main authority of Urdu language and education in India	New Delhi
Maharshi Sandeepani Rashtriya Veda Vidya Pratishthan	Preserve, conserve and develop the oral tradition of Vedic studies	Ujjain
Rashtriya Sanskrit Vidyapeetha	Higher learning in Sanskrit studies, Sastras and Pedagogy	Tirupati
Indian Institute of Science Education & Research (IISER)	To integrate education with research	Kolkata, Pune, Mohali, Bhopal, Thiruvananthapuram
National Institute of Technical Teachers' Training & Research	Training for faculty and staff of technical institutions and working professionals from industry	Kolkata, Chennai, Bhopal, Chandigarh
Board of Apprenticeship Training	Establish a liaison between the technical institutions and the industries in the respective Region	Mumbai, Kolkata, Kanpur, Chennai
Indian School of Mines University	Started as an institution to impart mining education. Now a multi-departmental technical university	Dhanbad
National Institute of Foundry and Forge Technology (NIFFT)	Teaching, training, research & development, consultancy and documentation and information retrieval services in metal casting and metal forming technology	Ranchi
National Institute of Industrial Engineering	Post Graduate programs in both Industrial Engineering and Industrial Management	Mumbai
Mahatma Gandhi Antarrashtriya Hindi Vishwavidyalaya	Promotion and development of Hindi language and literature	Wardha
Indira Gandhi National Tribal University	Higher education and research facilities for tribal population	Amarkantak

GOVERNANCE, POLITY AND ADMINISTRATION

Constitution of India

Some Salient Features of the Constitution of India

1. The Constitution of India is a comprehensive document and probably the lengthiest written constitution in the world. It contains 395 Articles and 12 Schedules.
2. It is designed to work as a federal Constitution in normal times, and as a unitary one in emergency.
3. It establishes a parliamentary system of government both at the Centre and in the States. The President is the constitutional Head of State and the Council of Ministers headed by the Prime Minister is the real executive which is responsible to the Lok Sabha. In the States, the Council of Ministers headed by the Chief Ministers is responsible to the Legislative Assembly.
4. It introduces adult franchise (*i.e.*, every adult of the age of 18 and above has been given the right to vote) and it also introduces the system of joint electorates.
5. It guarantees Fundamental Rights to all citizens of India.
6. It lays down the 'Directive Principles of State Policy' for the guidance of the governmental authorities in the country.
7. It provides for an independent judiciary; the Supreme Court acts as the guardian of the Constitution.
8. Another feature of the Constitution is that it makes India a Secular State. There is no State religion and no religion is given any privilege.
9. The Indian Constitution is neither very rigid nor very flexible. It is a unique combination of flexibility and rigidity. A major part of the Constitution can be amended by Parliament by a two-thirds majority of members of each chamber present and voting and that majority must also be the majority of total membership of each chamber. There are some important provisions for the amendment of which the consent of at least half of the states is also required. In special circumstances, the constitution can be adjusted without resorting to formal amendment. For example, the Rajya Sabha can transfer any state subject to the Centre in national interest. For this purpose, it has to pass a resolution by a two-thirds majority of members present and voting. Again, during an Emergency the President can suspend the autonomous status of the can be amended by a simple majority of parliament.

Framing the Indian Constitution

The present constitution of India was framed by the Constituent Assembly of India set up under the Cabinet Mission Plan of May 16, 1946.

A number of committees submitted reports to the Constituent Assembly on the different aspects of the constitution. On the basis of these reports the constitution was prepared by Constitutional Adviser, Sri B.N. Rao. The Drafting Committee under the chairmanship of Dr. Ambedkar worked on the draft and produced the Draft Constitution with 315 articles and 8 schedules. In its progress through the Constituent Assembly, the constitution grew in bulk and took its final shape with 395 articles and 8 schedules on November 26, 1949, "We, the people of India" gave ourselves the new constitution.

There have been 94 amendments to our Constitution so far.

Schedules of the Constitution

A Constitution or an Act often contains schedules which are generally given at the end. These Schedules are an integral part of the constitution. The device of including schedules in the constitution facilitates a reference to details because they are put in one place. The Indian Constitution contains 12 schedules. (The original Constitution contained eight schedules. Four were added later).

First Schedule. The State and the Union Territories that comprise the Union of India are listed in the first schedule.

States :

1. Andhra Pradesh	2. Assam	3. Bihar
4. Gujarat	5. Kerala	6. Madhya Pradesh
7. Tamil Nadu	8. Maharashtra	9. Karnataka
10. Orissa	11. Punjab	12. Rajasthan
13. Uttar Pradesh	14. West Bengal	15. Jammu & Kashmir
16. Nagaland	17. Haryana	18. Manipur
19. Himachal Pradesh	20. Tripura	21. Meghalaya
22. Sikkim	23. Mizoram	24. Goa
25. Arunachal Pradesh	26. Chhattisgarh	27. Uttaranchal
28. Jharkhand	29. Telangana	

Union Territories :

1. Delhi	2. Andaman and Nicobar Islands
3. Lakshadweep	4. Dadra and Nagar Haveli
5. Daman and Diu	6. Puducherry
7. Chandigarh	

Second Schedule. It prescribes the salary payable to the President, the Governor of a State, the Chief Justice of India, Judges of the Supreme Court and High Courts, the Comptroller and Auditor General, etc.

Third Schedule. It contains forms of oaths and affirmations.

Fourth Schedule. It allocates seats for each State of the Indian Union in the Rajya Sabha.

Fifth Schedule. It contains provisions as to the administration and control of Scheduled Areas and Scheduled Tribes.

Sixth Schedule. It contains provisions as to the administration of Tribal Areas in the States of Assam, Meghalaya, Tripura, Mizoram and Arunachal Pradesh.

Seventh Schedule. It gives the three lists of powers or subjects to be looked after by the Union (Centre) and the States. In the first place, there is the list of exclusively federal or central subjects. It is called the Union List and comprises 97 subjects. In the second place, there is the list of exclusive powers of the States. The list contains 66 subjects. In the third and the last place, there is the concurrent list comprising 47 subjects.

Eighth Schedule (Article 344(I) and 351). It contains a list of 22 languages of India recognised in the constitution. These are :

(1) Assamese	(2) Bengali	(3) Gujarati
(4) Hindi	(5) Kannada	(6) Kashmiri
(7) Konkani	(8) Malayalam	(9) Manipuri
(10) Marathi	(11) Nepali	(12) Oriya
(13) Punjabi	(14) Sanskrit	(15) Sindhi
(16) Tamil	(17) Telugu	(18) Urdu.

In 2004, four languages were added to the Eight Schedule vide the constitution (Ninety Second) Amendment Act, 2003. These were :

(19) Bodo	(20) Dogri
(21) Maithili	(22) Santhali.

Ninth Schedule. This schedule was added by the first Amendment Act of 1951. It contains a list of acquisition laws (*i.e.* laws under which property has been acquired) which cannot be declared invalid on the ground of inconsistency with any of the Fundamental Rights.
Tenth Schedule. This schedule was added by the 52nd Amendment Act of 1985. It contains provisions as to disqualification on ground of defection.
Eleventh Schedule. This schedule was added by the constitution (73rd Amendment) Act, 1992. It lays down 29 items on which Panchayats shall have powers and authority to function as institutions of self-government.
Twelfth Schedule. The schedule was added by the constitution (74th Amendment) Act, 1992. It lays down 18 items on which municipalities shall have powers and authority to function as institutions of self-government.

Indian Federation

India is federal in structure but unitary in spirit.
Federal Features.
- (a) It has a written constitution which clearly distributes powers between the Centre and the Units.
- (b) Like all other federations, India has a Supreme Court which acts as the guardian of the Constitution, and is also authorised to decide disputes between the Centre and the Units.

Unitary Features. The Indian Constitution has a distinctive unitary bias. Several provisions of the Constitution strengthen the Centre at the expense of the States. The Constitution, for example, provides for single citizenship, single integrated judiciary and unified administrative services. There is a large sphere of concurrent legislative power in addition to the long Union List. Residuary powers have been vested in the Centre. Again, subjects can be transferred from the State List to the Centre by the Rajya Sabha. The boundaries of the State units can be altered by Parliament. During an emergency, the government can assume a unitary character.

The States do not possess sufficient sources of income. They depend upon the Centre for financial aid. Financial dependence always brings along dependence in policy and administration.

Citizenship

The following are entitled to Indian Citizenship :
1. Any person born as well as domiciled in the territory of India with no consideration of the nationality of his parents;
2. Any person who or whose father was not born in India, but who has his domicile in India for not less than five years, immediately preceding the commencement of the Constitution;
3. Any person who has migrated to India from Pakistan before the 19th July, 1948.
4. Any person, who having migrated to Pakistan has returned to India under a permanent permit granted to him by the Indian authorities; or
5. Who has migrated to India after the 19th July, 1948 and has been registered as a citizen of India by a competent authority.

The Constitution adopts the principle of single citizenship for the whole of India. In a typical federation, there is generally double citizenship - Citizenship of the federation as a whole and citizenship of each federating State. In the USA, this principle has been adopted. A State (unit) there can grant its citizens or residents certain rights which it may deny to the citizens of other units.

Fundamental Rights

Certain rights are called fundamental or basic because they are essential for the realisation of the highest good of the citizens. These rights are to be looked upon as inalienable rights of an individual, which every human being is entitled to enjoy if he/she is to maintain human dignity. They are incorporated in the Constitution and are justiciable, *i.e.*, any violation of these rights can be questioned in a court of law. Some restrictions on the Fundamental Rights have been imposed in the interest of common good and the security of the country.

(1) **Right to Equality.** The principle of equality means that there are no special privileges and no distinctions based upon religion, caste, colour, creed or sex. In Public employment, the State provides equal opportunities to all people, if they are otherwise qualified; social equality has been secured by abolition of untouchability.

(2) **Right to Freedom.** The Constitution provides to every citizen the following rights :

(a) freedom of speech and expression,

(b) to assemble peacefully,

(c) to form associations and unions,

(d) to move freely throughout the territory of India,

(e) to reside and settle in any part of the territory of India,

(f) to practise any profession or carry on any active trade and profession.

(3) **Right to Freedom of Religion.** Except when it is not in the interest of public order, morality, health etc., every person is entitled to the freedom of conscience, and the right to profess, practise and propagate any religion freely.

(4) **Cultural and Educational Rights.** The Constitution provides that every community has full freedom to run its own educational institutions, to preserve its own language and culture. The 86th amendment, 2002 of the constitution provides for free and compulsory education to all children of the age of six to fourteen years.

(5) **Right against Exploitation.** Traffic in human beings, and forced labour and the employment of children under 14 years in a factory, mine, etc., are punishable offences.

FUNDAMENTAL DUTIES

A new chapter dealing with the fundamental duties of Indian citizens was added by the 42nd Amendment. It shall be the duty of every citizen of India :

(1) To abide by the constitution and respect its ideals and institutions, the National Flag and the National Anthem;

(2) To cherish and follow the noble ideals which inspired our national struggle for freedom;

(3) To uphold and protect the sovereignty, unity and integrity of India;

(4) To defend the country and render national service when called upon to do so;

(5) To promote harmony and the spirit of common brotherhood amongst all the people of India transcending religious, linguistic and regional or sectional diversities, to renounce practices derogatory to the dignity of women;

(6) To value and preserve the rich heritage of our composite culture;

(7) To protect and improve the natural environment including forests, lakes, rivers and wild life and to have compassion for living creatures;

(8) To develop the scientific temper, humanism and the spirit of inquiry and reform;

(9) To safeguard public property and to abjure violence;

(10) To strive towards excellence in all spheres of individual and collective activity so that the nation constantly rises to higher levels of endeavour and achievement.

(11) To provide opportunities for education to his child or, as the case may be, ward between the age of six and fourteen years.

The last Fundamental Duty [Article 51A(11)] was added through the 86th Constitutional Amendment Act, 2002.

(6) **Right to Constitutional Remedies.** When a citizen feels that any of his fundamental rights has been encroached upon, he can move the Supreme Court or High Court, or any other court empowered for the purpose by an Act of Parliament, for their enforcement and these courts are empowered to issue the usual writs of habeas corpus, mandamus, prohibition, quo warranto and certiorari for such enforcement.

Note. The right to property was also one of the fundamental rights, according to the original Constitution. This right has been taken away by the 44th Amendment Act passed in December, 1978. It is now only a legal right.

Directive Principles of State Policy

The Directive Principles of State Policy though not enforceable through a court of law are regarded as 'fundamental in the governance of the country.' They are merely instructions or directives to the legislatures and the executive authorities for the day-to-day administration of the country.

The State is directed to promote the welfare of the people. To achieve this aim, the State should strive:

(1) To provide adequate means of livelihood for all citizens.

(2) To have fair distribution of wealth and material resources among all classes.

(3) To ensure equal pay for equal work for men as well as for women.

(4) To provide early childhood care and educations for all children until they complete the age of six years (substituted by 86th Amendment).

(5) To provide work, education and public assistance during unemployment, old age, sickness, etc.

(6) To improve public health.

(7) To raise the level of nutrition and standard of living.

(8) To ensure just and humane conditions of work so as to offer full opportunity for enjoyment of leisure, and social and cultural progress.

(9) To reduce the inequalities of income.

(10) To secure protection of child and adult labour against exploitation and moral and material abandonment.

(11) To promote agriculture and animal husbandry; improving breed of cattle and preventing cow slaughter.

(12) To protect monuments of historical and national importance.

(13) To establish village panchayats and also to separate the judiciary from the executive.

(14) To safeguard and promote and educational and economic interests of the Scheduled Castes and Scheduled Tribes.

(15) To promote international peace and security, maintain just and honourable relations amongst nations and encourage the settlement of international disputes by arbitration.

These are some of the important Directive Principles of State Policy. The 42nd Amendment gave primacy to Directive Principles over Fundamental Rights. But the Supreme Court struck down Section 4 of the 42nd Amendment which gave primacy to Directive Principles over Fundamental Rights on the ground that it changed the basic features of the Constitution.

The President

The executive power of the Union is exercised by the President of India either directly or through officers subordinate to him. A council of Ministers headed by the Prime Minister aids and advises the President in the exercise of his functions. The 42nd Amendment made it explicit that he would always act on the advice of the Council of Ministers. However, under the 44th Amendment the President has been given the option of asking the cabinet to reconsider its advice. But he must act in accordance with the reconsidered advice.

Election of the President. He is elected by an electoral college comprising (a) the elected members of the Houses of Parliament and (b) the elected members of the Legislative Assemblies of the States by a system of proportional representation by means of a single transferable vote; voting is by secret ballot.

Qualifications for election as President :

(1) He must be a citizen of India,

(2) He must not be less than 35 year's of age,

(3) He must be qualified for election as a member of the Lok Sabha but shall not be a member; and

(4) He must not be holding any office of profit under the Government of India or any other Government. A Governor of State or a Minister of the Union or State or Vice-President of the Union will not, however, be considered as a person holding an office of profit.

Term of Office. The President holds office for five-years, unless he resigns earlier or he is removed from office by impeachment. He is eligible for re-election.

Salary and allowances. He is entitled to an official rent free residence and he draws a salary of Rs. 5 lakh per month.

Impeachment. The President may be impeached on a charge of "violation of the Constitution". Such impeachment can be moved in either House of the Parliament by means of a resolution. Such a resolution can be moved only, after at least fourteen days' notice in writing signed by not less than one-fourth of the total number of the members of the house has been given of their intention to move the resolution. Such a resolution must be passed by at least two-thirds of the total membership of the House concerned. The charges must be investigated by the other House. The President has the right to be heard and defended during the investigation of the charges against him. If the investigating House sustains the charges by a resolution, adopted by a two-third majority, the President must be removed from office at once.

Powers of the President

Executive Powers. He is vested with the power of making appointments, *i.e.*, he appoints State Governors, Judges of the High Courts and Supreme Court and their Chief Justices, members of the Union Public Service Commission, the Auditor General and the Comptroller General of India and the Attorney General; besides, he makes all diplomatic appointments. He is the Supreme commander of the armed forces of India. He governs the Union Territories through Lt. Governors or Chief Commissioners, who are appointed by him. He calls upon the party or a coalition of parties enjoying majority in the Lok Sabha to form the government.

Legislative Powers. He may address either House of Parliament, send messages to either House concerning those matters which he wants to be considered by the House. He can summon and prorogue either House of Parliament and dissolve the Lok Sabha, and order fresh elections. He can call joint sittings of the two Houses to resolve their differences over a bill. The first session of Parliament after each general election for the Lok Sabha and the first session of each year begins with an address of the President. Any Bill passed by Parliament must receive his assent, before it becomes an Act. He is empowered to make regulations for the Union Territories. He can promulgate an Ordinance when Parliament is not in session. He nominates 12 members to the Rajya Sabha and may nominate two Anglo-Indians to the Lok Sabha.

Financial Powers. No money bill or demand for grant can be introduced or moved in Parliament unless it has been recommended by the President.

Judicial Powers. He has the power to grant pardon, reprieve or remission of punishment or commute death sentences.

Emergency Powers. In any emergency caused by war, aggression, or armed rebellion or internal disturbance or by the failure of the constitutional machinery or by financial instability, the President can proclaim a state of emergency, and he can take under his direct charge the administration of any State of India.

The powers seem to be formidable. But, it must be remembered that these are only theoretical powers of the President. In fact, all these powers are exercised by the President on the advice of the Cabinet, and the advice of the cabinet is binding on the President. If in the Lok Sabha no party commands an absolute majority, the President has a real choice while appointing the Prime Minister. In this way he can determine the very complexion of the ministry.

Vice-President

He is the *ex-officio* Chairman of the Rajya Sabha. He acts in place of the President when the latter falls ill or vacates his office for any other reason, till a newly elected President assumes office. In case of the death of the President, the Vice-President can act for him till the new President is elected by the procedure laid down in the Constitution.

He is elected by the members of both Houses of Parliament according to the system of proportional representation, by means of a single transferable vote; voting is by secret ballot. He must be a citizen of India, not less than 35 years of age of qualified for election as member of the Rajya Sabha. His term of office is five years, unless he resigns earlier or he is removed from office.

Council of Ministers

The Constitution provides that a Council of Ministers with the Prime Minister as its head will aid and advise the President of the Indian Union in the exercise of his functions. The Council of Ministers is the real working executive and the pivot round which the whole political machinery revolves.

Formation. The President sends for the leader of the majority party in the Lok Sabha and appoints him or her as the Prime Minister. All other Ministers are appointed by the President on the advice of the Prime Minister.

Functions. The Cabinet formulates the general executive policy of the Indian Union, prepares legislative programme for Parliament, and also the budget and it decides upon money bills to be introduced in Parliament. It chalks out the foreign policy of the Indian Union. The President does not attend the meetings of the Cabinet. The Prime Minister conveys to him all decisions of the cabinet.

Prime Minister and his Functions

The leader of the majority party or Alliance of parties before and after general election in the Lok Sabha is appointed as the Prime Minister by the President. The President is the titular or constitutional head of the Union Executive and the Prime Minister is the real head. The Prime Minister and other Ministers form the real working executive. The Prime Minister is the chief confidential advisor to the President.

He presides over the meetings of the Cabinet. He co-ordinates the work of the various ministers and exercises general supervision and control over the work of the various departments of the Government. He can remove any Minister. When the Prime Minister resigns, the entire ministry resigns with him. He represents the cabinet as a whole in the Lok Sabha. He explains the policies, actions and decisions of the Government to Parliament.

Parliament

Parliament consists of two Houses, namely, the Council of States (Rajya Sabha, or the Upper House) and the House of the People (Lok Sabha, or the Lower House).

The Lok Sabha. Its maximum strength is 550 (Not more than 530 from the States to be elected directly and not more than 20 to represent U.Ts.) An Indian citizen of 18 and above is eligible to vote. A candidate for membership of the Lok Sabha must be a citizen of India and not less than 25 years of age. The normal term of the House is five years. The House can, however, be dissolved earlier by the President. The said period may, while a proclamation of emergency is in operation, be extended by Parliament by law for a period not exceeding one year at a time and not extending in any case beyond a period of six months after the proclamation has ceased to operate.

Members of the House elect the **Speaker** and the **Deputy Speaker** from among themselves. The Speaker acts as the presiding officer of the House and, in his absence, the Deputy Speaker acts for him.

The Rajya Sabha is a permanent body not subject to dissolution, elected indirectly, and its total strength cannot exceed 250. Twelve members, who have distinguished themselves in literature, arts, science or social service, are nominated by the President. The remaining seats are distributed among the States and Union Territories. The representatives of the States are elected by the members of the Legislative Assemblies of the States concerned by the method of single transferable vote. A candidate for membership of the Rajya Sabha must be a citizen of India and he should not be less than 30 years of age. One third of the members must retire once in two years, and their places be filled by fresh election. The Vice-President of India is the *ex-officio* Chairman of the Rajya Sabha.

Relations between the two Houses of Parliament. If a non-money bill is passed by one House, and the other House rejected it or the two Houses do not agree to the amendments, the President may summon a joint meeting of both Houses to resolve the deadlock. The decision of the majority prevails. As for money bills, every such bill must be introduced in the Lok Sabha. It cannot be introduced in the Rajya Sabha. Any such bill cannot be rejected by the Rajya Sabha though it may delay it for 14 days at the most. The Cabinet, which is the real working executive, is responsible to the Lok Sabha only.

Important Parliamentary Terms

(1) **Act.** A Bill passed by both Houses of Parliament/Legislature and assented to by the President/ Governor.

(2) **Ad hoc Committee.** A Committee constituted by the House or by the Chairman or by the presiding officers of both the Houses jointly to consider and report on specific matter and becomes functus officio as soon as the task is completed.

(3) **Adjournment of Debate.** Adjournment on a motion adopted by the House, of the debate on a Motion/Resolution/Bill on which the House is then engaged until a future day or sine die as specified in the motion.

(4) **Adjournment of the sitting of the House.** Termination of the sitting of the House which meets again at the time appointed for the next sitting.

(5) **Adjournment sine die.** Termination of a sitting of the House without any definite date being fixed for the next sitting.

(6) **Appropriation Bill.** A Money Bill passed annually (or at various times of the year) providing for the withdrawal or appropriation from and out of the Consolidated Fund of India, of moneys, voted by Lok Sabha and moneys charged on the Consolidated Fund for the services of a financial year or a part of a financial year.

(7) **Ballot.** A process to determine inter se priority of more than one notice through a draw of lot.

(8) **Bill.** The draft of a legislative proposal put in the proper form which, when passed by both Houses of Parliament and assented to by the President becomes an Act.

(9) **Budget.** Annual financial statement of the estimated receipts and expenditure of the Government of India in respect of a financial year. The Budget is laid in Rajya Sabha in two parts viz., the Railway Budget and the General Budget.

(10) **Bulletin.** Bulletin means the Bulletin of Rajya Sabha. It is published in two parts. Part I contains a brief record of the proceedings of the House at each of its sittings; and Part II contains information on any matter relating to or connected with the business of the House or Committees or other matter which in the

opinion of the Chairman may be included therein.

(11) **Casting Vote.** The vote cast by the Chairman, or a Member acting as such in the House and by the Chairman or a Member acting as such in a Committee, in the case of an equality of votes on a matter.

(12) **Crossing the floor.** Passing between the member addressing the House and the Chair which is considered breach of Parliamentary etiquette.

(13) **Demand for Grants.** Earmarking of budgetary allocation for meeting the plan and non-plan expenditure of a Ministry/Department.

(14) **Draw of lot.** A method applied to determine the relative precedence of private members' Bills and Resolutions, notices of questions, half-an-hour discussions or any other notice given by more than one member simultaneously for being taken up on the same day.

(15) **Expunction.** Deletion of words, phrases or expressions from the proceedings or records of Rajya Sabha by an order of the Chairman for being defamatory or indecent or unparliamentary or undignified.

(16) **Finance Bill.** A Bill ordinarily introduced every year to give effect to the financial proposals of the Government of India for the following financial year and includes a Bill to give effect to supplementary financial proposals for any period.

(17) **Half-an-Hour Discussion.** A Member with the permission of the Chairman may raise a discussion on a matter of sufficient public importance which has been the subject of a recent oral or written question and the answer to which needs elucidation on a matter of fact.

(18) **Leader of the Council.** The Prime Minister, if he is a member of the Council or a Minister who is a member of the Council and is nominated by the Prime Minister to function as the Leader of the Council.

(19) **Leader of the Opposition.** A Member of the House, who is, for the time being, the leader in that House of the Party in opposition to the Government having the greatest numerical strength and recognised as such by the Chairman.

(20) **Leave of absence.** A member wishing to obtain permission of the House for remaining absent from its sittings is required to make an application stating the reasons and the period for which he may be permitted to be absent from the sittings of the House.

(21) **Motion.** A formal proposal made to the House by a Minister or a member that the House do something, order something to be done or express an opinion with regard to some matter, and is so phrased that, if adopted, it will purport to express the judgment or will of the House.

(22) **Motion of Thanks.** A formal motion moved in the House, expressing its gratitude to the President for the Address delivered by him/her under article 87(1) of the Constitution to both Houses of Parliament assembled together.

(23) **Naming a Member.** The drawing of attention of the House by the Chairman to the conduct of a member who disregards the authority of the Chair or abuses the Rules of the House by persistently and willfully obstructing the business thereof, with a view to action being taken to suspend him from the service of the House for a period not exceeding the remainder of the session.

(24) **Ordinance.** A law made by the President in exercise of the powers vested in him under article 123 of the Constitution.

(25) **Point of Order.** A point relating to the interpretation or enforcement of the Rules of Procedure or such articles of the Constitution as regulate the business of the House raised in the House and submitted for the decision of the Chair.

(26) **Prorogation.** The termination of a session of Rajya Sabha by an order made by the President under article 85(2)(a) of the Constitution.

(27) **Question Hour.** The first hour of a sitting of the House allotted for asking and answering of questions.

(28) **Question of Privilege.** A question involving a breach of privilege either of a member or of the House or of a Committee thereof or a contempt of the House.

(29) **Quorum.** The minimum number of members required to be present at a sitting of the House or a Committee for valid transaction of its business, which is one-tenth of the total number of members of the House, as provided under article 100(3) of the Constitution.

(30) **Roll of Members.** A register in which newly elected members sign, after making and sub-

scribing the oath or affirmation and before taking their seats for the first time in the House.

(31) **Session.** A session of Rajya Sabha comprises the period commencing from the date and time mentioned in the order of the President summoning Rajya Sabha and ending with the day on which the President prorogues Rajya Sabha.

(32) **Short Notice Question.** A question relating to a matter of urgent public importance asked for oral answer by a Member with shorter notice than fifteen clear days by giving the reasons for asking the question with short notice.

(33) **Sitting of the House.** A sitting of the House is duly constituted when it is presided over by the Chairman or a member competent to preside over a sitting of the House under the Constitution or the Rules of Procedure of Rajya Sabha.

(34) **Special Mention.** A procedure available to a Member who wishes to mention a matter of public importance in the House by reading out from the text not exceeding 250 words.

(35) **Standing Committee.** Committee constituted by election by the House or nomination by the Chairman every year or from time to time which are permanent in nature.

(36) **Starred Question.** A question to which a member wishes to have an oral answer on the floor of the House and which is distinguished by an asterisk.

(37) **Statutory Resolution.** A resolution in pursuance of a provision in the Constitution or an Act of Parliament.

(38) **Supplementary question.** A Question asked by any member when called by the Chairman for the purpose of further elucidating any matter of fact regarding which an answer has been given during the question hour.

(39) **Unstarred Question.** A question which is not called for oral answer in the House and the written answer to such a question is deemed to have been laid on the Table.

(40) **Whips.** Members drawn from the party in power and the parties/groups in opposition to perform specified functions and form vital links in the internal organization of a party inside Parliament.

Legislative Process

A Bill

A Bill is a draft law that Parliament proposes to make. If approved and passed by Parliament, the Bill becomes an Act. A Bill is divided into clauses; these become sections when the Bill becomes an Act. There are three stages through which a bill has to pass in one house of the Parliament.

Different types of Parliamentary Bills

Bills may be classified on the basis of their content as Ordinary Bill, Money and Finance Bills, and Constitution Amendment Bills

Ordinary Bills. Any Bill which is not a Constitution Amendment Bill or a Money Bill is classified as an Ordinary Bill. Ordinary Bills are of five types.

- Original Bills (which embody new proposals, ideas or policies),
- Amending Bills (which modify, amend or revise existing Acts),
- Consolidating Bills (which consolidate existing law on a particular subject),
- Expiring Laws (Continuance) Bills (which authorise the continuation of an expiring Act), and
- Bills to replace Ordinances issued by the President.

Money and Financial Bills. A Bill is considered to be a Money Bill if it contains only provisions dealing with all or any of the following matters listed below. A Financial Bill may contain other proposals in addition to these. For example, a Bill that contains a taxation clause, but does not deal solely with taxation is a Financial Bill.

- The imposition, abolition, remission, alteration or regulation of any tax;
- The regulation of money borrowed by the Government of India or any guarantee given by the Government of India;

- The Bill can also consider amendment of the law with respect to any financial obligations undertaken or to be undertaken by the Government of India;
- The custody of the Consolidated Fund of India or the Contingency Fund of India , the payment of moneys into or the withdrawal of moneys from any such Fund;
- The appropriation of moneys out of the Consolidated Fund of India;
- The declaring of a new item to be expenditure charged on the Consolidated Fund of India. Also, if there is any increase in the amount of any such expenditure;
- The receipt of money on account of the Consolidated Fund of India or the Public Account of India or the custody or the issue of such money or the audit of the accounts of the Union or of a State.

The Supreme Court of India

It is the highest court of justice in India. It consists of a Chief Justice and not more than 30 other judges; they hold office till the age of 65. The President appoints the judges of the Supreme Court in consultation with the Chief Justice of India and such Judges of the Supreme Court and of High Courts as he may consider to be necessary .

Qualifications. Any person who has been a Judge of a High Court for 5 years or is an eminent jurist or who has been a practising advocate of a High Court or of two or more such courts in succession for a period of 10 years can be appointed as a judge of the Supreme Court.

The Judges of the Supreme Court draw Rs. 2.5 lakh per month and the salary of Chief Justice is Rs. 2.8 lakh per month.

Jurisdiction and Powers. Its powers are: (1) Original, (2) Appellate, and (3) Advisory.

(i) It has original jurisdiction (*i.e.* cases can begin in the Supreme Court itself) in a dispute between the Centre and any State or States or between the States themselves. The dispute must be regarding some legal right. Political questions cannot be brought before the Supreme Court.

(ii) It hears appeals in cases which involve an interpretation of the Constitution. In civil cases, an appeal lies to the Supreme Court from any judgement of a High Court if the High Court certifies that the case involves a substantial question of law of general importance. In the criminal field, it can hear an appeal if a High Court has an appeal reserved on order of acquittal of an accused person and sentenced him to death; if it has withdrawn for trial before itself any case from a subordinate court and sentenced the accused person to death; or the High Court certifies that the case is a fit one to be heard by the Supreme Court.

(iii) The President has the power to refer a question of law, or any fact of public importance for the opinion and report of the Supreme Court.

(iv) It acts as the guardian of Fundamental Rights, *i.e.*, when a citizen feels that his Fundamental Rights have been encroached upon, he can move either the Supreme Court or the High Court for the enforcement of his rights.

(v) The Supreme Court is empowered to entertain special appeals in its discretion from any judgement or order in any case passed by any court or tribunal in India.

The decisions of the Supreme Court are binding on the executive, and the judgements passed by it are binding on all the courts of the country.

Removal. A judge of the Supreme Court cannot be removed from office except by an order of the President passed after an address by each House of Parliament supported by a majority of the total membership of that House and majority of two-thirds of the members present and voting in the same session.

The removal can be on the grounds of proved incapacity and misbehaviour.

The Attorney General of India

The President of India appoints a person who is qualified to be appointed as a Judge of the Supreme Court to be the Attorney General of India for expert legal advice to the Government of India. He is to perform duties of legal character and such other functions as may be assigned to him by the President under the Constitution. In the performance of his duties, he has the right of audience in all Indian Courts.

Comptroller and Auditor General

The President appoints the Comptroller and Auditor General of India to perform all duties and exercise powers in connection with the accounts of the Union and the States. His main duty is to keep a vigilant watch on the finances of the Union and the States, to submit reports to the President and the Governor and to ensure that the moneys voted by the legislature are spent under appropriate heads, and they are not exceeded or varied.

The Governor

The executive head of each State is called 'Governor'. He is appointed by the President, holds office for five years, receives a salary of Rs. 3.5 lakh per month, and he is also entitled to a number of other allowances and privileges. Any Indian citizen who is not less than 35 years of age is eligible for appointment as Governor.

Powers of the Governor. No money bill can be introduced in the Legislative Assembly of the State except on the recommendation of the Governor. The Constitution empowers him to grant pardon, remit, suspend or commute any punishment.

He summons, fixes the time and place of the meeting of the legislature. He addresses the meeting of the legislature at the commencement of the session once in a year. He can send messages to the State legislature. Every bill passed by the legislature must have his assent. He has the power of promulgating an ordinance, whenever the legislature is not in session.

Council of Ministers

The Constitution provides a Council of Ministers, with a Chief Minister at his head, to aid and advise the Governor in the exercise of his functions. The Governor appoints the Chief Minister and other Ministers are appointed on the advice of Chief Minister. Usually all the Ministers must be members of the legislature of the State but sometimes even a non-member may be appointed as a Minister. In that case, he cannot retain his office for more than six months without getting elected as a member of the legislature of the State. The Council of Ministers is collectively responsible to the Legislative Assembly of the State. The Chief Minister presides over the meetings of the cabinet. In case of a breakdown of the Constitution, the President can authorise the Governor to administer the State on his behalf.

The State Legislature

Every State has a legislature. Some States have one House while others have two. Where there is one chamber, it is known as the Legislative Assembly (*Vidhan Sabha*) and where there are two Houses, the Upper House is called Legislative Council (*Vidhan Parishad*) and the Lower House is known as Legislative Assembly (*Vidhan Sabha*). Maharashtra, Bihar, Tamil Nadu, Uttar Pradesh, Karnataka and Jammu and Kashmir have two Houses, whereas other States have only one House.

Legislative Assembly (Vidhan Sabha). Total membership of a Legislative Assembly varies in each State according to its population. Generally, one member represents 75,000 people and no Legislative Assembly can have more than 500 of fewer than 60 members. Some seats may be reserved for the Scheduled Tribes and Scheduled Castes. The Assembly elects a Speaker and a Deputy Speaker from among its own members. The normal term of the Assembly is five years. While a proclamation of Emergency is in operation, the term of the Assembly may be extended by Parliament by law for a period not exceeding one year at a time and not extending in any case beyond a period of six months after the proclamation has ceased to operate. The qualifications for being a member of the Legislative Assembly are : The candidate should (1) be a citizen of India (2) be not less than 25 years of age, and (3) possess such other qualifications as may be prescribed by Parliament.

Legislative Council (Vidhan Parishad). The maximum strength of this Council must not be more than one-third of the total number of members of the Legislative Assembly of the State but it must not be less than 40. One-third of its members are elected by the local bodies; one third by the Legislative Assembly of the State (persons elected must not be members of the State Assembly); one-twelfth by the University graduates of at least three years standing, one twelfth by teachers of at least three years standing in secondary schools or the higher institutions of the State and one-sixth to be nominated by the Governor from among persons distinguished in Literature, Science, Art, Cooperative Movement and Social Service.

Centre-State Relations

It is often criticized that the Indian federation has a pronounced unitary bias. The Centre has been made very strong at the expense of the states or units of the Indian federation. The relationship between the Centre and the States can be discussed under the following heads :

Legislative. The Centre has been given a long list of exclusive powers. There are 97 subjects in the Union list. On these subjects Parliament can make laws. Then there is a fairly long list of concurrent powers. Subjects mentioned in concurrent list can be looked after by both the Centre and the States. But even here the laws passed by the centre override those passed by the States.

Residuary powers have been also given to the Centre. This is definitely a source of strength for the Centre.

The Centre can take over any State subject even in normal times if the Rajya Sabha approves by a two-thirds majority of its members present and voting on the ground that it is of national interest.

Administrative. The executive power of the State is to be exercised in such a way as to ensure compliance with the laws made by Parliament. Further, the Union executive is empowered to give such directions to the States as may appear to the Government of India to be necessary for the purpose. Not satisfied with these, the Constitution goes a step further. It calls upon every State not to impede the executive power of the Centre in the State. If any central agency finds it difficult to operate within a State, the Central executive is empowered to issue directions to the State Government to remove all obstacles.

Financial. The States in India do not possess sufficient sources of income. They are dependent on the Centre for financial aid. Financial dependence brings with it dependence in policy and administration in its wake.

During a proclamation of Emergency the President is empowered to transfer to the Centre all the legislative and executive authority of the State.

Special Provisions Relating to Minorities

Reservation of Seats. Scheduled Castes and Scheduled Tribes have certain seats reserved for them in the Lok Sabha. The President is empowered to nominate not more than two members of the Anglo-Indian community to the Lok Sabha, if he finds that the community has inadequate representation in the House. Scheduled Castes and Scheduled Tribes have a number of seats reserved for them in the Legislative Assemblies of the States also. The Governor is empowered to nominate members of the Anglo-Indian community to the Legislative Assembly of a State, if he finds that the community is inadequately represented.

Language of the Indian Union

The official language of the Union is Hindi in Devanagri script and the international form of Indian numeral is used for official purposes. For a period of fifteen years from the commencement of the Constitution, English was to continue for all official purposes of the Union. If at the end of 15 years, Hindi was not able to replace English, Parliament could provide for the use of English, for specific purposes. The Constitution also lays down that the legislature of a State may by law adopt any one or more of the languages for use in the state, but Hindi is to be used for all official purposes of the Union. The need for the use of English language in the proceedings of the Supreme Court, High Courts, etc., and in bills and enactments has been recognised.

The Official Languages Act of 1967 has provided for the use of English indefinitely. It has been provided that the Centre will carry on correspondence with the non-Hindi speaking states in English and with the Hindi-speaking States in Hindi.

Local Self Government in India

Local self-government implies the transference of the power to rule to the lowest rungs of the political order. It is a form of democratic decentralization where the participation of even the grass root level of the society is ensured in the process of administration.

History of Local Administration

The village panchayat, as a system of administration, began in the British days, as their offer to satisfy the demands for local autonomy. They opened up the governance of the lowest levels to the citizens. The GoI act, 1935 also authorizes the provinces to enact legislations.

How did the concept of local self-government evolve in India?

Even though such minor forms of local governance was evident in India, the framers of the constitutions, unsatisfied with the existing provisions, included Article 40 among the Directive Principles, whereby:

"The state shall take steps to organize village panchayats and endow them with such powers and authority as may be necessary to enable them to function as units of self-government."

Later, the conceptualisation of the system of local self-government in India took place through the formation and effort of four important committees from the year 1957 to 1986. It will be helpful if we take a look at the committee and the important recommendations put forward by them.

1. Balwant Rai Mehta Committee (1957)

Originally appointed by the Government of India to examine the working of two of its earlier programs, the committee submitted its report in November 1957, in which the term 'democratic decentralization' first appears.

The important recommendations are:

- Establishment of a three-tier Panchayati Raj system - gram panchayat at village level (direct election), panchayat Samiti at the block level and Zila Parishad at the district level (indirect election).
- District Collector to be the chairman of Zila Parishad.
- Transfer of resources and power to these bodies to be ensured.

The existent National Development Council accepted the recommendations. However, it did not insist on a single, definite pattern to be followed in the establishment of these institutions. Rather, it allowed the states to devise their own patterns, while the broad fundamentals were to be the same throughout the country.

Rajasthan (1959) adopted the system first, followed by Andhra Pradesh in the same year. Some states even went ahead to create four-tier systems and Nyaya panchayats, which served as judicial bodies.

2. Ashok Mehta Committee (1977-1978)

The committee was constituted by the Janata government of the time to study Panchayati Raj institutions. Out of a total of 132 recommendations made by it, the most important ones are:

- Three-tier system to be replaced by a two-tier system.
- Political parties should participate at all levels in the elections.
- Compulsory powers of taxation to be given to these institutions.
- Zila Parishad to be made responsible for planning at the state level.
- A minister for Panchayati Raj to be appointed by the state council of ministers.
- Constitutional recognition to be given to Panchayati Raj institutions.

Unfortunately, the Janata government collapsed before action could be taken on these recommendations.

3. G V K Rao Commitee (1985)

Appointed by the Planning Commission, the committee concluded that the developmental procedures were gradually being taken away from the local self-government institutions, resulting in a system comparable to 'grass without roots'.

- Zila Parishad to be given prime importance and all developmental programs at that level to be handed to it.
- Post of DDC (District Development Commissioner) to be created acting as the chief executive officer of the Zila Parishad.
- Regular elections to be held

4. L M Singhvi Commitee (1986)

Constituted by the Rajiv Gandhi government on 'Revitalisation of Panchayati Raj institutions for Democracy and Development', its important recommendations are:

- Constitutional recognition for PRI institutions.
- Nyaya Panchayats to be established for clusters of villages

Though the 64th Constitutional Amendment bill was introduced in the Lok Sabha in 1989 itself, Rajya Sabha opposed it. It was only during the Narasimha Rao government's term that the idea finally became a reality in the form of the 73rd and 74th Constitutional Amendment acts, 1992.

Panchayati Raj System under 73rd and 74th Constitutional Amendment acts, 1992

The acts of 1992 added two new parts IX and IX-A to the constitution. It also added two new schedules - 11 and 12 which contains the lists of functional items of Panchayats and Municipalities. It provides for a three-tier system of Panchayati Raj in every state - at the village, intermediate and district levels.

What are Panchayats and Municipalities?

- Panchayat and Municipality are the generic terms for the governing body at the local level. Both exist as three tier systems – at the lower, intermediate and upper levels.
- The 73rd Constitutional Amendment act provides for a Gram Sabha as the foundation of the Panchayati Raj system. It is essentially a village assembly consisting of all the registered voters in the area of the panchayat. The state has the power to determine what kind of powers it can exercise, and what functions it has to perform at the village level.

- The 74th Constitutional Amendment act provides for three types of Municipalities:
  1. Nagar Panchayat for a transitional area between a rural and urban area.
  2. Municipal Council for a small urban area.
  3. Municipal Corporation for a large urban area.
- Municipalities represent urban local self-government.
- Most of the provisions of the two acts are parallel, differing only in the fact that they are being applied to either a Panchayat or a Municipality respectively.
- Each Gram sabha is the meeting of a particular constituency called ward.
- Each ward has a representative chosen from among the people themselves by direct election.
- The chairperson of the Panchayat or Municipality at the intermediate and district level are elected from among these representatives at the immediately lower level by indirect election.

Types of Urban Local Government

There are eight types of urban local governments currently existing in India:

1. Municipal Corporations.
2. Municipality.
3. Notified area committee.
4. Town area committee.
5. Cantonment board.
6. Township.
7. Port trust.
8. Special purpose agency.

How are the elections held in the local government bodies?

- All seats of representatives of local bodies are filled by people chosen through direct elections.
- The conduct of elections is vested in the hands of the State election commission.
- The chairpersons at the intermediate and district levels shall be elected indirectly from among the elected representatives at the immediately lower level.
- At the lowest level, the chairperson shall be elected in a mode defined by the state legislature.
- Seats are reserved for SC and ST proportional to their population.
- Out of these reserved seats, not less than one-third shall be further reserved for women.
- There should be a blanket reservation of one-third seats for women in all the constituencies taken together too (which can include the already reserved seats for SC and ST).
- The acts bar the interference of courts in any issue relating to the election to local bodies.

Qualifications Needed to be a Member of the Panchayat or Municipality

Any person who is qualified to be a member of the state legislature is eligible to be a member of the Panchayat or Municipality.

"But he shall not be disqualified on the ground that he is less than 25 years of age if he has attained the age of 21 years"

This means that unlike the state legislature, a person needs to attain only 21 years of age to be a member of panchayat/municipality.

Duration of the Local Government Bodies

- The local governing bodies are elected for a term of five years.
- Fresh elections should be conducted before the expiry of the five-year term.
- If the panchayat/municipality is dissolved before the expiry of its term, elections shall be conducted within six months and the new panchayat/municipality will hold office for the remainder of the term if the term has more than six months duration.
- And for another five years if the remaining term is less than six months.

New Education Policy 2020

This policy will replace the 34-year-old National Policy on Education (NPE), 1986. This is the first education policy of the 21st century and replaces the thirty-four-year-old National Policy on Education (NPE), 1986. Built on the foundational pillars of Access, Equity, Quality, Affordability and Accountability, this policy is aligned to the 2030 Agenda for Sustainable Development and aims to transform India into a vibrant knowledge society and global knowledge superpower by making both school and college education more holistic, flexible, multidisciplinary, suited to 21st century needs and aimed at bringing out the unique capabilities of each student

What is NEP's 5+3+3+4 format to replace 10+2? One of the salient features of the new National Education Policy is shifting from decades-old 10+2 format to 5+3+3+4 keeping in mind a child's development and capabilities. The new NEP replaces the rules framed in 1986 and restructures school and higher education to make more flexible and with an integrated approach.

What does 5+3+3+4 mean? The new NEP has replaced school education 10+2 format with 5+3+3+4. Here's how school education will be approached according to the new and reformed education policy:

- **New school assessment scheme.** The new school assessment scheme will come in place from 2022-2023. As per the new assessment scheme, school exams in grades 3, 5, and 8 will test the child's basic learning with a 360-degree progress report card. The policy has emphasized mother tongue/local language/regional language as the medium of instruction at least till Grade 5, but preferably till Grade 8 and beyond. Sanskrit to be offered at all levels of school and higher education as an option for students, including in the three-language formula. Other classical languages and literature of India also to be available as options. No language will be imposed on any student. Students to participate in a fun project/activity on 'The Languages of India', sometime in Grades 6-8, such as, under the 'Ek Bharat Shrestha Bharat' initiative. Several foreign languages will also be offered at the secondary level. Indian Sign Language (ISL) will be standardized across the country and National and State curriculum materials developed, for use by students with hearing impairment.
- **Online Education and Digital Education.** The NEP 2020 aims at promoting online education consequent to the recent rise in epidemics and pandemics to ensure preparedness with alternative modes of quality education whenever and wherever traditional and in-person modes of education are not possible, has been covered. A dedicated unit to orchestrate the building of digital infrastructure, digital content and capacity building will be created in the MHRD to look after the e-education needs of both school and higher education.

Key Points of New Educational Policy 2020

School Education

- New Policy aims for universalization of education from pre-school to secondary level with 100 % Gross Enrolment Ratio (GER) in school education by 2030.
- NEP 2020 will bring 2 crores out of school children back into the mainstream through the open schooling system.
- The current 10+2 system to be replaced by a new 5+3+3+4 curricular structure corresponding to ages 3-8, 8-11, 11-14, and 14-18 years respectively. This will bring the hitherto uncovered age group of 3-6 years under the school curriculum, which has been recognized globally as the crucial stage for the development of mental faculties of a child. The new system will have 12 years of schooling with three years of Anganwadi/pre-schooling.
- Emphasis on Foundational Literacy and Numeracy, no rigid separation between academic streams, extracurricular, vocational streams in schools; Vocational Education to start from Class 6 with Internships.

- Teaching up to at least Grade 5 to be in mother tongue/ regional language. No language will be imposed on any student.
- Assessment reforms with 360-degree Holistic Progress Card, tracking Student Progress for achieving Learning Outcomes.

Higher Education

- Gross Enrolment Ratio in higher education to be raised to 50 % by 2035; 3.5 crore seats to be added in higher education.
- The policy envisages broad-based, multi-disciplinary, holistic Under Graduate education with flexible curricula, creative combinations of subjects, integration of vocational education, and multiple entries and exit points with appropriate certification. UG education can be of 3 or 4 years with multiple exit options and appropriate certification within this period.
- Academic Bank of Credits to be established to facilitate Transfer of Credits.
- Multidisciplinary Education and Research Universities (MERUs), at par with IITs, IIMs, to be set up as models of best multidisciplinary education of global standards in the country.
- The National Research Foundation will be created as an apex body for fostering a strong research culture and building research capacity across higher education.
- Higher Education Commission of India (HECI) will be set up as a single overarching umbrella body for entire higher education, excluding medical and legal education. HECI to have four independent verticals - National Higher Education Regulatory Council (NHERC) for regulation, General Education Council (GEC) for standard-setting, Higher Education Grants Council (HEGC) for funding, and National Accreditation Council(NAC) for accreditation. Public and private higher education institutions will be governed by the same set of norms for regulation, accreditation, and academic standards.
- Affiliation of colleges is to be phased out in 15 years and a stage-wise mechanism is to be established for granting graded autonomy to colleges. Over some time, it is envisaged that every college would develop into either an Autonomous degree-granting College or a constituent college of a university.
- An autonomous body, the National Educational Technology Forum (NETF), will be created to provide a platform for the free exchange of ideas on the use of technology to enhance learning, assessment, planning, administration.
- NEP 2020 emphasizes setting up of Gender Inclusion Fund, Special Education Zones for disadvantaged regions and groups.
- The Centre and the States will work together to increase the public investment in the Education sector to reach 6% of GDP at the earliest.

MULTIPLE CHOICE QUESTIONS

1. The first Open University in India was set up in the State of
   (A) Andhra Pradesh (B) Delhi
   (C) Himachal Pradesh (D) Tamil Nadu
2. Most of the Universities in India are funded by
   (A) the Central Government
   (B) the State Governments
   (C) the University Grants Commission
   (D) Private bodies and Individuals
3. Which of the following organizations looks after the quality of Technical and Management education in India ?
   (A) NCTE (B) MCI
   (C) AICTE (D) CSIR
4. The President of India is
   (A) the Head of State
   (B) the Head of Government
   (C) both Head of the State and the Head of the Government
   (D) None of the above
5. Who among the following holds office during the pleasure of the President of India ?
   (A) Chief Election Commissioner
   (B) Comptroller and Auditor General of India
   (C) Chairman of the Union Public Service Commission
   (D) Governor of a State
6. According to Radhakrishnan Commission, the aim of Higher Education is
   (A) To develop the democratic values, peace and harmony
   (B) To develop great personalities who can give their contributions in politics, administration, industry and commerce
   (C) Both (A) and (B)
   (D) None of these
7. The National Museum at New Delhi is attached to
   (A) Delhi University
   (B) a Deemed University
   (C) a Subordinate Office of the JNU
   (D) Part of Ministry of Tourism and Culture
8. Match **List-I** with **List-II** and select the correct answer from the code given below :

List - I (Institutions)	**List - II (Locations)**
(a) National Law Institute	(i) Shimla
(b) Indian Institute of Advanced Studies	(ii) Bhopal
(c) National Judicial Academy	(iii) Hyderabad
(d) National Savings Institute	(iv) Nagpur

Codes:

	(a)	(b)	(c)	(d)		(a)	(b)	(c)	(d)
(A)	(iii)	(ii)	(iv)	(i)	(B)	(i)	(ii)	(iii)	(iv)
(C)	(iv)	(iii)	(i)	(ii)	(D)	(iii)	(i)	(ii)	(iv)

9. Election of Rural & Urban local bodies are conducted and ultimately supervised by
   (A) Election Commission of India
   (B) State Election Commission
   (C) District Collector and District Magistrate
   (D) Concerned Returning Officer
10. Which opinion is not correct ?
   (A) Education is a subject of concurrent list of VII schedule of Constitution of India
   (B) University Grants Commission is a statutory body
   (C) Patent, inventions, design, copyright and trade marks are the subject of concurrent list
   (D) Indian Council of Social Science Research is a statutory body related to research in social sciences
11. Value education makes a student
   (A) Good citizen
   (B) Successful businessman
   (C) Popular teacher
   (D) Efficient manager
12. Networking of libraries through electronic media is known as
   (A) Inflibnet (B) Libinfnet
   (C) Internet (D) HTML
13. The University which telecasts interactive educational programmes through its own channel is
   (A) B. R. Ambedkar Open University, Hyderabad
   (B) I. G. N. O. U.
   (C) University of Pune
   (D) Annamalai University

14. The Government established the University Grants Commission by an Act of Parliament in the year
(A) 1980 (B) 1948 (C) 1950 (D) 1956

15. Universities having central campus for imparting education are called
(A) Central Universities
(B) Deemed Universities
(C) Residential Universities
(D) Open Universities

16. Which is the smallest North-east State in India ?
(A) Tripura (B) Meghalaya
(C) Mizoram (D) Manipur

17. India's first Defence University is in the State of
(A) Haryana (B) Andhra Pradesh
(C) Uttar Pradesh (D) Punjab

18. Most of the Universities in India
(A) conduct teaching and research only
(B) affiliate colleges and conduct examinations
(C) conduct teaching/research and examinations
(D) promote research only

19. Which one of the following is not a Constitutional Body ?
(A) Election Commission
(B) Finance Commission
(C) Union Public Service Commission
(D) Planning Commission

20. Which one of the following statements is not correct ?
(A) Indian Parliament is supreme.
(B) The Supreme Court of India has the power of judicial review.
(C) There is a division of powers between the Centre and the States.
(D) There is a Council of Ministers to aid and advise the President.

21. Which one of the following statements reflects the republic character of Indian democracy ?
(A) Written Constitution
(B) No State religion
(C) Devolution of power to local Government institutions
(D) Elected President and directly or indirectly elected Parliament

22. Who among the following appointed by the Governor can be removed by only the President of India ?
(A) Chief Minister of a State
(B) A member of the State Public Service Commission
(C) Advocate-General
(D) Vice-Chancellor of a State University

23. Who among the following can be asked to make a statement in Indian Parliament ?
(A) Any MLA
(B) Chief of Army Staff
(C) Solicitor General of India
(D) Mayor of Delhi

24. Which of the following institutions in the field of education is set up by the MHRD Government of India ?
(A) Indian council of world Affair, New Delhi
(B) Mythic Society, Bangalore
(C) National Bal Bhawn, New Delhi
(D) India International Centre, New Delhi

25. 'SITE' stands for
(A) System for International technology and Engineering
(B) Satellite Instructional Television Experiment
(C) South Indian Trade Estate
(D) State Institute of Technology and Engineering

26. What is the name of the Research station established by the Indian Government for 'Conducting Research at Antarctic ?
(A) Dakshin Gangotri (B) Yamunotri
(C) Uttari Gangotri (D) None of these

27. Ministry of Human Resource Development (HRD) includes
(A) Department of School Education and Literacy
(B) Department of Higher Education
(C) Both (A) and (B)
(D) None of the above

28. Parliament can legislate on matters listed in the State list
(A) With the prior permission of the President.
(B) Only after the constitution is amended suitably.
(C) In case of inconsistency among State legislatures.
(D) At the request of two or more States.

29. Indian Institute of Advanced Study is located at
(A) Dharmshala (B) Shimla
(C) Solan (D) Chandigarh

30. Who has signed an MOU for Accreditation of Teacher Education Institutions in India ?
(A) NAAC and UGC (B) NCTE and NAAC

(C) UGC and NCTE (D) NCTE and IGNOU

31. The recommendation of National Knowledge Commission for the establishment of 1500 Universities is to
   (A) create more teaching jobs
   (B) ensure increase in student enrolment in higher education
   (C) replace or substitute the privately managed higher education institutions by public institutions
   (D) enable increased movement of students from rural areas to urban areas

32. According to Article 120 of the Constitution of India, the business in Parliament shall be transacted in
   (A) English only (B) Hindi only
   (C) English and Hindi both
   (D) All the languages included in Eighth Schedule of the Constitution

33. The Parliament in India is composed of
   (A) Lok Sabha & Rajya Sabha
   (B) Lok Sabha, Rajya Sabha & Vice President
   (C) Lok Sabha, Rajya Sabha & President
   (D) Lok Sabha, Rajya Sabha with their Secretariats

34. The enrolment in higher education in India is contributed both by Formal System of Education and by System of Distance Education. Distance education contributes
   (A) 50% of formal system
   (B) 25% of formal system
   (C) 10% of the formal system
   (D) Distance education system's contribution is not taken into account while considering the figures of enrolment in higher education

35. Assertion (A) : The U.G.C. Academic Staff Colleges came into existence to improve the quality of teachers.
   Reason (R) : University and college teachers have to undergo both orientation and refresher courses.
   (A) Both (A) and (R) are true and (R) is the correct explanation.
   (B) Both (A) and (R) are correct but (R) is not the correct explanation of (A).
   (C) (A) is correct and (R) is false.
   (D) (A) is false and (R) is correct.

36. As per the NCTE norms, what should be the staff strength for a unit of 100 students at B.Ed. level ?
   (A) 1 + 7 (B) 1 + 9 (C) 1 + 10 (D) 1 + 5

37. The Right to Information Act, 2005 makes the provision of
   (A) Dissemination of all types of information by all Public authorities to any person.
   (B) Establishment of Central, State and District Level Information Commissions as an appellate body.
   (C) Transparency and accountability in Public authorities.
   (D) All of the above

38. The accreditation process by National Assessment and Accreditation Council (NAAC) differs from that of National Board of Accreditation (NBA) in terms of
   (A) Disciplines covered by both being the same, there is duplication of efforts.
   (B) One has institutional grading approach and the other has programme grading approach.
   (C) Once get accredited by NBA or NAAC, the institution is free from renewal of grading, which is not a progressive decision.
   (D) This accreditation amounts to approval of minimum standards in the quality of education in the institution concerned.

39. Which option is not correct ?
   (A) Most of the educational institutions of National repute in scientific and technical sphere fall under 64th entry of Union list.
   (B) Education, in general, is the subject of concurrent list since 42nd Constitutional Amendment Act 1976.
   (C) Central Advisory Board on Education (CABE) was first established in 1920.
   (D) India had implemented the right to Free and Compulsory Primary Education in 2002 through 86th Constitutional Amendment.

40. Which statement is not correct about the "National Education Day" of India ?
   (A) It is celebrated on 5th September every year.
   (B) It is celebrated on 11th November every year.
   (C) It is celebrated in the memory of India's first Union Minister of Education, Dr. Abul Kalam Azad.
   (D) It is being celebrated since 2008.

41. A sector plan in education indicates
   (A) overall planning
   (B) a limited area of planning
   (C) planning for a region
   (D) planning for a particular level of education

42. The ultimate purpose of comparative education is
(A) closely studying the patterns of education in other countries.
(B) finding similarities and differences between systems of education in different areas
(C) adapting feasible educational programmes by scientifically studying these in other regions.
(D) studying the educational problems of a region in comparison with those of other regions.

43. Education and socio-economic development are
(A) Related in direct proportion
(B) Related in an indirect proportion
(C) Sometimes related and sometimes not related.
(D) Not related.

44. Indicate the number of Regional Offices of National Council of Teacher Education.
(A) 04 (B) 05 (C) 06 (D) 08

45. The state in India spending the largest amount on primary education is
(A) Maharashtra (B) Kerala
(C) Gujarat (D) Tamilnadu

46. Which method is adopted in order to create social attitude among students ?
(A) teacher-centric method
(B) input-out method
(C) collective persuasive method
(D) all of these

47. Education and population are related as follows
(A) Expansion of education leads to developing trends of small size family among educated males and females
(B) Expansion of education can control growth-rate of population
(C) Expansion of education makes population more qualitative.
(D) All the above

48. Which of the following rights was considered the "Heart and Soul" of the Indian Constitution by Dr. B.R. Ambedkar ?
(A) Freedom of Speech
(B) Right to Equality
(C) Right to Freedom of Religion
(D) Right to Constitutional Remedies

49. Which categories of the following women appear in greater proportion in profession of nursing ?
(A) Christian (B) Hindu
(C) Muslim (D) No pattern is reported

50. From the point of view of population control through family planning there should be
(A) more literacy of males than females
(B) more literacy of women than men
(C) eradication of illiteracy of the old men
(D) emphasis on expansion of education

51. For raising the educational standards of the university
(A) students opting for higher education should be selected on the basis of intellectual tests
(B) occupational and industrial development is essential with higher education
(C) state policy should be effective
(D) Both (A) and (B)

52. Which one of the following is an important occupation of educated women ?
(A) teaching (B) medicine
(C) nursing (D) all of these

53. For reducing expenditure on technical education
(A) technical educational institutions should start to take donations;
(B) it is necessary to reduce expenses on instruments and equipments of technical education
(C) it is necessary to provide apprenticeship training through companies
(D) it is necessary to reduce the number of technical educational institutions.

54. The higher education is still dominated by
(A) Mother-tongue (B) English
(C) Hindi (D) All of these

55. The Fundamental Duties of a citizen include
1. Respect for the Constitution, the National Flag and the National Anthem
2. To develop the scientific temper.
3. Respect for the Government.
4. To protect Wildlife.

Choose the correct answer from the codes given below :

Codes :
(A) 1, 2 and 3 (B) 1, 2 and 4
(C) 2, 3 and 4 (D) 1, 3, 4 and 2

56. Which one of the following difficulties occur in the rural area for continuing secondary education of girls ?
(A) Parents do not desire to give co-education to their daughters alongwith boys
(B) Poverty of parents

(C) Help of girls in household work and work in agriculture
(D) All the above

57. The President of India takes oath
(A) to uphold the sovereignty and integrity of India.
(B) to bear true faith and allegiance to the Constitution of India.
(C) to uphold the Constitution and Laws of the country.
(D) to preserve, protect and defend the Constitution and the law of the country.

58. Match the List – I with the List – II and select the correct answer from the codes given below :

List – I (Commissions and Committees)	**List – II (Year)**
(a) First Administrative Reforms Commission	(i) 2005
(b) Paul H. Appleby Committee I	(ii) 1962
(c) K. Santhanam Committee	(iii) 1966
(d) Second Administrative Reforms Commission	(iv) 1953

Codes :	**(a)**	**(b)**	**(c)**	**(d)**
(A)	(i)	(iii)	(ii)	(iv)
(B)	(iii)	(iv)	(ii)	(i)
(C)	(iv)	(ii)	(iii)	(i)
(D)	(ii)	(i)	(iv)	(iii)

59. Constitutionally the registration and recognition of political parties is the function performed by
(A) The State Election Commission of respective States
(B) The Law Ministry of Government of India
(C) The Election Commission of India
(D) Election Department of the State Governments

60. The most desirable outcome of higher education is
(A) Training of individual
(B) Acquisition of general knowledge
(C) Increase in academic excellence
(D) Acquisition of higher order thinking skills

61. Open learning institutions differ from the formal education institutions in that
(A) the former offers more courses than the latter
(B) the former offers more flexibility in choice of course
(C) the latter implements more-flexible evaluation pattern
(D) the teaching process is given more importance than the learning by open learning institutions.

62. The education of primitive man was concerned with
(A) vocational element (B) religious element
(C) moral element (D) all of these

63. In India we are facing a problem of quantitative growth of higher education. The best solution could be to
(A) use satellites to teach all the courses
(B) accept the facts and maintain the status quo
(C) make higher education costlier so as to prevent students going for higher education
(D) provide alternative opportunities for life long learning.

64. What is your opinion about religious studies in educational institutions ?
(A) It should be prevented
(B) It should be discouraged
(C) it must be such that it should nourish humanitarian values
(D) Educational institutes should be non-secular.

65. Which of the following bodies grants funds for higher education ?
(i) UGC
(ii) State Government
(iii) Municipal Corporation and Zila Parishad
(iv) Central Government
(A) Only (i) (B) Only (iii) and (iv)
(C) (i), (ii) and (iv) (D) All of these

66. The Kothari Commission's report was entitled on
(A) Education and National Development
(B) Learning to be adventure
(C) Diversification of Education
(D) Education and socialization in democracy

67. Which of the following is not a Dualmode University ?
(A) Delhi University
(B) Bangalore University
(C) Madras University
(D) Indira Gandhi National Open University

68. Which part of the Constitution of India is known as "Code of Administrators" ?
(A) Part I (B) Part II
(C) Part III (D) Part IV

69. Which article of the constitution provides safeguards to Naga Customary and their social practices against any act of Parliament ?
(A) Article 371 A (B) Article 371 B
(C) Article 371 C (D) Article 263

70. Which one of the following difficulties occur in the rural area for continuing secondary education of girls ?

(A) Parents do not desire to give co-education to their daughters alongwith boys
(B) Poverty of parents
(C) Help of girls in household work and work in agriculture
(D) All the above

71. The most prominent difference between Informal Education and Non formal Education is that
(A) The former is organised, the latter is not organised
(B) The former is not organised, the latter is organised
(C) The former occurs within the institution, the latter occurs outside the institution
(D) The former is subjective, the latter is objective.

72. The phrase, "equal educational opportunity" means
(A) Providing equal opportunity to have the type of education for which one is suited
(B) Provision of the same type of education for all
(C) Providing opportunity for all to get education at any level
(D) Ensuring admission to all for the desired stream of education.

73. Which is not an important aim of educational guidance ?
(A) To help the students to find out their physical, mental and education handicaps.
(B) To help the students to know about further educational channels available
(C) To give speed coaching to selected students in various subjects.
(D) To help the students to adjust themselves to the curriculum, the college and the social life connected with it.

74. Which one of the following is *not* the tool of good governance ?
(A) Right to information (B) Citizens' Charter
(C) Social Auditing (D) Judicial Activism

75. Education as an investment aims at
(A) Enhancing productivity
(B) Cultural development
(C) Development of democratic outlook
(D) Satisfaction of learners

76. Curriculum planning is a part of the sub system of
(A) educational management
(B) educational facilities
(C) educational communication
(D) educational activity

77. Extension Education is understood as
(A) extending new knowledge to the doorstep of those who need it
(B) extending educational opportunities to the deprived.
(C) a programme for educating the farmers.
(D) education meant to spread knowledge among villagers

78. NAAC is an autonomous institution under the aegis of
(A) ICSSR (B) CSIR
(C) AICTE (D) UGC

79. National Council for Women's Education was established in
(A) 1958 (B) 1976
(C) 1989 (D) 2000

80. The most important factor in teaching in higher education is to
(A) Supply the relevant information to students
(B) Prepare students for the various competitive examinations
(C) Lead students to the sources of information
(D) Develop a spirit of competition for higher achievement in students.

81. In higher education, students are better motivated through
(A) Competition
(B) Personal achievements
(C) Co-operation
(D) Individual attention

82. Which one of the following is *not* situated in New Delhi ?
(A) Indian Council of Cultural Relations
(B) Indian Council of Scientific Research
(C) National Council of Educational Research and Training
(D) Indian Institute of Advanced Studies

83. Many individuals accept employment in educational fields, because of
(A) their zeal for imparting knowledge
(B) lack of job opportunities elsewhere;
(C) considering teaching profession as their aim
(D) lively interest in acquisition of knowledge

84. Approach towards education should be
(A) Imparting knowledge
(B) Investment in human resources
(C) Sacred mission
(D) Employment - oriented

85. Which of the following was not consisted in the recommendations of National Policy on Education - 1986.
(A) Redesigning courses
(B) Expansion of institutions
(C) Training of teachers
(D) Training of guardians

86. The National Policy of Education-1986 recommended for
(A) Reorganisation of education
(B) Use of English in wide range
(C) Use of Sanskrit in wide range
(D) None of the above

87. The Indira Gandhi National Open University came into existence in
(A) April, 1985 (B) September, 1985
(C) April, 1977 (D) September, 1977

88. Who among the following gave particular attention to establishment of comprehensive institutions for the rural people starting at the early childhood level going upto the highest.
(A) Mahatma Gandhi
(B) Rabindranath Tagore
(C) Vivekananda (D) Both (A) and (B)

89. IGNOU stands significantly apart from other universities because of
(A) national jurisdiction
(B) flexible admission rules
(C) student support services
(D) All of the above

90. Value education should help in
(A) Increasing states income.
(B) Increasing teachers income
(C) Controlling guardian's expenditure on child's schooling.
(D) Eliminating violence fanaticism.

91. Match List-I with List-II and select the correct answer from the code given below

List-I (Institutions)	**List-II (Locations)**
(a) Dr. Hari Singh Gour University	(i) Mumbai
(b) S.N.D.T. University	(ii) Baroda
(c) M.S. University	(iii) Jodhpur
(d) J.N. Vyas University	(iv) Sagar

Codes :

	(a)	**(b)**	**(c)**	**(d)**		**(a)**	**(b)**	**(c)**	**(d)**
(A)	(iv)	(i)	(ii)	(iii)	(B)	(i)	(ii)	(iii)	(iv)
(C)	(iii)	(i)	(ii)	(iv)	(D)	(ii)	(iv)	(i)	(iii)

92. The first Indian Satellite for serving the educational sector is known as
(A) SATEDU (B) INSAT - B
(C) EDUSAT (D) INSAT - C

93. Exclusive educational channel of IGNOU is known as
(A) Gyan Darshan (B) Gyan Vani
(C) Door Darshan (D) Prasar Bharati

94. Two ways of imparting value education are
(A) Incidental and accidental
(B) Systematic and non-systematic
(C) Direct and indirect
(D) None of the above

95. Sri Prakash committee was set up in
(A) 1970-71 (B) 1965-66
(C) 1984-85 (D) 1959-60

96. Which of the following is not recommended by Sri Prakash committee
(A) teaching moral values
(B) silent meditation
(C) co-curricular activities
(D) none of the above

97. The period of Indian Education Commission was
(A) 1965-66 (B) 1945-46
(C) 1964-66 (D) 1945-47

98. The Indian Education commission recommended for
(A) time-table (B) suitable teachers
(C) methods of moral teaching
(D) All the above

99. The head quarter of Mahatma Gandhi Antarrashtriya Hindi Vishwavidyalaya is situated in
(A) Sevagram (B) New Delhi
(C) Wardha (D) Ahmedabad

100. Patriotic values are included under the groups of
(A) social values (B) moral values
(C) health values (D) ultimate values

101. Educating health values includes
(A) Schools should have first aid box.
(B) Medical inspection of the students
(C) Ventilation in schools.
(D) All the above

102. The Ishvarbhai Patel Committee was set up in
(A) 1977 (B) 1985
(C) 1967 (D) 1992

103. The Ishvarbhai Patel Committee recommended for
(A) to integrate work experience
(B) value oriented education

(C) women legislation
(D) none of the above

104. Value oriented education develops
(A) cultural values
(B) vocational efficiency
(C) character (D) all these

105. The number of open universities and directorates of distance education whose courses are recognised by UGC as on August 9, 2018, is:
(A) 49 (B) 53
(C) 58 (D) 62

106. Self styled, unrecognized universities are termed as
(A) fake universities (B) open universities
(C) closed universities (D) None of these

107. The CPEPA stand for
(A) Centre with potency of education
(B) Centre with potential for excellence in particular area
(C) Centre with primary education excellence in public areas
(D) None of the above

108. NCTE as a statutory body functions under
(A) MHRD (B) MoE
(C) UGC (D) Ministry of textiles

109. As per HRD ministry's 'India ranking report 2016', the top ranking university in India is
(A) Indian Institute of Science, Bangalore
(B) JNU, New Delhi
(C) BITS, Pilani
(D) Punjab University, Chandigarh

110. What amount has been provided in the Eleventh Five Year Plan for Education Mission through ICT?
(A) Rs. 5000 crore (B) Rs. 550 crore
(C) Rs. 6000 crore (D) Rs. 650 crore

111. The Development objective of Higher Education during Tenth Five Year Plan (2002-07) was
(A) Sustainable Human Development
(B) Relevance in World Context
(C) Improvements in Quality of Teaching
(D) All the above

112. Which of the following are included in main feature of the UGC XIth Five Year Plan (2007-12) ?
(A) Incentives for resource mobilization
(B) Universities with potential for excellence
(C) Basic facilities for women
(D) All of the above

113. Indicate the number of Regional Offices of University Grants Commission of India.
(A) 10 (B) 07 (C) 08 (D) 09

114. The UGC reserved 10 per cent of the total allotted Budget during Tenth Five Year Plan for
(A) North-Eastern Universities and their Constituent Colleges
(B) East-Western Universities and their Constituent Colleges
(C) North-Southern Universities and their Constituent Colleges
(D) Border Universities and their Constituent Colleges

115. Ph.D. is also called
(A) D.Phil (B) Ph. Doctor
(C) Doctor of Psychology (D) D.Ph.

116. The National Institute of Education Planning and Administration has been converted into a Deemed University and is now called the
(A) NUEPA (B) ERNET
(C) CIEFL (D) INDEST

117. The UGC INFONET network is run and managed as
(A) ERNET (B) NUEPA
(C) INFLIBNET (D) None of these

118. Match List - I with List - II and select the correct answer using the codes given below

List - I (Institutes)	List - II (Locations)
(a) Central Institute of English and Foreign Languages	(i) Chitrakoot
(b) Gramodaya Vishwavidyalaya	(ii) Hyderabad
(c) Central Institute of Higher Tibetan Studies	(iii) New Delhi
(d) IGNOU	(iv) Dharmasala

Codes :

	(a)	(b)	(c)	(d)		(a)	(b)	(c)	(d)
(A)	(ii)	(i)	(iv)	(iii)	(B)	(iv)	(iii)	(ii)	(i)
(C)	(iii)	(iv)	(i)	(ii)	(D)	(i)	(ii)	(iv)	(iii)

119. The U.G.C. have launched Career Orientation Programme in
(A) 1994-95 (B) 2009-10
(C) 1986-87 (D) 1992

120. The main aim of Vocationalization in Higher Education is
(A) To control the enrolment of students in Post-graduation Courses
(B) To create repulsion towards Higher Education

(C) To shift the students attention from the problem of Unemployment

(D) To guard the students from continuing higher education without purpose

121. The abbreviation 'SCOVE' stands for

(A) Standing Committee of Vocational Education

(B) Supreme Court Ordinance on Vocational Employment

(C) State Committee on Vocational Education

(D) State Council of Virtual Education

122. The aim of U.G.C.'s Standing Committee of Vocational Education is

(A) To identify such institutions where vocational courses can be implemented

(B) To impart training to the teachers for vocational education

(C) To prepare study material for vocational courses

(D) All of the above

123. The UGC submitted a proposal to the World Bank for seeking grant in 2001-02 for the following plan

(A) To implement Vocational Courses in Higher Education

(B) To Co-ordinate the Vocational Courses in Intermediate classes

(C) To implement Scheme of Vocationalization in Primary Education

(D) To match the Vocationalization with the process of globalization.

124. The aim of Higher Education according to Radhakrishnan Commission is

(A) To develop the great personalities who can give their contributions in politics, administration, profession, industry and commerce

(B) To preserve the democratic values and develop a harmony between individual and society

(C) To pay respect to old beliefs and develop intellectual giants having faith in new beliefs and ideologies and their coordination with old ones.

(D) All the above

125. Which of the following is not an aim of Higher Education according to Kothari Commission?

(A) To explore new knowledge in context of truth and interpret it in terms of ancient knowledge and beliefs in contemporary needs

(B) To explore innate abilities in persons and develop them through training

(C) To promote social justice and equality

(D) To give right leadership in all the fields of life

126. On the basis of organisational structure the universities can be classified as

(A) Residential and Affiliating Universities

(B) Central and State Universities

(C) Unitary and Federal Universities

(D) None of the above

127. Delhi University is a

(A) Central University (B) State University

(C) Deemed University (D) Cannot say

128. The Residential Universities are the universities having

(A) Central Campus for Imparting Education

(B) Many Campuses for Imparting Education

(C) Both of the above are correct

(D) None of the above are correct

129. When a university has its separate campus for Teaching purposes and there are many autonomous and constituent colleges affiliated to it, then this organisational pattern is called

(A) A Federal University

(B) A Decentralized University

(C) An Unitary University

(D) None of the above

130. When a university runs some courses in its Central Campus and some other courses in its affiliating colleges, such University is called as

(A) Residential-Affiliating University

(B) Affiliating University

(C) Unitary Teaching University

(D) None of the above

131. On the basis of teaching process, the universities can be categorised as

(A) Traditional and Open Universities

(B) Central and State Universities

(C) Residential and Affiliating Universities

(D) None of the above

132. Open Universities are treated as Non-traditional Universities because

(A) Innovative methods of teaching and learning are used in these Universities

(B) Innovative methods of admission, curriculum and evaluation are followed in these universities

(C) Modern Communication Techniques are used in these universities

(D) All of the above

133. 'Complex of Colleges' is called
(A) Federal University
(B) Unitary University
(C) Central University
(D) State University

134. Generally in Federal type of Universities, the Organisational Pattern of Courses is
(A) Post graduate courses in university campus and graduate courses in constituent college
(B) Post graduate and graduate courses in university campus while graduate courses are only in its constituent colleges
(C) Special post graduate courses in university campus and in constituent colleges both types of the courses
(D) None of the above

135. Which of the following is not related to Indian Education Commission's (1964-66) recommendations?
(A) University's Autonomy and Income-Expenditure
(B) Role and Appointment of Vice-Chancellor
(C) University Legislation
(D) Role of Registrar

136. In 1969 the UGC had appointed a committee for
(A) Administrative of Universities
(B) Administrative Legislation of Colleges
(C) Administrative Legislation for both of the above
(D) None of the above

137. Who was the Chairman of the UGC Committee 1969 appointed for Administrative Legislation of the Universities?
(A) Dr. P.B. Gajendragadkar
(B) Dr. Laxman Swami Mudaliar
(C) Dr. Sarvapalli Radha Krishnan
(D) Dr. Zakir Hussain

138. The aim of value education to inculcate in students is
(A) the moral values (B) the social values
(C) the political values
(D) the economic values

139. The suggestion given by Dr. Gajendragadkar committee was
(A) To review the organisation structures of universities on regular basis
(B) To bring timely change in the University's organisation
(C) To bring change in Administrative wings of Universities
(D) All the above

140. A high level committee was set up in April 2009, headed by former UGC Chairman Yash Pal for
(A) Restructuring higher education in the country
(B) Formation of new universities
(C) Salary revision (D) None of these

141. The President of India is elected by
(A) Parliament (B) State legislatures
(C) By the people directly
(D) By an electoral college consisting of the elected members of the Lok Sabha, the Rajya Sabha and the State Legislative Assemblies

142. What is the minimum strength of a State Legislative Assembly?
(A) 40 (B) 60 (C) 50 (D) 70

143. Which of the following has not been laid down by the Indian Constitution?
(A) Direct election to the Lok Sabha
(B) Direct election to the State Legislative Assemblies
(C) Direct election of the President of India
(D) Creation of Supreme Court which is competent to interpret the Constitution

144. What is the age of retirement of the Supreme Court Judges?
(A) 60 years (B) 65 years
(C) 62 years (D) 70 years

145. The right of vote in India is given to all people on the basis of
(A) Age (B) Education
(C) Religion (D) Property

146. The most controversial amendment passed during the emergency was?
(A) 43rd (B) 41st
(C) 42nd (D) 44th

147. The Governor of a State in India is
(A) Directly elected by the people of the State
(B) Appointed by the Prime Minister
(C) Appointed by the President
(D) Appointed by the State Chief Minister

148. How many languages have been recognised by the Constitution?
(A) 13 (B) 14 (C) 22 (D) 16

149. To be eligible for election as President of India a person must have completed the age of
(A) 35 years (B) 40 years
(C) 30 years (D) 25 years

150. The Union Cabinet is responsible to
(A) The Rajya Sabha and the Lok Sabha

(B) The President of India
(C) The Lok Sabha only
(D) The electorate

151. Who among the following created the office of the District Collector in India ?
(A) Lord Cornwallis
(B) Warren Hastings
(C) The Royal Commission on Decentralisation
(D) Sir Charles Metcalfe

152. The number of Anglo-Indians who can be nominated by the President to the Lok Sabha is
(A) 2 (B) 3 (C) 4 (D) 5

153. The Attorney General of India is appointed by
(A) The Chief Justice of India
(B) The Prime Minister
(C) The President of India
(D) The UPSC

154. When does a Presidential Ordinance cease to operate?
(A) At the expiry of four-weeks from the reassembly of Parliament or earlier if both Houses disapprove it.
(B) At the expiry of six-weeks from the reassembly of Parliament or earlier if both Houses disapprove it
(C) At the expiry of six-months from the reassembly of Parliament or earlier if both Houses disapprove it
(D) None of these

155. The Indian Constitution has given a special status to the State of Jammu and Kashmir under Article
(A) 352 (B) 370 (C) 368 (D) 361

156. The drafting committee of the Indian Constitution was headed by
(A) Dr. Rajendra Prasad
(B) N. Gopalaswamy
(C) B.R. Ambedkar (D) None of these

157. The Supreme Commander of the Defence Forces of India is
(A) The Defence Minister
(B) The Prime Minister
(C) The Chief of the Army Staff
(D) The President of India

158. India is a republic because
(A) Every adult of the age 18 or more has been given the right to vote
(B) The Constitution guarantees fundamental rights of the people
(C) The Council of Ministers is responsible to the Lok Sabha
(D) Head of State is elected for a fixed term

159. The sanctioned strength of the sitting judges of Supreme Court of India is
(A) 13 (B) 31 (C) 16 (D) 26

160. Which of the following is not a Union Territory?
(A) Lakshadweep (B) Delhi
(C) Manipur (D) Daman & Diu

161. Article 370 of the Indian Constitution deals with
(A) The Emergency Powers of the President
(B) The special position of the State of Jammu and Kashmir
(C) The power to seek the advisory opinion of the Supreme Court on any matter of public importance
(D) Distribution of taxes between the Centre and the States

162. A Judge of the Supreme Court of India can be removed from office
(A) By the President of India according to his sweet will
(B) By the Prime Minister of India
(C) By the Chief Justice of India
(D) By the President on an address by each House of Parliament and supported by a majority of the total membership of that house and by a majority of not less than 2/3 of the members of that House present and voting

163. The vacancy in the office of the President must be filled within
(A) One year (B) Six months
(C) Four months (D) Three months

164. The Vice-President of India is elected by
(A) The same electoral college which elects the President of India
(B) The Rajya Sabha
(C) The Lok Sabha
(D) By an electoral college consisting of the members of both Houses of Parliament

165. When the two Houses of Parliament differ regarding a Bill then the deadlock is resolved by
(A) A joint sitting of the two Houses
(B) President of India
(C) Prime Minister of India
(D) By a special committee formed for the purpose

166. The maximum duration between two sessions of the Indian Parliament should not be more than

(A) 3 months (B) 6 months
(C) 9 months (D) one year

167. The maximum strength of the Lok Sabha and the Rajya Sabha is
(A) 525 and 250 respectively
(B) 552 and 250
(C) 535 and 275 (D) 500 and 250

168. The Comptroller and Auditor General of India is appointed by the
(A) Prime Minister of India
(B) President of India
(C) Finance Minister
(D) Lok Sabha

169. The Legislative Council of a State can be abolished or created by
(A) The President of India
(B) The Legislative Assembly of the State concerned
(C) By Parliament according to its will
(D) By Parliament provided the State Legislative Assembly passes a resolution to that effect

170. The total number of members in the Legislative Council of a State cannot exceed
(A) One fourth of the total number of members in the Legislative Assembly
(B) One-third of the total number of members of the Legislative Assembly
(C) One-sixth of the total members of the Legislative Assembly
(D) No such limit has been fixed

171. The total number of members of the Legislative Council can in no case be less than
(A) 40 (B) 60 (C) 50
(D) No minimum strength has been fixed

172. India has
(A) Parliamentary form of government
(B) Presidential form of government
(C) Both parliamentary and presidential forms of government
(D) None of these

173. If the Vice-President were to submit his resignation, he would notify to
(A) The President of India
(B) The Prime Minister
(C) The Chief Justice of India
(D) The Speaker of the Lok Sabha

174. Which of the following words were added to the Preamble of Indian Constitution under the 42nd Amendment?
(A) Democratic Republic
(B) Democratic Socialist
(C) Socialist Secular (D) Sovereign Secular

175. The Speaker of a State Assembly can be removed from his office by
(A) A resolution of the Legislative Assembly passed by a majority of all the members of the Assembly
(B) The President of India
(C) The Chief Minister (D) The Governor

176. The Governor of a state enjoys
(A) No discretionary powers
(B) Very extensive discretionary powers
(C) Discretionary Powers in certain matters
(D) None of these

177. Chief Minister is
(A) The Head of the State
(B) The Head of the Government
(C) An integral part of the legislature
(D) Always a member of the Lower House

178. Collective responsibility is the Hallmark of which form of Government?
(A) Parliamentary form
(B) Presidential form
(C) Military form (D) None of these

179. Which of the following exercises power to promulgate ordinances during the recess of the legislative?
(A) Chief Minister (B) Governor
(C) Speaker (D) Deputy Speaker

180. The Contingency Fund of the State is placed under the
(A) Secretary, Finance Dept.
(B) State Legislature
(C) Speaker (D) Chief Minister

181. The size of the Council of Ministers of a State
(A) Is fixed by the governor in accordance with the High Courts advice
(B) Is decided by the Chief Minister
(C) Is fixed by the Constitution (91st Amendment) Act, 2003
(D) Is dependent on the total strength of the assembly

182. Which one of the following cannot be dissolved but can be abolished any time?
(A) State Legislative Councils
(B) State Legislative Assemblies
(C) Rajya Sabha (D) Lok Sabha

183. The Election Commission of a state can be removed from office

(A) Only by the Governor
(B) In the same manner and on the same grounds as a judge of the Supreme Court
(C) Only by the President on the advice of the Chief Justice of the concerned State
(D) In the same manner as the Vice-President of India

184. 'Parliamentary Supremacy' is a definite feature of the political system in
(A) U.K. (B) India
(C) Canada (D) Australia

185. Cabinet government is based on
(A) Separation of legislature and executive
(B) Fusion of legislature, executive and judiciary
(C) Fusion of legislature and executive
(D) None of the above

186. When a State Government fails to comply with the directions of the Centre in the exercise of administrative power
(A) The Governor may be directed by the President to dismiss the ministry
(B) The President can declare a national emergency and convert the federal structure into a unitary one
(C) A Constitutional emergency can be declared in the State and the President can assume all the powers of the State Government
(D) The Supreme Court may be asked to intervene

187. Below are given two lists : One list contains officials and List-II refers to the person holding these posts. Match List-I with List-II by using the codes :

List-I (Presiding Officer)	List-II (House)
(i) Lok Sabha	1. Vice-President
(ii) Rajya Sabha	2. Speaker
(iii) Joint Session of Parliament	3. Deputy Speaker
	4. President

Code :

	(i)	(ii)	(iii)		(i)	(ii)	(iii)
(A)	1	2	4	(B)	4	2	1
(C)	3	1	2	(D)	2	1	4

188. _____ is the popular House of State Legislature.
(A) Legislative Assembly
(B) Legislative Council
(C) Legislative Sabha (D) Zila Council

189. Which one of the following is wrong?
(A) It is the duty of the Chief Minister to keep the Governor informed of all the decisions of the Cabinet
(B) The Governor has the Power to ask for any information from the Chief Minister regarding the administration of the State
(C) The Governor is the real head of the State administration
(D) As an agent of the Central Government the Governor may have to act sometimes independently of the advice of the Council of Ministers.

190. Which one of the following is not a function of the Chief Minister of a State?
(A) He allots business among his colleagues
(B) He can ask any Minister to resign and in case of his refusal advise the Governor to dismiss him
(C) He can dissolve the Legislative Assembly
(D) He presides over the meetings of the Cabinet and controls the agenda thereof

191. One-rupee currency note in India bears the signature of
(A) The President of India
(B) Finance Minister of India
(C) Governor, Reserve Bank of India
(D) Finance Secretary of Government of India

192. In case of death, resignation or removal of Governor, ________ acts as the Governor.
(A) The Chief Minister
(B) The President of India
(C) The Speaker
(D) The Chief Justice of High Court

193. If a Governor wants to resign, to whom does he address his letter of resignation?
(A) Prime Minister (B) Home Minister
(C) Chief Minister (D) President of India

194. A Governor can issue an ordinance
(A) Whenever he likes
(B) Whenever Chief Minister advises him
(C) Whenever the State Legislature is not in Session and the Governor is satisfied that immediate action is needed
(D) When the Union Government tells him to do so

195. The Governor of a State can
(A) Dissolve the Legislative Assembly
(B) Dissolve the Legislative Council
(C) Both the above
(D) None of the above

196. The Governor of a State can address the Legislature at the commencement of the
(A) New session after each general election
(B) First session every year

(C) Both of the above
(D) None of the above

197. Who appoints the Governor of a State?
(A) Home Minister of India
(B) President of India
(C) Chief Minister of that State
(D) Prime Minister of India

198. In ______ , the executive power of the State Government is vested
(A) The President of India
(B) The Chief Minister
(C) The Governor
(D) The Speaker of the Legislative Assembly

199. The Governor of a State holds his office only during the pleasure of
(A) Prime Minister (B) President
(C) Chief Minister (D) Home Minister

200. The right to freedom of speech and expression
(A) Does not include freedom of press
(B) Includes freedom of press
(C) Includes freedom of press only in certain respects
(D) None of the above

201. In India freedom of press is
(A) Specifically provided in the Constitution
(B) Implied in the right to freedom of expression
(C) Available to the people of India under Law of Parliament
(D) Available to the people of India under executive orders

202. The grant of franchise to women on equal terms with men is assertion of the principle of
(A) Political equality (B) Civil equality
(C) Natural equality (D) Social equality

203. The subordinate Civil Courts are headed by
(A) District Court (B) Session Court
(C) Board of Revenue (D) None of these

204. The report of the Public Accounts Committee is presented to the
(A) President (B) Prime Minister
(C) Rajya Sabha (D) Lok Sabha

205. A Parliamentary government cannot operate without
(A) A written constitution
(B) An independent judiciary
(C) Political parties
(D) A rigid constitution

206. Which of the following statements is correct regarding the procedure of passing of Bills in Parliament?
(A) A bill pending in Parliament shall not lapse because of the prorogation of the two Houses of Parliament
(B) A bill pending in the Rajya Sabha which has not been passed by the Lok Sabha shall lapse on its dissolution
(C) A bill pending in the Lok Sabha and pending in the Rajya Sabha shall not lapse on the dissolution of the Lok Sabha
(D) A bill pending in the Rajya Sabha which has been passed by the Lok Sabha shall not lapse on the adjournment of the Rajya Sabha

207. Parliamentary government was adopted in India
(A) By sheer accident
(B) Because it was made obligatory to adopt this government under Indian Independence Act of 1947
(C) Because of historical considerations and practical necessities
(D) On account of all the above reasons

208. Which one of the following statements is correct?
(A) The Chairman of the Rajya Sabha is elected by the elected members of the Rajya Sabha
(B) The Chairman of the Rajya Sabha presides over the joint session of both the Houses of Parliament
(C) The electoral college for the election of the Vice-President is the same as that for the election of the President
(D) The nominated members of both the Houses of Parliament have voting right in the election of the Vice-President but not in the election of the President.

209. The Constitution of India is
(A) One of the smallest constitutions in the world
(B) A medium sized constitution
(C) One of the most elaborate constitutions of the world
(D) None of the above

210. The subject on which the State Government enjoys exclusive powers are given in
(A) Concurrent List (B) State List
(C) Union List (D) Residuary List

211. To which one of the following categories does the Right to Property belong?
(A) Legal Right (B) Fundamental Right
(C) Human Right (D) Natural Right

212. Decisions on question about disqualification of members of the Lok Sabha are taken by the
(A) President (B) Prime Minister
(C) Minister for Parliamentary Affairs
(D) Secretary to Parliament

213. The members of Rajya Sabha are elected for a term of
(A) Three years (B) Five years
(C) Six years (D) Seven years

214. Which one of the following is not an essential qualification for contesting election to Lok Sabha?
(A) Citizenship of India (B) Age of 25 years
(C) Soundness of mind (D) Graduation

215. Which one of the following Lok Sabhas was dissolved before the expiry of its normal term?
(A) First Lok Sabha (B) Fourth Lok Sabha
(C) Sixth Lok Sabha (D) None of these

216. The Government in India is known as Parliamentary because
(A) Parliament is elected by the people
(B) Parliament consists of two houses
(C) Parliament is a sovereign body
(D) The executive is accountable to the Legislature

217. The Rajya Sabha
(A) is a permanent house
(B) has a maximum life of 6 years
(C) has a maximum life of 5 years
(D) has no fixed life

218. How many seats have been reserved for the Union Territories in Lok Sabha?
(A) 20 (B) 25 (C) 30 (D) 50

219. Which one of the following statements holds good in respect of the Rajya Sabha?
(A) One third of its members retire after every three years
(B) Two thirds of its members retire after every three years
(C) Two thirds of its members retire after every two years
(D) One third of its members retire after every two years

220. Who amongst the following acts as the presiding officer of the House without being its members?
(A) Vice-President of India
(B) Speaker of the Lok Sabha
(C) Chairman of the Legislative Council
(D) Speaker of the Legislative Assembly

221. Who among the following is considered to be the custodian of the Lok Sabha?
(A) The Prime Minister
(B) The Leader of the Opposition
(C) The Chief whip of the ruling party
(D) The Speaker

222. The Speaker of Lok Sabha has to address his letter of resignation to the
(A) Prime Minister of India
(B) Deputy Speaker of Lok Sabha
(C) President of India
(D) Vice-President of India

223. The "Fundamental Duties" of the Indian citizen have been
(A) Originally provided by the constitution
(B) Included in the constitution by the 44th amendment
(C) Included in the constitution by the 42nd amendment
(D) Inserted into the constitution by a judgement of the Supreme Court

224. The Presidential Government operates on the principle of
(A) Separation of Powers
(B) Division of Labour
(C) Fusion of Labour
(D) Centralisation of Power

225. Consider the following statements :
The Fundamental duties
1. Have always been a part of the constitution of India
2. Have been added through an amendment
3. Are applicable to all citizens of India
Which of these statements is/are correct?
(A) 1 and 3 (B) 1 only
(C) 2 only (D) 2 and 3

226. Indian Constitution reserves the residuary powers to
(A) The Union (B) The States
(C) The Parliament (D) The President

227. The Constitution amendment bills are initiated in
(A) The Lok Sabha
(B) The Rajya Sabha
(C) Either House
(D) The Lok Sabha with the prior approval of the State assemblies

228. The main feature of Presidential government is
(A) Stability (B) Irresponsibility
(C) Checks and balances
(D) Rigidity

229. Match List-I with List-II and select the correct answer from the codes given below :

List – I (Articles of the Constitution)	List – II (Institutions)
(a) Article 280	(i) Administrative Tribunals
(b) Article 324	(ii) Election Commission of India
(c) Article 323	(iii) Finance Commission at Union level
(d) Article 315	(iv) Union Public Service Commission

	(a)	(b)	(c)	(d)		(a)	(b)	(c)	(d)
(A)	(i)	(ii)	(iii)	(iv)	(B)	(iii)	(ii)	(i)	(iv)
(C)	(ii)	(iii)	(iv)	(i)	(D)	(ii)	(iv)	(iii)	(i)

230. Deemed Universities declared by UGC under Section 3 of the UGC Act 1956, are not permitted to
(A) offer programmes in higher education and issue degrees.
(B) give affiliation to any institute of higher education.
(C) open off-campus and off-shore campus anywhere in the country and overseas respectively without the permission of the UGC.
(D) offer distance education programmes without the approval of the Distance Education Council.

231. The aim of vocationalization of education is
(A) preparing students for a vocation along with knowledge
(B) converting liberal education into vocational education
(C) giving more importance to vocational than general education
(D) making liberal education job-oriented

232. The University Grants Commission was constituted on the recommendation of
(A) Dr. Sarvapalli Radhakrishnan Commission
(B) Mudaliar Commission
(C) Sargent Commission
(D) Kothari Commission

233. Which one of the following Articles of the Constitution of India safeguards the rights of Minorities to establish and run educational institutions of their own liking?
(A) Article 19 (B) Article 29
(C) Article 30 (D) Article 31

234. The Lok Sabha can be dissolved before the expiry of its normal five year term by
(A) The Prime Minister
(B) The Speaker of Lok Sabha
(C) The President on the recommendation of the Prime Minister
(D) None of the above

235. Match List - I (Institutions) with List - II (Functions) and select the correct answer by using the code given below :

List – I (Institutions)	List – II (Functions)
(a) Parliament	(i) Formulation of Budget
(b) C& A.G.	(ii) Enactment of Budget
(c) Ministry of Finance	(iii) Implementation of Budget
(d) Executing Departments	(iv) Legality of expenditure
	(v) Justification of Income

Code:

	(a)	(b)	(c)	(d)		(a)	(b)	(c)	(d)
(A)	(iii)	(iv)	(ii)	(i)	(B)	(ii)	(iv)	(i)	(iii)
(C)	(v)	(iii)	(iv)	(ii)	(D)	(iv)	(ii)	(iii)	(v)

236. Match List -1 with List-II and select the correct answer from the code given below :

List-I (Institutions)	List-II (Locations)
(a) The Indian Council of Historical Research (ICHR)	(i) Shimla
(b) The Indian Institute of Advanced Studies (HAS)	(ii) New Delhi
(c) The Indian Council of Philosophical Research (ICPR)	(iii) Bangalore
(d) The Central Institute of Coastal Engineering for fisheries	(iv) Lucknow

	(a)	(b)	(c)	(d)		(a)	(b)	(c)	(d)
(A)	ii	i	iv	iii	(B)	i	ii	iii	iv
(C)	ii	iv	i	iii	(D)	iv	iii	ii	i

237. Foundation training to the newly recruited IAS (Probationers) is imparted by
(A) Indian Institute of Public Administration
(B) Administrative Staff College of India
(C) L.B.S. National Academy of Administration
(D) Centre for Advanced Studies

238. Electoral disputes arising out of Presidential and Vice-Presidential Elections are settled by

(A) Election Commission of India
(B) Joint Committee of Parliament
(C) Supreme Court of India
(D) Central Election Tribunal

239. The difference between the University and the deemed University is that the former?
(A) is much bigger in size
(B) is established by the act of legislature
(C) is established by the central government
(D) looks after only affiliated colleges

240. Which of the following is not a Fundamental Right ?
(A) Right to equality
(B) Right against exploitation
(C) Right to freedom of speech and expression
(D) Right of free compulsory education of all children upto the age of 14

241. The idea of four Pillars of Education was suggested by
(A) UNICEF (B) UGC
(C) NCTE (D) UNESO

242. The name of the plan to increase enrolment in the higher education institutions is
(A) Rashtriya Uchchatar Shiksha Abhiyan (RUSA)
(B) Sarva Shiksha Abhiyan
(C) Both (A) and (B)
(D) None of the above

243. Which section of the UGC act provides for the promotion and coordination of university education and for the maintenance of standards of teaching, examination and research?
(A) Section 12 (B) Section 15
(C) Section 25 (D) Section 28

244. It is said that the present higher education system has its origin in Mountstuart Elphinstone's minutes, which stressed upon the need for establishing schools for teaching English and European science. This reported was presented in the year.
(A) 1823 (B) 1835
(C) 1858 (D) 1861

245. Which of the following committees recommended the spending of Rs. 500 crores to be spent on research in basic sciences every year by UGC every year?
(A) M.M. Sharma committee
(B) Kakodar committee
(C) Prof. Yashpal committee
(D) None of the above

246. A committee was set up in 1990 to review NPE (1986). Its report titled as 'Towards in Enlightened and humane Society' stated that system of higher education encourages memorization of facts and regurgitation rather than creativity. The head of the committee was
(A) Acharya Ramamurti
(B) Prof. Yashpal
(C) Prof. M.M. Joshi
(D) None of the above

247. Which of the following committee recommended the setting up of national Commission for Higher Education and Research (NCHER) for prescribed standard of academic quality and defining policies for advancement of knowledge in higher educational institutions?
(A) Sam Pitroda committee
(B) Prof. Yashpal committee
(C) M.M. Sharma committee
(D) Gnanam committee

248. Institutions of National Importance is an institution is higher education which serves as a pivotal player in developing highly skilled personal within the specified region of the country or state. This status can be conferred upon them by
(A) University grants commission
(B) An act of Parliament
(C) All Indian Council for Technical Education
(D) All the above

249. Commonwealth of learning (CoL) is the only official Commonwealth agency located outside Britain. It is located in
(A) New Delhi, India
(B) Vancouver, Canada
(C) Sydney, Australia
(D) Islamabad, Pakistan

250. The first inter university centre which was established by UGC in 1984 is
(A) Inter University Accelerator Centre (Nuclear Science Centre)
(B) Inter University for astronomy and astrophysics (IUCAA)
(C) Inter University Accelerator Centre (formerly Nuclear Science Centre)
(D) None of the above

251. Which of the following age groups is taken into consideration for constituting Gender Parity Index for higher education
(A) 15-22 years (B) 18-23 years
(C) 16-22 years (D) 18-25 years

252. There was a major announcement in Budget 2016-2017 in the form of Higher Education Funding Agency.

Which of the following statements are correct in this context?

I. An initial capital base of Rs. 1000 cr.

II. Joint participation of Government and philanthropic donors.

III. Quality infrastructure in IITs, NITs, IITs, etc.

Code:

(A) I and II (B) II and III
(C) I and III (D) All the above

253. According to 2011 Census Report, the difference between literacy rates of men and women in India is about

(A) 10% (B) 17% (C) 21% (D) 27%

254. For equality of educational opportunities among women, the Constitution has Provision under

(i) Article 45 (ii) Article 15(3)
(iii) Article 16(1) and (2) (iv) All the above

Which of the above is correct?

(A) Only (i) is correct
(B) (i) and (ii) are correct
(C) (i) and (iii) are correct
(D) (iv) is correct

255. Equality of educational opportunities is possible by

(A) Extending portals of educational institutions to all without any discrimination
(B) Opening more educational institutions
(C) Privatizing the education system in the country
(D) Public funding of Education

256. Who have signed MOU for recognition of Teacher Education in Special Education Programme in India?

(A) NCTE and NAAC (B) RCI and NCERT
(C) NCDS and RCI (D) RCI and NCTE

257. Which of the following statements are correct about the National Assessment and Accreditation Council ?

1. It is an autonomous institution.
2. It is tasked with the responsibility of assessing and accrediting institutions of higher education.
3. It is located in Delhi.
4. It has regional offices.

Select the correct answer from the codes given below :

Codes :

(A) 1 and 3 (B) 1 and 2
(C) 1, 2 and 4 (D) 2, 3 and 4

258. Which one of the following Councils has been disbanded in 2013?

(A) Distance Education Council (DEC)
(B) National Council for Teacher Education (NCTE)
(C) National Council of Educational Research and Training (NCERT)
(D) National Assessment and Accreditation Council (NAAC)

259. Which of the following is/are a minority institution(s) ?

1. Punjabi University, Patiala
2. Osmania University, Hyderabad
3. Kashmir University, Srinagar
4. St. Stephens College, Delhi

Select the correct answer from the code given below :

(A) 1 and 2 (B) 2 and 4
(C) 2 only (D) 4 only

260. Which of the following statements are correct about the National Advisory Council (NAC) ?

1. The National Advisory Council is a statutory body.
2. It is headed by the Prime Minister of India.
3. It facilitates constant interaction with the leaders of civil society.
4. It provides policy and legislative inputs to the Government of India.

Select the correct answer from the code given below :

(A) 1, 2 and 3 (B) 2, 3 and 4
(C) 1, 3 and 4 (D) 3 and 4

261. In which of the following categories the enrolment of students in higher education in 2010-11 was beyond the percentage of seats reserved ?

(A) OBC students (B) SC students
(C) ST students (D) Woman students

262. Which one of the following statements is not correct about the University Grants Commission (UGC)?

(A) It was established in 1956 by an Act of Parliament.
(B) It is tasked with promoting and coordinating higher education.
(C) It receives Plan and Non-Plan funds from the Central Government.
(D) It receives funds from State Governments in respect of State Universities.

ANSWERS

1. (A)	**2.** (C)	**3.** (C)	**4.** (A)	**5.** (D)	**6.** (C)	**7.** (D)	**8.** (D)	**9.** (B)	**10.** (C)
11. (A)	**12.** (A)	**13.** (B)	**14.** (D)	**15.** (A)	**16.** (A)	**17.** (A)	**18.** (C)	**19.** (D)	**20.** (A)
21. (D)	**22.** (B)	**23.** (C)	**24.** (C)	**25.** (B)	**26.** (A)	**27.** (C)	**28.** (D)	**29.** (B)	**30.** (B)
31. (B)	**32.** (C)	**33.** (C)	**34.** (B)	**35.** (A)	**36.** (A)	**37.** (D)	**38.** (B)	**39.** (A)	**40.** (A)
41. (D)	**42.** (C)	**43.** (A)	**44.** (A)	**45.** (B)	**46.** (C)	**47.** (D)	**48.** (D)	**49.** (A)	**50.** (B)
51. (D)	**52.** (D)	**53.** (C)	**54.** (B)	**55.** (B)	**56.** (D)	**57.** (D)	**58.** (B)	**59.** (D)	**60.** (D)
61. (C)	**62.** (D)	**63.** (D)	**64.** (C)	**65.** (C)	**66.** (A)	**67.** (D)	**68.** (C)	**69.** (A)	**70.** (D)
71. (B)	**72.** (A)	**73.** (C)	**74.** (D)	**75.** (A)	**76.** (D)	**77.** (D)	**78.** (D)	**79.** (A)	**80.** (C)
81. (B)	**82.** (D)	**83.** (B)	**84.** (B)	**85.** (D)	**86.** (A)	**87.** (B)	**88.** (D)	**89.** (D)	**90.** (D)
91. (A)	**92.** (C)	**93.** (A)	**94.** (C)	**95.** (D)	**96.** (D)	**97.** (C)	**98.** (D)	**99.** (C)	**100.** (A)
101. (D)	**102.** (A)	**103.** (A)	**104.** (D)	**105.** (B)	**106.** (A)	**107.** (B)	**108.** (A)	**109.** (A)	**110.** (A)
111. (D)	**112.** (D)	**113.** (B)	**114** (A)	**115.** (A)	**116.** (A)	**117.** (A)	**118.** (A)	**119.** (A)	**120.** (D)
121. (A)	**122.** (D)	**123.** (A)	**124.** (D)	**125.** (B)	**126.** (A)	**127.** (A)	**128.** (A)	**129.** (A)	**130.** (A)
131. (A)	**132.** (D)	**133.** (A)	**134.** (A)	**135.** (D)	**136.** (C)	**137.** (A)	**138.** (A)	**139.** (D)	**140.** (A)
141. (D)	**142.** (A)	**143.** (C)	**144.** (B)	**145.** (A)	**146.** (C)	**147** (C)	**148.** (C)	**149.** (A)	**150.** (C)
151. (B)	**152.** (A)	**153.** (C)	**154.** (B)	**155.** (B)	**156.** (C)	**157.** (D)	**158.** (D)	**159.** (B)	**160.** (C)
161. (B)	**162.** (D)	**163.** (B)	**164.** (D)	**165.** (A)	**166.** (B)	**167.** (B)	**168.** (B)	**169.** (D)	**170.** (B)
171. (A)	**172.** (A)	**173.** (A)	**174.** (C)	**175.** (A)	**176.** (C)	**177.** (B)	**178.** (A)	**179.** (B)	**180.** (A)
181. (C)	**182.** (A)	**183.** (B)	**184.** (A)	**185.** (C)	**186.** (C)	**187.** (D)	**188.** (A)	**189.** (C)	**190.** (C)
191. (D)	**192.** (D)	**193.** (D)	**194.** (C)	**195.** (A)	**196.** (A)	**197.** (B)	**198.** (C)	**199.** (B)	**200.** (B)
201. (B)	**202.** (A)	**203.** (A)	**204.** (D)	**205.** (C)	**206.** (A)	**207.** (C)	**208.** (C)	**209.** (C)	**210.** (B)
211. (A)	**212.** (A)	**213.** (C)	**214.** (D)	**215.** (C)	**216.** (D)	**217.** (A)	**218.** (A)	**219.** (D)	**220.** (A)
221. (D)	**222.** (C)	**223.** (C)	**224.** (A)	**225.** (D)	**226.** (A)	**227.** (C)	**228.** (A)	**229.** (B)	**230.** (B)
231. (A)	**232.** (A)	**233.** (C)	**234.** (C)	**235.** (B)	**236.** (A)	**237.** (C)	**238.** (C)	**239.** (D)	**240.** (D)
241. (D)	**242.** (A)	**243.** (A)	**244.** (A)	**245.** (A)	**246.** (A)	**247.** (B)	**248.** (B)	**249.** (B)	**250.** (C)
251. (B)	**252.** (B)	**253.** (B)	**254.** (D)	**255.** (A)	**256.** (D)	**257.** (B)	**258.** (A)	**259.** (D)	**260.** (D)
261. (A)	**262.** (D)								

ADDITIONAL MULTIPLE CHOICE QUESTIONS

1. Which organization is responsible for the development and implementation of SWAYAM in India?
   (1) UNESCO
   (2) NASSCOM
   (3) Ministry of Human Resource Development (MHRD)
   (4) World Bank
2. What is the primary objective of SWAYAM?
   (1) To provide free textbooks to students
   (2) To offer online courses to students across India
   (3) To establish physical learning centers
   (4) To promote private education institutions
3. SWAYAM courses are primarily aimed at which level of education?
   (1) Primary school
   (2) Secondary school
   (3) Higher education
   (4) Vocational training
4. SWAYAM PRABHA is an extension of SWAYAM that focuses on
   (1) Live classroom lectures
   (2) Recorded video lectures
   (3) Virtual reality simulations
   (4) Gaming for education
5. How are SWAYAM PRABHA lectures broadcasted to learners?
   (1) Through satellite TV channels
   (2) Through social media platforms
   (3) Through mobile apps
   (4) Through physical DVDs
6. Which of the following is NOT a common feature of MOOCs?
   (1) Open access to course materials
   (2) Certification upon completion
   (3) Live, in-person lectures
   (4) Interaction with instructors and peers
7. MOOCs typically attract learners from
   (1) A specific region or country
   (2) A single institution
   (3) A global audience
   (4) Only high-income households
8. Which platform is known for offering a wide variety of MOOCs from universities and institutions worldwide?
   (1) Coursera
   (2) SWAYAM
   (3) SWAYAM PRABHA
   (4) Khan Academy
9. What is the key advantage of MOOCs for learners?
   (1) Personalized face-to-face instruction
   (2) High cost of enrollment
   (3) Flexibility in learning schedules
   (4) Limited access to course materials
10. Which of the following is a primary challenge associated with MOOCs?
    (1) Lack of instructor expertise
    (2) Limited course variety
    (3) High enrollment fees
    (4) High dropout rates
11. SWAYAM PRABHA primarily broadcasts which type of content?
    (1) Live lectures
    (2) Pre-recorded video lectures
    (3) Interactive simulations
    (4) Virtual reality experiences
12. SWAYAM offers courses in which languages?
    (1) English only
    (2) Hindi only
    (3) Multiple languages including English and Hindi
    (4) Regional languages only
13. Which organization in India is responsible for accrediting and recognizing SWAYAM courses?

(1) All India Council for Technical Education (AICTE)
(2) University Grants Commission (UGC)
(3) National Board of Accreditation (NBA)
(4) Indian Institutes of Technology (IITs)

14. What is the primary mode of assessment for SWAYAM courses?
(1) Final exams held at physical centers
(2) Continuous assessment through quizzes and assignments
(3) Oral interviews with instructors
(4) Peer evaluations

15. Which government initiative in India focuses on using technology to improve the quality of education?
(1) SWAYAM
(2) SWAYAM PRABHA
(3) Digital India
(4) Skill India

16. Which of the following is a benefit of SWAYAM and MOOCs for learners?
(1) Limited access to course materials
(2) High cost of enrollment
(3) Increased access to quality education
(4) Limited interaction with instructors

17. In SWAYAM PRABHA, how many channels are dedicated to broadcasting educational content?
(1) 5 (2) 10
(3) 25 (4) 50

18. What is the primary source of funding for SWAYAM and SWAYAM PRABHA initiatives in India?
(1) Corporate sponsors
(2) International grants
(3) Government of India
(4) Private universities

19. Which of the following is NOT a goal of SWAYAM?
(1) To improve access to high-quality education
(2) To promote lifelong learning
(3) To increase the number of students enrolled in higher education
(4) To improve the quality of education in India

20. Which of the following is NOT a feature of SWAYAM Prabha?
(1) It is a free-to-air television channel
(2) It broadcasts educational content from SWAYAM
(3) It is available to all viewers in India
(4) It is only available in urban areas

21. Which of the following is NOT a benefit of MOOCs?
(1) They offer a flexible learning experience
(2) They are affordable
(3) They are accessible to students from all over the world
(4) They are a substitute for traditional classroom instruction

22. Which of the following is a drawback of MOOCs?
(1) They can be difficult to complete
(2) They do not provide students with the opportunity to interact with their peers
(3) They can be expensive
(4) All of the above

23. Which of the following is a way to overcome the drawbacks of MOOCs?
(1) Take MOOCs in conjunction with traditional classroom instruction
(2) Join a MOOC discussion forum or online community
(3) Seek out additional resources to support your learning
(4) All of the above

24. Which of the following is NOT a key consideration in the evaluation of CBCS?
(1) The extent to which students have the flexibility to choose courses that meet their interests and needs.
(2) The ease of transitioning between institutions.
(3) The effectiveness of the teaching and learning methods.
(4) The fairness of the evaluation system.

25. Which of the following is a potential advantage of using a grading system in CBCS?
(1) It allows for a more nuanced assessment of student learning.
(2) It is more transparent and easier to understand than other evaluation methods.
(3) It is more aligned with the demands of the workplace.
(4) All of the above.

26. Which of the following is a potential drawback of using a grading system in CBCS?
(1) It can lead to grade inflation.
(2) It can discourage students from taking challenging courses.

(3) It can be difficult to compare the performance of students from different institutions.
(4) All of the above.

27. Which of the following is a potential advantage of using a competency-based evaluation system in CBCS?
(1) It focuses on what students can do rather than on how well they perform on tests.
(2) It is more flexible and allows for students to demonstrate their learning in a variety of ways.
(3) It is more aligned with the needs of the workplace.
(4) All of the above.

28. Which of the following is a potential drawback of using a competency-based evaluation system in CBCS?
(1) It can be difficult to develop and implement competency-based assessments.
(2) It can be difficult to compare the performance of students from different institutions.
(3) It can be subjective and difficult to ensure fairness.
(4) All of the above.

29. What is the primary objective of the Choice Based Credit System (CBCS) in higher education?
(1) To eliminate choice for students and standardize the curriculum
(2) To provide flexibility and choice to students in selecting courses
(3) To reduce the number of credit hours required for graduation
(4) To prioritize vocational training over academic courses

30. In CBCS, what is a "credit" typically equivalent to?
(1) A fixed number of lecture hours
(2) The grade received in a course
(3) The cost of course materials
(4) The duration of a semester

31. Which of the following is a key advantage of CBCS in higher education?
(1) Limited student choice in course selection
(2) Rigidity in the curriculum structure
(3) Promotion of interdisciplinary learning
(4) Uniform grading system

32. Under CBCS, how are students evaluated for their performance in each course?
(1) Through a single final exam at the end of the program
(2) Through continuous assessment methods, including exams, assignments, and presentations
(3) Through standardized national tests
(4) Through a lottery system

33. What is the purpose of a Choice Based Credit System (CBCS) grading system?
(1) To rank students based on their intelligence
(2) To simplify administrative processes for universities
(3) To assess students' performance in a course
(4) To eliminate the need for examinations

34. In CBCS, what does the "Choice Based" aspect refer to?
(1) Students have no choice in course selection
(2) Students can choose their instructors
(3) Students can choose courses from a range of electives
(4) Students can choose their classmates

35. Which institution or organization is responsible for implementing and overseeing CBCS in higher education in a country?
(1) Local municipalities
(2) Individual universities
(3) Ministry of Education or similar government body
(4) Private companies

36. What is the primary aim of the credit system in CBCS?
(1) To make courses more challenging for students
(2) To measure the weight of textbooks
(3) To quantify the workload of a course
(4) To increase the number of holidays in the academic calendar

37. How does CBCS contribute to the internationalization of higher education?
(1) By limiting exposure to global perspectives
(2) By promoting isolation from international trends
(3) By facilitating credit transfers between institutions worldwide
(4) By discouraging collaboration with foreign universities

38. What is the role of Continuous Internal Assessment (CIA) in CBCS?

(1) To conduct surprise inspections of classrooms
(2) To monitor students' social activities
(3) To assess students' performance throughout the semester
(4) To determine the overall cost of education

39. Which of the following is an example of ICT used in data collection for research?
(1) Telephone interviews
(2) Field observations
(3) Handwritten surveys
(4) Printed questionnaires

40. Which software tool is commonly used for statistical analysis in research?
(1) Photoshop
(2) Microsoft Word
(3) SPSS (Statistical Package for the Social Sciences)
(4) Microsoft Excel

41. What is the term for the process of using ICT to search for and gather existing research literature and resources?
(1) Data analysis
(2) Literature review
(3) Primary data collection
(4) Hypothesis testing

42. Which ICT tool can help researchers organize and manage their references and citations?
(1) Microsoft PowerPoint
(2) EndNote
(3) Google Docs
(4) YouTube

43. How can ICT aid in collaboration among researchers from different geographic locations?
(1) By increasing travel opportunities
(2) By enabling virtual meetings and document sharing
(3) By decreasing communication altogether
(4) By relying on physical mail for collaboration

44. Which of the following is a benefit of using online surveys for research?
(1) Limited accessibility to participants
(2) Lower response rates
(3) Quick data collection and analysis
(4) Difficulty in data entry

45. What is the term for the practice of using ICT to create 3D models for research simulations?
(1) Virtualization
(2) Simulation modeling
(3) Augmented reality
(4) Social networking

46. How can Geographic Information Systems (GIS) be applied in research?
(1) To analyze climate change data
(2) To conduct literary reviews
(3) To organize research notes
(4) To edit research manuscripts

47. Which ICT tool can assist researchers in visualizing complex data sets?
(1) Google Search
(2) Virtual Reality (VR) headsets
(3) Excel spreadsheets
(4) Twitter

48. How can social media platforms like Twitter and Facebook be useful in research?
(1) To replace traditional research methods entirely
(2) To connect with peers and disseminate research findings
(3) To store and organize research data
(4) To replace academic journals

49. What is the primary advantage of using cloud computing in research?
(1) Increased data security
(2) Lower cost of data storage
(3) Reduced accessibility to research data
(4) Limited collaboration opportunities

50. In research, what does the term "Big Data" refer to?
(1) Small datasets with limited significance
(2) The volume of data that exceeds the processing capacity of traditional databases
(3) The absence of data in a research study
(4) Data collected from a single source

51. How can ICT assist in data visualization in research?
(1) By limiting data representation to tables and spreadsheets
(2) By providing tools for creating charts, graphs, and interactive visualizations
(3) By eliminating the need for data visualization
(4) By focusing on textual descriptions of data

52. What is the role of data mining in research?
(1) To extract valuable insights from large datasets
(2) To collect primary data through surveys
(3) To conduct literature reviews
(4) To validate research hypotheses

53. How can researchers use virtual labs in their work?
   (1) To conduct experiments in a physical laboratory
   (2) To replace traditional lab work entirely
   (3) To simulate experiments and collect data virtually
   (4) To publish research findings
54. Which ICT tool can be used to detect plagiarism in research papers?
   (1) Data visualization software
   (2) Social media platforms
   (3) Plagiarism detection software
   (4) Virtual labs
55. What is the term for the practice of using online repositories to share research data and publications openly?
   (1) Data hoarding
   (2) Open access publishing
   (3) Closed research sharing
   (4) Data piracy
56. How can virtual conferencing tools like Zoom and Skype benefit researchers?
   (1) By reducing the need for communication with peers
   (2) By facilitating international travel for conferences
   (3) By enabling remote collaboration and conference participation
   (4) By eliminating the need for research presentations
57. Which of the following is NOT an example of ICT used in research?
   (1) Online databases
   (2) Statistical software
   (3) Laboratory equipment
   (4) Cloud computing
58. Which of the following is a benefit of using ICT in research?
   (1) It can help researchers to collect and analyze data more efficiently.
   (2) It can help researchers to collaborate with others more effectively.
   (3) It can help researchers to disseminate their findings more widely.
   (4) All of the above
59. Which of the following is an example of how ICT can be used to collect data in research?
   (1) Using online surveys
   (2) Using social media
   (3) Using sensors and other wearable devices
   (4) All of the above
60. Which of the following is an example of how ICT can be used to analyze data in research?
   (1) using statistical software
   (2) using data mining tools
   (3) using machine learning algorithms
   (4) All of the above
61. Which of the following is an example of how ICT can be used to disseminate research findings?
   (1) publishing papers in academic journals
   (2) presenting research at conferences
   (3) using social media to share research findings
   (4) All of the above
62. What is the primary purpose of referencing in academic writing?
   (1) To add length to the paper
   (2) To make the paper look more professional
   (3) To give credit to the original sources and avoid plagiarism
   (4) To confuse the reader
63. Which style guide is commonly used for referencing in the fields of humanities and arts?
   (1) APA (American Psychological Association)
   (2) MLA (Modern Language Association)
   (3) Chicago Manual of Style
   (4) IEEE (Institute of Electrical and Electronics Engineers)
64. Which element is typically included in a full citation for a book in the APA style?
   (1) Publisher's location
   (2) Page numbers
   (3) Date of access
   (4) Volume and issue number
65. In APA referencing, how are in-text citations usually formatted for direct quotations?
   (1) (Author's last name, year, page number)
   (2) (Year, author's last name, page number)
   (3) (Author's last name, page number, year)
   (4) (Page number, author's last name, year)
66. Which style guide is commonly used in the social sciences for referencing?
   (1) MLA (2) Chicago
   (3) APA (4) Harvard
67. What is the primary difference between APA and MLA citation styles?
   (1) APA uses footnotes, while MLA uses in-text citations

(2) APA uses author-date format, while MLA uses footnotes
(3) APA uses numeric citations, while MLA uses author-page format
(4) APA and MLA are the same style with different names

68. In the Chicago Manual of Style, which type of citation includes a full bibliographic entry in a footnote or endnote?
(1) Author-date citation
(2) Parenthetical citation
(3) Bibliographic citation
(4) Numeric citation

69. Which of the following is a common feature of Harvard style referencing?
(1) Footnotes and endnotes
(2) Numeric citations
(3) In-text citations with author's name and year
(4) Parenthetical citations

70. In Harvard style, how is a reference to a book typically formatted in the reference list?
(1) Author's last name, first initial. (Year). Title of Book. Publisher.
(2) Title of Book (Year), Author's last name, first initial. Publisher.
(3) Year. Author's last name, first initial. Title of Book. Publisher.
(4) Publisher. Author's last name, first initial. (Year). Title of Book.

71. Which citation style is commonly used in scientific and engineering fields, particularly for journal articles?
(1) APA (2) MLA
(3) IEEE (4) Harvard

72. In IEEE citation style, how are in-text citations usually formatted for direct quotations?
(1) [Author's last name, year, page number]
(2) (Author's last name, year, page number)
(3) [Author's last name, page number]
(4) (Author's last name, page number)

73. What is the purpose of a bibliography or reference list at the end of an academic paper?
(1) To provide additional reading materials for the reader
(2) To list all sources consulted during research, whether cited or not
(3) To summarize the main points of the paper
(4) To include personal opinions and anecdotes

74. Which style guide is often used for legal citations in academic writing?
(1) APA (2) MLA
(3) Bluebook (4) Chicago

75. In the Bluebook citation style, what is typically used to refer to specific legal cases?
(1) Footnotes
(2) Parenthetical citations
(3) Volume and page number
(4) Ibid.

76. Which Pramana is often used to validate the existence of God in Indian philosophy?
(1) Anumana (2) Pratyaksha
(3) Upamana (4) Sabda

77. Which element is commonly included in a citation for an online source in various citation styles?
(1) URL (Uniform Resource Locator)
(2) Author's middle name
(3) Date of birth of the author
(4) Physical location of the source

78. In the MLA citation style, how are in-text citations typically formatted for paraphrased information?
(1) (Author's last name, page number)
(2) [Author's last name, page number]
(3) Author's last name (page number)
(4) Author's last name, page number

79. What is the primary purpose of a DOI (Digital Object Identifier) in a reference citation?
(1) To indicate the date of publication
(2) To provide a link to the author's website
(3) To identify and locate a specific online resource
(4) To display the author's credentials

80. Which citation style is commonly used for academic papers in the field of history?
(1) APA (2) MLA
(3) Chicago (4) IEEE

81. In the Chicago citation style, how are subsequent citations to the same source typically formatted?
(1) Ibid.
(2) (Author's last name, page number)
(3) [Author's last name, page number]
(4) (Author's last name, year, page number)

82. Which citation style is often used in business and management research?
(1) APA (2) MLA
(3) Chicago (4) Bluebook

83. Which of the following is NOT a common format for referencing?
(1) Harvard (2) MLA
(3) Chicago (4) Turabian

84. Which of the following is the most common format for referencing in the social sciences?
(1) APA (2) MLA
(3) Chicago (4) Turabian

85. Which of the following is the most common format for referencing in the humanities?
(1) APA (2) MLA
(3) Chicago (4) Turabian

86. Which of the following is the most common format for referencing in law and business?
(1) APA (2) MLA
(3) Chicago (4) Turabian

87. Which of the following is the most important consideration when choosing a referencing style?
(1) The discipline in which you are writing
(2) The audience for your writing
(3) The requirements of your instructor or publisher
(4) All of the above

88. What is the primary purpose of a thesis or dissertation?
(1) To summarize existing research on a topic
(2) To provide a brief overview of a subject
(3) To present original research findings and contribute to the field
(4) To entertain readers with anecdotes and stories

89. In academic writing, what is the standard format for citing sources within the text of a thesis or article?
(1) Endnotes
(2) Footnotes
(3) Parenthetical citations
(4) References at the beginning of the paper

90. Which section of a research article typically provides an overview of the study's main findings and their implications?
(1) Abstract
(2) Introduction
(3) Literature review
(4) Conclusion

91. What should be the primary focus of the introduction section in a research article?
(1) Detailed methodology
(2) A summary of the author's qualifications
(3) A clear statement of the research problem or question
(4) Personal anecdotes

92. Which statement is true regarding the use of passive voice in academic writing?
(1) It is always preferred for clarity.
(2) It should be used sparingly to emphasize the author's actions.
(3) It should be avoided entirely.
(4) It is primarily used in the conclusion section.

93. What does the term "literature review" refer to in academic writing?
(1) A summary of the author's personal experiences
(2) A critical analysis of existing research on the topic
(3) A list of recommended books for further reading
(4) A fictional story related to the research topic

94. Which of the following is a common goal of the discussion section in a research article?
(1) To restate the research question
(2) To present new research findings
(3) To interpret the results and their significance
(4) To provide an abstract summary of the study

95. What is the primary function of an abstract in a research article?
(1) To provide a detailed discussion of the research methodology
(2) To summarize the main points and findings of the study
(3) To introduce the author's personal opinions and biases
(4) To list the references used in the article

96. What is the term for the practice of acknowledging the sources and ideas of others in your writing?
(1) Plagiarism (2) Citation
(3) Paraphrasing (4) Self-plagiarism

97. Which section of a research article typically provides an overview of the relevant literature on the topic?
(1) Discussion (2) Introduction
(3) Methodology (4) Conclusion

98. What is the purpose of an appendix in a thesis or research article?
(1) To provide a list of references

(2) To include raw data, supplementary materials, or additional information
(3) To summarize the main findings of the study
(4) To introduce the author's personal opinions

99. Which of the following is a key element of effective thesis or article writing?
(1) Overloading the text with jargon and technical terms
(2) Using complex sentences to impress the reader
(3) Clarity and precision in conveying ideas
(4) Avoiding the use of citations and references

100. What is the primary goal of the methodology section in a research article?
(1) To summarize the main findings of the study
(2) To provide an in-depth analysis of the literature
(3) To describe the research methods and procedures used
(4) To list the author's personal experiences

101. Which statement is true regarding the use of anecdotes in academic writing?
(1) Anecdotes are essential to maintain reader interest.
(2) Anecdotes should be used sparingly and must relate to the research topic.
(3) Anecdotes are the primary focus of the methodology section.
(4) Anecdotes are discouraged in academic writing.

102. What is the term for the practice of reusing one's own previously published work without proper citation?
(1) Plagiarism (2) Self-plagiarism
(3) Citation (4) Paraphrasing

103. Which of the following is a key component of a strong thesis statement in a research article?
(1) Vague language and ambiguous terms
(2) A clear and specific research question or claim
(3) A lengthy and complex sentence structure
(4) Personal anecdotes and opinions

104. In a thesis or research article, what is the term for the section that lists the sources cited in the text?
(1) References (2) Appendices
(3) Abstract (4) Introduction

105. What is the primary purpose of peer review in academic publishing?
(1) To promote authors' works without critique
(2) To identify and correct errors in research articles
(3) To allow authors to publish without review
(4) To discourage the publication of new research

106. Which of the following is considered a reputable source for academic research?
(1) Personal blog posts
(2) Wikipedia articles
(3) Peer-reviewed journals
(4) Social media comments

107. In academic writing, what is the term for the practice of presenting someone else's work or ideas as your own?
(1) Plagiarism (2) Citation
(3) Paraphrasing (4) Abstracting

108. What is the primary function of mass media in society?
(1) To entertain (2) To educate
(3) To manipulate (4) To generate profits

109. Which of the following is an example of traditional mass media?
(1) Facebook (2) Television
(3) YouTube (4) Snapchat

110. How has the internet transformed the way people consume news?
(1) It has made news consumption more passive.
(2) It has reduced the availability of news sources.
(3) It has increased the speed and accessibility of news.
(4) It has eliminated the need for news reporting.

111. Which theory of mass media effects suggests that media can influence public opinion and behavior?
(1) Uses and Gratifications Theory
(2) Agenda-Setting Theory
(3) Cultivation Theory
(4) Gatekeeping Theory

112. In mass media, what does the term "gatekeeping" refer to?
(1) The process of selecting which stories to cover and which to ignore
(2) The legal regulations placed on media outlets

(3) The ownership of media companies
(4) The technology used in media production

113. What is the "fourth estate" in journalism and mass media?
(1) The advertising industry
(2) The government
(3) The judiciary
(4) The press

114. Which of the following is an example of a social media platform?
(1) CNN
(2) The New York Times
(3) Twitter
(4) National Geographic

115. What term is used to describe the merging of traditional media with digital platforms, creating new ways of delivering content?
(1) Convergence (2) Monopoly
(3) Fragmentation (4) Censorship

116. Which communication model suggests that mass media delivers messages directly to passive audiences?
(1) The Hypodermic Needle Model
(2) The Two-Step Flow Model
(3) The Cultivation Model
(4) The Limited Effects Model

117. What does the term "echo chamber" refer to in the context of social media?
(1) A room with soundproof walls
(2) A social media platform designed for private communication
(3) An environment in which people encounter only information that confirms their existing beliefs
(4) A space where social media influencers gather to create content

118. Which of the following is a characteristic of "fake news" or disinformation?
(1) It is always intentional and malicious.
(2) It is produced by reputable news organizations.
(3) It may contain false or misleading information.
(4) It is regulated by government agencies.

119. What term is used to describe the practice of selectively presenting information to influence public opinion?
(1) Censorship (2) Propaganda
(3) Journalism (4) Advertising

120. Which type of media ownership involves a single company owning multiple media outlets in various forms (e.g., newspapers, TV, radio)?
(1) Monopoly (2) Oligopoly
(3) Diversification (4) Decentralization

121. What is "media literacy"?
(1) The ability to control media content
(2) The ability to understand, analyze, and critically evaluate media messages
(3) The process of producing media content
(4) The ownership of media outlets

122. Which of the following is a potential positive effect of mass media on society?
(1) Promoting conformity and discouraging diversity of thought
(2) Encouraging critical thinking and informed citizenship
(3) Reducing access to information
(4) Limiting freedom of expression

123. What does the term "media convergence" refer to?
(1) The competition among media outlets
(2) The merging of different media forms and technologies
(3) The censorship of media content
(4) The decline of mass media

124. Which theory suggests that long-term exposure to media content can shape individuals' perceptions of reality?
(1) Uses and Gratifications Theory
(2) Cultivation Theory
(3) Gatekeeping Theory
(4) Agenda-Setting Theory

125. What is the primary purpose of media regulations and censorship by governments?
(1) To promote media convergence
(2) To protect freedom of the press
(3) To ensure accuracy and objectivity in reporting
(4) To control the flow of information and maintain authority

126. What is the term for a news story that emphasizes sensationalism and entertainment over informative content?
(1) Investigative journalism
(2) Tabloid journalism
(3) Editorial (4) Press release

127. Which communication model suggests that opinion leaders play a crucial role in influencing others' attitudes and behaviors?

(1) The Hypodermic Needle Model
(2) The Two-Step Flow Model
(3) The Cultivation Model
(4) The Limited Effects Model

128. In a democratic society, what role does the media often play?
(1) To reinforce government control
(2) To discourage public debate
(3) To provide a platform for diverse voices and hold the government accountable
(4) To limit access to information

129. What term is used to describe the deliberate spreading of false information with the intent to harm someone's reputation?
(1) Libel (2) Slander
(3) Defamation (4) Fair use

130. What is "media bias"?
(1) The practice of promoting unbiased reporting
(2) The tendency of media outlets to favor certain perspectives or ideologies
(3) The absence of opinion in news reporting
(4) The focus on sensationalism in journalism

131. In the context of media ethics, what does "objectivity" refer to?
(1) A complete absence of opinion in reporting
(2) A commitment to promoting a specific political ideology
(3) Fair and balanced reporting, free from bias
(4) The use of sensationalism to attract readership

132. Which of the following terms refers to the practice of advertisers paying for the placement of their products within media content?
(1) Product placement
(2) Subliminal advertising
(3) Sponsorship
(4) Propaganda

133. Which pramana (means of knowledge) is related to the direct sensory experience?
(1) Anumana (Inference)
(2) Upamana (Comparison)
(3) Pratyaksha (Perception)
(4) Shabda (Testimony)

134. Which Indian philosopher is known for his work on Nyaya Sutras?
(1) Adi Shankaracharya
(2) Ramanuja
(3) Gautama (4) Patanjali

135. What is the role of Anumana (Inference) as a means of knowledge?
(1) To provide direct sensory experience
(2) To draw conclusions based on reasoning
(3) To rely on authoritative testimony
(4) To compare different objects

136. Which pramana is related to language and communication?
(1) Anumana (Inference)
(2) Upamana (Comparison)
(3) Pratyaksha (Perception)
(4) Shabda (Testimony)

137. In Indian logic, what is Upamana (Comparison) used for?
(1) Establishing historical facts
(2) Drawing conclusions based on inference
(3) Recognizing similarities between objects
(4) Direct sensory experience

138. Who is credited with developing the Nyaya school of Indian philosophy?
(1) Adi Shankaracharya
(2) Ramanuja
(3) Gautama
(4) Patanjali

139. Which means of knowledge is based on the testimony of reliable sources?
(1) Anumana (Inference)
(2) Upamana (Comparison)
(3) Pratyaksha (Perception)
(4) Shabda (Testimony)

140. Which Nyaya philosopher wrote the Nyaya Sutra, a foundational text of Indian logic?
(1) Kanada (2) Patanjali
(3) Gautama (4) Nagarjuna

141. What is the primary source of knowledge according to the Nyaya school?
(1) Inference (2) Perception
(3) Testimony (4) Comparison

142. Which of the following is NOT one of the six pramanas (means of knowledge) in Indian philosophy?
(1) Anumana (Inference)
(2) Pratyaksha (Perception)
(3) Abhava (Non-existence)
(4) Shabda (Testimony)

143. Who is the proponent of the Advaita Vedanta school of Indian philosophy?
(1) Adi Shankaracharya
(2) Ramanuja

(3) Gautama
(4) Patanjali

144. What is the role of Anupalabdhi (Non-apprehension) as a means of knowledge?
(1) To establish the existence of an object
(2) To establish the absence or non-existence of an object
(3) To compare two objects
(4) To rely on authoritative testimony

145. In Indian logic, what is Yukti?
(1) Perception (2) Inference
(3) Testimony (4) Comparison

146. Which pramana is related to inference based on the absence of an object?
(1) Pratyaksha (Perception)
(2) Anupalabdhi (Non-apprehension)
(3) Shabda (Testimony)
(4) Upamana (Comparison)

147. Which school of Indian philosophy focuses on the concept of Shabda (Testimony) as a primary means of knowledge?
(1) Nyaya (2) Vedanta
(3) Samkhya (4) Mimamsa

148. What is the purpose of Pramanas in Indian philosophy?
(1) To establish the non-existence of objects
(2) To create logical paradoxes
(3) To provide valid means of acquiring knowledge
(4) To eliminate the need for reasoning

149. Who is known for his commentary on the Nyaya Sutra, which is considered a seminal work in Indian logic?
(1) Shankaracharya (2) Ramanuja
(3) Udayana (4) Nagarjuna

150. In Indian logic, what is the term used to describe the doubt or skepticism regarding the validity of a means of knowledge?
(1) Abhava (2) Vyapti
(3) Anumana (4) Agyaanta

151. Which of the following is the most authoritative means of knowledge in Indian logic?
(1) Perception (2) Inference
(3) Testimony (4) Comparison

152. Which of the following is the best example of inference in Indian logic?
(1) I see smoke rising from the chimney, so I infer that there is a fire in the house.
(2) I hear a loud noise, so I infer that there has been an accident.
(3) I see a footprint in the sand, so I infer that someone has walked by.
(4) All of the above

153. Which of the following is the best example of testimony in Indian logic?
(1) I see smoke rising from the chimney, so I infer that there is a fire in the house.
(2) I hear a loud noise, so I infer that there has been an accident.
(3) I see a footprint in the sand, so I infer that someone has walked by.
(4) My teacher tells me that the Earth is round, so I believe her.

154. Which of the following is the best example of comparison in Indian logic?
(1) I see smoke rising from the chimney, so I infer that there is a fire in the house.
(2) I hear a loud noise, so I infer that there has been an accident.
(3) I see a footprint in the sand, so I infer that someone has walked by.
(4) A swan is white, a peacock is white, and a dove is white. Therefore, all birds are white.

155. Which Pramana is based on the principle of cause and effect?
(1) Anumana (2) Pratyaksha
(3) Upamana (4) Sabda

156. What is the source of knowledge in Upamana Pramana?
(1) Sense perception
(2) Testimony
(3) Comparison and analogy
(4) Inference

157. Which Pramana relies on the words of authority or experts?
(1) Anumana (2) Pratyaksha
(3) Upamana (4) Sabda

158. What does the term "Sabda" in Indian philosophy refer to?
(1) Inference
(2) Testimony or verbal testimony
(3) Direct perception
(4) Comparison

159. Who is considered the primary proponent of Nyaya philosophy, which heavily relies on Pramanas?
(1) Adi Shankaracharya
(2) Ramanuja
(3) Gautama
(4) Patanjali

160. Which Pramana is often associated with linguistic knowledge and language?
(1) Anumana (2) Pratyaksha
(3) Upamana (4) Sabda

161. What is the Nyaya term for "error" or "false cognition"?
(1) Anumana (2) Pratyaksha
(3) Upamana (4) Anadhigata

162. Which Pramana is primarily used for gaining knowledge of past events?
(1) Anumana (2) Pratyaksha
(3) Upamana (4) Sabda

163. Which of the following is NOT considered one of the six traditional Pramanas in Nyaya philosophy?
(1) Anumana (2) Upamana
(3) Smriti (4) Arthapatti

164. What is the term for the valid cognition that arises from the absence of something?
(1) Anumana (2) Pratyaksha
(3) Upamana (4) Anupalabdhi

165. Which Pramana is associated with non-perception or negative cognition?
(1) Anumana (2) Pratyaksha
(3) Upamana (4) Anupalabdhi

166. What is the primary concern of Indian epistemology?
(1) Metaphysics (2) Ethics
(3) The nature of knowledge and its sources
(4) Aesthetics

167. Which Nyaya philosopher is known for his work on epistemology and Pramanas?
(1) Kapila (2) Patanjali
(3) Gautama (4) Uddyotakara

168. Which Pramana is associated with memory and recollection?
(1) Anumana (2) Pratyaksha
(3) Smriti (4) Sabda

169. Which Pramana is most closely related to testimony or the words of others?
(1) Anumana (2) Pratyaksha
(3) Upamana (4) Sabda

170. According to Nyaya philosophy, how many valid Pramanas are there?
(1) 3 (2) 4
(3) 5 (4) 6

171. What is the term for doubt or skepticism in Indian philosophy?
(1) Samshaya (2) Anumana
(3) Pratyaksha (4) Upamana

172. Which Pramana is often used to establish the authority of scriptures and religious texts?
(1) Anumana (2) Pratyaksha
(3) Upamana (4) Sabda

173. Which Pramana is considered the most reliable and direct source of knowledge in Nyaya philosophy?
(1) Anumana (2) Pratyaksha
(3) Upamana (4) Sabda

174. Which of the following is not an example of ICT tool commonly used in higher education?
(1) LMS (Learning Management System)
(2) Social media platforms
(3) Blackboard and chalk
(4) Video conferencing software

175. Which aspect of higher education has ICT significantly impacted?
(1) Campus architecture
(2) Student enrollment
(3) Teaching and learning
(4) Library design

176. What is the primary purpose of a Learning Management System (LMS) in higher education?
(1) Campus security
(2) Faculty recruitment
(3) Course management and delivery
(4) Financial management

177. Which ICT tool is commonly used for conducting online examinations in higher education?
(1) Social media
(2) Video conferencing
(3) Learning Analytics
(4) e-Assessment systems

178. What does the term "Blended Learning" refer to in the context of higher education?
(1) Learning that takes place only in physical classrooms
(2) Learning that combines face-to-face and online instruction
(3) Learning without any use of technology
(4) Learning through peer interactions only

179. Which of the following is an advantage of using ICT in higher education?
(1) Decreased access to educational resources
(2) Limited communication between students and teachers
(3) Enhanced flexibility in learning
(4) Reduced need for qualified educators

180. What is the term for the practice of providing educational content, such as lectures, online for self-paced learning?
(1) Synchronous learning
(2) Asynchronous learning
(3) Experiential learning
(4) Collaborative learning

181. Which type of software is used to track and analyze students' learning behaviors and performance?
(1) Social media
(2) Learning Analytics
(3) Video conferencing
(4) Virtual reality software

182. What is the role of MOOCs (Massive Open Online Courses) in higher education?
(1) Exclusive courses for elite students
(2) Affordable and accessible online courses for a wide audience
(3) Traditional on-campus courses
(4) Private tutoring services

183. Which ICT tool is most commonly used for collaborative projects and discussions in higher education?
(1) Learning Management System (LMS)
(2) Social media platforms
(3) Video conferencing software
(4) Learning Analytics tools

184. How can virtual reality (VR) be used in higher education?
(1) To replace physical classrooms entirely
(2) To provide realistic simulations for various subjects
(3) To limit student interactions
(4) To reduce the need for qualified educators

185. What is the term for the process of using ICT to adapt learning materials to individual students' needs and abilities?
(1) Personalized learning
(2) Traditional teaching
(3) Standardized testing
(4) Synchronous learning

186. Which ICT tool is used for real-time online meetings and discussions with students?
(1) Learning Management System (LMS)
(2) Social media platforms
(3) Video conferencing software
(4) Learning Analytics tools

187. In the context of ICT in higher education, what does "BYOD" stand for?
(1) Bring Your Own Device
(2) Buy Your Own Device
(3) Build Your Own Database
(4) Browse Your Online Documents

188. Which of the following is a potential challenge in implementing ICT in higher education?
(1) Enhanced accessibility for all students
(2) Increased cost of education
(3) Reduced flexibility in course delivery
(4) Limited access to online resources

189. What is the term for the practice of using ICT to deliver educational content to remote or geographically dispersed students?
(1) Traditional education
(2) Distance education
(3) On-campus education
(4) Blended learning

190. Which aspect of higher education has been positively influenced by e-books and digital libraries?
(1) Campus security
(2) Student enrollment
(3) Research and resource availability
(4) Faculty recruitment

191. What is the primary purpose of a Digital Whiteboard in higher education?
(1) Creating physical copies of lecture notes
(2) Enhancing faculty recruitment
(3) Facilitating interactive and dynamic presentations
(4) Monitoring student attendance

192. Which of the following is a benefit of using ICT in higher education?
(1) Reduced need for teacher-student interactions
(2) Limited access to educational resources
(3) Enhanced accessibility to quality education
(4) Decreased importance of physical campuses

193. What does "e-governance" stand for?
(1) Electronic Governance
(2) Efficient Governance
(3) Effective Governance
(4) Eco-friendly Governance

194. Which of the following best describes e-governance?
(1) The use of technology to improve government operations and deliver services to citizens

(2) A form of government run entirely by artificial intelligence
(3) A system of governance without any digital components
(4) The use of traditional communication methods in government

195. Which of the following is NOT a potential benefit of e-governance?
(1) Increased transparency
(2) Enhanced efficiency
(3) Decreased citizen engagement
(4) Improved accessibility to government services

196. What is the primary goal of a government portal in the context of e-governance?
(1) To provide a platform for citizens to voice their grievances
(2) To centralize access to government information and services
(3) To restrict access to government information
(4) To conduct online elections

197. Which term describes the practice of using the internet to engage citizens in the decision-making process?
(1) E-democracy (2) E-commerce
(3) E-surveillance (4) E-voting

198. What is the main purpose of an e-government website?
(1) To provide news and entertainment content
(2) To facilitate online shopping
(3) To offer government services and information to the public
(4) To promote political campaigns

199. Which of the following is an example of an e-governance application?
(1) Social media platforms
(2) Online banking services
(3) Digital marketing campaigns
(4) Electronic tax filing systems

200. What is the role of a citizen portal in e-governance?
(1) To gather information on citizens
(2) To provide a platform for citizens to interact with government agencies
(3) To restrict access to government services
(4) To facilitate international diplomacy

201. Which technology is commonly used for secure authentication and access control in e-governance systems?
(1) Artificial intelligence
(2) Blockchain
(3) Virtual reality
(4) Satellite communication

202. What does "Open Data" refer to in e-governance?
(1) Government data that is classified and unavailable to the public
(2) Government data that is freely available to the public in a machine-readable format
(3) Government data that is only accessible to government employees
(4) Government data that is encrypted for security reasons

203. Which of the following is a key challenge in implementing e-governance initiatives?
(1) Limited availability of internet access
(2) Lack of government transparency
(3) Excessive citizen engagement
(4) Decreased efficiency in government operations

204. What is the term for the process of using digital technologies to transform government operations and improve efficiency?
(1) Digital disruption
(2) E-revolution
(3) Digital transformation
(4) E-inefficiency

205. Which government function is typically NOT addressed through e-governance initiatives?
(1) Healthcare delivery
(2) Tax collection
(3) Social welfare programs
(4) Space exploration

206. What is a "Smart City" in the context of e-governance?
(1) A city with a large population
(2) A city with advanced digital infrastructure to enhance urban living
(3) A city with strict government control
(4) A city without any digital technologies

207. Which of the following is NOT a common e-governance application in the context of public service delivery?
(1) Online education platforms
(2) E-healthcare services
(3) E-voting systems
(4) E-tax filing systems

208. What is the main purpose of a Geographic Information System (GIS) in e-governance?

(1) To provide citizens with entertainment content
(2) To analyze and display spatial data for better decision-making
(3) To facilitate online shopping
(4) To regulate access to government information

209. Which of the following is a common security concern in e-governance systems?
(1) Excessive transparency
(2) Data breaches and cyberattacks
(3) Overuse of physical documents
(4) Lack of authentication mechanisms

210. What is "digital divide" in the context of e-governance?
(1) A government's preference for digital communication
(2) The gap between those who have access to digital technologies and those who do not
(3) The use of digital currencies in government transactions
(4) A type of government document

211. Which of the following is an example of an e-governance initiative aimed at enhancing civic engagement?
(1) Online tax payment system
(2) E-passport application process
(3) Citizen feedback and complaint portal
(4) Military intelligence operations

212. What does the term "m-government" refer to in e-governance?
(1) Government services delivered through mobile devices
(2) Government services delivered through the mail
(3) Government services delivered through media outlets
(4) Government services delivered through social media

213. Which government agency is responsible for overseeing e-governance initiatives in many countries?
(1) Department of Defense
(2) Ministry of Technology
(3) Office of Information and Regulatory Affairs
(4) Department of Transportation

214. What is the primary objective of "e-participation" in e-governance?
(1) To restrict citizen involvement in government decision-making
(2) To encourage citizens to use traditional communication methods
(3) To involve citizens in the policymaking process using digital tools
(4) To eliminate the need for government agencies

215. What is the term for the use of biometric data, such as fingerprints or iris scans, in e-governance for identification and verification purposes?
(1) Multi-factor authentication
(2) Facial recognition
(3) Biometric authentication
(4) Two-step verification

216. What is the role of a Chief Information Officer (CIO) in e-governance?
(1) To manage the country's military
(2) To oversee the implementation of digital technologies in government
(3) To handle public relations for the government
(4) To regulate the media

217. In the context of e-governance, what does "cloud computing" refer to?
(1) The practice of storing government data in physical filing cabinets
(2) The use of physical servers for data storage
(3) The use of remote servers accessed via the internet for data storage and processing
(4) The elimination of data storage in government operations

218. How can ICT improve transparency in government operations?
(1) By reducing access to government information
(2) By limiting citizen participation in decision-making
(3) By providing access to government data and processes
(4) By increasing bureaucratic barriers

219. Which of the following is NOT a common ICT tool used in good governance?
(1) E-voting systems
(2) Social media platforms
(3) Televisions
(4) Government websites

220. What is the primary role of ICT in promoting citizen engagement in governance?
(1) To restrict access to government information
(2) To reduce opportunities for public feedback
(3) To facilitate communication and participation in decision-making
(4) To limit access to government services

221. How can e-participation platforms enhance good governance?
(1) By discouraging public involvement in policy discussions
(2) By centralizing all government operations
(3) By providing citizens with opportunities to contribute to policymaking
(4) By limiting access to government data

222. What is the main purpose of an open data initiative in the context of good governance?
(1) To restrict access to government information
(2) To make government data available to the public in a usable format
(3) To limit government transparency
(4) To reduce citizen engagement

223. How can ICT improve the efficiency of public service delivery in governance?
(1) By increasing bureaucratic hurdles
(2) By decreasing access to government services
(3) By streamlining processes and reducing paperwork
(4) By discouraging citizen engagement

224. Which term is used to describe the practice of using digital technologies to transform government operations?
(1) Digital disruption
(2) E-transformation
(3) ICT revolution
(4) Digital governance

225. What is the role of a Chief Information Officer (CIO) in promoting ICT use in good governance?
(1) To limit access to government data
(2) To oversee the implementation of digital technologies in government
(3) To promote traditional communication methods
(4) To regulate the media

226. How can ICT support the monitoring and evaluation of government programs and policies?
(1) By limiting access to program data
(2) By providing real-time data collection and analysis tools
(3) By decreasing transparency in program outcomes
(4) By eliminating the need for program evaluation

227. What is the primary goal of an e-government website?
(1) To promote government secrecy
(2) To restrict access to government services
(3) To offer government services and information to the public
(4) To reduce citizen engagement

228. In the context of ICT use in governance, what is "digital inclusion"?
(1) The practice of excluding certain groups from accessing government services
(2) The effort to provide equal access to ICT and government services for all citizens
(3) The use of digital currencies for government transactions
(4) The elimination of digital technologies in government operations

229. Which of the following is NOT a potential benefit of using ICT in public administration?
(1) Improved access to government services for remote areas
(2) Enhanced transparency and accountability
(3) Increased bureaucracy and paperwork
(4) More efficient government operations

230. What term is used to describe the practice of using ICT to improve government-citizen interactions and services?
(1) E-transparency (2) E-democracy
(3) E-participation (4) E-governance

231. How can ICT enhance public accountability in good governance?
(1) By restricting access to government information
(2) By increasing government secrecy
(3) By providing mechanisms for citizens to hold officials accountable
(4) By limiting citizen engagement

232. What is the role of social media platforms in promoting good governance?

(1) To decrease transparency in government operations
(2) To limit public discourse on political issues
(3) To facilitate public discussions, information sharing, and feedback
(4) To discourage citizen engagement

233. What does the term "m-government" refer to in the context of ICT and governance?
(1) Government services provided through traditional means
(2) Government services provided through media outlets
(3) Government services delivered through mobile devices
(4) Government services provided through postal services

234. Which of the following is a common security concern in ICT use for good governance?
(1) Limited access to government data
(2) Inefficient government operations
(3) Data breaches and cyberattacks
(4) Excessive transparency

235. What is the primary objective of "e-democracy" in the context of ICT and governance?
(1) To reduce citizen engagement in political processes
(2) To centralize government operations
(3) To involve citizens in political decision-making using digital tools
(4) To eliminate government transparency

236. What term is used to describe the practice of using biometric data, such as fingerprints or iris scans, for identification and verification in governance processes?
(1) Multi-factor authentication
(2) Facial recognition
(3) Biometric authentication
(4) Two-step verification

237. Which of the following is an example of an e-governance application aimed at enhancing civic engagement?
(1) Online tax payment system
(2) E-passport application process
(3) Citizen feedback and complaint portal
(4) Military intelligence operations

238. In the context of ICT and governance, what is "cloud computing"?
(1) The practice of storing government data in physical filing cabinets
(2) The use of physical servers for data storage
(3) The use of remote servers accessed via the internet for data storage and processing
(4) The elimination of data storage in government operations

239. What is the term for the practice of using digital technologies to transform government operations and improve efficiency?
(1) Digital disruption
(2) E-revolution
(3) Digital transformation
(4) E-inefficiency

240. How can ICT contribute to disaster management and emergency response in governance?
(1) By limiting access to emergency information
(2) By providing real-time data on disasters and coordinating response efforts
(3) By decreasing transparency in emergency operations
(4) By discouraging citizen engagement during emergencies

241. What is the term for the use of ICT to transform traditional government services into digital formats?
(1) E-commerce (2) E-government
(3) E-revolution (4) E-society

242. When were the Millennium Development Goals (MDGs) adopted by the United Nations?
(1) 1995 (2) 2000
(3) 2005 (4) 2010

243. How many MDGs were there in total?
(1) 5 (2) 8
(3) 10 (4) 12

244. Which of the following was NOT one of the MDGs?
(1) Gender equality and women's empowerment
(2) Climate change mitigation
(3) Eradication of extreme poverty and hunger
(4) Universal primary education

245. Which organization played a central role in monitoring and promoting the achievement of the MDGs?
(1) World Trade Organization (WTO)
(2) World Health Organization (WHO)
(3) United Nations Development Programme (UNDP)
(4) International Monetary Fund (IMF)

246. Which MDG aimed to reduce child mortality?
(1) MDG 1 (2) MDG 2
(3) MDG 4 (4) MDG 6

247. The first MDG aimed to eradicate extreme poverty and hunger. What was the specific target year for achieving this goal?
(1) 2020 (2) 2015
(3) 2030 (4) 2040

248. Which MDG aimed to promote environmental sustainability?
(1) MDG 3 (2) MDG 5
(3) MDG 7 (4) MDG 8

249. Which region made the most significant progress in achieving the MDGs, particularly in reducing poverty and child mortality rates?
(1) Sub-Saharan Africa
(2) Latin America
(3) South Asia (4) Western Europe

250. Which MDG focused on improving maternal health?
(1) MDG 3 (2) MDG 4
(3) MDG 5 (4) MDG 6

251. The MDGs aimed to achieve universal primary education. What specific target was set for this goal?
(1) Ensure that all children complete primary school
(2) Ensure that all children complete secondary school
(3) Ensure that all children attend school at least one day per week
(4) Ensure that all children have access to vocational training

252. Which MDG aimed to combat HIV/AIDS, malaria, and other diseases?
(1) MDG 4 (2) MDG 5
(3) MDG 6 (4) MDG 7

253. Which of the following is NOT a component of MDG 8 (Global Partnership for Development)?
(1) Trade (2) Debt relief
(3) Technology (4) Space exploration

254. What was the overall deadline for achieving the MDGs?
(1) 2005 (2) 2010
(3) 2015 (4) 2020

255. Which MDG aimed to promote gender equality and empower women?
(1) MDG 2 (2) MDG 3
(3) MDG 5 (4) MDG 6

256. Which country was often cited as a successful case in achieving many of the MDGs, particularly in poverty reduction and gender equality?
(1) India (2) China
(3) Brazil (4) Nigeria

257. The MDGs were succeeded by a new set of global development goals known as
(1) Sustainable Development Goals (SDGs)
(2) Economic Growth Goals (EGGs)
(3) Global Poverty Eradication Goals (GPEGs)
(4) Millennium Development Priorities (MDPs)

258. How many years did the world have to work toward achieving the MDGs?
(1) 5 years (2) 10 years
(3) 15 years (4) 20 years

259. Which MDG focused on ensuring environmental sustainability, including access to safe drinking water and sanitation?
(1) MDG 1 (2) MDG 3
(3) MDG 6 (4) MDG 7

260. Which MDG aimed to reduce the under-five mortality rate?
(1) MDG 2 (2) MDG 4
(3) MDG 6 (4) MDG 8

261. Which international conference in 2000 marked the adoption of the Millennium Declaration and the MDGs?
(1) United Nations Climate Change Conference (COP)
(2) United Nations Millennium Summit
(3) United Nations Human Rights Council (UNHRC)
(4) United Nations Security Council (UNSC)

262. Which MDG aimed to develop a global partnership for development?
(1) MDG 4 (2) MDG 5
(3) MDG 6 (4) MDG 8

263. What is the main difference between the MDGs and the Sustainable Development Goals (SDGs)?
(1) The number of goals
(2) The focus on economic growth
(3) The inclusion of climate change as a standalone goal
(4) The absence of a timeline

264. Which MDG aimed to promote access to affordable and essential medicines?
(1) MDG 1 (2) MDG 5
(3) MDG 6 (4) MDG 8

265. Which MDG aimed to reduce the maternal mortality ratio?
(1) MDG 2 (2) MDG 4
(3) MDG 5 (4) MDG 7

266. What was the primary purpose of the MDGs?
(1) To address global political conflicts
(2) To promote cultural diversity
(3) To improve global health and living standards
(4) To advance space exploration

267. What is the primary driver of climate change?
(1) Deforestation
(2) Natural climate variability
(3) Human activities, particularly the burning of fossil fuels
(4) Solar radiation fluctuations

268. Which international agreement aims to combat climate change by limiting global warming to well below 2 degrees Celsius above pre-industrial levels?
(1) Paris Agreement
(2) Kyoto Protocol
(3) Montreal Protocol
(4) Copenhagen Accord

269. In the context of climate change, what is the term "mitigation" referring to?
(1) Adapting to changing climate conditions
(2) Reducing greenhouse gas emissions
(3) Preparing for extreme weather events
(4) Climate finance

270. Which greenhouse gas is the primary contributor to global warming?
(1) Methane (CH_4)
(2) Carbon dioxide (CO_2)
(3) Nitrous oxide (N_2O)
(4) Water vapor (H_2O)

271. What is the "greenhouse effect" in the context of climate change?
(1) The cooling of the Earth's atmosphere
(2) The natural process by which greenhouse gases trap heat in the Earth's atmosphere
(3) The cooling effect of increased forest cover
(4) The reflection of sunlight by polar ice caps

272. Which country is the largest emitter of greenhouse gases?
(1) India (2) Russia
(3) China (4) United States

273. What is the term for the gradual rise in global average temperatures due to increased greenhouse gas concentrations?
(1) Global cooling
(2) Climate oscillation
(3) Global warming
(4) Thermohaline circulation

274. How do rising sea levels contribute to the social impacts of climate change?
(1) By increasing agricultural yields
(2) By creating new opportunities for coastal development
(3) By displacing communities and causing coastal erosion
(4) By reducing the risk of flooding

275. What is climate adaptation?
(1) Actions to prevent the occurrence of climate change
(2) Strategies to reduce greenhouse gas emissions
(3) Measures taken to adjust to the impacts of climate change
(4) Efforts to mitigate the effects of climate change

276. Which of the following is a consequence of climate change on human health?
(1) Increased access to clean water and sanitation
(2) Reduced incidence of infectious diseases
(3) Heat-related illnesses and the spread of vector-borne diseases
(4) Improved food security

277. What is the term for the displacement of people due to climate change-related impacts, such as sea-level rise or extreme weather events?
(1) Environmental migration
(2) Climate relocation
(3) Green resettlement
(4) Eco-emigration

278. How can climate change exacerbate social inequalities?
(1) By reducing the cost of renewable energy
(2) By increasing access to education
(3) By disproportionately affecting vulnerable communities
(4) By promoting gender equality

279. Which group of people is often considered the most vulnerable to the social impacts of climate change?
(1) Urban populations
(2) Wealthy individuals
(3) Indigenous communities and low-income groups
(4) Climate scientists

280. What is the role of the Intergovernmental Panel on Climate Change (IPCC) in addressing climate change?
(1) Implementing climate adaptation projects worldwide
(2) Conducting research on renewable energy technologies
(3) Assessing scientific information related to climate change and its impacts
(4) Promoting international climate negotiations

281. How can climate change affect food security?
(1) By increasing crop yields due to higher temperatures
(2) By reducing the availability of freshwater resources for agriculture
(3) By decreasing the demand for agricultural products
(4) By improving soil quality

282. What is the term for the practice of offsetting greenhouse gas emissions by investing in projects that reduce emissions elsewhere?
(1) Carbon capture
(2) Carbon neutrality
(3) Carbon footprint
(4) Carbon trading

283. Which international climate conference led to the adoption of the Paris Agreement in 2015?
(1) COP21 (Conference of the Parties to the UNFCCC)
(2) COP15
(3) COP27
(4) COP10

284. What is the term for the financial support provided to developing countries to help them address climate change and reduce greenhouse gas emissions?
(1) Climate finance
(2) Carbon pricing
(3) Green taxation
(4) Adaptation funding

285. How can the "tragedy of the commons" concept be applied to climate change?
(1) It highlights the importance of international cooperation in addressing climate change.
(2) It suggests that individuals and nations should act in their self-interest to solve the climate crisis.
(3) It emphasizes the role of market forces in reducing greenhouse gas emissions.
(4) It promotes the idea that natural resources should be privatized to prevent overuse.

286. What is the main goal of the Green Climate Fund (GCF)?
(1) To promote green energy initiatives in developed countries
(2) To support climate adaptation and mitigation projects in developing countries
(3) To reduce greenhouse gas emissions from industrial processes
(4) To establish a global carbon market

287. Which term describes the phenomenon where certain groups, regions, or countries bear a disproportionate burden of the negative impacts of climate change despite contributing less to its causes?
(1) Climate justice (2) Carbon parity
(3) Environmental equity
(4) Sustainable development

288. What is the term for the concept that future generations have the right to inherit a planet that is not irreversibly damaged by the actions of the present generation?
(1) Intergenerational equity
(2) Carbon neutrality
(3) Ecological footprint (4) Carbon offset

289. Which international organization monitors and reports on global progress toward climate goals and agreements?
(1) United Nations Security Council (UNSC)
(2) World Trade Organization (WTO)
(3) United Nations Framework Convention on Climate Change (UNFCCC)
(4) International Monetary Fund (IMF)

290. What is the term for the practice of intentionally spreading false or misleading information to downplay or deny the reality of climate change?
(1) Climate denialism
(2) Environmental extremism
(3) Climate skepticism
(4) Greenwashing

291. How can civil society and grassroots movements contribute to addressing climate change?
(1) By negotiating international climate agreements
(2) By conducting climate research
(3) By raising awareness, advocating for policy changes, and holding governments and corporations accountable

(4) By implementing large-scale climate adaptation projects

292. When was the Montreal Protocol on Substances that Deplete the Ozone Layer adopted?
(1) 1985 (2) 1987
(3) 1988 (4) 1990

293. What is the primary goal of the Montreal Protocol?
(1) To address climate change
(2) To protect endangered species
(3) To reduce emissions of greenhouse gases
(4) To protect the ozone layer

294. Which ozone-depleting substances are controlled under the Montreal Protocol?
(1) Carbon dioxide (CO_2)
(2) Methane (CH_4)
(3) Chlorofluorocarbons (CFCs) and other ozone-depleting chemicals
(4) Sulfur dioxide (SO_2)

295. What is the ozone layer?
(1) A layer of smog in the atmosphere
(2) A layer of ozone gas in the Earth's stratosphere that absorbs and filters out harmful ultraviolet (UV) radiation from the sun
(3) A layer of oxygen gas in the troposphere
(4) A layer of carbon dioxide in the mesosphere

296. Which international organization administers the Montreal Protocol?
(1) United Nations Environment Programme (UNEP)
(2) United Nations Development Programme (UNDP)
(3) World Health Organization (WHO)
(4) International Atomic Energy Agency (IAEA)

297. What is the term for chemicals that break down ozone molecules in the stratosphere?
(1) Greenhouse gases
(2) Ozone-friendly chemicals
(3) Ozone-depleting substances
(4) Ultraviolet blockers

298. Which ozone-depleting substances were commonly used in refrigerants and air conditioning systems before being phased out under the Montreal Protocol?
(1) Methane (CH_4)
(2) Carbon dioxide (CO_2)
(3) Hydrochlorofluorocarbons (HCFCs) and Chlorofluorocarbons (CFCs)
(4) Nitrous oxide (N_2O)

299. What is the primary reason for the phase-out of ozone-depleting substances under the Montreal Protocol?
(1) To combat global warming
(2) To reduce the production of toxic chemicals
(3) To protect human health from skin cancer
(4) To prevent harmful UV radiation from reaching the Earth's surface

300. Which gas is used as a replacement for CFCs and HCFCs in many refrigeration and air conditioning systems to reduce their impact on the ozone layer?
(1) Sulfur hexafluoride (SF_6)
(2) Hydrofluorocarbons (HFCs)
(3) Methane (CH_4)
(4) Nitrous oxide (N_2O)

301. What is the "ozone hole," and where is it typically found?
(1) A hole in the ozone layer caused by human activities; it is found over Antarctica.
(2) A natural phenomenon where ozone levels decrease temporarily during winter months; it occurs over the Arctic.
(3) A region of the atmosphere where ozone levels are abnormally high; it is found over the equator.
(4) A gap in the ozone layer caused by volcanic eruptions; it can occur anywhere.

302. Which amendment to the Montreal Protocol accelerated the phase-out of HCFCs (hydrochlorofluorocarbons) due to their contribution to ozone depletion and global warming?
(1) Beijing Amendment
(2) Vienna Amendment
(3) London Amendment
(4) Copenhagen Amendment

303. What is the role of the Multilateral Fund for the Implementation of the Montreal Protocol?
(1) To finance research on ozone-depleting substances
(2) To provide grants and loans to developing countries to help them meet their obligations under the Protocol
(3) To enforce compliance with the Protocol's provisions
(4) To conduct ozone layer monitoring

304. How often do the parties to the Montreal Protocol meet to assess its progress and negotiate amendments?
(1) Every year

(2) Every two years
(3) Every three years
(4) Every five years

305. What is the term for the complete removal or destruction of ozone-depleting substances from the environment?
(1) Ozone depletion
(2) Ozone recovery
(3) Ozone layer restoration
(4) Ozone destruction

306. Which of the following is a phase-out schedule for ozone-depleting substances under the Montreal Protocol?
(1) Gradual reduction followed by a complete ban
(2) Immediate ban without a phase-out period
(3) A temporary increase in production
(4) An annual quota system

307. What is the "ozone-friendly" alternative to CFCs used in many aerosol propellants and refrigeration systems?
(1) Hydrochlorofluorocarbons (HCFCs)
(2) Hydrofluorocarbons (HFCs)
(3) Hydrobromofluorocarbons (HBFCs)
(4) Hydroxychlorofluorocarbons (HCFOs)

308. Which country was the first to ratify the Montreal Protocol?
(1) United States (2) Canada
(3) Norway (4) Australia

309. Which United Nations body established the Montreal Protocol?
(1) United Nations General Assembly
(2) United Nations Security Council
(3) United Nations Economic and Social Council
(4) United Nations Environment Programme (UNEP)

310. In addition to ozone layer protection, what other benefit is associated with reducing the use of ozone-depleting substances?
(1) Reduced air pollution
(2) Increased agricultural productivity
(3) Lower energy consumption
(4) Mitigation of climate change

311. What is the penalty for non-compliance with the Montreal Protocol?
(1) Economic sanctions
(2) Trade restrictions
(3) Fines and penalties
(4) Expulsion from the United Nations

312. What is the relationship between the Vienna Convention for the Protection of the Ozone Layer and the Montreal Protocol?
(1) The Vienna Convention is a separate treaty unrelated to ozone protection.
(2) The Vienna Convention established the framework for the Montreal Protocol, which is its protocol.
(3) The Vienna Convention and the Montreal Protocol are two independent treaties with no connection.
(4) The Vienna Convention is an earlier version of the Montreal Protocol.

313. Which chemical substance used in fire extinguishers and as a refrigerant was the first to be phased out under the Montreal Protocol?
(1) Carbon tetrachloride (CCl_4)
(2) Hydrochlorofluorocarbons (HCFCs)
(3) Halon-1211
(4) Methyl chloroform (CH_3CCl_3)

314. Which of the following statements about the Kigali Amendment to the Montreal Protocol is true?
(1) It addresses the phase-out of carbon dioxide emissions.
(2) It aims to phase out hydrofluorocarbons (HFCs) due to their high global warming potential.
(3) It focuses on reducing methane emissions from agricultural practices.
(4) It establishes a global carbon trading system.

315. Which of the following is NOT one of the four groups of chemicals controlled by the Montreal Protocol?
(1) Halons
(2) Chlorofluorocarbons (CFCs)
(3) Hydrochlorofluorocarbons (HCFCs)
(4) Methane (CH_4)

316. What event led to the discovery of the ozone hole over Antarctica and contributed to the urgency of addressing ozone depletion?
(1) A volcanic eruption
(2) A nuclear weapons test
(3) The explosion of the Space Shuttle Challenger
(4) Observations by scientists in the 1980s

317. What was the main theme of the Rio Earth Summit?
(1) Climate change mitigation
(2) Sustainable development

(3) Biodiversity conservation
(4) Human rights

318. Who was the Secretary-General of the Rio Earth Summit in 1992?
(1) Kofi Annan
(2) Javier Pérez de Cuéllar
(3) Gro Harlem Brundtland
(4) Maurice Strong

319. Which document was adopted at the Rio Earth Summit to provide a comprehensive framework for sustainable development?
(1) The Kyoto Protocol
(2) The Rio Declaration on Environment and Development
(3) The United Nations Framework Convention on Climate Change (UNFCCC)
(4) The Cartagena Protocol on Biosafety

320. What is the term used to describe the series of principles and recommendations on environmental protection and sustainable development adopted at the Rio Earth Summit?
(1) The Earth Charter
(2) The Earth Manifesto
(3) The Earth Accord
(4) The Earth Covenant

321. Which world leader was a prominent advocate for sustainable development at the Rio Earth Summit and played a key role in its success?
(1) Margaret Thatcher
(2) Mikhail Gorbachev
(3) Ronald Reagan
(4) Nelson Mandela

322. What major international treaty aimed at reducing greenhouse gas emissions was opened for signature at the Rio Earth Summit?
(1) The Paris Agreement
(2) The Kyoto Protocol
(3) The Montreal Protocol
(4) The Stockholm Convention

323. The Convention on Biological Diversity (CBD) was one of the key agreements reached at the Rio Earth Summit. What is the primary goal of the CBD?
(1) To address climate change
(2) To promote sustainable agriculture
(3) To conserve biodiversity and ensure its sustainable use
(4) To regulate fisheries

324. Which term describes the concept of meeting the needs of the present without compromising the ability of future generations to meet their own needs?
(1) Environmental protection
(2) Ecological sustainability
(3) Sustainable development
(4) Resource conservation

325. What is the name of the global action plan for sustainable development that was adopted at the Rio Earth Summit?
(1) The Earth Agenda
(2) The Agenda 21
(3) The Millennium Development Goals
(4) The Sustainable Development Goals

326. Which of the following topics was NOT a major focus of discussion at the Rio Earth Summit?
(1) Desertification
(2) Oceans and marine resources
(3) Nuclear disarmament
(4) Freshwater resources

327. The concept of "common but differentiated responsibilities" was emphasized at the Rio Earth Summit. What does it refer to?
(1) The idea that all countries should have equal responsibilities for environmental protection
(2) The recognition that developed countries bear a greater historical responsibility for environmental degradation and should take the lead in addressing it
(3) The need for stricter environmental regulations for developing countries
(4) The principle of shared management of natural resources

328. Which of the following is NOT one of the three pillars of sustainable development as defined at the Rio Earth Summit?
(1) Economic development
(2) Environmental protection
(3) Social equity
(4) Cultural preservation

329. What is the term for the process of integrating environmental, social, and economic considerations into decision-making to promote sustainable development?
(1) Sustainability assessment
(2) Greenwashing
(3) Triple bottom line
(4) Environmental impact assessment

330. What role did the Rio Earth Summit play in shaping international environmental governance?

(1) It established a new global environmental organization.
(2) It led to the creation of the World Trade Organization (WTO).
(3) It laid the foundation for the United Nations Environment Programme (UNEP).
(4) It reinforced the authority of the International Atomic Energy Agency (IAEA).

331. The term "Agenda 21" refers to
(1) A plan for global disarmament
(2) A comprehensive action plan for sustainable development
(3) A treaty on the protection of indigenous peoples' rights
(4) A protocol on the conservation of endangered species

332. Who was the President of Brazil during the Rio Earth Summit in 1992?
(1) Fernando Henrique Cardoso
(2) Jair Bolsonaro
(3) Luiz Inácio Lula da Silva
(4) Fernando Collor de Mello

333. Which major group of stakeholders at the Rio Earth Summit represented non-governmental organizations (NGOs) and played a significant role in advocating for environmental and social issues?
(1) Business and industry
(2) Indigenous peoples
(3) Youth organizations
(4) Women's groups

334. Which key document adopted at the Rio Earth Summit set out principles for the conservation and sustainable use of forests worldwide?
(1) The Earth Charter
(2) The Rio Declaration on Forests
(3) The Forest Principles
(4) The Kyoto Protocol on Forests

335. Which country hosted the Rio Earth Summit in 1992?
(1) United States (2) Brazil
(3) Switzerland (4) France

336. What term is often used to describe the series of environmental and sustainability goals and targets that were formulated at the Rio Earth Summit?
(1) The Rio Goals
(2) The Earth Objectives
(3) The Sustainable Development Targets
(4) The Rio Mandates

337. What term refers to the process of governments formally agreeing to be bound by an international treaty or agreement, often through a signature followed by ratification?
(1) Adoption
(2) Accreditation
(3) Accession
(4) Alliance

338. The Rio Earth Summit marked the beginning of a new era in international environmental cooperation. Which subsequent global summits have built on its outcomes?
(1) The G7 Summits
(2) The World Economic Forum (WEF) meetings
(3) The Earth Summits (Rio+5, Rio+10, etc.)
(4) The United Nations General Assembly sessions

339. What term describes the practice of promoting economic development and growth while minimizing the negative impacts on the environment and ensuring social equity?
(1) Sustainable development
(2) Environmentalism
(3) Economic globalization
(4) Capitalism

340. What major outcome document of the Rio Earth Summit outlined the Rio Principles and Agenda 21, the action plan for sustainable development?
(1) The Earth Charter
(2) The Rio Declaration on Environment and Development
(3) The Stockholm Declaration
(4) The Rio Declaration on Social Equity

341. What is the term used for the maximum amount of greenhouse gases a country is allowed to emit under the Kyoto Protocol?
(1) Emission quota (2) Carbon budget
(3) Emission target (4) Pollution cap

342. Which group of countries, under the Kyoto Protocol, is categorized as Annex I Parties and has legally binding emission reduction targets?
(1) Developing countries
(2) Least developed countries
(3) Industrialized countries
(4) Non-Annex I Parties

343. What is the commitment period of the Kyoto Protocol, during which countries are obligated to meet their emission reduction targets?
(1) 5 years (2) 10 years
(3) 15 years (4) 20 years

344. Which gas is the primary focus of the Kyoto Protocol's efforts to reduce emissions due to its significant contribution to global warming?
(1) Methane (CH_4)
(2) Carbon dioxide (CO_2)
(3) Nitrous oxide (N_2O)
(4) Sulfur hexafluoride (SF_6)

345. Which country hosted the Third Conference of the Parties (COP_3) where the Kyoto Protocol was adopted?
(1) Japan (2) United States
(3) Canada (4) Germany

346. What is the term for the process by which a country can earn emissions reduction credits by investing in greenhouse gas reduction projects in another country?
(1) Carbon offsetting
(2) Emission trading
(3) Carbon capture and storage
(4) Greenhouse gas accounting

347. The "flexibility mechanisms" under the Kyoto Protocol include all of the following EXCEPT
(1) Clean Development Mechanism (CDM)
(2) Joint Implementation (JI)
(3) Emission Reduction Fund (ERF)
(4) International Emissions Trading (IET)

348. Which country is the largest emitter of greenhouse gases that did not ratify the Kyoto Protocol?
(1) China (2) India
(3) United States (4) Russia

349. What is the "carbon sink" concept in the context of the Kyoto Protocol?
(1) A technology for capturing carbon emissions from power plants
(2) A method for measuring emissions from deforestation
(3) Natural or human-made systems that absorb more carbon dioxide than they release
(4) The process of converting carbon dioxide into a solid form for storage

350. Which of the following greenhouse gases is primarily associated with agriculture and livestock production?
(1) Carbon dioxide (CO_2)
(2) Methane (CH_4)
(3) Nitrous oxide (N_2O)
(4) Chlorofluorocarbons (CFCs)

351. What is the term for the process of "carbon trading" allowed under the Kyoto Protocol, where countries can buy and sell emissions credits?
(1) Emission offsetting
(2) Cap and trade
(3) Carbon taxation
(4) Carbon capture

352. The Kyoto Protocol's first commitment period lasted from 2008 to
(1) 2010 (2) 2012
(3) 2015 (4) 2020

353. Which of the following countries was a notable non-Annex I Party to the Kyoto Protocol and was not required to set emission reduction targets?
(1) Canada (2) Japan
(3) Australia (4) China

354. What is the role of the Clean Development Mechanism (CDM) under the Kyoto Protocol?
(1) To reduce emissions from industrial processes
(2) To promote sustainable development in developing countries through emissions reduction projects
(3) To enforce emission reduction targets for Annex I Parties
(4) To regulate emissions from the aviation industry

355. What major international conference resulted in the Kyoto Protocol being adopted as a legally binding treaty?
(1) Earth Summit in Rio de Janeiro (1992)
(2) Bali Climate Conference (2007)
(3) Paris Climate Conference (2015)
(4) Copenhagen Climate Conference (2009)

356. The Kyoto Protocol is an extension of which earlier international environmental treaty?
(1) The United Nations Framework Convention on Climate Change (UNFCCC)
(2) The Montreal Protocol on Substances that Deplete the Ozone Layer
(3) The Ramsar Convention on Wetlands
(4) The Basel Convention on Hazardous Waste

357. What is the primary greenhouse gas associated with land-use changes, such as deforestation and forest degradation?
(1) Carbon dioxide (CO_2)
(2) Methane (CH_4)
(3) Nitrous oxide (N_2O)
(4) Sulfur hexafluoride (SF_6)

358. Which city hosted the Fourth Conference of the Parties (COP4) to the United Nations Framework Convention on Climate Change (UNFCCC), where the Kyoto Protocol negotiations took place?
(1) Berlin, Germany
(2) Paris, France
(3) Kyoto, Japan
(4) Copenhagen, Denmark

359. What is the name of the amendment to the Kyoto Protocol that extended the second commitment period for emission reductions beyond the initial commitment period?
(1) The Bali Amendment
(2) The Copenhagen Amendment
(3) The Marrakech Amendment
(4) The Doha Amendment

360. Which of the following greenhouse gases has the highest global warming potential (GWP) over a 100-year period?
(1) Carbon dioxide (CO_2)
(2) Methane (CH_4)
(3) Nitrous oxide (N_2O)
(4) Sulfur hexafluoride (SF_6)

361. What is the term for the "basket of greenhouse gases" used to calculate a country's emissions under the Kyoto Protocol?
(1) Emission factors
(2) Carbon footprint
(3) Carbon equivalent
(4) Emission units

362. What is the long-term temperature goal of the Paris Agreement?
(1) Limit global warming to 1 degree Celsius
(2) Limit global warming to 2 degrees Celsius
(3) Limit global warming to 3 degrees Celsius
(4) Limit global warming to 4 degrees Celsius

363. What is the term for the process of increasing the ambition of climate action over time to achieve the goals of the Paris Agreement?
(1) Climate adaptation
(2) Climate mitigation
(3) Climate finance
(4) Ratcheting up

364. Under the Paris Agreement, countries submit and update their climate action plans. What are these plans called?
(1) Carbon budgets
(2) Nationally Determined Contributions (NDCs)
(3) Climate treaties
(4) Green New Deals

365. Which greenhouse gas is the primary focus of the Paris Agreement's efforts to reduce emissions due to its significant contribution to global warming?
(1) Methane (CH_4)
(2) Carbon dioxide (CO_2)
(3) Nitrous oxide (N_2O)
(4) Sulfur hexafluoride (SF_6)

366. How often are countries required to communicate their updated climate action plans under the Paris Agreement?
(1) Every year
(2) Every two years
(3) Every five years
(4) Every decade

367. Which term is used in the Paris Agreement to refer to the process of providing financial support to developing countries for climate adaptation and mitigation efforts?
(1) Green financing
(2) Climate investment
(3) Climate finance
(4) Sustainable development aid

368. Which international organization serves as the secretariat for the Paris Agreement, facilitating its implementation and tracking progress?
(1) United Nations Environment Programme (UNEP)
(2) International Monetary Fund (IMF)
(3) World Bank
(4) United Nations Framework Convention on Climate Change (UNFCCC)

369. What is the role of the Global Stocktake under the Paris Agreement?
(1) To regulate greenhouse gas emissions from industries
(2) To assess the progress of countries in meeting their climate commitments
(3) To oversee the Green Climate Fund
(4) To monitor deforestation rates

370. Which of the following countries announced its intention to withdraw from the Paris Agreement but later reversed that decision?
(1) China (2) Russia
(3) United States (4) India

371. What is the term for the goal of the Paris Agreement to achieve a balance between sources of greenhouse gas emissions and their removal by sinks in the second half of this century?

(1) Carbon neutrality
(2) Net zero emissions
(3) Emission reduction target
(4) Climate resilience

372. Which of the following is NOT a key principle of the Paris Agreement?
(1) Common but differentiated responsibilities
(2) Equity and justice
(3) Market-based mechanisms
(4) Transparency and accountability

373. What role did the 2015 United Nations Climate Change Conference (COP21) play in the adoption of the Paris Agreement?
(1) It resulted in the formal adoption of the Paris Agreement text.
(2) It was the first meeting to discuss climate change.
(3) It focused solely on adaptation measures.
(4) It rejected the Paris Agreement.

374. Which country initiated the formation of the International Solar Alliance (ISA)?
(1) India (2) China
(3) United States (4) Germany

375. Where is the headquarters of the International Solar Alliance (ISA) located?
(1) Paris, France
(2) New Delhi, India
(3) Geneva, Switzerland
(4) Washington, D.C., USA

376. What is the primary objective of the International Solar Alliance (ISA)?
(1) To promote wind energy
(2) To promote nuclear energy
(3) To promote solar energy adoption and facilitate cooperation among solar-rich countries
(4) To reduce greenhouse gas emissions

377. Which two key elements of solar energy are the focus of the ISA's efforts?
(1) Solar cooking and solar transportation
(2) Solar panels and solar batteries
(3) Solar power generation and solar water heating
(4) Solar air conditioning and solar farming

378. How many member countries were required to formally establish the International Solar Alliance (ISA)?
(1) 5 (2) 20
(3) 50 (4) 121

379. What is the significance of the Tropic of Cancer and the Tropic of Capricorn in the context of the International Solar Alliance (ISA)?
(1) They are the locations of the ISA's first solar projects.
(2) Countries located between these latitudes receive abundant sunlight and are the primary target of ISA initiatives.
(3) They are the geographical boundaries of ISA membership.
(4) They are the names of the two main branches of the ISA secretariat.

380. Which international climate agreement is closely associated with the work of the International Solar Alliance (ISA)?
(1) The Paris Agreement
(2) The Kyoto Protocol
(3) The Montreal Protocol
(4) The Rio Declaration

381. What is the ISA's target for the deployment of solar energy capacity by 2030?
(1) 50 GW (2) 100 GW
(3) 250 GW (4) 500 GW

382. What role does the ISA play in facilitating the deployment of solar energy projects in member countries?
(1) It provides funding for solar projects.
(2) It conducts research on solar technologies.
(3) It acts as a platform for collaboration and knowledge sharing.
(4) It enforces international solar energy regulations.

383. Which financial institution is closely associated with the International Solar Alliance (ISA) and supports solar projects in member countries?
(1) World Bank
(2) International Monetary Fund (IMF)
(3) Asian Development Bank (ADB)
(4) European Investment Bank (EIB)

384. What is the name of the ISA's program that aims to mobilize USD 1 trillion in investment for solar energy by 2030?
(1) Solar Futures
(2) One Sun, One World, One Grid
(3) Solar Financing Initiative
(4) Solar Power Revolution

385. Which key event in India marked the launch of the International Solar Alliance (ISA) in 2015?
(1) The inauguration of the world's largest solar power plant

(2) The hosting of the United Nations Climate Change Conference (COP21)
(3) The signing of the Kyoto Protocol
(4) The adoption of the Sustainable Development Goals (SDGs)

386. How many solar-rich countries are eligible for membership in the International Solar Alliance (ISA)?
(1) 52 (2) 121
(3) 195 (4) 30

387. What is the ISA's flagship initiative aimed at promoting solar energy collaboration among member countries and creating a global solar grid?
(1) Solar Revolution Initiative
(2) One Sun, One World, One Grid
(3) Solar Cooperation Network
(4) SunConnect Initiative

388. Which ancient Indian text is often considered the foundation of the traditional Indian education system?
(1) Bhagavad Gita
(2) Arthashastra
(3) Upanishads
(4) Manusmriti

389. Which ancient Indian city was known for its famous university, where scholars from various parts of the world came to study?
(1) Nalanda (2) Varanasi
(3) Pataliputra (4) Taxila

390. The ancient Indian education system was often referred to as the "Gurukula" system. What does "Gurukula" mean?
(1) School of Sages
(2) Teacher's Home
(3) Temple of Learning
(4) Assembly of Scholars

391. Which ancient Indian sage is credited with being the author of the first recorded textbook on economics, known as "Arthashastra"?
(1) Gautama Buddha
(2) Chanakya (Kautilya)
(3) Adi Shankaracharya
(4) Patanjali

392. In ancient India, what were the subjects of study primarily focused on in the education system?
(1) Mathematics and astronomy
(2) Medicine and surgery
(3) Philosophy and spirituality
(4) All of the above

393. The ancient Indian educational institutions, such as Nalanda and Takshashila, were known for their expertise in which field of study?
(1) Literature and poetry
(2) Mathematics and science
(3) Religious studies and philosophy
(4) Politics and governance

394. Who was the famous Buddhist scholar and philosopher associated with the ancient Nalanda University?
(1) Adi Shankaracharya (2) Nagarjuna
(3) Aryabhata (4) Kalidasa

395. In the ancient Indian education system, what was the role of a "Guru"?
(1) A student
(2) A teacher or mentor
(3) A king
(4) A farmer

396. Which ancient Indian mathematician is known for his contributions to the field of mathematics, including the concept of zero and the decimal system?
(1) Aryabhata (2) Brahmagupta
(3) Bhaskara I (4) Sushruta

397. Which ancient Indian text is a compilation of various subjects, including medicine, surgery, and other sciences?
(1) Arthashastra (2) Bhagavad Gita
(3) Charaka Samhita (4) Manusmriti

398. The ancient Indian education system emphasized the study of "Vedas." How many Vedas are there in total?
(1) Two (2) Four
(3) Six (4) Eight

399. What was the medium of instruction in ancient Indian educational institutions like Nalanda and Takshashila?
(1) Sanskrit (2) Pali
(3) Prakrit (4) Classical Tamil

400. Which ancient Indian sage is known for his work "Yoga Sutras," which became a foundational text for the practice of yoga?
(1) Adi Shankaracharya (2) Nagarjuna
(3) Patanjali (4) Chanakya

401. What was the primary purpose of ancient Indian universities like Nalanda and Takshashila?
(1) Religious training
(2) Military training
(3) Scientific research
(4) All of the above

402. Who was the famous Indian mathematician-astronomer who authored the "Aryabhatiya," a significant work in the field of mathematics and astronomy?
(1) Aryabhata (2) Brahmagupta
(3) Bhaskara II (4) Sushruta

403. What was the name of the ancient Indian practice of oral transmission of knowledge from one generation to the next, often associated with the recitation of sacred texts?
(1) Shruti (2) Smriti
(3) Guru-shishya parampara
(4) Varna system

404. In ancient India, what term was used to refer to the board or institution where scholars would gather for intellectual debates and discussions?
(1) Gurukula (2) Vedashala
(3) Sabha (4) Tapascharya

405. Who was the famous grammarian and linguist known for his work "Ashtadhyayi," a comprehensive treatise on Sanskrit grammar?
(1) Panini (2) Kalidasa
(3) Chanakya (4) Nagarjuna

406. What is the name of the ancient Indian system of medicine that emphasizes holistic healing, including herbal remedies and surgery?
(1) Ayurveda (2) Siddha
(3) Unani (4) Naturopathy

407. The ancient Indian education system encouraged students to lead a disciplined and virtuous life. What term describes this aspect of education?
(1) Dharma (2) Karma
(3) Moksha (4) Nirvana

408. Which ancient Indian university is known for its association with the great teacher Charaka and his contributions to Ayurvedic medicine?
(1) Nalanda (2) Takshashila
(3) Vikramashila (4) Pushpagiri

409. Who was the famous Indian philosopher and teacher known for his contributions to the Advaita Vedanta tradition?
(1) Shankaracharya
(2) Nagarjuna
(3) Chandragupta Maurya
(4) Sushruta

410. Which ancient Indian text, attributed to Chanakya, provides insights into statecraft, economics, and political philosophy?
(1) Bhagavad Gita (2) Manusmriti
(3) Arthashastra (4) Upanishads

411. In the ancient Indian education system, what was the term used to describe the final stage of life, where a student becomes a householder?
(1) Grihastha (2) Brahmacharya
(3) Sannyasa (4) Varnashrama

412. Which ancient Indian university was known for its expertise in the field of medicine and surgery, as described in texts like the "Sushruta Samhita"?
(1) Nalanda (2) Takshashila
(3) Vikramashila (4) Pushpagiri

413. What is the primary purpose of NAAC?
(1) To conduct university entrance exams
(2) To accredit and assess higher education institutions in India
(3) To provide scholarships to students
(4) To promote research and development in higher education

414. Which organization in India is responsible for setting up NAAC and overseeing its operations?
(1) Ministry of Education
(2) University Grants Commission (UGC)
(3) National Board of Accreditation (NBA)
(4) All India Council for Technical Education (AICTE)

415. What is the highest grade awarded to an institution by NAAC for accreditation?
(1) A (2) B
(3) C (4) D

416. Which of the following is NOT an accreditation status awarded by NAAC?
(1) Accredited (2) A+ Grade
(3) Not Accredited (4) Reaccredited

417. NAAC assesses and accredits various types of higher education institutions, including universities, colleges, and
(1) Polytechnics
(2) Hospitals
(3) Research institutions
(4) Schools

418. What are the primary criteria used by NAAC for assessing and accrediting institutions?
(1) Infrastructure and location
(2) Student enrollment and attendance
(3) Curriculum and faculty quality
(4) Cultural activities and sports facilities

419. How often does NAAC conduct accreditation assessments for institutions in India?
(1) Every 5 years
(2) Every 10 years

(3) Every 3 years
(4) Whenever the institution requests it

420. Which of the following aspects of an institution is NOT typically evaluated during a NAAC assessment?
(1) Teaching and learning
(2) Research and consultancy
(3) Student political activities
(4) Infrastructure and facilities

421. Which document serves as the basis for the assessment and accreditation process conducted by NAAC?
(1) Institution's financial statements
(2) Institution's self-study report (SSR)
(3) Institution's alumni records
(4) Institution's marketing materials

422. Who is responsible for preparing the self-study report (SSR) for a higher education institution seeking accreditation from NAAC?
(1) UGC officials
(2) NAAC assessors
(3) Institution's faculty and administrators
(4) Accredited institutions

423. NAAC assessors evaluate an institution's performance in various categories, such as
(1) Infrastructure, facilities, and support services
(2) Faculty and student demographics
(3) Marketing and advertising efforts
(4) National rankings and awards

424. What is the term used for the outcome of the NAAC accreditation process, which indicates the level of quality and excellence achieved by an institution?
(1) Accreditation status
(2) Institutional grade
(3) Quality index
(4) Evaluation report

425. In addition to institutional accreditation, NAAC also provides accreditation for which of the following?
(1) Educational programs
(2) Students
(3) Faculty members
(4) Hostels and canteens

426. Which of the following is a peer-reviewed, accredited journal published by NAAC that focuses on higher education quality assessment and improvement?
(1) Quality India
(2) Accreditation Chronicle
(3) Assessment Gazette
(4) Excellence Journal

427. Which Indian state was the first to implement NAAC accreditation for all its universities and colleges?
(1) Karnataka (2) Tamil Nadu
(3) Maharashtra (4) Kerala

428. What is the role of the NAAC Executive Committee in the accreditation process?
(1) To conduct on-site assessments
(2) To develop assessment criteria
(3) To grant or deny accreditation status
(4) To oversee the operations of NAAC

429. Which category of higher education institutions typically undergoes NAAC accreditation more frequently?
(1) Universities (2) Colleges
(3) Technical institutions
(4) Medical colleges

430. What is the minimum score required for an institution to be awarded an "A" grade by NAAC?
(1) 1.5 (2) 2.5
(3) 3.0 (4) 4.0

431. NAAC has introduced a new grading system that includes a Cumulative Grade Point Average (CGPA). What is the highest CGPA a higher education institution can achieve?
(1) 4.0 (2) 5.0
(3) 6.0 (4) 7.0

432. What is the term for the process by which an institution seeks NAAC accreditation for the first time?
(1) Initial accreditation
(2) Reaccreditation
(3) Renewal of accreditation
(4) Accreditation assessment

433. In addition to assessment and accreditation, what other role does NAAC play in India's higher education system?
(1) Providing scholarships to students
(2) Conducting entrance exams
(3) Promoting international partnerships
(4) Offering financial assistance to institutions

434. What is the name of the national-level conference organized by NAAC to discuss quality assurance and accreditation in higher education?
(1) NAAC Summit
(2) Quality Confluence

(3) Academic Excellence Forum
(4) Accreditation Symposium

435. What is the primary objective of NAAC's peer team visits during the accreditation process?
(1) To conduct examinations for students
(2) To verify the accuracy of financial statements
(3) To assess the institution's quality and infrastructure
(4) To promote faculty development

436. What is the primary objective of skill-based education in India?
(1) To promote theoretical knowledge
(2) To prepare students for competitive exams
(3) To equip students with practical skills for employment
(4) To encourage artistic and creative pursuits

437. Which government agency in India is responsible for promoting and regulating skill development and vocational education?
(1) Ministry of Education
(2) National Skill Development Corporation (NSDC)
(3) University Grants Commission (UGC)
(4) All India Council for Technical Education (AICTE)

438. Which initiative was launched by the Indian government to provide skill training to over 40 crore (400 million) people by 2022?
(1) Pradhan Mantri Jan Dhan Yojana
(2) Make in India
(3) Skill India
(4) Digital India

439. Which ministry is responsible for the implementation of the Skill India Mission?
(1) Ministry of Finance
(2) Ministry of Human Resource Development
(3) Ministry of Skill Development and Entrepreneurship
(4) Ministry of Labour and Employment

440. What is the flagship program of Skill India that focuses on providing industry-relevant training to youth across various sectors?
(1) PM-KISAN
(2) Pradhan Mantri Kaushal Vikas Yojana (PMKVY)
(3) Atal Innovation Mission
(4) Swachh Bharat Abhiyan

441. Which organization plays a pivotal role in conducting assessments and certification of skilled workers in India?
(1) National Board for Accreditation and Certification (NBAC)
(2) National Institute of Open Schooling (NIOS)
(3) National Skill Development Corporation (NSDC)
(4) National Council for Vocational Training (NCVT)

442. What is the primary objective of the National Apprenticeship Promotion Scheme (NAPS) in India?
(1) To provide free education to all
(2) To promote apprenticeships and on-the-job training
(3) To increase the number of universities
(4) To encourage entrepreneurship

443. Which government initiative focuses on providing entrepreneurship training and support to aspiring young entrepreneurs in India?
(1) Digital India (2) Stand-up India
(3) Skill India (4) Make in India

444. Under the PMKVY scheme, how are candidates assessed and certified for their skills?
(1) Through written exams
(2) Through interviews with industry experts
(3) Through practical assessments
(4) Through online quizzes

445. Which sector has been a major focus of skill development efforts in India, particularly under the "Hunar Se Rozgar" program?
(1) Information technology (IT)
(2) Tourism and hospitality
(3) Manufacturing
(4) Agriculture

446. What is the role of the Sector Skill Councils (SSCs) in India's skill development ecosystem?
(1) Conducting competitive exams
(2) Certifying schools and colleges
(3) Identifying skill gaps, creating curriculum, and assessing skilled workers
(4) Managing vocational training institutes

447. Which ministry launched the "National Policy for Skill Development and Entrepreneurship 2015" to guide skill development efforts in India?
(1) Ministry of Home Affairs
(2) Ministry of Commerce and Industry
(3) Ministry of Skill Development and Entrepreneurship
(4) Ministry of External Affairs

448. Which Indian state launched the "Mukhyamantri Yuva Swabhiman Yojana" to provide unemployed youth with skill training and financial assistance?
(1) Tamil Nadu (2) Kerala
(3) Madhya Pradesh (4) Uttar Pradesh

449. What is the role of the "Kaushal and Rozgar Mela" events organized under PMKVY?
(1) Career counseling for students
(2) Skill assessments for job seekers
(3) Cultural festivals
(4) Skill competitions

450. Which organization in India focuses on providing skill training and employment opportunities to people with disabilities?
(1) National Skill Development Corporation (NSDC)
(2) National Institute of Open Schooling (NIOS)
(3) National Handicapped Finance and Development Corporation (NHFDC)
(4) Ministry of Social Justice and Empowerment

451. What term is commonly used to describe the practice of learning a trade or skill through hands-on experience and on-the-job training?
(1) Apprenticeship (2) Internship
(3) Reskilling (4) Certification

452. Under PMKVY, what is the monetary reward given to candidates upon successful completion of skill training?
(1) Rs. 500 (2) Rs. 1,000
(3) Rs. 2,000 (4) Rs. 5,000

453. What is the main focus of the "Skill Saathi" initiative launched by the Indian government?
(1) Promoting digital literacy
(2) Providing scholarships to students
(3) Creating a network of career counselors
(4) Encouraging entrepreneurship

454. Which government scheme provides interest-free loans to individuals from economically weaker sections to pursue skill development courses?
(1) Stand-up India
(2) Pradhan Mantri Awas Yojana (PMAY)
(3) Pradhan Mantri Kaushal Vikas Yojana (PMKVY)
(4) Mudra Yojana

455. What is the main objective of the "Udaan" scheme launched by the Ministry of Home Affairs?
(1) Skill development for rural youth
(2) Skill development for minorities
(3) Skill development for women
(4) Skill development for unemployed youth in Jammu and Kashmir

456. What is the term for the process of updating and enhancing one's skills to remain competitive in the job market?
(1) Skill development
(2) Upskilling
(3) Apprenticeship
(4) Vocational training

457. Which Indian city is known for hosting the annual "India Skills Competition" to showcase the skills of young talent in various trades?
(1) Mumbai (2) Delhi
(3) Bengaluru (4) Jaipur

458. Which organization collaborates with the Ministry of Skill Development and Entrepreneurship to implement the "Rural Self Employment Training Institutes" (RSETIs) program?
(1) Indian Banks' Association (IBA)
(2) National Skill Development Corporation (NSDC)
(3) Indian Institutes of Technology (IITs)
(4) Ministry of Rural Development

459. What is the primary focus of the "Pradhan Mantri Kaushal Kendra" (PMKK) initiative?
(1) Promoting sports skills
(2) Providing skill training to women
(3) Skill development in rural areas
(4) Skill development for the elderly

460. Which initiative was launched by the government to provide short-term skill training programs to unemployed youth and school dropouts?
(1) Skill India
(2) Pradhan Mantri Gramin Awaas Yojana (PMGAY)
(3) Pradhan Mantri Kaushal Kendra (PMKK)
(4) Deen Dayal Upadhyaya Grameen Kaushalya Yojana (DDU-GKY)

461. What is the primary goal of the New Education Policy 2020?
(1) To promote vocational education
(2) To improve access to quality education for all
(3) To privatize higher education institutions
(4) To reduce government spending on education

462. Under NEP 2020, what is the recommended age for the introduction of formal schooling through a foundational stage?
(1) 3 years (2) 5 years
(3) 6 years (4) 8 years

463. According to NEP 2020, what is the medium of instruction for students up to Grade 5?
(1) English
(2) Hindi
(3) Mother tongue/regional language
(4) Sanskrit

464. What is the name of the proposed regulatory body for higher education in India, as outlined in NEP 2020?
(1) University Grants Commission (UGC)
(2) National Board of Accreditation (NBA)
(3) National Testing Agency (NTA)
(4) Higher Education Commission of India (HECI)

465. NEP 2020 aims to achieve 100% Gross Enrollment Ratio (GER) in higher education by which year?
(1) 2030 (2) 2040
(3) 2050 (4) 2060

466. What term is used in NEP 2020 to describe the system of education that encourages students to develop critical thinking and problem-solving skills?
(1) Rote learning
(2) Examination-oriented education
(3) Holistic education
(4) Traditional education

467. NEP 2020 emphasizes the integration of vocational education into mainstream education. What is the proposed name for vocational subjects at the school level?
(1) Vocational Studies
(2) Professional Studies
(3) Skills Education
(4) Vocationalization of Education

468. According to NEP 2020, what is the target for the allocation of GDP (Gross Domestic Product) to education by 2030?
(1) 3% (2) 5%
(3) 6% (4) 10%

469. NEP 2020 recommends the introduction of a National Curriculum Framework (NCF) for school education. How often is the NCF expected to be updated?
(1) Every 5 years (2) Every 10 years
(3) Every 15 years
(4) It will not be updated

470. Under NEP 2020, which board will administer the Common Aptitude Test (CAT) for university admissions?
(1) University Grants Commission (UGC)
(2) National Board of Accreditation (NBA)
(3) National Testing Agency (NTA)
(4) All India Council for Technical Education (AICTE)

471. NEP 2020 encourages the establishment of multidisciplinary institutions known as:
(1) Polytechnics
(2) Community colleges
(3) Research universities
(4) Colleges of Excellence

472. NEP 2020 promotes the use of technology in education. What term is used to describe the digital platform that will be developed for hosting educational content?
(1) E-Pathshala (2) E-Gurukul
(3) E-Shiksha (4) E-Pragati

473. Under NEP 2020, what is the recommended student-teacher ratio for early childhood care and education centers?
(1) 10:1 (2) 20:1
(3) 30:1 (4) 40:1

474. What is the name of the new education policy that aims to promote the use of Indian languages as a medium of instruction in schools and higher education?
(1) Language Preservation Policy
(2) National Language Policy
(3) Mother Tongue-based Multilingual Education Policy
(4) Hindi Language Promotion Policy

475. NEP 2020 proposes the establishment of a National Educational Technology Forum (NETF) to
(1) Regulate online education platforms
(2) Develop open educational resources
(3) Promote the use of chalk and board in classrooms
(4) Monitor teacher performance

476. What term is used in NEP 2020 to describe a flexible approach to choosing subjects and courses in higher education, allowing students to design their own curriculum?
(1) Rigid curriculum
(2) Fixed syllabus

(3) Multiple pathways
(4) Standardized learning

477. NEP 2020 suggests the development of a credit-based system for higher education. What is the proposed name for this system?
(1) Credit Accumulation and Transfer (CAT)
(2) Semester Credit System (SCS)
(3) Choice Based Credit System (CBCS)
(4) Education Credit Framework (ECF)

478. Which Indian state was the first to adopt the New Education Policy 2020?
(1) Tamil Nadu (2) Kerala
(3) Haryana (4) Gujarat

479. NEP 2020 envisions the establishment of a National Research Foundation (NRF) to fund and promote research in which sectors?
(1) Science and technology
(2) Humanities and social sciences
(3) Both (1) and (2)
(4) None of the above

480. What is the term used in NEP 2020 to describe a flexible approach to choosing subjects and courses in higher education, allowing students to design their own curriculum?
(1) Rigid curriculum
(2) Fixed syllabus
(3) Multiple pathways
(4) Standardized learning

481. NEP 2020 recommends the introduction of a National Assessment Center (NAC) to conduct what type of assessments?
(1) Student assessments
(2) Teacher assessments
(3) Institution assessments
(4) Skill assessments

482. Under NEP 2020, what is the minimum degree requirement for teaching positions in schools?
(1) Bachelor's degree
(2) Master's degree
(3) Ph.D.
(4) No specific degree requirement

483. What is the term used in NEP 2020 to describe the process of integrating arts and sciences in education?
(1) Interdisciplinary
(2) Vocational
(3) Extracurricular
(4) Specialized

484. NEP 2020 recommends the establishment of a new apex body for higher education in India. What is its proposed name?
(1) National Education Commission (NEC)
(2) Higher Education Commission of India (HECI)
(3) University Grants Commission (UGC)
(4) All India Council for Technical Education (AICTE)

485. Which aspect of education is addressed by the "Early Childhood Care and Education (ECCE)" component of NEP 2020?
(1) Primary education
(2) Secondary education
(3) Higher education
(4) Pre-primary education

486. What term is used in NEP 2020 to describe the practice of combining vocational education with academic education at the secondary level?
(1) Vocationalization of education
(2) Skill development
(3) Professional studies
(4) Multidisciplinary learning

487. NEP 2020 envisions the establishment of a National Educational Technology Forum (NETF) to
(1) Regulate online education platforms
(2) Develop open educational resources
(3) Promote the use of chalk and board in classrooms
(4) Monitor teacher performance

ANSWERS

1. (3) **2.** (2) **3.** (3) **4.** (2) **5.** (1) **6.** (3) **7.** (3) **8.** (1) **9.** (3) **10.** (4)
11. (2) **12.** (3) **13.** (2) **14.** (2) **15.** (3) **16.** (3) **17.** (4) **18.** (3) **19.** (4) **20.** (4)
21. (4) **22.** (4) **23.** (4) **24.** (2) **25.** (4) **26.** (4) **27.** (4) **28.** (4) **29.** (4) **30.** (1)
31. (3) **32.** (2) **33.** (3) **34.** (3) **35.** (3) **36.** (3) **37.** (3) **38.** (3) **39.** (1) **40.** (3)
41. (2) **42.** (2) **43.** (2) **44.** (3) **45.** (2) **46.** (1) **47.** (2) **48.** (2) **49.** (3) **50.** (2)
51. (2) **52.** (1) **53.** (3) **54.** (1) **55.** (2) **56.** (3) **57.** (3) **58.** (4) **59.** (4) **60.** (4)
61. (4) **62.** (3) **63.** (2) **64.** (1) **65.** (1) **66.** (3) **67.** (2) **68.** (3) **69.** (3) **70.** (1)
71. (3) **72.** (2) **73.** (2) **74.** (3) **75.** (3) **76.** (4) **77.** (1) **78.** (1) **79.** (3) **80.** (3)
81. (1) **82.** (1) **83.** (1) **84.** (1) **85.** (2) **86.** (3) **87.** (4) **88.** (3) **89.** (3) **90.** (4)
91. (3) **92.** (2) **93.** (2) **94.** (3) **95.** (2) **96.** (2) **97.** (2) **98.** (2) **99.** (3) **100.** (3)
101. (2) **102.** (2) **103.** (2) **104.** (1) **105.** (2) **106.** (3) **107.** (1) **108.** (2) **109.** (2) **110.** (3)
111. (2) **112.** (1) **113.** (4) **114.** (3) **115.** (1) **116.** (1) **117.** (3) **118.** (3) **119.** (2) **120.** (1)
121. (2) **122.** (2) **123.** (2) **124.** (2) **125.** (4) **126.** (2) **127.** (2) **128.** (3) **129.** (3) **130.** (2)
131. (3) **132.** (1) **133.** (3) **134.** (3) **135.** (2) **136.** (4) **137.** (3) **138.** (3) **139.** (4) **140.** (3)
141. (2) **142.** (3) **143.** (1) **144.** (2) **145.** (2) **146.** (2) **147.** (4) **148.** (3) **149.** (3) **150.** (4)
151. (2) **152.** (4) **153.** (4) **154.** (4) **155.** (1) **156.** (3) **157.** (4) **158.** (2) **159.** (3) **160.** (4)
161. (4) **162.** (4) **163.** (3) **164.** (4) **165.** (4) **166.** (3) **167.** (4) **168.** (3) **169.** (4) **170.** (3)
171. (1) **172.** (4) **173.** (2) **174.** (3) **175.** (3) **176.** (3) **177.** (4) **178.** (2) **179.** (3) **180.** (2)
181. (2) **182.** (2) **183.** (2) **184.** (2) **185.** (1) **186.** (3) **187.** (1) **188.** (2) **189.** (2) **190.** (3)
191. (3) **192.** (3) **193.** (1) **194.** (1) **195.** (3) **196.** (2) **197.** (1) **198.** (3) **199.** (4) **200.** (2)
201. (2) **202.** (2) **203.** (1) **204.** (3) **205.** (4) **206.** (2) **207.** (1) **208.** (2) **209.** (2) **210.** (2)
211. (3) **212.** (1) **213.** (3) **214.** (3) **215.** (3) **216.** (2) **217.** (3) **218.** (3) **219.** (3) **220.** (3)
221. (3) **222.** (2) **223.** (3) **224.** (4) **225.** (2) **226.** (2) **227.** (3) **228.** (2) **229.** (3) **230.** (4)
231. (3) **232.** (3) **233.** (3) **234.** (3) **235.** (3) **236.** (3) **237.** (3) **238.** (3) **239.** (3) **240.** (2)
241. (2) **242.** (2) **243.** (2) **244.** (2) **245.** (3) **246.** (3) **247.** (2) **248.** (3) **249.** (2) **250.** (3)
251. (1) **252.** (3) **253.** (4) **254.** (3) **255.** (2) **256.** (2) **257.** (1) **258.** (3) **259.** (4) **260.** (2)
261. (2) **262.** (4) **263.** (3) **264.** (4) **265.** (3) **266.** (3) **267.** (3) **268.** (1) **269.** (2) **270.** (2)
271. (2) **272.** (3) **273.** (3) **274.** (3) **275.** (3) **276.** (3) **277.** (1) **278.** (3) **279.** (3) **280.** (3)
281. (2) **282.** (2) **283.** (1) **284.** (1) **285.** (1) **286.** (2) **287.** (1) **288.** (1) **289.** (3) **290.** (1)
291. (3) **292.** (2) **293.** (4) **294.** (3) **295.** (2) **296.** (1) **297.** (3) **298.** (3) **299.** (4) **300.** (2)
301. (1) **302.** (2) **303.** (2) **304.** (4) **305.** (1) **306.** (1) **307.** (2) **308.** (3) **309.** (4) **310.** (4)
311. (2) **312.** (3) **313.** (3) **314.** (2) **315.** (4) **316.** (4) **317.** (2) **318.** (4) **319.** (2) **320.** (2)
321. (2) **322.** (3) **323.** (3) **324.** (3) **325.** (2) **326.** (3) **327.** (2) **328.** (1) **329.** (3) **330.** (3)
331. (2) **332.** (4) **333.** (2) **334.** (3) **335.** (2) **336.** (4) **337.** (3) **338.** (3) **339.** (1) **340.** (2)
341. (4) **342.** (3) **343.** (2) **344.** (2) **345.** (1) **346.** (2) **347.** (4) **348.** (3) **349.** (3) **350.** (2)
351. (2) **352.** (2) **353.** (4) **354.** (2) **355.** (4) **356.** (1) **357.** (1) **358.** (1) **359.** (3) **360.** (4)

361. (3)	**362.** (2)	**363.** (4)	**364.** (2)	**365.** (2)	**366.** (2)	**367.** (3)	**368.** (4)	**369.** (2)	**370.** (3)
371. (2)	**372.** (3)	**373.** (1)	**374.** (1)	**375.** (2)	**376.** (3)	**377.** (3)	**378.** (2)	**379.** (2)	**380.** (1)
381. (2)	**382.** (3)	**383.** (1)	**384.** (2)	**385.** (2)	**386.** (1)	**387.** (2)	**388.** (4)	**389.** (1)	**390.** (2)
391. (2)	**392.** (4)	**393.** (2)	**394.** (2)	**395.** (2)	**396.** (1)	**397.** (3)	**398.** (2)	**399.** (1)	**400.** (3)
401. (4)	**402.** (1)	**403.** (3)	**404.** (3)	**405.** (1)	**406.** (1)	**407.** (1)	**408.** (4)	**409.** (1)	**410.** (3)
411. (1)	**412.** (2)	**413.** (2)	**414.** (2)	**415.** (1)	**416.** (3)	**417.** (3)	**418.** (3)	**419.** (2)	**420.** (3)
421. (2)	**422.** (3)	**423.** (1)	**424.** (1)	**425.** (1)	**426.** (1)	**427.** (1)	**428.** (4)	**429.** (3)	**430.** (3)
431. (2)	**432.** (1)	**433.** (3)	**434.** (2)	**435.** (3)	**436.** (3)	**437.** (2)	**438.** (3)	**439.** (4)	**440.** (2)
441. (3)	**442.** (2)	**443.** (2)	**444.** (3)	**445.** (2)	**446.** (3)	**447.** (3)	**448.** (3)	**449.** (2)	**450.** (4)
451. (1)	**452.** (3)	**453.** (3)	**454.** (4)	**455.** (4)	**456.** (2)	**457.** (2)	**458.** (1)	**459.** (3)	**460.** (4)
461. (2)	**462.** (2)	**463.** (3)	**464.** (4)	**465.** (1)	**466.** (3)	**467.** (4)	**468.** (3)	**469.** (2)	**470.** (3)
471. (4)	**472.** (1)	**473.** (1)	**474.** (3)	**475.** (2)	**476.** (3)	**477.** (3)	**478.** (3)	**479.** (3)	**480.** (3)
481. (1)	**482.** (2)	**483.** (1)	**484.** (2)	**485.** (4)	**486.** (1)	**487.** (2)			

MODEL PAPERS
(New Pattern)

Model Paper 1

Note : This paper contains fifty (50) multiple choice questions of two marks each. All questions are compulsory.

1. Arrange the following in sequence as they are introduced in increasing order of age of the students

a. Taxonomy of Educational Objectives
b. Team Teaching
c. Personalised system of Instructions
d. Concept of Interaction model of Teaching

Choose the **correct** answer from the options given below :

(A) b, a, d, c
(B) c, a, d, b
(C) a, d, b, c
(D) c, d, a, b

2. What is the full form of ARPANET ?

(A) Advanced Resource Project Agency Network
(B) Advanced Research Project Agency Network
(C) Applied Research Project Agency Network
(D) American Research Project Agency Network

3. While presenting your ideas in a classroom it is better to

1. recognize that there can be other views
2. recognize that students are not a homogenous mass
3. take dissenting views also in consideration

(A) 1 and 3
(B) Only 3
(C) 2 and 3
(D) 1, 2 and 3

4. Arrange the following teaching process in order:

(i) Relate the present knowledge with previous one
(ii) Evaluation
(iii) Reteaching
(iv) Formulating instructional objectives
(v) Presentation of instructional materials

(A) (i), (ii), (iii), (iv), (v)
(B) (ii), (i), (iii), (iv), (v)
(C) (v), (iv), (iii), (i), (ii)
(D) (iv), (i), (v), (ii), (iii)

5. Some of your colleagues are busy in cracking filthy jokes during their leisure in college. You are also a member of that group but unable to stop them. What would you do to avoid it ?

(A) You advice your colleagues to mind their languages while cracking jokes in college
(B) You persuade them not to waste their leisure time in filthy jokes.
(C) You change the groups or live in isolation because you don't relish it.
(D) You remind them of their noble profession.

6. Research is conducted to

(I) Generate new knowledge
(II) Not to develop a theory
(III) Obtain research degree
(IV) Reinterpret existing knowledge

Which of the above are correct ?

(A) I, III & II
(B) III, II & IV
(C) II, I & III
(D) I, III & IV

7. Match **List - I** with **List - II** :

List - I	**List - II**
A. Asiddha	I. Irrelevant middle term
B. Badhita	II. Unproven middle term
C. Viruddha	III. Contrary middle term
D. Savyabhicharra	IV. Contradicted middle term

Choose the **correct** answer from the options given below :

(1) A-II, B-IV, C-III, D-I
(2) A-I, B-II, C-III, D-IV
(3) A-II, B-III, C-I, D-IV
(4) A-III, B-IV, C-II, D-I

8. Research reports should be reviewed in the light of
   1. investigator bias
   2. cultural context
   3. methodological factors

   Which of one of the following is correct ?

   (A) 1 and 3 (B) Only 1
   (C) Only 3 (D) 1, 2 and 3
9. Four problematic situations are given below
   (i) A student is abnormally withdrawing in nature
   (ii) A considerable number of students always score low in your subject
   (iii) Students of your class are found to create disturbances in the class of a particular teacher.
   (iv) In spite of warning most of the students of a class are irregular with assignments.

   Which of these warrant action research ?

   (A) All the four (B) (i), (ii) and (iv)
   (C) (ii) and (iii) (D) (ii) and (iv)
10. Generally at present the following tradition has been observed for doing research
    (A) The supervisor putting the problem to student's mind without considering his ability, interest etc.
    (B) The researchers themselves work hard to search a good problem
    (C) By doing slight changes in the existing topics, variables etc., new problems have been worked out easily
    (D) Both A and C in the above

Directions: *A passage of text be given. Questions be asked from the passage to be answered.*

Gandhi's overall social and environmental philosophy is based on what human beings need rather than what they want. His early introduction to the teachings of Jains, Theosophists, Christian sermons, Ruskin and Tolstoy, and most significantly the Bhagavad Gita, were to have profound impact on the development of Gandhi's holistic thinking on humanity, nature and their ecological interrelation. His deep concern for the disadvantaged, the poor and rural population created an ambience for an alternative social thinking that was at once far-sighted, local and immediate. For Gandhi was acutely aware that the demands generated by the need to feed and sustain human life, compounded by the growing industrialization of India, far outstripped the finite resources of nature. This might nowadays appear naive or commonplace, but such pronouncements were as rare as they were heretical a century ago. Gandhi was also concerned about the destruction, under colonial and modernist designs, of the existing infrastructures which had more potential for keeping a community flourishing within ecologically-sensitive traditional patterns of subsistence, especially in the rural areas, than did the incoming Western alternatives based on nature-blind technology and the enslavement of human spirit and energies.

Perhaps the moral principle for which Gandhi is best known is that ocf active non-violence, derived from the traditional moral restraint of not injuring another being. The most refined expression of this value is in the great epic of the Mahabharata, (c. 100 BCE to 200 CE), where moral development proceeds through placing constraints on the liberties, desires and acquisitiveness endemic to human life. One's action is judged in terms of consequences and the impact it is likely to have on another. Jainas had generalized this principle to include all sentient creatures and biocommunities alike. Advanced Jaina monks and nuns will sweep their path to avoid harming insects and even bacteria. Non-injury is a non-negotiable universal prescription.

11. Which one of the following have a profound impact on the development of Gandhi's holistic thinking on humanity, nature and their ecological interrelations?
    (A) Jain teachings
    (B) Christian sermons
    (C) Bhagavad Gita
    (D) Ruskin and Tolstoy
12. Gandhi's overall social and environmental philosophy is based on human beings'
    (A) need (B) desire
    (C) wealth (D) welfare
13. Gandhiji's deep concern for the disadvantaged, the poor and rural population created an ambience for an alternative
    (A) rural policy (B) social thinking
    (C) urban policy (D) economic thinking
14. Colonial policy and modernisation led to the destruction of
    (A) major industrial infrastructure
    (B) irrigation infrastructure
    (C) urban infrastructure
    (D) rural infrastructure
15. Gandhi's active non-violence is derived from
    (A) Moral restraint of not injuring another being

(B) Having liberties, desires and acquisitiveness
(C) Freedom of action
(D) Nature-blind technology and enslavement of human spirit and energies

16. Which one of the following statements is true for Journals ?
(A) They are not a part of the print media.
(B) They concentrate an industry-specific, stream-specific or trade-specific issues, which are defined before hand.
(C) They given all types of news, views, and entertaining events.
(D) They are not prepared under the guidance of expert editors, writers and researchers but by journalists and freelance writers from the open market.

17. In downward communication, messages
(A) flow form the bottom to the top of the organization structure.
(B) flow from the top to the bottom of the organization structure.
(C) are meant to be exchanged between the members of the top brass
(D) None of these.

18. **Assertion (A) :** To communicate well in the classroom is a natural ability.
Reason (R) : Effective teaching in the classroom demands knowledge of the communication process.
Code :
(A) Both (A) and (R) are true, and (R) is the correct explanation of (A).
(B) Both (A) and (R) are true, but (R) is not the correct explanation of (A).
(C) (A) is true, but (R) is false.
(D) (A) is false, but (R) is true.

19. Who is well known for his comment on communication : '*Who (says) What (to) Whom (in) What Channel (with) What Effect*'
(A) Frank F X Dance
(B) Harold Lasswell
(C) Marshall McLuhan
(D) Joseph A Devito

20. The Ability to understand, communicate with, motivate, and support other people, both individually and in groups, defines which of the following organizational skills?
(A) Hard skills (B) Soft skills
(C) Conceptual skills (D) Political skills

21. In covering a certain distance, the speed of A and B are in the ratio of 3 : 4. If A takes 20 minutes more than B to reach the destination, the time taken by A to reach the destination is
(A) $1\frac{1}{4}$ hrs (B) $1\frac{1}{3}$ hrs
(C) 2 hrs (D) $2\frac{1}{2}$ hrs

22. 80 50 130 100 180 150 230
900 (A) (B) (C) (D) (E)
Which number will come in the place of (C) ?
(A) 1050 (B) 920
(C) 1000 (D) 950

23. If it is possible to make a meaningful word from the first, second, fourth and fifth letters of the word FALSEHOOD then which will be the third letter from the right ? Mark M if it is possible to make more than one word and if it is impossible to make any word then mark your answer as X.
(A) M (B) X
(C) S (D) A

24. In a certain code language, QUEUE is written as Q22, CHURCH is written as 1UR1. Which of the following would be the most appropriate code for BANANA in that language ?
(A) B5A5A (B) B5A5
(C) B55A (D) BA5A5A

25. The post office is in the East of the school while my house is in the South of the school. The market is in the North of the post office. If the distance of the market from the post office is equal to the distance of my house from the school, in which direction is the market with respect to my house ?
(A) North (B) East
(C) North-East (D) South-West

26. Which of the following statements are false? Choose from the code given below :
1. Inductive arguments always proceed from the particular to the general.
2. A cogent argument must be inductively strong.
3. A valid argument may have a false premise and a false conclusion.
4. An argument may legitimately be spoken of as 'true' or 'false'.

Code :
(A) 2, 3 and 4 (B) 1 and 3
(C) 2 and 4 (D) 1 and 2

27. Among the following statements **two** are contradictory to each other. Select the correct code that represents them :
Statements:
(a) All poets are philosophers.
(b) Some poets are philosophers.
(c) Some poets are not philosophers.
(d) No philosopher is a poet.
Codes:
(1) (a) and (b) (2) (a) and (d)
(3) (a) and (c) (4) (b) and (c)

28. Which one of the following Venn diagrams correctly illustrates the relationship among the classes:
Carrot, Food, Vegetables

(A) 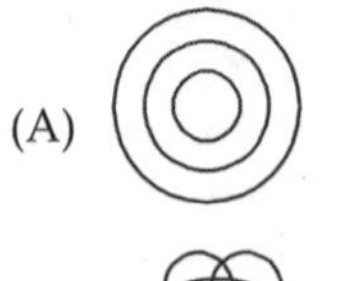 (B) 

(C) 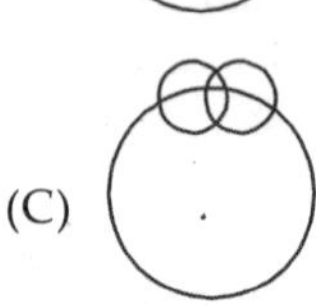 (D) 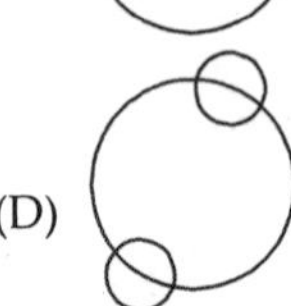

29. Choose the right code.
A deductive argument claims that
I. The conclusion does not claim something more than that which is contained in the premises.
II. The conclusion is supported by the premise/premises may be either true or false.
III. If the conclusion is false, then premise/premises may be either true or false.
IV. If premise/combination of premises is true, then conclusion must be true.
Codes :
(A) I and II (B) I and III
(C) II and III (D) All the above

30. Match the following

List-I	**List-II**
(a) Perception	(i) Ordinary
(b) Inference	(ii) Vyapti
(c) Comparison	(iii) Analogy
(d) Verbal testimony	(iv) Shalda

Codes :

	(a)	**(b)**	**(c)**	**(d)**
(A)	(i)	(ii)	(iii)	(iv)
(B)	(iv)	(iii)	(ii)	(i)
(C)	(i)	(iv)	(iii)	(ii)
(D)	(iii)	(iv)	(ii)	(i)

Directions. Study the graph and answer the questions 31-35 given below. In the following pie graph is marks obtain by a candidate in four subjects - Math, English, Hindi, Science, Social Science are given. Full marks of the examination is 540.

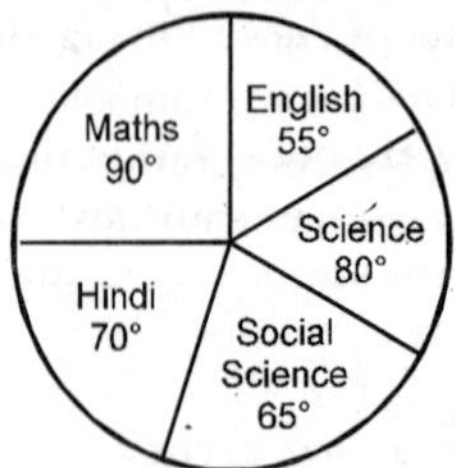

31. What is the percentage marks in math of the full marks ?
(A) 20% (B) 30%
(C) 35% (D) 25%

32. What is percentage marks of the total marks in English, Science and Social Science of the Full marks ?
(A) 45% (B) $44\frac{4}{9}\%$
(C) 55% (D) $55\frac{5}{9}\%$

33. In which subject student get 22.2% marks?
(A) Hindi (B) Science
(C) Social Science (D) English

34. In which subject student got 105 marks ?
(A) Math (B) Science
(C) Hindi (D) English

35. What percentage mark is more than the marks obtain in three subject: – English, Science and Social Science from the marks obtain in Hindi and Math ?
(A) 10% (B) 11%
(C) $11\frac{1}{9}\%$ (D) $10\frac{1}{9}\%$

36. A new Laptop has been produced that weighs less, is smaller and uses less power than previous Laptop models.
Which of the following technologies has been used to accomplish this ?
(A) Universal Serial Bus Mouse
(B) Faster Random Access Memory
(C) Blu Ray Drive
(D) Solid State Hard Drive

37. Given the following email fields, which of the email addresses will 'swami' be able to see when he receives the message ?

To... ram@test.com
Cc... raj@test.com; ravi@test.com
Bcc... swami@test.com; rama@test.com

(A) ram@test.com
(B) ram@test.com; raj@test.com; ravi@test.com
(C) ram@test.com; rama@test.com
(D) ram@test.com; rama@test.com; raj@test.com; ravi@test.com

38. Which of the following best explains RAM?
1. It is an acronym for Random Access Memory.
2. It is memory built from silicon chips that is used to store programs and data temporarily while they are being processed.
3. Read Access Memory.

(A) Only 1 & 3 (B) Only 2 & 3
(C) Only 1 & 2 (D) All of these

39. Put the following units of storage into the correct order, starting with the smallest unit first and going down to the largest unit :
(a) Kilobyte (b) Byte
(c) Megabyte (d) Terabyte
(e) Gigabyte (f) Bit
Give your answer from the following code :
(A) (f), (b), (a), (c), (d), (e)
(B) (f), (b), (a), (d), (e), (c)
(C) (f), (b), (a), (c), (e), (d)
(D) (f), (b), (a), (d), (c), (e)

40. With regard to computer memory, which of the following statement(s) is/are TRUE ?
P : Read Only Memory (ROM) is 'volatile' memory.
Q : Random Access Memory (RAM) is 'volatile' memory.
R : Secondary Memory is 'volatile' memory.
(A) P only (B) Q only
(C) P and Q only (D) P and R only

41. Match **List-I** with **List-II** and select the correct answer from the codes given below :

List - I (National Parks)	**List - II (States)**
(a) Periyar	(i) Orissa
(b) Nandan Kanan	(ii) Kerala
(c) Corbett National Park	(iii) Rajasthan
(d) Sariska Tiger Reserve	(iv) Uttarakhand

Codes :

	(a)	(b)	(c)	(d)
(A)	(ii)	(i)	(iv)	(iii)
(B)	(i)	(ii)	(iv)	(iii)
(C)	(iii)	(ii)	(i)	(iv)
(D)	(i)	(ii)	(iii)	(iv)

42. **Assertion (A):** Aerosols have potential for modifying climate
Reason (R): Aerosols interact with both short waves and radiation
(A) Both (A) and (R) are true, and (R) is the correct explanation of (A)
(B) Both (A) and (R) are true, but (R) is not the correct explanation of (A)
(C) (A) is true, but (R) is false
(D) (A) is false, but (R) is true

43. Sources of pollution which result in the disturbance of the earth or contamination of the surrounding land is called
(A) thermal pollutants
(B) industrial pollutants
(C) point pollution sources
(D) non-point pollution sources

44. Climate change has implications for
1. soil moisture 2. forest fires
3. biodiversity 4. ground water
Identify the correct combination according to the code :
(A) 1 and 3 (B) 1, 2 and 3
(C) 1, 3 and 4 (D) 1, 2, 3 and 4

45. **Assertion (A) :** In the world as a whole, the environment has degraded during past several decades.
Reason (R) : The population of the world has been growing significantly.
(A) (A) is correct, (R) is correct and (R) is the correct explanation of (A).
(B) (A) is correct, (R) is correct and (R) is not the correct explanation of (A).
(C) (A) is correct, but (R) is false.
(D) (A) is false, but (R) is correct.

46. Match **List-I** with **List-II** and select the correct answer from the code given below :

List - I (Institutions)	**List - II (Locations)**
(a) National Law Institute	(i) Shimla
(b) Indian Institute of Advanced Studies	(ii) Bhopal

(c) National Judicial Academy — (iii) Hyderabad

(d) National Savings Institute — (iv) Nagpur

Codes:

	(a)	(b)	(c)	(d)		(a)	(b)	(c)	(d)
(A)	(iii)	(ii)	(iv)	(i)	(B)	(i)	(ii)	(iii)	(iv)
(C)	(iv)	(iii)	(i)	(ii)	(D)	(iii)	(i)	(ii)	(iv)

47. Which one of the following statements is not correct ?

(A) Indian Parliament is supreme.

(B) The Supreme Court of India has the power of judicial review.

(C) There is a division of powers between the Centre and the States.

(D) There is a Council of Ministers to aid and advise the President.

48. The Fundamental Duties of a citizen include

1. Respect for the Constitution, the National Flag and the National Anthem
2. To develop the scientific temper.
3. Respect for the Government.
4. To protect Wildlife.

Choose the correct answer from the codes given below :

Codes :

(A) 1, 2 and 3 (B) 1, 2 and 4

(C) 2, 3 and 4 (D) 1, 3, 4 and 2

49. Match the List – I with the List – II and select the correct answer from the codes given below :

List – I (Commissions and Committees)	List – II (Year)
(a) First Administrative Reforms Commission	(i) 2005
(b) Paul H. Appleby Committee I	(ii) 1962
(c) K. Santhanam Committee	(iii) 1966
(d) Second Administrative Reforms Commission	(iv) 1953

Codes :

	(a)	(b)	(c)	(d)		(a)	(b)	(c)	(d)
(A)	(i)	(iii)	(ii)	(iv)	(B)	(iii)	(iv)	(ii)	(i)
(C)	(iv)	(ii)	(iii)	(i)	(D)	(ii)	(i)	(iv)	(iii)

50. Open Universities are treated as Non-traditional Universities because

(A) Innovative methods of teaching and learning are used in these Universities

(B) Innovative methods of admission, curriculum and evaluation are followed in these universities

(C) Modern Communication Techniques are used in these universities

(D) All of the above

ANSWERS

1. (A)	2. (B)	3. (D)	4. (D)	5. (B)	6. (D)	7. (A)	8. (C)	9. (D)	10. (D)
11. (C)	12. (A)	13. (B)	14. (D)	15. (A)	16. (B)	17. (B)	18. (D)	19. (B)	20. (B)
21. (B)	22. (B)	23. (D)	24. (C)	25. (C)	26. (C)	27. (B)	28. (A)	29. (A)	30. (A)
31. (D)	32. (D)	33. (B)	34. (C)	35. (C)	36. (D)	37. (B)	38. (C)	39. (C)	40. (B)
41. (A)	42. (A)	43. (D)	44. (D)	45. (B)	46. (D)	47. (A)	48. (B)	49. (B)	50. (D)

Model Paper 2

Note : This paper contains fifty (50) multiple choice questions of two marks each. All questions are compulsory.

1. If $(L)_M$ represents a number L in base-M number system, then identify the correct ascending order of the following numbers A-D when converted to decimal number system.
   a. $(11011.11)_2$ b. $(131.2)_4$
   c. $(25.5)_8$ d. $(16.6)_{16}$
   Choose the correct answer from the options given below:
   (A) c, d, b, a (B) a, c, d, b
   (C) c, d, a, b (D) b, a, c, d
2. Which of the following education methods are useful for students?
   (1) Idealism (2) Existentialism
   (3) Realism (4) Pragmatism
   Choose your answer by following codes:
   (A) 1 & 2 (B) 2, 3 & 4
   (C) 3 & 4 (D) 1, 2, 3 & 4
3. An effective teacher will ensure
   (A) cooperation among his students
   (B) laissez-faire role
   (C) competition among students
   (D) competition or cooperation as the situation demands
4. You are in class on the very first day of the opening session, and take introductions of the students, the primary objective of this introduction for you is
   (A) to know about students' potentialities along with their family status
   (B) selection of those students who can do the school job for you.
   (C) identification of potential
   (D) both (B) & (C)
5. Which of the following channel of SWAYAM Prabha deals with the social science and the education, Psychology, and Home Science?
   (A) Channel 01: VAGEESH
   (B) Channel 04: SAARASWAT
   (C) Channel 05: PRABANDHAN
   (D) Channel 06: VIDHIK
6. In Stratified sampling the units are selected
   (A) After dividing the population in different groups on the basis of specific standard and then taking an equal proportion of units from each group
   (B) After dissociating the population in different groups on the basis of specific standard and then the units are selected from these groups.
   (C) After dividing the population in different 'strata' and then selecting any one strata out of them
   (D) None of the above
7. Which of the following Statements is false in the context of research ?
   (A) It necessarily improves quality of functioning of the area in which it is conducted.
   (B) Inductive and deductive reasoning are applied in the research process.
   (C) Verifiable findings are derived by the research process.
   (D) Research is conducted to find answers of meaningful questions scientifically.
8. The need of philosophical research method is desired in
   (A) Philosophy related researches
   (B) All the researches involved in exploring the aims of social sciences
   (C) Explorations of *Atma* and *Paramatma*
   (D) Determining the role and extension of philosophy
9. The following steps of case-study have been jumbled with each other
   1. Focus of study
   2. Identification of cause-effect symptoms
   3. Remedy for adjustment
   4. Follow-up programme
   5. Data collection
   The correct sequence in above steps is
   (A) 1, 5, 2, 3, and 4 (B) 1, 4, 5, 2 and 3
   (C) 1, 2, 3, 4 and 5 (D) 5, 4, 3, 2 and 1

10. Match the following

(a)	Design will give an idea	(i)	Of its choice favouring his own methodological theoretical and personal orientation
(b)	Once the data through different techniques collected	(ii)	Testing different hypothesis
(c)	Each research will have a design	(iii)	Of time, money, personal budget, availability of data and nature of respondents
(d)	Different designs will help	(iv)	To what techniques will be used
(e)	Each design is bound i.e., have limitation	(v)	How will that be analysed

	(a)	(b)	(c)	(d)	(e)
(A)	iv	v	i	ii	iii
(B)	v	iv	iii	i	ii
(C)	i	iii	iv	v	ii
(D)	v	iv	iii	ii	i

Directions: *A passage of text be given. Questions be asked from the passage to be answered.*

The phrase "What is it like ?" stands for a fundamental thought process. How does one go about observing and reporting on things and events that occupy segments of earth space ? Of all the infinite variety of phenomena on the face of the earth, how does one decide what phenomena to observe ? There is no such thing as a complete description of the earth or any part of it, for every microscopic point on the earth's surface differs from every other such point. Experience shows that the things observed are already familiar, because they are like phenomena that occur at home or because they resemble the abstract images and models developed in the human mind.

How are abstract images formed ? Humans alone among the animals possess language; their words symbolize not only specific things but also mental images of classes of things. People can remember what they have seen or experienced because they attach a word symbol to them.

During the long record of our efforts to gain more and more knowledge about the face of the earth as the human habitat, there has been a continuing interplay between things and events. The direct observation through the senses is described as a percept; the mental image is described as a concept. Percepts are what some people describe as reality, in contrast to mental images, which are theoretical, implying that they are not real.

The relation of Percept to Concept is not as simple as the definition implies. It is now quite clear that people of different cultures or even individuals in the same culture develop different mental images of reality and what they perceive is a reflection of these preconceptions. The direct observation of things and events on the face of the earth is so clearly a function of the mental images of the mind of the observer that the whole idea of reality must be reconsidered.

Concepts determine what the observer perceives, yet concepts are derived from the generalizations of previous percepts. What happens is that the educated observer is taught to accept a set of concepts and then sharpens or changes these concepts during a professional career. In any one field of scholarship, professional opinion at one time determines what concepts and procedures are acceptable, and these form a kind of model of scholarly behaviour.

11. The problem raised in the passage reflects on
(A) thought process
(B) human behaviour
(C) cultural perceptions
(D) professional opinion

12. According to the passage, human beings have mostly in mind
(A) Observation of things
(B) Preparation of mental images
(C) Expression through language
(D) To gain knowledge

13. Concept means
(A) A mental image
(B) A reality
(C) An idea expressed in language form
(D) All the above

14. The relation of Percept to Concept is
(A) Positive
(B) Negative
(C) Reflective
(D) Absolute

15. In the passage, the earth is taken as
(A) The Globe
(B) The Human Habitat
(C) A Celestial Body
(D) A Planet

16. The function of mass communication of supplying information regarding the processes, issues, events and societal developments is known as

(A) content supply (B) surveillance
(C) gratification (D) correlation

17. "The reach of mass media is quite strong in India, but comparatively, the access to them is very weak." This statement is

(A) Definitely true (B) Probably true
(C) Definitely false (D) Probably false

18. The Library and information Science Department of Mysore University has taken up an ambitious project which aims to create an online data base of all doctoral theses and dissertations published by Indian Universities. The project sponsored by the Union Science and Technology Ministry is known as

(A) Vidya Bharti
(B) Vidya Bahini
(C) March Ahead
(D) Vidya Nidhi

19. Communication via New media such as computers, teleshopping, internet and mobile telephony is termed as

(A) Entertainment
(B) Interactive communication
(C) Developmental communication
(D) Communitarian

20. Self regulatory body of the television news channels in India is

(A) Press Council of India
(B) Television Council of India
(C) News Broadcasting Standards Authority
(D) Broadcast Authority of India

21. A 4 cm cube is cut into 1 cm cubes. What is the percentage increase in the surface area after such cutting?

(A) 4% (B) 300%
(C) 75% (D) 400%

22. In the following series if A and C, B and D and so on interchange their positions upto X, then which will be the fourth letter to the right of N in the new series formed ?

ABCDEFGHIJKLMNOPQRSTUVWXYZ

(A) W (B) J
(C) R (D) Q

23. If MATHEMATICS = 12345123678, then MAHATMA = ?

(A) 1242312 (B) 12425341
(C) 12345678 (D) 12345123

24. If P + Q means P is the brother of Q, P − Q means P is the mother of Q and P × Q means P is the sister of Q. Which of the following means M is the maternal uncle of R ?

(A) M − R + K (B) M + K − R
(C) M + K × R (D) None of these

25. Five boys were sitting in a circle facing to the centre. Salguna was to the left of Raman. Arul was to the right of Amit but between Amit and Narendra. Who was to the right of Salguna.

(A) Data inadequate
(B) Arul
(C) Amit
(D) Raman

26. **Assertion (A) :** The coin when flipped next time will come up tails.

Reason (R) : Because the coin was flipped five times in a row, and each time it came up heads.

Choose the correct answer from below :

(A) Both (A) and (R) are true, and (R) is the correct explanation of (A).
(B) Both (A) and (R) are false, and (R) is the correct explanation of (A).
(C) (A) is doubtful, (R) is true, and (R) is not the correct explanation of (A).
(D) (A) is doubtful, (R) is false, and (R) is the correct explanation of (A).

27. If the proposition "Vegetarians are not meat eaters" is false, then which of the following inferences is correct ? Choose from the codes given below :

1. "Some vegetarians are meat eaters" is true.
2. "All vegetarians are meat eaters" is doubtful.
3. "Some vegetarians are not meat eaters" is true.
4. "Some vegetarians are not meat eaters" is doubtful.

Codes :

(A) 1, 2 and 3 (B) 2, 3 and 4
(C) 1, 3 and 4 (D) 1, 2 and 4

28. The following question is based on the diagram given below. If the two small circles represent formal class-room education and distance education and the big circle stands for university system of education, which figure represents the university systems.

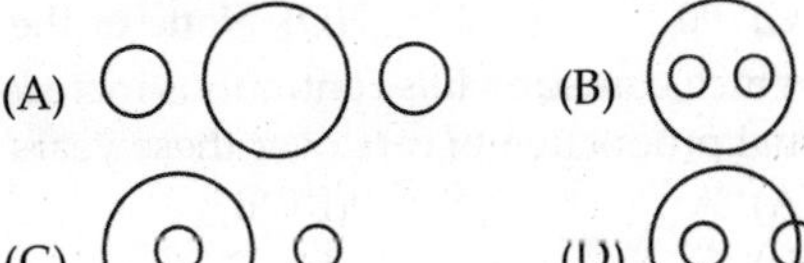

29. **Statement:** Most students are intelligent
Conclusions:
(i) Some students are intelligent.
(ii) All students are not intelligent.
Which of the following is implied ?
(A) Only (i) is implied
(B) Only (ii) is implied
(C) Both (i) and (ii) are implied
(D) Neither (i) nor (ii) is implied

30. **Assertion (A).** Buddhism accepts the pramanas.
Reason (R). He also believes in verbal testimony.
Codes:
(A) Both A and R are true and R is the correct explanation of A
(B) Both A and R are true, but R is not the correct explanation of A
(C) A is true, but R is false
(D) A is false, but R is true

Directions. Study the table carefully and answer the questions 31-35 given below.

Projected and Actual Production of Cars of 5 Different companies
(Numbers in '000)

Years	A		B		C		D		E	
	P	A	P	A	P	A	P	A	P	A
1987	22	20	16	12	21	20	22	16	22	20
1988	26	21	21	14	22	18	20	18	18	16
1989	24	22	15	14	26	20	22	21	20	18
1990	29	23	14	10	30	22	29	23	23	19
1991	28	21	18	15	34	28	26	24	21	17
1992	31	20	22	18	36	31	30	28	28	26

P = Projected; A = Actual

31. Which company has the highest actual production of cars over these years ?
(A) A (B) B
(C) C (D) D

32. Which year has the lowest projected production of cars of all the 5 companies ?
(A) 1987 (B) 1989
(C) 1990 (D) None of these

33. What is the percentage of actual production of cars compared to the projected production of cars of company D in the year 1988 :
(A) 85 (B) 86
(C) 90 (D) None of these

34. Which company has continuous increase in actual production of cars over these years ?
(A) A (B) B
(C) C (D) D

35. What is the approximate % actual production of cars compared to the projected production of cars of B over these years (1987-1991) ?
(A) 80 (B) 78
(C) 82 (D) 74

36. The part of a computer system containing the circuitry that does the adding, subtracting, multiplying dividing and comparing, is called as
(A) Arithmetic logic unit
(B) Memory
(C) CPU
(D) None of the above

37. Which of the following defines the term E-Banking?
1. It is the short form of Efficient Banking which means providing all banking related services to the customers in minimum required time during their visit to the branch.
2. E-Banking is providing banking facilities to all the customers through ATMs only which restricts their visits to a bank branch to a bare minimum.
3. E-Banking implies provisions of banking products and services through electronic delivery channels like ATMs, phone, internet, mobile phone etc.
(A) only 1
(B) only 2
(C) only 3
(D) only 1 & 3

38. Which of the following statements about 'outsourcing' are correct?
(1) Companies that are specialized time-sharing provide organisations with all their computational needs. This is called outsourcing.
(2) With outsourcing, time-sharing companies supply hardware and software to organisations for a fee and actually run program as service on a regularly scheduled basis.
(3) Outsourcing has become very popular for many companies that have own computers but find them inadequate and do not want to spend additional funds to upgrade them.
(A) Only (1) and (2)
(B) All of them
(C) Only (2) and (3)
(D) Either (1) or (3)

39. The term 'end-users' means
(A) employees who uses the server that has many computers connected to it.
(B) employees who need computer-produced information to analyses and summarize data and to help them in making decisions.
(C) people who use the computer in the end
(D) either (B) and (C)

40. ASCII and EBCDIC are the popular character coding systems. What does EBCDIC stand for?
(A) Extended Binary Coded Decimal Interchange Code
(B) Extended Bit Code Decimal Interchange Code
(C) Extended Bit Case Decimal Interchange Code
(D) Extended Binary Case Decimal Interchange Code

41. Which of the following statements is NOT true about the availability of water on the earth, the crisis for which is going to increase in the years to come?
(A) About 2.5 percent of the total water available on the earth is polluted water and cannot be used for human activities.
(B) Possibility is that some big glaciers will melt in the coming ten-fifteen years and sea level will rise by 3-4 metres all over the earth.
(C) 80 per cent of the water available to us for use comes in bursts as monsoons
(D) About 97.5 per cent of the total volume of water available on the earth is salty

42. Man's urge these days has been
1. to control communicable diseases.
2. to produce bumper crops where nothing grew earlier
3. increase of consumer facilities beyond the reach of man

(A) 1 alone (B) 1 and 2
(C) 1, 2 and 3 (D) 1 and 3

43. 'Fly ash' produced in thermal power plants is an ecofriendly resource for use in :
(a) agriculture as micro-nutrient
(b) wasteland development
(c) dam and water holding structures
(d) brick industry
Choose the correct answer from the code given below :
(A) (a), (b) and (d) only
(B) (b), (c) and (d) only
(C) (a), (c) and (d) only
(D) (a), (b), (c) and (d)

44. Sometimes secondary pollutants like ozone, PAN (Peroxy acylnitrate), HNO_3, H_2SO_4 formed from primary pollutants are more toxic than primary pollutants. This phenomenon of increased toxicity in pollutants is called
(A) Synergism
(B) Greenhouse effect
(C) Eutrophication
(D) Biomagnification

45. Match List I and II and select the correct answer using the codes given below the lists.

List I (Rivers)	List II (Dams)
P. Cauvery	1. Alamatti
Q. Krishna	2. Mettur
R. Narmada	3. Gandhi Sagar
S. Chambal	4. Sardar Sarovar

	P	Q	R	S
(A)	2	1	3	4
(B)	1	4	2	3
(C)	1	3	4	2
(D)	2	1	4	3

46. When a university has its separate campus for Teaching purposes and there are many autonomous and constituent colleges affiliated to it, then this organisational pattern is called
(A) A Federal University
(B) A Decentralized University
(C) An Unitary University
(D) None of the above

47. Below are given two lists : One list contains officials and List-II refers to the person holding these posts. Match List-I with List-II by using the codes :

List-I (Presiding Officer)	List-II (House)
(i) Lok Sabha	1. Vice-President
(ii) Rajya Sabha	2. Speaker
(iii) Joint Session of Parliament	3. Deputy Speaker
	4. President

Code :

	(i)	(ii)	(iii)
(A)	1	2	4
(B)	4	2	1
(C)	3	1	2
(D)	2	1	4

48. Match List - I (Institutions) with List - II (Functions) and select the correct answer by using the code given below :

List – I (Institutions)	List – II (Functions)
(a) Parliament	(i) Formulation of Budget
(b) C& A.G.	(ii) Enactment of Budget
(c) Ministry of Finance	(iii) Implementation of Budget
(d) Executing Departments	(iv) Legality of expenditure
	(v) Justification of Income

Code:

	(a)	(b)	(c)	(d)
(A)	(iii)	(iv)	(ii)	(i)
(B)	(ii)	(iv)	(i)	(iii)
(C)	(v)	(iii)	(iv)	(ii)
(D)	(iv)	(ii)	(iii)	(v)

49. A committee was set up in 1990 to review NPE (1986). Its report titled as 'Towards in Enlightened and humane Society' stated that system of higher education encourages memorization of facts and regurgitation rather than creativity. The head of the committee was

(A) Acharya Ramamurti
(B) Prof. Yashpal
(C) Prof. M.M. Joshi
(D) None of the above

50. Which of the following is/are a minority institution(s) ?

1. Punjabi University, Patiala
2. Osmania University, Hyderabad
3. Kashmir University, Srinagar
4. St. Stephens College, Delhi

Select the correct answer from the code given below :

(A) 1 and 2 (B) 2 and 4
(C) 2 only (D) 4 only

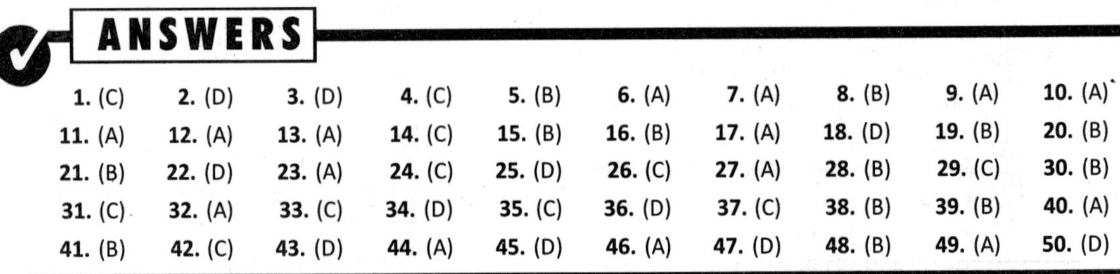

ANSWERS

1. (C)	**2.** (D)	**3.** (D)	**4.** (C)	**5.** (B)	**6.** (A)	**7.** (A)	**8.** (B)	**9.** (A)	**10.** (A)
11. (A)	**12.** (A)	**13.** (A)	**14.** (C)	**15.** (B)	**16.** (B)	**17.** (A)	**18.** (D)	**19.** (B)	**20.** (B)
21. (B)	**22.** (D)	**23.** (A)	**24.** (C)	**25.** (D)	**26.** (C)	**27.** (A)	**28.** (B)	**29.** (C)	**30.** (B)
31. (C)	**32.** (A)	**33.** (C)	**34.** (D)	**35.** (C)	**36.** (D)	**37.** (C)	**38.** (B)	**39.** (B)	**40.** (A)
41. (B)	**42.** (C)	**43.** (D)	**44.** (A)	**45.** (D)	**46.** (A)	**47.** (D)	**48.** (B)	**49.** (A)	**50.** (D)

PREVIOUS YEARS' PAPERS

December 2018

UGC NET – PAPER I

Note: This paper consists of fifty (50) multiple-choice-type of questions. All questions are compulsory.

1. Which of the following indicates the concept of Zone of Proximal Development (ZPD) as suggested by psychologist Lev Vygotsky?
   (A) A leaner's brain develops faster in childhood
   (B) A learner learns effectively when it is supported with real life examples
   (C) What a learner can do with help and without help
   (D) Friends interaction is very important for proper development of child
2. Which among the following is the correct set of four fundamental principles of Rabindranath Tagore's educational philosophy ?
   (A) Humans, Commercialization, Urbanization, Hinduism
   (B) Naturalism, Humanism, Internationalism, Idealism
   (C) Globalisation, Localisation, Transformation, Capitalism
   (D) Socialism, Spiritualism, Tourism, Commercialism
3. The field of study of the theory and practice of self-determined learning that focuses on the importance of knowing how to learn is known as:
   (A) Epistemology (B) Andragogy
   (C) Pedagogy (D) Heutagogy
4. The construction of thought process, which includes remembering, problem solving and decision making is called as:
   (A) Andragogy (B) Psychology
   (C) Pedagogy
   (D) Cognitive Development
5. The field of study dealing with methods and principles used in adult education is known as :
   (A) Pedagogy (B) Andragogy
   (C) Anthropology (D) Gerontology
6. The four approaches to knowing answers to research questions, according to Kerlinger, are:
   (a) Method of tenacity
   (b) Method of intuition
   (c) Method of authority
   (d) Method of science
   (e) Method of creativity
   (f) Method of non-functionality
   Codes:
   (A) (a), (b), (c) and (d) (B) (b), (c), (d) and (e)
   (C) (b), (d), (e) and (f) (D) (c), (d), (e) and (f)
7. One way to measure the extent to which a measure is free of random error is to compute its:
   (A) Content validity (B) Experimenter's bias
   (C) Test-retest reliability
   (D) Demand characteristics
8. Qualitative researchers criticise quantitative research for its tendency towards :
   (A) Emphasis on evidence
   (B) Focus on empiricism
   (C) Reductionism
   (D) Obsession with creativity
9. Which method is appropriate to reduce random error?
   (A) Select large sample size
   (B) Administer the test after a gap of one week
   (C) Administer the treatment in the same way every time
   (D) Administer manipulation checks

* Based on memory only. Please refer ugcnetonline.in

10. In relation to code of conduct in research what does APA stand for?
    (A) Advanced Psychological Authority
    (B) American Psychological Association
    (C) Australian Psychological Association
    (D) Association of Psychological Assessments

Directions-(Q. 11 to 15): Read the following passage carefully and answer questions.

For all the disagreement in the industry about the future of aviation, there is perfect accord on one point : There is going to be a lot more of it. The world's air passengers flew a combined 7.64 trillion kilometers in 2017. By 2037, that will rise to 18.97 billion kilometers, with about 40% of the increase happening within five intra-regional markets : China, India, North-America, Europe and South-east Asia. That is Sparking a battle over the biggest bottleneck holding back this growth airports. The governments that still own many of them should be more open to privatisation to cover a $ 78 billion funding gap in needed capital investments. Airlines, airports' biggest customers, see things differently. Costs at privatised terminals are higher and governments should be cautious about such actions in the interests of expanding the aviation sector as a whole. Privatising an airport does not necessarily make it more efficient. A study has found there was little difference between the performance of airports 100% owned by commercially-oriented government corporations and those majority controlled by private businesses. The key is instead to avoid structures where the incentives for managers are confused or misaligned, such as where private companies are brought in as minority investors or where managers are essentially bureaucrats swayed by political imperatives. There is a better solution of there, but it is not likely to be very attractive to incumbent airlines, airports, or passengers enamoured of the current generation of gleaming terminals : build more, cheaper airports.

11. What is the growth rate in aviation apart from the five intra-regional markets?
    (A) 10 per cent (B) 20 per cent
    (C) 30 per cent (D) 40 per cent
12. Why should the governments be open to privatisation of airports ?
    (A) Because they own many airports
    (B) Because there is a battle for growth
    (C) For necessary capital
    (D) To limit the government control of aviation industry
13. How do airlines see the move for privatisation of airports?
    (a) Feel that costs are high
    (b) Governments should be cautious
    (c) Interest of the aviation sector is important
    (d) It decentralises the authority to control

    Codes :
    (A) (a), (b) and (c) (B) (b), (c) and (d)
    (C) (c), (d) and (a) (D) (d), (a) and (b)
14. What is the key for making airports function efficiently?
    (A) Make private companies as minority shareholders
    (B) Provide misaligned incentives to managers
    (C) Recognise political imperatives of bureaucrats appointed as managers
    (D) Avoid structures of confused incentives to managers
15. Which of the following is the focal inference of the author in the passage ?
    (A) Private ownership of airports does not mean efficient management
    (B) Growth of the aviation industry is distorted
    (C) Airports are not an obstacle to the aviation industry
    (D) Government-owned airports are known for high performance
16. Signs are considered as secondary products of
    (A) Message (B) Channelisation
    (C) Semantic accuracy (D) Infotainment
17. The relational approach in classroom communication comes from
    (A) Intra-personal communication
    (B) Inter-personal communication
    (C) Organisational communication
    (D) Mass communication
18. Classroom speech is considered as a :
    (A) Technical medium
    (B) Non-technical medium
    (C) Mass medium
    (D) Unorganised medium
19. In a classroom, communication becomes effect when participants are:
    (a) Active (b) Empathetic
    (c) Heterophilous (d) Homophilous
    (e) Silent (f) Uncritical

    Codes :
    (A) (a), (b), (c) and (d) (B) (b), (c), (d) and (e)
    (C) (a), (b) and (d) (D) (c), (e) and (f)
20. The information seeking strategies of students are:

(a) Entropy-oriented (b) Overt
(c) Non-functional (d) Indirect
(e) Third party (f) Testing

Codes :

(A) (a), (b), (d) and (e)
(B) (b), (c), (e) and (f)
(C) (b), (d), (e) and (f)
(D) (a), (b), (c) and (f)

21. If DIVE is coded as IMYG, then the code for TAKE will be :

(A) XFMG (B) YENG
(C) TFMG (D) XENG

22. The next term in the series is :
56, 40,27, 17, 10, ...

(A) 6 (C) 8
(B) 7 (D) 5

23. The next term in the letter series is :
ME, KH, IK, GN, ... is

(A) EQ (B) CK
(C) BD (D) DF

24. Choose the word which is different from the rest

(A) Eyes (B) Nose
(C) Legs (D) Hands

25. Ram said, I am the only child of my mother", Next he pointed to a boy and continued, "This boy is the husband of the grandchild of my mother."
How is Ram related to the boy ?

(A) Father (B) Grandfather
(C) Brother-in-law (D) Father-in-law

26. Given below are two premises (a) and (b). Four conclusions are drawn from them. Select the code that states validity drawn conclusion(s) [taking the premises individually or jointly].

Premises :

(a) Some women are teachers.
(b) All teachers are hard-working.

Conclusions :

(i) All hard-working people are teachers.
(ii) All teachers are not women.
(iii) Some hard-Working teachers are women.
(iv) Some women are hard-working.

Codes :

(A) (i) and (ii) (B) (ii) and (iii)
(C) (i) and (iv) (D) (iii) and (iv)

27. In which of the following arguments the Conclusion can be no more than probable?

(A) Implicative (B) Analogical
(C) Deductive (D) Demonstrative

28. "To slow a beast, you break its limbs,
To slow a nation, you break its people."
Identify the argument involved in the above:

(A) Inductive (B) Deductive
(C) Analogical (D) Demonstrative

29. "The relation that exists between Premises and Conclusion is that of logical necessity" is the case with which of the following arguments?

(A) Inductive (B) Deductive
(C) Demonstrative (D) Analogical

30. Among the following statements, two are contradictory to each other. Select the code that represents them.

Statements:

(a) All surgeons are doctors.
(b) Some surgeons are doctors.
(c) Some surgeons are not doctors.
(d) No surgeons are doctors.

Codes:

(A) (a) and (b) (B) (a) and (d)
(C) (b) and (d) (D) (b) and (c)

Direction–(Q. 31 to 33)

Cab	Monday		Tuesday		Wednesday	
	Time (Hours)	Distance (kms)	Time (Hours)	Distance (kms)	Time (Hours)	Distance (kms)
A	16	656	12	480	10	410
B	10	700	14	490	18	720
C	11	770	13	650	16	640
D	12	744	15	825	14	840
E	14	826	14	728	12	840

The table given above gives the number of kilometers travelled and the number of hours taken by five cabs A, B, C, D, and E. Data on three days is given Monday, Tuesday and Wednesday."
Use the above data to answer the questions given below.

31. The average speed of cab A for the three days taken together is approximately :

(A) 10 km/hr (B) 20 km/hr
(C) 30 km/hr (D) 40 km/hr

32. The difference between the average speed of cab C and cab E on Monday is :

(A) 11 kms/hr (B) 21 kms/hr
(C) 31 kms/hr (D) 41 kms/hr

33. Which cab travelled the most in the three days taken together ?

(A) B (B) C
(C) D (D) E

34. Which of the following diagrams indicates the best relation between India, World and New Delhi ?

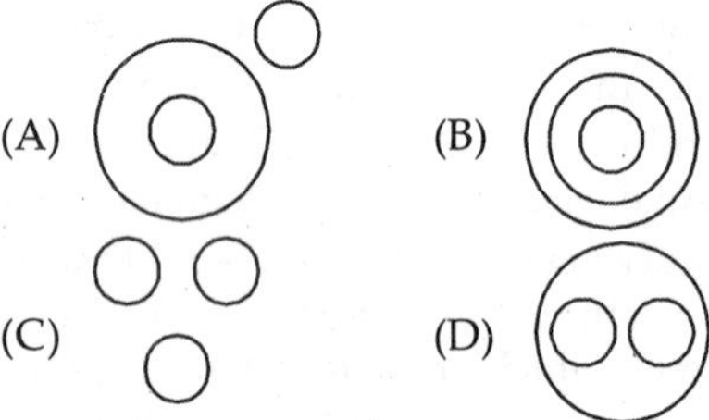

35. Which of the following diagrams best represents the relationship between, family, family member and domestic help?

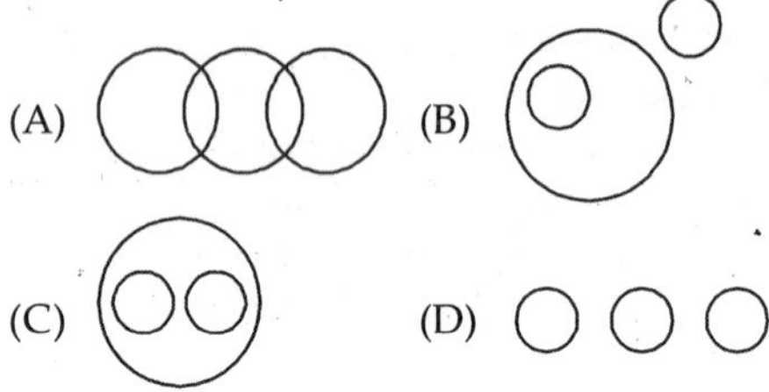

36. Which one of the following is not a Network Topology ?

(A) Ring (B) Chain
(D) Star (C) Bus

37. Match the following :

List-I	List-II
(a) Browser	1. Outlook
(b) Programming Language	2. DOS
(c) Operating System	3. Internet Explorer
(d) E-mail	4. Fortran

The correct code is:

Codes:

	(a)	(b)	(c)	(d)		(a)	(b)	(c)	(d)
(A)	1	3	2	4	(B)	3	4	2	1
(C)	2	3	4	1	(D)	4	3	2	1

38. Which of the following denotes the Internet hardware requirements ?

(a) Hub (b) Bridge
(c) Router (d) Gateway
(e) Modem

Codes :

(A) (e) only
(B) (a), (b) and (e)
(C) (b), (c), (d) and (e)
(D) (a), (b), (c), (d) and (e)

39. A set of rules used in communication in a network is called:

(A) Interface (B) Protocol
(C) Address (D) Reference

40. Which of the following are pointing devices?

(a) Trackball
(b) Touchscreen
(c) Graphic Tablet
(d) Joystick

Codes:

(A) (a) only
(B) (a) and (d)
(C) (a), (b) and (d)
(D) (a), (b), (c) and (d)

41. A study was carried out on the drought resilience in India. Which of the following States show highest level of handling drought?

(A) Telangana, Andhra Pradesh, Tamil Nadu
(B) Odhisha, Karnataka, Kerala
(C) Sikkim, Punjab, Arunachal Pradesh
(D) Jharkhand, Chhattisgarh, Jammu and Kashmir

42. The most harmful types of environmental pollutants are

(A) Human organic wastes
(B) Wastes from faecal matter
(C) Non-biodegradable chemicals
(D) Natural nutrients present in excess

43. Assertion (A) : Natural gas is very attractive eco-friendly fuel.

Reason (R) : It produces few pollutants and less carbon dioxide per unit energy than any other fossil fuel on Combustion,

Codes :

(A) Both (A) and (R) are true and (R) is the correct explanation of (A)
(B) Both (A) and (R) are true and (R) is not the correct explanation of (A)
(C) (A) is true, but (R) is false
(D) (A) is false, but (R) is true

44. What percentage of energy coming from the Sun is re-radiated towards the space ?
(A) 15% (B) 25%
(C) 30% (D) 50%

45. As per Central Forestry Commission (CFC), how many forest types are found in our country?
(A) 15 (B) 20
(C) 28 (D) 16

46. The number of open universities and directorates of distance education whose courses are recognised by UGC as on August 9, 2018, is:
(A) 49 (B) 53
(C) 58 (D) 62

47. Match the following :

List-I
(a) Open University
(b) Dual Mode University
(c) Mixed Mode University
(d) Deemed University
(e) Specialised University

List-II
1. Odisha State Open University, Odisha
2. Amity University
3. Indian Institute of Science, Bengaluru
4. University of Mumbai, Mumbai
5. School of Planning and Architecture, New Delhi

Codes :

	(a)	(b)	(c)	(d)	(e)
(A)	3	2	5	1	4
(B)	1	4	2	3	5
(C)	5	1	4	2	3
(D)	2	3	1	4	5

48. Which private institutions in the following list have been granted the status of "Institutes of Eminence" by the MHRD?
1. BITS, Pilani
2. MAHE, Manipal
3. Symbiosis, Pune
4. Amity University, Noida

Choose the correct answer from the code given below :

Codes :
(A) 1 and 2 (B) 1 and 3
(C) 2 and 3 (D) 2 and 4

49. One of the first states to establish a higher education council was :
(A) Sikkim (B) Goa
(C) Andhra Pradesh
(D) Jammu and Kashmir

50. State higher education councils are established under the instruction of :
(A) NITI Ayog (B) RUSA
(C) CABE (D) PUSA

1. (C)	**2.** (B)	**3.** (D)	**4.** (D)	**5.** (B)	**6.** (A)	**7.** (C)	**8.** (C)	**9.** (C)	**10.** (B)
11. (D)	**12.** (C)	**13.** (A)	**14.** (D)	**15.** (A)	**16.** (B)	**17.** (B)	**18.** (B)	**19.** (C)	**20.** (C)
21. (B)	**22.** (A)	**23.** (A)	**24.** (B)	**25.** (D)	**26.** (D)	**27.** (B)	**28.** (C)	**29.** (B)	**30.** (C)
31. (D)	**32.** (A)	**33.** (C)	**34.** (B)	**35.** (B)	**36.** (B)	**37.** (B)	**38.** (D)	**39.** (B)	**40.** (D)
41. (C)	**42.** (C)	**43.** (A)	**44.** (C)	**45.** (D)	**46.** (B)	**47.** (B)	**48.** (A)	**49.** (C)	**50.** (B)

June 2019

UGC NET – PAPER I

Note : **This paper consists of Fifty (50) objective type questions of Two (2) marks each. All questions are compulsory.**

1. When the learning outcomes of students are ensured with employment of less resources and effort on the part of a teacher and more initiative for self-learning is evident, which of the following expression will describe the teacher most appropriately?
   (A) Teacher is successful
   (B) Teacher is effective
   (C) Teacher is intelligent
   (D) Teacher is practical
2. A hypothesis should be conceptually
   (A) convoluted, complex and generic
   (B) complex, tough and general
   (C) simple, clear and specific
   (D) obscure, complicated and simple
3. Peer group interaction in a classroom helps in
   (A) Concept understanding
   (B) Realization of one's misunderstanding
   (C) Rapport Building
   (D) Questioning
4. Mailed questionnaire, observation, interview and collective questionnaire are instances of
   (A) Secondary sources (B) Personal sources
   (C) Primary sources (D) Tertiary sources
5. The study of 'why does stressful living result in heart attack'? can be classified as
   (A) Descriptive research
   (B) Explanatory research
   (C) Correlational research
   (D) Feasibility research
6. Listening is important for a teacher to
   (A) address the requirement of the learner.
   (B) gain knowledge.
   (C) keep the learner in good humour.
   (D) evaluate the learner for the progress made
7. Inclusive education implies
   (A) Ensuring learning outcome of every child to be the same
   (B) Including the disabled in the main stream
   (C) Provides compulsory education for children below 14 years
   (D) Ensuring that no child is left behind in education
8. During research, while recording observation if an observer rates an individual based on the rating given in another aspect of the interaction, this is termed as the
   (A) Evaluation effect
   (B) Error of central tendency
   (C) Halo effect
   (D) Categorical effect
9. The formulation of a research problem can be compared to
   (A) Laying the foundation of a building
   (B) Building the walls of a home
   (C) Polishing the doors of a building.
   (D) Constructing the ceiling of a house
10. Reflective Practice implies use of one's
    (A) Cognition (B) Metacognition
    (C) Metacognition on cognition
    (D) Reinforcement of learning

Directions (Q. 11-15): Read the following passage and answer the questions.

A business will usually go through a clear set of stages that will make up its organisational lie cycle. These stages include introduction, early growth, continuous growth, maturity and decline. The first stage, the introduction state, is the start-up phase where a business decides what its core strengths and capabilities are and starts selling its product or service. At this early stage, the founder or founders will be a part of every aspect of the daily process of the business. The main goal at this stage is to take off to a good start and make a place in the market. The next stage, the early growth phase, aims at increased sales and more development. The focus at this stage remains on the original product or service but the effort is to increase the market share and venture into related products or services. The main goal is to

* Based on memory only. Please refer ugcnetonline.in

move the founder to a more managerial role so more time is spent on managing and building the business. At this stage, documents and policies need to be developed so any member of the organisation can see the business any time. The third stage, the continuous growth stage, requires a systematic structure and more formal relationships among its participants. At this stage, the resource requirements of the business need careful handling. The focus is on the expansion of the business, keeping in mind its core strength and capability. A formal organisational structure and a clear delegation plan are important at this stage. At the fourth stage of maturity, a business often slows down as the level of innovative energy may have become weak and the formal structures may have become obstacles. A lot of care is required to prevent decline.

11. The resource requirements of a business need careful handling at which stage?
(A) Fourth (B) First
(C) Third (D) Second

12. Venturing into related products and services does not mean that a business will
(A) ignore the original product
(B) move the founder to a more managerial role
(C) delegate more responsibilities
(D) ignore the related products and services

13. The founder of a business does not move to a more managerial role at which stag
(A) Early growth stage (B) Maturity stage
(C) Decline stage (D) Start up stage

14. The slowing down of a business can happen if
(A) there is a decline in the market share
(B) the level of innovative energy weakens
(C) the managerial roles are not clear
(D) the level of investment declines

15. When will a business create its place in the market?
(A) At maturity (B) At introduction
(C) At early growth (D) At late growth

16. Which of the following is a characteristic of modern mass media?
(A) Capital intensive (B) Labour intensive
(C) Sustainable (D) Developmental

17. Which of the following signifies non-verbal communication in an essential way?
(A) Instructions written on a question paper.
(B) Learner attending an online class.
(C) The dress code followed by an individual.
(D) Yoga instructor teaching yoga poses to the pupils.

18. Which of the following is a stage of intrapersonal communication?
(A) Phatic stage (B) Intimate stage
(C) Personal stage
(D) Transcendental communication

19. Statements:
No Musicians are Japanese.
All Barbers are Musicians.
No Barbers are Japanese.
Identify the Middle Term in the above syllogism.
(A) Subject in the first premise and predicate in the second premise.
(B) Predicate in the first premise and subject in the second premise.
(C) Predicate in the both premises.
(D) Subject in both the premises

20. Consider the example given below:
Devadatta is growing fat.
He does not eat food during the day.
Therefore, He must be eating food during the night, other things being equal.
Identify the logic involved in the example provided above by choosing the correct answer from options given below:
(A) Arthapatti (B) Anupalabdi
(C) Anumana (D) Sabda

21. Consider the argument provided below:
"Sound is permanent because it is a product like the jar".
Identify the fallacy involved in the above argument on the basis of Indian logic from the options given below:
(A) Fallacy of contradictory reason
(B) Fallacy of wrong assertion
(C) Fallacy of irrelevant reason
(D) Fallacy of trivial reason

22. If RED is coded as 6720, then how would GREEN be coded?
(A) 16717209 (B) 1677209
(C) 9207716 (D) 1677199

23. Inductive argument proceeds from
(A) Universal to Particular
(B) Particular to Universal
(C) Universal to Universal
(D) Particular to Particular

24. Semantic barrier of communication is implied when the
(A) signal is lost before reaching the receiver.
(B) message transmitted by the source is unclear.
(C) receiver's attention is diverted.
(D) receiver does not understand the meaning of the message.

25. A trader mixes three varieties of refined oil costing Rs. 100, Rs. 40 and Rs. 60 per litre in the ratio 2:4:3 in terms of litre, and sells the mixture at Rs. 66 per litre. What percentage of profit does he make?
(A) 25% (B) 10%
(C) 9% (D) 8%

26. Among the five friends, Vineet is taller than Monika, but not as tall as Ram. Jacob is taller than Dalip but shorter than Monika. Who is the tallest in their group?
(A) Ram (B) Monika
(C) Vineet (D) Jacob

27. **Assertion (A):** Communication presupposes a shared, symbolic environment, a social relationship even among non-participants.
Reason (R): It leads to social interaction, which in combination with other factors contributes to a sense of community.
Choose the correct option given below:
(A) Both (A) and (R) are true and R is the correct explanation of A.
(B) Both (A) and (R) are true but R is not the correct explanation of A.
(C) (A) is true but (R) is false.
(D) (A) is false but (R) is true.

28. A man travelled from the village to the railway station at the rate of 20 Kmph and walked back at the rate of 5 kmph. If the whole journey took 5 hours, find the distance of the railway station from the village.
(A) 10 km (B) 15 km
(C) 20 km (D) 40 km

29. If 0.75 x = 0.02 y, then the value of (Y-X)/(Y+X) is
(A) 73/75 (B) 75/77
(C) 73/77 (D) 730/75

30. If the average of five numbers is (-20) and the sum of three of the numbers is 32, then what is the average of the other two numbers?
(A) (– 66) (B) (– 33)
(C) (– 34) (D) (– 132)

Direction (Q. 31-35):

Consider the following table that shows the production of fertilizers by a company (in 10000 tonnes) during the year 2011 to 2018. Answer the questions based on the data contained in the table:

Year	2011	2012	2013	2014	2015	2016	2017	2018
Production of Fertilizers:	35	50	70	55	75	60	85	90

31. What was the approximate percentage increase in production of fertilizers in 2018 compared to that in 2011?
(A) 157% (B) 165%
(C) 177% (D) 182%

32. In how many of the given years was the production of fertilizers more than the average production of the given years?
(A) 2 (B) 3
(C) 4 (D) 5

33. The average production of 2012 and 2013 was exactly equal to the average production of which of the following pairs of years?
(A) 2011 and 2012 (B) 2011 and 2017
(C) 2012 and 2014 (D) 2015 and 2016

34. In which year, the percentage increase in production as compared to the previous year was maximum?
(A) 2012 (B) 2013
(C) 2015 (D) 2018

35. What was the percentage decline in the production of fertilizers from 2013 to 2014?
(A) 20.4% (B) 21.4%
(C) 22.6% (D) 24.2%

36. Match the following :

Set-I	Set-II
(a) First Generation	(i) Transistor
(b) Second Generation	(ii) VLSI microprocessor
(c) Third Generation	(iii) Vacuum tube
(d) Fourth Generation	(iv) Integrated circuit

Codes:

	(a)	(b)	(c)	(d)		(a)	(b)	(c)	(d)
(A)	(iii)	(iv)	(i)	(ii)	(B)	(iii)	(i)	(iv)	(ii)
(C)	(iii)	(i)	(ii)	(iv)	(D)	(i)	(iii)	(iv)	(ii)

37. A/An ________ is a computer program that spreads by inserting copies of itself into other executable code or documents.
(A) Operating system (B) Computer Virus
(C) Firewall (D) Anti-virus

38. The expansion of SANKALP is
(A) Sanskrit Awareness and Knowledge Acquisition of Language Programme.
(B) kills Acquisition and Karatae Awareness for Livelihood Promotion.
(C) Skills Acquisition and Knowledge Awareness for Livelihood Promotion.
(D) Sanskrit Awareness and Knowledge Acquisition for Livelihood Promotion.

39. Which of the following is not a/an web browser?
(A) Internet Explorer (B) Mozilla Firefox
(C) Google Chrome (D) Yahoo

40. Which pollutant is the major source of marine pollution?
(A) Agricultural run-off
(B) Oil spill
(C) Industrial waste water
(D) Sewage

41. In Audio and Video compression, the term RGB means
(A) Red, Grey, Blue (B) Red, Green, Blue
(C) Red, Green, Black (D) Red, Grey, Black

42. The report of which of the following Education Commissions carries the sub-title 'Education for National Development'?
(A) Radhakrishnan Commission
(B) Mudaliar Commission
(C) Calcutta University Education Commission
(D) Kothari Commission

43. One Terabyte (TB) of memory is equal to
(A) 1024 KB (B) 1024 × 1024 KB
(C) 1024 × 1024 × 1024 KB
(D) 1024 × 1024 × 1024 Bytes

44. Permafrost is defining characteristic of which biome?
(A) Taiga (B) Tundra
(C) Grassland (D) Desert

45. The target set by Indian government for generating power from wind energy by the year 2022 is
(A) 60 GW (B) 50 GW
(C) 40 GW (D) 15 GW

46. The mangroves exist in
(A) Fresh water system
(B) Temperate areas
(C) Semi-arid areas (D) Saline waters

47. In which year the modern Indian University got established?
(A) 1957 (B) 1857
(C) 1947 (D) 1964

48. Which of the following statements best explains the concept of sustainable development?
(A) Use of natural resources minimally.
(B) Use of natural resources for our benefit.
(C) Use of natural resources judiciously so that they are available for further generations.
(D) Preserve our natural resources for our future generation.

49. Chemical oxygen demand in eutrophic water is
(A) Low (B) High
(C) Medium (D) Extremely low

50. In which era given below, higher education in India got a set back?
(A) British Era (B) Buddhist Era
(C) Mughal Era (D) Post-Independence Era

ANSWERS

1. (B)	2. (C)	3. (A)	4. (A)	5. (B)	6. (A)	7. (D)	8. (C)	9. (A)	10. (C)
11. (C)	12. (A)	13. (D)	14. (B)	15. (B)	16. (A)	17. (C)	18. (B)	19. (A)	20. (A)
21. (B)	22. (B)	23. (B)	24. (D)	25. (B)	26. (A)	27. (D)	28. (C)	29. (C)	30. (A)
31. (A)	32. (C)	33. (B)	34. (A)	35. (B)	36. (B)	37. (B)	38. (C)	39. (D)	40. (A)
41. (B)	42. (D)	43. (C)	44. (B)	45. (A)	46. (D)	47. (B)	48. (C)	49. (B)	50. (C)

December 2019

UGC NET – PAPER I

Note: This paper consists of fifty (50) multiple-choice-type of questions. All questions are compulsory.

1. Classroom Interactions are influenced largely by
(A) Student's commitment
(B) Teacher centric environment
(C) Organisational oversight
(D) Unsolicited interventions

2. A 50 year old man has a son whose age is 2/5 of his age. After how many, the ratio of the age of the man to his son will be 5/3?
(A) 10 Years (B) 15 Years
(C) 20 Years (D) 25 Years

3. "In this hospital, some nurses don't wear white dress, some doctors have private practice and medicines prescribed are of high cost. Therefore, treatment in this hospital is of poor quality". What fallacy does this argument make?
(A) Fallacy of composition
(B) Slippery slope
(C) Fallacy of accident (D) Fallacy of division

4. Which of the following is true with reference to anupalabdhi as a means of knowledge?
(A) I do not cognize the pot on the table, therefore it is absent there
(B) I directly perceive the absence of pot on the table
(C) I infer the absence of pot on the table since I do not find it to be there
(D) I know the absence of the pot on the table because I know its similarly with other

5. Bog is a wetland that receives water from
(A) nearby water bodies (B) melting
(C) rain fall only (D) sea only

6. Which one of the following is the characteristic feature of an argument?
(A) It is either valid or invalid
(B) It is neither valid nor invalid
(C) It is either true or false
(D) It is neither true nor false

7. In which of the following steps of research, the scope for creativity and imagination is utmost?
(A) Identifying the research problem and defining it
(B) Figuring out the related studies and the techniques used by other researchers
(C) Identifying variables and hypothesizing
(D) Data analysis and presentation of results

8. A college teacher does research with a view to depict the reality situations relating to home conditions of students and hostels provided for. Which of the following research format will be helpful to do so?
(A) Experimental Research
(B) Descriptive Research
(C) Participant observation based research
(D) Ethnographic Research

9. Which of the following is an example of maximum performance test?
(A) Projective personality test
(B) Interest inventory
(C) Aptitude test (D) Attitude scales

10. The length of the side of a square (5.0 cm × 5.0 cm) is increased by 1%. By what percentage (%), the area of the square increases?
(A) 1% (B) 2% (C) 5% (D) 4%

11. Consider the following statements and choose the right option
(1) Middle term should be distributed in atleast one premise
(2) Middle term should be present in the conclusion
(3) Both premises can be particular in a valid argument
(4) Both premises can be negative in a valid argument
(A) (3) and (4) (B) Only (3)
(C) Only (1) (D) (2) and (3)

12. When a large number of students with different performances levels are there in the class. For uniform imparting of educative interactions, a teacher should opt for a communication which is:
(A) Top-down and linear
(B) Technology - enabled
(C) Individual - centric (D) Self - projected

13. In case the population of research is heterogeneous in nature which of the following sampling techniques will ensure optimum representativeness of sample units?
(A) Simple random sampling
(B) Stratified random sampling
(C) Cluster sampling
(D) Systematic sampling

14. Given below are two statements one is labelled as Assertion (A) and the other is labelled as Reason (R)
Assertion (A): Classrooms communication is pre-decided by social and institutional demands.
Reasons (R): Positive educative actions should guide learners to acquire knowledge of social significance.
In the light of the above two statements, choose the correct option:
(A) Both (A) and (R) are true and is the correct explanation of (A)

* Based on memory only. Please refer ugcnetonline.in

(B) Both (A) and (R) true and is not the correct explanation of (A)
(C) (A) is true, but is (R) false
(D) (A) is false, but is (R) true

15. A person buys 3 items of Rs. 1500 each and 2 items of Rs. 1800 each from a shopping mall. On the total bill a discount of 10% is given. What is the average cost of the items?
(A) 1000 (B) 1458 (C) 1658 (D) 1550

16. The emphasis in memory level teaching is on which of the following?
(a) Organisation of thoughts and ideas
(b) Seeing of relationships among facts
(c) Systematic presentations to enable quick reproduction
(d) Critical thinking
(e) Mastery of concept sequencing of facts
(f) Segregating one feature from another
Choose the answer from the following options:
(A) (a), (b) and (c) (B) (a), (c) and (e)
(C) (b), (c) and (d) (D) (d), (e) and (f)

17. Classroom communication is
(a) Like a computer-program
(b) Dictatorial
(c) Purposeful (d) Pragmatic
Choose the correct option from those given below
(A) (a) and (c) (B) (b) and (c)
(C) (b) and (d) (D) (c) and (d)

18. Which of the following teaching method(s) is/are contributive to direct learning?
(a) Team teaching and lecturing
(b) Simulation and role playing
(c) Lecture with or without use of audio-visuals
(d) Participation in workshop and assignments
(e) MOOCs and heuristics
(f) Interactive presentation
Choose your answer from the following options:
(A) (b), (d) and (e) (B) (a), (b) and (c)
(C) (c), (d) and (f) (D) (d), (e) and (f)

19. Which of the following statistical technique will be appropriate for data analysis when the observations are available in the form of frequencies?
(A) Parametric 't' test
(B) Non-parametric 'u' test
(C) Non-parametric 'chi-square' test
(D) Parametric correlated 't' test

20. The most characteristic feature of an adolescent learner which determines his/her social and moral development is the
(A) Tendency to be away from parents
(B) Concern for hero worshipping for emulating values and standards
(C) Mixing up with peers in the neighborhood
(D) Identity crisis

21. "If it rains, then the drought will end. The drought has ended. Therefore, it rained". Which kind of fallacy does this commit?
(A) Deductive fallacy (B) Inductive fallacy
(C) Abductive fallacy (D) Informal fallacy

22. The smallest integer greater than 1 which is simultaneously a square and a cube of certain
(A) 8 (B) 9 (C) 36 (D) 64

23. Below are given two sets in which set I specifies the four behaviour modification techniques while set II indicates their exemplification. Match the two sets

Set I (Behaviour modification techniques)	Set II (Example)
(a) Positive reinforcement	i. Withdrawal of a pleasant stimulus or application of an aversive stimulus to stop the behaviour
(b) Negative reinforcement	ii. Painful or aversive stimulus is presented to stop the occurrence of behaviour
(c) Punishment	iii. The behaviour increases in frequency after the removal of the stimulus
(d) Extinction	iv. The behaviour increases in frequency after the presentation of a stimulus

Choose your answer from the following options:
(A) (a)-(i), (b)-(ii), (c)-(iii), (d)-(iv)
(B) (a)-(ii), (b)-(i), (c)-(iii), (d)-(iv)
(C) (a)-(iv), (b)-(iii), (c)-(ii), (d)-(i)
(D) (a)-(iii), (b)-(i), (c)-(ii), (d)-(iv)

24. Swapping of encoder- decoder roles in communication happens due to
(A) Cognitive disruptions'
(B) Semantic noise
(C) Feedback analysis
(D) Weak channelization

25. A research scholar while finally reporting the research results in the form of a thesis acknowledge the support of his/her supervisor in the preface. This will be treated as a
(A) Sheer formality (B) Needed formality
(C) Superfluous act (D) Part of ethically

Consider of the following table that shows the amount of exports (in crore) from three different companies A, B, and C over these years 2012-2018. Based on the date in the table.

Answer the questions 26-30

Year-wise amount of Exports from companies

Year	Amount of exports (In crore Rs) A	B	C
2012	40	90	70
2013	70	50	100
2014	50	70	130
2015	80	70	100
2016	110	90	70
2017	60	110	90
2018	130	150	110

26. In how many of the given years, were the exports from company A more than its average annual exports over the given years?
(A) 2 (B) 3 (C) 4 (D) 5

27. In which year, the absolute difference between the exports from companies A and B was the minimum?
(A) 2013 (B) 2014 (C) 2015 (D) 2016

28. What was the difference between the average exports of three companies in 2017 and the average exports of three companies in 2012?
(A) 15.33 crores (B) 18.67 crores
(C) 25 crores (D) 20 crores

29. For which of the following pairs of years, the total exports from the three companies put together are equal?
(A) 2014 and 2017 (B) 2015 and 2017
(C) 2016 and 2017 (D) 2014 and 2015

30. Average annual amount of exports during the given period for company B is approximately what percent (%) of the average annual amount of exports for company C?
(A) 64% (B) 21% (C) 3% (D) 33%

31. Which among the following is the flagship scheme of the Ministry of Skill Development and Entrepreneurship implemented by National Skills Development Corporation?
(A) Robotic India
(B) Artificial Intelligence @ schools
(C) Make in India
(D) Pradhan Mantri Kaushal Vikas Yojna

32. Which one of the following represents the correct order of sequence for reading skills in the context of research?
(A) Read, question, recall, review, survey
(B) Questions, survey, read, recall, review
(C) Recall, review, survey, question, read
(D) Survey, question, read, recall, review

33. Match the following study skills with their effective learning techniques:

Study Skills	**Learning Techniques**
(a) Elaborative interrogation	i. Mixing different kinds of problems together when studying
(b) Practice Testing	ii. Explaining what a section of text or an example problem means to you
(c) Self-Explanation	iii. Testing yourself on the material you are trying to learn
(d) Interleaved practice	iv. Answering why a fact is true

Choose the correct option:
(A) (a)-(iv), (b)-(iii), (c)-(ii), (d)-(i)
(B) (a)-(i), (b)-(ii), (c)-(iv), (d)-(iii)
(C) (a)-(ii), (b)-(iv), (c)-(i),(d)-(iii)
(D) (a)-(iii),(b)-(i), (c)-(ii), (d)-(iv)

34. Which among the following natural hazards has relatively slow onset?
(A) Volcanic eruptions (B) Droughts
(C) Wild free (D) Land and slides

35. Under Kyoto protocol, the parties, in the second commitment period, have to reduce their greenhouse gas emissions with reference to 1990 levels by atleast
(A) 10% (B) 12% (C) 15% (D) 18%

36. Match List-I with List-II in the context of computer networking:

List-I	**List-II**
(a) VOIP	i. Makes use of light pulses to transmit data
(b) Fibre-optic cable	ii. Use of internet to make phone calls
(c) URL	iii. Most appropriate to connect computers in a small building
(d) UTP cable	iv. Text used by web browsers to locate a web address on the Internet.

Choose the correct option:
(A) (a)-(iv), (b)-(i), (c)-(ii), (d)-(iii)
(B) (a)-(ii), (b)-(i), (c)-(iv), (d)-(iii)
(C) (a)-(ii), (b)-(iii), (c)-(iv), (d)-(i)
(D) (a)-(iv), (b)-(iii), (c)-(ii), (d)-(i)

37. Major Sources of oxygen demanding waste in fresh water systems are
(a) Agricultural run-off (b) Food Processing
(c) Ore Mining (d) Sewage effluent
(e) Landfill sites
Choose the correct options from these given below:
(A) (a), (d) and (e) (B) (b), (d) and (e)
(C) (a), (b) and (d) (D) (a), (b), (c) and (d)

38. The next term in the series
2, 5, 10, 17, 26, 37, _?_ is :
(A) 57 (B) 62 (C) 72 (D) 50

39. Select the option that includes file formats suitable for distributing sound files across the internet.
(A) Wmv,mp4,wma,mp3
(B) Avi,midi,wav,mp3
(C) Avi,mov,wmv,mp3
(D) Midi,wav,wma,mp3

40. Biomass fuels have the potential to form a sustainable carbon neutral energy source because they
(A) Produce carbon dioxide in combustion as much as they consume when they grow
(B) Produce less amount of carbon dioxide on combustion compared to the amount they use during their growth
(C) Have carbon dioxide content same as fossil fuels
(D) Do not produce hazardous emissions on combustion

41. Which of the following is/are major issues arising out of the growing reliance on information technology?

(a) Profitability (b) Security threats
(c) Privacy concerns
Choose the correct option:
(A) (a) and (b) only (B) (a) and (c) only
(C) (b) and (c) only (D) (a), (b) and (c)

42. In the age of four Vedas, students were admitted to the Vedic schools after performance of which ceremony, among the following:
(A) Upanayana ceremony
(B) Utsarjana ceremony
(C) Satapatha ceremony
(D) Dhanurvidya ceremony

43. Which of the following statements is/are correct?
(a) For the sequence of integers represented in binary as 00111, 01001, 01011, P.... the next integer P would be represented as 01101
(b) A byte is a binary number consisting of exactly 8 bits
Choose the correct option:
(A) (a) only (B) (b) only
(C) Both (a) and (b)
(D) Neither (a) and (b)

44. Which of the following communication technologies employ only asynchronous communication?
(A) Video conferencing (B) Email
(C) Forums (D) Instant messaging
Choose the correct option:
(A) (a) and (c) only (B) (b) and (d) only
(C) (b) and (c) only (D) (a) and (d) only

45. In order to meet the new demands of market economy and produce competent graduates, who can compete with their counterparts in international markets, the first and foremost change that needs to be introduced in the prevailing system of Indian higher education is related to:
(A) Admission process (B) Curriculum
(C) Educational technology
(D) Appointment of teachers

Read the passage and answer questions from 46 to 50.

Anyone who has ever been in a classroom where the teacher's presentation was lifeless, static and without vocal variety ran appreciate the commonsense value of the affective side of teaching. However, unlike the other behaviours, affect cannot be captured in transcripts of teaching or by classroom interaction instruments. Narrowly focused research instruments often miss a teacher's affective nature, which emerges from a more holistic view of the classroom. This affective nature is the foundation on which one can build a warm and nurturing relationship with his or her learness. What the instruments miss, the students see clearly. Students are good perceivers of the emotions and intentions underlying a teacher's actions and they often respond accordingly. A teacher who is excited about the subject being taught and shows it by facial expressions, voice inflection, gesture and movement thus communicating respect and caring for the learner- is more likely to hold the attention of students and motivate them to higher levels of achievement than one who does not exhibit these behaviours. Students take their cues from these affective signs and lower or heighten their engagement with the lesson accordingly. Enthusiasm is an important aspect of a teacher's affect. Enthusiasm is the teacher's vigour, power, involvement excitement, and interest during a classroom presentation and willingness to share this emotion with learners, who will want to respond in kind.

46. The affective nature of teaching is reflected in
(A) Deeper understanding of the classroom environment
(B) Other behaviours of the teacher
(C) The recording of classroom interaction
(D) The limited reliance on research instruments

47. The affective signs will provide students
(A) The basis for understanding contents
(B) Exhibitional behaviours
(C) Cues to hold attention
(D) A basis which triggers further enthusiasm

48. The passage focuses attention on
(A) Lifeless classroom presentation
(B) Affective factors of teaching
(C) Students as emotional learners
(D) Measuring teacher's affective nature

49. When does one feel the need for the value of affective aspects of teaching?
(A) When a teacher has a vocal variety
(B) When a teacher makes a dynamic presentation
(C) When a teacher's presentation is monotonous
(D) When a teacher's lecture is beyond expectation

50. Students respect a teacher who
(A) Is emotional
(B) Displays concern for students
(C) Has a powerful voice
(D) Has narcissitic attitude

ANSWERS

1. (A)	2. (D)	3. (B)	4. (A)	5. (A)	6. (A)	7. (C)	8. (C)	9. (C)	10. (B)
11. (C)	12. (B)	13. (B)	14. (A)	15. (B)	16. (B)	17. (D)	18. (A)	19. (C)	20. (C)
21. (A)	22. (D)	23. (C)	24. (C)	25. (D)	26. (B)	27. (C)	28. (D)	29. (D)	30. (C)
31. (D)	32. (D)	33. (A)	34. (B)	35. (D)	36. (B)	37. (C)	38. (D)	39. (D)	40. (A)
41. (C)	42. (A)	43. (C)	44. (C)	45. (B)	46. (A)	47. (D)	48. (B)	49. (C)	50. (B)

November 2020

UGC NET – PAPER I

Note: This paper consists of Fifty (50) objective type questions of Two (2) marks each. All questions are compulsory.

1. The modality of 'teaching' has to be differentiated from training or 'instructing' in terms of which of the following learning outcomes?
   (A) Disciplined and patterned behavior
   (B) Critical and creative thinking
   (C) Firm and durable association of ideas
   (D) Quick feedback
2. Which of the given learner characteristics are associated with field dependent (holistic/visual) learning style?
   (i) Focusing on facts and principles
   (ii) Relating concepts to personal experience
   (iii) Formal interaction with teacher related to tasks at hand
   (iv) Preferring to compete rather than cooperate
   (v) Preferring to cooperate rather than compete
   (vi) Perceiving global aspects of concepts and materials
   Choose the correct answer from the options given below:
   (A) (i), (ii) and (iii)
   (B) (ii), (iii) and (v)
   (C) (ii), (v) and (vi)
   (D) (iv), (v) and (vi)
3. Which of the following potential factors affecting teaching are related to instructional facilities and learning environment?
   (i) Praise and encouragement by teachers
   (ii) Non availability of textbooks/reading materials for use
   (iii) Proactive moves in the interactive processes
   (iv) Shortage of highly qualified teachers
   (v) Availability of smart classes
   Choose the correct answer from the following options:
   (A) (i), (ii) and (iii)
   (B) (ii), (iii) and (v)
   (C) (i), (iv) and (v)
   (D) (iii), (iv) and (v)
4. When the 'test data' tell us about a student's level of proficiency in a defined area the procedure of evaluation is called
   (A) Formative evaluation
   (B) Summative evaluation
   (C) Norm-referenced testing
   (D) Criterion-referenced testing
5. Which of the following is indicative of innovations in evaluation system at present'?
   (A) Semesterization system
   (B) Project based evaluation system
   (C) Choice based credit system
   (D) Objective based evaluation system
6. Identify the qualitative research designs from the list given below:
   (i) Exploring common experiences of individuals to develop a theory
   (ii) Controlling, manipulating, observing and measuring the effect
   (iii) Exploring the shared culture of a group of people
   (iv) Exploring individual stories to describe the lives of people
   (v) Extending generalizations from sample to population
   Select the correct answer from the following options:
   (A) (i), (iii) and (iv)
   (B) (i), (ii) and (iii)
   (C) (ii), (iii) and (v)
   (D) (ii), (iv) and (v)
7. Which of the following shows the correct sequence in undertaking Action Research based studies?
   (A) Planning, Acting on the plan, Observing and Reflecting
   (B) Acting on the plan, Observing, Planning and Reflecting
   (C) Reflecting, Planning, Acting on the plan and Observing
   (D) Acting on the plan, Reflecting, Planning and Observing
8. Application of ICT in research is relevant in which of the following stages?
   (i) Survey of related studies
   (ii) Data collection in the field

* Based on memory only. Please refer ugcnetonline.in

(iii) Data Analysis
(iv) Writing the thesis
(v) Indexing the references

Choose the most appropriate option from those given below:

(A) (ii), (iv) and (v)
(B) (i), (iii) and (v)
(C) (i), (ii) and (iv)
(D) (ii), (iii) and (iv)

9. Match List I with List II

List I (Key Terms used in Research)	List II (Description of Terms)
(a) Hypothesis	(i) Techniques used for collection of facts and information
(b) Sample	(ii) Devices for arriving at conclusions
(c) Research Design	(iii) A tentative statement indicating potential solution of the problem of study
(d) Research Tool	(iv) A subset drawn from a defined set
	(v) Conceptual framework for conducting research

Select the correct answer from the options given below:

(A) (a) - (i), (b) - (ii), (c) - (iii), (d) - (iv)
(B) (a) - (ii), (b) - (iii), (c) - (iv), (d) - (v)
(C) (a) - (i), (b) - (ii), (c) - (iv), (d) - (iii)
(D) (a) - (iii), (b) - (iv), (c) - (v), (d) - (i)

10. A researcher reports his/her research finding to the research audience in such a way that his/her personal views are necessarily getting supported. This would involves issues relating to

(A) Technical aberration
(B) Research ethics
(C) Scientific rigour
(D) Personal predilection

11. Given below are two statements, one is labelled Assertion (A) and the other is labeled Reason (R)

Assertion (A): Depending upon the classroom situation, some media of communication are more effective than others.

Reason (R): Selection of a medium is directly related to the nature of the message for students

In the light of the above, choose the correct answer from the options given below:

(A) Both A) and R) are true and R) is the correct explanation of A)
(B) Both A) and R) are true but R) is not the correct explanation of A)
(C) A) is true but R) is false
(D) A) is false, but R) is true

12. Communication skills of students can be improved by

(a) Asking general questions
(b) Exposure to new technology
(c) Fostering critical thinking
(d) Discriminant use of vocabulary
(e) Limited listening

Choose the most appropriate answer from the options given below:

(A) (a), (b) and (c)
(B) (b), (c) and (d)
(C) (c), (d) and (e)
(D) (a), (d) and (e)

13. Structured classroom communication can be categorized as

(A) Inter-personal communication
(B) Vertical communication
(C) Group communication
(D) Cross-purpose communication

14. For effective communication inside a classroom a teacher should embark upon

(A) Ideological leanings
(B) Innuendos
(C) Issuing attention commands
(D) Listener analysis

15. The concept of entropy as used in communication is related to

(A) Virtual reality
(B) Marketplace
(C) Order
(D) Communicative language

16. The next number in the given series is

196, 384, 736, ____

(A) 1344 (B) 1244
(C) 1434 (D) 1544

17. Find the missing letters in the series

BCA, YZX, EFD, _____, HIG

(A) UVW
(B) VWU
(C) WVU
(D) VUW

18. Vinod's mother-in-law is the mother of Amit's mother-in-law. How is Vinod related to Amit?

(A) Vinod is brother of Amit
(B) Vinod is father of Amit
(C) Vinod is uncle of Amit
(D) Vinod is father-in-law of Amit

19. In a certain code. FISH is written as EHRG. The code for JUNGLE will be
(A) ITNFKD
(B) KVOHMF
(C) ITMFKD
(D) TIMFKD

20. 63% of employees in a company are female. If the number of male employees is 111, then the total number of employees is
(A) 270 (B) 290
(C) 300 (D) 310

21. "Everyone believes that there is a soul Therefore you should also believe it." This inference commits which kind of fallacy
(A) Ad hominem
(B) Ad populum
(C) Fallacy of Accident
(D) Fallacy of Ambiguity

22. "God is great because He does great things". This inference commits which kind of fallacy?
(A) Ad populum
(B) Fallacy of Composition
(C) Fallacy of Division
(D) Petitio Principii

23. Anil's participation in classroom is indifferent. His parents do not find him to be active either. But his performance in examinations, ranges from being good to outstanding. Therefore, he must be studying privately, in a clandestine way. This is an example of which kind of Pramana?
(A) Upamana (Comparison)
(B) Anumana (Inference)
(C) Anupalabdhi (Non-apprehension)
(D) Arthapatti (Implication)

24. The distinction between purvavat and sesavat is made with reference to which of the following pramanas?
(A) Anumana (Inference)
(B) Pratyaksa (Perception)
(C) Comparison (Upamana)
(D) Abhava (Absence)

25. Which sentence cannot fit into the AEIO framework'?
(A) No salt has iodine
(B) The salt on the table has iodine
(C) All salt has iodine
(D) Some salt has iodine

Question Numbers : (26 to 30). Comprehension
Data in respect of Demand and Production of Computers of five companies. A - E are shown in the figure. Based on the data, answer questions that follow

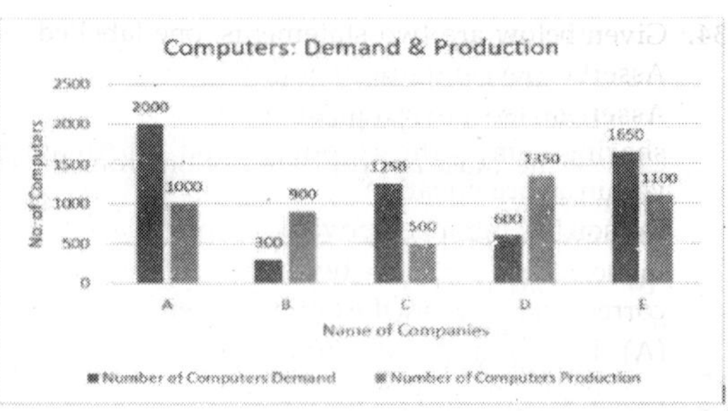

26. The ratio of the number of companies having more production than demand to that of companies having more demand than production is
(A) 3:2 (B) 1:4
(C) 4:1 (D) 2:3

27. Which company has minimum demand to production ratio?
(A) B (B) C
(C) D (D) E

28. The difference between average demand and average production of computers of all companies combined together is
(A) 950 (B) 190
(C) 180 (D) 850

29. The demand for computers is less than the production of computers in how many companies?
(A) 4 (B) 3
(C) 1 (D) 2

30. The demand of computers of Company D is more than that of the demand of the computers of Company B by
(A) 1.5 times (B) 2 times
(C) 2.5 times (D) 3 times

31. The term Plotter is best described as
(A) An input device to produce good graphics
(B) An output device to produce drawings and graphics
(C) A fast storage device for storing good quality graphics
(D) A multipurpose device for taking inputs as well as outputs

32. Which of the following is correct with respect to the size of the storage units?
(A) Terabyte < Petabyte < Exabyte < Zettabyte
(B) Petabyte < Exabyte < Zettabyte < Terabyte
(C) Exabyte < Zettabyte < Terabyte < Petabyte
(D) Zettabyte < Exabyte < Petabyte < Terabyte

33. E-commerce involves buying and selling of
(A) International goods
(B) Electronic goods
(C) Products related to computers
(D) Products and services over the Internet

34. Given below are two statements, one labelled as Assertion (A) and the other as Reason (R):

Assertion (A): An Intranet is a private network for sharing computing resources and information within an organization

Reason (R): Intranet is private version of the Internet

In the light of the above two statements, choose the correct answer from the options given below

(A) Both A) and R) are true and R) is the correct explanation of A)

(B) Both A) and R) are true but R) is not the correct explanation of A)

(C) A) is true, but R) is false

(D) A) is false, but R) is true

35. Which of the following devices allows a user to copy an external document and save it in electronic form onto a computer?

(A) Spammer (B) Scanner

(C) Printer (D) Plotter

36. From the following list, identify the sources of solid waste:

(i) Residential areas (ii) Oceans

(iii) Institutional areas (iv) Agriculture

(v) Dust storms

Select the correct answer from the options given below:

(A) (i), (ii) and (iii)

(B) (ii), (iii) and (iv)

(C) (iii), (iv) and (v)

(D) (i), (iii) and (iv)

37. Identify the sources of soil pollution from the following list:

(i) Industrial effluents

(ii) Eutrophication

(iii) Unscientific disposal of nuclear Waste

(iv) Off-shore oil drilling

(v) Improper management of septic systems

Choose the correct answer from the options given below:

(A) (i), (ii) and (iii)

(B) (ii), (iii) and (iv)

(C) (i), (iii) and (v)

(D) (ii), (iv) and (v)

38. Which of the following statements represents mangrove characteristics as a safety hedge?

(A) The mangrove trees are tall with dense canopies

(B) The mangrove trees provide both food and medicines

(C) The mangrove swamps separate the human settlement from the sea

(D) The mangrove trees protect vulnerable coastlines as they hold soil together

39. Which of the following statements about the Volatile Organic Compounds (VOCs) are correct?

(i) They cause acid rain

(ii) They may cause cancer

(iii) They play an important role in the formation of photochemical smog

Select the correct answer from the options given below:

(A) (i) and (ii) (B) (ii) and (iii)

(C) (i) and (iii) (D) (i), (ii), and (iii)

40. Which of the following was the central aim of the Paris Agreement?

(A) To reduce the CFCs emissions

(B) To strengthen the global response to the threat of climate change

(C) To address biological diversity issues

(D) To address the problem of ozone layer depletion

41. The ancient Indian University famous for specialized study in 'Hinayana' was

(A) Nadia University

(B) Nalanda University

(C) Vallabhi University

(D) Vikramsila University

42. Identify the non-conventional learning programmes:

(i) Gerontology

(ii) Psychology

(iii) Ethical hacking

(iv) Anthropology

(v) Pet Groomers

Choose the correct answer from the options given below:

(A) (i), (ii) and (iii)

(B) (ii), (iii) and (iv)

(C) (iii), (iv) and (v)

(D) (i), (iii) and (v)

43. Identify Key result areas of the Skill Acquisition and Knowledge Awareness for Livelihood Promotion (SANKALP) project:

(i) Institutional strengthening

(ii) Promotion of handicraft and carpet sector skills

(iii) Quality Assurance

(iv) Inclusion

(v) Overseas Employment through an agency

(vi) Expanding skills through Public Private Partnership (PPPs)

Choose the correct answer from the options given below:

(A) (i), (ii), (iii) and (iv)

(B) (i), (iii), (iv) and (v)

(C) (ii), (iv), (v) and (vi)

(D) (i), (iii), (iv) and (vi)

44. Identify reform related areas of governance listed by the NITI Aayog in the Three Year Action Agenda (2017-18 to 2019-20) exclusively:
(i) Environmental
(ii) Civil Services
(iii) Electoral
(iv) Corruption related
(v) Information and Communication Technology
Choose the correct answer from the options given below:
(A) (i), (ii) and (iii)
(B) (ii), (iii) and (iv)
(C) (iii), (iv) and (v)
(D) (i), (iv) and (v)

45. In the context of value education, which of the following stages will be considered a relatively advanced stage?
(A) Value collection through imitation
(B) Value assessment through inner evaluation
(C) Value clarification through exposure
(D) Value consolidation through integration

Question Numbers : (46 to 50). Comprehension
Read the following passage carefully and answer the questions that follow.

Two paradoxes inform and problematize every discursive and practical employment of "human rights". The first is substantive and directly political: it concerns the relation between "the human" and "the political", and belongs to the domain of political ethics in general. The other is more nearly epistemological and moral: it addresses the issue of how one understands and practices the relationship between idea and actuality, or moral universality and cultural relativity. Each stems from the fact that human rights would cobble together two kinds of concepts and practical relations that are not innately friendly and treats them as one, ignoring the inherent absence of complementarity in their relationship. Thus, the discourse of human rights synthesizes and occludes paradoxical features of the origins, history and character of human rights as an idea and a practice, making it far from self-evident as a conceptual "thing" or guide to moral and political practice. Paradox has always marked the invocation of human rights. Since their discursive inception, the initial paradoxes have not been solved so much as layered by new iterations of them – namely, that initiated in the UDHR (Universal Declaration of Human Rights), which identifies governments as the promissories for enforcement of human rights. Joining the paradoxes is an overarching feature that articulates human rights as a trans-political phenomenon besides being a political phenomenon designed to uplift all human societies.

46. The first important area of human rights paradox is concerned with
(A) Problematization
(B) Discursive employment
(C) Human practice
(D) Political ethics

47. The epistemological paradox of human rights refers to the understanding of
(A) Human aspects of rights
(B) Moral degradation
(C) Cultural dimension of human rights
(D) Political relations

48. What is ignored in comprehending two paradoxes of human rights?
(A) Innate friendliness of paradoxes
(B) Absence of complimentarity
(C) Relationship between idea and actuality
(D) Morality issues

49. What is missing in the discourse of human rights?
(A) Self evidence as a concept
(B) Paradoxical features
(C) Exclusion of human rights features
(D) Synthesis of concept and practice

50. What is added to the existing paradoxes of human rights?
(A) Iteration of UDHR
(B) Universality of human rights
(C) Invocation of human rights
(D) Political phenomenon across borders

ANSWERS

1. (B)	2. (C)	3. (B)	4. (D)	5. (C)	6. (A)	7. (A)	8. (B)	9. (D)	10. (B)
11. (A)	12. (B)	13. (C)	14. (D)	15. (C)	16. (A)	17. (B)	18. (D)	19. (C)	20. (C)
21. (B)	22. (D)	23. (D)	24. (A)	25. (B)	26. (D)	27. (A)	28. (B)	29. (D)	30. (B)
31. (B)	32. (A)	33. (D)	34. (B)	35. (B)	36. (D)	37. (C)	38. (D)	39. (B)	40. (B)
41. (C)	42. (D)	43. (D)	44. (B)	45. (D)	46. (D)	47. (C)	48. (B)	49. (A)	50. (D)

November 2021

UGC NET – PAPER I

Note: This paper consists of Fifty (50) objective type questions of Two (2) marks each. All questions are compulsory.

The following table embodies the details about the enrollment of students in five different activities namely Swimming, Singing, Drawing, Dancing and Handicraft in a School during the session 2020-21. A total number of 3000 students including 1750 girls have been enrolled in various activities in the school. Based on the data in the table, answer the **questions 1-5** :

Activity-wise Enrollment of Students

Activity	Percentage (%) of students enrolled (Out of 3000)	Percentage (%) of Girls enrolled (Out of 1750)
Swimming	16%	14%
Singing	21%	28%
Drawing	14%	16%
Dancing	24%	20%
Handicraft	25%	22%

1. What is the approximate percentage (%) of boys in the school?
(1) 42% (2) 28% (3) 34% (4) 50%

2. How many boys are enrolled in Singing and Handicraft taken together?
(1) 485 (2) 505 (3) 420 (4) 585

3. What is the total number of girls enrolled in Swimming and Drawing taken together'?
(1) 505 (2) 515 (3) 525 (4) 535

4. The number of girls enrolled in Dancing forms what percent (%) of the total number of students in the School? (Round-off to two digits)?
(1) 9.32% (2) 10.67%
(3) 11.67% (4) 14.67%

5. What is the ratio of the number of girls enrolled in Swimming to the number of boys enrolled in swimming?
(1) 59 : 49 (2) 23 : 29
(3) 33 : 43 (4) 49 : 47

6. Which of the following is designated as key behaviour of effectiveness of teaching as evident from researches?
(1) Using student ideas and contribution
(2) Structuring
(3) Teacher task-orientation
(4) Teacher affect

7. Identify the indirect teaching strategies from the following list :
(A) Gaining attention, informing the learner of the objective and presenting the stimulus material
(B) Concept building through examples and non-examples
(C) Explaining, exemplification and practice
(D) Problem based presentation with pair-share technique
(E) Encouraging students to use references from their own experiences

Choose the correct answer from the options given below :
(1) (B), (D) and (E) (2) (A), (B) and (C)
(3) (B), (C) and (D) (4) (C), (D) and (E)

8. Match List I with List II :

List I **Modalities of Teaching**	List II **Implementation**
(A) Instruction	(I) One way imposition of ideas from the teacher to the students
(B) Training	(II) Associative presentation of ideas from teacher to students
(C) Conditioning	(III) Disciplined drill conducted by teacher
(D) Indoctrination	(IV) Active interchange of ideas between teacher and students

Choose the correct answer from the options given below :
(1) (A)-(II), (B)-(I), (C)-(IV), (D)-(III)
(2) (A)-(I), (B)-(II), (C)-(III), (D)-(IV)
(3) (A)-(IV), (B)-(III), (C)-(II), (D)-(I)
(4) (A)-(III), (B)-(IV), (C)-(I), (D)-(II)

9. Given below are two statements :
Statement I : Computer based testing promotes objectivity in assessment processes.
Statement II : Choice-based credit system in Indian Higher Education is a new entry.
In the light of the above statements, Choose the most appropriate answer from the options given below :

* Based on memory only. Please refer ugcnetonline.in

(1) Both Statement I and Statement II are correct.
(2) Both Statement I and Statement II are incorrect.
(3) Statement I is correct but Statement II is incorrect.
(4) Statement I is incorrect but Statement II is correct.

10. Given below are two statements : One is labeled as Assertion A and the other is labeled as Reason R.
Assertion (A) : Teaching support system whether traditional or modern is purportedly put in place for effecting economy and ensuring quality in teaching-learning transactions.
Reason (R) : Learning outcomes in order to be congruent with stipulated instructional goals need scaffolds to begin with.
In the light of the above statements, Choose the most appropriate answer from the options given below :
(1) Both (A) and (R) are correct and (R) is the correct explanation of (A).
(2) Both (A) and (R) are correct but (R) is NOT the correct explanation of (A).
(3) (A) is correct but (R) is not correct.
(4) (A) is not correct but (R) is correct.

11. In which method of research an independent variable is manipulated with an intent to observe concomitant changes in dependent variable?
(1) ExPost Facto method
(2) Case study method
(3) Descriptive survey method
(4) Experimental method

12. Identify the features of empirico-inductive paradigm of research
(A) Research is concerned with the process rather than simply with outcomes or products
(B) Based on logical positivist philosophy which assumes a single objective reality
(C) Researchers are concerned with what are called 'participant perspectives'
(D) Attempts to establish universal context free generalizations
Choose the most appropriate answer from the options given below :
(1) (A) and (B) only (2) (B) and (C) only
(3) (C) and (D) only (4) (A) and (C) only

13. Match List I and List II

List I Sampling Methods	**List II** Procedure involved
(A) Simple Random Sampling	(I) The first member is used as an informant to identify other. The process goes on like this
(B) Stratified Random Sampling	(II) The units are chosen intact on the basis of their settings
(C) Cluster Sampling	(III) The units are chosen from defined groups /levels randomly
(D) Snowball sampling	(IV) The units are chosen by giving equal and independent chance to each

Choose the correct answer from the options given below :
(1) (A)-(I), (B)-(II), (C)-(III), (D)-(IV)
(2) (A)-(IV), (B)-(III), (C)-(II), (D)-(I)
(3) (A)-(III), (B)-(IV), (C)-(I), (D)-(II)
(4) (A)-(II), (B)-(I), (C)-(IV), (D)-(III)

14. Given below are two statements :
Statement I : Action Research is used primarily to improve a given situation by a practitioner.
Statement II : Applied research is directed at exploring applicability of principles already established.
In the light of the above statements, Choose the most appropriate answer from the options given below :
(1) Both Statement I and Statement II are correct.
(2) Both Statement I and Statement II are incorrect.
(3) Statement I is correct but Statement II is incorrect.
(4) Statement I is incorrect but Statement II is correct.

15. Given below are two statements : One is labeled as Assertion A and the other is labeled as Reason R.
Assertion (A) : A research thesis has to follow a prescribed format and style of referencing.
Reasons (R) : This ensures the observance of research ethics.
In the light of the above statements, Choose the most appropriate answer from the options given below :
(1) Both (A) and (R) are correct and (R) is the correct explanation of (A).
(2) Both (A) and (R) are correct but (R) is NOT the correct explanation of (A).
(3) (A) is correct but (R) is not correct.
(4) (A) is not correct but (R) is correct.

16. Which of the following is an example of physical barrier to communication?
(1) Cultural disparity (2) Inattention
(3) Verbalism (4) Ill health

17. When in a classroom communication, a teacher shows ability of creativity, correlation and analysis, it belongs to which category of skills?
(1) Thinking skills (2) Expression skills

(3) Media utilization skills
(4) Human skills

18. Why do we communicate?
(A) For social interaction.
(B) For happiness sake.
(C) For messages to be understood.
(D) For sharing of experience.
(E) For protection of traditions.
Choose the correct answer from the options given below :
(1) (A), (C), (E) only (2) (B), (C), (D) only
(3) (A), (C), (D) only (4) (A), (B), (E) only

19. Match List I with List II

List I **Types of communication**	**List II** **Function served**
(A) Mass communication	(I) Corridor discussion
(B) Intrapersonal communication	(II) Classroom Teaching
(C) Group communication	(III) For communicates with oneself
(D) Interpersonal communication	(IV) For mechanical message transmission

Choose the correct answer from the options given below :
(1) (A)-(IV), (B)-(III), (C)-(II), (D)-(I)
(2) (A)-(I), (B)-(II), (C)-(III), (D)-(IV)
(3) (A)-(II), (B)-(III), (C)-(IV), (D)-(I)
(4) (A)-(III), (B)-(II), (C)-(I), (D)-(IV)

20. Given below are two statements : One is labeled as Assertion A and the other is labeled as Reason R.
Assertion (A) : A man pulls a loaded truck by his hair which becomes news.
Reasons (R) : Unusual things make news called oddity and generate public interest.
In the light of the above statements, Choose the most appropriate answer from the options given below :
(1) Both (A) and (R) are correct and (R) is the correct explanation of (A).
(2) Both (A) and (R) are correct but (R) is NOT the correct explanation of (A).
(3) (A) is correct but (R) is not correct.
(4) (A) is not correct but (R) is correct.

21. Smita rode her scooty Northwards, then turned left and then again rode to her left 4 km. She found herself exactly 2 km West of her starting point. How far did she ride Northward initially?
(1) 2 km (2) 4 km (3) 5 km (4) 6 km

22. A 108 meter long train moving at a speed of 50 km/hr crosses a 112 meters long train coming from the opposite direction in 6 seconds. The speed of the second train is :
(1) 48 km/hr (2) 54 km/hr
(3) 66 km/hr (4) 82 km/hr

23. If a 30 meter ladder is placed against a 15 metre wall such that it just reaches the top of the wall, the angle of elevation of the wall is :
(1) 45° (2) 30° (3) 60° (4) 50°

24. The profit earned by selling a chair for Rs. 752 is 1.2 times the loss incurred when the same chair was sold for Rs. 400. What is the cost price of the chair?
(1) Rs. 540 (2) Rs. 592
(3) Rs. 560 (4) Rs. 640

25. Three men, four women and six children can complete a work in seven days. A woman does double the work a man does and a child does half the work a man does. How many women alone can complete this work in 7 days?
(1) 7 (2) 8 (3) 9 (4) 12

26. Given below are two statements :
Statement I : According to Nyaya philosophy an argument proceeds only on those issues that are completely unknown.
Statement II : According to Nyaya philosophy an argument does not proceed on those issues that are well established.
In the light of the above statements. Choose the most appropriate answer from the options given below :
(1) Both Statement I and Statement II are correct.
(2) Both Statement I and Statement II are incorrect.
(3) Statement I is correct but Statement II is incorrect.
(4) Statement I is incorrect but Statement II is correct.

27. With reference to Nyaya philosophy, which of the following statements is true?
(1) The linga or the middle term is not the Karana or operative cause of inference.
(2) The middle term may be a thing of the present but not of the past or the future.
(3) The middle term can function in an inference when past or future.
(4) The middle term can lead to the conclusion apart from the knowledge of vyapti or the universal relation between it and the major term.

28. Given below are two statements :
Statement I : Mimamsakas and Vedantins agree with the Naiyayikas that the syllogism consists of five members or propositions.
Statement II : Mimamsakas and Vedantins agree with the Naiyayikas that the syllogism is necessary only for parirthanumana or demonstrate inference and not for svarthanuniana or inference for oneself.

In the light of the above statements. Choose the most appropriate answer from the options given below :

(1) Both Statement I and Statement II are correct.
(2) Both Statement I and Statement II are incorrect.
(3) Statement I is correct but Statement II is incorrect.
(4) Statement I is incorrect but Statement II is correct.

29. Given below are two statements :

Statement I : A formal fallacy is one that may be identified through mere inspection of the form or structure of an argument.

Statement II : Formal fallacies are found only in deductive arguments that have identifiable forms.

In the light of the above statements, Choose the correct answer from the options given below :

(1) Both Statement I and Statement II are true.
(2) Both Statement I and Statement II are false.
(3) Statement I is true but Statement II is false.
(4) Statement I is false but Statement II is true.

30. "Whoever thrusts a knife into another person should be arrested. Surgeons thrust a knife into another person when operating. Therefore surgeons should be arrested".

Which fallacy is committed in the following argument?

(1) Hasty generalization
(2) Fallacy of accident
(3) Red Herring
(4) Appeal to unqualified authority

31. The next number P in the sequence of binary numbers 0, 10, 100, 110, P ..., is :

(1) 111 (2) 1000 (3) 1010 (4) 1001

32. Identify the correct order of following computer memory types ranked from slowest to fastest in terms of access time.

(A) Cache (B) CDROM
(C) Hard Disk (D) RAM
(E) Register

Choose the correct answer from the options given below :

(1) (C), (B), (A), (D), (E)
(2) (E), (A), (D), (C), (B)
(3) (B), (C), (D), (A), (E)
(4) (D), (A), (E), (B), (C)

33. Given below are two statements :

Statement I : CPU executes software directly from secondary memory.

Statement II : A software is termed as Open Source Software if it can be downloaded from the Internet.

In the light of the above statements, Choose the correct answer from the options given below :

(1) Both Statement I and Statement II are true.
(2) Both Statement I and Statement II are false.
(3) Statement I is true but Statement II is false.
(4) Statement I is false but Statement II is true.

34. Which of the following statements about wikis are True?

(A) Wiki pages can be locked by moderators to prevent vandlism.
(B) Every change that is made to a wiki page is logged and can be viewed in a history list.
(C) A wiki is designed to allow people to collaborate easily.

Choose the correct answer from the options given below :

(1) (A) and (B) only (2) (B) and (C) only
(3) (A) and (C) only (4) (A), (B) and (C)

35. Match List I with List II

List I (Digital Initiatives in Higher Education)	**List II (Purpose)**
(A) SWAYAM	(I) Online store and access of academic awards namely degrees, mark-sheets etc.
(B) SWAYAM PRABHA	(II) Store and access personal e-documents irrespective of physical location.
(C) Digilocker	(III) MOOCs for high-quality education anywhere and anytime.
(D) NAD	(IV) Free DTH channel for high-quality education.

Choose the correct answer from the options given below :

(1) (A)-(III), (B)-(IV), (C)-(II), (D)-(I)
(2) (A)-(IV), (B)-(III), (C)-(I), (D)-(II)
(3) (A)-(IV), (B)-(III), (C)-(II), (D)-(I)
(4) (A)-(II), (B)-(I), (C)-(III), (D)-(IV)

36. The waste component of waste categorized as "Trash" consists of

(A) Paper, Cardboard cartons
(B) Animal wastes
(C) Industrial process wastes
(D) Vegetable wastes
(E) Wood

Choose the correct answer from the options given below :

(1) (A) and (E) only
(2) (A), (C) and (E) only
(3) (A), (C), (D) and (E) only
(4) (A), (B), (D) and (E) only

37. Under Sustainable Development Goal 12- Sustainable Consumption and Production. one of the tar-

gets is to reduce per capita food Waste at the retail and consumer levels by

(1) 3/4 (2) 1/2
(3) 1/3 (4) 1/4

38. Small hydro power potential in India is estimated approximately as

(1) ~ 60 MW (2) ~ 100 MW
(3) ~ 10 GW (4) ~ 20 GW

39. The global environmental issue of Ozone depletion is due to emission of :

(A) Sulphur dioxide
(B) Chlorinated hydrocarbons
(C) Methane
(D) Carbone dixoide

Choose the most appropriate answer from the options given below :

(1) (A) and (B) only
(2) (B) only
(3) (B) and (D) only
(4) (A), (B) and (C) only

40. Which of the following natural disasters are accepted as landforms?

(1) Thunderstorm (2) Avalanche
(3) Storm (4) Flood

41. The NEP-2020 proposes to prepare which of the curriculum frameworks?

(A) National Curriculum Framework for School Education
(B) National Curriculum Framework for Adult Education
(C) National Curriculum Framework for Teacher Education
(D) National Curriculum Framework for Technical Education
(E) National Curriculum Framework for Vocational Education

Choose the correct answer from the options given below :

(1) (A), (C), (E) only (2) (B), (C), (D) only
(3) (A), (B), (C) only (4) (C), (D), (E) only

42. Which of the following values is related to self-transcendance?

(1) Security value
(2) Value of Universalism
(3) Value of freedom
(4) Value of conformity

43. NEP-2020 proposes to establish which of the following new bodies?

(A) SSSA (B) PARAKH
(C) IITI (D) NITI
(E) NTA

Choose the correct answer from the options given below :

(1) (A), (C), (D) only (2) (B), (C), (E) only
(3) (A), (B), (C) only (4) (B), (C), (D) only

44. Which of the following is an apex advisory and non statutory body?

(1) NITI Aayog (2) NCTE
(3) AICTE (4) MCI

45. Who among the following was the first Chairman of UGC?

(1) Sh Humayun Kabir (2) Sh C.D. Deshmukh
(3) Sh M. Moolgaokar (4) Moolchand Sharma

Read the passage carefully and answer the question that follow:

As the world is becoming increasingly interconnected, Global Citizenship Education (GCED), a response to contemporary global challenges, will be provided to empower learners to become aware of and understand global issues and to become active promoters of more peaceful, tolerant, inclusive, secure and sustainable societies. As a part of holistic education, students at all HEIs will be provided with opportunities for internships with local industry, businesses, artists, crafts person etc. as well as research internship with faculty and researchers at their own or other HEIs/research institutions, so that students may actively engage with the practical side of their learning and, as a by-product, further improve their employability. India will be promoted as a global study destination providing premium education at affordable costs thereby helping to rest its role as a Vishwa Guru. An international students office at each HEI hosting foreign students will be set up to coordinate all matters relating to welcoming and supporting students arriving from abroad. Research training collaboration and faculty/student exchanges with high quality foreign institution will be facilitated, and relevant mutually beneficial MOU with foreign countries will be signed. High Performing Indian Universities will be encouraged to set up campuses in other countries, and similarly, selected universities e.g. those from top 100 universities in the world will be facilitated to operate in India. A legislative framework facilitating such entry will be put in place and such universities will be given special dispensation regarding regulatory, governance and content norms on par with other autonomous institutions of India. Furthermore, research collaboration and student exchanges between Indian institutions and global institutions will be promoted through special efforts. Credits acquired in foreign universities will be permitted, where appropriate as per the requirements of each HEI, to be counted for the award of a degree.

46. New National Education Policy is grounded in the assumptions that :

(A) There is increasing interconnectedness among nations at the global level.

(B) Technical knowledge should replace traditional models of learning.

(C) HEIs must focus on promotion of desirable ethical values.

(D) There is need for changes in legislative framework to facilitiate free exchange of academic ideas and achievements.

Choose the correct answer from the options given below :

(1) (A), (B) and (D) only (2) (A) and (C) only
(3) (A), (C) and (D) only (4) (C) and (D) only

47. Given below are two statements :

Statement I : National Education Policy is framed with an objective of saving national HEIs from competition at the global level.

Statement II : National Education Policy is framed with an objective of encouraging exchange of knowledge and expertise both at local and global level.

In the light of the above statements, Choose the most appropriate answer from the options given below :

(1) Both Statement I and Statement II are correct.
(2) Both Statement I and Statement II are incorrect.
(3) Statement I is correct but Statement II is incorrect
(4) Statement I is incorrect but Statement II is correct.

48. Which of the following statements most appropriately represent one of the chief concerns regarding higher education?

(1) It argues for only local production and of knowledge and its implementation.
(2) It emphasizes only upon implementation of foreign higher education models in India.
(3) It argues for mutual exchange of knowledge and learning among national and international institutions of higher education.
(4) It argues for practical learning alone for employability putting social issues aside.

49. Holistic education at HEIs is aimed at :

(A) Research internship with researchers and faculty at different HEIs.

(B) Recyling of traditional knowledge systems.

(C) Providing opportunities for internships at local level.

(D) Keeping social sciences and natural sciences within distinct spheres of teaching and learning.

Choose the correct answer from the options given below :

(1) (B) and (D) only (2) (A) and (C) only
(3) (A) and (D) only (4) (C) and (D) only

50. Given below are two statements :

Statement I : National Education Policy envisages learning as a process of inculcating values of tolerance, inclusion and sustainability.

Statement II : National Education Policy lays stress on employability of learners in businesses and industries.

In the light of the above statements, Choose the most appropriate answer from the options given below :

(1) Both Statement I and Statement II are correct.
(2) Both Statement I and Statement II are incorrect.
(3) Statement I is correct but Statement II is incorrect
(4) Statement I is incorrect but Statement II is correct.

ANSWERS

1. (1)	**2.** (2)	**3.** (3)	**4.** (3)	**5.** (4)	**6.** (3)	**7.** (1)	**8.** (3)	**9.** (1)	**10.** (1)
11. (4)	**12.** (4)	**13.** (2)	**14.** (1)	**15.** (3)	**16.** (4)	**17.** (1)	**18.** (3)	**19.** (1)	**20.** (1)
21. (2)	**22.** (4)	**23.** (2)	**24.** (3)	**25.** (1)	**26.** (4)	**27.** (1)	**28.** (4)	**29.** (1)	**30.** (2)
31. (2)	**32.** (3)	**33.** (2)	**34.** (4)	**35.** (1)	**36.** (1)	**37.** (2)	**38.** (4)	**39.** (2)	**40.** (1)
41. (3)	**42.** (2)	**43.** (3)	**44.** (1)	**45.** (2)	**46.** (3)	**47.** (4)	**48.** (3)	**49.** (2)	**50.** (1)

September 2022

UGC NET – PAPER I

Note: This paper consists of Fifty (50) objective type questions of Two (2) marks each. All questions are compulsory.

The following table shows the percentage (%) distribution of number of students qualifying an Entrance Exam from seven schools A-G in the years 2020 and 2021. The number of students qualifying from School G in 2020 and 2021 are 90 and 135 respectively. Based on the data in the table, answer the questions 1-5:

School-Wise Distribution of Qualified Students

School	Distribution (%) of Qualified students	
	2020	2021
A	21%	23%
B	14%	8%
C	16%	11%
D	10%	14%
E	18%	16%
F	9%	18%
G	12%	15%

1. If P and Q are the average number of students qualifying from Schools B, C and D in 2020 and from Schools E, F and G in 2021, respectively, then Q – P is
(1) 32 (2) 35 (3) 38 (4) 41
2. Number of literate males of City E as a percentage of number of literate females of city F is
(1) 188.5 (2) 247.5
(3) 312.5 (4) 247.5
3. The ratio of the number of students qualifying from Schools B, C and D in 2020 to that of Schools E, F and G in 2021 is
(1) 2.3 (2) 51.75 (3) 3.2 (4) 25.33
4. The percent rise in the number of students qualifying from School D from 2020 to 2021 is
(1) 60% (2) 63% (3) 68% (4) 72%
5. The percentage of the number of students qualifying from Schools A-G together in 2021 with reference to 2020 is
(1) 140% (2) 120% (3) 135% (4) 112%
6. According to current estimate, the gross enrolment ratio in Higher Education in India is around 27%, which is expected to be increased to .... by the end of 2035.
(1) 30% (2) 40% (3) 50% (4) 60%
7. What is the concept of International Net-Neutrality?
(1) Imposed Invitations for end-to-end Internet access
(2) Broadband service providers can show preference to content
(3) Unimpeded end-to-end Internet access and usage
(4) All content that flows throughout the Internet should not be treated equally
8. In communication a high order of inference drawn from experience, direct or indirect, is responsible for
(1) Generalisation (2) Simplification
(3) Abstraction (4) Strong reaction
9. In which of the following methods of teaching, the student has to find out the answer to his/her own problem by unaided efforts?
(1) Case-study method
(2) Heuristic method
(3) Flipped classroom method
(4) Demonstration method
10. In the context of MOOCs in Higher Education in India, which of the following are CORRECT?
(A) They are learner - centric
(B) They can be delivered only through SWAYM portal
(C) They can benefit large number of learners
(D) They can be accessed anytime, anywhere and any number of times.
(E) All MOOCs are for earning credit
Choose the correct answer from the options given below :
(1) A & D Only (2) C & D Only
(3) A, B & E Only (4) A, C & D Only
11. A systematic review of literature adopts
(1) Explicit procedures
(2) Implicit procedures
(3) Personal-choice procedures
(4) Peer-suggested procedures
12. Given below are two statements : One is labelled as Assertion A and the other is labelled as Reason R.

* Based on memory only. Please refer ugcnetonline.in

Assertion (A): Chlorofluorocarbons (CFCs) are potent greenhouse gases.

Reasons (R): CFCs have the ability to catalytically destroy ozone in stratosphere.

In the Light of the above statements, choose the most appropriate answer from the options given below :

(1) Both (A) and (R) are correct and (R) is the correct explanation of (A)
(2) Both (A) and (R) are correct but (R) is NOT the correct explanation of (A)
(3) (A) is correct but (R) is not correct
(4) (A) is not correct but (R) is correct

13. There are three numbers in the ratio of 3:5:7 and the sum of these numbers is 975. Find the three members.

(1) 195, 325, 455
(2) 325, 195, 455
(3) 195, 310, 470
(4) 205, 315, 455

14. In a certain coding language, if 'CRICKET' is coded as 2632479. 'ROCKET' is coded as 612479, and 'KETTLE' is coded as 179907, then how 'LOCKER' shall be coded in that language?

(1) 102674 (2) 021647
(3) 120764 (4) 012476

15. Which of the following statements are correct regarding VoLTE?

(A) VoLTE stands for 'Voice over Long Term Evolution'.
(B) It is a digital packet voice service delivery over IP via an LTE access network.
(C) Provides more efficient use of spectrum than traditional voice.
(D) Eliminates the need to have voice on one network and data on another network.

Choose the *correct answer* from the options given below:

(1) A, B, C and D Only
(2) B, C and D Only
(3) A, B and C Only
(4) A, B and C Only

16. Which of the following statements are correct? Principal components of a CPU in a computer include:

(A) The Solid State Drive (SSD) that stores data persistently, typically using flash memory.
(B) The Arithmetic-Logic Unit (ALU) that performs arithmetic and logic operations.
(C) Processor registers that supply operands to the ALF and stores the results of ALU operation.
(D) The Control Unit (CU) that orchestrates the fetching (from memory), decoding and execution of instructions.

Choose the *correct answer* from the options given below:

(1) A, B and C Only
(2) B, C and D Only
(3) B and C Only
(4) A and D Only

17. Teacher 'A' uses chalk and board and dictates notes to students in classroom. Teacher 'B' uses Video-conferencing tool and LMS for providing digital resources. Which modes of teaching are used by teacher A and teacher B?

(1) Both online
(2) Both offline
(3) Teacher – A: online : Teacher – B : offline
(4) Teacher – A: offline : Teacher – B : online

18. Given below are two statements:

Statement I: Communication and socialisation are two non-convergent dimensions of any modern society.

Statement II: Communication enables the promotion of values that facilitate the process of enculturisation of people in a society.

In the light of the above statements, choose the correct answer from the options given below :

(1) Both Statement I and Statement II are true
(2) Both Statement I and Statement II are false
(3) Statement I is true but Statement II is false
(4) Statement I is false but Statement II is true

19. Given below are two statements :

Statement I: S megabytes = 213 gigabytes

Statement II: The decimal equivalent of the binary number $(11101.101)_2$ is $(29.625)_{10}$.

In the light of the above statements, choose the correct answer from the options given below :

(1) Both Statement I and Statement II are true
(2) Both Statement I and Statement II are false
(3) Statement I is true but Statement II is false
(4) Statement I is false but Statement II is true

20. Given below are two statements :

Statement I: Increasingly, photovoltaic panels are being used to supplement electrical energy from the power grid.

Statement II: One issue with grid-connected photovoltaics is that PV cells produce Alternating Current (AC) whereas powergrids use Direct Current (DC).

In the light of the above statements, choose the correct answer from the options given below:

(1) Both Statement I and Statement II are correct

(2) Both Statement I and Statement II are incorrect
(3) Statement I is correct but Statement II is incorrect
(4) Statement I is in correct but Statement II is correct

21. For which of the following forms of categorical propositions conversion is valid?
(A) Some S is P (B) Some S is not P
(C) No S is P (D) All S is P
Choose the correct answer from the options given below:
(1) A, B, C, D Only (2) A, C and D Only
(3) B, C and D Only (4) A, B and D Only

22. Find the next term in the following series: 1, 2, 4, 6, 7, 13, 10, 54, ?
(1) 162 (2) 13 (3) 64 (4) 72

23. Which of the following are useful tips in preparing questions for a structured interview?
(A) Introductory questions should be related to pleasantries.
(B) Introductory questions should be related to the research topic.
(C) Questions can be grouped, if the list of questions is long.
(D) General questions should precede specific questions.
(E) Repeat the personal questions again and again to test the truthfulness of the responses of the interviewee.
Choose the correct answer from the options given below:
(1) A, B, C Only (2) A, C, D Only
(3) B, C, D Only (4) A, D, E Only

24. Which of the following tools can be used for ICT enabled teaching?
(1) Paper chartsm (2) Physical models
(3) Projector (4) Black Board

25. Which of the following is considered as the highest scale in measurement?
(1) Nominal (2) Ordinal
(3) Interval (4) Ratio

26. Given below are two statements :
Statement I: Aristotelian syllogism is essentially verbalistic.
Statement II: Nyaya system recognizes the fact that the verbal form is the essence of inference.
In the light of the above statements, choose the most appropriate answer from the options given below :
(1) Both Statement I and Statement II are correct
(2) Both Statement I and Statement II are incorrect.
(3) Statement I is correct but Statement II is incorrect.
(4) Statement I is incorrect but Statement II is correct.

27. Depending on the intention which of the following logical informal fallacies may be involved in the following argument – 'I am shocked to hear you preaching atheism. Does your father know you believe that?'
(A) Appeal to authority
(B) Appeal to emotion
(C) Appeal to majority
(D) Appeal to force
Choose the correct answer from the options given below:
(1) A and D Only (2) A and B Only
(3) A and D Only (4) B and D Only

28. In India, much of the Central Government expenditure on general higher education is routed through
(1) Natural Council of Teacher Education.
(2) All India Council for Technical education
(3) University Grants Commission
(4) National Council for Educational Research and Training.

29. Broad parameters adopted by National Institutional Ranking Framework (NIRF) are
(A) Teaching, learning and Resources
(B) Graduation outcomes
(C) Outreach and Inclusivity
(D) Peer perception
(E) Low Carbon footprint
Choose the mast appropriate answer from the options given below :
(1) A, B, C, D Only (2) A, B, D, E Only
(3) B, C, D, E Only (4) A, C, D, E Only

30. Given below are two statements:
Statement I: All potential pollutants are synthetic chemicals.
Statement II: Many of the emerging contaminants have been observed to bioaccumulate in wildlife and humans.
In the light of the above statements, choose the correct answer from the options given below :
(1) Both Statement I and Statement II are true
(2) Both Statement I and Statement II are false
(3) Statement I is true but Statement II is false
(4) Statement I is false but Statement II is true

31. Which University in India was first to throw all University examinations open to girls?
(1). Punjab University
(2) Calcutta University
(3) Savitribai Phule University
(4) Bombay University

32. When it comes to knowledge-sharing, the important aspects of communication are:
(A) The supply side
(B) The demand side
(C) The policy currents
(D) The push and pull of policy makers
(E) The choice of filters
Choose the correct answer from the options given below:
(1) A, B, C Only (2) B, C, D Only
(3) C, D, E Only (4) A, D, E Only

33. A major focus in quantitative research is on
(1) Historicity (2) Causality
(3) Social reflections
(4) Creating an artificial environment

34. Given below are two statements:
Statement I: In Svartha Anumana (inference for oneself) we do not require a formal statement of the different members of inference, according to Nyaya view of inference.
Statement II: Svartha Anumana is a psychological process.
In the light of the above statements, choose the correct answer from the options given below:
(1) Both Statement I and Statement II are correct
(2) Both Statement I and Statement II are incorrect
(3) Statement I is correct but Statement II is incorrect
(4) Statement I is incorrect but Statement II is correct

35. Typhoid fever, a water born disease is caused by
(1) Virus (2) Bacteria
(3) Protozoan (4) Helminth

36. Miss Reena has been appointed by the Cyber Security Cell of Mumbai to break into the website of a terrorist organization to extract information. What among the following is a suitable description of Reena's profile?
(1) Hactivist (2) Ethical Hacker
(3) Troller (4) Black hat hacker

37. Given below are two statements :
Statement I: In India increasing access to higher education has been constrained by low completion rates at secondary education stage.
Statement II: By 2030, all multidisciplinary higher education institutions will be closed down.
In the light of the above statements, choose the correct answer from the options given below:
(1) Both Statement I and Statement II are true
(2) Both Statement I and Statement II are false
(3) Statement I is true but Statement II is false
(4) Statement I is false but Statement II is true

38. The simple interest accrued on a sum of certain principal is Rs. 1200 in 4 years at the rate of 8% per annum. What would be the simple interest accrued on thrice of that principle at the rate of 6% per annum in 3 years?
(1) 2150 (2) 2050
(3) 2025 (4) 2100

39. Which of the following are types of error in survey research?
(A) Sample error
(B) Source error
(C) Observational error
(D) Data collection error
(E) Data processing error
Choose the correct answer from the options given below :
(1) A, B, C Only (2) B, C, D Only
(3) B, D, E Only (4) A, D, E Only

40. In which context, the true effects of mass media communication on mass audience can be under stood?
(1) Economics (2) Social
(3) Political (4) Spiritual

41. Given below are two statements : One is labelled as Assertion A and the other is labelled as Reason R.
Assertion (A): Communication has the power to persuade, inform and disinform.
Reasons (R): The process of propaganda makes the line of distinction transparent between its elements for being persuasive.
In the Light of the above statements, choose the correct answer from the options given below:
(1) Both A and R are true and R is the correct explanation of A
(2) Both A and R are true but R is NOT the correct explanation of A
(3) A is true but R is false
(4) A is false but R is true

42. Given below are two statements :
Statement I: Often qualitative studies provide too many details of the setting that are investigated.
Statement II: Critics point out that qualitative research suffers from the issue of replication.
In the light of the above statements, choose the correct answer from the options given below:
(1) Both Statement I and Statement II are true
(2) Both Statement I and Statement II are false
(3) Statement I is true but Statement II is false
(4) Statement I is false but Statement II is true

43. If 'some men are vegetarians' is given as false, which of the following can be inferred to be true from it?
(A) All men are vegetarians.
(B) No men are vegetarians.

(C) Some men are not vegetarians.
(D) All non-vegetarians are men.
Choose the correct answer from the options given below:
(1) A, B and C Only (2) A, C, D Only
(3) B and C Only (4) C Only

44. Global warming can lead to/aggravate which of the following natural disasters?
(A) Drought (B) Earthquake
(C) Flood (D) Storm
Choose the correct answer from the options given below:
(1) A, B, C Only (2) S, C, D Only
(3) B, C, D Only (4) B, D Only

45. On allowing two successive discounts of 20% and 15%, the selling price of an article becomes Rs. 3060. What is the marked price of the article?
(1) 4000 (2) 4100
(3) 4200 (4) 4500

Read the following passage and answer questions from questions 46 to 50.

The conceptions and treatment of poverty were quite different before 1940. In colonial times the concern with poverty was conditioned by the belief that even if the natives could be somewhat enlightened by the presence of the colonizer, not much could be done about their poverty. It was because their economic development was pointless. The natives capacity for science and technology, the basis for economic progress was seen as nil. However, within Asian, African and Latin or Native American societies, vernacular societies had developed ways of defining and treating poverty that accommodated visions of community, frugality, and sufficiency. It is true that massive poverty in the modern sense appeared only when the spread of market economy broke down the communities. As a result, it deprived millions of people from access to land, water and other resources. With the consolidation of market economy, systemic issues became inevitable.

It is important to know the break that occurred in the conceptions and management of poverty first with the emergence of capitalism in Europe, and later with the advent of development in the Third world. The first break is described in terms of the advent in the nineteenth century of systems for dealing with the poor, based on assistance provided by impersonal institutions. Philanthropy occupied an important place in this transition. The transformation of the poor into the assisted had a profound consequence. The modernization of poverty invariably affected vernacular relations.

46. The market economy was responsible for
(1) Increased access to resources
(2) Massive poverty
(3) Enlightened development
(4) Idealisation of tradition

47. The Vernacular societies encountered economic poverty with
(1) Science and technology
(2) External aid
(3) Modern ideas
(4) Use of resources sparingly

48. Capitalistic development introduced the idea of
(1) Modernised poverty
(2) Impersonal institutions
(3) Third world
(4) Vernacular relations

49. The passage focuses on
(1) The merits of market economy
(2) The need for philanthropy to reduce poverty
(3) The ill-effects of capitalism
(4) The issue of redefining poverty in the Third World

50. Before 1940, colonisers believed that poor countries
(1) Can be changed
(2) Can be totally enlightened
(3) Cannot be changed
(4) Do not need their presence

ANSWERS

1. (1)	**2.** (4)	**3.** (4)	**4.** (3)	**5.** (2)	**6.** (3)	**7.** (3)	**8.** (3)	**9.** (2)	**10.** (4)
11. (1)	**12.** (2)	**13.** (1)	**14.** (4)	**15.** (1,2)	**16.** (2)	**17.** (4)	**18.** (4)	**19.** (4)	**20.** (3)
21. (2)	**22.** (2)	**23.** (3)	**24.** (3)	**25.** (4)	**26.** (3)	**27.** (1)	**28.** (3)	**29.** (1)	**30.** (4)
31. (4)	**32.** (1)	**33.** (2)	**34.** (1)	**35.** (2)	**36.** (2)	**37.** (3)	**38.** (3)	**39.** (4)	**40.** (2)
41. (3)	**42.** (1)	**43.** (3)	**44.** (2)	**45.** (1)	**46.** (2)	**47.** (1)	**48.** (1)	**49.** (3)	**50.** (3)

March 2023

UGC NET – PAPER I

Note: This paper consists of Fifty (50) objective type questions of Two (2) marks each. All questions are compulsory.

The following table presents the findings of a survey into how people travel to work:

Number of People Travelling to Work by			
Cycle	**Car**	**Bus**	**Walk**
72	18	35	55

Note: (a) 1 in 8 of the people who cycled to work were found to be over 65 years of age.

(b) 1 in 3 of the Cyclists stated that they travelled to work by bus on rainy days.

Based on the above, answer the question:

1. How many people cycled to work on a rainy day?
(1) 24 (2) 48 (3) 72 (4) 64

2. How many respondents indicated that they cycled to work and were over 65 years of age?
(1) 12 (2) 9 (3) 8 (4) 7

3. Which of the following statements is true?
(1) Slightly fewer than twice as many people indicated that they travelled to work by bus than by car.
(2) Slightly more than twice as many people indicated that they travelled to work by bus than by car.
(3) Slightly more people indicated that they travelled to work by bus than by car.
(4) Slightly fewer people indicated that they travelled to work by car than by bus.

4. The sum of which modes of travelling to work represents half the number of responses represented in the survey?
(A) Cycle and Car (B) Bus and Car
(C) Walk and Bus (D) Walk and Cycle
Choose the correct answer from the options given below:
(1) A and B Only (2) A and C Only
(3) B and C Only (4) B and D Only

5. How many more people indicated that they cycled to work compared with those who travelled by either bus or car ?
(1) 72 (2) 35 (3) 18 (4) 19

6. Given below are two statements:
Statement I: Learner centerd approach is centerd on teacher needs.
Statement II: Learner centerd approach is centerd on cooperative determination of subject matter.
In the light of the above statements, choose the most appropriate answer from the option given below:
(1) Both Statement I and Statement II are correct.
(2) Both Statement I and Statement II are incorrect.
(3) Statement I is correct but Statement II is incorrect.
(4) Statement I is incorrect but Statement II is correct.

7. Which of the following is a technique to provide right kind of support in right amount at right time to increase child's competence?
(1) Scaffolding (2) Assistance
(3) Accommodation (4) Schemas

8. SWAYAM PRABHA is an education learning platform initiated by DTH channels.
(1) Ministry of Human Resource and Development (Now Ministry of Education)
(2) University Grants Commission (UGC)
(3) Consortium for Educational Communication (CEC)
(4) All India Council of Technical Education (AICTE)

9. A learner combines her/his previous schemas or modifies them as per new experiences. The process of combining/ modifying existing schemas and to arrive at new schemas is known as
(1) Accommodation (2) Assimilation
(3) Adaptation (4) Equilibration

10. Which of the following curriculum development models come under Technical-Scientific Model?
(1) Open Classroom Model
(2) Taba's Model
(3) Weinstein and Fantini Model
(4) Roger's Model of Interpersonal Relations

11. Survey research is one of the key methods in
(1) Physics (2) History
(3) Sociology (4) Hermeneutics

12. Methods of social research are directly linked to different visions of
(1) Social reality

* Based on memory only. Please refer ugcnetonline.in

(2) Laboratory experiments
(3) Simulations (4) Virtual reality

13. Grand theories of social sciences operate at a
(1) Lower level
(2) Simplistic level
(3) Categorical level
(4) Higher level of abstraction

14. Which of the following are considered major types of qualitative research questions?
(A) Non-purposive
(B) Causes and consequences
(C) Predictive
(D) Evaluative (E) Descriptive
(1) A, B and C only (2) A, C and D only
(3) A, D and E only (4) B, C, D and E only

15. Given below are two statements:
Statement I: Time and cost are not relevant in determining the sample size.
Statement II: Unit non-response and item non-response do not matter in deciding the sampling error.
In the light of the above statements, choose the correct answer from the options given below.
(1) Both Statement I and Statement II are true
(2) Both Statement I and Statement II are false
(3) Statement I is true but Statement II is false
(4) Statement I is false but Statement II is true

16. The science of studying the feedback systems in humans, animals and machines is described as
(1) Feedback science
(2) Experience study
(3) Message Hermeneutics
(4) Cybernetics

17. De Saussure labelled language as a
(1) Technical code (2) Profusion of signs
(3) Verbalism (4) Macro generaliser

18. Which of the following are the criteria for public service communication?
(A) Personal bias (B) Ideological slant
(C) Accuracy (D) Comprehensiveness
(E) Separation of opinion and facts
Choose the correct answer from the options given below:
(1) A, B, C Only (2) B, C, D Only
(3) C, D, E Only (4) A, D, E Only

19. According to some experts like Marshal McLuhan, the following are considered hot media:
(A) Telephone (B) Television
(C) Radio (D) Cinema
(E) Print
Choose the correct answer from the options given below:
(1) A, B, C Only (2) B, C, D Only
(3) C, D, E Only (4) A, C, E Only

20. Given below are two statements:
Statement I: : Internet itself is a network and also a model for Cyberspace relations.
Statement II: Global interactive technologies, aided by the Internet, heralded the arrival of the 'second media age' by the end of the twentieth century.
In the light of the above statements, choose the correct answer from the options given below.
(1) Both Statement I and Statement II are true
(2) Both Statement I and Statement II are false
(3) Statement I is true but Statement II is false
(4) Statement I is false but Statement II is true

21. The monthly income of a person in the year 2020 was Rs. 65,000 and his monthly expenditure was Rs. 45,000. In the year 2021 his monthly income increased by 15% and his monthly expenditure by 7% What is the percentage increase in his savings?
(1) 33% (2) 31% (3) 35% (4) 28%

22. 5/9 of a number is equal to twenty five percent of a second number. Second number is equal to 1/4 of a third number. The value of the third number is 2960. How much is the 30% of the first number?
(1) 9.99 (2) 99.9 (3) 89.9 (4) 88.9

23. A man invested 1 / 3 of his retirement gratuity at 6% simple interest: 1/4 of his gratuity at 7% and the rest at 8% simple interest. If his annual return on these investments is Rs. 7012.5, find the total amount of gratuity invested by the man.
(1) Rs. 89,000 (2) Rs. 99,000
(3) Rs. 95,000 (4) Rs. 1,05,000

24. If in a certain, Coding language, 'Cheater' is coded as 'ejgcvgt', then how 'Preacher' will be coded in that language?
(1) 'rtgcejgt' (2) 'qsfbdifs'
(3) 'rtgbdjgt' (4) 'stgbdjgt'

25. What number should replace question mark (?) in the series given below? 7, 10, 19,46, 127, ?
(1) 202 (2) 192
(3) 173 (4) 370

26. Which fallacy is committed in the following argument?
"When I called you, you were neither in your class nor in the laboratory. Why are you avoiding me?"
(1) Circular argument (2) 'Red herring'
(3) Complex question (4) Slippery slope

27. Which of the following statements are logically equivalent?
(A) Some animals are birds.
(B) Some animals are not non-birds.
(C) Some non-birds are not non-animals.
(D) Some birds are animals.
Choose the correct answer from the options given below:

(1) B and C Only (2) B, C, D Only
(3) A, B and D Only (4) A, B and C Only

28. If the statement "no animals are fishes" is given as false, then which of the following statements can be immediately inferred to be true?
(A) All fishes are animals.
(B) Some animals are not fishes.
(C) All animals are fishes.
(D) Some animals are fishes.
Choose the correct answer from the options given below:
(1) B and D Only (2) A, C and D Only
(3) C and D Only (4) D Only

29. Which of the following propositions are contrary to each other?
(A) All fishes are mammals.
(B) Some fishes are mammals.
(C) No fishes are mammals.
(D) Some fishes are not mammals.
Choose the correct answer from the options given below:
(1) B and D Only (2) A and C Only
(3) A and D Only (4) B and C Only

30. According to Nyaya (Classical Indian School of Logic) which of the following argument involves the fallacy of Anupsamhari (non-exclusive middle term)?
(1) The hill has smoke because it has fire.
(2) Sound is eternal because it is audible.
(3) All things are non-eternal because they are knowable.
(4) Sound is eternal because it is produced.

Consider the following MS-Excel spreadsheet in which the population column represents the city's population in millions of people:

A	B	C	D	E	F
1. City	State	Population	Haryana	MP	UP
2. Patiala	Punjab	8.34			
3. Sonipat	Haryana	3.86			
4. Nmda	UP	2.71			
5. Indore	MP	2.16			
6. Mandi	HP	1.49			
7. Sagar	MP	1.38			
8. Panipat	Haryana	1.39			
9. Gwalior	MP	1.24			

31. Suppose the formula - IF ($B2=D$ 1, SA2,0) is entered into cell D2 and then the cell D2 is copied and pasted to D2:F9. How many cells in the range D2:F9 contains O?
(1) 0 (2) 6 (3) 12 (4) 18

32. Which of the following statements about email security best describes email encryption?
(1) This is a self-replicating program that can spread by email.
(2) This disguises the content of email messages in order to protect sensitive information.
(3) This consists of sending numerous duplicate mails to the same email address.
(4) The email header is changed so that the message appears to have come from someone else.

33. Given below are two statements about music files:
Statement I: A music clip stored in MP3 format would take up more memory than the same clip stored in WAV format.
Statement II: Music files stored in MP3 format are of better quality than files stored in WAV format.
In the light of the above statements, choose the correct answer from the options given below.
(1) Both Statement I and Statement II are true.
(2) Both Statement I and Statement II are false.
(3) Statement I is true but Statement II is false.
(4) Statement I is false but Statement II is true.

34. Which of the following statements are accurate?
(A) Web 2.0 is a simple static website without any interaction with its users.
(B) Web 2.0 brings people closer together with information using machines.
(C) Web 3.0 brings machines closer together using information.
Choose the correct answer from the options given below:
(1) A Only (2) B Only
(3) B and C Only (4) D only

35. Match List I with List II

LIST I (Output Device)	LIST II (Description)
A. Inkjet printer	I. Flat panel display that uses the light modulating properties of liquid crystals.
B. LCD screen	II. Flat panel display that uses an array of light-emitting diodes as pixels.
C. LED screen	III. Droplets of ink are propelled onto paper.
D. Laser Printer	IV. Electrically charged powdered ink is transferred onto paper.

Choose the correct answer from the options given below:
(1) A-IV, B-I, C-II, D-III
(2) A-IV, B-II, C-I, D-III
(3) A-II, B-I, C-III, D-IV
(4) A-III, B-I, C-II, D-IV

36. Atmospheric haze is mainly caused by?
(1) Ultra fine size particulate matters

(2) Oxides of nitrogen and Sulphur
(3) Ozone
(4) Carbon dioxide and Carbon monoxide

37. Given below are two statements:

Statement I: Nano scale metallic and bimetallic particles can efficiently remove common water pollutants such as Poly Chloro Benzenes (PCB), Organo chlorine pesticides and halogenated organic solvents.

Statement II: Nano scale metallic and bimetallic particles cannot reduce heavy metals such as nickel, arsenic, mercury etc.

In the light of the above statements, choose the most appropriate answer from the options given below.
(1) Both Statement I and Statement II are correct.
(2) Both Statement I and Statement II are incorrect.
(3) Statement I is correct but Statement II is incorrect.
(4) Statement I is incorrect but Statement II is correct.

38. Given below are two statements: One is labelled as Assertion A and the other is labelled as Reason R.

Assertion A: The change in sea level at any coastal location depends on the sum of global, regional and local factors.

Reason R: Therefore, the global mean sea level rise translates into an uniform rise in sea level around the world.

In the light of the above statements, choose the most appropriate answer from the options given below.
(1) Both A and R are correct and R is the correct explanation of A.
(2) Both A and R are correct but R is NOT the correct explanation of A.
(3) A is correct but R is not correct.
(4) A is not correct but R is correct.

39. Oxygen demanding wastes
(1) Decrease the oxygen level in water.
(2) Increase the oxygen level in water.
(3) Do not change the oxygen level in water.
(4) Increase the temperature of water.

40. Match List I with List II

LIST I (Sustainable Development Goal (SDG) number)	LIST II (Goal)
A. SDG 2	I. Sustainable cities and communities
B. SDG 3	II. Zero hunger
C. SDG 6	III. Good health and well being
D. DG 11	IV. Clean water and Sanitation

Choose the correct answer from the options given below:
(1) A-I, B-III, C-II, D-IV
(2) A-III, B-II, C-I, D-IV
(3) A-II, B-III, C-IV. D-I
(4) A-II, B-III, C-I, D-IV

41. What is the full form of 'SPARC'?
(1) Standard for Profession of Assessment and Research Communication
(2) Scheme for Promotion of Academic and Research Collaboration
(3) School for Promotion of Assessment and Right to commitment
(4) Social Protection of Advancement and Relationship Complex

42. According to NEP 2020, India will be promoted as a global study destination providing premium education at affordable costs thereby helping to restore its role as
(1) Economic power
(2) Knowledge Economy
(3) Vishwa Guru
(4) Shiksha Guru

43. What is the full form of 'NCIVE'?
(1) Non-Governmental course for the Initiation of Vocational Enhancement
(2) National Committee for the Integration of Vocational Education
(3) Non-Governmental Council for the Integration of Veterinary Education
(4) National Commission for the Information of Veterinary Education

44. The Government of India created Department of Science and Technology in the year:
(1) 1990 (2) 1985
(3) 1978 (4) 1971

45. The ancient system of education in India included education of which of the following ancient texts?
(A) Vedas (B) Brahmanas
(C) Upanishads (D) Dharma sutras
Choose the most appropriate answer from the options given below:
(1) A and C Only (2) B and D Only
(3) A, C and D Only (4) A, B, C and D

Read the following passage and answer the question given below:

Around the age of 2 children have a sense of intention, at least of their own intentions. They will announce, "I wanna peanut butter sandwich". As children develop a theory of mind, they also can understand that other people have intentions of their own. Older pre-schoolers who get along well with their peers can separate intentional from unintentional actions and react accordingly. For example, they will not get angry when another child accidentally knocks over their block tower. But aggressive children have more trouble assessing intention. They are likely to attack anyone who topples their tower, even accidently. As children mature, they are more able to assess and consider the intentions of others. With a developing theory of mind, children are increasingly able to understand that other people have different feelings and experiences and therefore may have a different viewpoint or perspective. This perspective-taking ability develops over time until it is quite sophisticated in adults. Being able to understand how others might think and feel is important in fostering cooperation and moral development, reducing prejudice, resolving conflicts, and encouraging positive social behaviours in general. Some coaching in perspective taking from the teacher might help if children mistreat peers and the mistreatment is not part of a deeper emotional or behavioural disorder.

46. Children of which of the following ages would generally have the best perspective taking ability?
(1) 3 years (2) 8 years
(3) 13 years (4) 18 years

47. Given below are two statements:
Statement I: Aggressive children can assess intention of others with ease.
Statement II: Different persons may have different viewpoints.
In the light of the above statements, choose the most appropriate answer from the options given below.
(1) Both Statement I and Statement II are correct.
(2) Both Statement I and Statement II are incorrect.
(3) Statement I is correct but Statement II is incorrect.
(4) Statement I is incorrect but Statement II is correct.

48. Understanding how others feel is important in
(A) Developing empathy
(B) Reducing prejudice
(C) Conflict resolution
(D) Encouraging Selfishness
(E) Enhancing cooperation
Choose the most appropriate answer from the options given below:
(1) A, B, C and D Only
(2) A, B, C and E Only
(3) B, C, D and E Only
(4) A, B, D and E Only

49. Given below are two statements: One is labelled as Assertion A and the other is labelled as Reason R.
Assertion A: Older pre-schoolers have better chances of getting along well with their peers as compared to young pre-schoolers.
Reason R: Older pre-schoolers generally have a better understanding of the intentions of others.
In the light of the above statements, choose the most appropriate answer from the options given below.
(1) Both A and R are correct and R is the correct explanation of A.
(2) Both A and R are correct but R is NOT the correct explanation of A.
(3) A is correct but R is not correct.
(4) A is not correct but R is correct.

50. Given below are two statements:
Statement I: A 2 years old child is likely to have a better understanding of his own intentions than those of others.
Statement II: It is always helpful to coach a child in perspective-taking if the child has the habit of mistreating others because of some behavioural disorder.
In the light of the above statements, choose the most appropriate answer from the options given below.
(1) Both Statement I and Statement II are correct.
(2) Both Statement I and Statement II are incorrect.
(3) Statement I is correct but Statement II is incorrect.
(4) Statement I is incorrect but Statement II is correct.

ANSWERS

1. (2)	**2.** (2)	**3.** (1)	**4.** (2)	**5.** (4)	**6.** (4)	**7.** (1)	**8.** (1)	**9.** (1)	**10.** (2)
11. (3)	**12.** (1)	**13.** (4)	**14.** (4)	**15.** (2)	**16.** (4)	**17.** (2)	**18.** (3)	**19.** (3)	**20.** (1)
21. (1)	**22.** (2)	**23.** (2)	**24.** (1)	**25.** (4)	**26.** (2)	**27.** (3)	**28.** (4)	**29.** (2)	**30.** (3)
31. (4)	**32.** (2)	**33.** (2)	**34.** (3)	**35.** (4)	**36.** (1)	**37.** (3)	**38.** (3)	**39.** (1)	**40.** (3)
41. (2)	**42.** (3)	**43.** (2)	**44.** (4)	**45.** (4)	**46.** (3)	**47.** (2)	**48.** (2)	**49.** (1)	**50.** (3)

OOO

December 2023

UGC NET – PAPER I

Note: This paper consists of Fifty (50) objective type questions of Two (2) marks each. All questions are compulsory.

Question Numbers : (1 to 5) – Comprehension

The following table shows the percentage (%) distribution of the number of candidates (Boys and Girls) and the number of boys who appeared in an entrance examination from six different cities A - F. A total of 78000 candidates appeared from all the six cities, in which the number of boys was 24000. Based on the data in the table, answer the questions that follow.

City-wise Details of Candidates who appeared in an exam.

City	Percentage Distribution	
	Candidates who appeared in the Exam	Boys who Appeared in the Exam
A	17%	23%
B	13.5%	20%
C	15%	17%
D	20%	10%
E	8.5%	21%
F	26%	9%

1. What is the total number of girls who appeared from City A?
   (1) 6420 (2) 6880
   (3) 7300 (4) 7740
2. What is the difference between the number of boys and the number of girls who appeared in the exam from City E?
   (1) 3450 (2) 3500
   (3) 3550 (4) 3650
3. Number of girls who appeared from City C is approximately ______ % of the number of candidates who appeared from City D.
   (1) 45 (2) 49
   (3) 54 (4) 57
4. Number of boys who appeared from City A is ______ % more than that from City B.
   (1) 8 (2) 12
   (3) 15 (4) 18
5. Number of girls who appeared from City F is approximately ______ % of the number of girls who appeared from all the six cities together.
   (1) 31.55 (2) 32.55
   (3) 33.55 (4) 34.55
6. The learning, in which a new behaviour is acquired but is not demonstrated until reinforcement is provided, is known as
   (1) Observational learning
   (2) Social learning
   (3) Latent learning
   (4) Moral learning
7. A teacher wants to assess the student's performance and wants to give immediate feedback. Which software you will select for the assessment?
   A. Kahoot
   B. Plotagon
   C. Screen-casto-matic
   D. Animaker
   E. Quizziz
   Choose the correct answer from the options given below:
   (1) A, B and D only
   (2) C, D and E only
   (3) B and C only
   (4) A and E only
8. Given below are two statements:
   Statement (I): As per Dewey's vision of learning, learners should demonstrate their knowledge through creativity and collaboration
   Statement (II): According to Piaget, learning is independent of the developmental stages of learner.
   In light of the above statements, choose the most appropriate answer from the options given below.
   (1) Both Statement (I) and Statement (II) are correct.
   (2) Both Statement (I) and Statement (II) are incorrect.

* Based on memory only. Please refer ugcnetonline.in

(3) Statement (I) is correct but Statement (II) is Incorrect.

(4) Statement (I) is incorrect but Statement (II) is correct.

9. Given below are two statements:

Statement (I): The non-directive model of teaching nurtures students rather than controlling the sequence of learning.

Statement (II): In the non-directive model of teaching the teachers role is that of a facilitator who has counselling relationship with students and who guides their growth and development.

In light of the above statements, choose the most appropriate answer from the options given below.

(1) Both Statement (I) and Statement (II) are correct.

(2) Both Statement (I) and Statement (II) are incorrect.

(3) Statement (I) is correct but Statement (II) is incorrect.

(4) Statement (I) is incorrect but Statement (II) Is correct.

10. In Charlotte Danielson's framework for teaching, the domain of Planning and Preparation' has the following components:

A. Organising physical space in classroom

B. Setting instructional outcomes

C. Designing student assessments

D. Demonstrating knowledge of content and pedagogy

E. Demonstrating knowledge of resources

Choose the correct answer from the options given below:

(1) C and E only

(2) A, B and D only

(3) B, C, D and E only

(4) A, B, C, D and E

11. Quantitative research can be construed as a research strategy that usually

(1) Entails a deductive approach to the relationship between theory and research.

(2) Emphasizes an inductive approach to the relationship between theory and research.

(3) Rejects the practices and norms of natural scientific model and of positivism in particular.

(4) Embodies a view of social reality as a constantly shifting emergent property of individual's creation.

12. Given below are two statements:

Statement (I): Qualitative research lays emphasis on contextual understanding.

Statement (II): Quantitative research is typically highly unstructured.

In light of the above statements, choose the most appropriate answer from the options given below.

(1) Both Statement (I) and Statement (II) are correct.

(2) Both Statement (I) and Statement (II) are incorrect.

(3) Statement (I) is correct but Statement (II) is incorrect.

(4) Statement (I) is incorrect but Statement (II) is correct.

13. In academic writing, the abbreviation 'fn.,' is used to represent

(1) forenoon

(2) footnote

(3) Forward page number

(4) Following page number

14. The mean and standard deviation of 75 observations are 45 and 15, respectively. If 2 is added to each observation, the new mean and standard deviation will be

(1) 47, 12 (2) 47, 14

(3) 47, 10 (4) 46, 12

15. A variable that has a causal impact on another variable is called

(1) Dependent variable

(2) Independent variable

(3) Confounding variable

(4) Extraneous variable

16. From the communication viewpoint, a completely predictable situation is considered to have

(1) Less fidelity (2) Negentropy

(3) Fluidity (4) Less sensitivity

17. The concept of framing is used to tailor political issues in election campaigns as part of communication strategy by

(1) Media audience

(2) Security agencies

(3) The Election Commission

(4) The Spin doctors

18. Which of the following are identified as roles of non-verbal communication in relation to verbal communication?

A. Accentuation B. Supervision

C. Repetition D. Substitution

E. Contradiction

Choose the correct answer from the options given below:

(1) A, B and C only

(2) B, C, D and E only
(3) A, C, D and E only
(4) A, B and E only

19. Which of the following are the examples of explicit meta communication?

A. Silent remorse
B. Avoidance of eye contact
C. Apologies
D. Excuses
E. Explanations

Choose the correct answer from the options given below:

(1) A, B and C only
(2) B, C and D only
(3) C D and E only
(4) A, B and E only

20. Given below are two statements:

Statement (I): Buddhists consider the language of communication as a divine gift.

Statement (II): Buddhists are of the view that the language for communication evolves according to social contexts and conditions.

In light of the above statements, choose the most appropriate answer from the options given below

(1) Both Statement (I) and Statement (II) are true.
(2) Both Statement (I) and Statement (II) are false.
(3) Statement (I) is true but Statement (II) is false.
(4) Statement (I) is false but Statement (II) is true.

21. Consider the following number series:

1, 3, 7, 15, 31, ?....

Identify the missing number (?) from the options given below

(1) 42 (2) 52
(3) 62 (4) 63

22. Consider the following letter series.

AA, BD, Cl, DP ?

The next term (?) in the series is

(1) ES (2) EV
(3) EY (4) EB

23. A sum of Rs 10,000.00 (ten thousand) is invested at rate of interest 8% per annum compounded half yearly. What will be the maturity amount in 1½ years?

(1) Rs 11248.64
(2) Rs 10816.28
(3) Rs 11200.00
(4) Rs 10108.64

24. In an organisation, there are a total of 40 employees consisting of 5 Executive officers, 15 Senior Staff and 20 Junior staff. The monthly salaries of an Executive officer, a Senior staff and a Junior staff are Rs 2,50,000, Rs 80,000 and Rs 45,000 respectively. What is the average salary of an employee of the organisation?

(1) Rs 20,000 (2) Rs 90,250
(3) Rs 82,750 (4) Rs 83,50

25. A train running at a speed of 90 km/hr starts slowing down at a constant rate of decrease in speed of 2.5 m/s. What is the distance covered by the train before it comes to a halt?

(1) 500 m (2) 750 m
(3) 250 m (4) 125 m.

26. Which of the following propositions are so related that they cannot both be false although they may both be true, as per square of opposition?

A. Some apes are monkeys.
B. All apes are monkeys.
C. Some apes are not monkeys.
D. No apes are monkeys.

Choose the correct answer from the options given below:

(1) B and D only
(2) A and B only
(3) A and C only
(4) C and D only

27. Which of the following statements are logically equivalent?

A. Some apes are not non-monkeys.
B. Some monkeys are not non-apes.
C. Some monkeys are apes.
D. Some apes are monkeys.

Choose the correct answer from the options given below:

(1) A and E only
(2) C and D only
(3) B, C and D only
(4) A, B, C and D

28. As per square of opposition, if the statement - "Some birds are apes" is given as false, then which of the following statements can be immediately inferred to be true?

A All birds are apes.
B. Some birds are apes.
C. No birds are apes.
D All birds are not apes.

Choose the correct answer from the options given below:

(1) C and D only
(2) A, C and D only
(3) B and D only
(4) B and C only

29. "It is so obvious that this world was created by an intelligent God. Just look at the amazing degree of organization that the world displays." Which fallacy is committed in this argument?
(1) Fallacy of composition
(2) Begging the Question
(3) Straw man
(4) False Cause

30. Given below are two statements, one is labelled as Assertion (A) and other one labelled as Reason (R).
Assertion (A): As per classical Indian view of logic the argument - 'Sound is quality because it is visible', is fallacious.
Reason (R): As per classical Indian view of logic the argument- 'Sound is quality because it is visible' involves a middle term that cannot by its very nature be present in the minor term.
In light of the above statements, choose the correct answer from the options given below.
(1) Both (A) and (R) are true and (R) is the correct explanation of (A).
(2) Both (A) and (R) are true but (R) is NOT the correct explanation of (A).
(3) (A) is true but (R) is false.
(4) (A) is false but (R) is true.

31. Alisha has agreed to send Khushi a 20-megabyte file. They both have a broadband internet connection. Alisha has to upload her file to a server and then Khushi needs to download it from the same server. The broadband data transfer rates (speeds) are: 1 megabit per second to upload a file and 8 megabits per second to download a file. If P and Q represent the time taken in seconds to upload and download Alisha's file respectively then (P, Q)=
(1) (20,160) (2) (144,18)
(3) (18,144) (4) (150,2)

32. Identify the correct order of the terms A-E to complete the following paragraph about computer devices and technology.
An ____ allows a user to write on a surface using a pen, and the text and drawings can then be captured and stored for later use. An ____ printer produces a hard copy of a document using ____ and piezoelectric technology. A ____ printer uses ____ a drum, and positive and negative charges, to produce a hard copy of a document.
A. inkjet
B. interactive whiteboard
C. laser
D. rotating
E. thermal bubble

Choose the correct answer from the options given below
(1) B, E, A, D C
(2) B, A, E, C, D
(3) A, B, E, C, D
(4) E, D, C, B, A

33. Given below are two statements:
Statement (I): An output device that creates an object by building layer upon player of material is called 3D printer. It is widely used In CAD applications.
Statement (II): Laptops can be used even when not plugged into an electricity socket.
In light of the above statements, choose the most appropriate answer from the options given below.
(1) Both Statement (I) and Statement (II) are true.
(2) Both Statement (I) and Statement (II) are false.
(3) Statement (I) is true but Statement (II) is false.
(4) Statement (I) is false but Statement (II) is true.

34. A computer uses RAM and ROM to store data. Which of the following statements describing ROM is/are true?
A. It stores the programs and data that are currently in use.
B. It is used to boot up the computer when power is turned on.
C. Its contents are retained when power is turned off.
Choose the correct answer from the options given below:
(1) A only (2) B only
(3) A and B only (4) B and C only

35. Match List-I with List-II

List I (Internet Term)	List II (Definition)
A. HTTP	I. A unique address given to a device on a network. It is provided by the manufacturer.
B. URL	II. The main protocol that governs the transmission of data using the Internet.
C. MAC address	III. An address given to each device on a network. It is provided by the network.
D. IP address	IV. The website address that is typed into the address bar.

Choose the correct answer from the options given below

(1) A - II, B - IV, C - I, D - III
(2) A - III, B - IV, C - I, D - II
(3) A - I, B - III, C - II, D - IV
(4) A - IV, B - II, C - I, D - III

36. Given below are two statements:

Statement (I): Exposure to mercury can be either through food chain or in the work place.

Statement (II): Poisoning by inorganic mercury (particularly vapours) results in the damage to the central nervous system.

In light of the above statements, choose the most appropriate answer from the options given below.

(1) Both Statement (I) and Statement (II) are true.
(2) Both Statement (I) and Statement (II) are false.
(3) Statement (I) is true but Statement (II) is false
(4) Statement (I) is false but Statement (II) is true

37. Given below are two statements:

Statement (I): Kyoto protocol only binds developed countries and places heavier burden on them

Statement (II): Kyoto protocol has nothing to do with United Nations Framework Convention on climate change (UNFCCC).

In light of the above statements, choose the most appropriate answer from the options given below.

(1) Both Statement (I) and Statement (II) are true.
(2) Both Statement (I) and Statement (II) are false.
(3) Statement (I) is true but Statement (II) is false.
(4) Statement (I) is false but Statement (II) is true

38. Match List-I with List-II

List I **Water Category**	**List II** **pH Value**
A. Normal Water	I. <5
B. Rain water	II. >7
C. Acid Rain Water	III. 5-6
D. Ocean Water	IV. 7

Choose the correct answer from the options given below

(1) A - IV, B - I, C- III, D - II
(2) A - IV, B - III, C - I, D - II
(3) A - IV, B - III, C - II, D - I
(4) A - III, B - II C - IV, D- I

39. Leachates are

(1) Persistent Organic Pollutants
(2) Algae found on eutrophic lakes
(3) Ozone depleting substances
(4) Contaminated liquid draining from landfills

40. Give below are two statements:

Statement (I): International Solar Alliance's vision: let us together make the sun brighter.'.

Statement (II): International Solar Alliance's mission: 'Every home how far away will have a light at home

In light of the above statements, choose the most appropriate answer from the options given below.

(1) Both Statement (I) and Statement (II) are true
(2) Both Statement (I) and Statement (II) are false.
(3) Statement (I) is true but Statement (II) is false.
(4) Statement (I) is false but Statement (II) is true.

41. In which of the colleges, the European education was imparted through the medium of mother tongue before independence?

(1) Mayo College, Ajmer
(2) St. Stephen College, Delhi
(3) St. Xavier College. Calcutta
(4) University College, Lahore

42. The policy on higher education during the eighth five-year plan was to encourage

(1) Expansion of public sector
(2) Involvement of private sector
(3) Establishment of foreign campuses
(4) Entry of foreign Universities

43. Which of the following Indian universities were modelled on the lines of University of London?

A. Calcutta B. Bombay
C. Madras D. Andhra
E. Mysore

Choose the correct answer from the options given below:

(1) A, B and C only
(2) B, C and D only
(3) C, D and E only
(4) A, B and D only

44. Which of the following subjects were taught at the University of Navadwip in ancient India?

A. Archaeology B. Physics
C. Logic D. Literature
E. Tantra

Choose the correct answer from the options given below:

(1) A, B and C only (2) B, C and D only
(3) C, D and E only (4) A, B and E only

45. Given below are two statements:

Statement (I): The rating system of higher educational institutions followed in India does not touch the structural diversity of such institutions.

Statement (II): A universal and holistic rating system is not feasible in India.

In light of the above statements, choose the most appropriate answer from the options given below.

(1) Both Statement (I) and Statement (II) are true.

(2) Both Statement (I) and Statement (II) are false.
(3) Statement (I) is true but Statement (II) is false.
(4) Statement (I) is false but Statement (II) is true.

Read the passage given below and answer the following questions:

India became the first country to land near the Moon's uncharted south pole region at 6.03 pm after 18 nail-biting minutes of descent ended in a perfect touchdown, offering irrefutable evidence of the astronomical abilities and galactic ambitions of a nation that on Wednesday announced itself as one of the world's foremost space powers.

Chandrayaan-3's touchdown which completed an extraordinary arc of decades of scientific perseverance also opened new vistas for the country's space programme in the lucrative market of space exploration and commerce. "India is on the Moon!" S. Somnath, the chief of Indian Space Research Organization (ISRO) said, as the Chandrayaan-3's lander Vikram, with the Pragyan rover contained within, made a safe and soft landing on the Moon.

The watershed moment came mere days after Russia – a space veteran - crashed its moon craft while attempting to reach the same territory. At an estimated budget of $75 million, Chandrayaan-3 was built at a fraction of the cost of not only previous American lunar missions but also this summer's cinema blockbusters Oppenheimer and Barbie. The Russian Luna-25 had cost $200 million.

"This is a victory cry of a new India," said Prime Minister Narendra Modi, waving the Indian flag as he watched the landing from South Africa. Beaming scientists and officials burst into applause and hugged each other in joy at ISRO's mission operations complex at Bengaluru after Vikram lander finally came to a rest on the rugged lunar terrain after 18 minutes that pushed millions in India on the edge of their seats.

46. India became the first country in the world to
(1) Land on the moon.
(2) Land a man on the moon.
(3) Land near the south pole of the moon.
(4) Orbit the moon.

47. Which of the following represents the estimated cost of building Ghandrayaan-3?
(1) 200 million dollars
(2) The same cost as the making of film *Barbie*
(3) More than the cost of making film *Oppenheimer*
(4) 75 million dollars

48. The words 'India is on the moon were spoken by
(1) The Indian Prime Minister
(2) The Russian President
(3) The Chief of ISRO
(4) The American President

49. The success of India's moon mission is significant because
A. It will make India a manufacturing hub.
B. It has made India one of world's foremost space powers.
C. It has opened new avenues for India's space exploration.
D. It has opened new vistas in the lucrative market of space exploration and commerce.

Choose the correct answer from the options given below:
(1) B, C and D only (2) A, B and C only
(3) C and D only (4) A and D only

50. Given below are two statements:
Statement (I): Chandrayaan-3's success was a result of years of scientific efforts.
Statement (II): Russia's Luna-25 landed on the moon minutes after Chandrayaan-3.
In light of the above statements, choose the most appropriate answer from the options given below.
(1) Both Statement (I) and Statement (II) are true
(2) Both Statement (I) and Statement (II) are false.
(3) Statement (I) is true but Statement (II) is false.
(4) Statement (I) is false but Statement (II) is true.

ANSWERS

1. (4)	**2.** (1)	**3.** (2)	**4.** (3)	**5.** (3)	**6.** (3)	**7.** (4)	**8.** (3)	**9.** (1)	**10.** (3)
11. (1)	**12.** (3)	**13.** (2)	**14.** (3)	**15.** (2)	**16.** (2)	**17.** (4)	**18.** (3)	**19.** (3)	**20.** (4)
21. (4)	**22.** (3)	**23.** (1)	**24.** (4)	**25.** (4)	**26.** (3)	**27.** (4)	**28.** (1)	**29.** (2)	**30.** (1)
31. (4)	**32.** (2)	**33.** (1)	**34.** (4)	**35.** (1)	**36.** (1)	**37.** (3)	**38.** (2)	**39.** (4)	**40.** (1)
41. (4)	**42.** (2)	**43.** (1)	**44.** (3)	**45.** (3)	**46.** (3)	**47.** (4)	**48.** (3)	**49.** (1)	**50.** (3)

June 2024

UGC NET – PAPER I

Note: This paper consists of Fifty (50) objective type questions of Two (2) marks each. All questions are compulsory.

Question 1 to 5: The following table shows the percentage (%) distribution of the number of readers of an IT magazine in the years 2019 and 2023, among the six different cities A-F. Based on the data in the table, answer the questions that follow.

City	2019	2023
A	10%	15%
B	14%	16%
C	17%	28%
D	9%	10%
E	24%	9%
F	26%	22%

1. If the number of readers from City-C in the year 2019 and that from City-E in the year 2023 were 73,100 and 51,300, respectively, then the number of readers from City-B in the year 2023 was approximately ___ % more than that in 2019.
(1) 53.7 (2) 50.3
(3) 52.8 (4) 51.5

2. If the number of readers from the City-D in the year 2019 and 2023 were 77,400 and 1,14,000 respectively, then what is the difference between the number of readers from City-F in the year 2019 and that in 2023 ?
(1) 24,800 (2) 27,200
(3) 28,400 (4) 33,600

3. If the total number of readers from all the six cities A-F together in the year 2023 was 50,000, then the number of readers was more than 7,400 in exactly ___ cities in the same year.
(1) 2 (2) 3
(3) 4 (4) 5

4. If the total number of readers from all the six cities A-F together in the years 2019 and 2023 were 4.3 lakh and 5.7 lakh, respectively, then what was the difference between the total number of readers from City-B and City-C together in the years 2019 and 2023 ?
(1) 1.175 lakh (2) 1.415 lakh
(3) 1.625 lakh (4) 1.596 lakh

5. If the ratio of the number of readers from City-A in the year 2019 to that in 2023 was 2 : 5, then what was the ratio of the number of readers from all the six cities together in the year 2019 to that in 2023?
(1) 3:5 (2) 4:5
(3) 4:9 (4) 2:5

6. Match List - I with List - II.

List - I (Types of toxicants)	List- II (Affected Organ)
A. Nephrotoxic	I. Kidney
B. Hematotoxic	II. Blood
C. Pulmonotoxic	III. Lungs
D. Hepatotoxic	IV. Liver

Choose the correct answer from the options given below:
(1) A-II, B-IV, C-I, D-III
(2) A-I, B-IV, C-III, D-II
(3) A-III, B-II, C-II, D-IV
(4) A-III, B-I, C-IV, D-II

7. What is the base-10 equivalent of the base-4 number 3013 ?
(1) 182 (2) 196
(3) 199 (4) 210

8. Mind to mind communication involves the communication of meanings through :
A.. Physical settings
B. Noise manipulation
C. Shared beliefs
D. Context
E. Values
Choose the correct answer from the options given below:
(1) A, B and D only
(2) B, C and D only
(3) A, B, C and E only
(4) C, D and E only

9. Identify the correct order of the following list of computer components ranked from slowest to fastest in terms of access time.

* Based on memory only. Please refer ugcnetonline.in

A. CPU cache B. RAM
C. SSD D. Optical Drive

Choose the correct answer from the options given below:

(1) D, C, B, A (2) C, B, A, D
(3) B, A, D, C (4) C, D, A, B

10. Match List -I with List - II.

List - I (Words)	List - II (Codes with same rule)
A. FIND	I. RGKC
B. CLOG	II. DGLB
C. SHOW	III. AJME
D. TIME	IV. QFMU

Choose the correct answer from the options given below:

(1) A-I, B-II, C-III, D-IV
(2) A-I, B-III, C-IV, D-II
(3) A-III, B-IV, C-I, D-II
(4) A-IV, B-I, C-II, D-III

11. Which fallacy is committed in the following statement?

"People with cases of flu should be kept in quarantine, because it has never been disproven as the best means of keeping the disease from spreading."

(1) Appeal to Ignorance
(2) Hasty Generalisation
(3) Slippery slope
(4) False cause

12. When communication helps a group to achieve its goals, it is known as :

(1) Disruptive role (2) Promotive role
(3) Counteractive role (4) Devotional role

13. Choose the correct statements:

A. $x\%$ of y is equal to $y\%$ of $100\,x$.

B. If 40% of 60% of $\left(\frac{3}{5}\right)$ a number is 504, then 25% of $\left(\frac{2}{5}\right)$ of that number is equal to 350.

C. If A is 15% more than B, then B is ~13.04% less than A.

D. 10% of 5 and 5% of 10 add-up to 0.1.

Choose the correct answer from the options given below :

(1) A and B only (2) B and C only
(3) C and D only (4) A and D only

14. Which of the following digital initiatives provides database of profiles of scientists/ researchers and other faculty members working at leading academic institutions and R&D organizations ?

(1) E-Vidwan
(2) National Academic Depository (NAD)
(3) SWAYAM prabha
(4) E-Shodhsindhu

15. A device used to convert a computer's digital signal to an analogue signal for communication is called a :

(1) bridge (2) modem
(3) switch
(4) Network Interface Card (NIC)

16. Match List -I with List - II.

List - I (Use)	List - II (Appropriate Computer Input Device)
A. To input voiceovers for a presentation	I. Microphone
B. To input a PIN	II. Number pad
C. To select options from a menu	III. Mouse
D. To operate a flight simulator	IV. Joystick

Choose the correct answer from the options given below :

(1) A-I, B-IV, C-III, D-II
(2) A-III, B-IV, C-I, D-II
(3) A-IV, B-II, C-I, D-III
(4) A-I, B-II, C-III, D-IV

17. Which of the following is the first Post-Independence education commission in India?

(1) Indian Education Commission
(2) Calcutta University Commission
(3) University Education Commission
(4) Indian Universities Commission

18. A motor boat covers a certain distance downstream in 5 hours but takes 6 hours to return upstream to the starting point. If the speed of the stream is 4 km/h, what is the speed of the motor boat in still water?

(1) 40 km/h (2) 42 km/h
(3) 44 km/h (4) 46 km/h

19. Which of the following statements A-D about computer memory size is/are true?

A. 25 KB is larger than 100 MB.
B. 999 MB is larger than 50 GB.
C. 3500 KB is smaller than 2 GB.
D. 2350 bytes is smaller than 2 KB.

Options

(1) A only (2) C only
(3) B and D only (4) B and C only

20. Which of the following approaches to the study of reality suggests that only knowledge gained through experience and the senses is acceptable?

(1) Constructionism (2) Ethnography
(3) Empiricism (4) Operationalism

21. Speed of a boat in still water is 5 km/hr and the speed of the stream is 1 km/hr. A man rows to a place at a distance of 24 km and comes back to the starting point. Find the total time taken by him.

(1) 8 hr (2) 10 hr
(3) 12 hr (4) 15 hr

22. Which of the following are essential requirements for the formation of photochemical smog?

A. Carbon monoxide (CO)
B. Nitrogen dioxide (NO_2)
C. Carbon dioxide (CO_2)
D. Volatile organic compounds (VOCs)
E. Sunlight

Choose the most appropriate answer from the options given below:

(1) A, C and E (2) B, D and E
(3) A, B, C, D and E (4) A, C, D and E

23. Knowing that you find algebra more difficult than your sister does, but that you could improve with practice, is an example of:

(1) Self-Regulation (2) Metacognition
(3) Self-discipline (4) Automation

24. Which of the following are the subdivisions of Implicit (Unconscious) memory?

A. Priming
B. Episodic Memory
C. Classical conditioning effects
D. Semantic Memory
E. Procedural Memory

Choose the most appropriate answer from the options given below:

(1) A, C and E (2) A, B, D and E
(3) B and D only (4) A, B, C, D and E

25. Match List-I with List-II

List-I (Concept)	List-II (Source)
A. Free commerce and communication	I. John Locke
B. Language as a conduit of communication	II. Karl Marx
C. Communication in economics	III. Adam Smith
D. Lines of communication	IV. Alfred Marshall

Choose the correct answer from the options given below:

(1) A-III, B-I, C-IV, D-II
(2) A-II, B-III, C-IV, D-I
(3) A-III, B-IV, C-I, D-II
(4) A-IV, B-I, C-II, D-II

26. Which of the following are true about breeder reactors?

A. They produce more fissile material than they consume.
B. There are no breeder reactors in India.
C. There are two types (Fast and Slow) of breeder reactors.
D. For breeding operation the conversion ratio (fissile material produced/fissile material consur be more than one.
E. Breeder reactors produce more nuclear waste than the conventional one.

Choose the correct answer from the options given below :

(1) A, C and D only (2) B, C and E only
(3) A, B and D only (4) A, C, D and E only

27. The media accountability system to improve media quality focuses on:

A. Evaluation B. Audience control
C. Monitoring D. Eduction
E. Feedback

Choose the correct answer from the options given below:

(1) A, B and C only (2) B, C and D only
(3) B, D and E only (4) A, C, D and E only

28. Identify the correct sequence of the following research organizations according to establishment.

A. Indian Council of Social Science Resarch (ICSSR)
B. National Council for Rural Institutes (NCRI)
C. Indian Council for Philosophical Research (JCPR)
D. Indian Council for Historical Research (ICHR)
E. Indian Institute of Advanced Studies (IIAS)

Choose the correct answer from the options given below:

(1) A, D, E, B, C (2) B, E, C, D, A
(3) E, A, D, C, B (4) C, B, A, E, D

29. When you try to predict the value of an outcome variable from one or more variables, you are likely to be using:

(1) The Pearson product-moment correlation
(2) Bivariate regression
(3) Multivariate regression
(4) Analysis of variance

30. According to the National Credit Framework (NCTF), after obtaining a Bachelor's Degree (Honours/ Research/ Engineering) of four years, the credit level earned is:

(1) 5.5 (2) 6

(3) 7.5 (4) 7

31. If a research project is set up so that everybody in the population of interest has an equal chance of being included in the sample, the research involves:

(1) Quota sampling

(2) Judgmental sampling

(3) Probability sampling

(4) Convenience sampling

32. What is the full form of POPs?

(1) Persistent Organic Pollutants

(2) Persistent Oxygenated Pollutants

(3) Polycyclic Organic Pollutants

(4) Polymerized Organic Pollutants

33. Match List-I with List-II

List-I (Abbreviation)	List-II (Meaning)
A. et.al.	I. in the same place
B. ante.	II. and others
C. cf.	III. compare
D. ibid.	IV. before

Choose the correct answer from the options given below:

(1) A-I, B-III, C-IV, D-II

(2) A-II, B-III, C-IV, D-I

(3) A-II, B-IV, C-III, D-I

(4) A-IV, B-II, C-III, D-I

34. Match List-I with List-II

List-I (Goals/Targets of MDGs and SDGs)	List-II (Number of Goals/Targets)
A. Goals in Millenium Development Goals	I. 8
B. Targets in Millenium Development Goals	II. 17
C. Goals in Sustainable Development Goals	III. 21
D. Targets in Sustainable Development Goals	IV. 169

Choose the correct answer from the options given below:

(1) A-I, B-III, C-IV, D-II

(2) A-I, B-II, C-IV, D-I

(3) A-I, B-I, C-IV, D-II

(4) A-I, B-II, C-I, D-II

35. Arrange the following in order of increasing connotation.

A. Fielder B. Ball player

C. Baseball player D. Athlete

Choose the correct answer from the options given below:

(1) B, C, A, D (2) B, A, C, D

(3) D, B, C, A (4) A, C, B, D

36. The Second Five Year Plan for implementation included the recommendations of the following:

A. University Education Commission

B. Languages Commission of India

C. Rural Higher Education Committee

D. Three-Year Degree Course Committee

E. Committee on Establishment of New Universities

Choose the correct answer from the options given below:

(1) C, D, and E only

(2) A, B, and C only

(3) B, C, and D only

(4) A, B, and E only

37. Which of the following statements are true?

A. The concept of truth can apply to single propositions.

B. The concept of truth can never apply to any single proposition by itself.

C. Propositions by themselves can be valid but not invalid.

D. A proposition cannot be valid by itself though it can be invalid on its own.

Choose the most appropriate answer from the options given below:

(1) D only (2) A and B only

(3) B and C only (4) B and D only

38. Which of the following statements is correct?

(1) Nyāya syllogism has three propositions.

(2) Nyāya syllogism has five terms.

(3) Nyāya syllogism has three propositions and three terms.

(4) Nyāya syllogism has five propositions.

39. Match List - I with List - II

List - I (Ancient Treatises)	List - II (Author)
A. Yoga-Sutras	I. Chanakya
B. Arthashastra	II. Gautama
C. Lilavati	III. Patanjali
D. Nyāya-Sutras	IV. Bhaskaracharya

Choose the correct answer from the options given below:

(1) A-IV, B-I, C-III, D-II
(2) A-II, B-IV, C-III, D-I
(3) A-III, B-I, C-IV, D-II
(4) A-I, B-III, C-II, D-IV

40. Which of the following statements is logically equivalent to the statement "No horses are feline"?
(1) No felines are horses.
(2) All non-horses are felines.
(3) No horses are non-feline.
(4) All non-felines are horses.

41. Which of the following is the National Coordinator of SWAYAM courses for non-technical graduation education?
(1) All India Council for Technical Education (AICTE)
(2) University Grants Commission (UGC)
(3) National Institute of Technical Teachers Training and Research (NITTTR)
(4) National Council of Educational Research and Training (NCERT)

42. Match List - I with List - II

List - I (Digital Initiative)	List - II (Purpose)
A. Shodh Sindhu	I. Hosts synopsis of research topics in Indian Universities
B. Shodh Gangotri	II. Provides access to e-resources to Universities and Colleges
C. Shodh Shuddhi	III. Free/Libre and open source software for Education
D. FOSSEE	IV. Plagiarism checking initiative aimed to ensure originality

Choose the correct answer from the options given below:
(1) A-IV, B-I, C-II, D-III
(2) A-II, B-I, C-IV, D-III
(3) A-I, B-II, C-III, D-IV
(4) A-I, B-IV, C-II, D-III

43. Arrange the following fractions in increasing order.
A. 6/11
B. 13/22
C. 19/32
D. 22/33
Choose the correct answer from the options given below:
(1) A, B, C, D
(2) D, C, B, A
(3) A, C, B, D
(4) B, D, A, C

44. Which technology first marked a separation between transportation and communication?
(1) Telegraph
(2) Projection
(3) Printing
(4) Photography

45. Arrange the different stages involved in the process of deduction in correct sequence.
A. Hypothesis confirmed or rejected
B. Data Collection
C. Revision of theory
D. Findings
Choose the correct answer from the options given below:
(1) A, B, D, C
(2) D, C, B, A
(3) A, C, B, D
(4) B, D, A, C

According to a World Health Organization report, about 80 percent of the world population uses traditional medicine systems in some or the other way. India has a distinctive and unique traditional medicine base, with each system having its own ancient philosophy, medicinal knowledge, perception and practices that align with the regional cultures, traditions and beliefs. The traditional medicine systems in India include Ayurveda, Yoga, Naturopathy, Unani, Siddha, Sowa Rigpa and Homeopathy which is known as Ayush. All these systems were fornmulated, practised and perfected in a continuum nuch before the advent of modern health science.

In many countries of the world, medical pluralism is the norm and traditional medicine is one of the surest means to achieve total healthcare coverage for the world population using acceptable, safe and economically – feasible methods. No system of medicine can single-handedly address all health The holistic patient-centered and individualised approach is the trademark of traditional systems and but an integrative approach incorporating Tthe positives of each can surely benefit mankind, enables the patient-physician partnership to design or customise treatment and lifestyle advice in order to achieve the highest potential for wel-being. This awareness combined with the increase in use of traditional medicine has brought the systems to the fore. The diverse activities ranging from the provision of prophylactic care to the management of disease and the effective implementation and integration of Ayush system to the public healthcare during the pandemic has garnered global attention to Ayush Systems, This has enabled the signing of the Host Country Agreement for the establishment of Global Centre for Traditional Medicine (GCTM) at Jamnagar.

46. In many countries of the world, medical pluralism is the norm because:

(1) Traditional systems of medicine are useless.
(2) Traditional systems of medicine befool the public.
(3) An integrative approach incorporating the positives of each system of medicine can in no way benefit mankind.
(4) No single system of medicine can single-handedly address all health concerns.

47. Which of the following facts about the traditional Indian medicine systems are false?

A. Each system is Unique.
B. They include Ayurveda, Naturopathy, Yoga, Unani, Siddha, Sowa Rigpa, and Homeopathy.
C. Each system has an essentially similar philosophy.
D. Modern Health Science preceded them.

Choose the most appropriate answer from the options given below:

(1) A, B, and D only
(2) B, and C only
(3) C and D only
(4) B, C, and D only

48. According to a World Health Organization report, the percentage of the world population that uses traditional medicine systems in some way or the other is:

(1) About 20% (2) About 50%
(3) About 100% (4) About 80%

49. The Global Centre for Traditional Medicine has been established in:

(1) World Health Organization
(2) Jamnagar
(3) New Delhi
(4) Haridwar

50. Choose the appropriate title for the passage.

(1) Allopathy
(2) Holistic Healthcare
(3) Ayurveda
(4) Homeopathy

ANSWERS

1. (4)	**2.** (4)	**3.** (3)	**4.** (1)	**5.** (2)	**6.** (2)	**7.** (3)	**8.** (4)	**9.** (1)	**10.** (1)
11. (1)	**12.** (2)	**13.** (4)	**14.** (1)	**15.** (2)	**16.** (4)	**17.** (3)	**18.** (3)	**19.** (2)	**20.** (3)
21. (3)	**22.** (1)	**23.** (2)	**24.** (4)	**25.** (1)	**26.** (4)	**27.** (1)	**28.** (4)	**29.** (3)	**30.** (2)
31. (3)	**32.** (1)	**33.** (3)	**34.** (1)	**35.** (3)	**36.** (1)	**37.** (1)	**38.** (3)	**39.** (3)	**40.** (1)
41. (2)	**42.** (2)	**43.** (3)	**44.** (1)	**45.** (3)	**46.** (4)	**47.** (3)	**48.** (4)	**49.** (2)	**50.** (2)

January 2025

UGC NET – PAPER I

Note: This paper consists of Fifty (50) objective type questions of Two (2) marks each. All questions are compulsory.

Question 1 to 5: Bakery shops in a city prepare three different varieties of hotcakes, namely, Cornmeal, American and Swedish. The following table shows the total number of hotcakes (three varieties together) sold by four different bakery shops, namely A, B, C and D on Monday along with the number of Cornmeal hotcakes sold and the difference between the number of American hotcakes and Cornmeal hotcakes sold. Based on the data in the table, answer the questions that follow.

Bakery-wise Sale Details of Hotcakes on Monday

Bakery	Total Number of Hotcakes sold	Number of Cornmeal Hotcakes Sold	Difference between the number of American and Cornmeal Hotcakes Sold
A	1200	320	40
B	1080	280	120
C	1000	360	80
D	1320	420	40

Note: (1) Total numbers of hotcakes sold = sum of sale of number of Cornmeal, American and Swedish hotcakes

(2) Number of American hotcakes sold is always greater than the number of Cornmeal hotcakes sold

1. What is the difference between the total number of Cornmeal hotcakes sold by bakery A and bakery D together, and the number of Swedish hotcakes sold by bakery A?

   (1) 175 (2) 200
   (3) 150 (4) 220

2. If the number of cornmeal hotcakes sold by bakery B on Tuesday (that is, the next day) is 20% more than that on Monday, the ratio of the number of American hotcakes to Swedish hotcakes by bakery B on Tuesday is 4:5, and the number of American hotcakes sold by bakery B on Tuesday is 320, then what is the total number of hotcakes sold by bakery B on Tuesday?

   (1) 1056 (2) 1150
   (3) 1200 (4) 1000

3. The number of American hotcakes sold by bakery A is _____ % more than the number of Swedish hotcakes sold by bakery C.

   (1) 20 (2) 80
   (3) 180 (4) 40

4. For another bakery E, if the total number of hotcakes sold is 120 less than that of bakery D, number of Cornmeal hotcakes sold is 40% of the total number of hotcakes sold by E, number of American hotcakes sold is 35% of the total number of hotcakes sold by E and the remaining are Swedish hotcakes sold by E, then what is the number of Swedish hotcakes sold by bakery E?

   (1) 210 (2) 300
   (3) 250 (4) 400

5. What is the ratio of the number of American hotcakes sold by bakery C to the number of Swedish hotcakes sold by bakery D?

   (1) 3:5 (2) 5:2
   (3) 1:1 (4) 4:3

6. Which of the following tools can be used to create a virtual science lab experience?

   A. Kahoot! B. Labster
   C. Turnitin D. Phet simulation
   E. Padlet

   Choose the correct answer from the options given below:

   (1) A, B and D Only (2) C and E Only
   (3) A and E Only (4) B and D Only

7. Which of the following are contrary propositions?

   A. All poets are visionaries
   B. Some poets are dreamers
   C. Some poets are not dreamers
   D. No square is a circle
   E. No poet is a dreamer

   Choose the correct answer from the options given below:

* Based on memory only. Please refer ugcnetonline.in

(1) D and E Only (2) C and D Only
(3) B and D Only (4) A and E Only

8. Android is a mobile operating system developed by ______.

(1) IBM (2) Apple
(3) Microsoft (4) Google

9. If a certain coding scheme, "DELHI" is coded as 5613910, then how is "MUMBAI" coded in this scheme?

(1) 1422143210 (2) 132113219
(3) 122012108 (4) 1523154311

10. Which of the following air pollutants causes serious health issue due to its greater affinity for hemoglobin in blood in comparison to oxygen?

(1) SO_2 (Sulphur dioxide)
(2) CO (Carbon Monoxide)
(3) CO_2 (Carbon dioxide)
(4) O_3 (Ozone)

11. Which of the following are impacts of a hydroelectric power plant?

A. Land degradation
B. Microseismicity
C. Greenhouse gas emission
D. Water pollution
E. Formation of smog

Choose the correct answer from the options given below:

(1) A, B, C and D Only
(2) A, C, D and E Only
(3) A, B, D and E Only
(4) B, C and E Only

12. Which of the following were the initiatives taken during the third five year plan?

A. Removal of the diploma course system.
B. Provision for correspondence courses.
C. Establishment of additional colleges including regional engineering colleges.
D. Appointment of working group on technical education.
E. Less emphasis on trained manpower.

Choose the correct answer from the options given below:

(1) A, B and C Only
(2) B, C and D Only
(3) C, D and E Only
(4) A, D and E Only

13. Match the LIST-I with LIST-II

LIST-I (Definition)	LIST-II (Characteristic)
A. Stipulative	I. They are used to eliminate ambiguity
B. Lexical	II. They encapsulate larger understanding of theory
C. Precising	III. It is neither accurate nor inaccurate
D. Theoretical	IV. It reports the meaning of the definiendum

Choose the **correct** answer from the options given below:

(1) A-II, B-IV, C-III, D-I
(2) A-I, B-III, C-IV, D-II
(3) A-IV, B-II, C-III, D-I
(4) A-III, B-IV, C-I, D-II

14. The committee for the establishment of a national open university was headed by

(1) G. Parthasarathy
(2) G. Rami Reddy
(3) Hari Gautam
(4) K. L. Srimali

15. If $(L)_M$ represents a number L in base-M number system, then identify the correct ascending order of the following numbers A-D when converted to decimal number system.

A. $(11011.11)_2$ B. $(131.2)_4$
C. $(25.5)_8$ D. $(16.6)_{16}$

Choose the correct answer from the options given below:

(1) C, D, B, A (2) C, D, A, B
(3) A, C, D, B (4) B, A, C, D

16. Situated cognition is ________.

(1) The idea that thinking is located in social and physical contexts, not within an individual's mind.
(2) A student's general knowledge about the world.
(3) The belief that one can master a situation and produce positive outcomes.
(4) A schema of an event.

17. If 7:x = 17.5: 22.5, find the value of x.

(1) 9 (2) 12
(3) 15 (4) 8

18. Which of the following are characteristics of computer-mediated mass communication?

A. One-way communication

B. Massification

C. Interactivity

D. Demassification

E. Asynchroneity

Choose the correct answer from the options given below:

(1) A, B, C Only (2) B, C, D Only

(3) C, D, E Only (4) A, B, E Only

19. The transfer of learning from one situation to another that is conscious and effortful is called

(1) Far-road transfer (2) High-road transfer

(3) Near-road transfer

(4) Long-road transfer

20. Which one of the following has highest turbidity?

(1) Drinking water (2) Muddy water

(3) Clear Lake water (4) Ocean water

21. Which of the following are the strategies of co-operative learning?

A. Rally coach B. Talking chips

C. Schedule D. Round table

E. Think-pair-share

Choose the correct answer from the options given below:

(1) A, B, D and E Only

(2) B and E Only

(3) A, C and E Only

(4) B and D Only

22. Which of the following is an independent malicious program that propagates itself across network by exploiting security flaws in widely-used services?

(1) Computer Worm (2) Computer Virus

(3) Trojan Horse (4) Logic Bomb

23. The tendency of researchers to subtly and inadvertently affect the behaviours of participants in a study, obscuring the true effect of the independent variable, is called

(1) Response bias (2) Experimenter bias

(3) Social desirability bias

(4) Hawthorne effect

24. Sound with frequencies below and above the audible frequency range are known as ______.

A. Feeble sound B. Infrasound

C. Parasound D. Ultrasound

Choose the correct answer from the options given below:

(1) A and C (2) B and C

(3) B and D (4) A and D

25. A man walks 12 km towards south and then 7 km towards north. From here he walks 5 km towards his left. How far and in which direction is the man with reference to his starting point?

(1) 5km, North-west

(2) 5km, south-west

(3) $5\sqrt{2}$, south-west

(4) $5\sqrt{2}$, south-east

26. Match the LIST-I with LIST-II

LIST-I (Population Mean (μ) and $\frac{1}{N}\Sigma x_i^2$)	LIST-II (Population Standard Deviation (σ))
A. $\mu = 3, \frac{1}{N}\Sigma x_i^2 = 90$	I. 12
B. $\mu = 4, \frac{1}{N}\Sigma x_i^2 = 116$	II. 11
C. $\mu = 5, \frac{1}{N}\Sigma x_i^2 = 146$	III. 9
D. $\mu = 6, \frac{1}{N}\Sigma x_i^2 = 180$	IV. 10

Choose the **correct** answer from the options given below:

(1) A-I, B-II, C-III, D-IV

(2) A-II, B-III, C-IV, D-I

(3) A-III, B-IV, C-II, D-I

(4) A-IV, B-III, C-II, D-I

27. Match the LIST-I with LIST-II

LIST-I (Scholar)	LIST-II (Expertise)
A. Brahmagupta	I. Political strategist
B. Kotilya	II. Sum
C. Patanjali	III. Doctor
D Charak	IV. Mathematician

Choose the **correct** answer from the options given below:

(1) A-I, B-II, C-III, D-IV

(2) A-II, B-III, C-IV, D-I

(3) A-III, B-IV, C-I, D-II

(4) A-IV, B-I, C-II, D-III

28. Find the number that can replace question mark (?) in the series given below"

21, 22, 26, 35, 51, ?

(1) 62 (2) 66
(3) 86 (4) 76

29. Identify the variables associated with interval scale of measurement:

A. Time of the day in 24-hour format
B. Date of birth
C. Weight
D. Height

Choose the correct answer from the options given below:

(1) A and B Only (2) C and D Only
(3) A, C and D Only (4) A Only

30. Match the LIST-I with LIST-II

LIST-I (Definition)	LIST-II (Characteristic)
A. Modelling	I. Helping learner in starting and gradually fading the support
B. Scaffolding	II. Searching for new information, verifying to accept it as authentic knowledge
C. Articulation	III. Observing the performance of an expert
D. Exploration	IV. Giving words to their understanding of the process and content

Choose the **correct** answer from the options given below:

(1) A-IV, B-III, C-II, D-I
(2) A-III, B-I, C-IV, D-II
(3) A-II, B-IV, C-I, D-III
(4) A-I, B-II, C-III, D-IV

31. According to the Naiyayikas, when we perceive a character, we perceive the general 'character' as its defining characteristic due to which of the following?

(1) Yogaj
(2) Inference
(3) Knowledge Characteristics
(4) General Characteristics

32. Arrange the following in the correct order of their appearance in the APA style of journal article referencing.

A. Name of journal in italics
B. doi
C. Initials of author
D. Title of article

Choose the correct answer from the options given below:

(1) A, B, C, D (2) B, C, D, A
(3) C, D, A, B (4) D, A, B, C

33. "Step on scale, please" represents which function of the language?

(1) Informative (2) Expressive
(3) Directive (4) Performative

34. Identify the chronological sequence of the following organisations:

A. Associated press
B. A. C. Nielsen
C. Academy of motion picture Arts and Sciences
D. Al Jazeera
E. Federal communications commission

Choose the correct answer from the options given below:

(1) A, B, C, E, D (2) B, D, E, C, A
(3) E, C, A, D, B (4) B, C, E, A, D

35. 'Fear of missing out' is part of

(1) Mass communication concentration
(2) Internet addiction
(3) Media control
(4) Media fragmentation

36. Match the LIST-I with LIST-II

LIST-I (Concept)	LIST-II (Description)
A. Media intrusion	I. Focuses on the practical use of knowledge
B. Social capital	II. Subversion of politics by media
C. Media literacy	III. The influence of potential leaders because of social group membership and participation
D. Pragmatism	IV. The ability to analyse media messages

Choose the **correct** answer from the options given below:

(1) A-I, B-II, C-III, D-IV
(2) A-II, B-III, C-IV, D-I

(3) A-III, B-IV, C-I, D-II
(4) A-IV, B-I, C-II, D-III

37. Find the value of the given expression correct upto 2 decimal places.

$$\frac{0.05\times0.05\times0.05+0.04\times0.04\times0.04}{0.05\times0.05-0.05\times0.04+0.04\times0.04}$$

(1) 0.19 (2) 0.09
(3) 0.90 (4) 0.85

38. The famous 'Wood's Dispatch' is often described as the _____ of English education in India.
(1) Bill of Rights
(2) People's Charter
(3) Preamble
(4) Magna Carta (Power of Attorney)

39. Match the LIST-I with LIST-II

LIST-I (Question)	LIST-II (Answer)
A. The speed of a CPU is measured in _____.	I. Inches
B. Storage capacity of data is measured in _____.	II. Hertz
C. Network bandwidth is measured in _____.	III. bits per second
D. Size of a computer monitor is measured in _____diagonally from corner to the opposite corner.	IV. Bytes

Choose the **correct** answer from the options given below:
(1) A-I, B-III, C-IV, D-II
(2) A-III, B-II, C-I, D-IV
(3) A-IV, B-I, C-II, D-III
(4) A-II, B-IV, C-III, D-I

40. Which of the following statements A-D are true with reference to high-level computer programming languages?
A. These need to be translated into machine code in order to run on a computer.
B. These are written using mnemonic codes.
C. These are specific to the computer's hardware.
D. These are portable languages.
Choose the correct answer from the options given below:
(1) B and C Only (2) A and B Only
(3) A and D Only (40 C and D Only

41. Knowledge is arrived at through the gathering of facts that provide the basis for laws. This refers to the principle of
(1) Deducitivism (2) Constructionism
(3) Objectivism (4) Inductivism

42. Identify the correct chronological sequence of the establishment of the following institutions in India.
A. Siddhartha college, Mumbai
B. Milind College
C. P.W.S. Arts and Commerce College
D. Khalsa College
E. Dr. Babasaheb Ambedkar College of Arts, Science and Commerce
Choose the correct answer from the options given below:
(1) A, E, C, D, B (2) B, C, E, A, D
(3) C, B, A, E, D (4) D, A, B, E, C

43. Match the LIST-I with LIST-II

LIST-I (Water Quality Parameters)	LIST-II (Explanation)
A. BOD	I. Amount of organic matter in water
B. DO	II. Acid/alkaline Neutral nature of water
C. COD	III. Oxygen absorbed by microorganisms
D. pH (pH)	IV. Amount of oxygen in water

Choose the **correct** answer from the options given below:
(1) A-III, B-IV, C-II, D-I
(2) A-III, B-IV, C-I, D-II
(3) A-I, B-II, C-III, D-IV
(4) A-I, B-II, C-IV, D-III

44. Which of the following is correct with reference to syllogism rules?
(1) From two negative premises, a negative conclusion is drawn
(2) Any term distributed in the premises must be distributed in the conclusion
(3) The middle term must be distributed in both premises
(4) A syllogism should have only three terms

45. When older media find new functions because their earlier functions are taken over by new technologies, the phenomenon is known as
    (1) Functional displacement
    (2) Alternative journalism
    (3) Existentialism
    (4) Experimentalism

Read the following passage and answer the questions that follow.

A radical new surgery procedure, laughed at not long ago, is holding out fresh hope for patients of cardiac myopathy, or enlargement of the heart. The technique, now in India, allows patients to go home two weeks after the operation, to lead a near-normal sedentary life. Cardiac myopathy is a condition that has a variety of causative factors. An attack from one of the 20 identified viruses, parasite infection, long-term alcohol abuse and blood pressure could bring it on, and in rare cases, it could follow child birth and is even known to run in families. The condition is marked by an increase in the size of the heart's chambers and a decrease in the efficiency of pumping.

46. Cardiac myopathy is a medical condition related to
    (1) The heart (2) The eyes
    (3) The muscles of the legs
    (4) Body movement

47. Which of the following is incorrect about the causative factors of cardiac myopathy?
    (1) Attack by certain identified viruses
    (2) Long-term alcohol abuse
    (3) Overeating
    (4) Heredity

48. Patients with cardiac myopathy have:
    (1) Increased heart rate
    (2) Slowing of the heart rate
    (3) Increased blood flow to the heart
    (4) Normal blood flow to the heart

49. Cardiac myopathy is a condition characterized by:
    (1) Shrinkage of the heart
    (2) Decrease in the size of the lungs
    (3) Limited air flow to the lungs
    (4) Heart enlargement

50. Which of the following is true about cardiac myopathy surgery?
    (1) The radical new surgery procedure is now available in India.
    (2) It was unsuccessfully tried in India in the past.
    (3) Earlier patients had to stay in hospital for 4 weeks after surgery.
    (4) Earlier the surgery was available in only a few cities in India.

ANSWERS

1. (4)	**2.** (1)	**3.** (2)	**4.** (2)	**5.** (3)	**6.** (4)	**7.** (4)	**8.** (4)	**9.** (1)	**10.** (2)
11. (1)	**12.** (2)	**13.** (4)	**14.** (1)	**15.** (2)	**16.** (1)	**17.** (1)	**18.** (3)	**19.** (2)	**20.** (2)
21. (1)	**22.** (1)	**23.** (2)	**24.** (3)	**25.** (3)	**26.** (3)	**27.** (4)	**28.** (4)	**29.** (1)	**30.** (2)
31. (4)	**32.** (3)	**33.** (3)	**34.** (1)	**35.** (2)	**36.** (2)	**37.** (2)	**38.** (4)	**39.** (4)	**40.** (3)
41. (4)	**42.** (4)	**43.** (2)	**44.** (4)	**45.** (1)	**46.** (1)	**47.** (3)	**48.** (2)	**49.** (4)	**50.** (1)

June 2025

UGC NET – PAPER I

Note: **This paper consists of Fifty (50) objective type questions of Two (2) marks each. All questions are compulsory.**

Study the table carefully and answer the questions :

The given data is regarding the number of paperback and hardbound books sold by four different book shops A, B, C and D :

Shops	Number of Hardbound books sold	Number of Paperback books sold
A	3500	2000
B	3900	5200
C	4400	5500
D	5500	6600

1. Number of hardbound books sold by shop A is approximately what percent less than the number of paperback books sold by shop C?

(1) 32 (2) 36

(3) 38 (4) 42

2. Number of total books (hardbound and paperback together) sold by the highest selling shop is what percent higher than the lowest selling shop ?

(1) 50% (2) 100%

(3) 120% (4) 150%

3. What is the ratio between total sale by shops A and C together to the total sale by shops B and D ?

(1) 77 : 106 (2) 73 : 102

(3) 17 : 33 (4) 21 : 27

4. What is the ratio between total number of hard bound books sold by shop C and D together and number of paperback books sold by shop D ?

(1) 2 : 1 (2) 5 : 4

(3) 3 : 2 (4) 9 : 7

5. What is the difference between the average number of hardbound books sold by shops A, B and D and the average number of paper back books sold by shops C and D ?

(1) 267 (2) 400

(3) 1570 (4) 1750

6. Match List - I with List - II

List - I	List - II
A. The source is not visible to the receiver because of Geographical distance	I. Technical Barriers to Communication
B. The people are having individual differences, motivation and attitude and anxiety and prejudice	II. Linguistic Barriers to Communication
C. With faulty expression, poor translation, ambiguous words	III. Psychological Barriers to Communication
D. With poor quality of audio and video signals, the message may not be sent to target group	IV. Physical Barriers to Communication

Choose the **correct** answer from the options given below :

(1) A-IV, B-III, C-II, D-I

(2) A-IV, B-I, C-III, D-II

(3) A-II, B-I, C-IV, D-III

(4) A-III, B-II, C-I, D-IV

7. CD-ROM stands for :

(1) Compressed Disk Read Only Memory

(2) Compact Device for Reading out Messages

(3) Compact Device for Read/Write Over Mobiles

(4) Compact Disk Read Only Memory

8. What are the factors to be considered while selecting a communication media ?

A. No need to think about receiver

B. Reliability

C. It should be costly

D. Confidentiality Availability

Choose the most appropriate answer from the options given below :

(1) A, B and C Only (2) B, C and D Only

(3) C, D and E Only (4) B, D and E Only

* Based on memory only. Please refer ugcnetonline.in

9. Under which section of The UGC Act, Inter-University Centres (IUCs) were established ?

(1) 12(ccc) (2) 12(B)
(3) 12(a) (4) 12(h)

10. Match **List - I** with **List - II** :

List - I	List - II
A. Asiddha	I. Irrelevant middle term
B. Badhita	II. Unproven middle term
C. Viruddha	III. Contrary middle term
D. Savyabhicharra	IV. Contradicted middle term

Choose the **correct** answer from the options given below :

(1) A-I, B-II, C-III, D-IV
(2) A-II, B-IV, C-III, D-I
(3) A-II, B-III, C-I, D-IV
(4) A-III, B-IV, C-II, D-I

11. Arrange the phases of life cycle analysis for information on environmental effects of products (from first to last) :

A. Inventory B. Initiation
C. Impact D. Improvement

Choose the correct answer from the options given below :

(1) A, B, D, C (2) C, D, A, B
(3) D, C, B, A (4) B, A, C, D

12. Arrange the following steps in model of listening in sequence

A. Interpreting B. Responding
C. Remembering D. Hearing
E. Understanding

Choose the correct answer from the options given below :

(1) E, C, A, B, D (2) D, E, C, A, B
(3) D, A, B, C, E (4) A, B, D, E, C

13. Arrange chronologically the establishment of given digital initiatives

A. National Digital Library (N.D.L.)
B. Shodhganga
C. Academic Bank of Credit (A.B.C.)
D. DIKSHA

Choose the **correct** answer from the options given below :

(1) C, D, B, A (2) D, B, C, A
(3) B, D, A, C (4) B, C, A, D

14. Major thrusts of National Policy on Education (NPE), 1986, were :

A. State level planning and coordination through state council for higher education
B. Expansion of open universities and distance education system
C. Establishment of National Assessment Centre PARAKH
D. Conferring autonomous status on selected colleges
E. Establishment of two multidisciplinary education and research universities (MERU) in each state

Choose the most appropriate answer from the options given below :

(1) A, C and D Only (2) C, D and E Only
(3) A, B and D Only (4) B, C, D and E Only

15. Arrange the following in sequence as they are introduced in increasing order of age of the students

A. Taxonomy of Educational Objectives
B. Team Teaching
C. Personalised system of Instructions
D. Concept of Interaction model of Teaching

Choose the **correct** answer from the options given below :

(1) A, D, B, C (2) B, A, D, C
(3) C, A, D, B (4) C, D, A, B

16. What is the full form of ARPANET ?

(1) Advanced Research Project Agency Network
(2) Advanced Resource Project Agency Network
(3) Applied Research Project Agency Network
(4) American Research Project Agency Network

17. Select correct order of finalising a research problem:

A. Defining the research problem
B. Selecting the area of research
C. Finding the research gap
D. Study of reference material and reports of previous researches
E. Identifying a research problem

Choose the **correct** answer from the options given below :

(1) B, C, D, A, E (2) D, B, C, E, A
(3) B, D, C, E, A (4) D, B, A, C, E

18. Match **List - I** with **List - II**

List - I (System Name)	List - II (Year/Time period)
A. The Mark I computer	I. 1951

B. IBM-701 II. 1953

C. IBM-650 III. 1937-44

D. The Universal Automatic Computer One (UNIVAC-1) IV. 1952

Choose the **correct** answer from the options given below:

(1) A-III, B-IV, C-II, D-I

(2) A-II, B-III, C-I, D-IV

(3) A-I, B-II, C-IV, D-III

(4) A-IV, B-l, C-II, D-III

19. Vyapti in Indian Logic refers to

(1) Logical contradiction

(2) Direct perception

(3) Invariable concomitance

(4) Verbal testimony

20. Choose the correct statements :

A. MS-Word saves the files in '.doc' format

B. SQL server is a local network server

C. 'MATLAB' is a mathematical software

D. Bootstrap loader is an example of entertainment software

Choose the **correct** answer from the options given below :

(1) A and B Only (2) A and C Only

(3) C and D Only (4) A and D Only

21. Which are the characteristics of research ?

A. It always aims to develop new theory.

B. It is a scientific process.

C. Logical reasoning is used in decision making during research process.

D. Hypothesis testing is done in every kind of research

E. It collects and analyses evidences to derive findings.

Choose the **most appropriate** answer from the options given below :

(1) B, C and D Only (2) A, B and C Only

(3) B, C and E Only (4) C, D and E Only

22. When was the Paris agreement adopted ?

(1) 5 October 2020 (2) 12 December 2015

(3) 7 November 2018 (4) 8 July 1998

23. In which conditions, Karl Pearson's correlation coefficient can be calculated ?

A. If means of both the variables are equal

B. If one variable is measured in interval scale and another is measured in ordinal scale

C. If there is linear relationship between two variables

D. If data are obtained in interval or ratio scale for both the variables

E. If direction of relationship between two valuables is known

Choose the most appropriate answer from the options given below :

(1) C and D Only (2) C, D and E Only

(3) B, D and E Only (4) A, C and E Only

24. Which of the following are considered as fallacies of relevance ?

A. Ad hominem B. False cause

C. Straw man D. Red herring

Choose the most appropriate answer from the options given below

(1) A and D Only (2) B and C Only

(3) A, C and D Only (4) A, B, and C Only

25. What is the sum of the first 15 terms of the following series ?

$2^2, 3^2, 4^2, 5^2$, ...

(1) 1261 (2) 1240

(3) 1239 (4) 1259

26. Match **List - I** with **List - II**

List - I	**List - II**
A. Goals are decided in the context of the needs of a nation	I. Modern Teaching Technology
B. Feedback is obtained at local level	II. Traditional Teaching Technology
C. Team Teaching	III. Instructional Technology
D. Time for completion of a task is same for all students	IV. Educational Technology

Choose the **correct** answer from the options given below:

(1) A-IV, B-II, C-I, D-III

(2) A-IV, B-III, C-I, D-II

(3) A-II, B-I, C-IV, D-III

(4) A-III, B-I, C-IV, D-II

27. In a categorical proposition, the subject and predicate are connected by :

(1) A question (2) A fallacy

(3) A copula (4) A mood

28. Choose the 'WRONG' statement:

A. Machine Language is a low level language

B. 'FORTRAN' is a high level language

C. 'C' is a low level language

D. 'SQL' is a low level language

Choose the correct answer from the options given below

(1) A and B Only

(2) B and C Only

(3) A and C Only

(4) C and D Only

29. How many Millenium Development Goals (MDG) were adopted by United Nations ?

(1) 8 (2) 7

(3) 5 (4) 10

30. Arrange the steps of evaluating a deductive argument:

A. Assess the truth of premises

B. Identify premises and conclusion

C. Test logical structure

D. Determine soundness

Choose the correct answer from the options given below

(1) A, B, C, D (2) A, C, B, D

(3) B, C, A, D (4) D, B, A, C

31. Match **List - I** with **List - II** :

List -I (Institutions of National Importance (INI) Acts)	**List - II (Year of Enactment)**
A. National Institute of Technology Act	I. 2017
B. Indian Institute of Management Act	II. 1961
C. Indian Institutes of Information Technology Act	III. 2007
D. Institutes of Technology Act	IV. 2014

Choose the **correct** answer from the options given below:

(1) A-III, B-I, C-IV, D-II

(2) A-II, B-III, C-IV, D-I

(3) A-IV, B-I, C-II, D-III

(4) A-II, B-IV, C-I, D-III

32. Which of the following is not an element of communication within the communication process cycle?

(1) Channel (2) Receiver

(3) Sender (4) Time

33. Arrange the areas for following shapes in descending order of then values :

A. The area of the curved surface of a cylindrical wire of radius 1.0 mm and length 3.5 cm

B. fire surface of a spherical ball of radius 3.5 mm

C. The area of a rhombus having diagonals 1.5 cm and 1.8 cm

D. The area of a circle of diameter 7.0 mm

Choose the **correct** answer from the options given below :

(1) D, B, C, A (2) A, B, C, D

(3) B, A, C, D (4) C, A, B, D

34. The study of how the mind creates knowledge has resulted in what are currently referred to as ________ view of Education.

(1) Pragmatic (2) Idealistic

(3) Metacognitive (4) Constructive

35. Identify the correct statement

A. If $2^x = \frac{256}{\sqrt{2}}$ then $x = \frac{15}{2}$

B. $\frac{1}{3}$ of 50% of 150 is greater than $\sqrt{576}$

C. In the merit list of an examination result, the rank of a student is 5th from the top among 20 students. His rank from the bottom of the list is at 15th position

D. In a class of 30 students, the average of weights of 20 students is 45 kg and the rest of students have an average weight of 40 kg. The average weight of the class is 42.5 kg

Choose the **correct** answer from the options given below :

(1) A, B and C Only (2) B, C and D Only

(3) A, B and D Only (4) A and B Only

36. An IP address consists of a

(1) 16- bit integer (2) 32- bit integer

(3) 64- bit integer (4) 96- bit integer

37. Find out the 'RIGHT' combinations below :

A. Learning a second language takes little time and efforts - Myth

B. All bilinguals easily maintain both languages - True

C. Learning a second language takes little time and efforts - True

D. All bilinguals easily maintain both languages - Myth

Choose the **correct** answer from the options given below :

(1) A and D Only (2) B and C Only
(3) A and B Only (4) C and D Only

38. Match **List - I** with **List - II**:

List - I (Context of Research)	**List - II (Method)**
A. Researcher continues data collection and analyses till the satisfactory findings are derived	I. Survey
B. Study of change in emotional maturity of the students with passage of lime	II. Experimental
C. Study of the effect of one variable on other variable in controlled situation	III. Develop mental
D. Study of social problems faced by working women	IV. Grounded theory

Choose the **correct** answer from the options given below :

(1) A-IV, B-III, C-I, D-II
(2) A-II, B-IV, C-II, D-I
(3) A-IV, B-III, C-II, D-I
(4) A-III, B-IV, C-I, D-II

39. A sum of Rs. 10,000 is invested for a term of $2\frac{1}{2}$ years at an interest rate of 8% compounded annually.

The amount on maturity will be :

(1) Rs. 12520.50 (2) Rs. 12024.62
(3) Rs. 12130.56 (4) Rs. 11664.48

40. Match List - I with List - II

List - I (Ecosystem)	**List - II (Biogeographic Realms)**
A. Eurasia	I. Neotropical realm
B. South and South East Asia	II. Palearctic realms
C. North America	III. Nearctic realm
D. South America	IV. Oriental realm

Choose the **correct** answer from the options given below:

(1) A-II, B-IV, C-III, D-I
(2) A-II, B-I, C-III, D-IV
(3) A-III, B-IV, C-I, D-II
(4) A-II, B-III, C-IV, D-I

41. To experience the educational value, one must extract its net meaning through

(1) Reflections (2) Communication
(3) Consequences (4) Decisions

42. Match **List -I** with **List - II**:

List - I	**List - II**
A. The numerator of a fraction is increased by 25% and the denominator is increased by 50% leading to a value of $\frac{5}{3}$. The original fraction is _____.	I. $\frac{1}{10}$
B. $4\frac{1}{3}-3\frac{1}{2}=$ ______.	II. $\frac{2}{5}$
C. The fraction equivalent to 40% is ______.	III. $\frac{5}{6}$
D. $\frac{0.064}{325 \times 3.20 - 3.20 \times 3.05}$	IV. $\frac{2}{1}$

Choose the **correct** answer from the options given below :

(1) A-II, B-III, C-IV, D-I
(2) A-III, B-II, C-IV, D-I
(3) A-IV, B-III, C-I, D-II
(4) A-IV, B-III, C-II, D-I

43. The Rigveda comprises hymns

(1) 1028 (2) 10600
(3) 1064 (4) 11300

44. Which of the following Statements is false in the context of research ?

(1) Inductive and deductive reasoning are applied in the research process.
(2) Verifiable findings are derived by the research process.
(3) Research is conducted to find answers of meaningful questions scientifically.
(4) It necessarily improves quality of functioning of the area in which it is conducted.

45. For disaster management, following processes must be adopted

A. Training B. Migration
C. Mitigation D. Response
E. Detection

Choose the **correct** answer from the options given below :

(1) B and C Only (2) B and E Only
(3) A, B and C Only (4) A, C, D and E Only

Read the following passage and answer the questions:

A person who takes the trouble to form his own opinions and beliefs, will feel that he owes no responsibility to the majority for Iris conclusions. If he is a genuine lover of truth, if he is inspired by a passion for seeing things as they are and an abhorrence of holding ideas which do not conform to facts, he will be wholly independent of the assent of those around him. When he proceeds to apply his beliefs in the practical conduct of life, the position is different. There are then good reasons why his attitude should be less inflexible. The society in which he is placed is an ancient and composite growth. The people from whom he dissents have not come by their opinions, customs and by a process of mere haphazard.

These opinions and customs all had their origin in a certain real supposed fitness. They have certain depth of root in the lives of a proportion of the existing generation. Their congruity with one another may have come to an end. That is only one side of the truth. The most zealous propagandism cannot penetrate to them. In common language, we speak of a generation as something possessed of a kind of exact unity, with all its parts and members homogenous. Yet, plainly it is not this. It is a whole but a whole in a state of constant flux, its factors and elements are eternally shifting. It is not one but many generations.

46. According to the passage, customs and traditions originate from
(1) Conflicts of life
(2) Ignorance
(3) The old generation
(4) Beliefs

47. A genuine lover of truth will:
(1) appreciate the quality of food
(2) make compromise with situation
(3) criticise what he does not like
(4) be wholly independent of the assent of those around him

48. According to the author, a generation is a whole but it is always
(1) Constant (2) Growing
(3) Homogeneous (4) Heterogeneous

49. One's position is usually different when a person ___________.
(1) turns a deaf ear to what others say
(2) pays attention to what people say
(3) proceeds to apply his beliefs in the practical conduct of life
(4) remains ignorant of happenings around him

50. According to the author, the attitude of self-opinionated person in the practical social life should be:
(1) flexible (2) rigid
(3) indifferent (4) proactive

ANSWERS

1. (2)	**2.** (3)	**3.** (1)	**4.** (3)	**5.** (4)	**6.** (1)	**7.** (4)	**8.** (4)	**9.** (1)	**10.** (2)
11. (4)	**12.** (2)	**13.** (3)	**14.** (3)	**15.** (2)	**16.** (1)	**17.** (3)	**18.** (1)	**19.** (3)	**20.** (2)
21. (3)	**22.** (2)	**23.** (1)	**24.** (3)	**25.** (4)	**26.** (2)	**27.** (3)	**28.** (4)	**29.** (1)	**30.** (3)
31. (1)	**32.** (4)	**33.** (2)	**34.** (4)	**35.** (4)	**36.** (2)	**37.** (1)	**38.** (3)	**39.** (3)	**40.** (1)
41. (1)	**42.** (4)	**43.** (1)	**44.** (4)	**45.** (4)	**46.** (3)	**47.** (4)	**48.** (2,4)	**49.** (3)	**50.** (1)

OOO

January 2026

UGC NET – PAPER I

Note: This paper consists of Fifty (50) objective type questions of Two (2) marks each. All questions are compulsory.

Study carefully the table given below and answer the question asked here under.

A college has four programs B.A., B.Sc., B.Com. and B.B. A.The results of the mid-semester and end-semester tests are shown in the table given below.

Results	Number of students			
	B.A.	B.Sc.	B.Com.	B.B.A.
Failed in both tests	28	23	17	27
Failed in mid-semester test but passed in end-semester test	14	12	8	13
Passed in mid-semester test but failed in end-semester test	6	17	9	15
Passed in both tests	64	55	46	76

1. If the number of students passing a test be considered a criterion for comparison of difficulty level of two tests, then mid-semester test of which of the following programs was the least difficult?

(1) B.A.
(2) B.Sc.
(3) B.Com.
(4) B.B.A.

2. Which program has the lowest passing percentage in end-semester test?

(1) B.A.
(2) B.Sc.
(3) B.Com.
(4) B.B.A.

3. Which program has the highest failure rate in the mid-semester test ?

(1) B.A.
(2) B.Sc.
(3) B.Com.
(4) B.B.A.

4. How many students are there in the four programs?

(1) 420
(2) 430
(3) 320
(4) 330

5. What is the ratio of number of students in B.Sc. program to the number of students in B.Com. program ?

(1) 80:107
(2) 107:131
(3) 107:80
(4) 80:131

6. Which of the following represents the ontological orientation of qualitative research strategies ?

(1) Deductive
(2) Positivism
(3) Objectivism
(4) Constructionism

7. Which term is NOT related to computer hardware?

(1) Bus
(2) Switch
(3) Windows
(4) Mouse

8. Arrange the following pairs of standard deviation (σ) and total number of samples (n) pertaining to different sampling distributions in the decreasing order of their standard error.

A. $\sigma = 1.6, n = 16$
B. $\sigma = 1.5, n = 25$
C. $\sigma = 0.6, n = 36$
D. $\sigma = 1.4, n = 49$

Choose the correct answer from the options given below:

(1) A, B, C, D
(2) A, B, D, C
(3) D, C, B, A
(4) C, B, D, A

* Based on memory only. Please refer ugcnetonline.in

9. Given below are two statements one is labelled as Assertion (A) and the other is labelled as Reason (R).

Assertion (A): The terms validity and invalidity do not apply to inductive arguments.

Reason (R): In an inductive argument, the conclusion does not have sufficient ground in the premises.

In the light of the above statements, choose the most appropriate answer from the options given below:

(1) Both (A) and (R) are correct and (R) is the correct explanation of (A)
(2) Both (A) and (R) are correct but (R) is not the correct explanation of (A)
(3) (A) is correct but (R) is not correct
(4) (A) is not correct but (R) is correct

10. Given below are two statements one is labelled as Assertion (A) and the other is labelled as Reason (R).

Assertion (A): People, who hold views contrary to those dominant in the media, keep those views to themselves.

Reason (R): Such people fear isolation or separation from those around them.

In the light of the above statements, choose the most appropriate answer from the options given below:

(1) Both (A) and (R) are correct and (R) is the correct explanation of (A)
(2) Both (A) and (R) are correct but (R) is not the correct explanation of (A)
(3) (A) is correct but (R) is not correct
(4) (A) is not correct but (R) is correct

11. Arrange the following in the ascending order of adoption in terms of Diffusion of Innovation among the masses:

A. Opinion Followers
B. Opinion Leaders
C. Early Adopters
D. Change Agents
E. Laggards

Choose the correct answer from the options given below:

(1) A, D, C, B, E
(2) D, C, B, A, E
(3) C, D, B, A, E
(4) A, B, C, D, E

12. The theory that argues that media can have a strong influence in deciding the small number of public problems or issues that people will think about at any given point in time, is:

(1) Agenda-Setting Theory
(2) Knowledge-Gap Theory
(3) Limited Effects Theory
(4) Personal Influence Theory

13. Arrange the following in increasing order in terms of their coverage:

A. PAN
B. MAN
C. WAN
D. LAN

Choose the correct answer from the options given below :

(1) D, B, A, C
(2) A, B, D, C
(3) A, D, C, B
(4) B, A, D, C

14. Match List-I with List-II:

List-I Ashram departments	**List-II** Subject
A. Vishnu place	I. Military education
B. tight space	II. Astrology
C. Garuna place	III. Politics
D. Mahendra place	IV. Travel and transportation

Select the correct answer from the options given below:

(1) A-II, B-IV, C-III, D-I
(2) A-I, B-III, C-II, D-IV
(3) A-III, B-II, C-IV, D-I
(4) A-I, B-II, C-III, D-IV

15. The issue related to 'traditional knowledge societies and their livelihood' is addressed in the National Mission for ______.

(1) Enhanced Energy Efficiency
(2) Sustaining the Himalayan Eco-system
(3) Sustainable Habitat
(4) A Green India

16. Which of the following are not true?

A. In the argument from ignorance fallacy, something is accepted as true because it is not proven false.

B. In Hasty generalisation fallacy, a general truth is applied to a particular case ignoring its uniqueness.

C. In Begging the question fallacy, an event is wrongly accepted as the cause of some other event.

D. The fallacy of Amphiboly occurs in arguing from premises whose formulations are ambiguous because of their grammatical construction.

Choose the correct answer from the options given below:

(1) A, B and C only
(2) A, B and D only
(3) B and C only
(4) A and D only

17. Active Audience Theories focus on assessing what _______.

(1) people do with media
(2) media does with people
(3) administration does with media
(4) regulations impact media

18. As per the recommendations of National Education Policy, 2020, all stand alone teacher education institutions will be required to convert into multidisciplinary institutions by:

(1) 2025
(2) 2030
(3) 2035
(4) 2040

19. Given below are two statements: one is labelled as Assertion (A) and the other is labelled as Reason (R).

Assertion (A): The projective techniques offer an approach to the measurement of the personality, which is different from the self-descriptive inventories.

Reason (R): Self-descriptive inventories require the subject to describe himself/herself while assessing personality.

In the light of the above statements, choose the most appropriate answer from the options given below:

(1) Both (A) and (R) are correct and (R) is the correct explanation of (A)
(2) Both (A) and (R) are correct but (R) is not the correct explanation of (A)
(3) (A) is correct but (R) is not correct
(4) (A) is not correct but (R) is correct

20. Identify the correct mathematical statements:

A. The value of $\frac{1}{4}+\frac{1}{4\times5}+\frac{1}{4\times5\times6}$ is equal to $\frac{37}{120}$.

B. $1+2\div\left\{1+2\div\left(1+\frac{1}{3}\right)\right\}$ is equal to $\frac{4}{5}$.

C. If the average of 6 numbers is 7, the average of 3 numbers of them is 5, then the average of remaining numbers is 9.

D. If 75% of a number is added to 75, then the result is number itself. Then the number is 300

E. Largest fraction from is $\frac{9}{31},\frac{6}{23},\frac{3}{17},\frac{4}{11}$ is $\frac{9}{31}$.

Choose the correct answer from the options given below:

(1) A and B only
(2) A, C and D only
(3) C and D only
(4) C, E and D only

21. Which of the following explains the fallacy (hetvābhāsa) of satpratipakṣa correctly?

(1) A fallacy where an inference is contradicted by perception or some other non-inferential prāmāṇa.
(2) A fallacy where one inference is contradicted by another inference.
(3) A fallacy that disproves the very proposition which it is meant to prove.
(4) A fallacy of the irregular middle

22. Match List - I with List - II.

List - I (Type of Development)	**List - II (Related with)**
A. Psycho-sexual Development	I. Identity vs. Role Confusion
B. Psycho-social Development	II. Anal Stage
C. Cognitive Development	III. Hypothetical-deductive reasoning
D. Moral Development	IV. Resolving ethical dilemma

Choose the correct answer from the options given below :

(1) A-II, B-III, C-I, D-IV
(2) A-III, B-I, C-IV, D-II

(3) A-I, B-IV, C-II, D-III

(4) A-II, B-I, C-III, D-IV

23. Identify the advantages of closed ended questions in survey research:

A. It is easy to process answers.

B. Respondents can answer in their own terms.

C. They are easy for the respondents to complete.

D. They allow unusual responses to be derived.

Choose the correct answer from the options given below :

(1) A and B only

(2) A and C only

(3) A, B and C only

(4) B, C and D only

24. Which of the following are application software ?

A. Spreadsheet

B. Word Processor

C. Operating system

D. Database

E. Compiler

Choose the correct answer from the options given below :

(1) A, C and D only

(2) B, C and E only

(3) A, D and E only

(4) A, B and D only

25. Measurement validity primarily relates to :

(1) Qualitative research

(2) Quantitative research

(3) Interpretivism

(4) Constructionism

26. Match List I with List - II.

List - I	List - II
A. Independent variable in true experimental design	I. Outcome variable
B. Dependent variable	II. Control variable
C. Intervening variable	III. Spurious variable
D. Confounding variable	IV. Stands between independent variable and dependent variable

Choose the correct answer from the options given below :

(1) A-IV, B-III, C-II, D-I

(2) A-II, B-I, C-IV, D-III

(3) A-I, B-II, C-III, D-IV

(4) A-II, B-III, C-IV, D-I

27. Match List - I with List - II.

List - I Successive discounts	List - II Equivalent discount
A. 10% and 15%	I. 28%
B. 20% and 30%	II. 32.5%
C. 10% and 20%	III. 23.5%
D. 10% and 25%	IV. 44%

Choose the correct answer from the options given below :

(1) A-I, B-II, C-IV, D-III

(2) A-II, B-III, C-I, D-IV

(3) A-III, B-IV, C-I, D-II

(4) A-IV, B-I, C-II, D-III

28. Given below are two statements one is labelled as Assertion (A) and the other is labelled as Reason (R).

Assertion (A): National Education Policy, 2020 (NEP-2020) visualized 'Research-Intensive Universities'.

Reason (R): NEP-2020 envisioned university as a place which lays equal emphasis on teaching and research.

In the light of the above statements, choose the most appropriate answer from the options given below:

(1) Both (A) and (R) are correct and (R) is the correct explanation of (A)

(3) (A) is correct but (R) is not correct

(2) Both (A) and (R) are correct but (R) is not the correct explanation of (A)

(4) (A) is not correct but (R) is correct

29. Match List-I with List-II:

List-I	List-II
A. Figurative	I. Communication is considered as a rational thought in relation to dominant ideological forces.
B. Semiotics	II. Considering communication as the ability to experience otherness through authentic dialogue
C. Phenomenologist	III. Treating communication as a practical art

D. Critical	IV.	Communication as an intersubjective practice through signs

Select the correct answer from the options given below:

(1) A-III, B-IV, C-II, D-I

(2) A-II, B-IV, C-III, D-I

(3) A-I, B-IV, C-II, D-III

(4) A-III, B-II, C-IV, D-I

30. Arrange the following greenhouse gases in the increasing order of their life time in the earth's atmosphere:

A. SF_6

B. N_2O

C. H_2O vapor

D. CH_4

Choose the correct answer from the options given below:

(1) C, D, B, A

(2) C, D, A, B

(4) B, A, D, C

(3) A, B, C, D

31. Arrange the following fractions in ascending order:

A. $\frac{2}{3}$

B. $\frac{7}{19}$

C. $\frac{9}{11}$

D. $\frac{8}{9}$

E. $\frac{7}{9}$

Choose the **correct** answer from the options given below :

(1) B, A, E, C, D

(2) B, E, A, D, C

(3) A, B, C, D, E

(4) B, C, A, E, D

3. Complete the following series :

N7V, K9T, H12R, __?__, B21N

(1) E14R

(2) E13Q

(3) E16P

(4) F16R

33. Match List - I with List - II.

List - I (Types Categorical propositions)	List - II (Explanation)
A. A proposition	I. Distributes both subject and predicate terms
B. E proposition	II. Distributes only predicate term
C. I proposition	III. Distributes only subject term
D. O proposition	IV. Distributes neither subject nor predicate term

Choose the correct answer from the options given below:

(1) A-II, B-I, C-IV, D-III

(2) A-III, B-I, C-IV, D-II

(3) A-I, B-II, C-III, D-IV

(4) A-IV, B-III, C-II, D-I

34. Match List I with List - II.

List - II	List - I
A. Phishing	I. Act of gaining unauthorized access
B. Hacking	II. Unsolicited email sent over the internet to a recipient on a mailing list
C. Spam	III. Small file or code stored on user's computer
D. Cookies	IV. The creator sends out legitimate-looking emails to target users

Choose the correct answer from the options given below :

(1) A-II, B-III, C-IV, D-I

(2) A-IV, B-I, C-III, D-II

(3) A-IV, B-I, C-II, D-III

(4) A-I, B-IV, C-II, D-III

35. Arrange the following senior functionaries of a central university in the correct hierarchal order:

A. Visitor

B. Dean of the faculty

C. Chancellor

D. Head of Department

E. Vice-Chancellor

Choose the correct answer from the options given below:

(1) A, C, E, D, B
(2) C, A, E, D, B
(3) A, C, E, B, D
(4) B, D, E, C, A

36. Which of the following is an example of biological motive?
(1) Achievement
(2) Hunger
(3) Power
(4) Affiliation

37. The smallest unit of information, a computer can understand and process is known as:
(1) Digit
(2) Byte
(3) Nibble
(4) Bit

38. Journals that prioritize self-interest at the expense of scholarship and are characterized by false or misleading information, deviation from best editorial/publication practices, lack of transparency and and/or use of aggressive and indiscriminate solicitation practices, are known as:
(1) Open access journals
(2) Proprietary journals
(3) Professional journals
(4) Predatory journals

39. Arrange the steps of creative thinking process in correct sequence :
A. Preparation
B. Evaluation
C. Illumination
D. Revision
E. Incubation

Choose the correct answer from the options given below :
(1) A, B, C, D, E
(2) E, D, C, B, A
(3) D, C, B, E, A
(4) A, E, C, B, D

40. Match List - I with List - II.

List - I	List - II
A. Primary Air pollutant	I. Peroxyacyl nitrate
B. Secondary Air pollutant	II. Carbon monoxide Aerosols
C. Ozone depleting Air pollutant	III. Aerosols
D. Cloud Condensation Nuclei	IV. Chlorofluorocarbons

Choose the correct answer from the options given below :
(1) A-I, B-II, C-III, D-IV
(2) A-II, B-I, C-IV, D-III
(3) A-I, B-II, C-IV, D-III
(4) A-II, B-I, C-III, D-IV

41. Given below are two statements one is labelled as Assertion (A) and the other is labelled as Reason (R).

Assertion (A): A wind mill will be more effective if it is placed at a higher elevation above the ground than a lower one.

Reason (R): Generally, the wind speed increases with altitude above the earth's surface.

In the light of the above statements, choose the most appropriate answer from the options given below:
(1) Both (A) and (R) are correct and (R) is the correct explanation of (A)
(2) Both (A) and (R) are correct but (R) is not the correct explanation of (A)
(3) (A) is correct but (R) is not correct
(4) (A) is not correct but (R) is correct

42. The oxygen consumed in the oxidation of an organic compound by microorganisms in the aquatic ecosystem is called ____.
(1) Dissolved oxygen
(2) Chemical oxygen demand
(3) Theoretical oxygen demand
(4) Biochemical oxygen demand

43. Which of the following is/are true :
A. The conversion of an O proposition is valid.
B. The conversion of an A proposition is an A proposition.
C. The conversion of an E proposition is conversion by limitation.
D. The conversion of an I proposition is valid.

Choose the correct answer from the options given below :
(1) A and D only
(2) A and B only

(3) C only

(4) D only

44. Two cyclists cover the same distance at 15 km/hr and 16 km/hr, respectively. If one cyclist takes 16 minutes longer than the other, then the distance travelled by each cyclist is:

(1) 64 km

(2) 16 km

(3) 68 km

(4) 12 km

45. Which among the following is the most liberal Open Education Resource license ?

(1) CC-BY

(2) CC-BY-SA

(3) CC-BY-ND

(4) CC-BY-NC

Read the following passage and answer the questions:

Organized endeavors directed by people responsible for planning, organizing, leading and controlling activities have existed for thousands of years. The Egyptian pyramids and the Great Wall of China, for instance, are tangible evidence that projects of tremendous scope, employing tens of thousands of people, were undertaken well before modern times. The pyramids are a particularly interesting example. The construction of a single pyramid occupied more than 100,000 workers for 20 years. Who told each worker what to do? Who ensured that there would be enough stones at the site to keep workers busy? The answer to such questions is managers. Regardless of what managers were called at the time, someone had to plan what was to be done, organize people and materials to do it, lead and direct the workers, and impose some controls to ensure that everything was done as planned.

Another example of early management can be seen during the 1400s in the city of Venice, Italy, a major economic and trade center. The Venetians developed an early form of business enterprise and engaged in many activities common to today's organizations. For instance, at the arsenal of Venice, warships were floated along the canals, and at each stop materials and riggings were added to the ship. Doesn't that sound a lot like a car "floating" along an automobile assembly line while components are added to it? In addition to this assembly line, the Venetians also used warehouse and inventory systems to keep track of materials, human resource management systems to manage the labor force, and an accounting system to keep track of revenues and costs.

46. According to the passage, the role of a manager includes all of the following, except:

(1) Stacking stones for the pyramids

(2) Planning what is to be done

(3) Organising people for the pyramids site

(4) Directing the pyramid work force

47. According to the passage, persons responsible for the control, organisation and planning have been directing organised endeavors :

(1) Since 1400's

(2) For 100,000 years

(3) For Twenty years

(4) For Thousands of years

48. According to the passage, the ancient equivalent of the assembly line was used in:

(1) Egypt

(2) China

(3) Venice

(4) Giza

49. The reader gets the following information from the given passage:

(1) Management is a recent creation.

(2) The title of management has been around since ancient times.

(3) The people who guide organized efforts can be seen through the ages.

(4) The assembly line system was prevalent in China, Egypt and Italy.

50. The passage documents that Egyptions involved in the construction of pyramids had :

(1) An inventary system to keep record of the stones.

(2) A plan for what was to be done.

(3) An accounting system to keep the record of money.

(4) A warehouse system to manage materials.

ANSWERS

1. (4)	**2.** (2)	**3.** (1)	**4.** (2)	**5.** (3)	**6.** (4)	**7.** (3)	**8.** (2)	**9.** (1)	**10.** (1)
11. (2)	**12.** (1)	**13.** (4)	**14.** (3)	**15.** (2)	**16.** (3)	**17.** (1)	**18.** (2)	**19.** (1,2)	**20.** (2)
21. (2)	**22.** (4)	**23.** (2)	**24.** (4)	**25.** (2)	**26.** (2)	**27.** (3)	**28.** (1)	**29.** (1)	**30.** (1)
31. (1)	**32.** (3)	**33.** (2)	**34.** (3)	**35.** (3)	**36.** (2)	**37.** (4)	**38.** (4)	**39.** (4)	**40.** (2)
41. (1)	**42.** (4)	**43.** (4)	**44.** (1)	**45.** (1)	**46.** (1)	**47.** (4)	**48.** (3)	**49.** (3)	**50.** (2)

❍❍❍